THE LEGAL ENVIRONMENT OF BUSINESS

THE LEGAL ENVIRONMENT OF BUSINESS

F. William McCarty
Western Michigan University

John W. Bagby
Pennsylvania State University

Second Edition

IRWIN

Homewood, IL 60430
Boston, MA 02116

Senior sponsoring editor:	Craig Beytien
Developmental editor:	Karen E. Perry
Marketing manager:	Ron Bloecher
Project editors:	Karen Murphy and Jean Roberts
Production manager:	Irene H. Sotiroff
Designer:	Stuart Patterson
Art coordinator:	Mark Malloy
Compositor:	Weimer Incorporated
Typeface:	10/12 Berkeley Old Style Medium
Printer:	Von Hoffmann Press

Library of Congress Cataloging-in-Publication Data

McCarty, F. William, date
The legal environment of business / F. William McCarty, John W. Bagby.—2nd ed.
p. cm.
ISBN 0-256-10628-2
1. Industrial laws and legislation—United States. 2. Commercial law—United States. 3. Law—United States. I. Bagby, John W. II. Title.
KF1600.M39 1993
346.73′07—dc20
[347.3067] 92–19956

Printed in the United States of America
1 2 3 4 5 6 7 8 9 0 VH 9 8 7 6 5 4 3 2

To students at Pennsylvania State University and Western Michigan University.

PREFACE

The legal environment is of concern to small business and to large multinational enterprises. Daily newspapers and weekly business magazines constantly include articles focusing on the legal environment's effect on business firms. From arbitration to product liability laws or antitrust provisions to securities regulations, business managers need to know how state, national, and international legal requirements are likely to affect business activities. The dramatic changes in the international environment clearly are changing the legal environment for global business activities.

The international changes that have occurred since the beginning of the decade were unimaginable only a few years ago. The most visible symbol of the differences between the communistic East and the capitalistic West, the Berlin Wall, is no more. The cold war between West and East ended as the Soviet Union collapsed. Countries such as Czechoslovakia, Poland, and even Bulgaria are moving toward democracy and new legal systems incorporating many Western concepts. East Germany disappears and Yugoslavia splits into several parts. The countries of the European Community move closer and closer together as laws are harmonized and trade barriers fall. Other countries on the European continent seek to align themselves with the Community. The "chunnel" between France and England moves toward completion, promising an unprecedented integration of the British Isles into Europe.

This edition of the text integrates some international perspectives into topical legal problem areas. The business manager who understands the legal environment, both at home and abroad, will be able to see opportunities and problems that others cannot envision. What are some of the differences in the legal systems that businesses encounter in different countries? Will an arbitration agreement in a contract reduce costly litigation and be enforced? What does the new Clean Air Act mean to a firm? Are there any changes in tort law that could affect a firm's liability for products it manufactures, sells, or services?

The approach of this text is based on a belief that a blending of the study of private and public law reflects the best method to understand the legal environment of business. Regulatory environmental and antitrust laws can be studied along with contract and tort principles. We have retained our use of introductory segments to provide an overview of chapter material along with a depiction of the past, present, and future developments related to the chapter's topic. The case and extracts illustrate important textual comments and concepts. The case questions and end-of-chapter summaries and problem questions enhance the review of legal principles in specific applications. In the previous edition, ethical dilemmas and problems were provided at the end of each part of the text. In this edition, we have integrated ethical considerations into each chapter because we feel that today both professors and students are deeply concerned with ethical problems.

We have designed this text to respond to the accreditation standards of the American Assembly of the Collegiate Schools of Business (AACSB). The new AACSB standards state:

Both undergraduate and MBA curricula should provide an understanding of perspectives that form the context for business. Coverage should include:

- Ethical and global issues
- The influence of political, social, legal, regulatory, environmental, and technological issues, and
- The impact of demographic diversity on organizations.

Thus, this text addresses the political, social, legal, regulatory, and environmental issues affecting business organizations. Antitrust, securities, and labor regulatory concerns are addressed in the chapters in Parts 5 and 6 of the text. Chapter 19 discusses the management of demographic diversity. Chapter 20 focuses on the environmental laws. In addition, ethical and global issues are integrated into the chapters by providing international perspective notes and ethical dilemma situations.

COVERAGE

This text provides historical information so that the student may better comprehend the context for the development of the law as it affects both today's and tomorrow's legal environment. The integration of ethical dilemmas into each chapter enhances the ability of students to see the relationship between how ethical problems arise in business and the legal regulatory response. The international perspectives ensure that some attention to differing legal environments will be considered when studying global business activities. In both the beginning and ending chapters, the relationship between law and ethics is explored. Similarly, the international aspects of law are introduced in the text's first chapters while a more detailed discussion is the focus of the next to last chapter.

This is a comprehensive text. We have built upon the chapters in our first edition, but have added new sections to chapters, expanded sections into complete chapters, and where appropriate, have condensed materials into fewer pages and chapters. New cases have been added and many reliable cases from the first edition have been edited. While most instructors will find more material than they can cover in one course, each professor should find adequate text and case materials for the topics he or she determines is most important for the students at a particular college or university.

TEXT ORGANIZATION

This text is organized into six parts, based on six concepts important to an understanding of the social, political, legal, and regulatory environment of modern, competitive business firms. Throughout the chapters contained in each part there are discussions of ethical, international, and controversial matters.

Part 1 introduces the legal systems of the United States and contrasts this with systems in other nations. This focuses on topics concerning legal process and institutions, dispute resolution techniques, and constitutional laws.

Part 2 focuses on the private law concerns of property, contracts, and torts. Property law is fundamental to nations with a tradition of market economics, capitalism, and democracy, like the United States. Contract law is the basis of all transactions and provides the foundation for international commerce. The discussion of torts addresses the responsibilities between individuals. Private law profoundly affects the obligations and liability of all business firms.

Part 3 addresses several particular legal problems that business firms face. The United States offers consumers more legal redress than most other nations. However, product liability and consumer financing laws are spreading throughout the world, changing the relationship between consumers and producers of goods and services.

Part 4 discusses the formation, financing, operation, and internal and external problems of operating business organizations. A wide variety of forms are discussed: sole proprietorships, Subchapter S corporations, and corporations. Regulations of the securities markets govern firms' access to the public capital markets.

Part 5 addresses the competition laws known as antitrust in the United States. While antitrust enforcement diminished during the 1980s, there are signs of its resurgence. The European Economic Community (EC), Japan, and other industrial nations are now beginning to adopt and enforce anti-monopoly laws largely based on the U.S. model. These considerations are likely to become more important considerations as the 21st century approaches.

Part 6 addresses the important considerations of employee relations. In recognition of the reduced impact of labor-management relations (trade unionism), this edition has reduced this coverage from two chapters to one. However, the expanding direct regulation of employment by the federal, state, and local governments has led to somewhat greater coverage of these areas in this edition. Workplace safety, compensation matters, employment contract conditions, and equal employment laws are discussed in two separate chapters.

Part 7 provides an integrative capstone to the study of the legal environment. This part focuses on environmental law, international law, and the social responsibility of business. These matters have received increasing attention during the 1980s but are placed last to highlight how they apply concepts discussed earlier. This also provides an opportunity for students to integrate other concepts learned earlier into a more complex framework.

CASE FEATURES

The text combines our analysis of important legal principles with extracts from court cases that apply some of the principles to specific situations. Each chapter includes three to six cases. All cases are introduced by a factual summary in the authors' language so that the reader can understand the situation being discussed by the court. Both recent and later cases are used to portray both a historical context for the development of the law and the current conditions in which legal problems occur. New cases have been added in almost every chapter so that students can see how contemporary legal problems are being addressed.

Because the law is subject to individual opinions and different interpretations, some dissenting opinions are included. They present contrasting legal views and often pose different approaches to solving particular problems. We continue to include case questions so that vital concepts of each situation are addressed by the reader.

CHAPTER PEDAGOGY

Each major topic is introduced with contextual matters covering the historical, social, political, and economic influences that have shaped the legal environment of business. The text employs the SQ3R study method that is introduced more fully in Chapter 1. This method enhances students' critical thinking skills by emphasizing the survey, question, read, recite, and review method of study.

Each chapter begins with several survey techniques to engage student interest. First, "key concepts" open each chapter, identifying important topics. Next, the "Introduction . . . Past, Present, Future" section offers contextual matters that provide integrative perspective for the issues that have been addressed by law and regulation. An overview follows to tie the various subtopics to the key concepts and the context.

Within the chapters are pertinent questions addressing important expressed or implied concerns raised by the cases. Boxed presentations and visuals offer relevant and concise presentation of the material, enhancing study. Commentary and business press coverage of key controversies enhance students' ability to question critically the important contemporary issues.

Each chapter concludes with a list of key terms and end-of-chapter problems designed to reinforce the SQ3R method with a mixture of actual cases, hypotheticals, and analytical expositions that review the concepts introduced.

ADDITIONAL FEATURES

The text includes both a brief and a detailed table of contents to enhance the survey features of the text. The glossary, which is more detailed than that in many texts, defines each term that is boldfaced or italicized in the text. This frees the reader from constantly consulting outside references and legal dictionaries. The appendixes present excerpts from important laws and regulations, as well as from the U.S. Constitution, which are relevant to the legal environment of business.

SUPPLEMENTS

The Study Guide for Students provides a summary of important chapter topics, a brief of each case, and objective and essay problems for review. Professor James Jurinski of the University of Portland has prepared the *Study Guide. The Instructor's Manual,* prepared by the authors, contains answers to case and problem questions, transparency masters, and other pertinent information for professors adopting the text. Computest 3, a computerized text bank, is also available to enhance the preparation of quizzes or examinations.

ACKNOWLEDGMENTS

We wish to acknowledge the collegial support received from faculty, staff, and administrators at Pennsylvania State University and the Haworth College of Business at Western Michigan University. The insights and recommendations of our colleagues have been useful. We also wish to thank the following reviewers for their valuable suggestions as they reviewed our draft manuscripts for this and the earlier edition of this text:

William Burke, *Trinity University*
Sandra Burns, *Arkansas State University*
Larry Clark, *Louisiana State University*
Theodore M. Dinges, *Longview Community College*

Michael Engber, *Ball State University*
Gamewell Gant, *Idaho State University*
James Hill, *Central Michigan University*
Jack Hires, *Valparaiso University*
Susan Jarvis, *Pan American University*
Paul Lansing, *University of Iowa*
Nancy Mansfield, *Georgia State University*
Keith Maxwell, *University of Puget Sound*
John Norwood, *University of Arkansas*
Steve Palmer, *Creighton University*
Sheelwant Pawar, *Idaho State University*
Daniel Reynolds, *Middle Tennessee State University*
Ira Schwartz, *Towson State University*
Burke T. Ward, *Villanova University*
William Wines, *Boise State University*
Larry Zacharias, *University of Massachusetts at Amherst*

We wish to give a special acknowledgment to Janice Loutzenhiser at California State University—San Bernardino. Her keen eye for detail and perceptive comments helped fine-tune this edition.

Our special thanks and gratitude go to our developmental editor, Karen Perry, our production editor, Karen Murphy, and our sponsoring editor, Craig Beytien, at Richard D. Irwin, Inc. Each of these talented individuals gave wise counsel and extended their efforts to bring this edition to publication.

We also wish to acknowledge the assistance provided by Patricia Brown and graduate student Richard Laaksonsen at Western Michigan University. Finally, we appreciate the patience, support, and encouragement of our families. Many thanks to Alma McCarty, Robin Bagby, and our children: Laura, Carolyn, Chris, David, Dianne, Julia Marie, and Jack.

F. William McCarty
John W. Bagby

CONTENTS IN BRIEF

CONTENTS

Part 5
Antitrust Law, 453

Part 6
Employment Law, 525

LIST OF CASES

Part 1

THE AMERICAN LEGAL SYSTEM

This first part of the text introduces the reader to the law and the legal system, providing the reader with an overview of the institutions and processes used to make law in the United States. The initial chapters focus on the nature of law and the legal system and on the significant characteristics and institutions in the American legal system.

Subsequent chapters review the civil litigation process from the time before filing a case through the appeal stage. Since alternative dispute resolution methods have become increasingly important, arbitration, mediation, and other means of dispute resolution are noted.

Chapters 5 and 6 deal with areas of law that shape the American legal environment. Constitutional provisions, from the commerce clause to protection of free speech, press, and assembly, significantly affect individual and business activities. Administrative law and regulations are more recent elements of the legal environment that contribute vital government regulation of business activities.

Chapter 1

INTRODUCTION TO LEGAL AND ETHICAL ANALYSIS

KEY CONCEPTS

Law refers to a society's established standards or guidelines for action or behavior and originates from a higher authority or from common practices and customs.

Legal analysis combines deductive and inductive reasoning. Inductive reasoning looks at specific cases to determine general legal concepts, whereas deductive reasoning looks at general principles and applies them to different cases.

In a common law legal system, *stare decisis* requires that precedent decisions be followed in subsequent cases.

The natural law and legal positivism theories of law look differently at the relationship of law to human actions. Understanding these and other theories helps us to understand different views about the role of law in a society.

Law and ethics are separate but related norms used as guides for personal and business conduct. The two major ethical theories are the consequence-oriented, or teleological, utilitarian theory and the duty-based, or deontological, universalism theory.

INTRODUCTION . . . PAST, PRESENT, FUTURE

The importance of law in society is not new. Hundreds and even thousands of years ago, some societies sought to codify local customs and practices so that individuals and businesspeople would know what they were expected to do and not to do. Today, these codes constitute the most important source of law in countries that have *civil law* legal systems. In other societies, customs and practices evolved into legal standards when courts resolved disputes by referring to those practices. Countries in which court decisions predated attempts to codify the law developed *common law* legal systems based on those *precedent* court decisions grounded in common law.

In many societies, religion has played an important role in the development of both ethical standards and legal rules. Today, the Islamic legal system, based on the *Koran* and teachings from it, predominates in many countries. Similarly, ethical precepts such as the Golden Rule form the basis for the universal ethical theory, which, along with the utilitarian theory, may be used for examining the ethical nature of business decisions and individual actions. Today, corporations are becoming more aware of the responsibilities they have to customers, suppliers, employees, and local citizens. Therefore, the importance of conducting ethical as well as legal analysis of proposed action is growing.

Increasingly, actions in one part of the world have consequences elsewhere. The transfer of a firm's operations from the United States to Mexico may prompt U.S. workers to protest the loss of jobs. The destruction of Kuwaiti oil fields causes environmental pollution in dozens of neighboring countries. The development of an "abortion pill" in France leads to demands for the drug in some countries and protests against its use in others. As the world thus becomes smaller, both ethical standards and legal rules will harmonize, and international norms will gradually develop. For example, the level of protection afforded to patents, copyrights, and trademarks (intellectual property) is becoming more similar across countries, as are ethical standards regarding gifts to public and private officials. The future is likely to require business managers to become more aware of their corporation's ethical behavior and to increase their knowledge of the legal environment surrounding their firm and industry.

OVERVIEW

The study of law begins with a realization of the importance of law to both personal and business activities. Law can be viewed as emanating either from the commands of a higher authority in a society or from common customs and practices. However, whereas both law and ethical standards are based on moral norms, only those rules or standards for behavior that are explicitly enforced by the society are considered laws.

Legal analysis requires the use of both deductive and inductive reasoning. General principles of law referred to in the text can be reviewed by using the SQ3R method of study. In the common law legal system found in the United States, the role of court decisions is important because according to the doctrine of *stare decisis,* similar prior court decisions from the same jurisdiction must be followed in subsequent cases. Case briefs help the reader to analyze the main components of a case.

Several theories seek to explain the nature of law and to answer questions regarding its origin. The theories of natural law, legal positivism, sociological, legal realism, critical legal study, and economic school, all help to enhance our understanding of the role of law in our society.

Because there is a close relationship between a society's legal rules and its moral values, the relationship between law and ethics is reviewed. Ethical analysis involves a process of examining motives and actions from the perspective of moral principles. Both the utilitarian and the universal theories provide a method of analysis that can be used to evaluate the ethical nature of many business decisions.

LAW AND THE LEGAL ENVIRONMENT

This book describes and analyzes the legal environment of business. Laws affect businesses in many ways. Contract, property, and tort laws directly influence business agreements, real estate purchases, and liability concerns. Laws also regulate a wide range of business activities, from the hiring of employees to the warranties that accompany the sale of products. Securities regulations influence business financing decisions. Environmental laws, employee safety regulations, and consumer protection rules attempt to limit the harmful side effects of economic activity by imposing penalties for violations and, therefore, requiring compliance from business firms.

Law in Today's Society

Both national and local news stories focusing on legal matters appear almost every day. For example, constitutional provisions in many states require governments to begin each year with a balanced budget. States and cities are frequently forced to cut services, lay off employees, and seek ways to raise revenue without overtaxing citizens in order to meet this legal obligation.

One of the longest-running national stories, the failure of thousands of savings and loan institutions across the country, raises numerous legal questions. Can depositors use the law to retrieve their money from failing firms? Are the directors and officers of a firm personally liable to individual depositors or to the federal insurance agency for losses the firm suffered? Can the shareholders of failing firms recoup their losses? The answers to these questions are found in the laws that make up a part of our legal environment. Contract laws and insurance regulations determine the protection offered to depositors. Agency, tort, and corporation laws must be consulted to assess the degree of legal liability to depositors or shareholders based on fraud or a lack of reasonable care and judgment on the part of officers and directors.

In 1990, over 40 percent of banks responding to a survey reported that one or more suits were filed that year against their officers and directors. Even President Bush's son agreed to make payment to some shareholders who claimed that he should be held accountable for failing to adequately perform his legal duty as a savings and loan director. In addition to failing to meet their civil obligations, some individuals may have broken criminal laws. In April 1990, the former chairman of a Dallas savings and loan was convicted of 13 counts of bank fraud; he was sentenced to 30 years in prison.

A second national story concerns the changing attitude regarding the copyright and patent law protection provided to computer software manufacturers. "Don't copy that floppy" is the cry of software makers who are stepping up efforts to crack down on illegal copying by software "pirates" worldwide. Personal computer manufacturers claim they lose billions of dollars in sales annually due to unauthorized copying. As enforcement of copyright laws tightens, businesses and institutions will need to develop software copying policies. Business managers in the 1990s must be aware of what is legal and what is not.

Even on college campuses, the law has made its presence known. Ivy League universities were accused of violating antitrust law by collaborating to set common tuition charges and financial aid packages for students. They settled out of court and agreed to disband their annual meetings. Stanford University's practices for billing federal research projects were questioned when yachts and parties appeared to have been financed by the taxpayers. Students, too, are more aware of the law's intrusion into their lives. As society comes to recognize that many rapes and assaults are committed by acquaintances and dates, young people on campus realize that they may face both criminal and civil liabilities if they don't heed the "no" of their friends. Fraternities at Colgate were sued for their part in the hazing of new members, in which some students died or were injured. Some fraternity members at the University of Virginia were indicted on charges stemming from a drug raid.

In addition to the headline stories, hundreds of less visible cases affect the livelihood of many businesspeople each day: an arbitration provision inserted in contracts between stockbrokers and their clients is upheld; a court determines that under certain conditions, accountants can be held liable for negligence in reviewing corporate annual reports; a sexual harassment case is decided in favor of a female attorney with the Securities and Exchange Commission. Furthermore, many legal problems are resolved without going to trial—in part due to the precedent represented by other cases. Johnson and Johnson settled out of court in one of the Tylenol-tampering cases. Rutgers University settled a suit brought by the parents of a student who died at a fraternity initiation party. Local residents opposing the development of green space in Kalamazoo reached an accord with the developer after the residents forced the developer to modify his original plan. The law is clearly part of our environment, so we must understand how it affects our business activities.

What Is Law?

The term **law** has several different meanings, each of which captures a different sense of the source of law, its legitimacy, and its use as a process.

Law: Definition One

That which is laid down, ordained or established. A rule or method according to which phenomena or actions coexist or follow one another.

Black's Law Dictionary

Law: Definition Two

A binding custom or practice of a community. A rule or mode of conduct or action that is prescribed or formally recognized as binding by a supreme controlling authority or is made obligatory by a sanction made, recognized, or enforced by the controlling authority.

Webster's Third New International Dictionary

Each of these definitions emphasizes several different aspects of law. The definition from *Black's Law Dictionary* notes that law refers to a result regardless of the process used to bring it about, that is, whether the result was ordained or established. Therefore, this definition focuses on the behavior that results from the establishment, creation, or recognition of the law. Actions or phenomena, whether particles of matter or people in a society, may be expected to occur as they do because of law.

According to the *Webster's* definition, law is not generated by an outside source or higher authority; rather, it flows from the customs and practices followed by the people in a society. The second segment of this definition emphasizes that sanctions are needed to make law effective. Therefore, only those societal customs or practices that are recognized as binding and are enforced by the authorities can be called laws.

By combining these two definitions, we can conclude that **law** refers to established standards or guidelines for action or behavior in a society, whether they originate from a higher authority or from the common practices and customs of people. To be law, however, the standards must be "binding"; they must be made obligatory by the authorities in a society.

Why Study Law?

As the stories noted above make clear, law reaches pervasively into our personal and professional lives. From arbitration awards and bankruptcy proceedings to securities fraud and waste disposal requirements, the law and the legal environment cannot be ignored by business managers. One of the primary reasons that business students in particular study law is to gain the knowledge necessary to plan the numerous activities that hinge on what the law allows or requires. The legal environment in the 1990s is not the same as in the 1960s or even in the 1980s. The legal institutions and methods commonly used to resolve disputes are changing, as is the role played by administrative agencies. For example, Chapter 4 discusses several emerging methods of dispute resolution: the minitrial and rent-a-judge, as well as arbitration and mediation. Also indicative of the shifting legal environment, some administrative agencies, such as the Interstate Commerce Commission, have lost significant regulatory powers, whereas in other areas, such as with securities regulations and environmental concerns, enforcement activities seem certain to increase. State courts and local regulatory bodies make thousands of decisions that determine where a business locates and, for certain industries (e.g., insurance, public utilities), what services can or must be offered and what rates can be charged for them.

In addition, as economic ties between countries have multiplied and strengthened, the world has shrunk. Many companies find that their domestic market has become too small. Even the biggest companies in the biggest countries cannot survive if their activities are limited to one or two countries when they compete in global industries. Thus, international sources of law must be consulted. In the 21st century, business managers must take into consideration regulations and legal decisions made in Tokyo and Brussels as well as those coming from Lincoln, Nebraska; Charleston, South Carolina; and Washington, D.C. when determining tomorrow's legal environment.

Thus, it is important that business managers have a general knowledge of the legal system and the most important laws affecting their activities. A society's laws embody and reflect its customs and values. Since the laws of a society change and evolve, the legal environment of business is dynamic. Business managers must be aware of those changes and the forces that cause them. Businesspeople who are aware of important legal rules and emerging legal developments can perform more efficiently and effectively than those who lack such knowledge.

What Is the Legal Environment of Business?

Many studies have attempted to define the legal environment of business. The term suggests something more than merely memorizing rules of law. The **legal environment of business** is generally concerned with the study of the legal, regulatory, and political institutions and processes affecting business activities. In essence, the legal environment of business relates primarily to those laws that affect the atmosphere in which business activities are conducted. Although public regulatory laws are central to a study of the legal environment, certain areas of private law, such as contract, tort, and property law, also require attention.

Finally, ethical problems should also be discussed as part of the legal environment of business because law and ethics guide behavior in tandem. Several of the legal cases referred to earlier, for example, raise ethical questions. Are directors of savings and loan institutions who spend corporate funds on lavish art and vacation hideaways or who invest in risky junk bonds acting ethically? Is insider trading not only illegal but also ethically improper? Other business cases involving pollution, misleading advertising, and unconscionable contracts clearly raise ethical concerns.

Legal Environment of Business Concerns

- An introduction to the fundamental legal institutions and processes.
- An overview of the primary private law fields of contract, tort, and property law, which directly affect many business transactions.
- An examination of specific areas in which there is significant regulation of business activities. These include labor and employment laws, securities regulation, consumer protection laws, antitrust concerns, and environment policies.
- An analysis of the relationship between law and ethics, including an examination of ethical problems as they relate to specific fields of law and a discussion of the social responsibility of business firms.

LEGAL ANALYSIS

Legal analysis involves the study of court cases that solve specific disputes by applying general legal principles. Throughout this text, extracts from court opinions are presented in conjunction with the text material. This mixture permits the study of law and the legal environment to combine both inductive and deductive reasoning.

Inductive Reasoning

Inductive reasoning is the process of examining specific situations to determine if they have some common attributes. A reader who studies several related cases gains an understanding of how the application of legal principles in similar cases leads to the formation of general legal rules. Case summaries reveal the logic used by a court to decide specific legal problems. Generalizations from those specific situations become the basis for solutions to other, similar problems. By reviewing different cases related to the same topic, a reader can see how individual decisions lead to the establishment of general legal principles.

The common law legal system of the United States relies on decisions in prior cases as an important source of law. At the center of the common law legal system is the doctrine of ***stare decisis***, which means "let the decision stand." Courts within the same jurisdiction are required to follow the legal principles set forth in earlier cases. Thus, the law applied to one case not only decides the case for the parties involved but also establishes a legal "precedent" for future similar cases. It is for this reason that legal analysis in the United

States involves the study of cases. This text includes end-of-chapter problems requiring the application of legal concepts based on situations to others that are similar.

Deductive Reasoning

Deductive reasoning is the process of examining general principles derived from induction or legislation and applying them to specific situations. Many countries of the world use a civil law legal system based on a code of law that contains the society's most important general principles. By examining those general principles, one can deduce how to apply them to other specific problems.

For example, consider the general principle that all real estate contracts must be in writing to be enforced. A specific real estate contract between the ABC firm and the XYZ firm can, therefore, be enforced only if it is written. The same principle should apply equally for a contract between the XYZ firm and John Jones or for one between John Jones and Mary Brown. To fully understand a general legal concept, its application to several different situations or cases must be examined. This text presents numerous legal principles and cases illustrating how judges apply general legal principles to solve specific problems. After reading and understanding the court's opinion in a specific case, generalizations can be made and used to resolve other, similar problems and cases.

Thus, in order to solve the questions and problems you see on examinations and in professional activities, you must go beyond memorizing important legal principles. You must be able to determine if a principle fits the test problem or the business situation in the same way in which it fit the case you studied. Legal analysis requires you to understand how specific case decisions give rise to general principles and how general principles apply in specific case situations.

Reading the Text Material

The study of law calls for a different approach than reading a newspaper, magazine, or book. A widely used study method known as *SQ3R* can be very effective in improving your ability to retain and comprehend the information presented in this text. SQ3R stands for survey, question, read, recite, and review. The organization of this text, and of each of its chapters, has been prepared in a manner intended to facilitate the use of the SQ3R method of study.

Your first task should be to *survey* the material assigned. Thus, if you are reading a chapter, look carefully at the content and organization of the material presented. The key concepts, introduction, and overview sections at the beginning of each chapter facilitate this process. Take a few minutes to read each section heading and one or two subsequent sentences. Remember that you are surveying what topics are addressed in the chapter. You are not yet seeking to comprehend the details.

The second segment of study focuses on *questioning*. Before you begin each section, formulate questions about the subject matter and about the key terms in order to focus your reading. In this way, the relevant points are more readily apparent. The questions following each case assist in highlighting important aspects of the court's opinion.

After you *read* the material, return to the questions you formulated and *recite* the answers to them. If you asked what was the meaning of a certain term, recite the definition for it. If you asked how to differentiate between two concepts, recite how each concept applies to particular situations.

The last step consists of *reviewing* the material studied. A review helps you to retain the information presented. Again, asking questions may be helpful. What were the major points addressed by the cases? Which legal concepts do they illustrate? How do the section headings relate to each other? A summary, key terms, and chapter exercises are presented at the end of each chapter to assist your review.

Reading Case Opinions

The court opinions found in this text are taken from the decisions of the various state and federal courts. Some are recent cases dealing with problems affecting contemporary business managers. Others are classic cases that represent important developmental changes in the application of law to certain activities. Some cases include both majority and dissenting opinions. Dissenting judges often provide insight into the terms of a conflict or the range of economic, social, or political views on an issue. Furthermore, dissenting opinions sometimes pave the way for later changes in the law.

At first, cases can be difficult to read and understand. It helps to look for certain elements that facilitate the review of a case's important aspects. It is often useful to write a short summary of the case, known as a **brief.** A brief helps to clarify the opinion and helps you to understand the issues addressed by the court. The next section contains a sample case, a discussion of items to include in a brief, and a sample brief.

READING A CASE AND WRITING A BRIEF

The following case is presented to sharpen your skills in case analysis and brief writing. Carefully read the *Katko v. Briney* case and the review questions that follow. Next, read the section on what items to include in a case brief. Prepare your own brief of the *Katko* case based on the format suggested. Finally, compare your brief with the sample brief. Although your brief should be similar to the sample, it need not be identical.

If you take the time to brief many of the cases in this text, both your understanding of the cases and your writing of briefs will improve. Writing a brief also helps to improve your analytical skills. It is almost impossible to write a good brief for a case unless you have first thought about the important facts, determined how the legal principle is applied, and analyzed the court's reasoning and decision.

A Sample Case

Katko v. Briney
183 N.W. 2d 657 (1971)
Supreme Court of Iowa

Plaintiff Katko sued for damages resulting from serious injury caused by a shot from a 20-gauge spring shotgun set by defendant Briney in a bedroom of an old uninhabited farmhouse. Briney had set the shotgun because there had been numerous housebreakings in the area. The shots from the gun hit Katko, who had broken into and entered the house to find and steal old bottles and dated fruit jars that were considered valuable antiques. Briney claimed he had a right to protect his property against thieves such as Katko. Katko claimed that Briney's shotgun trap was wrongful and illegal. At the trial, the jury returned a verdict for Katko against Briney for $20,000 actual damages and $10,000 punitive damages. The trial judge approved the jury's verdict, and Briney appealed to the Iowa Supreme Court.

Moore, Chief Justice

The primary issue here is whether an owner may protect personal property in an unoccupied boarded-up farmhouse against trespassers and thieves by a spring gun capable of inflicting death or serious injury. We are not here concerned with a man's right to protect his home and the members of his family. Defendant's home was several miles from the scene of the incident to which we refer.

For about ten years there occurred a series of trespassing and housebreaking events with loss of some household items, the breaking of windows, and messing up of the property in general. Through the years the defendant boarded up windows and doors in an attempt to stop the intrusions. He also posted a no trespassing sign some 35 feet from the house. On June 11, 1967, defendant set a shotgun trap in the north bedroom. It was rigged with wire from the doorknob to the gun's trigger so it would fire when the door was opened. Briney first pointed the gun so an intruder would be hit in the stomach, but at his wife's suggestion it was lowered to hit the legs. He admitted he did it "because I was mad and tired of being tormented," but he "did not intend to injure anyone." The spring gun could not be seen from the outside, and no warning of its presence was posted.

Plaintiff entered the old house by removing a board from a porch window. . . . [P]laintiff went to open the north bedroom door, the shotgun went off striking him in the right leg above the ankle bone. Much of his leg was blown away. He crawled to his vehicle and was then rushed to a doctor and the hospital, where he remained for forty days.

Plaintiff . . . pled guilty to the criminal charge of larceny in the nighttime of property of less than $20 value from a private building . . . [H]e was fined $50 and costs and paroled . . . from a 60-day jail sentence.

The main thrust of the defendant's defense is that the law permits the use of a spring gun in a dwelling or warehouse for the purpose of preventing the unlawful entry of a burglar or thief. The trial court instructed the jury that the law allows one to "use reasonable force in the protection of his property, but such right is subject to the qualification that one may not use such means of force as will take human life or inflict great bodily injury. Such is the rule even though the injured party is a trespasser and is in violation of the law himself."

The trial court also stated that "an owner of premises is prohibited from willfully or intentionally injuring a trespasser by means of force that either takes life or inflicts great bodily injury. The fact that the trespasser may be acting in violation of the law does not change the rule. The only time when such conduct of setting a spring gun or like dangerous device is justified would be when the trespasser was committing a felony of violence or when the trespasser was endangering human life by his act."

The overwhelming weight of authority, both textbook and case law, supports the trial court's statement of the applicable principles of law. Prosser on Torts, third edition, pages 116–18, states:

> The law has always placed a higher value upon human safety than upon mere rights in property; it is the accepted rule that there is no privilege to use any force calculated to cause death or serious bodily injury to repel the threat to land or chattels, unless there is also such a threat to the defendant's personal safety as to justify a self defense. . . . Spring guns and other mankilling devices are not justifiable against a mere trespasser, or even a petty thief.

Restatement of Torts, Section 85, page 180, states:

> The value of human life and limbs, not only to the individual concerned but also to the society, so outweighs the interest of a possessor of land in excluding from it those he is not willing to admit thereto that a possessor of land has no privilege to use force intended or likely to cause death or serious harm against another . . . unless the intrusion threatens death or serious bodily harm to the occupiers or users of the premises.

In *Allison v. Fiscus* (1951), the facts were very similar to [this case]. There, plaintiff's right to damages was recognized for injuries received when he broke a door latch and started to enter defendant's warehouse with intent to steal. As he entered, a trap of two sticks of dynamite buried under the doorway by defendant owner was set off and plaintiff seriously injured. The Ohio Supreme Court recognized the plaintiff's right to recover punitive damages in addition to compensatory damages.

The judgment of the trial court is affirmed.

Case Questions

1. Could Briney, as the owner of this unoccupied farmhouse, do anything to protect his property against thieves such as Katko?
2. Would this case be decided differently if Briney had posted a notice outside the house that there was a shotgun rigged to one of the bedroom doors?

3. What would be the decision in a case in which attack dogs are used to protect a jewelry store from burglars?

4. Would the case be decided differently if Briney were living in the house?

Items to Include in a Case Brief

Case Title and Citation In reading cases, look at the first several lines preceding the court's opinion. The first line states the title of the case and identifies the parties to the suit. Most of the cases cited in this text are appellate cases, not trial court cases, so generally the first party named is the **appellant**, the one who is bringing the appeal. The second party, known as the **appellee**, is the party who is satisfied with the trial court's decision. Some courts do not put the name of the appellant first; instead, they continue to place the names in the sequence used by the trial court.

If the court is a trial court, the name of the party bringing the case to trial, the **plaintiff**, appears first, whereas the name of the party against whom the suit was brought, the **defendant**, appears last. These two sets of litigation designations (appellant/appellee and plaintiff/defendant) indicate different characteristics about the parties, but sometimes the terms are used together. A plaintiff-appellee, such as Katko in the preceding case, is the party who originally brought the case to trial and who was satisfied with the trial court's decision. Briney, the defendant-appellant, is the party who was sued and was dissatisfied with the trial court's decision because he lost.

The second line contains the **citation**, which tells the reader and legal researcher where the case may be found. Court opinions are collected and bound together in books known as *reporters*. The numbers and abbreviations in the citation indicate in which book and on what page to find a case. The *Katko* case begins on page 657 of volume 183 of the second series of *North Western Reporter* books. The date indicates when the case was finally decided by the reviewing or appellate court. Several years may pass between the original trial and the decision by the reviewing court.

The third line gives the name of the court that wrote the opinion. Generally, this is an appellate court, which reviews the decision made by a lower court. In some cases, it may be a trial court, a state's supreme court, a federal court, or even an administrative agency. Chapter 2 discusses the organization of state and federal courts.

Facts Only those facts that provide information needed to resolve the problem confronting the court should be stated in a brief. You should read the entire case before beginning the brief so that you can distinguish salient facts important to deciding the issue from irrelevant or tangential facts. Notice in the sample brief how unimportant facts are omitted and the important facts are summarized.

Issue Court opinions frequently resolve several issues. Cases in this text are generally edited to present only the issue considered most important to the context of a discussion. The issue identifies the legal problem that must be answered to determine which of the disputing parties wins the case. Generally, the issue should be posed in the form of a question permitting a yes-or-no answer.

Holding The holding contains the court's answer to the question posed by the issue. The holding comprises the legal rule and precedent for which that case stands. It may also be useful to note which party won the lawsuit. The holding is the opinion of the majority of the judges of the court. It may not be the holding of all of the judges and you may disagree with it.

Rationale The court's reasoning explains the decision it reached. Be careful not to simply restate the decision as the rationale. In order to extract general rules from the court's decision, you must understand the court's reasoning. Ask yourself, "If the facts in this case were changed slightly, would the case be decided the same way? Why? Which facts or policies would lead a court in a slightly different case to reach the same opinion?" The premises used and the chain of reasoning form the basis for the court's decision.

Dissent Some cases that contain both a majority and dissenting opinion are presented to highlight controversies. A good brief should include a few sentences to summarize the views of the dissenting judges. Your comments should address the reasoning used to reach the dissenting opinion. When no dissent appears but there are obvious criticisms to the holding, you may voice these criticisms independently.

Comment and Rule of Law In your briefs, it may be helpful to include a section expressing your thoughts about the case. In this section, you may comment on the court's reasoning and on the consequences of the decision or the holding when it is later used as precedent. You may also want to summarize the rule of law from the case. The rule of law is generally limited to a one- or two-sentence statement that could be used as precedent in similar cases. Writing such a rule at the end of every case highlights the importance of that particular case to the development of law as well as to the litigating parties.

A Sample Brief

Katko v. Briney

Supreme Court of Iowa (1971)

Facts

Katko entered a boarded-up and uninhabited farmhouse owned by Briney with the intent of stealing some old bottles he believed to be there. Although a No Trespassing sign had been posted in front of the farmhouse, there was no notice that Briney had rigged a shotgun to go off when a bedroom door in the farmhouse was opened. When Katko opened that door, the shotgun went off, blowing away part of his leg. Katko sued Briney for damages caused by the shotgun blast. Briney claimed that he was not liable because he did not intend to seriously injure anyone and he is entitled to protect his property against thieves.

Issue

May an owner protect private property in an unoccupied house against trespassers and thieves by a spring gun capable of inflicting serious injury or death?

Holding

No. An owner cannot use deadly force in protecting personal property; the person using such force is liable for damages for any injury caused.

Rationale

The law places a higher value on human safety than on property rights. Deadly or dangerous force is permitted to protect property only if there is a threat of death or serious injury to those on the premises. Because these premises were unoccupied, deadly force could not be used. Although Briney said he did not intend to injure anyone, he should know that a shotgun can cause serious injury or death, and what he should know, not his stated intent, is the basis for judging his actions.

Comments

Even if there had been notice of the danger to an intruder, such as a sign indicating there was a shotgun trap, the law would hold the person who injures another liable for doing so. The case does not deal with the force that a person may use to protect both people and property because no one inhabited the premises. The law seeks to balance the interests of the property owner against a person's interest in being free from injury by others. Even when committing a trespass or larceny, people have an interest in being free from injury by others. Human life is given a higher priority than property.

THE NATURE OF LAW AND LEGAL THEORIES

Theories concerning the nature of law attempt to answer questions about the source of law, the extent of an individual's obligation to observe the law, and the adequacy and justice of particular laws. No single set of answers to these questions receives general acceptance. Rather, several theories contribute various perspectives that enhance our understanding of the role of law in society.

Natural Law Theory

Natural law theory holds that nature ordains the law independently from human action. In the U.S. Declaration of Independence, the second and most famous sentence provides a good example of natural law: human beings are "endowed by their Creator with certain inalienable rights," including "Life, Liberty and the pursuit of Happiness." The theory of natural law assumes that people will find rational justice by using their natural reasoning abilities.

The primary concerns of natural law theory are laws that deal with the human condition and with situations relating to fundamental human rights, including laws that guarantee the right to life, laws that guarantee a person's civil rights, laws that promote equal housing opportunities, and laws that protect a person's freedom of speech. According to the theory, natural law establishes fundamental human rights for all people, regardless of their culture or society. Natural law is the same for peasants in Afghanistan, steelworkers in Germany, and businesswomen in the United States.

People have espoused many variations of the natural law theme. Underlying each is the belief that certain higher principles of justice exist for all people, regardless of their present situation. Thus, the U.S. Constitution's Bill of Rights protects all people, even the criminals and hatemongers in society. Natural law theorists believe these principles can and should be implemented through legal institutions. Natural law theory continues to influence some laws today, particularly in right-to-life laws. Sometimes natural law is described as normative, prescribing what "ought to be," because it emphasizes a body of higher law that individuals must attempt to understand and obey.

Legal Positivism Theory

In the 18th century, scholars developed a positivist philosophy of law that continues to influence the teaching of law in many universities today. Legal positivism theorists contend that any accurate explanation of the nature of law should be based on what actually occurs in society, not what ought to be. Legal positivism theory analyzes law and legal institutions as they actually exist. Legal positivists regard as law only those rules that the state adopts to obligate people generally to do (or to refrain from doing) particular activities. This view emphasizes law as being the commands of a sovereign power. In some countries, sovereign power resides with a monarch or dictator, whereas in other societies it is vested in elected officials, legislators, or even the people at large. Regardless of the type of sovereign power, a just legal system, according to legal positivist criteria, is one that applies logical principles, clearly and formally stated, without bias.

Note that legal positivism theory emphasizes both the commands of the sovereign and the analysis of law based on observations of what occurs in the application and enforcement of those commands. This analytical approach presents an important contrast to natural law theory. The focus of legal positivism is on the here and now (what is), not on a normative objective (what ought to be). Some legal scholars criticize legal positivism for its lack of concern for moral content of laws.

Natural Law and Legal Positivism Compared

The first casualty in the battle over Justice Clarence Thomas's nomination to the Supreme Court in 1991 was the venerable concept of natural law—the idea that human rights are based on universal moral principles not limited by the letter of the law. Judge Thomas frequently refers to natural law in his academic writings. Some senators expressed significant concern as to whether then-Judge Thomas would invoke natural law rather than a combination of legal positivism, natural law, and conventionalism (which holds that judicial interpretation should reflect the community's moral judgment), in deciding some constitutional cases. Although he had written about natural law's place in the development of some legal concepts, Justice Thomas answered that he saw "little or no role for natural law" in matters of constitutional interpretation.

In the United States the debate over the relative merits of natural law and legal positivism dates from the early days of the nation. In 1798, Chief Justice John Jay, an author of the Federalist papers, and Justice James Iredell, a member of the Constitutional Convention, debated natural law in *Calder v. Bull.* Jay maintained that the legislature did not have the power to enforce laws that were "against all reason and justice." Iredell countered that "the ideas of natural justice" are too indefinite a basis for legal decisions.

Belief in natural law cuts across the ideological categories of left and right. Justice Thurgood Marshall, for example, invoked natural law in his briefs in *Brown v. Board of Education* in 1954. Justice Thomas's espousal of natural law is intriguing because in recent years, conservative jurists have primarily favored positivism. Appeals Court Justice Robert Bork and Supreme Court Chief Justice William Rehnquist are positivists, though liberals like Justice Hugo Black have been positivists as well.

In practice, virtually all judges decide cases on the basis of some mixture of legal positivism and natural law. Thus, Judge Bork failed to be confirmed as a Supreme Court justice because his theoretical writings urged a purely positivistic approach. Most judges hew to the positive law whenever it is tolerably clear, interpreting ambiguities in light of the traditions and consensus of the nation. Natural law is generally reserved for those unusual cases where the political branches, backed by community consensus, embark on a course of serious injustice.

Clarence Thomas appears to mix these stands judiciously. He has stated that "[i]n interpreting the Constitution, I would apply the approaches which the Supreme Court has used and I would be governed by Supreme Court precedents on those matters that come before me as a judge." He has never invoked natural law in a judicial opinion. His discussions of natural law have been in the context of academic arguments that the Constitution must be understood in light of the natural law principles held by the Founders.

Sociological Theory

Sociological theory is the principal legal theory developed during the 20th century. It views law as society's response to economic, political, historic, and social pressures. For example, in the late 19th century, the United States and many countries in western Europe reacted to the social turmoil that accompanied the Industrial Revolution by passing laws and using legal institutions to provide remedies for those in need. Antitrust laws restricted certain anticompetitive business practices, and child labor laws limited the use of children as workers in factories and offices. Sociological theorists believe the legal system and laws of a society are closely integrated into its social structure. They reject both the relationship between law and logic suggested by legal positivists and the universal truths of natural law. Instead, the law is examined and understood by observing how the law operates in society's legal institutions.

Sociological theory inspired several important concepts of 20th century legal thought. For example, the focus on the interaction between law and society recognizes that both society and laws are dynamic. Society changes as the balance of power shifts between various interests. Laws, in turn, change to reflect the changes taking place in society. Conversely, the legal system and the laws also influence society. Law can resolve conflicts between public and private interests or between the interests of groups and individuals. Because law can balance competing interests in a society, it can be used to assert social control. A society's governmental authorities use law to encourage, direct, change, or repress certain behavior. For example, tax law makes retirement earnings contributions exempt from income tax to encourage savings; licensing rules prohibit other behaviors as harmful or unprofessional conduct (selling real estate without a license); and criminal laws impose penalties such as fines and jail sentences to discourage socially undesirable conduct.

Legal Realism Theory

Legal realism theory is a variation of the sociological theory. Both consider law and legal institutions as reflections or implementations of economic, political, and social influences. However, legal realists are more concerned with how the legal system actually operates than with the more theoretical relationship between laws and the interests of society. Oliver Wendell Holmes's definition of law illustrates the legal realist point of view: "The prophecies of what the courts will do in fact, and nothing more pretentious, are what I mean by the law." To the legal realist, the law is determined not just by looking at a written statement, but also by examining the behavior of judges, lawyers, police officers, sheriffs, and administrative enforcement personnel in the legal system. The legal realist views law not as a mere set of established rules, but as a system of rules that fluctuate as the people in the legal system and the society itself change.

The legal realist studies the actions of legal officials rather than either existing or normative rules. Therefore, no unified concept of law underlies the theory of legal realism. Instead, the realist is concerned with the operation of an ever-changing legal system. Article 2 of the Uniform Commercial Code (UCC) reflects adherence to this philosophy of law. The UCC was drafted on the basis of observed business practices, and it mandates the most desirable practices of merchants. In many instances, the code requires merchants to follow "commercially reasonable" practices. Although such practices are not set in concrete and are subject to change, the UCC reflects the legal realist view.

The Economic School Theory

The economic school of thought was developed in 1970 by Richard Posner, a former law professor at the University of Chicago Law School and now a judge on the United States Court of Appeals for the Seventh Circuit. This theory holds that most laws may be evaluated according to economic theory since people are assumed to seek to maximize their own welfare. If you are injured in an accident, you may decide to seek compensation from the party at fault through mediation or litigation. The choice you make may depend on your view as to which forum offers you the best chance of receiving the most money.

Critical Legal Study Theory

Critical legal study theorists believe that law, like literary criticism, is the product of political and moral values. To critical legal theorists, law is not stable and predictable, but rather, is subject to interpretations by those involved in the legal system (legislators, judges, lawyers) and by ordinary people who behave according to what they believe the law means. The interpretation of law is based not only on logic and reason, but also on political and moral beliefs.

LAW AND ETHICS

Both law and ethics prescribe guidelines for behavior. Some people believe that obeying the law means they are also behaving ethically. Others believe that laws establish minimum standards whereas a system of ethics may actually impose stricter obligations. Thus, some argue that in certain situations, ethical standards may require people to violate the law. As Figure 1–1 notes, legal actions may be unethical and illegal actions may be ethical. For example, the principle of civil disobedience, as practiced by Mahatma Ghandi and Martin Luther King, Jr., is based on the belief that people should actively oppose unethical laws.

Although law and ethics are closely related, both reflecting moral judgments, they are fundamentally different. Legal rules require all people to follow certain clearly defined standards or face explicit consequences. If we violate criminal rules, we could be prosecuted and imprisoned. If we do not adhere to contract requirements, our agreements may

FIGURE 1–1
The Interplay of Laws and Ethics

	Legal actions (L)	Illegal actions (I)
Ethical actions (E)	(L) + (E)	(I) + (E)
Unethical actions (U)	(L) + (U)	(I) + (U)

be unenforceable and of little value. Ethical standards, by contrast, are subjectively determined on an individual and institutional basis. Unethical behavior often goes unpunished by society. In some groups unethical behavior is tolerated or accepted; in others, it is frowned upon and discouraged.

One of the areas in which the relationship between law and ethics arises concerns the imposition of a legal duty to provide information or even assistance. Consider the following ethical dilemmas.

ETHICAL DILEMMA

Today, some parties on both sides of the pro-life/pro-choice abortion debate believe so strongly in their positions that they are willing to violate the law. Pro-life advocates have chained themselves to the entrance of clinics where legal abortions are performed in order to prevent those abortions from taking place. Pro-choice activists in some jurisdictions are subject to laws that require clinics not to provide abortion information to pregnant clients; the activists nevertheless provide that information because they believe their ethical duty overrides the legal rules they are supposed to follow. Do you think it is acceptable to violate laws if ethical action is promoted in doing so? Are the actions of pro-life and pro-choice activists ethical?

Next, consider a chemical plant outside the United States. Some employees are exposed to toxic substances on a daily basis. Does the U.S. firm that is the controlling owner of the foreign plant have a legal duty to warn the foreign employees of the potential danger from the toxic chemicals? Should the firm consider laws of the United States or the foreign country or both? Is there an ethical obligation even if there is no legal duty?

Finally, say you are walking along a beach on a small lake when you spot a person in the water about 100 meters from shore. As you look closer, you see that the person in the water appears to be drowning. You look around, see no one else nearby, and knowing that you are a good swimmer and that the water is not too cold or too deep, you consider whether to rescue the drowning person who you now hear crying for help. Do you have a legal obligation to begin the rescue? If you begin the rescue, whether you have to or not, does the law impose on you a duty of care? Do you think the law would be the same in the United States as it is in another country, such as the Netherlands? Do you have an ethical duty to help the drowning person who is a complete stranger to you?

ETHICAL ANALYSIS

Ethics is a field of philosophy that examines motives and actions from the perspective of moral principles. *Morality* refers to human behavior that is found to be good and just. *Moral reasoning* involves the process of moving from premises to conclusions in determining the right course of action. The moral principles that form the basis for evaluating behavior are generally drawn from several different sources. Religious principles, such as the Golden Rule, the Ten Commandments, or similar precepts from the Buddhist or Muslim religions, frequently provide the starting point from which ethical analysis proceeds. Other ideals come from principles espoused by philosophers.

Like legal analysis, ethical analysis involves studying concepts and theories and applying them to particular situations. Ethical analysis cannot be accomplished simply by instinctively trying to determine what is right. Instead, using ethical theories, you must ask questions, examine alternatives, and seek solutions that coincide with ethical goals. Several ethical theories exist, each of which determines what is good or right in a different manner. It is up to you to determine which approach will be most helpful to guide you in different situations.

Even people who follow the same approach may apply moral standards to specific problems in different ways. Some people argue that because different cultures have varied customs and moral codes, no universal moral truth can be defined. According to this view, a practice that is considered morally wrong in one society may be commonly accepted in another. Critics voice strong objections to this belief. If, for example, there is discrimination based on race in South Africa, is the practice acceptable because it is permitted and approved by the dominant group in that country? From either viewpoint, ethical truths are conclusions that are backed by reasons and values, not merely subjective opinions of good and bad.

Two important ethical theories influence the formation of our moral concepts today. They are the teleological, or consequence-oriented, utilitarian theory and the deontological, or duty-based, universalism theory.

Utilitarian Theory

Utilitarian theory examines the consequences of a given action and defines an action as morally right and ethical if it produces the greatest amount of good for the greatest number of people. In order to reach this goal, there must be agreement on what is good and on the number of people affected by different actions. Different philosophers have reached varying conclusions about what is good (individual happiness, the common good, or material wealth) and about the number of people affected (focusing on those most directly affected, on anyone even slightly affected by a given act, or on no one being worse off).

The utilitarian does not focus on the inherent correctness of a given action, but rather, examines its consequences. In order to maximize the good from a given action or course of conduct, we must measure the costs and benefits from possible alternative activities. Thus, the utilitarian ethical analysis may require the performance of a societal cost-benefit analysis. Consider the decision to close a plant in Ohio and invest in a new one in South Carolina. This action may permit the company to produce at a lower cost, benefiting its customers. If production expands, the company may provide more employment, though at lower wages, and increase profit for the firm, its managers, and its owners. These benefits may outweigh the adverse affect on the community in Ohio, the Ohio workers, and the company's suppliers in that region.

Utilitarian theory is the dominant ethical theory used in business today. When used at the microlevel of the firm rather than at the macrolevel of the society, the firm seeks to maximize the benefit to the firm without considering the effects of its actions on society. Theories that focus on the consequences of actions, as does utilitarian theory, are known as teleological theories. There are no basic principles of good or right; good is determined by maximizing the good consequences of an action and minimizing the bad ones.

Kantian or Universal Theory

The second major ethical theory is referred to as the **Kantian or universal theory.** Immanuel Kant (1724–1804) is commonly considered the father of modern philosophy.

Unlike the utilitarian, Kant did not look at the consequences of actions to determine if they were ethical. Instead, Kant argued that a commitment to universal principles (the categorical imperative) should guide people. He believed that actions are moral only if those actions can be undertaken by everyone in good conscience. Thus, your actions should be guided by determining if your conduct could serve as the standard for universal conduct.

The Golden Rule exemplifies this duty-based standard: You are to act in the way you expect others to act toward you. Kant also focused on ends rather than means. Other people should be treated as individuals with worth, not as means to an end. This duty-based theory is known as a deontological theory. Conduct should be guided not by looking at its resulting consequences, but rather, by whether it coincides with pre-existing duties. Consider a business situation. What is ethical behavior for a person who sells a product knowing of some defect in it? Kant would examine the need for the seller to disclose to a potential buyer what he or she knows about the product by asking universal-based questions:

Using Kantian Ethical Analysis

1. Would I want everyone, regardless of the product being sold, to be able to refrain from disclosing what they know about a defect in the product? Does it matter what product is being sold, whether it is a used car with defective brakes, a ladder with a defective rung or step, or a bookshelf that lacks support on one of its shelves?
2. Would I want the principle of nondisclosure applied if I were the buyer instead of the seller?
3. Am I treating the other people involved (the buyer) as an end, according them respect, not as a means (to achieve a sale and profit for me.)

Business Ethics

Business ethics can be viewed as an application of traditional ethical analysis to business decisions. However, although decisions made by individuals in a business organization obviously affect that organization's actions, a business organization often has its own history, tradition, rules, and ethical standards. The actions of a business firm may be influenced by values, interests, and principles that differ from those of its individual managers. Ethical analysis, therefore, can sometimes be difficult to implement in a business context. Problems arise in: (1) identifying common values within a firm or industry, (2) deciding how much emphasis to place on collective benefits, (3) projecting side effects, and (4) defining the extent of a firm's responsibilities to outside groups.

Numerous business decisions require managers not only to know the law, but to make ethical decisions as well. For example, a beer manufacturer had planned to target its advertising for selling a beer with a high alcoholic content in predominantly low-income neighborhoods. By using such terms as "bold" and "high-performance," the manufacturer sought to increase sales of the product to consumers who might want a little extra "kick" from the beer. The campaign promised additional sales and profit, but were the ethical aspects of the advertising aimed at low-income consumers and distributed only in certain neighborhoods sufficiently analyzed? How would a universalist or a utilitarian analyze this venture? McDonald's offers a lean hamburger that has lower fat content and cholesterol than its other menu items. Did McDonald's respond to the marketplace's demand for such items, or did it determine what it should try to offer and then have the market respond?

Public opinion regarding the honesty and ethical standards of business executives, politicians, and even religious leaders has become less favorable in recent years. For example, in the United States, people recently have read about several scandals: insider trading by Wall Street executives (the Boesky and Milken cases), the receipt of campaign contributions that may have influenced important decisions by leading politicians (the Keating Five), and the misuse of funds by ministry representatives (Jim and Tammy Bakker of the PTL). The allegations regarding the fraud, deception, bribery, money laundering, and even assaults and murders by people associated with the bank formed by a Pakistani financier (BCCI) involve both legal and ethical violations.

TEXTUAL TREATMENT OF ETHICS

Law is often based on ethics. The area of business ethics is a growing concern to the public and to lawmakers. Therefore, it is important for future business managers to be able to examine the relationship between their actions and ethical standards. This text uses three approaches to study business ethics. First, this chapter provides an overview of the relationship between law and ethics that should guide your reading of cases and text material in later chapters. Second, the text incorporates ethical dilemmas pertaining to particular legal areas into the chapters and includes end-of-chapter ethical exercises. Third, Chapter 22 is devoted to a discussion of corporate social responsibility and business ethics. After reviewing the laws noted throughout the text, this final chapter provides an opportunity to summarize the social and business ethics problems that influence the legal environment of business.

SUMMARY

The study of law involves the study of court cases and textual materials. The law plays an important role in all societies, and its role in the United States is very significant. Law affects both personal and business activities. In the business world, an understanding of the legal environment of business is vital for managers taking part in financing, advertising, product development, and human resource decisions. The legal environment of business concerns not only the rules of law, with particular attention to the areas in which there is significant regulation of business conduct, but also the study of legal institutions and legal processes affecting business activities.

Legal analysis combines inductive reasoning, based on individual case study, with deductive reasoning, which focuses on general legal concepts. By looking at numerous similar specific cases, you can inductively formulate general principles, and by examining general concepts and applying them to different situations, you can deduce whether the general principles are indeed valid. This text incorporates a variety of items so that the reader can use the SQ3R method of study. In this method, you survey and formulate questions about the material, read the assigned material, recite questions and answers about your reading, and review what you have read. The cases in the text can be studied by preparing a brief that contains the important elements of the court's decisions. Your brief should include the facts, the central issue, the holding, the rationale, and for some cases, a dissent and commentary.

A number of theories attempt to explain the nature

of law. Natural law theory sees law as ordained by nature and separate from the customs of a particular society. Legal positivism theory emphasizes both the commands of the sovereign power and the analysis of law based on its application and enforcement in particular situations. Sociological theory views law and legal systems as an inherent part of a society, whereas the legal realism theory views law as emerging from the existing legal institutions of a society.

Both law and ethics prescribe guidelines for behavior. Ethics is concerned with examining motives and actions from the perspective of moral principles. Religious precepts and philosophical theories are common sources of such principles. Among the most influential ethical theories are utilitarian theory, which looks at the consequences of actions to determine their costs and benefits, and the Kantian or universalist theory, which examines whether moral standards can be universalized. Business ethics can be viewed as an application of traditional ethical analysis to business decisions. Because business organizations often have their own history, tradition, and values, the actions of a business firm may be influenced by values that differ from those of its managers.

KEY TERMS

law, p. 5
legal environment of business, p. 6
inductive reasoning, p. 7
stare decisis, p. 7
deductive reasoning, p. 8
brief, p. 9
appellant, p. 11
appellee, p. 11
plaintiff, p. 11
defendant, p. 11
citation, p. 11
ethics, p. 17
utilitarian theory, p. 18
universal theory, p. 19

CHAPTER EXERCISES

1. Give three definitions of law, and give an example of the application of each.

2. Write a short statement describing each of the legal theories discussed in the text. Give an example illustrating the views of each theory.

3. Three sailors and a cabin boy were adrift in an open lifeboat, 1,000 miles from land. On the 20th day, having been without food for 9 days and without water for 7 days, two of the sailors killed the cabin boy, who was in a very weak condition. He would probably have died had he not been killed. The three sailors ate his body and drank his blood for three days. Four days later, the sailors were rescued, and the two who killed the cabin boy were subsequently tried for murder. How do you decide this case as the judge? Under what jurisprudential theory? (*Regina v. Dudley & Stephens,* 14 Q.B.D. 273, 1884).

4. Describe each of the elements of a case brief. What is the citation? What terms are used to describe the parties involved in a case?

5. What is the difference between deductive and inductive reasoning? How is each used in the study of law?

6. Mary, a sixteen-year-old high school student, had an opportunity to sing with a small band. To enhance her singing abilities, she entered into a contract with Mrs. Thompson for a course of vocal music lessons. The lessons were scheduled to occur for fifteen weeks, and Mary agreed to pay Mrs. Thompson $1,500. She paid $500 at the beginning and was to pay the remaining $1,000 when the lessons were finished. Mary quit after completing 12 lessons and notified Mrs. Thompson that she was disaffirming the contract. She asked for the $500 she had paid to be returned, but Mrs. Thomp-

son refused. Mary then sued Mrs. Thompson for the return of the $500. Assume that the law entitled Mary to have the $500 returned. Was it ethical for her to seek it? Do you think Mary had any ethical duty to pay Mrs. Thompson for the lessons she did have? Why?

7. You are the Vice-President for International Sales of A-One AirSeat Corporation, which manufactures seats used in airplanes. Recently you have been discussing your product with an airline representative from Chinan Express, the government-subsidized airplane manufacturer in a heavily populated country in Asia. In order to sell products to this firm, you need a license from the government. In your discussion with the representative from Chinan Express, you learn that if you pay a certain individual $100,000, and have him apply for the license on behalf of your firm, it is very likely that the license will be granted within two months. On the other hand, if you apply directly, it may take up to two years for your firm to obtain the license. You hope to sell over $5 million in seats to Chinan Express. The president asks what you think would be the right thing for the company to do. What would be your recommendation to the president regarding this transaction? Consider both the Kantian and utilitarian ethical theories in formulating your answer.

8. Alpha Construction Company is considering who to promote to the position of regional sales manager for its heavy equipment division, which sells equipment to firms engaged in highway construction activities. In the past, the person promoted has usually been the top sales person from the various branch offices in the region. You are the Vice-President of Human Resources and need to make a recommendation to the company's Board of Directors concerning this position. Two candidates are being considered. Bob is a good salesperson from the company's New York office, well-liked by the customers, and knows many of the salespeople who he would have the responsibility to manage. Susan has been a salesperson with the firm for six years, and for the last three years has been the top salesperson. Some of the salespeople in the region are not sure how they would like having a woman as their manager. They suggest that customers with whom the regional manager would have to meet, entertain, and negotiate may not want to do business with a woman sales manager. Who will you recommend? Use ethical analysis to explain your decision.

9. Discuss the relationship between law and ethics. Give examples of acts that may be both legal and unethical and acts that may be both illegal and ethical.

10. Solar Sights, Inc. manufactures solar panels to be used in small office buildings and residences. Although the firm can demonstrate an energy savings if there is a specified amount of sunlight on the panel, many firms are reluctant to purchase the panels because trees on neighboring property may block out the sunlight. There is no law to protect access to the sun for solar panels in any of the states in which the firm does business. Refer to four legal theories noted in the chapter and explain why you think there should or should not be such a law.

Chapter 2

LAW AND THE LEGAL SYSTEM

KEY CONCEPTS

Law performs numerous tasks in a civilized society: law maintains order, provides a place to resolve disputes, and maintains a political authority while accommodating change.

The United States has a common law legal system. Countries with a common law legal system use more deductive reasoning and a method of trial different than that used in a civil law legal system. Islamic law, which recognizes no difference between the religious and the secular aspects of life, is followed in approximately 25 countries.

Substantive laws define rights and impose duties on members of society, whereas procedural laws detail the methods by which those rights and duties are enforced.

The supremacy clause of the U.S. Constitution generally resolves conflicts between state and federal laws in favor of the federal law.

Each of the three branches of the federal government has law-making powers. As chief of the executive branch, the president has both implied and expressed powers that can serve as the basis for executive orders. The legislature makes laws through the legislative process, whereas the judicial branch makes laws by applying law from prior cases, by interpreting statutory laws, and by deciding novel cases.

The federal and state court systems generally comprise trial courts, appellate courts, and a supreme court, although particular titles may differ.

INTRODUCTION . . . PAST, PRESENT, AND FUTURE

Law is not simply a set of rules that can be classified, memorized, and written for exams or for solving specific problems. The nature of law, and our understanding of it, has changed through the ages. Codes of law date back to 2000 B.C., when Hammurabi codified the practices and rules of ancient Babylon. In the United States, law is based on the "common" law, derived from England, whereas the "civil" law in many western European countries is derived from the codified Roman law.

In the 20th century, the United States has seen many changes in both the rules and sources of law. For example, rules that a buyer had to beware of purchasing possibly defective goods were abandoned. Instead, new statutory laws and court decisions now protect consumers by imposing implied warranty obligations on sellers. Administrative agencies concerned with consumer protection, employee safety, and environmental problems provide a new source for rules and orders affecting many business activities.

Internationally, the legal system of many countries has changed dramatically in the last few years. The eastern European countries have adopted some of the property and contract concepts from the West. The former Soviet Union has split to such an extent that, as the communist system focusing on state ownership of property is being discarded, each of the republics may now have the freedom to design its own legal system. In western Europe, the European Community (EC) is close to achieving its goal of integrating the economies of its member countries and unifying its laws on product liability, product labeling, intellectual property, and consumer protection. Who could have predicted that these changes would occur so rapidly?

In the future, it seems likely that legal systems will be in a state of change worldwide. On the one hand, some countries will seek to transfer significant law-making powers to international regional organizations (European Community countries) while at the same time other areas within some nations (e.g., Yugoslavia and the former Soviet Union) will shift law-making authority from the national level to the subnational, province, state, or republic level. In the United States, the tug-of-war between those favoring deregulation and those favoring reregulation will likely continue. Although individual freedom is important in the contract and property fields, environmental hazards, financial activities, and consumer concerns will likely be subject to governmental regulation. The legal environment will continue to be a significant concern for small and large business firms as we move into the 21st century.

OVERVIEW

In the first chapter, we discussed the role of law in today's society, methods of legal and ethical analysis, and the relationship between law and ethics. In this chapter, we study the components that comprise a legal system and examine the functions that legal systems perform in a society. All legal systems have similar components, such as the presence of institutions that create, change, or interpret the law. Of course, the specific institutions and the procedural and substantive laws created in one society differ dramatically from those in societies with a different legal system. Nevertheless, all legal systems seek to perform certain tasks, such as maintaining order and providing a forum for resolving disputes. In this chapter, the multiple sources of law in the United States are analyzed to develop a better understanding of their interrelationships. To differentiate among various types of law, several classifications are presented.

THE LEGAL SYSTEM

A society's legal system comprises several components. The institutions that create or amend the laws in a society constitute one component. The complexity and method of organizing legal institutions vary greatly from one society to another. The substantive laws regulating conduct constitute a second component. Some societies allow individuals and businesses significant freedom concerning their activities, whereas others scrutinize even minor aspects of business and personal life. Procedural laws, a third component, also differ greatly among societies. For example, the U.S. legal system has numerous trial procedural laws aimed at providing fair and impartial civil and criminal trials. The trial procedural laws in some other countries are less comprehensive.

Components of a Legal System

The origin of the institutions that create or apply a society's laws presents important questions for business. Does a society establish many institutions, such as legislative bodies, administrative agencies, governmental bureaus, and judicial entities? Or does the law-making power reside in one person (a dictator, premier, or king) or in one small group (the House of Saud or the mullahs of Iran)?

A second component of a society's legal system is the **substantive law** that regulates the activities of the people in that society. As noted later in this chapter, substantive law answers fundamental questions about the rights and responsibilities of a society's members. What criminal activities are prohibited? How formal must contractual agreements be to be considered valid? What business activities are subject to government control? The scope of the substantive law's regulation of individual conduct differs according to the society's political, economic, and cultural values.

A third component of a society's legal system is the **procedural law** that enforces that society's substantive laws. Procedural law answers questions about the processes used to enforce substantive laws. Does the legal system guarantee that a person charged with a crime has the right to be represented by an attorney at a trial? Will the trial allow the accused to offer testimony? In civil disputes, are the parties required to testify? These questions concern procedural laws that are important in determining the characteristics of a society's legal system.

Common Law Legal System

The legal system of the United States is a *common law* legal system. Because this legal system originated in England, it is sometimes known as the Anglo-American legal system. Over two dozen countries, such as the United States, Australia, New Zealand, and most of Canada, use a common law legal system. In common law systems, the courts are recognized not only as interpreters of the law but also as creators of law.

Origin of the Common Law In England, the courts existed long before the legislative body known as the parliament. Furthermore, since no written constitution existed, it was the courts that first began to create, interpret, and apply laws. These interpretations, found in written court decisions, reflected local customs and practices. After the Norman Conquest in 1066, the King and his successors used the King's courts to unify the country under a common, or uniform, set of customs. The common rules applied by these courts replaced local customs and formed the basis from which the common law evolved.

***Stare Decisis* Concept** As court decisions became recognized as a primary source of law, the doctrine of *stare decisis* developed. According to this concept, a judge's decision in a case not only constitutes the interpretation and application of the law to the controversy between the litigating parties, but it also sets a precedent for future cases.

The concept of *stare decisis* brings predictability to the law. By reading a prior case based on essentially the same facts, the decision for later cases can be predicted. However, *stare decisis* is applicable only within a given court system. Thus, a decision by the Michigan Supreme Court has to be followed by lower courts in Michigan, but not by lower courts in Pennsylvania. Only the lower courts in the same jurisdiction are bound by the precedents set by a given higher court.

Even within the same court system, applying the concept of *stare decisis* is difficult. Often several precedent cases exist which bear upon some aspect of the case under consideration. For example, in the *Cohen* case that follows, both the majority and dissenting judges on the United States Supreme Court seem to be following the precedent of prior cases. They disagree, however, on which cases and concepts should guide them in deciding the case under review.

Cohen v. Cowles Media Company

111 S. Ct. 2513 (1991)
Supreme Court of the United States

During the closing days of the 1982 Minnesota gubernatorial race, Dan Cohen, an active Republican, approached reporters from two newspapers and offered to provide documents relating to a candidate in an upcoming election. Cohen made clear to the reporters that he would provide the information only if he was given a promise of confidentiality. Reporters from both papers promised to keep Cohen's identity anonymous, and Cohen turned over copies of two public court records concerning Marlene Johnson, the Democratic-Farmer-Labor candidate for lieutenant governor. The first record indicated that Johnson had been charged in 1969 with three counts of unlawful assembly, and the second that she had been convicted in 1970 of petit [petty] theft. As it turned out, the unlawful assembly charges arose out of Johnson's participation in a protest of an alleged failure to hire minority workers on municipal construction projects, and the charges were eventually dismissed. The petit theft conviction was for leaving a store without paying for $6.00 worth of sewing materials. The incident apparently occurred at a time during which Johnson was emotionally distraught, and the conviction was later vacated.

After consultation and debate, the editorial staffs of the two newspapers independently decided to publish Cohen's name as part of their stories concerning Johnson. In their stories, both papers identified Cohen as the source of the court records. . . . The same day the stories appeared, Cohen was fired by his employer.

Cohen sued the newspaper publishers in Minnesota state court, alleging fraudulent misrepresentation and breach of contract. The trial court rejected the newspapers' argument that the First Amendment barred Cohen's lawsuit; a jury awarded Cohen $200,000 in compensatory damages and $500,000 in punitive damages. The Minnesota Court of Appeals, in a split decision, reversed the award of punitive damages but upheld the $200,000 compensatory damage award. A divided Minnesota Supreme Court reversed the compensatory damages award, and Cohen appealed to the United States Supreme Court.

Justice White delivered the opinion of the Court.

The question before us is whether the First Amendment prohibits a plaintiff from recovering damages . . . for a newspaper's breach of a promise of confidentiality given to the plaintiff in exchange for information. We hold that it does not.

Respondents rely on the proposition that "if a newspaper lawfully obtains truthful information about a matter of public significance then state officials may not constitutionally punish publication of the information, absent a need to further a state interest of the highest order." That proposition is unexceptionable, and it has been applied in various cases that have found insufficient the asserted state interests in preventing publication of truthful, lawfully obtained information.

This case however, is not controlled by this line of cases, but rather by the equally well-established line of decisions holding that generally applicable laws do not offend the First Amendment simply because their enforcement against the press has incidental effects on its ability to gather and report the news. As the cases relied on by respondents recognize, the truthful information sought to be published must have been lawfully acquired.

It is therefore beyond dispute that "the publisher of a newspaper has no special immunity from the application of general laws. He has no special privilege to invade the rights and liberties of others." Accordingly, enforcement of such general laws against the press is not subject to stricter scrutiny than would be applied to enforcement against other persons or organizations.

There can be little doubt that the Minnesota doctrine of promissory estoppel is a law of general applicability. [Promissory estoppel serves as a substitute for consideration when a person makes a promise that is expected to induce another person to act based on the promise.] It does not target or single out the press. . . . The First Amendment does not forbid its application to the press.

Respondents and amici (friends of the court) argue that permitting Cohen to maintain a cause of action for promissory estoppel will inhibit truthful reporting because news organizations will have legal incentives not to disclose a confidential source's identity even when that person's identity is itself newsworthy. Justice Souter makes a similar argument. But if this is the case, it is no more than the incidental, and constitutionally insignificant, consequence of applying to the press a generally applicable law that requires those who make certain kinds of promises to keep them. . . . [W]e conclude that the First Amendment does not confer on the press a constitutional right to disregard promises that would otherwise be enforced under state law. . . . Accordingly, the judgment of the Minnesota Supreme Court is reversed, and the case is remanded for further proceedings not inconsistent with this opinion.

Justice Blackmun, with whom Justice Marshall and Justice Souter join, dissenting.

The majority concludes that this case is not controlled by the decision in *Smith v. Daily Mail Publishing Co.,* to the effect that a State may not punish the publication of lawfully obtained, truthful information "absent a need to further a state interest of the highest order." Instead, we are told, the controlling precedent is "the equally well-established line of decisions holding that generally applicable laws do not offend the First Amendment simply because their enforcement against the press has incidental effects on its ability to gather and report the news."

I do not read the decision of the Supreme Court of Minnesota to create any exception to or immunity from the laws of that state for members of the press. In my view, the court's decision is premised, not on the identity of the speaker, but on the speech itself. Thus, the court found it to be of "critical significance," that "the promise of anonymity arises in the classic First Amendment context of the quintessential public debate in our democratic society, namely, a political source involved in a political campaign." . . .

Contrary to the majority, I disregard our decision in *Hustler Magazine, Inc. v. Falwell,* to be precisely on the point. There, we found that the liability for the publication of a satirical critique violated the First Amendment. There was no doubt that Virginia's tort of intentional infliction of emotional distress was "a law of general applicability" unrelated to the suppression of speech. Nonetheless, a unanimous Court found that, when used to penalize the expression of opinion, the law was subject to the strictures of the First Amendment. . . .

The majority attempts to distinguish *Hustler* on the ground that there the plaintiff sought damages for injury to his state of mind, whereas the petitioner here sought damages "for a breach of a promise that caused him to lose his job and lowered his earning capacity."

I perceive no meaningful distinction between a statute that penalizes published speech in order to protect the individual's psychological well-being or reputational interest, and one that exacts the same penalty in order to compensate the loss of employment or earning potential. Certainly, our decision in *Hustler* recognized no such distinction. . . .

To the extent that truthful speech may ever be sanctioned consistent with the First Amendment, it must be in furtherance of a state interest "of the highest order." Because the Minnesota Supreme Court's opinion makes clear the State's interest in enforcing its promissory estoppel doctrine in this case was far from compelling, I would affirm that court's decision.

I respectfully dissent.

Case Questions

1. What was the holding of the precedent case relied on by the majority? What was the holding of the precedent cases relied upon by the dissenting judges?
2. Do you find the two precedent cases conflicting? Which do you think is more applicable to this case?
3. What right of Mr. Cohen does this case protect?

Stare Decisis and Changing Circumstances A further, limiting aspect of *stare decisis* is that in some cases, the circumstances surrounding the decision made in the earlier case may have drastically changed. Thus, the same court when faced with a similar case years later could decide to make a different decision. In such a case, the court generally expressly notes that it is overruling the prior case and it explains why. Consider, for example, the historic 1954 *Brown v. Board of Education* case in which the United States Supreme Court clearly rejects the "separate but equal" doctrine it had earlier spelled out in the 1896 *Plessy v. Ferguson* case.

> In approaching this case, we cannot turn the clock back to 1868, when the [14th Amendment to the U.S. Constitution] was adopted, or even to 1896, when *Plessy v. Ferguson* was written. We must consider public education in the light of its full development and its present place in American life throughout the Nation. . . .
>
> We come then to the question presented: Does segregation of children in public schools solely on the basis of race, even though the physical facilities and other "tangible" factors may be equal, deprive the children of the minority group of equal educational opportunities? We believe that it does.
>
> . . . Whatever may have been the extent of psychological knowledge at the time of *Plessy v. Ferguson*, this finding is amply supported by modern authority. Any language in *Plessy v. Ferguson* contrary to this finding is rejected.

Review the *Brooks* case that follows to see why the Supreme Court of Alaska changed the law regarding prenuptial agreement.

Brooks v. Brooks

733 P.2d 1044 (1987)
Supreme Court of Alaska

Leora and Vern Brooks were married on August 5, 1978. It was each party's third marriage. At the time of their divorce, the Brookses had been married approximately 5½ years. Leora was 57 and Vern 54. The Brookses had no children together, but each has adult children from prior marriages.

At the time of their divorce, Leora was a resource management officer with the state of Alaska and a licensed real estate agent. Vern was an engineer with the FAA for 22 years and worked shortly for the Coast Guard in Juneau. He is currently retired on a medical disability and receives disability benefits.

On July 31, 1978, five days before their marriage, the Brookses executed a prenuptial (or premarital) agreement. It provides in pertinent part:

> During their marriage each of them shall be completely independent of the other as to all property owned by either of them before said marriage, and shall be subject to his or her disposition as his or her separate property in the same manner as if said proposed marriage had never been celebrated. Any and all property or monies acquired after said marriage shall be considered the joint property of husband and wife and in the event of termination of said marriage shall be divided equally.

The trial court granted the Brookses a divorce . . . and held that the parties' "[pre]nuptial agreement was validly entered into" and would be "enforced in its entirety." Leora Brooks appealed to the Supreme Court contending that the trial court improperly valued some of the parties' mutual property. The Supreme Court of Alaska decided it first had to review the validity of the prenuptial agreement. "We have yet to pass upon the validity of prenuptial agreements in this state. Thus, even though neither party challenges the agreement here, we must address this threshold issue."

Burke, Justice

The traditional common law view was that prenuptial agreements in contemplation of divorce (hereinafter prenuptial agreements) were inconsistent with the sanctity of marriage and the state's interest in preserving marriage and maintaining the financial security of divorced persons. Courts uniformly viewed these agreements as inherently conducive to divorce and as allowing a husband to circumvent his legal duty to support his wife. Thus, prior to 1970, prenuptial agreements that stipulated terms regarding alimony and property settlements upon divorce were almost universally considered *void ab initio* [void from inception] as contrary to public policy. The reason prenuptial agreements were thought to promote divorce was stated in *Crouch v. Crouch,* (Tenn. App. 1964):

> [S]uch [a] contract is promotive of divorce and void on grounds of public policy. Such contract[s] could induce a mercenary husband to inflict on his wife any wrong he might desire with the knowledge that his pecuniary liability would be limited. In other words, a husband could through abuse and ill treatment of his wife force her to bring an action for divorce and thereby buy a divorce for a sum far less than he would otherwise have to pay.

The policy grounds most frequently cited by the courts were that prenuptial agreements (1) are incompatible with and denigrate the marital relation, (2) tend to facilitate and induce divorce, and (3) burden the state by casting indigent spouses on public charity.

Since 1970, however, public policy has changed markedly. With the advent of no-fault divorce laws and the changes in society such laws represent, the traditional rule has rapidly given way to the more realistic view that prenuptial agreements are not *void ab initio* but are valid and enforceable if certain standards of "fairness" are met. Although the standards vary from state to state, the following three criteria are typically considered:

1. Was the agreement obtained through fraud, duress or mistake, or misrepresentation or nondisclosure of material fact?
2. Was the agreement unconscionable when executed?
3. Have the facts and circumstances changed since the agreement was executed, so as to make its enforcement unfair and unreasonable?

If none of the above factors are present, prenuptial agreements have generally been accorded judicial recognition.

As the West Virginia Supreme Court recently noted:

> The older rule was grounded in yesteryear's sound public policy: in general, thirty years ago women did not work in the market economy; society enjoyed a consensus that favored lifetime marriage and disfavored divorce; and prenuptial agreements that limited the support obligation in favor of former wives encouraged divorce and made divorced women potential charges of the state.

Circumstances have changed dramatically in the last three decades, however . . . [T]oday 58.7 percent of all married women are gainfully employed. [W]e no longer have a society-wide consensus on the sanctity of marriage: . . . . Currently divorces are being granted at the rate of approximately 1,200,000 per year.

Today, divorce is a "commonplace fact of life." As a result there is a concurrent increase in second and third marriages, often of mature people with substantial means and separate families from earlier marriages. The conflicts that naturally inhere in such relationships make the litigation that follows even more uncertain, unpleasant, and costly. Consequently, people with previous "bad luck" with domestic life may not be willing to risk marriage again without the ability to safeguard their financial interests. In other words, without the ability to order their own affairs as they wish, they may simply forgo marriage for more "informal" relationships. "This society's staggering divorce rate can only place any reasonable person on notice that divorce is as likely an outcome of any marriage as a permanent relationship."

Prenuptial agreements, on the other hand, provide such people with the opportunity to ensure predictability, plan their future with more security, and most importantly, decide their own destiny. Moreover, allowing couples to think through the financial aspects of their marriage beforehand can only foster strength and permanency in that relationship. In this day and age, judicial recognition of prenuptial agreements most likely "encourages rather than discourages marriage." . . .

In sum, both the realities of our society and the policy reasons favor judicial recognition of prenuptial agreements. . . . Therefore, we join those courts that have recognized that prenuptial agreements legally procured and ostensibly fair in result are valid and can be enforced. "The reasoning that once found them contrary to public policy has no place in today's matrimonial law."

For the reasons set forth above, the trial court's decision is affirmed in part, reversed in part, and remanded for reconsideration not inconsistent with the instructions set forth in the body of this opinion.

Case Questions

1. Why did prior case law hold that prenuptial agreements were illegal, contrary to public policy?
2. What changes have occurred since those cases were decided?
3. What benefits could people realize if prenuptial agreements were declared generally valid and enforceable?

Civil Law Legal System

Civil law is based on written statutes or codes. Civil law legal systems can trace their origin back to around 1750 B.C., when Hammurabi codified the laws of Babylon. From that time on, Babylonian laws were derived from the codes rather than from the society's common past practices. Thus, the codification of law represents a reformation of the legal system, breaking with previous use of societal practices as a basis for the law.

Most of the civil law legal systems in the world today are based on Roman law. Although Roman law existed as early as A.D. 100, its influence was minimal for centuries. By the 18th century, however, the codified Roman law had become the basis of the legal system in over 60 countries in western Europe, Asia, South America, and Africa.

Today, many countries have a hybrid system of civil and common law. For example, in Egypt, the modern legal system is influenced by both French civil law and English common law. In addition, Islamic law, discussed later, plays an important role in Egypt's legal system.

Differences in Civil and Common Law Legal Systems

Several differences exist between common law and civil law legal systems. The civil law legal system places greater importance on the governmental or administrative interpretation of law than does the common law legal system. The common law system relies on courts to interpret the law. The trial procedures of the two systems are also different. Litigation in the civil law legal system is like an investigation conducted by all parties. The judge whose powers are inquisitorial heads the investigative team, but both attorneys have duties to assist the judge and the court in determining the facts in dispute. In contrast, the common law legal system uses an adversarial trial process. Each party looks after its own interests, and the judge acts somewhat like a neutral umpire or a referee. Neither party must divulge information that harms its own case if the opposing party does not request that information.

Finally, common law legal systems make greater use of juries than do other legal systems. Each of these characteristics is discussed in subsequent sections of this chapter.

Distinctive Features of the Common Law Legal System

1. The development of law by a system of judicial precedent (*stare decisis*).
2. The use of an adversarial trial process.
3. The use of a jury to decide issues of fact in court cases.

CLASSIFICATION OF LAW

Law can be classified in a variety of ways. Some laws fit into more than one classification. For example, contract laws are generally private, substantive civil laws.

Substantive Law and Procedural Law

Substantive law is the part of the law that defines rights and imposes on members of society the duty to respect those rights. The part of the law that details the means or methods by which those rights or duties will be enforced is known as *procedural law.*

For example, substantive law defines the elements necessary to create an enforceable contract. However, procedural law determines how that substantive law will be enforced. Will the person who seeks to enforce another person's contractual commitment be entitled to a trial? Should a jury be used at the trial? These questions can be answered by reference to procedural laws.

Criminal Law and Civil Law

Another method of categorizing laws focuses on the rights that the law seeks to protect. If the purpose of a law is to protect the society as a whole, rather than one of its members, the law is a *criminal law.* If the conduct addressed by a law is conduct that affects individuals or persons in the society, the law is a *civil law.* Essentially, civil law focuses on wrongs against individuals, whereas criminal law focuses on wrongs against the whole society.

Note that one action may involve both a criminal wrong and a civil wrong. Thus, a person accused of committing improper acts may face both a criminal case and a civil case. The two cases would involve different parties and distinct and separate problems. Furthermore, both the substantive and procedural laws involved in the civil case would differ from those involved in the criminal case. For example, some officials of defunct savings and loan firms face both criminal prosecution and civil suits. If there was criminal fraud, the state or federal government, or both, can prosecute and seek to have the officials jailed and/or fined. The officials could also face civil suits brought by shareholders of the bankrupt firms. A shareholder would sue for his or her loss, claiming the negligence of the officer caused the loss of value to the firm's stock.

Who Initiates the Case? In a criminal case, the society initiates the legal action. This happens because the society, rather than the individual victim, is the primary victim of the wrong. The commission of a crime makes all people, not just the victim of the crime, feel less safe and secure. Thus, the society acts on behalf of all of its members (including, of course, the victim). Generally, the attorney representing the society may hold the office of district attorney, prosecuting attorney, state's attorney, or U.S. attorney. In a civil case, the lawsuit is brought by an individual person who claims that his or her rights have been infringed. The individual plaintiff selects and pays an attorney to represent him or her. The society is not a party to such lawsuits between two or more of its members.

Frequently, the title of a case identifies whether it involves a criminal or civil action. A criminal case, brought by the society, will be titled *People v. Smith,* or *United States v. Smith,* or *Michigan v. Smith.* Of course, since the United States or Michigan could be either a plaintiff or a defendant in a civil case, a case with the society named as one of the parties is not always a criminal case. However most of the cases in which the society is the plaintiff are criminal cases. A civil case, on the other hand, would be titled *Jones v. Smith* or *ABC Corporation v. Smith,* because individuals or organizations are parties on both sides.

Purpose The purpose of a criminal case is to determine whether the defendant committed a criminal act and whether the court must therefore impose some punishment. A person convicted of a crime might face a fine or be sent to jail or prison. That penalty should punish the wrongdoer and help the society. The criminal may be temporarily removed from the society by imprisonment. The example of that criminal's punishment may deter would-be criminals from committing similar acts. The punishment may even rehabilitate the criminal, so that he or she will be less likely to commit future wrongs against the society.

A civil lawsuit seeks not to punish the wrongdoer, but to compensate the person who has been wronged. If Laura breaks a contractual agreement that she made with David, he may bring a civil lawsuit against her. Generally, David would seek an award of damages as a remedy. He would want the court to order Laura to pay him a sum equal to the money he lost when she did not perform as agreed in their contract. Suppose that Laura had agreed to sell David 50 desks for his furniture store, each priced at $100, or a total of $5,000, and that at the last minute she refused to sell the desks as promised. If, to get similar desks for his store, David had to pay $125 each, or a total of $6,250, his lawsuit against Laura would seek $1,250 as damages.

Differences in Substantive Laws Substantively, the law specifying what acts constitute robbery differs from the law specifying what acts must occur in order to have an enforceable contractual agreement. In criminal cases, most actions considered criminal are defined by legislative enactments, such as federal or state statutes and municipal ordinances. In civil actions, a person's rights or duties toward other persons can be based either on statutory laws or on the common law of court decisions.

Differences in Procedural Laws The procedures followed in the two types of lawsuits also differ. In the *criminal lawsuit,* the accused defendant is presumed innocent until proven guilty. The individual defendant will win unless the society can prove *beyond a reasonable doubt* that he or she committed the criminal act. In the *civil lawsuit,* it is only necessary for the plaintiff to prove the case against the defendant *by the preponderance of the evidence.* These legal standards are the *burden of proof* necessary for the prosecutor or plaintiff to win a case.

For example, suppose that in a given civil case both the amount and quality of the evidence is a little more in the plaintiff's favor than in the defendant's favor. Because a preponderance of the evidence is in the plaintiff's favor, the plaintiff would win the case. However, the same amount and quality of evidence in the plaintiff's (prosecutor's) favor in a criminal case would not be sufficient to convince a jury or a judge of the defendant's guilt beyond a reasonable doubt. Thus, the defendant, not the plaintiff, would win the criminal case. The amount and quality of evidence required of the plaintiff to win a criminal case exceeds what is required to win a civil case. The differences in these burdens of proof highlight the controversy surrounding some laws with both civil and criminal provisions. For example, the racketeering laws (RICO), discussed in Chapter 22, encourage civil suits because the burden of proof is lighter.

Common Law and Statutory Law

The terms *common law* and *statutory law* are used to indicate the general source of law within a society. Although the common law of the United States originated in the customs and practices of the people in England, today in the United States the term **common law** generally refers to the case law that results from court decisions.

Where does one find the common law? Consider the following excerpt from a famous U.S. Supreme Court case, *Erie R. Co. v. Tompkins,* 304 U.S.64 (1938):

Erie Doctrine

Except in matters governed by the Federal Constitution or by acts of Congress, the law to be applied in any case is the law of the state. And whether the law of the state shall be declared by its Legislature or by its highest court in a decision is not a matter of federal concern. There is no federal general common law. Congress has no power to declare substantive rules of common law applicable in a state whether they be local in their nature or "general," be they commercial law or a part of the law of torts. And no clause in the Constitution purports to confer such a power upon the federal courts.

Of course, there is federal common law applicable to federal questions, interpreting constitutional provisions, federal statutes, and regulations. The Erie Doctrine prohibits separate federal common law that concerns matters that states regulate.

The term **statutory law** generally refers to the laws that have been formally adopted by legislative bodies. In the United States, legislative bodies include the U.S. Congress, the state legislatures, and local city councils or commissions. Although the laws and regulations of municipal bodies are sometimes referred to more specifically as *ordinances,* they are in fact a type of statutory law.

Law and Equity

Historically, England first organized the courts solely as *courts of law* under a writ system. There was a specific writ and a specific remedy for each specified problem. If you had unusual problems or wanted a unique remedy, the law courts would not help you. As the society of England evolved, it found the rigid legal system for addressing grievances and resolving disputes unresponsive to many legitimate claims.

In response, the king of England appointed his spiritual adviser as the chancellor, and eventually separate courts known as *courts of chancery* or *equity courts* were established to hear such cases. In these courts, the judges or chancellors could decide disputes with greater discretion than that exercised by the law courts. They could base their decisions on concepts of justice and equity, not just the provisions of the law. Further, the equity courts could grant remedies not available to the law courts. The *equitable remedies,* such as specific performance or an injunction, are used when the traditional legal remedies are not adequate to serve justice.

These two systems of courts, each with their own procedures, existed for hundreds of years in England before being brought to the United States. Law and equity courts continued to exist separately for years after the United States first formed its legal system, but eventually these two types of courts were merged into one.

Today, except for the lowest level of courts, judges in federal and state courts hear both legal and equity cases. The distinction between law and equity cases, however, still has some importance in our legal system. For example, juries hear and decide law cases but not equity cases. The plaintiff seeking an equitable remedy must first prove that the normal legal remedies are inadequate to properly remedy the injury in question.

Public and Private Law

Public law concerns the relationships between people and their governments. Thus, criminal law is classified as public law because it involves a wrong against the society. Both constitutional law and administrative law, discussed in Chapters 5 and 6, are also types of public law. Constitutional law concerns the power of government to perform certain activities, whereas administrative law concerns the law-making powers of administrative agencies.

Private law concerns the relationships between individuals and firms within the society. The private law topics of property, contracts, and torts are discussed in Chapters 7–9. While private law may seem more relevant to business firms than public law, public law has become increasingly important to many businesses because it regulates and often restricts business activities.

TASKS OF A LEGAL SYSTEM

Each society organizes its legal system to perform several different tasks. The institutions and functions of the legal system vary greatly from one society to the next. In both China and Japan, for example, business institutions often provide the means for resolving disputes, whereas in the United States that function is performed primarily by the legal system. Despite the differences among the legal systems in various societies, these systems generally perform certain similar functions. Maintaining order and providing a forum for resolving disputes are functions common to most legal systems. Other common functions, such as protecting expectations and maintaining a political authority while accommodating change, are briefly noted below.

To Maintain Order

Probably the most important function of a legal system is maintaining order within the society. For example, although societies as diverse as those in Poland, South Africa, China, and the United States have different laws concerning the activities of their people, each of these societies uses the legal system to maintain order. In a society without order, people cannot function efficiently because they must spend more time and energy protecting themselves and their property than in productive pursuits.

To Provide a Forum for the Resolution of Disputes

A society's legal system usually provides methods and places for individuals and organizations to resolve disputes. Without such forums, individual quarrels or disputes may incite such violence as brute force or gang or tribal wars. In the United States, the legal system provides numerous local, state, and federal courts that assist parties in resolving their disputes. Of course, courts are not the only forums for settling disputes. Numerous alternatives that are beginning to flourish are discussed in Chapter 4.

Other Tasks

Protecting Expectations The legal system protects expectations by providing a framework of rules on which people in the society can rely. When a consumer buys a ladder, the legal system reinforces the consumer's expectation that he or she will not suffer injury because the ladder is defective. The legal system cannot guarantee that the consumer will not be injured. Instead, it requires the maker of a defective ladder to compensate the consumer who has been injured as a result of the defect. The legal system thus encourages the use of reasonable care by the ladder manufacturer while assuring the consumer that it will protect his or her expectations for the use of a nondefective ladder. The legal system may also set minimum design or performance standards for products that are to be sold in the society.

Maintaining a Political Authority In almost all societies, the legal system maintains a dominant political authority. That authority generally punishes or expels people who turn over secret governmental documents to its opponents. It may even permanently imprison or execute its opponents. In the 1980s, for example, the then established political authority in Poland and in China used the legal system to protect itself against those who sought to challenge its power. The United States tolerates significantly more political discussion and dissent than do most other countries.

Social Change Decisions of a legal institution such as a court, a state agency, or a legislative body may bring about social change because people generally support such decisions. Of course, not everyone in society agrees with each new court decision, administrative regulation, or statute. However, once a decision is made, most people generally conform their behavior to its requirements. For example, the Occupational Safety and Health Administration (OSHA) imposed new safety standards on many factories and firms. Generally, court interpretations requiring the use of safer equipment have been adhered to, even when some of the rules and interpretations do not seem to make sense in certain situations.

Similarly, in recent years state legislatures have adopted anti-abortion laws that vary rather significantly from state to state. Obviously, in each state some people believe their state law is appropriate while others think they are very wrong. Nevertheless, with few exceptions, most people within the state will follow the decision of their legislature.

ETHICAL DILEMMA

Are judges who are faced with prior cases that seem to dictate the settlement for the dispute under consideration free to ignore those decisions if they believe that the precedent cases are not well-reasoned? Under what circumstances should judges who disagree with prior court decisions ignore them or seek to distinguish them in any possible manner rather than following their holdings? Would you give different answers if the judges are on trial courts rather than on a state supreme court? Why? Suppose judges believe that the laws are "behind the times" and not current with the wishes and needs of society? Is that a reason for prior court precedents to be ignored? What about cases in which the judge believes the majority of the citizens want to follow the prior law, but the judge believes that a change should be made in that law? Is it appropriate to make changes in the law even if neither the prior cases nor the wishes of the society desire a change? What factors should be considered by judges in reviewing the applicability of precedent cases to the case under review? Do you think either the universalist or utilitarian ethical theories help in answering these questions? Why?

INTERNATIONAL PERSPECTIVE AND COMMENTARY

> "The totalitarian government has long overstayed its welcome. Reformers insist that the ruler no longer use arbitrary power. . . . Functionaries of the central government tried intimidation but the top official eventually lost the support of almost every group in society."

The introduction of the proposed legal reforms became fatal to the accepted ideology in this country.

If asked to identify when these comments were made and what they were discussing, most people would think of the former Soviet Union. However, the commentary, which is from *The Wall Street Journal,* in fact refers to a different era and concerns a different country. A further portion of this article appears below:

Soviet Coup Blocked the Planned All-Union Runnymede

. . . The place was Runnymede in England, the year was 1215 and it was King John who was forced to submit to the Magna Carta and its revolutionary idea of legalized political and economic liberty. The king's promises included more power to regional lords, trials by juries of peers, due process and a ban on expropriation of private property. . . .

The closest the Soviets ever came to the Magna Carta was scheduled for last week, when the All-Union Treaty was supposed to be signed. The treaty was canceled during the coup that couldn't. . . . It hasn't been widely noted that the treaty and implementing laws also threatened the power of the Communist Party by introducing counterrevolutionary legal reform.

The treaty would have been the first Soviet charter of rights for the people, not for the state. The treaty, which does not mention the word socialism, would have created a new Union of Soviet Sovereign Republics. The republics and central government would pledge to "create a rule-of-law state which would serve as a guarantor against any tendencies to totalitarianism and arbitrariness." . . .

. . . These legal reforms may have posed an even greater threat to totalitarian rule than the treaty plan to spread power to the republics. It's one thing to lessen the grip of Moscow, it's another also to strip local party officials of their arbitrary power to block licenses, jail "black marketers" or seize property.

By blocking the All-Union Treaty, the hard-line communists gambled that they could block the double whammy of a rule of law that protects private property. Instead, many republics now refuse to join any union, confederation or commonwealth for fear that some other group of communists will again try to block reforms. It's no wonder many leaders of the republics and democratic parliamentarians this week asked why there should be a Soviet Anything.

. . . [T]he coup plotters were entirely right to understand that introducing modern legal concepts to the Soviet Union would be fatal to communism. Assuming that the Communist Party's over, it will be fascinating to watch the newest adherents to the rule of law join the Western world.

L. Gordon Crovitz, "Soviet Coup Blocked the Planned All-Union Runnymede," *The Wall Street Journal,* August 28, 1991.

SIGNIFICANT CHARACTERISTICS OF U.S. LEGAL SYSTEM

The U.S. Constitution provides the framework for the organization of the U.S. legal system. Two significant characteristics determine which governmental authority has law-making powers in a given situation. **Federalism** is the division of powers among federal, state, and local governments. The **separation of powers** is the splitting of law-making authority among the three branches of government: legislative, judicial, and executive. Each branch has separate powers to perform its specific functions and each provides checks and balances on the other branches. Together, these characteristics shape the sources of law in the U.S. legal system. The legislative, executive, and judicial branches, along with administrative agencies, constitute the four sources of law in the U.S. legal system.

The U.S. Constitution determines whether the state or federal legal system has the law-making powers to handle particular problems. Each state also has a constitution that describes the organization of its government and legal system. Although state constitutions differ in many ways, each separates the powers of governmental branches and preserves federalism by dividing power between the central state authority and local units of government, such as cities and counties.

Federalism

The term *federalism* describes a dual form of government, in which powers are divided between the states and the federal government. Before the Constitution was signed, state governments had shared law-making powers under a confederative form of government. Soon after the Revolutionary War, however, the states began to experience problems in building a common defense, conducting foreign affairs, and maintaining economic stability. Nevertheless, the states did not want to return to a strong central government like the one that had ruled over the colonies. Their compromise solution created a federalist government dividing law-making powers between the states and the central federal government.

Businesses and individuals often find this sharing of law-making authority confusing. What if there are different laws at the state and federal level or at the state and local level? Sometimes rules from different sources impose conflicting requirements. For example, the federal Environmental Protection Agency monitors air pollution emitted by new plants. However, state or local laws generally impose conditions on the construction of new plants and factories. These two sources of law may impose inconsistent requirements regarding the construction of new plants. Another example concerns corporate

FIGURE 2–1 Sharing of Federal and State Law-Making Powers

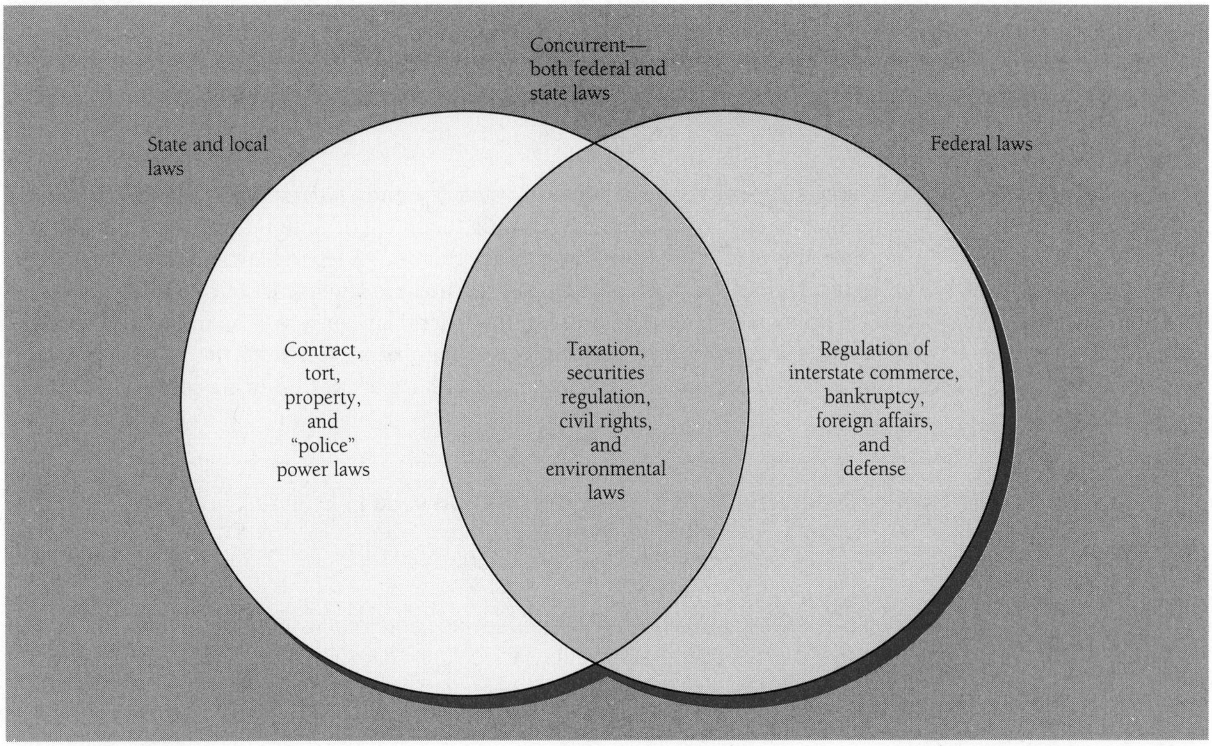

directors. While state law governs their actions, that law is not displaced by the federal law regulating investment advisers, even if those advisers are also directors of a corporation.

Despite the problems that result from the existence of two major legal systems, federalism has substantial benefits. First, state legal systems can deal with many problems within the states more effectively than can a distant federal government. Second, the division of power between the state and federal legal systems reduces the authority of each system. Consequently, special interest groups are less likely to dominate at all levels of those legal systems. Figure 2–1 illustrates the sharing of law-making powers between the federal and state legal systems.

Federal Supremacy

Sometimes a state law conflicts with a federal law. As a result, the state law may be preempted or nullified by the federal law. However, since state and local laws may have purposes other than those of federal laws or regulations, both sources of law may be enforced in certain circumstances. In such cases, the fact that a business complies with federal law generally does not exempt it from also meeting the separate requirements imposed by state and local law.

Where Congress enacts a statute or enters into a treaty with another country or where, pursuant to congressional mandate, a federal administrative agency regulates a specific activity, the supremacy clause of the U.S. Constitution prohibits state law from contradicting federal law.

The Supremacy Clause of the U.S. Constitution

This Constitution, and the Laws of the United States, which shall be made in Pursuance thereof; and all Treaties made, or which shall be made, under the Authority of the United States, shall be the supreme Law of the Land.

The existence of a conflict between a state law and a federal law is not always obvious. Courts analyze such conflicts by examining the intent of Congress in passing a statute or in authorizing an administrative agency's regulation. A federal law *preempts* a state law if a court determines that there was legislative intent to supersede state law. The intent may be based on explicit language found in the federal law, or it may be implicitly contained in the structure and purpose of the federal regulation. Consider the following case involving a federal regulation that conflicted with a state of California court decision.

Fidelity Federal Savings & Loan Association v. de la Cuesta

458 U.S. 141 (1982)
United States Supreme Court

The Federal Home Loan Bank Board, which regulates savings and loan associations, passed a regulation that permitted the associations to include "due-on-sale" clauses in their home mortgage loans. These clauses permit the lending association to require a homeowner who sells a home to pay the full loan balance to the association at that time. The homeowner is not permitted to transfer his or her mortgage liability to the buyer of the home without the association's consent.

A California case, *Wellenkamp*, had prohibited savings and loan associations in that state from enforcing such clauses. Therefore, buyers could assume the seller's mortgage without the lender's consent. If the interest rate charged the seller was lower than the interest rates prevailing when the buyer purchased, the buyer could lock in that lower interest rate. Fidelity Federal sought to enforce a due-on-sale clause in de la Cuesta's mortgage when he sold his home. The case then made its way to the United States Supreme Court to determine if the federal regulation preempted the state of California law.

Justice Blackmun delivered the opinion of the Court.

The pre-emption doctrine, which has its roots in the Supremacy Clause, requires us to examine congressional intent. Pre-emption may be either express or implied, and "is compelled whether Congress' command is explicitly stated in the statute's language or implicitly contained in its structure and purpose."

Absent explicit pre-emptive language, Congress' intent to supersede state law altogether may be inferred because "[t]he scheme of federal regulation may be so pervasive as to make reasonable the inference that Congress left no room for the States to supplement it," because "the Act of Congress may touch a field in which the federal interest is so dominant that the federal system will be assumed to preclude enforcement of state laws on the same subject," or because "the object sought to be obtained by federal law and the character of obligations imposed by it may reveal the same purpose."

Even where Congress has not completely displaced state regulation in a specific area, state law is nullified to the extent that it actually conflicts with federal law. Such a conflict arises when "compliance with both federal and state regulations is a physical impossibility," or when state law "stands as an obstacle to the accomplishment and execution of the full purposes and objectives of Congress."

These principles are not inapplicable here simply because real property law is a matter of special concern to the States: "The relative importance to the State of its own law is not material when there is a conflict with a valid federal law, for the Framers of our Constitution provided that the federal law must prevail."

Federal regulations have no less pre-emptive effect than federal statutes. Where Congress had directed an administrator to exercise his discretion, his judgments are subject to judicial review only to determine whether he has exceeded his statutory authority or acted arbitrarily.

When the administrator promulgates regulations intended to pre-empt state law, the court's inquiry is similarly limited:

> "If [h]is choice represents a reasonable accommodation of conflicting policies that were committed to the agency's care by the statute, we should not disturb it unless it appears from the statute or its legislative history that the accommodation is not one that Congress would have sanctioned."

Thus, we conclude that the Board's due-on-sale regulation was meant to pre-empt conflicting state limitations on the due-on-sale practices of federal savings and loans, and that the California Supreme Court's decision in *Wellenkamp* creates such a conflict.

Case Questions

1. What is the conflict between the federal regulation and the state law in this case?
2. Why does the Court determine whether a federal regulation was intended to pre-empt state law?

Shared Law-Making Authority Even though there may be both federal and state laws affecting a particular activity, on some occasions, courts find the federal law does not intend to crowd out or preempt the state law. In these areas of concurrent jurisdiction, both state and federal laws may exist together. For example, there are federal and state laws regulating taxation, antitrust, environmental, work safety, and securities matters. The federal legislation in these areas permits the states to also make and enforce laws that must be followed. Thus, a person who violates an antitrust law or an environmental requirement could, in some cases, be found liable in both federal and state courts. In other cases, the enforcement of shared laws is the responsibility of either the federal or the state regulators.

You may recall that in the *Cohen* case on page 27, the court was faced with a question of whether the first amendment's free speech provision crowded out a state law allowing for damages resulting from broken contractual agreements. The majority of that court concluded the federal law there did not displace the state law.

Separation of Powers

The government's powers, at both the federal and state levels, are separated into the executive, legislative, and judicial branches. Each branch is authorized to exercise only the powers that it possesses. Generally, the legislative branch makes the law, the judicial branch interprets the law, and the executive branch executes and enforces the law. The separation of powers is designed to provide checks and balances among the three branches of government. The framers of the Constitution included this principle because there was little accountability by the despotic English crown to the American colonies. Although checks and balances are cumbersome and inefficient at times, they prevent tyranny by any one branch of government.

No one branch has enough power to dominate the entire government. Each branch exercises some powers over the other branches, so that a checking mechanism exists. For

FIGURE 2–2 Separation of Powers in the Federal Legal System

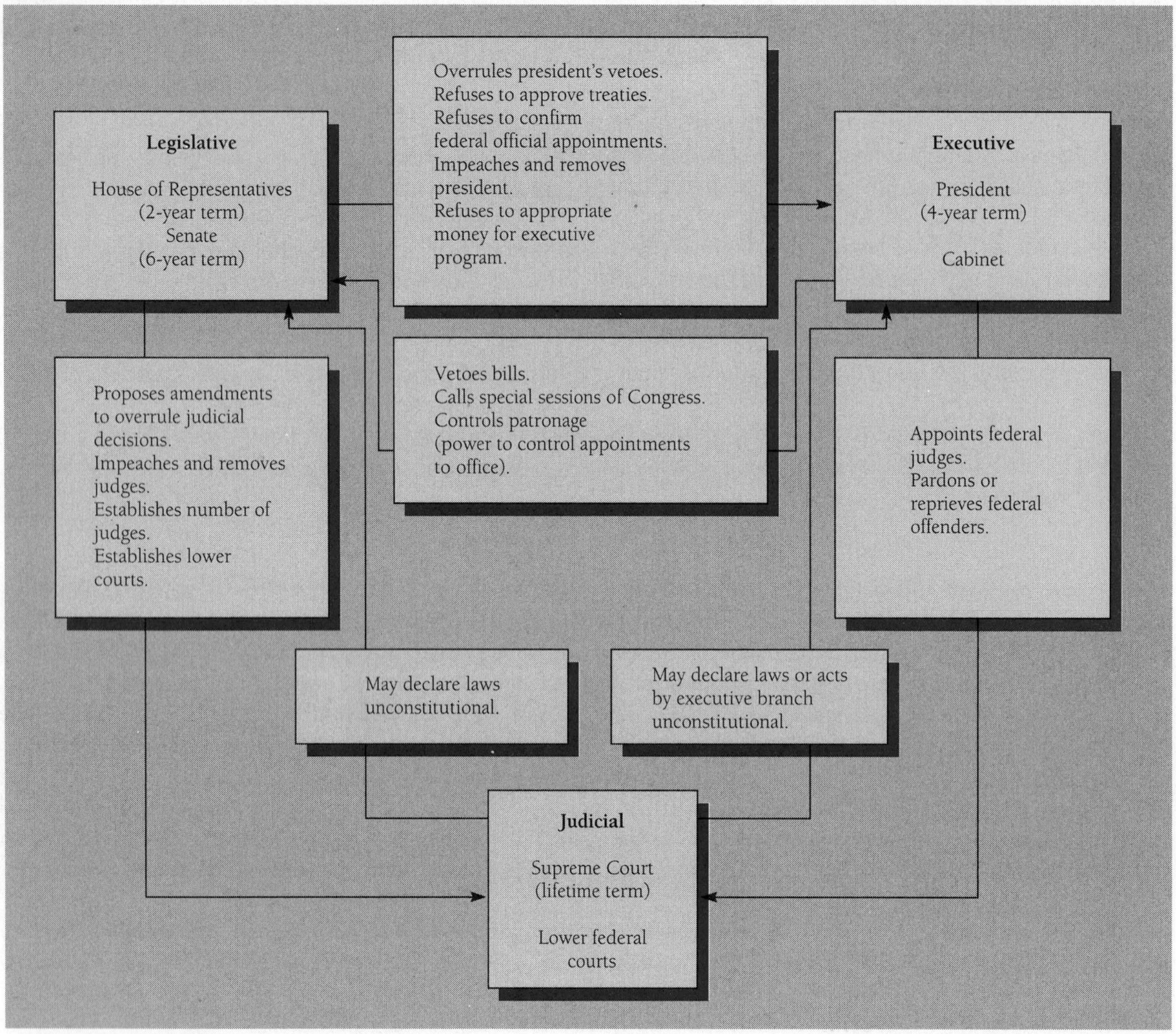

example, as Figure 2–2 portrays, the president, as chief of the executive branch, can veto the laws passed by the legislative branch. The legislative branch confirms many federal officials, has the "power of the purse," and can refuse to appropriate money for a program that the executive branch wants to encourage. The judicial branch has the authority to interpret and even declare void unconstitutional laws enacted by the legislative branch.

The principle of the separation of powers has been used to restrict the actions of both the legislative and executive branches of the federal government. In the case that follows, the Supreme Court examined a federal statute that granted significant budget-cutting authority to the comptroller general. Several congressmen claimed that since the comptroller is under congressional control, he could not perform executive branch functions without violating the separation of powers.

Bowsher v. Synar

478 U.S. 714 (1986)
United States Supreme Court

This case arose when Congress passed the Balanced Budget and Emergency Deficit Control Act of 1985 in an attempt to balance the federal budget. That law requires the comptroller general (Bowsher) to prepare a report projecting the federal budget deficit so that the spending reductions necessary to reach annual budget reduction targets could be made. The law gave the comptroller general the ultimate authority to determine the budget cuts to be made if Congress could not agree on them. Congressman Synar asserted that the law violated the separation of powers. He argued that the comptroller general, who was under the control of Congress, could not be given executive branch functions, such as determining how much spending to cut from the federal budget. The trial court held for Synar, and Bowsher appealed.

Burger, Chief Justice

. . . We noted recently that "[t]he Constitution sought to divide the delegated powers of the new Federal Government into three defined categories, Legislative, Executive, and Judicial." The declared purpose of separating and dividing the powers of government, of course, was to "diffus[e] power the better to secure liberty." Justice Jackson's words echo the famous warning of Montesquieu, quoted by James Madison in The Federalist No. 47, that " 'there can be no liberty where the legislative and executive powers are united in the same person, or body of magistrates'. . . ."

Even a cursory examination of the Constitution reveals the influence of Montesquieu's thesis that checks and balances were the foundation of a structure of government that would protect liberty. The Framers provided a vigorous and legislative branch and a separate and wholly independent executive branch, with each branch responsible ultimately to the people. The Framers also provided for a judicial branch equally independent with "[t]he judicial Power . . . extend[ing] to all Cases, in Law and Equity, arising under this Constitution, and the Laws of the United States." Art. III, § 2.

Other, more subtle, examples of separated powers are evident as well. Unlike . . . parliamentary systems, the President, under Article II, is responsible not to the Congress but to the people, subject only to impeachment proceedings which are exercised by the two Houses as representatives of the people. Art. II, § 4. And even in the impeachment of a President, the presiding officer of the ultimate tribunal is not a member of the legislative branch, but the Chief Justice of the United States. Art. I, § 3.

That this system of division and separation of powers produces conflicts, confusion, and discordance at times is inherent, but it was deliberately so structured to assure full, vigorous, and open debate on the great issues affecting the people and to provide avenues for the operation of checks on the exercise of governmental power.

The Constitution does not contemplate an active role for Congress in the supervision of officers charged with the execution of the laws it enacts. The President appoints "Officers of the United States" with the "Advice and Consent of the Senate. . . ." Article II, § 2. Once the appointment has been made and confirmed, however, the Constitution explicitly provides for removal of Officers of the United States by Congress only upon impeachment by the House of Representatives and conviction by the Senate. An impeachment by the House and trial by the Senate can rest only on "Treason, Bribery or other high Crimes and Misdemeanors." Article II, § 4. A direct congressional role in the removal of officers charged with the execution of the laws beyond this limited one is inconsistent with separation of powers.

This was made clear in debate in the First Congress in 1789. . . . This Court first directly addressed this issue in *Myers v. United States.* At issue in *Myers* was a statute providing that certain postmasters could be removed only "by and with the advice and consent of the Senate." The President removed one such postmaster without Senate approval, and a lawsuit ensued. Chief Justice Taft, writing for the Court, declared the statute unconstitutional on the ground that for Congress to "draw to itself, or to either branch of it, the power to remove or the right to participate in the exercise of that power . . . would be . . . to infringe the constitutional principle of the separation of governmental powers."

. . . [I]n Humphrey's Executor v. United States, . . . Justice Sutherland's opinion for the Court also underscored the crucial role of separated powers in our system:

> "The fundamental necessity of maintaining each of the three general departments of government entirely free from the control or coercive influence, direct or indirect, of either of the others, has often been stressed and is hardly open to serious question.". . .

In light of these precedents, we conclude that Congress cannot reserve for itself the power of removal of an officer charged with the execution of the laws except by impeachment. To permit the execution of the laws to be vested in an officer answerable only to Congress would, in practical terms, reserve in Congress control over the execution of the laws. The structure of the Constitution does not permit Congress to execute the laws; it follows that Congress cannot grant to an officer under its control what it does not possess. . . .

Appellants suggest that the duties assigned to the Comptroller General in the Act are essentially ministerial and mechanical so that their performance does not constitute "execution of the law" in a meaningful sense. On the contrary, we view these functions as plainly entailing execution of the law in constitutional terms. Interpreting a law enacted by Congress to implement the legislative mandate is the very essence of "execution" of the law. Under § 251, the Comptroller General must exercise judgment concerning facts that affect the application of the Act. He must also interpret the provisions of the Act to determine precisely what budgetary calculations are required. Decisions of that kind are typically made by officers charged with executing a statute. . . .

. . . By placing the responsibility for execution of the Balanced Budget and Emergency Deficit Control Act in the hands of an officer who is subject to removal only by itself, Congress in effect has retained control over the execution of the Act and has intruded into the executive function. The Constitution does not permit such intrusion. . . .

No one can doubt that Congress and the President are confronted with fiscal and economic problems of unprecedented magnitude, but "the fact that a given law or procedure is efficient, convenient, and useful in facilitating functions of government, standing alone, will not save it if it is contrary to the Constitution. Convenience and efficiency are not the primary objectives—or the hallmarks—of democratic government. . . ."

We conclude the District Court correctly held that the powers vested in the Comptroller General under § 251 violate the command of the Constitution that the Congress play no direct role in the execution of the laws. Accordingly, the judgment and order of the District Court are affirmed.

Case Questions

1. Is there a way to rewrite the duties of the comptroller general that would make the Act constitutionally valid?
2. If the aspect of the Act that allowed Congress to appoint and remove the comptroller general were deleted, would the law then be constitutional?
3. In designing the Constitution, why did the Founders want to separate the powers of the legislative and executive branches?
4. If the Supreme Court hands down a decision that part of a statute is unconstitutional, is the entire statute then invalid?

Role of the Jury

Another characteristic of the common law legal system is in its use of the jury. The jury is used to determine facts; the questions of law in a case are determined by a judge. Although the jury is not unique to common law legal systems, it is more prominent in common law countries than in civil law legal systems. In the United States, the jury's role

FIGURE 2–3
Arguments Advanced When Debating the Role of the Jury

Advantages of Using a Jury

- Deliberations by a jury tend to expose the biases of any one individual; the result is less biased than if only one judge were used.
- The public has become accustomed to the jury and accepts it as an integral part of the U.S. legal system.
- The law is written in general terms—reasonable doubt in criminal cases and reasonable conduct in negligence cases—and it is a jury, drawn from a cross section of the community, which can best apply those standards.
- Juries offer a sense of involvement in the legal system.
- The role of the jury balances the power of the judge.

Disadvantages of Using a Jury

- The jury selection process and trying cases to juries greatly increases the length of trials.
- A jury is no more capable of applying community standards for a particular case and party than is a judge.
- Juries have not been shown to have less bias than judges.
- Juries may be less qualified in complex and technical cases than a judge; if one or more jurors does not understand the problem, the jury's verdict may not make sense.

in both civil and criminal cases is constitutionally protected under Amendments 6 and 7. Therefore, the right to trial by jury is a fundamental right.

Historically, the jury has had an important place in the American legal system since the union's inception. The colonists brought the jury with them as a measure to prevent royal abuses in the judicial systems. The Stamp Act of 1765 stated that the trial by jury was an inherent and invaluable right of every British colonist. Then, in 1774, the First Continental Congress declared that the colonies were adopting the common law of England, including the right to be tried by a jury of one's peers.

While the right to trial by jury in the United States thus sprang from the existence of the jury in 18th-century England, the first popular use of the jury dates back to 590 B.C. in Athens, Greece. Modern critics of the jury system note the ancient origin of the jury and assert that its use as a trier of fact in today's society is outdated. They note that in modern English civil cases the jury is used only on rare occasions. The debate over the advantages and disadvantages of a jury trial usually rests on several arguments, such as those listed in Figure 2–3.

Sources of Law

As Figure 2–2 depicts, each of the three branches of government in the U.S. legal system has certain law-making powers. In addition, administrative agencies at both the federal and state levels have been created by the legislative branch and granted significant law-making authority. A review of the sources of law, therefore, must also focus on the rules and decisions coming from agencies, bureaus, and commissions at the federal, state, and local levels.

THE LEGISLATIVE BRANCH

A *legislature* is an officially selected body of persons vested with the responsibility to make laws for a political unit such as a nation or a state. The federal legislature in the United States is the Congress. Most state legislatures consist of two houses, which together have the authority to make laws known as statutes, enactments, or legislation.

The legislative process at the federal level is similar to that used in most states. Potential legislation begins when a bill is introduced in either the House of Representatives or the Senate. After a bill is introduced, it is referred to one of the specialized committees with responsibility for reviewing legislation regarding certain subjects. Most bills die when a committee refuses to take action. The committee can act on a bill by holding hearings, by submitting it to staff members for research and review, and by "marking it up," reviewing it line by line and rewriting its terms.

Once a committee recommends a bill, it is forwarded to the floor of the house of Congress in which it was introduced. The committee attaches its report, which focuses on the policy for the proposal and its intended effect. A minority report may be included if some members of the committee disagree with the majority's recommendations. The bill will be voted on in that house of Congress and if approved, it will be sent to the other house of Congress.

The other house pursues the same process: committee consideration study, review, and eventual vote by that full house. If the bills approved by each house of Congress differ, a conference committee consisting of members of both houses will seek to find a compromise that satisfies both houses. The compromise version must then be approved by votes of each house. Once both houses of Congress approve a bill, it is sent to the president for review. This is one of the checks that the executive branch has on the actions of the legislative branch.

The president may approve the bill or veto it. If the president vetoes the bill, it is returned to the house from which it originated and may be reviewed again. Congress may then seek to override the veto, but a two-thirds vote from each house of Congress is necessary for an override. During his first term, President Bush vetoed over two dozen bills sent to him by Congress; none of them was overturned by subsequent congressional action.

One other option is open to the president; he or she can take no action for a period of 10 days after receiving the bill. In that case, the bill becomes law unless Congress adjourns and thus prevents the president from returning the bill. If Congress adjourns, inaction by the president will be considered a *pocket veto,* preventing the bill from becoming law.

THE EXECUTIVE BRANCH

The executive branch consists of the chief executive (the president or state governor), the cabinet, and those administrative agencies that derive their authority from the executive. Section 1 of Article II of the Constitution states that "The executive Power shall be vested in a President of the United States of America." Other provisions of the Constitution give the president the power to make treaties (with the advice and consent of two thirds of the Senate) and the authority to act as Commander in Chief of the Armed Forces.

The *executive order* is the most common method by which the executive branch makes law. Executive orders may be based on powers expressly granted to the president, from powers implied from the Constitution, or by powers delegated to the president from the

Congress. For example, the president's authority to negotiate trade agreements with other countries is based on powers granted to the president by Congress in the Tariff and Trade Act, while the authority to send military personnel within the country, and perhaps on a limited basis outside the country, to provide assistance in times of emergency or to defend the country is based on constitutional powers. An executive order that has had significant impact on business is the executive order requiring federal contractors to take affirmative action to ensure that their employment practices are not discriminatory. This executive order is discussed in Chapter 19.

Administrative Agencies

Although administrative agencies are generally housed in the executive branch of government, they are created by the legislative branch. Agencies are frequently granted extensive law-making powers, which may include executive functions such as conducting investigations and administering governmental programs. An agency may also be granted legislative functions such as rulemaking, and judicial functions such as adjudicating individual cases or claims. Administrative agencies at the state level include the Workman's Compensation Bureau, the Secretary of State, and the Department of Commerce, while the Social Security Administration, the Customs Bureau, and the Internal Revenue Service are federal agencies which have a variety of law-making powers.

Administrative agencies must use certain uniform procedures, which are generally specified by the legislature in an Administrative Procedures Act (APA). If the required procedures are followed, the rules and regulations of the administrative agencies have the force of law. While courts may review administrative agency actions, agency decisions are often deferred to by a court exercising its judicial review. Chapter 6 discusses administrative agencies and their functions in greater detail.

THE JUDICIAL BRANCH

Article III, Section 1 of the U.S. Constitution

The judicial Power of the United States, shall be vested in one supreme Court, and in such inferior Courts as the Congress may from time to time ordain and establish.

Courts are also a source of law. However, laws emerging from the judicial branch are different from legislative acts. Whereas statutory law is usually general and prospective, the common law of court decisions is particular and retrospective. Thus, legislative bodies usually make laws affecting future norms of society, while courts make decisions affecting past events. Of course, important judicial decisions, through precedent cases, can affect many people who are not parties to an actual case.

State Judicial Systems

A court's power to hear and decide cases is referred to as its **jurisdiction**. The term jurisdiction also refers to the political entity (e.g., state) that exercises the power to hear cases. The jurisdiction of various courts, both at the state and federal levels, is established by statute. Since cases are originally heard by trial courts, these courts are courts of

FIGURE 2–4 A Multi-Level State Court System

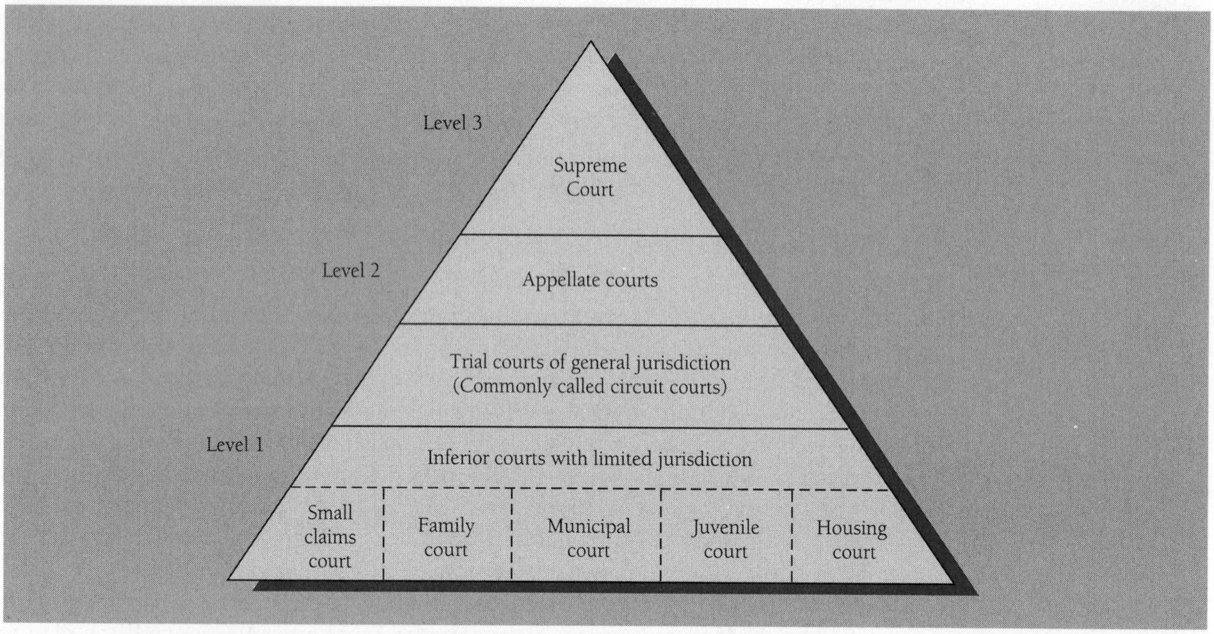

original jurisdiction. Appellate courts do not hear trials; instead, they review trial court decisions. These courts are said to have *appellate jurisdiction.* Figure 2–4 depicts a multilevel state court system. Courts at level 1 are courts with original jurisdiction, while courts at levels 2 and 3 are courts with appellate jurisdiction. Some states have fewer than 3 levels of courts and the names of courts in each level differ among the states. A trial court's jurisdiction to hear a case involves both *jurisdiction of the person* (jurisdiction over both participants) and *jurisdiction of the subject matter* (jurisdiction over the problem that a case concerns).

A general trial court has the power to hear almost any type of dispute. Thus, it has subject matter jurisdiction over almost all cases, except for minor or special disputes heard by inferior courts. Personal jurisdiction requires that the parties to the dispute be properly before the court. The plaintiff who files a complaint with a court thereby agrees to have that court resolve the dispute and grants it personal jurisdiction over the plaintiff. Personal jurisdiction over the defendant is acquired by using a document known as a *summons* to serve notice of the lawsuit on the defendant.

Most state laws allow for other methods of obtaining personal jurisdiction over the defendant. Occasionally, publication in a local newspaper provides sufficient notice to the defendant. When a potential defendant is outside the state where the court is located, a *long arm statute* is used. For example, if a citizen of Florida is involved in an accident in Michigan that injures a Michigan citizen, the Michigan long arm statute grants personal jurisdiction over the Florida defendant to a Michigan court even if summons is served on the defendant in Florida. As long as some minimum contact exists between the out-of-state defendant and the state with the long arm statute, the notification to the defendant need not take place inside the state where the court is located. Without some minimum contact, it would offend traditional notions of fairness and justice to pull an out-of-state defendant into court.

An *inferior trial court* is generally limited to hearing certain kinds of cases or minor disputes that might otherwise have to be brought into the general trial courts. For example, the district court in the Michigan judicial system hears minor criminal cases and civil disputes involving less than $10,000. This court is much like a municipal court, its jurisdiction and power being limited to a given geographic area, such as a city. Pennsylvania has a comparable court, known as the court of common pleas.

Probate courts sometimes hear juvenile cases as well as estate cases involving a deceased person's will. Some states have family courts that hear divorce and child custody cases. Traffic courts and housing courts are also inferior courts that decide only certain types of cases.

Many states have special courts to handle cases not requiring regular court proceedings. For example, a small claims court generally hears civil cases involving less than a certain dollar amount, such as $3,000. Parties usually appear in such courts without an attorney, and the decisions of these courts generally cannot be appealed. "The People's Court" television program is based on actual disputes that qualify for presentation in a California small claims court.

Federal Judicial System

As Figure 2–5 depicts, the basic three-tier system is used by the federal judiciary, with trial courts at the bottom, appellate courts in the middle, and the U.S. Supreme Court at the top. In addition to the regular three-tier courts, the federal judicial system includes several special courts, including: the Court of Claims (determines monetary claims against the United States), the Tax Court, Bankruptcy Courts, and the Court of International Trade. As these courts hear only certain types of cases, their jurisdiction is called *limited subject matter* jurisdiction.

As noted, the Supreme Court of the United States is expressly referred to in Article III of the U.S. Constitution. It hears appeals from the federal appellate courts and from the highest state courts. The Constitution also provides that a few cases, such as disputes between two states, may originate in the Supreme Court.

The federal appellate courts are called the *circuit courts of appeal.* These courts are organized into 13 circuits, spread geographically across the nation. There is one circuit for the District of Columbia, one for appeals from the Court of International Trade and the Court of Claims, and the remainder for appeals from federal trial courts within each of 11 circuits or regions encompassing several states.

At the trial level of the federal judicial system is the *federal district court.* There is at least one district court, often with numerous judges, in each state, and many states have several district courts. While state courts at the trial level can generally hear any type of dispute, the power of a federal trial court is limited. This is because its jurisdiction regarding the subject matter of disputes is limited to two basic types of cases: cases involving federal questions and cases involving diversity of citizenship.

Federal question cases focus on the source of law that governs the case. Such cases are resolved by reference to federal statutes, the U.S. Constitution, a U.S. treaty, a federal administrative regulation, or an executive order of the president.

On the other hand, *diversity of citizenship cases* focus on the parties' citizenship, regardless of the nature of their problem. Such cases require all plaintiffs to have state citizenships diverse or different from those of all defendants. Diversity of citizenship cases also require that the damages being sought exceed $50,000. A corporation is considered a citizen of either the state where it was incorporated or where it has its principal place of business. Thus, the General Motors Corporation, incorporated in Delaware, could

FIGURE 2–5 The Federal Judicial System

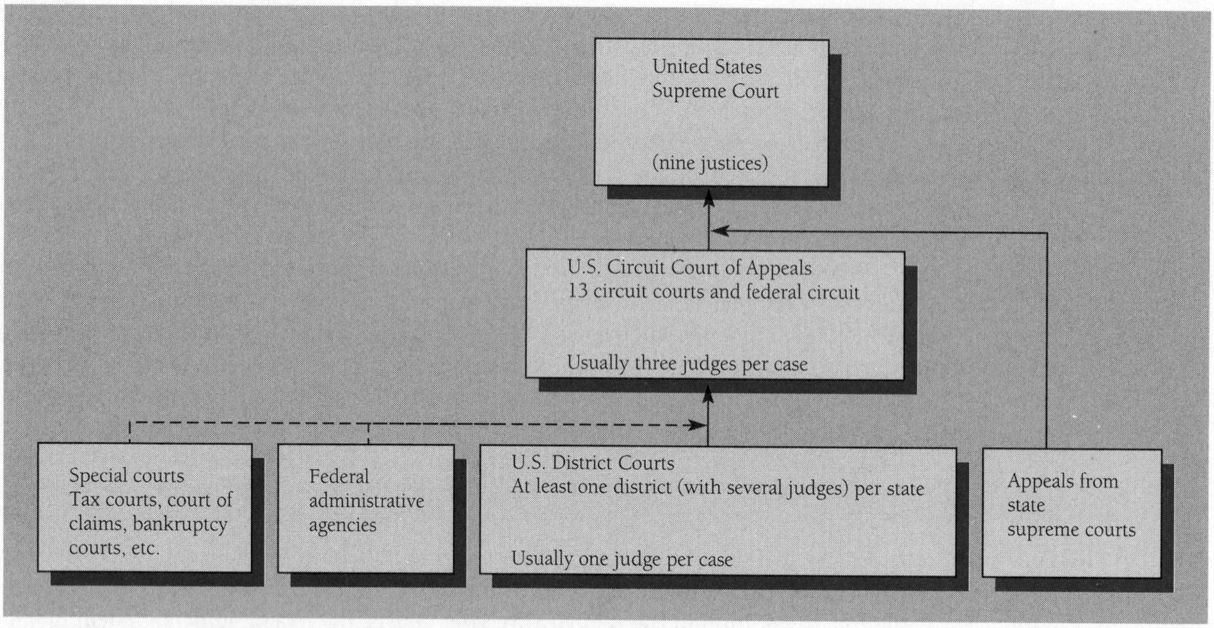

be a citizen of either Delaware or Michigan. For this reason, if General Motors sues a citizen of Georgia, the dispute, regardless of its subject matter, may be brought in a federal district court. However, if it sues a citizen of Delaware or Michigan, it cannot use the federal court system unless the case concerns a federal question.

Certain special aspects of the federal district court's diversity of citizenship jurisdiction should be noted. First, the federal district court's jurisdiction is not exclusive; it is concurrent or shared with that of the state courts. A plaintiff who wishes to sue defendants from other states may do so in either a state court that has jurisdiction or in a federal district court. If the suit is started in the state's judicial system, the defendants may be able to remove the case to a federal district court for trial. In most cases, however, the plaintiff controls the court system used.

Second, if a case is brought in a federal district court solely because of diversity of citizenship, that court must apply substantive state law (such as the contract law of Georgia) to resolve the parties' dispute. However, the federal district court will apply federal procedural rules.

Finally, some cases must be filed in either the federal or state court system. For example, bankruptcy or patent cases must be heard in special courts in the federal court system. These subjects are covered only by federal laws. Conversely, a contract dispute between two California residents with no federal questions must be heard in the California state courts. In such a dispute, there would be no subject matter jurisdiction for a federal court and probably no personal jurisdiction for the courts of other states.

Thus, you should distinguish between concerns focused on bringing a case in the federal or state legal system and concerns regarding the rules that determine the proper substantive law. Just as the federal courts apply state laws in most diversity of citizenship cases, the state courts sometimes apply federal law in resolving disputes brought to them. Determining where a case is heard and decided is not the same as determining which substantive laws apply. The latter determination is governed by *conflict of law rules,* which establish criteria to aid the judge in applying the most appropriate law.

How Courts Make Law

Laws emerging from the judicial branch are different from legislative acts. Legislative bodies can usually respond to political, social, and economic change more quickly than the judiciary. Because judges act only when a case or controversy is presented, they cannot react directly to such change. Further, whereas statutory law is general and prospective, the common law of judicial decisions is particular and retrospective. Of course, exceptions exist. Some statutes are intended to affect only a few companies or individuals, and important judicial decisions, through precedent, affect many people who are not parties to an actual case.

Courts make law by deciding cases and controversies. The law controlling a particular case may originate from prior court decisions, from statutory laws, from administrative regulations, or occasionally from the court itself if a law is made for that case. When a court uses a prior decision as a source of law for a later case, it is adhering to the concept of *stare decisis.* A court may also decide a case by interpreting statutory law. In so doing, it attempts to determine the legislature's intent in passing the statute so that the statute can be properly applied to the case. Sometimes a court confronts a new problem, one not addressed by prior cases, administrative regulations, or existing legislation. When that happens the court's determination decides the case for the litigating parties and also establishes a precedent for later cases.

Applying Law from Prior Cases One purpose of applying law from prior cases is to promote stability and predictability in the law. If a court changed the rule of law or applied it differently when confronted with facts similar to those at issue in a prior case, the law would be unpredictable. Frequent changes in the law would make it impossible for people to base their future conduct on existing interpretations. More litigants might appeal court decisions in the hope that appellate judges would use a different interpretation. Consistent application of the same law to different people facing similar problems promotes uniformity in the law.

The concept of *stare decisis* does require a court to follow the decision made in an earlier similar case. However, in some situations, a court finds that the overall circumstances of a present case are not the same as those in earlier situations. Although adherence to precedent is needed to promote stability and predictability in the law, the law must also be flexible enough to change as society encounters changes in technology, science, morals, economics, or politics. The *Brooks* case discussed earlier provides an example of the Supreme Court of Alaska's determination that a change was needed regarding the law governing the enforceability of prenuptial agreements.

Interpreting Statutory Laws Many cases require courts to interpret the meaning of language in a statute. One aspect of that activity focuses on determining what an informed reader would understand from the text. A second aspect focuses on determining the legislature's intent; what did the drafters of the statute have in mind when they selected certain words or phrases? In general, courts use a combination of these methods in interpreting statutes.

Courts have established several rules to aid them in interpreting statutes. Generally, they begin by looking at the *plain meaning* of a statute. If the plain meaning of a word or phrase used in a statute is obvious, no further analysis is required. However, the legislature may use the same word in different contexts to mean different things. For example, does the term *person* include a corporation? Corporations are not commonly thought of as persons. Yet some statutes, such as the Uniform Partnership Act, intentionally include a corporation as a person. Thus, the plain meaning of the term *person* in one statute may differ from its plain meaning in another statute.

If the plain meaning of statutory words or phrases is unclear, courts frequently turn to the *legislative history* to determine the legislature's intent in selecting those words or phrases. Several questions are asked to determine that intent. What were the words in the original draft of the bill? How were those words changed in the version of the bill that became law? Is there any record from a legislative committee regarding why certain changes were made? Did the sponsors of the statute make any comments concerning the inclusion of particular words or phrases? Inquiries of this kind assist a court in determining the legislative intent of an unclear or ambiguous statute.

Another method of determining the meaning of words or phrases in a statute is to analyze the policy or *purpose* behind the statute. Why was this particular statute passed? The questionable words or phrases should be interpreted in a manner that furthers the purpose of the statute. Courts also examine the context of such words or phrases.

Which of the methods of statutory interpretation referred to above were used in the following case? Note the court focused on several specific phrases in the statute, such as "place of public accommodation" and "deny access."

Quinnipiac Council, Boy Scouts of America, Inc.
v.
Commission on Human Rights and Opportunities, et al.
528 A2d 352 (1987)
Supreme Court of Connecticut

Catherine Pollard requested, first in 1974, and again in 1976, that she be appointed scoutmaster of Boy Scout troop 13 in Milford. Pollard had had a long history of active involvement in scouting as a merit badge counselor, a cub scout den mother, and as a troop 13 committee member. In this latter capacity, she had acted as de facto scoutmaster for troop 13 when it lacked a functioning scoutmaster and an assistant scoutmaster during the years 1972 to 1976. Nonetheless, Pollard's application to be scoutmaster was turned down because of the policy of the Boy Scouts of America that scoutmasters be men at least 21 years of age. Although the official policy statement of the Boy Scouts of America imposes no gender qualification for employment, and encourages women to undertake volunteer leadership roles, the national organization does not permit women to serve in certain positions: scoutmaster, assistant scoutmaster, webelos den leader, assistant webelos den leader, and lone scout friend and counselor. The plaintiff rejected Pollard's application solely because of this national policy, without making any judgment whatsoever about her individual qualifications to perform the duties required of a scoutmaster.

Ms. Pollard filed a complaint with the Commission on Human Rights, and after a hearing, it determined that the Quinnipiac Council, a local council chartered by the Boy Scouts of America serving central Connecticut, was statutorily obligated to offer Pollard a position as scoutmaster. Quinnipiac appealed that agency's decision to the Superior Trial Court, which reversed the agency's decision. Pollard and the Commission on Human Rights appealed that decision to the state Supreme Court.

PETERS, Chief Justice.

The dispositive issue in this case is whether the refusal to permit a woman to serve as a scoutmaster for a Boy Scout troop is a violation of our public accommodation statute. . . .

I

In our determination of the merits of the defendants' appeals, it is important to identify, at the outset, what is and what is not at issue. The central question before us is whether the defendants can sustain their *statutory* claim that § 53-35(a), our public accommodation statute, forbids the plaintiff from denying to Pollard, because of her gender, the opportunity to serve the plaintiff as a scoutmaster. . . .

It is a discriminatory accommodation practice, under § 53-35(a), to deny any person within the jurisdiction of this state "full and equal accommodations in every place of public accommodation, resort or amusement . . . by reason of . . . sex. . . ." The phrase "place of public accommodation, resort or amusement" is itself defined "within the meaning of this section [as] any establishment, which caters or offers its services or facilities or goods to the general public. . . ."

In deciding whether § 53-35(a) makes a gender based refusal to consider an application for scoutmaster a discriminatory public accommodation practice, we operate under well established principles of statutory construction designed to assist us in ascertaining and giving effect to the apparent intent of the legislature. "If the language of a statute is plain and unambiguous, we need not look beyond the statute because we assume that the language expresses the intention of the legislature." When we are faced with ambiguity in a statute, however, we turn for interpretive guidance to its legislative history, the circumstances surrounding its enactment, and the purpose the statute is to serve. . . .

We first address the question whether § 53-35(a), in any and all circumstances, entirely excludes the Boy Scouts of America. The plaintiff urges us to hold that the concept of "*place* of public accommodation" necessarily involves a specific physical site and hence automatically excludes its organization from the coverage of the statute. . . .

The statute, in § 53-35(a), defines a "place of public accommodation" as "any establishment, which . . . offers its services. . . ." The legislature has itself linked its definition of "place" not with a site, but rather with "any establishment." The meaning of this linkage is sufficiently ambiguous on its face to require us to look further to determine what the legislature intended to encompass within its prohibition of discriminatory accommodation practices.

Inquiry into the statute's legislative history makes it exceedingly doubtful that linkage to a physical site is a necessary element of the present definition of a "place of public accommodation." Public accommodation statutes in general have their origins in the common law duties of innkeepers and common carriers to offer their services to the general public without discrimination. In Connecticut, as the trial court correctly observed, our public accommodation statutes have repeatedly been amended to expand the categories of enterprises that are covered and the conduct that is deemed discriminatory. . . .

. . . In 1953 . . . the definition came to be, as it remains today, "any establishment which caters or offers its services or facilities or goods to the general public."

In order to draw appropriate implications from this legislative history we must consider the remedial purpose that the public accommodation statute was designed to implement. . . .

. . . [T]he unconditional language of the statute, the history of its steadily expanded coverage, and the compelling interest in eliminating discriminatory public accommodation practices persuade us that physical situs is not today an essential element of our public accommodation law. [O]ur statute now regulates the discriminatory conduct and not the discriminatory situs of an enterprise which offers its services to the general public.

Our conclusion that our public accommodation statute does not automatically exclude the plaintiff from coverage because it does not have a fixed physical situs does not, however, end our inquiry. The next question that we must address is whether its conduct in denying Pollard an opportunity to become a scoutmaster was a discriminatory public accommodation practice. We hold that it was not.

In the decision of whether a discriminatory public accommodation practice has occurred, the determinative issue is whether an "establishment" that serves "the general public" has denied access to its goods and services to a member of a protected class. . . . Unlike the statutes in some other jurisdictions, our statute does not expressly limit its coverage to "business enterprises" nor does it expressly exclude private clubs or organizations.

We can discern no reason to interpolate a "business" limitation into the legislature's unadorned reference to "any establishment." Like the question of situs, the question of coverage must reflect the legislative purpose of eliminating discriminatory conduct by those who serve the general public. From that vantage point, the organizational status of the enterprise that is the service provider cannot be the determinant of statutory coverage. . . . Although no private organization is duty-bound to offer its services and facilities to all comers, once such an organization has determined to eschew selectivity, under our statute it may not discriminate among the general public. This construction accords with that of other courts in our sister states construing similar legislation. . . .

. . . All of our antidiscrimination law is essentially fact-bound. As the Supreme Court of the United States has frequently reminded us, and as we have repeatedly stated in our own opinions, the *individual* is the focal point of the legislation that defines and prohibits discriminatory practices. The purpose of antidiscrimination legislation is to afford access to opportunity on the basis of individual abilities rather than on the basis of stereotypical generalizations.

In considering the opportunity of which an individual claims to have been deprived, the focus is equally on the particular opportunity, the particular position, rather than on access to an organization or an industry as a whole.

The corollary to these well established principles is that a person seeking recovery for discriminatory practices must demonstrate that he or she has personally been deprived of access to goods or services or positions in a manner forbidden by the statute governing access to public accommodations.

The issue in this case therefore is whether the record sustains Pollard's claim that she has personally been deprived of a public accommodation when she was denied the opportunity to become a scoutmaster. . . .

It is important to note the precise claim that the defendants advance. They maintain that Pollard was denied access to an "accommodation" because the plaintiff denied her the opportunity *to be of service* to the plaintiff. This claim raises an issue of first impression not only in this state but apparently in the country as a whole.

We observe first that a statute that addresses a discriminatory denial of *access to goods and services* does not, on its face, incorporate an allegedly discriminatory refusal by an enterprise to avail itself of a claimant's desire to *offer services*. . . .

Our public accommodation statute, § 53-35(a), gives no indication that it was intended to encompass the proffer of services within its definition of discriminatory accommodation practices. The absence of a statutory exception for a "bona fide occupational qualification or need" in the text of § 53-35(a) is more consistent with a legislative intent to leave such practices to be regulated by statutes that address employment discrimination rather than by statutes directed to discrimination in public accommodations. We therefore conclude that, in denying Catherine Pollard the opportunity to serve as scoutmaster of Boy Scout troop 13, the plaintiff did not deprive her of an "accommodation" as that term is used in our public accommodation statute.

Case Questions

1. What part of the statute does the Court examine to determine if its meaning is ambiguous? What does it decide?
2. What does the Court conclude after reviewing the legislative history? Which party does this favor?
3. What is the difference between what the statute protects regarding discriminatory action and the activity complained of by Ms. Pollard?

SUMMARY

Although a society's laws may be viewed as determining the nature of the society's legal system, the institutions in a society that create or apply laws are also an important part of its legal system. The role of the courts in making or applying law differs significantly between the common law and civil law legal systems. Other differences in these legal systems lead judges and lawyers to use different reasoning processes to determine the law that should apply to resolve a specific problem.

Despite their differences, all legal systems perform similar functions. Probably the most important of these functions is the maintenance of order within the society. They also provide a forum for the resolution of disputes and provide some certainty and stability while accommodating changes in society.

Laws can be classified in various ways. Substantive law defines rights and duties; procedural law details the methods by which those rights and duties are enforced. Significant differences in the parties, procedures, rules, and purposes distinguish criminal law cases from civil law cases. Both common law and statutory law are sources of law. Laws can also be classified by the extent to which the problems with which they deal affect the public rather than private parties.

Two distinctive features of the U.S. legal system are the division of law-making authority vertically between the states and the federal government and horizontally among the legislative, judicial, and executive branches of government. The twin bases of federalism and separation of powers shape the structure of the U.S. legal system. The *Synar* case illustrates the application of the separation of law-making powers among the branches of government. The supremacy clause, which resolves most of the conflicts between state and federal laws in favor of the federal laws, also shapes the legal environment in the United States.

Each of the three branches of government performs distinct roles in the federal and state legal systems. The legislature, generally consisting of two houses, is the primary law-making branch of government. Although both the federal and state legislatures make law through a process that begins with the proposal of a bill, much of the work is done through committees.

The executive branch consists of the chief executive, his or her staff advisers, and the departments of government that administer and enforce the laws. Administrative agencies are sometimes also considered a part of the executive branch. The chief executive, who has express and implied law-making authority, uses executive orders to implement certain executive policies.

The federal and state judicial branches are usually organized into trial courts, appellate courts, and a supreme court. Both federal and state courts can hear some similar types of cases. For example, diversity of citizenship cases that do not involve special federal laws can generally be filed in either federal or state courts. The federal and state court systems each also have exclusive powers to resolve certain legal questions. Patent, bankruptcy, and federal tax cases must be brought to the federal courts. Property matters or contract disputes involving citizens of the same state generally must be brought to the state courts.

Courts make law by applying laws from prior cases, by interpreting constitutional and legislative provisions, and by deciding cases that raise novel questions. Although the precedent of prior cases is usually followed, in some situations a court declines to follow prior case law. When this happens, as in the *Cohen* case, the court's decision sets a new precedent for future case decisions.

Courts follow several principles when seeking to interpret statutes. The plain meaning of words or phrases, the legislative history of statutes, and analysis of the context surrounding questionable words or phrases are used by courts to determine statutory intent. Even when deciding a question that has not been answered by prior cases or existing legislation, a court makes law. In such instances, an appellate or supreme court's decision and statements of law will be followed by other courts in the same jurisdiction in future years.

KEY TERMS

substantive law, p. 26
procedural law, p. 26
civil law, p. 32
common law, p. 34
statutory law, p. 34
federalism, p. 38
separation of powers, p. 38
jurisdiction, p. 47

CHAPTER EXERCISES

1. How would you describe the components of the U.S. legal system to a student from Poland who is enrolled in your school?
2. Compare and contrast the common law and civil law legal systems.

3. Distinguish between *(a)* procedural and substantive law, *(b)* criminal and civil law, and *(c)* common law and statutory law.

4. Federalism and the separation of powers are fundamental in the U.S. legal system. The term *separation of powers* refers to the notion that lawmaking power in our government is divided among the executive, judicial, and legislative branches. Each branch acts as a check on the others, thus preventing one branch from exercising too much power. What is the idea behind federalism? What similarities are there between federalism and the separation of powers?

5. If your manufacturing company sells its product in 20 states, would you prefer regulation by state law or by federal law? What are the problems if your company is sued?

6. What is the major advantage of *stare decisis* in a precedent-oriented system?

7. The basic characteristic of common law is that the courts will follow a case that establishes a precedent when similar issues arise in later cases. However, the courts do not always follow precedent. Why?

8. Mrs. Plaintiff sues the defendant church to recover damages for injuries sustained when she tripped on a loose stair tread at the church. For many years prior to this suit, the courts of the state have followed the rule that nonprofit organizations, such as churches, are not to be liable in such situations even where the injury is a result of their own carelessness. You are a judge of the court deciding whether or not the defendant church should be held liable. In deciding the issue of charitable immunity, should you apply the rule of *stare decisis*, overrule the old precedent, or let the legislature resolve the issue through the legislative process?

9. Give an example of rulemaking through the legislative process. How is this process different from the making of rules by a court?

10. A state statute prohibits the "carrying on one's person of any gun, knife, or other concealed weapon or implement of violence." Several women who were suspected of prostitution were arrested outside a large hotel in a major city. After a search of their handbags, several small cannisters of mace were found. Have these women violated the statute's terms? What principles would be used to interpret the statute?

Chapter 3

LITIGATION

KEY CONCEPTS

There is greater litigation in the United States than in most other countries. The frequency of litigation may be due to the openness of courts to a wide variety of problems, to the high number of lawyers in the society, or to individualism and the willingness among individuals and firms to litigate in order to resolve disputes.

The civil litigation process comprises several stages, from prepleading concerns to postjudgment problems. Pretrial activities are important in civil cases because most such cases are settled without a trial.

During a trial, the judge determines the law that is applied to the disputed issues and, to prevent bias, screens the evidence that the litigants will present. The jury determines the facts and draws conclusions based on the judge's instructions as to the law.

Attorneys perform different functions for their clients. They act as counselors, negotiators, drafters of documents, and litigators. The attorney-client privilege is intended to encourage full and frank communication between attorneys and their clients. The privilege allows attorneys to prohibit third parties from accessing confidential information communicated by clients to their attorneys.

The jury in civil litigation acts as a check on the powers granted to the judge and parties. Juries are selected from the community through a process that seeks a representative and impartial jury.

INTRODUCTION . . . PAST, PRESENT, FUTURE

In the past, the civil litigation system handled far fewer cases than it does today. In almost all fields of business litigation, from advertising and bankruptcy to contract and tort law, the number of cases litigated has increased dramatically over the past several decades. Both individuals and firms are more likely to bring disputes to the courts than they were in the past. In addition, recent changes in the environmental, civil rights, and product liability fields have increased the potential for litigation. An increased familiarity with the legal system may also be making it easier for people to resort to litigation.

As a result of the increased caseload, the legal system has become overburdened. Administrative agencies and local, state, and federal courts are all swamped with a backload of cases. Civil cases throughout the country are being pushed aside as criminal cases take priority on court dockets due to the requirement that defendants accused of crimes be given a prompt trial. The increasing costs and delays associated with litigation have led many firms to better manage their legal costs.

In the future, attempts to manage and control the cost of litigation are likely to increase. The alternative dispute methods referred to in the next chapter may stall or even reverse the trend of increasing litigation. Limits on the access to litigation or the compensation awarded to an injured party may be imposed by society before the end of the century.

OVERVIEW

Litigation is a process whose primary objective is the settling of disputes. Through court determinations of disputes, laws are interpreted, applied, and created. Most disputes do not wind up in courts for resolution but are resolved through negotiations. In some cases, the parties to disputes turn to outside authorities for assistance in resolving them. Although a variety of methods are used to settle disputes, the most visible and formal method is the litigation process. Unlike the decisions in mediation, arbitration, and other alternative methods, judicial decisions beyond the trial level generally must be explained in written opinions that become public information. It is through such opinions, exemplified by the cases in this text, that laws are applied to specific facts and legal principles are established.

Although more publicity is given to criminal litigation than to civil litigation, civil litigation is of greater concern to both the average citizen and the business manager. Sometimes business managers use litigation as a part of their management strategy. In the United States, there is little stigma to litigation, and perhaps more willingness to use it to solve problems that are not satisfactorily resolved through negotiation than there is in Japan, where the confrontation that litigation brings is not encouraged. Consensus practices aimed at harmonizing conflicting goals are such a part of the Japanese business environment that litigation between business firms is viewed as disruptive to long-term trust building.

Firms incurring rising legal costs are also likely to more carefully scrutinize legal costs in general and litigation expenses in particular. Attorneys who are employees of corporate firms (in-house counsel) may be given more of the legal work of the firm to perform and may act as managing supervisors on projects requiring the use of outside law firms.

FIGURE 3–1 Civil Suits Filed in Federal Courts

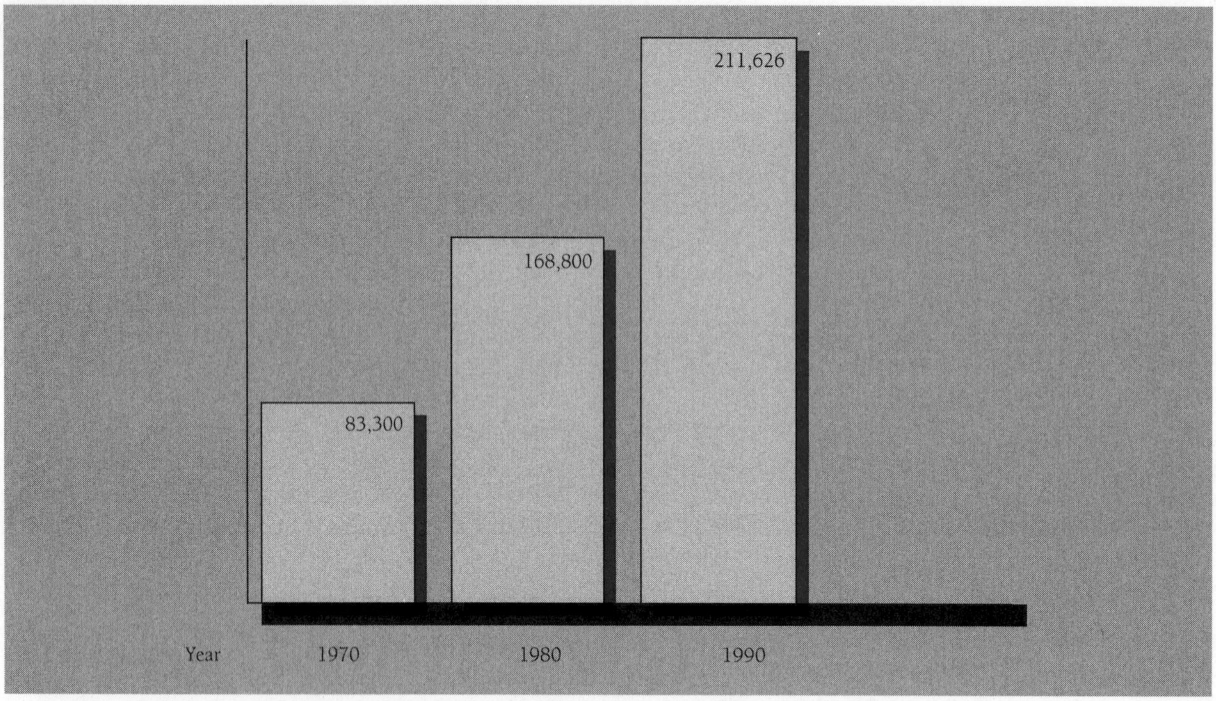

Source: U.S. Department of Commerce. Bureau of the Census, *Statistical Abstract of the United States, 1990* (Washington, D.C.: U.S. Government Printing Office, 1991), p. 189.

LITIGATION IN THE U.S. LEGAL SYSTEM

The United States is a litigious society—that is, a society in which people often prefer to sue rather than settle disputes by other methods. As Figure 3–1 shows, over 210,000 civil suits were filed in federal courts in 1990; less than 5 percent of these suits reached trial. However, because most civil cases involve questions of state law, such as contract, real estate, and personal injury law, they are generally litigated in state courts rather than federal courts. In 1989, over 17 million civil cases were filed in our state courts. Figure 3–2 portrays these court filings. In 1990, 211,626 civil cases were filed in U.S. district courts. While total civil filings have declined from 1985 (278,778), much of the decrease has occurred in less complex cases (recovery of debts and social security filings) while complex case filings (civil rights and labor cases) continue to rise. Cases filed in the U.S. bankruptcy courts continue to grow at an alarming rate. In 1990, almost 783,000 bankruptcy cases were filed. That number represents an increase of over 200 percent from the 331,000 cases filed in 1980.[1]

The causes and effects of the increase in litigation are varied. Some suggest that one cause may be the weakening of such social units as the family, church, and neighborhood.

[1]Administrative Office of the United States Courts, *Federal Judicial Workload Statistics* (U.S. Government Printing Office, Washington D.C., 1991).

FIGURE 3–2 Filings in State Courts in 1989*

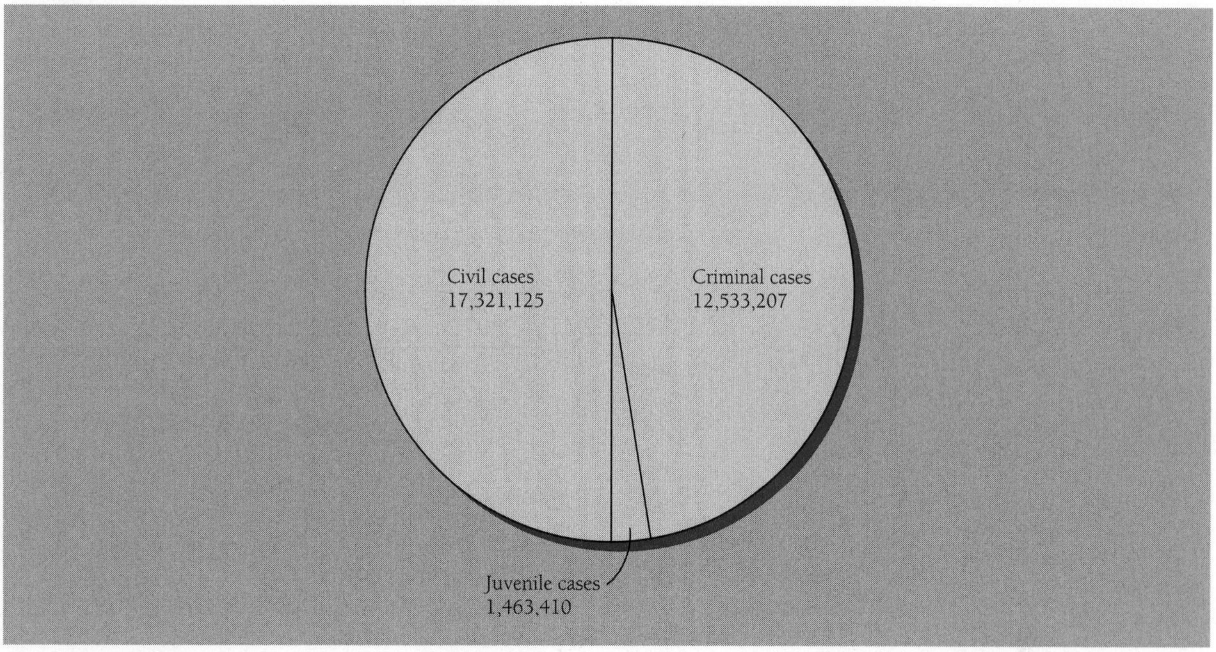

*Does not include traffic cases

Source: *Guidebook to the Use of State Court Caseload Statistics*, National Center for State Courts (Williamsburg, Va., 1991) Table 1, p. 9.

In earlier times, these social units often helped people resolve their disputes without court intervention. Others argue that greater numbers of more severe injuries have resulted from technological changes in our complex society. And some note that the increase in the number of civil lawsuits parallels the increase in the number of lawyers. Figure 3–3 shows the increase in the number of attorneys employed in the United States since 1970.

A noticeable effect of the increase in civil litigation is the increase in the cost of liability insurance. Less noticeable are the effects of civil litigation on entrepreneurial risk taking. Is fear of product liability lawsuits making companies more conservative in developing new products? Are the expense and aggravation of malpractice claims causing doctors to shy away from emergency or surgical fields? Is the prospect of litigation increasing the time it takes to open new chemical plants or to place innovative drugs on the marketplace?

Litigation can grow out of almost any problem and can be employed by world leaders as well as workers in low-level jobs. An Israeli politician, for example, brought suit against *Time* magazine because he felt that it had libeled him in an article. General Westmoreland sued a broadcasting network when one of its television programs stated that he had presented deceptive information to political leaders during the Vietnam War. A federal judge ordered an airline to pay over $50 million to 3,364 women, former flight attendants,

FIGURE 3–3 Attorneys Employed in the United States

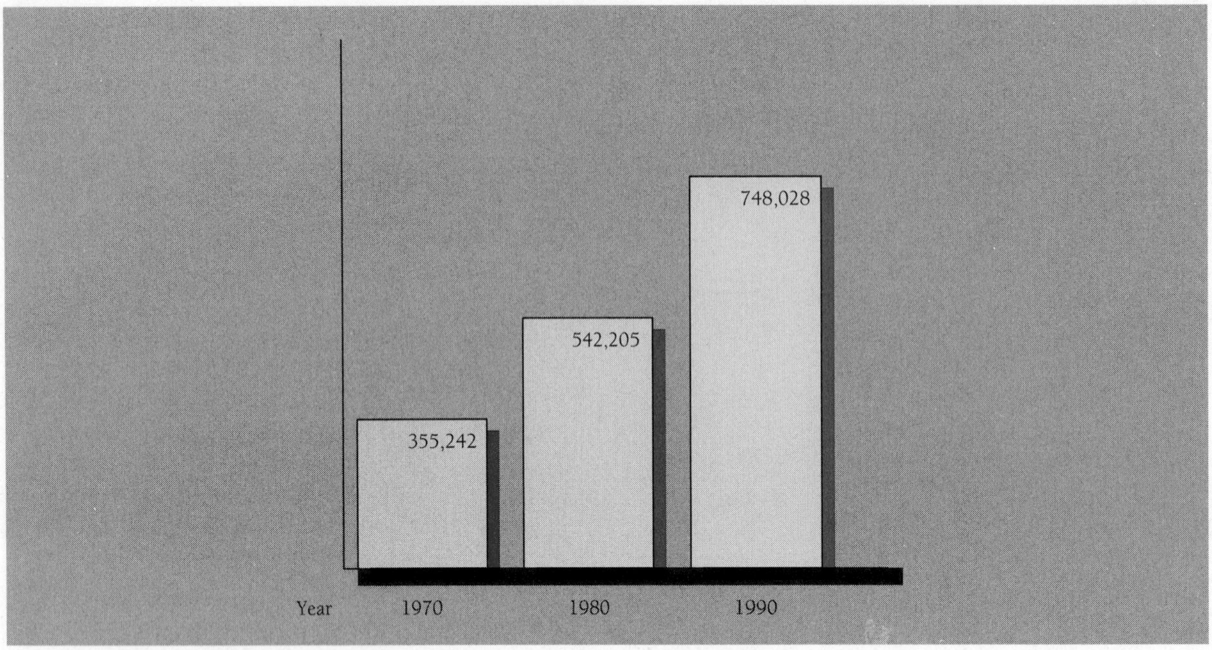

Source: U.S. Department of Commerce. Bureau of the Census, *Statistical Abstract of the United States, 1991* (Washington, D.C.: U.S. Government Printing Office, 1991), p. 395.

who proved that they had been paid less than male stewards in similar jobs. Thousands of lawsuits involving a vast variety of problems are brought to various courts in the United States every day.

Criminal and Civil Litigation

Criminal cases are brought by a public official representing the society at large; civil cases are brought by individuals and business enterprises. As noted in Chapter 2, criminal litigation and civil litigation differ significantly in their use of a jury and in their parties, purpose, and processes. Thus, in examining any court opinion, legal process, or principle of law, it is important to bear in mind the differences between criminal and civil litigation.

Adversarial Process

In the legal system of the United States, all litigation is modeled on the **adversarial principle**, which charges the parties with responsibility for the development and proof of their claims. In the adversarial process, the parties, not the judges, must decide what evidence to present, which witnesses to use, and when to object to something that the opposing party seeks to do. Because most people are not familiar with the complexities of litigation, the parties to litigation generally hire attorneys to represent them and present their case.

INTERNATIONAL PERSPECTIVE

Many other nations do not employ the adversarial principle in conducting litigation. Instead, they employ the **inquisitorial principle**, which requires all parties to assist the judge in investigating the facts of the controversy before the court. In the inquisitorial process, the judge, somewhat like an orchestra leader, takes an active part in determining the facts. By contrast, the judge in a trial using the adversarial process is more like a referee in a sports event, essentially reacting to objections posed by the attorneys.

The rationale for the use of the adversarial process is that truth and justice are more likely to emerge if each litigant is responsible for preparing, presenting, and defending his or her case. A neutral judge brings impartiality to the process, and the biased parties are expected to bring greater concern and dedication than that of parties who are assisting in an investigation.

Critics of the adversarial system argue that winning or losing a case too often depends on the skill of the attorneys rather than the merits of the case. It is also argued that the adversarial process leads parties to hide or distort facts in order to strengthen their positions. Accordingly, legal reforms adopted in recent decades have sought to lessen the impact of the adversarial principle in litigation. In addition, the usage of the adversarial principle has decreased as a result of increased use of administrative tribunals and alternative methods of dispute resolutions such as are noted in the following chapter.

THE CIVIL LITIGATION PROCESS

Since many of the civil cases that are filed never reach trial, it is necessary to look at the entire civil litigation process, not just the trial itself, to understand the nature of civil litigation. The civil litigation process can be divided into stages that begin before a case has been filed and end after a trial has been decided.

Stages of the Litigation Process

- Prelitigation concerns
- Pleadings stage
- Pretrial activities
- Trial procedures
- Appellate process

Prelitigation Concerns

Before any litigation begins, the disputing parties should consider a number of matters. Several important questions relate to the attorney's role. Should the party consult an attorney as soon as there is the possibility of litigation? Can the disputing parties investigate the facts and settle the dispute without seeking the assistance of attorneys? Would turning the dispute over to attorneys at an early stage take too much control away from the parties themselves? If the parties try to work things out themselves, will their discussions, notes, and documents hurt their cases if the dispute later appears in civil litigation? Answering such questions helps determine when an attorney should be consulted.

Even after a decision to consult and retain an attorney has been made, several matters must be addressed before any litigation begins. These matters are the who, what, when, and where of the dispute.

Questions to Ask Before Litigation

- *Who* are the parties that could be sued? Often there are multiple defendants and the plaintiff has to decide whether to sue some or all of the parties that might be liable.
- *What* is the basis of the suit? A party who may be able to sue on the basis of a contract, breach of warranty, or tort may need to determine the advantages to pursuing one theory rather than another.
- *When* will the litigation begin? Should the party seek to file suit as soon as possible, or should the onset of litigation be delayed in the hope of achieving a settlement?
- *Where* could the litigation take place? If a party has a choice of several courts, the place of suit may affect the applicable law or who can be sued.

These and other questions should be answered before litigation begins. In the following section, the description of the litigation process suggests some answers.

Pleadings Stage

A civil lawsuit is begun by filing a complaint with a court that has jurisdiction. Typically, the plaintiff's attorney files the complaint with the court and has a copy of the complaint and a summons delivered to the defendants.

The **complaint** is a document that gives the plaintiff's version of the *historical facts*—allegations about the circumstances that led to the claimed wrongful acts by the defendant. It also generally includes *jurisdictional facts*—statements showing why the case is being brought before this particular court. Finally, the complaint concludes with a *prayer or request for relief.* This specifies the remedy that the plaintiff wants the court to impose. If the plaintiff is seeking to be compensated for loss, the prayer for relief will request damages. A copy of a complaint appears in Figure 3–4.

The **summons** is a court order that gives the defendant notice of the lawsuit and requires the defendant to respond within a prescribed period of time (frequently 20 days). If no response is filed within that time period, a *default judgment* will be entered. This judgment is entered as a result of the defendant's nonappearance.

The response to the plaintiff's complaint is generally found in the defendant's answer. The **answer** is a document that responds point by point to the allegations and statements of the plaintiff's complaint. If the defendant agrees with a statement, the defendant may admit that the statement is true. If the defendant disagrees with an allegation, the answer will show that the defendant denies the allegations. In this way, the defendant addresses each essential segment of the plaintiff's claim.

The answer may also include an affirmative defense. An *affirmative defense* provides a legal justification for the defendant's conduct. It states a legal reason why the defendant would be found not liable even if the plaintiff's claims were found to be true. A *counterclaim,* which is essentially a suit by the defendant against the plaintiff, may also be a part of the defendant's answer.

In addition to the answer, the defendant's response to the plaintiff's complaint, the defendant may also make a variety of other responses by motions. A *motion* is a request to the court for some type of court order. Motions may be made throughout the pleading,

FIGURE 3–4 Complaint

State of Michigan
Kalamazoo County Circuit Court

Network Computers, Inc. Plaintiff(s)	Judge R. S. Jones (Assigned Judge)
v.	
GMNI Computers Company Defendant(s)	Civil Action No. 92—123456—NI (Year-File-Code)
Charles Brown (98765) Attorney(s) for the Plaintiff	
580 N. Main St., Kalamazoo, MI 49003 Address	
(616)—345—5442 Phone Number	

There is no other civil action between these parties arising out of the same transaction or occurrence as alleged in this complaint pending in this court, nor has any such action been assigned to a judge.

COMPLAINT

Plaintiff. Network Computers, Inc., by its attorneys, Charles Brown states:

1. Between the dates of July 1, 1991 and October 10, 1991 Plaintiff sold and delivered certain goods, wares, and merchandise to the Defendant, upon open account, upon the promise of Defendant to pay for these goods.
2. There is now unpaid upon this account the sum of $12,250.00.
3. The account has become stated between the parties.
4. As a consequence, Defendant is justly indebted to Plaintiff in the amount of $12,250.00 plus interest from and after October 10, 1991 plus costs of suit.
5. A copy of the account and an affidavit verifying the account are attached as Plaintiff's Exhibits A and B.

PLAINTIFF REQUESTS judgment in its favor and against Defendant in the amount of $12,250.00 plus interest, cost, and attorneys' fees.

Brown & Black, P. C.
(Firm Name)
By Charles Brown
(Typed Name of Attorney)
580 N. Main St., Kalamazoo, MI 49003
(Address)
(616)—345—5442
(Phone Number)

Dated: July 12,1992

pretrial, trial, and posttrial stages of litigation. During the pleadings stage, most motions are made in writing. Before the court acts on a motion, notice is provided to the opposing party and oral arguments on the motion are presented to the judge. The judge either grants or overrules motions before litigation continues.

If the defendant's answer raises facts not addressed in the plaintiff's complaint, the plaintiff files a reply document. A *reply* either admits or denies the new facts raised by the defendant's answer. Once all of the pleadings have been filed, the framework or outline of the litigation emerges. Matters that the defendant has admitted in the answer are not at issue and need not be proved at trial. The disputed facts and allegations form the basis for further investigation during the pretrial stage and at the trial.

Pretrial Activities

Discovery Procedures After the pleadings have been filed, but before the trial begins, each party seeks to discover as many important facts as possible about the dispute. The U.S. legal system has a very open approach to litigation in general and to discovery procedures in particular. Because both of the parties to a lawsuit have access to the same information, documents, and potential witnesses, any surprise at the time of trial is usually eliminated.

Discovery procedures are the methods used by each of the parties in a lawsuit to uncover facts, documents, or other things, that are in the exclusive knowledge or possession of the opposing party or that party's witnesses and may be used as evidence. Discovery is less significant in criminal litigation than in civil cases because in criminal litigation some of the defendant's information does not have to be made available to the prosecution. A variety of discovery procedures are used in civil suits.

Depositions A *deposition* is transcribed testimony that a witness gives under oath and outside court. The witness is examined by the attorney for one party and then cross-examined by the attorney for the other party; all of the questions and answers are recorded by a court reporter. Depositions enable the parties to find out prior to a trial, when the witness's recall is fresh, what that person might say when called on to testify at the trial. If a witness is unable to appear at the trial, his or her deposition may be used and the testimony preserved. Because both deposition and trial testimony are given under oath, conflicts between a deposition statement and trial testimony can be used to discredit a trial witness. Clearly, before testifying at a trial, a well-prepared witness will carefully review his or her deposition statement.

Examinations A doctor hired by the opposing party may conduct physical examinations of a party to determine the extent of a claimed injury. A psychiatrist may conduct mental examinations to assist in determining a party's mental state. Examinations of buildings by contractors, engineers, and architects may reveal hidden defects in design or construction.

Inspections and Production of Documents Bookkeeping records, correspondence, medical files, and financial documents in the possession of either party may be requested and must be made available for inspection and review by the opposing party. Only privileged or totally irrelevant information is exempt from such a request.

Interrogatories Written questions submitted to the opposing party must be answered under oath. Although the opposing party need not provide answers that go beyond the questions asked, this discovery device sometimes uncovers information that only the opposing party has. A question might ask, for example, if the opposing party has or knows of any correspondence relating to defects in products sold to the plaintiff.

Pretrial Conference A *pretrial conference* is a meeting of several persons, such as the attorneys and the judge, held prior to trial to enhance the interchange of opinions and eliminate differences or disputes. Pretrial conferences seek to narrow the issues in dispute and to move the controversy toward either trial or settlement. Some pretrial conferences are quite formal: the judge, attorneys, and perhaps the parties meet in court and review outstanding issues. Other pretrial conferences are informal: the attorneys and judge discuss the case in the judge's office, and no formal record of their conversation is kept.

A judge may ask the parties to submit documents, such as briefs, showing the sources of law that back up their claims. If a trial is to be conducted, the use of expert witnesses may be discussed and the possible date and length of the trial determined. Settlement options that could resolve the controversy without a trial are also reviewed. For example, if an injured party is seeking compensation, the parties may agree that the plaintiff's medical expenses incurred since the injury amount to $100,000. The defendant may not admit liability and the plaintiff may be seeking additional compensation, but the question of what medical expenses have been incurred will not need to be proven at the trial.

INTERNATIONAL PERSPECTIVE; DISCOVERY OR DISCLOSURE

Two different systems exist in the United States and in most European countries for obtaining information needed for trial. In the United States, a civil suit may be filed even though the plaintiff has very little information regarding potential witnesses and what their testimony may indicate about the issues in the trial.

In the U.S. system, the filing of the case generally occurs first and then the parties seek to *discover* information from the other party that will enhance their case. The discovery entails interrogatories to the opposing parties, numerous depositions from the parties and their witnesses, and frequent requests for files and documents that might have any possible bearing on the case. The objective of the discovery process is laudable—it seeks to produce all relevant evidence—but it often becomes too extensive, repetitive, and expensive for the parties.

In the European countries (including England, a common law country), a case is investigated before it is filed. The potential litigants *disclose* documents and possible witness information before the case is filed. Once suit is filed, preliminary pleadings are filed to see if the case has legal merit. If it does, a trial date is set and the parties exchange their witness lists and a short statement of what the witnesses will say. Exhibits to be used are exchanged and the trial proceeds. Depositions may not be used at trials unless a witness is outside the court's jurisdiction.

Although each system has merit, there is a growing belief that the discovery procedure currently used in most U.S. courts is too cumbersome, expensive, and time-consuming. Whether it will be modified or completely discarded is unclear; the disclosure system is being carefully reviewed to see how it might apply in the U.S. legal environment.

Trial Procedures

Most civil cases do not result in a trial; instead, they are settled by the parties outside the courtroom. Approximately five percent of the civil cases filed in federal courts are tried. Usually, when a trial does occur, this is because the parties are unable to agree about what actually happened. Thus, the primary purpose of most civil trials is to determine from the information submitted by the parties what actually happened. In the American legal system, questions of fact are usually determined by a jury. However, in some civil cases, the parties do not have a right to a jury trial. The Seventh Amendment to the United States Constitution provides: "In suits at common law, where the value in controversy shall exceed twenty dollars, the right to trial by jury shall be preserved . . ." Thus, suits which were tried in the chancery or equity courts (without benefit of a jury) instead of "at common law" are not covered by the seventh amendment's jury trial guarantee. Equity cases include cases in which the plaintiff asks the court to grant an unusual remedy, such as an injunction or a specific performance order. Those remedies are equitable remedies which historically were not available in common law suits; suits asking for such relief are not tried before a jury.

In some cases, the parties agree to waive their rights to a jury trial. In non-jury trials, the judge not only determines the legal questions, but also decides the facts. In the *Palmer* case that follows, a third party defendant in the case (a third-party defendant is a party whom the original defendant brings into the case) claims he is entitled to a jury trial, whereas the government claims a case like his is not guaranteed a jury trial by the Seventh Amendment. The court also considers whether that party has waived the right to a jury trial.

Palmer v. United States
652 F.2d 893 (9th Cir. 1981)
United States Court Of Appeals

Palmer was injured after being struck by an automobile driven by an employee of the United States. At the time of the accident, Palmer had been standing in a public highway directing traffic around Fisher's automobile, which had been disabled after colliding with another vehicle. Fisher, who later admitted having had an alcoholic beverage prior to his collision, had left the scene of the accident prior to the time Palmer was struck by the government vehicle.

Palmer sued the government under the Federal Tort Claims Act seeking damages for negligence. The government impleaded Fisher as a third-party defendant, demanding indemnity in the event the government was held liable to Palmer. Although both Palmer and Fisher asked for a jury trial, no jury was impaneled. During the trial, neither Palmer nor Fisher objected to the court's apparent failure to rule on the jury demands.

The trial court found that the negligence of both the government and Fisher had contributed to the injuries sustained by Palmer. Under California's doctrine of comparative negligence, the court held the government responsible for 30 percent and Fisher responsible for 70 percent of the negligence causing Palmer's injuries. Damages were determined to be $88,600. Because the government was the only named defendant in the plaintiff's actions, the court ordered it to pay the entire amount to Palmer. It then held the government was entitled to a judgment against Fisher for 70 percent of the damages it paid. Fisher appealed, contending that the court erred in denying him a jury trial. Fisher argued the government's claim is a tort claim under the common law and therefore warranted a jury trial. The government argued its claim for compensation due from Fisher derives from the doctrine of contribution, an equitable doctrine, and therefore does not warrant a jury trial under the Seventh Amendment.

Ferris, Circuit Judge

Whether the Seventh Amendment authorizes a jury trial in a particular case does not depend on the character of the overall action, but instead is determined by "the nature of the issue to be tried." An issue is considered "legal" when its resolution involves the ascertainment and determination of legal rights or justifies a remedy traditionally granted by common law courts.

Here, the government's claim against Fisher requires a determination of the extent to which Fisher's negligence contributed to Palmer's injuries, the relative fault between Fisher and the government, and whether the government has in fact satisfied the judgment rendered against it in Palmer's original negligence suit. Each of these issues involves determinations of rights and liabilities traditionally arising in common law suits for negligence. Moreover, the government seeks to recover from Fisher a portion of the damages which it was required to pay to Palmer. Recovery of damages is a remedy traditionally granted by common law courts. Accordingly, we hold that Fisher, as a third-party defendant who was not joined as a defendant in Palmer's original action, had a right to a jury trial on the government's claim for partial comparative indemnity.

There is no dispute here that Fisher filed a timely demand for a jury trial. Federal Rule of Civil Procedure 38(d) specifically provides that, once a timely demand is filed as required by Federal Rule of Civil Procedure 5(d), the demand can only be withdrawn by consent of the parties. Hence, the precise issue here is whether Fisher waived his right to jury trial by withdrawing his demand. Under Federal Rule of Civil Procedure 39(a), a consensual withdrawal of a jury demand can be effected by the parties through either (1) written stipulation filed with the court or (2) oral stipulation made in open court and entered in the record. The record before us reveals neither an oral nor a written stipulation by the parties to withdraw Fisher's jury demand. Under the terms of the procedural rules applicable here, then Fisher's jury demand was never properly withdrawn.

The government argues, however, that Fisher withdrew his jury demand by failing to object and by otherwise acquiescing to the bench trial format of the district court proceedings. We decline to create an exception to the precise terms of Federal Rules of Civil Procedure 38(d) and 39(a), although we recognize that other courts have done so. Because the constitutional right to a jury trial is fundamental, we must indulge every reasonable presumption against its waiver. A party's acquiescence to the district court's maintenance of a bench trial, without more, is insufficient to establish a withdrawal of a jury demand.

We hold, therefore, that there was no withdrawal of Fisher's demand for a jury trial.

Reversed and remanded.

Case Questions

1. What is the criterion used to determine whether a party in a civil case is entitled to a jury trial? When is an issue a legal issue?
2. What are the two reasons the court gives for why Fisher is entitled to a jury trial?
3. If a party in a federal case wants to waive the right to a jury trial, how can he or she make that waiver?

Selection of a Jury Usually, the first step in any trial is the selection of the jury. In most states, the number of jurors varies with the type of case. Approximately three fourths of the states have civil case juries consisting of from six to eight people. In many states, the jury's decision or **verdict** need not be reached by unanimous vote. In Michigan, for example, all civil case juries consist of six people and a decision on which five of the six agree constitutes the jury's verdict. A *hung jury* occurs if less than the minimum required to make a valid decision agree.

Prospective jurors are chosen from various sources in the community. The selection process is intended to obtain a cross section of the community. Of course, some of the people selected may not be impartial with regard to the matters at issue in specific cases. If it can be shown that a person's biases might influence his or her decision in a particular case, the judge will grant a challenge to exclude that person from serving as a juror on that case. Challenges to potential jurors and other aspects of the jury's role are discussed in a subsequent section of this chapter.

Presentation of Evidence Once the jury has been selected, the presentation of evidence begins. First, each party is given a chance to make an *opening statement,* an overview of the case to be presented. This statement indicates to the judge and jury what testimony, documents, and exhibits the party intends to present as evidence. Opening statements are not considered evidence.

The plaintiff, who begins the presentation, has the burden of proving the complaint's allegations by the preponderance of evidence. Most of the evidence presented is the oral testimony of witnesses who are questioned by the attorneys. Documents, charts, or other exhibits are also submitted. After a witness has answered the questions of the plaintiff's attorney on direct examination, the defendant's attorney asks that witness questions through cross-examination.

Direct examination is the questioning of a witness by the party on whose behalf the witness has been called, while *cross-examination* is the questioning of a witness called by the opposing party. The questioning of a witness can continue through redirect and recross-examination if new issues are brought out in the witness's answers.

Once the plaintiff has called all of the witnesses who are to testify and has introduced the exhibits to be considered by the jury, the plaintiff's primary case is complete. If the testimony presented is not sufficient to allow a jury to decide for the plaintiff, the defendant can present a motion to the judge to direct the verdict and dismiss the case. If the judge agrees with the request, the judge will grant the *motion to direct the verdict* in favor of the defendant. When this occurs, the jury has nothing to do; the case is over and has been decided in the defendant's favor. If the judge does not grant the motion, the trial continues and the defendant presents evidence.

Oral testimony of witnesses called by the defendant and cross-examined by the plaintiff is presented to the jury and the judge. If a party believes that the rules of evidence prohibit the introduction of certain evidence, that party may object to the evidence. The judge then makes a legal decision to allow the evidence (*overruling* the objection) or to prohibit its use (*sustaining* the objection). Each major decision that the judge makes concerning the admissibility of evidence can later be reviewed by an appellate court.

Rules of Evidence The rules of evidence assure that information presented during a trial is relevant, unbiased, and reliable. Testimony that has been determined to be unreliable or irrelevant should not be presented. For example, the fact that a witness committed several traffic offenses in the past five years would be irrelevant in a civil trial involving a contract dispute. If one of the parties seeks to ask the witness a question concerning those offenses, the other party can object to such evidence as irrelevant to the trial. The judge would then rule on the objection and should exclude the evidence by sustaining the objection.

Similarly, information contrary to a rule of evidence may be offered at a trial. One such rule concerns *hearsay* testimony. This rule of evidence, which has many exceptions, excludes as unreliable any testimony based on what a person has heard other people say. Testimony is restricted to statements based on the witness's knowledge and observation. For example, if Chris witnesses a fight between Dave and Jim, Chris may testify as to what he saw. However, if Chris tells Dianne about that fight, Dianne may not testify as to what she heard Chris say. Hearsay testimony is excluded because the opposing party cannot probe Chris's perceptions if only Dianne is available to report the hearsay.

Concluding the Trial After the plaintiff and defendant have finished presenting evidence, each is usually given a chance to offer rebuttal evidence contradicting the evidence that was presented by the opposing party. The parties are then usually allowed to make *closing statements*, or summations that organize the evidence to assist the jury's logic in arriving at that party's desired conclusion. Like the opening statements, these statements are not evidence and the jury cannot consider them facts in reaching its decision.

After the closing statements have been presented, the judge gives the jury *instructions* as to the law that it should apply to the dispute and as to the evidence presented by the parties. The judge's instructions summarize the law, and the jury reviews the evidence and determines the facts. On the basis of these two components, law and facts, the jury reaches its *verdict*.

Although people often think of the jury's verdict as the end of a trial, the trial judge may legally set aside or change a verdict. Most judges are hesitant to alter a jury's verdict, but if a judge believes that a jury's verdict is not based on the evidence presented or does not follow the instructions of law, the judge may reverse the verdict by granting a *judgment notwithstanding the verdict (JNOV)*. Of course, a judge's reversal of a verdict may be appealed.

Postjudgment Concerns

It is the court's *judgment* or decision that ends the trial court proceedings. If either party considers the judgment wrong, that party can appeal the judge's legal errors. Such errors may arise if the judge admits or denies the use of certain testimony or exhibits as evidence, or makes mistakes in instructing the jury as to the law. If the judgment is not appealed within a specified period, it becomes final.

A plaintiff may obtain a judgment against a defendant for $100,000, yet fail to receive that amount. The judgment is a legal determination of the amount of money owed. If the defendant does not pay the determined amount voluntarily, the plaintiff may require legal means to enforce the judgment.

One method used to enforce a judgment is garnishment. *Garnishments* of wages or bank accounts are court orders to other persons, such as the defendant's employer or bank, to pay the plaintiff some of the defendant's money. They are discussed in Chapter 11.

Another method is to attach assets of the defendant, such as a car or other personal property. An *attachment* is an order allowing one person, such as the plaintiff, to sell personal property of the defendant, such as equipment, inventory, or furnishings, so that the proceeds may be used to pay off a judgment. A *lien* grants the plaintiff an interest in real estate owned by the defendant. If that real estate is sold, some of the sale proceeds will be paid to the plaintiff.

The judgment of a court usually remains in effect for several years and may be renewed. Anytime during that period, property acquired by the defendant can be garnished, attached, or subjected to a lien so that it can be used to satisfy the judgment. Only after the judgment has been fully paid or satisfied does the defendant's legal obligation to the plaintiff terminate.

Appellate Process

An appellate court reviews the legal rulings that one or both of the parties think were incorrectly made by the trial court judge. The trial court is charged primarily with deciding factual discrepancies between the parties. In an appeal, therefore, a determination of the facts is unnecessary because all of the factual issues were decided prior to or at the trial. Because of the difference in function between the trial court and the appellate court, the appellate process varies substantially from the trial process.

The *trial court record* consists of the transcript of the testimony of all the witnesses, the exhibits used as evidence, the judge's rulings on all objections to the introduction of evidence, the judge's instructions to the jury, the jury's verdict, and the judgment of the court. The comments of the parties generally consist of oral arguments, supported by written presentations called *briefs*. A *brief* used in an appeal highlights the claims made by a party at the trial. It usually provides references to other cases that support those claims.

Appellate court judges make decisions based on the trial court record, the oral arguments, written briefs of the parties, and research and discussion conducted by the appellate court itself. An appellate court generally consists of three judges who act by a majority vote. If the appellate court agrees with the trial court's judgment, it affirms that court's determination. If the appellate court determines that the trial court's judgment was incorrect, it reverses the judgment. Finally, the appellate court can either modify the legal remedy provided by the trial court or remand (return) the case to the trial court for some redetermination.

Suppose an appeal is made because the plaintiff that lost the case wanted to use certain testimony at the trial that the judge excluded. If the appellate court determines that the judge's interpretation was wrong and that the plaintiff's testimony should have been allowed as evidence, the appellate court would probably remand (return) the case to the trial court. If the excluded testimony was critical to the plaintiff's case, the verdict of the jury (which was against the plaintiff) might have been different. Because there is no way to tell whether the jury's decision would have been different, the case is sent back to the trial court, which must now allow the plaintiff to use the excluded testimony.

PARTICIPANTS IN CIVIL LITIGATION

The framework of civil litigation is provided by the principle of separating or decentralizing power among different parties, which, as Chapter 2 noted, is built into the U.S. legal system. Attorneys, as representatives of the parties, are given significant responsibilities for investigating facts and presenting evidence. Control of this part of the litigation process rests with the parties, not with the judge. The jury's power to render a verdict balances the power given to the judge. The judge, jury, attorney, and parties involved in civil litigation each have distinct roles to play. Each of them complements the others, and each also balances and checks the power granted the others.

The Trial Judge

Judges are selected in several ways. Federal judges are appointed by the president, with the advice and consent of the Senate. The states use a mixture of appointive and elective processes to choose judges. A judge in the American legal system must perform several functions. The parties in a case have a right to a judge who is able to act as an impartial decision maker at the trial by deciding legal issues based on existing laws, not on the basis of individual beliefs or because of bias towards one of the parties. In the *Easley* case, the impartiality of the judge is questioned and reviewed by the Court. Both before and during a trial, the judge must rule on numerous motions. The judge must also instruct the jury regarding the law that it is to use in arriving at its verdict. After the trial, other judges, who act as an appellate court, provide a check on the trial court judge by reviewing the judgment. The Court of Appeals judges in the *Easley* case review the decisions made by Judge Feikens, the trial court judge who heard the District Court case Easley brought against The University of Michigan Board of Regents.

Easley v. University of Michigan Bd. of Regents
906 F.2d 1143 (5th Cir. 1990)
United States Court of Appeals

On November 21, 1984, appellant Easley, formerly a student at The University of Michigan School of Law, but who was suspended for plagiarism, filed complaint in the United States District Court for the Eastern District of Michigan against a number of officials of the University.

In addition, Easley filed a motion to disqualify Judge Feikens based upon the Judge's association with the University's Law School and "his well-publicized Negrophobia."

After this court denied Easley's subsequent petition for a writ of mandamus directing Judge Feikens to disqualify himself, the district court held as a matter of law, that since Easley had never completed his degree requirements, he, therefore, never obtained a property interest in a J.D. degree.

Easley renewed his motion to disqualify Judge Feikens and also moved for a new trial before an unbiased judge.

Judge Feikens subsequently denied Easley's motions to disqualify and for a new trial. . . . , granted defendants' motion for summary judgment on Easley's equal protection and first amendment claims and dismissed Easley's search and seizure claim for failure to plead brief, simple, and clear facts showing a basis for relief. This appeal followed.

Ryan, Circuit Judge

Assuming that Judge Feikens should not have disqualified himself, we find no error in the court's disposition of Easley's equitable and legal claims. However, given the strong interest in promoting public confidence in the integrity of the judicial process, we must look more closely at the affiliations alleged by Easley to determine if Judge Feikens abused his discretion in denying Easley's two motions for disqualification.

We observed that Easley made a number of allegations in support of his motion for recusal relating to Judge Feikens' alleged association with The University of Michigan and his alleged racial bias. We rejected Easley's claim of racial bias as entirely unwarranted and then turned to the allegations of Judge Feikens' association with The University of Michigan.

We noted that while some of the grounds advanced for seeking Judge Feikens' disqualification on the basis of his own and his sons' affiliation with The University of Michigan are patently meritless, out of an abundance of caution, others deserved scrutiny on remand. That "abundance of caution," we said, derived principally from "the strong interest in promoting public confidence in the integrity of the judicial process." To fully protect that "strong interest," we reserved our decision on the recusal issue as it relates to Judge Feikens' alleged association with the University and remanded the matter to the district court.

> [T]he district court shall conduct an evidentiary hearing for the limited purposes of (1) enlarging the record regarding the nature of Judge Feikens' associations and affiliations with the Law School, its faculty, and its administrators; (2) determining whether Judge Feikens acquired extra-judicial knowledge of matters material to this controversy through these associations, particularly the Law School's Committee of Visitors; and (3) determining, notwithstanding the court's findings regarding (2) above, whether, because of such associations, Judge Feikens' impartiality in this matter might "reasonably be questioned."

Judge Feikens submitted an affidavit defining the scope of his affiliations with The University of Michigan. He stated that he is an alumnus of the Law School; that he was a volunteer fundraiser for the Law School Fund in 1964; that since 1981 he has been a member of the Committee of Visitors of The University of Michigan Law School, the purposes of which are essentially social and informational; that he did not participate in board affairs during the period in which Easley's case was pending before him; and that he is a member of The University of Michigan Club of Detroit through which he participates in athletics-related social events.

In response to Easley's interrogatories, the six individual defendants, administrators and faculty members at The University of Michigan, candidly detailed their associations with Judge Feikens. And, The University of Michigan, as a defendant, produced materials describing the purpose and activities of the Committee of Visitors, corroborating the disclosures Judge Feikens made in his affidavit.

On April 17, 1989, Judge Hackett conducted an evidentiary hearing. In a written "Findings and Conclusions" issued that same day, she stated, in relevant part:

> Nothing in this record supports a finding that Judge Feikens acquired actual or constructive extra-judicial knowledge of matters material to this controversy through his various associations with The University of Michigan or its law school; 4) Nothing in this record supports a finding that the judge's impartiality might reasonably be questioned, other than plaintiff's conclusory allegations.

We turn, therefore, to the final issue left unresolved in *Easley:* Whether Judge Feikens abused his discretion in denying appellant's motion for recusal on the basis of the Judge's alleged associations with The University of Michigan. We consider the issue, having in mind the rule that:

> Recusal is mandated . . . only if a reasonable person with knowledge of all the facts would conclude that the judge's impartiality might reasonably be questioned.

Instructions to the district court . . . were formulated with particular concern for the provisions of U.S.C. § 455, which states in pertinent part:

> (a) Any justice, judge, or magistrate of the United States shall disqualify himself in any proceeding in which his impartiality might reasonably be questioned.
> (b) He shall also disqualify himself in the following circumstances:
> (1) Where he has a personal bias or prejudice concerning a party, or personal knowledge of disputed evidentiary facts concerning the proceeding;

We now hold that Judge Feikens did not abuse his discretion in refusing to recuse himself from Easley's litigation with The University of Michigan. Without more, the amicable feelings Judge Feikens undoubtedly has for his alma mater, The University of Michigan, fail to demonstrate a sufficient basis for his recusal.

Nothing in the expanded record suggests that Judge Feikens was privy to extra-judicial information relating to Easley's situation at The University of Michigan Law School or to his claim against the University based on his affiliations with the Law School.

Hence, the district court complied with our second instruction on remand.

Nor does the current record support Easley's unsubstantiated assertion that Judge Feikens' impartiality should be questioned. Judge Hackett specifically found:

> Nothing in this record supports a finding that the judge's impartiality might reasonably be questioned, other than plaintiff's conclusory allegations.

For the foregoing reasons, we affirm the decision of the district court.

Case Questions

1. What were the two reasons Easley claimed as a basis for disqualifying Judge Feikens from deciding the case he filed?
2. What did the Court of Appeals require a different trial court judge to do in order to determine if Feikens was biased? What was the result of those actions?
3. Did Judge Feikens discuss this case with any of the administrators from The University of Michigan? What result would occur if there were such discussions?

The Jury

The jury's primary role in the American legal system is to determine the disputed facts. Either of the parties involved in a civil trial can request a jury. Nevertheless, waiving of the right to a jury trial is quite frequent in civil cases. In many of the world's legal systems, no jury is available for most civil lawsuits. Thus, the role of the jury is most often discussed as a part of the criminal trial process rather than the civil trial process. The following commentary presents an unusual situation; the prosecutor desiring a jury trial which the defendants want to waive.

Judge or Jury? Federal Prosecutor Wants Lay People to Hear Insider-Trading Case

By Stephen J. Adler

NEW YORK—In a surprise move, the U.S. attorney's office has refused to allow defendants in the Marcus Schloss & Co. insider-trading case to have a judge, rather than a jury, decide their case.

While defendants in criminal cases have a constitutional right to trial by jury, ordinarily they can waive that right and allow a judge to hear the case in a so-called bench trial. But under federal procedural rules, both the judge and the prosecutor have to consent to the waiver. And in this case, the prosecutor refused.

In his letter Friday opposing the bench trial, Manhattan U.S. Attorney Benito Romano said, "Jury trials occupy a special place in the framework of our government and therefore, absent extraordinary circumstances not present here, it is the general policy of this office not to consent to a defendant's waiver of a jury."

Defense lawyers said . . . that juries are likely to be unsympathetic to well-to-do defendants, particularly in cases involving alleged abuses on Wall Street.

Stanley S. Arkin, attorney for defendant D. Ronald Yagoda, said, . . . "A jury is not going to understand the professional's advantage in trading stocks as opposed to the advantage that a crook gets."

In the case, Mr. Yagoda, the former head of trading at Marcus Schloss, was charged with conspiring with members of the "Yuppie Five" ring, allegedly to trade on inside information. He was also charged with perjury and obstruction of justice in connection with his testimony before the Securities and Exchange Commission. Marcus Schloss was charged with insider trading in connection with its arbitrage activities. Both defendants pleaded innocent.

. . . Mr. Romano extolled trial by jury in general and added that there was a particularly important reason for such a trial in this case. "It is not secret that certain recent indictments charging securities law violations and related offenses have engendered a great deal of public debate and controversy," he wrote. "The public interest in the prosecution of these 'white-collar' criminal cases suggests to us that primary responsibility for deciding such cases should be placed in the hands of a jury drawn from the lay community."

Defense lawyers in the case agree that they have no legal appeal available because the federal rules and court cases clearly give the prosecution the right to veto their request for a bench trial.

Two major types of juries are a part of the American legal system. The *grand jury* (discussed in Chapter 22) generally has from 17 to 23 members and investigates possible criminal activity. It plays no role in the civil litigation process. The more common type of trial jury, which has 12 or fewer members, is known as the *petit jury* because it is smaller than the grand jury.

Selection of Potential Jurors Potential jurors are generally selected from the adult population of the community in which the court hearing the case is located. The pool of available people is usually drawn from voter registration or drivers' license lists. Although state laws differ, most eligible adults called are required to serve if selected. If some community group is excluded from jury service, then the jury does not adequately reflect the community.

The Impartiality of the Jury Several special concerns have been expressed regarding the use of a jury in the American legal system. In some cases, there is such pretrial publicity surrounding a case that it may be difficult or impossible to find an impartial jury. Is an impartial jury obtainable if a case being tried is the subject of intense pretrial publicity? Can potential jurors who read the papers, watch television, or listen to the radio be impartial? Consider the answers suggested to these questions in the following extract from *United States v. Haldeman*,[2] a criminal case involving several Watergate participants.

It is fundamental that "the right to jury trial guarantees to the criminally accused a fair trial by a panel of impartial 'indifferent' jurors." To be indifferent a juror need not be ignorant. In these days of swift, widespread and diverse methods of communication, an important case can be expected to arouse the interest of the public in the vicinity, and scarcely any of those best qualified to serve as jurors will not have formed some impression or opinion as to the merits of the case. To hold that the mere existence of any preconceived notion as to the guilt or innocence of an accused, without more, is sufficient to rebut the presumption of a prospective juror's impartiality would be to establish an impossible standard; *it is sufficient if the juror can lay aside his impression or opinion and render a verdict based on the evidence presented.*

We find the pretrial publicity in this case, although massive, was neither inherently prejudicial nor unforgettable. We therefore turn to an examination of the voir dire itself. . . .

After determining the venireman's degree of interest in and exposure to the case, the court inquired whether he had formed or expressed an opinion of the guilt or innocence of any defendant. If the venireman had formed an opinion, the judge attempted to determine whether that opinion was firmly held or could be set aside. In closing he was asked whether he could return a fair and impartial verdict based solely on the evidence presented at trial and the court's instructions on the law. . . .

Mere familiarity with the facts and issues involved in the case would not have rendered a venireman unqualified to sit.

Case Questions

1. Can jurors who have opinions about a defendant's guilt or innocence be impartial?
2. Can potential jurors who are already familiar with some of the facts and issues of a case be impartial jurors?

The Representative Nature of the Jury Another concern regarding the jury focuses on its representative nature. Is a jury that does not reflect the community's racial, economic, social, or educational makeup still qualified? Potential jurors who have been brought into a court to determine whether they can serve on a specific case go through a process called *voir dire*, which means "to speak the truth." The judge and each of the parties have a right to question the potential jurors to determine whether they have any bias that would prevent them from rendering an impartial verdict.

A party that considers a juror biased will challenge that person by using either a challenge for cause or a peremptory challenge. A *challenge for cause* cites a legal reason for not selecting the person, such as the person's being related to one of the parties, having a financial interest in the case, or holding a firm opinion about the case. If the judge agrees with the party's reason, the challenge for cause is granted and the person is dismissed. An unlimited number of challenges for cause can be granted. A *peremptory challenge* does not cite any reason for dismissing a potential juror. A limited number of potential jurors may be dismissed through the use of such challenges.

In 1986, the U.S. Supreme Court decided the *Batson* case.[3] The court determined that Batson, a black defendant, was denied equal protection of the law when the prosecutor used peremptory challenges to strike all black veniremen (potential jurors) from the panel. The court found the State's privilege to strike individual jurors through peremptory challenges was subject to the equal protection clause and that when those challenges were used in a discriminatory manner, they violated the rights of the defendant. Following the

---

[2]559 F.2d 31, (D.C. Cir., 1976).

[3]*Batson v. Kentucky*, 476 U.S. 80 (1986).

Batson case, attorneys and litigants in civil cases wondered about the right of a private party in a civil case to use peremptory challenges to exclude jurors on account of their race. The answer to that question came five years later, in the *Edmonson* case.

Edmonson v. Leesville Concrete Company, Inc.

Ill. S. Ct. 2077 (1991)
United States Supreme Court

Edmonson, a black construction worker, was injured in a job site accident at Fort Polk, Louisiana, a federal enclave. Edmonson sued Leesville Concrete Co. for negligence in the federal district court claiming it permitted one of the company's trucks to roll back and pin him against some construction equipment. Edmonson invoked his Seventh Amendment right to a trial by jury. During *voir dire,* Leesville used two of its three peremptory challenges authorized by statute to remove black persons from the perspective jury. Referring to our *Batson* decision, Edmonson asked the court to require Leesville to provide a race-neutral explanation for the peremptory challenges. The trial court judge denied the request on the grounds that *Batson* does not apply to civil cases.

The jury found for Edmonson in the amount of $90,000, but as it determined he was 80 percent at fault, it reduced his award to $18,000. Edmonson appealed and the Court of Appeals reversed, holding that *Batson's* decision that peremptory challenges could not be used to exclude jurors on the basis of race also applies to civil cases. On an en banc (full panel) rehearing, the Court of Appeals upheld the District Court. Edmonson then appealed to the Supreme Court.

Justice Kennedy delivered the opinion of the Court

We must decide in the case before us whether a private litigant in a civil case may use peremptory challenges to exclude jurors on account of their race. Recognizing the impropriety of racial bias in the courtroom, we hold the race-based exclusion violates the equal protection rights of the challenged jurors

In *Powers v. Ohio,* we held that a criminal defendant, regardless of his or her race, may object to a prosecutor's race-based exclusion of persons from the petit jury. Our conclusion rested on a two-part analysis. First, following our opinions in *Batson* and in *Carter v. Jury Commission of Greene County,* we made clear that a prosecutor's race-based peremptory challenge violates the equal protection rights of those excluded from jury service. Second, we relied on well-established rules of third-party standing to hold that a defendant may raise the excluded jurors' equal protection rights.

Powers relied upon over a century of jurisprudence dedicated to the elimination of race prejudice within the jury selection process. Indeed, discrimination on the basis of race in selecting a jury in a civil proceeding harms the excluded juror no less than discrimination in a criminal trial. In either case, race is the sole reason for denying the excluded venireperson the honor and privilege of participating in our system of justice.

That an act violates the Constitution when committed by a government official, however, does not answer the question whether the same act offends constitutional guarantees if committed by a private litigant or his attorney. The Constitution's protections of individual liberty and equal protection apply in general only to action by the government. Racial discrimination, though invidious in all contexts, violates the Constitution only when it may be attributed to state action. Thus, the legality of the exclusion at issue here turns on the extent to which a litigant in a civil case may be subject to the Constitution's restrictions.

. . . This fundamental limitation on the scope of constitutional guarantees "preserves an area of individual freedom by limiting the reach of federal law" and "avoids imposing on the State, its agencies or officials, responsibility for conduct for which they cannot fairly be blamed." One great object of the Constitution is to permit citizens to structure their private relations as they choose subject only to the constraints of statutory or decisional law.

To implement these principles, courts must consider from time to time where the governmental sphere ends and the private sphere begins.

We begin our discussion within the framework for the state action analysis set forth in *Lugar.* There we considered the state action question in the context of a due process challenge to a State's procedure allowing private parties to obtain prejudgment attachments. We asked first whether the claimed constitutional deprivation resulted from the exercise of a right or privilege having its source in state authority, and second, whether the private party charged with the deprivation could be described in all fairness as a state actor.

There can be no question that the first part of the *Lugar* inquiry is satisfied here. By their very nature, peremptory challenges have no significance outside a court of law. Their sole purpose is to permit litigants to assist the government in the selection of an impartial trier of fact. . . . Peremptory challenges are permitted only when the government, by statute or decisional law, deems it appropriate to allow parties to exclude a given number of persons who otherwise would satisfy the requirements for service on the petit jury.

. . . Today in most jurisdictions, statutes or rules make a limited number of peremptory challenges available to parties in both civil and criminal proceedings. In the case before us, the challenges were exercised under a federal statute that provides, "In civil cases, each party shall be entitled to three peremptory challenges." Without this authorization, granted by an Act of Congress itself, Leesville would not have been able to engage in the alleged discriminatory acts.

Given that the statutory authorization for the challenges exercised in this case is clear, the remainder of our state action analysis centers around the second part of the *Lugar* test, whether a private litigant in all fairness must be deemed a government actor in the use of peremptory challenges. Although we have recognized that this aspect of the analysis is often a fact-bound inquiry, our cases disclose certain principles of general application. Our precedents establish that, in determining whether a particular action or course of conduct is governmental in character, it is relevant to examine the following: the extent to which the actor relies on governmental assistance and benefits, whether the actor is performing a traditional governmental function, and whether the injury caused is aggravated in a unique way by the incidents of governmental authority. Based on our application of these three principles to the circumstances here, we hold that the exercise of peremptory challenges by the defendant in the District Court was pursuant to a course of state action.

It cannot be disputed that, without the overt, significant participation of the government, the peremptory challenge system, as well as the jury trial system of which it is a part, simply could not exist. As discussed above, peremptory challenges have no utility outside the jury system, a system which the government alone administers. In the federal system, Congress has established the qualifications for jury service, and has outlined the procedures by which jurors are selected. To this end, each district court in the federal system must adopt a plan for locating and summoning to the court eligible prospective jurors. This plan, as with all other trial court procedures, must implement statutory policies of random juror selection from a fair cross section of the community, and nonexclusion on account of race, color, religion, sex, national origin, or economic status.

At the outset of the selection process, prospective jurors must complete jury qualification forms as prescribed by the Administrative Office of the United States Courts. . . . In a typical case, counsel receive these forms and rely on them when exercising their peremptory strikes. The Clerk of the United States District Court, a federal official, summons potential jurors from their employment or other pursuits. . . . Whether or not they are selected for a jury panel, summoned jurors receive a per diem fixed by statute for their service.

The trial judge exercises substantial control over *voir dire* in the federal system. In some cases, judges may even conduct the entire *voir dire* by themselves, a common practice in the District Court where the instant case was tried.

When a lawyer exercises a peremptory challenge, the judge advises the juror he or she has been excused.

As we have outlined here, a private party could not exercise its peremptory challenges absent the overt, significant assistance of the court. The government summons jurors, constrains their freedom of movement, and subjects them to public scrutiny and examination. The party who exercises a challenge invokes the formal authority of the court, which must discharge the prospective juror, thus effecting the "final and practical denial" of the excluded individual's opportunity to serve on the petit jury. Without the direct and indispensable participation of the judge, who beyond all question is a state actor, the peremptory challenge system would serve no purpose. By enforcing a discriminatory peremptory challenge, the court "has not only made itself a party to the [biased act], but has elected to place its power, property and prestige behind the [alleged] discrimination." In so doing, the government has "create[d] the legal framework governing the [challenged] conduct," and in a significant way has involved itself with invidious discrimination.

In determining Leesville's state-actor status, we next consider whether the action in question involves the performance of a traditional function of the government. A traditional function of government is evident here.

In the federal system, the Constitution itself commits the trial of facts in a civil cause to the jury. Should either party to a cause invoke its Seventh Amendment right, the jury becomes the principal factfinder, charged with weighing the evidence, judging the credibility of witnesses, and reaching a verdict. The jury's factual determinations as a general rule are final. These are traditional functions of government, not of a select, private group beyond the reach of the Constitution. . . .

The principle that the selection of state officials, other than through election by all qualified voters, may constitute state action applies with even greater force in the context of jury selection through the use of peremptory challenges. Though the motive of a peremptory challenge may be to protect a private interest, the objective of jury selection proceedings is to determine representation on a governmental body. Were it not for peremptory challenges, there would be no question that the entire process of determining who will serve on the jury constitutes state action. The fact that the government delegates some portion of this power to private litigants does not change the governmental character of the power exercised.

Race discrimination within the courtroom raises serious questions as to the fairness of the proceedings conducted there. Racial bias mars the integrity of the judicial system and prevents the idea of democratic government from becoming a reality. To permit racial exclusion in this official forum compounds the racial insult inherent in judging a citizen by the color of his or her skin.

A civil proceeding often implicates significant rights and interests. Civil juries, no less than their criminal counterparts, must follow the law and act as impartial factfinders. And, as we have observed, their verdicts, no less than those of their criminal counterparts, become binding judgments of the court. Racial discrimination has no place in the courtroom, whether the proceeding is civil or criminal. The Constitution demands nothing less. We conclude that the courts must entertain a challenge to a private litigant's racially discriminatory use of peremptory challenges in a civil trial.

It may be true that the role of litigants in determining the jury's composition provides one reason for wide acceptance of the jury system and of its verdicts. But if race stereotypes are the price for acceptance of a jury panel as fair, the price is too high to meet the standard of the Constitution.

The quiet rationality of the courtroom makes it an appropriate place to confront race-based fears or hostility by means other than the use of offensive stereotypes. Whether the race generality employed by litigants to challenge a potential juror derives from open hostility or from some hidden and unarticulated fear, neither motive entitles the litigant to cause injury to the excused juror.

The judgment is reversed, and the case is remanded for further proceedings consistent with our opinion.

Case Questions

1. Do the constitutional guarantees of individual liberty and equal protection usually apply to private parties? Why?
2. What are the reasons the court gives for finding that the use of peremptory challenges to jurors in a civil case constitute "state action"?
3. What are the sequences of steps in the selection of a jury that are outlined in the case?

The Attorney

An **attorney-at-law** is a person who acts for someone else in legal matters that may concern real estate, tax, contract, or civil litigation problems. In the United States, the license to practice law is granted by the states and not by the federal government. The requirements differ somewhat among the states, but graduation from an approved law school and the successful completion of a state-approved bar examination are generally prerequisites to obtaining a license to practice law.

Attorney's Office Environment Some attorneys have their own law offices. Others are members of firms with 2 or 3 and up to 400 or more attorneys. Still others are salaried employees of corporations. Many attorneys are employed by federal, state, and local governmental agencies. A significant number of attorneys do not even practice law; they work as bankers, business managers, or educators.

Businesses that constantly use attorneys to perform a variety of functions have developed several organizational means for working with their attorneys. Many businesses hire attorneys as employees and either disperse them among operational units or centralize them into a separate legal department. A staff of lawyers who work as attorneys for a business is generally referred to as *corporate counsel* or *inside counsel.* The lawyers on such a staff work inside a corporation as corporate employees, not as members of a separate firm of lawyers that contracts with a corporation. This is the role played by Mr. Thomas in the *Upjohn* case, which appears on page 82.

A different type of business-attorney relationship exists when a business retains a lawyer or a law firm. This relationship is usually based on a contract specifying the fee that the business will pay in exchange for the services provided for the business by the lawyer or law firm. A business may not want to hire a lawyer each time it has a legal problem. Instead, it may agree to pay a set sum to retain a law firm and thus ensure that when it needs that firm's services, it can consult with the firm's lawyers. The attorney-client relationship is formed once the retainer agreement has been made, and it remains in effect whenever the law firm performs work for the business.

Many businesses work both with attorneys who are employees and with attorneys in law firms. The inside counsel usually perform functions while some legal specialized services are provided by the attorneys in law firms. In many cases, an outside law firm is hired to act as a litigator if the legal problems of a business involve court proceedings. Some companies bargain with law firms to reduce their fees for the services they provide. Figure 3–5 depicts some of the methods being used by business to reduce legal fees.

FIGURE 3–5
Methods Used by Business Firms to Reduce Legal Fees

- **Bidding on proposals** Clients send proposals to several law firms; the law firms detail their plans, specify attorneys who will be used, and state the fee to be charged.
- **Blended rates** Clients pay an hourly rate that blends the rates normally charged by senior level partners and junior level associates; the law firm then determines who to assign to the client.
- **Flat fees** Law firms agree to handle a project for a flat fee, no matter how many attorney hours are needed.
- **Mix of hourly and contingent fees** Some portion of the firm's hourly fees is dependent upon success in the case.
- **Volume discount** A business agrees to send a law firm all of a specific kind of work (e.g., environmental litigation) and the law firm agrees to discount its normal fees.

INTERNATIONAL PERSPECTIVE: LAWYERS AND GLOBAL BUSINESS

Business firms engaged in international business rely on the advice of those attorneys who have the knowledge of the rules of international trade and investment. These attorneys may be employees of the business firm itself or may be practicing in a law firm. Many U.S. law firms have followed their clients overseas and they are now located in cities like Beijing, Moscow, Tokyo, and Mexico City.

Some nations, like Japan, admit very few foreign attorneys, while others, like France, allow foreign attorneys in their country to do only those activities which their lawyers could do in the foreigner's home country. The restrictions on attorneys most often affect the attorney's representation of a client in court; few nations allow foreign attorneys to represent a client without assistance from a local attorney. There are also some restrictions imposed for foreign attorneys who seek to negotiate with government or business representatives.

In the European Community, attorneys from one member nation are allowed to move freely among the member nations to establish law firms and to provide legal services. It may be that this freedom will expand beyond the Community's borders. However, even in the Community, the restrictions on court appearances and formal representation of a client are enforced.

The growth of international business activities has led to an expansion of multinational legal departments and international law firms. The mixture of lawyers from different nations who work side by side on international business matters is leading to the development of an international legal practice.

Functions Performed by Attorneys Most of the time spent by practicing attorneys on legal matters does not relate to the conduct of trials. The attorney acting as litigator performs the most visible type of legal work, but counseling, negotiating, and drafting functions are the predominate and most time-consuming activities of many attorneys.

An attorney acting as a *counselor* for a firm gives the firm advice regarding its activities. How do tax laws affect the firm's decision to purchase or lease a building? What should the contract forms say when the firm sells products to consumers? Should the firm organize a separate corporate entity to sell its products internationally? Although the officers and directors of a firm are responsible for such decisions, they generally seek the counsel of both inside and outside attorneys concerning the laws that affect the firm's activities.

Attorneys also work as *negotiators*. If a business is purchasing a sizable real estate parcel, developing a mall, or contracting to install computers in a university, specialized attorneys may be called on to negotiate contract terms. Businesses having contractual relations with labor unions frequently hire attorneys to negotiate collective bargaining agreements. Attorneys often negotiate with governmental representatives. For example, an attorney for a business may negotiate with a local government about a variance in the zoning code or a reduction in the local property taxes. Negotiations at the state level may focus on agency investigations, licenses, permits, or compliance reports. At the national or international level, attorneys may negotiate a joint venture or license agreement for a business firm.

Attorneys are also drafters of documents. They often write wills for clients, prepare contracts regarding the purchase and sale of businesses, or draft partnership agreements. An attorney who drafts documents seeks to ensure that their language addresses and resolves as many legal problems as possible. Given this objective, it is not surprising that the contract terms for what appears to be a simple transaction are often detailed and complex. The parties expect attorneys to draft documents that cover all of the essential concerns and foreseeable problems, including concerns of which the parties may be unaware.

The attorney who works as a *litigator* in a trial is engaged in the most visible of legal tasks. Because of the publicity given to certain types of lawsuits (product liability, environmental protection, and securities regulation), many people assume that a business is almost invariably the defendant when it is in court. In fact, the bulk of business litigation involves corporations as plaintiffs. Generally, lawsuits in the fields of contract and commercial law involve suits between two businesses. Because the American legal system is an adversary system, the attorney's role in a civil trial is clearly that of an advocate for the client's interests from the prepleadings stage through the trial.

Functions Performed by Attorneys

Attorney Function	Examples
Counselor	Advises business on whether to incorporate Counsels on whether tax laws favor a lease rather than a purchase of property
Negotiator	Negotiates labor contract for business with employees' representative Negotiates a contract for a major purchase—such as a new computer system
Drafter	Prepares contracts regarding sale of business Drafts will
Litigator	Represents individual or business acting as plaintiff in lawsuit Defends business or individual being sued by other parties

Attorney-Client Privilege A business firm wants to select an attorney who can be trusted, whether as an employee or by means of a retainer agreement. The attorney-client relationship is based on trust. Frequently, the attorney requires confidential information in order to perform his or her function. To counsel, negotiate, draft, or litigate, the attorney must be informed about business activities relating to that function. The **attorney-client privilege** provides that an attorney cannot be forced to divulge such confidential information regarding his or her client. In the *Upjohn* case, which follows, the U.S. Supreme Court reviews the role of Upjohn's attorney. Is a corporate attorney permitted to keep confidential information obtained from employees about questionable payments made to foreign officials, or must the attorney reveal that information to the Internal Revenue Service (IRS)?

Upjohn v. United States

449 U.S. 383 (1981)
United States Supreme Court

After Thomas, the general counsel for Upjohn, was informed that one of its foreign subsidiaries had made questionable payments to foreign government officials in order to secure business, he began an internal investigation of such payments. He sent all of Upjohn's foreign managers a questionnaire and also interviewed them and other company officials and employees. Subsequently, based on a voluntarily submitted report, the IRS began an investigation to determine the tax consequences of the questionable payments. It demanded that Upjohn furnish it with the replies to the questionnaire, notes of the interviews, and the memoranda regarding the payments. Upjohn refused on the ground that these documents were protected from disclosure by the attorney-client privilege. The United States then sued to obtain them. The trial court concluded that the summons should be enforced. Upjohn appealed to the Court of Appeals, which affirmed the trial court's decision, and Upjohn then filed for review by the Supreme Court.

Justice Rehnquist delivered the opinion of the Court

The attorney-client privilege is the oldest of the privileges for confidential communications known to the common law. Its purpose is to encourage full and frank communications between attorneys and their clients and thereby promote broader public interests in the observance of law and the administration of justice. The privilege recognizes that sound legal advice or advocacy depends upon the lawyer's being fully informed by the client. Admittedly complications in the application of the privilege arise when the client is a corporation, but this Court has assumed that the privilege applies when the client is a corporation, and the Government does not contest the general proposition.

In the case of the individual client, the provider of the information and the person who acts on the lawyer's advice are one and the same. In the corporate context, however, it will frequently be employees beyond the control group (officers and agents responsible for directing the company's action in response to legal advice) who will possess the information needed by the corporation's lawyers. Middle-level and indeed lower-level employees can embroil the corporation in serious legal difficulties, and it is only natural that these employees would have relevant information needed by corporate counsel if he is adequately to advise the client.

The communications at issue were made by Upjohn employees to counsel for Upjohn acting as such, at the direction of corporate superiors in order to secure legal advice from counsel. . . . Information, not available from upper-echelon management, was needed to supply a basis for legal advice concerning compliance with securities and tax laws, foreign laws, currency regulations, duties to shareholders, and potential litigation in each of these areas. The communications concerned matters within the scope of the employees' corporate duties. The questionnaire identified Thomas as "the company's General Counsel" and referred in its opening sentence to the possible illegality of payments such as the ones on which information was being sought. Consistent with the underlying purpose of the attorney-client privilege, these communications must be protected against compelled disclosure.

Application of the attorney-client privilege to communications such as those involved here puts the adversary in no worse position than if the communication had never taken place. The privilege only protects disclosure of communications; it does not protect disclosure of the underlying facts by those who communicated with the attorney.

"A fact is one thing and a communication concerning that fact is an entirely different thing. The client cannot be compelled to answer the question, 'What did you say or write to the attorney?' but may not refuse to disclose any relevant fact within his knowledge merely because he incorporated a statement of such fact into his communication to his attorney." . . .

Our decision that the communications by Upjohn employees to counsel are covered by the attorney-client privilege disposes of the case so far as the responses to the questionnaires and any notes reflecting responses to interview questions are concerned. The summons reaches further, however, and Thomas has testified that his notes and memoranda of interviews go beyond responses to his questions. To the extent that the material subject to the summons is not protected by the attorney-client privilege as disclosing communication between an employee and counsel, we must reach the ruling by the Court of Appeals that the work-product doctrine does not apply to the summonses issued. While conceding the applicability of the work-product doctrine, the Government asserts that it has made a sufficient showing of necessity to overcome its protection.

We think a stronger showing of necessity and

unavailability by other means than was made by the Government in this case would be necessary to compel disclosure. Accordingly, the judgment of the Court of Appeals is reversed, and the case remanded for further proceedings.

Case Questions

1. What is the difference between the attorney-client privilege and the work product rule?
2. What is the purpose of the attorney-client privilege?

The Litigating Parties

A person who may become a party in a civil lawsuit should know action to take that would help to avoid litigation, action that should be taken when there is the potential for litigation, and action to take as a party involved in litigation.

How to Avoid Litigation One midwestern law firm suggests to its clients that the following steps may help to avoid litigation.[4] First, important transactions should be reduced to a signed writing. The writing should be prepared before any performance is required. Where possible, written promises should be secured (i.e., payment assured), either by property or by an indemnification clause, one that makes the promising party liable for actual expenses and damages incurred by the other party if the first party breaches the agreement.

Second, the person who is about to sign a written agreement should make sure that he or she understands it before signing. Although this may seem elementary, many people are more prone to simply sign an agreement, particularly one that uses rather specific legal terms, than to ask questions about it. The more complex the transaction, the more important it is to review and question the meaning of terms used in the written agreement.

Finally, it is important to be alert to situations with high litigation potential. Transactions that have a substantial value or especially difficult consequences to one of the parties (such as with an employee discharge) require planning before action. In these situations, consideration of the legal consequences regarding words spoken, letters written, or actions taken need to be carefully reviewed before any such action occurs.

Actions Anticipating the Potential for Litigation People who are owners or managers of business firms may want to have a formal program of procedures to follow when their employees become aware of circumstances that might lead to litigation. In order to document a claim or properly defend one, there are several steps that should be followed in most cases.[5] Figure 3–6 highlights some of those different steps.

Actions to Take after Becoming a Party to Civil Litigation A party in a civil lawsuit must be aware of how his or her role relates to the roles of the judge, jury, and attorney. During the trial, the judge's role is to be an impartial decision maker. Thus, neither party should try to discuss a pending case with the judge. During the trial the judge must allow only legally proper evidence to be presented for the jury's consideration. Accordingly, a party should not volunteer information while testifying during a trial.

Each of the parties in a civil lawsuit aids in selecting the jury. Acting in cooperation with his or her attorney during the *voir dire*, a party may seek information from potential

---

[4]*Understanding Litigation*, a booklet by Howard & Howard Attorneys, P.C., September 7, 1983.

[5]Ibid.

FIGURE 3–6 Documenting or Defending a Potential Claim

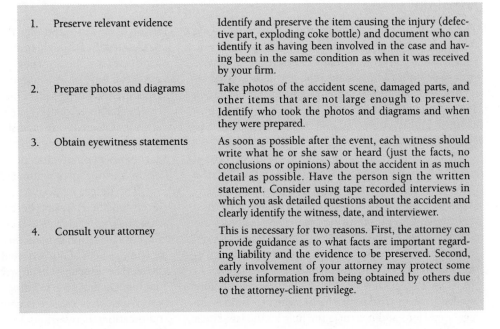

1.	Preserve relevant evidence	Identify and preserve the item causing the injury (defective part, exploding coke bottle) and document who can identify it as having been involved in the case and having been in the same condition as when it was received by your firm.
2.	Prepare photos and diagrams	Take photos of the accident scene, damaged parts, and other items that are not large enough to preserve. Identify who took the photos and diagrams and when they were prepared.
3.	Obtain eyewitness statements	As soon as possible after the event, each witness should write what he or she saw or heard (just the facts, no conclusions or opinions) about the accident in as much detail as possible. Have the person sign the written statement. Consider using tape recorded interviews in which you ask detailed questions about the accident and clearly identify the witness, date, and interviewer.
4.	Consult your attorney	This is necessary for two reasons. First, the attorney can provide guidance as to what facts are important regarding liability and the evidence to be preserved. Second, early involvement of your attorney may protect some adverse information from being obtained by others due to the attorney-client privilege.

jurors that may help ensure the selection of a sympathetic jury. Although impartial juries are an objective of our legal system, the parties each seek a jury that is more sympathetic to their position than to that of the other party. If a party is testifying in a case, he or she must try to answer questions persuasively. Most experienced observers believe that jurors are adept at telling when a witness is lying. Thus, truth is not merely the best policy; it is the only policy.

ETHICAL DILEMMAS IN LITIGATION

Although the alternative dispute resolution methods referred to in the following chapter sometimes offer meaningful cost and time savings when compared to litigation, parties still often choose to pursue litigation. Is it ethical for a party to seek to litigate a questionable case or to harass the opponent into settlement by threatening or conducting costly pretrial procedures? If a large firm has significant resources and easy access to legal counsel, is it ethical for that firm to pursue litigation if it suspects its small firm opponent will be unable to bear the time and cost such litigation will require? Similarly, if the cost of litigation for a defendant is significantly more than the cost of settlement of a minor claim, is it ethical to file a nuisance claim against that party?

Before bringing a suit, a client should have a reasonable belief that wrongful conduct has occurred, that damages have resulted, and that genuine issues exist. Litigation can be an ethical method of settling disputes, but unfounded or vindictive litigation wastes scarce societal resources and brings about disrespect for the law. The law provides remedies for victims of unfounded litigation. Thus, the fraudulent use of legal processes is both unethical and illegal.

SUMMARY

The American legal system provides a variety of ways in which parties to a dispute can seek to resolve it. Litigation in the United States is based on the adversarial principle, which makes the parties and their attorneys responsible for presenting needed information and arguments about the law. The parties, pretrial procedures, and trial practices of criminal and civil litigation are quite dissimilar.

The civil litigation process consists of several stages. Many of the concerns of civil litigation must be addressed before a trial begins: Who can be sued? Where can the suit be brought? What would be the best theory to use in pursuing the case? The pleadings and pretrial stages are often crucial to the outcome of civil litigation since most cases never reach trial but are settled during these preliminary stages.

Civil cases that do go to trial may be tried before a judge alone or with both a judge, who determines the legal questions and instructs the jury on the law, and a jury, which determines the facts. Each party in a civil case has a role in selecting prospective jurors through the use of challenges. The plaintiff begins the presentation of evidence and then the defendant follows. Witnesses testify through direct and cross examination conducted by the attorneys. Rules of evidence determine the type of information presented at a trial; the rules are intended to prohibit use of irrelevant, biased, or unreliable evidence. The jury verdict occurs after closing statements are made but before the judgment is rendered. Postjudgment collection methods include garnishment or attachment. If legal errors in a trial are made, a trial court's judgment may be appealed.

The judge, jury, attorneys, and parties each perform specific roles in the civil litigation process. To some degree, each acts as a check on the others. Thus, the civil litigation process incorporates the check-and-balance system of our national and state legal environment. The attorney-client privilege protects the information clients give to attorneys in confidence. The privilege exists so as to encourage full and frank communications between attorneys and their clients and thereby promote broader interest in the observance of law and the administration of justice.

KEY TERMS

adversarial principle, p. 62
inquisitional principle, p. 63
complaint, p. 64
summons, p. 64
answer, p.64
discovery procedures, p. 66
verdict, p. 69
judgment, p. 71
garnishment, p. 71
attorney-at-law, p. 79
attorney-client privilege, p. 82

CHAPTER EXERCISES

1. Distinguish the adversarial system from the civil law inquisitorial system of litigation.
2. Describe the progress of a case through the U.S. state and federal court systems beginning at the trial level and ending at the U.S. Supreme Court or the highest appellate court in a state system.
3. Identify each of the following and place them in the proper order of their sequence in civil litigation: motion to direct the verdict, counterclaim, answer, deposition, motion to dismiss for lack of jurisdiction, verdict, complaint, direct examination of plaintiff's witness.
4. Evaluate the role of the jury in the U.S. legal system. Should that role be changed? What problems are presented by the jury selection process?
5. Thiel sued Southern Pacific Company for injuries he received from a moving train. The jury in the case returned a verdict for Southern Pacific, but Thiel appealed claiming the jury had not been properly selected. The jury selection process deliberately excluded from the jury list anyone who worked for a daily or hourly wage. Should the judgment and jury verdict at the trial level be upheld? *Thiel v. Southern Pacific Co.*, 328 U.S. 217 (1946).

6. Assume that several employees of your company inform in-house counsel of their concern about your company's safety violations. Should those communications be protected by the attorney-client privilege? How does this contact differ from the attorney-client contact in the *Upjohn* case?
7. Nancy sues Martha in Kentucky and recovers a judgment for $25,000. The decision of the trial court was not appealed. Martha has not paid Nancy any of the money; what can Nancy do to collect from Martha?
8. Defendant Guzman was charged with violating the federal selective service laws because he refused to report for a physical examination and to report for induction into the armed services. Before trial, Guzman claimed the jury selection system used by the court, which was to determine his guilt or innocence, violated his right to jury representation by a cross section of the community because it excluded persons under the age of 21 from serving on the jury. At the time of the indictment, Guzman was 20. Further, defendant claims using the voter registration list as the sole source of names causes a substantial underrepresentation of young persons (such as those below the age of 30) on the jury because these persons have a significantly lower registration rate. How should the court decide this claim? See *United States v. Guzman,* 337 F. Supp. 140 (S.D., N.Y., 1972), aff'd. 468 F 2d 1245, Cert. den. 410 U.S. 937.
9. USF, a real estate development firm, expanded and grew from a small accounts receivable financing firm to an international conglomerate from 1962 to 1971. It began having financial problems in 1972. When it crashed in 1973, numerous criminal, administrative, and civil cases were filed against it. Because there were common legal issues based on contract, tort, and securities laws in most of the civil cases, they were consolidated and scheduled to be tried together. The trial court judge ruled that the legal and factual issues were so complex as to be beyond the abilities of a jury; thus, he denied all demands for a jury trial. Should the complexity of a case be a basis for denying a party's right to a jury trial in a civil case? See *In re U.S. Financial Securities Litigation,* 609 F 2d 411 (9th Cir., 1979).
10. Some scholars have suggested that lawyers have both ethical and legal duties to inform their clients who are considering litigation about alternative dispute resolution methods.[6] These scholars believe lawyers have an obligation to fully inform their clients of all available options before pursuing litigation. Discuss how the teleological and deontological ethical theories could guide a lawyer who is discussing litigation, and alternatives to it, with a client.

---

[6]D. Burkhardt and F. Conover, "The Ethical Duty to Consider Alternatives to Litigation," *The Colorado Lawyer* (February 1990), p. 249.

Chapter 4

ALTERNATIVE DISPUTE RESOLUTION

KEY CONCEPTS

Dispute resolution can be costly for individuals and firms. Business managers should consider various dispute resolution methods and assess costs and benefits of alternatives to litigation.

The use of alternative dispute resolution methods such as arbitration, mediation, minitrial, and private courts has been growing rapidly. Some methods are alternatives to litigation whereas others are used within the litigation system.

In arbitration, a dispute is heard by someone other than a judge; arbitrators usually have authority to make a binding decision that is enforceable through the courts.

Mediation is a process in which a third person attempts to reconcile a dispute between two parties by persuading them to adjust or settle their differences. Mediators generally have no authority to order resolutions. A minitrial is an informal presentation of a dispute by the parties and their attorneys to senior executives of each party or to an independent adviser.

Private trials use the paid services of retired judges or attorneys to hear cases. Although many of these judges have no legal authority, some states do recognize the judgments of these rent-a-judges.

INTRODUCTION . . . PAST, PRESENT, FUTURE

The concept of alternatives to court litigation has been studied and supported since early in the 20th century. Congress passed the Federal Arbitration Act in 1925, and the American Arbitration Association was founded a year later. However, it was not until the 1970s that the emphasis on alternative dispute resolution (ADR) increased as the legal system began to become so crowded and expensive that it was nearly inaccessible for poor and even middle-class individuals.

Today, the term alternative dispute resolution covers a broad range of options to the adversarial system of litigating disputes. These options generally include arbitration, mediation and conciliation, the minitrial and summary trial, and the private court or rent-a-judge methods. The term alternative not only contrasts these methods with litigation, but it also conveys a sense of choice and selection for the disputing parties. In some cases, this sense of choice is no longer true due to statutes or court rules that require ADR to be used for certain problems. In some jurisdictions, civil cases of less than a specified dollar amount and divorce property matters must be submitted to mediation before being litigated. When contract clauses require arbitration, the contracting parties may have no other choice of how to resolve disputes. Contracts requiring the use of arbitration, commonly used in international business transactions, are becoming more common for health care providers, landlords, and securities brokers.

By the middle of the 1980s, ADR was being embraced by large corporations as a means to solve complicated disputes while cutting burgeoning legal costs. State legislatures also began to require the use of mediation, minitrials, and arbitration within the judicial system. Thus, ADR has become mandatory in some cases rather than being voluntarily chosen by the parties. By the beginning of the 1990s, both the former chief justice of the Supreme Court and a vice president of the United States had spoken out about the costs of litigation and the adversarial process. Awareness about and use of ADR are increasing both in corporate boardrooms and in academic institutions.

In the future, alternatives to litigation for both individuals and firms will become a part of our interaction with the legal environment. Neighborhood mediation centers, mandatory arbitration of many contract disputes, and increased use of minitrials will lead to the mainstreaming of these dispute resolution methods. In the first edition of this text, alternative dispute resolution was only a small part of the dispute resolution chapter. In this edition, we have completely separated it from the litigation chapter to highlight its importance. Perhaps in a future edition, the title *alternative* will be eliminated from ADR because arbitration, mediation, et al. will be seen as mainstream methods for resolving disputes.

OVERVIEW

The use of alternative dispute resolution methods has been growing rapidly, both as a part of the civil litigation process and as an alternative to it. **Arbitration** is the most recognized form of alternative dispute resolution and is commonly used in international contracts, labor disputes, and most commercial transactions. Parties select arbitration by inserting clauses in a contract to govern future disputes or by agreeing to use arbitration after a dispute arises. An arbitrator, or arbitration panel, generally has authority to make a binding decision of the dispute. Courts generally recognize and enforce the disputing parties' choice of arbitration and the arbitrator's decision.

Mediation is a process of dispute resolution whereby a third party seeks to persuade the disputing parties to settle their differences. Mediation is used in international conflicts, labor-management disagreements, and in numerous contract disputes. The Federal Mediation and Conciliation Service has experienced mediators who serve in labor-management disputes. Unlike the arbitrator, the mediator usually has no authority to resolve the dispute.

Minitrials are informal presentations of disputes before senior executives of the disputing parties who often rely on an independent adviser. Once the senior executives have heard the presentations, settlement of the dispute becomes more likely because the strengths and weaknesses of the parties' cases become evident. Sometimes the adviser is asked to render an advisory opinion as to how a court might decide the dispute.

Private trials use retired judges or attorneys to resolve disputes. The parties can avoid crowded court calendars and are able to select judges with specialized expertise rather than the randomly assigned judges in the courts. Decisions at private trials generally are not recognized and enforced. However, some states, like California, recognize these **rent-a-judge** decisions as valid trial judgments.

Other alternatives to civil litigation that have developed include the small claims court, summary jury trial, and administrative hearing. Although litigation may be pursued as part of a business strategy in some cases, in many situations ADR techniques offer a less expensive and more effective means of resolving disputes. Business managers need to recognize the existence of these alternatives to litigation so that they are able to select and employ the most appropriate method for any given dispute.

CIVIL LITIGATION AND ADR

Both litigation and ADR constitute important segments of the U.S. legal system. The courts are established in the Constitution as a forum for resolving disputes. The courts are open to all people (although difficult to access for poor people), and they involve citizens in dispute resolution through juries. Although litigation is costly and inefficient, the courts play an important role as a check on the other branches of our government. Through the application of the Bill of Rights and due process guarantees (discussed in the next chapter), the courts enforce the rights of the minority. Most people support a strong and independent court system because it forces the government and other people in society to act according to rule of law.

ADR techniques are generally fairly quick, not too expensive, and private. None of those attributes are common to litigation. ADR involves the parties in a nonadversarial environment, encouraging each party to participate in seeking a solution that both parties can live with in both short and long-term periods. Business managers need to be cognizant of different ADR techniques so that an optimal method is selected for any dispute the business confronts. Effective dispute resolution management is too important to be ignored either by individuals or by firm managers.

ADR essentially refers to less adversarial methods of dispute resolution, whether used as a part of a court process or as an alternative to it. There are several basic differences between the adversarial method of dispute resolution followed in civil litigation and the ADR processes. First, in the adversarial process, the neutral party (judge) makes a decision after hearing from the disputing parties, whereas in ADR, the hearing officer may help formulate the result during the process. Second, in adversarial litigation, one party wins and the other loses. By contrast, ADR methods allow for each party to benefit from the resolution. Third, whereas ADR requires communication and trust between the parties, the adversarial system nurtures distrust and animosity. Finally, the parties in liti-

FIGURE 4–1
Litigation (Adversarial) and ADR (Problem-Solving) Comparisons

	Litigation	ADR*
Neutral party's role	Decides case after hearing from parties via adversarial process	Helps parties' conciliation while hearing from them
Outcome	One winner—one loser	No winner/loser Parties agree to solution
Party's view of other party	Opponent not to be trusted	Parties need to communicate and perhaps trust
Rule of law	Usually governs outcome of individual cases	May play no role in determining result

*These are less true of arbitration than with other ADR methods.

gation expect their case will be governed by a general legal principle found in a statute, administrative regulation, or court decision. In an ADR matter, the outcome of the dispute need not be based on general legal principles. Although legal rules are followed in most arbitration hearings, most ADR methods do not require the decision or result to be based on recognized legal rules. Figure 4–1 compares litigation's adversarial nature with ADR's emphasis on creative problem-solving.

ADR COMES OF AGE

ADR has come into its own in the last decade. In 1980, Congress enacted the Federal Dispute Resolution Act. The legislation encourages state and local agencies to establish forums that provide arbitration, mediation, conciliation, or similar procedures to resolve minor disputes. Although these provisions expired in 1984, by that time other voices and actions to increase the use of ADR were occurring. In 1984, Warren Burger, then the chief justice of the U.S. Supreme Court called attention to the drawbacks of litigation: "Trials by the adversarial contest must in time go the way of the ancient trial by battle and blood. Our system is too costly, too painful, too destructive, too inefficient for a truly civilized people."[1]

Built-In Protection Against the Litigation Blues

By James F. Henry

If you want to do business with General Mills, then you'd better be willing to forgo formal litigation of any future dispute. Why? Because this Fortune 500 company will not sign a contract unless you agree that conflicts will be resolved through the use of a minitrial, mediation or another alternative dispute resolution (ADR) procedure.

ADR is not brand new. Lawyers have deployed it in countless disputes, often with great success. Some creative managers and lawyers are institutionalizing the use of ADR. They

[1]The remarks of the chief justice were given at the 1984 midyear meeting of the American Bar Association. See J. Carnaham, "What Chief Justice Burger Had to Say," in *Ohio Bar Association Report* (1984).

are making these techniques a permanent element of corporate strategy—in relations with customers, with suppliers and with employees. Some examples:

- Deere & Co., the heavy equipment maker, routinely mediates its product liability cases through a company that provides ADR services. In 1990, Deere lawyers directed 36 cases to mediation; by early this year [1991], 20 had settled.
- Grappling with the banking crisis, the FDIC has trained 100 "dispute coordinators" in its offices nationwide. Directed by FDIC lawyers, these staffers negotiate and mediate certain bank loan disputes. In 1990, they saved the FDIC $3 million in legal costs.
- General Motors has devised a two-step ADR system for resolving disputes with its many dealers, encompassing such common issues as termination, service obligations and product allocation.
- When work-related disputes arise in the ranks of its 42,000 nonunion employees, Northrop uses four different ADR methods to resolve them.
- The main mission of IBM's industry relations department, which consists of 16 staffers with sales and marketing backgrounds, is to prevent and resolve disputes between IBM and other companies in the computer industry.

Despite the diversity of processes and disputes, there are common themes to these varied programs. One, a feature of IBM and FDIC initiatives and many others, is the central role assigned to the business manager. No longer does a manager simply tell his lawyers to sue, and then wait for the call to a deposition. It is a main tenet of ADR that the talents and skills of executives are invaluable in dispute resolution. In minitrials, mediations and other ADR procedures, senior business executives participate as fully as their lawyers in resolving disputes.

The flip side of this development is that lawyers are viewing disputes in a more businesslike, managerial fashion. According to Motorola general counsel Richard H. Weise, "Our product is the resolution of disputes, and with ADR we think we can deliver a higher-quality product with less cost and in a shorter time."

But despite the compelling rationale underlying the use of ADR, the task of instituting it within a corporation is difficult.

Clearly, rooting out the litigation habit is arduous, piecemeal and prone to setbacks. Many lawyers and top managers, inured to litigation, look with distaste on the so-called ADR "wimp" factor. Old habits die hard, especially when substantial effort is needed to learn the new ones. Lawyer Marguerite Millhauser, who counsels companies about ADR, compares it to another revolution: computers. In winning over a person wedded to his typewriter or pencil, the computer advocate must confront the former's "fear of the unknown, fear of making a mistake, fear of failure and fear of being judged," Ms. Millhauser says.

But the effort is worth it. . . . The promise of ADR—in saving time and money, in preserving business relationships, in better "win-win" results—far exceeds the cost of institutionalizing it.

Source: This article is excerpted from *The Wall Street Journal*, July 22, 1991, p. A8.

ADR in the Corporate Arena

In 1977, the first minitrial was used by Telecredit, Inc., and TRW, Inc., to settle a patent dispute.[2] The parties had spent two years and over $1,000,000 in their pretrial activities. Telecredit claimed TRW had infringed its patents and TRW wanted a showing of how the

[2]*Business Week*, October 13, 1980, p. 170.

patents had been infringed. Telecredit asked TRW whom it would believe and TRW said it wanted the opinion of a neutral outside expert. A former Court of Claims judge was picked by the parties to be an adviser, but not to act as a judge or arbitrator. Gradually they agreed to procedural rules and the minitrial method of dispute resolution was born. The parties settled their dispute less than three months after the minitrial agreement, no doubt saving another $1 million in legal fees to the disputing firms.

In 1985, IBM demanded arbitration in a long-standing dispute with Fujitsu. Two arbitrators were chosen and they soon became mediators and negotiated new agreements between the parties. The parties followed the lead of the arbitrators/mediators and resolved their existing problems without litigation. Further, the two firms also agreed to use the ADR method for resolving any future problems. These firms used alternate dispute resolution techniques to solve problems when they realized they had not moved toward resolution in their prelitigation maneuvers.

In 1987, the U.S. Supreme Court pointed to the Federal Arbitration Act as its basis for determining that customers of a brokerage house, Shearson/American Express, Inc., were required to arbitrate claims charging violation of several federal securities laws. The broker had a compulsory arbitration agreement provision in the contract with the customer:

> The Federal Arbitration Act provides that arbitration agreements "shall be valid, irrevocable, and enforceable, save upon such grounds as exist at law or in equity for the revocation of any contract. . . . The Act thus establishes a 'federal policy favoring arbitration.' "[3]

ADR in the Neighborhood

In the last several years, a network of diverse dispute resolution programs have evolved to mediate, arbitrate, and facilitate conflicts into agreement with a minimum of stress on the disputing parties and the courts. Today, these programs may be found in state, city, or county agencies. Trade associations have consumer action panels. University systems often use student volunteers and employ ombudsmen to serve as mediators. Some cities have independent organizations that provide mediation service for the community as a whole.

In Michigan, for example, the Community Dispute Resolution Program was established by the legislature in 1988 and funded by an increase of filing fees at the circuit court trial level. Presently, 12 dispute resolution centers provide conciliation, mediation, or other forms of voluntary dispute resolution to persons as an alternative to litigation. Several common questions about neighborhood dispute resolution centers are answered below.

1. **Who are the mediators?** Mediators are community volunteers who receive at least 25 hours of specialized training in conflict resolution techniques and communication skills. They are laborers, counselors, attorneys, senior citizens, and employees at various community organizations.
2. **What kind of matters are appropriate for mediation?** Each center has guidelines that generally include neighborhood disputes (fences/driveways), consumer/merchant disputes, business and contract disputes, landlord/tenant problems, family disputes, and small claims. Disputes involving controlled substances and serious violence are not appropriate for mediation.

---

[3]The *Shearson/American Express, Inc.* case is excerpted on p. 98 of this chapter.

FIGURE 4–2
Arbitration Offer Found in Patient Information Booklet

Michigan Medical Arbitration Program
Standard Offer

Arbitration is a method of deciding disputes without going to court. The offer of this agreement is authorized under Michigan law to provide the patient with a choice between arbitration or going to court to resolve any health care complaint which may arise.

In arbitration, a 3-person panel made up of a doctor or other health care professional, a lawyer, and a member of the public will hear and decide your case. In most cases a decision made by the arbitration panel is final and cannot be appealed to court.

Please take a moment to review the agreement. Signing the agreement is your choice. You will receive the same quality of health care whether or not you sign. If you do sign, you have 60 days after you are discharged to change your mind.

The patient information booklet you receive should answer any questions you may have. Questions can also be answered by calling the American Arbitration Association's toll-free number in the booklet.

This provision appears in booklets approved by the Michigan Commissioner of Insurance. It was written by the Michigan Arbitration Advisory Committee, a group of consumers, doctors, hospital administrators, nurses, and lawyers.

3. **Why do people use mediation?** Mediation is quick, usually occurring within 10 days from the time both parties have agreed to mediate. The mediation usually lasts less than two hours. It is inexpensive, since the centers provide free mediation to indigent people and low costs to others. It is successful because the goal is to have all parties satisfied. Mediation aims at a win/win situation. It offers privacy, since all discussions related to the subject of mediation remain confidential and cannot be used in a lawsuit. Its effectiveness rates high, with approximately 80 percent of all mediations ending in agreement.[4]

ARBITRATION

Arbitration is probably the best known of the alternative dispute resolution methods. Arbitration is commonly used in international commercial transactions, in health-care provider contracts with patients, in settling disputes between professional athletes and their team owners, and in contracts between securities brokers and their clients. A sample arbitration offer found in a Patient Information Booklet given to health-care patients is shown in Figure 4–2. In arbitration, a dispute is heard by someone other than a judge. One person or a panel of people gather evidence from the contending parties under generally less complicated procedures than those followed in court.

The arbitrator is usually a specialist familiar with the type of problem underlying the dispute. Because the arbitrator handles fewer cases than a judge does, the dispute can be resolved more quickly than if it went through the courts. Further, arbitrators are often familiar with the nature of the dispute and the commercial practices of firms in the same or similar industries. By contrast, judges who are randomly assigned to the controversy may not have the specialized expertise permitting appropriate decisions.

[4] "Win or Lose—Mediation: Where the Winning Solution Is Up to You" (Michigan State Court Administrator's Office, Lansing, Mich.), 1991.

Voluntary Agreements to Arbitrate

The most important first step in initiating arbitration is the agreement to arbitrate. That agreement may be one of two kinds: (1) a future dispute arbitration clause in a contract; or (2) where the parties did not agree in advance, a submission of an existing dispute to arbitration. If the parties agreed in advance to arbitrate a dispute, the party initiating the action serves a Demand for Arbitration on the other party and also files it with an arbitration association, such as the American Arbitration Association (AAA). The AAA rules of arbitration generally require the other party be given a certain time period in which to respond to the claim before any documents are submitted or a hearing occurs.

Parties who have not agreed in a contract to arbitrate may nevertheless use arbitration. They both sign a submission to arbitration agreement, which constitutes a contractual obligation of the parties that will be enforced by the courts as long as it is not contrary to public policy or illegal. Both a future dispute arbitration clause and a submission agreement, which needs to be signed by both parties, are depicted below.

For the Arbitration of Future Disputes:

Any controversy or claim arising out of or relating to this contract, or the breach thereof, shall be settled by arbitration in accordance with the Commercial Arbitration Rules of the American Arbitration Association, and judgment upon the award rendered by the arbitrator(s) may be entered in any court having jurisdiction thereof.

For the Submission of Existing Disputes:

We, the undersigned parties, hereby agree to submit to arbitration under the Commercial Arbitration Rules of the American Arbitration Association the following controversy: (cite briefly). We further agree that the above controversy be submitted to (one) (three) arbitrator(s) selected from the panels of arbitrators of the American Arbitration Association. We further agree that we will faithfully observe this agreement and the rules, and that we will abide by and perform any award rendered by the arbitrator(s) and that a judgment of the court having jurisdiction may be entered upon the award.

INTERNATIONAL PERSPECTIVE

Although courts in the United States were at one time hesitant to allow arbitrators to oust the jurisdiction of courts in resolving international disputes, there are now a number of sources that ensure the recognition and enforcement of arbitration agreements. First, statutes in every state of the United States recognize arbitration. Second, several recent decisions of the U.S. Supreme Court have eliminated all obstacles to U.S. enforcement of agreements to arbitrate made by parties in international contracts. The *Mitsubishi* case excerpted following is one of these cases.[5] Finally, the United Nations Convention on the Recognition and Enforcement of Foreign Arbitral Awards, ratified by most of the world's leading commercial nations, is a multilateral treaty that provides

[5]This case is also excerpted in slightly different form in Chapter 21's discussion of international dispute resolution.

for the recognition of arbitral awards and prevents courts from litigating disputes the parties agreed to arbitrate. Arbitration is common in international business situations for several reasons. Each party fears bringing its dispute to hostile foreign courts with unfamiliar and perhaps bewildering procedures. Each party believes the judges or jurors in a foreign court will be partial towards the party from that country. Finally, each party generally perceives that prior disputes resolved through arbitration were regarded more favorably than those resolved through litigation.

Mitsubishi Motors Corp. v. Soler Chrysler-Plymouth, Inc.

473 U.S. 614 (1985)
United States Supreme Court

Mitsubishi Industries, Inc., a Japanese corporation, and Chrysler International, a Swiss corporation, formed a joint venture company, Mitsubishi Motors, to distribute through Chrysler dealers outside of the United States vehicles manufactured by Mitsubishi and bearing Chrysler and Mitsubishi trademarks. Soler Chrysler-Plymouth, an automobile dealer incorporated in Puerto Rico, and Chrysler entered into a Distributor Agreement that provided for the sale by Soler of Mitsubishi-manufactured vehicles within Puerto Rico. Paragraph VI of the Agreement, labeled "Arbitration of Certain Matters," provided:

> All disputes, controversies, or differences which may arise between Mitsubishi and Soler out of or in relation to . . . this Agreement or for the breach thereof, shall be finally settled by arbitration in Japan in accordance with the rules and regulations of the Japan Commercial Arbitration Association.

Initially, Soler maintained brisk sales, but following a slump in the new-car market in 1981, Soler requested Mitsubishi to delay or cancel shipment of several orders. A year later, Soler disclaimed any responsibility for failing to sell cars under its contract. Mitsubishi brought suit in the United States in Puerto Rico, seeking an order to compel arbitration in accord with Paragraph VI of the Agreement. The district court ordered Soler to arbitrate, even as to its antitrust claims. The Court of Appeals reversed because it felt Soler's antitrust claim should not be subject to arbitration because of public policy concerns. Mitsubishi appealed to the Supreme Court.

Justice Blackmun delivered the opinion of the Court.

We granted certiorari primarily to consider whether an American court could enforce an agreement to resolve antitrust claims by arbitration when that agreement arises from an international transaction. Soler reasons that, because it falls within a class of whose benefit the federal and local antitrust laws were passed, the clause cannot be read to contemplate arbitration of these statutory claims.

We do not agree, for we find no warrant in the Arbitration Act for implying in every contract a presumption against arbitration of statutory claims. The "liberal federal policy favoring arbitration agreements," manifested by the Act as a whole, is at bottom a policy guaranteeing the enforcement of private contractual arrangements: the Act simply "creates a body of federal substantive law establishing and regulating the duty to honor an agreement to arbitrate."

There is no reason to depart from these guidelines where a party bound by an arbitration agreement raises claims founded on statutory rights. Of course, courts should remain attuned to well-supported claims that the agreement to arbitrate resulted from the sort of fraud or overwhelming economic power that would provide grounds "for the revocation of any contract." But, absent such compelling considerations, the Act itself provides no basis for disfavoring agreements to arbitrate statutory claims.

By agreeing to arbitrate a statutory claim, a party does not forgo the substantive rights afforded by the statute; it only submits to their resolution in an arbitral, rather than a judicial, forum. It trades the procedures and opportunity for review of the courtroom for the simplicity, informality, and expedition of arbitration.

We now turn to consider whether Soler's antitrust claims are nonarbitrable even though it agreed to arbitrate them. As in *Scherk v. Alberto-Culver Co.*, we conclude that concerns of international comity, respect for the capacities of foreign and transnational tribunals, and sensitivity to the need of the international commercial system for predictability in the resolution of disputes require that we enforce the parties' agreement, even assuming that a contrary result would be forthcoming in a domestic context.

There is no reason to assume at the outset of the dispute that international arbitration will not provide an adequate mechanism. To be sure, the international arbitral tribunal owes no prior allegiance to the legal norms of particular states; hence, it has no direct obligation to vindicate their statutory dictates. The tribunal, however, is bound to effectuate the intentions of the parties. Where the parties have agreed that the arbitral body is to decide a defined set of claims that includes, as in these cases, those arising from the application of American antitrust law, the tribunal therefore should be bound to decide that dispute in accord with the national law giving rise to the claim.

As international trade has expanded in recent decades, so too has the use of international arbitration to resolve disputes arising in the course of that trade. The controversies that international arbitral institutions are called upon to resolve have increased in diversity as well as in complexity. Yet the potential of these tribunals for efficient disposition of legal disagreements arising from commercial relations has not yet been tested. If they are to take a central place in the international legal order, national courts will need to "shake off the old judicial hostility to arbitration," and also their customary and understandable unwillingness to cede jurisdiction of a claim arising under domestic law to a foreign or transnational tribunal. To this extent, at least, it will be necessary for national courts to subordinate domestic notions of arbitrability to the international policy favoring commercial arbitration.

Accordingly, we "require this representative of the American business community to honor its bargain," . . . by holding this agreement to arbitrate "enforce[able] in accord with the explicit provisions of the Arbitration Act." The judgment of the Court of Appeals is affirmed in part and reversed in part, and the cases are remanded for further proceedings consistent with this opinion.

Case Questions

1. Does U.S. policy favor or disfavor arbitration agreements?
2. What is the difference in arbitration panels and courts regarding an "allegiance" to the norms of particular states?
3. What are the benefits of litigation that are "traded off" by an agreement to arbitrate?

Court-Mandated Arbitration

In some cases, courts require litigating parties to submit their cases to arbitration. California is one of the leading states requiring the use of court-annexed arbitration. For example, cases seeking damages of less than $50,000 may be ordered to arbitration. In these cases, the parties are still involved in selecting the arbitrators and the hearing is similar to that used in voluntary arbitrations, but there is no judge nor jury, and no written decision with reasons is provided. Instead, the arbitrator issues an award that is binding if it is not appealed. There are several procedural differences, involving the use of subpoenas and the discovery methods, between the court-mandated arbitration and the voluntary arbitration. Nevertheless, even court-mandated arbitration is generally quicker and less expensive than a trial.

Enforcement of Arbitration Agreements

In recent years, the Supreme Court has upheld arbitration provisions in a number of different circumstances. In the *Shearson/American Express* case referred to earlier, arbitration of a claim brought under the 1934 Securities and Exchange Act (Exchange Act) and the Racketeer Influenced and Corrupt Organizations Act (RICO) was found not to be too complicated for arbitration. Later that year, the Court found that a federal court could not refuse to enforce an arbitration agreement rendered under a collective-bargaining agreement.[6]

In 1991, the Court returned to a lower court the question of whether arbitration of a stockbroker's sex discrimination claim is excluded by the Federal Arbitration Act's specific exclusion of "contracts of employment" from its provision.[7] The court's opinion in the *Shearson/American Express* case is noted below.

Shearson/American Express, Inc. v. McMahon

482 U.S. 220 (1987)
United States Supreme Court

The McMahons were customers of Shearson/American Express, Inc. (Shearson), a brokerage firm registered with the Securities and Exchange Commission (SEC), under customer agreements providing for arbitration of any controversy relating to their accounts. They filed suit in Federal District Court against Shearson alleging violations of § 10(b) of the Securities Exchange Act of 1934 (Exchange Act) and SEC Rule 10b-5, and of the Racketeer Influenced and Corrupt Organizations Act (RICO). Shearson moved to compel arbitration of the claims pursuant to the Federal Arbitration Act, which requires a court to stay its proceedings if it is satisfied that an issue before it is arbitrable under an arbitration agreement. The district court held the Exchange Act claims were arbitrable, but that their RICO claim was not. The Court of Appeals found neither claim arbitrable. Shearson then appealed to the Supreme Court.

Justice O'Connor delivered the opinion of the Court.

This case presents two questions regarding the enforceability of predispute arbitration agreements between brokerage firms and their customers. The first is whether a claim brought under § 10(b) of the Securities Exchange Act of 1934 must be sent to arbitration in accordance with the terms of an arbitration agreement. The second is whether a claim brought under the Racketeer Influenced and Corrupt Organizations Act (RICO) must be arbitrated in accordance with the terms of such an agreement.

Between 1980 and 1982, respondents Eugene and Julia McMahon were customers of Shearson/American Express, Inc. (Shearson), a brokerage firm registered with the Securities and Exchange Commission (SEC or Commission). Two customer agreements signed by Julia McMahon provided for arbitration of any controversy relating to the accounts the McMahons maintained with Shearson. The arbitration provision provided in relevant part as follows:

> "Unless unenforceable due to federal or state law, any controversy arising out of or relating to my accounts, to transactions with you for me or to this agreement or the breach thereof, shall be settled by arbitration in accordance with the rules then in effect of the National Association of Securities Dealers Inc., or the Board of Directors of the New York Stock Exchange, Inc., and/or the American Stock Exchange, Inc. as I may elect."

The Federal Arbitration Act provides the starting point for answering the questions raised in this case. The Act was intended to " revers[e] centuries of judicial hostility to arbitration agreements," by "plac[ing] arbitration agreements 'upon the same footing as other

[6] *United Paperworkers Intern. Union v. Misco, Inc.*, 108 S.Ct. 364 (1987).

[7] *Dean Witter Reynolds, Inc. v. Alford*, 111 S.Ct. 2050 (1991).

contracts' " (*Scherk v. Alberto-Culver Co.*) The Arbitration Act accomplishes this purpose by providing that arbitration agreements "shall be valid, irrevocable, and enforceable, save upon such grounds as exist at law or in equity for the revocation of any contract." The Act also provides that a court must stay its proceedings if it is satisfied that an issue before it is arbitrable under the agreement. The Arbitration Act thus establishes a "federal policy favoring arbitration."

This duty to enforce arbitration agreements is not diminished when a party bound by an agreement raises a claim founded on statutory rights. As we observed in *Mitsubishi Motors Corp. v. Soler Chrysler-Plymouth, Inc.* "we are well past the time when judicial suspicion of the desirability of arbitration and of the competence of arbitral tribunals" should inhibit enforcement of the Act "'in controversies based on statutes.' "

The Arbitration Act, standing alone, therefore mandates enforcement of agreements to arbitrate statutory claims . . . To defeat application of the Arbitration Act in this case, therefore, the McMahons must demonstrate that Congress intended to make an exception to the Arbitration Act for claims arising under RICO and the Exchange Act, an intention discernible from the text, history, or purposes of the statute.

When Congress enacted the Exchange Act in 1934, it did not specifically address the question on the arbitrability of § 10(b) claims. The McMahons contend, however, that congressional intent to require a judicial forum for the resolution of § 10(b) claims can be deduced from § 29(a) of the Exchange Act, which declares void "[a]ny condition, stipulation, or provision binding any person to waive compliance with any provision of [the Act]."

First, we reject the McMahons' argument that § 29(a) forbids waiver of § 27 of the Exchange Act. Section 27 provides in relevant part:

> "The district courts of the United States . . . shall have exclusive jurisdiction of violations of this title or the rules and regulations thereunder, and of all suits in equity and actions at law brought to enforce any liability or duty created by this title or the rules and regulations thereunder."

We do not read *Wilko v. Swan,* (1953), as compelling a different result. In *Wilko,* the Court held that a predispute agreement could not be enforced to compel arbitration of a claim arising under § 12(2) of the Securities Act. *Wilko* must be understood as holding that a plaintiff's waiver of the "right to select the judicial forum" was unenforceable only because arbitration was judged inadequate to enforce the statutory rights created by § 12(2).

Indeed, any different reading of *Wilko* would be inconsistent with this Court's decision in *Scherk v. Alberto-Culver Co.* In *Scherk,* the Court upheld enforcement of a predispute agreement to arbitrate Exchange Act claims by parties to an international contract. The *Scherk* Court assumed for purposes of its opinion that *Wilko* applied to the Exchange Act, but it determined that an international contract "involve[d] considerations and policies significantly different from those found controlling in *Wilko.*" The Court reasoned that arbitration reduced the uncertainty of international contracts and obviated the danger that a dispute might be submitted to a hostile or unfamiliar forum. At the same time, the Court noted that the advantages of judicial resolution were diminished by the possibility that the opposing party would make "speedy resort to a foreign court." The decision in *Scherk* thus turned on the Court's judgment that under the circumstances of that case, arbitration was an adequate substitute for adjudication as a means of enforcing the parties' statutory rights.

The second argument offered by the McMahons is that the arbitration agreement effects an impermissible waiver of the substantive protections of the Exchange Act.

Initially, they contend that predispute agreements are void under § 29(a) because they tend to result from broker overreaching. They reason that *Wilko* is premised on the belief "that arbitration clauses in securities sales agreements generally are not freely negotiated." . . . We decline to give *Wilko* a reading so far at odds with the plain language of § 14 or to adopt such an unlikely interpretation of § 29(a).

The other reason advanced by the McMahons for finding a waiver of their § 10(b) rights is that arbitration does "weaken their ability to recover under the [Exchange] Act." That is the heart of the Court's decision in *Wilko,* and respondents urge that we should follow its reasoning. *Wilko* listed several grounds why in the Court's view, the "effectiveness [of the Act's provisions] in application is lessened in arbitration."

It is difficult to reconcile *Wilko's* mistrust of the arbitral process with this Court's subsequent decisions involving the Arbitration Act. See e.g., *Mitsubishi Motors Corp. v. Soler Chrysler-Plymouth, Inc.; Dean Witter Reynolds Inc. v. Byrd, (1985); Southland Corp. v. Keating,* (1984); *Moses H. Cone Memorial Hospital v.*

Mercury Construction Corp., (1983); *Scherk v. Alberto-Culver Co.*, (1974).

Indeed, most of the reasons given in *Wilko* have been rejected subsequently by the Court as a basis for holding claims to be nonarbitrable. In *Mitsubishi,* for example, we recognized that arbitral tribunals are readily capable of handling the factual and legal complexities of antitrust claims, notwithstanding the absence of judicial instruction and supervision. Likewise, we have concluded that the streamlined procedures of arbitration do not entail any consequential restriction on substantive rights.

. . . Even if *Wilko's* assumptions regarding arbitration were valid at the time *Wilko* was decided, most certainly they do not hold true today for arbitration procedures subject to the SEC's oversight authority. Since the 1975 amendments to § 19 of the Exchange Act, the Commission has had expansive power to ensure the adequacy of the arbitration procedures employed by the SROs (Self-Regulating Organizations, the National Securities Exchanges, and Registered Securities Associations). In short, the Commission has . . . the power to mandate the adoption of any rules it deems necessary to ensure that arbitration procedures adequately protect statutory rights.

In the exercise of its regulatory authority, the SEC has specifically approved the arbitration procedures of the New York Stock Exchange, the American Stock Exchange, and the NASD, the organizations mentioned in the arbitration agreement at issue in this case. We conclude that where, as in this case, the prescribed procedures are subject to the Commission's § 19 authority, an arbitration agreement does not effect a waiver of the protections of the Act.

We conclude, therefore, that Congress did not intend for § 29(a) to bar enforcement of all predispute arbitration agreements. In this case, where the SEC has sufficient statutory authority to ensure that arbitration is adequate to vindicate Exchange Act rights, enforcement does not effect a waiver of "compliance with any provision" of the Exchange Act under § 29(a). Accordingly, we hold the McMahons' agreements to arbitrate Exchange Act claims enforceable and in accord with the explicit provisions of the Arbitration Act.

(Note that discussion of the RICO claim is omitted as the court's reasoning on that question was similar to the reasoning excerpted here.)

Case Questions

1. What two statements about arbitration agreements can be found in the Federal Arbitration Act?
2. The McMahons' claim that the Arbitration Act does not apply to this case conflicts with the provisions of the Securities Exchange Act; explain what language in that Act supports McMahons' claim and what the Court decides about the alleged conflict.
3. Is the *Wilko* case referred to by the McMahons still valid as it applies to arbitration matters? Why? How does the *Mitsubishi* case relate to this question?

MEDIATION

Mediation, like arbitration, is used to resolve disputes. While it is somewhat similar to arbitration, there are important differences. Mediation is a process in which a third person, the mediator, attempts to reconcile a dispute between two parties by persuading them to adjust or settle their differences. The mediator usually acts as a go-between who encourages the parties to modify their positions. He or she usually has no authority to resolve the dispute.

The mediator's role is not to judge but to persuade and seek compromise and reconciliation. While the arbitrator renders a decision and thus acts as a substitute for the judge, the mediator merely emphasizes the reasonableness of the parties' demands. Generally, if the contract or agreement between the parties provides for arbitration, the arbitrator's decision is final. By contrast, the mediator's recommendations are not binding and usually do not have to be accepted by the contending parties. In most cases, those recommendations are not directly enforceable through the legal system.

Mediators have been used to settle international boundary disputes, baseball strikes, and numerous contract disputes. The Federal Mediation and Conciliation Service has experienced mediators who serve in labor-management disputes. For example, they assist in disputes between local school boards and teachers' unions. The Magnuson-Moss Product Warranty Act authorizes mediation in disputes regarding malfunctioning consumer products.

Mediators are used for a variety of reasons. A mediator can defuse emotions between parties who may be angry or upset with each other. Mediators may suggest alternative strategies to the parties and encourage the use of unforeseen compromise positions. Mediators may point out weaknesses to each party in their respective positions, thereby encouraging more realistic settlement discussions.

Court-Annexed Mediation

In many state trial courts, mediation is used as a part of the pretrial litigation procedure. For example, in Michigan, rules of procedure dictate that all eligible actions will be considered for mediation if not resolved by a certain point, normally at the close of discovery. An action may be selected for mediation by the court, by agreement of the parties, or by motion of one of the parties and an order of the court.

THE MINITRIAL

Some corporations use the minitrial, an informal presentation of a dispute by the parties and their attorneys to senior executives of each party or to hired independent outsiders. A neutral party is often present as a moderator or adviser. In some situations, the adviser is asked for his or her opinion, while in others the senior executives of the disputing firms meet to discuss settlement as soon as the presentation has been completed. Once the senior executives have heard both sides of the dispute and become aware of the relative strengths and weaknesses of their positions, settlement may be more likely to occur.

The minitrial requires all of the parties to agree to its use. The minitrial allows the parties to resolve questions of law and fact in complex disputes through the use of an abbreviated discovery process. The abbreviated discovery procedure, requiring exchange of documents and names of witnesses, gives the parties fuller knowledge of the facts involved in the dispute and makes them more ready to reach a settlement. After the discovery stage, the adviser meets with the parties and seeks to resolve procedural issues. The actual trial generally lasts only a day or two and occurs months, not years, after the case begins.

The adviser at the hearing does not take the role of the judge, but instead derives his or her authority from the parties. In some cases, the minitrial will be presented to the respective parties and the adviser will merely conduct the hearing. In other cases, the adviser may be given authority to render an advisory opinion as to the outcome of the case if in fact it went to trial.

The Michigan program is instructive. The mediation panel generally consists of three persons. Generally there is an attorney associated primarily with plaintiff's cases, an attorney normally associated with defendant's cases, and an attorney not normally associated with either. Only 28 days' notice is required before a mediation hearing can occur. At the hearing, each side generally has 15 minutes to orally argue its position to the panel. The statements made at the mediation hearing are not admissible evidence in any court. The panel has 14 days to evaluate the case and inform the attorneys of its evaluation. Each party then has 28 days to accept or reject the mediation award; the failure to file a written acceptance or rejection is treated as an acceptance.

FIGURE 4–3
Comparison of Dispute Resolution Methods

Method of Dispute Resolution	Binding/Reviewable	Decision Maker	Nature of Decision	Public/Private
Civil trial	Yes–can appeal	Judge not selected by parties	Written decision with reasons	Public
Arbitration	Yes–limited review	Selected by parties; generally has expertise on subject in dispute	Sometimes a written decision with reasons	Private except when court reviews
Mediation	No, but can be enforced if in contract	Selected by parties	Generally based on agreement by parties; sometimes required	Private
Minitrial	No, but can be enforced if in contract	Selected by parties; sometimes has expertise on subject in dispute	Based on agreement by parties	Private
Private trial/ rent-a-judge	Sometimes–then subject to appeal	Selected by parties	Written decision; sometimes with reasons	Private unless enforcement needed

If all parties accept the award, a judgment is entered in accordance with the panel's recommendation. If all or a part of the award is rejected, the trial may proceed. The mediation award and the acceptance or rejection of the parties is sealed and may not be opened until after the judge enters a judgment. If a party has rejected a mediation award and the case proceeds to trial, that party must pay the opposing party's actual costs, including attorneys' fees, unless the verdict is more favorable to the rejecting party than the mediation award.

Minitrials have been used in patent disputes, product liability cases, unfair competition, and antitrust claims. The advantages of the minitrial include:

1. The parties can design the processes and rules to be used.
2. The process may allow for influence of mediation and creative problem-solving.
3. The use of some discovery techniques allows each party to learn the facts and pertinent issues about its opponent; this promotes an informed settlement.
4. The adviser can be selected for his or her expertise and can be granted varying degrees of authority.
5. Both the preparation for the trial and the trial itself are relatively brief.
6. The case is generally presented to the executives of the parties themselves; the people with authority to settle the dispute.
7. The hearings are confidential; the parties and the adviser agree not to disclose information regarding the proceedings to others.

A comparison of the different methods of dispute resolution should consider a number of factors. Among those depicted in Figure 4–3 are:

1. Is the decision reached through each method binding? Can the decision be reviewed?

2. How is the decision maker selected? Does that person generally have expertise in the particular type of dispute?
3. Is the decision written? Are reasons given? Do the parties have to agree with the decision?
4. Is the process by which the dispute is resolved public or private?

PRIVATE TRIALS OR RENT-A-JUDGE

Some businesses have sought to resolve disputes by using the paid services of retired judges or lawyers who assume the role of judge. The parties to such cases are able to select the judge who will hear the case and to have their case heard whenever they are ready to present it. In this dispute resolution method, referred to as the rent-a-judge or private trial method, society does not vest the judge with the legal authority to impose a binding decision on the disputing parties. However, the parties frequently agree to accept the judge's determination.

A California statute originating in the early 1900s permits the parties to bypass the formal court system and use paid judges or referees. This statute allows the decision of the rent-a-judge to have the finality of trial court judgments. Although some of the problems with civil litigation are overcome by using these private trials, some people believe private trials also pose problems. The commentary that follows discusses some of the common questions about private courts.

ETHICAL DILEMMAS AND ADR

The goal of dispute resolution is equity. Whether they choose a civil trial, arbitration, mediation, minitrial, or rent-a-judge, most people want what is rightfully theirs. The cost of alternative dispute resolution methods may vary from one type to the next. Mediation through community dispute resolution centers generally is the least expensive method. Arbitrators are a bit more expensive, and rent-a-judges are generally the most expensive. If you pay for a more expensive method of dispute resolution, are you going to receive a better result? If the job of deciding cases is taken out of the hands of judges, what standards will be imposed on the parties who instead perform that task? What types of checks and balances will guarantee that they are doing an equitable job? Will poorer people get an inferior quality of justice merely because they cannot afford to use certain methods of dispute resolution?

Would the universalist and the utilitarian both find private trials ethical? For one perspective, see the following commentary.

Private Court Alternatives to the Public Court Logjam

Surely more than a few Americans serving on civil juries have asked themselves why private disputes are litigated at public expense. What public interest is served, for example, when lawyers bid for big settlements, and big fees, in class-action suits they themselves organized? What entitles such entrepreneurs to a taxpayer subsidy and a claim on the valuable time of jurors? Or why should public facilities be used to resolve big-money disputes between corporate giants over a contract they willingly signed?

Those questions, interesting as they are, are not threatening to bring down civil justice. But that edifice is tottering a bit from overload, without any clear enthusiasm among taxpayers for expanding it to meet a seemingly insatiable demand. As a result, some litigants, to save time and legal costs, are turning to private justice, and it seems to serve quite well.

If "Alternative Dispute Resolution," or ADR, continues to expand, it might well stimulate serious debate over privatization of some civil litigation as a means of freeing up the public courts for faster administration of criminal justice. The broad public clearly has a direct and significant interest in that, what with bailed-out criminals awaiting trial, roaming the streets to commit new crimes. . . .

The American Arbitration Association . . . has provided ADR services for many years, as have similar groups. But while arbitrators often have special expertise, some lawyers complain of an absence of legal precedents and procedures and the tendency of some arbitrators to merely split differences.

A newer and more fascinating development is the private court. One of the most ambitious private-court enterprises is Judicate, Inc., set up in Philadelphia in 1985 to offer services nationwide. . . . Jay D. Seid, a 28-year-old lawyer-business administrator, was called in as president to put the company on a sounder financial footing. . . .

Judicate courtrooms are miniature public courtrooms, with a bench for the judge, a chair for the witness and chairs on either side for the litigants. Many of the judges are retirees from the public bench. Unlike a public court, Judicate allows litigants to choose the judge they want from a panel. Trials use public-court processes, but the rules are simpler and things move faster. Most cases, however, are dispatched with a simple settlement hearing, which can be held almost anywhere and may cost disputants as little as $75 each.

Private courts have sometimes been tabbed as "justice for the rich," but Mr. Seid says that is not the real life experience. "Many of our clients are low-income people. For an insurance company to get a dollar to a plaintiff in a normal case, it's going to cost them two dollars out of pocket because of delays, litigation costs and court fees. If this system works right, you can get more money to the plaintiff with less cost to the defendant and everybody benefits."

A more serious charge is that private justice contributes nothing to the total body of law. "The criticism is that we are not helping the court system and the system of justice, because some cases should be in a public forum," says Mr. Seid. "The fact is that not every case should go to us. We're not here for the cutting edge, for the case that's breaking new ground, for novel, complex legal arguments. Those cases should be tried in public courts. What we're trying to do is free the public courts of routine existing law cases or cases where liability isn't really in question but you're just trying to figure out how much the case is worth."

Public courts are so seldom challenged as institutions because of their long and honorable English common-law tradition. There is widespread agreement that anyone, however humble, deserves a day in court if wronged. This assurance contributes to a sense of fairness that prevents private resentments from becoming widespread public discontents that might threaten the social and political order. . . .

While the beauties of English common law are well accepted, the U.S. court systems—federal, state and local—are faced with new practical realities. Judges must try to cope with new conflicts arising out of scientific advances—whether a computer microcode can be copyrighted—that might best be settled by someone with technical expertise. Corporate lawyers sometimes practice "strategic litigation," just to tie up competitors in court. Tort litigation has exploded.

Given the old saying, "Justice delayed is justice denied," there clearly is room for new thinking about dispute resolution.

OTHER ALTERNATIVES

Several additional alternatives to resolving disputes through civil litigation exist. These include small claims courts, summary jury trials, and specialized administrative agency hearings. Additional alternatives, often featuring combinations of different ADR methods, are also being used in some situations.

Small Claims Courts

Small claims courts exist in most states to resolve minor civil disputes, particularly those where money damages are sought. Several significant differences exist between the procedures found in these courts from those in use in the general courts. Although the decision maker may be the same judge who presides over the general court, that is not always the case. Other characteristics vary from state to state.

Characteristics of the Small Claims Court

1. Only claims for money may be brought to the small claims court, and usually a limit, varying from $1,000 to $5,000, depending on state laws, is placed on the amount that can be recovered.
2. Attorneys cannot represent parties in the small claims court; the parties must represent themselves.*
3. No jury trial is available; the judge decides both legal and factual questions.
4. Informal procedures are used, and most of the evidence rules do not apply.
5. No appeal is possible; the judge's decision is final.*

*Some states do allow attorneys in small claims courts and some do allow appeals.

Summary Jury Trial

The summary jury trial first appeared in 1983 in a Cleveland federal district court.[8] The procedure, now used in many federal and state courts, normally lasts only a day and involves using a jury and a summary of the evidence that would be presented. The judge gives preliminary instructions on the law to the jury, the attorneys for each side make short opening statements and then, in a limited time period, each summarizes the evidence that would be used at the trial. The jury in fact plays only an advisory role, but the judge generally does not inform them of the fact until after a verdict is rendered.

Although there is no actual trial, the jury, generally consisting of no more than six people, does render a verdict. The parties, including an executive with settlement authority from a corporation, must attend the entire trial. Immediately after the verdict, the parties are sent to a settlement negotiation, normally without their attorneys. If no settlement is reached, neither the occurrence nor the result of the summary jury trial is admissible when the case later goes to court. Approximately 95 percent of all cases are settled quickly after the jury's verdict, making this form of mock trial quite successful.

[8]See Allison, J., "Five Ways to Keep Disputes out of Court," *Harvard Business Review*, January–February, 1990, p. 172.

Administrative Agency Hearings

State and federal legal systems delegate significant dispute resolution roles to *administrative agencies*. The workings of these agencies are discussed in detail in Chapter 6; here, their roles in resolving disputes are briefly noted. Numerous agencies have been given judicial responsibilities; they hear cases, conduct trial-type proceedings, and make enforceable orders or decisions. For example, all of the states have some type of workers' compensation agency. This agency determines the eligibility for benefits of workers who have been injured at work or laid off. The Administrative Procedures Act generally establishes the procedures followed at agency hearings.

An agency is given power to hear and determine certain types of disputes because its specialization is believed to result in more informed decisions and perhaps more efficient hearings than are obtainable in the state or federal courts that normally handle civil litigation. Thus, the IRS and a special tax court, not the civil courts, hear most tax liability disputes.

In 1990, two laws intended to increase administrative agency use of ADR were passed. The Administrative Dispute Resolution Act and the Negotiated Rulemaking Act require the use of ADR techniques in the adjudicatory and rulemaking tasks being performed by federal administrative agencies. These laws specifically authorize agencies to use arbitration, mediation, and other ADR methods.

ADR: PROS AND CONS

ADR has grown because each of the methods possesses some advantage when compared to litigation. The text has referred to the lower cost and the quicker resolution of the dispute as significant advantages usually attributed to the ADR methods. Figures 4–1 and 4–3 noted several comparisons between litigation and ADR techniques; those and others are summarized in Figure 4–4. Litigation sometimes is selected because the cost or delay associated with it may be an advantage to one of the parties. Thus, if you might be held responsible for damages suffered by the other party, you'd prefer to pay those damages later, after going through litigation, rather than at an earlier time. Similarly, the cost of litigation may be a deterrent. A large firm may prefer to litigate with a small firm, hoping that the small firm's lack of financial resources will make it more prone to settlement. Litigation is generally more appropriate in cases where a new legal policy is at stake because only the courts can establish the policy as precedent for future decisions.

In the case that follows, the U.S. Supreme Court rejects the claim that arbitration of an age-discrimination complaint is contrary to the policies promoted in the Age Discrimination in Employment Act of 1967 (ADEA). Note the Court's analysis of the various disadvantages to arbitration that the plaintiff Gilmer raises.

Gilmer v. Interstate/Johnson Lane Corp.

111 S Ct 1647 (1991)
United States Supreme Court

Interstate/Johnson Lane Corporation (Interstate) hired Gilmer as a Manager of Financial Services in May 1981. As required by his employment, Gilmer registered as a securities representative with several stock exchanges, including the New York Stock Exchange

FIGURE 4–4
Pros and Cons of ADR

Pros: Advantages of ADR over litigation

1. Less time from beginning of controversy to resoluton of dispute.
2. Less cost because of lower attorney fees, less time away from work by corporate employees, lower "court" costs for the prevailing party.
3. Parties can select a more experienced decision-maker or facilitator rather than being randomly assigned to a judge.
4. Parties are able to select where the dispute will be heard; they are not bound to use the court system where each party does business.
5. The nonadversarial nature of ADR makes it easier to do business in the future with an opponent. The parties are actively involved in solving a problem and are not passive participants.
6. The informality of ADR methods is less formidable than are the evidentiary rules governing court procedures.
7. ADR is more confidential than litigation, which becomes a matter of public record.

Cons: Disadvantages of ADR as compared to litigation

1. The longer time frame for litigation may be advantageous to one of the parties if it will have to make a payment to the other party once the dispute is resolved. Passage of time naturally decreases both the cost to the defendant and the value of the plaintiff's recovery.
2. The use of discovery in litigation allows each party to obtain valuable information from the other party.
3. The rule of law generally governs the dispute; if the law is on one party's side, the case is more likely to be decided in that party's favor.
4. Only the courts can establish precedent. If a party has concern about future cases as well as the present controversy, litigation may establish the needed precedent.
5. Litigation is generally preferred if the case involves new or complex legal theories.
6. Litigation is more public and thus may be used to let other parties know that disputes will not be settled for their nuisance value.

(NYSE). His registration application, entitled "Uniform Application for Securities Industry Registration or Transfer," provided, among other things, that Gilmer "agreed to arbitrate any dispute, claim or controversy" arising between him and Interstate "that is required to be arbitrated under the rules, constitutions or by-laws of the organizations with which I register." Of relevance to this case, NYSE Rule 347 provides for arbitration of "any controversy between a registered representative and any member or member organization arising out of the employment or termination of employment of such registered representative."

Interstate terminated Gilmer's employment in 1987, at which time Gilmer was 62 years of age. After first filing an age discrimination charge with the Equal Employment Opportunity Commission (EEOC), Gilmer sued in the United States district court alleging that Interstate had discharged him because of his age, in violation of the Age Discrimination in Employment Act (ADEA). In response, Interstate filed a motion to compel arbitration of the ADEA claim. The district court denied Interstate's motion, but the United States Court of Appeals for the Fourth Circuit reversed, finding "nothing in the text, legislative history, or underlying purposes of the ADEA indicating a congressional intent to preclude enforcement of arbitration agreements." Gilmer appealed to the Supreme Court.

Justice White delivered the opinion of the Court.

The question presented in this case is whether a claim under the Age Discrimination in Employment Act of 1967 (ADEA), can be subjected to compulsory arbitration pursuant to an arbitration agreement in a securities registration application. The Court of Appeals held that it could, and we affirm.

The Federal Arbitration Act (FAA) was originally enacted in 1925, and then reenacted and codified in 1947 as Title 9 of the United States Code. Its purpose was to reverse the longstanding judicial hostility to arbitration agreements that had existed in English common law and had been adopted by American courts, and to place arbitration agreements upon the same footing as other contracts. Its primary substantive provision states that "[a] written provision in any maritime transaction or a contract evidencing a transaction involving commerce to settle by arbitration a controversy thereafter arising out of such contract or transaction . . . shall be valid, irrevocable, and enforceable, save upon such grounds as exist at law or in equity for the revocation of any contract." The FAA also provides for stays of proceedings in federal district courts when an issue in the proceeding is referable to arbitration. . . . These provisions manifest a "liberal federal policy favoring arbitration agreements."

It is by now clear that statutory claims may be the subject of an arbitration agreement, enforceable pursuant to the FAA. Indeed, in recent years we have held enforceable arbitration agreements relating to claims arising under the Sherman Act, of the Securities Exchange Act of 1934, the civil provisions of the Racketeer Influenced and Corrupt Organizations Act (RICO), and § 12(2) of the Securities Act of 1933. See *Mitsubishi Motors Corp. v. Soler Chrysler-Plymouth, Inc.,* (1985); *Shearson/American Express Inc. v. McMahon,* (1987); *Rodriguez de Quijas v. Shearson/American Express, Inc.,* (1989). In these cases we recognized that "by agreeing to arbitrate a statutory claim, a party does not forgo the substantive rights afforded by the statute; it only submits to their resolution in an arbitral, rather than a judicial, forum." *Mitsubishi, supra,* at 628.

Although all statutory claims may not be appropriate for arbitration, "having made the bargain to arbitrate, the party should be held to it unless Congress itself has evinced an intention to preclude a waiver of judicial remedies for the statutory rights at issue." Throughout such an inquiry, it should be kept in mind that "questions of arbitrability must be addressed with a healthy regard for the federal policy favoring arbitration."

Gilmer argues that compulsory arbitration of ADEA claims pursuant to arbitration agreements would be inconsistent with the statutory framework and purposes of the ADEA. Like the Court of Appeals, we disagree.

As Gilmer contends, the ADEA is designed not only to address individual grievances, but also to further important social policies. We do not perceive any inherent inconsistency between those policies, however, and enforcing agreements to arbitrate age discrimination claims. It is true that arbitration focuses on specific disputes between the parties involved. The same can be said, however, of judicial resolution claims. Both of these dispute resolution mechanisms nevertheless also can further broader social purposes. The Sherman Act, the Securities Exchange Act of 1934, RICO, and the Securities Act of 1933 all are designed to advance important public policies, but, as noted above, claims under those statutes are appropriate for arbitration. "So long as the prospective litigant effectively may vindicate [his or her] statutory cause of action in the arbitral form, the statute will continue to serve both its remedial and deterrent function." *Mitsubishi, supra,* at 637.

We also are unpersuaded by the argument that arbitration will undermine the role of the EEOC in enforcing the ADEA. An individual ADEA claimant subject to an arbitration agreement will still be free to file a charge with the EEOC, even though the claimant is not able to institute a private judicial action. Indeed, Gilmer filed a charge with the EEOC in this case. In any event, the EEOC's role in combating age discrimination is not dependent on the filing of a charge; the agency may receive information concerning alleged violations of the ADEA "from any source," and it has independent authority to investigate age discrimination.

In arguing that arbitration is inconsistent with the ADEA, Gilmer also raises a host of challenges to the adequacy of arbitration procedures. Initially, we note that on our recent arbitration cases we have already rejected most of these arguments as insufficient to preclude arbitration for statutory claims. Such generalized attacks on arbitration "rest on suspicion of arbitration as a method of weakening the protections afforded in the substantive law to would-be complainants," and as such, they are "far out of step with our current strong endorsement of the federal statutes favoring this method of resolving disputes."

Gilmer first speculates that arbitration panels will be biased. However, "we decline to indulge the presumption that the parties and arbitral body conducting a proceeding will be unable or unwilling to retain competent, conscientious and impartial arbitrators."

Gilmer also complains that the discovery allowed in arbitration is more limited than in the federal courts, which he contends will make it difficult to prove discrimination. . . . There has been no showing in this case that the NYSE discovery provisions, which allow for document production, information requests, depositions, and subpoenas, will prove insufficient to allow ADEA claimants such as Gilmer a fair opportunity to present their claims. Although those procedures might not be as extensive as in the federal courts, by agreeing to arbitrate, a party "trades the procedures and opportunity for review of the courtroom for the simplicity, informality, and expedition of arbitration." *Mitsubishi, supra,* at 628. Indeed, an important counterweight to the reduced discovery in NYSE arbitration is that arbitrators are not bound by the rules of evidence.

A further alleged deficiency of arbitration is that arbitrators often will not issue written opinions, resulting, Gilmer contends, in a lack of public knowledge of employers' discriminatory policies, an inability to obtain effective appellate review, and a stifling of the development of the law. The NYSE rules, however, do require that all arbitration awards be in writing, and that the awards contain the names of the parties, a summary of the issues in controversy, and a description of the award issued. In addition, the award decisions are made available to the public.

It is also argued that arbitration procedures cannot adequately further the purposes of the ADEA because they do not provide for broad equitable relief and class actions. As the court below noted, however, arbitrators do have the power to fashion equitable relief. Indeed, the NYSE rules applicable here do not restrict the types of relief an arbitrator may award, but merely refer to "damages and/or other relief."

An additional reason advanced by Gilmer for refusing to enforce arbitration agreements relating to ADEA claims is his contention that there often will be unequal bargaining power between employers and employees. Mere inequality in bargaining power, however, is not a sufficient reason to hold that arbitration agreements are never enforceable in the employment context. . . . The FAA's purpose was to place arbitration agreements on the same footing as other contracts. Thus, arbitration agreements are enforceable "save upon such grounds as exist at law or in equity for the revocation of any contract."

We conclude that Gilmer has not met his burden of showing that Congress, in enacting the ADEA, intended to preclude arbitration of claims under that Act. Accordingly the judgment of the Court of Appeals is affirmed.

Case Questions

1. What purpose was the Federal Arbitration Act intended to accomplish?
2. What two arguments does Gilmer suggest make arbitration of age-discrimination claims inappropriate?
3. Discuss three arguments that Gilmer suggests should preclude arbitration of statutory claims.

SUMMARY

Alternative dispute resolutions (ADR) are generally nonadversarial methods of dispute resolution that are used instead of civil litigation. Arbitration, mediation, minitrial, and private trials are among the more common ADR methods. In addition, small claims courts, summary jury trials, and administrative agencies are also options that are used instead of litigation.

Firms engaged in international business, such as those involved in the *Mitsubishi* case, have used arbitration to resolve disputes for many years, and arbitration is widely used in many commercial cases. Arbitrators can usually make final and binding decisions. Voluntary arbitration occurs as a result of a contract clause governing future disputes or a submission agreement signed by both parties concerning an existing dispute. Some courts also require the use of arbitration. Agreements to arbitrate and arbitration awards are enforceable through courts, as the *Shearson/American Express* and *Gilmer* cases indicate. Because arbitrators usually handle fewer cases than judges and work primarily with certain types of business transactions, arbitration can be a quicker and more efficient method of dispute resolution than civil litigation.

Mediation is used by parties seeking an informal and nonbinding method of resolving disputes. It is also used both with the civil litigation process and as an alternative to it. When used with civil litigation, mediation is often required before a party proceeds to trial. The trial takes place only if the mediation decision is not accepted. However, if a party proceeds to trial after rejecting the mediation award, that party must pay the opposing party's costs unless the trial verdict was more favorable than the mediation award. The mediator's role is not to judge but to persuade and seek to reconcile differences. Court-mandated arbitration and mediation procedures vary among the states.

The minitrial features a presentation to the executives of the parties and the use of a neutral adviser. After the presentation, the parties seek a settlement. Sometimes, the adviser gives an opinion as to how a court would likely resolve the dispute. The minitrial process usually allows the parties limited discovery before the trial and only a one- or two-day presentation at the trial. Generally, it is the executives of the parties, not the adviser, who have the authority to settle the dispute. Thus, the minitrial, like mediation, is nonbinding in nature. In the private trial, a retired judge or attorney is hired to hear and decide a case. The parties can select the judge and will have their case heard more quickly than if they had used litigation. While the private trial is generally nonbinding, statutes in some states, such as California, do allow the decision of this rent-a-judge to be as final as trial judgments.

Other alternatives include the small claims court, the summary jury trial, and various administrative agency actions. ADR may not always be preferable to litigation; instead, there are pros and cons to each. The informed business manager will be aware of the variety of methods for resolving disputes and select the method that is most likely to accomplish his or her objectives.

KEY TERMS

arbitration, p. 89
mediation, p. 90
minitrial, p. 90
private trials/rent-a-judge, p. 90
ADR, p. 90
summary jury trial, p. 105

CHAPTER EXERCISES

1. What are the four most common methods of alternative dispute resolution?
2. Explain how the term *alternative* in ADR has more than one meaning.
3. Describe three situations in which a manager might prefer to use litigation rather than an ADR method to solve a dispute.
4. Compare and contrast the role of the parties toward each other, the role of the parties in determining the process and rules to be used, and the role of the decision maker in litigation with his or her role in the ADR methods.
5. Construct a scenario in which it would be best to use each of the various methods of alternative dispute resolution.
6. A contract between the general contractor and the electrical subcontractor on a construction contract provides that if they were unable to agree on any matter with respect to the contract or if a dispute arose between them, they would submit the dispute to arbitration. The general contractor files a complaint against the electrical subcontractor in a trial court of general jurisdiction. What decision should that court make? Why?
7. The firm where you work is a large firm that is involved in a multimillion-dollar antitrust and breach of contract suit with another large firm. The two firms are competitors in the same industry but each also has license agreements and a joint venture with the other. Each firm expects to spend several hundred thousand dollars in attorney's fees and other costs to prepare for the suit. The case is scheduled to come before the court in about a year. The executives of your firm are upset with the slow pace of litigation and the long time period it will

take to get the case into and out of court. If appeals occur, several years could come and go before the case is resolved.

You are invited to a brainstorming session called by one of the executives who is in charge of managing the litigation. He has asked a group of people to gather together to pose suggestions for ways in which this dispute could be solved without going to court. Which of the alternative resolution techniques would you recommend and why?

8. AMF Inc. and Brunswick Corp. each manufacture automatic scoring devices for use in bowling. Brunswick advertised that its automatic scoring device was more reliable than any others in use and AMF brought suit claiming the advertisement was false and deceptive. AMF sued Brunswick and the litigation was resolved by an agreement whereby each party would submit any future disputes regarding advertising claims to an arbitration panel for nonbinding arbitration. Later, Brunswick ran several advertisements that claimed its laminated lanes were more durable than the wood lanes manufactured by AMF. AMF sued to have Brunswick submit its information to the arbitration panel, but Brunswick refused. Should the court force Brunswick to provide the arbitration panel with information on its laminated lanes?

9. Rodriguez de Quijas signed a standard arbitration agreement with Shearson/American Express brokerage house when he opened an account with that firm. The contract obligates the parties to settle any controversies through binding arbitration. De Quijas brought suit against Shearson alleging that the broker made false and fraudulent transactions in his account, and he claims the broker violated the 1933 Securities Act. The Securities Act authorizes a person who is injured by a breach of that act to sue for damages, and de Quijas asserts that language allows him to bypass the arbitration. Do you agree?

10. Careful Construction Company entered into a contract with All-Right Electric Company whereby All-Right agreed to do electric work on several commercial office buildings Careful had contracted to build. Their contract provided that any dispute between the parties was to be submitted to a private court. A dispute arose as to whether All-Right's work conformed to the standards it had agreed to in the contract. All-Right wanted to bring the dispute to trial, but it made a token appearance before a private judge. It presented no evidence, called no witnesses, but simply read statements indicating that its work did conform to the contract. The private judge decided in favor of Careful Construction Company, but All-Right refuses to abide by that judge's decision. Would a court enforce the private judge's decision and decline to hear a case if All-Right sues?

Chapter 5

CONSTITUTIONAL LAW

KEY CONCEPTS

The U.S. Constitution establishes the structure of the federal government, clarifies the relationship between the governments of the separate states and the federal government, and sets limits to governmental encroachment on the personal lives of individuals and their business affairs.

The judicial branch has significant lawmaking powers to interpret legislative, constitutional, and common laws at both the state and federal government levels.

The federal government's power to regulate interstate and foreign commerce is the basis for most of the federal laws affecting business activities. The powers to tax and spend facilitate this regulation.

Freedom of speech guaranteed by the First Amendment protects individuals and business entities from state and federal government actions that might attempt to restrain the free market for ideas.

The Fifth and Fourteenth Amendments provide for due process in state and federal governmental processes and in substantive laws. The equal protection clause prohibits government from discrimination.

INTRODUCTION . . . PAST, PRESENT, FUTURE

Nearly every major provision of the U.S. Constitution reflects a reaction to the tyrannical rule that the English crown exercised over the American colonies. The Constitution restricts the potential misuse of governmental powers by the central government, which was experienced by the colonies. The federal system created by the Constitution spreads governmental powers among separate branches at each level of government and separates powers between the federal and local governments. The colonies first organized into a confederation to confine the central government's powers. However, the confederation could not coordinate the states' activities, resulting in protectionism and conflicting policies that were harmful to the whole country's strength. The Constitution was then developed as a compromise between the Federalists, who desired a strong central government, and the Anti-Federalists, who supported stronger states' rights.

The courts have reinforced the federal government's pervasive power to regulate business and interstate commerce. Nevertheless, there are still disputes over the relative roles of the states in our federal system. Many cases hold that the federal powers to regulate business activities are so pervasive that they preempt any state interference with interstate commerce. By contrast, other cases have carved out pockets of states' rights to regulate the local incidents of local business activity. However, state laws that interfere excessively with the federal government's enumerated lawmaking powers are held unconstitutional under the supremacy clause.

In the future, constitutional law will probably focus more on relations between individuals and government. Conflicts may arise between the rights of individuals as stated in the Bill of Rights and reinforced by numerous antidiscrimination and privacy statutes and other laws intended to cure social problems. The new federalism movement of the 1980s put greater financial and regulatory responsibilities on the states. The renewed regulatory activism of the states' legislatures, administrative agencies, and attorneys general may challenge the present concept of resolving conflicts in federalism.

OVERVIEW

The U.S. Constitution is the basis of American law and the foundation for power at all levels of government. As the supreme law of the land, the Constitution establishes the basic structure of the federal government, provides for the states' self-government, and limits the encroachment of government on business and personal activities.

The Constitution consists of two major parts and several subparts. The first part contains the Preamble and seven substantive articles. Article I establishes the Congress and defines its powers. Article II creates the executive branch and confers its powers. Article III establishes the judiciary and empowers Congress to create the federal courts. Article IV defines the basis for the states' relations with one another. Article V authorizes the procedures for amending the Constitution. Article VI is a catchall provision, and Article VII provides for the original ratification (adoption) of the Constitution.

The second part of the Constitution contains the constitutional amendments. The first 10 amendments, the Bill of Rights, were ratified in 1791 to protect fundamental freedoms and liberties. Since then, over 5,000 amendments have been proposed, but only 17 have passed. These deal with liquor prohibition, taxation, the abolition of slavery and its effects, congressional pay, and election matters. Amendment proposals in recent years have sought to require equal rights for women, balance the federal government budget, outlaw desecration of the American flag, and establish the right to life for unborn fetuses.

THE BASIS FOR CONSTITUTIONAL POWERS

The Historical Perspective

Conflict over the separation of powers has dominated the history of American constitutional law since the Revolutionary War. Our government represents a compromise between opposing views of where the most legitimate, efficient, and responsible places for governmental power should reside. America has continually struggled between two political forces in the search for the optimal model of government. The *Federalists* advocated the unitary form of central or national government. The *Anti-Federalists* represented regional interests that advocated stronger local governments. A general theory of government, known as **federalism** or *dual federalism,* recognizes that it is legitimate for power to reside at both the central levels and at local levels. Much of American history and the contemporary legal issues affecting business depend on the fundamentals of federalism and on the separation of powers in both state and federal governments.

Constitutional Development during the Revolutionary War The original impetus for the Revolutionary War was the pervasive and tyrannical rule of the English crown over the American colonies. The English crown was dictatorial and abusive in its governance, failing to respect the opinions of the American colonists. The Constitution restricts potential misuse of central governmental power by separating governmental powers into distinct branches. Although the separation of powers into many governmental units may not seem economically efficient, it provides a more effective system for avoiding tyranny.

The original 13 colonies derived their political powers from colonial charters granted by the English crown. These documents eventually developed into separate state constitutions that were ultimately modeled on the U.S. Constitution. The English crown's unified control promoted similar structures in the colonial governments. Nevertheless, the colonies had divergent social and economic interests and considered themselves separate, distinct, and sovereign political entities. The colonies united during the Revolutionary War because of their opposition to English tyranny. Their only motivation for doing so was their common and immediate need for defense.

The Articles of Confederation The colonies' first attempt to unify was a reaction to the strong central government of England. In 1776, soon after the Declaration of Independence, the states devised a confederation form of government that was no more than a loose aggregation of the states. It was similar to the confederation experiments of early Switzerland, the Germanic states, and the Papal states. A *confederation* is a loose alliance of independent entities that seek to retain their respective autonomies and self-determination. Confederating states join together for some limited common goal, such as defense. They reject stronger forms of central government.

The *Articles of Confederation* created the first American confederation. It provided a benchmark for the strongest form of states' rights in American federalism. Since the Articles were ratified between 1777 and 1781, the trend has clearly been toward an increase in the powers of the central government and a decrease in the powers of the states, despite intermittent periods of states' rights sentiment.

The Articles gave the new American Congress very limited power to conduct foreign affairs, raise armed forces, and levy taxes. It did not create branches of government with executive or judicial power. The early Congress was not empowered to raise money and could only request the states to contribute money for their collective efforts. However, the states had different currencies creating havoc in interstate commerce and runaway inflation. As a result, the central government found it difficult to maintain domestic peace and prevent violent outbreaks reflecting political, social, and economic problems. These incidents of domestic unrest caused a general loss of prestige for the U.S. government under the Articles. In response, the states attempted to revise the Articles; instead, they wrote an entirely new document, the U.S. Constitution.

Development of the Constitution The Constitution reflects several compromises between the two dominant political groups. Initially, the Federalist party succeeded by securing a strong national government in the areas of international affairs, interstate commerce, and taxation. The Federalists were largely well-to-do merchants from the Northeast who stood to gain most from unfettered interstate commerce. The Anti-Federalists represented the states' rights interests, which insisted that the states should retain some governmental powers. The Anti-Federalists were largely populists representing the agrarian interests of the South who distrusted both the Federalists and central governments. The struggle for power between these two groups resulted in a compromise. The U.S. government reserves the police power to the states and provides for the exercise of regional strength through state representation in the U.S. Congress. The premise of the Constitution is that the states were originally separate and sovereign colonial polities. Their ratification of the Constitution relinquished some control over their own destiny, permitting the central government to control in matters affecting all the states. This allocation of legal powers between the state and federal governments establishes the structural design for the legal environment of business.

INTERNATIONAL PERSPECTIVE: OTHER NATIONS' CONSTITUTIONS

The U.S. Constitution is a truly remarkable document in world history. No other nation's constitution in existence today has survived longer than the U.S. Constitution. Several factors have probably contributed to this success: the promise of freedom, the vastness of U.S. natural resources, the rugged individualism and motivation of immigrants from all over the world, and the rejection of rigid feudal class systems then used in other nations. Nevertheless, the U.S. Constitution provides the blueprint for minimum government intervention while permitting fundamental democratic principles. It balances efficiency with freedom and rewards individual achievement while protecting individual rights. The U.S. Constitution accommodates the powers of numerous competing economic, social, and political interests unlike in the ethnically dominated governments of most other nations.

The U.S. Constitution reflects influences from several other nations. The founders drew principles of democracy from experiences of the Greek and Roman Empires. The English provided not only the fundamental common law tradition, but also stimulated the rejection of monarchies and excessive central government control. The lack of a written English constitution inspired the American founders to rely on more than just the English unwritten customs and conventions. The Magna Carta, reluctantly issued by England's King John in 1215, was the forerunner to the U.S. Constitution's due process provisions. It guaranteed fundamental personal liberties such as the enjoyment of life, liberty, and property except after judgment by one's peers. There was also considerable influence from the French, who were concurrently rejecting feudal monarchy. Montesquieu's writings on the shortcomings of monarchy and despotism also inspired the design of the U.S. republic.

Today, Europeans stand to benefit from the United States' experience under the Constitution. The nations of the European Community (EC) are lowering their mutual borders and will soon confront many of the collective problems inherent in central governance of diverse sovereignties. The EC can learn from the United States' economic harmonization in matters of instituting a common currency, encouraging intra-EC commerce, integrating their varying laws and traditions, and interacting with outside nations. The EC has the benefit of the United States' experience in designing the new EC confederation. The post-World War II occupation of Japan led to that nation's adoption of its constitution and other laws based on U.S. law. As the communist and socialist systems of Eastern European nations crumble, the U.S. Constitution will stand as a model for designing their forms of democracy, preference for free markets, and adoption of private property. The U.S. Constitution provides a workable pattern for encouraging economic activity throughout the world.

The Powers of Government

A number of governmental powers are found in the U.S. Constitution. The *enumerated powers* are expressly *delegated* to the federal government by the states. The *implicit powers* expand the power of the U.S. Congress to legislate where this is "necessary and proper" to implement particular enumerated powers. The *reserved powers* of the states include the *police power* to look after the general health, safety, welfare, and morals of their people.

Not all powers are given exclusively to either the federal or state government. Both governments share or have *concurrent powers* to make laws in several areas (e.g., taxation). Certain potential powers are *prohibited* to both the state and federal governments. For example, neither government may make laws that establish a religion. Finally, the supremacy clause denies to the states the power to legislate in areas where the powers of the federal government are exclusive. These relative powers are better visualized, as in Figure 2–1 in Chapter 2.

Enumerated, Delegated, or Exclusively Federal Powers The Constitution enumerates certain powers that the states originally delegated to the federal government. The regulation of interstate commerce is an exclusively federal concern. Under the Articles of Confederation, the states could isolate themselves economically from one another by imposing tariffs, tolls, and taxes and by issuing separate currencies.

Two aspects govern the federal power over interstate commerce. First, the states are prohibited from making laws that would unduly burden interstate commerce. Second, Congress has the power to regulate interstate commerce. The commerce clause, to be explored in detail later, is generally regarded as the most important constitutional power affecting business.

The federal government has several exclusive powers. Only the federal government may act in foreign affair matters. The states have no power to make war, sign treaties, naturalize citizens, or regulate aliens. The federal government has power over the post office and the construction of post roads, which has given rise to the federal road system.

Reserved and Concurrent Powers The Tenth Amendment reserves the powers not delegated to the federal government to the states.

The Tenth Amendment

The powers not delegated to the United States by the Constitution, nor prohibited by it to the States, are reserved to the States respectively, or to the people.

Despite the reservation to the states of the residual or remaining governmental powers, the states share most of their powers with the federal government. Examples include the power to tax and the powers of eminent domain.

The primary source of the states' power is the **police power**, which permits each state to protect its citizens' "health, safety, welfare, and morals." The police power is very significant because it enables the states to legislate in the areas of criminal law, tort law, contract law, commercial law, divorce law, regulatory law, and property rights. However, the U.S. Constitution limits the states' powers over property rights. For example, the power of eminent domain permits any level of government to execute a **taking**; that is, the government can condemn private land for public purposes, such as to build a highway, government building, or flood farmland under a lake. The U.S. Constitution requires the government to pay "just compensation." This clause was included as a response to England's practice of confiscating colonists' property for use by the English crown.

What constitutes a taking, and what rights does a property owner have if the government wants to use the power of eminent domain to take that owner's property? The following case discusses this dilemma while emphasizing the extent of the "taking" experienced by the private owner.

Penn Central Transportation Co. v. New York

438 U.S. 104 (1978)
United States Supreme Court

In 1965, New York City enacted a Landmarks Preservation law that attempted to prevent the destruction of historic structures when developers and city officials failed to consider the value or productive economic uses of landmarks. Historic places enhance the general quality of life due to their historical significance, their contribution to our cultural heritage, and their workmanship. The law assumes New York is a worldwide tourist center, a capital of business, and a center for culture and government that could be endangered if historic places were not protected. The law did not authorize the city to purchase landmarks. Instead, it used services, standards, controls, and incentives to encourage preservation by owners, yet permit them a "reasonable return" on their investment. The New York Landmarks Preservation Commission had 11 members and a technical staff. Where the Commission had a special character or historic or aesthetic interest or value, it might designate the property as a "landmark." After correlation with the city's master zoning plan by the Board of Estimate, the owner might appeal this designation. The Commission designated the Grand Central Station as a landmark, frustrating its owner, the Penn Central Railway Corporation, from destroying the aboveground structure to build a high-rise building on the site. Penn Central claimed that this action was a taking of private property for public use without payment of "just compensation."

Justice Brennan delivered the opinion of the Court.

"Government hardly could go on if to some extent values incident to property could not be diminished without paying for every such change in the general law," and this Court has accordingly recognized, in a wide variety of contexts, that government may execute laws or programs that adversely affect recognized economic values. Exercises of the taxing power are one obvious example. A second are the decisions in which this Court has dismissed "taking" challenges on the ground that, while the challenged government action caused economic harm, it did not interfere with interests that were sufficiently bound up with the reasonable expectations of the claimant to constitute "property" for Fifth Amendment purposes.

This Court has upheld land-use regulations that destroyed or adversely affected recognized real property interests. Zoning laws are, of course, the classic example.

Goldblatt v. Hempstead is a recent example. There, a 1958 city safety ordinance banned any excavations below the water table and effectively prohibited the claimant from continuing a sand and gravel mining business that had been operated on the particular parcel since 1927. The Court upheld the ordinance against a "taking" challenge, although the ordinance prohibited the present and presumably most beneficial use of the property. A use restriction on real property may constitute a "taking" if not reasonably necessary to the effectuation of a substantial public purpose, or perhaps if it has an unduly harsh impact upon the owner's use of the property.

Pennsylvania Coal Co. v. Mahon is the leading case for the proposition that a state statute that substantially furthers important public policies may so frustrate distinct investment-backed expectations as to amount to a "taking." There the claimant had sold the surface rights to particular parcels of property, but expressly reserved the right to remove the coal thereunder. A Pennsylvania statute, enacted after the transactions, forbade any mining of coal that caused the subsidence of any house, unless the house was the property of the owner of the underlying coal and was more than 150 feet from the improved property of another. Because the statute made it commercially impracticable to mine the coal, and thus had nearly the same effect as the complete destruction of rights claimant had reserved from the owners of the surface land, the Court held that the statute was invalid as effecting a "taking," without just compensation.

Finally, government actions that may be characterized as acquisitions of resources to permit or facilitate uniquely public functions have often been held to constitute "takings." In holding that direct overflights above the claimant's land, that destroyed the present use of the land as a chicken farm, constituted a "taking," *Causby* emphasized that Government had not "merely destroyed property [but was] using a part of it for the flight of its planes."

[Appellants] observe that the airspace above the Terminal is a valuable property interest. They urge that the Landmarks Law has deprived them of any gainful use of their "air rights" above the Terminal and that, irrespective of the value of the remainder of their parcel, the city has "taken" their right to this superjacent airspace, thus entitling them to "just compensation" measured by the fair market value of these air rights.

"Taking" jurisprudence does not divide a single parcel into discrete segments and attempt to determine whether rights in a particular segment have been entirely abrogated. In deciding whether a particular governmental action has effected a taking, this Court focuses rather both on the character of the action and on the nature and extent of the interference with rights in the parcel as a whole—here, the city tax block designated as the "landmark site."

. . . Appellants, moreover, exaggerate the effect of the law on their ability to make use of the air rights above the Terminal in two respects. First, it simply cannot be maintained, on this record, that appellants have been prohibited from occupying *any* portion of the airspace above the Terminal. While the Commission's actions in denying applications to construct an office building in excess of 50 stories above the Terminal may indicate that it will refuse to issue a certificate of appropriateness for any comparably sized structure, nothing the Commission has said or done suggests an intention to prohibit *any* construction above the Terminal. The Commission's report emphasized that whether any construction would be allowed depended upon whether the proposed addition "would harmonize in scale, material, and character with [the Terminal]." Since appellants have not sought approval for the construction of a smaller structure, we do not know that appellants will be denied any use of any portion of the airspace above the Terminal.

Case Questions

1. Does the U.S. Constitution prohibit the "taking" of private property? What is a taking, and what might justify a governmental taking of private property?
2. What examples of government takings of private real property are there?
3. Is there an alternative method for fulfilling the public use purpose that does not involve a partial or complete taking?

The *Penn Central* case illustrates how the takings clause can be of particular interest to business. It illustrates a *partial taking*, that is, a loss incidental to government regulation. For example, a partial taking may be at issue where: (1) a landowner is prevented from exploiting the property's greatest economic value, (2) a landowner must let others somehow use the property, or (3) a landowner does not receive just compensation, usually appraised at fair market value, for the taking. Government regulations generally involve no compensable taking where the property is simply restricted from some uses. To do otherwise would severely restrict government's ability to regulate. However, since 1987 the Supreme Court now considers some partial takings as compensable. For example, compensation was required when a government body took an easement for public beach access and when the use of property in a flood plain was temporarily restricted.[1] The Supreme Court balances the economic impact of a regulation against its anticipated public benefits.

Judicial Review

The American legal heritage of common law has evolved into a hybrid of the common law and civil law legal systems. Both types of law periodically require interpretation, a function historically provided by the courts.

Constitutional Interpretation Many constitutional provisions are precise enough to make interpretation unnecessary. For example, most of the numerical limitations seem clear enough. The minimum age for the president and for members of Congress and the majority vote required to pass legislation, override vetoes, or amend the Constitution all seem quite precise. However, several vague terms were deliberately placed in the Constitution to permit flexibility as society changed. Because the founders knew that they could not anticipate the whole range of potential human behaviors, they left some prohibitions intentionally vague to permit the courts flexibility and discretion in interpretation. This helps to prevent compliance with only the "letter" but not the "spirit" of the law.

Judicial Restraint The Supreme Court's power to interpret the Constitution is important because the formal constitutional amendment process is cumbersome. Since the original Bill of Rights was ratified, the Constitution has been amended only 17 times. By contrast, the Supreme Court has decided questions of constitutional law thousands of times, effectively changing the Constitution.

A court's power to make laws is limited in several important ways. First, a federal court and the courts of most states may adjudicate and interpret only after a real *case or controversy* has arisen; advisory opinions are not permitted. A few states permit their

[1]*First English Evangelical Lutheran Church of Glendale v. Los Angeles County,* 482 U.S. 304 (1987); *Nollan v. California Coastal Commission,* 107 S. Ct. 3141 (1987).

courts to provide advisory opinions. Second, most judges exercise judicial restraint by trying not to make new or sweeping changes in the law. Most judicial decisions must be made in conformance with established precedents. The common law rule of precedent ensures consistency, provides some notice, and restricts judges from imposing their own economic or social beliefs.

Numerous constraints have been placed on the judiciary's power to make new laws. **Strict constructionism**, a narrow view, assumes that the legislature is better suited than the judiciary to consider the societal or economic problems that require pervasive new laws. Although courts have significant law-making powers, they are powerless to enforce their decisions. Without the appropriation of funds by the legislature or enforcement by the executive, there is no mechanism for the enforcement of judge-made law. Legal precedents are also subject to later changes imposed by the legislature. In 1944, for example, the Supreme Court first applied the antitrust laws to insurance companies. Immediately, Congress passed the McCarran-Ferguson Act, which reversed the decision giving the insurance industry an antitrust exemption. Today, there are pressures on Congress to abolish that exemption.

Supreme Court Review of Legislation Prior to 1803, the judicial review of legislation was unknown in all nations. In the United States, where conflict arises between the Constitution and a statute, the legislation is subject to **judicial review.** The power of judicial review flows naturally from both the common law of precedent and from the supremacy clause. There is no specific constitutional provision conferring this power on the Supreme Court. Instead, the Supreme Court conferred the power of judicial reviews on itself in the landmark 1803 case of *Marbury v. Madison.*[2]

In the last few days of his administration, President John Adams made several special appointments to federal office before the new president, Thomas Jefferson, could take office. The Senate confirmed these appointments. Marbury was appointed as a justice of the peace for the District of Columbia. Jefferson told James Madison, the new secretary of state, not to grant several of Adams' appointments, including Marbury's commission. Marbury brought suit in the Supreme Court for a *writ of mandamus,* a court order to force Madison to deliver his commission. Chief Justice John Marshall ruled that a judge's duty is to interpret the law and apply it to the facts of a controversy. When the controversy involves the constitutionality of legislation, the courts have the power to invalidate the legislature's enactments if they are unconstitutional. This case established the doctrine of judicial review, permitting the courts to interpret legislation and declare whether laws are constitutional.

Commentary:
The Supreme Court: Ideology and Politics

From time to time, throughout American Constitutional history, the Supreme Court's political independence has been questioned. Supreme Court judges are appointed by the president with the "advice and consent" of the U.S. Senate. This provides a check on the power of the executive branch balancing the executive and judiciary's powers. However, critics often charge the nomination process is too political, thereby assuring the appointment of political ideologues. For example, when the president and a Senate majority are from the

[2]*Marbury v. Madison,* 1 Cranch 137 (1803).

same political party, the president can appoint and the Senate confirm justices who are clearly sympathetic to their own party's ideology. Observers charge Franklin D. Roosevelt, a Democrat, had a politically sympathetic Senate majority of Democrats. This permitted him to appoint liberal judges supportive of the New Deal and FDR's more aggressive form of regulatory government.

Supreme Court justices' political and ideological leanings become important in close questions. A single swing vote on Constitutional questions is decisive, possibly changing established Constitutional interpretations. For example, *Roe v. Wade* inferred the abortion rights rule from a constitutional right to privacy. However, the right to privacy is not expressly stated in the U.S. Constitution. A conservative court majority is likely to overturn the abortion right, leaving the matter to be settled in the state legislatures.

When the presidency is held by a member of one party and the Senate is controlled by the other party, any new Supreme Court members will probably reflect some ideological or political balance. Senate hearings usually reveal whether the nominee has extremist philosophies. This suggests the president should nominate moderate candidates more acceptable to the Senate. This conflict emerged in President Reagan's failed 1989 nomination of Robert Bork to the Supreme Court. Judge Bork's conservative free market ideology was well documented in his writings and speeches. He clearly reinforced this perception with testimony given before the Senate Judiciary Committee, the committee that screens nominees before the full Senate votes. Judge Bork was not confirmed allegedly because he was portrayed by liberal interest groups as a strict constructionist and hostile to privacy, civil rights, and antitrust enforcement. Critics charge that subsequent Supreme Court nominations by Presidents Reagan and Bush were chosen because their ideological views were not well known. Because their writings were scarce and their ideologies relatively unknown, they avoided being "Borked," that is, defeated by lobbying pressure on Senate members. Political grandstanding on nationwide television by several senators from both parties contributed to public discontent over the advice and consent process during Judge Clarence Thomas' 1991 confirmation.

The advice and consent process was designed to permit open debate of a nominee's ideology and qualifications. The president should be given some free reign to select ideologically compatible individuals for the cabinet. These people must regularly work with the president's team and harmonize with the administration. However, judges and other independent government officials, like SEC or FTC Commissioners, are independent of the administration. Their experience and job qualifications are more important than ideological conformity. The nomination and confirmation process has permitted a shift of emphasis from ideological compatibility to qualifications as necessary to suit the position. The president and Senate should return to the true spirit of the U.S. Constitution's "advice" provision, which requires the president to first seek counsel from the whole Senate. This could help avoid the divisiveness of nominating an ideologically unacceptable candidate. Future replays of the destructive treatment of Judges Bork and Thomas may weaken public faith in the nomination process applicable to all federal judges, cabinet members, and other important federal officials.

SPECIFIC POWERS OF GOVERNMENT

Commerce Clause

The power over commerce, an enumerated power of the federal government, forms the basis for nearly all economic regulation. The commerce clause is the most important constitutional provision with impact on business.

The Commerce Clause

The Congress shall have the Power . . . To regulate Commerce with foreign Nations, and among the several States, and with the Indian Tribes.

Two major aspects of the commerce clause concern the regulation of business. First, it affirmatively grants Congress the power to regulate interstate commerce. Second, by implication, it denies the states the power to regulate or impede interstate commerce. This does not mean that the states cannot regulate the intrastate or local incidents of all commerce. States may validly use their police power to protect the health, safety, welfare, and morals of their citizens. In some areas, both federal and state laws may regulate commerce as long as the purposes of the state laws are proper.

Regulation of Foreign Commerce Regulation of trade with foreign nations is an exclusively federal power under the U.S. Constitution, whereas under the Articles of Confederation, the states made inconsistent compacts with foreign nations. This provision of the Constitution is based on the theory that the power to make treaties, conduct foreign relations, and regulate foreign commerce should be determined by a single, unified entity representing the will and needs of the whole nation.

The definition of foreign commerce becomes a problem because foreign commerce necessarily begins or ends within a state. State regulation of imports or exports with foreign nations is invalid if it restricts trade or requires any special treatment of foreign goods. The states may exercise limited regulation over foreign goods once these goods are in the hands of a retailer and the bulk of a wholesale lot has been broken down into smaller commercial units. This happens, for example, if the international bulk unit, a large container or pallet, has been broken down into cases. Nevertheless, a state regulation may be invalid if it discriminates between domestic and foreign commerce, even if the regulation is arguably based on public welfare concerns. Some other nations permit their political subdivisions to affect foreign commerce. For example, the Canadian provinces regulate Canada's securities markets. Provincial regulators can make international enforcement agreements with other nations' regulators.

Federal Regulation of Commerce The original intention of the commerce clause was to grant Congress sufficient power to govern all areas of economic activity. In 1824, however, the Supreme Court in *Gibbons v. Ogden,*[3] restricted Congress from regulating *intrastate* matters, that is, matters wholly within only one state, by interpreting the word *interstate* more narrowly.

Interstate Commerce

Commerce, undoubtedly, is traffic, but it is something more: it is . . . commercial intercourse between nations, and parts of nations, in all its branches, and is regulated by prescribing rules for carrying on that intercourse.

[3]*Gibbons v. Ogden,* 6 L. Ed. 23 (1824).

At the beginning of the 20th century, the Supreme Court made its most restrictive interpretations of the interstate commerce powers of Congress. The Court stated that interstate commerce must include some transportation of goods across state lines. Therefore, almost all manufacturing was considered intrastate and not subject to federal regulations.

Commerce Power and the New Deal New Deal economics influenced the Supreme Court's interpretation of the commerce clause. During the Great Depression, there were mounting public pressures for federal solutions to the economic devastation. The efforts of President Franklin D. Roosevelt and Congress to enact such solutions pitted them against the Supreme Court's laissez-faire pre-disposition. After the 1937 power struggle between the Supreme Court and President Roosevelt, the Supreme Court validated nearly all of the remedial legislation regulating commerce that Congress had enacted, including such major laws as the National Labor Relations Act, the Securities acts, and the Fair Labor Standards Act. Since 1937, the commerce clause has become the most significant source of congressional power to regulate business. Federal legislation has been upheld under the commerce clause even where its purpose has been to develop a federal police power to preserve health, safety, and welfare.

Today, the federal power over interstate commerce extends to nearly all facets of life, even where economic benefits and burdens are readjusted. Only two general limitations restrict this power to regulate. First, the power of Congress over wholly intrastate activities is expressly limited by the Constitution. Second, the *affectation doctrine* requires that the activity regulated must affect interstate commerce in some way. This means that some reasonable link must exist between that activity and some aspect of interstate commerce. The determination by Congress that such a link exists is usually sufficient to satisfy the courts, even though the link may be tenuous. How strong must the link be between interstate commerce and the activity to validate the regulation? The next case illustrates this link in instances that might at first glance appear to be wholly intrastate.

Perez v. U.S.

402 U.S. 146 (1971)
United States Supreme Court

Perez was alleged to be a "loan shark," a profession that Congress found to be largely controlled by organized crime. Loan sharks enter into extortionate credit transactions characterized by the use of threat or violence to enforce repayment. Perez, a local loan shark, lent Miranda $1,000 to be repaid in $105 installments for 14 weeks, which was increased to $130 after 6 weeks. An additional $2,000 loan was to be repaid in $205 installments, which Perez increased to $330 after threatening Miranda. Perez increased the payment until Miranda sold his butcher shop, unable to make further payments. Perez continued to threaten violence to Miranda and his family, suggesting that collections would soon be made by Perez' more violent associates. Perez was charged with loan-sharking, a federal crime.

Justice Douglas delivered the opinion of the Court.

The Commerce Clause reaches, in the main, three categories of problems. First, the use of channels of interstate or foreign commerce which Congress deems are being misused, as, for example, the shipment of stolen goods or of persons who have been kidnapped. Second, protection of the instrumentalities of interstate commerce, as, for example, the destruction of an aircraft, or persons or things in commerce, as, for example, thefts from interstate shipments. Third, those activities affecting commerce. It is with this last category that we are here concerned.

Chief Justice Marshall in *Gibbons v. Ogden* said: "government . . . action is to be applied to all the external concerns of the nation, and to those internal concerns which affect the States generally; but not to those which are completely within a particular State. The completely internal commerce of a State, then, may be considered as reserved for the State itself."

Chief Justice Stone wrote for a unanimous Court in 1942 that Congress could provide for the regulation of the price of intrastate milk, the sale of which, in competition with interstate milk, affects the price structure and federal regulation of the latter. The commerce power, he said, " extends to those activities intrastate which so affect interstate commerce, or the exertion of the power of Congress over it, as to make regulation of them appropriate means to the attainment of a legitimate end, the effective execution of the granted power to regulate interstate commerce."

Wickard v. Filburn soon followed in which a unanimous Court held that wheat grown wholly for home consumption was constitutionally within the scope of federal regulation of wheat production because, though never marketed interstate, it supplied the need of the grower which otherwise would be satisfied by his purchases in the open market . . .

In *United States v. Darby,* the decision sustaining an Act of Congress which prohibited the employment of workers in the production of goods "for interstate commerce" at other than prescribed wages and hours, *a class of activities* was held properly regulated by Congress without proof that the particular intrastate activity against which a sanction was laid had an effect on commerce. That case is particularly relevant here because it involved a criminal prosecution, a unanimous Court holding that the Act was "sufficiently definite to meet constitutional demands." Petitioner is clearly *a member of the class* which engages in "extortionate credit transactions" as defined by Congress and the description of that class has the required definiteness.

It was the "class of activities" test which we employed in *Heart of Atlanta Motel, Inc. v. United States* to sustain an Act of Congress requiring hotel or motel accommodations for Negro guests. The Act declared that " 'any inn, hotel, motel, or other establishment which provides lodging to transient guests affects commerce *per se.*" That exercise of power under the Commerce Clause was sustained.

In a companion case, *Katzenbach v. McClung,* we ruled on the constitutionality of the restaurant provision of the same Civil Rights Act which regulated the restaurant "if . . . it serves or offers to serve interstate travelers or a substantial portion of the food which it serves . . . has moved in commerce." Apart from the effect on the flow of food in commerce to restaurants, we spoke of the restrictive effect of the exclusion of Negroes from restaurants on interstate travel by Negroes. . .

Extortionate credit transactions, though purely intrastate, may in the judgment of Congress affect interstate commerce. In an analogous situation, Mr. Justice Holmes, speaking for a unanimous Court, said, "[W]hen it is necessary in order to prevent an evil to make the law embrace more than the precise thing to be prevented it may do so." It appears, instead, that loansharking in its national setting is one way organized interstate crime holds its guns to the heads of the poor and the rich alike and syphons funds from numerous localities to finance its national operations.

Case Questions

1. What is the link between loan-sharking and interstate commerce?
2. If local activities may affect interstate commerce, what might be left as wholly intrastate activities beyond federal control?

The broad commerce power to regulate business can be further implemented through the *necessary* and *proper* clause, a catchall phrase following the list of delegated powers in Article I, Section 8. This permits regulation even beyond an enumerated power such as regulating commerce. Legislation covering such additional matters is valid when it makes regulation of an enumerated power more effective. For example, a limit on tort remedies against nuclear power generators was based on the necessary and proper clause as a way to encourage development of the nuclear power industry.

The Necessary and Proper Clause

The Congress shall have Power . . . To make all Laws which shall be necessary and proper for carrying into Execution the foregoing Powers.

State Regulation of Commerce The Constitution does not specifically deny the states the power to regulate interstate commerce. However, an examination of the case law illustrates that the states' powers are limited. The dual-federalism concept permits the states to regulate intrastate activities even if they impose a minor effect on interstate commerce.

Today, a "balancing test" is applied to state laws that regulate commerce. First, the state regulation must bear a rational relationship to a valid state goal. Second, the effect of the state regulation on interstate commerce must be slight. Third, the extent to which the state regulation discriminates against interstate commerce must be small. Fourth, the necessity for the state regulation must be great. These four factors draw a balance between the state's interests in regulating and the need for federal uniformity. If a state law regulating commerce is reasonably related to a strong and necessary state goal and the burdens and discrimination that it places on interstate commerce are small, the law should be valid.

Through a long line of cases, the states' powers to regulate interstate commerce have been refined. These cases can be divided into three basic groups, each of which will be briefly discussed: (1) restriction of state regulation of interstate transportation, (2) control of state regulation of production and trade, and (3) tolerance of state taxation of multistate and multinational businesses.

State Regulation of Transportation In the 1925 case of *Buck v. Kuykendall,*[4] a Washington State common carrier licensing statute was invalidated as a burden on interstate commerce. Buck was refused permission to use the Washington State highways to operate an "auto stage line" because the territory was "already being adequately served." The Supreme Court found that the state was attempting to unconstitutionally regulate interstate commerce, and not simply the safety of its highways. In the 1938 case of *South Carolina State Highway Dept. v. Barnwell Bros.,*[5] the state restricted the width and weight of truck traffic. This was upheld as a legitimate safety concern, despite the incidental burden that the restrictions placed on interstate commerce. Long trucks presented similar safety concerns to Iowa, which validly restricted double trailers over 60 feet long.[6]

State safety concerns must be actual and not conjectural, a problem addressed by the arbitrary train-length restrictions in the 1945 case of *Southern Pac. Co. v. Arizona.*[7] Arizona attempted to collect penalties from Southern Pacific Railway for violating the 14-car passenger-train maximum limit and the 70-car freight-train limit. This case introduced the "balancing test" that the Supreme Court then used to invalidate the Arizona

---

[4]*Buck v. Kuykendall,* 267 U.S. 307 (1925).

[5]*South Carolina State Highway Dept. v. Barnwell Bros.,* 303 U.S. 177 (1938).

[6]*Kassel v. Consolidated Freightways Corp. of Delaware,* 450 U.S. 662 (1981).

[7]*Southern Pac. Co. v. Arizona,* 325 U.S. 761 (1945).

statute as arbitrary. *Bibb v. Navajo Freight Lines, Inc.*[8] presented a similar problem in 1959. Illinois attempted to require all trucks to use a particular type of curved mudguard for their wheels. The statute was found unconstitutional because the mudguards, manufactured by an Illinois company, were expensive and offered little additional protection over the equipment used by most trucking companies. There must be compelling local interest before local regulations imposing a burden on interstate commerce will be upheld as constitutional.

Discriminatory State Regulation of Production Most state restrictions on out-of-state products are discriminatory, placing an undue burden on interstate commerce. An exception exists for state quarantine restrictions. For example, laws imposing liability on persons bringing diseased cattle into Iowa were upheld, as were state regulations prohibiting the delivery of diseased cattle to New York. Today, to protect their fruit trees from disease, Arizona and California may legitimately restrict the fruit brought into those states.

Some state statutes are offered to prevent the spread of disease or unwholesome foods, although in reality they are intended to favor in-state producers. A state or local economic interest in maintaining domestic products, conserving local resources, or retaining favorable prices for state citizens generally does not justify placing a burden on interstate commerce. Most state restrictions on the export of commodities or products outside the state are also invalid.

The celebrated milk import cases have been particularly troublesome. Although states may use the police power to assure food safety, several milk regulations have been invalidated. States have attempted to control the price, place of production, or distance that milk travels to market on the pretext of maintaining the milk's wholesomeness. The New York State Milk Control Act of 1933 established minimum prices for milk in order to ensure sanitary conditions. Madison, Wisconsin, restricted milk sales in the city to milk produced within 25 miles of the city. A Mississippi regulation allowed the sale of milk produced out-of-state only if the state of origin permitted the import of Mississippi's milk. The Supreme Court found these state laws to be excessive regulations for their limited objective because other means existed to control milk purity.

State Taxation of Interstate Business States may impose burdens on interstate commerce by taxing out-of-state businesses. Taxation is justifiable if the out-of-state business has some connection, or *nexus,* with the taxing state. The nexus is a valid basis for taxation because all residents should pay for the use of governmental benefits. These benefits include the protection of the state's laws, police, fire department, and courts, as well as the use of its public facilities, such as the direct use of roads or the indirect use of parks or schools by employees.

Several types of tax may be valid. Each must apply fairly to both in-state and out-of-state businesses. For example, *property taxes* are legitimate if they are levied on real estate or personal property residing within the state on "tax day." *Use taxes* are legitimate if the seller is exempt from paying sales tax but the purchaser resides within the taxing state.

Some difficulties have arisen with the "unitary" income taxes levied by some states on multistate and multinational businesses. States may validly tax only the portion of a business's income that is derived from property or activities within the state. For example, an auto assembly plant might be located in the taxing state, but all of the component parts might be produced in other states. The taxing state may tax only the assembly

---

[8]*Bibb v. Navajo Freight Lines, Inc.*, 359 U.S. 520 (1959).

operations and not the manufacture of the components. However, it is difficult to accurately compute the portion of income derived within a particular state if companies do a substantial amount of out-of-state business. Income taxes on multistate or multinational businesses, both foreign and domestic, are valid if they meet modified criteria for interstate commerce. First, a reasonable formula must apportion the tax. Second, a nexus or minimum contact must be established between the state and the business being taxed. Third, the tax must not discriminate against or place an unconstitutional burden on interstate commerce.

Contract Clause

The *contract clause* prohibits states from impairing private contracts. This limitation restricts the states, but not the federal government, from passing statutes or administrative regulations that modify the duties owed under existing contracts. The contract clause was interpreted to prohibit the states from imposing economic regulations during the 19th century.

The Contract Clause

No State shall . . . pass any . . . Law impairing the Obligation of Contracts.

The framers of the Constitution included the contract clause in response to the economic chaos that existed under the Articles of Confederation. The major purpose of the clause was to prevent popular pressures for the passage of *debtor relief laws*. Because more people were debtors than creditors, the framers feared that the debtors might elect legislators pledged to pass laws releasing all debts. The contract clause was intended to forbid such actions.

Some early interpretations of the contract clause restricted public grants by the states to individuals and institutions (colleges). Modern interpretations of the contract clause permit the states to modify existing contracts only in emergency situations, for example, where this is necessary to protect the public health, safety, or welfare.

Should the contract clause be interpreted literally to prohibit all state regulation of business? The following case illustrates how the Supreme Court may be beginning to reevaluate the growing intervention of state governments into business affairs, signaling a possible return to laissez-faire attitudes.

Allied Structural Steel Co. v. Spannaus
438 U.S. 234 (1978)
United States Supreme Court

A Minnesota statute required most employers to pay a "pension funding charge" if its pension plan was terminated or if the firm permanently closed its Minnesota offices. The charge applied if pension funds were insufficient to cover liabilities for employees who worked at least 10 years. Allied notified the state of its intention to close its Minnesota office. It discharged nine employees who had no pension plan but qualified as pension obligees under the statute. Minnesota assessed Allied a $185,000 pension-funding charge. The statute created a contract liability for pensions that had not previously existed.

Justice Stewart delivered the opinion of the Court.

First of all, it is to be accepted as a commonplace that the Contract Clause does not operate to obliterate the police power of the States. "It is the settled law of this court that the interdiction of statutes impairing the obligation of contracts does not prevent the State from exercising such powers as are vested in it for the promotion of the common weal, or are necessary for the general good of the public." The first inquiry must be whether the state law has, in fact, operated as a substantial impairment of a contractual relationship. The severity of the impairment measures the height of the hurdle the state legislation must clear. Minimal alteration of contractual obligations may end the inquiry at its first stage. Severe impairment, on the other hand, will push the inquiry to a careful examination of the nature and purpose of the state legislation.

The severity of an impairment of contractual obligations can be measured by the factors that reflect the high value the Framers placed on the protection of private contracts. Contracts enable individuals to order their personal and business affairs according to their particular needs and interests. Once arranged, those rights and obligations are binding under the law, and the parties are entitled to rely on them.

Here, the company's contracts of employment with its employees included as a fringe benefit or additional form of compensation, the pension plan. The company's maximum obligation was to set aside each year an amount based on the plan's requirements for vesting. The plan satisfied the current federal income tax code and was subject to no other legislative requirements. And, of course, the company was free to amend or terminate the pension plan at any time. The company thus had no reason to anticipate that its employees' pension rights could become vested except in accordance with the terms of the plan. It relied heavily, and reasonably, on this legitimate contractual expectation in calculating its annual contributions to the pension fund.

The effect of Minnesota's Private Pension Benefits Protection Act on this contractual obligation was severe. The company was required in 1974 to have made its contributions throughout the pre-1974 life of its plan as if employees' pension rights had vested after 10 years, instead of vesting in accord with the terms of the plan. Thus a base term of the pension contract—one on which the company had relied for 10 years—was substantially modified. The result was that, although the company's past contributions were adequate when made, they were not adequate when computed under the 10-year statutory vesting requirement. The Act thus forced a current recalculation of the past 10 years' contributions based on the new, unanticipated 10-year vesting requirement.

Not only did the state law thus retroactively modify the compensation that the company had agreed to pay its employees from 1963 to 1974, but also it did so by changing the company's obligations in an area where the element of reliance was vital—the funding of a pension plan.

Moreover, the retroactive state-imposed vesting requirement was applied only to those employers who terminated their pension plans or who, like the company, closed their Minnesota offices.

Entering a field it had never before sought to regulate, the Minnesota Legislature grossly distorted the company's existing contractual relationships with its employees by superimposing retroactive obligations upon the company substantially beyond the terms of its employment contracts. . . .

The statute in question here nullifies express terms of the company's contractual obligations and imposes a completely unexpected liability in potentially disabling amounts. There is not even any provision for gradual applicability or grace periods. Yet there is no showing in the record before us that this severe disruption of contractual expectations was necessary to meet an important general social problem. It did not operate in an area already subject to state regulation at the time the company's contractual obligations were originally undertaken, but invaded an area never before subject to regulation by the State. It did not effect simply a temporary alteration of the contractual relationships of those within its coverage, but worked a severe, permanent, and immediate change in those relationships—irrevocably and retroactively. And its narrow aim was leveled, not at every Minnesota employer, not even at every Minnesota employer who left the State, but only at those who had in the past been sufficiently enlightened as voluntarily to agree to establish pension plans for their employees.

Case Questions

1. Is the contract clause given literal meaning in this case?
2. What is the most important initial factor that must be determined in a contract clause case? How is this factor determined?
3. In what instances might a state's impairment of contract be justified?

Full Faith and Credit Clause

An important element of federalism is that each state must recognize the laws and legal processes of the other states. Without this recognition, some of the states could become a refuge for persons seeking to evade their legal obligations elsewhere. To prevent such misuse of the states' borders, the framers of the Constitution formulated the *full faith and credit clause.*

Full Faith and Credit Clause

Full Faith and Credit shall be given in each State to the public Acts, Records, and judicial Proceedings of every other State.

Full faith and credit is distinguished from *stare decisis,* the rule of precedent. Precedents are previous cases that establish rules of law applicable to other similar disputes arising later. Full faith and credit does not require states to adopt other states' precedents, only to enforce their laws or judgments between particular disputing parties when suit is brought in another state. The full faith and credit clause requires application of the doctrines of *res judicata* and *collateral estoppel.* These doctrines require that when a competent court with jurisdiction over the subject matter renders a final decision, there can be no further litigation, except for appeals. The doctrines are similar to the criminal law doctrine of *double jeopardy,* which prohibits the prosecution of an individual twice for the same crime. All of these doctrines require a halt to litigation so that a defendant cannot be subjected to repeated suits on the same issues. The courts of other states must recognize and enforce the final decisions of all sister states. For example, if a creditor wins a judgment against a debtor in one state and the debtor flees to another state, the creditor may enforce that decree in the second state. This is true even if the second state does not have the same law as the state rendering the decree. Thus, Indiana need not require the payment of alimony in divorce actions between its citizens. However, it must enforce the alimony awards decreed in other states. Otherwise, Indiana could become a haven for alimony defaulters from other states.

Another important effect of the full faith and credit clause is that the courts of each state must apply the law of the state having the closest relationship to the events at issue in a suit. For example, parties may form a contract in one state, but one of the parties might bring suit for breach of the contract in another state. The *forum state* (the state in which the suit is brought) must apply the law of the state with the closest connection to the contract. The Supreme Court has approved several definitions of "closeness," although a complex *conflicts of law* analysis is often required to predict the proper choice of law if the forum state's substantive law differs from that of the other states involved. Similar problems exist in tort and domestic relations litigation. Conflicts of law rules often prevent a party from *forum shopping,* that is, shopping for a state court with law favorable to that party.

Privileges and Immunities

The *privileges and immunities clause* is another aspect of federalism that prohibits the states from erecting barriers at their borders.

Privileges and Immunities Clause

The Citizens of each State shall be entitled to all Privileges and Immunities of Citizens in the several States.

No state may discriminate against the citizens of other states by prohibiting travel or denying access to its courts. Note here, however, that corporations are not considered citizens under the privileges and immunities clause. Thus, out-of-state corporations may be charged higher taxes than domestic corporations as long as the taxes are not confiscatory. Similarly, since state taxes support state educational institutions financially, nonresident students may pay higher college tuition at state universities than do resident students. The commerce, full faith and credit, and privileges and immunities clauses work together to unify the nation while preserving states' rights.

Taxing and Spending Power

The federal government has the power to tax to raise revenue or to discourage certain activities. Even if Congress does not have a specific power to directly regulate a particular activity, the taxing and spending power may be used for that purpose. Earlier cases invalidated taxes intended only as indirect regulation rather than for revenue raising. However, today the Supreme Court focuses less on Congress' motives to levy the tax and more on whether or not the tax is valid as a regulatory measure. For example, taxes have been validated on sales of marijuana, firearms, and gambling, which are in reality indirect regulations of these activities.

Congress also has the power to spend tax receipts. Spending is legitimate on matters connected to an enumerated power and also on items not directly related to an enumerated power. Funds raised by taxes may be spent on nearly any policy Congress chooses, so long as it does not violate another constitutional provision. Both the taxing and spending powers of the federal government may be used to expand its powers to regulate in many areas not originally specified as federal powers in the U.S. Constitution.

CONSTITUTIONAL RIGHTS OF BUSINESSES AND INDIVIDUALS

The adoption of several fundamental rights known as the *Bill of Rights* amended the Constitution during its initial ratification process. The Fourteenth Amendment reinforces these rights. The *First Amendment* contains several rights, most notably freedom of speech, freedom of the press, freedom of assembly, and freedom of religion. The *Fourth Amendment* ensures the right to be secure from searches and seizures except on the issuance of a warrant. The *Fifth Amendment* includes several provisions ensuring fair judicial process, such as protection against self-incrimination, the right to a grand jury indictment, protection against double jeopardy, and the right to due process. The *Sixth Amendment* guarantees a speedy trial, an impartial jury, the confrontation of witnesses, subpoena powers, process to obtain witness testimony, and the right to legal counsel. The *Seventh Amendment* preserves the right to a trial by jury in actions at common law. The *Eighth Amendment* prohibits excessive fines.

These constitutional rights are not absolute; they have been interpreted and refined over the last 200 years. Courts balance the need for constitutional protection against other important policy considerations. The Bill of Rights protections specifically apply to natural persons, but they frequently extend to other entities, such as corporations, that are considered artificial persons. Corporations may validly claim protection of most of the Bill of Rights, particularly during criminal investigations and proceedings. The next sections examine these rights, with particular emphasis on the impact they have on business operations and business personnel.

The First Amendment

The First Amendment comprises the fundamental rights of free speech, press, assembly, and exercise of religion. Although the First Amendment specifically protects citizens from congressional action, under the absorption doctrine the Fourteenth Amendment's due process limitation applies most of the constitutional protections to governmental action by all levels and branches of government. Its application to religion in the business context is discussed further in Chapter 19.

The First Amendment

Congress shall make no law respecting an establishment of religion, or prohibiting the free exercise thereof; or abridging the freedom of speech, or of the press; or the right of the people peaceably to assemble, and to petition the Government for a redress of grievances.

Freedom of Speech The freedom of speech guaranteed by the First Amendment provides society with access to the general marketplace of ideas. This protection ensures that speakers have expressive access to the public and improves the quality and quantity of available ideas. Speech includes both verbal and nonverbal methods of expression. For example, the courts uphold union picketing for lawful purposes as nonverbal speech. However, laws may regulate some of the incidents of speech to preserve safety and public order. For example, the number of pickets and the manner of picketing may be controlled to preserve safety and order.

Not all types of speech are protected because society's need for some types of expression does not outweigh the social costs of allowing them. Obscenity, defamatory statements, incitement to riot, fraudulent statements, and subversive speeches are not protected under the First Amendment. The courts are particularly sensitive to the prior restraint laws that prohibit certain classes of speech. *Prior restraint* arises, for example, if a city denies a permit to assemble or a court prohibits a public meeting even though that activity's potential for violence is quite low. Prior restraint may arise if a governmental entity restricts speech that might oppose the politicians in power.

Commercial Speech Initially, the courts were not sympathetic to the protection of commercial speech. They approved legislation regulating advertising on the principle that commercial speech was less justifiable than other forms of speech because it resulted only in personal gain for the advertiser. Commercial speech was not thought to have the same legitimate social purpose as political speech. However, more recent cases have recognized that commercial speech performs an important function of information dissemination. By making adequate information available to all market participants, the free exercise of commercial speech helps ensure more efficient operation of the market.[9]

Commercial speech may be restricted as to time, place, and manner, but only where society's need for regulation outweighs the speaker's interest in making the speech. The criteria below are used to regulate commercial speech. How do these apply to restrictions on the advertising of tobacco or alcohol?

Criteria to Regulate Commercial Speech

- The commercial speech must concern lawful activity and not be misleading.
- The degree of restriction must directly relate to the degree of governmental interest.
- The restriction must reach no further than necessary to protect the governmental interest, and no other practical method exists to protect this interest.
- The time, place, and manner of the speech may be regulated, provided that no change is made in the substance of the speech.

Should problems such as the energy crisis outweigh an electric utility's right to advertise? The following case established the analysis that is used to evaluate restrictions on commercial speech.

Central Hudson Gas & Electric Corp. v. Public Service Commission

447 U.S. 557 (1980)
United States Supreme Court

In response to the energy crisis, the New York Public Service Commission ordered all electric utilities to cease advertising that promoted electricity use. Only informational advertising that encouraged shifts of consumption from peak to off-peak times was permitted. Central Hudson Gas and Electric opposed the ban on First Amendment grounds.

Justice Powell delivered the opinion of the Court.

The Commission's order restricts only commercial speech, that is, expression related solely to the economic interests of the speaker and its audience. The First Amendment, as applied to the States through the Fourteenth Amendment, protects commercial speech from unwarranted governmental regulation. Commercial expression not only serves the economic interest of the speaker, but also assists consumers and furthers the societal interest in the fullest possible dissemination of information. In applying the First Amendment to this area, we have rejected the "highly paternalistic" view that government has complete power to suppress or regulate commercial speech. "[P]eople will perceive their own best interests if only they are well enough

[9] *Virginia Pharmacy Board v. Virginia Citizens Consumer Council*, 425 U.S. 746 (1976).

informed, and . . . the best means to that end is to open the channels of communication, rather than to close them. . . ." Even when advertising communicates only an incomplete version of the relevant facts, the First Amendment presumes that some accurate information is better than no information at all.

If the communication is neither misleading nor related to unlawful activity, the government's power is more circumscribed. The State must assert a substantial interest to be achieved by restrictions on commercial speech. Moreover, the regulatory technique must be in proportion to that interest. The limitation on expression must be designed carefully to achieve the State's goal. . . . First, the restriction must directly advance the state interest involved; the regulation may not be sustained if it provides only ineffective or remote support for the government's purpose. Second, if the governmental interest could be served as well by a more limited restriction on commercial speech, the excessive restrictions cannot survive. . . .

In commercial speech cases, then, a four-part analysis has developed. At the outset, we must determine whether the expression is protected by the First Amendment. For commercial speech to come within that provision, it at least must concern lawful activity and not be misleading. Next, we ask whether the asserted governmental interest is substantial. If both inquiries yield positive answers, we must determine whether the regulation directly advances the governmental interest asserted, and whether it is not more extensive than is necessary to serve that interest.

The Commission offers two state interests as justifications for the ban on promotional advertising. The first concerns energy conservation. Any increase in demand for electricity—during peak or off-peak periods—means greater consumption of energy. The Commission argues, and the New York court agreed, that the State's interest in conserving energy is sufficient to support suppression of advertising designed to increase consumption of electricity. In view of our country's dependence on energy resources beyond our control, no one can doubt the importance of energy conservation. Plainly, therefore, the state interest asserted is substantial.

The State's interest in energy conservation is directly advanced by the Commission's order at issue here. There is an immediate connection between advertising and demand for electricity. Central Hudson would not contest the advertising ban unless it believed that promotion would increase its sales. Thus, we find a direct link between the state interest in conservation and the Commission's order.

We come finally to the critical inquiry in this case: whether the Commission's complete suppression of speech ordinarily protected by the First Amendment is no more extensive than necessary to further the State's interest in energy conservation. The Commission's order reaches all promotional advertising, regardless of the impact of the touted service on overall energy use. But the energy conservation rationale, as important as it is, cannot justify suppressing information about electric devices or services that would cause no net increase in total energy use. In addition, no showing has been made that a more limited restriction on the content of promotional advertising would not serve adequately the State's interest.

The Commission's order prevents appellant from promoting electric services that would reduce energy use by diverting demand from less efficient sources, or that would consume roughly the same amount of energy as do alternative sources. In neither situation would the utility's advertising endanger conservation or mislead the public. To the extent that the Commission's order suppresses speech that in no way impairs the State's interest in energy conservation, the Commission's order violates the First and Fourteenth Amendments and must be invalidated.

Case Questions

1. What steps are taken to justify bans on commercial speech?
2. What types of commercial speech are presumed to be unjustified?

Political Speech First Amendment protection also extends to the political speech of commercial entities. Corporations may validly disseminate ideas and influence political thought as long as they do not violate the campaign finance laws, discussed more fully in Chapter 22. However, the subject of the political speech should be general, and not identify specific political parties or candidates.

In *First National Bank of Boston v. Bellotti,*[10] a Massachusetts statute prohibited a corporation from making expenditures or contributions for the purpose of influencing the vote on questions submitted to voters unless the questions materially affected the corporation. The statute also prohibited corporate advocacy on legislation involving taxation. Corporate violators could be fined up to $50,000, and the corporate officer who authorized the expenditures could be fined and imprisoned for up to one year. First National Bank of Boston and others desired to publicize their views that a ballot question on a graduated individual income tax was unconstitutional. The court held:

> [The First] Amendment protects the free discussion of governmental affairs. . . . The inherent worth of the speech in terms of its capacity for informing the public does not depend upon the identity of its source, whether corporation, association, union, or individual. . . . The press does not have a monopoly on either the First Amendment or the ability to enlighten. . . . The First Amendment goes beyond protection of the press and the self-expression of individuals to prohibit government from limiting the stock of information from which members of the public may draw.
>
> If a legislature may direct business corporations to "stick to business," it also may limit other corporations—religious, charitable, or civic—to their respective "business" when addressing the public. Such power in government to channel the expression of views is unacceptable under the First Amendment. Especially where, as here, the legislature's suppression of speech suggests an attempt to give one side of a debatable public question an advantage in expressing its views to the people, the First Amendment is plainly offended.

ETHICAL DILEMMA: THE THREAT OF LITIGATION CHILLS FREEDOM OF SPEECH

The Bill of Rights includes constitutional freedoms most Americans consider to be sacred and fundamental rights. They are the product of the accumulation of political struggles over several millennia which mark the evolution of human civilization. However, the First Amendment freedom of speech often appears to conflict with other civil rights and property rights. This problem has arisen in recent years with public participation by individuals and interest groups. They may write editorials, give speeches, organize boycotts, or otherwise become involved in political participation (e.g., complaints to regulators, testimony before legislatures) that arguably harasses a particular business. For example, some interest groups have made public attacks on real estate developers alleging environmental or aesthetic destruction. In other cases, citizens have complained to regulators about a manufacturer's allegedly unsafe products. As a result of these attacks, the targeted business can suffer declining sales, a loss of reputation, or face tough new regulations. Some of these targeted businesses have responded by suing for damages or to enjoin the speech. Such responses are termed *SLAPP* suits, *Strategic Litigation Against Public Participation.* These actions by either side may involve an ethical dilemma of constitutional proportions. Either an unfair pressure is brought on the targeted business or costly litigation is brought by affluent firms, chilling the free speech or government participation by individuals and thereby frustrating these fundamental constitutional rights.

Some businesses targeted by such public participations have brought SLAPP suits alleging one or more of several torts: defamation (libel, slander), trade disparagement, trademark infringement, misrepresentation or fraud, tortious interference with contract relations, interference

[10] 435 U.S. 765 (1978).

with prospective advantage, and/or violation of privacy. In many cases, the target's mere initiation of suit intimidates the public participant and silences the public participation. However, public participants who have challenged SLAPP suits are usually successful in blunting the SLAPP and vindicate their right to participate. Indeed, in some SLAPP-back suits the public participants have won damages for abuse of process or malicious prosecution against the originally targeted business. Targeted businesses should never be denied judicial access to redress malicious damage by a public participant acting in bad faith. However, public participants should not be intimidated from exercising their First Amendment rights, free speech and petitioning the government for redress of grievances, when their cause is legitimate. Vindicating constitutional rights and abusing the political and legal systems pose ethical dilemmas for all persons and firms involved.

The Fifth and Fourteenth Amendments

The Fifth and Fourteenth Amendments contain two major provisions to maintain fundamental fairness: the due process clause and the equal protection clause. The Fifth Amendment applies its protections to actions taken by the federal government.

Fifth Amendment Due Process Clause

No person shall be . . . deprived of life, liberty, or property, without due process of law.

The Fourteenth Amendment applies the Fifth Amendment to the states under the *absorption* or *incorporation* doctrine. This doctrine assures that the Fourteenth Amendment incorporates the fundamental protections offered by the Fifth Amendment and extends them to the governmental actions taken by the states.

Fourteenth Amendment: Due Process and Equal Protection Clauses

. . . nor shall any State deprive any person of life, liberty, or property, without due process of law; nor deny to any person within its jurisdiction the equal protection of the laws.

Equal Protection of the Laws The need for equality under the law after the abolition of slavery demanded a definitive constitutional statement. The equal protection clause of the Fourteenth Amendment provided blacks with protection from arbitrary legislative distinctions. Today, that clause applies to all types of arbitrary and unreasonable classifications in legislation. By its very nature, legislation must delineate the persons or entities that are subject to the law, based on such classifications as conduct, size of business, or level of income. Establishing fair classifications of this kind is difficult, requiring careful statutory design. For example, only murderers should receive punishment under criminal statutes prohibiting murder. Similarly, the Uniform Commercial Code imposes special obligations on merchants; it requires a higher level of conduct in commercial transactions from merchants than from nonmerchants. These classifications are fair only when they adequately discriminate.

Legislative classifications with no reasonable purpose are unconstitutional under the equal protection clause. Under the rational basis test, laws should have general applicability unless there is sufficient reason to discriminate against certain people. This test applies in many situations, but it seldom invalidates legislation. Another test, the strict scrutiny test, applies in situations involving discrimination against suspect classes of persons or discrimination in matters of fundamental rights. When strict scrutiny applies, many statutes are held unconstitutional. An intermediate test, quasi-strict scrutiny, can also be important in business contexts.

Rational Basis The equal protection clause does not disturb the constitutionality of a statute if there is a rational connection between the statute's classification scheme and a permissible governmental purpose. Under this **rational basis** test, the statute is first presumed constitutional. Government may regulate in areas that are normally and legitimately the role of government. For example, Congress may pass laws pursuant to an enumerated power, such as the regulation of interstate commerce. State legislatures may pass criminal laws implementing the police power. Any classifications used in statutes enacted for such purposes must have a reasonable basis and not be arbitrary.

In *Minnesota v. Clover Leaf Creamery Co.*,[11] the Supreme Court found that a Minnesota statute provided adequate equal protection even though it prohibited only plastic disposable packaging for milk. The statute sought to diminish the solid-waste problem and save energy by banning nonreturnable plastic milk containers, yet it permitted the use of nonreturnable plastic containers for other products. The rational basis test, which was used here, invalidates only the most outrageously arbitrary classification schemes. States may implement a regulation program step by step by eliminating evils only partially at first and deferring complete elimination to future regulations.

Strict Scrutiny In more recent years, courts have used the **strict scrutiny** test to invalidate legislation that violates certain fundamental rights or discriminates against suspect classes. When the rigorous criteria of the strict scrutiny test are applied, legislation is seldom acceptable if any conceivable alternatives can achieve the same legitimate regulatory end. Under strict scrutiny, the suspect legislation must be necessary to and be the only means to achieve a compelling governmental interest. To survive a strict scrutiny attack, a statute must relate to the governmental interest more closely than is required under the rational basis test, and the governmental purpose must be more important. The defenders of the statute must prove actual legislative intent to reach the legitimate governmental goal.

Strict scrutiny applies only to fundamental rights and to discrimination against suspect classes. *Fundamental rights* include voting rights, interstate travel, immunity from mandatory sterility, and criminal procedural protections. *Suspect classes* are demographic classifications of people who deserve greater protection because they have been subjected to intentional discrimination and because they are nearly powerless to overcome the discrimination. Suspect classes include classifications based on race, national origin, and alien status. Discrimination in employers' hiring, firing, and promotion decisions is governed by separate antidiscrimination laws, discussed in greater detail in Chapter 19.

Quasi-Strict Scrutiny A third classification, *quasi-strict scrutiny,* has arisen in recent years. It falls between the rational basis and the strict scrutiny tests. This standard applies where the rights involved are clearly important but not quite considered fundamental rights, or where the classifications in the statute are only partially suspect. For example, classifications based on sex, gender, or legitimacy must be substantially related to an important government objective. This forms a middle ground between rational basis and

---

[11]*Minnesota v. Clover Leaf Creamery Co.*, 449 U.S. 456 (1981).

strict scrutiny. The quasi-strict scrutiny test validates some classifications while invalidating others. Clearly the equal protection inquiry is quite fact specific.

Equal protection issues arise most often in cases of racial segregation. Equal protection has required reapportionment of state legislatures under the principle of "one man, one vote," as when two nearby congressional districts in a state have grossly unequal numbers of citizens. The courts have ruled as unconstitutional military regulations affording spouses of servicewomen lesser benefits than the spouses of servicemen. The denial of voting rights in school district elections to nonparents or non-property owners was found unconstitutional under strict scrutiny.

Due Process of Law The intent of the due process clause was to prevent unfair and predetermined outcomes of criminal trials such as occurred when American colonists appeared before English judges. Due process requires government to observe at least a minimum level of fairness in trial procedures. This fairness doctrine prohibits arbitrary, biased, and unreasonable outcomes in trials and administrative hearings. The due process clause applies to a wide variety of criminal, civil, and administrative hearings. Certain private determinations by nongovernmental entities are also subject to some form of due process. However, due process rights are not identical in all cases: criminal defendants usually receive more specific and extensive protections than do civil or administrative litigants.

Due process prohibits government from depriving any person of life, liberty, or property without due process of law. A *person* in this context is broadly construed to include both natural persons and artificial persons, such as corporations or unincorporated associations. A *deprivation of life* usually denotes capital punishment and arises in right to die or euthanasia cases. A *deprivation of liberty* occurs when one is denied the ability to move freely in public areas, that is, while not trespassing on private property. A *deprivation of property* occurs when a person must pay a fine or money damages or when property is taken by government. Due process permits government deprivations of life, liberty, or property, but only if due process is followed.

Due process has developed into two separate limits on unreasonable governmental action. *Procedural due process* incorporates the traditional issues regarding the processes of investigation, arrest, detainment, trial, and appeal. *Substantive due process* involves issues concerning the fairness of legislation that defines rights and duties. These due process issues arise whenever government attempts to vindicate rights, whether those attempts are prosecuted by government attorneys, initiated in court or administrative agencies, or conducted by private entities affected with a public character (e.g., private universities). To successfully claim a due process right, some form of *state action* or governmental process must be in question.

Procedural Due Process Two basic rights in litigation involve due process protections. The first right is intended to assure defendants a fair opportunity to offer a defense and the use of fair trial procedures. This is why in some cases a notice of suit must be personally delivered to the defendant (service of summons). *Substituted service* of process is a valid alternative method of notifying the defendant whenever it is impossible to deliver a notice of suit personally.

The second basic due process right in litigation concerns the conduct of the trial. The precise fair trial procedures vary according to the rights adjudicated, the type of trial, and the severity of the penalties. The trial procedures should afford the utmost protection to a criminal defendant charged with a capital crime. At the other extreme, an administrative proceeding to discipline a college student provides due process even if many of the procedural technicalities of a criminal trial are not followed. The Fifth, Sixth, and Seventh Amendments are also read to require several fair trial procedures.

Defendant's Due Process Rights

1. Confront witnesses with cross-examination.
2. Present evidence.
3. Subpoena witnesses.
4. Have an impartial decision maker.
5. Appeal the trial decision.

Is a full trial by jury necessary to review a university's dismissal of a student for poor scholarship? Informal administrative processes need not include the full spectrum of evidentiary rules yet must provide the minimum due process required by the U.S. Constitution. In *Board of Curators of the University of Missouri v. Horowitz,*[12] Horowitz was dismissed from the University's medical school for failure to meet academic standards. She had been fully informed of the faculty's dissatisfaction with her progress and the adverse impact this could have on her timely graduation. The ultimate dismissal decision was deliberate and careful. Horowitz sued the university, claiming a lack of due process in the dismissal process. The Supreme Court compared academic dismissal to disciplinary proceedings, reserving traditional due process steps like notice and opportunity to present evidence only for disciplinary proceedings.

> Justice Rehnquist held that: "The decision to dismiss respondent rested on the academic judgment of school officials that she did not have the necessary clinical ability to perform adequately as a medical doctor and was making insufficient progress toward that goal. Such a judgment is by its nature more subjective and evaluative than the typical factual questions presented in the average disciplinary decision. Like the decision of an individual professor as to the proper grade for a student in his course, the determination whether to dismiss a student for academic reasons requires an expert evaluation of cumulative information and is not readily adapted to the procedural tools of judicial or administrative decision making."

Substantive Due Process The substantive due process doctrine allows a court to declare a statute unconstitutional if the statute fails to provide due process. In the late 19th and early 20th centuries, the *economic due process* doctrine was applied to early regulatory statutes that required minimum wages or maximum working hours or allowed union membership. Most of these statutes were declared unconstitutional as unjustifiably restricting the freedom of business to contract or as depriving business of its property without due process. Today, the economic substantive due process doctrine is inapplicable.

In the area of personal liberty and rights, the substantive due process doctrine retains some validity. It requires that legislation meet two tests. The first test is an ends-means

[12] 435 U.S. 78 (1978).

test similar to that found in equal protection cases. This test requires that legislation be directed toward a legitimate governmental purpose and that the means used be closely connected to that purpose.

Second, the test prohibits vague legislation. A statute is unconstitutional if it does not provide ascertainable criteria for the identification of unlawful conduct. For example, a law enforcement officer cannot arrest someone based on the officer's interpretation of what constitutes wrongdoing. Laws permitting this level of discretion are vague. In *Coates v. City of Cincinnati*,[13] the city passed a criminal ordinance prohibiting "three or more persons to assemble . . . on any of the sidewalks . . . and there conduct themselves in a manner *annoying* to persons passing by . . ." (emphasis added). On the basis of this ordinance, the Cincinnati authorities prosecuted Coates for participating in a student demonstration. The ordinance violated Coates's right to due process because it subjected his constitutional right of assembly to an imprecise standard embodied in the term *annoying conduct*. Conduct that some people find "annoying" does not annoy others, so people of common intelligence must necessarily guess at the word's meaning. The substantive due process right also protects business from prosecution under vague laws.

Punitive Damages There is a widespread perception that juries are awarding increasingly larger punitive damage awards. *Punitive damages* are an additional component of damages above and beyond compensatory damages, the amount that compensates the plaintiff for the losses actually suffered. Advocates of punitive damages argue they are necessary to deter business activities with adverse side effects on society. Without the threat of severe penalties, business managers have little incentive to avoid endangering the public with harmful products, manufacturing processes, or business practices. Managers are well insulated from lawsuit pressures, and they seldom bear the wealth effects of their decisions directly because the firm, not individuals, must pay. Advocates of punitives argue that highly visible punitive awards signal managers to more carefully consider the impact of their decisions on others.

Punitive damages could have an adverse impact on companies. Critics charge punitives are unpredictable and counterproductive for the economy. For example, a multimillon-dollar punitive award could wipe out a company's profitability for years, force it to drop products, slow its innovation, force the closing of facilities, cause the loss of jobs, or even drive the company into bankruptcy. Recent challenges to punitive damages have alleged they violate two fundamental constitutional rights. First, punitives are allegedly excessive fines prohibited by the Eighth Amendment. Second, unbridled jury discretion to assess punitive damages violates the defendant's right to due process under the Fourteenth Amendment.

In *Browing-Ferris Indus. v. Kelco Disposal*,[14] the Supreme Court rejected the Eighth Amendment argument. A regional BFI executive instructed the local BFI office to cut prices and drive Kelco, a competing waste collector, out of business. A jury awarded Kelco $51,146 in compensatory damages and $6 million in punitives in Kelco's monopolization suit. The Eighth Amendment was intended to protect convicted defendants from excessive punishment by government, not from civil actions between private parties. Should the due process clause apply to restrict punitive damages? The following case reexamines the constitutionality of punitives.

---

[13]*Coates v. City of Cincinnati*, 402 U.S. 611 (1971).

[14]492 U.S. 257 (1989).

Pacific Mutual Life Ins. Co. v. Halsip

111 S.Ct. 1032 (1991)
United States Supreme Court

The health insurance for Halsip and other employees of Roosevelt City, Alabama, lapsed after health and life insurance premiums were misappropriated by Ruffin acting as agent for both Union Fidelity Life Insurance Co. and Pacific Mutual Life Insurance Co. Premiums for this coverage were to be deducted from city employee paychecks and remitted by the city clerk to Ruffin and then to the insurers. Ruffin misappropriated the premiums and never forwarded the insurer's notice warning the insureds that their health insurance coverage would lapse. After hospitalization, Halsip was forced to pay her hospital bill. Her physician placed her unpaid account with a collection agency that obtained a judgment against her, adversely affecting her credit. Halsip sued Ruffin for fraud. The jury held Pacific Mutual vicariously liable under *respondea superior,* that is, responsible for its agent's wrongful acts. Halsip was awarded $1,040,000, approximately $840,000 of which was in punitive damages.

Justice Blackmun delivered the opinion of the Court.

Alabama's common-law rule is that a corporation is liable for both compensatory and punitive damages for fraud of its employee effected within the scope of his employment. We cannot say that this does not rationally advance the State's interest in minimizing fraud. Alabama long has applied this rule in the insurance context, for it has determined that an insurer is more likely to prevent an agent's fraud if given sufficient financial incentive to do so.

Imposing exemplary damages on the corporation when its agent commits intentional fraud creates a strong incentive for vigilance by those in a position "to guard substantially against the evil to be prevented."

Under the traditional common-law approach, the amount of the punitive award is initially determined by a jury instructed to consider the gravity of the wrong and the need to deter similar wrongful conduct. The jury's determination is then reviewed by trial and appellate courts to ensure that it is reasonable.

So far as we have been able to determine, every state and federal court that has considered the question has ruled that the common-law method for assessing punitive damages does not in itself violate due process. In view of this consistent history, we cannot say that the common-law method for assessing punitive damages is so inherently unfair as to deny due process and be *per se* unconstitutional.

One must concede that unlimited jury discretion—or unlimited judicial discretion for that matter—in the fixing of punitive damages may invite extreme results that jar one's constitutional sensibilities.

We need not, and indeed we cannot, draw a mathematical bright line between the constitutionally acceptable and the constitutionally unacceptable that would fit every case. We can say, however, that general concerns of reasonableness and adequate guidance from the court when the case is tried to a jury properly enter into the constitutional calculus.

To be sure, the instructions gave the jury significant discretion in its determination of punitive damages. But that discretion was not unlimited. It was confined to deterrence and retribution, the state policy concerns sought to be advanced. And if punitive damages were to be awarded, the jury "must take into consideration the character and the degree of the wrong as shown by the evidence and necessity of preventing similar wrong." The instructions thus enlightened the jury as to the punitive damages' nature and purpose [and] identified the damages as punishment for civil wrongdoing of the kind involved.

Before the trial in this case took place, the Supreme Court of Alabama had established post-trial procedures for scrutinizing punitive awards. In *Hammond v. City of Gadsden,* it stated that trial courts are "to reflect in the record the reasons for interfering with a jury verdict, or refusing to do so, on grounds of excessiveness of the damages." Among the factors deemed "appropriate for the trial court's consideration" are the "culpability of the defendant's conduct," the "desirability of discouraging others from similar conduct," the "impact upon the parties," and "other factors, such as the impact on innocent third parties." The *Hammond* test ensures meaningful and adequate review by the trial court whenever a jury has fixed the punitive damages.

Also before its ruling in the present case, the Supreme Court of Alabama had elaborated and refined the *Hammond* criteria for determining whether a punitive award is reasonably related to the goals of deterrence and retribution. It was announced that the following could be taken into consideration in determining whether the award was excessive or inadequate: (a) whether there is a reasonable relationship between the punitive damages award and the harm likely to result from the defendant's conduct as well as the harm that actually has occurred; (b) the degree of responsibility of the defendant's conduct, the duration of that conduct, the defendant's awareness, any concealment, and the existence and frequency of similar past conduct; (c) the profitability to the defendant of the wrongful conduct and the desirability of removing that profit and of having the defendant also sustain a loss; (d) the "financial position" of the defendant; (e) all the costs of litigation; (f) the imposition of criminal sanctions on the defendant for its conduct, these to be taken in mitigation; and (g) the existence of other civil awards against the defendant for the same conduct, these also to be taken in mitigation.

The application of these standards, we conclude, imposes a sufficiently definite and meaningful constraint on the discretion of Alabama fact finders in awarding punitive damages. The Alabama Supreme Court's post-verdict review ensures that punitive damages awards are not grossly out of proportion to the severity of the offense and have some understandable relationship to compensatory damages.

Pacific Mutual thus had the benefit of the full panoply of Alabama's procedural protections.

We are aware that the punitive damages award in this case is more than 4 times the amount of compensatory damages, is more than 200 times the out-of-pocket expenses of respondent Halsip, and, of course, is much in excess of the fine that could be imposed for insurance fraud. . . . in the criminal context. While the monetary comparisons are wide and, indeed, may be close to the line, the award here did not lack objective criteria. We conclude, after careful consideration, that in this case it does not cross the line into the area of constitutional impropriety. Accordingly, Pacific Mutual's due process challenge must be, and is, rejected.

The judgment of the Supreme Court of Alabama is affirmed.

It is so ordered.

Justice O'Connor, dissenting.

Punitive damages are a powerful weapon. Imposed wisely and with restraint they have the potential to advance legitimate state interests. Imposed indiscriminately, however, they have a devastating potential for harm. Regrettably, common-law procedures for awarding punitive damages fall into the latter category. States routinely authorize civil juries to impose punitive damages without providing them any meaningful instructions on how to do so. Rarely is a jury told anything more specific than "do what you think best."

In my view, such instructions are so fraught with uncertainty that they defy rational implementation. Instead, they encourage inconsistent and unpredictable results by inviting juries to rely on private beliefs and personal predilections. Juries are permitted to target unpopular defendants, penalize unorthodox or controversial views, and redistribute wealth. Multimillion-dollar losses are inflicted on a whim.

Due process requires that a State provide meaningful standards to guide the application of its laws. A state law that lacks such standards is void for vagueness. The void-for-vagueness doctrine applies not only to laws that proscribe conduct, but also to laws that vest standardless discretion in the jury to fix a penalty.

I have no trouble concluding that Alabama's common-law scheme for imposing punitive damages is void for vagueness.

"The touchstone of due process is protection of the individual against arbitrary action of government." Alabama's common-law scheme for awarding punitive damages provides a jury with "such skeletal guidance," that it invites—even requires—arbitrary results. It gives free reign to the biases and prejudices of individual jurors, allowing them to target unpopular defendants and punish selectively. In short, it is the antithesis of due process. It does not matter that the system has been around for a long time, or that the result in this particular case may not seem glaringly unfair. The common-law scheme yields unfair and inconsistent results "in so many instances that it should be held violative of due process in every case."

Case Questions

1. What procedures does Alabama provide to assure due process in the assessment of punitive damages?
2. In what situations does the Supreme Court suggest that punitives could violate the defendant's due process rights?
3. Justice O'Connor's dissent suggests a potential for due process violations remains under Alabama's punitive damage process. What are these potential defects in the Alabama process?

Several states now limit punitives by statute; Alabama "caps" punitive damages at no more than $250,000 per case. The "tort reform" discussed further in Chapter 9 and "product liability reform" discussed in Chapter 10 are part of this. Courts after *Halsip* are in conflict, some have narrowed punitives, some have invalidated limits on damage awards, and others continue awarding punitives without any arbitrary dollar limitation. Critics of the tort reform movement charge that stories about punitive damages are distorted to advocate statutory limitation. Most large punitive awards are newsworthy but are eventually reduced on appeal through *remittitur.* Most tort reformers fail to concede this fact.

A recent comprehensive empirical study of punitives awarded between 1965 and 1990 in both state and federal courts made several findings rebutting the false claims of tort reformers. The researchers found most large awards: (1) were made in asbestos cases, (2) declined since 1986, (3) are made by state courts, (4) predominate in the South, (5) are usually based on the failure to warn consumers of known defects, and (6) the plaintiffs are victims of catastrophic injuries. [15] Although the uncertainty of punitives has been reduced drastically in recent years, they will probably remain of importance to business in the future.

Self-Incrimination The protection of witnesses from compelled self-incrimination constitutes one of the best-known aspects of the Fifth Amendment. By "pleading the Fifth," witnesses may refrain from giving evidence that might tend to show their own guilt. The Fifth Amendment constrains the investigatory activities of administrative agencies, prosecutors, police, and Congressional committees.

An important limitation on the protection against self-incrimination has developed. That protection is a personal right, so it protects only a natural person from whom testimony is sought. Therefore, corporations and other business entities do not receive protection against incriminating evidence taken from an employee's testimony in matters involving the corporation. Employees may assert the privilege of protection against self-incrimination to protect their own interest. However, they may not use the privilege to protect their business employer from incrimination.

In many instances, evidence that incriminates one party is in the hands of another party. For example, accountants or attorneys often hold tax documents for their clients, and when government officials seek these documents, the clients may try to claim that the Fifth Amendment privilege against self-incrimination applies to the documents. This

[15] Michael Rustad, *Demystifying Punitive Damages in Product Liability Cases: A Survey of a Quarter Century of Trial Verdicts,* Research Monograph Paper of the Roscoe Pound Foundation, Washington, D.C., 1991.

argument usually fails on the grounds that the privilege is testimonial, so it protects only verbal, not documentary, evidence.

Other types of evidentiary privileges have developed under the common law. These privileges protect the accused from the release of confidential information by close associates. Such associates include spouses, attorneys, priests or ministers, and, in some states, accountants.

The Fourth Amendment

Of all the constitutional provisions discussed, the Fourth Amendment provides business with the greatest protection from unfair administrative investigations. Typically, the Fourth Amendment protection arises before a criminal defendant has been indicted or before a civil administrative case is filed. The Fourth Amendment prohibits unreasonable searches and seizures of both natural persons and corporations.

Fourth Amendment: Unreasonable Searches and Seizures

The right of the people to be secure in their persons, papers, and effects, against unreasonable searches and seizures, shall not be violated, and no Warrants shall issue, but on probable cause, supported by Oath or affirmation, and particularly describing the place to be searched and the persons or things to be seized.

The administrative regulation of business often involves several methods of investigation. After suit has been filed, an administrative agency may use discovery devices to access information providing its case. Discovery devices include interrogatories and depositions used to question litigating parties and other witnesses. The production of document request permits the examination of private files. Before suit has been filed, administrative investigators may get information from required reports, on-site inspections, and subpoenas. After assessing this information, the agency may decide whether there is sufficient evidence to prosecute or sue.

Statutes require that many types of records be kept. These records are maintained for the public's benefit, so they are considered *public* records with no right to privacy. Accordingly, no Fifth Amendment privilege protects them from disclosure. Administrative agencies may share with other agencies the nonprivileged evidence that they gather. Most federal agencies may refer investigative files to the Justice Department for criminal prosecution. For example, the Securities and Exchange Commission may inform the Justice Department about the information it has on inside trading that could lead to criminal charges.

Subpoenas The statute creating administrative agencies usually gives them the power to subpoena documents. **Subpoenas** require pretrial and trial testimony from witnesses. A *subpoena duces tecum* requires the production of documents. Agencies may not abuse the subpoena power for ulterior motives. For example, agencies may not harass a particular business by issuing excessive subpoenas and they may not publicly disclose trade secrets and other private matters subpoenaed in private records. To ensure that agencies do not exceed their subpoena powers, administrative subpoenas are not *self-executing*. This means the recipient of an administrative subpoena may validly refuse to either testify or to produce the documents requested until ordered to do so by a court.

FIGURE 5–1
U.S. Constitution's Bill of Rights

Amendment Number	Rights Established
First Amendment	Freedom of religion, speech, press, assembly, petition government for redress of grievances
Second Amendment	Right to bear arms
Third Amendment	Limits on quartering soldiers in private homes
Fourth Amendment	No unreasonable searches and seizures without warrant issued on probable cause
Fifth Amendment	Indictment required for serious crimes; no double jeopardy for crimes; no compelled self-incrimination; no deprivation of life, liberty, or property without due process; no takings without just compensation.
Sixth Amendment	Criminal trial rights: speedy and public trial, trial by impartial jury, notice of trial, confront adverse witnesses, subpoena witnesses, representation by counsel
Seventh Amendment	Civil trial rights: jury trial, limited appeal of jury verdict
Eighth Amendment	No excessive bail or fines, no cruel and unusual punishment
Ninth Amendment	Enumerating these rights does not make an exclusive list, other rights are retained by the people
Tenth Amendment	Powers not delegated to federal government are retained by states or the people

An agency must justify a subpoena before a court will order enforcement. Four fairness standards, established in *United States v. Powell,* [16] require the agency to prove that its investigation is legitimate and that the information it seeks is relevant.

United States v. Powell Subpoena Enforcement Standards

1. The agency must have a legitimate purpose to investigate.
2. The inquiry must be relevant to that legitimate purpose.
3. The agency must not already have the requested information in its possession.
4. The agency must follow all of its own administrative procedures in issuing the subpoena.

The subpoena recipient will be required to comply if the agency satisfies the *Powell* criteria. The extent to which law enforcement officials may search private business premises for evidence of wrongdoing is also limited by the Fourth Amendment. This topic is discussed in Chapter 6 on the powers of administrative agencies. Figure 5–1 summarizes the Bill of Rights.

SUMMARY

The U.S. Constitution is the basic and supreme law that establishes the structure and limits of American government. It represents compromises on the centralization and separation of government powers. This is effected through a system of checks and balances (separation of powers) and the sharing of power between

[16]*United States v. Powell,* 379 U.S. 48 (1964).

the federal and state governments (federalism). Through adoption of the Constitution, the federal government gained broad enumerated powers over foreign affairs, interstate commerce, and taxation. Federal law prevails if it conflicts with state laws. However, states may exercise the reserved police power to protect the health, safety, welfare, and morals of its citizens, if for a legitimate objective.

Several specific governmental powers derived from the Constitution may affect business. The commerce clause permits the federal government to regulate trade and commerce with foreign countries and among the states. The states cannot erect protectionist trade barriers against other states or in foreign trade. Since most commercial activities have some impact on interstate commerce, state regulation may impose only minor burdens as determined by the "balancing test."

Although the contract clause has restricted the states from regulating business activity, today most courts use the due process clause to invalidate unreasonable state economic regulations. The full faith and credit clause requires each state to respect and give effect to the laws and court decisions of other states. The privileges and immunities clause prohibits a state from discriminating against the citizens of other states. The states do not consider out-of-state corporations citizens under this clause.

The Bill of Rights comprises the first 10 amendments to the U.S. Constitution. These were originally passed to assure fundamental rights for individuals, but they also apply to business. The First Amendment guarantees freedom of the press, speech, religion, and assembly. However, the First Amendment does not prevent reasonable governmental restraints on obscenity, defamation, incitement, fraud, subversion, and commercial speech necessary to protect society.

The equal protection clause of the Fifth and Fourteenth Amendments requires that all individuals receive equal protection of the law without arbitrary legislative distinctions or discrimination. No equal protection problem exists if there is a rational connection between a statute's classification scheme and a permissible governmental purpose. In discrimination cases, however, legislation must survive a strict scrutiny of its purpose and effect if an unequal protection claim arises. The due process clauses of the Fifth and Fourteenth Amendments protect both individuals and corporations from deprivation of life, liberty, or property without due process. Procedurally, due process requires notice of litigation, fair trial procedures, and an impartial tribunal. Substantively, it requires that legislation have a legitimate objective and use only reasonable means to achieve it.

The Fifth Amendment prohibits government from requiring self-incriminating testimony from an accused individual. This protection against self-incrimination cannot be invoked by corporations because they are not natural persons. The Fourth Amendment protects both individuals and corporations from unreasonable searches and seizures that usually arise before a suit has been filed. An administrative agency may seek testimony or the production of personal or corporate records if the inquiry is legitimate and the agency has carefully followed its own procedures. A court will enforce administrative subpoenas requiring testimony or the production of documents, but only where the information sought is relevant and not already in the agency's possession.

KEY TERMS

federalism, p. 114
police power, p. 117
taking, p. 117
strict constructionism, p. 120
judicial review, p. 120
rational basis, p. 136
strict scrutiny, p. 136
subpoena, p. 143

CHAPTER EXERCISES

1. Is there any limit to the ability of Congress to regulate intrastate activity under the commerce clause? Consider the case of an Ohio farmer, Filburn, who was fined $117.11 for exceeding his 1941 acreage allotment for wheat under the Agricultural Adjustment Act of 1938. Filburn was allotted 11.1 acres for this purpose, but he sowed and harvested 23 acres. He sold some of his wheat

but used most of it as food for his family and as feed for his cattle. Filburn sued for an injunction against the enforcement of the fine. He argued that his activity had been completely intrastate and that Congress could not regulate it under the commerce clause. How should the Supreme Court decide the case? Why? *Wickard v. Filburn*, 317 U.S. 111 (1942).

2. An Arkansas statute requires that all motor vehicles sold in the state be equipped with radial tires. A federal statute requires that all automobiles sold in interstate commerce be equipped with a new mechanism that substantially improves wheel alignment. Both statutes have been passed for the purpose of safety and obtaining better gas mileage. Are both statutes enforceable? Why or why not?
3. The Georgia legislature passes a law that requires interstate truckers and moving vans to stay off Georgia highways from 7 A.M. to 10 A.M. and from 4 P.M. to 6 P.M. so that local traffic will move better during rush hour. What constitutional issues does this statute trigger?
4. Harry Homeowner resides within the city boundaries of Lake City, which the state recently granted a huge sum to erect a civic center. To build this civic center as planned, Lake City condemned the property and residence owned by Harry Homeowner, mailed Harry a check for an amount equal to 25 percent of the appraised value, and ordered Harry and his family to leave the premises with all of their belongings within two weeks. Lake City conducted no hearing concerning this matter. What constitutional issues does this situation raise?
5. Pennsylvania passes a statute requiring all unemployed non-Pennsylvanians present in the state to leave Pennsylvania. What is the problem with this statute?
6. The city of Atlanta passes an ordinance banning the sale of all toys with toxic paint and sharp edges. The effect of this ordinance is to ban the sale of foreign toys, which amount to 70 percent of the toys sold in the Atlanta area. The Atlanta ordinance is much stricter than the federal statutes governing toy safety. Answer the following questions:
   a. Where does the city of Atlanta get the power to ban hazardous toys?
   b. Is a problem presented by the fact that the Atlanta ordinance is more stringent than the federal statutes?
   c. Does the city of Atlanta have the power to regulate the sale of foreign toys?
7. What is meant by judicial review? Does this give the Supreme Court the final word on what the law and the Constitution mean?
8. Explain the constitutional foundation for state and federal government regulatory power.
9. New Hampshire enacted a commuters' income tax that taxed the New Hampshire-derived income of nonresidents. New Hampshire did not tax the income of New Hampshire residents. Residents of Maine and part of New Hampshire challenged the validity of the tax. The case was transferred directly to the New Hampshire Supreme Court, which upheld the statute. The case was then heard by the U.S. Supreme Court on appeal. What was the result and why?
10. Under an Alabama state law regarding divorce, a wife may recover alimony from her husband if cause is shown. When Mr. and Mrs. Orr filed for a divorce, Mr. Orr claimed alimony from his wife and was denied it under the state statute. He appealed, claiming that the statute denying alimony to husbands was unconstitutional. On what grounds is his claim based? What was the result, and why? *Orr v. Orr*, 440 U.S. 268 (1980).
11. The plaintiffs, consumers of prescription drugs, claimed that they would benefit from the advertising of prescription drugs. They brought a suit against the Virginia State Board of Pharmacy in which they challenged the constitutionality of a Virginia statute declaring it unprofessional conduct for a licensed pharmacist to advertise the price of prescription drugs. The board had the power to revoke a license or to impose a fine for violation of the statute. As a result of the statute, all advertising of the price of prescription drugs was effectively forbidden. The Citizens Consumer Council sued the Virginia State Board of Pharmacy. On what grounds would its lawsuit be brought? With what result, and why? *Virginia State Board of Pharmacy v. Virginia Citizens Consumer Council*, 425 U.S. 748 (1976).

12. Constitutional law is the history of judicial interpretation and modification of the U.S. Constitution. Constitutional cases usually arise when someone challenges long-established constitutional precedents. Constitutional law experts often put low probabilities of success on cases in which the Supreme Court is required to change its interpretation of the U.S. Constitution. For example, many observers considered *Roe v. Wade* to be just such a losing case, yet it profoundly changed abortion and privacy law. Pivotal cases of this kind pose an ethical dilemma in constitutional areas. In addition, the Federal Rules of Civil Procedure give judges the power to punish lawyers and their clients for frivolous filings in litigation.

Is it ethical for plaintiffs to attack well-established precedents if most experienced observers consider the litigation frivolous? Is it ethical for plaintiffs' lawyers to pursue such cases if their main motivation is to establish their reputation in highly visible court actions? Is it ethical for plaintiffs, their lawyers, and special interest groups to set up situations simply to test or challenge laws that they consider undesirable? Are the judicial restraints against frivolous litigation sufficient to remove these questions regarding the motives of litigation from the area of ethical analysis?

Chapter 6

ADMINISTRATIVE LAW

KEY CONCEPTS

Administrative law concerns the procedures used by administrative agencies to perform rulemaking, adjudicatory, and informal activities. Federal and state administrative procedure statutes establish the procedures governing most of these agencies.

Rulemaking involves agency actions that affect a large number of people and do not depend on facts about people's individual circumstances. Notice, comment, and publication procedures are generally used in rulemaking.

Adjudication occurs when an administrative agency determines existing facts, applies rules or laws to those facts, and reaches a conclusion or decision by some type of hearing process. An adjudicatory hearing usually follows trial-type procedures.

The majority of administrative agency activities are informal, such as granting permits, determining eligibility for governmental benefits, or collecting information. The procedures used in informal activities vary, and only rarely is there judicial review of these activities.

Although most of the actions of administrative agencies are potentially subject to judicial review, several factors limit the number of actions actually reviewed. Some of the discretionary actions of these agencies are not reviewable; in other cases, policy factors may lead a court to decline to review an administrative action. Finally, the scope of judicial review differs according to the nature of the administrative activity.

INTRODUCTION . . . PAST, PRESENT, FUTURE

Administrative law concerns the organization and operation of what is known as the fourth branch of government—the administrative agencies. An *administrative agency* is a governmental body that is not included in the Constitution as part of the legislative, executive, or judicial branches. Congress established the first administrative agencies in 1789 to deal with foreign imports and to provide pension fees to disabled soldiers. These agencies, and their modern successors, are known as *executive agencies* because they are subject to control by the executive branch of the government. The first independent administrative agency, the Interstate Commerce Commission, was created in 1889.

The federal agencies, and their state and local counterparts, were created to meet the changing needs of the country. In the early years of the United States, there was little regulation of business by government. However, as the United States grew and prospered, the industrial revolution changed the country from an agrarian to an industrial society. A few businesses began to dominate in certain industries, and their use of power and certain monopoly practices led to the establishment of independent federal regulatory agencies.

More recently, in the 1960s and 1970s, laws were passed creating agencies to deal with social problems in such fields as civil rights, consumer protection, the environment, and employee safety. Subsequently, the social regulation of the 1960s and 1970s gave way to policies of deregulation and regulatory reform. In the 1980s, the downsizing and restructuring of firms in the airline, trucking, communication, and financial services industries led to dramatic changes in the regulatory environment. It is likely that global competition will force even more regulatory changes to occur during the remaining years of the 20th century. In the future, a shift to regulation by private groups and by regional or international bodies may replace some of the state and federal regulation of business.

OVERVIEW

Today, businesses are regulated in many ways by a variety of administrative agencies at the federal, state, and local levels of government. This government regulation occurs through the *administrative process,* a variety of activities performed by administrative agencies. **Administrative law** is at the heart of that process; it governs the grant of powers to agencies, specifies the procedures that agencies must use in carrying out their operations, and determines the extent to which agency activity is reviewed by the courts.

Administrative agencies deal with many different problems and operate in different ways. This chapter examines the creation of administrative agencies and the legislative delegation of their powers. Then, it reviews the functions performed by these agencies as they make rules, adjudicate cases, and perform numerous informal activities. The role that courts play in reviewing agency functions is also noted. After briefly reviewing the interaction between administrative agencies and the businesses they regulate, the chapter concludes with an evaluation of the future of government regulation by administrative agencies.

ADMINISTRATIVE AGENCIES: GENERAL CONCERNS

Congress created the Interstate Commerce Commission as the first independent federal regulatory agency for reasons similar to those that later led to the establishment of thousands of other federal, state, and local administrative agencies. Most administrative agencies are created to deal with specific problems. Each of the three branches of government has some control over the actions of administrative agencies.

Creation of Administrative Agencies

In the late 19th century, Congress wanted to institute a fair system for establishing the rates charged by railroads. However, it lacked the expertise needed to establish such rates. Should the rates throughout the country be equal on a per mile basis? Should the rates differ with the amount of freight or passenger traffic or with the distance traveled? How could Congress draft one law that would apply to many different situations?

In addition, if Congress did somehow establish fair rates, what would happen if conditions changed? If railroad costs went up and traffic decreased, should the rates decrease? What if some railroads made a profit and others did not? Congress realized that it would be unable to constantly monitor the railroad industry and that an organization capable of examining the industry's problems over a period of years was needed.

Finally, if general railroad rates were established, the courts would have to determine how the rates should apply to specific situations. But the courts were already very busy, and they had little expertise regarding the specific problems of the railroad industry. Thus, the Interstate Commerce Commission was created and granted both the power to determine general rates, a rulemaking or legislative type of power, and the power to resolve disputes regarding the application of those rates, an adjudicative type of power.

As the years passed, Congress created other administrative agencies to deal with other specialized problems. In 1914, the Federal Trade Commission was created to help curb monopolistic practices that the Sherman Act, passed in 1890, had failed to address. As radio transmission became common, the need to allocate the available bandwidths led to the creation of the Federal Communications Commission. The airplane brought us the Federal Aviation Agency, now the Federal Aviation Administration (FAA), and the Food and Drug Administration (FDA) was established to deal with impure foods and quack medicines. The stock market crash of 1929 led to the creation of the Securities and Exchange Commission (SEC), and the development of atomic energy led first to the creation of the Atomic Energy Commission (AEC), and then its conversion to the Nuclear Regulatory Commission (NRC). Some of the functions performed by selected federal agencies are listed in Figure 6–1.

In recent years, new agencies have been created as additional problems emerged that appeared too complicated for Congress to address and monitor. In 1970, for example, the Environmental Protection Agency (EPA) and the Occupational and Safety Health Administration (OSHA) were created. The Consumer Product Safety Commission (CPSC) emerged in 1972 to protect the consumer against unreasonable risks associated with consumer products. This text discusses the laws and regulatory powers of these and other administrative agencies.

Role of Administrative Law

Administrative agencies, created to deal with specific societal problems, clearly illustrate the connection between law and the changing society. However, administrative law is not concerned with the substance of regulatory laws or with the specific regulations promulgated by these agencies. The substantive rules of the agencies are dealt with in other chapters. Thus, regulatory concerns of the Federal Trade Commission are discussed in Chapters 15 and 16; concerns of the Securities and Exchange Commission, in Chapter 14; and concerns of the Environmental Protection Agency, in Chapter 20.

FIGURE 6–1
Functions of Selected Administrative Agencies

Consumer Product Safety Commission (CPSC)	Protects the public against risk of injury from consumer products
Environmental Protection Agency (EPA)	Administers laws related to water and air pollution, solid wastes, and other environmental concerns
Equal Employment Opportunity Commission (EEOC)	Enforces civil rights and equal opportunity laws regarding discrimination in employment
Federal Trade Commission (FTC)	Protects the public from anticompetitive behavior and unfair and deceptive business practices
Food and Drug Administration (FDA)	Administers laws that prohibit distribution of adulterated, misbranded, or unsafe foods, drugs, and cosmetics
Interstate Commerce Commission (ICC)	Regulates interstate surface transportation
National Labor Relations Board (NLRB)	Conducts union certification elections and holds hearings on alleged unfair labor practices
Occupational Safety and Health Administration (OSHA)	Enforces laws seeking to provide all workers with a safe and healthy work environment
Securities and Exchange Commission (SEC)	Enforces federal securities laws regulating the sale of securities to the investing public

Instead, administrative law is concerned with the procedures that the agencies use to perform the tasks delegated to them by legislative bodies. This chapter concerns the processes that administrative agencies generally use to make rules and regulations and to apply laws and those rules and regulations in the cases that they adjudicate and in their informal activities.

Delegation of Authority to Administrative Agencies

Since administrative agencies are not mentioned in the U.S. Constitution, their powers must originate from one of the three branches of government expressly granted powers by the Constitution. Administrative agency powers originate with legislation known as *enabling acts*.

As noted in Chapter 2, the Constitution grants Congress legislative powers while assigning other powers to the executive and judicial branches. These powers are intentionally separated to prevent the concentration of power. However, because administrative agencies may have all three types of governmental powers, several constitutional questions were raised when Congress first created them. If an agency had the power to make rules and regulations, was Congress giving away its legislative power? Could legislative power, granted to Congress by the Constitution, be exercised by other governmental organizations? Was the separation of powers violated if agencies possessed legislative, judicial, and investigative authority?

Some of the early cases dealing with such questions determined that the delegation of authority from Congress to administrative agencies did violate the separation of powers. However, since early in the 20th century, the courts have generally upheld the legislature's delegation of authority to administrative agencies.

Delegation is the transfer of power by one governmental body (such as the legislature) to another (such as an administrative agency). Although it is unconstitutional for the legislature to transfer *all* of its legislative powers to an administrative agency, it is permissible for the legislature to delegate part of its authority to make rules and regulations to an agency. *Enabling legislation* grants some authority to an agency and specifies the activities that the agency may perform.

In the Federal Trade Commission Act, for example, the Federal Trade Commission was created and was given authority to protect the public from uncompetitive behavior and unfair and deceptive acts or practices. Similarly, the Securities and Exchange Act of 1934 granted the Securities and Exchange Commission authority to regulate the securities markets.

The activities that specify the concerns to be addressed by an agency are commonly referred to as *standards.* If the legislature does not adequately define the standards by which agency actions are guided, the courts may find that the grant of authority to the agency is unconstitutional.

A congressional delegation of legislative powers to administrative agencies was held unconstitutional in *Schechter Poultry Corp. v. United States.*[1] In that case, Congress delegated to industry associations the authority to make "codes of fair competition" that the president could approve. That delegation of authority did not supply the industry associations or the executive branch with the necessary standards:

> Section 3 of the Recovery Act is without precedent. It supplies no standards for any trade, industry, or activity. It does not undertake to prescribe rules of conduct to be applied to particular states of fact determined by appropriate administrative procedures. Instead of prescribing rules, it authorizes the making of codes to prescribe them. For the legislative undertaking, section 3 sets up no standards, aside from the statement of the general aim of rehabilitation, correction, and expansion described in section 1. In view of the scope of that broad declaration, and of the nature of the few restrictions that are imposed, . . . [w]e think that the code-making authority thus conferred is an unconstitutional delegation of legislative power.

In the years since the *Schechter* decision, the U.S. Supreme Court and most of the state supreme courts have allowed very broad and general standards to be used in delegating authority to administrative agencies. For example, the Occupational Safety and Health Administration (OSHA) was given the authority to make rules to assure, so far as possible, every worker in the nation "safe and healthful" working conditions. That authority gives OSHA the power to establish safety and health standards for furniture, computer, and automobile manufacturing plants. Obviously, such a broad delegation of power to the agency gives it great discretion. However, each of the three branches of government does exercise some control over administrative agency activities.

Controls over Administrative Agencies

Administrative agencies are not directly accountable to the people. Administrators, unlike legislators, judges, and the president, are not elected. Thus, controls over administrative agencies are needed to ensure that the agencies are responsive to the country's needs. The legislature that delegates power to an administrative agency maintains some control over the agency's activities. Similarly, the executive that appoints a person to head an agency and the courts that review its activities also exercise some control. Finally, some controls over agencies are exercised by the public through access to agency information.

---

[1]295 U.S. 495 (1935).

FIGURE 6–2
Amendments to the Administrative Procedure Act (1946)

Date	Act	Purpose
1966	Freedom of Information Act	Provides public access to agency records
1976	Sunshine Act	Allows public access to public meetings—requires meetings to be open unless reason for closing is explained
1980	Regulatory Flexibility Act	Directs agencies to take into account the size of businesses when preparing rules and seeking information
1990	Negotiated Rulemaking Act	Requires agencies to consider and employ alternative dispute resolution methods in rulemaking and enforcement

Legislative Controls In the enabling legislation, Congress generally specifies which activities an agency may perform. If the agency acts beyond that authority, the judicial branch may find the agency action illegal. Congress also establishes the procedures an agency must follow in making rules and adjudicating cases. The **Administrative Procedures Act** (APA) specifies these procedures for most federal agencies. Most of the states have a similar act. Figure 6–2 depicts the amendments to the Administrative Procedures Act. The Freedom of Information Act is discussed later in this chapter.

In many states, an automatic periodic review of agencies is provided by *sunset laws*. Under such laws, the legislature reexamines the records of agencies and determines whether to continue their authority. When agencies request funding, special *legislative oversight committees* may carefully scrutinize their activities.

Congress has also attempted to preserve some direct legislative control over the rulemaking powers of administrative agencies. Typically, the *legislative veto power* gives it the chance to veto administrative rules that it finds objectionable. Although Congress as a whole has the power to revoke rules of administrative agencies, courts have found the separation of powers principle is violated if only a part of Congress seeks to exercise the legislature's power and there is no presentment to the president for signature. In the *Chada* case, the House of Representatives passed a resolution to veto the decision of an administrative law judge in the Immigration and Naturalization Service suspending Chada's deportation. The U.S. Supreme Court found that action unconstitutional:

> The Framers were acutely conscious that the bicameral requirement and the Presentment Clauses would serve essential constitutional functions. The division of the Congress into two distinct bodies assures that the legislative power would be exercised only after the opportunity for full study and debate in separate settings. The President's unilateral veto power, in turn, was limited by the power of two thirds of both Houses of Congress to overrule a veto, thereby precluding final arbitrary action of one person. . . . The Constitution sought to divide the delegated powers of the federal government into three defined categories, legislative, executive, and judicial, to assure, as nearly as possible, that each branch of government would confine itself to its assigned responsibility.
>
> Examination of the action taken here . . . reveals that it was essentially legislative in purpose and effect. The one-House veto operated in this case to overrule the Attorney General and mandate Chada's deportation. Disagreement with the Attorney General's decision on Chada's deportation—that is, Congress's decision to deport Chada—no less than Congress's original choice to delegate to the Attorney General the authority to

> make that decision, involves determination of policy that Congress can implement in only one way: bicameral passage followed by presentment to the President. The {legislative} veto doubtless has been in many respects a convenient shortcut: the sharing with the Executive by Congress of its authority over aliens in this manner is, on its face, an appealing compromise. In purely practical terms, it is obviously easier for action to be taken by one House without submission to the President . . . The choice we discern as having been made in the Constitutional Convention imposes burdens on governmental processes that often seem clumsy, inefficient, even unworkable, but those hard choices were consciously made by men who had lived under a form of government that permitted arbitrary governmental acts to go unchecked.[2]

The legislature also has significant control over administrative agencies through its control of the budget. The budget for an agency whose mission or recent action is not popular with the legislature may be cut back. At both the federal and state levels, legislatures are willing to exercise their "power of the purse" to signal their concerns to administrative agencies. This fiscal power is shared with the executive branch because the president proposes the annual budget.

Executive Controls The executive branch has the clearest line of authority over administrative agencies. Most agency heads are appointed to their positions by the president, who retains the authority to hire and fire them. Subject to the civil service system and Senate approval, the president can control the policies of many agency administrators. The administrators of independent agencies do have some independence from the executive; they have fixed terms of office, and they can generally be removed only *for cause.* The Securities and Exchange Commission, Federal Trade Commission, and Federal Reserve Board are among the independent agencies. Agencies may also be reorganized by the president with the consent of Congress. Thus, functions and powers of one agency can be transferred to other agencies.

Judicial Controls The courts have the authority to review the rules, informal actions, and adjudications of administrative agencies. Judicial review of agency actions by the judicial branch is discussed in a subsequent section of this chapter. Today, it is these controls, not the constitutional challenge to the legislative delegation of authority, that are most important in ensuring that administrative agencies do not act in an arbitrary manner.

Public Controls Concern over secret agency activities and the misuse of information led to passage of the Freedom of Information Act (FOIA) in 1966. Congress sought to increase the accountability of agencies to the public by mandating that agency files be open to public interest groups, scholars, journalists, and other interested parties. Businesses sometimes use the FOIA to review agency information about competing firms. Cases have sought to limit this use of agency files, but the courts have held that the FOIA requires all agencies, departments, and independent commissions to make all agency documents publicly available unless the documents qualify for one of the statute's nine exemptions.

---

[2] *I.N.S. v. Chada*, 462 U.S. 919 (1983).

Freedom of Information Act Exemptions

1. Documents classified by the president in the national interest.
2. Documents related to agency internal personnel practices.
3. Documents whose disclosure is prohibited by other statutes.
4. Documents containing trade secrets or financial data.
5. Documents reflecting the deliberative process of agency policy formulation or containing advisory opinions.
6. Personnel, medical, and similar files whose disclosure would be an unwarranted invasion of privacy.
7. Selected law enforcement records.
8. Documents regarding the operation of financial institutions.
9. Geological and geophysical maps and data.

Functions of Administrative Agencies

Administrative agencies perform activities at all levels of government in the United States. Local government agencies coordinate transportation facilities and schedules and establish zoning regulations for business and residential land use. State agencies often include mental and public health boards, departments of commerce and labor, and commissions for employment, construction, natural resources, insurance, and liquor control. Of the more than 100 agencies at the federal level, the two that affect the most people are the Internal Revenue Service and the Social Security Administration. The Internal Revenue Service interprets the tax statutes, collects taxes, and makes rules and regulations that specify how taxpayers are to compute the taxes they owe to the federal government. The Social Security Administration determines eligibility for social security benefits and issues millions of checks to eligible recipients.

Administrative agency activities can be classified into three general functions that are discussed in the remainder of the chapter. The first of these functions is **rulemaking.** Many administrative agencies are authorized to make rules and regulations that have the effect of law.

The second general function of administrative agencies is adjudicatory in character. Many agencies conduct **adjudicatory hearings** to determine whether a particular individual or business has violated a legislative statute or an administrative regulation. In a hearing, an agency finds facts and applies laws or rules to those facts. Generally, the procedures of administrative hearings are similar to but less formal than those used in the courts. The federal courts process several hundred thousand cases each year, whereas several million claims are processed annually by federal agencies, and even more are processed by state and local agencies.

The activities comprised by the third general function of administrative agencies are referred to as **informal actions.** Agencies administer grants and assistance programs, undertake investigations, gather and analyze data, and issue reports. Some agencies grant patents, and others regulate immigration, classify grain, or review waste disposal plans.

ETHICAL DILEMMA FOR ADMINISTRATORS

Regulators, administrative law judges, and case workers in administrative agencies hold powerful positions due to their role in making, interpreting, and enforcing the law. An administrator engaged in rulemaking may assign greater importance to the public comments made by parties in favor of a proposed rule than to those made by parties opposed to the ruling. Administrators may decide to proceed to a hearing in some cases while declining to initiate cases based on individual complaints in other situations. Administrative law judges may consider individual circumstances in one situation where a rule or statute is not followed but refuse to overlook violations in other cases. Some case workers may apply one administrative policy in certain cases and another in different cases even though the facts of the problems appear to be similar. When there is a lack of impartiality or fairness or when policies are not applied evenly, the actions of administrators are unethical.

ADMINISTRATIVE RULEMAKING

The line between rulemaking and adjudication is occasionally blurred because both involve hearings. However, an agency action that affects a large number of people and does not depend on facts about individual circumstances is generally regarded as rulemaking rather than adjudication.

Rulemaking Power

The power to make rules originates with the legislature, which then delegates some of its rulemaking power to an administrative agency. Of course, the legislature also can later limit or revoke the agency's rulemaking power. In the early 1980s, for example, the Federal Trade Commission (FTC) began to make rules requiring used car dealers to disclose certain information regarding the defects of the cars they sold. After the dealers lobbied Congress, it specifically revoked the FTC's authority to make such rules.

Imposing Procedural Requirements

The legislature specifies an agency's rulemaking procedures. Sometimes the legislature tailors those procedures to a specific agency in the enabling legislation. More frequently, the legislature refers to another statute that governs rulemaking as well as a variety of other administrative activities. Both Congress and state legislatures have passed special laws detailing the procedural requirements that agencies must follow in making rules and in performing adjudicative functions. The APA establishes such procedures for federal agencies.

Providing Notice An agency engaged in rulemaking must provide public notice that it will hold a hearing to receive comments about a particular problem or a specific rule proposal. Such notice must generally be provided at least 30 days before the hearing date.

Holding a Hearing to Receive Comments Unlike a court trial or an administrative adjudicatory hearing, at a rulemaking hearing there is usually no trial or adversarial proceeding. Instead, people affected by the proposed rule offer oral or written comments on the proposals and the agency is represented by people who listen to those comments.

Preparing the Final Rule After the hearing, the administrative agency reviews the comments offered by interested parties and affected businesses. It is required to provide a general and concise summary of the comments. It may revise or withdraw the proposed rule to reflect those comments, but it has no legal obligation to do so. If only a few people with a similar view offered comments, the hearing alone would not provide enough diversity of views. The agency is free to prepare its final rule in the most appropriate form, and it must then publish the rule. All federal rules appear in the *Federal Register* and are later compiled into the *Code of Federal Regulations (CFR)*. Rules adopted by state administrative agencies may sometimes be found in sources such as the *Michigan Register,* although most state compilations are less well organized.

In the following case, the agency concerned did not follow the rulemaking procedures established by the Administrative Procedure Act. Heckler, secretary of health and human services, sought to establish a policy that would impose additional duties on hospitals. The court discussed the agency's duty to consider "relevant factors to prevent arbitrary and capricious decision making and to assure rational consideration of the impact of the contemplated regulatory action." What concerns did the court have regarding the establishment of agency policy?

American Academy of Pediatrics v. Heckler
561 F. Supp. 395 (D.C.D.C. 1983)
United States District Court

This case involved the validity of an administrative rule published without benefit of public comment by Heckler, secretary of the Department of Health and Human Services. The rule concerned the care and treatment of newborn infants in hospitals receiving federal funds. The rule was sparked by a case involving an infant born with Down's syndrome (mongolism) and a surgically correctable blockage of his digestive tract that precluded normal feeding. The infant's parents refused to consent to surgery, and the hospital turned to the state for guidance. Despite the appointment of a special guardian, no judicial intervention occurred. Because the infant needed immediate surgery, he died within six days of birth.

The rule published by Heckler required hospitals and other medical institutions receiving federal aid to post a sign warning that failure to feed and care for handicapped infants violated federal law. It authorized an immediate investigation by a squad from the Health and Human Services office to protect the health of such an infant, and it required institutions receiving federal aid to give 24-hour access to hospital records and facilities during the investigation. Physicians, hospital staff members, and families were to be questioned.

The American Academy of Pediatrics sued Heckler, contending that the rule was arbitrary and capricious and that no justification existed for dispensing with public comment in the rulemaking process as required by the Administrative Procedure Act.

Gesell, Judge

The Administrative Procedure Act was designed to curb bureaucratic actions taken without consultation and notice to persons affected. Broad delegations of rulemaking authority from the Congress were intended to be tempered by assuring a degree of due process for those to be governed by the rule. The greater the impact of the regulation upon established practices or the greater the number of people directly affected, the more the courts have insisted that the right of comment by those affected be preserved.

Thus the Act has been generally construed to curtail rulemaking without comment. Moreover, the Act requires that all regulations shall issue only after the rulemaker has considered relevant factors to prevent arbitrary and capricious decision making and to assure rational consideration of the impact of the contemplated regulatory action. The instant regulation offends these established precepts to a remarkable extent.

The Court is well aware that the agency rulemaking must be considered deferentially and that this Court is prohibited from substituting its own judgment for that of the agency's decision. Nevertheless, this Court may not, on the other hand, "rubber-stamp" challenged agency decisions and must inquire whether the agency's action was based on a consideration of the relevant factors. Lacking such consideration, the regulation fails to satisfy the test of rationality and cannot be sustained because it is arbitrary and capricious.

The record tendered in support of the Secretary's action here clearly establishes that many highly relevant factors central to any application of section 504 to medical care of newborn infants were not considered prior to promulgation of the challenged rule.

All matters considered by the Secretary are documented in Court Exhibit A. However, that record reflects no consideration whatsoever of the disruptive effects of a 24-hour, toll-free "hotline" upon ongoing treatment of newborns. As indicated, any anonymous tipster, for whatever personal motive, can trigger an investigation involving immediate inspection of hospital records and facilities and interviewing of involved families and medical personnel. In a desperate situation where medical decisions must be made on short notice by physicians, hospital personnel and often distraught parents, the sudden descent of "Baby Doe" squads on the scene, monopolizing physician and nurse time and making hospital charts and records unavailable during treatment, can hardly be presumed to produce higher quality care for the infant.

It is clear that a primary purpose of the regulation is to require physicians treating newborns to take into account only wholly medical risk-benefit considerations to prevent parents from having any influence upon decisions as to whether further medical treatment is desirable. The Secretary did not appear to give the slightest consideration to the advantages and disadvantages of relying on the wishes of the parents who, knowing the setting in which the child may be raised, in many ways are in the best position to evaluate the infant's best interests.

None of these sensitive considerations touching so intimately on the quality of the infant's expected life were even tentatively noted. No attempt was made to address the issue of whether termination of painful, intrusive medical treatment might be appropriate where an infant's clear prognosis is death within days or months or to specify the level of appropriate care in futile cases.

. . . Even if the regulation could withstand the requirements of [the APA], it must be declared invalid due to the Secretary's failure to follow procedural requirements in its promulgation. It is undisputed that the rule was not issued in accordance with either the public notice or 30-day delay-of-effective date requirements of the APA. The Secretary argues that the rule is either a "procedural" or "interpretative" rule not subject to the requirements of these provisions, or that waiver of these requirements is appropriate given the need "to protect life from imminent harm." Neither of these arguments has merit.

This regulation cannot be sustained. It is arbitrary and capricious. . . . At the minimum, wide public comment prior to rulemaking is essential. Only by preserving this democratic process can good intentions be tempered by wisdom and experience.

Case Questions

1. What two requirements does the Administrative Procedure Act impose on agencies contemplating rulemaking actions?
2. What are some of the appropriate factors that the agency did not consider in this case?
3. If the agency had considered the appropriate factors, would the regulation have been legal?

ADMINISTRATIVE ADJUDICATION

In many instances, administrative agencies are authorized to perform adjudicative functions. They may determine facts, apply rules or laws to those facts, and reach a decision. In performing adjudicative functions, both federal and state agencies generally follow court-type procedures. However, there are several important differences between agency adjudicative procedures and those used in traditional court trials. A jury trial is not possible in administrative hearings, and most hearings do not observe all of the traditional rules of evidence. Many of the procedures governing administrative adjudications are specified in applicable administrative procedures law.

Most administrative adjudications follow the traditional sequence of (1) investigation, (2) complaint, (3) hearing, and (4) decision or order. Of course, many of the matters that are investigated never reach the complaint stage. And even after a complaint has been filed, most controversies are settled without a full hearing. Most administrative hearings follow the procedures used in court trials for notice, presentation of evidence by witnesses, introduction of documents, cross-examination, and arguments to the administrative law judge or hearing examiner.

At the end of a hearing, the administrative law judge issues an order based on the application of relevant law to the facts presented at the hearing. Frequently, that order may be appealed to some other person or group of persons within the agency. For example, the order of an administrative law judge in the Federal Trade Commission can be appealed to the the commissioners themselves. In rendering its decision, the commission has broad powers to modify the order. If a party wishes to appeal the commission's final decision, the case proceeds to the federal Court of Appeals.

Thus, the courts have the power to review the decisions of administrative agencies. Administrative agencies and the businesses they regulate frequently have different views regarding what procedures the agencies should follow in carrying out their activities. If an agency plans to revoke a license held by a business, does it first have to hold a trial-type hearing? This issue is addressed in the following case.

Gallagher & Ascher v. Simon

678 F. 2D 1007 (1982)
Seventh Circuit Court of Appeals

The Customs Service, a division in the Department of the Treasury, determined that Gallagher, an importing business, should lose its license as a customs broker because it had violated a "timely entry" Treasury Department regulation. Gallagher argued that before suspending its license, the Treasury Department should have held an adjudicatory hearing and granted it all the rights and procedures generally available in a trial. Since the Customs Service was a division of the Department of the Treasury, Gallagher sued Simon, the Secretary of the Treasury. After the federal district court decided in Simon's favor, Gallagher appealed to the Court of Appeals.

Cudahy, Circuit Judge

At the time this case began, Gallagher was a licensed customs broker in Chicago. It had been issued a special permit by the Treasury Department which allowed it to secure the immediate release of imported goods by submitting invoices to customs inspectors for examination at the point of entry. Gallagher was allowed to complete the entry documents and pay the duty at a later time, referred to as making a "timely entry." Regulations defined timely entry as being within 10 days after the day on which the imported merchandise was first released under a special permit.

If a broker fails to make timely entry, the District Director of the Customs Service initiates a claim for liquidated damages. Generally, warning letters are then sent to offending brokers. Notice of the suspension of the special permit follows if brokers continue not to make timely entries.

On July 23, 1976, District Director Hertz issued a warning letter to Gallagher, accusing it of making 9 late entries in the preceding month. The warning letter stated the number of violations was unacceptably large and advised that if Gallagher's performance did not improve, its special term permit would be suspended in September. Gallagher took no action. . . . When Gallagher made 21 untimely entries in August, District Director Hertz, in a September 12 letter, issued an order suspending Gallagher's special term permit for a period of 30 days commencing . . . September 17, 1976. . . . Gallagher then filed suit in district court.

The APA provides that the formal adjudicatory procedures described in sections 556 and 557 must be followed "in every case of adjudication required by statute to be determined on the record after opportunity for an agency hearing. . . ." The APA, as many courts have recognized, does not itself mandate that a trial-type hearing be held where none is required under the administrative agency's own governing statute; the APA simply dictates the procedures to be followed when another statute provides for a hearing. Thus, if the governing statute does not require that a hearing be conducted in connection with a particular agency action, [the adjudicatory provisions] "do not come into play." In the instant case, the regulation authorizing the District Director to suspend a broker's special term permit does not provide an opportunity for an agency hearing. Consequently, . . . the APA does not require that a permit suspension comply with the procedures to be used in an adjudicatory hearing.

The plaintiffs argue that all license suspension and revocation cases [include] an independent right to an adjudicatory hearing. Section 558(c) of the APA provides in pertinent part:

> When application is made for a license required by law, the agency . . . shall set and complete proceedings required to be conducted in accordance with sections 556 and 557 of this title or other proceedings required by law and shall make its decision. Except in cases of willfulness or those in which public health, interest, or safety requires otherwise, the withdrawal, suspension, revocation, or annulment of a license is lawful only if, before the institution of agency proceedings therefore, the licensee has been given—(1) notice by the agency in writing of the facts or conduct which may warrant the action; and (2) opportunity to demonstrate or achieve compliance with all lawful requirements.

The instant case involves an agency decision to suspend a license and thus is governed by the second sentence in section 558(c). Read literally, all that this sentence requires of an agency proposing the suspension of a license is that the licensee receive prior written notice of the facts warranting the suspension and an "opportunity to demonstrate or achieve compliance" with all legal requirements. It does not mandate any sort of hearing, let alone a trial-type hearing described in sections 556 and 557. The legislative history . . . indicates that the special treatment accorded licensees was not intended to trigger a right to an adjudicatory hearing meeting the requirements of sections 556 and 557. The district court concluded that the District Director had met his obligations under this section, and we agree. The notice requirement was satisfied in the instant case by the warning letters sent by the District Director to Gallagher.

The second requirement—an opportunity to demonstrate or achieve compliance—was also met in the instant case. An opportunity to achieve compliance was, indeed, the very purpose of the warning letters, which threatened suspension of the term special permits only if the broker's conduct did not improve. Such a notice of violations and a request to comply in the future meet the requirements of section 558(c). We conclude that the impact of the two suspensions, relatively short in duration and affecting only a portion of the customs broker's business, was not so great as to require more formal procedures than were afforded. We conclude that these government interests outweigh the factors supporting additional procedural safeguards, the costs of which would be unduly great. Affirmed.

Case Questions

1. Under what circumstances should an administrative agency consult the Administrative Procedure Act to determine whether a trial-type hearing is required?
2. What provision of the APA controlled the need for a trial-type hearing in this case?
3. What procedures does the APA require an administrative agency to follow in suspending or revoking a license? How were those procedures followed here?

INFORMAL ADMINISTRATIVE ACTIVITIES

General Activities

Most agency actions are informal rather than adjudicative or legislative. Administrative agencies engage in a wide variety of informal actions, many of which are not subject to court review. In some instances, however, such decisions are reviewed informally within the agency. Frequently, the action taken by the initial decision maker is reviewable by an immediate supervisor and again by a person at the agency's highest level. Critics suggest that such reviews are merely perfunctory and perhaps not impartial. It is important, however, that all of the expert agency personnel consider decisions affecting regulated business so as to assure consistency in matters affecting similar firms.

Information-Gathering Activities

Administrative agencies gather information through three different types of activities. First, many agencies gather and analyze information as they engage in rulemaking or adjudication. Many legislative statutes and administrative regulations require regulated companies to submit reports, financial records, and other documents. As such records are usually considered public documents, the Fifth Amendment privilege against self-incrimination does not protect them from disclosure. Further, an agency may share documents in the public record with other agencies. Since various agencies require many different reports, the cost of complying with agency requests for information can be a significant burden for businesses, particularly small firms. This has led to the Paperwork Reduction Act and to the regulatory cost-benefit analysis discussed later in this chapter.

Second, administrative agencies hold informal hearings in order to gather information. Many agencies use subpoena power to compel the testimony of witnesses or the production of needed documents at such hearings. The secretary of the Department of Health and Human Services could have held informal hearings with hospital administrators, doctors, and parents to determine whether the department should respond to the situation mentioned in the *Pediatrics* case.

Third, agencies often have the power to inspect the books and records or the premises of regulated businesses. For example, the Securities and Exchange Commission (SEC) investigates complaints against securities brokers. If some basis for such a complaint exists, the SEC may want to inspect a broker's books and records. In 1987, the SEC began to conduct numerous investigations about possible violations of insider trading laws and stock manipulations. The investigations led to both criminal and civil charges against individuals and securities firms.

OSHA inspectors visit factories and plants to determine whether conditions are unsafe or whether OSHA's safety rules are being violated. Because regulatory inspections serve the public interest, should courts give special interpretations to the Fourth Amendment with regard to administrative inspections? Should the probable cause requirement usually followed in criminal cases be relaxed in dealing with administrative warrant procedures? The following case illustrates the dilemma posed by on-site searches in administrative investigations.

Marshall v. Barlow's, Inc.

436 U.S. 307 (1978)
United States Supreme Court

An OSHA inspector sought to inspect and search Barlow's plumbing business in Idaho. The inspector said that OSHA was simply conducting a routine inspection of the premises. Barlow's refused to permit the inspection, claiming the Fourth Amendment protected it against unreasonable searches, and required that OSHA obtain a warrant before conducting an inspection. The trial court granted Barlow's an injunction to prevent OSHA from conducting a warrantless search, and Marshall, the Secretary of Labor who oversees OSHA, appealed to the Supreme Court.

Justice White delivered the opinion of the Court.

The Occupational Safety and Health Act of 1970 (OSHA) empowers agents of the Secretary of Labor (Secretary) to search the work area of any employment facility within the Act's jurisdiction. The purpose of the search is to inspect for safety hazards and violations of OSHA regulations. No search warrant or other process is expressly required under the Act.

The Secretary urges that warrantless inspections to enforce OSHA are reasonable within the meaning of the Fourth Amendment. . . . The Warrant Clause of the Fourth Amendment protects commercial buildings as well as private homes. To hold otherwise would belie the origin of that Amendment, and the American colonial experience. The Fourth Amendment's commands grew in large measure out of the colonists' experience with the writs of assistance [that] granted sweeping power to customs officials and other agents of the King to search for smuggled goods.

Against this background, it is untenable that the ban on warrantless searches was not intended to shield places of business as well as of residence. This Court has already held that warrantless searches are generally unreasonable, and that this rule applies to commercial premises as well as to homes.

> "As we explained in *Camara,* a search of private houses is presumptively unreasonable if conducted without a warrant. The businessman, like the occupant of a residence, has a constitutional right to go about his business free from unreasonable official entries upon his private commercial property. The businessman, too, has that right placed in jeopardy if the decision to enter and inspect for violation of regulatory laws can be made and enforced by the inspector in the field without official authority evidenced by a warrant."

The Secretary submits that warrantless inspections are essential to the proper enforcement of OSHA because they afford the opportunity to inspect without prior notice and hence to preserve the advantages of surprise. While the dangerous conditions outlawed by the Act include structural defects that cannot be quickly hidden or remedied, the Act also regulates a myriad of safety details that may be amenable to speedy alteration or disguise. The risk is that during the interval between an inspector's initial request to search a plant and his procuring a warrant following the owner's refusal of permission, violations of this latter type could be corrected and thus escape the inspector's notice.

We are unconvinced, however, that requiring warrants to inspect will impose serious burdens on the inspection system or the courts, will prevent inspections necessary to enforce the statute, or will make them less effective. In the first place, the great majority of businessmen can be expected in normal course to consent to inspection without warrant; the Secretary has not brought to this Court's attention any widespread pattern of refusal.

Whether the Secretary proceeds to secure a warrant or other process, with or without prior notice, his entitlement to inspect will not depend on his demonstrating probable cause to believe that conditions in violation of OSHA exist on the premises. Probable cause in the criminal law sense is not required. For purposes of an administrative search such as this, probable cause justifying the issuance of a warrant may be based not only on specific evidence of an existing violation but also on showing that "reasonable legislative or administrative standards for conducting an . . . inspection are satisfied with respect to a particular [establishment]."

A warrant showing that a specific business has been chosen for an OSHA search on the basis of a general administrative plan for the enforcement of the Act derived from neutral sources such as, for example, dispersion of employees in various types of industries across a given area, and the desired frequency of searches in any of the lesser divisions of the area, would protect an employer's Fourth Amendment rights. We doubt that the consumption of enforcement energies in the obtaining of such warrants will exceed manageable proportions.

We hold that Barlow's was entitled to a declaratory judgment that the Act is unconstitutional insofar as it purports to authorize inspections without warrant or its equivalent and to an injunction enjoining the Act's enforcement to that extent. The judgment of the District Court is therefore affirmed.

Case Questions

1. What would OSHA have had to do if it still wanted to search the Barlow's premises?
2. How does the need for a warrant protect the business person if a government official determines that a search is necessary?
3. Does the requirement of an administrative search warrant make it more difficult and expensive for OSHA to conduct inspections?

JUDICIAL REVIEW AND ADMINISTRATIVE AGENCIES

The scope of judicial review of administrative decisions is limited because administrative agencies are considered experts in the activities assigned to them. Since courts, unlike agencies, hear a wide diversity of cases, they seldom have the specialized knowledge possessed by agencies.

Determining Whether an Agency Activity Is Reviewable

Before a court reviews an activity of an administrative agency, it must answer three questions about the propriety of its review:

Judicial Review Questions

1. Is the agency activity subject to judicial review?
2. If so, are there reasons not to review this particular problem or decision?
3. What standards or criteria should be used to determine the legality or propriety of the agency's activity?

Agency Activities That Are Not Reviewable Before undertaking a judicial review of an administrative agency's activity, a court must decide whether the activity is, in fact, subject to review. Some agency activities are not subject to judicial review; in such instances, the agency's decision is considered final. For example, the Food and Drug Administration was asked to investigate a state's use of drugs in administering capital punishment. The agency declined to do so, and the court refused to review this agency action. Thus, an agency's decision not to act, not to investigate, or not to file a complaint against a firm is often considered an unreviewable decision. This stance is justified because the agency has discretion to make decisions on the use of its resources to carry out the policies set by the legislature. These *discretionary activities* of agencies are not reviewable by the courts and are immune from private tort liability.

A second category of agency activities is also exempt from judicial review. If the legislature clearly specifies that the agency has the final authority over a matter, the courts

FIGURE 6–3
Reasons Why a Court Might Not Review Agency Activities

Concern of Courts	Topic	Reasons for a Court Not to Review
Who seeks review?	Standing	If the person is not an aggrieved party, injured in some way, there may not be a disputed case.
When will problem be ready for review?	Ripeness	If the agency's activity is not yet final, the court should not act.
When is the party seeking review?	Exhaustion of remedies	If the person affected has remedies available in agency, the court should not review.
Where is review to take place?	Primary jurisdiction	If both court review and administrative review are possible, maybe the court should defer to agency.

will follow the *statutory preclusion* of judicial review. For example, the administrator of veterans affairs has the final authority to determine the benefits due to veterans:

Example of Statutory Preclusion of Judicial Review

[T]he decisions of the administrator on any question of law or fact under any law administered by the Veterans Administration providing benefits for any veterans and their dependents or survivors shall be final and no other official or any court of the United States shall have the power or jurisdiction to review any decision.[3]

Reasons Not to Review The second judicial review question focuses on whether there are reasons why a court should not review an administrative agency action, even though it could do so. Answering these questions depends on: (1) the person seeking review (a matter of *standing*), (2) the finality of the agency's decision (a matter of *ripeness*), (3) the extent to which the agency has reviewed the activities (a matter of *exhaustion of administrative remedies*), and (4) whether the agency should review before a court does so (a matter of *primary jurisdiction*). The questions that address the propriety of court intervention in agency activities are summarized in Figure 6–3.

Standards for Review The third question that a court must answer is: What standards should it use to judge or measure the administrative agency's activity? In general, courts examine whether an agency has clearly explained why and how it reached a decision. However, courts do not second-guess agency decisions.

Review of Agency Legislative Activities

As noted in the *Overton Park* case, which appears at the end of this section, "The court is not empowered to substitute its judgment for that of the agency." However, the scope of a court's review generally depends on the type of activity being reviewed. When an agency performs a legislative function, such as rulemaking, the reviewing court seeks to answer several specific questions.

[3] 38 U.S.C.A. Section 211(a).

Questions Affecting Review of Agency Legislative Actions.

1. Is the delegation of legislative authority to the agency sufficiently limited?
2. Did the agency's action fall within the powers granted to the agency by the legislature?
3. Did the agency's action violate any constitutional or statutory requirements imposed on the agency?
4. Did the agency follow proper procedures (usually specified by statute)?
5. Is the action of the agency "arbitrary or capricious"?

Courts will uphold an agency legislative action if these five questions are answered satisfactorily. In the *Vermont Yankee* case that follows, the lower court found the agency's rulemaking procedures improper. The U.S. Supreme Court's review clearly indicates that judicial review has a limited role with regard to the rulemaking of administrative agencies.

Vermont Yankee Nuclear Power Corporation v. Natural Resources Defense Council, Inc.

435 U.S. 519 (1978)
United States Supreme Court

This case involved the granting of a construction permit and later an operating permit for the Vermont Yankee nuclear power plant. Under the provisions of the Atomic Energy Act, the Atomic Energy Commission was authorized to make decisions regarding applications for such a permit. The commission's decision making process required a three-member Atomic Safety and Licensing Board to conduct a public adjudicatory hearing. At that hearing, the Natural Resources Defense Council (NRDC) unsuccessfully sought to require the board to consider the environmental effects of plant operations concerned with reprocessed nuclear fuel. The commission did, however, begin rulemaking proceedings to examine the concern raised by the NRDC.

During those proceedings, the commission indicated that it would not allow cross-examination of the participants' testimony, but that any person giving oral testimony would be subject to questioning by the commission. After the rulemaking hearing, the commission adopted a rule dealing with the impact of fuel reprocessing in licensing procedures. The NRDC objected to the rulemaking process and appealed the decision of the commission to the Court of Appeals. Even though the APA commission had followed rulemaking requirements, that court found its rulemaking procedure inadequate. Vermont Yankee then appealed to the Supreme Court.

Justice Rehnquist delivered the opinion of the Court.

In 1946, Congress enacted the Administrative Procedure Act, which, as we have noted elsewhere, was not only a "new, basic and comprehensive regulation of procedures in many agencies," but was also a legislative enactment which settled "long-continued and hard-fought contentions, and enacts a formula upon which social and political forces have come to rest."

Section 4 of the Act, dealing with rulemaking, requires in subsection (b) that "notice of proposed rulemaking shall be published in the Federal Register . . . ," describes the contents of that notice, and goes on to require in subsection (c) that after notice, the agency "shall give interested persons an opportunity to participate in the rulemaking through submission of written data, views, or arguments with or without opportunity for oral presentation. After consideration of the relevant matter presented, the agency shall incorporate in the rules adopted a concise general statement of their basis and purpose."

In interpreting this provision of the Act, we [have] held that generally speaking this section of the Act establishes the maximum procedural requirements which Congress was willing to have the courts impose on agencies in conducting rulemaking procedures. Agencies are free to grant additional procedural rights in the exercise of their discretion, but reviewing courts are generally not free to impose them if the agencies have not chosen to grant them. . . .

Much of the controversy in this case revolves around the procedures used in the rulemaking hearing which commenced in February 1973. In a supplemental notice of hearing the Commission indicated that while discovery or cross-examination would not be utilized, the Environmental Survey would be available to the public before the hearing along with the extensive background documents cited therein. All participants would be given a reasonable time to present their position and could be represented by counsel if they so desired. . . . More than 40 individuals and organizations representing a wide variety of interests submitted written comments.

The Licensing Board identified as the principal procedural question the propriety of declining to use full formal adjudicative procedures. . . . In some circumstances additional procedures may be required in order to afford the aggrieved individuals due process. But, this much is absolutely clear. Absent constitutional constraints or extremely compelling circumstances the "administrative agencies should be free to fashion their own rules of procedure and to pursue methods of inquiry capable of permitting them to discharge their multitudinous duties."

NRDC argues that § 4 of the Administrative Procedure Act, merely establishes lower procedural bounds and that a court may routinely require more than the minimum when an agency's proposed rule addresses complex or technical factual issues. We think the legislative history does not bear out its contention. The Senate Report explains what eventually became § 4 thus:

"The bill is an outline of minimum essential rights and procedures. . . . It affords private parties a means of knowing what their rights are and how they may protect them. And the Attorney General's Manual on the Administrative Procedure Act . . . further confirms that view. In short, all of this leaves little doubt that Congress intended that the discretion of the agencies and not that of the courts be exercised in determining when extra procedural devices should be employed.

There are compelling reasons for construing §4 in this manner. In the first place, if courts continually review agency proceedings to determine whether the agency employed procedures which were, in the court's opinion, perfectly tailored to reach what the court perceives to be the "best" or "correct" result, judicial review would be totally unpredictable. And the agencies, operating under this vague injunction to employ the "best" procedures and facing the threat of reversal if they did not, would undoubtedly adopt full adjudicatory procedures in every instance. Not only would this totally disrupt the statutory scheme through which Congress enacted "a formula upon which opposing social and political forces have come to rest," but all the inherent advantages of informal rulemaking would be totally lost.

Secondly, it is obvious that the court in these cases reviewed the agency's choice of procedures on the basis of the record actually produced at the hearing, and not on the basis of the information available to the agency when it made the decision to structure the proceedings in a certain way. This sort of Monday morning quarterbacking not only encourages but almost compels the agency to conduct all rulemaking proceedings with the full panoply of procedural devices normally associated only with adjudicatory hearings.

Finally, and perhaps most importantly, this sort of review fundamentally misconceives the nature of the standard for judicial review of an agency rule. Thus, the adequacy of the "record" in this type of proceeding is not correlated directly to the type of procedural devices employed but rather turns on whether the agency has followed the statutory mandate of the Administrative Procedure Act or other relevant statutes. If the agency is compelled to support the rule which it ultimately adopts with the type of record produced only after a full adjudicatory hearing, it simply will have no choice but to conduct a full adjudicatory hearing prior to promulgating every rule. In sum, this sort of unwarranted judicial examination of perceived procedural shortcomings of a rulemaking proceeding can do nothing but seriously interfere with that process prescribed by Congress. (*Reversed and remanded.*)

Case Questions

1. What element of the rulemaking procedures was questioned by the Court of Appeals?
2. What are the sources of law that might be consulted to determine the rulemaking procedures that an agency should use?
3. What source does the Supreme Court indicate should generally determine the appropriate agency rulemaking procedures?

Review of Agency Adjudicatory Activities

When an agency performs a review of a judicial function, such as the holding of an adjudicatory hearing, the court's review process is somewhat different from its review of rulemaking. The following questions are generally examined when a court reviews an agency adjudicatory action.

Questions Affecting Review of Agency Adjudicatory Actions

1. Did the agency violate any constitutional or statutory provisions imposed on it?
2. Does the agency have proper jurisdiction to decide the case?
3. Did the agency follow proper procedures (usually established by statute)?
4. Is the agency's decision supported by "substantial evidence" in its record?

Review of Agency Informal Activities

Courts sometimes review an agency's informal activities. Many of those activities are discretionary, not subject to review by the courts. In the *Overton Park* case that follows, the court first examines the question of reviewability. Once a court determines that an agency's action is subject to review, what other factors influence that review? Read the case and see how the court determines the answers to other questions affecting the judicial review of informal agency activities.

Questions Affecting Review of Agency Informal Actions

1. Is the action in question subject to judicial review?
2. Did the agency act within the scope of its authority?
3. Did the agency follow the procedural requirements?
4. Was the agency's action "arbitrary and capricious"?

Citizens to Preserve Overton Park v. Volpe
401 U.S. 402 (1981)
United States Supreme Court

Volpe, secretary of the Department of Transportation, determined that a federal highway (Interstate 40) could be built through a park in Memphis, Tennessee. Several federal laws prohibited him from authorizing the use of park property to construct a highway if feasible and prudent alternative locations were available. A citizens' group—

Citizens to Preserve Overton Park—sued in federal district court, claiming that the secretary's decision was invalid because he did not make formal findings of fact in support of the decision. This group also claimed that the secretary's decision was unsound and argued that it should be reviewed and considered by the courts.

Both the district court and the appellate court rejected the group's claim because they found the secretary's decision to be unreviewable by the courts. The group then appealed to the Supreme Court, asking whether the secretary's decision was reviewable and, if so, what standard of review should determine whether his decision was lawful.

Justice Marshall delivered the opinion of the Court.

A threshold question—whether petitioners are entitled to any judicial review—is easily answered. . . . The Administrative Procedure Act provides that the action of "each authority of the Government of the United States," which includes the Department of Transportation, is subject to judicial review except where there is a statutory prohibition on review or where "agency action is committed to agency discretion by law." In this case, there is no indication that Congress sought to prohibit judicial review and there is most certainly no "showing of 'clear and convincing evidence of a legislative intent" to restrict access to judicial review.

Similarly, the Secretary's decision here does not fall within the exception for action "committed to agency discretion." This is a very narrow exception.

The very existence of the statutes indicates that protection of parkland was to be given paramount importance. The few green havens that are public parks were not to be lost unless there were truly unusual factors present in a particular case or the cost or community disruption resulting from alternative routes reached extraordinary magnitudes. If the statutes are to have any meaning, the Secretary cannot approve the destruction of parkland unless he finds that alternative routes present unique problems.

Plainly, there is "law to apply" and thus the exemption for action "committed to agency discretion" is inapplicable. But the existence of judicial review is only the start: the standard for review must also be determined. For that we must look [again] to . . . the Administrative Procedure Act, which provides that a "reviewing court shall hold unlawful and set aside agency action, findings, and conclusions found" not to meet six separate standards. In all cases agency action must be set aside if the action was "arbitrary, capricious, an abuse of discretion, or otherwise not in accordance with law" or if the action failed to meet statutory, procedural, or constitutional requirements.

The generally applicable standards . . . require the reviewing court to engage in a substantial inquiry. Certainly, the Secretary's decision is entitled to a presumption of regularity. But that presumption is not to shield his action from a thorough, probing, in-depth review.

The court is first required to decide whether the Secretary acted within the scope of his authority. . . . The reviewing court must consider whether the Secretary properly construed his authority to approve the use of parkland as limited to situations where there are not feasible alternative routes or where feasible alternative routes involve uniquely difficult problems. And the reviewing court must be able to find that the Secretary could have reasonably believed that in this case there are no feasible alternatives or that alternatives do involve unique problems.

Scrutiny of the facts does not end, however, with the determination that the Secretary has acted within the scope of his statutory authority. [The APA also] requires a finding that the actual choice made was not "arbitrary, capricious, an abuse of discretion, or otherwise not in accordance with law." . . . To make this finding the court must consider whether the decision was based on consideration of the relevant factors and whether there has been a clear error of judgment.

Although this inquiry into the facts is to be searching and careful, the ultimate standard of review is a narrow one. The court is not empowered to substitute its judgment for that of the agency.

The final inquiry is whether the Secretary's action followed the necessary procedural requirements. Here the only procedural error alleged is the failure of the Secretary to make formal findings and state his reason for allowing the highway to be built through the park. Here, there is an administrative record that allows the full, prompt review of the Secretary's action that is sought without additional delay which would result from having a remand to the Secretary. That administrative record is not, however, before us.

Thus it is necessary to remand this case to the District Court for review of the Secretary's decision. That review is to be based on the full administrative record that was before the Secretary at the time he made his decision.

Case Questions

1. What was the Court's answer to the allegation that the administrative action was not subject to judicial review?
2. How did the Court determine whether the agency's actions were arbitrary and capricious?
3. Why did the Court send this case back to the district court for further review?

BUSINESS INTERACTION WITH AN ADMINISTRATIVE AGENCY

Information and Influence through Trade Associations

Since administrative agencies perform a variety of functions, businesses interact with them in different ways. Almost all businesses seek to keep informed about relevant agency rulings and regulations. Small businesses frequently rely on trade associations to alert them to agency proposals. Trade associations also offer conventions, training courses, and programs that keep members abreast of current political developments. Today, over 2,500 trade associations are based in Washington, D.C., and hundreds more are found in each of the state capitals and in major cities. Trade associations generally seek the adoption of administrative rules and legislation favorable to their members.

Cost-Benefit Analysis

Every business must comply with administrative requirements, orders, and regulations, whether or not it is able to keep informed about and comment on their development. What is the cost of such compliance? Several executive orders issued in the 1980s require executive agencies to make a cost-benefit analysis on all new rules. In addition, some of the independent agencies perform cost-benefit analyses.

Executive Order 12,291, which provides for the evaluation of major regulations on a cost-benefit basis, requires agencies to comply with the following principles:

1. Obtain adequate information in formulating rules.
2. Perform an initial cost-benefit analysis on all rule proposals to determine whether a major rule is present.
3. Maximize the net benefits to society by adopting a regulation only when the social benefits of regulation outweigh the costs of regulation.
4. Consider alternative proposals.
5. Correlate all regulatory proposals to reduce conflicts.

Although the direct cost of compliance with agency regulations can be estimated, it is more difficult to assess the benefit gained from administrative agency activities. What effect do EPA regulations mandating cleanup of air, water, and land pollution have on the health of individuals? If the FDA prevents drugs with significant side effects from being marketed, how many deformities, injuries, or even deaths are prevented? If the FAA requires increased maintenance on commercial airplanes, how many crashes are prevented? What is the value to society of less pollution, fewer dangerous drugs, safer air travel and even reduced injuries and deaths? Moreover, the costs and benefits of specific regulations do not accrue to the same people, further complicating the measurement of their relative values. Finally, it is impossible to assign objective values to the social benefits, and sometimes even the costs. Thus, cost-benefit analyses are but imperfect attempts to assess the efficiency of government regulation.

INTERNATIONAL PERSPECTIVE

The institutions of the European Community (EC) include an administrative Commission. It consists of 17 members who represent the Community, not national interests (national interests are represented by the Council of Ministers). The Assembly or Parliament and the European Court of Justice are the other major EC institutions. Each commissioner supervises and directs a directorate encompassing a functional area such as transportation, energy, or agriculture. The Commission proposes regulations and directives to the Council and seeks to ensure that Community laws are followed. Regulations are directly applicable in EC countries, whereas directives leave to the member country the method of achieving the aims noted in the directive.

The administrators or bureaucrats of the European Community are referred to as *Eurocrats*. Brussels is home to over 12,000 Eurocrats who draft rules, bring enforcement actions, and recommend changes in the legislation of member countries. Rule-writers are divided into 22 administrative directorates-general. They, and the staff of the 17 commissioners, are at the center of the Brussels bureaucracy. Rules affecting mergers, worker participation on corporate boards of directors, and telecommunication standards are drafted, discussed, redrafted, voted on, and implemented. In addition, rules on local content requirements and exemptions from antitrust laws are currently being rewritten in response to changing trade problems and court decisions.

Accounting firms, management consultants, law firms, trade associations, and state officials from the United States have active Brussels offices from which they lobby the administrators. Those who are successful say they do not try to have the American rules and practices transferred to Europe. Instead, they demonstrate that the interests of their U.S. clients are compatible and consistent with the European interests.

Criticism and Commentary

A criticism directed at administrative agencies concerns the relationship between their structure and the performance of their functions. In some agencies, rulemaking and adjudication are not completely separated—the personnel who make the rules may also decide whether those rules have been violated in certain cases. In other instances, agency personnel not only establish rules and serve as judges, they also perform the prosecutorial function of deciding when to charge someone with violating the rules. When an agency acts as rulemaker, judge, and prosecutor, the separation of powers within the agency is more real than apparent. Many of the criticisms directed at administrative agencies are partially valid, and most authorities agree that steps should be taken to improve the performance of these agencies.

Today, most administrative law judges, in fact, have quasi-independent roles. They are separated from the head of the agency in which they serve and have no responsibility or influence with regard to rulemaking or prosecutorial decisions of the agency. Because administrative law judges generally serve for some time within one agency, they offer a degree of specialization not found in most courts. Agency administrators also perform valuable functions that relieve the courts and legislatures from monumental burdens. Without their expertise and efficiency, activity in the traditional three branches of government would have come to a standstill long ago.

Federal, state, and local agencies appear to be the most effective organizations for administering the complex laws necessary to regulate numerous societal activities. As some form of governmental regulation is desired by most people, administrative agencies appear to be inevitable. They have developed in almost all independent nations and are likely to increase in importance as technology expands and society becomes more complex. Given the constant tension between the demand for regulation and business criticism of regulatory burdens, the cycle of alternating regulation and deregulation is apt to continue.

SUMMARY

Administrative agencies perform many functions in all legal systems. Agencies at the federal, state, and local levels derive their powers from the legislature. Both federal and state legislatures grant agencies the power to make rules, to hear and decide certain types of controversies, and to perform a variety of informal investigative and administrative tasks.

In making rules, administrative agencies are required to follow procedures usually specified in a federal or state administrative procedures act. Generally, an agency must first provide public notice that it intends to engage in rulemaking and then hold a hearing to receive public comment. A rulemaking hearing is not a trial; it is a forum at which the agency presents its views and receives, in oral or written form, the comments of the public. After a hearing, the agency usually provides a summary of the comments offered at the hearing, and its reaction to them, before adopting a rule. That rule need not, however, be based on those comments. Still, the *Pediatrics* case indicates that a rule is likely to be held invalid if it is adopted without input from the public through comment at a hearing. Furthermore, an administrative agency's adoption of a rule contrary to the public's views may be found arbitrary and capricious when reviewed by a court.

Administrative agencies also make individual determinations concerning possible violations of agency rules or statutory laws. In performing this adjudicatory function, an agency is required to conduct a hearing using procedures similar to those used in a court trial. If the courts do not find substantial evidence in the record that supports an agency decision, the decision can be overturned.

Many informal activities, such as investigating compliance with statutes or agency rules by regulated businesses, are performed by administrative agencies. Administrative agencies may also grant permits, determine client eligibility for benefits, or approve the expenditure of governmental funds for selected projects. Such informal activities are less subject to review by the courts than the rulemaking or adjudicatory activities of administrative agencies. The *Overton Park* case illustrates the limited nature of judicial review of these activities.

Businesses interact with administrative agencies in numerous ways. Many businesses and trade associations become involved in agency rulemaking activities. Numerous industries and individual businesses find that the activities of some administrative agencies are vital to them. Some critics of government regulation suggest leaving to the marketplace many of the functions performed by administrative agencies. However, because the citizen, worker, or investor is usually unable to deal effectively with environmental concerns, safety requirements, or investor protection matters, administrative regulation of business is likely to remain a vital part of the American legal environment.

KEY TERMS

administrative law, p. 149
enabling acts, p. 151
Administrative Procedures Act, p. 153
sunset laws, p. 153
rulemaking, p. 155
adjudicatory hearings, p. 155
informal actions, p. 155

CHAPTER EXERCISES

1. Define and give examples of the rulemaking and adjudicatory functions of an administrative agency in your local or state government.
2. Compare and contrast administrative rules and administrative orders on the basis of the procedures followed and their effect.
3. Describe the sources of controls on administrative agency action.
4. The federal Mine, Safety, and Health Act of 1977 requires federal mine inspectors to inspect underground mines at least twice a year. The inspection is intended to ensure compliance with health and safety standards. The act also grants inspectors the right to enter any mine without advance notice of an inspection. If a mine operator refuses to allow a warrantless inspection, the secretary of labor is authorized to bring a civil action for an injunction. When a federal mine inspector attempted a follow-up inspection of one company's stone quarries, an officer of the company refused to allow the inspection. The company relied on the *Marshall v. Barlow's* case as authority for denying the inspector admission to the quarries without a search warrant. Was the company's action legal?
5. Describe an agency adjudicatory proceeding. What is the main difference between an agency proceeding and a court trial?
6. A Florida administrative rule permits a warrantless search of child day-care facilities, including private homes used as day-care centers, at any time of day. The Florida legislature's concern is to protect the health and safety of children at these centers by eliminating such hazards as inadequate capacity, accessibility to poisonous materials, open pools, and sexual abuse. Is the Florida warrantless search scheme constitutional as applied to private homes?
7. The state of Georgia has regulations granting compensation to employees for work-related injuries. The Workers Compensation Board awards compensation after conducting hearings. The findings of the Workers Compensation Board are subject to judicial review and reversal only if the board acts outside its powers or if the award is not supported by substantial evidence on the record taken as a whole. Does the Workers Compensation Board exercise legislative or adjudicatory powers in making awards? Explain.
8. The Interstate Commerce Commission (ICC) published a general notice in the *Federal Register* outlining proposed legislation to be submitted to Congress. The notice asked for comments from the general public. Following a period allowed for written comments, instead of submitting legislation to Congress, the ICC issued final rules that affected tour brokers. These regulations put new, expensive "tour broker surety bond" requirements on tour brokers. The National Tour Brokers' Association sued the ICC, claiming the notice provided was inadequate under the APA. Did the ICC comply with the procedural requirements under the Administrative Procedures Act? (*National Tour Brokers' Association v. United States*, 591 F. 2d 896, 1978.)
9. The National Traffic and Motor Vehicle Safety Act requires the secretary of transportation to consider "relevant motor vehicle safety data" in making regulations. In 1977, the secretary promulgated a safety regulation that required new motor vehicles produced after September 1982 to have passive restraints (either continuous pull automatic seat belts or air bags). The regulation left the choice of passive restraints to the manufacturer. In February 1981, the secretary of transportation reopened the rulemaking process because of changes in the economy and problems in the auto industry. Two months later, the secretary proposed rescinding the regulation. The public then submitted comments on this proposal. State Farm Mutual Automobile Insurance sought review of the rescission, claiming the rescission of the safety standard was arbitrary and capricious. Do you agree? Why? (*Motor Vehicle Manufacturers' Association v. State Farm Mutual*, 463 U.S. 29, 1983.)
10. The government obtains people with expert knowledge for its regulatory agencies from the very industries that they are supposed to regulate. This often gives rise to conflicts of interest. This revolving door problem is a concern of almost

every government agency. The best place to get experts for the Food and Drug Administration is from either the food or the pharmaceutical industries. If an executive from ABC Drug Company is appointed director of the Food and Drug Administration, how should he or she treat a product that ABC is trying to convince the FDA to approve? The reverse of that situation is equally perplexing. If a top-ranking official of the Food and Drug Administration quits and is hired by ABC Drug Company, how should that person's prior affiliation with the FDA influence its approval of ABC's drugs? How could government regulations limit the potential conflicts of interest from the revolving door?

Part 2

PRIVATE LAW

Part 2 focuses on the fundamental aspects of private law: property, contracts, and torts. Private law concerns the responsibilities of an individual or firm toward other individuals or firms.

Property rights vary from one society to the next; in the United States, the individual's property rights in both real and personal property are significant. Although some contend that property law is based on ancient practices, in fact it is an evolving and dynamic area that affects most people in the society.

Contract law and tort law are commonly identified as private law. Each concerns the rights and duties of individuals in the society. Whereas contracts concern voluntary rights and duties, torts concern duties that the law imposes. Even if you do not voluntarily agree to assume obligations, the law imposes tort obligations that you have toward others.

Individuals and businesses must understand the basic concepts of private law: Businesses must know how to acquire and protect property interests, and they must be aware of procedural laws affecting individuals with defined property interests. Familiarity with consent, illegality, and performance issues can enhance the enforceability of contracts. Chapter 9 explores the basic concepts affecting liability for intentional, negligent, and strict liability torts.

Chapter 7

PROPERTY

KEY CONCEPTS

Property is a bundle of rights in physical and intangible interests permitting the holder to possess, transfer, pledge, or otherwise use property.

Property, whether tangible or intangible, is generally classified as either real property or personal property. Intellectual property is intangible personal property created primarily by mental efforts.

Both real and personal property may be co-owned by two or more individuals or businesses. Different forms of ownership, joint tenancy with survivorship, tenancy in common, and community property confer distinct rights on co-owners.

Intellectual property consists of copyrights, patents, trademarks, and trade secrets.

Transfers of real estate generally use contract of sale and warranty deed documents. The seller provides adequate title, and the buyer, after securing financing, pays the established price.

Both common law nuisance concepts and legislative regulations provide controls over the use of real property. Governmental control extends to the eminent domain power, which permits the taking of private property for a public purpose upon payment of reasonable compensation. Reasonable private restrictions or restrictive covenants are generally enforceable.

INTRODUCTION . . . PAST, PRESENT, FUTURE

Property rights form the foundation of our free enterprise system. The U.S. Constitution (Fifth Amendment) recognizes the importance of property by protecting people from being deprived of property without due process of law and by requiring compensation if private property is taken for a public purpose. Property rights are not the same in every society; the recognition of such rights often evolves within a society. In developing countries, technology must usually be imported to make local businesses competitive on a global scale. The imported patented, copyrighted, and trademarked products drain the scarce resources of these countries. Thus, regulations encourage the transfer of foreign technology and its use by the licensee rather than protecting the foreign property owner. As developing countries industrialize, their concern for the protection of intellectual property rights generally increases.

For many years, property in the United States consisted primarily of land and tangible items of personal property closely associated with land. The owner of land had nearly absolute rights regarding its use. In fact, a person's property interest in other persons—slaves—was once recognized and enforced. The abolition of slavery not only changed the nation, it also changed the relative importance of land and the property rights of landowners.

In the 20th century, property rights began to conflict with individual rights. Could a restaurant owner prohibit some individuals from using a restaurant open to the public? If pollutants from an owner's use of land fouled the air or water, did neighbors or society have remedies against the landowner? Such questions entail conflicts between enforcement of an owner's property rights and recognition of the rights of other individuals and of society. At the same time, increasing congestion in urban areas led to a variety of regulations affecting landowners. The conflict between property rights and individual rights eventually resulted in a limitation of the law's recognition of the absolute rights of real property owners, thus diminishing the relative role of such property as a source of wealth and status.

Yet, at the same time, many new forms of personal property have been recognized. In the world of investments, warrants and options give investors the right to purchase stock at some future date. A newly recognized real property right, time-sharing, allows a number of persons to have rights to use one piece of real estate, each at a specified time. Resorts in the Caribbean, Mexico, and throughout the United States sell interested purchasers the right to use homes, condominiums, and even luxury yachts. Further, owners of time-sharing rights in different properties subscribe to networks that permit them to exchange their rights with each other.

Finally, the law now recognizes property interests in previously unprotected intangible items. A person may have a property interest in obtaining future employment with a firm or in receiving governmental benefits. A license to practice a profession or to sell such products as securities or liquor is being recognized as property. The recognition of a property interest in computer chips and in specific computer operating systems or programs is vital to create the incentive to innovate.

The concept of property has undergone significant change in our nation. Land and real estate no longer constitute the most important part of a person's property. Property rights based on such intangibles as status, reputation, and intellectual acquisitions have moved to the fore. It is likely that these newly recognized property rights will be subject to significant future local, state, or federal regulation.

OVERVIEW

When property is discussed, most people think of physical things, such as a book, a boat, or a home. From the legal viewpoint, **property** is not constituted by the things themselves but rather by the relationship between the individual and those things. Property is defined as a bundle of rights that people have in things. The law creates these rights to prevent others from interfering with the owner's use and enjoyment of property.

Ownership interests are recognized by enforcing the right of a person or a business to use property. For example, the owner of a boat may use the boat, let others use it, or prevent others from using it. If someone takes the boat without the owner's permission, the law may punish this as theft. The courts enforce the owner's right to the boat by ordering the thief to return it or pay damages to the owner. The owner has the right to remodel the boat or even destroy it. The owner can use the boat as collateral for a loan. If the owner sells the boat or leases it to other people, the rights of ownership or possession of the boat will be transferred and recognized by law.

The key concept of property is the law's recognition and enforcement of the rights of people with regard to items considered to be property. Without the law's protection of these rights, property has meaning only to the extent that the possessor can exclude others by force. Property law describes a legally enforceable relationship between people or businesses and certain things as a **property interest.**

This chapter discusses the nature of property and the classification of property into real and personal property. Because the use of computers in the business world has become so significant, a section on computer law is also included. Although computer law cuts across several different legal areas, property law is an important portion of the emerging computer law. The chapter also examines the methods used to transfer ownership or possession of both personal property and interests in real property. Because the sale or transfer of real property is an important event for many people and for businesses the chapter outlines the primary steps and legal documents involved in a typical transaction of this kind. The chapter concludes with a section detailing the legal controls imposed on the owner of real property.

CLASSIFICATION OF PROPERTY

The ways in which the law classifies property are reflected in the laws and procedures that affect ownership rights. For example, the classification of property as real or personal affects how that property is transferred. The transfer of real property, such as a house, requires a formal document as a deed. To inform other parties of the buyer's interest in the property, the deed must be recorded in a government office. By contrast, the buyer of personal property does not need to use a formal deed or to record it in a government office. Instead, delivery of personal property, such as a book, is sufficient to transfer title to the buyer. Despite the different methods used to transfer property, the new owner of real or personal property obtains all the rights that belonged to the former owner.

Real Property

Real property (also known as realty) is land and everything attached to it, including the air above it and the minerals below the surface. Historically, the owner of land has received extensive legal protection. A person wrongfully thrown off his or her land may sue to recover it. A person who contracts to buy land may sue the seller to require specific performance of the contract and to force transfer of the title to the land. In contrast, a person who contracts to purchase personal property may generally sue only for damages. Thus, if a buyer contracts to purchase a vacant lot and the seller decides not to sell it, the buyer may sue and force transfer of the title upon payment of the contract price. But if a buyer contracts to purchase an item of personal property, such as a boat, the buyer is able to sue only for damages unless the boat is a unique item. All real property is unique, but most personal property is not unique.

Items attached to land are considered real property, even if they were once classified as personal property. *Fixtures* are personal property that have become real property through attachment to land or buildings. To determine whether an item of personal property has become a fixture, the courts will examine several factors: the intent of the party who attaches the item, the manner in which the item is attached, and the use of the item with that or other real property.

These questions arise when someone sells a home. Which items in the home are personal property that generally will not be transferred to the purchaser, and which are fixtures that will be transferred to the purchaser? Would the following items be classified as personal property or as fixtures?

Fixtures (Real Property) or Personal Property?

1. A refrigerator plugged into the wall with an electric cord but otherwise unattached to the walls of the house.
2. A dishwasher built into a cabinet and inserted under a kitchen counter.
3. An area rug on the floor just inside the front door.
4. Wall-to-wall carpeting that completely covers the floor of the main bedroom and is attached to the floor with large staples.
5. A decorative light fixture in the hallway that the seller informs the buyer will be replaced with a standard light fixture.
6. Keys to the house door.

Item	Typical Classification	Determinative Characteristic
1. Refrigerator	Personal Property	Not attached and not usually intended to be sold with realty
2. Dishwasher	Fixture	Attached to realty
3. Area rug	Personal property	Not attached and easily usable in another residence
4. Wall-to-wall carpeting	Probably a fixture	Attached like a fixture, but intent of parties is important
5. Decorative light fixture	Personal property	Intent converts typical fixture to personal property; even though fixture is attached, it can be removed easily without leaving damage
6. Keys	Fixtures	Intended to be sold with realty

Personal Property

Personal property (also known as personalty) that has a physical existence, such as this textbook, a shirt, a boat, or a pair of shoes, is called **tangible property** because it can be seen, touched, and felt. Unless converted to fixtures, as just discussed, most movable property is considered tangible personal property. **Goods** are tangible personal property items that are movable at the time they are identified in a sales contract. Items attached to the land, such as crops or minerals, become personal property once they have been detached or extracted.

Personal property that has no physical existence is referred to as **intangible property.** As with tangible property, the law recognizes the owner's right to sell, pledge, use, or give away such property. A stock share, copyright, trademark, account receivable, or bank account is intangible property. Thus, intangible property includes both economic interests in property, as with a bank account or a share of stock, and intellectual property, such as copyrights, patents, and trademarks. However, because the owner of intellectual property has special statutory rights that determine who can copy the author's book, use a patented computer chip, or sell goods affixed with the owner's trademark or symbol, intellectual property is discussed in a subsequent section.

The federal Constitution and most of the state constitutions prohibit government from taking "property" without due process of law. This makes the determination of what constitutes property an important issue in numerous court cases. Generally, cases of this kind concern items of intangible personal property, such as the right to continued employment. Does the expanded determination of intangible property apply to a college professor's interest in having his employment continued beyond an established term?

Board of Regents of State College v. Roth
408 U.S. 562 (1972)
United States Supreme Court

Roth was hired by the Board of Regents to teach political science at Wisconsin State University on the Oshkosh campus. His appointment specified employment for one year. After completing that term, Roth was notified that he would not be rehired. Because he had been hired for a one-year term and had not been granted tenure, the university claimed that it had no obligation to give him notice of cause for the decision not to rehire him. Roth claimed that due process of law required that he be notified of the reason for not rehiring him.

Justice Stewart delivered the opinion of the Court.

The only question presented to us at this stage in the case is whether the respondent had a constitutional right to a statement of reasons and a hearing on the University's decision not to rehire him for another year. We hold that he did not.

The requirements of procedural due process apply only to the deprivation of interests encompassed by the Fourteenth Amendment's protection of liberty and property. When protected interests are implicated, the right to some kind of prior hearing is paramount. But the range of interests protected by procedural due process is not infinite. To determine whether due process requirements apply in the first place, we must look not to the "weight" but to the *nature* of the interest at stake. We must look to see if the interest is within the Fourteenth Amendment's protection of liberty and property.

"Liberty" and "property" are broad and majestic terms. They are among the "[g]reat [constitutional] concepts . . . purposely left to gather meaning from experience. . . . [T]hey relate to the whole domain of social and economic fact, and the statesmen who founded this Nation knew too well that only a stagnant society remains unchanged."

The Court has also made clear that the property interests protected by procedural due process extend well beyond actual ownership of real estate, chattels, or money. By the same token, the Court has required due protection for deprivations of liberty beyond the sort of formal constraints imposed by the criminal process.

The Fourteenth Amendment's procedural protection of property is a safeguard of the security of interests that a person has already acquired in specific benefits. These interests—property interests—may take many forms.

Thus, the Court has held that a person receiving welfare benefits under statutory and administrative standards defining eligibility for them has an interest in continued receipt of those benefits that is safeguarded by procedural due process.

Similarly, in the area of public employment, the Court has held that a public college professor dismissed from an office held under tenure provisions, and college professors and staff members dismissed during the terms of their contracts, have interests in continued employment that are safeguarded by due process.

Certain attributes of "property" interests protected by procedural due process emerge from these decisions. To have a property interest in a benefit, a person clearly must have more than an abstract need or desire for it. He must have more than a unilateral expectation of it. He must, instead, have a legitimate claim of entitlement to it.

Property interests, of course, are not created by the Constitution. Rather they are created and their dimensions are defined by existing rules or understandings that stem from an independent source such as state law—rules or understandings that secure certain benefits and that support claims of entitlement to those benefits.

Just as the welfare recipient's "property" interest in welfare payments was treated and defined by statutory terms, so the respondent's "property" interest in employment at Wisconsin State University–Oshkosh was created and defined by the terms of his appointment. Those terms secured his interest in employment up to June 30, 1969. But the important fact in this case is that they specifically provided that the respondent's employment was to terminate on June 30. They did not provide for contract renewal absent "sufficient cause." Indeed, they made no provision for renewal whatsoever.

Thus, the terms of the respondent's appointment secured absolutely no interest in re-employment for the next year. They supported absolutely no possible claim of entitlement to re-employment. Nor, significantly, was there any state statute or University rule or policy that secured his interest in re-employment or that created any legitimate claim to it. In these circumstances, the respondent surely had an abstract concern in being rehired, but he did not have a *property* interest sufficient to require the University authorities to give him a hearing when they declined to renew his contract of employment.

Reversed and remanded.

Case Questions

1. Could a person have a property interest in employment that would be entitled to due process protection?
2. What determines whether a person has a property interest in something? Where does that interest come from?
3. What sources would you consult to determine whether you have a property right in your continued employment?

INTELLECTUAL PROPERTY

Intellectual property is intangible property created primarily by mental rather than physical efforts. The most common types of intellectual property are patents, trade secrets, trademarks, and copyrights. Figure 7–1 summarizes the many types of property, including intellectual property. Several types of intellectual property are protected under the common law; however, for all of these except trade secrets, compliance with special federal statutory registration requirements ensures the fullest property rights.

In some countries, laws do not protect certain property, particularly intellectual property such as copyrights, patents and trademarks. Thus, a country might not grant or recognize patents on certain products. In India, patents for any invention intended for use as a food, medicine, or drug are prohibited. Many U.S. drugs are widely reproduced in India and other developing countries because patent protection is not available. Often

FIGURE 7–1
Different Types of Property

Real property—interest in land	One acre of land along with the house, garage, and fixtures on it
Real property—fixture	The furnace and built-in dishwasher in a house
Personal property—tangible	A chair and sofa in a house
Personal property—intangible	Fifty shares of Exxon stock
Personal property—intellectual	Copyright of a book or magazine article

intellectual property is not protected in developing countries because it is easy to misappropriate and difficult to protect, because the property is often in great demand, and because the lack of physical substance to the property weakens its exclusivity.

Other countries have laws that recognize property rights but do not commonly enforce them. In Brazil, copyright laws are similar to those in other countries, but piracy of videocassettes and computer software and unauthorized translation of literary works is widespread. In Singapore, "Lotus 1–2–3™" copies sell for approximately $5, and fake Rolex™ watches can be found for $25.

In other countries, the legal processes that affect property rights are slow and cumbersome. Whereas trademark applications in the United States are processed in a little over a year, in Japan the processing period is almost four years. During the time the application is pending, there is no penalty for trademark infringement.

Licensing of Intellectual Property

A *license* is a permit to sell, assemble, manufacture, or use property belonging to another firm. Franchisors such as McDonald's and Holiday Inn license to franchisees the right to use their trademark on the hamburgers and hotel rooms that the franchisees sell. Patented drugs may be licensed by one pharmaceutical firm to another, sometimes in exchange for a license on other products (referred to as *cross-licensing*).

The evolution of intellectual property laws is exemplified by changes in Japanese laws. In the 1960s, each licensing agreement required government approval; the government sought to negotiate better terms for Japanese firms who were importing technology. By the 1970s, the government only had to be notified of the licensing. Today, the government in Japan is more concerned with the export of technology than with its import.

Firms competing internationally need to be aware of the steps required to protect international property. As the case stories in the accompanying international perspective indicate, failure to consider the legal consequences of actions that may seem innocent can be disastrous. Intellectual property is often the subject of a licensing agreement in international business transactions. Thus, this topic is discussed in greater detail in Chapter 21, which focuses on the International Legal Environment.

INTERNATIONAL PERSPECTIVE: CASE STORIES ON PROTECTING INTELLECTUAL PROPERTY

According to a recent article prepared by officials at the Patent and Trademark Office of the U.S. Department of Commerce, U.S. firms competing internationally need to protect their intellectual property. The difference between an advantageous competitive arrangement and commercial disaster may depend on forethought and planning regarding intellectual property. Recent examples of successes and failures drawn from composite experiences of U.S. firms include:

- Company A sent product literature to a potential foreign business partner. Soon, the would-be partner cornered the market for the product in its region. Although company A had a U.S. patent, its public disclosure made its product unpatentable in most foreign countries.
- Company B knew pirated copies of its computer programs were being sold in some foreign countries. It blocked commercial importation of its product in those countries, enforced its copyright country by country, and was successful in stopping infringements in its major markets.
- Company C did business on a handshake. Its closely guarded technology was very useful to its competitors.
- Company D believed its exclusive rights to inventions and writings were very valuable and it sought the best protection in each country in which it did business. If adequate protection was not available, it avoided investing there.

Source: U.S. Department of Commerce, "An Introductory Guide for U.S. Businesses on Protecting Intellectual Property Abroad," *Business America*, July 1, 1991.

Patents

A *patent* is issued by the Patent Office for products that are original, novel, useful, and nonobvious. For example, patents have been issued for the ballpoint pen, new drugs, and photographic equipment. The owner of a patent has a legal monopoly, generally for a period of 17 years, to make, sell, and use the patented product or process. Obtaining a patent is often time consuming and expensive, usually requiring a patent search by a patent attorney. The search must prove that the product is new and significantly different from any previously patented products.

The owner of a patented product may assign this property interest in a license to others. This is frequently done in exchange for royalty payments. Typically, the patent is assigned to a firm that agrees to manufacture and market the patented product. Research scientists and engineers at corporations are often requested, as part of their employment contract, to transfer to the corporation the rights to any products that they develop. The patents for these products are then issued to the corporation.

A patent gives its owner a monopoly; its unauthorized use is a patent *infringement*. The patent owner may sue the infringer for damages and seek an injunction prohibiting future infringements by the wrongdoer. For example, Polaroid Corporation won a patent infringement case that it brought against Kodak, thus forcing Kodak out of the instant photography market.[1] After the patent on a product expires, the product is considered to be in the public domain. Thereafter, any firm or individual may freely use the patented information. For example, the drug Motrin, used to treat arthritis, was a product patented by the Upjohn Company. After the patent expired, other pharmaceutical firms were free to manufacture similar products, such as Advil, based on the Ibuprofen ingredient originally described in the Motrin patent.

[1] *Eastman Kodak Company v. Polaroid Corporation*, 479 U.S. 850 (1986).

Trade Secrets

A *trade secret* is a valuable formula, process, or compilation of information known only to its developer. To obtain legal protection for a trade secret, two elements must be present. First, there must be some valuable information, such as a special recipe, a customer list, or a manufacturing process. For example, "the Colonel's secret ingredients" used in preparing Kentucky Fried Chicken and the secret formula for Coca-Cola are considered valuable information.

Second, the owner must attempt to keep the information secret. Information that becomes widely known to competitors or the general public cannot remain a trade secret. For example, a competitor of Du Pont obtained aerial photographs of the layout of a newly built Du Pont manufacturing facility, and the competitor's photographer claimed that Du Pont had not kept secret its manufacturing process for producing methanol. However, the court ruled that even though Du Pont's process was discoverable through aerial photography, Du Pont had made considerable effort to maintain confidentiality. Thus, the information was not freely available to the public and was therefore protected by trade secret law.[2]

No time limit is placed on trade secrets. As long as information is valuable and kept secret, it is protected. The absence of a time limit on trade secret protection sometimes makes a trade secret more valuable than a patent. However, reliance on trade secret protection is much riskier than reliance on patent protection because lawful discovery of the secret information terminates the protection, whereas patent protection generally exists for 17 years. Trade secrets are protected by state tort laws, discussed further in Chapter 9. By contrast, as a Supreme Court case notes, federal laws protect patents.

A Comparison of Patents and Trade Secrets

Trade secret law and patent law have coexisted in this country for over one hundred years. Each has its particular role to play, and the operation of one does not take away from the need for the other. Trade secret law encourages the development and exploitation of those items of lesser or different invention than might be accorded protection under the patent laws, but which items still have an important part to play in the technological and scientific advancement of the Nation. Trade secret law promotes the sharing of knowledge and the efficient operation of industry; it permits the individual inventor to reap the rewards of his labor by contracting with a company large enough to develop and exploit it. Congress, by its silence over these many years, has seen the wisdom of allowing the States to enforce trade secret protection.[3]

ETHICAL DILEMMA IN MISAPPROPRIATING INTELLECTUAL PROPERTY

Industrial espionage has received increasing attention in recent years. In high-technology industries, numerous attempts have been made to steal trade secrets. Although the federal patent and copyright laws provide some protection for trade secrets, these laws have several limitations.

[2] *E.I. Du Pont de Nemours & Co. v. Christopher,* 431 F.2d 1012 (1970).

[3] *Kewance Oil Co. v. Bicron Co.,* 416 U.S. 470, 493 (1974).

The formal procedure for patenting a machine, process, or design is expensive. Moreover, there are often long delays in securing a patent, and some designs may be useful for only a short time. Sometimes the costs of patent infringement litigation outweigh the benefits of the patent. Patents provide insufficient protection because some foreign firms can ignore U.S. patent laws. Some new processes are very complex, requiring many separate patents and many years for development into commercial viability. During this time, the public and competitors of the patent holder may have access to the information on which the patents are based. To avoid the costs and the loss of privacy that patenting entails, many of the fruits of research and development are not patented.

It is not improper to use "reverse engineering." This is a method of discovering trade secrets (but not copyrights or patents) hidden in a finished product that is already being marketed. For example, in the early 1980s, GM bought 10 Volvos to disassemble and learn how to make safer cars. GM could validly use any trade secret information learned from this reverse engineering. However, any patented technology discovered in such a process must be licensed to legitimately use. When the owner is taking reasonable precautions to preserve secrecy, others are prohibited from using devious methods to misappropriate trade secrets if no reasonable defense is available. In *Du Pont v. Christopher,* the court said: " Our devotion to freewheeling industrial competition must not force us into accepting the law of the jungle as the standard of morality expected in our commercial relations. Our tolerance of the espionage game must cease when the protections required to prevent another's spying cost so much that the spirit of inventiveness is dampened."

Trademarks

A ***trademark*** is a distinctive mark on goods that distinguishes them from those of competitors. The mark may be a picture, a design, words, or a combination thereof. The golden arches design used by McDonald's and the words Coca-Cola, and *Xerox* are trademarks. They are used on storefronts and packages and in advertisements to show consumers that products originate from a particular firm.

Like patents, trademarks are registered under a special federal statute—in this case, the *Lanham Act.* The trademark owner first applies to the Patent and Trademark Office for registration and then conducts a search of existing trademarks to determine whether the intended use of the trademark conflicts with the use of existing trademarks. Owners of existing trademarks may challenge an application for a new trademark if they consider it too similar to their trademarks or confusing to the public. Four different types of marks are protected by federal law.

Types of Marks Protected under the Lanham Act

1. Trademarks—identify goods originating from particular companies, such as IBM or Pepsi.
2. Service marks—identify services provided by particular companies, such as Holiday Inn or Hilton.
3. Certification marks—certify that certain standards have been met by the manufacturer of the products on which a seal is displayed, such as the Good Housekeeping Seal of Approval, the seal of the American Meterological Service, the designation of approval from Underwriters Laboratories (UL approved).
4. Collective marks—used by associations such as the Boy Scouts of America to identify products that they manufacture, approve, or endorse.

Registered marks of all four types are generally referred to as trademarks. They are valid for 20 years and may be renewed for a second 20 years. To qualify for registration, a trademark must be associated by the public with the firm or source from which it originates. For example, if the public associates Coke, a registered trademark, with any cola drink, the trademark may eventually become generic, and able to be used by anyone.

The term *LITE* was first used by the Meister Brau company in 1967 to designate a low-calorie, low-carbohydrate beer. The company registered the trademark and later sold the name and trademark to the Miller Brewing Company. Later, other brewers began to manufacture low-calorie beers, and Miller sued to protect its trademark. In 1977, the Court of Appeals determined that the term *light beer* had become associated in the minds of the public with generic products rather than the products of a particular producer. Accordingly, trademark protection became unavailable to the manufacturer of any light beer.[4] A somewhat similar problem is discussed in the following case. Should trademark protection be granted for a product whose trade name represents the initials for a generic term?

Anheuser-Busch, Inc. v. Stroh Brewery Co.

750 F.2d 631 (1984)
8th Circuit Court of Appeals

In January 1984, Anheuser-Busch applied for registration of the trademark "LA" for a low-alcohol beer that it had developed. It began marketing the beer in March 1984. That month, Stroh Brewery announced its plans to market two beers using the "LA" label, one for Schaeffer beer and the other for Old Milwaukee. In April 1984, Anheuser-Busch sued Stroh for trademark infringement, trademark dilution, and unfair competition. Stroh argued that the mark "LA" was generic and descriptive of products, so that trademark laws could not protect it. The trial court found for Anheuser-Busch, and Stroh appealed.

Gibson, Circuit Judge

Stroh first argues that the initials of a generic term such as "low alcohol" cannot assume trademark status.

Rather, the question in the instant case is whether, when a party seeks to protect initials alone which are also the initials of a generic or descriptive phrase, the initials are to be equated with that phrase. The key issue, as the case demonstrates, is the nature of the relationship or tie between the initials and the generic or descriptive phrase and the relationship or tie between the initials and the product. As the district court properly held, if some operation of the imagination is required to connect the initials with the product, the initials cannot be equated with the generic phrase but are suggestive in nature, thereby rendering them protectible. Stroh also refers us to some thirteen cases in support of their contention. We have examined these cases carefully and find that in none is it stated as a matter of law that initials of generic or descriptive phrases are unprotectible. We conclude that the district court did not err as a matter of law in engaging in a factual determination of the proper classification to be accorded the initials LA.

Stroh next argues that the district court erred as a matter of law in relying primarily on consumer perceptions in its classification of LA. It asserts that consumer perceptions should not be used as the principal test for "terms that have started out as generic category descriptors." Stroh's assertion assumes that LA is a "generic category descriptor." As discussed above, the

[4]*Miller Brewing Co. v. G. Heileman Brewing Co.*, 561 F.2d 75 (1977).

district court specifically found LA to be neither generic or descriptive. Thus *Miller Brewing Co. v. Jos. Schlitz Brewing Co.,* the case Stroh cites as authority, is not on point: that case deals with the irrelevance of a survey of the responses of 988 beer drinkers to "the meaning of a familiar word of Anglo-Saxon heritage" (i.e., "light"). The mark LA in a beer-drinking context obviously is not so familiar. As the *Miller* case itself points out, when "a coined word for a commercial product" is involved, the proper test becomes "what 'buyers understand by the word.' "

In *WSM, Inc.* we specifically stated that "[t]he test for deciding whether a word has become a generic title of a product or service is one of buyer understanding: 'What do the buyers understand by the word for whose use the parties are contending.' " The same test applies when deciding whether a word is descriptive.

Stroh argues that since the term LA was merely generic or descriptive, the district court improperly relied on the consumer survey offered into evidence. Stroh further attacks the methodology of the survey. . . .

In determining the viewpoint of the prospective purchasers in trademark and unfair competition cases, substantial weight may be accorded the result of a properly conducted survey. Courts have frequently relied upon properly conducted surveys in determining whether marks are generic or descriptive. Indeed, survey evidence may be the most practical manner of approaching the evaluation of public reaction in such cases.

Stroh also argues that the consumer survey was improperly designed. The survey was designed by Dr. Yoram Wind, Professor of Marketing and Management, Wharton School, University of Pennsylvania. The district court found that the consumer survey was fairly and scientifically conducted by qualified experts and impartial interviewers, that the study drew responses from a sample of a relevant portion of potential consumers, that the questions upon which the results relied did not appear to be misleading or biased, and that the recordation of responses was handled in a completely unbiased manner. Stroh . . . argues the survey was defective because respondents who were familiar with low alcohol beer were not asked what LA meant.

Dr. Wind also stated that if a student of his had included such a question in "a research design he would have gotten an F in the course." We believe the district court did not err in finding Dr. Wind's defense of his research design persuasive. The district court therefore properly looked to the consumer survey in reaching its conclusion that "LA . . . stands for an idea which requires some operation of the imagination to connect it with the product."

As we observed before, the district court grounded its analysis of the protectibility of LA on four mutually exclusive categories: the generic, descriptive, suggestive, and arbitrary or fanciful. The district court found the term LA to be suggestive in nature.

Stroh argues that the term is generic. We have addressed above and found wanting Stroh's contention that initials of generic phrases must similarly be so classified.

We affirm the issuance of the injunction by the district court.

Bright, Circuit Judge, dissenting

In this case, a major beer brewer, Anheuser-Busch, invokes federal jurisdiction seeking trademark protection for its brand name "LA." I would deny protection because its claim to the mark "LA" reflects a preemptive and anticompetitive intent to capture the emerging market for low alcoholic content beer by converting the initials of "low alcohol" (l.a.) into a trademark.

The objectives of the trademark law are: (1) to prevent confusion among the consuming public as to the source of goods or services and (2) to indicate ownership and permit the trademark owner to control the product's reputation. To realize these objectives, a trademark must distinguish a product from similar products and identify its owner or producer. Consequently, only those marks characterized as distinctive may receive trademark protection. Thus, to gain trademark protection for the mark "LA," Anheuser-Busch must demonstrate by clear and convincing evidence that LA primarily serves to designate its source (from Anheuser-Busch) rather than to describe or indicate a characteristic that it shares with other beers of low alcoholic content produced by other brewers.

The majority relies heavily on the district court's determination that the initials "LA" do not describe but merely suggest the beer's low alcoholic content. This finding rested upon a market survey, conducted at the behest of Anheuser-Busch in contemplation of this litigation. The survey concluded that consumers perceived LA as the brand name of the product and not as a description for low alcohol beer.

. . . However, the market survey introduced by Anheuser-Busch in the district court suffers several fatal defects. . . . The perceptions of a group of wholly uninformed consumers are, however, simply legally irrelevant. Dr. Wind's approach essentially measures consumer perception in an abstract, hypothetical context: what does a mark convey immediately to a consumer who has never before seen the product and who might not even know that such a product category exists.

Thus, a legally relevant test of consumer perceptions must reflect the real world and a real market. In this case, then, the appropriate group of consumers to survey would have been an informed group of consumers, familiar with low alcohol beer.

Examination of the market survey reveals serious defects—namely, that the conclusion that LA does not connote low alcohol beer was drawn from the legally irrelevant sample group of uninformed consumers asked to draw meaning from an isolated product label, and that the survey was otherwise insufficient because of the questionable structure and make-up of the questions asked. Thus, upon analysis, this survey does not, in my view, support the district court's finding that LA is suggestive.

Case Questions

1. If the term *low alcohol* is a generic term that cannot be trademarked, what was the court's basis for granting trademark protection to "LA" beer?
2. What test did the court use to determine whether a word was generic?
3. What was the basis of the dissenting judge's argument?
4. What should be the role of consumer attitude surveys in similar trademark cases?

Copyrights

Copyrights protect the original work of authors, musicians, and painters who produce works of artistic or intellectual merit. This book has been copyrighted, making it illegal to take the authors' words without permission. Like corporate researchers who invent patentable products, authors who contract to write a book generally transfer their copyright to the publishing firm that seeks to sell it.

Copyright protection exists under the common law once a work has been created. However, if the work is widely distributed without federal statutory copyright registration, it becomes part of the public domain and loses copyright protection. A registration process simpler than those for patents or trademarks is used if the work is published and distributed with a copyright notice. With copyrights, unlike patents or trademarks, no one conducts a search to determine originality or the absence of conflict. This means that a copyright holder may be subject to a copyright infringement suit by another copyright holder.

The required copyright notice may take the form of the word *copyright,* the abbreviation *copr,* or the symbol ©, followed by the year and the name of the copyright holder. The copyright for this book is located on the page following the title page. Copyright protection under the Copyright Act of 1976 lasts for the life of the creator plus 50 years. If there is more than one creator, as with this book, the copyright lasts for 50 years beyond the life of the longest surviving creator. Copyrights protect the words, tunes, or composition of the author, compose or painter, but not the ideas expressed in the copyrighted material. Thus, you have the right to read a portion of a book, take some of the author's ideas, and use them to create new, noninfringing text. However, as the term *copyright* suggests, you do not have the right to copy the particular words, the "form of expression," that the author uses or to photocopy material in the book without permission unless the purpose is exempt. Does the developer of a computer operating system have a right to copyright that system, or does the system represent an idea not subject to copyright protection? The case presented at the end of this section indicates how the copyright law applies to computer programs.

Some use of copyrighted material is permitted. The *fair use doctrine* allows the quotation of several paragraphs in a book for use in a report or in a published review or

FIGURE 7–2
Important International Treaties Affecting Intellectual Property: Patents, Trademarks, and Copyrights

Treaty & Membership	Type of Property	Protection
Paris Convention United States and 90 other countries	Patents Trademarks	National treatment (No discrimination against foreigners) Priority rights (Provides protection for one year after initial filing)
Patent Cooperation United States and 40 other countries	Patents	Provides for international application (File internationally and then nationally)
Berne Convention United States and 80 other countries	Copyrights	Works published in one country are automatically eligible for protection in other countries without registration
Universal Copyright Convention United States and 90 other countries	Copyrights	Excuses registration in foreign country if adequate notice of claim if given

commentary. This doctrine also permits taping for personal use songs played on the radio. Similarly, a 1984 Supreme Court case, determined that television shows could be copied onto a VCR for later personal enjoyment without violating the rights of the copyright owners.[5] However, as the broadcasters of professional sports events remind us, further use is prohibited.

A Typical Copyright Notice Announcement

No rebroadcast or other use of this copyrighted game and the play-by-play announcement of it is permissible without the consent of major league baseball and the competing teams.

There is a variety of international treaties affecting intellectual property. The protection of intellectual property is becoming a greater concern for many western firms and there is increased negotiation regarding this topic in both bilateral and multilateral treaties. Several of the more important multilateral treaties to which the United States is a party are depicted in Figure 7–2.

Apple Computer, Inc. v. Franklin Computer Corp.

714 F.2d 1240 (1983)
3rd Circuit Court of Appeals

Apple filed suit against Franklin, charging it with copyright infringement of 14 of its computer operating system programs and patent infringement, unfair competition, and

[5]*Sony Corp. v. Universal City Studios*, (464 U.S. 417 1984).

misappropriation. Franklin admitted copying Apple's programs, but asserted that these programs were not eligible for copyright protection. The district court found for Franklin, and Apple appealed.

Sloviter, Judge

In 1976, after considerable study, Congress enacted a new copyright law to replace that which had governed since 1909. Under the law, two primary requirements must be satisfied in order for a work to constitute copyrightable subject matter—it must be an "original wor[k] of authorship" and must be "fixed in [a] tangible medium of expression." The statute enumerates seven categories under "works of authorship" including "literary works," defined as follows:

> "Literary works" are works, other than audiovisual works, expressed in words, numbers, or other verbal or numerical symbols or indicia, regardless of the nature of the material objects, such as books, periodicals, manuscripts, phonorecords, film, tapes, disks, or cards, in which they are embodied.

A work is "fixed" in a tangible medium of expression when:

> its embodiment in a copy or phonorecord, by or under the authority of the author, is sufficiently permanent or stable to permit it to be perceived, reproduced, or otherwise communicated for a period of more than transitory duration. A work consisting of sounds, images, or both, that are being transmitted, is "fixed" for purposes of this title if a fixation of the work is being made simultaneously with its transmission.

Although section 102(a) does not expressly list computer programs as works of authorship, the legislative history suggests that programs were considered copyrightable as literary works.

Under the statute, copyright extends to works in any tangible means of expression "*from which they can be perceived,* reproduced, or otherwise communicated, either directly or *with the aid of a machine or device.*" Further, the definition of "computer program" adopted by Congress in the 1980 amendments is "sets of statements or instructions to be used *directly or indirectly* in a computer in order to bring about a certain result."

The amendments also substituted a new section 117, which provides that "it is not an infringement for the owner of a copy of a computer program to make or authorize the making of another copy or adaptation of that computer program" when necessary to "the utilization of the computer program" or "for archival purposes only." The language of the provision, by carving out an exception to the normal proscriptions against copying, clearly indicates that programs are copyrightable and are otherwise afforded copyright protection.

We considered the issue of copyright protection for a computer program in *Williams Electronics, Inc. v. Arctic International, Inc.,* and concluded that "the copyrightability of computer programs is firmly established after the 1980 amendment to the Copyright Act." Thus a computer program, whether in object code or source code, is a "literary work" and is protected from unauthorized copying, whether from its object or source code version. . . .

Franklin argues that an operating system program is either a "process," "system," or "method of operation" and hence uncopyrightable. Franklin correctly notes that underlying section 102(b) and many of the statements for which *Baker v. Selden* is cited is the distinction which must be made between property subject to the patent law, which protects discoveries, and that subject to copyright law, which protects the writing describing such discoveries. . . . Both types of programs instruct the computer to do something. Therefore, it should make no difference for purposes of section 102(b) whether these instructions tell the computer to help prepare an income tax return (the task of an application program) or to translate a high-level language program from source code into its binary language object code form (the task of an operating system program such as "Applesoft"). Since it is only the instructions which are protected, a "process" is no more involved because the instructions in an operating system program may be used to activate the operation of the computer, than it would be if instructions were written in ordinary English in a manual which described the necessary steps to activate an intricate complicated machine. There is, therefore, no reason to afford any less copyright protection to the instructions in an operating system program than to the instructions in an application program. . . .

Franklin's other challenge to copyright of operating system programs relies on the line which is drawn between ideas and their expression. *Baker v. Selden* remains a benchmark in the law of copyright for the reading given it in *Mazer v. Stein,* where the Court stated, "Unlike a patent, a copyright gives no exclusive right to the art disclosed: protection is given only to the expression of the idea—not the idea itself."

The expression/idea dichotomy is now expressly recognized in section 102(b), which precludes copyright for "any idea." This provision was not intended to enlarge or contract the scope of copyright protection but "to restate . . . that the basic dichotomy between expression and idea remains unchanged."

Many of the courts which have sought to draw the line between an idea and expression have found difficulty in articulating where it falls. As we stated in *Franklin Mint Corp. v. National Wildlife Art Exchange, Inc.*:

> Just as a patent affords protection only to the means of reducing an inventive idea to practice, so the copyright law protects the means of expressing an idea; and it is as near the whole truth as generalization can usually reach that, *if the same idea can be expressed in a plurality of totally different manners, a plurality of copyrights may result,* and no infringement will exist (emphasis added).

We adopt the suggestion in the above language and thus focus on whether the idea is capable of various modes of expression. If other programs can be written or created which perform the same function as an Apple's operating system program, then that program is an expression of the idea and hence copyrightable.

In summary, Franklin's contentions that operating system programs are *per se* not copyrightable is unpersuasive. . . . We believe that the 1980 amendments reflect Congress' receptivity to new technology and its desire to encourage, through the copyright laws, continued imagination and creativity in computer programming. . . . [W]e reverse the denial of the preliminary injunction and remand for reconsideration.

Case Questions

1. Why are computer programs subject to copyright laws that are intended to protect original works of authorship fixed in a tangible medium of expression?
2. Compare the matters subject to copyright protection with those subject to patent protection.
3. Did the court reach its decision by looking at the common law from prior cases or by interpreting a statute?

ETHICAL ANALYSIS OF PROPERTY RIGHTS

The law of intellectual property rights—patents, copyrights, trademarks, and trade secrets—is designed to encourage innovation in areas that could eventually affect society. These property rights are based on an implied contract between the innovator and the government. To encourage the development of new products, the innovator is given a monopoly for a limited time. In exchange, the innovator must share the innovation's benefits with society.

The major ethical problem with intellectual property arises from its intangible nature. It is easy to understand that stealing tangible property is unethical and illegal. The owner immediately knows of the loss, and society generally condemns the misappropriation. By contrast, intangible property (e.g., information, ideas, inventions, designs) appears to be inexhaustible. When one person misappropriates a copy of intangible property, the owner still has the original property. However, this misappropriation diminishes the owner's opportunity to fully exploit the intangible property right. There is a common misunderstanding that nothing has been misappropriated because the owner still has the original. However, an ethical problem clearly arises because the misappropriator has gained value without expending development efforts to earn it or pay the owner for it. Misappropriation or infringement of intellectual property is a tempting act because it is often easy to do and may go undetected. Unauthorized photocopying and software duplication exemplify this unethical misappropriation.

COMPUTER LAW

Computers are used by millions of business firms to accomplish a wide variety of tasks. From word processing to data storage to product scanning, the computer has become ubiquitous in both the back rooms and executive office suites of most business organizations. Of course, some people who use computers may do so for unauthorized and illegal purposes. Such crimes as fraud, embezzlement, and sabotage are easy to commit for knowledgeable computer users. Businesses therefore need to be vigilant and informed about actions they may take to prevent computer crimes or to prosecute if necessary.

Laws Applicable to Computer Hardware and Software

The unique aspect of computer law deals more with software than with hardware. *Software* concerns the programming involved with a computer. As the *Apple* case notes, software is often divided into operational and application programs. *Computer hardware* is regarded as equipment. In most cases, the hardware is movable and so it is tangible personal property. Contract law is applicable when it is purchased, leased, or sold; the relationship between these laws is discussed in Chapter 8.

Even if software is sold with the hardware, courts have held that a sale of goods takes place. However, if only software is sold, such as to a business that already has its computer hardware, many courts have held that no goods are involved. Thus, contract law, not sales law, applies to that transaction. Other courts, referring to the existence of a tangible disk or tape and manuals, have applied sales law to the lease or sale of computer software. The *Apple* case presents one of the problems the law has had to face with regard to computers: Are computer programs property that can be copyrighted? Another problem the law faces with regard to this new technology is whether the theft, unauthorized use, or destruction of the data in a computer's memory violates criminal laws. A variety of different computer crimes may be committed. Someone may enter false data into a computer's memory (indicating a fictitious person has a bank account or insurance policy), alter or destroy files (erase records of loans owed, records of telephone calls made), make unauthorized use of a computer system (access a competitor's data or classified military information), or commit theft by computer (have bank funds transferred to an account in a thief's name and then withdraw the funds from the bank).

Computer Crime

A **computer crime** is any illegal act requiring knowledge of computer technology or involving the use of a computer. As both the ethical and criminal aspects of computer crime are discussed in Chapter 22, this chapter provides only a brief review of computer crime. There are two categories of computer crimes. First, a computer may be used as a tool in committing a crime. In one case involving insurance fraud, employees of an insurance company entered fictitious names of new policy holders into their company's computer system. The company then used the computer's list of its policy holder names to obtain financing. When the fraudulent scheme was uncovered, the value of the company's stock declined and several company officials were convicted for their criminal actions.

A second category of computer crime occurs when information stored on a computer is stolen or damaged. As computer microchips allow thousands of pages of data to be stored in a computer's memory, many businesses store customer account information, financial data, and product inventory records in computer files. Like other valuable property, the records and data may be damaged or stolen. Damage may occur when someone introduces a computer virus program into the computer records. The virus may alter or destroy existing records. A theft occurs when there is any unauthorized entry into a computer system. As the *McGraw* case in Chapter 22 notes, the theft of computer time may be regarded as a criminal act. Access to a computer system by illegal means may allow the thief to find out financial, personnel, or trade secret information about a company.

Laws Affecting Computer Crime Computer crimes are addressed several ways by the law. The definitions of some general criminal acts, such as the unauthorized taking of property, have been interpreted to apply to computer crimes as well as to other crimes. Thus, the definition of property in a theft statute may not be amended to specifically refer to software, business information, and customer lists.

Similarly, many states have enacted specific laws addressing specific computer-related crimes. The term *scavenging* refers to crimes perpetrated by collecting data from discarded material. By looking at discarded carbon paper copies used in a credit card transaction, the name, credit card number, and expiration date of a credit card holder can be obtained. That information can then be used to acquire goods and services. Many state laws now include theft of services or labor under false pretenses to specifically target the unauthorized use of credit cards.

There is also some protection against computer crimes in the federal laws. The Fair Credit Reporting Act (discussed in Chapter 11) makes illegal the unauthorized access to credit reporting information. The Semiconductor Chip Protection Act provides a special system of legal protection for mask works used in the production of semiconductor chips. It confers the exclusive right to reproduce and distribute mask works for ten years, subject to registration by the Copyright Office. As noted in the *Apple* case, the copyright law applies to computer programs; the unauthorized use or reproduction of copyrighted material is both a tort and a crime.

Finally, the Counterfeit Access Device and Computer Fraud and Abuse Act of 1984 makes it a crime to use or access federal or private computers without authorization in several situations. Accessing a computer to get classified military or foreign policy information is a felony if done with the intent to harm the United States or to benefit another country. Unauthorized access to financial records of federal financial institutions (banks, savings and loans, credit unions, and registered securities brokers are covered) is also prohibited by this law.

ETHICAL DILEMMA: ENTERTAINMENT AND COMPUTER SOFTWARE

Ethical dilemmas have been emerging in other areas of intangible property. For example, should television, movie, or record performers have the right to control when and where their movies are viewed or their records are heard? The question seemed to be settled before videocassette recorders (VCRs) began selling widely. Music broadcast over the radio may be recorded legally by listeners for replay later, so long as they do not attempt to pirate the music by reselling it for profit.

Now that stereo manufacturers are selling digital audiotape (DAT), this question is again becoming clouded. The video- and audiotaping techniques of the past produced imperfect copies of the original. Static and distortion introduced in the broadcasting and recording processes made copies less desirable than the original. However, DAT and recordable CDs permit an exact copy to be produced. This may give pirates an incentive to reproduce a copyrighted work, which, in turn, would prevent the copyright holder from receiving "just" compensation. An ethical dilemma arises because the property rights of the copyright holder are outside the copyright holder's exclusive physical control. This motivates pirates to misappropriate the copyrighted work. Music companies are apparently not planning to follow the strategy that was used in the *Betamax* case. Instead, they have made an arrangement requiring DAT recorder manufacturers to include a device making such recordings impossible.

A similar problem arises with computer software. The ability of personal computers to precisely duplicate software has led many software companies to include devices that make unauthorized copying difficult (copy protection). An ethical dilemma confronts software owners whose private access to the computer source code enables them to duplicate the software. If they make duplicate copies for their backup purposes, the copyright owner suffers no loss. However, if the copies are used by others who might have purchased the software, the copyright owner may be deprived of revenue. A tougher ethical question arises when the software duplicator simply seeks to test a software program before actually purchasing it. If the duplicator is favorably impressed with the software and purchases it, this may actually benefit the software owner. Despite this potentially favorable impact on software owners, software piracy is illegal unless the license permits duplication or the software is in the public domain. Both civil and criminal penalties can be imposed on those who violate the software copyright law. Many corporations are strictly enforcing rules prohibiting software pirating by their employees.

OWNERSHIP AND TRANSFER OF PERSONAL PROPERTY

Transferring the possession of personal property does not necessarily transfer its ownership. When a person transfers only the possession and custody of personal property to another person for a specific purpose, a *bailment* is created.

Bailments

For example, a **bailment** arises if one person transfers or loans personal property to another person for a specific purpose. For example, if John gives a watch to a jeweler for repair, a bailment occurs. The jeweler is the *bailee* (custodian of the property transferred) who must exercise reasonable care over the *bailor's* property (John's watch) while it is in the bailee's custody. By contrast, transfer of the possession of personal property that is also intended to transfer its title (the right to ownership of the property or evidence thereof) is either a sale or a gift. A valid will may postpone the transfer of personal property until after death.

Transfer of Title

A Sale The most common method of transferring the title to personal property is a *sale*. State contract laws generally regulate the methods for effecting sales of goods. Article 2 of the Uniform Commercial Code, enacted into law in 49 states, is the primary source of such regulation. Most of the states also have special statutory provisions for the sale of motor vehicles, such as cars, trucks, or motor homes. Such contracts are discussed further in Chapter 8.

A Gift Personal property may also be transferred by a gift. A gift made by a living person is referred to as an *inter vivos gift*. A gift of personal property is valid if the donor intends to make the gift and delivers possession of the item. Actual delivery of the item is not necessary if something is done to evidence the transfer of ownership. For example, transferring the keys and title certificate of a car is sufficient to transfer the title to the car, and putting the donee's name on a savings account book is sufficient to transfer the money in the account.

Transfer at Death An owner of personal property may transfer it at death by making a valid will. The will may specify who is to take specific personal property owned by the decedent: "I give my automobile to my sister Susan." The will may also make a general statement such as " I give all the furniture in my home to my wife Sally." Even a statement like "all the remainder of the property I own, I give to my daughter Julie" will transfer the title to personal property at a person's death. If a person dies without a valid will, state law provides a method for distributing the decedent's property to the surviving heirs. The law of the state where the decedent was domiciled (had a primary residence) is applied to the disposition of personal property. The laws governing the transfer of personal property differ from those that govern the descent of real property. The law of the state where the real property is located controls that transfer.

OWNERSHIP OF REAL PROPERTY

The law recognizes different interests in real property. For example, the ownership of things under, on, or above land may be separated. Several interests in the same piece of land may exist at the same time. Those interests can be grouped into three categories: possessory interests, nonpossessory interests, and undivided interests.

Possessory Interests

Estates in land and leasehold interests concern rights that relate to the possession of land. The term *estate* is used in real property law to indicate the nature, quantity, and quality of an ownership interest. The extent of an estate is determined by its duration and by the time when the rights to possess and enjoy it begin. These rights may include life estate, leasehold estate, and dower rights.

Life Estate

A person may use the property during his or her life (the life could also be that of another person). After that time, the owner loses any interest in the property and another person receives the remainder of the ownership interest. For example, if an elderly parent transfers a residence to a child while retaining a life estate, the parent has the use of the residence for life, but the child will receive the ownership when the parent dies.

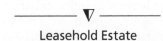

Leasehold Estate

A person known as the lessee or tenant may possess and control the property during the term of the lease. Leases are commonly used in business for both personal and real property. Where law prevents a person or a company from owning property, long-term leases (such as 99-year leases) are quite common.

Dower Interest

An interest in land granting a surviving spouse (either spouse is usually eligible) either a life interest in or full ownership in some portion of the deceased spouse's real property.

The leasehold estate or lease is the most common possessory interest in real property. The tenant's interest in the property is called a *leasehold,* and the landlord's interest is called a *reversionary interest.* Both the landlord and the tenant may transfer their interests to other people unless their lease agreement restricts this right. Residential leases commonly require the landlord's written approval of any transfer by the tenant.

Assignment of Lease If the lease does not prohibit assignment, a tenant may assign a leasehold interest in property by transferring that interest to an assignee. However, the assignee does not replace the tenant on the lease agreement. A lease *assignment* grants the assignee all the rights that the tenant had, such as the right to live in an apartment. An assignment also imposes the tenant's duties on the assignee, such as the duty to pay the rent. However, the tenant must pay the rent if the assignee does not.

Suppose that Cari, who leases and manages a frozen yogurt store on Main Street, decides to leave that location for a better location on North Rose Street, and that John contracts with her to take over her lease on the Main Street store in an assignment. John is the *assignee,* the person to whom the assignment is made, and Cari is the *assignor,* the person who makes the assignment. John becomes a party to the original lease agreement with the owner. He must pay the rent on the Main Street store, but Cari remains secondarily liable if he fails to do so.

Sublease In a *sublease,* the subtenant has a contract only with the tenant, not with the owner, and the subtenant does not receive all of the tenant's rights. Subleases are for a shorter period than that of the original lease. For example, assume that Cari, who has a two-year lease on a yogurt shop, decides to vacation in the Bahamas for 10 months and therefore subleases the shop to John for one year. After that year, Cari will still have one year left on her lease. In this sublease, John is not a party to the lease made with the owner. Cari still owes the rent for the entire two years of her lease, but the sublease entitles her to receive from John the rent due under the sublease agreement. John's rights are based only on the sublease terms, not on the lease between Cari and the owner. Figure 7–3 illustrates the differences between an assignment and a sublease.

An assignee receives the rights granted in the original lease between the landlord and the tenant, while a subtenant receives none of those rights. The subtenant's rights and duties arise solely from the sublease agreement. In the following case, a clause in the lease between Conklin and Acme prohibited Acme from assigning its lease without obtaining written permission from Conklin. However, the lease agreement did not expressly prohibit a sublease. What factors did the court examine to determine whether Acme's transfer was a permissible sublease or a prohibited assignment?

FIGURE 7–3 Comparison of Assignment and Sublease of Real Property

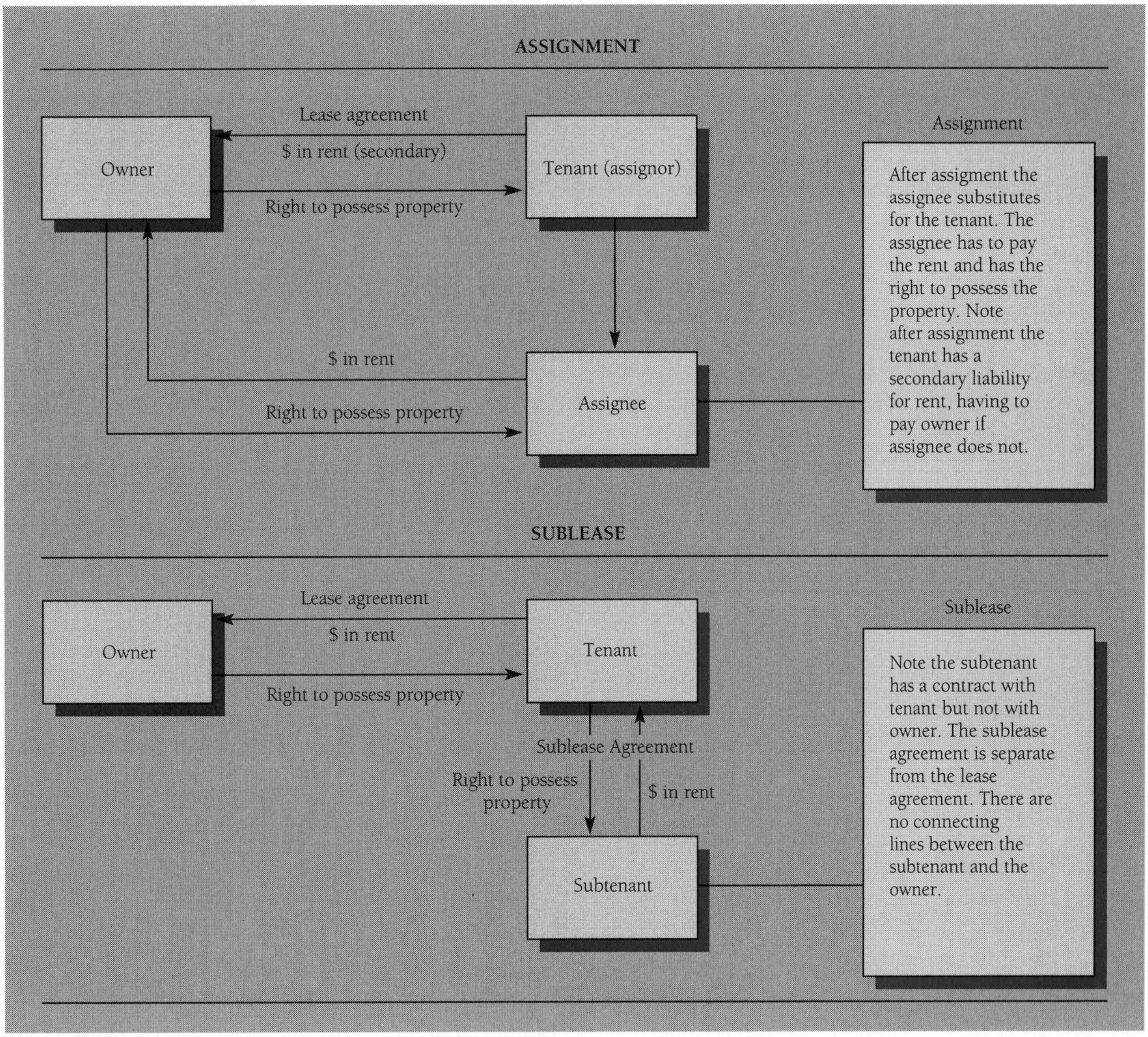

Conklin Development v. Acme Markets, Inc.

453 N.Y.S. 2d. (1982) 930
Supreme Court, Appellate Division

The Plaintiff, Conklin Development, signed a contract leasing space in a shopping mall to the defendant, Acme Markets. The lease agreement prohibited assignment of the lease by Acme but allowed Acme to sublease the space. Conklin claimed that Acme had violated the lease by assigning its lease interest to P & C Markets (P & C). Acme asserted that its agreement with P & C was a permitted sublease because Acme's lease term expired on May 31, 1983, whereas P & C's term expired on May 1, 1983.

Memorandum Decision

There is no question that the agreement between Acme and P & C was a sublease, not an assignment. In order to constitute an assignment, the transfer from the original lessee must convey the entire interest of the lessee. If he retains a reversionary interest in the real property transferred, privity of estate does not arise between the landlord and the transferee. [*Privity of estate* is the mutual or successive relationship to the same rights in property.] . . . The transfer under such circumstances constitutes a sublease, and the relation of landlord and tenant does not exist between the original lessor and the transferee.

The instrument between Acme and P & C specifically reserves unto Acme the right to exercise the renewal options in the prime lease, distinctly and explicitly subordinates any renewals of the sublease to Acme's right to exercise renewal options of the prime lease and recites that Acme remains liable to plaintiff for the performance of the obligations of the prime lease. Based on these provisions, Special Term correctly found the instrument to be a sublease.

Having found that the Acme-P & C agreement was a sublease and not an assignment, no privity of contract or estate between plaintiff and . . . P & C could exist.

Affirmed.

Case Questions

1. What is the essential characteristic of a lease assignment?
2. What is meant by the term *privity of estate* as it applies to this case?
3. If the agreement between Acme and P & C was a sublease, what rights did Conklin have in the sublease?

Nonpossessory Interests

A second category of real property interests grants a limited use or enjoyment of property that does not involve exclusive possession.

Easements An *easement* is a nonpossessory interest permitting its owner to make limited use of some portion of a property. An easement might allow a gas or electric utility company to install and service underground cable. It might also grant an adjoining landowner access to a landlocked parcel. For example, if Anna owns land that backs onto a lakefront and Brad's land is across the street from Anna's front yard, Brad might have an easement over a portion of Anna's land, permitting him to cross her land to get to the lakefront.

Licenses A *license* also allows one party to use another party's land for a limited purpose, but unlike an easement, a license is generally personal in nature and revocable by the property owner. A license is granted, not to the owner of a specific lot (say, the owner of the property across the street), but to a specific person. When land is sold, an easement is generally transferred to the new owner, but a license is not. Thus, a license might permit a neighbor to cut wood on the owner's property or to use the lakefront at the back of the owner's lot. However, it does not grant that privilege to the purchaser of the licensee's property and it can be disregarded by the purchaser of the licensor's property.

Liens A *lien* gives one person a nonpossessory, collateral-like interest in another person's property. Typically, a lien is granted to a lender who accepts it as security against a borrower's promise to repay a debt. A *mortgage* is a common type of lien on real property. Liens also exist on personal property. For example, when a mechanic does repair work on a car, a *mechanic's lien* is generally created by statute. If you do not pay the repair cost, the mechanic can sell the car and use the proceeds to pay the repair bill. In most types of personal property, security interests such as liens are governed by Article 9 of the UCC, which is discussed in Chapter 11.

Undivided Interests

The third category of real property interests comprises those held by several parties jointly. Some methods may be selected by the parties; others are imposed by law.

Co-ownership Property may be co-owned by taking title to it either as joint tenants or as tenants in common. If joint tenancy is selected, each of the joint tenants has an equal right to possess the entire property and no joint tenant can exclude the others from possession. If there are only two tenants and either dies, the survivor becomes the sole owner of the property. Such joint tenancy, referred to as *joint tenancy with rights of survivorship,* generally must be intentionally created.

A *tenancy in common* also allows each co-owner an undivided right to possess the entire property. It does not, however, include a right of survivorship. If one tenant dies, the court generally partitions the property, giving a portion of it to each cotenant and also to the deceased co-owner's heirs. For example, assume two people own an apartment building, a boat, or a store as tenants in common. If one of the co-owners dies, the decedent's heirs, not the surviving cotenant, usually inherit his or her share.

Community property ownership The laws of several states, mostly in the Southwest, consider a husband and wife co-owners of all property acquired during their marriage, regardless of whose labor made the acquisition possible. For example, if cars, furniture, or jewelry are purchased by one spouse and title is placed in only that spouse's name, community property law treats the property as belonging equally to both spouses. Gifts, individually inherited property, and separate property owned prior to or after the marriage are generally not considered community property: such items may be kept separately by each of the spouses.

Condominium and cooperative ownership Many people desire to share ownership in real property yet maintain their own living space. This may be done through condominium or cooperative ownership. For example, individual control over a specific area (an apartment) may be given to each owner of an apartment building, while the common areas (the pool, lobby, hallways, and outside lawn area) may be co-owned by all the owners. Each owner of a *condominium* owns an individual apartment unit and agrees to share the upkeep expenses of the common areas. Owners may sell individual units at will.

By contrast, a corporation usually owns *cooperative* buildings or developments. Occupants of individual units buy shares in the corporation and then lease a unit from it. In many cooperatives, each shareholder-owner must obtain the approval of the other shareholder-owners before selling or subleasing an individual unit.

SALE OR TRANSFER OF REAL PROPERTY

Transfer by sale is the most common and the most important method of obtaining title to real estate. Contract law, discussed in Chapter 8, plays an important role in most real estate transactions because a purchase and sale of real estate is based on the contract made by the parties.

Most people participate in several real estate transactions during their lives. Lease provisions and landlord-tenant laws are most relevant to apartment tenants. The purchase of a home may occur several times during a person's life. Small firms often buy buildings for office space, and larger firms often build and develop numerous parcels of real estate in locations across the country and perhaps throughout the world. Because numerous legal documents must be prepared and reviewed in any real estate transaction, the advice of an attorney and the assistance of real estate agents should be sought before any of the steps discussed below are taken.

The Sales Agreement

A seller of real estate usually contacts a real estate broker to establish the terms of sale. The seller and broker must agree on how long the broker will have the right to list the property for sale. The seller may give the broker the exclusive right to list the property. Such listing contracts usually require the payment of a commission to the broker after the broker produces a person who is "ready, willing, and able" to purchase the property. Even if the seller later decides not to sell to that person, the broker may usually collect the commission because he or she has successfully performed the obligations of the listing contract.

A contract to sell real property is generally prepared in one of two ways. For many residential real estate transactions, the seller or the seller's broker prepares a document known as the *purchase agreement* or *offer to purchase.* Standardized form contracts which have blanks for the insertion of variable information are often used. This document becomes the contract after being signed by the purchaser and accepted and signed by the seller.

The contract must be in writing to be enforceable. It details the purchase price to be paid, the type of deed to be provided by the seller, the seller's obligations regarding the title to the property, and the financing terms. As the purchaser generally must obtain mortgage financing, the purchase agreement is usually contingent on obtaining the mortgage on specified terms. Any personal property that is to be included in the sale, such as drapes, major appliances, or furniture, also is listed in this agreement.

For most commercial real estate transactions, the parties do not begin with a formal contract or a document prepared by one of them. Instead, they first negotiate the terms and then one of them prepares a contract reflecting the negotiated terms. The terms of their agreement are usually found in the contract they sign at the end of negotiations.

The Legal Documents

After the contract has been signed by the parties, both the seller and the purchaser must perform certain actions to consummate their transaction. The seller must provide satisfactory proof of title to the property being sold. Depending on local custom, either title insurance (an insurance company's policy that the seller has title to the property) or an abstract of title (a history of the transactions transferring title to property), with an attorney's opinion of its appropriateness, generally satisfies this requirement. A survey of the property or a termite inspection may be required. A certificate showing that the local property taxes have been paid is usually needed. The seller's mortgage lender must be notified so that its loan balance is paid and its security interest in the property is discharged.

Generally, the purchaser will use the time following execution of the contract to obtain a lender's commitment to finance some portion of the purchase price needed for the payment to the seller. After the lender commits to lend the money needed for the purchase price, it will require the purchaser-borrower to sign a promissory note and mortgage agreement.

The Mortgage A *mortgage* gives the lender an ownership interest in the property being purchased. It creates a security interest to provide collateral for the *promissory note* that evidences the purchaser's debt. The purchaser-borrower is known as the *mortgagor,* and the lender is known as the *mortgagee.* If the proof of title and other documents furnished by the seller are acceptable to the mortgagor and the mortgagee, a closing date for the sale is set.

The Deed The *closing* of the real property sale is an event at which the parties sign and exchange several documents. The seller provides the purchaser with a deed to the property. Generally, the deed is a *warranty deed,* one that warrants or guarantees that the title is good and free of any liens or encumbrances by others who might have an interest in the property. A warranty deed must include certain words to effectively transfer the property. A typical warranty deed appears in Figure 7–4.

If the purchaser agrees, the seller may instead promise to transfer only whatever interest the seller has in the property by using a *quitclaim deed.* Such deeds are not used in most sales because if it turns out that the seller does not own the property, then a quitclaim deed transfers nothing to the purchaser. Quitclaim deeds are used in transactions between spouses, partners, or joint tenants. A quitclaim deed is sufficient to transfer the legal interest in property owned by the seller to the purchaser where the parties know each other and know what interest each party owns.

Other Documents Along with the warranty deed, the seller and the mortgage lender provide a closing statement itemizing what amounts the purchaser is to pay. After reviewing the deed, the proof of title documents, and the closing statement, the purchaser and the mortgagee-lender pay the purchase price, less any credits for money paid.

Recording Then, the lender or the purchaser records the deed. All important documents affecting the title to real property must be *recorded*—entered into the public record. Deeds, mortgages, long-term leases, easements, liens, and assignments are generally recorded to provide notice to other parties of the various interests in specific parcels of real property. An unrecorded deed is effective between the purchaser and the seller, but it has no effect on the rights of any third parties to their transaction. Recording a document such as a deed or a mortgage gives notice to the world that a certain person has an interest in particular real estate. Thus, persons interested in purchasing must consult the record to determine who claims an interest in the property to be purchased.

FIGURE 7–4 Warranty Deed

The Grantor(s) ROBERT A. BROWN AND MARILYN B. BROWN, HUSBAND AND WIFE AS JOINT TENANTS, whose address is 4488 S. 15th ST., GRAND JUNCTION, MI convey(s) and warrant(s) to THOMAS A. STEVENSON AND MARY R. STEVENSON, HUSBAND AND WIFE AS JOINT TENANTS whose address is 1803 W. PARK ST., LANSING, MI the following described premises situated in the CITY of GRAND JUNCTION, County of MASON and state of Michigan:

LOT 47 OF THE WEST PORT PLAT IN THE CITY OF GRAND JUNCTION, MASON COUNTY, MICHIGAN, EXCEPT THE WEST 20 FEET THEREOF, ACCORDING TO THE PLAT THEREOF AS RECORDED IN LIBER 1 OF PLATS ON PAGE 69, MASON COUNTY RECORDS

for the sum of SEVENTY-FIVE THOUSAND AND NO/100 DOLLARS ($75, 000.00) subject to easements and building and use restrictions of record and further subject to

NO OTHER ENCUMBRANCES.

Dated this 8TH day of JANUARY, 1992

Signed in the presence of:	Signed by:
* MARTHA BLACK	* ROBERT A. BROWN
* JAMES GREEN	* MARILYN B. BROWN
	*
	*

STATE OF MICHIGAN
COUNTY OF MASON } SS

The foregoing instrument was acknowledged before me this 8TH day of JANUARY, 1992 by

ROBERT A. BROWN AND MARILYN B. BROWN .

* PATRICIA SAEL
Notary Public, MASON County,
Michigan
My commission expires DECEMBER 13, 1992

County Treasurer's Certificate	City Treasurer's Certificate

When recorded Return To:	Send Subsequent Tax Bills To	Drafted by JOHN ALLEN
JOHN ALLEN & BOOTH P. C. (name)	THOMAS A. STEVENSON	Business Address
433 W. STATE STREET (Street address)	4488 S. 15TH ST.	ALLEN & BOOTH P. C.
GRAND JUNCTION, MI (city and state)	GRAND JUNCTION, MI	433 W. STATE ST.
		GRAND JUNCTION, MI

Tax Parcel * ______ Recording Fee ______ Transfer Tax ______

* TYPE OR PRINT NAMES UNDER SIGNATURES.

LEGAL CONTROL OF REAL PROPERTY

The most stringent control on real property regulates who can own it. Such control is uncommon in the United States, but some governments restrict the right of aliens to own real property. In Mexico, for example, foreign businesses or individuals are usually not allowed to own real property within 100 kilometers of a border or 50 kilometers of a seacoast. They must lease it from Mexican owners, or have a trust hold title for their benefit. In the United States, state laws generally prohibit minors from owning real property while permitting them to own personal property. Some of the states limit the ownership of certain real estate by foreigners.

Most of the controls over real property are found in tort and local land use regulations. For example, nuisance laws grant relief to persons adversely affected by another person's use of property. Zoning ordinances and development regulations restrict the types of buildings that property owners may erect or the activities that they may engage in on their property. Such ordinances and regulations are imposed primarily by local units of government to benefit the public. Private restrictions, though not favored by the law, are enforced if they are reasonable and if they benefit other property owners. Finally, property may be taken by the government through its power of *eminent domain*, if the property is needed for a public purpose and the owner is adequately compensated.

Nuisance Laws

An owner of real property cannot use it in a way that injures others. A *private nuisance* exists if an owner's use of real property deprives others of their right to use and enjoy their own property. The playing of a loud stereo through the night might be a private nuisance to a neighbor. A *public nuisance* involves conduct that affects a broad group of people. A back-to-school block party attracting thousands of students and other individuals to several residences might constitute both a private nuisance and a public nuisance. A private nuisance might occur because neighbors are unable to use and enjoy their property. A public nuisance might occur because members of the public are unable to use streets and walkways for travel. Public nuisance cases are usually brought by the government, whereas private nuisance cases are brought by individuals.

How should a court resolve a dispute when residents in an apartment complex complain that the periodic rock music concerts in the neighboring shopping center interfere with their right to peace and quiet?

McQuade v. Tucson Tiller Apartments, Ltd.
543 P.2d 150 (1975)
Arizona Court of Appeals

Tucson Tiller Apartments (Tiller) is located next to the McQuade shopping center, Plaza Antigua. The trial court found that in the past two years McQuade has held 5 to 10 rock music events that attracted between 3,000 and 7,000 people. The court found that the noise from these events was so loud as to interfere with the reasonable use of Tiller's property and that the McQuade premises could not accommodate such large crowds without interfering with the reasonable use of Tiller's property. The trial court enjoined McQuade from holding concerts with loud music and from holding mass attendance events larger than its property could handle. McQuade, referred to in the opinion as the appellant and defendant, sought review by the Court of Appeals.

Hathaway, Judge

It is undisputed that appellants intend to continue holding mass music events. The purpose of these concerts is to promote the businesses in Plaza Antigua. As this is a continuing business practice, we will treat this case as one involving a continuing nuisance rather than an anticipated nuisance. The fact that the injury is only occasional does not prevent an injunction.

Music does not constitute nuisance per se, but it may become a nuisance because of loud noise or the attraction of large crowds. Noise, to be enjoined, must produce substantial injury and annoy the normal person.

In determining whether the acts constitute a nuisance, the court should consider all the circumstances, including the locality and character of the surroundings, the nature of the defendant's business and the manner in which it is conducted, the value to the community of the defendant's activities, the defendant's ability to reduce the harm, and the extent to which the defendant would be damaged by an injunction and the plaintiff damaged by the failure to enjoin. The court can also consider priority of use.

In sum, the court looks at the reasonableness of the defendant's activities in the locality. This involves a balancing test.

Here the area is neither residential nor industrial. Appellants' mass musical events are not of great utility to the community. Although appellants can take steps to reduce the harm, any improvements will be minor so long as the loud music and large crowds continue. Appellants are not greatly harmed by this injunction. The mass events are not necessary to running the shopping center, and appellants are free to engage in other activities which advertise their shopping center.

On the other hand, if the injunction is not upheld, appellee's tenants will continue to suffer from the long days of loud noise, parking problems, trespass, and other annoyances.

Applying a balance test, we have no hesitancy in holding appellee's right to use and enjoyment outweighs appellants' interest in continuing to hold loud, mass attendance events.

It is conceded that appellants held events at their shopping center before appellee's apartments were built. However, coming to the nuisance is not a complete defense, but only one factor to consider along with the others. That portion of the injunction prohibiting loud noise and crowds greater than appellants' property can accommodate is upheld.

The injunction is affirmed as modified.

Case Questions

1. What test was used by the court to determine whether the rock music events at the plaza constituted a nuisance?
2. If the shopping center was there before the apartments were built, does the shopping center have the right to continue using the property as it did previously?

Zoning and Development Restrictions

Local governments have **police power**, the power to impose reasonable regulations that promote the public health, safety, morals, and general welfare of their community. *Zoning ordinances* are laws that restrict the use of real property in furtherance of these objectives. Such ordinances generally regulate the structure, size, and design of buildings, the density of population, the size of lots, the setback requirements for the placing of buildings, aesthetics, and the use of property for commercial, residential, or industrial purposes.

Many local governments also have ordinances that impose regulations on the development of vacant real property within their jurisdiction. For example, sewer and water requirements must be met and street or road plans must be approved before any development can begin. In some cases, open spaces must be set aside by real estate developers for use as parks and public facilities. Some large planned developments have been allowed to combine various uses of the entire property, such as residential and commercial uses, in one area despite the limitations that zoning ordinances impose in other areas. Such developments are known as *planned unit developments (puds)*. As people have become more aware of the limitations of land use controls at the local level, there has been a trend to move some of these legal controls to the regional or state level.

Enforcement of Private Restrictions

A private agreement limiting the use of real property is called a *restrictive covenant.* Such covenants are usually written directly into the deeds to properties when these are sold by the real estate developer so that purchasers of properties in a development are bound to the consistent use of the properties. Thus, purchasers of any parcel of property will receive a deed requiring them to abide by the restrictions imposed for the benefit of the owners of the remaining properties in the development. For example, a deed may require that all garages be attached to houses or that all buildings on lots be set back a stipulated distance from lot lines.

Restrictive covenants generally *run with the land.* This means that the restrictions are imposed on whoever buys the land and are not canceled by its sale. Restrictive covenants commonly require that houses built on property be at least a certain size and limit the use of property to residential purposes. Thus, restrictive covenants are often similar to zoning regulations in the limits that they impose on the owners of property.

However, because restrictions originate from an owner of private property and limit the use of property by other owners, they are not favored by the law. Nevertheless, they are generally enforced if they benefit the other property owners whom they were intended to benefit. At one time, some deeds contained restrictions prohibiting persons of certain races from owning the deeded property. A 1947 U.S. Supreme Court decision made such restrictions unenforceable. The *Jayno* case, which follows, concerns the enforcement of a restrictive covenant. How did the court determine whether to enforce this private agreement or a public policy? Did the dissenting judge disagree with the majority regarding the application of the restriction in question to the subject property?

Jayno Heights Landowners Association v. Preston

271 N.W.2d 268 (1978)
Michigan Court of Appeals

On land that he owned in the Jayno Heights subdivision, Preston built a house that he leased to others who used it as a residence for elderly women. A restrictive covenant in all deeds to property in the subdivision limited the use of the property to single family residences. Jayno Heights sued Preston, claiming the property was not being used by a "family." A state statute, however, provides that six or fewer persons in a residential care facility is a residential use of property for zoning purposes. The trial court upheld the validity of the deed restriction and found that the occupants of the house were not a family unit. Preston appealed to the Court of Appeals.

J. H. Gillis, Judge

"The word 'family' is one of great flexibility. In *Carmichael v. Northwestern,*" it was said by Chief Justice Graves, speaking for the Court:

> "Now this word 'family,' contained in the statute, it is an expression of great flexibility. It is applied in many ways. It may mean the husband and wife having no children and living alone together, or it may mean . . . any group constituting a distinct domestic or social body."
>
> "We discover nothing in the statute implying a narrow sense, and we should not be inclined to attribute one where the result would cause injustice." *Boston-Edison Protective Association v. The Paulist Fathers, Inc.*

However, *Boston-Edison* and its definition of family does not apply here. The restrictive covenant in the instant case specifically limits the occupation of the residence to not more than one single family unit. The restrictive covenant in *Boston-Edison* is silent in respect to who shall occupy the dwelling.

Moreover, the dwelling at issue in the instant case is being used for commercial purposes while the Paulist Fathers in *Boston-Edison* made no commercial use of their residence. There is nothing in the record to indicate that the residents of the property at issue are anything more than a group of unrelated individuals sharing a common roof. Accordingly, we cannot conclude that the property in this case is being used by a single family unit.

Defendants also argue that public policy forbids the enforcement of the restrictive covenant. Defendants direct us to the recent change in the township zoning act which defines adult foster care facilities as single family residences for purposes of zoning ordinances. While this statute certainly expresses public policy, the Michigan Supreme Court has held that definitions employed in housing codes and zoning ordinances do not control the interpretation of restrictive covenants. In addition, the township zoning act is expressly directed towards zoning restrictions, not private restrictive covenants.

A careful reading of the statute reveals that the Legislature did not intend to impinge upon the enforcement of private deed restrictions. Private deed restrictions are contractual rights and should not be impaired by state legislative action absent the lawful exercise of the police power.

We find no such exercise of the police power by the Legislature in respect to private restrictive covenants. We also note that private residential restrictions, if established by proper instruments, are favored by public policy.

This Court does not believe that the public policy in favor of providing adult foster care facilities, under the facts of this case, outweighs the public policy favoring the rights of property owners to restrict the use of their property to single family dwellings occupied by single family units.

McGregor, Judge (Dissenting)

The *Bellarmine* Court described the policy conflict between enforcing the covenant and permitting the described use of the property before reaching the basis of its decision.

> "Unquestionably, promoting the development and maintenance of quality programs and facilities for the care and treatment of the mentally handicapped is a settled public policy of our state. That policy has both a constitutional and legislative foundation. But we must also recognize that restrictive covenants may constitute valuable property rights. Further, it has been the policy of our judiciary to protect property owners who have complied with the restrictions from violations of the covenants by others."

I would conclude that six unrelated elderly women residing together in an adult foster care facility constitute "one single family unit" within the meaning of the restrictive covenant in question. The basis of affiliation of these elderly women is their mutual need for foster care. By providing these services in a small dwelling in a residential community, defendants are preserving for their patients many of the benefits of family life which are absent in more institutionalized settings. There is a powerful public policy which supports this use of the property. For these reasons, the use of defendant Preston's home as an adult foster care facility should be permitted.

In applying with the utmost caution the principle that restrictive covenants which violate public policy may not be enforced, I would find that the public policy favoring the establishment of residential adult foster care facilities outweighs the policy supporting the enforcement of residential restrictive covenants and that the covenant in question may not be enforced to enjoin defendants' use of this property as a licensed foster care facility.

Case Questions

1. What key provision in the deed was in question here?
2. Which legal policies conflicted in this case, and how did the court resolve the conflicts?
3. Who benefits from a restrictive covenant in a deed?

The Power of Eminent Domain

Eminent domain is the power of the government to take private property without the owner's consent. There is clear constitutional authority for acquisitions of private property by the government—including federal, state, and local units and even private corporations that have been delegated this power by the appropriate government. However, several limitations are imposed on the exercise of eminent domain.

First, the property must be taken for a public purpose. Clearly, this requirement is met if the property is needed for the building of a school, a new road, or a prison facility. Second, the property owner must be adequately compensated. This requirement is a firm component of the concept of eminent domain in the United States, though not in some other countries. Third, the property owner is entitled to due process of law before the property is taken. Thus, a hearing regarding the need for the property and the adequacy of the compensation must be held prior to its taking. Finally, the government may be considered to have "taken" privately owned property if it imposes significant limitations on the uses of that property. In such a case, the owner will be entitled to compensation for that taking.

SUMMARY

The law defines property as a bundle of rights. These rights are recognized and enforced by law when other people interfere with the owner's use or enjoyment of property. For example, the due process clauses of the U.S. Constitution's 5th and 14th Amendments protect people from governmental action that would deprive them of property without due process.

Property can be classified as real or personal, usually based on whether it is attached to land or movable. Although fixtures may have originally been personal property, permanently attaching them to real property transforms them into real property. Both tangible objects and intangible rights are recognized as property. Copyrights, trademarks, patents, and trade secrets are types of intellectual property. The first three are generally protected by federal registration and some treaties provide means for intellectual protection. The common law offers some protection for copyrights, trademarks, and trade secrets.

Because law sometimes grants special protection to property, the courts must determine what constitutes an interest in property. In some situations, rights to governmental benefits or job security may be recognized as intangible property.

The transfer of personal property may create a bailment or constitute a delivery of title. A bailment transfers only possession and custody to the bailee, whereas a delivery of title transfers ownership. Title to personal property may be transferred by sale or gift; a gift may be made during life or after death.

Both possessory and nonpossessory interests in real estate are recognized. A lease agreement creates a possessory interest in real property. Frequently, the lessee or tenant is prohibited from transferring all of his or her possessory rights through an assignment. A sublease differs from an assignment because in a sublease the transferor keeps some rights. A subtenant's rights are based on the sublease agreement, not on the rights of the lease.

Easements, licenses, and liens are nonpossessory interests in real property. An easement usually runs with the land and gives its owner the right to perform specific activities on someone else's real property. A license permits someone to perform an activity on another's real property; unlike easements, licenses are personal in nature and are not automatically transferred to other parties. A lien provides a security interest in property for a mortgage lender; such liens as the mechanic's lien can exist in personal property.

Co-ownership of personal property may take several forms. The joint tenancy, tenancy in common, and community property methods of sharing real property provide different rights to co-owners. Condominium and cooperative ownership of real property provide methods for individually owning or possessing specific space while sharing ownership of common areas.

The sales contract is the basic document governing the sale of real estate. A deed, usually a warranty deed, actually transfers title to property, while a mortgage protects the interest of the lender of some or all of the property's purchase price. All documents transferring interests in real estate must be recorded to indicate to third parties the owner's interests in the property.

Real property is subject to control from both common law and regulatory statutes or ordinances. Nuisance laws and zoning restrictions regulate the use of real property so that it is consistent with the uses of other property. Although private restrictions on real property are not favored by the law, reasonable restrictive covenants are enforceable. Upon payment of adequate compensation, government may exercise its power of eminent domain and take private property for a public purpose.

KEY TERMS

property, p. 178
property interest, p. 178
real property, p. 178
tangible property, p. 179
fixtures, p. 179
goods, p. 179
intangible property, p. 180
intellectual property, p. 181
computer crime, p. 192
bailment, p. 194
mortgage, p. 199
police power, p. 204

CHAPTER EXERCISES

1. Apply the chapter's information on intellectual property to the software industry. Compare and contrast copyright protection and patent protection for software. What arguments could you make supporting the position that, for protecting the software industry and the public, trade secret protection may have greater advantages than copyright or patent protection?
2. Five years after graduation, you decide to purchase your first home. List the legal documents that you will review and sign as part of the purchase of real estate.
3. John signed a contract to purchase a home from Bill. When John took possession of the property, he noticed that Bill had removed several antique lighting fixtures, a built-in double self-cleaning oven, a furnace, and planter boxes on the deck. If the contract was silent as to who was entitled to these items, who would win if John sued Bill for their return? Why?
4. Allen, Bob, and Charles own a piece of real estate as joint tenants with right of survivorship. What would be the result if Charles transferred his interest to Don? How would Allen, Bob, and Don now concurrently own this property?
5. Jane and Joe were business partners who owned real estate as joint tenants and not as tenants in common. At the time of Jane's death, a dispute arose between her heirs and Joe as to who owned her half interest in the property. Who is entitled to the property interest that she had? Explain.
6. A residential developer owned property that fronted a small pond and property just across the street. All of the property was developed except for one front lot on the pond that was used as a means of access to the pond for property owners across the street. What is the best way for the property owners across the street to gain access to the pond if the remaining front lot is sold?
7. Although delivery to the grantee of a valid deed to real estate normally transfers title between the grantor and the grantee, the deed should also be recorded in the county where the real estate is located. Why?
8. Beard owned an apartment building and leased an apartment to Frances. Subsequently, Frances sublet the apartment to Jane and went on a long vacation. Beard then began eviction proceedings because the landlord-tenant document prohibited subletting the apartment. Is there a difference between the rights under a sublease and the rights under an assignment? May a landlord prohibit a sublease?
9. The California Portland Cement Company manufactures cement in a plant built on land that it has owned for 20 years. When the company bought the land and built the plant, the surrounding land was vacant and unimproved. Colbert, who owns land near the plant on which he lives and raises citrus crops, files suit to have the plant enjoined as a nuisance because of the dust and smoke that it produced. Is he entitled to an injunction? (*Hulbert*

v. California Portland Cement Co., 118 P. 928, 1911)

10. Carl purchased two adjoining lots. A restrictive covenant accompanying the sale of the lots stated that "no lot shall be used for a nonresidential purpose." On one of the lots, Carl constructed a large garage in which he refurbished expensive classic cars. Did construction of the garage violate the restrictive covenant? Who can enforce the covenant?

11. With the phenomenal growth rate of computer technology, it is not surprising that this industry is also the most controversial area of property law. Most software packages are protected by a copyright. Most software companies also place a lock on the program to prevent its duplication. Usually, however, someone, or some company, finds a way to unlock the program shortly after it hits the market. There are legitimate companies that design software that helps duplicate copyrighted packages. However, such duplication may be illegal as a violation of copyright laws and counterproductive, since it reduces the profitability of designing new programs.

People may rationalize the duplication of software because of the high prices charged for it. What they do not consider is the time and money spent in designing the software. The illegal duplication of software actually increases its price because its developers know that the sales (and profit) of duplicated software will dramatically decline. Thus, software companies must artificially inflate the price charged to the legitimate buyer to make a profit on the sale of fewer products. With the profit incentive taken out of software development, the industry may become stagnant. By purchasing a legitimate software package you are not only obeying the law but you are also promoting the development of new and improved packages.

Are consumers willing to give up the development of new and better products in order to get current ones cheaper? Is the software company that circumvents copyright protection of other companies acting ethically?

Chapter 8

CONTRACTS

KEY CONCEPTS

Contracts are the basis for most business relationships. Valid and enforceable agreements require: (1) genuine mutual assent, (2) legal contractual capacity, (3) consideration supporting the parties' promises, and (4) a legal contractual purpose.

Mutual assent of the parties exists when a valid, definite, and intentional offer is communicated by the offeror and accepted by the offeree. The acceptance must usually mirror the offered terms, though minor differences may exist in the sale of goods.

Contracts must be supported by consideration or have a legal substitute, such as promissory estoppel. Consideration separates idle, unimportant, or social promises from the more serious ones that deserve legal enforcement because people expect to rely on them.

Some contracts may be voidable by one party because the law protects minors, drunken, drugged, and insane persons. Victims of coercive negotiations may rescind their contracts due to mistake, misrepresentation, fraud, duress, undue influence, or unknown illegality.

Generally contracts need not be in writing unless they involve the sale of land, guarantee the debt of another, must last more than one year, or involve the sale of $500 or more of goods. Evidence that would modify written contract terms may be excluded from trial.

Outside third parties may have rights in the contracts of others if these parties are intended to benefit by the contracts or receive their rights by way of assignment. The assignment of contract rights or delegation of contract duties is usually permissible unless the transfer would materially change the expected performance.

INTRODUCTION . . . PAST, PRESENT, FUTURE

Modern contract law has its origins in the evolution of common law court decisions. As early as the ancient Egyptians, contract-like devices were recognized. However, the early English law perceived no need to enforce promises, holding persons liable only for defective performances. Modern contract law developed later as a result of the theory of laissez-faire capitalism, which coincided with the industrial revolution. The growing number of transactions and the physical remoteness of contracting parties dictated the need for greater certainty in commercial transactions. The U.S. Constitution expresses libertarian ideals that emphasizes individual free will, as in such provisions as the contract clause, discussed in Chapter 5, which limits states from interfering with existing contracts. When these ideals are applied to commercial contracts, they create the freedom of contract principle. Today, parties are not completely free to contract for anything, particularly illegal objectives. However, freedom of contract encourages free enterprise by increasing the certainty of the parties' expectations, permitting better planning.

The common law of contracts is collected and rephrased by legal scholars into a compilation known as the *Restatement (Second) of Contracts.* Many courts cite the *Restatement* as if it were legislation. Today, the contract law of most states has evolved into a combination of common law precedents, the *Restatement,* and statutory contract law.

The most important statutory law of contracts is the Uniform Commercial Code (UCC). The UCC governs many types of contracts and now applies in all states. The UCC is based on the **law merchant**, which evolved from the trading practices and conventions adopted by European merchants during the Middle Ages. The UCC Article 2 governs contracts for the sale of goods and has other provisions applicable to specialized transactions indicated in Figure 8–1. The UCC holds commercial parties to a higher level of duty than consumers. Commercial parties are known as *merchants* if they "deal in goods of the kind" or provide services as expert agents.

In the future, contract law is likely to evolve from inflexible requirements to reflect real-world business practices; the UCC is a prime example of this trend. The law will need to respond to the mechanization of commercial contracting through computer communications, a process known as electronic data interchange (EDI). For example, parties will adopt common contract terms and use electronic communications of offer and acceptance. The rule of consideration may be further weakened as the courts recognize that the parties to contracts are in the best position to know how serious their expectations are. The rights of incapacitants may be further eroded as minors become more sophisticated.

In the future, many more contract disputes will be resolved by alternative dispute resolution, particularly arbitration, now commonly used in international contracts. There will be an increase in regulation of consumer contract problems, which are discussed in Chapters 10 and 11. However, the need for greater trust and good faith by commercial parties, perhaps reducing contract formalities, may lead to emulation of Japanese contracting conventions. This would permit the discipline of the market to replace some aspects of legal enforcement.

INTERNATIONAL PERSPECTIVES: THE VARIOUS CONCEPTIONS OF "CONTRACT"

Contract law varies, often quite widely, between nations and even among their political subdivisions, states, or provinces. Although international custom has influenced national laws somewhat toward uniformity, there are often some fundamental differences in each nation's historical

Figure 8–1
Uniform Commercial Code (UCC)

Article Number	Title	Coverage
1	General Provisions	Definitions common to the whole UCC
2	Sales	Contract rules for sales of goods
2A	Leases	Contract rules for leases of goods
3	Commercial Paper	Negotiations & transfer of checks, notes, drafts, & certificates of deposit
4	Bank Deposits & Collections	Relationships between banks & depositors; collection process for commercial paper
4A	Funds Transfers	Relationships among commercial entities & banks in processing funds transfers by wire [electronic funds transfers for consumers is governed by federal law]
5	Letters of Credit	Parties' obligations & process for using letters of credit to finance international sales of goods
6	Bulk Transfers	Notice & protection of creditors from merchant selling all inventory & absconding with sale proceeds
7	Warehouse Receipts Bills of Lading, Documents of Title	Negotiation & transfer process for evidence of title to goods in transit or storage
8	Investment Securities	Negotiation & transfer of investment securities (e.g., stock, bonds)
9	Secured Transactions	Creation & enforcement of liens on goods; priorities among secured creditors

and cultural view of commercial transactions. International commercial law reflects concern over the heightened risk affecting cross-border transactions, the arbitrary and protectionist intervention of some governments, foreign currency fluctuations, and the greater physical distances involved. Details of international commercial transactions are discussed further in Chapter 21, including a discussion of the specialized documents used, international contract law, and the problems of performance.

Certainty in international transactions is complicated because there are varying approaches to contracting that reflect different legal systems: (1) the common law system applicable in the United States and some nations of the former British empire, (2) the civil law system applicable in nations with a European continental heritage, (3) Islamic law, (4) socialist law, and (5) law in developing countries. Each system has unique cultural, political, and historical differences that impact contract duties, formation, performance, and expectations. For example, uncertainties will probably increase in dealings with Eastern bloc nations as they evolve away from the socialist system. Socialist theory has been antagonistic to profit, contracts have been made exclusively with highly bureaucratic foreign government agencies, written contracts are always necessary, and terms must be exhaustively specified, particularly the price term. Socialist governments were inflexible about supplementing vague contracts with trade customs or "market prices." These practices are changing as socialist nations embrace democracy and capitalism. Civil law nations fill in contract gaps with statutory terms common to all contracts, a concept embraced by the UCC in the United States.

Trade between developing countries (LDCs) and industrialized nations reflects the LDCs' disadvantage in bargaining power and less developed legal systems. The United Nations' Vienna Convention for the International Sale of Goods (CISG), discussed further in Chapter 21, reflects the LDCs' concerns over these problems. Dealings between firms in LDCs and developed nations raise ethical concerns because contracts are negotiated with foreign government officials. In some cases, foreign officials have expected special favors before granting business to companies from other nations. Concern over these practices led the United States to adopt the Foreign Corrupt Practices Act (FCPA) to prohibit U.S. firms from making corrupt payments. The FCPA is discussed in Chapter 22.

Dealings between U.S. and Japanese companies stand in contrast to contracts with LDCs or socialist nations. The Japanese hold dear long-term relations built on trust, long-term commitment, and superior performance. They do not rush into contracts with foreign firms. Instead, Japanese firms rely on a drawn-out negotiation focusing on the prospects for harmonious future relations rather than on the favorability of particular terms, such as price. Extensive socializing is used in Japan to probe the intentions of another firm's representatives before a deal is finalized. This practice appears extremely time-consuming to the more impatient American contract negotiators. However, sound relationships of trust and "saving face" are essential to successful business dealings with the Japanese. Today, most nations' international commercial contracts seek to foresee and resolve disputes with a choice of law provision or with binding international arbitration. By contrast, the Japanese prefer to solidify relationships between firms and resolve disputes through consensus. They do not welcome the intrusion of an outside arbitrator or the embarrassing visibility of public adversariness.

OVERVIEW

This chapter examines the formation and performance of contracts by discussing the events and conditions affecting their validity. First, contracts are classified according to several criteria. Next, the analytic steps that determine the existence of a contract are covered. The four following sections discuss problems affecting the validity of contracts and the agreement process: lack of consideration, incapacity, misrepresentation, mistake, duress, and illegality. Then, the need for contracts to be made in writing and the effects of the written terms are discussed. This is followed by an exploration of the rights of third parties who may benefit by the contracts of others or whose contract rights or duties are transferred from others. Finally, problems arising during the performance or breach of contracts are discussed.

IMPORTANCE OF CONTRACT LAW

Contracts are the most basic of all business relationships. All sales of personal property, real estate, services, and employment result from contracts. The interactions of businesses with suppliers, customers, and employees are all based on various contracts for services, sales of land, and sales of goods. Even less formal relations that many college students encounter are contracts. For example, the following involve enforceable contracts whether or not they are in writing: dormitory and food service agreements, apartment leases, textbook purchases and sales, party commitments such as hiring a band or DJ, charitable fundraisers, student organization sponsored events such as plant tours or office visits, and outside speaker engagements. Contracts are intangible relationships among parties that provide for enforceable duties that the parties voluntarily assume. Many contracts are put into written documents to provide evidence of such relationships. There is no tangible "contract," however, but only the legally enforceable rights resulting from the agreements of parties. A *contract* may be defined as an enforceable set of mutual obligations for which the law provides a remedy, recognizes a duty, or provides for court enforcement.

Contracts are enforced so that commerce may proceed in an orderly fashion. If businesses could not rely on their reasonable expectations that contracts will be performed, commerce might be reduced and it would become less stable. In such an uncertain world, only face-to-face agreements could be made with reasonable certainty and many agreements would be breached. Because contracts create legally enforceable obligations, businesses may plan for future purchases, production, and sales. Contracts assure business a reasonable remedy when an obligation is breached. Such commercial disputes comprise a rising proportion of the current boom in litigation.

CLASSIFICATION OF CONTRACTS

Contracts are classified in several ways. *Express contracts* arise from the parties' outward expressions of mutual assent (either oral or written statements or gestures). *Implied in fact contracts* are inferred from the parties' actions. For example, a written employment agreement is an express contract, whereas the contract between a taxi driver and a passenger is implied. Contracts implied in law are quasi contracts, discussed later in this section.

Bilateral contracts exist where there are two promises, one from each party. A *unilateral contract* arises where one of the parties does not look for a return promise but instead asks for the other party's actual performance. For example, a reward poster is an offer to enter into a unilateral contract; the offeror of the reward promises to pay if some other party provides the information sought. The other party does not accept the reward contract by promising to provide the needed information but instead accepts the reward offer by performing the act of providing information. Section 2–206 of the UCC permits both bilateral and unilateral contracts. It permits acceptance of an order (offer) with either a prompt promise to ship or a prompt shipment of goods that conform to the order's specifications. Most contracts are bilateral.

A *valid contract* is completely enforceable by either party if it meets all of the necessary legal requirements; a *void contract* is invalid and unenforceable. A void contract arises when a contract has an illegal objective or when one party is adjudged to have been insane or incompetent before contracting. A *voidable contract* allows one or both of the parties to rescind or cancel because of a problem such as incapacity, fraud, misrepresentation, duress, undue influence, or mistake. *Executed contracts* are contracts that have been fully performed by both parties. *Executory contracts* are those in which some duties are not yet performed.

The original author of a contract proposal or offer is the *offeror*. The person to whom the offer is made is the *offeree*. Only the offeree may create a binding contract by communicating an acceptance. Because a bilateral contract contains at least one promise from each party, each party is a *promisor*, a maker of each promise. As a result of making contractual promises, each party owes a duty to the other party as an *obligor*. Of course, each party is also the recipient of the other party's promise, so each promisor is also a *promisee*. Usually, each party is also an *obligee* to whom the duty or obligation is owed unless the rights of third parties are involved.

Contracts Implied in Law

A **quasi contract**, though not a real contract, is treated like a contract for many purposes. Quasi-contractual agreements do not arise from agreements between the parties. Instead, certain obligations are *implied-in-law* under special circumstances. If one of the parties is *unjustly enriched* because the other party *confers benefits*, then quasi-contractual liability may arise. A quasi contract frequently occurs where a benefit is conferred accidentally and the recipient could have prevented the mistake. Quasi-contractual liability may also arise in an emergency, such as one in which a doctor supplies lifesaving services to an unconscious victim. In situations of this kind, even though there is no actual agreement and thus no actual contractual liability arises, the courts often require that compensation be paid because it is unjust to receive benefits without paying for them. For example, suppose that an adult knowingly permits a neighborhood child to cut the adult's lawn by mistake. Although there is no contract for the child's services, it would be unjust for the adult to keep the benefits without paying if the adult could have prevented the work.

MUTUAL ASSENT: THE AGREEMENT

Before a bilateral contract arises, the parties must agree to the contract's terms, a step known as *mutual assent*. In most cases, the parties begin preliminary negotiations of the contract by communicating their expectations about the terms. For example, an advertisement or the initial sales pitch of a salesperson may start the negotiations. The contract terms usually include an identification of the parties, an adequate description of the subject matter, the price (i.e., the cash, property, or services) to be exchanged, the quantity of the property or services, the time for the parties to perform their obligations, and any other key terms (e.g., credit terms, warranties). These early communications may be in the form of offers and counteroffers, or they may be merely informational.

A fine line distinguishes informational communications from the operative contracting communications of offer, acceptance, revocation, or rejection. This distinction is based on the **objective theory of contracts**, which holds that the reasonable interpretation of the parties' communications, as they would appear to an objective observer, determines whether an offer has been made, accepted, or terminated. The following subsections explain and exemplify how to identify the five operative contracting communications: offer, counteroffer, acceptance, revocation, and rejection. Keep in mind that ordinary communications merely convey information; they do not make or destroy a binding contract. By contrast, contracts are created or destroyed by the five operative contracting communications because these fall within the objective theory of contracts. Figure 8–2 depicts the communications possible between parties A and B.

Offer

An *offer* is a proposal to contract that contains all of the necessary contract terms. The proposal must be intended by the offeror to confer a power of acceptance on the offeree. It becomes effective when communicated to the offeree. The offer is usually made in an oral or written manner, but occasionally it can be communicated by gestures, such as the bids made in auctions.

Objective Theory of Contracts All expressions of the contracting parties are judged by how a reasonable person would respond. If a reasonable person would conclude that the offeror's communications were clearly intended to confer a power of acceptance on the offeree and the offeree need only accept to create a contract, then the offeror's statement is a legal offer. The offeror's hidden intent or secret hesitation is irrelevant if the average reasonable person would believe that the offeror intended to make an offer.

The objective theory of contracts applies to all communications between parties, including offers, counteroffers, acceptances, revocations, rejections, preliminary negotiations, and inquiries regarding terms. Thereby, what is apparent to a reasonable person,

FIGURE 8–2 Potential Communications between Contractors

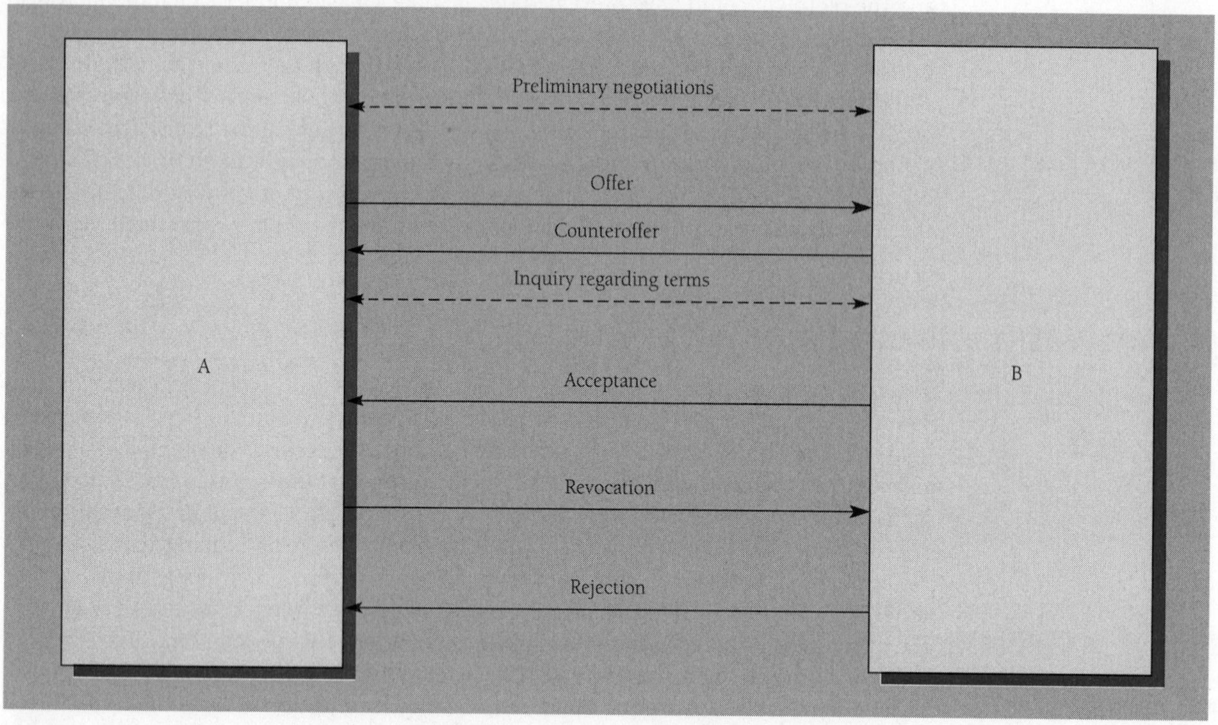

After preliminary negotiations, there are five possible types of operative contracting communications. The offer confers a power of acceptance on the offeree. An acceptance exercises that power, creating a contract. A revocation or rejection terminates the power of acceptance, so that no contract results. Like preliminary negotiations, the offeree's inquiry regarding terms does not affect the power of contracting; it only transfers information. A counteroffer rejects the offer and substitutes a different offer.

and not the subjective or innermost thoughts or intentions of the offeror, determines the existence of an offer. For example, an emotional person may make a proposal, but only in jest. Such a proposal might be an offer irrespective of the emotional person's intent if a reasonable person concludes that the offeror intended to make an offer.

Definite Terms Usually, a reasonable person will definitely express all or nearly all of the proposed contracts essential terms when making an offer. In some circumstances, however, the parties may assume that reasonable or customary terms should be included even if they are not expressed. Under UCC 2-204, for example, terms of a contract may be left open for future determination and later inferred from the circumstances. The contract will be enforced as long as a "reasonably certain basis" exists "for giving an appropriate remedy." For example, the price of goods may be determined later if the parties leave the price term open, if they say nothing about price, or if they intend to use the market price. In these cases, UCC 2-304 infers a reasonable price determined as of the time for delivery.

Preliminary Negotiations Problems may arise in interpreting whether business communications are really offers. Generally, advertisements for goods or services are intended to be merely invitations to deal; they are not actual offers. This is so because most reasonable persons would presume that advertisements, solicitation letters, catalogs, and price lists are intended merely to solicit the buyer's interest. These communications seldom confer a power of acceptance because most people expect to negotiate after receiving such information.

FIGURE 8–3 Offer and Acceptance

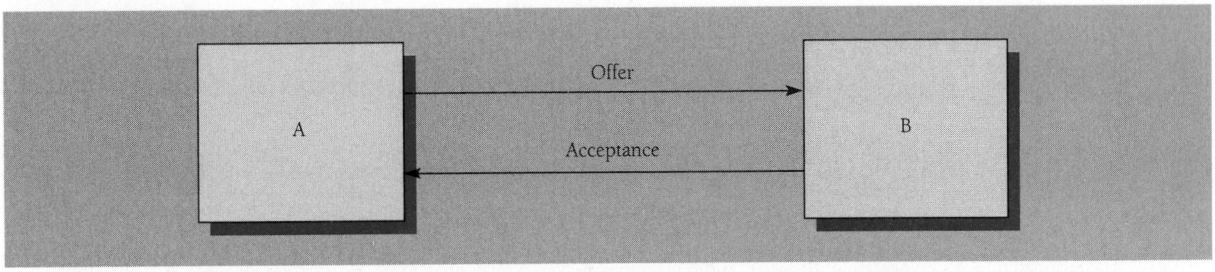

A's offer passes a power of acceptance to B, who exercises that power and a contract results when B dispatches an acceptance to A. For example, if A offers to purchase B's house and B mails an acceptance to A, an enforceable contract exists.

FIGURE 8–4 Counteroffer

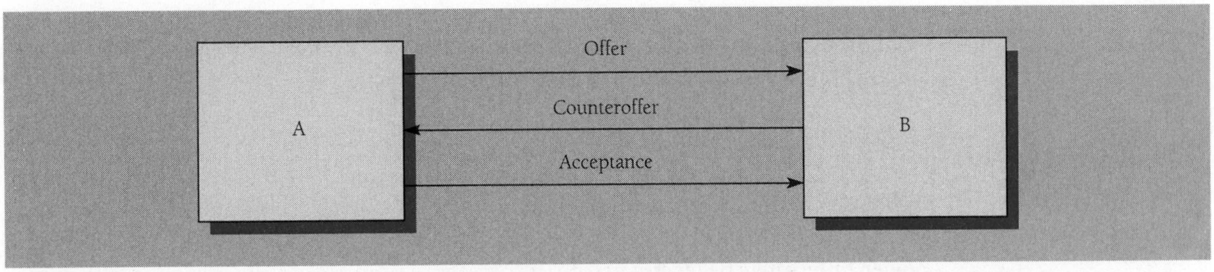

A's offer is terminated by B's counteroffer or conditional acceptance, but it extends a new offer to A. The contract results when A dispatches an acceptance in response to B's counteroffer. For example, if A offers to purchase B's house but B counteroffers at a higher price, then no contract exists until A accepts B's counteroffer.

If advertisements were routinely considered offers, many problems could arise because a contract might be created if the prospective purchaser merely accepted an advertisement. For example, many sellers would not be prepared with sufficient inventory if too many of these "offerees" responded to a particular advertisement. It is reasonable to assume that advertisers do not want this result so their advertisements are not offers, only preliminary negotiations. However, if the wording in an advertisement clearly indicates that it is an offer, the advertiser may be inviting immediate acceptance. For example, language such as "while they last" in an advertisement creates an offer.

Acceptance

For a contract to be formed, the offeree must accept the offer, as illustrated in Figure 8–3. A contract comes into existence when the offeree accepts the exact terms proposed. This results in an exact agreement, a *meeting of the minds*. In one form of negotiating, informal communications between the parties take place before either actually makes an offer. Later, a formal offer, containing all of the terms already acceptable to both parties, is made by one party and formally accepted by the other. Businesses often use this form when contracting with suppliers or commercial customers.

In another form of negotiating, the parties exchange several offers, none of which are accepted. Instead, each response to the previous offer is a *counteroffer*. Eventually, when one of the counteroffers is finally accepted, a contract results. This second form is used most often in sales of residential real estate and is illustrated in Figure 8–4.

FIGURE 8–5 Revoked Offer

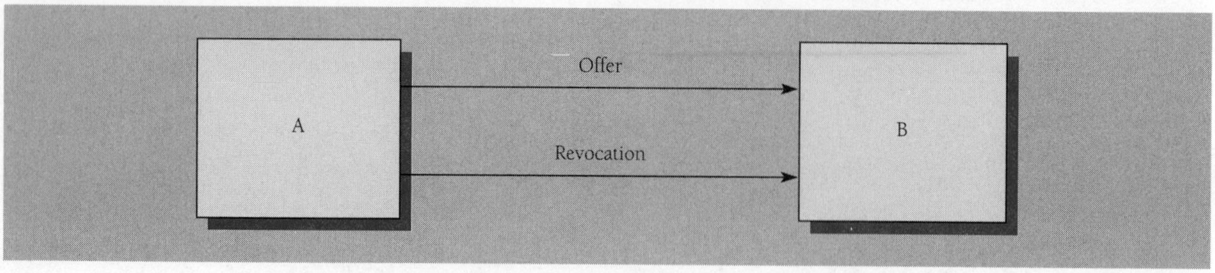

A's offer is terminated by A's revocation of the offer, and if made before B responds, no contract results. For example, if A offers to purchase B's house but has a change of heart before B responds, A may withdraw the offer by revocation and no contract result.

In either form of negotiating, a binding contract is formed when the last offer made is unconditionally accepted by the offeree. The *mirror-image rule* of contracts requires that the acceptance correspond in all respects to the terms proposed in the offer. Aside from the exception in UCC 2–207 discussed later, a contract may be formed only through an acceptance that exactly mirrors the offered terms.

Termination of Offers

As long as an offer remains open, the offeree is free to accept and create a contract. However, offers may be terminated, ending the offeree's ability to exercise the contracting power. Offers may be terminated by the passage of time, revocation, rejection, acceptance, the death of either party, or the destruction of the contract's subject matter.

Lapse of Time Offers do not confer a permanent power of acceptance. Offers are terminated by the passage of a reasonable time, a period that varies depending on the circumstances. In volatile markets, such as the stock, currency, or commodities markets, the reasonable duration of the offer is extremely short, perhaps just a matter of minutes. By contrast, in more stable markets, such as the real estate market, the reasonable duration of the offer may be measured in weeks or even months.

An offeror who wants the offer to terminate in an even shorter time may limit its duration. In such a case, the offer will lapse *under its terms* after the specified time passes. For example, prospective home buyers often specify that their offers are to lapse in a few hours or days. This tactic creates an imminency that may induce a reluctant seller to accept a lower price.

Revocation Usually, the offeror may withdraw an offer by the act of *revocation.* A revocation is expressed when the offeree hears directly from the offeror. However, a revocation may be implied, as when the offeree receives reliable knowledge that the offered property was sold to another person. Revocation is illustrated in Figure 8–5.

Option Contracts In some instances, an offeror may promise not to revoke an offer. Such *irrevocable offers* are useful, for example, when the offeree needs to expend significant sums to survey or research the subject matter before agreeing. If the offer is held open, the offeree has more time to study it without fear of losing the deal.

There are two ways to make an offer irrevocable: option contracts and firm offers. An **option contract** is formed when the offeree pays a price (consideration) for irrevocability. The option becomes a separate contractual commitment in which the offeror

FIGURE 8–6 Rejected Offer

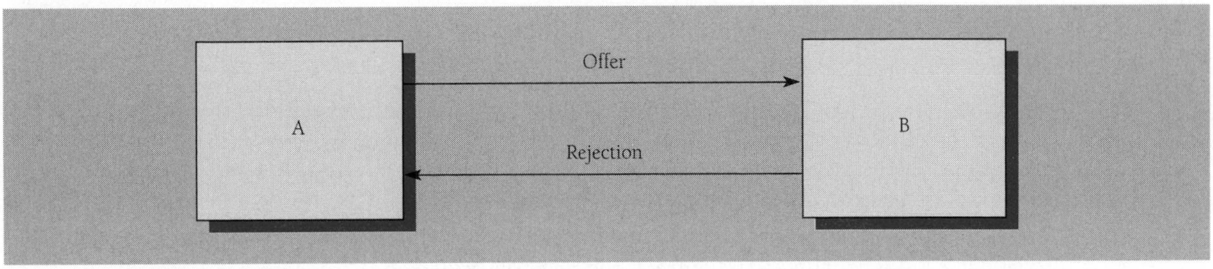

A's offer is terminated by B's rejection of the offer; no contract results. For example, if A offers to purchase B's house and B immediately rejects the offer, no contract results.

gives up the right to revoke. Under the UCC, a *firm offer* can result in an irrevocable offer even without payment of consideration. An offeror who revokes a firm offer or sells optioned property to another person will be liable for damages for breach of contract. For example, assume that in a signed writing a goods merchant makes an offer to sell a buyer 500 widgets at $30 each. If the merchant promises to keep the offer open for two weeks but then withdraws it the next day, the buyer may enforce the contract to get damages.

Firm Offer (UCC 2–205)

An offer made by "a merchant to buy or sell goods in a signed writing which by its terms gives assurance that it will be held open is not revocable . . . [even without consideration] during the time stated or . . . for a reasonable time, but in no event . . . [for longer than three months]."

[Note that some civil law nations require offers to stay open for a minimum period, such as three days.]

Rejection The offeree may respond to the offer by communicating a *rejection* that terminates the offeree's power of acceptance. Rejection is illustrated in Figure 8–6. However, an offeree's response to an offer may not be an unequivocal rejection. For example, the offeree, while stating that the offer is accepted, might attach additional or different conditions to the acceptance. This type of response is often called a *conditional acceptance.* If the offeree revises the offer in any way, then it is considered a *counteroffer.* Because both conditional acceptances and counteroffers show a lack of exact agreement between the offered terms and the allegedly "accepted" terms, they are considered rejections. Where deviations are found between the offered terms and the accepted terms, no contract results because the parties have failed to agree and have not arrived at a mirror-image meeting of their minds.

Mirror-Image Rule The requirement that the acceptance mirror the offered terms is known as the *mirror-image rule.* This common law rule applies to contracts for land sales, services, or employment. When parties correspond about a possible contract, how do they know when a binding contract arises? The following case illustrates the problem of obtaining an exact mirror image between offered and accepted terms.

J. Apablasa v. Merritt & Co.

1 Cal. Rept. 500 (1959)

The plaintiff and the defendants wrote three letters to each other concerning the marketing of the plaintiff's invention. On August 24, 1955, the defendants wrote the first letter to the plaintiff. The plaintiff responded to that letter with a response dated August 27, 1955. The defendants did not reply to the plaintiff's August 27 letter, so the plaintiff wrote to the defendants on September 20, 1955. The plaintiff alleged that the first and last letter constituted a contract; the defendants denied that a contract was formed by these communications.

Defendants' August 24 letter:

> "I think you have a very fine invention. Undoubtedly with the right design worked out for the various models, proper sales brochures, and a concentrated direct-sales effort, the returns should be most gratifying. I feel confident that 50,000 units at $50.00 each could be sold within the first year.
>
> "For us to work out the proper sales program and devote ourselves one hundred percent to the adaptability and perfection of various designs is, in itself, going to involve a great deal of time and money. I feel if the enterprise is going to be a success we should use all the money we have to develop and market the product, and pay you your fee out of the operating profits.
>
> "Should you decide to give us a try in merchandising and marketing the item, instead of the $50,000 cash you mentioned as your selling price, I should suggest $100,000 as a bonus payment to be paid from a fixed percentage of the earnings and when this has been paid, that you should receive a continuing graduated percentage of the profits thereafter.
>
> "Trusting something like this would be acceptable to you, and looking forward to hearing from you quite soon, I am
>
> "Sincerely yours,"

Plaintiff's August 27 letter:

> "After due consideration, and in view of my age and other circumstances, I would like to sell the invention outright as I have already expressed to you, possibly taking less down payment—$5,000 instead of $10,000 and the balance on or before five years to make up the $50,000, which I have no doubt would be fair to assume would be available from the profits.
>
> "I hope that within the different views we have expressed, something of mutual interest may be worked out."

Plaintiff's September 20 letter:

> "After careful consideration I have decided to accept your proposition as outlined in your letter to me of August 24th, 1955, with this proviso: that you agree to put this product in production within a definite period of time from the date of the signing of any agreement between us."

An analysis of the writing fails to disclose the definite terms necessary to constitute it an offer to manufacture or have manufactured, merchandise and market plaintiff's invention—for an offer must be certain and definite.

It is well settled that if the offer is so indefinite as to make it impossible for a court to decide just what it means, and to fix exactly the legal liability of the parties, its acceptance cannot result in an enforceable agreement. The letter, a definite rejection by defendants of the idea of an outright sale of the device and an invitation to consider their services in merchandising and marketing the same, omits any reference to manufacturing; indeed, nothing therein relates to how or by whom the article is to be produced; production cost and who shall bear the same; how raw materials, patterns, designs and samples will be supplied; in what manner plaintiff's invention and patent if one exists, shall be transferred and to whom; and when production is to begin. Likewise, as to the marketing of the item, absent is any reference to territory, whether distribution is to be exclusive, who is to set the price, and the minimum amount to be sold in what period of time. Relative to the $50 figure mentioned, it appears to be only a suggested possible sales price used as a basis for speculation as to within what time, how many, and at what amount the items could be sold; and far from fixing the selling price, the figure constitutes no more than an expression of opinion of what possible returns "could" be expected and what "could" be done if sufficient time and money are expended on a proper program. Nor is there mention of how much out of any established sales price defendants are to receive on each item for their services, and how much is to be paid plaintiff. The "suggested percentage" is exactly what it purports to be—a suggestion of what "could" be worked out in the future "should (plaintiff) decide to give (them) a try to merchandising and marketing the item." That this letter was by no means intended to constitute an offer is found in the last paragraph wherein defendants expressed their hopes that "*something like this*" would be acceptable to plaintiff. (Emphasis added.)

Herein plaintiff rejected consideration of any arrangement to market and merchandise his invention and professed interest only in its outright sale. Appellant does not dispute that defendants' August 24 letter relates only to marketing and merchandising; and it is obvious his reply actually proposes a plan altogether different than that suggested by defendants, revealing an absence of any meeting of the minds and complete lack of interest in any program excluding outright sale. At most his letter of August 27 amounted to no more than a counter-proposal by him rejecting any plan heretofore proposed by defendants.

Where a person offers to do a definite thing and another introduces a new term into the acceptance, his answer is a mere expression of willingness to treat or it is a counter-proposal, and in neither case is there a contract; if it is a new proposal and it is not accepted it amounts to nothing.

Case Questions

1. Did the defendants intend to confer a power of contracting on the plaintiff in the August 24 letter? What language in the August 24 letter indicates that the defendants had mental reservations?
2. What could have been the practical effects of the plaintiff's August 27 and September 20 letters?

UCC Battle of the Forms Commercial organizations often fail to adhere strictly to the mirror-image rule. In sales of goods contracts, there is often a "**battle of the forms.**" Buyers and sellers, with the aid of their attorneys, construct invoices, order forms, and confirmation forms containing very favorable terms for themselves. Inevitably, there are differences between terms found in the offer forms and the terms found in the acceptance forms. Minor differences usually go unnoticed unless a dispute arises. UCC 2–207 provides a more practical solution to this problem than the common-law mirror-image rule.

Additional Terms in Acceptance or Confirmation (UCC 2–207)

1. A definite and seasonable expression of acceptance or a written confirmation which is sent within a reasonable time operates as an acceptance even though it states terms additional to or different from those offered or agreed upon, unless acceptance is expressly made conditional on assent to the additional or different terms.
2. The additional terms are to be construed as proposals for addition to the contract. Between merchants such terms become part of the contract unless:
   (a) the offer expressly limits acceptance to the terms of the offer;
   (b) they materially alter it; or
   (c) notification of objection to them has already been given or is given within a reasonable time after notice of them is received.
3. Conduct by both parties which recognizes the existence of a contract is sufficient to establish a contract for sale although the writings of the parties do not otherwise establish a contract. In such case the terms of the particular contract consist of those terms on which the writings of the parties agree, together with any supplementary terms incorporated under any other provisions of this Act.

UCC 2–207 applies to forming a contract when there are only minor deviations between the parties' written documents in sales of goods. Slight differences between the offer and the acceptance do not always cause a contract to fail. A contract is formed if there are no material differences on key terms in the parties' communications, though either party may reimpose the mirror-image rule. Counteroffers are possible only if highly material terms are in dispute between the writings. *Highly material terms* include the terms essential to the contract: the identities of the parties, the price, the quantity, or the subject matter. For example, differences in the size, color, or grade of goods would be highly material, resulting in a counteroffer.

Material additions, deletions, or changes found in the acceptance or confirmation form do not destroy the contract, so the parties have a binding agreement. If different terms appear in the second communication, they are considered mere proposals to modify the contract that exists on the originally offered terms. Such proposals may be accepted or rejected by the offeror. *Material terms* are those that would cause surprise to either party, such as changes in standard warranty protection or customary credit terms.

When both of the parties are merchants, immaterial differences generally become part of the contract, as long as the offeror does not object. If the parties' conduct impliedly recognizes that the contract exists, then it is enforceable. In that case, the contract's terms are those on which the writings agree, together with other terms automatically supplied by the UCC. For example, a contract exists even if the parties' forms do not agree if the buyer pays for the goods or the seller delivers them.

Auctions

Auction sales present a problem of identifying which party is the offeror and which is the offeree. Under the common law of auction sales, the identities of the offeror and offeree are defined by the apparent intent of the parties. Sellers at an auction usually desire to retain the right to withdraw goods from the auction block if the bids are inadequate. In that case, the bids are considered offers and the auctioneer's final act of knocking down the goods to the highest bidder is the acceptance. Under UCC 2–328, an auction of this kind is called an *auction with reserve* because the seller is considered to reserve the right to withdraw goods from the auction block before final sale.

Of course, it is possible to switch the offeror-offeree designations in an auction, so that the bidder accepts the auctioneer's offer of the goods. Each higher bid replaces the previous bid as the acceptance until bidding stops and the contract is formed. An auction of this kind is called an *auction without reserve* because the auctioneer does not reserve the right to withdraw the goods after bidding starts. Auctions are usually with reserve unless the auction notice explicitly indicates otherwise. Auctions without reserve often draw bargain hunters who expect the goods to be sold even if only low bids are made.

The Parties' Communications

For one party's communications to confer, exercise, or terminate the power of acceptance, the communications must be intended to affect the power of contracting. Most of the communications between contracting parties are effective only when actually received. There is one exception—the *mailbox rule* of acceptances. Unless the offeror states otherwise, a *dispatch* occurs when the offeree has done everything that can be done to send off the acceptance. For example, a contract immediately comes into existence when the offeree drops a properly addressed, stamped letter of acceptance into a Postal Service mailbox. The acceptance is effective even if a rejection or revocation arrives before the

FIGURE 8–7 Mutual Promises

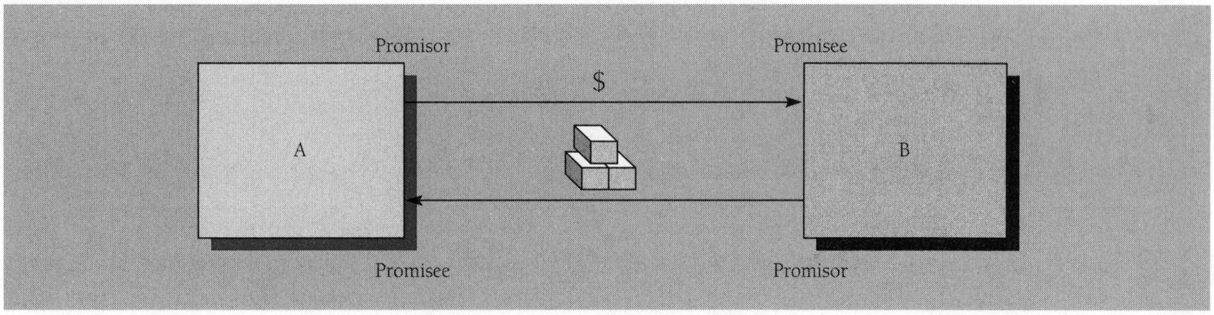

In the contract resulting from mutual assent between A and B (offer and acceptance), A promises to pay for goods that B promises to deliver. Each of them is a promisor and each a promisee on the two respective promises

acceptance arrives. However, if the offeree uses an unreasonable means of communication, the offeree's acceptance is effective only when received. In addition, the offeror may require actual receipt of the offeree's acceptance before the contract becomes effective. Acceptances are generally effective only upon receipt in civil law nations.

UCC 2–206 is more lenient than the mailbox rule; under that provision, absent an agreement to the contrary, an acceptance is effective if it is communicated by any means reasonable under the circumstances, if it is in common use, and if it is as fast as or faster than the means used by the offeror.

CONSIDERATION

The law does not enforce all agreements. There are two reasons why mutual promises must go beyond a certain minimum threshold to create a contract. First, many promises are made idly or lightly, with no intention of creating binding obligations. For example, promises to make a gift, to do a favor for another, or to participate in a social arrangement are considered less serious than business promises. Second, only sufficiently important cases should burden the judicial system. Although it might be socially desirable to rely on all promises, there must be some limit on the enforceability of promises, a limit corresponding to the seriousness and motivation of the promisor and the reasonableness of the promisee's expectations. These reasons justify the *consideration* requirement. Consideration distinguishes serious, enforceable promises from less serious and unenforceable promises. The rule of consideration, which requires that the parties mutually give value or make obligations, is the principal measure of the significance of promises. The mutual promises necessary for adequate consideration are illustrated in Figure 8–7.

Tests for the Presence of Consideration

Several tests are used to determine the presence of consideration. These tests are cast in terms of value, benefits, detriments, mutuality of obligation, and the exchange of promises. One common misconception is that the consideration requirement means that value must pass physically between the parties. There is a similar misconception that a real

FIGURE 8–8 Consideration: Detriments and Benefits

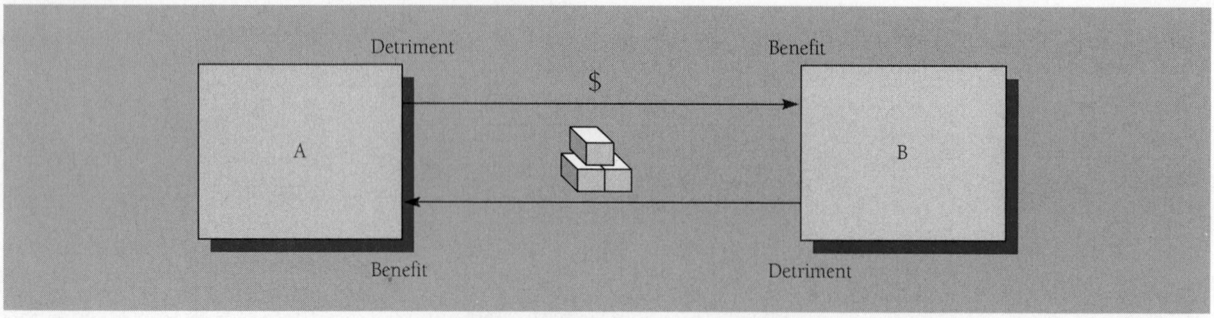

Consideration exists for a contract when the two parties exchange new promises. A promises to pay money to B because B promises to deliver goods to A, and B promises to deliver goods to A because A promises to pay money to B. A's promise to pay B for the goods that B delivers is a benefit to B and a detriment to A. B's promise to deliver goods to A is a benefit to A and a detriment to B.

detriment to the promisor and a real benefit to the promisee must occur. Although consideration generally exists if property or labor is exchanged, the consideration requirement is often satisfied with less, such as when the parties merely promise new things.

For the purposes of determining the presence of consideration, only *legal detriments* or *legal benefits* need be present in the promises. These legal measures of value do not require the exchange of real value. Instead, consideration is present if the parties make promises that obligate them in the future. A promise to do something new, something that the promisor was not previously obligated to do, is sufficient consideration to support a contract. A promise is quite different from the actual transfer of the property or services pledged in it. All that is necessary is that the promise create the legally binding obligation and satisfy the test for consideration. Promises alone have sufficient legal value to test an agreement's seriousness. Actual performance is not required to satisfy the consideration element.

A *forbearance* is a promise not to do something or to refrain from doing something; it also constitutes sufficient consideration. In the settlement of a dispute over an automobile accident, for example, the party at fault usually promises to pay money in exchange for the victim's promise to refrain from suing for damages. This explains why contracts to release a negligent driver are enforceable to prevent suit by the victim who accepts an insurance company settlement. The proper test of consideration is whether the parties make mutually binding new promises. Enforceable promises may be either promises to do something new or promises to refrain from doing something previously permissible. Both parties must change their legal obligations for consideration to exist as illustrated in Figure 8–8.

Mutuality of Obligation

The exchange element of consideration is a very important concept. Parties that exchange promises are more likely to intend to be legally bound. Each party makes a promise "on the condition" that the other party make an acceptable return promise. With few exceptions, the mutual or bilateral nature of the promises clearly indicates their seriousness and the parties' intent to be bound. Each party makes a promise "in consideration" of the other party's promise, so the promises are mutually given in exchange for each other. Each party is induced or motivated to promise something new because the other party

FIGURE 8–9 Consideration: Detriment to the Promisee

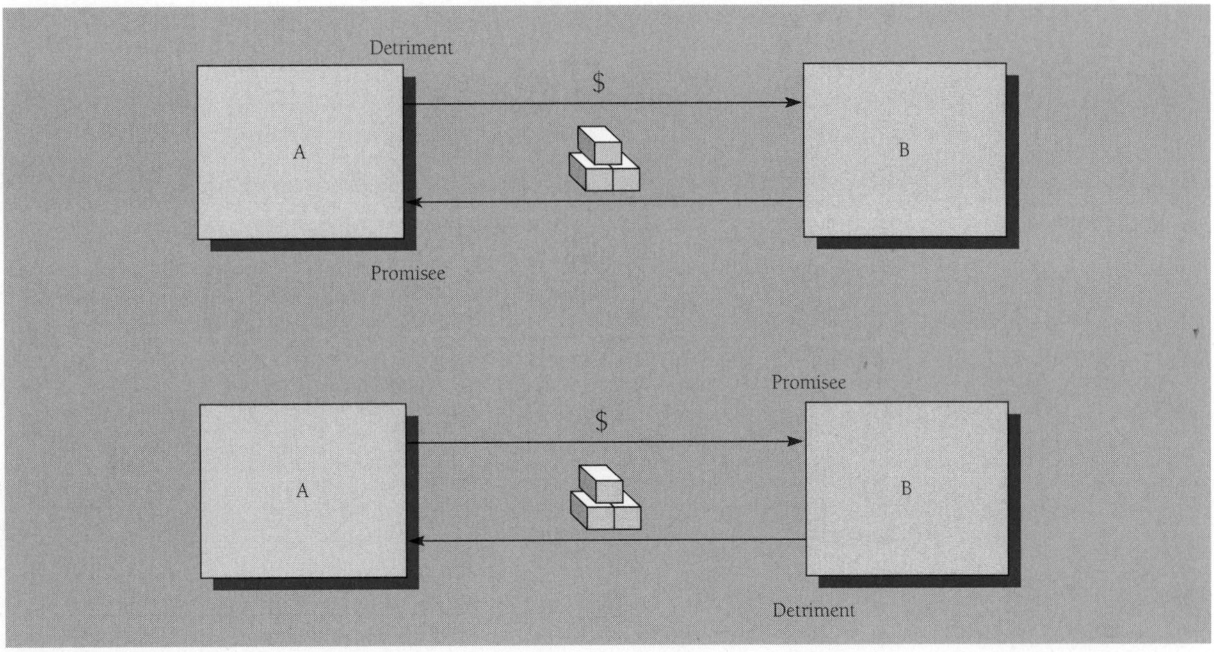

Consideration exists for the whole contract because, from A's perspective, there is a "detriment to the promisee." A's detriment is the promise to pay money to B, made in exchange for B's promise to deliver goods to A.

Consideration exists for the whole contract because, from B's perspective, there is a "detriment to the promisee." B's detriment is the promise to deliver goods to A, made in exchange for A's promise to pay money to B.

has made a new promise in return. Stated another way, each party's promise must be supported by the consideration found in the other party's counterpromise.

The classic formulation of consideration holds that there must be a legal *detriment to the promisee* or a legal *benefit to the promisor* when the promises of the parties are analyzed. Detriment to the promisee is illustrated in Figure 8–9, and benefit to the promisor is illustrated in Figure 8–10. Each of these efficient tests demonstrates that two promises have been made and that each party has given and received legal value. Another formulation holds that each party must consciously give legal value in an outgoing promise in return for the incoming promise. Still another formulation holds that consideration will exist whenever the offer and acceptance result in two new promises made in exchange for each other. Each formulation includes elements of legal value given for and legal value received from the conscious mutual exchange of interdependent promises. The theoretical nature of consideration need not pose great problems of interpretation or detection because the following situations indicate where consideration is usually absent.

Unenforceable Promises: Consideration is Lacking

In several common situations, consideration is found lacking, and the alleged agreement is therefore unenforceable. If either party's promise is subject to that party's wish, will, or desire, then the promise is *illusory.* For example, an unlimited right to cancel the contract permits the promisor to "back out" at any time. Such illusory promises are never binding, so these contracts lack consideration. However, if the cancellation right is limited,

FIGURE 8–10 Consideration: Benefit to the Promisor

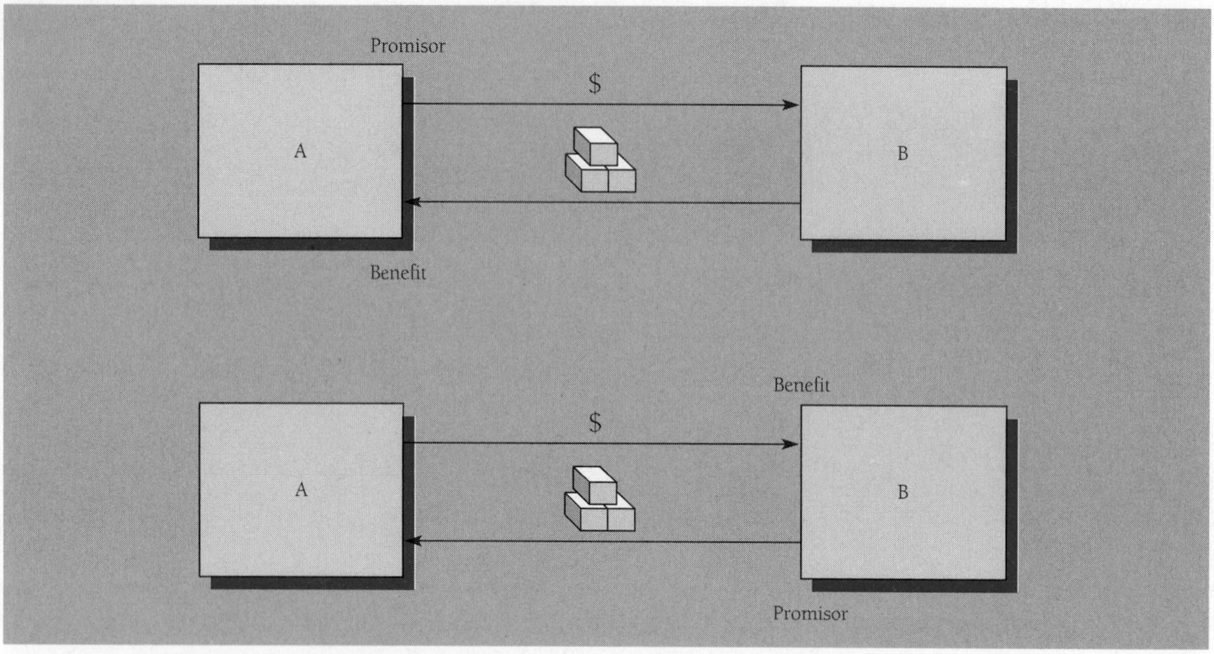

Consideration exists for the whole contract because, from A's perspective, there is a "benefit to the promisor." A's benefit is the expectation of receiving goods from B, made in exchange for A's promise to pay money to B.

Consideration exists for the whole contract because, from B's perspective, there is a "benefit to the promisor." B's benefit is the expectation of receiving payment from A, made in exchange for B's promise to deliver goods to A.

perhaps by requiring 30 days' notice before cancellation, then the promise provides good consideration.

If one party is already legally bound to perform an obligation and then simply repromises it, the second promise is merely stale repetition. There is nothing new given in exchange for the promisee's return promise. Since there is a **preexisting legal duty**, the promisor is already legally obligated to do or refrain from doing the activity repromised. In that case, consideration is lacking and a contract based on the restated promise is unenforceable. Thus, if a jockey under contract to ride a horse in the Kentucky Derby pressures the horse's owner for more pay when the odds become more favorable for the horse to win, the owner's promise to pay more is not supported by any new consideration. The jockey has a preexisting legal duty to ride in the Derby under the original contract terms.

There is sufficient consideration in an **accord and satisfaction** when a debtor agrees to settle a disputed or unliquidated debt. For example, a client may not have agreed to a doctor's or lawyer's price before the services were rendered, so the bill may be in dispute. By contrast, agreements to settle undisputed debts with the debtor promising to pay less are usually not supported by consideration because the debt amount is the debtor's preexisting legal duty. However, if the debtor promises to pay the amount sooner or in a different medium, then the creditor receives something different than originally promised so consideration will be present.

Promises Enforceable without Consideration

It is not always necessary to prove that a promise is supported by consideration. In a few unusual cases, a single, one-way, or gratuitous promise, though unsupported by consideration, becomes enforceable on the basis of fairness and equity. The doctrines of *promissory estoppel* and *charitable subscriptions* can provide a means of enforcement. In such cases, the courts examine the promisee's detrimental reliance and the courts attempt to balance fairness between the parties.

Elements of Promissory Estoppel

1. Under the circumstances, should the promisor reasonably expect that the promisee will rely on the promise and then act in some definite and substantial way? This is known as a *detrimental reliance.*
2. Has the promisee *in fact relied* on the promise to his or her own detriment?
3. In *balancing the equities* of enforcing or not enforcing the promise, would substantial unfairness be avoided if the promise is enforced?

The doctrine of charitable subscriptions applies when a charitable institution relies on a donor's promise to make a contribution. Typically, the promisor pledges to make a donation to the charity and the promisee relies on that pledge to its detriment by changing its position. For example, if a member's promise to make a big contribution induces a church to remodel its building, the one-way charitable subscription becomes enforceable when the church contracts with a builder. Should private businesspersons be given a similar protection? The following case illustrates that promissory estoppel protects a promisee's expectations when no remedy exists under traditional contract law.

Hoffman v. Red Owl Stores, Inc.

133 N. W. 2d 267 (Wis. 1965)

During 1960, Hoffman had numerous conversations with representatives of Red Owl Stores, Inc. concerning his establishment of a Red Owl food store in Wautoma, Wisconsin. At their urging, he bought a small independent store to gain experience in grocery retailing. After three months, his store was operating profitably. Again at the urging of Red Owl representatives, he sold the store to his manager. Hoffman was assured that if he sold his bakery business, Red Owl would set him up in a new Red Owl store. He leased a building site for the Red Owl store. He was advised on successive occasions that he needed more investment capital than the Red Owl representatives had previously suggested. Hoffman's negotiations with Red Owl finally broke down when Red Owl insisted that his father-in-law make him a $13,000 gift for use as investment capital.

Sec. 90 of Restatement, 1 Contracts provides:

> "A promise which the promisor should reasonably expect to induce action or forbearance of a definite and substantial character on the part of the promisee and which does induce such action or forbearance is binding if injustice can be avoided only by enforcement of the promise."

Because we deem the doctrine of promissory estoppel . . . is a needed tool . . . we endorse and adopt it.

The record here discloses a number of promises and assurances given to Hoffman by Lukowitz on behalf of Red Owl upon which plaintiffs relied and acted upon to their detriment.

Foremost were the promises that for the sum of $18,000 Red Owl would establish Hoffman in a store. After Hoffman had sold his grocery store and paid the $1,000 on the Chilton lot, the $18,000 figure was changed to $24,100. Then in November 1961, Hoffman was assured that if the $24,100 figure were increased by $2,000, the deal would go through. Hoffman was induced to sell his grocery store fixtures and inventory in June 1961, on the promise that he would be in his new store by fall. In November, plaintiffs sold their bakery building on the urging of defendants and on the assurance that this was the last step necessary to have the deal with Red Owl go through.

We conclude that injustice would result here if plaintiffs were not granted some relief because of the failure of defendants to keep their promises which induced plaintiffs to act to their detriment.

Case Questions

1. What are the elements of promissory estoppel?
2. How could Red Owl have avoided liability in this case?
3. What consideration would have been given by Hoffman if Red Owl's actions were construed as an offer for a unilateral contract?

The consideration requirement is waived in several other, but limited, situations. For example, a debt barred by either the statute of limitations or the debtor's discharge in bankruptcy may be revived if the debtor reaffirms the original promise to pay the debt or makes partial payment. Debts barred by bankruptcy must be approved by the bankruptcy court judge. *Composition* agreements entered into by several creditors and a debtor are enforceable without new consideration because the parties have a mutual interreliance similar to actual consideration. A common law modification contract lacks consideration unless both parties' obligations are changed.

Under UCC 2–209, there is no need for consideration if both parties agree to modify an existing sale of goods even if only one party's obligation is changed. As discussed previously, no consideration is required for merchants that make firm offers in a signed writing. UCC firm offers are irrevocable for up to three months.

CAPACITY

Not all persons are legally capable of entering into contracts. Some persons lack the mature judgment, experience, cognitive development, or ability needed to understand the effects of their promises. Minors, drunken, drugged, and insane persons are protected from the possibility that the other party will deal too harshly with them. The law determines that such persons lack contractual capacity.

The mental and negotiating capabilities of incapacitated persons are not evaluated in every case. Rather than invalidating outright all the contracts of incompetents, the law gives each incompetent the right to avoid unfair contracts. An incompetent may usually withdraw or *disaffirm* a contract. This protection lasts until the minor reaches the age of majority, usually 18, or the drunken, drugged, or insane person becomes lucid.

In most of the states, both deserving and shrewd minors are protected by the right to disaffirm a contract. For example, a minor can disaffirm a reasonable contract even if the adult party is damaged by the disaffirmance. Adults can protect themselves by assuring the other party is not a minor or by insisting an adult parent or guardian join in or cosign the contract. Adults do not have the right to disaffirm contracts with minors.

Voidability of an Incompetent's Contracts

Before attaining majority status, minors may disaffirm their contracts at any time. If that is done, most of the states require the minor to return the contractual benefits still in his or her possession. The fact that some of these benefits are missing or have depreciated is usually irrelevant. Many of the states now limit the minor's absolute right of disaffirmance by making minors who have misrepresented their age liable for the adult's losses.

After a minor attains majority status or after an incompetent becomes lucid, any decision to disaffirm must be made within a reasonable time. During this grace period, the minor may assess the fairness of contracts made during minority and decide to either disaffirm or ratify them. Once the minor who reaches majority ratifies the contract, the right to disaffirm ends.

The contracts of minors and other incompetents are not automatically considered void; they are voidable. Only an intentional act of disaffirmance by the minor will release liability. Because a minor cannot make a legally binding contract during minority, so too it is impossible to ratify a contract during minority. A voidable contract may be ratified only after the incapacity is removed. This occurs when a minor reaches majority or when a drunken, drugged, or insane person becomes lucid. The law may imply ratification if the incompetent either refrains from disaffirming beyond a reasonable time after the incapacity is removed or acts in a manner inconsistent with disaffirmance. For example, if after reaching 18 a person continues to use property bought during minority, the courts will usually infer that ratification should be implied from the person's conduct.

Necessaries

In some instances, an incompetent's right to disaffirm is limited and he or she must pay for *necessaries,* the necessities of life: food, clothing, and shelter. Necessaries may also include contracts for services and property that aid in sustaining life, such as tools of the trade, employment placement services, vocational education, and medical services or supplies.

The possibility of an unfair bargain may still exist in such instances, such as when necessaries are overpriced. The law implies a quasi-contractual obligation of the incompetent to pay only the reasonable value of the necessary items, an amount that may be less than the originally agreed price. However, if the incompetent's parent or guardian is able to provide these items, they are not necessary and so a contract for them is voidable by the minor.

REALITY OF CONSENT AND THE DEFENSES TO FORMATION

In some cases, the parties' mutual assent is not genuine. Either or both of the parties may have been unwillingly coerced or induced into an agreement. The law generally favors the stability and reasonable expectations of contractors, so it is difficult to cancel an agreement. However, if the level of misunderstanding or coercion is so great that it would be too unfair to enforce it, an agreement can be canceled. Such situations usually arise when one party misrepresents material facts to the other, when certain mistakes are made, or when one party is coerced.

Misrepresentation and Fraud

It is unjust for either party to provide incorrect information to the other about the contract's subject matter. From an economic perspective, the allocation of resources is not optimal if contractors have inaccurate information. The law will not permit the wrongful party to benefit by enforcing a contract based on misrepresentation. The innocent victim may rescind a contract induced by the misrepresentation of a material fact on which the victim has justifiably relied, suffering damages as a result of doing so. A good faith requirement of "honesty in fact in the conduct or transaction concerned" applies to every contract or duty covered by the UCC.

The initial focus in a misrepresentation case is on the person making the representations and on the representations themselves. Not all representations are facts that can be misrepresented. *Facts* are matters susceptible to exact knowledge, such as past events or conditions. Usually, predictions of future events are merely opinions. Unless the representer is a recognized expert, such as an appraiser, statements of opinion or future application cannot be misrepresented. For example, a salesperson's use of generalized statements concerning the value of goods is known as *puffing*. Reasonable people realize that puffing statements are usually too vague to be misrepresented as facts.

If the person making representations of facts knows, or should know, that the representations are false, then the inequity is fraudulent and more serious. *Fraud* is not only a reason to rescind or cancel a contract; it may also provide the basis for monetary damages under the tort of *deceit*. Fraud is also a criminal act.

The second focus in a misrepresentation case is on the victim. In negotiating a contract, the victim's reliance on the other party's representations must be reasonable. Sometimes the victim should not believe a particular representation. If the victim has superior experience with the subject matter of the contract, then the victim should independently investigate. If there is no actual reliance by the victim, then there is no causal link between the misrepresentation and the alleged damage. This releases the misrepresenter from liability, because contract law aids only victims damaged as a direct result of another's wrongdoing. However, if the victim of fraud honestly and reasonably believed the misrepresenter's statements, the contract may be canceled. For example, if an expert truck salesperson promises that a delivery truck will hold 5,000 pounds of cargo, the buyer may rescind if the truck is designed to hold only 3,000 pounds.

Mistake

In most instances, the law refuses to aid those who blunder in contract negotiations by making mistakes of judgment in assessing either the contract's value or their own capabilities. However, some mistakes concern such key terms as the identity, existence, or character of the contract's subject matter. When both parties are mistaken about the subject matter, a *bilateral* or *mutual mistake* occurs, permitting either party to rescind. If only one party is mistaken, a *unilateral mistake,* the contract is voidable only if the nonmistaken party takes advantage of the other party's mistake.

Duress

The terms of most contracts are dictated by market forces or by one party's business needs. Freedom of contract prevents the law from changing the terms of freely negotiated contracts. However, if one party unduly pressures the other party, the resulting contract may be voidable. The threat or actual use of force is the most obvious coercion that might cause a person to agree to unfavorable contract terms. This constitutes *duress,* and the victim may rescind the contract. The threat of criminal prosecution is duress, but the threat of civil suit is not duress unless the claim is unfounded and malicious. *Economic duress* arises if one party threatens to breach an existing contract unless the victim agrees to another, usually unfavorable, contract. However, economic duress is not a justifiable basis for cancellation if the economic circumstances are imposed by the market or if the victim makes mistakes of judgment.

UCC 2–302 permits the court hearing a contract dispute to modify adhesion contracts, those with unfair provisions, under the **unconscionability** doctrine. The parties may present evidence of the purpose and commercial setting of any clause brought into question. However, some consumer contracts may be designated unconscionable if they are one-sided and oppressive, cause unfair surprise, and show an allocation of risks due to one side's superior bargaining power. Courts are increasingly applying unconscionability beyond the UCC context to achieve fairness in common law contracts. The courts seldom apply unconscionability to commercial parties, reserving it for the uniquely vulnerable position of consumers. Commercial parties are generally better informed, have better access to legal counsel, have stronger bargaining power, and negotiate contracts more carefully than consumers.

A subtle form of coercion exists where *undue influence* is exerted by someone having a fiduciary or family relationship with the victim. Undue influence will form the basis for contract rescission if a position of trust is used to divert property from its normal course. For example, a young boy's grandmother became his guardian after his parents died. He was heir to a considerable block of corporate stock that the grandmother induced him to sign over to her. Since undue influence deprived him of the stock, he was later able to disaffirm the stock transfer to the grandmother, requiring the corporation to reissue it to him.

ETHICAL DILEMMA: ECONOMIC DURESS

The use of threats or intimidation to coerce someone to agree to an unfavorable contract is unethical. If the coercion amounts to duress or undue influence, the contract may also be unenforceable under contract law. However, many contracting activities that are not illegal may nevertheless pose ethical dilemmas. The decision-maker should analyze the type of coercion used in negotiating a contract. If the pressures employed are typical of market forces, they are legal and probably also ethical. For example, supply and demand pressures that relate to price, quantity, or other standard contract terms would seldom pose an ethical issue unless one party had the power to corner a market or single-handedly change supply or demand. Tactics may be unethical if they are clearly coercive, are not tied directly to contract terms, or threaten, coerce, or intimidate.

It is considered commercially reprehensible to threaten a breach of contract to coerce the other party into an undesirable agreement. Market outcomes are optimal only if participants have reasonable expectations their contracts will be performed. Consider the case of *Totem Marine Tug & Barge, Inc. v. Alyeska Pipeline Service Co.*[1] Alyeska became dissatisfied with Totem's slow progress in moving construction materials up to the trans-Alaska pipeline, so Alyeska commandeered the vessels while en route. This voided Totem's insurance and Alyeska terminated Totem's contract. Totem billed Alyeska for expenses exceeding a half million dollars. Alyeska knew that

[1]584 P.2d 15 (Ala. 1978).

without cash to pay other creditors soon Totem would go bankrupt. Alyeska delayed making payment and eventually coerced Totem to settle for less than 20 percent of the billings. Alyeska's nonpayment illustrates how unethical conduct is distinguished from simply taking advantage of market conditions. An act is both illegal and unethical if the stronger party creates a business compulsion in bad faith to exact more favorable terms than possible without the coercion.

ILLEGALITY

The common law doctrine of *illegality* holds that the law should not aid lawbreakers; therefore, the courts may not aid either party to an illegal contract. Illegality arises if the principal contract objective calls for the commission of a criminal or tortious act, making the contract illegal and unenforceable. The problem of applying the illegality doctrine becomes more complex if the contract calls for acts that do not initially appear illegal, but nevertheless an illegal performance seems likely. When the most likely method of performing the legal acts is illegal, the contract may be illegal. However, an otherwise legal contract is not made illegal by the mere possibility that one of the parties to the contract might do an illegal act while performing the contract. The court must determine the legality of the subject matter and assess how the principal duties will probably be performed.

Because the courts refuse to enforce the duties of either party to an illegal contract, it is often said that the parties must be left as the court finds them. For example, if one party has already paid for an executory illegal act, the other party will not be required to perform that act. The party that paid for the unperformed illegal act may not seek court assistance to have the money returned. Illegal contracts cannot be rescinded or enforced, despite the unfairness to a blameless party. However, this harsh outcome is tempered in some of the common types of illegal contracts discussed next.

Types of Illegality

The courts generalize about four common illegality areas in which they modify the rule prohibiting enforcement of illegal contracts. These areas are licensing, gambling, public policy, and restraints of trade.

Licensing Statutes Many states and municipalities require certain professionals and most businesses to obtain licenses before entering into contracts to do the licensed activity. Before a court will refuse to enforce the contracts of unlicensed persons, there must be a determination about the type of license involved. Some licensing statutes, such as municipal business licenses, have only a *revenue raising* objective. Such statutes and ordinances do not usually test the expertise or qualifications of licensed individuals. If the objective of a license is revenue raising, contracts made by unlicensed persons or businesses are generally enforceable even if they have neglected to obtain the required license. However, they may be liable for a penalty.

On the other hand, all of the states require the licensing of certain professions. The primary objective of these statutes is to protect the public from unscrupulous and unskilled practitioners. These *regulatory licensing statutes* require satisfaction of certain professional qualifications for lawyers, doctors, engineers, teachers, real estate brokers, barbers, and others to demonstrate their good character and skill. Contracts of an unlicensed person to provide regulated services are unenforceable and illegal. Because licensing statutes are designed to protect the public from unskilled and unscrupulous persons, customers or clients are usually permitted to rescind contracts with unlicensed professionals and regain funds paid because clients are the class of persons to be protected.

Gambling In all of the states, the free exercise of gambling is illegal except in licensed casinos, at licensed pari-mutuel racetracks, at licensed off-track betting parlors, at sales locations for state lotteries, or at limited charitable functions (e.g., bingo games). Contracts to pay illegal gambling debts are unenforceable.

One of the most perplexing problems with gambling is determining what activities constitute illegal gambling. *Gambling* is the creation of a risk with no prior existence primarily for the purpose of shifting the risk to expose the parties to gain or loss. If two parties bet on the price level that a particular stock will reach on a particular day, an unenforceable gambling contract arises. Although a similar economic event seems to occur if one party sells a stock and another party buys it, there is a fundamental difference between this transaction and a bet. Stock carries the risk of uncertain price movements with its ownership. By contrast, a bet on the price of a stock creates a brand-new risk that is not associated with stock ownership but is created with the gambling contract.

Insurance contracts are also susceptible to gambling. If the beneficiary or loss payee (the person designated to receive the policy proceeds) has a close connection with the insured person or property, then the insurance contract is legal because the beneficiary's risk preexisted that contract. This close connection or nexus, called an *insurable interest,* indicates that the insurance policy is not illegal gambling.

An insurable interest in a person's life exists where there is a close family relationship (i.e., spouse, child, parent) or where the insured is a key employee of a business. An insurable interest in property exists where the beneficiary owns, leases, or holds a lien on the property (collateral) or where a seller identifies specific goods as destined for shipment to a particular buyer. If the purchaser of insurance has no insurable interest, the insurance contract is like illegal gambling; in that case, if a loss occurs, only the premiums are returned to the purchaser.

Public Policy As a matter of public policy, the courts usually do not enforce agreements that violate society's ethical and moral norms as found in statutes and court decisions. Public policy prohibits contracts that seek to bribe or unduly influence public officials, fiduciaries, agents, or law enforcement officials in the performance of their duties. Such contracts are illegal and unenforceable. For example, public policy prohibits certain terms in the contracts of parking lot operators, pawn shops, or checkrooms. These parties are *bailees* because they hold custody of the property of others. Bailees often use **exculpatory clauses** to escape liability for losses of the owner's property while it is in the bailee's custody. Such clauses are generally unenforceable if the bailee seeks to be free of liability for willful misconduct. Exculpatory clauses are valid only to relieve the bailee of liability for negligence. The terms must also be communicated to the property owner.

Restraints of Trade Many contracts that attempt to restrain trade are illegal because they violate public policy. For example, contracts prohibiting the transfer of property and contracts made between competitors to fix prices, divide markets, allocate customers, or create monopolies are illegal under contract law and under federal antitrust law, both of which are discussed in Chapters 15 and 16. In some limited situations, however, trade restraints are economically useful, justifying their enforcement.

Employment Contracts An employer may have a legitimate interest in restricting former employees from quitting to work for a direct competitor. Employers often give their salespeople confidential customer lists, teach them innovative sales tactics, or provide them with secret new product information that could damage the employer if a salesperson quit to join a competitor. Designers, engineers, and persons in upper management may learn trade secrets whose disclosure would damage the competitive position of their employer. To protect these legitimate confidential interests, an employer may restrain an employee from immediately working for a direct competitor by insisting that the employee sign a *covenant not to compete*. The restraints imposed by the covenant must be limited to a geographic region and must last for only a reasonable time after the employee has left the employer, usually two or three years.

Employment contract covenants not to compete are not favored by the law, particularly if they deprive the employee of a reasonable livelihood. There has been a trend toward refusing their enforcement if they are too broad or vague or if they damage the employee. There is a trend to limit overbroad covenants not to compete to reasonable periods of time and to reasonable geographic regions in which the employee had a direct impact. Some overbroad covenants are completely unenforceable, suggesting that employers should draft them carefully or lose all protection. Employers may still use confidentiality agreements to protect valuable trade secrets, and patent assignments to clarify ownership.

Sale of a Business In the sale of a business or a professional practice, a similar need arises to protect the intangible property rights transferred. The purchaser of a business often pays a premium price for its "going concern" value, an amount that often exceeds the fair market value of its tangible assets. This premium paid for the goodwill of a business needs protection by a covenant not to compete.

Typically, a buyer is willing to purchase a seller's business only if the seller promises not to compete with the buyer. This helps assure that the seller's customers, clients, or patients will not simply follow the seller to a new location. Covenants not to compete that are intended to protect either goodwill or business trade secrets are considered *ancillary* (closely connected) to the sale of business contract and are therefore enforceable if drafted reasonably. Such covenants must cover only a limited geographic region, but they may last indefinitely in the sale of business context.

What unique risks does an employer have if a salesperson quits to join a competitor? The following case illustrates the types of interests that legitimately deserve protection.

Eastern Dist. Co., Inc. v. Flynn

567 P. 2d 1371 (Kan. 1977)

Flynn became dissatisfied with his job at Eastern Distributing Company, a wholesale liquor distributor in Kansas City, Kansas, and joined a competitor. He immediately began to service the same customers previously served as Eastern's route salesman. Flynn's written contract of employment with Eastern restricted him from disclosing Eastern's list of customers to a competitor or from soliciting those customers if he ceased to be associated with Eastern for any reason. The contract also restricted him from any connection with a competitor of Eastern's within a 50-mile radius of his former sales territory for one year following his termination from Eastern. Eastern sought an injunction ordering Flynn to cease from competing with Eastern.

It has become well established that a noncompetition clause is valid if it is ancillary to any lawful contract, but it is subject to the test of reasonableness of the covenant and whether it is inimical to the public welfare.

Professor Blake points out that if contacts are infrequent and irregular there may be no sufficient risk to the employer to support any degree of restraint and further that frequency of contact may also affect the permissible period of restraint; the important consideration being that the employer should be given a reasonable period of time in which to overcome the former employee's personal hold over the customers. With respect to locale of the contact the important factor is whether the contact is made at the employer's place of business, which involves less risk to the employer, or at the customer's home or business establishment, which is more likely to direct the customer's loyalty primarily to the employee and support some degree of restraint.

It is also generally recognized that the "customer contacts" theory gains added weight where the business is one in which the employee is the sole or primary contact with the customers and in which a close personal relationship with them is fostered, enabling the employee to control such business as a personal asset.

It is well-settled law that the mere desire to prevent ordinary competition does not qualify as a legitimate interest of an employer and a restrictive covenant is unreasonable if the real object is merely to avoid such ordinary competition.

However, it is also a well-recognized principle that "customer contacts" is a legitimate interest to be protected by an employer. It is clear from the import of the language of the instant contract that "customer contacts" was the principal incident which Eastern intended to protect.

While the names of customers and their places of business are matters of public record, Baird testified that the hours a licensee is available, the names and ordering habits of their clerks are not. The evidence disclosed that a salesman's calls on customers were frequent and regular; that they were made at the customer's place of business rather than at Eastern's; and that the salesman was Eastern's principal, if not its sole, contact with customers. Defendant was hired away from Eastern to continue to serve the same customers he knew while employed by Eastern. There is ample evidence to support the trial court's findings which viewed in the light of the foregoing authorities establishes a legitimate interest subject to protection by a court of equity.

We think the trial court in the exercise of its equitable powers fairly and reasonably reduced the area restriction to only that which was necessary to protect plaintiff's interest. We find no public policy or public interest involved under the facts and circumstances of this case sufficient to avoid or render unenforceable a reasonable restraint.

Case Questions

1. When is a noncompetition clause ancillary to an employment contract?
2. What interests can be protected by a reasonable covenant not to compete?
3. How would a court enforce a covenant not to compete if it were worded so broadly as to include an unreasonable geographic area or an unreasonable duration?

WRITTEN CONTRACTS

Contrary to the popular misconception, most oral contracts are fully enforceable and legally binding. Generally, contracts do not have to be in writing. Of course, it may be difficult to prove the precise contract terms unless there is a written document. To reduce the possibility of inaccurate fact findings in court, the law requires that some contracts be in writing. For contracts that fall into several special classes, the *statute of frauds* requires a written contract signed by the party to be charged. It is this party who usually denies the existence of a contract and usually is alleged to be in breach. Written contracts need only be signed by the party against whom the plaintiff seeks enforcement.

To be effective, a written contract must appear in a certain form, known as a **memorandum.** A memorandum may be an informal document or even a collection of several documents referring to the same transaction. It may be pieced together from separate documents, receipts, telegrams, letters, order forms, confirmations, addressed envelopes, and the like. The signature may be any tangible sign that is used to authenticate a writing. A cursive signature is usually sufficient, but so is a stamp, seal, initial, printing, typing, or even an *X* if it is intended by the party for authentication.

Written contracts are necessary in four major business-related activities: (1) sales of land, (2) guarantees to pay the debts of others, (3) contracts incapable of performance within one year, and (4) sales of goods of $500 or more.

Sales of Land

A contract that calls for the transfer of any *interest in land* must be in writing to be enforceable. This requirement applies to contracts that transfer a variety of real estate interests, including a fee simple, easement, covenant, mortgage, condominium ownership, mineral rights, growing vegetation, and leases lasting more than one year in most states, three years in others (e.g. Pennsylvania).

An exception permits enforcement of a *part performance* of an oral land sale contract if the buyer has (1) paid part or all of the purchase price, (2) taken possession of the property with the seller's knowledge, and (3) made valuable improvements on the land. Enforcement of oral land sales is justified because it would be unfair to let the seller use the technicalities of the statute of frauds to back out of an unattractive oral deal if the buyer has taken possession. In such instances, most courts grant a *specific performance*, ordering the seller to deed the property over to the buyer even though a written sale contract is missing.

Guarantee Contracts

If an outsider promises a creditor that he or she will pay the original debtor's debt, the promise must be in writing. Such promises are known as collateral contracts of *guarantee*. The original debtor's contract of debt need not be in writing, but the guarantor's promise to pay if the debtor defaults *must* be in writing. A true collateral contract of guarantee is enforceable only if the debtor defaults. For example, assume that C, a creditor, is willing to extend credit to D, the debtor, only if G, the outside guarantor, provides additional assurance that the debt will be repaid. G's promise to pay D's debt if D defaults is a collateral contract of guarantee that must be in writing.

An exception to this requirement exists when the guarantor's *main purpose* or *leading object* is merely to protect the guarantor's own interests. An oral guarantee is enforceable in this situation because fraud is less likely to be present. For example, a corporation in financial difficulty may be able to borrow money only if its president agrees to guarantee the loan. Because the president's main purpose in guaranteeing the loan is to protect the presidency, the guarantee need not be in writing.

The guarantee contract should be carefully distinguished from collateral and security arrangements that need no writing to be enforceable. Since loan cosigners or comakers are both primarily liable on the debt, their promises are not collateral guarantee contracts and need not be in writing.

Contracts Incapable of Performance within One Year

Long-term and complex contracts are the most susceptible to problems of proof. If a suit for breach of contract is brought long after the original day of contracting, witnesses may forget the facts. Therefore, a contract that is incapable of being performed within one year must be in writing. This requirement is less onerous than it may seem to be. In many instances, the parties choose to take longer than a year to perform contracts that are capable of full performance within a year. But the fact that a contract might take longer than a year to perform is immaterial and does not require a writing. Contracts that set specific starting and ending dates longer than one year must be written. The time begins to run when the contract is made, and it ends with the last required performance. Similarly, contracts that require a number of years for full performance must be in writing.

Sales of Goods

The common law statute of frauds has been amended by the UCC for contracts involving the sale of goods for $500 or more. However, the UCC provisions are less restrictive than the common law statute of frauds. The memorandum required by the UCC need not state all the terms of the contract accurately, but it is enforceable only up to the quantity stated in the writing. The UCC has special "gap filling" provisions that infer the terms needed to complete a contract. For example, oral testimony may supply terms of price, delivery, quality, or industry customs. There are four major exceptions to the UCC statute of frauds.

One of the UCC exceptions holds that if both parties to an oral contract are merchants and one party sends a written confirmation of an oral agreement to the other party, then no writing is necessary if the receiver fails to object within 10 days. This *receiver bound* exception provides an incentive for merchants to carefully read and quickly respond to all mail. A second UCC exception exists for *specially manufactured* goods, defined as goods unsuitable for sale in the seller's ordinary course of business. An oral telephone order for $1,000 of unique manufactured goods becomes enforceable as soon as the seller makes a substantial beginning in procuring or making the goods. Goods requiring special printing, embossing, or unusual colors would be specially manufactured.

A third UCC exception permits enforcement of an oral contract if the party seeking to deny the contract nevertheless substantiates the agreement by making an *admission*. The admission may appear in testimony, in pleadings, or otherwise in a court proceeding. The statute of frauds will not aid a party that seeks to use the writing requirement to renege on a contract actually entered into orally. The final UCC exception permits enforcement of oral contracts if there has been either a *part payment* for goods or acceptance of a *partial delivery*. However, a contract will be enforced under this part performance doctrine only for the quantity of goods paid for or accepted. The next case illustrates the receiver bound exception for merchants.

Thompson Printing Machinery Co. v. B.F. Goodrich Co.

714 F.2d 744 (7th Cir. 1983)
U.S. Court of Appeals, Seventh Circuit

James Thompson made an oral contract with Ingram Myers, a Goodrich agent, to purchase approximately $9,000 worth of used equipment displayed at the B.F. Goodrich surplus machinery department in Akron, Ohio. Thompson confirmed the oral purchase with a written purchase order sent to Goodrich four days later including Thompson's name, address, phone, and information about the purchase. Copies of the document were distributed within Goodrich but not to Myers and the machinery was sold to another purchaser. Thompson claimed that Goodrich received the confirmation letter and was bound by it. Goodrich claimed the statute of frauds was not satisfied by any memorandum it signed.

Cudahy, Justice

Uniform Commercial Code section 2–201(2) provides:

> "Between merchants if within a reasonable time a writing in confirmation of the contract and sufficient against the sender is received and the party receiving it has reason to know its contents, it satisfies [the statute of frauds] against the [receiver] unless written notice of objection to its contents is given within 10 days after it is received."

We must emphasize that the only effect of this exception is to take away from a merchant who receives a writing in confirmation of a contract the statute of frauds defense if the merchant does not object. The sender must still persuade the trier of fact that a contract was in fact made.

Goodrich argues Thompson's confirmation cannot qualify for the exception. Thompson erred in not specifically designating on the envelope, check, or purchase order that the items were intended for Myers or the surplus equipment department. Goodrich was unable to "find a home" for the check and purchase order in accordance with its regular procedures of sending copies of the documents to several of its departments.

The literal requirements are met that a writing is received and that Goodrich has reason to know its contents. There is no specific or express requirement that the "receipt" be by any Goodrich agent in particular. Section 1–201 provides that notice received by an organization is effective for a particular transaction from the time when it would have been brought to [the proper individual's attention] if the organization had executed due diligence.

The question comes down to whether Goodrich's mailroom, given the information it had, should have notified the surplus equipment manager of Thompson's confirmatory writing. If Goodrich had exercised due diligence in handling Thompson Printing's purchase order and check, these items would have reasonably promptly come to Myers' attention. The purchase order on its face should have alerted the mailroom that the documents referred to a purchase of used printing equipment. Since Goodrich had only one surplus machinery department, the document's home should not have been difficult to find. Even [with difficulty in identifying the transaction] the purchase order had Thompson Printing's phone number printed on it. Thus, we think Goodrich's mailroom mishandled the confirmatory writings. This failure should not permit Goodrich to escape liability by pleading nonreceipt.

Case Questions

1. The "receiver bound" rule discussed places what two important duties on all merchants about mail they receive? Considering the size and geographic dispersion of many corporations, is 10 days a reasonable time?
2. What could a merchant like Goodrich do in its contracts to avoid the problem encountered in this case? What other procedures should be adopted?

INTERPRETATION OF CONTRACTS

When disagreements arise over the meaning of contract terms, they are resolved with the objective rule of contracts. These terms are interpreted by how a reasonable person would understand the words used. Common words are given their general meaning unless the particular line of business applies a unique *usage of trade* to the words in question. For example, the word *gross* commonly means large, shameful, or out of proportion, but among wholesalers and retailers it refers to twelve dozen, a quantity of 144. The UCC permits the parties to define the words used in their contract by custom or precedent found in a recognized *course of dealing*, from previous conduct, or through the *course of performance* of a single contract with repeated performances (e.g., several installment payments or deliveries). For example, a buyer who has failed to object to consistently late deliveries may not claim breach of contract unless the seller is notified that late deliveries will no longer be tolerated. Any ambiguity arising in a written contract is resolved against the drafter, who is responsible for using clear terms. This is particularly important to businesses that use their own form contracts, because the ambiguities in such contracts cannot burden consumers.

Parol Evidence Rule

Before a contract is finalized, the parties frequently negotiate or "dicker" about its terms. The negotiation process often involves the proposal of alternative terms that replace previously withdrawn terms, either by using counteroffers or by inquiring about the acceptability of terms. As the proposed terms change, advantages are granted to one side and burdens are imposed on the other. The final agreement usually represents a compromise in which both parties have given up some of their original expectations so as to find an agreeable middle ground. This process of give-and-take through negotiation has fostered the parol evidence rule.

Under the **parol evidence rule**, neither party may prove that the contract has terms different from those stated in the written document. The parol evidence rule excludes from the jury's consideration oral or written evidence that would alter or vary the terms in the written contract. Thereby, neither party may seek the jury's sympathy by introducing evidence of a contract term that may have only been proposed during preliminary negotiations but was omitted when the parties reached their final agreement.

If the parties intend the written contract to embody all the terms of their agreement, the law presumes that they expect it to "tell the whole story." Such an intentionally complete document is known as an *integration*. It should be distinguished from the memorandum required to "satisfy" the statute of frauds. Conceivably, a memorandum might be neither intended nor complete enough to be considered an integration.

The parol evidence rule is also distinguished from the statute of frauds because it is "triggered" by a memorandum. The parol evidence rule tends to protect the integrity of written contracts and the parties' expectations of performance as specified in the writing. As a practical matter, the rule requires the party that did not prepare the writing to read it carefully before signing. This extra care will assure that all of the terms the parties finally agreed on actually appear in the written contract.

The parol evidence rule does not exclude evidence that clarifies ambiguities or shows fraud, duress, mistake, illegality, incapacity, or later contract modifications. What policies are furthered by the parol evidence rule? The following case illustrates the admissibility of parol evidence that might alter the written contract.

Masterson v. Sine

436 P.2d 561 (Cal. 1968)

Dallas Masterson and his wife, Rebecca, transferred their ranch to Dallas' sister Medora and her husband, Lu Sine, with a grant deed. The deed reserved to the Mastersons an option right to repurchase the ranch within the next two years for the sale price plus the depreciated value of improvements added by the Sines. After the sale, Dallas was adjudged bankrupt. Both the trustee in bankruptcy and Rebecca brought suit to establish their right to enforce the option.

The parol evidence rule precluded admission of extrinsic evidence offered by defendants to show that the parties wanted the property kept in the Masterson family and that the option was therefore personal to the grantors and could not be exercised by the trustee in bankruptcy.

When the parties to a written contract have agreed to it as an " integration"—a complete and final embodiment of the terms of an agreement—parol evidence cannot be used to add to or vary its terms. When only part of the agreement is integrated, the same rule applies to that part, but parol evidence may be used to prove elements of the agreement not reduced to writing.

The crucial issue in determining whether there has been an integration is whether the parties intended their writing to serve as the exclusive embodiment of their agreement. The instrument itself may help to resolve that issue. It may state, for example, that "there are no previous understandings or agreements not contained in the writing," and thus express the parties' "intention to nullify antecedent understandings or agreements." . . . Circumstances at the time of the writing may also aid in the determination of such integration.

In formulating the rule governing parol evidence, several policies must be accommodated. One policy is based on the assumption that written evidence is more accurate than human memory. This policy, however, can be adequately served by excluding parol evidence of agreements that directly contradict the writing. Another policy is based on the fear that fraud or unintentional invention by witnesses interested in the outcome of the litigation will mislead the finder of facts.

McCormick has suggested that the party urging the spoken as against the written word is most often the economic underdog, threatened by severe hardship if the writing is enforced. In his view the parol evidence rule arose to allow the court to control the tendency of the jury to find through sympathy and without a dispassionate assessment of the probability of fraud or faulty memory that the parties made an oral agreement collateral to the written contract, or that preliminary tentative agreements were not abandoned when omitted from the writing.

Evidence of oral collateral agreements should be excluded only when the fact finder is likely to be misled. The rule must therefore be based on the credibility of the evidence. [T]he Restatement of Contracts permits proof of a collateral agreement if it "is such an agreement as might *naturally* be made as a separate agreement by parties situated as were the parties to the written contract."

The draftsmen of the Uniform Commercial Code would exclude the evidence in still fewer instances: "If the additional terms are such that, if agreed upon, they would certainly have been included in the document in the view of the court,then evidence of their alleged making must be kept from the trier of fact."

The option clause in the deed in the present case does not explicitly provide that it contains the complete agreement, and the deed is silent on the question of assignability. Moreover, the difficulty of accommodating the formalized structure of a deed to the insertion of collateral agreements makes it less likely that all the terms of such an agreement were included. Moreover, even when there is no explicit agreement—written or oral—that contractual duties shall be personal, courts will effectuate a presumed intent to that effect if the circumstances indicate that performance by substituted person would be different from that contracted for.

In the present case, defendants offered evidence that the parties agreed that the option was not assigned in order to keep the property in the Masterson family. The trial court erred in excluding that evidence.

The judgment is reversed.

Case Questions

1. What is an integration agreement?
2. What kinds of evidence does the parol evidence rule make inadmissible at trial?
3. What is the purpose of the parol evidence rule?

Title and Risk of Loss

Before the UCC, the concept of *title* or ownership of property triggered numerous concerns: the right to insure the property, the risk of financial loss if the property was damaged or destroyed in transit, and legal remedies against the seller or a wrongdoer. However, the UCC provides for separate treatment of these concerns: insurable interest, risk of loss, and title. Today, the title to goods affects ownership, rights of the owner's creditors, and the responsibility to pay taxes. Title cannot pass from the seller to the buyer until after the goods have been identified, either in the contract or at the time that the seller ships them or designates them as for the buyer. Title passes when the agreement dictates that it pass. However, if the contract does not mention title transfer, then the title to goods passes when the seller completes the obligation to deliver: (1) when they are delivered to the carrier in a contract requiring the seller to "ship," (2) when they are

FIGURE 8–11
Mercantile Terms

Mercantile Abbreviation	Mercantile Term	Mercantile Term Meaning
FOB	Free on board	Requires payment of freight charges: (1) by buyer if FOB (named place of seller's shipment), (2) by seller if FOB (named place of buyer's destination), (3) by seller if FOB (named carrier vessel, car, or vehicle). Title and risk of loss pass from seller to buyer at the named place.
FAS	Free alongside	Requires seller to deliver goods alongside vessel designated by buyer. Title and risk of loss pass from seller to buyer alongside the vessel.
CIF (CF)	Cost, insurance, freight	Seller's price includes cost of goods, loading, transit insurance, and freight charges for transport to the named destination. Seller must contract for the transportation. Title and risk of loss pass from seller to buyer when the goods are delivered to the carrier.
C&F	Cost & freight	Seller's price includes cost of goods, loading, and freight charges for transport to the named destination. Seller must contract for the transportation. Title and risk of loss pass from seller to buyer when the goods are delivered to the carrier.
Ex-Ship	Ex-Ship	Requires unloading of goods from ship at named port, title and risk of loss pass from seller to buyer when unloaded.

delivered to the buyer in a contract requiring the seller to "deliver," or (3) at the time of contracting if delivery occurs without moving the goods, such as when the goods are held in an independent warehouse.

Risk of loss is still important because goods can be damaged or lost in shipment, sometimes as a result of natural catastrophes. After risk of loss has passed to the buyer, the purchase price must be paid even if the goods have been damaged or lost. By contrast, the seller is liable for breach of contract to deliver if a loss occurs before risk of loss passes to the buyer. Therefore, the parties have conflicting incentives to alter the risk of loss by the use of favorable contract language and should both consider insuring the goods during transit.

The parties may specifically designate when title or risk of loss passes; otherwise, passage is made according to numerous technical determinations. Generally, it passes at either the point of the shipment's origin or at the point of arrival at the destination when these are designated by the use of *mercantile terms* such as: FOB, FAS, CIF, C&F, or Ex-Ship. Consider the example of goods shipped from a Philadelphia manufacturer to a Detroit wholesaler. In an "FOB Philadelphia" contract, risk and title pass when the seller tenders the goods to the carrier in Philadelphia. In an "FOB Detroit" contract, risk and title pass when the carrier delivers the goods to the buyer in Detroit. If mercantile and risk of loss terms are absent in the contract, then risk passes when the buyer receives the goods from a merchant seller or when the goods are tendered by a nonmerchant seller. Common mercantile terms are summarized in Figure 8–11.

FIGURE 8–12 Third-Party Beneficiary

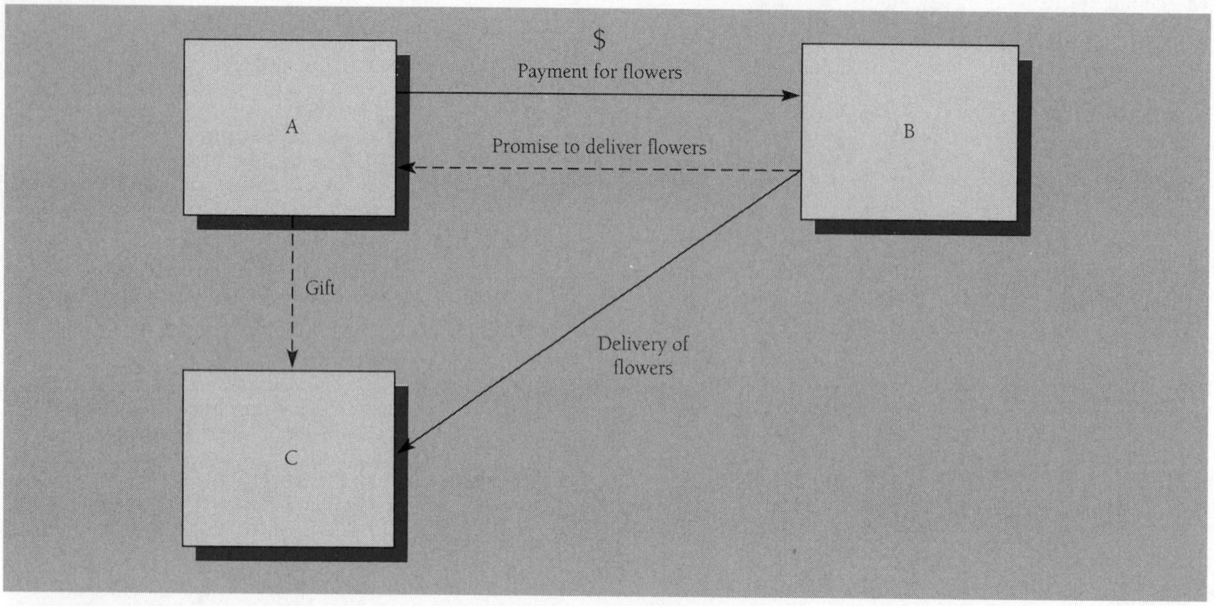

A buys flowers from B to be delivered to C, and the contract between A and B identifies C as the recipient of B's performance. Thus, C is a donee third-party beneficiary of the contract between A and B. C may require B, but not A, to perform the contract.

THIRD-PARTY RIGHTS

It seems logical that only contracting parties may seek judicial enforcement of contracts. In four distinct situations, however, outsiders have legally enforceable rights or responsibilities in the contracts that others make. The first two situations involve contracts specifically identifying an outside third party that is intended to receive the contract benefits. Such third parties are either creditor beneficiaries or donee beneficiaries. The third and fourth situations arise when either contracting party transfers contractual rights or obligations under an existing contract to an outsider. In such situations, the outsider may enforce the contract or be required to perform a contractual duty if transferred from one of the original contracting parties.

Third-Party Beneficiaries

An outsider intentionally identified as a beneficiary or obligee in the original contract is known as a *third-party beneficiary,* illustrated in Figure 8–12. A third-party beneficiary may enforce the contract against the original obligor. If the person to whom the promise of performance was originally made intended the contract to be a gift to the third party, the third party has no right to sue this promisee. For example, if a person purchases flowers from a florist for a spouse, the recipient spouse, as a *donee third-party beneficiary,* can enforce the contract against the florist (the obligor) but has no right to sue the spouse who purchased the flowers. The spouse conferring the gift simply used the florist's services to make the gift.

A different case arises where the third party was previously owed a duty by the promisee and the promisee uses the obligor to discharge this duty. Here, the outsider, a

FIGURE 8–13 Assignment of Rights

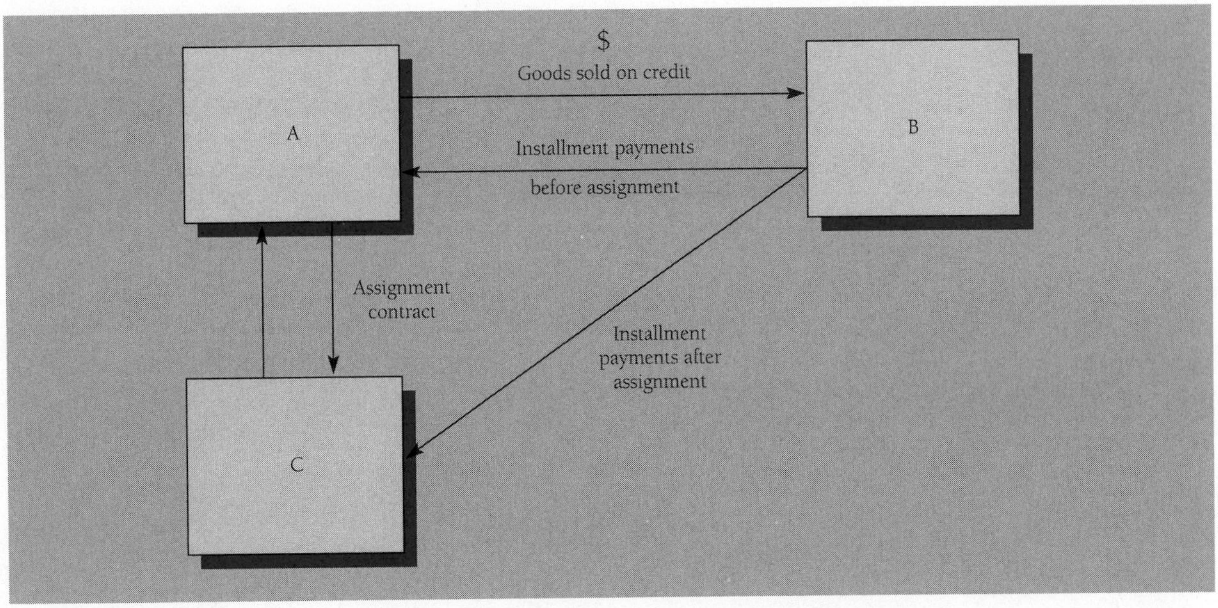

A's account receivable is factored to C, an assignment of rights. C is the factor that obtains the right to receive the installment payments that B originally promised to A. B's consent is necessary only for the assignment of personal services.

creditor third-party beneficiary, may enforce the obligation against either of the original contracting parties. The promisee is liable to the third party because the duty existed prior to and independently of the third-party beneficiary contract. For example, a home sale contract may identify the lending bank as a creditor third-party beneficiary. The buyer assumes the seller's mortgage, thereby promising to repay the original mortgage loan. Unless the bank releases the seller from making the payments, the bank may sue either the seller or the buyer if the loan goes into default, because the seller originally borrowed the money.

Incidental Beneficiaries

Some outsiders, *incidental beneficiaries,* benefit only by coincidence from the contracts of others. They have no rights to enforce a contract because they are neither identified in the contract nor intended to benefit from it. For example, contracts for the construction of new factories often generate significant economic benefits for the surrounding community. However, these community members cannot enforce the construction contracts because these people are merely unintended and incidental beneficiaries.

Assignment and Delegation

Contract rights and duties are sometimes transferred to an outsider in a separate contract. Such transfer contracts are usually made after the original contract. The law distinguishes between the *assignment of a right* to enforce the original contract, illustrated in Figure 8–13, and the *delegation of a duty* to perform under the original contract, illustrated in Figure 8–14. In the sale of an ongoing business, for example, assignments of

FIGURE 8–14 Delegation of Duty

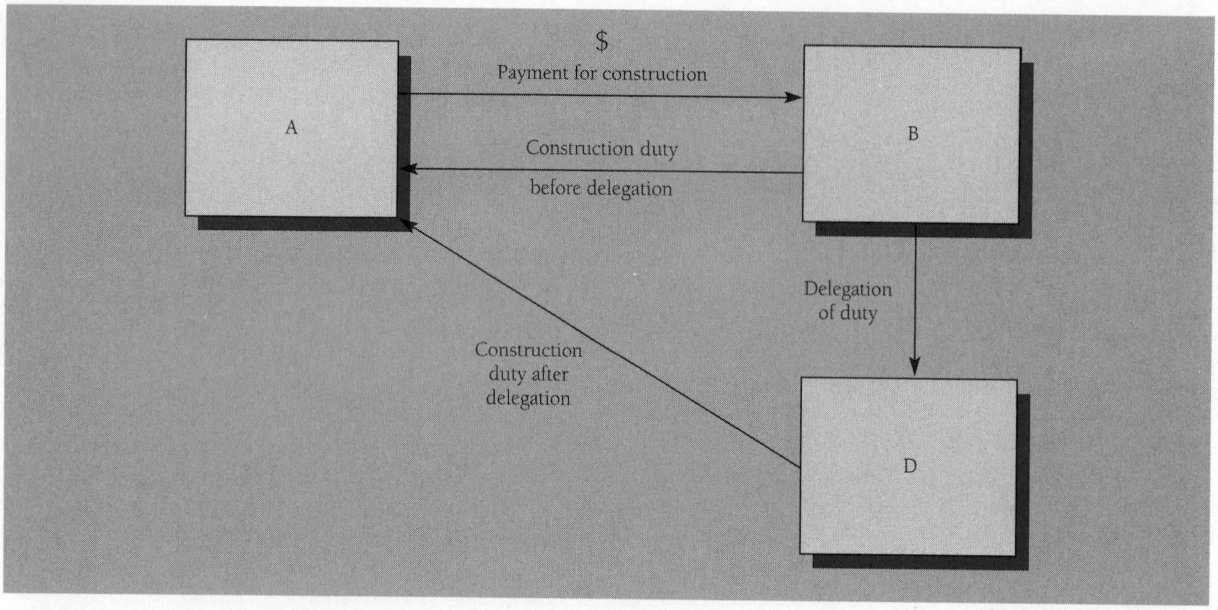

B's obligation to perform construction services is delegated to D. In this delegation of a duty, D is the delegate that is obligated to perform the construction services for A. A's consent is necessary only for the delegation of personal services.

rights to enforce contracts with others (e.g., accounts receivables) are often combined with delegations of duties previously undertaken with others (e.g., accounts payables). The purchaser of the business may collect on contract rights formerly owed to the seller and the purchaser must perform contract duties the selling firm formerly owed to its customers.

The transfer of rights or duties is sometimes accomplished without the permission of the other party to the original contract. Such transfers are effective only when they do not materially change the obligations or rights of the nonconsenting party. For example, a wholesaler may assign past-due accounts receivables to a collection agency (a factor). The debtors may not complain because as long as the assignee notifies them of the assignment, the change of payee does not materially affect their original payment obligation. Rights and duties are freely transferable if they involve obligations to pay money or are standard repair and construction contracts. The test for transferability focuses on the nonconsenting contracting party. A transfer is unenforceable if the nonconsenting party suffers a material change in duty or right. Personal service contracts are typical of the assignments or delegations that are not effective unless the other original contractor consents to substitute the new party as assignee or delegate. The original contract can limit later delegation.

What is the distinction between personal service contracts that involve a material change and contracts that are fully assignable or delegable? The next case illustrates how to identify duties or rights that are freely transferable without imposing a material change on the nonconsenting contractor.

Macke Co. v. Pizza of Gaithersburg, Inc.

270 A 2d 645 (Md. 1970)

Virginia Coffee Service, Inc. contracted with Pizza of Gaithersburg, Inc. to provide cold-drink vending machines for each Pizza location. The Macke Company later purchased all of Virginia's assets and received its contracts by assignment, including the contract with Pizza. Pizza attempted to terminate these contracts, and Macke brought suit to determine its rights under the combined assignment and delegation.

In the absence of a contrary provision—and there was none here—rights and duties under an executory bilateral contract may be assigned and delegated, subject to the exception that duties under a contract to provide personal services may never be delegated nor rights be assigned.

[This court has] held that the right of an individual to purchase ice under a contract without its terms reflected a knowledge of the individual's needs and reliance on his credit and responsibility could not be assigned to the corporation which purchased his business. In *Eastern Advertising Co. v. McGaw & Co.,* our predecessors held that an advertising agency could not delegate its duties under a contract which had been entered into by an advertiser who had relied on the agency's skill, judgment, and taste.

We cannot regard the agreements as contracts for personal services. . . . The appellees earnestly argue that they had dealt with Macke before and had chosen Virginia because they preferred the way it conducted its business. Specifically, they say that service was more personalized, since the president of Virginia kept the machines in working order, that commissions were paid in cash, and that Virginia permitted them to keep keys to the machines so that minor adjustments could be made when needed. Even if we assume all this to be true, the agreements with Virginia were silent as to the details of the working arrangements and contained only a provision requiring Virginia to "install . . . the above listed equipment and . . . maintain the equipment in good operating order and stocked with merchandise." We think the Supreme Court of California put the problem of personal service in proper focus a century ago when it upheld the assignment of a contract to grade a San Francisco street:

> "All painters do not paint portraits like Sir Joshua Reynolds, nor landscapes like Claude Lorraine, nor do all writers write dramas like Shakespeare or fiction like Dickens. Rare genius and extraordinary skill are not indispensable to the workmanlike digging down of a sand hill or the filling up of a depression to a given level, or the construction of brick sewers with manholes and covers, and contracts for such work are not personal, and may be assigned."

Moreover, the difference between the service the Pizza Shops happened to be getting from Virginia and what they expected to get from Macke did not mount up to such a material change in the performance of obligations under the agreements as would justify the appellee's refusal to recognize the assignment.

Restatement, Contracts § 160(3) (1932) reads, in part:

> "Performance or offer of performance by a person delegated has the same legal effect as performance or offer of performance by the person named in the contract, unless, (a) performance by the person delegated varies or would vary materially from performance by the person named in the contract as the one to perform, and there has been no . . . assent to the delegation. . . ."

Uniform Commercial Code § 2–210(5) permits a promisee to demand assurances from the party to whom duties have been delegated.

As we see it, the delegation of duty by Virginia to Macke was entirely permissible under the terms of the agreements.

Case Questions

1. What is a personal service?
2. Why would it be unjust or inefficient to require an obligee to accept a personal service performance from someone other than the original obligor?
3. How could either party to the original agreement have avoided this outcome?

CONTRACT PERFORMANCE AND REMEDIES FOR BREACH

Sometimes one party to a valid contract finds performance is no longer advantageous, either because of their personal incapability or because the contract's value has disappeared. The law usually enforces such contracts. There are several degrees of performance quality. An executory contractual duty can be discharged if it becomes impossible to perform. However, in most cases if one party breaches, the other party may be entitled to a legal remedy such as damages or specific performance.

Certain events or **conditions** are often necessary before the parties' rights are enforceable. Some contracts contain *conditions precedent,* events which must happen before a duty is owed. For example, a home buyer is usually not required to purchase the house until sufficient financing is obtained. Financing is a condition precedent to the buyer's obligation to purchase. *Concurrent conditions* arise when each party's performance is conditioned on the other party's near simultaneous tender of counterperformance. For example, in most retail sales the buyer's payment is concurrently conditioned on the seller's delivery and the seller's delivery is concurrently conditioned on the buyer's payment. Occasionally, *conditions subsequent* arise to provide warranty repairs until a condition subsequent occurs, such as the expiration of the warranty period or consumer abuse such as the failure to make necessary oil changes. Contract remedies are usually granted after the parties establish the occurrence of one or more conditions.

Discharge by Performance

Each party's performance is judged by the degree of perfection that the obligee can objectively expect to receive. To fully discharge contractual duties in most situations, each party must perform exactly as promised or be guilty of a **material breach.** In the event of a material breach, the innocent party may suspend counterperformance and sue for a remedy. However, when a complex performance is required, something less than *full performance* may suffice. In building construction contracts, for example, a contractor acting in good faith may deviate slightly from the plans and specifications if the deviation is minor and unintentional. If the required materials are unavailable and a reasonable substitute is used, the contractor should still be paid. However, it may be necessary to adjust the purchase price to reflect the lesser quality of this **substantial performance.**

Late deliveries, payments, or performances of services are also judged in this way. If the performance delay is so serious that it constitutes a material breach, then the innocent party is relieved from performance and may sue for breach. By contrast, slight delays must be tolerated, perhaps with a price adjustment made. However, at the time of contracting either party may insist that *time is of the essence,* requiring a timely performance.

Either party may notify the other party of inability to perform in the future; this is an *anticipatory breach,* known as an *anticipatory repudiation* under the UCC. Such a preannounced breach permits the innocent party to immediately sue for breach or pursue other remedies without waiting for the time originally set for performance. The UCC permits a contract to be reinstated after anticipatory repudiation if the innocent party has not yet sought a remedy. In addition, either party may at any time demand *adequate assurances of performance* from the other party. If the other party fails to give these assurances within a reasonable time, the innocent party may pursue remedies for breach even if the time for performance has not yet arrived.

Impossibility of Performance

The doctrines of delegation and impossibility are fundamentally interrelated. Sometimes an obligor becomes ill and cannot perform services or an obligor cannot deliver goods because the goods were destroyed or a factory halted production. A strike or a boxcar shortage may also prevent performance. In such situations, the contract becomes *subjectively impossible* to perform. That is, the obligor cannot perform as promised, but perhaps others could be substituted as delegates to perform.

Consider the contrast between a contract for the services of a famous portrait painter and a contract for the manufacture of standard goods. If the painter becomes ill, there is no substitute for the quality of his or her performance. Because no one else can paint the portrait as specified, the painter's duty is either justifiably delayed or excused by impossibility. By contrast, if a manufacturer of standard goods or a building contractor suffers a strike, there is no objective legal impossibility. Since the services of the manufacturer and the building contractor are not unique, some other manufacturer could produce the goods or some other contractor could construct the building. In such cases, the obligor is required to delegate the duty or risk paying damages. The doctrine of impossibility applies only when unique services are excused or unique subject matter is destroyed after the contract has been made but before performance is due.

There are other variations of this defense: *frustration of purpose* and *commercial impracticality*. Some courts release an obligor if, after the contract has been made, events occur that render the other party's performance worthless. The UCC releases parties from performing if an unforeseen event makes the obligor's performance highly impractical. For example, if an obligor's cost of goods increased by 10 times or more, then the contract might be discharged for commercial impracticality.

Force Majeure Clauses

The parties may agree to define the particular events that trigger the impossibility defense. *Force majeure clauses* are often used in contracts if one or both parties could be exposed to uncertain and debilitating events. *Force majeure clauses* are enforceable as privately bargained for impossibilities. Oil and gas contracts typically contain force majeure clauses. These excuse performance if, through no fault of either party, performance becomes impossible due to labor troubles, war, transportation failures, acts of God, or any other listed event.

Damages

Contract law is intended to satisfy the parties' reasonable expectations of performance. In most cases, money damages are efficient and satisfactory remedies. *Compensatory damages* are the most typical damage awards because they represent the losses actually suffered in obtaining a replacement, realizing the promisee's original expectations, or securing a substitute performance. Of course, the promisee has a *duty to mitigate damages* by avoiding and minimizing such damages. The UCC specifically permits the recovery of *consequential damages,* those additional damages that flow naturally from the breach, including lost income or profits. *Punitive damages* are rarely awarded in breach of contract cases unless the promisor is also guilty of tortious and willful misconduct.

FIGURE 8–15
Comparison of Common Law with UCC Article 2 "Sales"

Provision or Characteristic	Common Law	UCC Article 2 "Sales"
Application	Land sales, employment, services	Sales of goods (e.g., personal property)
Source of law	State case law precedent Restatement	Uniform state adopted code
Acceptance of unilateral offer	Perform act requested	Prompt shipment of conforming goods
Terms left open in offer? Essential terms	All essential terms must be present in offer	Enforceable contract possible even with certain terms left open for future determination or inference; quantity term is essential
Option contracts	Consideration required	No consideration required if firm offer made in merchant's signed writing (valid up to 3 months)
Mirror image rule	Offered terms must exactly match acceptance terms	Mirror image unnecessary unless highly material terms differ (price, quantity, subject matter, parties' identity)
Mailbox rule	Contract formed when acceptance dispatched using offeror's means of communication	Contract formed when acceptance dispatched using any reasonable means under the circumstances
No consideration required	Barred debts, promissory estoppel, charitable subscription, composition	Modification of existing contract, merchant's firm offer (option)
Adhesion contract	Freedom of contract and consideration requirement usually not helpful to victim	Unconscionability prohibited mainly in consumer contracts
Statute of frauds, written contract requirement	Sales of land, contracts incapable of performance within 1 year, guarantees of other's debts (see exceptions below)	Sales of goods for $500 or more (see exceptions below)
Statute of frauds exceptions	Land sale part performance, main purpose (leading object) in guarantees	Merchant receiver bound, specially manufactured goods, admissions, partial payment/delivery
Memorandum	All terms must be stated somewhere in the assembled documents	UCC gap filling terms may provide any term except quantity; UCC memo enforceable only up to quantity stated
Remedies	Anticipatory breach, damages, impossibility, frustration of purpose, rescission	Anticipatory repudiation, demand adequate assurance of performance, cancellation, damages, cure, cover, specific performance

Damages for breach can be made more certain if the parties agree to a *liquidated damage* provision in which the parties specify a damage sum payable if one party breaches. Liquidated damage provisions are enforceable only if they are a legitimate estimate of uncertain future damages. Any attempt to use liquidated damages as a penalty to discourage breach will not be enforced. For example, if a wholesaler presold a quantity of goods to be acquired from a manufacturer, an unreasonably large liquidated damage provision in the manufacturer's supply contract would be unenforceable as a penalty because the wholesaler's potential loss is limited to the difference between actual and resale price. However, if the wholesaler had not presold the goods and the market for the goods was uncertain, a liquidated damage provision might still be reasonable.

Specific Performance

Although damages are the most typical remedy, a *specific performance* of the contract may be ordered in cases involving unique property (e.g., land, collectibles, or goods previously designated for purchase). This is a court order requiring the parties to perform as originally promised. When money damages are inadequate to satisfy the promisee's expectations, the extraordinary remedy of specific performance may be ordered. However, no specific performance will be ordered for personal services.

UCC Remedies

Under the UCC, a seller who delivers *nonconforming goods* (goods that do not meet the contract specifications) may *cure* the breach by notifying the buyer that the seller is substituting conforming goods if they are delivered before the time for performance. A buyer may *cover* by purchasing substitute goods from another seller if the seller fails to deliver conforming goods by the time set for performance. A full comparison of the differences between the UCC and common law are summarized in Figure 8–15.

LEASES OF GOODS

Increasingly, the tax law and the incentive to reduce debt has made leasing an attractive substitute to purchasing goods for both consumers and businesses. The UCC has been amended with Article 2A, which fills a gap in the law with a more reliable and uniform treatment of leases. Each lease contract is known as a *lease agreement* in which the *lessor* grants to a *lessee* the right to possess and use goods for a term of time in return for consideration. UCC Article 2A treats leases of goods more like sales of goods than like leases of real property (e.g., apartment, storefront). Article 2A "Leases" contains provisions that generally parallel Article 2 "Sales" covering issues like: firm offers, contract formation, statute of frauds, the parol evidence rule, performance, assignment and delegation, remedies, warranties, cure, and cover. Article 2A is currently adopted in several states and will probably be adopted more widely in the future.

SUMMARY

Contracts are the most basic and important business relationship. They are made up of legally enforceable obligations arising from mutual promises. Contracts are enforced to permit orderly business, satisfying the parties' reasonable expectations. Contracts for service and land sales are governed by the common law of each state. The UCC governs sales of goods. Valid and enforceable contracts arise when the parties (1) have legal capacity and (2) mutually assent to a single agreement that is (3) supported by consideration and (4) has a legal objective.

Mutual assent is based on the parties' communications. The offer confers the power to contract and must include key terms: parties' identity, subject matter, description, quantity of goods, price, and time for performance. A contract results when the offeree unconditionally accepts the offeror's precise proposal. Slight differences between the written form used by buyers and sellers of goods are often permissible. Except for acceptances, which are usually effective when dispatched, all communications are effective when received.

Contracts may be unenforceable, particularly those that are unimportant or not serious. Contracts become enforceable if consideration exists, as where two parties make promises in reliance on each other's counterpromise. Promises to do something or to refrain from doing something are sufficient. However, a repromise of a previously made promise is unenforceable under the preexisting legal duty rule. Some promises made without consideration are enforceable under promissory estoppel.

Minors, drunken, drugged and insane persons are protected from unwise contracts. Minors can usually disaffirm a contract until a reasonable time after reaching majority. Then, the law implies a ratification of the contract, eliminating the right to disaffirm. Minors must usually pay the reasonable value of necessaries.

A contract obligation may be avoided if either party's assent is obtained by coercion, including duress, the threat or actual use of force. If one party to a contract misrepresents material facts to the other, the victim may cancel the contract. Mistakes concerning the identity, existence, or subject matter of a contract permit rescission. Where both parties to a contract are mistaken or where one party knowingly takes advantage of the other's mistake, the contract is voidable.

A contract is unenforceable if its primary objective violates a criminal or tort law. A contract is also unenforceable if its objective appears legal but will probably involve an illegal act. Contracts made by unlicensed professionals are illegal if the licensing statute is regulatory but not if it is revenue raising. Most gambling contracts are illegal and unenforceable. Public policy disfavors exculpatory clauses in which one party attempts to avoid all responsibility. Restraints of trade are illegal unless they are reasonably worded to protect valid interests arising in an employment contract or the sale of a business.

Not all contracts must be in writing to be enforceable. The statute of frauds requires a simple written memorandum, signed only by the party denying the contract, and only if the contract involves: (1) land sale, (2) guarantee, (3) contracts incapable of performance within one year, and (4) sales of goods of $500 or more. The following exceptions may permit enforcement of oral contracts: part performance of land sales or sales of goods, contracts whose main purpose protects the loan guarantor, specially manufactured goods, or admissions.

If the parties put their agreement into a complete and formal writing (integration), neither party can alter that agreement with testimony of different terms. . . . Evidence of misrepresentation, fraud, duress, undue influence, illegality, incapacity, or later modifications or clarifications is still admissible.

Third parties may have enforceable rights or duties in the contracts of others, but only if one or both of the contracting parties specifically intend it. Incidental and unintended beneficiaries have no rights in contracts. A contracting party may transfer contract rights or duties by assignment or delegation. The transferee may enforce the transfer if the other contracting party suffers no material change in duty or right.

A contract obligor that is unable to perform as promised should find a substitute to perform. Parties may be relieved of their duty to perform contract obligations if performance of those obligations becomes impossible or too burdensome. Innocent parties may sue for a remedy such as damages or specific performance.

KEY TERMS

law merchant, p. 211
quasi contract, p. 214
objective theory of contracts, p. 215
option contract, p. 218
"battle of the forms," p. 221
preexisting legal duty, p. 226
accord and satisfaction, p. 226
unconscionability, p. 231
exculpatory clauses, p. 233
memorandum, p. 235
parol evidence rule, p. 239
conditions, p. 246
material breach, p. 246
substantial performance, p. 246

CHAPTER EXERCISES

1. The plaintiff, a real estate developer, requested that the defendant utility company extend power lines to a new subdivision but never signed a contract promising to pay for the installation. After the utility company completed the installation of the new lines, the plaintiff sought a declaratory judgment that it was not liable for the cost of extending the lines. Is the real estate developer liable?
2. Larry and Bo were playing a friendly game of golf at Callaway Gardens. As Larry was about to drive from the tee, Bo said: " If you make a hole in one, I'll give you $500." Larry made a hole in one. Does Bo have to pay?
3. Nancy had a contract to work for Ace Construction for two years when financial difficulties developed at the company. In oral conversation with the owner of Ace Construction, Nancy offered to resign. The owner did not accept that oral offer. Later, the owner wrote Nancy a letter accepting her oral offer to resign. Has the offer lapsed?
4. The plaintiff purchased an option to buy the defendant's hunting lodge. The written option agreement stated that the option to purchase was to expire on May 1. On April 15, the plaintiff refused to exercise the option in a notification to the defendant. Subsequently, on April 29, the plaintiff attempted to exercise the option. Where an offeree (the plaintiff in this case) refuses to exercise an option and subsequently decides to exercise it, does the first refusal extinguish the offer? Does it make a difference if the offeror (the defendant/seller in this case) has not changed his position after the refusal?
5. The plaintiff and the defendant are merchants in the carpet business. The defendant (Carpet Mart), a carpet retailer in Tennessee, purchases carpets from the plaintiff (Carpet Company in Dalton, Georgia). The parties have been involved in a series of transactions over a period of six years. Typically, their arrangements involved the following steps. The defendant would make an oral offer to buy from the plaintiff. The plaintiff would then send a written acknowledgment to the defendant. The defendant would then send a written purchase order.

   The plaintiff's acknowledgment form contained the following language: "The acceptance of your order is subject to all of the terms and conditions on the face and reverse side hereof, including *arbitration,* all of which are accepted by the buyer; it supersedes contrary terms on the buyer's order form, if any."

   The defendant's purchase order made no objection to any of the terms in the plaintiff's acknowledgment form. Later, the defendant refused to pay for a shipment of carpet, claiming that the shipment did not meet its specification since some of the carpets in the shipment were not manufactured from a 100 percent Kodel polyester fiber but from a cheaper and inferior carpet fiber. The plaintiff sued to compel arbitration. Was there an agreement to arbitrate, or was the arbitration provision a "material alteration" of the contract within UCC 2–207? (*Dorton v. Collins, Aikman Corp.*, 453 F.2d 1161, 1972.)
6. Jane contracted for the purchase of a house. Before the closing, she discovered that the house had a leaky roof. At the closing, she would not pay until the seller promised to repair the roof. The seller promised to repair, and she paid the purchase price. Is the seller's promise enforceable? Why or why not?
7. The plaintiff, a 14-year-old, purchased a bicycle from her next-door neighbor, who was 25. The plaintiff sought to return the bicycle, but the defendant seller refused to return the purchase price. Is the contract avoidable?
8. John was employed by Acme Development Company as a commercial real estate salesman. His employment contract provided that if he left Acme's employment, he could not engage in the real estate business for five years within 10 miles of its offices. He brought an action for declaratory judgment to determine his rights under the contract. Acme counterclaimed and sought an injunction to prevent him from working for a competitor. Can an employer automatically enforce a restrictive covenant in an employment contract?
9. The office manager of your company purchased a computer after a computer salesperson assured her that it would be more than adequate for the

particular purposes of the company. Later, the office manager discovered the printer was too slow to meet the company's needs. She seeks to rescind the sales contract on the basis of misrepresentation. With what result, and why?

10. Jones had an oral agreement to purchase 1.3 acres of land in a 10-acre tract owned by seller. Seller refused to close on the contract. If the buyer sues for specific performance, will the statute of frauds be a valid defense?

11. Jane purchased a life-cycle exercise machine at Body Works. The written installment sales contract disclaimed any warranty obligations to the seller. Jane experienced several problems with the exercise machine that Body Works refused to repair. Jane sued the Body Works on its oral promise that if problems arose, it would "take care of them." Is this oral promise admissible in court?

12. The plaintiff/purchaser bought a sporting goods store located near the athletic field of a major university. As part of the contract, the defendant/seller agreed that he would not open a competing business in the university town for the next three years. The following summer, the seller opened a competing sporting goods store on the other side of town. The plaintiff/purchaser claimed that he was entitled to money damages for breach of contract. Can the seller of the sporting goods store open a competing store and solicit business from his former customers?

13. SupplyCo's sales representative, Jack Jenkins, has made numerous sales calls on ABC Manufacturing, usually negotiating with Henry Smith, ABC's purchasing manager. SupplyCo sells industrial solvents that could be used in ABC's manufacturing processes. ABC's solvent needs currently amount to several hundred thousand dollars annually and are fulfilled by IndusSolvCo, under a long-term supply contract. Henry suggested to Jack that if SupplyCo would permit Henry's family to use the SupplyCo corporate beach house for Henry's family vacation, he would terminate the IndusSolvCo contract prematurely to make future purchases from SupplyCo. None of this is put in writing, and Henry's family used the beach house for their two-week summer vacation. Thereafter, Henry did not terminate the IndusSolvCo. supply contract and never makes any orders from SupplyCo, although he is apologetic when Jack again visits ABC. What ethical issues are apparent for both men and their companies? Comment on the role of the statute of frauds in controlling the unethical behavior of these parties.

Chapter 9

TORTS

KEY CONCEPTS

Torts are civil wrongs involving failure to act with due care or to refrain from intentional aggression on others. Tort victims may bring suit for compensation for their injuries independently of any criminal charges or breach of contract suits concerning the same acts.

Employers may be liable for torts committed by their employees if the tortious acts occur while the employees are acting within the scope of their employment.

Intentional torts include false imprisonment, placing the victim in apprehension of battery, harmfully or offensively touching the victim, falsely injuring the victim's reputation, intruding on the victim's privacy, or interfering with the victim's property or business interests. Punitive damages may be assessed if the tort is part of a course of conduct or a pattern of malicious action.

Individuals and businesses must conduct themselves with due care to guard against the foreseeable harm that their acts may cause. An injured plaintiff may be compensated with money damages if the defendant breached the duty of reasonable care and if the negligent act is the proximate cause of injury.

Plaintiffs in negligence suits who endanger themselves through contributory negligence or voluntary assumption of risk may not recover damages even if the defendant caused the injury. Many states allow a negligent plaintiff to recover damages, but they reduce the compensatory award by the amount that the plaintiff is at fault.

Strict liability in tort holds the defendant liable regardless of fault. Although strict liability was originally limited to ultrahazardous activities, it is now also applied in defective product cases.

Proposals to reform tort law include modifying joint and several liability and setting limits on the recovery of noneconomic damages.

INTRODUCTION . . . PAST, PRESENT, FUTURE

In the past, tort law was primarily concerned with protecting people from wrongful acts causing personal injury or damage to property. Assault, battery, and trespass were considered clearly tortious acts for which the victim could seek compensation. Over the years, tort law has also become concerned with protecting people's reputation, right to privacy, and freedom from tortious actions causing mental distress. Today, interference with personal rights (sexual harassment) and economic relations (interference with contracts) is of greater concern to many people than are actions that interfere with property rights (trespass).

In the negligence area, many of the states have switched from the "all or nothing" contributory negligence defense to a comparative negligence standard. This ensures that minor negligence on the plaintiff's part will not completely bar recovery for injuries caused by the defendant's negligence. Although the negligence requirements have not changed, arguments in several recent cases have sought to impose new duties on governments, business firms, and individuals for injuries to plaintiffs.

In the future, tort law will probably be more closely tied to the increasing use of the strict liability theory in defective product cases than with intentional or negligence tort concepts. Product liability is discussed in detail in Chapter 10, but this chapter covers several possible tort reforms that may diminish the size and frequency of tort recoveries.

OVERVIEW

All individuals and corporations are responsible for harm caused by their activities. A person who is injured as a result of some action (or inaction) of a business or another person has a legal right to be compensated. **Tort law** is the legal system's recognition of an injured party's right to seek damages that compensate for personal injuries. This chapter focuses on the application of tort law to the business firm.

Whereas crimes are wrongs against society, torts are civil wrongs against individuals. The two major types of civil wrongs, torts and breach of contract, generally require compensation of the injured parties. There are three types of torts: intentional, negligence, and strict liability. Although each of these types has distinct requirements for proof by an injured party, all three require both proof of a causal connection between the tortious act and the injury and proof that the injury is compensable.

Intentional torts may involve actions that interfere with personal rights, property rights, or economic relations. Infliction of mental distress and invasion of privacy exemplify intentional torts that interfere with personal rights. Trespass and interference with contractual relations are intentional torts that interfere, respectively, with property rights and economic relations.

Negligence requires proof of four elements. The existence of a duty to act carefully is the first element. The remaining three elements are proved by showing that the nonperformance of that duty (second element) is the proximate cause (third element) of another's injury (fourth element). Contributory or comparative negligence, usually the latter, may be a whole or partial defense to negligence. Assumption of risk is also usually a defense, though it overlaps somewhat with comparative negligence.

Strict liability is an increasingly important theory of tort law. The use of extrahazardous products, such as chemicals or explosives, brings with it liability without fault. Recently, many product liability cases have been based on strict liability. Some possible tort reforms related to strict liability are noted at the end of this chapter.

BUSINESS AND VICARIOUS LIABILITY

Tort law is an important legal concern of businesses because they may be held liable for the actions of their employees. Most businesses act through other people: officers, employees, and independent agents. Corporations, partnerships, and most sole proprietorships (discussed in Chapter 13) employ people and other firms to implement their activities. The law holds a business responsible for the actions that it has the right to control.

Vicarious Liability: The Agent and the Independent Contractor

If an agent commits torts while working on behalf of a business, the injured person can sue the business and/or the agent. The liability of the business is known as *vicarious liability.* The business is called a *master* or *principal,* and its agents are known as *servants* or *agents.* Vicarious liability arises when an agent causes injury to a third party, an individual or another business, while acting on behalf of a principal.

A business is not held vicariously liable for the act of an agent if the business has no right to control that agent's means of conducting the act. For example, if a person is employed by a business solely to do a particular job without the business having any control over how the job is to be done, only that person is responsible for his or her acts. The business is not generally liable for the torts of such a person, referred to as an *independent contractor.* The vicarious liability of businesses for the acts of agents or contractors is discussed in greater detail in Chapter 12.

Vicarious Liability and Individual Direct Liability

Although a business is held vicariously liable for an employee's torts, this fact does not alter the direct liability of the employee. All persons are directly liable for their tortious acts. The vicarious liability imposed on a business for employee torts is in addition to this direct liability. For example, if ABC Trucking Company employs John to drive a delivery truck and John's negligent driving causes injury to pedestrians, John will be directly liable and ABC vicariously liable to the pedestrians for their injuries.

There are several reasons why the vicarious liability of a business is generally more significant than the direct liability of an employee. First, because both the business and the employee may be held liable, the injured party usually sues both of them. The injured person may be unsure whether the employee is solely responsible as an independent contractor or whether the business is also liable because the employee is a servant. By suing both, the injured plaintiff forces the business and the employee to determine the extent of the control that the business can exercise over the employee. Second, the business usually has greater financial resources than the employee; this basis for suing the business is known as the *deep pocket theory.* Whereas the business usually secures insurance to cover its potential liability to injured parties, the wages or other financial resources of the employee are frequently insufficient to satisfy large damage awards. Given this disparity in resources, the business, with its deep pocket, is often the primary target of the injured person.

CLASSIFICATION OF TORTS AND BUSINESS ACTIVITIES

Torts are civil wrongs that may also give rise to criminal charges. In tort cases, it is the injured party, not society, that seeks compensation from the wrongdoer. Tort law is a part

FIGURE 9–1 Relationship of Tort Law to Criminal Law and to Other Branches of Civil Law

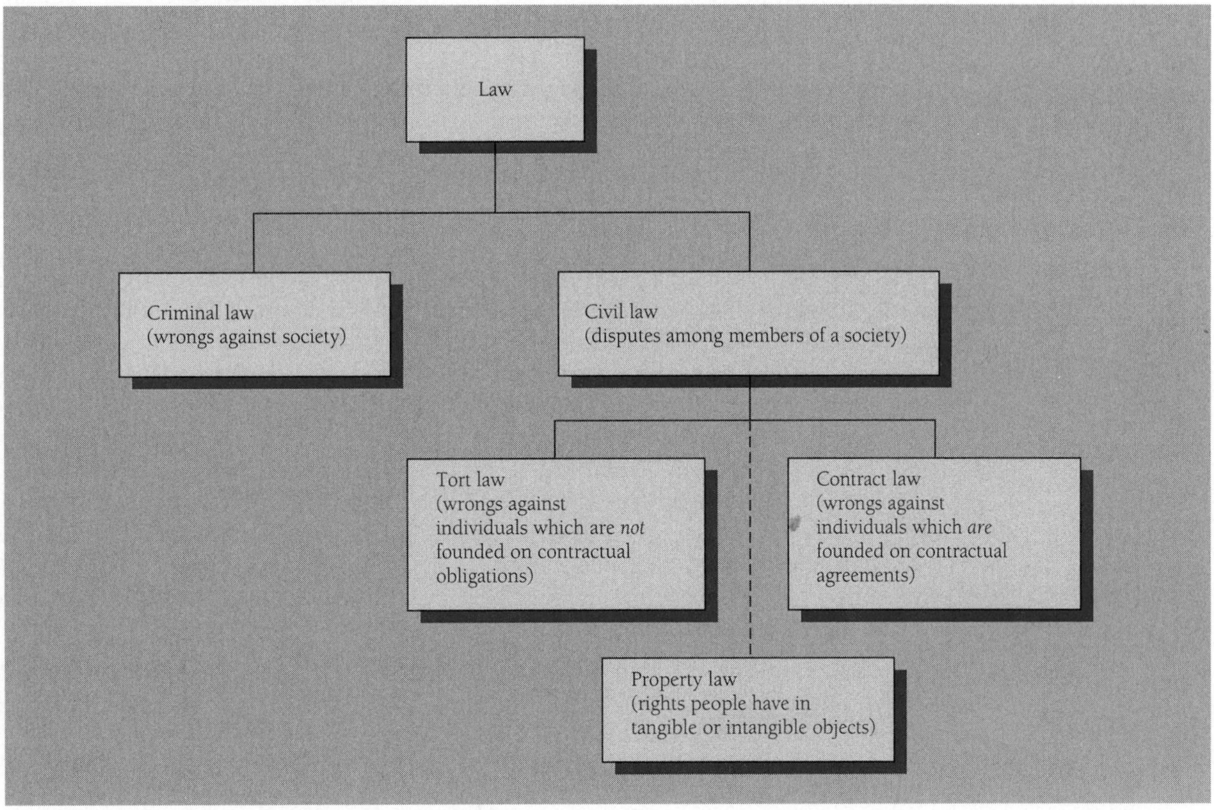

of the civil segment of our legal system. As Figure 9–1 illustrates, it may also be contrasted with the civil law of contracts discussed in the preceding chapter.

Tort Law and Criminal Law

An action that results in personal injury may also constitute a criminal action. Torts are wrongs committed against individuals or businesses, whereas crimes are wrongs committed against society. The tort case is primarily concerned with compensating the victim of a legal wrong, whereas the criminal case is primarily concerned with punishing the person who commits a wrong against society. Although criminal law originally depended on common law precedents, it is now based primarily on statutory laws passed by the federal and state legislatures. By contrast, tort law principles emerge primarily from common law precedents, though some statutes affect tort law liability.

There is no double jeopardy if a person is tried for a civil tort and a criminal act, even if both arise out of the same wrongful act. *Double jeopardy* occurs only when a person is tried twice for the same crime. The substantive law, trial procedures, and burdens of proof are different for tort cases than for criminal cases. Thus, although a tortious action could be a crime, it need not be; it is a wrong for which the injured party can be compensated.

Suppose that a tenant in an apartment causes damage to the apartment owner's property. If the tenant intentionally causes the damage, say by writing on the walls, the tenant would be committing both a tort and a crime. The tenant could be guilty of the crime of malicious destruction of property and also liable to compensate the owner for the damage. A prosecutor could sue the tenant for the criminal act, and the owner could sue the tenant for the tort that damaged the property. However, if the damage caused by the tenant was unintentional and resulted from negligence or carelessness, such as allowing water to spill over from the bathtub onto the floor, the tenant would be held liable only for the tortious action. The owner could bring a civil damage suit against the tenant, but the prosecutor could not bring a criminal action.

Tort Law and Contract Law

If a business or an individual breaches a contractual obligation while also committing a tort, the injured party may bring both a breach of contract case and a tort case. Since both cases involve civil (noncriminal) actions arising from the same events and involving the same parties, the two actions must usually be brought together in one legal proceeding. For example, suppose a consumer purchases a coffee mug and later notices that the inside is chipped, so that pieces of the mug float into the liquid he or she drinks from it. The contract of purchase was that the mug was fit for the ordinary purpose; since the mug did not meet that standard, the seller breached the contract. However, the purchaser could also sue the manufacturer of the mug in tort because the manufacturer breached its responsibility for being reasonably careful in the manufacture of its mugs. Both the manufacturer and the seller could be sued in one suit, alleging a negligent tort against the manufacturer and a breach of contract by the seller.

A plaintiff may recover damages if either the nonperformance of a contract or the commission of a tortious act is proved against the defendant. Whether the plaintiff proves that one or both wrongs has occurred, the compensation to the plaintiff is generally based on the seriousness of the injury. Because the injury is the same, the compensation due, whether from both or either of the defendants, is also generally the same. In tort cases involving intentional torts, however, the law permits the plaintiff to collect punitive damages in addition to compensatory damages. Punitive damages are not available in a breach of contract action.

INTERNATIONAL PERSPECTIVE: WHERE TO HEAR A TORT CASE AND WHAT LAW TO APPLY

The general legal principle governing a tortious act is that the law of the place where the tort occurs is usually applied. Of course, it is not always easy to determine where a tort action occurs. In the *Union Carbide*[1] case, a U.S. court was asked to hear a tort case against Union Carbide Ltd. (an Indian corporation) and Union Carbide, Inc. (a U.S. corporation), which owned a majority of the Indian corporation. The plaintiffs alleged that the lack of supervision by the U.S. firm made it responsible for the deaths and damage caused by an explosion at the Indian manufacturing facility. It asked the U.S. court to hear the case and to apply U.S. tort law in determining liability.

The U.S. court refused to hear the case because the parties, witnesses, and documentary evidence were primarily in India. The court applied the concept of *forum non conveniens*, determining that the U.S. court was not a convenient forum in which to hear and decide the case. Likewise, the court looked at the *conflict of law* rules and determined that the substantive law to apply in determining liability for the explosion should be the law of the place where the wrong occurred, India.

[1] *In Re Union Carbide Corp. Gas Plant Disaster* 809 F 2d 195 (2d Cir., 1987)

FIGURE 9–2
Requirements for Proof in Different Types of Torts

Type of Tort	Requirements	Examples
Intentional tort	Intent to commit act Causal connection of act to injury	Battery—hitting a person in the face Trespass—stepping on the property of another person without permission
Negligent tort	Duty to act in a reasonable manner Breach of duty Proximate causation connecting act to injury Injury to plaintiff	Driving a car carelessly and causing injury Improperly cleaning a floor in a store, causing a customer to slip and fall
Strict liability in tort	Ultrahazardous activity or inherently defective product The activity or defect causes plaintiff's injury The defect exists when the product is left under the defendant's control	A company dynamiting an old building causes injury to a person across the street A person is injured while drinking from a defective and chipped coffee mug.

Types of Torts

There are three different types of torts: intentional torts, negligence, and strict liability. Each type imposes liability on individuals or businesses that injure others. Yet, as Figure 9–2 illustrates, each type of tort has distinctive requirements for proof. In some situations, however, there may not be a clear line differentiating the requirements of one type of tort from another.

INTENTIONAL TORTS

An **intentional tort** is an intentional, wrongful act of the person committing the tort (the *tortfeasor*). The plaintiff must prove that the defendant intended to do the act that caused the injury. Tortious actions that interfere with personal rights may pertain to physical or mental injury, interference with private property (such as trespassing), and interference in economic relations.

General Requirements

Intentional torts require the plaintiff to prove only that the defendant intended to do the *act* that caused the injury; it is not necessary to prove that the defendant intended to cause the injury. If, however, the plaintiff can prove evil motive or desire to harm, he or she may collect punitive damages in addition to compensatory damages. *Compensatory damages*, such as damages for medical expenses, lost income, and pain and suffering, compensate the injured person for the loss actually suffered. *Punitive damages* punish the wrongdoer for his or her actions and are intended to deter others from committing similar actions. Punitive damages are usually available only in intentional tort cases where there is proof of malice or a clear disregard of the rights of others.

Required Elements of Intentional Torts

1. The defendant *intended* to do the act.
2. The act committed, not something else, *caused* the plaintiff's injury.
3. The plaintiff suffered *injury*, such as personal injury, property damage, or the deprivation of a right.

The clearest cases of intentional torts generally occur in situations in which one person causes physical injury to another person. For example, a punch in the nose can be the basis for an intentional tort if it causes injury. The law requires that people refrain from intentional actions that injure others. It allows recovery of damages for an injury caused by someone's intentional interference with the right not to be injured. The compensation depends on the amount needed to restore the injured person to the state in which he or she would have been if no tort had been committed.

Several kinds of intentional acts interfere with personal rights and are therefore torts. Torts may arise from physical or mental injury, from interference with property rights, and from interference with economic relations. Inducing a supplier to breach a contract with a business is an example of tortious interference with economic relations.

Categories of Intentional Torts

Category	Example
Interference with personal rights	Assault, battery, defamation, false imprisonment
Interference with property rights	Conversion or trespass
Interference with economic relations	Interfering with contract rights or with a prospective business advantage

Intentional Torts That Interfere with Personal Rights

Assault Assault is the intentional act of putting someone in apprehension of immediate offensive harmful touching. The victim need not be frightened; apprehension here means expectation. Words alone do not typically constitute an assault because they are not sufficient to make an ordinarily reasonable person apprehensive of immediate harm. Words coupled with a menacing gesture, however, can constitute an assault. The relevant intent in assault is that of the actor. The apprehension is based on the victim's state of mind, judged by a reasonable standard. Note that actual physical contact need not take place for an assault to occur. A person who points a gun or a knife at another person in a threatening manner commits an assault, even though the victim is not actually touched.

Battery Battery is the intentional offensive touching of another person without justification or consent. Battery also includes the unprivileged touching of another with some instrumentality put in motion by the aggressor. For example, shooting with a bullet that hits someone constitutes a battery. "Reasonable justification" is usually the key to determining whether a battery has been committed. Minimal, social, or unavoidable touching, such as occurs on a crowded bus or at a sporting event, is usually not considered battery because it is expected, justified, and not offensive to a reasonable person.

A person imminently threatened or battered by another may respond in self-defense with similar force without incurring liability. However, if a third party or a person's property is threatened, it is less likely that the "defensive battery" will be justified.

False Imprisonment False imprisonment is the intentional confinement of a nonconsenting individual within a bounded area for an appreciable time. False imprisonment may be charged against a business that attempts to deal with suspected shoplifters or with employees suspected of dishonest behavior. Under common law, a storekeeper could be held liable for detaining a suspected shoplifter if that person was later found to be innocent. Most of the states now have statutes that limit the liability of storekeepers for false imprisonment to unreasonable actions or bad faith detentions. If storekeepers have probable cause or act in good faith in detaining a suspected shoplifter, they will not be liable. The privilege is a qualified one; if it is abused, the storekeeper could be held liable for detention without reasonable cause.

Defamation A defamation is the publication of an untrue statement about another person that injures the person's reputation or character. *Slander* is oral defamation, and *libel* is written defamation. The reason for the publication requirement is that a person's good name exists only in terms of evaluations by others. If the audience does not consider the statement derogatory or if no one hears or reads the statement, there is no injury to the person's reputation or character and thus no defamation. Truth constitutes an absolute defense; true statements are considered legally justified. Certain statements are defamatory per se (automatically)—for example, accusing a person of murder or alleging that a person has a loathsome communicable disease such as syphilis.

Another defense to defamation exists if the person who makes the statement has a qualified or absolute privilege to do so. During litigation, judges, attorneys, and witnesses have an absolute privilege. A qualified privilege exists for private matters if the statement is made by someone who has a duty to make statements and if the statement is communicated only to those with an immediate interest in the information. For example, if a prospective employer asks a former employer about a former employee's character, the former employer's statement is privileged. Thus, if the former employer acts in good faith and not in malice, there is no defamation even if the statement is untrue.

Another exception occurs with public figures. No defamation of a person who is a public figure exists unless the statement is both untrue and made with malice. Malice is often difficult to prove. However if, for example, a reporter writes an untrue story about a public figure, the defamation may be regarded as malicious if the reporter did not take reasonable steps to substantiate the statements of his or her sources.

Infliction of Mental Distress The courts are beginning to recognize that the intentional infliction of emotional harm is a separate tort. Liability is usually limited to outrageous acts that cause detectable emotional injury. Although courts frequently hold that there has to be some physical injury to allow recovery for mental distress, some courts allow recovery even in the absence of physical injury.

Invasion of Privacy The right of privacy protects a person from unwarranted interference with the right to be left alone. Recent cases have involved the unauthorized revelation of private facts about a person's intimate life. For example, a television portrayal of a person's life, even if disguised as fiction, is wrongful if the viewers are likely to know whose life has been portrayed. The use of a person's commercial endorsement without consent is an unlawful appropriation. Unlike defamation, truth is not a defense to an invasion of privacy.

An important issue regarding the right of privacy arises with regards to victims of AIDS (acquired immunodeficiency syndrome). How should the right of privacy be balanced against public protection when a person with AIDS seeks the names and addresses of blood donors whom he suspects caused his disease? The case that follows discusses the right of privacy and the competing public interest in maintaining a volunteer-based blood supply.

Rasmussen v. South Florida Blood Service

500 So. 2d 533 (1987)
Supreme Court of Florida

In 1982, Donald Rasmussen suffered injuries when struck by an automobile while sitting on a park bench. While hospitalized as a result of those injuries, he received over 50 units of blood by transfusion. In July 1983, he was diagnosed as having AIDS; he died a year later. In his suit for negligence against the driver who caused his original injuries, he attempted to prove the source of his aggravated AIDS injury. He served South Florida Blood Service (Blood Service) with a subpoena requesting its records and documents indicating the names and addresses of blood donors. There was no allegation of negligence against Blood Service, and it was not a defendant in Rasmussen's negligence suit.

Blood Service asked the trial court to bar it from disclosing the requested information, but the trial court ordered it to comply with Rasmussen's subpoena. The Court of Appeals reversed, concluding that the requested material should not be discovered. Rasmussen's heirs appealed to the Florida Supreme Court.

Barkett, Justice

The Supreme Court first recognized a right of privacy based on the United States Constitution in *Griswold v. Connecticut* (1965). This right of privacy has been described as "the most comprehensive of rights and the right most valued by civilized man." In recent cases, the Court has discussed the privacy right as one of those fundamental rights that are "implicit in the concept of ordered liberty such that neither liberty nor justice would exist if they were sacrificed."

In *Whalen v. Roe* (1977), the Supreme Court specifically recognized that the right to privacy encompasses at least two different kinds of interest, "the individual interest in avoiding disclosure of personal matters, and . . . the interest in independence in making certain kinds of important decisions." In *Nixon v. Administrator of General Services* (1977), the Supreme Court reaffirmed the confidentiality strand of privacy.

Moreover, in Florida, a citizen's right to privacy is independently protected by our state constitution. In 1980, the voters of Florida amended our state constitution to include an express right of privacy. In approving the amendment, Florida became the fourth state to adopt a strong, freestanding right of privacy as a separate section of its state constitution, thus providing an explicit textual foundation for those privacy interests inherent in the concept of liberty which may not otherwise be protected by specific constitutional provisions.

A principal aim of the constitutional provision is to afford individuals some protection against the increasing collection, retention, and use of information relating to all facets of an individual's life.

It is now known that AIDS is a major health problem with calamitous potential. At present, there is no known cure and the mortality rate is high. As noted by the court below, medical researchers have identified a number of groups that have a high incidence of the disease and are labeled "high-risk" groups. Seventy-two percent of all AIDS victims are homosexual or bisexual males with multiple sex partners and seventeen percent are intravenous drug users.

As the district court recognized, petitioner needs more than just the names and addresses of the donors. His interest is in establishing that one or more of the donors has AIDS or is in a high risk group. Petitioner argues that his inquiry *may* never go beyond comparing the donors' names against a list of known AIDS victims, or against other public records (e.g., conviction records in order to determine whether any of the donors is a known drug user). He contends that because a limited inquiry *may* reveal the information he seeks, with no invasion of privacy, the donors' privacy rights are not yet at issue.

However, the subpoena in question gives petitioner access to the names and addresses of the blood donors with no restrictions on their use. There is nothing to prohibit petitioner from conducting an investigation without the knowledge of the persons in question. We cannot ignore, therefore, the consequences of disclosure to nonparties, including the possibility that a donor's coworkers, friends, employers, and others may be queried as to the donor's sexual preferences, drug use, or general life-style.

The threat posed by the disclosure of the donors' identities goes far beyond the immediate discomfort occasioned by third party probing into sensitive areas of the donors' lives. Disclosure of donor identities in any context involving AIDS could be extremely disruptive and even devastating to the individual donor. If the requested information is released, and petitioner queries the donors' friends and fellow employees, it will be functionally impossible to prevent occasional references to AIDS. As the district court recognized:

> AIDS is the modern day equivalent of leprosy. AIDS, or a suspicion of AIDS, can lead to discrimination in employment, education, housing and even medical treatment.

By the very nature of this case, disclosure of donor identities is "disclosure in a damaging context." We conclude, therefore, that the disclosure sought here implicates constitutionally protected privacy interests.

. . . Society has a vital interest in maintaining a strong volunteer blood supply, a task that has become more difficult with the emergence of AIDS. The donor population has been reduced by the necessary exclusion of potential blood donors through AIDS screening and testing procedures as well as by the unnecessary reduction in the donor population as a result of the widespread fear that donation itself can transmit the disease. In light of this, it is clearly "in the public interest to discourage any disincentive to volunteer blood donation." Because there is little doubt that the prospect of inquiry into one's private life and the potential association with AIDS will deter blood donation, we conclude that society's interest in a strong and healthy blood supply will be furthered by the denial of discovery in this case.

In balancing the competing interests involved, the probative value of the discovery sought by Rasmussen is dubious at best. The potential of significant harm to most, if not all, of the fifty-one unsuspecting donors in permitting such a fishing expedition is great and far outweighs the plaintiff's need under these circumstances.

Accordingly, we approve the decision of the Third District.

Case Questions

1. State the competing interests that were involved in the search for information in this case.
2. Why did the court determine that the disclosure of the requested information would do greater harm than its nondisclosure?

Intentional Torts That Interfere with Property Rights

Interference with property rights concerns one person's unauthorized appropriation or use of another person's property. The person owning or possessing the property may be injured even if the property is not damaged. Trespass and conversion are torts that interfere with property rights. The right to possess real property is violated by trespass; the right to possess personal property is violated by a conversion, destruction, or taking of that property.

Trespass A person who enters someone else's real property without consent is committing a trespass. The intentional act of entering the possessor's property causes the injury. Even if the property is not damaged, the possessor is harmed by the unpermitted entry. A person who owns real property, such as land and the trees attached to it, has the right to have that property remain free from interference. Of course, if the property is also damaged, there is need for greater compensation.

Conversion Conversion occurs when one person appropriates property that is rightfully in another person's possession. The theft of goods from someone's house represents not only a crime but also the tort of conversion. Thus, the defendant may be held responsible both for the criminal act of larceny and for compensatory damages. Conversion also occurs when a person fails to return borrowed property or property placed in a bailment for a specific purpose. For example, if Joe lends Sue his computer for one month but she keeps it for three months, Sue commits conversion. Sue has wrongfully denied Joe the use and enjoyment of his computer for two months. Generally, a successful conversion suit requires proof of the owner's demand for the return of property, followed by an intentional refusal to return it.

The victim of conversion may sue for damages measured by the rental value of the converted property. Thus, in the above example, Joe could sue for damages based on two months' rental value of a similar computer. If the defendant destroys or permanently deprives the owner of property, the damages would equal the market value of the property.

Intentional Torts That Interfere with Economic Relations

Both individuals and businesses are protected from unreasonable interference with their economic relations. The intentional torts of disparagement, interference with contract rights, and interference with prospective business relations all pertain to the area of economic relations.

Disparagement The tort of disparagement comprises disparaging statements regarding the business activities of a person or a business. This tort arises if the plaintiff can prove that specific business losses occurred as a result of the statements. For example, if the advertising of a business states that the products of another business are not of normal quality, that another business buys stolen goods, or that another business does not pay minimum wages to covered employees, the disparaged business could sue in tort.

Disparagement is sometimes referred to as *trade libel*. Unlike traditional libel, disparagement concerns only an individual's business or trade; it does not concern an individual's personal activities. Further, the plaintiff in a disparagement suit must prove that the disparagement is false. In a libel case, however, the defendant must prove that the libelous statements are true.

Interference with Contract Rights The tort of interference with contract relations involves intentional tampering with the contract of a person or a business. The contract may be between an employer and an employee, a business and a supplier, or a business and a customer. Intentionally causing the breach of a valid contract constitutes wrongful interference with contractual relations. The tort occurs if the defendant, knowing of a contract between the plaintiff and another party, intentionally induces that other party to breach the contract, thus causing injury to the plaintiff.

Interference with Prospective Business Relations The tort of interference with the prospective economic advantage of an individual or a business is similar to the tort of interference with contract relations. Individuals and firms have a legal duty not to tamper with the business relations of others. This is true whether those business relations involve currently enforceable contracts or merely the expectancy of contracts. The following case discusses the Pennzoil–Texaco fight over Getty Oil Company. Pennzoil sued Texaco for its wrongful interference with an agreement between Pennzoil and Getty Oil. Texaco claimed that it did not knowingly interfere with their agreement.

Texaco, Inc. v. Pennzoil Co.
729 S.W.2d 768 (1987), certiorari denied 108 S.Ct. 1305 (1988)
Texas Court of Appeals

In December 1983, Pennzoil announced an unsolicited offer for 16 million shares of Getty Oil at $100 per share. Subsequent to that offer, discussions between Gordon Getty, who, as trustee, owned over 40 percent of Getty Oil's stock, and Pennzoil progressed, and a Memorandum of Agreement was signed by Pennzoil and Getty, who, with others, owned a majority of the Getty Oil stock.

However, the Getty Oil board of directors voted to reject the Pennzoil offer, requesting instead a revised offer of slightly more than $110 per share. At the same time, Gordon Getty began to seek offers from other firms. Meanwhile, Pennzoil agreed to the Getty Oil request, and on January 4, 1984, Getty Oil's lawyers and public relations staff began to draft a press release describing the terms of the agreement with Pennzoil, and Pennzoil's lawyers began to draft a more detailed transaction agreement.

On January 5, Texaco's board of directors authorized its officers to make an offer for 100 percent of Getty Oil. Gordon Getty that day agreed to sell his shares of stock to Texaco for $125 per share. The next day, Getty Oil's board of directors voted to withdraw its counterproposal to Pennzoil and to accept Texaco's offer. After Texaco announced that it would merge with Getty Oil, Pennzoil sued Texaco for wrongful interference with its merger contract with Getty Oil. Texaco claimed that no binding contract existed between Pennzoil and Getty Oil and that if such a contract did exist, it had not knowingly interfered with the contract.

The trial court found for Pennzoil. It awarded Pennzoil $7.53 billion in damages as a result of Texaco's interference. It also found that Pennzoil should receive $3 billion in punitive damages. Texaco appealed to the Texas Court of Appeals.

Warren, Justice

First, Texaco asserts that Pennzoil failed to prove that Texaco had actual knowledge that a contract existed. New York law requires knowledge by a defendant of the existence of contractual rights as an element of the tort inducing a breach of that contract. However, the defendant need not have full knowledge of all the detailed terms of the contract.

There is even some indication that a defendant need not have an accurate understanding of the exact legal significance of the facts giving rise to a contractual duty, but rather may be liable if he knows those facts, but is mistaken about whether they constitute a contract. . . . Since there was no direct evidence of Texaco's knowledge of a contract in this case, the question is whether there was legally and factually sufficient circumstantial evidence from which the trier of fact reasonably could have inferred knowledge.

Texaco argues that the writings known to Texaco and the verbal assurances it was given are matters of undisputed fact that do not add up to actual knowledge of a binding contract. It states that the only written evidence known to Texaco was the Memorandum of Agreement, the January 4 press release, and the January 2 "Dear Hugh" letter from Gordon Getty to Hugh Liedtke, Pennzoil's CEO. Texaco contends that these writings confirm the absence of a binding agreement.

Based on the other evidence at trial, different inferences could have been drawn from the fact that the press release did not state exactly the same information contained in the Memorandum of Agreement.

It was for the jury to decide what weight to give to the evidence, and where conflicting inferences were possible from the evidence, it was the jury's task to choose between them.

Texaco's next contention is that the unambiguous wording of the press release, i.e., the "subject to" and agreement "in principle" language, demonstrated that there was no contract. We disagree that the press release is unambiguous, and our discussion above of the press release's use of the terms: agreement "in principle," and "subject to" a definitive agreement applies equally here. That language did not in itself preclude the existence of a contract, nor a jury finding of Texaco's knowledge of one.

We find that an inference could arise that Texaco had some knowledge of Pennzoil's agreement with the Getty entities, given the evidence of Texaco's detailed studies of the Pennzoil plan, its knowledge that some members of the Getty board were not happy with Pennzoil's price, and its subsequent formulation of strategy to "stop the [Pennzoil] train" and "take care of Liedtke."

Pennzoil contends that the jury could also draw an inference of Texaco's knowledge of its agreement from the evidence relating to a *Wall Street Journal* article dated January 5. That article reported on the terms of the Pennzoil/Getty merger and referred to an "agreement" 17 times.

Finally, Pennzoil points out that certain demands made by the [Getty] Museum and the [Getty] Trust also gave Texaco knowledge of their contractual obligations to Pennzoil. The jury could reasonably infer that Texaco was given knowledge of the Pennzoil agreement from this evidence. . . .

The jury was not required to accept Texaco's version of events in this case, and this Court may not substitute its own interpretation of the evidence for the decision of the trier of fact. There was legally and factually sufficient evidence to support an inference by the jury that Texaco had the required knowledge of an agreement.

From the evidence, the jury could have concluded that Texaco deliberately seized upon an opportunity to wrest an immensely valuable contract from a less affluent competitor, by using its vast wealth to induce the Museum, Gordon Getty, and Getty Oil to breach an existing contract. The evidence shows that the wrongful conduct came not from servants or mid-level employees but from top-level management. Apparently the jury believed that the conduct of Texaco's top-level management was less than the public was entitled to expect from persons of such stature. There is no evidence that Texaco interfered with the contract to injure Pennzoil, but the jury could reasonably conclude from the evidence at trial that Texaco cared little if such injury resulted from its interference.

Considering the type of action, the conduct involved, and the need for deterrence, we are of the opinion that the punitive damages are excessive and that the trial court abused its discretion in not suggesting a remittitur.

If within thirty days from the date of this judgment, Pennzoil files in this Court a remittitur of two billion dollars, as suggested above, the judgment will be reformed and affirmed as to the award of $7.53 billion in compensatory damages and $1 billion in exemplary damages; otherwise the judgment will be reversed and remanded.

Case Questions

1. What "knowledge" of the Pennzoil–Getty Oil contract by Texaco was required to prove that Texaco committed the tort of inducing a breach of contract?
2. What facts showed that Texaco could have had some knowledge of that contract?

NEGLIGENT TORTS

Under the law of negligence, a person or a business must act responsibly and will be held liable for breach of the duty of care when others are injured because of such a breach. Whereas an intentional tort is actionable only if there is intent to do the act causing injury, a **negligent tort** occurs if a careless act causes injury to others. Thus, negligence is based on fault. People have an obligation to act reasonably. When the carelessness of an individual or a business causes injury to others, tort law holds that individual or business liable to compensation for the injury.

General Requirements

Four requirements must be proved by a plaintiff in a negligence case.

Required Elements of Negligence

1. The defendant owes a *duty of care* to the plaintiff.
2. The defendant *breached* or did not perform that duty.
3. The nonperformance or breach of the duty was the *proximate cause* of the plaintiff's injury.
4. The plaintiff suffered *injury,* and damages can be determined to compensate the plaintiff for the injury.

Cases often focus on particular elements of negligence. However, the *Williams* case, which follows, reviews each of the four major elements. Note, however, that it has combined into one the last two elements listed above—proximate cause and injury. Which of the four required elements was found to be lacking in the *Williams* case?

Williams v. Jackson Co.

359 So. 2d 798 (1978)
Court of Civil Appeals of Alabama

The Williamses purchased a house and later found that serious defects in the subflooring had led to termite infestation. The Williamses then sued both the real estate company (the Jackson Company) that had prepared the deed transferring ownership of the house to them and the firm (Pest-Ex) that had inspected the house for termites. Both firms claimed that they were not liable because they owed no duty to the Williamses. The trial court agreed with the firms and the Williamses appealed.

Wright, Presiding Judge

In every action in tort three elements must be present: (1) a duty of defendant to protect plaintiff from the injury of which he complains; (2) a failure to fulfill that duty; and (3) an injury to the plaintiff proximately caused by the failure of defendant. Plaintiff contends that when defendant [Jackson Company] drew the deed for the transfer of title in the purchase of the house and lot, it undertook the practice of law. By such undertaking it assumed the duty of not only properly drawing a legal instrument but also the duty of giving full legal advice to plaintiffs concerning the purchase, including informing them that the doctrine of caveat emptor applied. We are unable to accept this contention for recovery.

There is no contention that Jackson Company represented to plaintiffs that they were skilled or qualified to give legal advice, or assumed any contractual obligation to provide such advice. Assuming that the preparation and furnishing of the deed by Jackson Company constituted the unauthorized practice of law in violation of statute and was negligence as a matter of law, the duty arising thereby was only to provide a proper and legal deed resulting in transfer of title. Jackson Company could not thereby be said to have assumed the duty of providing full legal advice. . . .

We further consider that plaintiff's theory breaks down as to the third element necessary, that of proximate cause. The negligent act charged is drawing of the deed. The injury complained of is the purchase of a defective house. There is no conceivable chain of causation between the breach of a duty to draw a valid deed and the purchase of a house with holes in the floor. The decision to purchase has been made before a deed is drawn. In fact, it is stated in the claim that the contract to purchase was executed before Jackson Company was ever contacted. Even if that were not so, it is not reasonably foreseeable that the preparation of a deed would result in the purchase of a defective house. The test of reasonable foreseeability is not met.

The claim of plaintiffs against Pest-Ex alleged that on July 15, 1976, plaintiffs signed a contract with a real estate agent for the purchase of a house and that after signing the contract of purchase, they applied for a commitment from the Federal Housing Administration to guarantee a loan for the purchase. A commitment letter was subsequently issued by F.H.A. but was subject to inspection for termites by an approved termite control company and a report thereof on a form furnished by F.H.A.. Defendant Pest-Ex did perform the inspection and submitted the report, a copy of which was required by F.H.A. to be furnished the buyer and seller. The claim is that Pest-Ex negligently failed to inspect and state in the report that there was damage to the subflooring and that as a proximate sequence of the failure to report the presence of damage, plaintiffs suffered injury. The issue on appeal is whether the court was correct in finding that Pest-Ex owed no duty to plaintiffs because they were not a party to the contract for inspection.

In dismissing the claim through a finding that Pest-Ex owed no duty to plaintiffs because they were not parties to the contract Pest-Ex made with F.H.A., the court erred. Privity of contract is not a required basis of duty in such cases. It has now been expressly stated by our supreme court that duty may arise from a social relationship as well as from a contractual relationship; that a duty to use care may arise from the reasonable man test of foreseeability of injury. Thus one who undertakes to perform a contract may be determined to owe a duty to others not privy to the contract to perform his obligations under the contract without negligent injury to such others. Such duty may arise from the foreseeability that such others may be injured by negligent performance, or duty may arise from the knowledge that others are relying upon a proper performance. This latter source of duty could surely be shown by evidence in support of the claim against Pest-Ex in this case. The trial court was incorrect in its holding that plaintiffs could not recover from Pest-Ex because there was no privity of contract.

Case Questions

1. Which of the four elements that must be proved in a negligent tort case were found to be lacking in the Williamses' case against Jackson Company?
2. How does the court's analysis of the case that the Williamses brought against Pest-Ex differ from the case against Jackson Company?

Duty of Care The law imposes a duty on all individuals and businesses to act carefully toward others when it is foreseeable that a lack of reasonable care could cause injury. The duty of care is based on the premise that many actions involve a predictable danger of injury. It is not necessary to foresee the precise harm that could occur if reasonable care is not exercised, but only that the failure to exercise reasonable care poses an unreasonable risk of some harm. However, if no risk of harm is foreseen, there is no duty to use reasonable care. In such situations, causing an injury to someone would not constitute a negligent tort.

Certainly, it is reasonable to foresee that driving a car too fast risks harm to other drivers and pedestrians. Therefore, a duty to use reasonable care requires the driver to guard against such harm. A driver who fails to perform the duty of driving carefully may be committing a negligent tort. Some of the states apply no-fault laws to motor vehicle accidents. In those states, in most cases the injured party need not prove the driver's negligence to be entitled to compensation.

Breach or Nonperformance of Duty The plaintiff must prove that the defendant did not perform the duty of care or is responsible for the nonperformance of that duty. For example, if you have a party in your home, the law imposes on you a duty to use reasonable care in maintaining the property and in conducting the party so as to protect guests from foreseeable risks. Does a room have loose rugs on which a guest could slip and fall or loose ceiling tiles that could fall on someone? If the homeowner or apartment tenant does not take precautions with regard to such items of foreseeable danger, the duty of care is not performed (and thus is breached). Thus, nonperformance of the duty of care occurs if a person acts in a careless, reckless, or unreasonable manner.

For example, in a case filed against the Los Angeles International Airport,[1] no liability was placed on the airport for the death of a person who was killed when a bomb that had been placed in a public coin-operated locker exploded. The court found the airport itself was not in dangerous condition and that the city that operated the airport had taken reasonable steps to guard against terrorism: "The complaint here sets forth no facts which give rise to the duty on the part of the City to expand its policing of the airport terminal."

The law does not require that a person or a business be an insurer or a guarantor of the absolute safety of others. Negligence is based on a comparison of a person's actions with the standard for the actions expected from the mythical, ordinary, reasonable person. Sometimes a person or a business acts reasonably yet still causes injury to others. For example, a company that manufactures room heaters uses a process to ensure that they do not overheat, risking fire. If the company has acted reasonably, as compared to the standard expected of manufacturers of similar products, there would be no negligence even if the heater became defective and caused injury to its user. In such a case, the company could not be held liable for negligence, though it might be held liable on some other basis, such as an implied warranty or strict liability.

Proximate Cause Once the plaintiff has shown that the defendant breached the duty of care, the defendant's act must also be shown to be the proximate cause of the plaintiff's injury. *Proximate cause* is the standard used in negligence cases to establish the required causal relationship between the defendant's nonperformance or breach of duty and the plaintiff's injury. Only injuries with a close (proximate) causal connection to the actions of the defendant, or injuries caused by actions whose consequences can be reasonably foreseen, can trigger the defendant's liability. The law does not impose unlimited liability on the defendant whose actions are only weakly linked to the plaintiff's injury.

For example, suppose that a person standing on a curb and seeking to board a bus takes a big stride to reach the bus step and then falls and is injured. The proximate cause of the person's injury would probably not be the distance of the bus from the curb. The proximate cause would probably be the person's act of striding too far to reach the bus instead of walking off the curb and then climbing onto the bus. If the causal connection is not close, there is no liability on the bus company.

There is no negligence in situations in which happenstance or intervening events lead to unforeseen consequences. For example, suppose that Adams, who is camping in the woods, fails to carefully extinguish a campfire. If the fire spreads from the campground to a nearby building, Adams would probably be liable because there would be a close causal connection between his breach of duty and the damage to the building. However, if soon after the building begins to burn, an unusually strong wind causes the fire to spread for miles and miles, the rule of proximate cause would excuse Adams from liability for damage caused to more distant property.

Even if a duty of care is not performed, there must be a close connection between the plaintiff's injury and the nonperformance. In the *Moncur* case against Los Angeles

[1] *Moncur v. City of Los Angeles Dept. of Air,* 137 Cal. Rptr. 239 (1977).

International Airport, the court examined whether the explosion was sufficiently connected to the alleged lack of reasonable care by the Airport Commission. Courts traditionally look to the defendant's actions to see whether *but for* those actions the injury to the plaintiff would still have occurred.

This "but for" test is generally used to determine proximate cause. "But for" the actions of the defendant, would the injury to plaintiff have occurred? In the case that follows, the court considers both the requirement of duty and the requirement of proximate cause. If Kmart was not responsible for the injury to the plaintiffs, who was? The court also notes that even if it assumed Kmart should have a crosswalk, Kmart might not be liable. Why not? Note, however, the Commentary on the California Supreme Court decision, which replaces the "but for" test with the "substantial factor" test. The latter is easier for plaintiffs to meet.

Flowers v. Kmart Corp.

616 P.2d 955 (1980)
Court of Appeals of Arizona

Robert and Charlotte Flowers were both struck by an automobile driven by a third party (Ruch) as they were walking to their car in Kmart's parking lot. They sued Kmart, alleging that it had negligently failed to adequately regulate pedestrian and vehicular traffic in its parking lot. Kmart responded that the alleged hazardous condition was not the proximate cause of the appellants' injuries. The trial court granted Kmart's motion for summary judgment. This appeal followed.

Donofrio, Judge

The question of whether a duty exists is one for the court to decide; the question of whether such a duty has been breached is ordinarily reserved for a jury to determine; and the question of whether such negligence is the proximate cause of an injury is also usually a question for the jury. The absence of a breach of care can be decided by the court as a matter of law only if the court can say that reasonable persons could come to no other conclusion. Similarly, the question of whether negligence is the proximate cause of an injury is one for the court, if after reviewing all the facts and circumstances, there is no reasonable chance or likelihood that the conclusions of reasonable persons would differ.

While Kmart was not the insurer of the safety of the appellants, it did owe them a duty of reasonable care to protect them from physical harm caused by the accidental, negligent, or intentional acts of third persons.

Kmart contends that . . . it did not breach its duty to the appellants by failing to provide a crosswalk for their use. On the present record, we agree. Our courts have often held than an invitor should not be obligated to anticipate that invitees would fail to appreciate dangers generally known to be inherent in conditions which are obvious.

Even if we were to have held that Kmart had owed a duty to the appellants, we would affirm the granting of the summary judgment on the additional ground that the appellants failed in their burden to show that the acts and omissions of Kmart constituted the proximate cause of the accident. The proximate cause of an injury is that which in a natural and continuous sequence, unbroken by any efficient intervening cause, produces an injury, and without which the injury would not have occurred.

There is only limited testimony as to causation. In his deposition, appellant Robert Flowers stated that he really didn't know how Kmart should have acted differently to regulate and control traffic in its parking lot. He said that he believed that if there had been a crosswalk then defendant Ruch would have stopped and not struck them. This belief is sheer speculation. Appellants' statement that if a crosswalk had been available then they would have used it does not address the issue of whether the presence of a crosswalk would have prevented the accident.

We conclude that the trial court correctly decided that there were no genuine issues of material fact and that appellees were entitled to judgment as a matter of law.

Affirmed.

Case Questions

1. Why did the Flowers sue Kmart rather than Ruch, the driver of the car?
2. Which of the four elements of negligence were proved in this case? Which were not proved?

Commentary: Will the Proximate Cause Requirement Be Changed?

By Amy Stevens and Junda Woo

The California Supreme Court has made it easier for victims to win personal-injury and product-liability lawsuits, in a technical decision with wide implications.

The ruling will affect virtually all jury trials statewide in which it has been alleged that there were multiple causes for a person's injuries. The 6–1 ruling struck down the state's traditional jury instruction on negligence liability, substituting one that would permit juries to find that there can be more than one cause of harm.

The court's decision requires an instruction that asks the jury to determine instead whether the defendant's conduct was a "substantial factor" in bringing about harm, and would allow a jury to hold defendants liable even if their behavior was only a contributing factor in the injury.

The rejected jury instruction required a jury to find that harm wouldn't have occurred "but for" the defendant's actions. "Proximate cause," the rejected standard, has been criticized by legal scholars and disapproved by many state courts nationwide, because it tended to mislead juries into thinking that the defendant had to be physically near the injured party, or that the defendant's actions had to have occurred close in time to the harm. The decision by the influential California high court could encourage even more states to move away from the "but for" test.

The "substantial factor" test developed as an alternative, discretional instruction about 25 years ago. The effect of the new ruling is to make that instruction mandatory.

Source: Amy Stevens and Junda Woo, "California Eases Standards on Negligence," *The Wall Street Journal*, December 12, 1991, p. B5.

Injury The final element of a negligence case requires proof that the plaintiff's injury is compensable by some amount of damages. The injury need not be physical. Legal injury occurs whether the plaintiff sustains pain, suffers embarrassment, or loses money. The trier of fact—this is normally the jury in a negligence case—determines the amount of damages necessary to compensate the plaintiff.

The plaintiff generally has the burden of proving the injury and the extent of damages necessary to compensate for it. In a negligence trial, both the plaintiff and the defendant frequently use expert witnesses to aid them in presenting evidence related to the damage issue. For example, the plaintiff may have a doctor testify regarding the extent of the injuries suffered and the likelihood of permanent disability. The defendant usually has a doctor testify that the plaintiff's injuries are less severe than claimed.

The plaintiff also has an economic or financial expert testify that based on his or her calculations and projections, and taking the doctor's testimony into account, the plaintiff will have a diminished earning capacity in the future. This expert usually concludes that the jury should award the plaintiff a sum of money computed as the present value of the plaintiff's future earnings loss. The defendant can, of course, cross-examine the plaintiff's financial expert and can produce an expert witness who testifies that a smaller amount of damages would compensate for the plaintiff's earnings loss, and the plaintiff's attorney can, of course, cross-examine the defendant's expert witness. It is for the jury to determine the believability of these conflicting economic projections.

Negligence Per Se and Res Ipsa Loquitur In two circumstances—negligence per se and *res ipsa loquitur*—the burden of proof on the plaintiff is less than it is in most negligence cases. *Negligence per se* applies when the plaintiff uses the defendant's violation of a criminal statute as proof of the defendant's negligence. For example, if a statute requires a moving firm to have certain safety equipment on its trucks and the defendant moving firm did not have such equipment, the statute creates a conclusive presumption that the defendant was negligent. In some of the states, the presumption is not conclusive but can be rebutted by other evidence.

Res ipsa loquitur means "the thing speaks for itself." In some situations, circumstantial evidence is used to establish a prima facie (first impression) case of negligence. Unless the defendant counters this evidence, the doctrine of *res ipsa loquitur* is sufficient to prove negligence. This doctrine is used in situations in which the plaintiff cannot know the exact cause of negligence, as in cases involving product liability or negligent building construction. A building will not usually crumble or collapse unless there was some negligence in its design or construction; thus, even though the exact cause of the failure is not known, circumstantial evidence suggests that there was negligence.

ETHICAL DILEMMAS FOR INTENTIONAL AND NEGLIGENT TORTS

The intentional and negligent state of mind accompanying a tortious act can be exposed to ethical analysis. Clearly, when a tortfeasor knows that an act will injure others, performing that act is unethical. Intentional aggression on another person illustrates an ethical conflict between the actor's self-interest and the victim's rights. Fraud is a classic form of ethical dilemma, in which the perpetrator breaches the victim's trust. For example, a salesperson who has gained the trust of a potential customer knows that the customer is likely to rely on the salesperson's statements. This salesperson commits fraud by intentionally making a statement contradictory to fact.

Negligent actions can also be analyzed with ethical principles. To the extent that wrongdoers have had sufficient experience with harmful or damaging instrumentalities, they should know when extra precautions are necessary to avoid injury. Evidence of carelessness, recklessness, or a wanton disregard of the consequences of an act indicates that the actor is making an unethical decision to ignore the dangers. This is not to say that all negligent acts are unethical. However, when the actor should know that an outcome could cause injury and fails to adequately guard against it, the actor's reckless disregard of consequences approximates intentional misconduct, an unethical act. For example, society increasingly believes that driving under the influence of alcohol is both an unethical act and an illegal criminal act. The person knows, or should know, that his or her conduct can cause injury to others but, disregarding the possible consequences, he or she operates a motor vehicle.

FIGURE 9–3
Comparative Negligence: Recovery Under Different State Standards

	State A	State B
Recovery for plaintiff who is 85% at fault and whose injuries amount to $100,000	$15,000	0 (Plaintiff cannot recover if more than 50% at fault.)
Recovery for defendant who is 15% at fault and whose injuries amount to $50,000	$42,500	$42,500

In State A, the court would actually award the plaintiff nothing and the defendant would receive the net amount of $27,500, the difference between the amount due the plaintiff and the amount due the defendant.

Defenses to Negligent Torts

There are three basic defenses to negligence claims: contributory negligence, comparative negligence, and assumption of risk.

Contributory Negligence The **contributory negligence** defense, which must generally be raised by the defendant, alleges that even though the defendant may have been negligent, the plaintiff was also somewhat negligent. In the past, the law prohibited any recovery by the plaintiff from the defendant if the defendant proved any contributory negligence by the plaintiff. This is commonly known as the *all-or-nothing rule* because the plaintiff wins all if contributory negligence is not proved and nothing if contributory negligence is proved.

Comparative Negligence Because of the harsh effect of contributory negligence on plaintiffs who were only slightly at fault, most states now use comparative negligence as the most common defense in negligence cases. **Comparative negligence** weighs the relative negligence on the plaintiff and the defendant. In some states, it does not matter how much negligence is attributable to the plaintiff. Even if the plaintiff can prove that the defendant is only 15 percent negligent in causing the plaintiff's injuries, the plaintiff (who would be 85 percent negligent) can still recover damages equal to 15 percent of the money needed to totally compensate for those injuries. For example, suppose that a two-car accident occurs in a state using this type of comparative negligence defense. Assume that the plaintiff (the driver of Car 1) is found to be 85 percent at fault for his own injuries. If $100,000 is needed to totally compensate the plaintiff for his injuries, the plaintiff would be able to recover $15,000 from the defendant (the driver of Car 2), who was 15 percent at fault.

Other states permit the plaintiff to recover damages from the defendant only if the defendant is responsible for at least 50 percent of the plaintiff's injuries. In the states that follow this interpretation of comparative negligence, the plaintiff in our example would recover nothing from the defendant.

However, suppose that the defendant was also injured in this accident, in the amount of $50,000. Figure 9–3 compares the amount that each party would recover under both systems of comparative negligence if the plaintiff was 85 percent at fault and suffered $100,000 in injuries and the defendant was 15 percent at fault and suffered $50,000 in injuries.

Assumption of Risk Like comparative negligence, the **assumption of risk** defense is based on the concept of fault. If the plaintiff knew, or should have known, of the risk inherent in a particular situation and voluntarily assumed that risk, the defendant should not be responsible for the plaintiff's injuries even if the defendant is negligent. A classic example of this defense occurs when a plaintiff is injured while riding in a car with an intoxicated driver. Although the defendant driver is negligent in driving while intoxicated, the plaintiff, who knows the risk of riding with an intoxicated driver yet voluntarily does so, may be denied recovery due to his or her assumption of that risk.

Some of the states that accept the defense of comparative negligence do not also accept the defense of assumption of risk. In their view, the plaintiff's assumption of risk is a form of negligence comparable to the defendant's negligence. In these states, the assumption of risk and comparative negligence defenses are viewed as one defense. As is indicated in the case that follows, there is significant overlap between the two concepts. However, even when a state has dropped the use of contributory negligence in favor of comparative negligence, a distinction generally exists between comparative negligence and assumption of risk.

Assumption of risk occurs when a person who knows of a risk nevertheless proceeds in the face of that risk. Contributory or comparative negligence compares the action of the one person to the action of the reasonable person (to determine whether there is any negligence) and of the defendant (to determine the relative negligence of the parties). A person's actions can contribute to causing an injury even if he or she does not know of the risk involved. In the following case, what was the basis for the distinction between these two defenses in Mississippi?

McGowan v. St. Regis Paper Co., Inc.

419 F. Supp. 742 (S.D. Miss. 1976)
United States District Court

McGowan was injured while unloading wood chips for his employer, Columbia, at the St. Regis paper mill. He had performed similar work at the paper mill before, so he knew that oil or grease often built up on the ramp that he used. In fact, he admitted that he had seen the oil and grease that caused him to fall. When McGowan sued St. Regis for negligence, St. Regis claimed that he had assumed the risk when he continued to use the ramp after knowing it to be in a dangerous condition. The trial court's decision follows.

Nixon, District Judge

The owner or occupier of business premises owes invitees, such as plaintiff, the duty to exercise reasonable or ordinary care to keep its premises in a reasonably safe condition and to warn them of any dangers which are known or should be known to the owner through the exercise of reasonable care. However, in the interest of his own safety, an invitee is required to use that degree of care and prudence which a person of ordinary intelligence would exercise under the same or similar circumstances, and in the usual case, there is no obligation to protect him against dangers which are known to him or which are obvious and apparent. Against such conditions it may normally be expected that the visitor will protect himself, and for this reason it is frequently held that reasonable care requires nothing more than a warning of danger.

In this case, although the defendant did not post any warning signs or give any other type of warning to plaintiff or other truck drivers unloading the wood chips on the defendant's ramp, they nevertheless knew, or in the exercise of reasonable care, should have known, of the probable existence of oil or grease being present on the ramp, which lifted many trucks while unloading chips therefrom; in fact, the plaintiff testified that he actually saw the oil or grease which subsequently caused him to slip and fall and realized that it constituted a dangerous condition. Therefore, the defendant was under no duty to warn him of that obvious and known danger.

There is no proof that the defendant caused the oil or grease to be present on the ramp, that they had knowledge thereof, or that it had existed for such a period of time that they were charged with such knowledge. As a matter of fact, ten trucks had unloaded on this ramp on the morning in question prior to the time that the plaintiff was injured, and one had just left the ramp after unloading. Thus, the plaintiff has failed to prove by a preponderance of the evidence that the defendant was guilty of any negligence which proximately contributed to cause the plaintiff's injuries.

. . . The Mississippi Supreme Court has held that where assumption of the risk overlaps and coincides with contributory negligence, the contributory negligence or comparative negligence rule of Mississippi is applicable. However, the Court refused to abolish the doctrine of assumption of the risk as a bar to recovery and recognized that the application of the rule of comparative negligence, which is not a complete defense, where it overlaps and coincides with contributory negligence, "does not prevent a defense on the ground that the plaintiff's injury was caused by his negligence, if his negligence was the sole proximate cause of the injury." The defense of assumption of the risk is in fact quite narrowly confined and restricted by two requirements: first, that the plaintiff must know and understand the risk he is incurring, and second, that his choice to incur it must be entirely free and voluntary. As the Mississippi Supreme Court pointed out in the case of *Daves v. Reed,* the significant difference between assumption of the risk and contributory negligence is between risks which were in fact known to the plaintiff and risks which he merely might have discovered by the exercise of ordinary care. The former defense is governed by the subjective standard of the plaintiff himself, whereas the latter is measured by the objective standard of the reasonable man. Assumption of the risk is a jury question in all but the clearest cases.

The undisputed facts of the instant case constitute one of the rare instances where the doctrine of assumption of the risk as a complete bar to recovery is applicable, inasmuch as the plaintiff subjectively knew, as admitted in his sworn testimony, that the oily or greasy substance was present on the unloading ramp, that it constituted a dangerous condition, and that he voluntarily and freely was walking through the substance with a chain in his hand in an attempt to "tie down" his truck prior to tilting the ramp and unloading wood chips from the truck. He did not notify the employee of the defendant who was on duty in the control house a short distance away of this condition or ask that anything be done in connection therewith, but freely and voluntarily subjected himself to the danger which he recognized. Thus, he is barred from recovery by the doctrine of assumption of risk as it has been enunciated by the Mississippi Supreme Court.

Case Questions

1. Why wasn't St. Regis obligated to warn McGowan of the danger presented by the oil and grease on the ramp?
2. Did the court find that St. Regis was negligent in maintaining the ramp?
3. How did the court differentiate assumption of risk from contributory or comparative negligence?

INTERNATIONAL PERSPECTIVE: TORT LAW AND THE EUROPEAN COMMUNITY

In the European Community, (EC), Article 215 of the Treaty of Rome provides that the noncontractual liability of the Community is governed by the "general principles common to the laws of the member states." Much of the work of the European Court of Justice is now handled by the European Court of First Instance. This court was authorized by the 1987 Single European Act, and its jurisdiction is limited to actions or proceedings by individuals or legal persons (firms).

When damages are sought in litigation involving Community law, the European Court of Justice and the Court of First Instance must determine what principles of noncontractual liability (tort law) are common to the laws of member states. This is not easy, as there are now 12 member nations. Two members are common law jurisdictions, whereas the others are civil or code law countries. The European Community tort liability principles are not based on those national laws which impose the highest duty. Instead, it is common law national principles, such as fault being required for finding of negligence, that create Community liability principles. Although the laws of many EC member states base liability for defective products on negligence, today the EC uses a no-fault liability standard for damages caused by defective products.

STRICT LIABILITY TORTS

The traditional view of strict liability is that a person engaging in inherently dangerous or ultrahazardous activities is liable to any injured party, regardless of the actor's intent or fault. Therefore, strict liability is different from intentional torts and negligence because strict liability requires neither a finding of intentional wrongdoing nor a finding of fault.

General Requirements

Strict liability recovery is relatively easy to establish compared to either the negligence or intentional tort standards. A **strict liability** tort occurs if one person does something dangerous that injures another person who is within the scope of risk. The determination of whether an activity is extrahazardous is the important question in strict liability cases. By reading past cases, we can make a list, though not an exhaustive one, of activities that courts find to be extrahazardous. The dusting of crops, the keeping of wild and vicious animals, and the use of explosives and certain chemicals are activities that have been found to be ultrahazardous. On the other hand, such activities as mining coal, driving automobiles, and keeping gasoline in service station tanks have been found not to be ultrahazardous.

In the last several decades, an increasing number of suits involving defective products have been decided on the basis of strict liability. There is strict liability for a product found to be defective if the product is unreasonably dangerous and the danger is not readily apparent to the buyer. Typical strict liability cases have involved such products as foods and drinks, playground equipment, defective consumer appliances, and automobiles. In these cases, the plaintiff must meet the following three requirements which will be discussed further in Chapter 10.

Required Elements of a Strict Liability Defective Products Case

1. There was a *defect* in the product.
2. The defect *caused* the plaintiff's *injury.*
3. The defect existed when the product left the defendant's *control.*

Defenses

Because proof of negligence is not required in strict liability cases, the contributory or comparative negligence defenses are not available. However, most states do recognize as defenses the assumption of risk and *misuse*, which is a form of assumption of risk based on improper product use. If a cigarette manufacturer warns the purchaser or user of cigarettes of a specific risk associated with their use, the manufacturer is generally not liable to compensation for injuries resulting from that risk to a person who knowingly assumed it. A recent Supreme Court case discussing this issue is found in Chapter 10. If a product that is intended to be used to kill ants or insects outside the house is used to kill household insects, despite a clear warning on the product, and the product injures the plaintiff, the defense of misuse could be used against the injured plaintiff.

Policies

Several policies underlie the allowance of recovery on the basis of strict liability. First, such liability tolerates an extrahazardous activity if it has some social value. Second, compensation for a victim is more likely in strict liability cases than in negligence cases. Allowing the defendant to spread the costs of the injury among many users enables society to receive the benefits of the extrahazardous activity while sharing the cost of compensating the injured party. For example, society benefits from allowing miners and road or bridge builders to have explosives available for their work. Society also shares in the cost of compensating a party injured by the use of such explosives because blasting insurance obtained by the miners and the road or bridge builders is expensive, due to strict liability laws, and that affects the cost of our minerals, roads, and bridges.

On the other hand, there are some policy reasons against the concept of strict liability. The most obvious is that the defendant can escape liability only by forgoing the extrahazardous activity. Thus, the law does not distinguish between a good and bad business that performs an extrahazardous activity except to the extent that good users undertake extra precautions.

TORT LAW REFORM

Because so many cases involving strict liability have applied to sales of products that cause injuries, many manufacturers have sought federal and state legislative changes in the area of product liability law. This area involves not only the strict liability and negligence tort concepts but also warranty and misrepresentation laws. Because product liability laws are important to consumers of products as well as their manufacturers and sellers, Chapter 10 is devoted to this subject, although this section discusses some possible areas of product liability reform.

The Future of Tort Law

The 1980s were a period of dramatic growth in litigation. Tort law expanded as more extensive duties were recognized by the courts. Juries became more sympathetic to victims of accidents, product failures, and unsafe conditions, applying the deep pocket theory to hold accountable corporate defendants that were perceived to have extensive financial resources. Eventually, insurers of these firms claimed that they were unable to accurately predict the outcome of tort litigation. As a result, insurance premiums skyrocketed, some types of insurance became unavailable, and both insurers and potential corporate defendants called for tort reform in the media, through various legislatures, and in the courts.

Proponents of tort reform claimed that it would create a fair, predictable, and equitable fault system while reducing the costs of litigation. They asserted that the tort crisis had increased the cost of goods and services, stifled innovation in new products, delayed the introduction of new drugs, and postponed the sharing of benefits in many research breakthroughs. The tort reforms that have been sought include: changes in the allocation of liability among several defendants, limits on certain types of damages, restriction of double recoveries by plaintiffs, reduction of the contingency fee incentives of plaintiff attorneys, sanctions against frivolous suits, and periodic payments of damages over a number of years. The first two areas of potential reform are noted in subsequent sections. In the years ahead, astute managers will closely monitor both legislative and judicial endeavors to address this important segment of the legal environment.

Joint and Several Liability

Joint and several liability requires the complete satisfaction of a plaintiff's damage award from any or all of the responsible defendants, regardless of the degree of fault of any single defendant. A defendant may be required to pay more than its share of the damage award if the other defendants are *judgment-proof* (uninsured or unable to pay). This provides an incentive to plaintiffs to sue a deep pocket defendant that may be only slightly at fault because the whole compensatory and punitive amount must be paid by any defendant with sufficient financial resources. For example, drivers injured in traffic accidents often sue the state as well as the other driver because the state is responsible for road conditions. If the other driver is at fault but has insufficient insurance to satisfy the plaintiff's damages, the state's deep pocket is liable for the remainder. Most proposals to limit joint and several liability would apply only to certain torts or for defendants that are only slightly at fault while retaining joint and several liability for more serious torts.

Damage Caps

Tort reform efforts usually attempt to significantly limit or eliminate such *noneconomic damages* as (1) pain and suffering, (2) lost of consortium with a spouse, (3) emotional distress, (4) embarrassment, and (5) punitive damages. For example, some states have imposed specific dollar amount ceilings for noneconomic damages in all negligence cases. Other states have such ceilings only for specific types of suits, most notably medical malpractice or product liability cases. Still other states require "clear and convincing evidence" before allowing noneconomic damages to exceed the ceilings. Efforts have been increasing to establish more precise standards of misconduct before punitive damages are awarded, as discussed in Chapter 5.

SUMMARY

Tort law is an important area of legal concern to businesses. Liability is imposed on a business for the actions of its employees, agents, and even its contractors if they are acting within the scope of their authority and are subject to control by the business. Since a business usually has greater insurance coverage and financial resources, the deep pocket approach generally leads tort victims to make more and larger claims on businesses than on individual wrongdoers.

Three classes of torts can form the basis for the liability of a business to an injured party. Intentional torts are based on actions that have been committed intentionally. Negligent torts result from the wrongdoer's carelessness or lack of reasonable care. Strict liability torts require no proof of fault or of intent to act in a wrongful manner; instead, they are based on dangerous or ultrahazardous activities. Since many strict liability torts involve product liability concerns, this area is treated in greater detail in the next chapter.

Intentional torts require, not proof of intent to harm, but proof of intent to commit the act that causes harm. Among the intentional torts are actions that interfere with personal rights, such as battery or false imprisonment, and actions that impair a person's reputation or state of mind, such as defamation, the infliction of mental distress, and invasion of privacy. Other intentional torts are those that interfere with property rights, such as trespass and conversion, and those that interfere with economic relations, such as interference with contract rights.

Negligent torts occur when a person or a business having a duty to act reasonably toward others does not perform that duty and that nonperformance is a proximate cause of the injuries of others. In negligence cases, the presence of each of the four elements of negligence—duty, nonperformance, proximate cause, and injury—must be proved. Several defenses may be asserted by a business sued in a negligence case. The defenses of contributory and comparative negligence examine whether the plaintiff contributed to causing the injuries suffered. In contributory negligence, any negligence on the plaintiff's part prevents recovery whereas in comparative negligence, which is a defense in most of the states, the negligence of the injured plaintiff reduces, but does not totally bar, the compensation that the defendant must pay to the plaintiff. The assumption of risk defense is used in a negligence case if the plaintiff performed some activity closely associated with a specific risk of which he or she was, or should have been, aware.

In strict liability cases, no proof of the defendant's fault is required. A defendant that makes dangerous products, such as firearms or caustic chemicals, is liable for any injuries resulting from the use of those products. Strict liability cases were originally concerned only with wild animals or inherently dangerous products, but today almost any defective product can be the basis for such a case. The only defenses to a product liability case are the plaintiff's assumption of risk or misuse of the product.

The chapter also notes some of the proposals for reforming tort law that have been advanced so as to alert the reader to potential changes in this legal area.

KEY TERMS

tort law, p. 255
intentional tort, p. 259
negligent tort, p. 266
contributory negligence, p. 273
comparative negligence, p. 273
assumption of risk, p. 274
strict liability, p. 276

CHAPTER EXERCISES

1. Susan left work after dark one evening. She was assaulted and battered in the parking lot. The security guard detained the assailant. Both Susan and the local district attorney brought separate cases against the defendant. Did their cases cause double jeopardy for the defendant? Compare and contrast the causes of action Susan brought on the basis of tort assault and battery with the causes of action the district attorney brought on the basis of criminal assault and battery.

2. What four requirements must a plaintiff prove in order to recover damages in a suit based on negligence?

3. Mrs. Davis was in debt to a finance company. She informed the company that she was no longer employed, that she was on public aid, and that she was unable to make payments on her loan. Over an eight-month period, in attempting to collect the debt, employees of the finance company called her several times a week, sometimes more than once a day, using obscene and threatening language. Employees of the finance company visited her home weekly to demand payments on the debt. On one occasion, an agent from the finance company even telephoned her at a hospital where she was visiting her sick daughter. Mrs. Davis sued the finance company for damages, alleging severe emotional distress. Was the finance company's conduct toward her tortious? Explain.

4. John, a novice skier, brought a negligence action against Big Bear Ski Resort for injuries that allegedly occurred when he became entangled in underbrush concealed by loose snow. John was skiing on the resort's novice trail. No warning signs re-

garding the underbrush were posted. What would be the basis for holding Big Bear Ski Resort liable?

5. The plaintiff was injured in an automobile accident caused entirely by the defendant driver. The plaintiff was not wearing his seat belt. He was thrown from the car and sustained a head injury when he landed on the pavement. The defendant offered evidence that had the plaintiff been wearing his seat belt, he would not have been thrown from the car. If the doctrine of comparative negligence is followed, will this reduce the damages to which the plaintiff is entitled? Explain.

6. Black sued a retail store for injuries. He slipped on rainwater as he stepped on a mat just inside the door to the store. Prior to the fall, a store employee placed a "Caution: Wet Floor" sign approximately 5 feet in front of the door. In accordance with store procedure, the employee mopped the entrance area periodically on rainy days. What defense will the retail store assert? Is this defense different from contributory negligence?

7. Explain the concept of joint and several liability, how it is applied, and the grounds on which it is criticized.

8. The defendant company has been a bicycle manufacturer for 50 years. It has always used reputable raw material suppliers. During the manufacturing process, it always follows quality control standards, making safety checks on every 10th bicycle that comes off the assembly line. Jane purchased a new bicycle from the company. While riding under normal conditions, she jumped a low curb. Because three spokes of the front wheel were defective, the wheel collapsed, and Jane was injured. As a result of the accident, she is now paralyzed from the waist down. Discuss the liability of the company on the grounds of negligence and strict liability.

9. A man ran to catch a commuter train in Grand Central Station. An employee of the Long Island Railroad negligently tried to assist the man as he jumped for the train, causing the man to drop a package he was carrying. The package, which contained legal fireworks, exploded. The explosion shook the train platform, causing a weighing scale to fall over and injure Mrs. Palsgraf and her daughter, who were standing some distance away from the explosion. Mrs. Palsgraf sued the Long Island Railroad. What was the result, and why? (*Palsgraf v. Long Island Railroad Co.*, 248 N.Y. 339, 1928.)

10. The plaintiff (a salesman) sought damages for statements that were alleged to have been made by his former employer. He alleged that following the termination of his employment, the sales manager of his former employer made statements to his friends, business associates, and customers accusing him of theft of company property and that the sales manager knew these statements to be false. The plaintiff's wife testified that the sales manager's statements caused her husband to become depressed and to have more sleepless nights than he had had before he learned of the statements. The plaintiff testified that the accusations caused him anxiety, depression, humiliation and many sleepless nights. Has the plaintiff made out a cause of action for slander? Is the truth a defense to a cause of action based on defamation? Is the truth a defense to a cause of action based on invasion of privacy? (*Hennis v. O'Connor*, 388 N.N. 2d 470, 1986.)

11. The plaintiffs were homeowners near a uranium milling facility operated by the defendant corporation. Unknown to the plaintiffs, for years, the defendants had placed "mill tailings" in and around the foundation of the land that later became the foundation for the plaintiff's home. As a result, the plaintiffs were exposed to very high levels of radiation. They brought suit for chromosomal damage, increased risk of cancer, and mental suffering. Should the plaintiffs have to prove that chromosomal changes in their body have occurred? How should the court decide if there is any likelihood that such damage could be reversed in the future if they move away from the danger? The judge determined that the plaintiffs could not recover for "increased risk of cancer" because they could not show any present physical injury. Should the plaintiffs accept such risk because "there are always some risks in life"? Some courts reason that recognizing and compensating injuries based on increased risk would "create a flood of speculative injuries" from people who fear they might be injured. Do you agree that the burden of deciding such cases would be too great for the legal system? Should the law focus instead on those who are injured rather than those who might be injured? See

Bradford v. Susquehanna Corporation 586 F. Supp. 14 (D. Colo., 1984) and *Anderson v. W.R. Grace & Co.* 628 F. Supp. 1219 (D. Mass., 1986).

12. Consider the following cases related to drug-testing by employers. On May 26, 1986, the city of Plainfield, N.J., orders all its firefighters to submit to a surprise urinalysis while under the surveillance and supervision of bonded testing agents employed by the city. A similar process was repeated on two separate occasions until over 100 employees were tested. There was no notice of the intent to conduct the mass urinalysis. Later, sixteen firefighters were informed they had tested positive for the presence of controlled dangerous substances; they were immediately terminated without pay. The plaintiff firefighters claim their right to privacy and their freedom from unreasonable searches and seizures were violated. Do you agree? What torts would you argue have been committed? See *Capua v. City of Plainfield* 643 F. Supp. 1507 (1986).

Recall that while government employees are protected by the federal Constitution against unreasonable searches and seizures, employees in the private sector have no such protection. Would your answer be different if the employees worked for Disney World? What if the employees worked for a non-profit agency such as the Boy Scouts or the Red Cross? Should it matter if the private firms receive substantial federal funds? Analyze these cases from an ethical perspective. See C. Stone, "Corporate Vices and Corporate Virtues: Do Public/Private Distinctions Matter?" 130 *Univ. of Penn. Law Review* 1441 (1982).

Part 3

CONSUMER LAW

This part covers the public and private law that affects a business's consumer relations. Public law generally facilitates consumer choice by requiring disclosure about products and services or by preventing the sale of unsafe products or deceptive services. Private law gives consumers a remedy for their damages when public law fails to protect them adequately.

The private and public law approaches to defective product liability and prevention are covered in Chapter 10. First, the business's exposure to product liability under tort and contract law theories is explored. Next, the preventative governmental regulation of product safety is discussed.

Chapter 11 discusses the public laws that protect consumers from incomplete or deceptive information about products and services. The Federal Trade Commission (FTC) defines deceptive advertising, polices advertisers' claims, and administers consumer financing disclosures, requiring lenders to provide comparable information. Additionally, there is a discussion of the credit granting and collection process.

Chapter 10

PRODUCT LIABILITY

KEY CONCEPTS

There are four primary theories of product liability: breach of warranty, negligence, strict liability, and misrepresentation.

Express warranties arise when the seller makes affirmations of fact or provides a description, sample, or model of the goods. Implied warranties are imposed by the UCC on merchants and on any seller that selects goods for the buyer.

Negligent product liability is usually based on the seller's failure to properly design, inspect, or package the goods or the failure to warn users of known dangers.

Under strict liability, the burden of proving that a product's defects render it unreasonably dangerous is generally easier to prove than negligence or breach of warranty.

Nearly any seller in the distribution chain may be liable for product liability. However, sellers may have affirmative defenses: contributory or comparative negligence, assumption of risk, or misuse.

Government agencies promote product safety by regulating the design, manufacture, and distribution of goods.

INTRODUCTION . . . PAST, PRESENT, FUTURE

Historically, product liability suits were brought infrequently and were usually unsuccessful. Two basic legal principles limited liability for unsafe products. First, *caveat emptor,* or "let the buyer beware," protected sellers from buyers' suits, requiring buyers to inspect each product for defects prior to purchase. Before the 20th century, products were simple and buyers had a basic understanding of most materials and mechanisms. However, the industrial revolution changed these basic underlying assumptions. First, products became more complex, utilizing electronics and new materials with unknown characteristics: plastics, composites, metal alloys, dangerous chemicals, and synthetics. These new materials often have new and unknown mechanisms, with capabilities outside most buyers' general experience. Common people largely understood products made of wood, leather, natural fabrics, and simple metals. Second, after the West was settled, the work skills became increasingly specialized. The capabilities and rugged individualism of the jack-of-all-trades became unsuitable for the increasingly specialized factory work. Third, complex new products are mass-produced in distant factories, breaking the traditionally close contact buyers had with the local craftsmen. As a result of these structural changes, buyers had greater difficulties comparing the safety and quality of products to their own experience with similar products or through familiarity with the product.

The second legal principle limiting liability for defective products was the doctrine of **privity of contract.** Privity denies the victim the right to sue the seller of an unsafe product unless the victim contracted directly with the seller. Typically, suits against manufacturers were barred because the victim purchased from a retailer. The assembler/manufacturer, wholesaler, or component part manufacturer lacked privity with the victim and was thus shielded from liability. Privity was also absent if the victim was a bystander, such as a pedestrian in an auto accident or a member of the purchaser's family. The trend today—one of the most significant legal trends of this century—is to relax privity in product liability cases based on tort theories. However, there are still many vestiges of privity, particularly when the breach of warranty theory is used.

OVERVIEW

This chapter discusses the theories, remedies, litigation, and regulatory environment of product liability laws. The first section examines the historical development of suits against sellers of products. Next, the chapter explores the breach of warranty, negligence, strict tort liability, misrepresentation, and criminal theories of product liability cases. The risk exposure of business is directly related to several procedural concerns: who may sue, who may be liable, the burden of proof required, and affirmative defenses. The last section discusses product safety regulation by government agencies, preventive regulatory programs to avert product liability harms by enforcing minimum standards. This is consistent with the old adage that "an ounce of prevention is worth a pound of cure." Tort concepts developed in Chapter 9 and in the following sections are also applicable to services and malpractice.

Does the fact that an automobile was purchased from a retailer prevent the manufacturer's liability for personal injuries caused by defects in the automobile? The next case started the inroads on the privity doctrine that later permitted development of more liberal theories of product liability, such as strict liability.

MacPherson v. Buick Motor Co.

217 N.Y. 382, 111 N.E. 1050 (1916)
New York Court of Appeals

MacPherson bought a new Buick from a retail dealer that had originally purchased the car from the manufacturer, Buick Motor Company. The spokes of the car's wooden wheel crumbled, causing the car to collapse and injure MacPherson. The wheel was purchased from a component part manufacturer. A reasonable inspection would have disclosed the defect.

Cardoso, Judge

For a neglect of ordinary care or skill whereby injury happens, the appropriate remedy is an action for negligence. The right to enforce this liability is not to be confined to the immediate buyer. The right extends to the persons or class of persons for whose use the thing is supplied. It is enough that the goods "would in all probability be used at once . . . before a reasonable opportunity for discovering any defect which might exist," and that the thing supplied is of such a nature "that a neglect of ordinary care or skill as to its condition or the manner of supplying it would probably cause danger to the person or property of the person for whose use it was supplied, and who was about to use it."

We hold that the principle of *Thomas v. Winchester* is not limited to poisons, explosives, and things of like nature, to things which in their normal operation are implements of destruction. If the nature of a thing is such that it is reasonably certain to place life and limb in peril when negligently made, it is then a thing of danger. Its nature gives warning of the consequences to be expected. If to the element of danger there is added knowledge that the thing will be used by persons other than the purchaser, and used without new tests, then, irrespective of contract, the manufacturer of this thing of danger is under a duty to make it carefully.

We have put aside the notion that the duty to safeguard life and limb, when the consequences of negligence may be foreseen, grows out of contract and nothing else. We have put the source of the obligation where it ought to be. We have put its source in the law.

From this survey of the decisions, there thus emerges a definition of the duty of a manufacturer which enables us to measure this defendant's liability. Beyond all question, the nature of an automobile gives warning of probable danger if its construction is defective. This automobile was designed to go 50 miles an hour. Unless its wheels were sound and strong, injury was almost certain. It was as much a thing of danger as a defective engine for a railroad. The defendant knew the danger. It knew also that the car would be used by persons other than the buyer. This was apparent from its size; there were seats for three persons. It was apparent also from the fact that the buyer was a dealer in cars, who bought to resell. The maker of this car supplied it for the use of purchasers from the dealer. The dealer was indeed the one person of whom it might be said with some approach to certainty that by him the car would not be used. Yet the defendant would have us say that he was the one person whom it was under a legal duty to protect. The law does not lead us to so inconsequent a conclusion. Precedents drawn from the days of travel by stagecoach do not set the conditions of travel today. The principle that the danger must be imminent does not change, but the things subject to the principle do change. They are whatever the needs of life in a developing civilization require them to be.

In this view of the defendant's liability there is nothing inconsistent with the theory of liability on which the case was tried. It is true that the court told the jury that "an automobile is not an inherently dangerous vehicle." The meaning, however, is made plain by the context. The meaning is that danger is not to be expected when the vehicle is well constructed.

There is nothing anomalous in a rule which imposes upon A., who has contracted with B., a duty to C. and D. and others according as he knows or does not know that the subject-matter of the contract is intended for their use.

We think the defendant was not absolved from a duty of inspection because it bought the wheels from a reputable manufacturer. It was not merely a dealer to automobiles. It was a manufacturer of automobiles. It was responsible for the finished product. It was not at liberty to put the finished product on the market without subjecting the component parts to ordinary and simple tests.

Case Questions

1. What is the doctrine of privity? What does this doctrine mean in product liability suits?
2. What is the duty of care for a manufacturer of goods? To whom is the duty owed?
3. What impact is there on the liability of a manufacturer if component parts of that manufacturer's products are made by other manufacturers?

Limitations on Product Liability Suits

The manufacturing industry has been plagued by expansive new product liability theories. One such area of changing law concerns how to deal with *delayed manifestation* of injuries, a very complex issue. In some cases, a product has unknown hazards when made. The victim's injury cannot be detected until several years after using the defective product. Meanwhile, the statute of limitations may run out and the victim's suit is prohibited. In other cases, delayed manifestations of injuries, such as the side effects of new medications, make it difficult to later identify the precise manufacturer of the defective product.

Recent decisions have addressed both of these concerns. In many states, the statute of limitations period begins to run when the injury occurs rather than earlier when the product was purchased. This exposes the seller to potential liability for a longer time after the sale. A few states have reacted to this greater exposure by enacting *statutes of repose*. These limit the time that products must remain defect free. These and other product liability reforms are discussed at the end of the chapter.

Some drug cases, such as *Sindell v. Abbott Laboratories,*[1] have introduced new theories to address the difficulty of identifying the manufacturer of the particular product causing the victim's damage. To prevent miscarriage, Sindell's mother took a prescription drug, DES, while pregnant with Sindell. Many years later, Sindell developed cervical cancer due to her mother's use of DES. Sindell could not identify which one of the several manufacturers that made the drug actually produced the prescription her mother used. The court developed the concept of **market share liability** to permit victims to bring suit against any or all producers of DES. This concept makes it unnecessary to precisely identify the brand of drug in the actual prescription used. Instead, the extent of a manufacturer's liability may be based on the defendant's actual market share in the drug sales at the time the drug was used. Recent cases have prohibited third generation plaintiffs (granddaughters) from recovery.

A limitation on victims' product liability suits has arisen in the asbestos and IUD product liability litigation. Manville, the predominant asbestos producer and a profitable company, filed for bankruptcy reorganization under Chapter 11. Manville continued operations and delayed suits by creditors and liability claimants until it emerged from reorganization. Eventually, the product liability claimants approved a plan to settle their claims without forcing Manville into liquidation. Claimants generally received less money damages than they could have if not for bankruptcy protection.

In recent years, a great increase in business litigation related to product liability has occurred. Product liability laws have a profound impact on manufacturers, wholesalers,

[1] *Sindell v. Abbott Laboratories,* 163 Cal. Reptr. 132, 607 P.2d 924 (1980).

and retailers. The cost of product liability planning, insurance, and defense has skyrocketed, creating a cost containment crisis affecting both the manufacturing and insurance industries. Reactions to the product liability crisis by courts, juries, government, insurers, and manufacturers assure that product liability concerns will continue to influence the decisions of business managers profoundly.

Many innovative new products may be withheld from the market in anxiety over the prospects for product liability suits. This possibility is particularly troublesome for national public policy as the need increases for new drugs to treat dangerous and debilitating diseases such as AIDS and cancer. Excessive apprehension over potential product liability may chill America's technological competitiveness in world markets. Legislatures and the courts have been both broadening and restricting product liability duties, making it difficult to accurately estimate product liability insurance premiums. This uncertainty may have contributed to the liability insurance crisis discussed in Chapter 9. As a result of these problems, several states have been "rolling back" the trend toward higher and unpredictable product liability awards. Although federal product liability legislation is currently stalled in Congress, emphasis will continue to be placed on these problems for the next few years. Product liability reform is discussed further at the end of this chapter.

THE PRODUCT LIABILITY THEORIES

There are several theories of product liability under state law. Managers should be aware of the range of legal theories available to plaintiffs and should understand the limitations and special features of each theory. Contract theories of express and implied warranty usually apply if the goods are purchased. Negligence and strict liability expose sellers to the greatest potential liability. Each theory, as applied in different states, may have different substantive and procedural requirements.

Warranty Liability

A **warranty** is an affirmation of fact or a promise of performance made in any product sale governed by the Uniform Commercial Code (UCC). In either warranty or strict liability cases, it is unnecessary to determine who is "at fault." Many states apply warranty liability to any business in the chain of distribution. However, some privity requirements still exist for warranty actions in about one third of the states.

Warranty provisions are often contract terms that impose additional duties on the seller. There are three types of product quality warranties: (1) express warranty, (2) implied warranty of merchantability, and (3) implied warranty of fitness for a particular purpose. The UCC also implies a warranty of title requiring sellers to have rights to pass full ownership to buyers unless the possibility of adverse claims is evident to the buyer.

Express Warranties Express warranties are contractual promises relating to the future performance of goods. Goods are defective if they fail to meet the express warranty standards. Warranty liability arises if the seller agrees to provide a remedy to the purchaser. The buyer need not prove any seller misrepresentation or fault. An express warranty arises under UCC 2-313 if the seller's promise forms a *basis of the bargain*. This means that the parties must consider the warranty a part of the description of the goods. No particular reliance needs to be proved for the warranty to become enforceable. The promises that form the terms of the express warranty may come from (1) an affirmation

FIGURE 10–1 Express Warranty

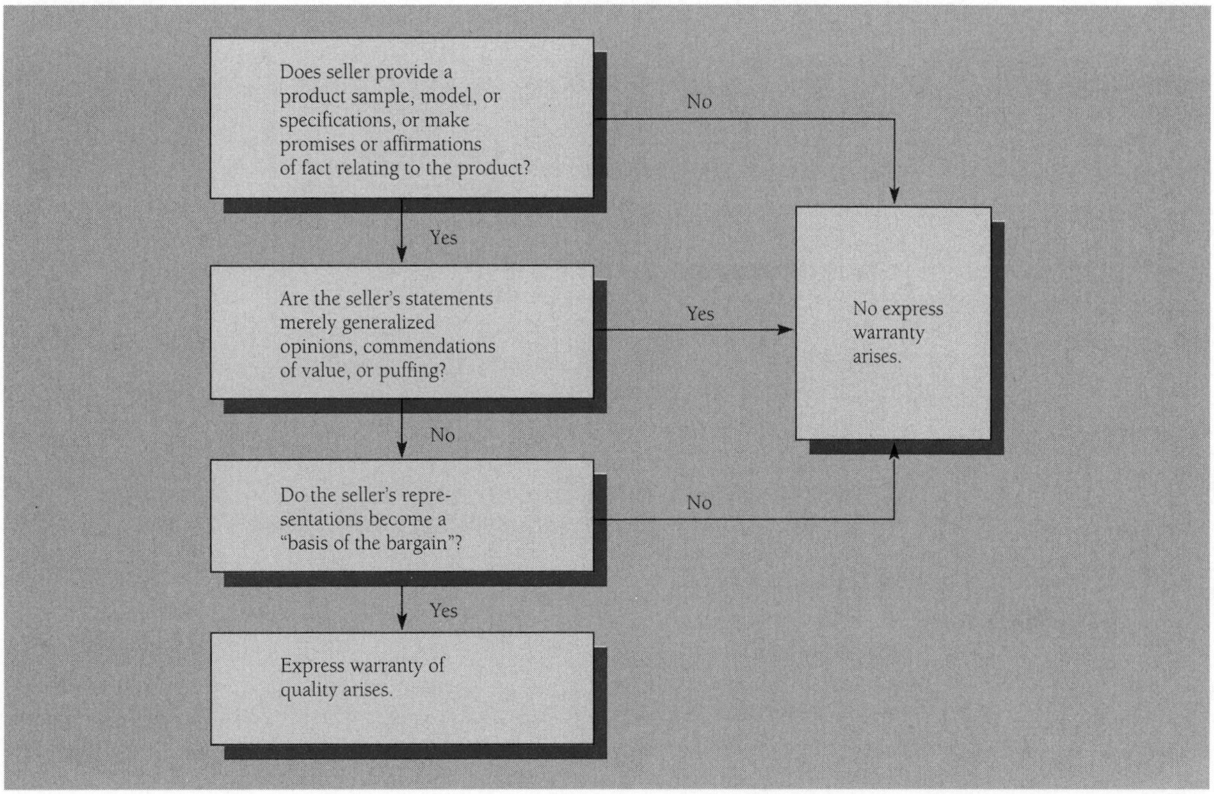

of fact or any promise relating to the goods, (2) a description, (3) a sample, (4) technical specifications, or (5) a model used by the seller in making representations to the buyer.

Express warranties are formed by the seller's promises or by other conduct. For example, an express warranty is formed if the seller presents technical specifications or a blueprint to the buyer. An express warranty may also be inferred from past deliveries that lead the buyer to assume that future deliveries will involve similar goods. A sample of the goods, such as grain or chemicals drawn from a larger bulk, may represent the expected average quality. A model may be used when the actual goods to be delivered are not available. The making of an express warranty is illustrated in Figure 10-1.

Generalized statements of value are usually too vague to be warranty promises; such expressions are a seller's *puffing*. For example, when an auto dealer claims that an automobile is "great" or "a bargain," no warranty arises. For a warranty to be valid, however, warranty statements need not be in any special format, nor labeled as a *warranty* or *guarantee,* nor must the seller intend to create warranty obligations. Express warranties are enforceable to the extent that the seller promises satisfaction. The precise timing of the seller's promise or the seller's display of a sample is not important; even promises made after the sale can create or modify the warranty. What is important is that the statement becomes part of the contract description.

An express warranty may be made in written or oral form as long as the parol evidence rule does not require that it be in writing. As explained in Chapter 8, the parol evidence

FIGURE 10–2 Implied Warranty of Merchantability

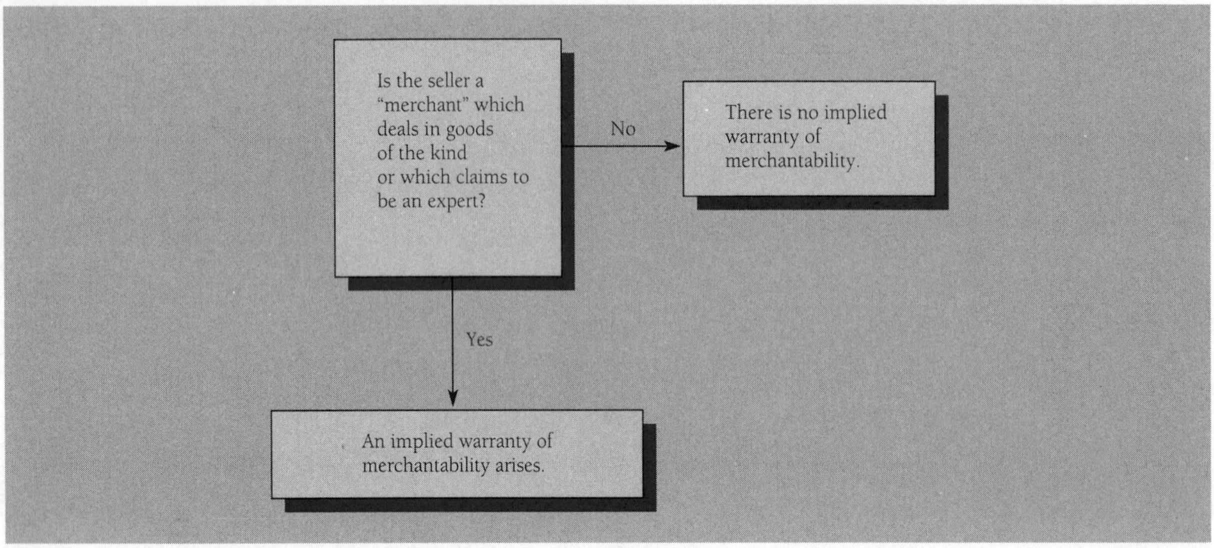

rule applies when a written contract of sale is intended to be the complete contract between buyer and seller. If the written contract is considered an integration and it contains no written warranty, then no oral evidence of an express warranty is admissible. However, because promises create a warranty, a car dealer's statements made while showing a car are considered a warranty, even if there is no formal written contract.

Implied Warranty of Merchantability A warranty of merchantability is implied under UCC 2-314 whenever goods are sold by a merchant. A *merchant* is a seller or buyer who deals in goods of the kind involved in the contract or who professes to be an expert in the particular trade. Sellers are considered merchants when they employ agents who are merchants. Even secondhand goods must conform to the merchantability standard when sold by a merchant. In isolated sales, those occurring out of the ordinary course of business, no merchantability warranty applies. For example, if a person sells his or her personal car to a neighbor, there is no implied warranty of merchantability. Merchantability warranties are illustrated in Figure 10-2.

Characteristics of Merchantability

1. Pass without objection in the trade under the contract description.
2. Are of fair average quality if *fungible* (i.e., all units equivalent or interchangeable, as with grains or chemicals, and lose their identity when mixed together).
3. Are fit for the ordinary purposes for which they are used.
4. Are of even kind, quality, and quantity within the variations permitted.
5. Are adequately contained, packaged, and labeled as required by the agreement.
6. Conform to the label or container description.

An implied warranty may be inferred from trade customs. A *usage of trade* is a common practice among most of the firms in a particular business. A *course of dealing* refers to a common practice followed by two contracting partners from their previous dealings. For example, an obligation to provide pedigree papers to substantiate the lineage of a show dog or a blooded bull may arise from a usage of trade. The trade might consider an animal merchantable only where adequate pedigree is demonstrated. Merchantable goods must at least conform to the UCC characteristics of merchantability.

The various definitions for merchantable goods may also provide guidance for the interpretation of an unclear express warranty. Should products be fit for the ordinary uses expected by consumers? The following case illustrates how the implied warranty of merchantability establishes minimum consumer expectations for performance.

McCabe v. L. K. Liggett Drug Co.

330 Mass 177, 112 N.E.2d 254 (1953)
Massachusetts Supreme Court

The plaintiff purchased a coffee maker from L. K. Liggett Drug Company. After a few uses, the plaintiff noticed that the water failed to boil up fully from the lower chamber to the upper chamber. The coffee maker injured the plaintiff when it exploded in her face as she examined it more closely.

Williams, Justice

Merchantable quality means that goods are reasonably suitable for the ordinary uses for which goods of that description are sold. Whether this coffee maker was of such quality depended on its capability, when properly used, to make coffee. This presented a question of fact for the jury. The evidence consisted of the coffee maker and the testimony of the plaintiff concerning the so-called explosion. The jury could find that she assembled the parts [and used it to make coffee] in accordance with instructions and in the manner that an ordinary person would be expected. The evidence, we think, was sufficient to warrant them in finding why the coffee maker blew up when so used. The appliance had a circular metal filter which fitted over the upper end of the tube in the upper bowl and obviously was intended to hold the coffee grounds in the upper bowl while permitting the water to come up from the lower bowl. This filter was similar in shape to an ordinary metal bottle cap. It had thirty-six small notches in its lower edge which rested on the bottom of the bowl and encircled the opening of the tube. The filter was held in position over the tube by a plunger equipped with springs which reached down into the tube. The plaintiff offered in evidence the opinion of an expert that the area of the notches of the filter was inadequate to provide for the release of the pressure which developed from the boiling water; that this area could be further decreased by the "congealing" of the coffee grounds; and that the pressure in the bottom section, having inadequate release, would build up to a point where it would have an explosive effect.

The fact that the apparatus violently burst apart in the manner described showed that the accumulating pressure was not being released and in the absence of explanation was itself evidence of a defective condition.

If the coffee maker was so imperfect in design that it could not be used without the likelihood of an explosion it could be found that the appliance was not reasonably fit for making coffee and therefore not merchantable.

The plaintiff was not deprived of her right to rely upon the implied warranty either by a failure to inspect or by an inspection before use, as it could have been found that the defect in design would not be obvious to an ordinary person on inspection.

Case Questions

1. When does an implied warranty of merchantability arise?
2. What minimum performance may be expected from merchantable goods?
3. What was the effect of the buyer's opportunity to inspect the goods before using them?

FIGURE 10–3 Implied Warranty of Fitness for a Particular Purpose

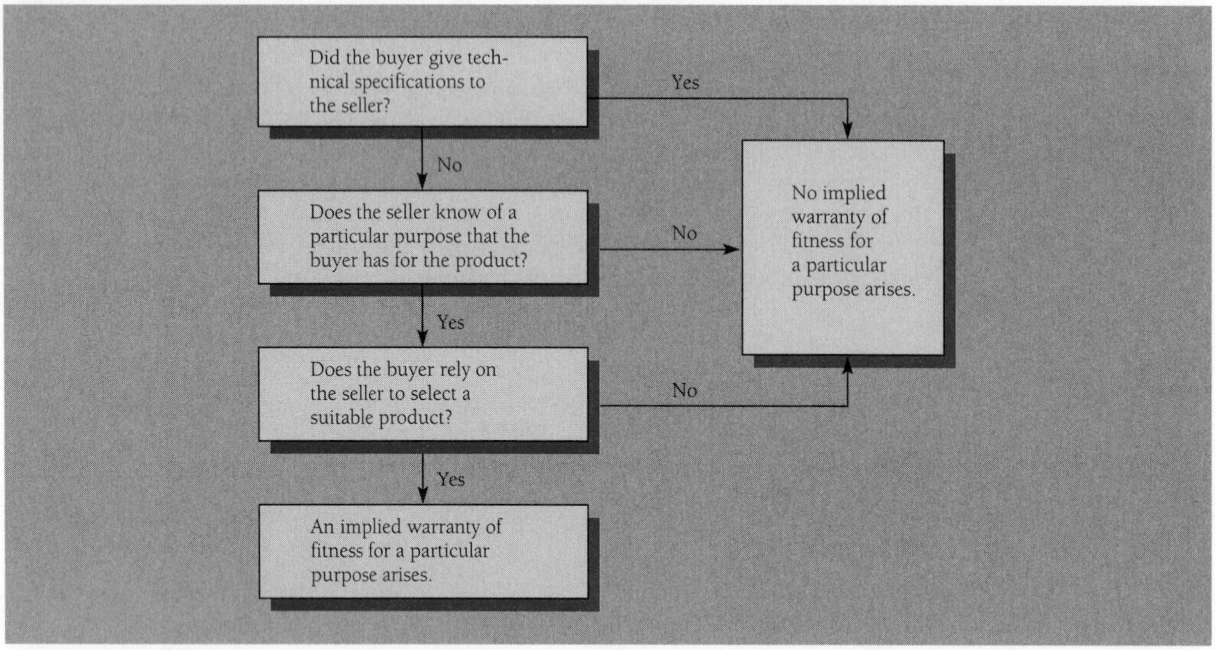

Implied Warranty of Fitness for a Particular Purpose The *implied warranty of fitness for a particular purpose* may be made by any seller, whether or not the seller is a merchant. This "fitness" warranty arises under UCC 2-315 whenever the buyer relies on the seller's expertise to select goods to suit the buyer's intended use. For example, if a paint dealer is asked to select nontoxic paint for use in a child's room, this implies a warranty that the paint contains no lead. Even if the buyer does not directly communicate the particular purpose to the seller, the fitness warranty arises if the seller has reason to know the purpose. The buyer must actually rely on the seller's expertise and selection decision before there is a fitness warranty (see Figure 10-3).

The particular purpose at issue in a fitness warranty is distinguished from an ordinary purpose under the merchantability warranty. Particular purposes are specific and planned uses peculiar to the buyer's household or business. Ordinary purposes are the uses customarily made by most buyers. For example, shoes are ordinarily made for walking on normal ground, but a special pair might be necessary for mountain climbing, a particular purpose. A buyer who relies on the seller's selection of a particular pair for this purpose has the benefit of a fitness warranty. However, no fitness warranty arises if the buyer ignores the seller's suggestions and insists on a particular brand or model of goods, because in that case there is no buyer reliance on the seller's expertise.

What circumstances might surround a seller's understanding of the buyer's business, permitting an inference that the buyer is relying on the seller's selection expertise? In *Northern Plumbing Supply, Inc. v. Gates,*[2] Gates sought to purchase pipe from Northern Plumbing Supply for use in making a farm implement. Northern's president, Luxem, knew of Gates' purpose because he had visited Gates' farm. Gates showed Luxem a section of

---

[2]*Northern Plumbing Supply, Inc. v. Gates*, 196 N.W.2d 70 (N. Dak. 1972).

pipe with a wall thickness of 0.133 inch as a model for the pipe he desired but simply requested "standard" pipe. Northern supplied Gates with "standard" pipe with a thinner wall thickness of 0.116 inch which was too weak for the farm implement attachments that Gates made. Even though Luxem conceded the thinner wall pipe would not hold up to the stress of Gates' use, he insisted it was not his responsibility to second-guess Gates' request for "standard" pipe. The court held Gates was a farmer with no way of knowing "standard" pipe had an insufficient wall thickness for his purposes. As a seller, Luxem should know all about pipes and about Gates' intended use. All the elements of an implied warranty of fitness were present in this case.

Warranty Exclusions Although it would seem advisable for sellers to exclude warranties whenever possible, the seller may intentionally offer a warranty to distinguish its products from competitors'. Some sellers may orally claim warranty coverage, but a fine print provision in the sales contract excludes the oral warranty. To prevent such misunderstandings UCC 2-316 requires the seller act in good faith in excluding warranties. A warranty remains in force if a seller engages in any unconscionable conduct in excluding a warranty.

All implied warranty exclusions must be conspicuous in the sale contract. An exclusion must be written in common language that draws the buyer's attention to the exclusion. The exclusion of the implied warranty of merchantability must mention the word *merchantability* or otherwise clearly exclude the warranty. The wordings *as is* or *with all faults* are examples of language that in common understanding call the buyer's attention to the warranty exclusion so all warranties of quality are excluded.

Typical Warranty Exclusion

THE SELLER HEREBY DISCLAIMS ALL OTHER WARRANTIES, EITHER EXPRESS OR IMPLIED, INCLUDING ANY IMPLIED WARRANTY OF MERCHANTABILITY OR FITNESS FOR A PARTICULAR PURPOSE.

Buyer's Inspection of Goods A warranty is automatically excluded to the extent that the seller gives the buyer a reasonable opportunity to inspect the goods prior to contracting and the inspection would reveal the defect. The seller can demand the buyer make an inspection. For example, if a salesclerk requests the buyer of a stereo unit to test its FM reception while the unit is on display, but the buyer refuses, no warranty on FM reception will arise. The scope of the examination necessary is based on the buyer's opportunity to inspect and on the buyer's expertise in discovering a particular type of defect. A usage of trade, a course of dealing, or a course of performance may also exclude a warranty.

Inconsistent Warranties and Exclusions Where the terms of an express warranty are inconsistent with an exclusion or a disclaimer, the inconsistency is resolved in favor of the buyer. For example, a two-year express warranty in bold typeface is inconsistent with a fine print exclusion of an express warranty. In that case, the buyer will have the benefit of the express warranty. However, it is completely consistent to provide a warranty on some aspect of the goods while disclaiming warranty on other aspects. For example, automobile manufacturers often provide warranties limited to the car's drive train (engine and transmission) and expressly exclude any warranty on the tires and battery. The excluded parts are usually covered by warranties from their separate manufacturers, so the buyer must make warranty claims against the separate manufacturers. The warranty exclusion process is illustrated in Figure 10-4.

FIGURE 10–4 Exclusion of Warranties

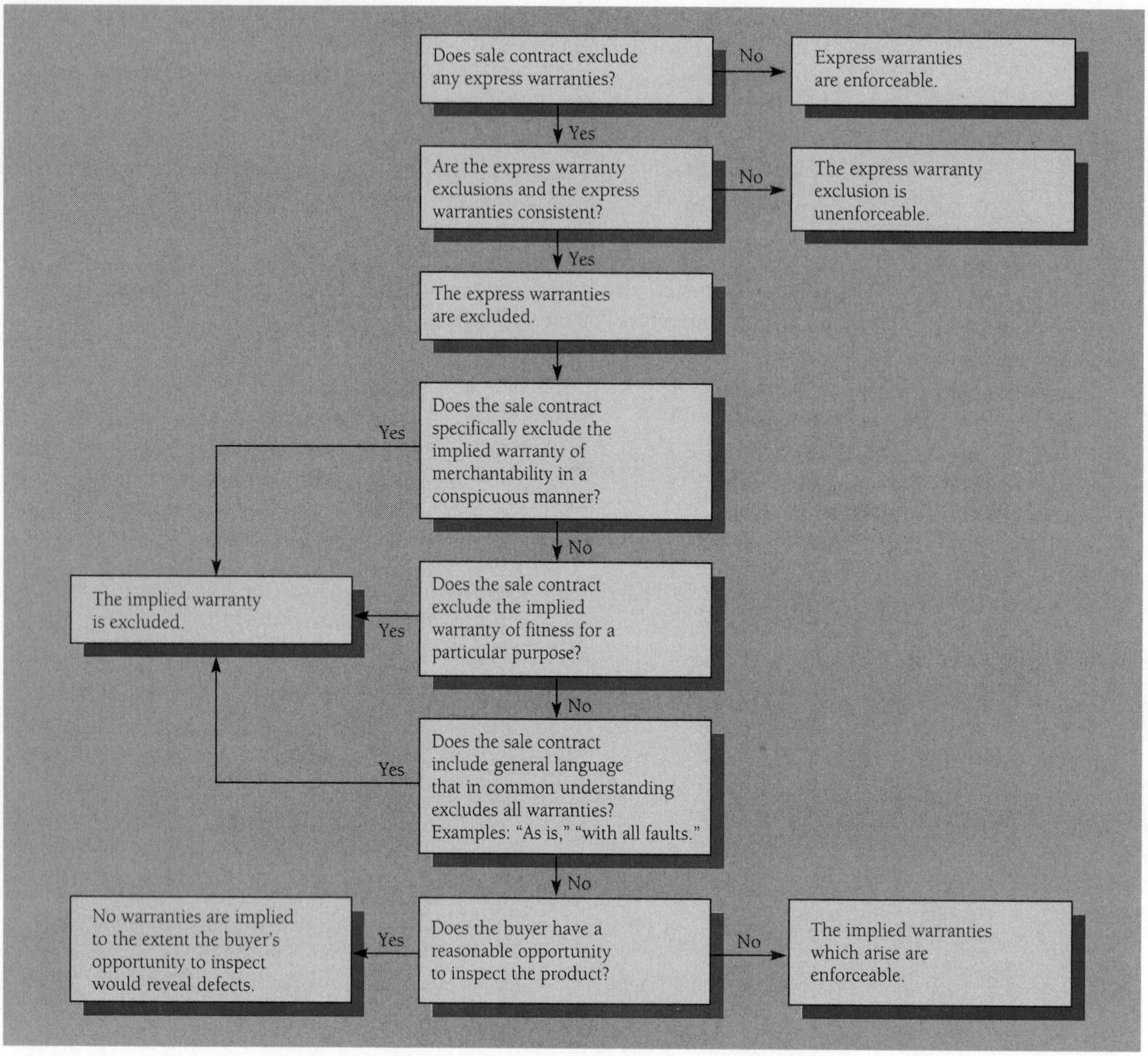

Magnuson-Moss Warranty Act Some sellers make outlandish claims about the performance or characteristics of goods. Some sellers have promoted warranties as a major inducement to purchase, calling them "full" warranties when they are not. This led Congress in 1975 to pass the Magnuson-Moss Warranty Act to increase consumer information, prevent deception, and improve consumer product competition. The Federal Trade Commission (FTC) is responsible to implement the Act.

FTC warranty regulations apply to consumer product sales of $15 or more. The FTC does not require any express warranty. Any warranty given must be (1) conspicuous, (2) found in a single document, and (3) written in readily understood language. A warranty must also identify the parties it covers and clearly describe the parts or characteristics excluded from coverage. If a warranty claim is made, the warrantor must state precisely the services provided. The dates of the warranty's commencement and cessation, along with step-by-step procedures for warranty claims, must be stated. If informal dispute settlement procedures such as arbitration are used, the procedures must be described. Usually, the consumer must attempt to resolve the claim through these procedures before taking further action. If the seller provides an express warranty, limitations on implied warranties are invalid, with the exception that implied warranties can be limited to the duration of the express warranty.

If consumer merchandise costing over $10 is sold and a warranty is given, the warranty must be conspicuously classified as "full" or "limited." A **full warranty** must provide the consumer with reasonable replacement or repair rights without other charges or conditions. Return of the warranty registration card is not a condition to honor the warranty. *Consequential damages,* those that replace lost profits or earnings if the user is injured by a defective product, may be limited with conspicuous language. If the consumer makes repeated unsuccessful attempts to remedy defects, a refund or free replacement option must be available. This avoids the seller's attempt to "wear down" the buyer and sets minimum standards for "lemons." Full warranties are so costly that few sellers provide them. Consequently, most warranties are either limited or are provided as extra-cost options. Several states have enacted various *lemon laws* that require refund or replacement of certain consumer goods that the dealer is unable to fix after repeated attempts.

ETHICAL DILEMMA IN CONSUMER CONFUSION ABOUT WARRANTIES

The UCC warranty exclusion/disclaimer provisions are an important example of legislated ethics in the warranty area. The UCC requires all parties to exercise good faith and observe fair dealings to meet consumers' reasonable expectations. Sellers have strong incentives to win sales by promising extensive warranties. However, the rising cost of defect claims gives sellers a conflicting incentive to limit warranties.

In the past, some unethical sellers promised warranties in sales literature, in the salesperson's representations, and even in the sale contract. Fine print warranty disclaimers were also included in the contract to prevent the seller's warranty liability. This problem is reinforced by the parol evidence rule, which effectively prevents consumers from proving that a warranty claim was made. Sellers can avoid this ethical dilemma by: (1) complying with the UCC warranty exclusion provisions, (2) prohibiting sales personnel from making outlandish claims, and (3) providing an effective repair and replacement process.

Negligence

Negligence was the first tort theory used in product liability cases. The plaintiff must prove the damage sustained was the "fault" of the defendant's negligent conduct and the prima facie case of negligence, discussed in Chapter 9.

The plaintiff must prove the defendant had a duty to exercise due care and to foresee any unreasonable risk of harm posed by the goods sold. The seller must minimize risks of injury by adequately designing, building, or inspecting the goods. Primary responsibility to minimize product defects rests with the product manufacturer or assembler. In some situations wholesalers and retailers should inspect, assemble, or prepare the goods before delivery. For example, auto dealers have the duty to inspect new cars sold to consumers. Manufacturers must warn consumers and give instructions for safe use. **Failure**

to warn is now the most prevalent negligence product liability theory. Breach of these duties may result in liability to any person who might reasonably be expected to use or be affected by a defective product. For example, it is negligent not to inspect empty beverage bottles before filling them because it is reasonable to expect that foreign substances may injure a consumer.

A wide range of injured victims may sue under negligence, including the purchaser, members of the purchaser's family, the purchaser's guests, and even bystanders if they fall within the zone of foreseeability. Foreseeable bystanders are persons reasonably expected to be affected by defective products. For example, it is foreseeable to expect a defective automobile to injure a pedestrian.

Defenses to Negligence Affirmative defenses ordinarily available to a negligence defendant may also be asserted in product liability suits. If the plaintiff contributed to the negligence by not using due care to guard against dangers, the defendant may be partially or completely relieved of liability by comparative or contributory negligence. If the plaintiff misused the product or voluntarily assumed a known risk in using the product or if the risk of injury was unknown or unknowable, then the defendant will be relieved of negligence liability. The statute of limitations for negligent torts, often a two-year period, is usually applied in negligence product liability actions.

Strict Liability

The most common theory of product liability used today is based neither on fault nor on the provisions in the sales contract. Under the strict liability in tort theory, a manufacturer, wholesaler, or retailer that is in the business of selling products may be liable for injuries resulting from defects that render the products unreasonably dangerous. Many states have judicially adopted the version of strict liability found in Section 402A of the *Second Restatement of Torts.*

Restatement of Torts Second, Section 402A

1. One who sells a product in a defective condition unreasonably dangerous to the user or consumer or to his property is subject to liability for physical harm thereby caused to the ultimate user or consumer, or to his property, if
   (a) the seller is engaged in the business of selling such a product, and
   (b) it is expected to and does reach the user or consumer without substantial change in the condition in which it is sold.
2. The rule stated in Subsection (1) applies although
   (a) the seller has exercised all possible care in the preparation and sale of his product, and
   (b) the user or consumer has not bought the product from or entered into any contractual relation with the seller.

Unreasonably Dangerous and Defective The strict liability claimant must prove the product's (1) defectiveness and (2) unreasonably dangerous condition. These standards are purposely vague to cover a wide variety of products and situations.

Defectiveness generally depends on the customer's expectations for product performance. Products with weak parts or mechanical limitations are defective. The merchantability standards provide some guidance for defectiveness. Products with inadequate safety warnings, which are unfit for ordinary purposes, with inadequate packaging or labeling, or which would not pass without objection in the trade are probably defective for strict liability purposes.

Unreasonable danger is closely tied to customer expectations. A product dangerous beyond what an ordinary consumer would expect is unreasonably dangerous. Consider alcohol, caffeine, and tobacco, common substances with dangerous side effects when used improperly or excessively. Most consumers know the risks, so they are not unreasonably dangerous unless adulterated with foreign substances.

The strict liability theory exposes business to the broadest potential liability of all product liability theories because of its lesser burden of proof. The privity doctrine and the defenses of contributory and comparative negligence are inapplicable. Some states recognize defenses such as product misuse, assumption of risk, and failure to discover a defect the plaintiff should have discovered. Commonly, plaintiffs allege all three product liability theories against all sellers in the chain of distribution.

Misrepresentation

Merchants and others engaged in the business of selling goods to the public may be liable for misrepresentations of the quality or characteristics of products. Unlawful misrepresentations may result from either negligence or conscious and knowing misstatements. Section 402B of the *Second Restatement of Torts* is a common basis for the misrepresentation theory of product liability.

Misrepresentation by Seller of Chattels to Consumer (Restatement of Torts Second, Section 402B)

One engaged in the business of selling chattels who, by advertising, labels, or otherwise, makes to the public a misrepresentation of a material fact concerning the character or quality of a chattel sold by him is subject to liability for physical harm to a consumer of the chattel caused by justifiable reliance upon the misrepresentation, even though

(a) it is not made fraudulently or negligently, and
(b) the consumer has not bought the chattel from or entered into any contractual relation with the seller.

Although the misrepresentation theory is similar to a breach of express warranty, the two differ in several important respects. Misrepresentation is a tort; it is not based on the UCC or other contract principles. The tort statute of limitations applies, and contractual limitations of remedy, exclusions of warranty, or exclusions of consequential damages are ordinarily inapplicable. There is no privity requirement making the manufacturer, wholesaler, retailer, or other distributor potentially liable. *Consumers* entitled to sue are broadly defined to include employees who use the goods on the job and family members with permission to use the goods.

The misrepresentation must be material and must concern the goods' characteristics. In one case, a windshield misrepresented as "shatterproof" shattered after a stone hit it. The matter misrepresented must be factual and susceptible to exact knowledge. Mere statements of opinion and dealer puffing are not misrepresentations. However, if the consumer is unaware of the misrepresentation, it is not actionable. Only publicly made misrepresentations or advertisements are actionable; individual misrepresentations made only to a particular consumer are not covered by Section 402B.

In one case, a mace weapon was represented in a brochure as capable of "instantaneous incapacitation . . . [of] entire groups." The manufacturer was held liable for injuries suffered by a motel's night auditor who was attacked when the mace weapon failed to repel attackers. In another case, a wire rope failed, permitting a hoisted weight to fall on a consumer. The manufacturer's manual was distributed to dealers for review by buyers. It misrepresented the rope's strength, and formed the basis for liability.

Misrepresentations may be inferred from the way goods are merchandised, even if the marketing efforts are only directed toward a segment of the population. A policeman purchased a riot helmet from his department, relying on a package illustration showing a motorcyclist wearing the helmet. The policeman wore the helmet while riding his motorcycle. The helmet was designed to release quickly on impact and came off his head in a motorcycle accident. The manufacturer was held liable based on the misrepresentation because the helmet was unsuitable for motorcycling. The various product liability theories are compared in Figure 10-5.

Criminal Product Liability

In recent years, considerable attention has focused on criminal product liability. In several states, both state and municipal prosecutors may bring criminal actions against certain product sellers. An Indiana statute makes it criminal to negligently cause a death. Most homicide statutes require proof the defendant intended the act that causes death. However, the Indiana statute predicates guilt on unintentional death resulting from a negligent failure to exercise due care.

In an Indiana case, Ford Motor Company was charged with negligent design of the Pinto gas tank. Three young girls died when their Pinto burst into flames after being rear-ended. Although Ford was acquitted in this case, the case broke new ground in potential punishment for criminal product liability. This area has become increasingly important because the fines, punishment, and adverse publicity resulting from criminal prosecutions or regulatory investigations are harmful to corporate goodwill. Criminal punishment may penalize both businesses and individual employees. However, at this time the extent of criminal product liability sanctions is unclear.

LIABILITY OF PARTIES IN DISTRIBUTION CHAIN

Selection of the proper parties as plaintiffs and defendants is an important part of product liability cases. Substantive and procedural laws applicable in the state where the wrong occurs and in the forum state may restrict or expand the number of parties that are potential plaintiffs and defendants. Nevertheless, the clear trend has been to recognize the injuries of more classes of persons as compensable if caused by defective products. This trend exposes business to increasing risks. Possible plaintiffs include both the purchaser and others who are affected by the use of such products. Mass torts and class action suits brought by one person representing all injured plaintiffs has also raised the risk of business and its insurers.

After final distribution of products to the ultimate consumers, there are three classes of persons who may be affected by a defective product. The first group consists of the purchaser and the purchaser's family. The second group consists of the employees of a

FIGURE 10–5 Comparison of Product Liability Theories

Theory	Eligible Defendants	Eligible Plaintiffs	Damages Recoverable	Prima Facie Elements Required	Defenses
Negligence	Manufacturer primarily liable; some jurisdictions hold retailers to a duty to discover and disclose defects that are discoverable upon an inspection Franchisors of negligent designs	Any person within the traditional negligence risk perimeter as determined by the concepts of duty and proximate cause; i.e., those within the zone of foreseeability	General and special damages that result directly from the breach Punitive if negligence is "willful," trend to limit Trend to limit non-economic damages (pain and suffering)	Duty Breach of Duty Actual cause Proximate cause Damages *Res ipsa loquitur* may establish duty and breach	Contributory negligence Comparative negligence Assumption of risk Misuse of product Statute of limitations State-of-the-art
Strict liability (*Second Restatement of Torts*, Section 402A)	Sellers, manufacturers, retailers, suppliers, or lessors if in the business Franchisors if control retained over defective manufacture or misrepresentations in advertising	Users and consumers; bystanders included increasingly	General and special damages for personal injury, physical harm, or property destruction No punitives Trend to limit non-economic damages (pain and suffering)	Defect Unreasonably dangerous Consumer expectations Causation Damages	Assumption of risk Misuse of product Should have discovered unreasonable danger (similar to contributory negligence) Statute of limitations
Breach of warranty (UCC)	Merchants as to implied warranties of merchantability; any seller as to fitness or express warranties	All natural persons who might reasonably be expected to use, consume, or be affected by defective product; most states: only family, guests, or those in household; some states have wider coverage	Trend to limit to purely commercial economic losses, but strongly resisted in some states No punitives	Contract of sale Warranty Breach of warranty Warranty not excluded Damages	Most contract defenses: Failure to notify of breach Lack of privity Misrepresentation Fraud Duress Undue influence Statute of limitations
Misrepresentation (*Second Restatement of Torts*, Section 402B)	Sellers, manufacturers, retailers, suppliers, or lessors if in the business	User, consumer, or bystander if relying on misrepresentation	General and special damages for physical harm	Merchant seller Misrepresentation to public Justifiable reliance Causation Damages	Misrepresentation not made publicly Dealer puffing No reliance Statute of limitations

FIGURE 10–6 Chain of Distribution

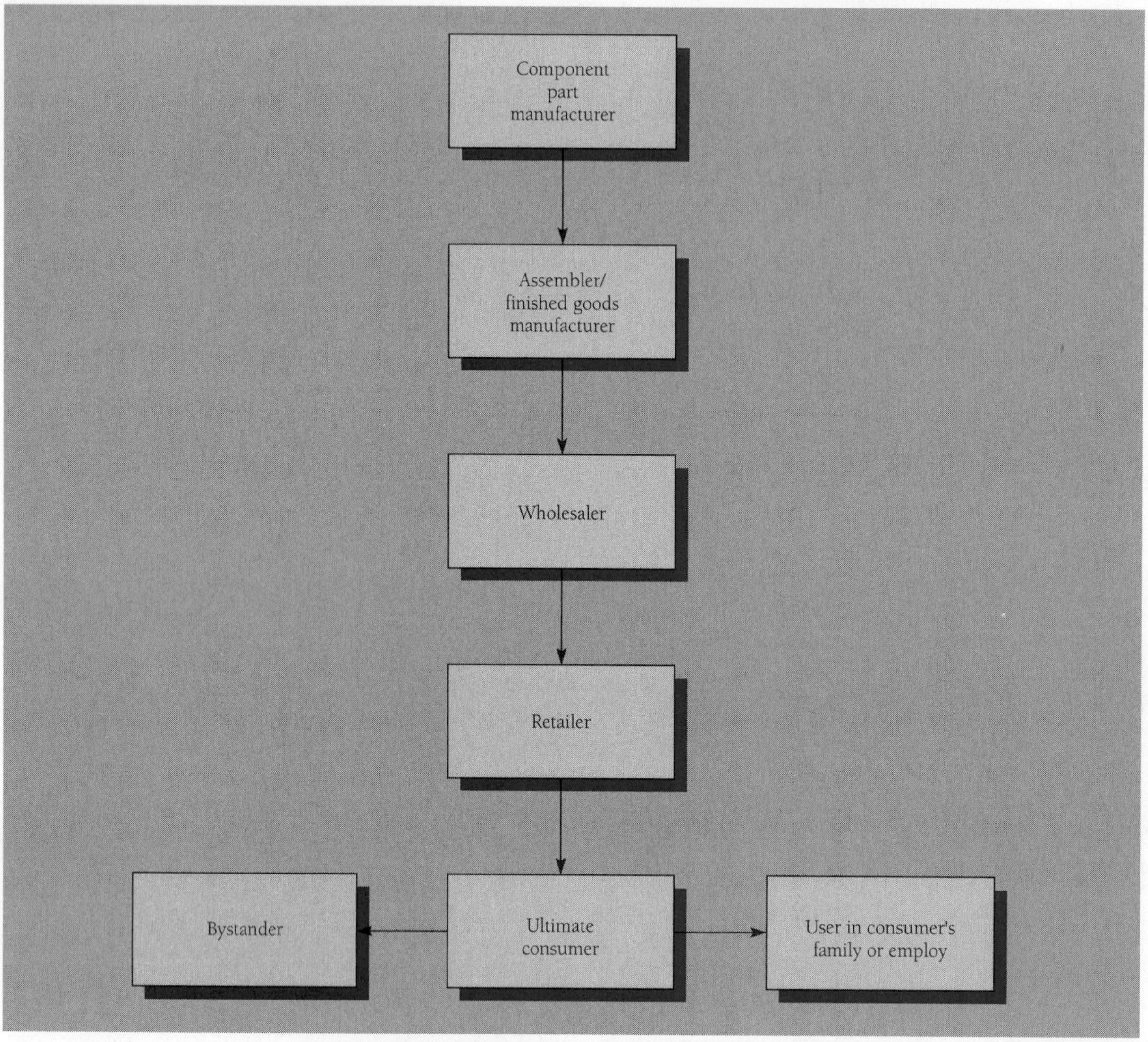

Privity of contract for the sale of products exists only between each level in the chain of distribution. No privity exists between bystanders or users and any seller. No privity exists between the ultimate consumer and any seller other than the retailer.

commercial consumer who use or may be affected by the product. The third group consists of bystanders who may be affected by the product if it fails.

Product liability law has significantly expanded the number of defendants potentially liable for defective products. Most entities in the chain of distribution, illustrated in Figure 10-6, are potential defendants, including component part manufacturers, assemblers, wholesalers, and retailers. Most products begin with the refinement of raw materials or the manufacture of component parts. The manufacturer or assembler combines components into finished products. A wholesaler may then purchase the products for resale to retailers who purchase with a view to resell to ultimate consumers.

Manufacturers

Component part manufacturers and assemblers of finished products can be held liable under all product liability theories. Component part manufacturers may be shielded from liability if (1) the finished product assembler converted the component to an unexpected use or (2) the component reached the consumer after the assembler, dealer, or buyer made substantial changes in it. In one example, a punch press manufacturer sold a machine without safety devices, expecting the industrial customer to add the safety devices best suited to the specific work application. The punch press manufacturer was not held liable when the customer safety device failed, causing injury to an employee.

Wholesalers

While wholesalers are not usually named as defendants in product liability actions, they may be held liable under any of the product liability theories. Typical suits against wholesalers are brought against the domestic distributors of foreign-made goods. For example, the domestic subsidiaries of foreign automakers have been held liable for injuries resulting from automobile defects.

Retailers

Retailers are the most likely to be sued because they have privity with the buyer. Retailers are held liable under all product liability theories. However, some vestiges remain of a defense known as the *sealed container doctrine.* Under this theory, the retailer has no duty to discover concealed or latent defects. For example, some states relieve retail food stores from liability if a sealed container (e.g., bottled liquids or soft drinks) explodes or leaks out, causing injury or slippery conditions. Certainly, it would be impractical for a retailer to conduct scientific tests or regularly dismantle all goods for inspection. The retailer's duty arises when the sealed container is opened, when the retailer suspects poor quality, or when the retailer provides some assembly or installation service, a dealer-introduced defect. Manufacturers may also be liable for defects introduced by a dealer if final production steps are delegated to the dealer, a common practice in the automobile industry.

Franchisors

Increasingly, patented product designs are licensed by franchise owners to franchisees for manufacturing. Because the franchisee actually manufactures the product, the franchisor may be shielded from warranty or strict liability suits. However, if the design is defective, the franchisor may be held liable for negligent design. Additionally, many franchise agreements reserve to the franchisor control over the franchisee's quality control, approval of product modifications or adaptations, and oversight of product advertising. Such increased control over the franchisee manufacturer may expose the franchisor to the various product liability laws.

Allocating Product Liability among Sellers

As just discussed, most parties in the distribution chain may be held responsible for product liability. Several other legal doctrines affect the liability of participants in the distribution chain, including market share liability, discussed previously, and joint and several liability, a tort reform discussed in Chapter 9. Other doctrines include subrogation, indemnification, and successor liability.

Employees who are injured while using industrial machinery for their employers' operations may have a product liability claim against the machinery manufacturers and a workers' compensation claim, as discussed in Chapter 18. Employers or workers' compensation insurers who are required to pay these claims are given the right of *subrogation* to sue the defective equipment manufacturer. For example, if the injured employee's claim is paid by workers' compensation, the insurer is substituted as the claimant in the product liability suit against the defective equipment manufacturer. Thereby, subrogation is a form of reimbursement from the equipment manufacturer for the workers' compensation claim paid by the insurer. Any party ordered to pay a product liability judgment may have the right of *indemnification* from the responsible seller. For example, if a wholesaler was held liable for a defectively manufactured product, it could seek indemnification from the manufacturer who was ultimately responsible for a defect in design, manufacture, handling, or warnings.

The trend in the 1980s to restructure businesses has led to mergers, acquisitions, and corporate breakups involving the sale of various product lines. This raises the question of *successor liability:* are the purchasers of these businesses liable for defective products manufactured or designed by the selling corporation? Generally, business purchasers are liable only for debts they consciously assume, so defective product claims remain the selling corporation's liability. However, if a corporation files for bankruptcy or the seller of a product line is liquidated, product liability claimants could be left with nothing. Some states hold the purchasing corporation liable for product liability risks, requiring it to inherit these liabilities irrespective of the acquisition contract terms. For example, the purchaser may be liable where the transaction is designed as a sham to avoid liability, the transaction in substance amounts to a merger, or the purchasing corporation continues with the same management and owners that the seller had.

Service Liability

Providers of services can be liable if injuries result from their activities. As the service provider is held to a duty of due care, most service liability cases are based on negligence. To avoid liability for negligence or other *malpractice,* professionals who are doctors, lawyers, accountants, and engineers must perform services that are at least equal to the reasonably prudent professional standard. Suits alleging medical malpractice, audit failures, and attorney malpractice have increased at alarming rates in recent years.

The service provider could also be liable for failing to meet a contractual warranty of satisfaction or success. For example, few doctors would promise perfect success in a medical operation and few lawyers would promise perfect success in litigation. Such promises would obligate them to provide that success and therefore give the patient or client an enforceable contract right. However, strict liability is generally inapplicable to sales of services unless they are closely tied to sales of goods. For example, strict service liability is generally limited to such things as a restaurant's defective service of adulterated food or a hairdresser's misuse of hair chemicals that physically injure a client.

DEFECTIVENESS

The central issue in a product liability suit is proof of the product's defect. In a negligence case, the seller must have failed to exercise due care in the product design, manufacturing, handling, inspection, packaging, instructions, or warnings. Under strict liability, there must be proof the product was rendered unreasonably dangerous by its defect. Under a warranty theory, the plaintiff must prove that the goods failed to conform to the warranty. The plaintiff must always prove the defect caused the injury.

Defective Designs

Products must be designed to eliminate defects that could lead to injury. Under warranty or strict liability, a defective design is considered a condition of the product. By contrast, negligently designed products result from a lack of due care by the designer or manufacturer. The practical difference is that in negligence suits the design process is examined closely for the foreseeability of danger. The inquiry is simpler in strict liability suits because it is only necessary to find the presence of a defect; the question of foreseeability or fault is irrelevant. A reasonably acting designer may escape negligence liability if the design appeared reasonable at the time of design. However, reasonable design activities are still subject to absolute liability for unreasonably dangerous products.

Interaction between the warranty and negligence theories also creates some apparent conflicts. If a buyer provides specifications to the seller, then the warranty of fitness arises. In such a situation, the manufacturer may nevertheless be negligent, because during the manufacturing process the manufacturer is in the best position to assure that a design is not faulty. By contrast, a useful design that is inherently dangerous may nevertheless be free from defects. For example, although knives are inherently dangerous, they are not defective simply because they can cut things effectively. The manufacturer may limit its liability for such obvious dangers by providing safety devices or warnings where practical. For example, chain saws are inherently dangerous because of a tendency to "kick back," so chain saw manufacturers must issue warnings or install chain-stop safety devices to limit their liability.

How much misuse must the manufacturer foresee and guard against to avoid a defective design? The following case limits the defective design concept.

Westinghouse Electric Corp. v. Nutt

407 A.2d 606 (1979)

District of Columbia Court of Appeals

Dirickson Nutt, an 11-year-old child, was injured after falling down an elevator shaft built and maintained by Westinghouse. The elevator had stopped between floors, and one rider pulled the doors open to let occupants jump down to the fifth floor below. Nutt slipped through the open doorway, between the floor and the underside of the elevator, injuring his arm, which was eventually amputated. He claimed Westinghouse was negligent in designing the elevators so the doors could be opened in this manner.

Gallagher, Judge

Without question Westinghouse, as manufacturer, was under a duty to design a reasonably safe elevator. This duty did not require Westinghouse "to adopt every possible new device which might possibly have been conceived or invented." In a design case, as in other areas of tort law, liability is imposed only for the creation of an unreasonable danger. Thus, Westinghouse's duty was one of reasonableness in designing the elevator "so as to make it not accident-proof, but safe for the use for which it was intended."

This duty of care includes the adoption of reasonable safety devices. What constitutes "reasonable care" will vary with the circumstances, and involves "a balancing of the likelihood of harm, and the gravity of harm if it happens, against the burden of precaution which would be effective to avoid the harm."

Westinghouse points to its compliance with existing industry-wide standards as dispositive of the question of due care. Two professional engineers, experts in elevator design, testified at trial that the elevator complied with all applicable safety codes and regulations. An elevator inspector for the District of Columbia government established conformance with the local elevator code. However, compliance with legislative or industry standards "does not prevent a finding of negligence where a reasonable man would take additional precautions."

Similarly, industry-wide custom influences, but does not conclusively determine, the applicable standard of care. As Justice Holmes put it, "What usually is done may be evidence of what ought to be done, but what ought to be done is fixed by a standard of reasonable prudence, whether it is usually complied with or not." Evidence of industry custom, however, may be conclusive when a plaintiff fails to introduce *any* evidence that the product was not reasonably safe for its intended use. Thus, the elevator's conformity to industry and legal standards established Westinghouse's due care unless the Nutts proffered contrary evidence that the product, as designed, created an unreasonable danger.

The sole evidence produced by the Nutts to establish a departure from the standard of care was the testimony of Mr. Foote. In effect, Mr. Foote gave his opinion that a longer toe guard or a different latch placement would have prevented the accident. However, evidence of a design alternative, by itself, is not sufficient to impose liability on the manufacturer.

A finding of unreasonable danger most often turns on the absence of a safety device that was available at the time of manufacture. Adoption of the suggested design alternative by other manufacturers for use in the same or similar equipment would be persuasive evidence. Customary use of another safer design is also relevant to establish the standard of care, and that the defendant's design is unreasonably dangerous. Evidence of available safety mechanisms illustrates what is feasible, and suggests a body of knowledge of which the defendant should be aware. As the court stated in *Moren v. Samuel M. Langston Co.:*

> A manufacturer is held to the degree of knowledge and skill of experts. This standard imposes upon the manufacturer the duty of an expert to keep abreast and informed of the developments in his field, including safety devices and equipment used in his industry with the type of products he manufacturers.

Here, testimony of customary safety features was not introduced. In addition, appellee's evidence failed to establish that an elongated toe guard is known to be feasible, even though not utilized by other manufacturers. This would seem to be the furthest courts have gone in imposing a duty on the manufacturer to keep abreast of recent scientific developments. Mr. Foote admitted on cross-examination that he had no knowledge of the factors involved in design of a toe guard, nor of the feasibility of his suggestions.

Against Westinghouse's evidence that the equipment was reasonably safe as designed, the Nutts mustered little contrary evidence. Mr. Foote's safety suggestions were not competent evidence that Westinghouse, the manufacturer, created an unreasonable danger. Thus, appellees failed to prove Westinghouse's deviation from the applicable standard of care in designing the elevator.

Case Questions

1. What is the function of safety regulations and industry-wide standards in determining the duty of care under negligence law?
2. What is the plaintiff's burden of proof if the defendant shows compliance with industry standards and safety regulations?

The *state-of-the-art defense* has been successfully asserted by manufacturers where all known safety improvements have been included in products and further refinements are unknown at the time of manufacture. While the state-of-the-art defense might relieve a seller from liability based on negligence, it usually has no applicability to strict liability. The wording of Section 402A of the *Second Restatement of Torts* clearly provides for liability whenever a defect exists, irrespective of the manufacturer's fault. Therefore, products manufactured many years ago are judged by today's technology. This added liability exposure suggests why states are experimenting with **statutes of repose** that would enable manufacturers to innovate without fear that any improvements must be installed into all products previously sold.

ETHICAL DILEMMA: BALANCING RISKS AND BENEFITS

The ethical problems of product safety can be evaluated with a risk-benefit/analysis similar to cost-benefit/analysis. Some recent cases have used this technique to project risks and benefits by assessing the feasibility and economic impact of safer designs. On one side of this analysis are the projected costs of additional safety features, societal decline if fewer useful products are brought to market, and the loss of utility if existing and unmodified products are withdrawn. These costs of product liability and safety regulation are contrasted with the benefits of reducing injuries and reduction of the attendant burdens placed on society. Such benefits arise from the lowered risk of injuries, reduced medical and insurance costs, and the work time saved with less dangerous designs. The risk-benefit/analysis always involves trade-offs between the product's utility and the societal costs of compensating injuries and avoiding accidents. Society increasingly views it as unethical when manufacturers fail to conduct risk-benefit/analyses in good faith.

Several manufacturers have suffered costs by carelessly considering a product's risk-benefit/analysis. For example, evidence showed that Ford Motor Co. management knowingly permitted use of a faulty-designed fuel tank filler neck for the Ford Pinto making the car dangerously vulnerable to explosion in a rear-end collision.[3] Ford executives knowingly postponed making a costly correction in the design to save $100 million in corporate profits. Confronted with such evidence, at least one jury assessed punitive damages of $125 million, although it was reduced on appeal. Ford suffered goodwill and reputational losses in the 1970s and 1980s from: adverse publicity about the Pinto, Ford's managerial approach to safety and profits, and its malfunctioning automatic transmissions. Management has an ethical responsibility to consider the social impact of its decisions. The cost of product liability litigation is not the only negative factor for manufacturers.

Sellers can improve safety particularly when the cost to the seller is low, such as in warning users of known dangers. Adequate product designs and high quality control is always necessary. From time to time society reevaluates the utility and social costs of certain products. For example, the manufacturers of 3-wheel all terrain vehicles (ATVs) could not prevent them from flipping over when maneuvered abruptly. Some consumers used their ATVs irresponsibly by refusing to heed warnings; others were too unskilled to appreciate the dangers. After widespread negative publicity, and under pressure from the Consumer Product Safety Commission, manufacturers halted production of the more dangerous 3-wheeled ATVs and all children's ATVs. Although ATV use was popular, society refused to accept the level of ethical judgments by both manufacturers and consumers. This risk-benefit/analysis resulted in complete elimination of the more dangerous models.

The most effective defense to product liability litigation is also the moral high ground: selling safer products. Short-sighted decisions to "cut corners" for profitability, justified as the only survival technique, ignore the adverse impact of selling defective products: product liability financial exposure, reputational losses, and increased regulation. Increasingly, responsible corporations are instituting some form of "Total Quality Management" (TQM). These firms create a fundamental corporate culture conducive to quality and the production of safe products. These firms are more likely to remain competitive in the long run. TQM has the added advantage of improving the firm's reputation and employee morale and pride.

Duty to Warn

Sellers are shielded from liability where adequate directions and warnings of known dangers are provided. However, warnings alone do not replace the manufacturer's duty

[3] *Grimshaw v. Ford Motor Co.*, 119 Cal. App. 3d 757, 174 Cal. Rptr. 348 (Cal. Ct. App. 1981).

to provide obvious safeguards. For example, a conspicuous warning about the dangers of a punch press would be insufficient if a simple guard device would protect the operator from serious injury.

To be effective, warnings must be understandable and conspicuous. Sellers are often reluctant to place too many warnings on products because this might alarm purchasers. This is not an adequate justification for a failure to warn of known dangers or known allergic reactions. If serious danger would arise when directions are disregarded, then the warning must be made more conspicuous. A warning must be calculated to reach the likely users of the product. In one case, employees used machinery purchased by their employer, but a separate warning to users was required in addition to the warnings to the employer. In the case of a machine tool used in a factory, the warnings must be conspicuously noted on the machine tool and be understandable by the average worker. Warnings placed in a bulky user's manual may be insufficient if users are unlikely to ever see or consult the manual.

Hazardous processing machinery is often covered with many warnings. Manufacturers should foresee and warn against dangers attendant to all uses and even to the service procedures. In *Nelson v. Hydraulic Press Mfg. Co.*,[4] a maintenance worker was injured while attempting to repair an injection molding machine. Melted plastic was placed through a feed tube and forced into molds to manufacture various plastic parts. Nelson climbed a ladder to observe a hardened plastic plug when molten plastic suddenly erupted causing him severe injury. No warnings appeared on the machine. The court said:

> The jury, as reasonable persons, could have concluded that the defendant manufacturer knew or should have known of the danger to maintenance men from exposure to hot plastic material erupting through the feed hole during maintenance operations to purge the machine of hardened plastic, and that as a result of the failure to warn or instruct concerning said danger the machine in question was unreasonably dangerous and in a defective condition when it left the control of the defendant and that the defective condition was a proximate cause of plaintiff's injuries and damages.

Warnings are mandated by product safety, discussed at the end of this chapter.

Establishing Defectiveness

Proof of a product's defects may come from several sources. Conflicting expert testimony is often heard from engineers, scientists, designers, and production experts concerning the product's performance and design characteristics. Many documents from the seller's files must be produced during discovery. These may show whether a particular design or warning was considered and rejected as too costly by the manufacturer's designers or production managers.

The legal doctrine ***res ipsa loquitur***, which stands for "the facts speak for themselves," permits an injured plaintiff to prove that the defects caused the injury even if there is no proof of causation. An injured plaintiff may sometimes prove a defect even if the failure destroys the product. In *Escola v. Coca-Cola Bottling of Fresno*,[5] a waitress was injured when a bottle of Coca-Cola exploded in her hand because of carbonation pressure and/

[4]404 N.E.2d 1013 (Ill. Ct. App. 1980).

[5]150 P.2d 436 (Cal. 1944).

or weakness of the bottle. The injured plaintiff's burden of proof under *res ipsa loquitur* was established for product liability actions:

> Defendant is not charged with the duty of showing affirmatively that something happened to the bottle after it left its control or management; . . . to get to the jury the plaintiff must show that there was due care during that period. Plaintiff must also prove that she handled the bottle carefully. The reason for this prerequisite is . . . to eliminate the possibility that it was the plaintiff who was responsible. . . . It is not necessary, of course, that plaintiff eliminate every remote possibility of injury to the bottle after defendant lost control, and the requirement is satisfied if there is evidence permitting a reasonable inference that it was not accessible to extraneous harmful forces and that it was carefully handled by plaintiff or any third person who may have moved or touched it. Upon an examination of the record, the evidence appears sufficient to support a reasonable inference that the bottle here involved was not damaged by any extraneous force after delivery to the restaurant by defendant. It follows, therefore, that the bottle was in some manner defective at the time defendant relinquished control.
>
> An explosion such as took place here might have been caused by an excessive internal pressure in a sound bottle, by a defect in the glass of a bottle containing a safe pressure, or by a combination of these two possible causes. The question is whether under the evidence there was a probability that defendant was negligent in any of these respects. If so, the doctrine of *res ipsa loquitur* applies.
>
> The bottle was admittedly charged with gas under pressure, and the charging of the bottle was within the exclusive control of defendant. As it is a matter of common knowledge that an overcharge would not ordinarily result without negligence, it follows under the doctrine of *res ipsa loquitur* that if the bottle was in fact excessively charged, an inference of defendant's negligence would arise. If the explosion resulted from a defective bottle containing a safe pressure, the defendant would be liable if it negligently failed to discover such flaw. . . .
>
> A pressure test is made by the bottle manufacturer by taking a sample from each mold every three hours—approximately one out of every 600 bottles—and subjecting the sample to an internal pressure of 450 pounds per square inch, which is sustained for one minute. (The normal pressure in Coca-Cola bottles is less than 50 pounds per square inch.) The sample bottles are also subject to the standard thermal shock test. The witness stated that these tests are "pretty near" infallible.
>
> It thus appears that there is available to the industry a commonly used method of testing bottles for defects not apparent to the eye, which is almost infallible. Since Coca-Cola bottles are subjected to these tests by the manufacturer, it is not likely that they contain defects when delivered to the bottler which are not discoverable by visual inspection. Both new and used bottles are filled and distributed by defendant. The used bottles are not again subjected to the tests referred to above, and it may be inferred that defects not discoverable by visual inspection do not develop in bottles after they are manufactured. Obviously, if such defects do occur in used bottles there is a duty upon the bottler to make appropriate tests before they are refilled, and if such tests are not commercially practicable the bottles should not be re-used.

AFFIRMATIVE DEFENSES

Sellers may assert several defenses to prevent or lessen their liability. Disclaimers of warranties and lack of privity are defenses to a breach of warranty suit. Situations in which plaintiffs place themselves in peril are the most widely recognized defenses. These defenses include contributory and comparative negligence, assumption of risk, and misuse of the product. If the plaintiff failed to exercise due care in using the product, contributory or comparative negligence may completely or partially bar recovery in a negligence or warranty case.

Since strict liability and breach of warranty are not based on fault, the courts are hesitant to apply the negligence doctrines of contributory or comparative fault. However, assumption of risk and product misuse are recognized defenses to both strict liability and warranty actions. In many cases involving latent (hidden) defects or the delayed manifestation of injuries, the plaintiff may have trouble proving causation. Successful defendants challenge the plaintiff's weak evidence that the defect led directly to the injury. This is particularly true in novel areas where scientific research is inconclusive to link the use of some drug or substance to an injury like that of the plaintiff's.

Should sellers of products be held liable for injuries sustained by people who have knowingly exposed themselves to danger? The following case illustrates the assumption of risk doctrine in a warranty case.

Hensley v. Sherman Car Wash Equipment Co.

520 P.2d 146 (Colo. 1974)
Colorado Supreme Court

The plaintiff, an employee at a car wash, was injured when she fell into a hole in the floor used for a hookless conveyor. The conveyor moved the cars through the wash area. Although a pivoting safety hood swung down over the hole to permit the cars' tires to pass over it, it reopened after a car passed.

Pierce, Judge

To establish the express warranty, plaintiff relies on the following language contained in an information sheet provided by defendant:

> "3. SAFE WORKING CONDITIONS. Car wash personnel are assured safe working conditions on all areas of the vehicle by the pivoted safety hood at exit end, over drive box which swings down as tire rides over, and then swings back up to cover the opening after tire has passed over; eliminates all possibility of persons stepping into an open pit."

Defendant contends that plaintiff's inattentiveness amounted to contributory negligence and barred recovery, and that plaintiff "assumed the risk" as she was aware that the safety hood had not been operating properly since the installation of the equipment approximately one month earlier. However, plaintiff testified that on the morning of the accident, a representative of Sherman had worked on the equipment and, specifically, had adjusted the safety hood, assuring her and the manager of the car wash that the device was working properly. Furthermore, she testified that she had observed the hood through the morning; that it operated properly each time a car came through the process; and that, therefore, she assumed that it had been properly repaired.

Other jurisdictions have held that the concept of contributory negligence, as it is known in negligence case law and as distinct from the doctrine of assumption of risk, has no place in actions premised on breach of warranty. In the absence of established Colorado law, we adopt that view.

This case presents a clear example of the distinctions between warranty and negligence theories. While the conduct of plaintiff in looking backwards as she stepped into the opening at the end of the conveyor might well constitute negligence on her part, this part was within the scope of the risk warranted against by defendant. It is uncontested that the purpose of the safety hood was to prevent a person from stepping into the opening at the end of the conveyor unit. As the language relied on by the plaintiff makes clear, the safety hood was designed to assure safe working conditions for employees and to "eliminate all possibility" of persons stepping into the opening. The very risk which defendant warranted not to exist was encountered by plaintiff, and her negligence or lack of due care is irrelevant. Contributory negligence is not a defense where plaintiff's conduct only puts the warranty to the test.

The most common accepted affirmative defense to a warranty claim is unreasonable use of the product by the plaintiff with knowledge of the defective condition and the risk it creates. Defendant was entitled to an instruction to the effect that plaintiff could not recover if she unreasonably exposed herself to a known defective condition. Such activity on her part would be disregard of a known danger, and she would not be proceeding in reliance upon defendant's warranty.

It is uncontested that plaintiff was aware of the fact that the safety hood had not been operating properly at all times. However, if her testimony is to believed, the fact of her knowledge is attenuated by her apparent reliance on the assurances from the defendant's representative that the safety hood had been repaired and her own observation of the hood just prior to the accident. The issue is her awareness of a defect in the mechanism *at the time of the accident.* Whether or not her reliance on the statements of the repairman and her own observations was justifiable would be a question for the jury to determine.

Case Questions

1. What representations created the warranty in question?
2. What are the differences between the contributory negligence, assumption of risk, and product misuse defenses?

Abnormal use or misuse of the product by the plaintiff is similar to the assumption of risk defense. A *misuse* is an unreasonable use of the product in a manner that was not intended by the seller or designer. A misuse is sometimes foreseeable by the seller, so warnings or design changes may be necessary. The courts have not been consistent in their application of the misuse defense. Some courts have recognized this defense in strict liability cases, whereas others have refused to apply it. In one case, the manufacturer of a chair claimed that it was misuse for the buyer to stand on the chair and use it as a stepladder. The court found this use to be foreseeable and required that the chair be designed to remain stable even under the pressures of a person standing on it.

ETHICAL DILEMMAS IN CONSUMER RESPONSIBILITY FOR PRODUCT SAFETY

Consumers also face ethical dilemmas when they misuse products. Sellers are increasingly considered principally responsible for safety. Consumers may be lulled into complacency and not use products responsibly. Safety is a concern for all parties: the manufacturer, dealer, and user. Consumers have common sense duties to avoid exposing themselves, their families, and bystanders to potential dangers. Some states are applying concepts of comparative fault, reducing recoveries paid to plaintiffs whose injuries are increased by not wearing seatbelts.[6]

PRODUCT SAFETY REGULATION

The product liability recovery system is supplemented by product safety regulations requiring certain products to maintain minimal safety levels. Food products, drugs, consumer products, and motor vehicles must meet safety specifications. Regulators have both

[6] *Waterson v. General Motors Corp.*, 544 A.2d 357 (N.J. 1988).

protective and curative remedies. The product liability system compensates victims, whereas the regulatory system attempts to prevent the sale of unsafe products.

Food and Drug Safety and Purity

One of the first areas of product safety to develop was in consumable foods and drinks. Early state statutes concerned the wholesomeness of milk. Today, state and local governments exercise police power to regulate the impact of food and drugs on the health, safety, and welfare of citizens. Regulated foods include bread, milk, milk products, imitations of milk products, soft drinks, intoxicating liquors, fruits, fruit products, grains, grain products, and eggs. Commonly, the production, manufacturing, processing, sale, marketing, and transportation of food are subject to regulatory oversight, often through licensing.

The Food and Drug Administration The Food and Drug Administration (FDA) and the U.S. Department of Agriculture (USDA) also regulate the purity of foods and drinks. Federal statutes dating back to 1906 enable these agencies to regulate filled milk, meat, poultry, bottled drinking water, vitamins, infant formulas, eggs, food additives, and tea. The federal agencies have the power to control adulterated and misbranded foods, food-level tolerances for poisonous ingredients, and the use of pesticides and additives in foods or raw agricultural commodities. Labeling standards require disclosure of the contents of food products and nutritional profiles.

Drug Safety The Federal Food, Drug, and Cosmetic Act of 1938 empowers the FDA to regulate drugs and devices: any article or component intended to diagnose, cure, mitigate, treat, or prevent disease, or to affect the bodily structure of humans or animals. *Devices* include most medical instruments and apparatus such as an IUD or prosthesis.

The states also regulate drugs, including drugs sold over-the-counter and prescription drugs sold by state-licensed pharmacists. Municipal boards of health have similar regulatory power over drugs as the FDA. Misbranding and adulteration are common classifications of defects.

The FDA and the states may prohibit some types of drug advertising. In one case, for example, claims that a tranquilizer could cure "the anxiety that comes from not fitting in" were found misleading. In another case, a manufacturer was held to have overpromoted an antibiotic drug that effectively concealed its warning, leading to liability. State regulatory schemes usually provide remedies to consumers and local boards of health, including the power to ban, seize, condemn offending articles and substances. The regulation of advertising is discussed in Chapter 11.

Consumer Product Safety

The most pervasive federal statute covering defective consumer products is the Consumer Product Safety Act of 1972 (CPSA). The CPSA created the Consumer Product Safety Commission (CPSC) to administer the Act. The Injury Information Clearinghouse compiles product failure statistics, collects research on defects, and funds research to discover defects. Public disclosure of the defects discovered is controlled to minimize undue adverse publicity about particular manufacturers. The CPSC has power to establish minimum product standards and to enforce regulations for noncomplying products. The CPSC also administers the Federal Hazardous Substances Act and the Poison Prevention Packaging Act, which cover the labeling and misbranding of poisons and hazardous substances, and the Flammable Fabrics Act, which sets minimum standards for the fire-retardant qualities of fabrics.

Motor Vehicle Safety

The federalization of automobile safety regulations began with the National Traffic and Motor Vehicle Safety Act of 1966. Congress sought to reduce traffic accidents, deaths, and injuries by establishing vehicle safety standards, supporting related research, and providing mechanisms to remedy defective vehicles. Two major systems were designed to prevent injuries. The first system empowers the Department of Transportation (DOT) to promulgate practical safety standards for motor vehicles. All newly manufactured domestic and foreign vehicles sold in the United States must be certified as complying with these standards. Extensive civil fines may be imposed for noncompliance. The second system requires remedies for defects arising after sale, such as nonfunctioning or malfunctioning auto parts. These defects are often discovered by customers, testing agencies, manufacturers, or DOT. The manufacturer may be required to (1) recall and repair defective vehicles, (2) replace defective vehicles, or (3) refund the purchase price.

Other state and federal statutes and agencies regulate the safety of particular products. The Federal Aviation Administration (FAA) sets private and commercial aircraft safety standards. The Occupational Safety and Health Administration, discussed in Chapter 18, indirectly regulates tool and workplace defects by setting minimum safety standards for tools.

The Administrative Remedies

Safety regulations establish standards and minimum specifications for the structural integrity and performance of products. Sample products are tested to evaluate their "breaking point." This can facilitate the redesign. A product's resistance to typical operating stresses and patterns must hold within a range reasonably expected under normal use. A hammer, for example, might be required to withstand a minimum pounding pressure before fracturing. Its claw might be required to withstand a normal prying pressure.

Agencies are often empowered to "rule in" as legal all safe products and thereby to "rule out" unsafe products. Drugs and food additives may not be sold or used unless they appear on the "legal list." The FDA has established several lists of approved food additives. For example, the *Generally Recognized as Safe (GRAS)* list includes foods and/or food additives that were considered safe for consumption when the list was first published in 1958. The artificial sweetener NutraSweet was separately approved for use in certain goods. The FDA also lists drugs acceptable for prescription and over-the-counter sales. Experimental drugs, such as several AIDS drugs, may not be prescribed or sold until placed on the list after extensive testing.

Certain products and food additives are excluded from distribution. The FDA, USDA, CPSC, and Congress have each banned the sale of certain new items. A product ban may be implemented simply through the issuance of a new rule creating the ban or through withdrawal of the authority from manufacturers to produce and sell an existing product. For example, the use of cyclamates as artificial sweeteners was banned in the 1969 Delaney Amendment, which Congress passed after evidence mounted about their health hazards.

Warning Labels and Advertising Nearly all safety regulators require that products be branded and that they include instructions for use. Warnings may be necessary to prevent product misuse consistent with the duty to warn. Foods, drugs, cosmetics, and toys are typical of products required to carry conspicuous warnings of known dangers and directions for safe use. Warning labels may help prevent misuse. Mandatory warning labels may also help manufacturers establish misuse by consumers who disregard a conspicuous and known warning. The *Cipollone* case, discussed later, illustrates this controversy.

Several advertising issues arise under product safety regulations. Electronic media advertising of cigarettes is banned, relegating tobacco ads only to the print and billboard media. The surgeon general has required that a warning about the dangers of cigarettes be placed on cigarette packages. Listerine's false claim that it could cure colds led to an FTC curative advertisement order to "uncondition" the market by stating that Listerine could not cure or lessen the severity of colds. Consumer groups oppose the Camel cigarette character because of its appeal to children.

Searches, Seizures, Forfeitures, and Condemnations Speedy action is often critical in food and drug cases. To avert widespread disaster, the various food and drug regulators have immediate powers to search for adulterated foods and drugs. The Tylenol and other tamperings justified such immediate and summary action. The administrative remedies of seizure, forfeiture, condemnation, and impoundment are used when speedy action is necessary.

Repair, Refund, or Replacement Both the Consumer Product Safety Act and the National Traffic and Motor Vehicle Safety Act require manufacturers and sellers to remedy defects commonly with a repair following public announcement of recall. Although recalls are intended to cure defects, the repairs also prevent injuries. Recalls often follow consumer complaints or failure reports. Because recalls enable manufacturers to repair defective products, they probably decrease product liability suits based on product failure.

Interactions between Product Liability and Safety Systems

There are numerous interactions between the state product liability compensation systems and the various administrative product safety systems. Evidence from product liability trials showing negligent design, manufacture, or failure to warn often triggers action by a product safety administrative agency. Whenever a recovery suit creates adverse publicity concerning unsafe products, public opinion may force regulators to consider further action. Ford Pinto fuel tank failures led to several highly publicized damage suits causing publicity and the Pinto recall.

Regulatory Noncompliance and Damage Suits Plaintiffs in traditional product liability recovery actions can lessen their burden of proof by simply proving the product fails to meet regulatory standards. In a case involving a poisonous chemical, for example, the manufacturer's failure to include the skull and crossbones or other warning symbol required by regulations triggered liability even though a textual warning was provided. The package failed to adequately warn two migrant workers who could not read English.

Negligence liability may also be established under the doctrine of *negligence per se*. Whenever a statute or regulation is violated, the product liability plaintiff may have a lighter burden of proof if the plaintiff is the type of person that the statute is intended to protect. Some courts hold that negligence per se provides only a rebuttable presumption of the manufacturer's negligence. A violation may be justified if some other protective measure, safety device, or warning is sufficient. Negligence per se only establishes negligence and the plaintiff must still prove causation.

Several state and some federal statutes provide for private damage suits. For example, the CPSA has an additional private right of action independent of common law product liability theories. The Swine Flu Act relieved the manufacturers of the swine flu vaccine from liability for mass inoculations in the 1970s. The U.S. government was substituted as the defendant in place of the drug manufacturers.

Regulatory Compliance as Due Care Product liability defendants often show their compliance with safety regulations as evidence of their due care. Many courts reject this contention because government regulations are only minimum standards above which there may still be negligence, breach of warranty, or unreasonably dangerous defects. However, compliance with regulations may be evidence of reasonable care. Some product liability reform laws limit damages recoverable against drug manufacturers if they comply with government regulations. The next case illustrates the impact that federal cigarette warning requirements may have on various state product liability theories and which may apply to various other products requiring federal or state warnings, including alcoholic beverages, automobiles, pharmaceuticals, medical devices, and pesticides.

Cipollone v. Liggett Group, Inc.

(No.90-1039)—U.S.—(1992)
United States Supreme Court

Mrs. Rose Cipollone smoked cigarettes from 1942 until she died shortly after removal of a cancerous lung in 1984. Thereafter, Antonio Cipollone, her husband, continued her product liability suit against three cigarette manufacturers. Cipollone presented extensive evidence that she was addicted to smoking and that the cigarette manufacturers made misleading advertisements assuring smokers of safety and made advertisements favorably depicting smokers. The cigarette manufacturers alleged that the Federal Cigarette Labeling and Advertising Act of 1965 as amended by the Public Health Cigarette Smoking Act of 1969 preempted state law, thus displacing the product liability laws on which Rose's claims were based. A jury awarded Antonio $400,000 for breach of warranty for advertising before the 1965 warning label requirement, but found that Rose was 80 percent comparatively negligent, denying her any damages. After Antonio's death, the couple's son Thomas appealed a U.S. Circuit Court of Appeals decision overturning the jury's damage award.

Justice Stevens delivered the opinion of the Court.

"WARNING: THE SURGEON GENERAL HAS DETERMINED THAT CIGARETTE SMOKING IS DANGEROUS TO YOUR HEALTH." A federal statute enacted in 1969 requires that warning (or a variation) to appear in a conspicuous place on every package of cigarettes sold in the United States.

Article VI of the Constitution provides that the laws of the United States "shall be the supreme Law of the Land . . . any Thing in the Constitution or Laws of any state to the Contrary notwithstanding." State law that conflicts with federal law is "without effect." Consideration "start[s] with the assumption that the historic police powers of the States [are] not to be superseded by . . . Federal Act unless that [is] the clear and manifest purpose of Congress." In the 1965 preemption provision regarding advertising (§5(b)), Congress spoke precisely and narrowly: "No statement relating to smoking and health shall be required in the advertising of [properly labeled] cigarettes." A warning requirement promulgated by the FTC and other requirements under consideration by the States were the catalyst for passage of this act, which reflected Congress' efforts to prevent "multiplicity of State and local regulations pertaining to labeling of cigarette packages."

The plain language of the preemption provision in the 1969 Act is much broader than that of its predecessor. First, the later act bars not simply "statements," but rather "requirement[s] or prohibition[s] . . . imposed under State law." Second, the 1969 act reaches beyond statements "in the advertising" to obligations "with respect to the advertising or promotion" of cigarettes. The 1969 Act worked substantial changes in the law: rewriting the label warning, banning broadcast advertising, and allowing the FTC to regulate print advertising. The phrase "[n]o requirement or prohibition" sweeps broadly and suggests no distinction between positive enactments and common law. We must look to each of petitioner's common law claims to determine whether it is in fact preempted. The central inquiry in each case is straightforward: We ask whether the legal duty that is the predicate of the common law damages action constitutes a "requirement or prohibition based on smoking and health . . . imposed under State law with respect to . . . advertising or promotion."

Failure to Warn

Petitioner offered two closely related theories: first, that respondents "were negligent in the manner [that] they tested, researched, sold, promoted, and advertised" their cigarettes; and second, that respondents failed to provide "adequate warnings of the health consequences of cigarette smoking." Petitioner's claims are preempted to the extent that they rely on a state law "requirement or prohibition . . . with respect to . . . advertising or promotion." [Petitioner's] claims that respondents' post-1969 advertising or promotions should have included additional, or more clearly stated, warnings, are preempted. The Act does not, however, preempt petitioner's claims that rely solely on respondents' testing or research practices or other actions unrelated to advertising or promotion.

Breach of Express Warranty

A manufacturer's liability for breach of an express warranty derives from, and is measured by, the terms of that warranty. The "requirements" imposed by an express warranty claim are not "imposed under State law," but rather imposed by the warrantor. While the general duty not to breach warranties arises under state law, the particular "requirement . . . based on smoking and health . . . with respect to the advertising or promotion [of] cigarettes" in an express warranty claim arises from the manufacturer's statements in its advertisements. In short, a common law remedy for a contractual commitment voluntarily undertaken should not be regarded as a "requirement . . . imposed under State law" within the meaning of §5(b). To the extent that petitioner has a viable claim for breach of express warranties made by respondents, that claim is not preempted by the 1969 Act.

Fraudulent Misrepresentation

Petitioner alleges two theories of fraudulent misrepresentation. First, respondents, through their advertising, neutralized the effect of federally mandated warning labels based on a state law prohibition of advertising that tends to minimize health hazards of smoking. Such a prohibition, however, is merely the converse of a state law requirement that warnings be included in advertising and promotional materials. Section 5(b) of the 1969 Act preempts both requirements and prohibitions; it therefore supersedes petitioner's first fraudulent misrepresentation theory.

Petitioner's second theory alleges intentional fraud and misrepresentation both by "false representation of a material fact [and by] conceal[ment of] a material fact." Petitioner's claims that respondents concealed material facts are not preempted insofar as those claims rely on a state law duty to disclose such facts through channels of communication other than advertising or promotion. Thus, for example, if state law obliged respondents to disclose material facts about smoking and health to an administrative agency, §5(b) would not preempt a state law claim based on a failure to fulfill that obligation.

Petitioner's fraudulent misrepresentation claims that do arise with respect to advertising and promotions are not preempted by §5(b). Such claims are not predicated on a duty "based on smoking and health" but rather on a more general obligation—the duty not to deceive. Congress offered no sign that it wished to insulate cigarette manufacturers from longstanding rules governing fraud. To the contrary, both Acts explicitly reserved the FTC's authority to identify and punish deceptive advertising practices—an authority that the

FTC had long exercised and continues to exercise. This indicates that Congress intended the phrase "relating to smoking and health" to be construed narrowly, so as not to proscribe the regulation of deceptive advertising.

State law prohibitions on false statements of material fact do not create "diverse, nonuniform and confusing" standards. Unlike state law obligations concerning the warning necessary to render a product "reasonably safe," state law proscriptions on intentional fraud rely only on a single, uniform standard: falsity. The phrase "based on smoking and health" fairly but narrowly construed does not encompass the more general duty not to make fraudulent statements. Petitioner's claim based on allegedly fraudulent statements made in respondents' advertisements are not preempted by §5(b) of the 1969 Act.

Conspiracy to Misrepresent or Conceal Material Facts

Petitioner's final claim alleges a conspiracy among respondents to misrepresent or conceal material facts concerning the health hazards of smoking. This duty is not preempted by §5(b) for it is not a prohibition "based on smoking and health."

The judgment of the Court of Appeals is accordingly reversed in part and affirmed in part, and the case remanded. It is so ordered.

Case Questions

1. What product liability theories are preempted by the federal warning requirement?
2. Discuss the immunity a manufacturer receives for compliance with all regulations.

PRODUCT LIABILITY REFORM

The product liability crisis is closely related to the general tort reform movement discussed in Chapter 9. Many of the same forces have been at work to expand the theories of liability and the growth of damage awards. These developments have triggered similar responses by manufacturers and insurers seeking tort reform changes to joint and several liability, the imposition of damage caps, and collateral source information. Specific product liability reforms have emerged in over half of the states, though federal reform is still under consideration by Congress. Juries have given huge compensatory awards. Large punitive damages have increased the cost of defending product liability cases. The lack of reliable product liability data from manufacturers, trade associations, and government agencies has compounded the uncertainties faced in calculating insurance premiums. Manufacturers have passed additional insurance and redesign costs on to consumers. This crisis has led several state legislatures to change the product liability system so as to make it more predictable.

Some states have imposed exclusive product liability theories such as defective design, failure to warn, or the manufacturer's deviation from the design, thereby limiting the growth of new theories. Other states have reduced the limitations period by redefining when the statute of limitations accrues (begins to run) or by establishing statutes of repose. States have enacted damage caps on punitive damages and non-economic damages (pain and suffering). Some states permit only one punitive damage award per product defect, effectively encouraging plaintiffs to rush their cases. Another alternative is to bifurcate product liability trials so that punitive damages are determined in a less impassioned proceeding, separate from the main trial. Some states exempt human blood and tissue products from the strict liability theory. A few states recognize the unavoidably unsafe conditions of products with inherently risky characteristics (e.g., knives) by recognizing these are not design defects.

Most of the product liability reforms have expanded or confirmed the affirmative defenses: contributory negligence, comparative negligence, and assumption of risk. Some states have adopted the misuse defense or expanded assumption of risk to include situations in which the plaintiff failed to observe reasonable precautions in using the product or should have appreciated an open and obvious risk or danger in failure to warn cases.

A few states have modified the privity concept by exempting retailers and other sellers from liability unless the manufacturer was beyond the state's jurisdictional powers or the reseller modified the product. The state-of-the-art defense has been adopted in a few states, and other states have limited drug liability suits if FDA regulations are met. Some states prohibit evidence of product design changes that eliminated the defective condition in products produced later. The state legislatures will probably continue to experiment with limitations on product liability suits. To minimize the adverse impact of product liability, businesses should remain aware of these developments and adhere to industry's standards.

INTERNATIONAL PERSPECTIVE: MAINTAINING U.S. COMPETITIVENESS

Critics charge the United States is becoming uncompetitive in world markets because the product liability system imposes excessive costs on U.S. industry. Many foreign nations impose safety, packaging, labeling, and warranty regulations on imported products. Some civil law nations have more extensive statutory liability provisions, similar to implied warranties, than common law nations. The EC has product safety regulations that parallel those in the United States.

Other nations' liability systems are not as financially favorable to injured plaintiffs as the U.S. system. For example, New Zealand prohibits common law tort actions against the sellers of goods. Instead, New Zealand's government has instituted a state-run no-fault compensation system for most types of defective product injuries.

The burden of product liability laws arguably falls evenly on foreign and U.S. manufacturers when selling in the United States. However, differences in safety and testing standards can impose greater costs in selling abroad. Foreign nations may impose more stringent standards on imported goods than on those domestically produced. For example, the U.S. automobile industry has long argued that U.S.-built vehicles are priced 40 percent higher in Japan than in the United States because of discriminatory and specious Japanese requirements for imported automobile inspections.

Ethical issues arise in product liability when a domestic manufacturer withdraws a defective product from the home market and turns to foreign markets to dispose of existing inventories. For example, critics charge that after U.S. manufacturers were prohibited from selling the IUD birth control device in the United States they cut their losses by unloading excess inventories in the lesser developed countries. As information spreads about business's global social responsibility, the impact of defective products will become both an international and ethical dilemma for manufacturers from all nations.

SUMMARY

As a result of the inroads that have been made on the privity doctrine, businesses have been increasingly held liable to victims when products fail or cause injury. This has caused a product liability litigation crisis. Product liability suits have been altered by changes in substantive and procedural legal doctrines such as statutes of limitations, the identification of the precise defendant, the use of bankruptcy reorganization to avoid liability, and tort reform.

Product liability suits may be based on the contract theory of warranty. Express warranties may arise from models, specifications, oral promises, or other contractual promises. Merchants who regularly sell or act as agents make an implied warranty of merchantability.

The implied warranty of fitness for a particular purpose arises when a seller selects goods for the buyer's special purpose.

Sellers may exclude express and implied warranties with conspicuous and consistent language. The federal Magnuson-Moss Warranty Act prohibits labeling a warranty as a "full" warranty unless the warranty permits repair, refund, or replacement of defective goods at the buyer's option. All other warranties must be labeled as "limited."

There is even greater expense for torts of negligence and strict liability. The negligence theory holds a manufacturer, wholesaler, or retailer of a defective product liable if the injury should have been foreseen. Sellers must design, manufacture, assemble, and handle products with reasonable care and warn users of reasonably foreseeable and known dangers. Sellers are strictly liable for defective and unreasonably dangerous products. Lack of privity or proof of fault is not a barrier to strict liability suits. Many victims allege liability under all three product liability theories.

Product liability may also be based on the seller's misrepresentations of the product's quality or characteristics in advertising, sales representations, or an owner's manual. Some states permit criminal prosecution of sellers of defective goods.

Both the federal government and state governments have supplemented the state common law product liability system with product safety regulations. Fresh and packaged foods must be handled in specified ways, and certain food producers must be licensed. Administrative agencies may recall adulterated or misbranded foods and may seize, condemn, or impound tainted foods or foods and drugs that have been tampered with. Dangerous food additives may be banned. Similar regulations exist for prescription and over-the-counter drugs.

Similar protective regulations exist for consumer products and automobiles. The CPSC and the NHTSC regulate the safety characteristics of these products. These agencies may set minimum safety standards for products and may rule in (license, legal list) and rule out (ban) products. Manufacturers of automobiles may be ordered to repair defective vehicles after a recall, to replace such vehicles, or to refund the purchase price. Manufacturers may also be required to provide warning labels or curative advertisements.

Failure to meet the minimum standards for administrative product liability regulations may lead to traditional product liability under the theories of warranty, negligence, or strict liability. Compliance with government standards is generally not a defense to traditional product liability suits unless pre-empted.

KEY TERMS

privity of contract, p. 285
market share liability, p. 287
warranty, p. 288
full warranty, p. 295
failure to warn, p. 296
statute of repose, p. 304
res ipsa loquitur, p. 307

CHAPTER EXERCISES

1. For the most part, privity of contract is invalid as a defense in product liability cases, except in the Uniform Commercial Code. Why is this so? Does the *McPherson v. Buick Motor Co.* case provide insight into this question?
2. In many product liability lawsuits, the plaintiff is suing because the goods purchased had some inherent defect and did not work at all. For other product liability theories discussed in the chapter, goods that may be satisfactory for normal purposes may still be the subject of a product liability lawsuit. Identify as many situations as you can that illustrate the second type of lawsuit.
3. Define what is meant by *strict liability.* How does this theory differ from liability based on a contractual promise or warranty liability? How does it differ from liability based on fault?
4. Read the following three examples. Identify which type of warranty applies to each.

a. The seller of new boats shows a sample sailboat claiming boxed-up sailboats on the back lot are just like the sample. The boxed sailboat purchased is not like the sample at all. There is no written contract of sale.

b. If a "full warranty" is given, a malfunctioning product must be replaced without charge.

c. A new sailboat sold from the back lot has leaks in the hull, and the sailboat sinks to the bottom of the lake.

5. What type of warranty is involved in the following fact pattern? A customer asked for a pair of hiking boots that would be suitable for mountain climbing above the timberline of the Rockies. The customer said that she would be carrying packs with a weight of over 75 pounds. The salesperson recommended a pair of traditional hiking boots with waffle soles and no extra support. As a result of wearing the boots (which lacked adequate support), the customer became crippled while on the climb and was helicoptered out of the wilderness. What is the best ground to sue on?

6. A man was severely injured when an automobile, left unattended on a hill, struck him as he was playing golf. The car had been left with the gearshift in the "park" position, but the gears became disengaged. The plaintiff brought an action against both the manufacturer and the owner of the car. On what grounds can a "bystander" who receives personal injuries bring action against the manufacturer?

7. Harry Handyman, an accountant, prides himself on doing all the work on his home himself. When the floor in his kitchen needed replacing, he went to the local hardware store and purchased a roll of linoleum and, after a lengthy discussion with the owner, a can of Super-Bind Linoleum Glue. Harry followed all of the warnings and instructions on the can. He left all the windows in the kitchen open, and he positioned a fan to blow the toxic fumes out of the room. Nevertheless, while he was spreading the glue, an explosion ripped through the kitchen, severely burning him and damaging his home. Later investigation revealed that the cause of the fire was the ignition of the fumes from the glue by the pilot light of a hot-water heater in the utility room outside the kitchen. What cause of action does Harry have, and against whom? Explain.

8. Jones purchased a steel-belted radial tire. The tire had a design defect that caused it to separate, but she was not warned of this defect even though the manufacturer had received several complaints. The tire blew out when she was driving the car on rough terrain. Is Jones entitled to recover for injuries from the manufacturer?

9. The plaintiff received a transfusion of blood supplied by a blood bank. She tested HIV positive for the AIDS virus as a result of the transfusion. Is the blood bank liable by reason of strict liability and breach of implied warranty?

10. What is the relationship between government regulation of product liability and the traditional common law theories of recovery for product liability?

11. BabyFoodCo is a major processor of infant formula sold in the United States and in many third world countries. Most infant formula makers use primarily soybean protein to make their products. Motivated by soybean price increases due to recent crop failures, BabyFoodCo decided to use the corn protein residue that remains after the oil is extracted from corn as an alternative to soy protein. Although this mixture is rich in certain types of protein, it is dangerously deficient in lyposine, an amino acid essential for the development of infants' vision. Initially, BabyFoodCo scientists were unaware of this problem, and the newly formulated infant formula was rushed to the market. After two years of sales, the American Science Foundation reported on the lyposine deficiency and BabyFoodCo recalled huge quantities of their corn-based infant formula. To avoid a massive income loss for that year, BabyFoodCo secretly marketed the recalled infant formula to several third world countries by mislabeling it as soybean-based. What ethical duties does BabyFoodCo have toward the American babies who were fed the formula and have underdeveloped vision? What ethical problems exist for the international sales of the mislabeled corn-based infant formula?

Chapter 11

ADVERTISING AND FINANCING REGULATION

KEY CONCEPTS

The Federal Trade Commission regulates unfair and deceptive trade practices in advertising, direct marketing, retail sales, and consumer financing.

The Consumer Credit Protection Act protects consumers by imposing numerous duties on business sellers and financing firms. The disclosure of credit terms, credit billing practices, discriminatory lending practices, and unreasonable credit collection activities are regulated.

Secured financing provides the secured party with a security interest in the debtor's property to satisfy a defaulted debt. When the debtor agrees to the security interest, that interest attaches, and the creditor gains priority over other creditors.

The bankruptcy laws permit an overburdened individual or business debtor to obtain a fresh start free of most prior debts. The debtor's assets are liquidated and distributed to creditors in straight bankruptcy. Under wage earner's and reorganization plans, prior debts are changed by extending repayment or altering their character.

INTRODUCTION . . . PAST, PRESENT, FUTURE

Before the 1930s, common law contract and tort principles of misrepresentation, warranty, and interference with economic relations provided the primary legal protections for consumers. Since 1938, Congress has addressed consumer desires by expanding Federal Trade Commission (FTC) authority to regulate consumer affairs. The FTC's regulatory fervor has varied with the political climate. The Consumer Credit Protection Act as amended expands FTC powers to regulate consumer sales, financing, and credit practices.

By today's standards, some creditors' past actions seem arbitrary, oppressive, and unrelated to the borrower's ability to repay. Creditors used unsuitable information and criteria to withhold credit from otherwise creditworthy individuals. Decisions not to grant credit often reflected views held by some niche of society about credit risks or were made to achieve social engineering. Many loan decisions were based on: (1) the lender's personal biases, (2) distorted information about borrowers' business, lifestyle, associates, or family, and (3) credit reports containing unsubstantiated, defamatory, and false allegations of impropriety (gossip). For example, many creditors ignored the income stability of working women and blacks, believing they had only a limited work ethic and were unable to "hold down a job." As this attitude appeared to become pervasive among creditors, major regulations of the credit granting process followed.

In reaction against the jailing of debtors under English law, the founders of the United States favored a more helpful attitude toward overburdened debtors. The U.S. Constitution specifically empowers Congress to provide for debtor relief with a uniform system of bankruptcy law. Both individuals and businesses may use the bankruptcy laws to obtain relief from excessive debt entanglement. The procedures of straight bankruptcy and the special arrangement plans for wage earners and corporate reorganizations create an environment for balancing the interests of individuals and their families with shareholders, secured creditors, and unsecured creditors. Bankruptcy laws have evolved slowly over the years, and the current stability of these laws suggests that drastic changes will not occur in the near future. In the corporate debt area, however, there has been increased concern over the debt financing of takeovers. Reactions to this trend by lawmakers and creditors and an apparent blurring of the distinction between debt and equity may lead to restricting "excessive debt."

OVERVIEW

Businesses have had to deal increasingly with a labyrinth of state and federal disclosure laws intended to benefit consumers. Businesses should carefully consider the penalties and other burdens imposed by these laws before advertising or extending consumer credit.

Initially, this chapter considers the regulatory powers of the FTC and other agencies over unfair and deceptive trade practices, deceptive advertising, and consumer protection. The consumer financing relationship is then analyzed; special emphasis is given to the lender's obligations in disclosing credit terms, granting credit, reporting on the credit history of borrowers, and collecting debts. The following section discusses how the lender obtains rights to use collateral as partial repayment of the debtor's defaulted debts. Bankruptcy, the last resort in debt collection procedures, is covered next, followed by lender liability problems.

CONSUMER PROTECTION BY THE FEDERAL TRADE COMMISSION

The FTC is the independent regulatory agency that Congress entrusts to promote a competitive business environment. Originally created in 1914 to enforce the antitrust laws, the FTC obtained consumer protection authority in the Wheeler–Lea Act of 1938. The Consumer Credit Protection Act grants extensive powers to enforce consumer credit protection regulations. There is considerable overlap between the FTC's consumer protection function and its powers to promote competition. The FTC fosters competition by monitoring business practices and prohibiting those found deceptive and which might divert sales from honest competitors. Deceptive advertisements distort consumers' information, making their purchase decisions inferior, and thus undermine the goals of perfect competition.

The FTC also has the power to prosecute violations of Section 5 of the Federal Trade Commission Act. That Act prohibits unfair methods of competition and unfair or deceptive trade practices. The courts have interpreted trade practices to be "unfair" if they offend established public policy and if they are immoral, unethical, oppressive, unscrupulous, or will substantially injure consumers. FTC interpretations may be different from those of the courts, reflecting the prevailing ideology of the FTC and the judiciary. Trade practices have traditionally been found "deceptive" if they tend to deceive the consumer, even if no actual deception is proved. Figure 11–1 summarizes the FTC's powers under the consumer protection laws.

FTC Powers

The FTC exercises several powers that facilitate the enforcement of the consumer protections laws. The FTC defines unfair and deceptive trade practices by issuing *trade regulation rules,* which have the force of law. These rules prohibit deceptive activity in one or more industries. For example, there are trade regulation rules that address abuses in door-to-door sales, bait and switch sales tactics, direct marketing schemes, and used car sales. The FTC also may issue *advisory opinions* to individual firms seeking to avoid charges of unfair or deceptive trade practices in their proposed activities. More comprehensive advice is sometimes available through *industry guides* addressing the trade practices of an entire industry. FTC advisory opinions and industry guides do not bind the courts and they may be amended later by the FTC itself.

FTC investigations and enforcement actions are initiated after complaints are heard from consumers, business competitors, administrative agencies, or Congress. The FTC may also initiate its own investigations. The FTC's Bureau of Consumer Protection monitors consumer sales practices to obtain evidence of potential violations. The FTC then conducts an investigation to determine whether there is sufficient evidence to bring an enforcement action. The FTC may issue *cease and desist orders* or settle charges with *consent decrees,* without going to trial, in which the defendants usually agree to eliminate the deception.

The FTC may also issue an *affirmative disclosure order* requiring an offender to provide information in future advertisements or a *corrective advertising order,* requiring advertisements to correct past misleading advertisements. Corrective advertisements are discussed in the next section. A *multiple product order* prohibits future deceptive advertising by a firm with a history of false advertising in selling any of its' numerous products. The FTC has also successfully sought rescission of contracts, returns of property, refunds of the consumer's purchase price, and damage payments to consumers.

FIGURE 11–1
FTC's Powers under Consumer Protection Laws

Federal Trade Commission Act, 1914	Prohibits unfair or deceptive trade practices
Wheeler-Lea Act, 1938	Prohibits deceptive advertising
Truth-in-Lending Act, 1968	Regulates creditor advertising and the disclosure of credit terms
Fair Credit Reporting Act. 1970	Regulates contents and provisions of credit history reports
Equal Credit Opportunity Act, 1975	Prohibits discrimination in the extension of consumer credit
Fair Credit Billing Act, 1975	Prescribes procedures for billing debtors
Magnuson-Moss Warranty Act,* 1975	Regulates warranties on consumer goods
Fair Debt Collection Practices Act, 1978	Prohibits deceptive and abusive debt collection practices
Electronic Funds Transfer Act, 1978	Requires disclosure of EFT transactions and processes; provides for detection and correction of errors
Fair Credit and Charge Card Disclosure Act, 1988	Requires disclosure of credit card account terms
Home Equity Loan Consumer Protection Act, 1988	Requires disclosure of home equity loan terms

*Covered in Chapter 10.

If the business under investigation disputes the charges, an administrative hearing may be held before an administrative law judge (ALJ). Appeals of the ALJ's decision go first to the five FTC commissioners and then to the U.S. Circuit Courts of Appeals for judicial review. Violators of FTC regulations or cease and desist orders may be fined up to $10,000 per violation.

The FTC commissioners are appointed by the president with approval by the Senate. There must be political balance on the FTC, with nearly equal representation from both of the two major political parties. Some industries are exempt from FTC regulation if regulated by another federal, state, or local agency, such as public utilities and the securities industries. However, a few industries, like consumer creditors, are regulated by both the FTC and another agency.

ETHICAL DILEMMAS IN CONSUMER PROTECTION

Consumer activist groups view product marketing as involving excessive sales pressure and some unfair practices. When goods are oversold, there may be evidence of unethical conduct. The ethical dilemma presented is whether the selling organization, individual salesperson, or advertising consultant has made a conscious decision to mislead prospective purchasers. Unethical conduct arises when a sales presentation or an advertisement makes untrue, fraudulent, or exaggerated claims. Misrepresentations or intentional fraud may appear in documents, sales literature, catalogs, price lists, "certified" test results, testimonials, advertising, or verbal sales talk provided by the seller or made in response to the buyer's inquiry.

Even where there is no misrepresentation during contracting, a transaction may be viewed as unethical during its performance. The conscious delivery of poor quality goods or goods unsuitable for the buyer is unethical unless the seller notifies the buyer the substandard delivery is an accommodation. Unfair advantage taken of uneducated consumers is also unethical.

ADVERTISING REGULATION

The advertising of consumer products has contributed to the tremendous industrial expansion of the 20th century. A legitimate function of advertising is to inform consumers; however, that function is subverted when advertising is used to deceive them by false statements and misleading practices.

Common Law Remedies

Although the common law provides remedies for victims of deceptive advertising, there are significant stumbling blocks to the effectiveness of these remedies. Chapter 8 noted that since the buyer is usually considered an offeror under contract law, the seller's advertisement is seldom treated as an offer. If the product's actual specifications or its price at the store is different from the advertised specifications or price, there is no breach of contract because no enforceable contract yet exists. However, Chapter 10 noted warranties and actionable misrepresentations may arise from advertising and other language in the sales materials or contract. Such warranties may form the basis for a consumer's complaint about deception.

The tort of deceit or fraud may exist if an advertiser knowingly makes material misrepresentations of fact on which an injured purchaser justifiably relies. Protection of trademarks and trade names exists under both common law and federal statutes. If an advertiser makes untrue statements in comparing its goods with the goods of a competitor, the defamed competitor may sue for trade libel, slander, or disparagement.

Deceptive Advertising

Congress believed that these common law remedies did not protect consumers adequately, so it passed the Wheeler–Lea Act in 1938 to deal with **deceptive advertising.** This statute authorizes the FTC to prosecute unfair or deceptive trade practices in advertising. To measure deception, the FTC's deception policy statement assesses advertisements from the perspective of the total impression created in the consumer's mind. To be deceptive, an advertisement need only have a capacity to mislead consumers about some material aspect of the product. This test is interpreted in a reasonable manner by a hypothetical "typical ordinary consumer." It is not necessary to prove either that the advertiser intended to deceive or that actual deception occurred. However, the deceptiveness must be so strong that a reasonable person, not a gullible one, would be deceived.

Unsubstantiated Claims The FTC views advertisements as having deceptive elements if the claims made are not supported by a reasonable basis in scientific evidence. For example, demonstrations must accurately depict the performance of the advertised product. Test results that create the impression of the product's superiority must be based on studies or surveys with a scientific basis. The demonstrations must illustrate some relevant or meaningful product attribute.

Puffing A seller's opinion or generalized commendation of value is not a misrepresentation under contract law (Chapter 8), nor does it form the basis for an express warranty (Chapter 10). Puffing would probably not be deceptive advertising unless it accompanied more concrete but false statements about the product's characteristics or performance.

Mock-Ups A *mock-up* is a false demonstration to improve an advertisement's appearance or effect, and it is deceptive if the viewer believes it represents the real thing. A mock-up that fails to disclose important facts or clearly acknowledge that the demonstration is not genuine is an unfair or deceptive practice. For example, Volvo's ad agency chose to tout the structural integrity and crashworthiness of Volvo cars in a mock-up of a "big-wheel" car crushing event. The ad showed a Volvo surviving uncrushed as it was driven over by a "big-wheel" four-wheel drive vehicle as other brands of cars were being crushed. Volvo's ad agency could have cited extensive valid scientific evidence of the Volvo's safety. However, the agency decided the repeated trials necessary to adequately catch the event on film would eventually crush even the Volvo. Later Volvo fired the ad agency when it was discovered the Volvo in the film had been extensively reinforced to survive the many film "takes" necessary to shoot a successful commercial. This ad was a mock-up because viewers were led to believe the Volvo in the ad was standard.

Colgate-Palmolive used a series of one-minute commercials allegedly showing Rapid Shave enabling a razor to "cut right through this tough, dry sandpaper." Actually, a mock-up was used in which loose sand was applied to plexiglass. Real sandpaper would require 80 minutes of soaking with shaving cream to soften enough to be shaved as shown. The U.S. Supreme Court acknowledged the FTC's expertise in determining the deceptiveness of ads and held: "We think it inconceivable that the ingenious advertising world would be unable to conform to the FTC's insistence that the public be not misinformed."[1]

Omissions and Half-Truths Clearly advertisers must refrain from making directly false or misleading claims about product quality, price, or composition. However, it is also deceptive to tell some truths while omitting clarification. An *omission* or *half-truth* is deceptive if more information is necessary to keep the ad from being misleading. For example, the selective use of data, comments, or conclusions from scientific studies may be a deceptive half-truth. The FTC ordered P. Lorillard to stop advertising that Old Gold cigarettes were lower in tar and nicotine than the six leading brands because the differences were statistically negligible. The ads cited selective data from a *Reader's Digest* article concluding Old Gold's lower tar and nicotine content was not meaningful for smokers' health. Only the article's most favorable portion was extracted, whereas the more negative conclusion was omitted, creating an "entirely false and misleading impression" in the ad about the article's content and Old Gold's health impact.[2]

Endorsements Endorsements by sports figures or celebrities, such as those found in shaving, beer, and medical insurance commercials, should reflect the actual opinions of these persons. An advertiser may use such an endorsement only while the sports figure or celebrity actually uses the product. By contrast, fictional dramatizations using unknown actors are usually not endorsements and do not require a heartfelt opinion or

---

[1] *FTC v. Colgate-Palmolive Co.*, 380 U.S. 374 (1965).

[2] *P. Lorillard v. FTC*, 186 F.2d 52 (4th Cir. 1950).

actual use by the actor. Such actors have been used, for example, in the Bartles and James wine cooler ads. In such situations, the consumer is less likely to purchase the product due to respect felt for the endorser. Some responsible advertisers indicate that their commercials are fictional dramatizations. False endorsements may trigger liability for fraud for the advertiser and the celebrity.

Corrective Advertisements When an advertiser makes misstatements in advertisements, the FTC assumes that the misconception will remain in the consumer's mind. Only further advertising of a similar magnitude, duration, and creativity can correct such "durable" false impressions. In some cases, a court-approved consent decree is used to order the advertiser to conduct **corrective advertising** rebutting the misleading claims of prior advertising. The FTC has used corrective advertising orders since the well-known *Listerine* case in which Warner-Lambert was ordered to begin advertising that corrected its former claims that Listerine killed millions of "germs" because these germs did not cause colds as consumers might expect from the ads. The U.S. Circuit Court of Appeals dismissed Warner-Lambert's challenge to FTC power to order a corrective ad stating: "Contrary to our prior advertising, Listerine will not help prevent colds or sore throats or lessen their severity."[3]

FTC Corrective Advertising Standard

[I]f a deceptive advertisement has played a substantial role in creating or reinforcing in the public's mind a false and material belief that lives on after the false advertising ceases, there is clear and continuing injury to competition and to the consuming public as consumers continue to make purchasing decisions based on the false belief. Since this belief cannot be averted by merely requiring respondent to cease disseminating the advertisement, we may appropriately order respondent to take affirmative action designed to terminate the otherwise ill effects of the advertisement.

Source: Federal Trade Commission

Comparative Ads and the Lanham Act The FTC favors the recent trend toward scientifically verifiable comparative advertising because it encourages competition. The "Pepsi Challenge" blind taste tests use large random samples from nationwide independent testing so its comparisons showing consumer preference over other cola brands is valid. However, invalid comparisons may be false and deceptive, exposing the advertiser to damages under the common law tort of trade disparagement and for lost profits under §43(a) of the Lanham Act, the federal trademark registration statute. The disparaged competitor may sue if the comparison makes false or misleading statements of fact or representations about the nature, characteristics, geographic origin, or quality of a competitor's products, services, or commercial activities.

Comparison advertising was long condemned by most U.S. businesses as ultimately harmful to their whole industries. However, comparative ads are appearing with greater frequency particularly as surveys proliferate from independent research firms. Japanese businesses try to avoid active comparison ads because they disturb the traditional appearance of industrial harmony important to Japanese culture.

---

[3] *Warner-Lambert Co. v. FTC,* 562 F.2d 749 (D.C. Cir. 1977).

ETHICAL DILEMMAS IN ADVERTISING

If advertising creates demand and additional use of some dangerous products, or exposure to them increases accidents, then safety may be enhanced by restricting the advertising. This type of ethical dilemma has been reduced somewhat for sellers of guns, cigarettes, and alcohol because advertising of these items is restricted. Some groups believe promoting dangerous products is unethical, such as ads for 3-wheel all terrain motorcycles or ads showing the glamour of smoking or drinking.

Children are a particularly vulnerable audience for certain types of advertising. The use of hero advertising and the merging of children's programming into advertising also pose ethical dilemmas. Advertisers must carefully consider how the audience will receive the advertising claims or the lifestyle and activities presented. An ethical dilemma is presented by advertisements that overreach the consumer's ability to appreciate the risks or costs of the product.

Packaging and Labeling

Congress empowered the Commerce Department to regulate product packaging and labeling in the Fair Packaging and Labeling Act in 1966. As increased packaging obscures the consumer's actual view of the product, accurate label descriptions become increasingly important for product evaluation. Labels must: (1) identify the product, (2) identify the name and address of the manufacturer, packer, or distributor, and (3) list the quantity and serving size in a specific manner. FTC rules require particular labeling of numerous diverse products. For example, accurate octane numbers must appear on gasoline pumps. Numerous additional laws regulate packaging and labeling of wool products, cigarettes, flammable fabrics, textiles, food, drugs, and cosmetics empowering various agencies to regulate labeling and other deceptive practices.

ETHICAL DILEMMAS IN PRODUCT LABELING

Recent trends toward better nutrition have generated a flurry of new and repackaged foods and nutritional products. Unfortunately, some food producers began pandering to the public's newfound obsession with healthy eating by taking advantage of consumers' limited nutrition knowledge. Many undertook large-scale advertising that made exaggerated claims of product performance and confused consumers. Such activities pose ethical dilemmas when advertisers misinform consumers by preying on their fears of ill health, their prejudices about body image, and their ignorance about nutritional facts. The FDA, which monitors unfair and deceptive trade practices in marketing food, drugs, and nutritional products, suddenly became more active regulators in the early 1990s. The FDA now more closely scrutinizes product claims about food contents, fad diets, and product descriptors such as "diet," "light," "fresh," "natural," and "low-fat."

The promotion of some products as "no-cholesterol" or "low-cholesterol" falsely suggest that similar products from other manufacturers do contain cholesterol. For example, no major national brand of peanut butter contains cholesterol. There is no cholesterol in peanuts and no one adds cholesterol-laden lard to peanut butter as done many years ago. Also, even when factual, a producer's claim that its food is low in cholesterol may be an unethical half-truth. This is so because high blood cholesterol levels are more closely linked to eating foods high in saturated fat than simply in eating foods high in cholesterol. Similar ethical abuses occur with the terms "biodegradable" and "recyclable." The meaning of these terms is unclear because products may decompose very slowly or be difficult to process. For example, composite materials, such as the aluminum foil and plastic used in some juice boxes, are hard to separate.

Health claims that products contain lower amounts of suspected unhealthy substances can also be misleading because the comparative descriptors "diet," "lower," or "light" have no meaning except when compared with similar foods that regularly contain more of that substance. For example, the term "light" beer is meaningless unless it contains significantly fewer calories than the average beer. "Light" can also be understood as suggesting lighter flavor, smell, or color.

The FDA has responded to this perceived unethical behavior by requiring more accurate and meaningful nutritional labeling. These rules, scheduled to become effective in 1993, permit the use of such terms only in accurate comparisons or when the descriptor has a legal definition. For example, "low-cal" foods must contain less than 40 calories per serving; "sodium-free" products must contain less than 5 milligrams per serving; "sugar free" foods must contain less than .5 gram per serving; "reduced fat" may contain no more than half the fat of an identified comparison item. Foods advertised as "high" in some substance must contain 20 percent more per serving of the substance than the recommended daily intake. Although additional regulation to curb further ethical abuses is opposed by the food industry, proposed legislation would empower the FDA to inspect company records, subpoena documents in investigations, and raise penalties.

TRADE REGULATION RULES AND DECEPTIVE TRADE PRACTICES

The FTC may use the notice and comment rulemaking procedures discussed in Chapter 6 to issue consumer protection regulations. The following sections discuss some of the significant trade regulation rules the FTC has issued under section 18 of the FTC Act and deceptive practices challenged under section 5.

Holder-in-Due-Course Rule

Under the UCC commercial paper law, a special rule applies when a person endorses a negotiable check or a promissory note and delivers it to another person. Even if defective goods are purchased by the consumer-debtor who wrote the check or agreed to pay the loan, the consumer has no right to withhold payment from the new holder of the check or note (the transferee). For example, after a consumer purchases a refrigerator on an installment loan contract, the seller may assign (sell) the loan contract (promissory note) to a finance company. If the refrigerator is defective, the consumer is not permitted to stop making installment payments so as to pressure the seller into fixing it. The finance company acquires a special legal status as a **holder in due course** and may demand payment from the consumer.

The holder-in-due-course rule was developed to make the use of negotiable instruments and commercial paper more reliable. The rule encourages financial institutions to regard checks and notes as the "equivalent of cash." Potential purchasers of checks and notes are more likely to accept these "negotiable instruments" if they know that the seller's breach or defective goods purchased will not affect their right to collect the money due.

In 1976, the FTC issued a regulation suspending the holder-in-due-course rule for an individual consumer's purchase or lease of goods and services. This rule requires that any consumer credit contract contain a boldface clause permitting the consumer to stop paying on debts if the seller committed fraud or breached the contract or if the goods are defective.

FTC Holder-in-Due-Course Rule Disclosure

NOTICE: ANY HOLDER OF THIS CONSUMER CREDIT CONTRACT IS SUBJECT TO ALL CLAIMS AND DEFENSES WHICH THE DEBTOR COULD ASSERT AGAINST THE SELLER OF THE GOODS OR SERVICES OBTAINED PERSUANT HERETO OR WITH THE PROCEEDS HEREOF

Purchases made on credit cards are still subject to the special protections given endorsees under the holder-in-due-course rule. If consumer goods are purchased on a credit card, the loan balance must still be paid off. The consumer must settle any disputes over the defective goods directly with the seller without stopping payment unless the purchase is made within 50 miles of the consumer's home.

Bait and Switch

Some sellers stock a limited supply of inexpensive "loss leader" merchandise as "bait" to lure potential buyers into the store intending that sales personnel can "switch" them into purchasing more expensive products. This **bait and switch** tactic violates FTC guidelines if a sales person refuses to show the cheaper merchandise, represents that the bait will be out of stock for a long time, holds an inadequate supply of the bait, or is following instructions to actively switch customers to alternative goods. For example, it is illegal to advertise an inexpensive color TV when insufficient inventory is available and salespeople are instructed to encourage buyers to switch to more expensive models.

Direct Marketing/Mail Order

The FTC has promulgated a *30-day rule* for mail-order merchandisers. Sellers of mail-order merchandise are prohibited from soliciting orders for goods that cannot be shipped within 30 days after receiving a prepaid order. This prevents sellers from "sitting" on orders and forces prompt shipment. When faced with unanticipated delays, the seller has the choice of (1) canceling the orders and refunding the payments or (2) informing the consumers of the delays and providing them with the option of waiting for the shipment or rescinding the sale. Many high-quality mail-order retailers wait until shipment to charge customers' credit cards, notify customers of the status of their orders, and remind customers of their alternatives.

Door-to-Door Sales

The FTC imposes a cooling-off period for door-to-door sales. The *cooling-off period* provides consumers with an opportunity to reassess purchases during the three days following a door-to-door purchase. This helps counteract the high pressure often present in such sales. For example, high-pressure tactics are often used to sell encyclopedias door-to-door to parents of high-school students. The cooling-off period permits recision of the sale after the sales representative pressure is removed.

Door-to-door sales contracts must have a warning addressed to the buyer about this cancellation right and must include a cancellation form. The sale of real estate, insurance, securities or commodities from a registered broker, and many types of sales solicited by the buyer are exempt from this regulation but may be covered under state law.

Other Trade Regulations

The FTC has promulgated other trade regulation rules to counter unfair and deceptive trade practices. The *Used Car Rule* requires a window sticker or buyer's guide on used cars. Sellers must clearly state what warranties are given, whether the car is sold "as is," what the consumer must pay for repairs after the sale, advising consumers to seek an independent mechanical inspection, and reminding consumers that oral promises are difficult to prove. The insulation rule requires standardized testing and disclosure of home insulation "R-value" to facilitate comparison shopping. The *Funeral Rule* requires the disclosure of itemized funeral costs and provides consumer information about various funeral services in the FTC Funeral Guide.

While the FTC's initial challenges mostly centered on "deceptive" trade practices, it is now also focusing on "unfairness," the other prohibited element in section 5. The FTC initially defined unfairness as immoral, unethical, oppressive, or unscrupulous activity that violates the legal standard of fairness and causes substantial consumer injury. Subsequently, the FTC refined this definition and said *unfairness* was conduct causing substantial and unavoidable consumer injury that is not outweighed by consumer benefits or by competition. Is it unfair for a company to raise a fixed fee it had agreed to in consumer contracts? Unfairness is illustrated in the following case.

Orkin Exterminating Co. v. F.T.C.

849 F. 2d 1354 (11th Cir. 1988)
United States Court of Appeals

Orkin offered lifetime continuous protection guarantees on termite extermination services it provided to over 200,000 customers. For a fixed annual fee these customers could have their homes retreated if the home at any time became reinfestated with termites. When Orkin discovered it was losing money on the retreatments, it raised the fees by approximately 40 percent. Orkin's sales personnel feigned a computer billing error if a surprised customer referred to the fixed price language in their contracts. The FTC issued a cease and desist order to Orkin and Orkin appealed, claiming the FTC exceeded its section 5 authority because FTC precedents had applied only the deception standard, not the unfairness standard it applied to Orkin.

Clark, Judge

We must decide whether the Commission exceeded its authority in deciding that one company's unilateral breach of over 207,000 consumer contracts could meet the Commission's definition of unfairness. The policy statement's consumer injury standard was the focus of its analysis. The unfairness standard requires a finding of substantial injury to consumers. "The harm resulting from Orkin's conduct consists of increased costs for services previously bargained for and includes the intangible loss of the certainty of the fixed price term in the contract." The Commission's finding of "substantial" injury is supported by undisputed fact that Orkin's breach generated more than $7,000,000 in revenues from renewal fees to which the Company was not entitled. Although the actual injury to individual customers may be small on an annual basis, this does not mean such injury is not "substantial." Because the "increase in the fee was not accompanied by an increase in the level of service provided or enhancement of its quality," no consumer benefit had resulted from Orkin's conduct. Customers could not have reasonably avoided the harm caused by Orkin's conduct. The Commission generally relies on free and informed consumer choice as the best regulator of the market.

Nothing indicates that the Commission did anything other than that which it purported to do: apply the unfairness standard contained in its Policy Statement.

The Commission's conclusion was simply that it was an "unfair" practice to breach over 200,000 contracts. We think that this was a reasonable application of the Commission's unfairness standard. Section 5 by its very terms makes deceptive and unfair practices distinct lines of inquiry. While a practice may be both deceptive and unfair, it may be unfair without being deceptive. The Commission's policy statement assumes the unfairness doctrine differs from, and supplements, the prohibition against deception. For the foregoing reasons, we affirm the Commission's cease and desist order.

CASE QUESTIONS

1. Define "unfairness" as used by the FTC in enforcement actions based on section 5 of the FTC Act.
2. Does an agency lose the right to enforce certain offenses if most of its prior enforcement efforts focused on other offenses?
3. Would breach of contract alone be a sufficient basis for a finding of "unfairness"? What more proof might be necessary?

State Laws Prohibiting Unfair Competition

States have legislation paralleling the FTC Act, the so-called *Mini-FTC Acts*. These laws typically empower the state attorney general or a special administrative agency to enforce prohibitions against unfair and deceptive trade practices and unfair methods of competition. Several states permit private rights of action by damaged consumers for damages, treble damages, punitive damages, attorney's fees, injunctions, rescission of contracts, and class action suits. Attorneys general may seek injunctions, restitution, civil penalties, criminal punishment, and other remedies. One of the most notable developments in the 1980s was the coordination of enforcement efforts by various states' attorneys general through their National Association of Attorneys General organization. Various other state statutes regulate particular aspects of consumer fraud such as lemon laws, door-to-door sales, and use of plain English in insurance contracts. Business must remain aware of this expanding area of federal and state consumer protection.

CONSUMER FINANCING

There is such a widespread use of consumer credit in the United States that it can be difficult to rent a car or hotel room without using a credit card. An increase in loan defaults has accompanied the business and consumer debt binge of the 1980s. This section discusses several laws passed as amendments to the Consumer Credit Protection Act to curb abuses in the business of extending, reporting, and collecting consumer loans.

Consumer Credit Protection

The Truth-in-Lending Act, passed in 1968, is the basic component of the Consumer Credit Protection Act. It was designed to facilitate the consumer's comparison of creditors' loan terms and thereby encourage competition among lenders. The Fair Credit Reporting Act, requiring consumer credit reports to contain accurate information, was added in 1970. The Fair Credit Billing Act, added in 1975, requires accuracy in consumer credit billings. The Equal Credit Opportunity Act of 1975, prohibits making discriminatory credit decisions. The Fair Debt Collection Act passed in 1978 prohibited creditors from using unreasonable debt collection tactics. Finally, in 1988, the Fair Credit and Charge Card Disclosure Act and the Home Equity Loan Consumer Protection Act required additional disclosures.

Truth-in-Lending Act The Truth-in-Lending Act authorizes the Federal Reserve Board to implement the Act with *Regulation Z,* which requires a uniform presentation of credit terms to assist borrowers in comparing the costs of credit. The act requires that creditors use a uniform computation method to explain its credit terms.

Creditors A *creditor,* as defined by the act, regularly extends or arranges credit for consumers. Such creditors include sellers of consumer goods that hold their own accounts or that arrange the consumer's credit through creditors not regularly engaged in the consumer credit business. Thus, a Ford dealer that arranges a car buyer's credit through the Ford Motor Company Credit Corporation is relieved from making the Truth-in-Lending disclosures, but the disclosures must then be made by the Ford Motor Company Credit Corporation.

Most consumer financial institutions (i.e., banks, savings and loan associations, credit unions), consumer retailers, and credit card issuers are considered creditors who must comply with the Act. Service businesses, that regularly grant or arrange credit such as contractors, plumbers, lawyers, doctors, dentists, clinics, and hospitals, must also make the Truth-in-Lending disclosures.

Consumer Credit The Truth-in-Lending Act requires disclosure from creditors whenever a loan is made for personal, family, or household purposes. The Act covers loans of less than $25,000 that are repayable in four or more installments. Real estate loans have no dollar limit; thus, disclosure is required for all consumer real estate mortgages. Specifically exempt are loans made to government units, businesses, corporations, and broker-dealer loans to investors buying securities or commodities.

Credit Term Disclosures Creditor must conspicuously disclose all the key loan terms including sale price, total of deferred payments, finance charges, and the **annual percentage rate of interest (APR).** The finance charges include interest, loan application fees, points, finder's fees, time/price differential, credit life insurance premiums if required by the lender, credit investigation report fees, and miscellaneous service fees. This itemized information illustrated in Figure 11–2 permits the borrower to easily compare credit costs with competing lenders.

Advertised loan terms must be typical of the credit transactions that the lender makes regularly. For example, most 48-month loans have a higher interest rate than 12-month loans. If most borrowers use 48-month loans, then the 12-month loan is not "typical" and should not be the one advertised. All loan terms must be conspicuously indicated if any one loan term is advertised (e.g., interest rate).

The Home Equity Loan Consumer Protection Act was passed in 1988 in response to a lack of disclosures in the expanding market for tax-deductible home equity loans (second mortgages). The required disclosures of this act are more extensive than the disclosures required for most other loans. The Act requires more detail about the APR (fixed- or variable-rate terms), a clear statement of all additional fees and repayment options, and the observance of certain standards in advertising. The Act also has requirements that go beyond mere disclosure, including prohibitions against (1) the use of obscure indexes in setting variable rates and (2) the lender's unilateral termination of the loan or acceleration of principal repayment unless the borrower is guilty of fraud, acts adversely affecting the collateral, or is in payment default.

What fees are actually considered finance charges? The next case shows that credit transactions not labeled as such must still comply with the Truth-in-Lending requirements.

FIGURE 11–2 Sample Truth-in-Lending Disclosure

Big Wheel Auto Alice Green

ANNUAL PERCENTAGE RATE The cost of your credit as a yearly rate.	FINANCE CHARGE The dollar amount the credit will cost you.	Amount Financed The amount of credit provided to you or on your behalf.	Total of Payments The amount you will have paid after you have made all payments as scheduled.	Total Sale Price The total cost of your purchase on credit, including your downpayment of $ 1500–
14.84 %	$ 1496.80	$ 6187.50	$ 7604.30	$ 9124.30

You have the right to receive at this time an itemization of the Amount Financed.

☐ I want an itemization. ☒ I do not want an itemization.

Your payment schedule will be:

Number of payments	Amount of Payments	When Payments Are Due
36	$211.23	Monthly beginning 6-1-81

Insurance

Credit life insurance and credit disability insurance are not required to obtain credit, and will not be provided unless you sign and agree to pay the additional cost.

Type	Premium	Signature	
Credit Life	$120	I want credit life insurance.	Alice Green Signature
Credit Disability		I want credit disability insurance.	Signature
Credit Life and Disability		I want credit life and disability insurance.	Signature

Security: You are giving a security interest in:

☒ the goods being purchased.

☐ ______________________

Filing fees $ 12.50 Non-filing insurance $ ________

Late Charge: If a payment is late, you will be charged $10.

Prepayment: If you pay off early, you

☐ may ☐ will not have to pay a penalty.

☒ may ☐ will not be entitled to a refund of part of the finance charge.

See your contract documents for any additional information about nonpayment, default, any required repayment in full before the scheduled date, and prepayment refunds and penalties.

I have received a copy of this statement.

Alice Green 5-1-81

Signature Date

*means an estimate

Joseph v. Norman's Health Clubs, Inc.

532 F. 2d 86 (8th Cir. 1976)
United States Court of Appeals, Eighth Circuit

Norman's Health Clubs sold most of its memberships on installment terms. The lifetime memberships cost $360, payable in 24 equal monthly installments, though a few were sold for cash at a discount of 24 percent to 46 percent. The customers choosing installments signed a note that Norman's resold at a discount to finance companies which sent members coupon books for making payments directly to them.

Lay, Circuit Judge

The fundamental purpose of the Truth-in-Lending Act is to require creditors to disclose the "true" cost of consumer credit, so that consumers can make informed choices among available methods of payment.

The Act was intended to change the practices of the consumer credit industry, and the statute reflects Congress' view that this should be done by imposing disclosure requirements on those who "regularly" extend or offer to extend consumer credit. In interpreting the Act, the Federal Reserve Board and the majority of courts have focused on the substance, rather than the form, of credit transactions, and have looked to the practices of the trade, the course of dealing of the parties, and the intention of the parties in addition to specific contractual obligations. "Some creditors would attempt to characterize their transactions so as to fall one step outside whatever boundary Congress attempted to establish."

The finance companies operated under a definite working arrangement with the Club. The evidence discloses that (1) the finance companies were alerted almost simultaneously with the customer's execution of a note; (2) an immediate credit check was then made by the finance companies; (3) if the customer's note was accepted, the finance companies paid the Club the amount of the note less the discount; (4) the finance companies accepted assignments without recourse to the Club, thus relying solely on the customer for payment; (5) the finance companies often contacted the customer the same day and upon approving him, the companies would send out their payment book describing the manner of payment and notice of late charges (not mentioned in the note assigned); (6) the finance companies carried the note on their books as a "loan" and listed a "finance charge"; and (7) thereafter, the finance companies treated the club member in the same manner as they did their direct consumer loan customers. The situation was no different than if the finance companies had gone to the Club with the prospective member, paid the Club for the membership and then taken the customer's note just as they did take it.

The Act defines "finance charge" as:

> the sum of *all* charges, payable directly or *indirectly by the person to whom the credit is extended,* and imposed directly or *indirectly* by the creditor as an incident to the extension of credit, including . . . any amount payable under a . . . discount . . . system.

"Finance charge" under TILA was intended to include not only "interest" but many other charges for credit.

All of the discount originally agreed upon by the Club and the finance companies was passed along to the customers as a charge for use of credit. It may be, however, that some portion of the subsequent increases in the discount was not passed along to the customers and was rather absorbed by the Club as a reduction in its profit. On the other hand, adding more members may have permitted the seller so to reduce cost per member that it could provide the same services without increasing the face amount of the note. [The Truth-in-Lending disclosure must be made by finance companies.]

Case Questions

1. What is the purpose of applying the Truth-in-Lending Act to finance companies?
2. What would disclosure of the credit terms indicate was the real cost of the installment contracts here?

Credit Cards Credit cards are a form of open-ended credit or revolving charge account covered by the Truth-in-Lending Act. Credit cards may be issued only on request or on application by the cardholder, though many credit card issuers actively solicit applications. A cardholder becomes liable for the use of a credit card upon accepting the card, usually by signing, using, or authorizing use of the card. The Truth-in-Lending Act limits the cardholder's liability to $50 for unauthorized charges; there is no cardholder liability for unauthorized use after the cardholder has notified the card issuer that the card has been lost or stolen. Private credit card protection services are available to insure cardholders against the potential $50 losses and notify card issuers.

The Fair Credit and Charge Card Disclosure Act of 1988 added several disclosure requirements for charge card issuers. These requirements vary, depending on whether the consumer is solicited by telephone, by mail, or by a "take one" application form. When accounts are solicited by mail and variable interest rates apply, this fact, as well as how the rates are determined, must be disclosed. Membership fees, account maintenance fees, minimum finance charges, cash advance fees, late payment fees, and grace periods during which the customer may pay without additional fees must be disclosed.

The terms of an open-credit account must be disclosed when the account is opened and periodically thereafter (billing inserts). For example, the creditor must state the conditions that trigger the finance charge, the balance on which it is computed, the method of computation, and the interest rates used. A statement of customer rights must be provided, including the amount of the minimum payment required and a description of how additional charges or liens are incurred. Monthly or other periodic statements must disclose the amounts of balances due, finance charges, unpaid balances on which finance charges are computed, the APR, and the periodic rates (monthly rates) applied to unpaid balances. Billings must include an address for billing inquiries and state the customer's rights.

Penalties and Enforcements Both criminal and civil liabilities may be imposed for violations of the Truth-in-Lending Act. Willful violators can be imprisoned for up to one year and fined up to $5,000. The civil liability to consumers is set at double the amount of the damage sustained ($100 minimum and $1,000 maximum) plus costs and reasonable attorney's fees.

ETHICAL DILEMMAS IN DEBTOR-CREDITOR RELATIONS

The creditor-debtor relationship has evolved significantly over the years. Both the creditor and the debtor face ethical dilemmas in negotiating the terms of their contract, performing the debt payment, and confronting the default and collection process. The costs of defaulting debtors are borne by all debtors because higher interest rates and more stringent collection and security terms are used to cover the costs of defaults. Debtors with no reasonable intention or hope of repaying act irresponsibly if they seek credit or if they misrepresent sources of income or their assets. Is it ethical for debtors with good credit histories to pay for the expenses of defaulters through higher interest rates?

Some people view the social cost of a creditor's strict collection procedures as intrusive and unfair. If a debt is used to pay for necessities of life, it seems unfair for the creditor to repossess these necessities after the debtor defaults. How should society balance the unfairness of passing the costs of default risk on to responsible debtors against society's other considerations of fairness? Creditors should continue to refine their methods of screening debtors before granting credit, so that they make loans only to creditworthy debtors. A seller that grants credit to uncreditworthy individuals only to increase product sales imposes a burden on society.

Fair Credit Billing The Fair Credit Billing Act provides mechanisms to resolve billing disputes with creditors. Creditors must comply with the Act if the credit is payable in more than four installments or if a financing charge is imposed. Creditors are required to inform consumers of their rights and provide an address for billing inquiries.

The consumer may make inquiries regarding billing errors, such as incorrect amounts of improperly billed purchases. Such inquiries must be made in writing within 60 days after receipt of a disputed bill. The creditor must acknowledge an inquiry within 30 days and must explain an error within the next two billing cycles (usually two months). The error must be investigated and corrected if the consumer is correct. The debtor must be informed of the creditor's position and receive copies of documents requested.

While the parties attempt to resolve the disputed debt, the creditor may not attempt to collect the debt, threaten the debtor, make adverse credit reports about the disputed debt, or restrict or close the debtor's account. The creditor may continue to issue bills reflecting the disputed debt and may reduce the debtor's credit line by the disputed amount. The notice and delay provisions of the Act are designed to enable the debtor to respond to the creditor's actions and to encourage investigation and informal settlement. A creditor violating the Act loses the right to collect both the disputed debt and the finance charges and can be fined $50 for each disputed billing item.

Fair Credit Reporting Act The keystone to assuring fair credit is the protection of the debtor's "good credit rating." Although the ultimate responsibility for a good rating lies with the debtor, many people can affect a debtor's credit rating. Approximately 1,900 credit reporting agencies (credit bureaus) throughout the nation investigate, archive, and report on many personal aspects of debtors. The private services of these agencies enable creditors to evaluate the creditworthiness of loan applicants. Credit standing is also used as an indicator of character and general reputation used in employment, bonding, and insurance decisions. Congress passed the Fair Credit Reporting Act to assure the fairness of the credit reporting process to applicants for credit without unduly burdening the credit reporting system.

Credit Histories Credit reporting agencies collect information on debtors' credit history: the promptness and fullness of installment repayments on loans and credit cards. Credit reporting agencies also collect information about the reputation and character of debtors. Congress permits debtors to correct past debt-paying mistakes and requires the removal of obsolete information from the debtor's file. For example, bankruptcies over 14 years old and bad debt information over 7 years old may not be reported.

Credit Reporting Agency Duties Any entity in interstate commerce that is regularly engaged in the collection or evaluation of consumer credit information provided to third parties must comply with the Act. Reports used only by the reporting agency are exempt. Reports concerning transactions between the consumer and the reporter are not covered.

Credit reporting agencies must verify information to assure its accuracy. If a consumer disputes information in agency files, whether or not that information has been reported, the agency must reinvestigate unless the consumer's dispute is frivolous. If the objectionable information is not deleted, the consumer may include a brief statement of his or her version of the dispute. For example, if two consumers have the same name, but with different spellings (e.g., Johnson versus Johnsen), an inaccurate report might be made.

Each of these consumers is permitted to include a statement in the files concerning this confusion. If adverse information on a consumer is not deleted from an agency's files, all reports on that consumer sent out from the agency must include the consumer's statement or an accurate abstract of it. The consumer may insist that the statement be given to anyone who received the adverse information within the prior two years for employment purposes or within the prior six months for any other purposes.

Users Entitled to Credit Reports The customers of credit reporting agencies, usually potential creditors, insurers, or employers, are the ultimate users of credit reports. A user must have a legitimate purpose to request a report. Reports may be legitimately supplied pursuant to a court order, upon written request of the consumer, or to any entity reasonably expected to use the reports in making decisions on such matters as (1) the granting of consumer credit, (2) the issuance of insurance policies, (3) employment, (4) the granting of governmental licenses, or (5) other legitimate purposes.

Remedies The Act and state common law provide remedies for unconscionable conduct in credit investigations. The FTC may designate particular activities of violators as unfair and deceptive trade practices or issue cease and desist orders. Users who obtain information from credit reporting agencies under false pretenses may be criminally liable. For example, falsification of the prospective debtor's request for credit information is criminal.

Credit reporting agencies that knowingly provide information for illegitimate purposes may also be held criminally liable, with fines of up to $5,000 and/or imprisonment up to one year. Agencies that willfully or negligently violate the Act may have civil liability for actual damages, reasonable attorney's fees, and court costs. Punitive damages may be assessed for willful violations.

Credit reporting agencies may be held liable for negligence if they do not install and maintain reasonable procedures to ensure the accuracy of reports and supply the reports only for legitimate purposes. The common law torts of defamation and invasion of privacy may also be used by a damaged consumer. Users, credit reporting agencies, and those who supply inaccurate information to credit reporting agencies may be held liable for damages if the information is false or violates the right of privacy.

Commentary: Integrity of Personal Financial Privacy

Personal financial data about most individuals is available increasingly from confidential creditor records and from publicly available court filings, mortgages, personal property liens, and other matters. Personal profiles can be compiled from mailing lists, financial surveys, buying patterns, and interviews with acquaintances. For example, banks regularly examine the notes customers write on their checks, ask for additional numbers such as credit cards, driver's license, and telephones, and examine customer deposits to determine income. This information is compiled to determine buying patterns and sold to information services which resell this data to marketers, lenders, employers, and others. The numbers of calls made to 800 and 900 numbers are captured and matched with reverse phone directories. Clearly this information could be used for other undisclosed purposes.

Many privacy experts believe the information explosion unduly threatens individual privacy and cannot be addressed by the current consumer credit protections. There is no scientific evidence linking debt repayment problems with poor job performance, yet credit reports are used increasingly in place of prohibited lie detector tests as a job screening technique. Credit reports are the number one area of consumer complaints to the FTC.

In the early 1990s, evidence surfaced that sloppy procedures at credit reporting agencies showed individuals' records full of inaccuracies causing damage to their prospects for credit, insurance, licenses, and employment. The FTC and 19 states' attorneys general settled charges with TRW, the giant credit reporting agency, based on allegations it sold sensitive data to junk mailers, permitted errors to recur, and inadequately investigated customer complaints. The TRW settlement pressures the other two major credit reporting agencies, TransUnion and Equifax, to adopt similar protections or risk further federal regulation.

New legislation could: (1) penalize creditors who supply errors, (2) establish tougher penalties, (3) require distribution of corrected reports if employers or creditors were supplied errors, (4) require a free annual credit report to all consumers, (5) require consumer authorization for reports not used for credit, insurance, licenses, or employment, and (6) ban selling data to junk mailers.

Equal Credit Opportunity Act The Equal Credit Opportunity Act is intended to assure that the creditor's decision to extend or deny credit is not based on the consumer's membership in one of the suspect classes that have historically experienced discrimination. Credit cannot be denied on the basis of race, color, sex, religion, national origin, age, or marital status or on the basis of the fact that public assistance is the source of a person's income. In addition, credit cannot be denied in retaliation against the consumer for exercising rights under the Consumer Credit Protection Act.

Generally, the creditor is prohibited from inquiring whether income is derived from separate maintenance, child support, or alimony and from inquiring as to the race, color, religion, or national origin of the applicant. For example, *redlining,* a practice of refusing home mortgage loans in declining neighborhoods, is prohibited. There are a few exceptions to these prohibitions. A creditor may inquire into marital status to determine whether a spouse might assert a state dower right or a community property interest which gives priority over the collateral. If public assistance is the source of income, the creditor may make inquiries regarding the stability of that income. For example, a creditor considering an applicant's ability to repay a long-term loan may validly inquire whether unemployment compensation is limited in time.

Under the Equal Credit Opportunity Act, creditors are civilly liable for actual and punitive damages if they deny credit on the basis of suspect class membership. Private parties and certain government agencies may seek an injunction against future violations. These regulations concern only unlawful discrimination in the granting of credit; employment discrimination is discussed in Chapter 19.

Electronic Funds Transfer

Debt and other payments are being made increasingly by paperless **electronic fund transfers (EFT)** using automated teller machines (ATM), electronic or direct deposits, telephone or computer terminal transfers, point-of-sale machines, and automatic payments. To assure that payments are made accurately, that personal privacy is maintained, and that computer hackers do not tamper with electronic payments, Congress passed the Electronic Funds Transfer Act in 1978. This act amends the Truth-in-Lending Act, requiring financial institutions to make disclosures to customers, resolve errors, and provide customer remedies.

Financial institutions must notify EFT customers of their rights and send them monthly statements. These statements must show the date and amount of each transfer, the retailer's name, and the terminal used. Receipts must be provided for transactions using terminals but not for phone transfers. Allegations of errors must be investigated by the financial institution, and the institution must give the customer notice in writing within 10 days. Treble damages may be assessed against the financial institution if it does not resolve errors quickly and accurately.

Financial institutions are liable for damages if a customer's account has sufficient funds but the EFT transaction is not made. Customers may recover punitive damages between $100 and $1,000 and there are criminal penalties. Consumers are liable for unauthorized use of their ATM cards up to $50 if the bank is notified within two days after the consumer learns the card is lost and up to $500 if notice is given within 60 days. Consumers can be liable up to their available balance and credit line limit if withdrawals are made by someone given the consumer's personal identification number (PIN).

Debt Collection

The debt relationship is a consensual one between creditors and debtors. In return for the advancement of cash or goods, the debtor voluntarily promises to repay the debt principal and the interest in fixed or variable installments. As long as payments are timely made, the relationship is usually amicable. If the debtor defaults, however, the creditor will probably take steps to collect the debt. Many promissory notes (IOUs) contain an acceleration clause permitting the creditor, after the debtor has defaulted on a single payment, to declare the entire principal balance due immediately. This facilitates the collection of the whole debt in a single suit or foreclosure against the collateral without the need to bring a new collection suit for each periodic payment. As long as the creditor or debt collector fairly but tenaciously pursues the debtor, the debtor has little basis for legal action.

Debt Collection Practices If unfair debt collection practices are followed, the debtor has several remedies under the common law. Defamation (libel and slander) may be used where the debt collector publishes untrue statements about the debtor. The right of privacy makes it unlawful to use unreasonable collection tactics that intrude on the debtor's solitude or that place the debtor in a false light in the public eye. In some states, the intentional infliction of emotional distress also protects debtors from outrageous actions by creditors.

Creditors have a number of methods and devices to assure repayment of loans. Consumer loans are often secured by (1) the cosignature of another debtor, (2) credit insurance, (3) bonding, or (4) forfeiture of rights in the collateral (foreclosure). If a debt is backed by collateral, the debtor grants the creditor a legal right to repossess and sell the collateral upon default. The creditor must first attempt to satisfy the debt out of the proceeds from the sale of the collateral. Real estate mortgages and automobile security arrangements create security interests of this type.

If a creditor is forced to bring suit on a defaulted loan, the *execution process* is used. This process is somewhat similar to a foreclosure sale. It permits the forced sale of the debtor's noncollateral assets. Execution is available only after a court order, and it typically requires the assistance of the sheriff.

The creditor may also use the statutory right of **garnishment**. This is a court order requiring a third party, which holds the debtor's property, to turn it over to the creditor, the sheriff, or the court. The creditor serves a *writ of garnishment* on the debtor's employer or bank, which must deduct a sum of money from wages or a bank account to pay the creditor directly. Because of numerous abuses, Congress amended the Consumer Credit Protection Act to restrict garnishment. With some exceptions, the amount garnished may not exceed 25 percent of the debtor's after-tax income. Employers may not fire garnished employees, under the assumption that they are irresponsible, merely because their wages are garnished.

Fair Debt Collection Practices Act In an effort to end invasion of privacy, harassment, and other abuses in the debt collection process, Congress amended the Consumer Credit Protection Act with the Fair Debt Collection Practices Act in 1978 and again in 1986. Consumer debts for personal, family, or household purposes must be collected in conformity with the Act's provisions. The Act applies to all parties in the business of collecting debts for others; it does not apply to attorneys or to creditors collecting their own debts.

Debtors may be contacted by a debt collector only between the hours of 8 A.M and 9 P.M. or at other convenient times. The acceptable methods of contact include telephone, mail, telegram, or visits in person. The debtor may send the debt collector a written request to cease contact within 30 days after the first contact. After receiving this notice, the debt collector must stop all contacts except for simple notices that indicate further legal action. Within five days of the debt collector's first contact with the debtor, the debt collector must send the debtor a written notice. That notice must include the debt amount, the original creditor's identity, a copy of the debt or judgment, and a statement of the debtor's rights if the debt is not genuine.

A debt collector that violates the Act by using any prohibited collection method may be held civilly liable for actual damages, pain and suffering, emotional distress, invasion of privacy, court costs, and reasonable attorney's fees. Several collection practices are specifically prohibited under the Act: threats of violence to person, property, or reputation; obscenities; repeated and annoying use of the telephone; false statements about the debtor to anyone; the use of documents falsely appearing to be official statements (e.g., court orders); and contacts at the debtor's worksite if the employer prohibits them. Debt collectors may not contact anyone other than the debtor, except that the debtor's attorney must be contacted if the collector knows about the attorney. Debt collectors may investigate a missing debtor's whereabouts by contacting third parties. The FTC can enforce the Act with penalties, and debtors may seek monetary damages.

Usury Laws

States have passed and revised *usury laws* regulating the highest interest rates that can be charged to consumer debtors. These laws are in direct conflict with the free market theory, which suggests that the market for credit should set interest rates by forces of supply and demand. However, the legislative history of the states' usury laws reveals that these laws address several abuses. First, they perform a consumer protection function by limiting the cost of credit. Second, they counteract the criminal activity that excessive interest rates induce through loan sharking.

Usury law is best known for the credit-like transactions that it does not cover. Usury applies only to consumer loans and not to commercial loans made to businesses, because businesses are expected to adequately protect themselves. Credit card interest rates are governed by separate interest rate ceilings. *Time/price differentials,* in which cash prices are listed separately from deferred payment prices for the purchase of merchandise, are also exempt. These differentials arise when an outright cash price is listed at a lower level than if the price is paid in installments. The penalty for charging usurious interest rates varies among the states, ranging from a small penalty, through forfeiture of some or all of the interest, to complete forfeiture of the loan principal. From time to time, some states have imposed such low usury ceilings that credit has become scarce. However, as a result of the high inflation of the early 1980s, most states' usury ceilings are above 20 percent.

Secured Financing

The creditor's willingness to extend credit often depends on how adequately the debtor assures repayment. The debtor's promissory note provides a legal right to sue for the unpaid debt, but this is inadequate if the debtor becomes insolvent. However, there are other repayment assurances: investigation of the debtor's creditworthiness beforehand, credit insurance, guarantee contracts made by others, and the creditor's rights in collateral. Many loans to individuals and businesses are made on the condition the debtor grants legal rights in some property permitting the creditor to foreclose on the collateral to satisfy defaulted debts. The land mortgages discussed in Chapter 7, new car liens, and a corporate bondholder's security interest in machinery are common examples of security interests.

The UCC provides the legal machinery for securing loans with collateral other than real estate. UCC Article 9 establishes the procedures for creating a **secured transaction** in personal property. The *secured party,* usually the lender, is given special rights to keep or sell the collateral on default. Commonly, the loan proceeds are used to purchase the collateral, so a *purchase money security interest (PMSI)* arises. The security interest *attaches,* or is created, when the borrower (1) signs a security agreement or the creditor holds possession of the collateral, (2) the secured party gives value (consideration) for the security interest (usually advances the loan principal), and (3) the borrower has rights in the collateral.

Perfection The creditor is responsible for making the security interest effective by assuring attachment with a *security agreement,* a writing, signed by the debtor, describing the collateral. This makes the security interest effective between the debtor and the creditor. However, debtors are usually free to grant security interests in the same collateral to other secured parties. This may cause disputes among the various secured parties, particularly if the collateral becomes worth less than the total outstanding debts. Therefore, secured parties must usually *perfect* their security interests to put the world on notice. Perfection usually occurs when the secured party files a *financing statement,* describing the collateral and the security interest, at an appropriate local government office required by state law. Alternatively, the secured party may perfect by taking possession of the collateral, a practice certain to alert third parties of a potential security interest. Most vehicles have title certificates so that notice of the security interest is written directly on the title certificate, a document necessary to transfer ownership.

Priorities Disputes can arise among competing secured parties when the debtor becomes insolvent and defaults on the secured loan payments. If the collateral sale value will be less than the claims of all the secured parties, then questions arise about *priority.* Generally, the secured party that perfected first can have the debt completely satisfied first out of the foreclosure sale proceeds. Among unperfected parties, the first party to attach a security interest will win. Article 9 provides for many complex additional priority rules that depend on a number of factors about the types of secured parties, the types of collateral (e.g., inventory, consumer goods, farm products, equipment), whether the loan created a PMSI, whether the debtor is in bankruptcy, and whether the collateral was purchased by a good faith purchaser for value.

Default After these problems have been resolved, the secured party is often given the choice of simply keeping the collateral in complete satisfaction of the debt or of selling it in a public or private sale. If the sale brings more than the secured party's debt, the surplus will be used to pay for expenses of the repossession and sale and to repay other debts secured by the collateral; the remainder belongs to the debtor. If the sale brings an amount insufficient to satisfy these claims, the debtor is still responsible for the deficiency.

Uniform Consumer Credit Code

The Uniform Consumer Credit Code (UCCC) is a single, uniform, and comprehensive state law governing consumer credit transactions. The controversial UCCC is adopted by only a few states. It is largely superseded by other laws, such as the Consumer Credit Protection Act, in regulating credit contract terms, credit disclosures, retail installment sales, usury, door-to-door sales, garnishment, and creditor remedies.

Consumer Leasing

Leasing has fast become a viable alternative to consumer credit purchases because lease payments are usually lower than loan payments, and the 1986 Tax Act eliminated the deduction for loan interest except on home mortgages and home equity loans. In recognition that consumer leases of goods are often a substitute for credit transactions, the Consumer Leasing Act has provisions similar to the Truth-in-Lending Act. The act empowers the Federal Reserve Board to issue Regulation M and provides liability for violations. It applies to all consumer leases of personal property with a total contract obligation of under $25,000. Auto rentals, business leases, and land leases are not covered.

The act requires disclosures similar to the Truth-in-Lending Act concerning the number, amount, and period of payments; warranties; maintenance responsibilities; purchase options, if any; and premature termination obligations. For example, people who now lease autos rather than finance their purchase must be given a disclosure form indicating typical terms: the lease payments, the purchase option price (residual value), that warranties are limited to the auto manufacturer's express warranty, that the lessee must service the auto and keep it insured, and that early termination will cost the lessee the present value of all remaining lease payments.

BANKRUPTCY

The Constitution empowers Congress to pass uniform bankruptcy laws. The Bankruptcy Act of 1898, which governs bankruptcy in the United States, has been revised several times. The latest amendments were made in the Bankruptcy Reform Acts of 1978, 1984, and 1986. After a bankruptcy filing, the debtor may lose control and ownership of many assets. These are liquidated (sold), and the proceeds are eventually distributed to creditors. Usually, most of the unpaid portion of the bankrupt's debts are *discharged,* or eliminated altogether, resulting in a "clean slate." Thus, bankruptcy law provides the overextended debtor with a "fresh start" and assures fair and equal treatment to creditors. There are several forms of bankruptcy that may be used by individuals, businesses, and certain government units.

Straight Bankruptcy

The most well-known form of bankruptcy is found in Chapter 7 of the bankruptcy law; it is known as *straight bankruptcy.* It provides for a complete liquidation of the debtor's assets and partial satisfaction of most debts. The bankruptcy courts administer the process of (1) collection and sale of the debtor's assets, (2) verification of creditor claims, (3) distribution of the liquidation proceeds, and (4) granting the debtor a discharge of most debts.

Insolvent individuals, partnerships, and corporations may be liquidated. However, several highly regulated industries such as banks, savings and loan associations, railroads, most governmental units, and insurance companies in financial distress do not receive this traditional liquidation treatment in bankruptcy. Instead, they may be merged with financially healthy entities or assisted through their financial crisis by regulators.

Under bankruptcy law, insolvency is determined on either the cash flow basis or the balance sheet basis. When the bankrupt is unable to pay debts as they become due, insolvency exists on the cash flow basis. If the bankrupt's liabilities exceed its assets, insolvency exists on the balance sheet basis.

The Bankruptcy Process

From the time that the bankruptcy petition is filed until the final disposition of the case by the bankruptcy court, a stay or suspension order is in effect. The *stay* prevents creditors from collecting debts or foreclosing on collateral. During the bankruptcy proceedings, the bankrupt, its creditors, the bankruptcy court, and the bankruptcy trustee each play a particular role.

Voluntary and Involuntary Petitions A debtor may file a *voluntary petition* with the bankruptcy court, or creditors may "throw" a debtor into bankruptcy by filing an *involuntary petition.* A minimum number of creditors is required to file an involuntary petition. If the debtor has more than 12 creditors, at least 3 must join in the involuntary petition. If there are 12 or fewer creditors, only 1 creditor needs to file the involuntary petition. The creditors that file an involuntary petition must also have *unsecured claims* (debts without collateral) amounting to at least $5,000. These requirements are intended to prevent creditor misuse of bankruptcy in retaliation or intimidation.

Duties of the Debtor In order to qualify for a discharge from debts, the debtor must perform several duties and cooperate in good faith during bankruptcy proceedings. Within a reasonable time after the petition is filed, the debtor must file documents with the bankruptcy court, including (1) a list of creditors, (2) a schedule or list of assets and liabilities, and (3) other financial statements. The debtor must give up all nonexempt property to the bankruptcy trustee, who becomes the legal owner until liquidation. All tangible and intangible property, such as goods, real estate, patent rights, copyrights, trademarks, accounts receivables, must be surrendered. The debtor must appear at creditor meetings and at the final hearing.

The Bankruptcy Trustee Soon after the petition has been filed, the bankruptcy court appoints an interim trustee to call the first meeting of the creditors, at which a permanent trustee is elected by majority vote. The debtor is examined (questioned) at this first meeting to determine such things as the whereabouts of the debtor's property. The permanent trustee carefully collects and disposes of the property to accumulate a fund to pay off creditor claims. The trustee determines whether each creditor's claim is genuine and may challenge any fraudulent claims against the debtor. The trustee may also sue for property and debts owed to the debtor.

The trustee has the power to set aside (invalidate) both preferential and fraudulent transfers. *Preferential transfers* are payments or property transfers made in the 90 (ninety) days prior to the filing of the petition that give a particular creditor a greater percentage of the assets than would be distributed to that creditor in normal bankruptcy proceedings. For example, if the debtor paid off an old debt in the month before filing bankruptcy, the trustee may recover the payment, thus requiring equal treatment for all creditors. *Fraudulent transfers* are sales or gifts for unfair value that the debtor made to closely related third parties, such as relatives, partners, or corporate officers, at any time within the year before filing the petition.

The trustee must keep adequate accounting records and must file detailed statements of the disposition of assets with the bankruptcy court. Professionals, such as accountants, appraisers, attorneys, and auctioneers, are hired as necessary to assist the trustee. The proceeds from liquidation of the bankrupt's property (the bankrupt's estate) are used to pay these and other costs of bankruptcy.

Exemptions Individual bankrupts may keep certain property necessary to continue life after liquidation of the bankrupt's estate.

Property Exempt from Bankruptcy Liquidation (Federal)

1. Not more than $7,500 equity in the homestead.
2. Not more than $1,200 equity in one automobile.
3. Not more than $200 per item in all household items.
4. Not more than $500 in jewelry.
5. Not more than $400 worth of other property not listed above, including any unused portion of the $7,500 homestead equity.
6. Not more than $750 in tools of the debtor's trade.
7. Life insurance interests (i.e., whole life cash value and dividends).
8. Prescribed health aids.
9. Government benefits (e.g., social security, veteran's benefits, alimony).

When a husband and wife go bankrupt as joint petitioners, they may add their separate individual exemptions together. Unless a state prohibits it, the bankrupt may choose the federal exemptions listed above or any other exemptions applicable under the state's law of execution, whichever is preferable for the bankrupt. State exemptions and amounts vary greatly, although some are *considerably* more generous.

Distribution There are three basic types of creditors in bankruptcy proceedings. *Secured creditors* have security interests, such as mortgages or liens on specific property.

Security interests give these creditors a preference on the sale proceeds after the secured items have been sold in liquidation, but only up to the liquidation value of the collateral. To the extent that the collateral is insufficient to satisfy secured creditor claims, they are unsecured. Secured creditors may demand assurances from the trustee that their security will not be impaired during bankruptcy or reorganization.

Unsecured or *general creditors* have no security interests to protect their debts. They must take their shares of the distribution proceeds equally as a group on a pro rata basis. For example, trade creditors that supply inventory or equipment to the debtor without retaining a lien are unsecured. Credit card issuers are also unsecured.

Priority creditors gain priority over unsecured creditors, but not over secured creditors, as to their specially defined claims. Each of the classes of priority creditors may have its claims totally repaid before the next class receives payment. If there are insufficient funds to pay all the claims of a particular class of priority creditors, they share pro rata and all lower-priority creditors receive nothing.

Priority Creditor Classes

1. Administration expenses of bankruptcy; accountant and attorney's fees, court costs, trustee's fees, costs of preserving bankrupt's property.
2. Debts incurred after the filing of an involuntary petition and before appointment of a trustee.
3. Wages up to $2,000 per employee of the bankrupt in the 90 days preceding the petition or cessation of business, whichever is first.
4. Unpaid employer contributions to employee benefit plans within the 180 days preceding the petition or business cessation, to the extent that the $2,000 in wages per employee is unused.
5. Consumer claims up to $900 in deposits or prepayments for undelivered goods or unperformed services.
6. Taxes of local, state, and federal governments with various limitations.

Discharge of Debts After liquidation, a discharge in bankruptcy will be ordered, giving the bankrupt a clean slate for preexisting debts. However, if the bankrupt has concealed assets, made fraudulent transfers, destroyed books or records, disobeyed a bankruptcy court order, failed to explain the loss of assets, or made fraudulent statements in the bankruptcy proceeding, a discharge can be denied. If no discharge is granted the bankrupt will lose its assets in the liquidation but will still owe the unpaid portion of all debts. Some debts, such as alimony, child support, federal taxes, and federally insured student loans are not discharged.

Alternatives to Liquidation

It is not necessary for all debtor-bankrupts to submit to a complete liquidation and discharge in bankruptcy. If the debtor is in a moderate state of financial health and suitable arrangements can be worked out with creditors, then alternative procedures are available.

Wage Earners Under Chapter 13, individuals with regular income from salary, wages, or commissions as employees may have their debts readjusted but not discharged. The Chapter 13 adjustment procedure is available if the income earner has aggregate unsecured debts of less than $100,000 and aggregate secured debts of less than $350,000. The debtor remains in possession of his or her assets during the proceedings and after the approval of an adjustment plan. The *plan* provides a cash flow and payment schedule to repay all debts. If the readjustment is ultimately approved, creditors may not involuntarily force the debtor into liquidation during or after the initiation of the Chapter 13 process. Debtors unable to adhere to the plan may later switch to straight bankruptcy.

In most Chapter 13 proceedings, the individual debtor, sometimes with counseling, devises and files the debt repayment plan with the bankruptcy court. Under the plan, the debtor has flexibility to combine debt compositions and/or extensions of existing debts so as to facilitate repayment. The terms of the debts are usually readjusted by the bankruptcy court to enable the debtor to make the payments without going into liquidation. *Composition* arrangements allow for the payment of a lesser principal and/or interest rate. *Extension* terms permit the debtor to make smaller payments by extending the maturity date and/or the number of debt payments. Most such plans must be completed within three years unless the court approves a longer period. The bankruptcy court must approve any new debts taken on after the plan has been implemented and before all debts are repaid.

The plan must be approved by the bankruptcy court, but not necessarily by the creditors. As long as the plan provides that unsecured creditors will receive as much as they would under a liquidation, their approval is unnecessary. Secured creditors need not approve the plan if the debtor surrenders the secured property to them or if they retain a lien at least equal to the debt amounts. Priority claimants must receive full payment or agree to accept a lesser sum.

The debtor's employer or the debtor pays a certain sum periodically (usually monthly) to the bankruptcy trustee. The trustee has the responsibility of apportioning that sum among the creditors pro rata in accordance with the plan. If the debtor has complied, the debtor is discharged after the conclusion of the plan, even if some creditors have received less than the original amount of their debts plus interest and penalties.

Corporate Reorganizations Corporations, and now individuals, may take advantage of Chapter 11, a **reorganization** process similar to the Chapter 13 arrangement. This process permits businesses with going-concern value to continue operation during financial difficulties. The purpose is to minimize the negative impact of business failures on the economy and on creditors, customers, suppliers, employees, and the community. In a Chapter 11 proceeding, a debtor corporation is reorganized pursuant to a voluntary or involuntary petition. Individuals who do not quality for Chapter 13 may use Chapter 11.

The reorganization process is usually more complex and time consuming than the Chapter 13 wage earner's adjustment. Each *class* or group of similar creditors and shareholders forms a separate committee to propose, modify, and approve a master *plan of reorganization*. After a thorough investigation into the debtor corporation's business prospects, financial condition, and activities, these committees meet and attempt to negotiate an acceptable plan. The plan may include elements of composition, extension, and/or reduction or *cram down*, which means that the debtor corporation's shareholders, bondholders, and creditors will receive less than the stated value of their claims. Some creditors may be converted into shareholders, preferred shareholders may be converted into common shareholders, and common shareholders may lose shares of stock. All of the claimants generally have smaller claims after a cram down of their original claims.

If the debtor corporation's management is unable to continue the business, the committees may require that a special trustee be appointed. This trustee will operate the business without interference from the debtor's former management. Alternatively, if the debtor's management is considered capable of successfully continuing the business, no trustee is appointed and the debtor's management proposes a reorganization plan.

The reorganization plan must be presented within the first 120 days after the bankruptcy court orders relief. In more complex reorganizations, the creditor committees consider the merits of various proposed plans. Approval occurs when a majority of the creditors in a committee, holding at least two thirds of the aggregate debt in that class, vote for it. Stockholder committees must also approve plans with a two-thirds vote of the members of each class (common or preferred stock). Some Chapter 11 proceedings are referred to as "pre-packs" in which the various claimants negotiate the plan before filing the petition. When the plan can be worked out amicably and the bankruptcy court approves the plan as fair to all parties, the pre-pack can be more efficient and avoid goodwill losses because the proceeding is so swift.

If the bankruptcy court finds that a particular plan is fair and equitable to all the classes of creditors, then the whole plan may be approved even if some committees have not approved it. The final court approval of the plan discharges the corporation from its former debts and equity interests and substitutes the new claims defined in the plan. A corporate reorganization can be converted into a liquidation if this appears to be in the best interest of all involved.

Chapter 11 has been used recently to reduce the impact of labor union contracts, product liability claims, and court judgments. For example, Texaco declared bankruptcy to avoid paying Pennzoil $11 billion because of Texaco's alleged interference with Pennzoil's takeover of Getty Oil Company. Eventually, the two companies agreed to a $3 billion settlement, later approved as a reorganization plan by Texaco's creditors, stockholders, and the bankruptcy court. The asbestos product liability claims against Manville were delayed and probably reduced by its Chapter 11 filing. In these cases Chapter 11 bankruptcy is not used by insolvent corporations; it has been used by solvent corporations to avoid going out of business due to huge claims. How should a costly labor contract be reconciled with a bankruptcy reorganization? The next case illustrates the interplay between Chapter 11 and federal labor law. Recent amendments in the Bankruptcy Reform Act make the action taken in the following case more difficult.

N.L.R.B. v. Bildisco

466 U.S. 513 (1984)
United States Supreme Court

Bildisco, a building supply distributor, filed for protection under Chapter 11 of the bankruptcy laws. Approximately 45 percent of Bildisco's employees were covered by a collective bargaining agreement between the Teamsters union and Bildisco due to expire in two years. Bildisco failed to make health and pension benefit payments, schedule wage increases, and remit dues collected to the union. Bildisco was charged with an unfair labor practice under the federal labor law.

Justice Rehnquist delivered the opinion of the Court.

Section 365(a) of the Bankruptcy Code provides in full:

> "(a) Except as provided in sections 765 and 766 of this title and in subsections (b), (c), and (d) of this section, the trustee, subject to the court's approval, may assume or reject any executory contract or unexpired lease of the debtor."

This language by its terms includes all executory contracts except those expressly exempted, and it is not disputed by the parties that an unexpired collective-bargaining agreement is an executory contract.

Although there is no indication in § 365 of the Bankruptcy Code that rejection of collective-bargaining agreements should be governed by a standard different from that governing other executory contracts, all of the Courts of Appeals which have considered the matter have concluded that the standard should be a stricter one.

The Bankruptcy Court should permit rejection of a collective-bargaining agreement under § 365(a) of the Bankruptcy Code if the debtor can show that the collective-bargaining agreement burdens the estate, and that after careful scrutiny, the equities balance in favor of rejecting the labor contract. The standard which we think Congress intended is a higher one than that of the "*business judgment*" rule, but a lesser one than that embodied in the *REA Express* opinion of the Court of Appeals for the Second Circuit.

Since the policy of Chapter 11 is to permit successful rehabilitation of debtors, rejection should not be permitted without a finding that the policy would be served by such action. The Bankruptcy Court must make a reasoned finding on the record why it has determined that rejection should be permitted. Determining what would constitute a successful rehabilitation involves balancing the interests of the affected parties—the debtor, creditors, and employees. The Bankruptcy Court must consider the likelihood and consequences of liquidation for the debtor absent rejection, the reduced value of the creditors' claims that would follow from affirmance and the hardship that would impose on them, and the impact of rejection on the employees. In striking the balance, the Bankruptcy Court must consider not only the degree of hardship faced by each party, but also any qualitative differences between the types of hardship each may face.

The Bankruptcy Court is a court of equity, and in making this determination it is in a very real sense balancing the equities. Nevertheless, the Bankruptcy Court must focus on the ultimate goal of Chapter 11 when considering these equities. The Bankruptcy Code does not authorize free-wheeling consideration of every conceivable equity, but rather only how the equities relate to the success of the reorganization. The Bankruptcy Court's inquiry is of necessity speculative and it must have great latitude to consider any type of evidence relevant to this issue.

Our determination that a debtor-in-possession does not commit an unfair labor practice by failing to comply with § 8(d) prior to formal rejection of the collective-bargaining agreement does undermine the policy of the NLRA, for that policy, as we have noted, is to protect the process of labor negotiations not to impose particular results on the parties. Nevertheless, it is important to note that the debtor-in-possession is not relieved of all obligations under the NLRA simply by filing a petition for bankruptcy. A debtor-in-possession is an "employer" within the terms of the NLRA, and is obligated to bargain collectively with the employees' certified representative over the terms of a new contract pending rejection of the existing contract or following formal approval of rejection by the Bankruptcy Court. But while a debtor-in-possession remains obligated to bargain in good faith under NLRA § 8(a)(5) over the terms and conditions of a possible new contract, it is not guilty of an unfair labor practice by unilaterally breaching a collective-bargaining agreement before formal Bankruptcy Court action.

Case Questions

1. Which is given priority, the bankruptcy law or collective bargaining agreements sanctioned by the labor law. Why?
2. What might happen to the debtor corporation if the union contract were rigidly enforced?
3. Will bankruptcy be a viable alternative for any corporation seeking to avoid its labor contracts?

ETHICAL DILEMMAS IN BANKRUPTCY AND INSOLVENCY

Bankruptcy presents ethical dilemmas to both creditors and debtors. The framers of the Constitution intended the bankruptcy laws to eliminate the English practice of imprisoning defaulting debtors. Although such imprisonment was a strong disincentive to avoid default, it prevented debtors from earning money to repay their debts. Society believes that fairness demands that debtors who have borrowed more than they can repay should be given another chance through bankruptcy. On the other hand, debtors who misuse bankruptcy increase the cost of credit and limit the availability of credit to others. Both creditors and debtors face ethical dilemmas in relation to bankruptcy.

Some people argue that protection under the bankruptcy reorganization provisions is too readily available to solvent corporations. The bankruptcy stay is imposed after a corporation voluntarily files for reorganization under Chapter 11, preventing creditors from collecting their debts. The stay forces negotiation for a reduction of their collective claims, is a costly process, and it raises fairness issues for creditors with legitimate claims, because they will most certainly receive less than originally expected. Should the threat of bankruptcy filings be used as a bargaining point in negotiations with liability claimants, labor unions, or judgment claimants? Is it ethical for profitable business corporations to avoid their debt responsibilities under government protection? Can claimants actually receive more in reorganization than in straight bankruptcy?

In the 1980s, the managers of some publicly traded corporations purchased all the outstanding corporate stock in a transaction called a *leveraged buyout (LBO)* or *management buy-out (MBO)*. Most companies had unused borrowing capacity that was used to finance the purchase of shares from public shareholders. Some LBO companies were restructured by selling off profitable divisions to pay down this new debt. As a result of this leveraging, many LBO companies became excessively debt-laden. When the business cycle turned down and the recession hit in the early 1990s, some LBO corporations were forced into bankruptcy. Creditors have charged that MBO managers sold off the only profitable divisions, leaving the company insolvent. Is such activity unethical and an unlawful fraudulent conveyance under the bankruptcy laws? Some observers argue managers of solvent MBO companies acted unethically because they kept secret their plans for expansion or new products when shares were purchased from the former shareholders. Is it unethical for corporate managers with fiduciary duties to shareholders to hide positive information so they can purchase the stock more cheaply?

LENDER LIABILITY

Creditors have become increasingly liable for damages to debtors resulting from misjudgments affecting the debtor's business. The traditional common law theories of tort law and breach of contract are used to hold lenders accountable for fraud, bad faith, breach of fiduciary duty, breach of contract, or interference with contract relationships, or for making mistakes in imposing managerial decisions on the debtor.

Most of the **lender liability** lawsuits have involved troubled farm loans and business borrowers. Many farmers borrowed heavily when farmland values were high. When these values later declined, their farms had insufficient value as collateral for the hefty farm equipment loans that they had secured. This triggered the right of banks to call due or renegotiate the loans, and many banks insisted on changes in the farm's management. Similarly, during bad economic times, some banks were less willing to work out overdue business loans. Banks have been held liable for environmental cleanup costs for foreclosed land.

Lenders may occasionally risk liability if managerial decisions imposed on the debtor cause the debtor's business to decline. Such decisions usually arise in two contexts: (1) the selection or veto of particular managers, officers, or directors; and (2) the veto of particular business decisions. In one celebrated case, a bank had loan agreements with Farah Manufacturing Company, a clothing manufacturer. These agreements permitted the bank to veto any changes in executive management that "for any reason whatever" impaired the debtor's ability to repay the loan. The bank threatened to bankrupt and padlock the company if William Farah took control. Under the management of the chief executive officer selected by the bank, Farah's assets were partially liquidated to pay the bank debts. Much of Farah's equipment was sold to a competitor, and the purchase was financed by another of Farah's lenders. The court found that Farah was entitled to have its affairs managed by competent officers and directors. It determined that the bank's actions were inconsistent with standards of fair play.[4]

The Uniform Commercial Code imposes a duty of good faith in every loan contract governed by its provisions. In one case, a bank failed to advance funds to a debtor under a line of credit agreement. A *line of credit* commits the lender to lend up to a specified amount unless the borrower becomes uncreditworthy. The debtor had come to expect the bank to make advances based on prior dealings. The court stated that the lender was required to give sufficient notice of its intention to discontinue giving advances, so that the debtor could find financing elsewhere.[5]

When a lender undertakes to provide business management advice to a troubled borrower, the lender may become a fiduciary obligating the lender to exercise the highest and utmost good faith in dealings with the debtor. Liability can arise if the lender pressures the borrower to fire its management consultant and the lender's managerial advice causes the borrower's financial condition to deteriorate. In one instance, a bank promised to provide more long-term financing if the troubled borrower would provide more collateral. After the additional collateral had been given, the bank refused further loans and the borrower failed. The bank was held liable for the failure.

SUMMARY

Numerous state and federal consumer protection regulations apply to businesses that advertise products or services or that grant credit. The FTC regulates this field through informal settlements, corrective advertisements, and litigation.

Advertising claims must have a reasonable basis in scientific evidence, must demonstrate relevant product features, must be accurate, and may not omit important facts. Endorsements by celebrities must be based on actual product use, though fictional dramatizations by unknown actors are permissible. Comparison tests should be conducted scientifically.

The FTC holder-in-due course rule permits consumers to stop making installment loan payments if the seller breaches the contract. Sellers are prohibited from luring consumers into showrooms with bait and switch tactics. Mail-order marketers must inform the buyer of a stockout or shipment delay, refund the purchase price, or ship the goods within 30 days after an order has been received. Many door-to-door sales may be rescinded within a three-day cooling-off period.

Consumer credit transactions are regulated by the Consumer Credit Protection Act. The Truth-in-Lending Act requires standardized disclosure of loan terms. The APR, sales price, total deferred payments, and finance charges must be disclosed in a uniform format. Charges for unauthorized credit card use are limited to $50 per card account. Cardholders must be notified of the credit terms for card use, and periodic billings must disclose the balance due, the finance charges, the APR, and the monthly interest rates applied to unpaid balances. Violators are subject to criminal fines or imprisonment and civil liability.

The Fair Credit Billing Act provides consumers with notice of billing disputes and with mechanisms for resolving them. Creditors must respond quickly to debtors' inquiries and investigate disputes. The Electronic Funds Transfer Act regulates paperless payments. The Fair Credit Reporting Act requires that reported credit information be accurate or be revised. Credit reporting agencies must reinvestigate information the consumer claims is inaccurate. Only bona fide users of credit history may access credit files, and only for legitimate purposes. It is illegal to discriminate against a credit applicant on the basis of race, color, sex, religion, national origin, age, marital status, or welfare status. The Fair Debt Collection Practices Act prohibits harassing debt collection methods.

Secured transactions permit secured creditors to keep or sell the collateral if the debtor defaults. The

---

[4]*State National Bank of El Paso v. Farah Manufacturing Co.*, 678 S.W.2d 661 (1984).

[5]*K.M.C. Co. v. Irving Trust Co.*, 757 F.2d 752 (6th Cir. 1985).

secured interest must first attach and then gain priority over other secured parties by perfection by filing or possession.

Bankruptcy laws give debtors a fresh start after nonexempt assets are liquidated and creditors paid. Either the debtor or its creditors may initiate proceedings. Creditors may not collect their debts or foreclose during bankruptcy. The bankrupt debtor must cooperate with the bankruptcy court. The bankruptcy trustee is responsible for the bankrupt's property and the validation of all creditors' claims.

Individual bankrupts may keep certain necessities of life or exempt property even after liquidation. Secured creditors have priority to be paid the liquidation value of their collateral. Priority creditors are given priority over all other creditors. The remaining unsecured creditors have no priority but may receive a pro rata share of the liquidation proceeds. Bankrupts that cooperate fully and are innocent of fraud are granted a discharge of most debts.

Alternatives to bankruptcy liquidation exist for both corporations and individuals. Debtors in moderate financial distress have their debts readjusted in a plan. In Chapter 11 reorganizations, all claimants may have their claims reduced.

Lenders may have lender liability to the borrower for negligence or bad faith. If the lender imposes poor managerial decisions or insists on particular managers who mismanage the business, there may be liability. Lenders must act in good faith based on reasonable expectations derived from past experience.

Key Terms

deceptive advertising, p. 324
corrective advertising, p. 326
holder in due course, p. 328
bait and switch, p. 329
annual percentage rate of interest (APR), p. 332
electronic fund transfers (EFT), p. 338
garnishment, p. 339
secured transaction, p. 341
reorganization, p. 346
lender liability, p. 349

CHAPTER EXERCISES

1. The Smell Fresh Company claims that its new aerosol spray will "eliminate all noxious fumes within a one-mile radius of paper mill plants in the area." The Federal Trade Commission doubts that this claim is correct. What will the FTC probably demand that the company do?

2. What remedies are available when an advertiser makes misstatements in advertisements?

3. Identify the following laws, and state the reasons for their enactment:
   a. The Truth-in-Lending Act.
   b. The Fair Credit Reporting Act.
   c. The Equal Credit Opportunity Act.
   d. The Fair Debt Collection Practices Act.

4. The chapter outlines four areas in which the Federal Trade Commission issues rulemaking procedures to promulgate consumer protection regulations. Define the holder-in-due-course rule, and give an example of its application.

5. Downtown Department Store advertises an inexpensive compact disc player when an insufficient inventory is available. In response to the advertisement, hundreds of customers come into the store to purchase the compact disc player. The salespeople in the store encourage these customers to purchase more expensive models of the compact disc player, which are available. Does this present a legal problem?

6. A door-to-door salesman sells Mary $450 worth of gardening equipment. Mary pays $100 down and signs an installment contract for the balance. Two days later, she decides that she really doesn't need all of the equipment. Does she have a remedy, or is she bound by the installment contract?

7. Under the Truth-in-Lending Act, what is a "finance charge"? What charges are included as finance charges?

8. The Plaintiff Furniture Company sold a television set and a stereo to a customer and retained a

security interest in these items to secure the payment of the purchase price. The furniture company did not file a financing statement. The customer pledged the television set and stereo to a pawnbroker as security for a loan. The customer defaulted on the debt to the furniture company after making four payments. There was a contest between the pawnbroker and the furniture company as to who had a prior security interest in the items. Why is it important for the creditor to file a financing statement? Is the furniture company protected in this case?

9. Some of Dan's creditors want to petition him into involuntary bankruptcy. What proof do the creditors need to obtain an order or a release? Are there any alternatives for debtor Dan other than to submit to the bankruptcy court?

10. Eastern Airlines has lost millions of dollars in recent years. One cause of the loss is that Eastern competitors have had lower labor costs and have been able to charge lower fares. Eastern is entitled by law to file a bankruptcy petition requesting a reorganization. In such a petition, Eastern can seek to have the court reject its collective bargaining agreements and other employee contracts. If the request is granted, Eastern would no longer be bound by its collective bargaining agreements. Under such a bankruptcy reorganization, Eastern can continue to do business while arrangements are being made by the court to adjust Eastern's contractual obligations.

    Would Eastern be morally justified in filing for protection under the bankruptcy laws in an effort to avoid its costly labor contracts?

11. The economy in the southwestern United States is closely tied to the oil industry. A drop in the price of oil during the 1980s played havoc with the economy of the Southwest and caused massive layoffs and lost income for many families. The overall housing market plunged, lowering home prices below what many people still owed on their home mortgages. Some homeowners, confronted with little income and the inability to sell their homes, simply moved out and left the mortgage lenders with large unpaid debts and insufficient collateral value in the homes. Foreclosures locked the lenders into big losses on these loans, leading several lenders to become bankrupt. This created a domino effect, contributing to the Savings and Loan failure problem. What are the ethical issues for (1) home buyers/borrowers, (2) loan officers, and (3) real estate speculators who purchased these homes cheaply at foreclosure sales?

Part 4

BUSINESS ORGANIZATIONS

This part focuses on laws affecting business organizations. Chapter 12 discusses the agency principles governing relations between employers and their employees, agents, and contractors. The extent of the employer's right to control the employee, agent, or contractor and the scope of authority given to the employee's representative affects the liability of the employing firm for torts committed and contracts negotiated by such business agents. Chapter 13 highlights the different types of business organizations: proprietorships, partnerships, and corporations. Other organizational firms such as the limited partnership and the limited liability company are also noted. Since many businesses invest in securities and need capital to finance their activities, the final chapter of this part reviews the securities regulations affecting the issuance and sale of corporate securities. The agency, business organization, and securities laws affect the organization of business firms as well as many of its operational activities.

Chapter 12

AGENCY

KEY CONCEPTS

Agency relationships are created through mutual consent. An act or expression of the principal is needed to authorize an agent to act on the principal's behalf; the authority of an agent may be actual or apparent, or it may be based on subsequent ratification of an originally unauthorized act.

An agent owes the principal loyalty and has the obligation to obey the principal's instructions and to use reasonable care in the performance of the principal's business.

The principal generally must compensate the agent, reimburse the agent's expenses, and indemnify losses incurred by the agent in operating the principal's business.

The master-employer is generally liable for the torts of the servant-employee, but not for the servant-employee's contractual commitments.

The principal is liable for an agent's torts if the wrongful acts are within the scope of the agent's authority and for an agent's contracts if the principal is disclosed to the third party.

The employer is generally not liable for either the tort actions or contractual commitments of an independent contractor.

INTRODUCTION . . . PAST, PRESENT, FUTURE

The agency relationship is more important today than it has been in the past century. At the beginning of the 20th century, most business transactions were based on personal relationships. Buyers and sellers usually knew each other and dealt with one another face to face. Today, a significant percentage of the world's business is transacted by large corporate organizations that act only through agents, employees, and contractors.

In many instances, an employer today exercises less direct supervision over its employees than it did in the past. Today, fewer people are working in large manufacturing plants in which their actions are overseen by foremen representing the principal. Instead, current workers are sales representatives, computer operators, customer service agents, and specialized secretaries who perform more highly skilled activities on behalf of their principals or employers. Similarly, separate firms often provide technical service representatives, cleaning assistants, part-time word processors, data entry clerks, nurses, and office assistants for other firms.

In the future, as firms contract for more services instead of hiring additional employees, agency law is more likely to concern the employer-independent contractor relationship than the employer-employee relationship. Accordingly, the law may reexamine the duties of the various parties toward one another. The imposition of liability on the principal for the wrongs of "its" agents and perhaps some of its contract personnel is likely to be viewed as a cost of doing business.

OVERVIEW

Most business activities are carried on by people who work on behalf of business firms. Business firms may hire persons to act as employees, may appoint persons as general agents, or may contract with independent contractors who agree to do specific work. This chapter first examines how these agency relationships are created and terminated. Then, it discusses the duties of the agent and the principal to each other. Finally, it considers the relationships between the principal-employer and the employee, agent, and independent contractor.

No one person is able to perform all of the activities that are required to operate a business. Therefore, businesses select agents to represent them in their activities with suppliers, employees, and customers. In this context, the term *agent* refers to any person who acts on behalf of or represents a *principal*. The nature of the relationship between an employer or principal and its employees, agents, and independent contractors affects its liability for the tortious acts of those representatives. The greater control the principal has, the more likely the principal will be held liable for torts of its agents. A principal's liability for contracts that its agent agrees to with third parties depends on whether the agent's action was authorized and whether the third party knew of the principal's existence and identity.

CREATION AND TERMINATION OF AN AGENCY RELATIONSHIP

The agency relationship is a consensual relationship because it is based on the consent of both agent and principal. Neither can force the other to accept an agency relationship. An agency relationship between a principal and an agent arises once the relationship is created. The duties and rights of the parties as principal and agent are separate from those created by an agreement or employment contract between them.

FIGURE 12–1
Types of Agency Relationship

Type of Relationship	Degree of Control	Example
Master-servant	Direct control over servant's physical activities	Foreman/factory worker, farmer/farm hand
Principal-agent	Control over general scope of activities but not over details	Owner/manager department head/sales clerk
Employer-independent contractor	Control of results but not of how tasks are performed	Homeowner/plumber client/attorney

There are three types of agency relationships, each of which involves different controls and responsibilities for both principal and agent; the three types are depicted in Figure 12–1. As a result of differences in the right of the principal to control the activities of the agent, the principal's contract and tort liability, discussed near the end of the chapter, differs with the type of relationship that it has with the agent.

The **master-servant relationship**, generally referred to today as the **employer-employee relationship**, occurs between an employer and an employee whose physical conduct is subject to the employer's control and direct supervision. The factory worker, household employee, and farmhand typify the servant or employee in this type of relationship.

The **principal-agent relationship** involves an agent who is authorized by a principal to carry out a broad range of activities on the principal's behalf. A store manager, a sales agent, and a corporate officer are examples of agents who act in a variety of ways on behalf of their principal-employer.

In the **employer-independent contractor relationship**, the independent contractor is not subject to the control of the employee-principal. The employer who contracts with an independent contractor, such as a plumber or an attorney, to perform certain activities has no right to control the method of performance used by the contractor.

The principal-agent relationship is separate from the employer-employee relationship. Although all employees are agents, not all agents are employees. For example, although an employer and an independent contractor have a type of agency relationship, the independent contractor is not an employee. Similarly, a person may allow someone to act on his or her behalf without creating an employment relationship. One roommate does errands for another, or one friend consents to help another in a building, repairing, or cleaning project. The roommate and friend acting for others are agents but not employees.

Creation of an Agency Relationship

An agency relationship may be created by conduct less formal than the conduct necessary for a contract relationship. For example, express statements or actions of the principal are sufficient to indicate that an agency relationship has been created. If a purchasing firm tells an IBM salesperson that "the computer will be picked up by a Miss Jones from our firm," the purchasing firm creates an agency relationship permitting Miss Jones as its agent to take delivery of the computer.

Similarly, a manager asks an office messenger to deliver documents to another firm, and that request creates an agency relationship even though the manager did not talk

FIGURE 12–2 Creation of Agent's Authority

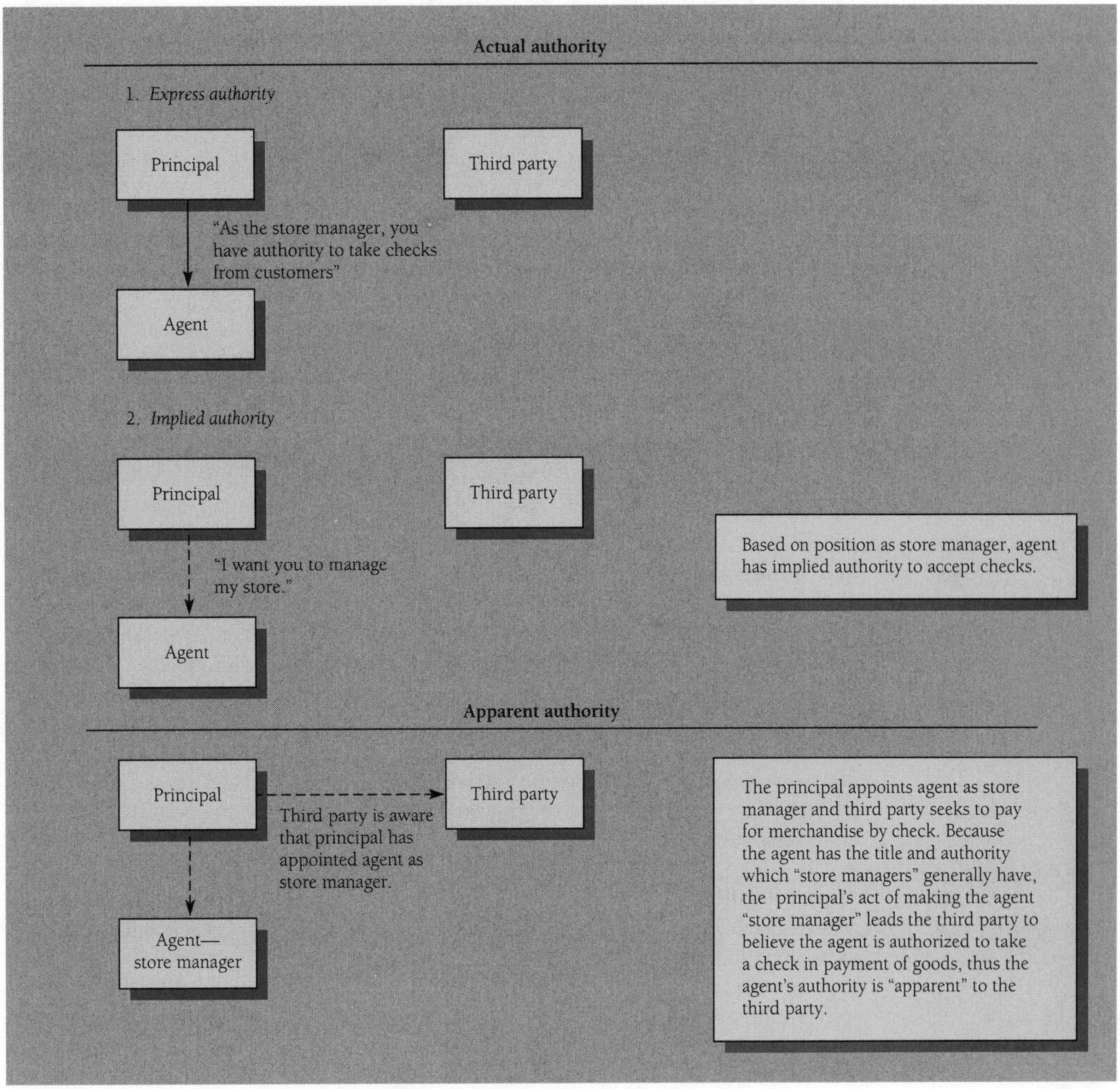

directly with anyone from the firm receiving the documents. The messenger is the sending firm's agent while performing the errand. Whenever two people agree that one of them, the agent, is acting on behalf of the other, the principal, an **agency relationship** has been created.

The burden of proving an agency relationship is on the person who claims that it exists. This may be a third party that dealt with an agent and seeks to hold the principal liable on a transaction of the agent. To prove that the principal is liable for the acts of the agent, the third party must show that the agent was authorized to act for the principal. That authority may arise in several ways: actual authority, which is either express or implied; apparent authority; or ratification. These methods of creating the agent's authority are illustrated in Figure 12–2.

FIGURE 12–2 *(continued)*

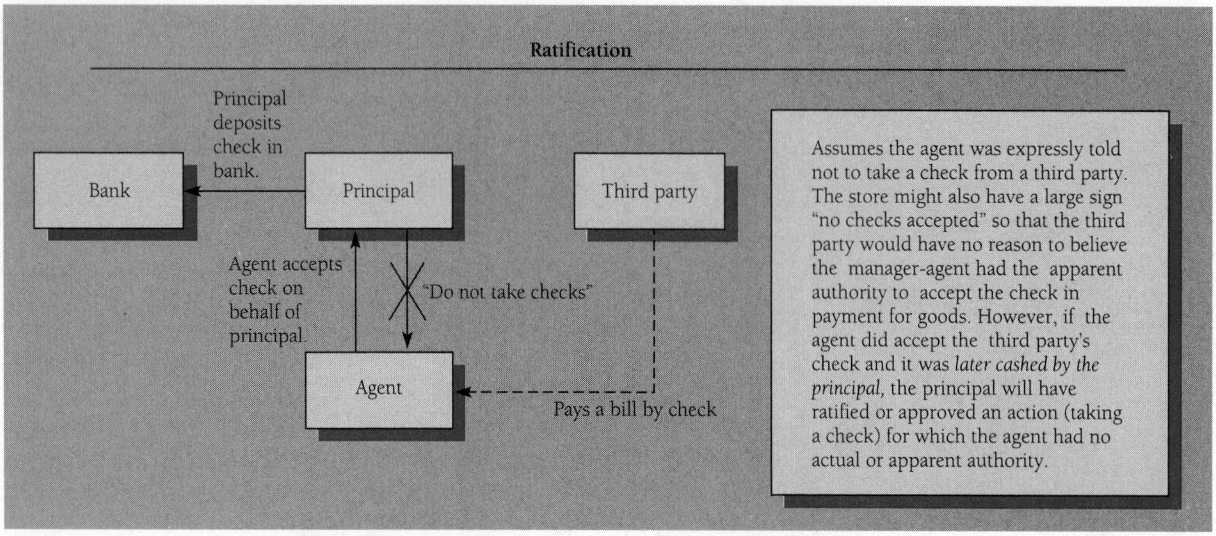

Actual Authority The principal gives the agent *actual authority* through express statements such as "Sell my IBM stock" or by implication from circumstances. For example, a person who has been given the express authority to manage a store has the additional implied authority to do whatever else is necessary to accomplish that task. If one of the clerks quits, the store manager has the implied authority to hire a replacement. The manager can also accept deliveries made to store or send someone to pick up needed supplies, even if the owner of the store did not expressly grant such authority. Actual implied authority adds details to a vague or general grant of actual express authority that enable the agent to implement the powers expressly granted as others in that trade normally have such additional powers.

Apparent Authority *Apparent authority* exists when the principal creates the appearance of authority in an agent, even though it does not grant the agent actual authority. If the principal does something that leads a third party to reasonably believe that an agent has authority, the principal is liable for the agent's actions. For example, if you go to a store and the person who is acting as the manager of the store approves the cashing of your check, it is reasonable for you to assume that the owner has authorized the store manager to give such approval on its behalf. Even if the owner did not expressly give the manager that authority, the manager may have the apparent authority to act on the owner's behalf.

Of course, if the check is unusually large or is drawn on an out-of-town bank, it may not be reasonable for you to assume that a manager has the authority to approve the check. The question is whether the principal has put the agent in a position that would lead a reasonable person to believe that the agent is authorized to do certain acts for the principal. The principal is the source of the agent's apparent authority. If the principal does not make it apparent to the third party that the agent can act for the principal, the agent lacks apparent authority.

In the case that follows, Thomas, the chief executive officer of the Commerce Bank of Plano, Texas, signed a letter of credit on behalf of Grant Curtis, one of its customers, to the Bank of Garland. The letter of credit committed the Bank of Plano to pay $100,000 to the Bank of Garland when it presented the letter of credit (LOC) to the Bank of Plano for payment (an LOC is a letter issued by a bank that indicates the bank will make payments under specific circumstances).

However, the Bank of Plano did not pay and, after it was taken over by the Federal Deposit Insurance Corporation (FDIC), the Bank of Garland sued. The FDIC claims Thomas did not have the actual authority to issue the letter of credit. What is the basis for the court's finding regarding Thomas's apparent authority to issue the letter of credit?

Federal Deposit Insurance Corporation v. Texas Bank of Garland

783 Swd 604 (1989)
Court of Appeals of Texas

The facts of the case are undisputed. On July 28, 1987, Grant Curtis personally delivered the letter of credit (LOC) signed by Sam Thomas to Texas Bank of Garland (TBG), naming TBG as the third-party beneficiary. The LOC, together with a pledged $200,000 certificate of deposit, was collateral for the renewal of a $300,000 note, payable to TBG by Curtis. The LOC reads:

Sam Thomas, III
Chairman of the Board
Chief Executive Officer

Commerce Bank Plano
P.O. Box 865499
Plano, Texas 75086

IRREVOCABLE LETTER OF CREDIT NUMBER 0056

DATE: JULY 28, 1987

FOR THE ACCOUNT OF: GRANT CURTIS
3008 Milton Avenue
Dallas, Texas 75205

TO BENEFICIARY: TEXAS BANK GARLAND
1919 S. Shiloh
Garland, Texas 75042

AMOUNT: $100,000.00

EXPIRATION: NOVEMBER 28, 1987

Gentlemen:

We hereby establish our irrevocable Letter of Credit in your favor, available by your draft at sight, on us, accompanied by this Letter of Credit. All drafts must be marked: "DRAWN UNDER LETTER OF CREDIT #0056."

This Letter of Credit is transferable without limitations as to the number of transfers or the r.umber of transferees. Except as expressly stated herein, this Letter of Credit is governed by the Uniform Customs and Practices for Documentary Credits (198 revision), International Chamber of Commerce Publication #400.

We hereby engage with you, your transferees, endorsers, and assigns, that all drafts drawn under and in compliance with the terms of this Credit will be duly honored if drawn and presented for payment at our office at 901 W. Parker Road, Plano, Collin County, Texas, on or before 1:00 o'clock P.M., Plano, Texas time, not prior to October 28, 1987, and not subsequent to November 28, 1987.

This Letter of Credit can be renewed for an additional period of time if mutually agreed by both Texas Bank Garland and Commerce Bank Plano prior to maturity.

Sincerely,

/s/ Sam Thomas

Sam Thomas
Chairman of the Board
Chief Executive Officer

Curtis defaulted on the note, and on November 23, 1987, TBG presented the LOC, a letter of instruction, and a $100,000 draft drawn against the LOC to Commerce Bank of Plano (CBP). On the same day as presentment, CBP notified TBG that it would dishonor the LOC. CBP provided TBG with a written notice of dishonor on November 24,

1987. On or about November 25, 1987, TBG sued CBP to recover under the LOC. In January 1988, the FDIC was appointed receiver of CBP, and it filed a plea in intervention. The trial court rendered a summary judgment for TBG and the FDIC appealed.

Ovard, Justice

1. Thomas's Authority

The FDIC contends that the trial court erred in granting summary judgment in favor of TBG because Thomas had no actual or apparent authority to sign the LOC. The FDIC argues that the LOC was not issued by CBP but by Thomas personally.

A corporation can act only through its agents. It is elementary that a bank is bound by the acts of its officers while acting in the scope of their authority, either actual or apparent.

a. Actual authority

Actual authority can be either express or implied. The record shows that Thomas was denied actual authority to issue the LOC. However, even so, we sustain the trial court's judgment because the record conclusively establishes Thomas's apparent authority.

b. Apparent Authority

The FDIC argues that Thomas did not have the apparent authority needed to issue the LOC, and that even if Thomas possessed the necessary apparent authority, TBG did not exercise reasonable due diligence to ascertain such authority. The doctrine of apparent authority to act as an agent is based on the law of estoppel. The doctrine does not apply unless the person dealing with the agent was misled by the representation or conduct of the principal. The person dealing with the agent must have been induced to act to his prejudice by reason of the principal's conduct, after exercising due diligence to ascertain the truth.

Apparent authority may arise by a principal's action which lacks such ordinary care as to clothe an agent with the indicia of authority, thus leading a reasonably prudent person to believe that the agent has the authority he purports to exercise.

Thomas was CBP's chief executive officer and chairman of the board. Appointing a person to such a position may, in itself, create apparent authority in an employee. Appointing a person as an executive officer impliedly grants in him the authority to issue letters of credit. . . . As TBG's senior vice president for loans testified, "Someone who is chairman of the board and chief executive officer would certainly have the power to issue a letter of credit."

We hold that issuing a letter of credit is within the scope of apparent authority ordinarily entrusted to the chief executive officer of a bank. Thomas had the apparent authority necessary to act as an agent for his bank in issuing the LOC to Curtis.

We will now turn to the question of whether TBG exercised due diligence in ascertaining whether Thomas possessed the necessary apparent authority to issue the LOC. Due diligence is sufficient when it is shown that persons are dealing with bank officers in good faith, without notice of want of authority, and when the officer appears to be acting within the apparent scope of his authority. In a prior transaction, a TBG officer ascertained that Thomas was the chief executive officer and chairman of the board for CBP. Thomas continued in this position on the date that the LOC was issued to Curtis. In addition, an officer of TBG examined the Texas Banking Red Book, a reference manual for the banking industry, and verified Thomas's position with CBP. We hold that TBG exercised due diligence under these facts and that Thomas had the apparent authority to issue the LOC.

c. Thomas as Agent

The FDIC further argues that CBP's operating policy prohibited Thomas from issuing the LOC and that Thomas did not follow CBP's policy requirements. An agent's authority is presumed to be coextensive with the business entrusted to his care. That authority is not diminished at the expense of a third party by private instructions or limitations imposed by the principals, which are not communicated to third parties dealing with the agent.

There is no evidence that CBP communicated its letter of credit policy, or any of the limitations placed on Thomas, to its customers or the banking community. We hold that, before FDIC is entitled to rely upon those policies to diminish an agent's apparent authority, it was CBP's responsibility to communicate its operating policies to the banking public. TBG, as a third-party beneficiary, had no notice of these policies or limitations and was allowed to rely on the validity of Thomas's signature. The chief executive officer and chairman of the board of CBP had the apparent authority to sign and to issue the LOC.

In conclusion, we hold that after considering all of the evidence and the motions, the LOC was a letter of credit; Thomas had the apparent authority to sign and issue the LOC; and federal common law does not bar TBG's recovery because TBG strictly complied with the terms of the LOC.

Consequently, we affirm the judgment of the trial court.

Case Questions

1. Can apparent authority to act as an agent arise because of actions or words the agent conveys to the third party?
2. What is it that the Bank of Plano (FDIC) did that led the Bank of Garland to reasonably believe that Thomas did have the authority to issue a letter of credit for the Bank of Plano? Would your answer be different if Thomas was the Vice-President of the Bank, not its Chairman of the Board?
3. For the Bank of Plano to be successful in its claim that Thomas lacked apparent authority, what would it had to have done?

Ratification When a principal approves an act performed by an agent without authority, *ratification* occurs. The ratification may be expressed or implied. If a principal agrees to be bound by a contract negotiated by an agent who acted without authority or who exceeded the bounds of his or her authority, an express ratification occurs. If the principal accepts the benefits of the contract and does nothing more, an implied ratification occurs.

What source of authority gives a business manager the power to offer a certain salary to a prospective employee? The following case considers the concepts of actual, apparent, and ratification authority in an employment situation.

Schoenberger v. Chicago Transit Authority

405 N.E.2d 1076 (1980)
Appellate Court of Illinois

Schoenberger sued the Chicago Transit Authority (CTA) to recover contract damages. At issue was whether the CTA might be held liable under agency principles for a promise, allegedly made by its employee ZuChristian when Schoenberger was hired, that he would receive a $500 increase in salary within a year after beginning work. Schoenberger stated that he never inquired into ZuChristian's authority to discuss salary with him but believed that ZuChristian's authority overrode the authority of the Placement Department, which he thought had only a "perfunctory" role in hiring.

ZuChristian testified that his supervisor had told him to make informal offers to prospective employees. However, ZuChristian stated that when he told Schoenberger of his desire to hire him, he intended Schoenberger to regard this as an offer. He also stated that he lied to Schoenberger when he told him that the $19,300 salary offer was a clerical error. This story, he said, was agreed upon by his superior, John Hogan, and was intended to ensure Schoenberger's acceptance of the lower salary approved by the Employee Relations Department.

When the increase was not given at the promised time, Schoenberger resigned and filed this suit. The trial court ruled in favor of the CTA, and Schoenberger appealed.

Campbell, Justice

The main question before us is whether ZuChristian, acting as an agent of the C.T.A., orally contracted with Schoenberger for $500 in compensation in addition to his $19,300 salary. The authority of an agent may only come from the principal and it is therefore necessary to trace the source of an agent's authority to some word or act of the alleged principal. Authority may be actual or apparent, actual being either express or implied. The authority to bind a principal will not be presumed, but rather, the person alleging authority must prove its source unless the act of the agent has been ratified.

Both Hogan and Bonner, ZuChristian's superiors, testified that ZuChristian had no actual authority to either make an offer of a specific salary to Schoenberger or to make any promise of additional compensation. Furthermore, ZuChristian's testimony corroborated the testimony that he lacked the authority to make formal offers. From this evidence, it is clear that ZuChristian lacked the actual authority to bind the C.T.A. for the additional $500 in compensation to Schoenberger.

Nor can it be said that the C.T.A. clothed ZuChristian with the apparent authority to make Schoenberger a promise of compensation over and above that formally offered by the Placement Department. Here Schoenberger's initial contact with the C.T.A. was with the Placement Department where he filled out an application and had his first interview. There is no evidence that the C.T.A. did anything to permit ZuChristian to assume authority, nor did they do anything to hold him out as having the authority to hire and set salaries. ZuChristian was not at a management level in the C.T.A., nor did his job title of Principal Communications Analyst suggest otherwise. The mere fact that he was allowed to interview prospective employees does not establish that the C.T.A. held him out as possessing the authority to hire employees or set salaries. Moreover, ZuChristian did inform Schoenberger that the formal offer of employment would be made by the Placement Department.

Our final inquiry concerns the plaintiff's contention that irrespective of ZuChristian's actual or apparent authority, the C.T.A. is bound by ZuChristian's promise because it ratified his acts. Ratification may be expressed or inferred and occurs where the principal, with knowledge of the material facts of the unauthorized transaction, takes a position inconsistent with nonaffirmation of the transaction. Ratification is the equivalent to an original authorization and confirms that which was originally unauthorized. Ratification occurs where a principal attempts to seek or retain the benefits of the transaction.

Upon review of the evidence, we are not convinced that the C.T.A. acted to ratify ZuChristian's promise. According to Bonner's testimony, when he took over the supervision of ZuChristian's group in the fall of 1976 and was told of the promise, he immediately informed ZuChristian that the promise was unauthorized and consequently would not be honored. Subsequently, he informed Schoenberger of this same fact. Mere delay in telling Schoenberger does not, as the plaintiff contends, establish the C.T.A.'s intent to ratify.

For the reasons we have indicated, the judgment in favor of the defendant, C.T.A., is affirmed.

Case Questions

1. Explain why the court found that the CTA did not authorize ZuChristian to offer Schoenberger a salary increase.
2. What did Schoenberger have to prove to show that ZuChristian was acting as the CTA's agent when he discussed Schoenberger's employment at $19,800 instead of $19,300?
3. Who had the authority to commit the CTA to a definite salary for a prospective employee?

Termination of an Agency Relationship

The principal-agent relationship and the agent's authority to bind the principal may be terminated either by the parties or by operation of law.

Termination by the Parties The parties themselves may provide when the relationship ends—for example, "This agency terminates six months after the date of this agreement." Even if nothing about termination is expressed, the agency terminates once the agent has completed the activities spelled out in the agreement creating the agency.

At any time, the parties may mutually agree that they will terminate the agency relationship. In most cases, either party may terminate the relationship. However, if the agent has a property interest in the business, the agency may not be terminated without mutual consent. This is because an agent whose reimbursement depends on the continuation of his authority to act as an agent has an *agency coupled with an interest.* Agents who represent media personalities or well-known speakers often have a property interest in the money paid to the principals. The agent's commission comes from the money paid to the principal that the agent collects from third parties.

Termination by Operation of Law The agency relationship may also be terminated by the destruction of its subject matter. For example, if a homeowner's agreement with a real estate agent authorizes the agent to list a home for sale for six months, the agency relationship automatically terminates if a flood or fire destroys the home three months later. Death of either the agent or the principal also terminates the agency relationship. Finally, if the law makes illegal the performance of the agent's acts, the agency relationship terminates when the change in the law occurs.

Termination and Notice to Third Parties Even though an agency relationship has been terminated, the principal may still be bound by the agent's subsequent acts if appropriate notice is not given to the third parties with which the agent has dealt. For example, if a company terminates an employee's authority to charge purchases on its behalf at a store where it regularly purchases supplies, the company must inform the store of that termination. Although an agent's actual authority ends when an agency has been terminated, third parties with which the agent has dealt must be informed of the termination for the agent's apparent authority to end.

DUTIES OWED BY PRINCIPAL AND AGENT TO EACH OTHER

Once an agency relationship exists, the parties owe certain duties to each other. An agent and principal have a special *fiduciary relationship,* one based on trust and confidence. This relationship constitutes the basis for many of the legal and ethical problems in business relations. A fiduciary duty arises in every transaction that an agent undertakes.

Duties of the Agent to the Principal

Fiduciary Duties Law imposes **fiduciary duties,** which are duties above and beyond those assumed by the parties in their contract. Fiduciary duties are imposed on the agent (the fiduciary) because he is given power and authority over the property and interests of another party (the principal) that places its trust in him. As a fiduciary, the agent must act on behalf of the principal, not in his own interest.

The fiduciary duty is a special form of trust that requires the employee-agent to act in good faith, based on the utmost loyalty and due care for the principal's interest. The agent may not allow conflicts of interest to modify a decision regarding the principal's business. For example, the purchasing agent of a firm cannot allow a conflict of interest to affect his or her selection of automobiles purchased for the firm. The agent's brother may own a car dealership, or a car dealer may promise the agent the use of a personal car in exchange for purchases on the firm's behalf, but the agent's purchasing decisions must be based on the best interests of the firm and not on family loyalty or on self-interest.

The following passage describes the fiduciary duty:

Classic Characterization of the Fiduciary Duty

Joint adventurers, like copartners, owe to one another, while the enterprise continues, the duty of the finest loyalty. Many forms of conduct permissible in a workaday world for those acting at arm's length, are forbidden to those bound by fiduciary ties. A trustee is held to something stricter than the morals of the marketplace. Not honesty alone, but the punctilio of an honor the most sensitive, is then the standard of behavior. As for this there has developed a tradition that is unbending and inveterate. . . . Only thus has the level of conduct for fiduciaries been kept at a level higher than that trodden by the crowd.

Source: Justice Benjamin Cardozo, in *Meinhard v. Salmon,* 164 N.E. 545, 546 (N.Y. 1928).

INTERNATIONAL PERSPECTIVE

Selling products internationally generally involves using either an agent or a distributor. Although both of these parties represent a seller, they do so in different capacities. It is important that firms seeking to transact international business determine which type of representative will suit its purposes.

An agent firm acts on the seller's behalf in selling products; the agent is paid by the seller on a commission basis and thus is paid when a sale occurs. The agent does not purchase the goods of the seller, but agrees to use its best efforts to try to sell the goods. In many countries, agents may represent several different manufacturers, although generally they agree not to sell goods of one seller that compete directly with goods of other sellers they represent. The agent generally has no risk with regard to the goods. If they are damaged while in the agent's possession, through no fault of the agent, the seller, not the agent, must assume the loss.

A distributor firm acts on the seller's behalf in selling products. The distributor purchases the products of the seller and then resells those products to international buyers. The distributor deals with the principal-seller at arm's length and does not owe the seller fiduciary duties, as does the agent. However, the distributor does often have contract obligations to use its best efforts to promote the seller's products. The distributor assumes the risk of ownership of the goods. If the goods are lost or damaged while owned by the distributor, it is the distributor's loss, not the seller's. The distributor is more like an independent contractor than an agent.

As the International Perspective suggests, it is sometimes difficult to determine whether there is a fiduciary relationship between parties. In the Boeck case, which follows, Boeck claims that Merrill Lynch had a fiduciary duty towards him in his role as a customer who was buying soybean futures. Merrill Lynch claims that Boeck traded on his own account and that as his broker, it merely executed the purchases and sales of commodities he wished to trade. This case has both a majority and dissenting opinion for your review; which do you agree with? Why?

Merrill Lynch, Pierce, Fenner & Smith, Inc. v. Boeck

377 N.W. 2D 605 (1985)
Supreme Court of Wisconsin

Merrill Lynch commenced this action to recover $21,712 that Boeck owed on his investment account for soybean futures transactions made during May, 1978. Boeck denied liability and counterclaimed for the losses he sustained on the transactions.

Boeck was an experienced commodities investor who had dealt with two other brokerage houses before opening a commodities account with Merrill Lynch in February, 1977. Before he began trading with Merrill Lynch, Boeck subscribed to several publications and services concerned with commodities investments. Boeck signed a commodities account agreement that set forth the risky and speculative nature of investing in commodities futures contracts and that warned of the possibility of significant losses. Merrill Lynch had no authority to decide what trades to make in Boeck's account.

Boeck was drawn to Merrill Lynch by an advertisement placed by Merrill Lynch in the Wall Street Journal. He stated that he opened the account at Merrill Lynch because the company had a good reputation for financial services and a strong research program in the commodities field.

Douglas Terrill, Boeck's broker at Merrill Lynch, testified that during March, April, and May of 1978, Boeck regularly asked what information Merrill Lynch's research department had about particular commodities. Boeck claims that he based his commodities investment decisions on the information and advice given to him by Merrill Lynch.

The critical time period in the relationship between Boeck and Merrill Lynch was May 15, 1978, through June 1, 1978. On May 15, Boeck claims Terrill told him that Merrill Lynch's soybean expert, David Bartholomew, had just returned from a trip to Brazil and that he had sharply reduced his estimate of the size of the Brazilian soybean crop. Bartholomew was reputed to be a world-renowned expert in the soybean industry and Terrill advised Boeck of that fact. Terrill allegedly told Boeck that news of Bartholomew's trip and Bartholomew's estimate of Brazil's crop had not been made public and that based on this news, Merrill Lynch's research department soon would make a very strong recommendation to buy, among other things, bull spreads in soybeans and soybean meal.

Terrill denied telling Boeck about a visit by Bartholomew to Brazil or that Bartholomew had sharply reduced his estimate of the Brazilian soybean crop. Bartholomew also testified that he never lowered his estimate of the 1978 Brazilian soybean crop below the April estimate and that the crop, in fact, was higher than the April estimate. He denied traveling to Brazil during 1978. However, Merrill Lynch never denied telling Boeck the crop estimate was going down.

On May 17, 1978, Boeck claims that Terrill learned that the Brazilian government had increased, not decreased, its soybean crop estimate. Terrill never told Boeck about this information even though Terrill handled numerous soybean and soybean meal trades for Boeck between May 17 and 30. Over 98 percent of Boeck's losses were sustained as a result of investments he made after May 17. Terrill, however, argues that the May 17 information did not indicate a change in Merrill Lynch's estimate, and, in fact, the reports were not consistent or conclusive. Nonetheless, Merrill Lynch's estimate of Brazil's soybean crop was higher than Terrill's alleged representation of Bartholomew's estimate.

The trial court found Merrill Lynch owed no fiduciary duty to Boeck and the Court of Appeals affirmed.

Steinmetz, Judge

Both parties rely on *Schweiger v. Loewi & Co., Incorporated,* to support their respective claims concerning a broker's fiduciary duty. In that case, this court held that a broker who is "handling" a customer's financial investments owes that customer a fiduciary duty. Boeck argues that this holding imposes a fiduciary duty in broker-customer relationships, such as the one in the present case. Merrill Lynch contends that Schweiger only imposes a fiduciary duty in the case of discretionary accounts. We agree that a broker does not have a fiduciary duty to a customer with a nondiscretionary account absent an express contract placing a greater obligation on the broker or other special circumstances.

We are persuaded by the decisions from other jurisdictions refusing to impose a fiduciary duty in the case of nondiscretionary accounts. In *Robinson v. Merrill Lynch, Pierce, Fenner & Smith, Inc.,* (1971), that court held that a fiduciary duty did not arise to require the transmission of all extrinsic facts or opinions related to the market in question unless there was an express contract or special circumstances which required defendant to transmit to plaintiff such information.

"To make this defendant or any other broker the guardian of a customer such as the plaintiff would destroy an important part of the marketplace. In every case a trader could recover damages from his broker merely by proving non-transmission of some fact which, he could testify with the wisdom of hindsight, would have affected his judgment had he learned of it." In the instant case, there is no indication of any express agreement or special circumstances between Merrill Lynch and Boeck for the provision of investment decision services. . . .

The record in this case reveals that Boeck had a nondiscretionary account and that he made all the investment transaction decisions on his Merrill Lynch account. Terrill merely placed the orders at Boeck's request. Boeck was an experienced commodities trader who was aware of the risks and uncertainties of that type of investing. There is no express agreement on special circumstances to provide investment advice other than as an incident to brokerage activities. Upon these facts, we hold that a broker does not owe a fiduciary duty to an investor-customer who makes all of the investment decisions, unless there is an express agreement placing a greater obligation on the broker or other special circumstances. We are unpersuaded by the decisions of the Commodities Futures Trading Commission which Boeck construes as reaching a contrary result.

We are also unpersuaded by the concurrence's argument that a broker may become a fiduciary for a person with a nondiscretionary account by gaining the person's trust and confidence and purporting to advise that person with the other's interest in mind. A fiduciary relationship does not arise merely because a broker offers advice and counsel upon which a customer has a right to place trust and confidence. The right to place trust and confidence in the reliability of representations involving commercial transactions already is protected by the law of misrepresentation. A fiduciary relationship arises from a formal commitment to act for the benefit of another (for example, a trustee) or from special circumstances from which the law will assume an obligation to act for another's benefit. The mere fact of reliance on representations, therefore, does not necessarily create a relationship of trust and confidence leading to a fiduciary duty. Thus, we do not hold that a fiduciary duty may arise out of every circumstance where there is a relationship of trust and confidence between the parties.

Here, Merrill Lynch did not formally agree to make investment decisions for Boeck. In fact, Boeck always remained ultimately responsible for making investment decisions, as required by his nondiscretionary account. Also, no special circumstances exist from which we could find that Merrill Lynch should be responsible as a fiduciary for Boeck's investment decisions. Moreover, if we held that a broker is a fiduciary in these circumstances, then an investor could allege that the broker exercised poor judgment when advising the investor. This is because the duty of a fiduciary is greater than simply the duty not to misrepresent. A professional fiduciary, like a broker, also would be held to a higher degree of skill and care than a man of ordinary prudence. Recognizing the full implications of treating a broker as a fiduciary, we refuse to hold that a broker is liable as a fiduciary for representations to an investor with a nondiscretionary account. We would make a broker a guarantor of a customer's investments if we held otherwise. . . . Although the trial court and the court of appeals correctly ruled that Merrill Lynch did not owe Boeck a fiduciary duty and that strict responsibility is not an issue in this case, we conclude that Boeck is entitled to a new trial on the negligent misrepresentation theory of liability. We base this conclusion on the fact that the real controversy was not fully and fairly tried.

Louis, Judge and Ceci, Judge (dissenting)

Although no express contract existed between Merrill Lynch and Boeck regarding investment advisory services, there is no doubt that Merrill Lynch undertook to provide such advice and market information to Boeck as an incident to the commodities account agreement. Disputed testimony indicates that Merrill Lynch's soybean expert subsequently reduced sharply his previous estimate of the Brazilian soybean crop.

It is undisputed, however, that Merrill Lynch never denied telling Boeck that the crop estimate was going down. Nor is it questioned that Merrill Lynch failed to inform Boeck that the Brazilian government had increased its estimate to the country's soybean crop. And no one, not even the majority, disputes that "the size of the Brazilian soybean crop was a significant, material factor affecting the price of soybean futures."

Boeck established that he sustained over ninety-eight percent of his losses in soybean futures as a result of investments made after the critical date of May 17, 1978, the date when Boeck asserts that Terrill first learned that the Brazilian government's soybean estimate directly varied with the Merrill Lynch estimate. Merrill Lynch, through Terrill, never relayed this critical information to Boeck. In other words, the jury found, and nowhere does the majority disagree, that Merrill Lynch undertook to provide its client Boeck with material investment advice and failed to provide Boeck with critical information in its possession which varied with its earlier information. This constitutes a breach of Merrill Lynch's fiduciary duty owed to Boeck. The breach caused Boeck to sustain substantial losses in the soybean market.

The extent of a broker's fiduciary duty in this situation would require that it disclose to the client all significant, material information in its possession regarding the transactions involved. Here, Merrill Lynch would be required to disclose to Boeck all significant, material information regarding the status of the Brazilian soybean crop. Merrill Lynch's fiduciary duty subsumes, at the very least, a responsibility to disclose information it possesses which is contrary to the significant, material information it originally gave to the client. A finding that Merrill Lynch breached its fiduciary duty owed to Boeck would not make Merrill Lynch "a guarantor of [Boeck's] investments." Rather, such a finding would merely make a broker liable for its fiduciary breaches. . . .

The trust and confidence which Boeck placed in Merrill Lynch became legally significant when Merrill Lynch undertook to inform Boeck of the status of the soybean commodities market and of its own decreased projections for the Brazilian soybean crop. Merrill Lynch breached its fiduciary duty when it failed to inform Boeck of the significant, material information of the Brazilian government's promising forecasts for the crop. The jury was correct in its verdict determination regarding breach of fiduciary duty; I disagree with the majority's contrary conclusion.

Case Questions

1. According to the majority opinion, does a broker generally have a fiduciary obligation to customers who use the broker to purchase and sell securities? Is that also true if the customer is buying and selling commodities, futures, or options?
2. If Merrill Lynch had a fiduciary relationship with Boeck, would the broker be able to prove he performed the fiduciary duty if he proved he did not misrepresent any information to Boeck?
3. According to the dissenting opinion, what is the reason for imposing a fiduciary duty on Merrill Lynch and how did it breach that duty?

Note that the fiduciary duty may also be imposed by regulation. For example, the New York Stock Exchange has recently indicated that "discount" stock brokers who simply execute customer directed trades without providing investment advice may nevertheless be held to the "suitability" duty. This is a derivative of the fiduciary duty requiring brokers to "know their customers' " financial condition and risk preferences and make only "suitable" trades, for example, no risky commodity futures for widows and conservative investors.

INTERNATIONAL PERSPECTIVE: LEGAL & ETHICAL LAPSES FOR JAPANESE FIRMS

Ten Japanese securities firms provided over one billion dollars in investment losses to favored clients. Between October 1987 and March 1990, the Big Four Japanese firms, Nomura Securities, Nikko Securities, Daiwa Securities, and Yamaichi Securities, admitted spending over $900 million on behalf of 229 customers. Six more firms provided $260 million to favored clients.

The securities firms sought to make up losses suffered by the clients as the Japanese stock market declined sharply in 1990. The firms also reported they had recorded the compensation to clients as losses for tax purposes. The Japanese Ministry of Finance asked the firms to revise their financial accounts to accurately reflect the compensation paid to the clients.

The securities firms of course not only represented the favored clients, but regular clients as well. How could the firms, as an agent working for all clients, compensate some clients for losses they suffered while not compensating others? Do the securities firms owe ethical and legal obligations to potential clients to disclose their payments to favored clients? Who is injured by these practices?

The Duty of Loyalty Loyalty is the most important fiduciary duty imposed by law on the agent. The agent must honestly represent the principal's interests. Any conflicts between the principal's interests and the agent's interests must be disclosed to the principal or avoided by the agent. For example, the law requires a stockbroker to disclose the brokerage firm's role in underwriting a new issue of a company's stock to its clients. A stock underwriter receives compensation for selling stock, so it cannot also receive compensation from a client-buyer unless it discloses its dual role to the client-buyer.

The agent's duty of loyalty also prohibits representation of two principals that are contracting together unless these principals know of the agent's dual role and agree to it. Some professions prohibit any *dual agencies*. For example, an attorney cannot represent opposing parties in a case. One of the parties can go unrepresented while the attorney represents the other party, but it must be made clear that the attorney is working on behalf of only one party. However, if an agent is merely a broker seeking to bring two parties together and neither party relies on the broker for advice and assistance in negotiation, the courts will allow the agent-broker to perform this limited, *middleman* or *finder* function.

The Corporate Opportunity Doctrine The *corporate opportunity doctrine* applies the fiduciary duties, such as the duty of loyalty, to corporate agents. It prohibits the diversion of business opportunities by corporate directors, officers, or key employees if the corporation has an expectancy in the opportunities. These people may not use their positions in the corporation to identify promising business opportunities for themselves if the corporation might have an interest in those opportunities. The misuse of such opportunities for personal benefit constitutes a breach of fiduciary duty.

Guth, president of the Loft retail store chain, borrowed the company's money and used its office personnel and credit to purchase Pepsi-Cola stock for himself. Loft's board of directors claimed that the corporate opportunity to purchase the stock should have been offered to the company first. Guth had been alerted to the availability of the stock because he was the president of Loft. Since cola products were sold in the Loft stores, Loft would probably have been interested in the purchase. The Supreme Court of Delaware found that the purchase of the Pepsi-Cola shares was a corporate opportunity belonging to Loft that Guth had wrongfully misappropriated for his own benefit.[1]

Of course, corporate fiduciaries may undertake personal business activities without breaching their fiduciary duties. The key determination is whether the corporation has an interest or expectancy sufficient to establish a "beachhead" in the type of opportunity involved. If the opportunity is in the same "line of business" as existing corporate activities, then the agent's duty is to present it to the corporation. Must a corporate fiduciary present business opportunities to the corporation if the fiduciary learns of them outside his or her business capacity? The following case explores the uncertainties of the opportunities in which the corporation has an expectancy.

---

[1]*Guth v. Loft, Inc.*, 5 A.2d 503 (1939).

Science Accessories v. Summagraphics

425 A.2d 957 (1980)
Supreme Court of Delaware

Three employees of Science Accessories (SAC) quit to develop and market a new product with Summagraphics Corporation. Although the product that Summagraphics sold was conceived by a Dr. Brenner, who had not been associated with SAC, SAC claimed that these employees acquired secret information from it that they later used to develop Brenner's product on behalf of Summagraphics. Each of the employees had signed a contract with SAC stipulating that inventions or discoveries made while they were employees of SAC belonged to it. SAC claimed that the employees could not use that secret information without breaching their contractual and fiduciary duties to SAC and without taking a corporate opportunity from SAC. The trial court found for the employees and SAC appealed to the Supreme Court of Delaware.

Horsey, Justice

The basis of defendants' alleged breach of contractual duties to SAC was a technology disclosure agreement which each of them had signed as an employee of SAC and which, in pertinent part, provided:

> Any invention or discovery which I may make or conceive, either alone or jointly with others, while employed by the Company, for any improvement in process, machine, manufacture or composition of matter, which relates to the Company's business . . . shall be the property of the Company, whether patentable or not and whether made or conceived during regular business hours or otherwise. I will fully and promptly disclose to the Company . . . all information known to me concerning such improvement. . . .

SAC claims that defendants' conduct was in breach of fiduciary duties defendant owed SAC under agency law principles. It is true, of course, that under elemental principles of agency law, an agent owes his principal a duty of good faith, loyalty, and fair dealing. Encompassed within such general duties of an agent is a duty to disclose information that is relevant to the affairs of the agency entrusted to him. There is also a corollary duty of an agent not to put himself in a position antagonistic to his principal concerning the subject matter of his agency.

However, agency law is not without its limitations as to both duty to disclose and duty not to act adversely to a principal's business. Thus, an agent is not under a duty to disclose to his principal information obtained in confidence, the disclosure of which would be a breach of duty to a third person. Similarly, an agent is not prevented from acting in good faith outside his employment even though it may adversely affect his principal's business. Further, an agent can make arrangements or plans to go into competition with his principal before terminating his agency, provided no unfair acts are committed or injury done his principal.

These principles and limitations of agency law carry over into the field of corporate employment so as to apply not only to officers and directors, but also to key managerial personnel. They reflect competing policy interests in the law as to employer-employee relationships. On the one hand, there is ". . . concern for the integrity of the employment relationship [which] has led courts to establish a rule that demands of a corporate officer or employee an undivided and unselfish loyalty to the corporation."

However, there is an offsetting policy "recognized by the Courts . . . of safeguarding society's interest in fostering free and vigorous competition in the economic sphere . . . This policy in favor of free competition has prompted the recognition of a privilege in favor of employees which enables them to prepare or make arrangements to compete with their employers prior to leaving the employ of their prospective rivals without fear of incurring liability for breach of their fiduciary duty of loyalty."

The doctrine of corporate opportunity represents one aspect of the law's effort to reconcile these competing policy interests. The doctrine of corporate opportunity is a species of the duty of a fiduciary to act with undivided loyalty. Thus, the law of corporate opportunity is clearly pertinent, if not decisive, to the issue of whether defendants breached any fiduciary duty owed SAC.

Briefly summarized, the law is that if a business opportunity is presented to a corporate executive, the officer cannot seize the opportunity for himself if: (a) the corporation is financially able to undertake it; (b) it is within the corporation's line of business; (c) the corporation is interested in the opportunity. *Guth v. Loft, Inc.* A corollary of the Guth rule is that when a business opportunity comes to a corporate officer which . . . is not one which is essential or desirable for his corporation to embrace, the officer is entitled to treat the business opportunity as his own and the corporation has no interest in it.

Whether the Guth rule or its corollary applies depends, of course, on the facts and the reasonable inferences to be drawn therefrom. Here, the uncontradicted findings of the Court below were: that SAC was "neither inclined nor able to develop new products" in the digitizer field by reason of its poor financial condition and its evident unwillingness during the period in question "to develop products suggested by Whetstone." Those findings are clearly sufficient to support the Trial Court's conclusion that Brenner's concept was not an opportunity available to SAC but one that defendants could legally embrace as their own; and SAC does not claim otherwise.

Since Brenner's concept was found to be an outside opportunity not available to SAC, defendants' failure to disclose the concept to SAC, and their taking it to themselves for purposes of competing with SAC, cannot be found to be in breach of any agency fiduciary duty. Affirmed.

Case Questions

1. What "competing policy interests" in the law concerning employer-employee relationships were noted by the court?
2. How does the corporate opportunity doctrine relate to the agent's duty of loyalty to the corporation?
3. Why did the court find that the agent employees had not violated the corporate opportunity doctrine?

Duty to Communicate Information One of the essential aspects of the principal-agent relationship is that a third party can provide information to an agent and assume that the agent will provide the information to the principal. For example, if an insurance policyholder informs an insurance agent about changes in the insured property, the policyholder assumes that the agent will pass the information on to the insurer. The agent has the duty to pass along information concerning the insured property and can be liable for losses to the principal (insurer) resulting from his or her failure to do so. This duty is sometimes seen as an extension of the duty of loyalty that the agent owes to the principal.

The duty to disclose information was at issue when a savings and loan association, which ordered a termite inspection conducted on a home that it was mortgaging for a potential buyer, was informed by the inspector the home was infested with termites. Although the savings and loan association argued that the termite inspection had been conducted for its benefit, not for that of the home purchaser-principal, the Supreme Court of Ohio found that it had violated its duty to disclose the information obtained from the inspection to its principal:

> One who acts as an agent for another becomes a fiduciary with respect to matters within the scope of the agency relation. . . . An agent owes his principal a duty to disclose all material information which the agent learns concerning the subject matter of the agency relation and about which the principal is not apprised. Furthermore, where a principal suffers loss through his agent's failure to function in accordance with his duty, the agent becomes liable to the principal for the resulting damages.
>
> We conclude that appellant, through its president, Russell, assumed the role of appellees' agent for the purpose of securing the termite inspection. From that relation-

ship arose a duty to inform them of the results of the inspection, and the breach of that duty resulted in the damages found by the jury to have been sustained by appellees. In reliance that the inspection would be conducted and the results made available to them, no separate inspection was initiated by appellees. Appellant was duty-bound to disclose the material facts relating to the termite infestation before recording the deed.[2]

Duty of Obedience The principal has the right to direct the agent how to perform certain activities, and the agent must obey all reasonable instructions regarding the agency. For example, a firm may direct its employees not to accept personal checks in payment for merchandise that they sell for it. Then, if an employee accepts an uncollectible check on the firm's behalf, the employee can be held liable to the firm. Of course, the agent does not have to follow the principal's instructions to commit illegal acts. And there are even instances in which the agent may act contrary to the principal's instructions.

In an emergency, the agent is allowed to disregard the principal's instructions if doing so is in the principal's best interest. Suppose that a truck driver hauling perishable foodstuffs for a firm was instructed to use the firm's credit card only for gas and oil purchases. If as a result of an emergency situation, such as a flooded roadway or a freak ice storm, the driver has to do something to keep the foodstuffs from spoiling, despite the instructions the driver could use the credit card to pay for their storage during the emergency.

Duty to Use Reasonable Care The agent has the duty to use reasonable care in the performance of his or her duties. The extent of an agent's duty of care is determined by the type of work that the agent performs. An accountant performing an audit must use the care that reasonable accountants would use in performing similar work. The agent must use reasonable care in looking after the principal's property. If goods are damaged, lost, or destroyed while in an agent's possession, the agent could be held liable if he or she did not exercise reasonable care. However, the agent is not an insurer of the goods or a guarantor of their safety; only reasonable care is required.

Duty to Account If the agent receives money or property for the principal's business, the agent must provide an accounting to the principal regarding the items received. If the agent is authorized to use the funds for certain expenditures, then the agent must keep receipts and record expenditures. One aspect of the duty to account is the agent's duty to give the principal anything of value that the agent receives from third parties in connection with the principal's business. If the agent receives special gifts or money from parties dealing with the principal, the agent must turn over those items to the principal.

Companies usually have policies regarding the amount of personal gifts that key employees, such as purchasing agents, may keep. For example, a company might allow the agent to retain items valued at less than $50. Absent such a policy, the agent must account for all items received while he or she is acting on the principal's behalf. This duty to account even applies to the president of the United States. The president cannot keep for personal uses valuable items received from foreign countries or representatives. Cars, expensive jewelry, and similar gifts to the president become the property of the United States.

---

[2]*Miles v. Perpetual Savings & Loan,* 380 N.E.2d 1364 (1979).

Duties Owed by the Principal to the Agent

The principal's duties to the agent are based on the contract between them and on agency law, but not on the fiduciary relationship. This is because the agent, acting for the principal, is the fiduciary, but not vice versa. The principal is usually obligated by contract to compensate the agent. Further, if the agent spends money on the principal's behalf, the principal must reimburse the agent for those outlays. Finally, the agent who suffers losses due to legal action by a third party is entitled to be indemnified for those losses by the principal.

Duty to Compensate Although generally the principal must compensate the agent, it is possible for the principal and the agent to agree that the agent will not be compensated for activities performed on the principal's behalf. This creates a relationship known as *gratuitous agency.* A salesperson, truck driver, or stockbroker who acts as an agent on behalf of someone else usually has the right to receive compensation for services performed. The details of the terms of compensation are generally expressed in a contract.

The employment contract generally indicates how the compensation is to be paid: by a salary, commission, or bonus arrangement or by some combination thereof. Although it is not uncommon for people to begin an agency relationship without a written contract, using such an agreement can eliminate many future problems. For example, settling the form of compensation ahead of time can prevent disputes; likewise, a clarification of the expenses that will be reimbursed should be included in any agent's contract.

Sometimes an agent's compensation depends on the occurrence of a special event. If the event does not occur, the agent has no right to compensation. For example, attorneys representing personal injury plaintiffs frequently agree to be paid a *contingency fee;* the fee is due only if compensation is awarded to the plaintiff by the court or through settlement. Stockbrokers and salespeople are frequently paid on a commission basis. Brokers are paid a commission for selling stock to customers or obtaining orders from them. Otherwise, they have a right to reimbursement from their employers for expenses, but no right to compensation.

If there is no contract between the principal and the agent detailing the terms and conditions affecting the agent's right to compensation, the law implies that reasonable compensation will be paid for services that the agent renders.

Duty to Reimburse Expenses The agent who advances his or her funds in conducting business for the principal is entitled to be reimbursed by the principal if the principal has authorized the agent's activities. A salesperson instructed to attend a meeting on the principal's behalf would be entitled to reimbursement for registration fees and travel and lodging expenses incurred while attending the meeting. On the other hand, if a salesperson attended a meeting without first notifying the principal, the principal would not be legally obligated to reimburse the agent for these expenses.

Duty to Indemnify The principal's duty to reimburse the agent for expenses extends to indemnifying the agent for losses that the agent incurs while conducting the principal's business. For example, if the agent loses money while performing a contract, the principal must compensate the agent for the loss. The duty to indemnify also applies to expenses that the agent incurs in defending claims brought against the agent while performing authorized acts for the principal. For example, if a third party claims that a pizza delivery driver damaged that party's property, expenses incurred by the driver-agent in defending the litigation are reimbursable.

Duty to Provide Safe Working Conditions The law requires the principal to provide safe premises and equipment for its agents and employees. The principal has to inspect the workplace and warn the agent of any unsafe conditions. Chapters 18 and 20 discuss specific obligations of employers with regard to employee safety and environmental hazards.

ETHICAL DILEMMA: YOUR AGENT'S OBLIGATION—TO YOU?

"Let's call our travel agent to see where she can find the best price for our trip."

"We've looked at a number of office sites with our real estate agent; do you think he can help us determine which one we can get for the best price?"

"Ted, our insurance agent, says the life insurance policy offered by the Rock Solid Insurance Firm is the best one for us; should we go ahead and get that policy or do you want to look around some more?"

Each of these statements assumes that a person looking to purchase travel services, real estate, or insurance products can call on an agent to look after their interest. In each case, the agent the potential purchaser is planning to deal with represents the provider of the services, not the purchaser. The travel agent is paid by hotels and by airlines when they sell a room or a ticket to you. As agents, they have legal duties to their principal, not to you, the third party. The real estate agent represents the seller and is paid a commission by the seller if the agent gets the purchaser to contract to buy the seller's property. The insurance agent does not have an obligation to search for the best policy to fit your needs. Instead, the agent's obligation is to the insurance company(s) he or she represents.

As a possible purchaser of these services, you need to understand that the agent is not working on your behalf. An agent has an ethical obligation to inform third parties that he or she does not represent them. Of course, the agent can and should, in promoting the interest of its principal, be helpful to potential customers. Firms that use agents to deal with third parties should take the responsibility for the acts of the agent. If travel agents, realtors, or insurance representatives make mistakes or cause problems, it is the firm they represent, not the customer, who has the obligation to rectify the problems.

AGENCY RELATIONSHIPS AND THE LIABILITY OF THE PRINCIPAL

The liability of the principal for the contractual and tortious activities of its representatives depends on the nature of the relationship between the principal and the representative and on the knowledge and perceptions of third parties regarding their relationship. The knowledge and perception of the third party regarding the relationship determines the principal's liability for contracts agreed to between an agent and a third party. Determining whether the agent acts within the scope of his or her authority is critical in assessing the principal's liability for torts committed by an agent. This section examines the three basic agency relationships and the attendant liability of the principal or employer for the agent's contracts or torts.

Contract Liability

Master-Servant Relationship With a master-servant relationship, in which the master has the right to control the physical acts of the servant-employee, the servant generally has no authority to make contracts for the master. No third party should expect a factory employee at General Motors to be able to contract for that corporation. A third party who does contract with such a person would not be able to hold the principal (General Motors) liable because the third party should know that the agent has no authority to act on behalf of the firm.

Employer–Independent Contractor Relationship Similarly, with an employer–independent contractor relationship, the independent contractor usually has no authority to contract on behalf of the employer. If one person contracts to hire another person as a plumber, dentist, or accountant, the employer does not thereby authorize that person to make contracts for the employer. Further, the hiring of such a person does not give any third party reason to believe that the person has authority to make contracts for the employer. Since the independent contractor does not receive actual or apparent authority from the principal-employer, the principal-employer will not be liable for contracts that the independent contractor makes with third parties.

Principal-Agent Relationship Difficulties regarding the liability for contracts negotiated by an agent with third parties occur when the relationship is between a principal and an agent. The principal's liability for contracts that the agent makes with third parties depends on the third party's knowledge of the agency relationship. Principals may be classified as disclosed, partially disclosed, or undisclosed.

A **disclosed principal** is one whose existence and identity is known by the third party when it contracts with the agent. If the agent discloses the existence and identity of the principal to the third party and the agent acts within the scope of his or her authority, the principal is liable for the contract the agent makes with the third party. Only the principal is liable to the third party; the agent has no contractual liability. For example, when IBM sells computers to a university, a representative of IBM negotiates with a representative of the university. These employees are agents who have disclosed the identity and existence of their principals. Thus, the university as a third party cannot hold the IBM employee personally liable for the performance of the contract. Likewise, IBM cannot hold the employee of the university personally liable for the university's performance of the contract.

If the agent acts beyond his or her authority and the third party has no reason to know that the agent is exceeding that authority, the agent, not the principal, is liable to the third party. The agent's liability in this case is based on a breach of the implied warranty of authority given to the third party, not on the contract itself.

A **partially disclosed principal** is one whose existence is known by the third party, but whose identity is unknown; the third party knows the agent is acting for someone else, but does not know the identity of the principal. If an agent discloses the existence of a principal, but not the principal's identity, the contracting third party may hold either the principal or the agent liable if the contract is not performed. For example, if a real estate development firm is seeking to build a new shopping mall or an amusement park in an area, it may seek to purchase the needed property by acting through agents. If the developer discloses its intention to buy many different parcels of property, after it has purchased some property, the price of the remaining property it hopes to buy will increase significantly in price. Thus, a developer might ask five or ten different agents to seek to buy the desired property, instructing each not to disclose the developer's identity to the sellers. The owners who are approached by agents interested in buying their property would know the agents were representing someone else; they would know there is an agency relationship between the agent and the undisclosed principal. However, they would not know the identity of the principal.

If the contracts made between the third parties and the agents obligate the agent to pay money over a period of several years, the third party can hold either the agent or the principal liable if the money is not paid as promised. The agent is liable because that is the person with whom the third party negotiated and with whom that party thought he or she was contracting. The principal is liable because the agent was acting within the scope of his or her authority in contracting to purchase the property. The third party's *election* (seeking to hold either the principal or the agent liable on the performance of the contract) usually occurs once he or she discovers the identity of the principal. The principal, although undisclosed at the time of the contract, can also enforce the contract against the third party.

An **undisclosed principal** is one whose existence and identity is unknown to the third party. The third party thinks the contract is being made by the agent on his or her own behalf, not as an agent for an unknown principal. If the agent is acting for a totally undisclosed principal, the third party is not aware of an agency relationship. In this case, the third party holds the agent liable on the contract. It is the agent who has to perform the contract because the third party reasonably believed that the agent, not some unknown person whom the agent in fact represented, made the contract.

Most agents do not want to be held personally liable on contracts they make for their principal's behalf. The agent who does not want to be held liable for such contracts can clearly indicate the principal party that is to be held liable. If a person signs a contract as "Mike Sleaford," there is no reason to think that he is acting as an agent. He has signed his own name and will be held liable. If he signs the contract as "Mike Sleaford, agent for First Southern Bank," it is unclear whether Mike or the bank will be held liable. If Mike wants to be clearer, he can sign as follows: "First Southern Bank, by Mike Sleaford, its agent." Here, Mike has indicated that First Southern Bank is the principal to be held liable and that he signed for it as an agent, not as the principal contracting party.

Tort Liability

Liability of Master-Employer for Torts of Servant-Employee Since the employer has the right to control the activities of the servant-employee, the employer will be liable to third parties who are injured by the employee's actions. This vicarious liability of the employer is in addition to the liability of the employee-servant who commits the tort. A person is not excused from liability for a tort merely because the tort occurs while the person is working for an employer.

As a practical matter, the injured third party will usually turn to the employee-principal firm, rather than to the employee, for compensation. If the employee is acting to further the employer's business, rather than acting solely on his or her own behalf, the employer will be liable.

Principal's Liability for Torts Committed by Its Agents The firm as principal is liable for the tortious acts of its agent if the activities of the agent are within his or her scope of authority. This rule of ***respondeat superior,*** "let the superior respond," holds the principal liable regardless of the principal's fault or lack of fault. The principal's liability is based on the agent's tort; it is the agent's tort, not that of the principal, that is the basis for the vicarious liability imposed on the principal.

For example, if a negligent driver for Pizza Hut causes injury to a pedestrian, the driver is liable, but the injured party can sue both the driver and Pizza Hut. However, the injured party can collect only once, whether totally from one party or partially from each of the parties. The fact that Pizza Hut is liable does not displace the liability of the driver. Liability is imposed on the principal because the principal directed or authorized the agent to act in its place. Essentially, in exchange for enabling the principal to do business through the agent, the law imposes liability on the principal when that agent, while acting within the scope of his or her employment, commits torts.

Because "the scope of authority" limits the principal's liability for the agent's torts, it is important to determine what acts are outside the agent's authority. When the agent acts on his or her own and not in furtherance of the principal's business, the principal is not held liable. The acts of the agent are then beyond the scope of the agent's authority. Because the law often leans toward compensation for the injured party, the liability of the principal for acts of an agent is likely to increase. Consider the following commentary.

Commentary: Employer's Liability for Injuries Caused by Employee's Drunk Driving

Case law appears to be moving in the direction of holding the employer-principal liable for the torts of its agents even when the agent's activities do not occur at the workplace. For example, employers are held liable if an employee's drinking causes injuries to others. In the past, court cases have found companies liable for accidents that have resulted after drunken Christmas parties, picnics, or other company-sponsored events.

Employers cannot ignore the drinking of employees at work. Almost a half-dozen states recognize employer liability for the actions of intoxicated employees who have been generally drinking in the workplace with the complicity of the employer. But, if the employee or agent was not at work or at a company event and had not been directed to meet clients or prospective customers, courts generally would not hold the employer liable for torts of the agent.

However, in August of 1991, *The Wall Street Journal* reported that a Tampa, Florida, jury returned a verdict against a salesman and his employer for $85,000 in compensatory damages and $800,000 in punitive damages because the salesman got drunk while entertaining clients and later killed two people in an automobile accident.[3] Although both the agent and the employer are held liable, the employer generally ends up paying most of the tab. The salesman had been attending a convention at a hotel and had been drinking while entertaining guests; the drinks were paid for by the president of his company. After he left the convention, he rear-ended another car, causing the deaths of two people.

The case suggests that any time agents of a firm are acting within the scope of their authority, such as entertaining clients at a convention, the employer may be held liable for the agents' torts. It may no longer matter whether the activities occur on the premises of the employer or after normal work hours have finished.

Employers might avoid liability by directing agents not to drive after they have been drinking. Perhaps a policy mandating a "two-drink limit and then you call a taxi to leave" is necessary to avoid vicarious liability for the firm.

Employer's Liability for Contracts Negotiated by an Independent Contractor In the employer–independent contractor relationship, the employer generally does not have the right to tell the independent contractor how to perform the work. Because the employer

[3] "Drunk-Driving Liability Widens for Employers," *The Wall Street Journal,* August 27, 1991, p. B1.

FIGURE 12–3
Agency Relationships

Type of Relation	General Characteristics	Examples
Master-servant, referred to as employer-employee	Employee is under direct control of employer. Master or employer gives detailed directions to servant or employee.	Restaurant manager supervises dishwashers. Foreman supervises assembly line worker.
Principal-agent	Principal has right to control actions of agent but does not exercise detailed control over all of the agent's physical activities.	Sales manager tells sales agent what route to cover and what policies to use. Vice president of bank manages bank activities.
Employer-independent contractor	Independent contractor is *not* subject to employer's control. Contractor agrees to results, but determines how to achieve those results.	Roofing contractor determines how to roof, and homeowner agrees to end result. Business firm employs messenger service to deliver messages in town, and messenger service determines how deliveries are to be made.

does not have the right to control the independent contractor's performance of the contract, the employer is generally not in a good position to ensure that the independent contractor performs with due care. If a roofing contractor repairs the roof on a person's home and some shingles blow off the roof and injure a neighbor, the roofing contractor is liable for the damage caused, but the homeowner is not. The roofing contractor determines how to repair the roof, and the homeowner does not control, or have the right to control, how the roofing contractor goes about doing so.

There are some exceptions to this general principle. An employer may by law be prohibited from delegating certain tasks to independent contractors. Employers who use independent contractors to perform such tasks will be held liable if the actions of the independent contractors are tortious toward third parties. Figure 12–3 portrays the general characteristics of the three major types of agency relations, the master-servant, principal-agent, and the employer-independent contractor. The last paragraph of the case that follows discusses the circumstances under which an employer can be held liable for the torts of the independent contractor.

Similarly, because it is the absence of the employer's right to control that makes the employer–independent contractor relationship different from the other relationships between the employer and its representatives, the courts will closely examine the possible control of the employer. If the employer could have exercised some control but did not do so, the employer may be held liable for the torts of the independent contractor. How much control must an employer be able to exercise over an agent-contractor before being liable for the torts of that agent-contractor? The next case illustrates how the employer's right to control determines whether there is an employer–independent contractor relationship or either a principal-agent or employer-employee relationship.

Massey v. Tube Art Display, Inc.

551 P.2d 1387 (1976)
Court of Appeals of Washington

Tube Art was to move a sign it provided for its client, McPherson Realty, to a new location. It hired Redford, a backhoe operator, to dig a hole at a spot that it marked. While digging the hole, Redford struck a gas pipeline. Finding no leak, he left the site. The next morning, an explosion in the building served by the pipeline killed several people and injured others. Massey, a tenant in the building, sued Tube Art for injuries caused to his property, claiming that it was liable for Redford's negligence as its employee-agent. The trial court agreed with Massey, and Tube Art appealed to the Court of Appeals, which affirmed the trial court's determination.

Swanson, Judge

Traditionally, servants and nonservant agents have been looked upon as persons employed to perform services in the affairs of others under an express or implied agreement, and who, with respect to physical conduct in the performance of those services, is subject to the other's control or right of control. An independent contractor, on the other hand, is generally defined as one who contracts to perform services for another, but who is not controlled by the other nor subject to the other's right to control with respect to his physical conduct in performing the services.

In determining whether one acting for another is a servant or independent contractor, several factors must be taken into consideration [as] listed in Restatement (Second) of Agency:

a. the extent of control which, by the agreement, the master may exercise over the work details;
b. whether or not the one employed is engaged in a distinct occupation or business;
c. the kind of occupation, with reference to whether, in the locality, the work is usually done under the direction of the employer or by a specialist without supervision;
d. the skill required in the particular occupation;
e. whether the employer or the workman supplies the instrumentalities, tools, and the place of work for the person doing the work;
f. the length of time for which the person is employed;
g. the method of payment, whether by the time or by the job;
h. whether or not the work is a part of the regular business of the employer;
i. whether or not the parties believe they are creating the relation of master and servant; and
j. whether the principal is or is not in business.

All of these factors are of varying importance in determining the type of relationship involved and, with the exception of the element of control, not all the elements need be present. It is the right to control another's physical conduct that is the essential and oftentimes decisive factor in establishing vicarious liability, whether the person controlled is a servant or a nonservant agent.

Our review of the evidence supports the trial court's evaluation of both the right and exercise of control even though Redford had been essentially self-employed for about 5 years at the time of trial, was free to work for other contractors, selected the time of day to perform the work assigned, paid his own income and business taxes and did not participate in any of Tube Art's employee programs. The testimony advanced at trial, which we find determinative, established that during the previous three years Redford had worked exclusively for sign companies and 90 percent of his time for Tube Art. He had no employees, was not registered as a contractor or subcontractor, was not bonded, did not himself obtain permits or licenses for his jobs, and dug the holes at locations and in dimensions in exact accordance with the instructions of his employer. In fact, Redford was left no discretion with regard to the placement of the excavations that he dug. Rather, it was his skill in digging holes pursuant to the exact dimensions prescribed that caused him to be preferred over other backhoe operators. We therefore find no disputed evidence of the essential factor—the right to control—nor is there any dispute that control was exercised over the most significant decisions—the size and location of the hole.

Assuming for the sake of argument that Redford acted as an independent contractor, this court does not accept Tube Art's argument that its liability is, therefore, negated. In the present case, Tube Art exercised control over where the hole was to be dug, the day it was to be dug and how deep the hole was to be. Moreover, it was not unreasonable to expect Tube Art to know that gas pipes might very well be lurking in the vicinity of the proposed excavation. In such a case it was incumbent upon Tube Art to ascertain where other service pipes might be. Failing this, Tube Art cannot now disclaim liability. Rather, where the danger to others is great, a duty is imposed upon an employer to make such provision against negligence as may be commensurate with the obvious danger. It is a duty which cannot be delegated to another so as to avoid liability for its neglect.

Affirmed.

Case Questions

1. Which of the factors suggested in the *Restatement (Second) of Agency* are most important in determining an employee's status as a servant or independent contractor?
2. Would the court have decided for Tube Art if Redford had been designated as an independent contractor?
3. In what way was Redford negligent? Could Massey have held him liable for that negligence? In what way was Tube Art negligent? Could Tube Art be held liable for its negligence and for the negligence of Redford?

SUMMARY

There are three different types of agency relationships: master-servant relationships, principal-agent relationships, and employer–independent contractor relationships. Agency relationships are generally created by contract. Even in the absence of a contract, however, an agency relationship may arise if the parties consent to it. The burden of proving an agency relationship rests with the person who claims that it exists. For the agent's acts to be binding on the principal, there must be actual authority, apparent authority, or ratification from the principal. An agency relationship can be terminated by agreement of the parties or by operation of law.

Once an agency relationship exists, each of the parties owes certain duties to the others. The duties of the parties are usually specified in a contract. Even in the absence of an express agreement, however, the agent owes the principal several fiduciary duties: the duty of loyalty, the duty to communicate information, the duty to use reasonable care, and the duty to account. The principal also owes the agent several duties: generally, the principal must compensate the agent, reimburse the agent's expenses, indemnify the agent for losses, and provide the agent with a safe workplace.

Most agency problems spring from the agent's activities with third parties. Usually, the concern focuses on whether a principal can be held liable for the torts committed or the contracts negotiated by its agent. The liability of the principal depends on the type of agency relationship that exists and on the knowledge and perception of third parties regarding that relationship.

In the master-servant or employer-employee relationship, the employer has the right to control the employee's physical activities. Usually, the employee is under the direct control of the employer, which supervises and directs the employee's work. The employer is liable for torts of the employee that cause injury to third parties, but since the employee has very limited authority to negotiate contracts for the employer, the employer is not liable for the employee's contracts.

The principal-agent relationship arises when a principal, such as a business firm, hires an agent to represent it and to work according to guidelines and procedures established by the principal. The principal may not always be in direct control of the agent's physical activities, but it retains the right to direct how the agent is to perform assigned tasks. The principal is liable for tortious acts of the agent that are within the agent's scope of authority and for contracts made by agents who disclose (fully or partially) the principal to third parties.

In the employer–independent contractor relationship, the employer contracts with another party, the independent contractor, to have that party perform certain tasks. The independent contractor, not the employer, determines how those tasks are performed. Since the employer has no right to control the independent contractor's performance, the employer is usually not liable for tortious acts of the independent contractor. Unless otherwise agreed, the independent contractor has no authority to commit the employer to contracts.

KEY TERMS

master-servant relationship or employer-employee relationship, p. 356
principal-agent relationship, p. 356
employer–independent contractor relationship, p. 356
agency relationship, p. 357
fiduciary duty, p. 363
disclosed principal, p. 374
partially disclosed principal, p. 374
undisclosed principal, p. 375
respondeat superior, p. 375

CHAPTER EXERCISES

1. When may an agent be personally liable on the contracts he or she signs with third parties?
2. Assume that an insurance company has fired a life insurance salesman who worked for it for 15 years in a rural community. It does not notify the community at large or any of its former customers that this agent no longer works for it. The agent keeps his rate book, life insurance policies, and other documentation that he received from the insurance company. Three weeks after being fired, he sells a $100,000 term life insurance policy to a former customer. Is the insurance company bound by the agent's actions?
3. Roberts, who lived in Boston, owned 10 acres of land in Florida that he decided to sell. He wrote Johns to inquire whether Johns would act as his agent in attempting to find a buyer. After some correspondence, it was agreed that Johns would act as Roberts' agent. Roberts relied completely on Johns' judgment with respect to the value of the land. After Johns wrote Roberts that $1,000 per acre was a reasonable price for it, Roberts agreed to a sale at that price and a firm purchased the land for $10,000. A short time later, Roberts learned that Johns was a partner in that firm and that the land was reasonably worth $30,000. Assume that the other partners knew the facts as stated above. What are Roberts' rights?
4. Jeff Reynolds is a project administrator of a high-tech corporation. His wife, a former computer programmer, is now raising two small children while she develops software in an office at home. Jeff and his wife dream of having their own company someday. Meanwhile, Jeff likes his job and his boss and works hard at the corporation. A software developer demonstrates a terrific new software package that he wants Jeff's company to use and promote. Jeff is impressed. He indicates that the program is not exactly in line with his company's business but that the company might be interested if the package were seen by the right people. However, Jeff does not offer the software package to his company. Instead, he and his wife strike a deal with the software developer to market the package on a free-lance basis on their own. Does this present any legal problems?
5. A principal employed an agent as a commercial real estate salesman on a commission basis. The principal allowed the agent to draw $1,500 a month as base pay. The salesman/agent worked for the principal six months, but his commissions averaged less than $500 a month. The principal then terminated the agent's employment and sought to recover the payment on the draw that it had made over and above commissions. Will the principal recover?
6. The defendant, a general contractor, entered into a contract to build a house for the plaintiff. The defendant subcontracted all of the carpentry work to Joe. Joe failed to enclose a stairwell, and the plaintiff fell through it, suffering injuries. Is the general contractor responsible?
7. Al's Ice Cream hired Bob to drive its Good Humor truck during the summer months. While making his rounds, Bob fell asleep and the truck hit a telephone pole. The truck was damaged in the amount

of $3,000. Can Al's Ice Cream recover this amount from its agent? Explain.

8. Which party, the master or the servant, is ultimately liable for torts that are the servant's rather than the master's fault? Would your answer change if the servant's torts were caused by the master's improper instructions?

9. Stokely-Van Camp, Inc. hires Lennen & Newell as its advertising agent. Lennen and Newell contracts with CBS for the purchase of advertising time. The contract Lennen and Newell makes with CBS is not signed by Stokely-Van Camp. If CBS is not paid for the advertising time, can it hold Stokely-Van Camp liable? *CBS v. Stokely-Van Camp, Inc.* 456 F. Supp. 539 (1977).

10. Davis was a salaried traveling salesman for Playtex. He had no set hours and worked only when necessary, including evenings and weekends. On a Sunday, he was planning to go to a girlfriend's house to have dinner and do some paperwork. On the way he was involved in an auto accident with Barnum. Barnum died, and Rappaport, his executor, brought suit against Playtex. Is Playtex liable for Davis' action? *Rappaport v. Playtex Corp.*, 352 N.Y. S.2d 241 (1974).

11. Haven had minor surgery but was paralyzed due to what he claims was negligence on the part of his surgeon. Haven wants to sue both the surgeon and the hospital where the surgery was performed. Dr. Randolph, the surgeon, was not employed by the hospital and the hospital did not control the way in which Dr. Randolph performed the surgery on Haven. Is there a principal-agency relationship between Dr. Randolph and the hospital, such that Haven can hold the hospital liable for Randolph's negligence? *Haven v. Randolph* 342 F. Supp. 538 (1972).

12. A personnel or human resources director at a firm may be given the responsibility for setting the salary level for new employees. Frequently, that person has a salary ceiling or range and, based on the qualifications of the candidate, has the authority to make an offer within those guidelines. Suppose you were the person with such authority and were interviewing a candidate for a position which normally pays $25,000 annually. After discussing the terms of employment with a candidate you'd like to hire, you ask the candidate: "What salary would you expect for this position?" If the candidate replies: "I'd like to be paid at least $20,000," what salary would you offer? Would it make a difference if you know that your performance will be more highly regarded if you hire for the lowest possible salary?

    Do you have legal or ethical obligations to your firm and to the candidate for employment, or to just one of them? If you knew that the candidate likely would later find out that he or she could have asked for $5,000 more in salary, would this change your answer? Does it matter whether the candidate is the sole support of a family and needs the higher salary?

Chapter 13

BUSINESS ORGANIZATIONS

KEY CONCEPTS

Proprietorships and partnerships are easily created forms of business organization. Owners of these organizations are liable in contract and tort for activities of agents and employees.

Partners have fiduciary duties to the partnerships and to the other partners. Authorized acts of a partner bind the partnership and expose both the partnership and the personal assets of the partners to liability.

As agents, corporate officers and directors must exercise reasonable care and be loyal to the firm. Unreasonable business judgments or conflicts of interest may form the basis for damages to the corporation and its shareholders.

Although a corporation is owned by its shareholders, the board of directors generally exercises managerial control over most corporate activities; only extraordinary concerns need shareholder approval. The separation of ownership and control permits corporations to raise capital from passive investors and to employ professional managers as corporate officers who run day-to-day corporate activities.

The critical features that distinguish a corporation from a proprietorship and a partnership are a corporation's perpetual life, the transferability of ownership interests in a corporation, and the limited liability of a corporation for acts of its agents and employees. In extraordinary cases, however, individual owners of a corporation may be held liable for corporate activities.

INTRODUCTION . . . PAST, PRESENT, FUTURE

The sole proprietorship is the oldest and most common form of business organization. No special legal formalities are needed to establish a sole proprietorship, and no special legal rules, since it has a single owner, regulate relations among its participants.

Like the sole proprietorship, the partnership form of business organization has existed for thousands of years. Although no special requirements must be met to form a partnership, it is customary and desirable to prepare a partnership agreement. Current state partnership laws are based on the Uniform Partnership Act, which was drafted about 80 years ago. A Revised Uniform Partnership Act that is being developed is becoming more important in the 1990s. The limited partnership came into use in the early 19th century. It arose as a result of difficulties encountered in obtaining corporate charters and as a result of concerns over the unlimited liability of partners in a general partnership. The limited partnership is generally viewed as a mixture of the partnership and corporate forms of business organization. Most of the states have adopted the Uniform Limited Partnership Act.

The corporation is the dominant form of business organization in the United States. The association of individuals in a single legal organization has existed since ancient times. Under Roman law, corporations were able to do many of the things that individuals could do, such as own, sell, or inherit property; acquire assets; and incur liabilities. These early forms of corporations influenced the development of English law, which is the basis for corporate law in the United States.

Corporations as we know them today date back to the late 1700s, when state legislatures began to authorize their formation and operation. The separate entity concept of the corporation is at the heart of its distinct legal status. Most state corporation laws are based on the Revised Model Business Corporation Act which was drafted in 1984.

Future regulation of business organizations is likely to concentrate on the corporation. In the last several decades, numerous proposals have suggested the development of federal corporate law to displace state regulation of corporations. Supporters of these proposals argue that the states are more interested in attracting corporations than in regulating them and that the country needs a uniform corporate law. Although there has been little movement toward the adoption of such proposals, federal securities and environmental laws increasingly affect corporate activities.

Amid this discussion of increased regulation, corporations, beset by dramatic increases in hostile takeovers in recent years, have sought protection in state antitakeover laws. The states, concerned with possible losses of jobs and tax revenues, have responded by passing legislation aimed at protecting their corporations. As the 20th century draws to a close, many U.S. corporations, as well as corporations in other countries, seem to be engaged in significant restructuring. Corporations merge with each other; divisions are sold off or realigned; employees are laid off; contributions to pension plans and health care costs are reduced; new management groups purchase control of corporate segments and affiliates; and joint ventures with foreign corporations are actively pursued. As the structure and concerns of the corporate world change, major modifications in corporation law will inevitably follow.

OVERVIEW

The sole proprietorship, partnership, and corporation are the basic forms of business organizations in the United States. More specialized entities, such as the joint venture, the limited partnership, the Subchapter S corporation, the professional corporation, and the limited liability company have evolved from these three basic forms. After reviewing the proprietor and the partnership forms of business organizations, the chapter notes the unique role of franchises in business organizational concerns. Then, it examines the corporation form of business organization.

The numerous types of corporations are discussed, and the functions performed by corporate shareholders, directors, and officers are reviewed. Finally, the proprietorship, partnership, and corporate forms of business organizations are compared.

As you read this material, keep in mind the discussion of the primary characteristics and the formation processes of each form of business organization. Table 13–1 (p. 408) provides some of this information, but you may want to prepare your own chart as you compare and contrast the different forms of business organizations.

THE PROPRIETORSHIP FORM OF BUSINESS ORGANIZATION

An individual who owns a business is called a **sole proprietor.** Of course, as the business of a sole proprietor grows, he or she must hire employees to perform the work and hire agents to conduct transactions with other businesses.

Characteristics of a Proprietorship

A sole proprietorship is not considered to be an entity separate from its owner. If the business is sued, the suit is filed against the owner, though the name of the business is usually also indicated. For example, "Charles Smith, doing business as (D/B/A) Charley's Crabhouse" is a form often used. Charles Smith, not just the business organization, is the defendant, so all of his assets, whether derived from the business or from other sources, are exposed to liability for any legal judgment. A sole proprietorship has no legal status apart from that of its owner.

All the profits of a sole proprietorship belong to the owner. Thus, a sole proprietor generally does not need to file a separate income tax return for the business. Instead, income derived from the business is determined on a separate schedule (Schedule C for the federal income tax) of the owner's individual tax return. The income or loss from the business is combined with any other income of the owner to determine the owner's income tax liability. Approximately 80 percent of U.S. business organizations are sole proprietorships or partnerships.

Creation of a Proprietorship

A sole proprietorship is easier to form than any other kind of business organization. A special name may be used for the business, provided that a certificate for doing business under an assumed name is filed. Generally, the certificate is filed in the county in which the business operates. For example, Charles Smith's restaurant might do business under the name of "Charley's Crabhouse." If an owner wants to open several stores or branches of the same business, the certificate must generally indicate the location of each store. Registration of such trade names is discussed in Chapter 7.

Numerous local, state, and federal laws require the owner of any business, regardless of its form of organization, to comply with certain governmental regulations. For example, permits may be needed from state authorities if the business emits pollutants or manufactures hazardous products. Federal and state taxes must be withheld from the wages of employees, and local ordinances may govern certain activities. Nevertheless, the sole proprietorship is easier to form and usually subject to less government regulation than is any other kind of business organization.

THE PARTNERSHIP FORM OF BUSINESS ORGANIZATION

Although partnership law was developed through case-to-case decisions under common law, today almost all of the states have adopted the provisions of the Uniform Partnership Act (UPA). The UPA has been in effect since 1914, but difficulties have led to the drafting of a revised law.

Revised Uniform Partnership Act

The Revised Uniform Partnership Act (RUPA) amends the old UPA by following case law and simplifying partnership law with common provisions found in most well-planned partnership agreements. RUPA adopts the entity theory except to the extent necessary to retain the favorable "flow-through" tax treatment of the Internal Revenue Code. Partnership dissolutions are treated as " breakups" under RUPA, abandoning the confusing "dissolution" process. After a partner withdraws, the other partners can more readily choose either to continue or discontinue business operations without concern the business must be liquidated. Finally, RUPA permits the partnership agreement to vary the partners' rights among themselves and achieve a mutually acceptable governance structure. RUPA will probably be adopted by most states during the 1990s and eventually replace the UPA.

Characteristics of a Partnership

The Uniform Partnership Act defines a **partnership** as an association of two or more persons who intend to carry on a business for profit as co-owners. The designation of business associates as partners has an important impact because each partner is both a principal, as a part of the partnership, and an agent, when acting on behalf of the partnership. The UPA defines corporations and other partnerships as persons; thus, these entities can join with other persons or other entities to form a partnership. The law does not require the parties to sign a written agreement, but partners must consent to work together. Of course, sound business practice should lead the parties to set out their rights and responsibilities in writing. Through consultation with an attorney, the parties can focus their attention on the problem areas that the partnership agreement should address.

Second, the partners must carry on their business as co-owners. This requirement does not mean that the parties must contribute equal amounts of property and capital to the business. Rather, the parties have a community of interest in sharing the management responsibilities and the profits and losses of the business. If the owner of a business hires a manager to run the business and the manager does not share in the profits or losses of the business, these parties are not partners. Even if an employee receives a bonus based on business profits, there is no partnership because the employee does not also share in business losses. Although partners can make their own agreements regarding the sharing of profits, in the absence of special provisions, the law presumes partners will share profits and losses equally, even if their work or capital contributions are unequal.

Third, the objective of the parties must be to make a profit. People who act together in a nonprofit organization are not considered partners. Of course, the law does not require that a profit be made; it only requires that profit making be the intent or motive of the parties. If the partnership incurs losses, each partner must share those losses in some proportion. Should a married couple automatically be considered partners if they conduct business operations together? The following case illustrates the application of the criteria for a partnership to the business activities of a married couple.

Skaar v. Wisconsin Department of Revenue

211 N.W.2d 642 (1973)
Supreme Court of Wisconsin

Mr. and Mrs. Skaar farmed property together in Wisconsin. Under the federal income tax law, married people such as the Skaars were permitted to file a joint return and effectively split their income even though all of the income and deductions belonged to only one spouse. Under the Wisconsin income tax law in effect at the time of this case, even though married people could file one income tax return, each spouse was taxed individually on his or her income. Mr. and Mrs. Skaar claimed that their farm income was partnership income shared equally by both of them as partners. Despite their claim, the Wisconsin Department of Revenue found that the Skaars were not partners. The Wisconsin Tax Appeals Commission reversed that decision, and the Department of Revenue appealed to the Supreme Court of Wisconsin.

Hanley, Justice

The sole issue is whether the Wisconsin Tax Appeals Commission (WTAC) erred in affirming the Department of Revenue's denial of the taxpayers' application for abatement of the additional income tax assessment by concluding that, as a matter of law, no bona fide partnership existed.

While the Wisconsin income tax is modeled upon the federal system, the personal income tax treatment of married individuals under the federal and Wisconsin tax provisions is dissimilar. Under the federal system, married individuals are permitted to file a joint return and effectively split their income even though all income and deductions belong to only one spouse. Wisconsin, on the other hand, while permitting married individuals to file jointly, taxes each spouse individually on his income, and deductions and income splitting is not allowed.

Since Wisconsin has adopted the Uniform Partnership Act, we must initially look there for guidance. Sec. 178.03(1), Stats. defines a partnership as an "association of two or more persons to carry on as co-owners a business for profit." More specifically, it is recognized that four elements need be met so as to qualify as a partnership. Initially, the contracting parties must intend to form a bona fide partnership and accept the legal requirements and duties emanating therefrom. Secondly, there must exist a community of interest in the capital employed. Thirdly, there must be an equal voice in the management of the partnership. Finally, there must be a sharing and distribution of profits and losses. Applying these elements to the case at bar, we hold that a bona fide partnership was not created. While the taxpayers may have desired to create a marital financial relationship similar to a partnership, it is clear they did not intend to create a bona fide partnership.

Initially, the parties to a partnership must intend to contractually form the legal relationship of a partnership. Such an intent is not shown here. While the W.T.A.C. found that the parties had reached an oral understanding, such oral understanding does not show the necessary intent. The oral understanding is more consistent with their marital relationship than with the existence of a bona fide partnership.

There do exist many indications that the taxpayers did not intend to create a bona fide partnership. They did not file partnership tax returns as required both federally and in Wisconsin. We think that if the taxpayers had intended to form a bona fide partnership they would not have violated the federal and Wisconsin legal requirement of filing. Likewise, the taxpayers failed to pay the federal self-employment tax for Mrs. Skaar, which would have been required had said business arrangement been a partnership. Such tax surely would have been paid had the taxpayers intended to form a partnership and fulfill the legal requirements. The record discloses they were familiar with such requirements.

There are other indications the taxpayers did not intend to form a partnership. There was no automobile liability insurance coverage for Mrs. Skaar even though had a bona fide partnership been created, Mrs. Skaar would be liable for the tortious acts of her partner.

Similarly, the books of the farm operation were not kept in a manner consistent with a bona fide partnership in that there was no division of the farming operation profits between the taxpayers. In fact, the lower court found that the taxpayers did not consider themselves partners in a legal sense.

The taxpayers argue that their desire to own everything together . . . established the fact that they intended a partnership. Such is not the case. A partnership is not implied merely from a common ownership of property. The facts that the community recognized Mrs. Skaar as possessing the authority to bind the farming enterprise and that Mrs. Skaar helped manage and operate the farm are not in themselves controlling. Such facts are as common to a marital relationship as they are to a partnership.

Proof as to the fourth element of the partnership—the division of profits—is also insufficient to show the existence of a bona fide partnership. In fact, there was no proof whatsoever that the taxpayers agreed to divide and did in fact distribute the profits of the farming enterprise. The fact that the account books fail to show any division of profits between the taxpayers creates an inference that the taxpayers never intended to so distribute said profits. . . .

Consistent with our finding that the relationship in question was not a bona fide partnership, we likewise hold that their relationship failed to qualify as a joint venture because of the scope and period of time which such a relationship encompasses.

Judgment is reversed and cause remanded with directions to affirm the decision of the Wisconsin Tax Appeals Commission.

Case Questions

1. Which of the four elements required of a partnership by the Uniform Partnership Act adopted in Wisconsin was missing here?
2. What evidence indicated whether the Skaars agreed to divide the profits from the business?

Formation of a Partnership

Because a partnership involves at least two people, there is a sharing of rights and responsibilities. A partnership is usually created by the parties through a partnership agreement that defines their respective rights and duties. Such businesses as accounting firms and law firms frequently choose the partnership form of business organization. Some partnerships involve numerous parties with complex business transactions, whereas others involve only a few parties sharing in the operations of a single small business. As a result, the formalities of creating a partnership vary greatly, ranging from complex written articles of partnership to a simple verbal agreement between two partners.

Partnerships Compared to Similar Entities

Both the joint venture and the limited partnership have characteristics that are similar to those of partnerships. However, each of these specialized entities also has features that distinguish it from the partnership.

Partnerships and Joint Ventures The partnership and joint venture are similar in that both involve two or more persons who join together in some business activity. However, they differ in their scope and duration. A partnership is created to carry on business activity for an indefinite period, whereas a joint venture is limited to a specified time period. Further, the joint venture, unlike the partnership, does not envision cooperation of the parties as associates in a number of different, but perhaps related, projects. Joint adventurers seek to cooperate in one specific venture and are not considered associates or partners in other ventures.

For example, General Motors and Toyota operate a large-scale joint venture to manufacture automobiles at a plant in California (NUMMI). This single venture does not make the two corporations partners in other activities. Once their commitment with regard to this venture has expired, they may elect to cease working together on any business activity. Meanwhile, they will continue to compete on other projects involving the manufacture and sale of motor vehicles. Because the joint venture is limited in scope and duration, it is not used for long-term business activities.

Corporations from different countries often form joint ventures. Such corporations do not intend to be partners in all of their business transactions. Instead, they act together in a limited setting for a specified time. Although an international joint venture can be formed by contract, typically it is formed by means of a separate corporate organization. A further discussion of the role of joint ventures in international business transactions is provided in Chapter 21.

Partnerships and Limited Partnerships In a limited partnership, unlike a general partnership, some of the partners are allowed to limit their liability to the amount of their original investment. Each limited partnership must have at least one general partner with unlimited liability and at least one partner with limited liability. The limited partner, like the corporate shareholder, has limited liability, but unlike the corporate shareholder, the limited partner has no voice in the control or management of the business. In fact, if the limited partner does participate in the management of the business, the *legal* protection of limited liability may be lost.

Limited partnership ownership interests can be made transferable, so the death or withdrawal of one limited partner does not affect the continuity of the partnership. The general partner or partners in a limited partnership have essentially the same status as the partners in a general partnership. Each general partner may act on behalf of the limited partnership, and each can be held personally liable for partnership activities. However, the general partner or partners in a limited partnership do not have the authority to admit new general partners without the consent of the limited partners unless the limited partnership certificate gives them this authority.

Limited partnerships are frequently used to raise capital for the development of special projects. This enables, for example, a wealthy limited partner to invest significant funds in such a project without risking his or her other assets to creditors of the project. Oil wells, drilling ventures, Broadway shows, shopping centers, movies, and other rather risky ventures are often organized as limited partnerships.

The general partnership and the limited partnership also differ in the requirements for their creation. General partnerships can be created by the parties without a written agreement, whereas the Uniform Limited Partnership Act (ULPA) and the Revised Uniform Limited Partnership Act (RULPA) require the filing of a certificate. The certificate must contain information regarding the partnership business, the names of the partners, and the amount of their capital contributions. Either the ULPA or the RULPA has been adopted in all of the states except Louisiana.

The ULPA also states that a limited partner's name may not be used in the partnership name. Moreover, the partnership name must include the words *limited partnership* or the abbreviation *l.p.* so that third parties will realize that it comprises one or more limited partners who are not liable for partnership activities beyond their capital contributions.

The Role of Partnership Participants

Each partner in a partnership has both rights and duties toward the other partners. Essentially, each partner acts both as an agent for other partners and as a principal when other partners are agents for partnership purposes. A partner's relations with third parties is based on agency law. In dealing with a third party, the responsibilities of a partner are based on the authority, actual or apparent, given the partner by the partnership.

A Partner's Duties toward Other Partners The duties of a partner to other partners and to the partnership are defined in the partnership agreement and are inferred from the agency relationship between the partnership as principal and the partners as agents. Each partner is both an agent and a principal for the other partners. The partnership is regarded as the principal, and each partner, as a part of the partnership, has the obligations of a principal with regard to the activities of other partners. For instance, the partnership must reimburse a partner who spends personal money in buying supplies for the partnership. The partners as a group owe the expenses incurred by an individual partner.

As an agent, each partner owes the partnership the fiduciary duties that an agent owes to his or her principal:

Fiduciary Duties Owed by the Partner as an Agent of the Partnership

1. The duty of loyalty.
2. The duty to communicate information.
3. The duty to obey instructions.
4. The duty to use reasonable care.
5. The duty to render an account.

If a partner violates any of the fiduciary duties owed to the partnership, the other partners can require that partner to account for any damages or for any profits. What duty do partners owe the partnership for a profit that only some of the partners received in the conduct of business activities? The following case illustrates the trust that is expected of all partners as fiduciaries of the partnership and of one another.

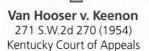

Van Hooser v. Keenon

271 S.W.2d 270 (1954)
Kentucky Court of Appeals

Van Hooser, the defendant, and Keenon, the plaintiff, were partners with several other parties in the operation of a bus line. Several years after the partnership began business, Van Hooser began discussions with a representative from Greyhound, Inc. about the possible acquisition of the partnership business by Greyhound. As a result of these discussions, Greyhound gave Van Hooser $37,500 to be used as a partial payment for a controlling interest in the partnership business if that business could be converted into a corporation.

An agreement with Greyhound specified that if Greyhound later decided not to purchase the business, the money could be retained by Van Hooser and several of his partners. Van Hooser induced his partners to convert their partnership into a corporation, but Greyhound later decided not to purchase the bus line. When Keenon found out that Van Hooser and others had personally retained the Greyhound payment, he sued Van Hooser, claiming that the money given to Van Hooser belonged to the partnership. The trial court found for Keenon, and Van Hooser appealed.

Stewart, Justice

The case was referred to the master commissioner of the Fayette Circuit Court, who found that when Greyhound, Inc., paid $37,500 for an option to purchase a 60 percent interest in the partnership this included 60 percent of every partner's interest therein and that the money paid for the option inured to the benefit of all the members of the partnership in proportion to their ownership. . . . This finding was approved by the circuit judge and he rendered judgment solely against defendants Van Hooser and Utter, for the 25 percent due plaintiffs. We should state, at the outset, that there is no relation of trust or confidence known to the law that requires of the parties a higher degree of good faith than that of a partnership. Each partner is the confidential agent of all the others and each has a right to know all that the others know. Nor will one partner be permitted to benefit at the expense of the firm. No undue advantage of one over another by misrepresentation or concealment will receive the approval of the law. A court of equity will always grant relief to the partner who has suffered from a breach of the obligation. One partner will not be permitted to obtain secretly any right that should belong to the partnership and put it to his own individual profit. Of such character is the securing of a contract. The criterion is not an actual evil motive, for the courts look to the results of any such action regardless of evil intent. If such action results in profit or advantage, the courts will require an accounting.

Applying the foregoing basic rules of the common law to the admitted facts of this case, we conclude as did the lower court, and the evidence abundantly supports our conclusion, that the five defendants were and are under a legal obligation as partners to share proportionately with plaintiffs the option money which was obtained by the optioners by virtue of the partnership relationship. The important factor is that these defendants received money which should have gone into the partnership treasury and then should have been divided proportionately among all of the partners. The excuse advanced by them that they were compelled to keep the Keenons in the dark, in order for their plan to work, certainly furnishes no legal basis under the circumstances for their retention of all the money.

Furthermore, we believe it was proper to render judgment against the two appealing defendants alone for the full amount due plaintiffs. They initiated and consummated the option deal with Greyhound, Inc., and they collected and divided up among the five optioners the cash benefits from the transaction. . . . The mere fact that the five optioners have already apportioned the $37,500 among themselves does not relieve the appealing defendants of their obligation to settle with plaintiffs for their proportionate part.

We therefore conclude the lower court correctly disposed of the issues raised.

Wherefore, the judgment is affirmed.

Case Questions

1. Why did the court decide that the money received from Greyhound belonged to the partnership?
2. If a partner obtains a right that should belong to the partnership but uses that right for individual profit, does the profit belong to the partnership even if the partner did not intend to benefit at the partnership's expense?

Partners' Rights in a Partnership The rights and responsibilities of the partners in the operation of a partnership are generally established in their partnership agreement. If not, the UPA grants certain property rights to each partner.

A Partner's Property Rights

- Rights in specific partnership property.
- An interest in the partnership.
- The right to participate in the management.

Partnership activities generally involve the use of property, either furnished by the partners or purchased by partnership resources. For example, a partnership of lawyers needs desks, books, telephones, file cabinets, computers, and other items of property. It is important to distinguish the property of the partnership from the personal and individual property that is owned by each partner but is used in the activities of the partnership.

Rights in Specific Partnership Property If property is owned by the partnership, its use by an individual partner may be restricted. Further, if partnership property is sold, the proceeds may be retained by the partnership or distributed according to the partnership agreement. For example, if a partnership sells its desks, the proceeds belong to the partnership and are distributed according to the partnership agreement. The proceeds from a desk used by a partner will not necessarily be distributed to that partner. On the other hand, if a partner owns a desk that the partnership uses, the proceeds from the sale of that desk belong to the individual partner, not to the partnership.

Each partner has an equal right with the other partners to possess and use partnership property for partnership purposes. On the death of a partner, that partner's right to partnership property passes to the surviving partners, not to the partner's heirs.

An Interest in the Partnership The second aspect of a partner's property rights concerns the partner's interest in the partnership itself. The UPA states that a partner's interest in the partnership is "his share of the profits and surplus, and the same is personal property." This interest is an asset that can be transferred, that can be seized by creditors of the individual partner, and that becomes a part of the individual partner's estate at death.

Partnership agreements often prohibit the transfer of an individual partner's interest to someone outside the partnership until the partnership or other partners have been given the opportunity to purchase it. Even when that interest is transferred, the transferee receives only a right to participate in the firm's profits; he or she does not have a right to participate in the firm's management or to become a partner. For example, if one of the three partners in a pizza business transfers her interest to you, you receive only the right to share in the profits or losses of the business. You do not have a right to make decisions about the operation of the business or to act on behalf of the other partners. Furthermore, the transferor remains obligated to perform services for the business unless the remaining partners consent to the delegation of that duty to you and you agree to assume it.

Partnership creditors, not the creditors of an individual partner, have first claim on partnership property needed to satisfy debts. Creditors of an individual partner may seize that partner's share of the profits, but not any specific partnership property. Through a court approved *charging order,* the creditor may take the individual partner's share of the business but may not interfere in the operations of the business.

Right to Participate in the Management The third aspect of a partner's property rights is the partner's right to participate in the management of the partnership business. If no contrary agreement is made by the partners, each partner has an equal right to manage and conduct the partnership business. By majority rule, the partners may make decisions regarding the operational aspects of running the business. The majority cannot, however, exclude the other partners, and it must act in good faith. Extraordinary changes, such as admitting a new partner, entering a different business, or relocating the business, cannot be made without the unanimous consent of all the partners. Generally, partnerships of more than several people alter these rules in the partnership agreement. For example, the partnership agreement of a large accounting or law firm typically specifies that new partners may be admitted by majority vote of the senior partners, that one partner may make most of the day-to-day management decisions for the firm, or that a small committee has the authority to change the firm's location.

A Partner's Relations with Third Parties Partnership law can be viewed as an extension of agency law. Under the UPA, a partner has the implied authority to engage in transactions for carrying on the normal partnership business. A partner can contract to hire employees, borrow money, and purchase items needed to operate the business. Thus, a third party that negotiates with a partner in selling goods, lending money, or transacting other normal business of a partnership can look to the partnership for payment. The contract made by a partner is the contract of the partnership, not the contract of the individual partner.

The partnership must inform third parties of any restrictions imposed on a partner's ability to make such contracts. Otherwise, the UPA provides that third parties are not affected by such limitations. For example, if only specific partners are authorized to purchase furniture for a partnership, the partnership must inform the furniture stores with which it deals. If it does not, and if an unauthorized partner makes a purchase from a furniture store, the furniture store can still look to the firm for payment.

A partnership and all of its partners are liable to injured third parties for the torts of any partner who acts in the ordinary course of business or with the authority of the other partners. If a partner commits a tort outside the carrying on of his or her normal business activities, the partnership is not liable. Thus, the general rules of *respondeat superior* affecting the principal-agent relationship, as discussed in Chapter 12, determine a partnership's liability for the torts of individual partners.

Because partners are individually liable to third parties for all of the firm's financial obligations, a partnership must be careful about its commitments. When a partnership leases property for its office, it is committing each of the partners to pay the rent obligation it agrees to. Sometimes that obligation becomes greater than the partners ever envisioned.

Personal Risk Becomes a Major Worry for Partnerships

By Eugene Carlson

Lots of people dream of becoming partners in their own business or professional firm. But Frank Cihlar learned the hard way that joining the fold carries an enormous risk. . . .

Mr. Cihlar, 48 years old, is being squeezed by the unlimited liability principle that undergirds the partnership form of business. It is a problem that's emerging as a major concern for professionals and many entrepreneurs in these hard economic times. Problems often involve office leases. . . .

In a general partnership, the form of organization for most service professionals and many small businesses, partners are individually responsible for all of the firm's financial obligations. (By contrast, the amount that a creditor can recover from a corporation is limited to its assets.)

Specialists say Mr. Cihlar's tale should serve as a warning flag to newly formed partnerships that may be tempted to commit their firms to long-term office leases at current bargain-basement rates. They suggest instead that partners should exploit the glut of empty office space nationwide to escape the liability hammerlock.

Landlords anxious to fill their buildings may be willing to limit the extent of an individual partner's financial obligation in case of default, they say. And small firms can sometimes strike short-term office-sharing arrangements with larger partnerships with excess space to avoid the liability risk altogether. . . .

Washington lawyer Austin Frum's three-person firm has tried to sidestep the problem by subleasing about 1,500 square feet of excess space on a two-year, nonrenewable basis, from a large law firm. "For most lawyers, making partner in a law firm has been like winning some sort of medal, but it has its dark side," Mr. Frum observes.

Source: Eugene Carlson, "Personal Risk Becomes a Major Worry for Partnerships," *The Wall Street Journal*, January 3, 1992, p. B2.

Termination of a Partnership

Termination of a partnership is a two-stage process involving dissolution and winding up. The Uniform Partnership Act defines dissolution as "a change in the relation of the partners caused by any partner ceasing to be associated in the carrying on . . . of the business." Thus, the death, withdrawal, or retirement of a partner technically dissolves the original partnership. In most cases, however, the dissolution does not affect the continuation of the business because the remaining partners wish to carry on. Instead, the books and records of the partnership are revised to reflect the dissolving of the old partnership and the beginning of a new one; meanwhile, the normal business of the partnership continues.

When dissolution occurs and a new partnership is not going to continue the business, a winding up of the business takes place. In these cases, the existing partnership must wind up, or terminate, the business by paying its debts, liquidating or selling its assets, and distributing the remaining proceeds among the partners. All third parties must be notified of the firm's dissolution and creditors with whom the business has dealt are entitled to specific notice. The general notice is usually accomplished by one or more newspaper advertisements, while the specific notice requires that a notice be mailed to the firm's creditors. The partners involved in winding up a business have no authority to continue the business; they are only authorized to complete the transactions that have been started, collect assets, and pay off debts. When the business is wound up, assets are distributed, as specified by the UPA, to (1) creditors who are not partners; (2) creditors who are partners; (3) partners to repay capital contributions; (4) partners entitled to profits.

FRANCHISES AND BUSINESS ORGANIZATIONS

A franchise may be considered a type of business organization because it defines how a firm's assets are financed, controlled, and distributed. However, a **franchise** is a privilege granted or sold, such as the privilege of using a name or process to sell products or services agreed upon between two parties, the franchisor and the franchisee. The *franchisor* develops a product or service, often protected by a trademark or a trade name, and then licenses this product or service to *franchisees* as a uniform method of doing business. Each of the parties to a franchise generally has its own form of business organization. Frequently, the franchisor consists of several commonly owned corporations. Franchisees invest in their own business operations and usually organize their own corporations.

Distinctive Characteristics of a Franchise

The most distinctive characteristic of a franchise is the franchisor's exercise of substantial control over a business owned by the franchisee. In exchange for allowing the franchisee to use the franchisor's unique trade name, trademarks, and special products and techniques, the franchisee permits the franchisor to establish the products that may be sold, the hours of operation, and the types of equipment that are to be used. Although fast-food franchises such as Wendy's, Little Caesar's Pizza, and Burger King are highly visible, franchises are common in many service businesses, such as the motel industry (Holiday Inn and Hilton), the tax preparation business (H & R Block), the muffler business (Midas and Tuffy), and even the legal business (Hyatt Legal Services). A franchise agreement usually provides that the franchisee will pay an established percentage of its gross sales to the franchisor as compensation for the use of the franchisor's trademark and business methods. Chapter 16 discusses the antitrust aspects of other forms of franchise compensation and the level of control that franchisors may exercise. Chapter 16 includes the *Principe v. McDonald's* case, which discusses why such control is important.

Typically, the franchise contract requires that the franchisee conform to the standard operating procedure specified by the franchisor. For example, the hamburgers must be cooked in a specified manner, and only certain kinds of potatoes can be used for the french fries. Failure to follow those requirements is usually grounds for termination of the franchise. In the franchise agreement, the franchisor (generally a large corporation such as Pillsbury, the owner of the Burger King trademark) frequently agrees to provide managerial assistance to the franchise, to select the site for operating the franchise, and to regulate the purchasing, advertising, and record keeping of the franchise. The franchisee, generally a local firm, agrees to provide the monetary investment in the business, to establish the desired business organization, and to operate the franchise in accordance with the terms of the franchise agreement.

Franchise Legislation

Many of the states have enacted legislation aimed at protecting the franchisee from unilateral termination of the franchise by the franchisor. Although the statutes vary, typically they require the franchisor to notify the franchisee of problems with the franchisee's operations prior to termination. Many of these statutes limit the franchisor's right to cancel the franchise agreement. The Automobile Dealer Day in Court Act and the Petroleum Parties Act are specific laws aimed at particular industries.

At the federal level, Federal Trade Commission regulations seek to protect prospective franchisees from misrepresentations in the initial sale of franchises. For example, certain franchisors must disclose specific information regarding franchises to potential franchisees at least 10 days prior to entering into any agreement with them. Further, the franchisor's estimates of potential earnings must be supported by documents showing the basis for its estimates of gross sales and income. This helps prevent potential franchisees from purchasing franchises whose prices are based on overly optimistic estimates. State securities laws also are applicable to franchises because the franchises are viewed as involving the marketing of securities.

THE CORPORATION FORM OF BUSINESS ORGANIZATION

Although the corporation is now the dominant form of business organization in the United States, it did not arrive on the U.S. scene until the late 18th century. The **corporation**, a separate entity distinct from its owners, is sometimes traced to ancient Greece or Rome. The early use of corporations influenced English law, which eventually became the basis for corporate law in the United States. Although the American colonists originally did not favor incorporations, the right of individuals to form a common business organization eventually became recognized in this country.

The Role of the Corporation Today

Although corporations account for less than 20 percent of the number of business organizations in the United States, they are responsible for over 80 percent of sales and annual revenue. The size and dominance of the U.S. corporation as a business organization could not have been envisioned 100 years ago. In recent years, mergers between such firms as

Warner Communications and Time, Inc. have created even larger corporate entities. In banking, communications, transportation, and pharmaceuticals, larger corporations have acquired smaller ones. In countries such as Japan, Canada, Australia, and the countries of the European Community, corporations have become dominant through mergers within and across national boundaries.

INTERNATIONAL PERSPECTIVE: ESTABLISHING FOREIGN CORPORATIONS

Although each state in the United States has its own laws for establishing business organizations, the various state laws do not differ dramatically from each other. However, a U.S. firm considering international investment will meet significantly different corporation laws. If the investment occurs in a developing country without a firmly established market economy, there may be significant restrictions imposed on entry into particular industries, controls on operations, and restrictions imposed on the withdrawal of capital or profits. What if the investment occurs in a developed country with a market economy, such as Germany?

In many European countries, there are two forms of business organizations, one for closely held corporations and one for public corporations. Thus once a firm has decided to use the corporate form of business organization, it then must decide which form of organization will best fit its purposes (these are briefly discussed in Chapter 21). The laws and regulations governing each are quite different. For example, a U.S. firm contemplating establishing a German subsidiary corporation will find that Germany has two forms of corporations, the GmbH and the AG. The GmbH is used for small corporations, whereas the AG is for public corporations. Several basic differences between the two forms are noted below:

	GmbH	AG
Minimum capital	50,000 marks	100,000 marks
Minimum number of incorporators	1	5
Transfer of Shares	Cannot be traded on stock exchange	Can be traded on stock exchange
Board of directors	No special requirements if fewer than 500 employees	Required to have both a supervisory board (representing employees and employers) and a management board
Accounting procedures	No special requirements	Public disclosure

Characteristics of the Corporation

At least four essential characteristics make the corporate form desirable for firms that have large capital needs and want to create a separate entity that can endure for many years. State laws determine how corporations must be formed; the documents generally required to form a corporation are noted below. Later sections discuss several types of corporations and examine the various roles of shareholders, directors, and corporate officers.

Separate Entity The first characteristic of the corporation is its status as a **separate entity** or person. The law gives the corporation a legal life of its own. It is responsible for paying its own taxes, and it can be held accountable for its own torts and in some cases for the commission of crimes. Several of the U.S. Constitution's provisions protecting persons also apply to corporations, including the due process clause, the prohibition of unreasonable searches and seizures of property, the access to courts, and the ability to buy, sell, and hold property rights.

Limited Liability A second corporate characteristic, the **limited liability** of each individual shareholder who owns a portion of the corporation, is frequently the primary reason for incorporation as distinguished from organizing as sole proprietorships and general partnerships. The corporation's status as a separate entity shields its owners from personal liability for corporate debts. Although shareholders may lose their investment if the shares of stock they hold in the corporation become worthless, generally they cannot be held personally liable for corporate debts.

In some unusual cases, the concept of limited liability is disregarded. These cases usually involve closely held corporations in which the dominant shareholder is also active as a director or officer of the corporation. In such cases, the courts may *pierce the corporate veil* of liability and hold some individual, often a shareholder, liable for acts of the corporation. For example, a court held that a cab driver who was the sole owner, officer, and employee of a corporation that owned two cabs could not escape individual liability for his negligent operation of a cab owned by the corporation.[1]

What conditions might permit a court to disregard the limited liability of an individual shareholder? The next case illustrates such conditions and reviews the theories used to pierce the corporate veil.

Mills Co. v. Crawfish Capitol Seafood

569 So. 2d 1108 (1990)
Court of Appeals of Louisiana

Henry Mills Company, Inc., filed suit against Crawfish Capitol Seafood, Inc. and its incorporators, Champagne, Melancon and Peltier for money due for work done in renovating a building that the corporation planned to use in processing seafood. The individual defendants, who were also the corporation's only members of the board of directors and officers, claimed that the contract was made by the corporation and that as individuals they could not be held liable for the corporation's debts. The trial court found for Mills against the corporation, but held that the individuals were not liable for the corporation's debts. Mills appealed.

Domengeaux, Chief Judge

The general rule that corporations are distinct legal entities, separate and distinct from the individuals who compose them, is statutory in origin and well recognized in Louisiana jurisprudence. Thus, shareholders are not individually responsible for the debts due by the corporation.

In *American Bank of Welch,* this court discussed the limited exceptions to the rule of nonliability of shareholders for the debts of corporations. One exception

---

[1] *Walkovszky v. Carlton,* 18 N.Y. 2d 414 (1966).

involves the corporation's failure to conduct its business on a corporate footing, thereby disregarding the corporate entity to such an extent that the corporation ceases to be distinguishable from its shareholders. In such situations, the corporation is referred to as the *alter ego* of its shareholders, and the court may *pierce the corporate veil* and impose personal liability on the shareholders.

In deciding whether to pierce the corporate veil, the totality of the circumstances must be examined. This determination is primarily a factual finding for the court to make. In deciding whether to pierce the corporate veil, the factors to be considered by the court include, but are not limited to: commingling of corporate and shareholder funds, failure to follow statutory formalities for incorporation and the transaction of corporate affairs, undercapitalization, failure to provide separate bank accounts and bookkeeping records, and failure to hold regular shareholder or directors' meetings. . . .

In the case before us, Mills must prove that Champagne and Peltier disregarded the corporate entity to such an extent that it ceased to be distinguishable from themselves. This is a heavy burden of proof. When fraud or deceit is absent, other circumstances must be so strong as to clearly indicate that the corporation and shareholders operated as one.

. . . In reaching a determination of whether the corporate veil should be pierced in the instant case, the trial court discussed the five factors listed in *Daley.* Concerning the commingling of corporation and shareholder funds, the record reflects corporate funds were used to renovate a restaurant where the crawfish would be cooked prior to processing and packaging for resale. The restaurant was leased to Melancon individually. Before the crawfish operations began, Melancon used the facility as a restaurant business in which Crawfish Capitol Seafood had no interest. The operation lasted two to three weeks. We, like the trial judge, find this insignificant. . . . While it is true that the restaurant was renovated with corporate funds, we do not believe Melancon's personal use of the facility for two to three weeks constitutes commingled assets to the extent required to pierce the corporate veil.

Considering other relevant circumstances, the trial judge found, and the record supports her finding, that the statutory formalities required for incorporation and the transaction of corporate affairs were met. The Certificate of Incorporation and the Articles of Incorporation were included in the record.

Although bylaws were not written, bylaws are not required by law. The failure to issue stock certificates is likewise insignificant; each shareholder owned a one-third interest in the corporation in exchange for services to be rendered to the corporation, which can include management, labor, and technical expertise, as well as supplies or equipment.

The testimony reveals that the shareholders met regularly; although minutes of these meetings were not kept, minutes are not required by law. Crawfish Capitol Seafood had its own bank account from which numerous checks were drawn. Bookkeeping records were not available, but because the corporation never actually started doing business, its bookkeeping records would be sparse, if existent at all.

The remaining factor discussed by the trial court is Mills' contention that Crawfish Capitol Seafood was undercapitalized. The record does not support that contention. Crawfish Capitol Seafood obtained interim financing of $160,000.00 from Breaux Bridge Bank and Trust. The State of Louisiana approved a loan application for permanent financing. For reasons which were not made a part of the record, the permanent financing fell through. . . . Furthermore, when its permanent financing fell through, Crawfish Capitol Seafood ceased operations and incurred no additional financial obligations.

The circumstances presented in this case are insufficient to clearly indicate that the shareholders and the corporation were acting as one and therefore do not justify piercing the corporate veil.

In light of the totality of the circumstances of this case, and after reviewing the testimony of Champagne, Melancon, and Peltier, we cannot conclude that the corporation and the shareholders were indistinguishable. Therefore, the trial court did not err in failing to disregard the corporate entity of Crawfish Capitol Seafood.

AFFIRMED.

Case Questions

1. What does the court find regarding each of the five factors it reviews to determine if the individuals can be held liable for the corporation's debts?
2. Explain what is meant by the terms *alter ego* and *pierce the corporate veil.*

Freely Transferable Ownership A third corporation characteristic is the *freely transferable* nature of its ownership. An interest in a corporation, represented by shares of stock, can usually be transferred without disrupting business activities. The sale of an interest in a partnership or the sale of a proprietorship often does interrupt normal business activities.

Perpetual Life Finally, the *perpetual life* of a corporation is another characteristic that distinguishes it from the sole proprietorship or partnership. Unlike the sole proprietorship or partnership, the corporation's existence is not dependent on the lives of its owners. Changes in ownership generally do not affect the operations of the firm's business.

Characteristics of a Corporation

1. Separate entity.
2. Limited liability of owners.
3. Freely transferable ownership.
4. Perpetual life distinct from owners.

Corporate Formation

A corporation is formed when the state of incorporation grants a corporate charter. The first decision affecting the formation of a corporation is the selection of the state in which to incorporate. Although the Model Business Corporation Act provides some degree of similarity in the corporation laws of the states, there are distinct differences among them.

Many corporations choose to incorporate in the state where their business originates. However, they may choose to incorporate in a state whose corporate laws they view more favorably, such as Delaware. Delaware's legislative provisions and court decisions enable corporations to conduct their internal affairs with few restrictions. The law of the state of incorporation is usually applied in litigation concerning a corporation's internal activities and its relations with its shareholders, so choosing the state in which to incorporate is an important aspect of forming a corporation.

The persons who apply to the state for incorporation are called *incorporators*. They are required to pay certain filing fees and to file a document, called the *articles of incorporation*, that is reviewed by the secretary of state or the state commerce department. Incorporators generally have to comply with several requirements before the articles of incorporation or corporate charter is approved. To avoid confusing parties that deal with the new corporation, its name cannot be too similar to that of another corporation. The corporate name must include a special term such as *incorporated, limited,* or *company,* or an abbreviation of one of those terms, to indicate that the firm is a corporation. This requirement is imposed so that people dealing with the firm will know that it has limited liability.

Other requirements include the naming of a registered agent for the corporation and the designation of the corporation's principal place of business. These requirements permit all persons dealing with the corporation to contact it by mail and to deliver legal papers to its agent. Many states require that the officers and directors of the corporation be listed in the articles of incorporation. The corporation must begin with a minimum capitalization, typically $1,000. Its capital structure must indicate the rights of each class of shareholders.

After the articles of incorporation have been approved, the shareholders attend an organizational meeting. At this meeting, they elect the board of directors, which establishes corporate policies. Either the shareholders or the board of directors adopts *bylaws,* rules governing the internal aspects of the corporation's activities. The officers who will conduct the business of the corporation are then selected by the board of directors, and stock certificates are issued to the shareholders.

TYPES OF CORPORATIONS

Although this chapter focuses on the business corporation, which is created to make a profit, most of the state corporation laws provide for a number of types of entities that can be organized in the corporate form. A corporation may be public or private, organized for profit or nonprofit, publicly or closely held, professional or nonprofessional, and foreign or domestic. Each of these categories focuses on some special characteristic of the corporate form of organization.

Public and Private Corporations

This classification refers to the purpose for which the corporation has been created. Business corporations such as IBM, Xerox, and General Motors are private corporations that were created by private individuals for private purposes. The Federal Home Loan Bank, many of the state universities, and numerous municipal water or school districts are public corporations that governments created and funded to serve public purposes.

Profit and Nonprofit Corporations

This classification focuses on the operational objectives of the corporation. A profit-oriented corporation seeks to make money for its shareholders. The corporation distributes profits to the shareholders as dividends or retains them for its further growth. If the corporation's assets are sold, the net assets are divided among the shareholders.

A nonprofit corporation does not have shareholders and does not seek to pay dividends or operate at a profit. The League of Women Voters, the Boy Scouts, and the Sisters of Saint Joseph are examples of nonprofit corporations. Such corporations carry over any surplus of receipts over disbursements to the following year.

Publicly or Closely Held Corporations

This classification concerns the degree to which the stock ownership of a for-profit corporation is spread among owners. The ownership of a publicly held corporation, such as ATT or IBM, is widely diffused rather than concentrated among a few individuals. Publicly owned stock can be traded from one owner to another through stock exchange transactions. In order to issue stock to the public, a corporation must comply with federal and state laws and regulations imposed on the issuing and trading of corporate securities. These problems are discussed further in Chapter 14.

A closely held corporation, such as one formed by the owners of a local department store, has stock that is not sold to or traded by the public at large. The stock of a closely held corporation is owned by only a few people who are generally active in the management or relatives of the founder. In closely held corporations, unlike publicly held corporations, management and ownership are not separated.

Most state laws affecting private corporations apply equally to public and closely held corporations. However, in recent years, as the commentary following the next section indicates, a number of states have authorized the creation of **limited liability companies** (LLCs). The LLC offers its owners limited liability and taxation of the owners' earnings, not that of the corporate entity. Although it is like the Subchapter S corporation described in the next section, the LLC allows the owners to annually reallocate income and deductions among themselves to fit their individual needs, a practice that the Subchapter S provisions do not permit, and avoids some of the restrictions imposed on the number of "S" corporation shareholders.

The Subchapter S Corporation The **Subchapter S corporation**, or **S corporation**, is a creature of the federal income tax laws. For tax purposes, it is viewed as a hybrid between the corporation and the general partnership. It can be formed by only a limited number of stockholders, each of whom must agree to use the S corporation form of business organization. It has two important attributes: (1) it is viewed as a corporation for purposes of liability; and (2) it is taxed like a partnership. With few exceptions, the shareholders of an S corporation cannot be held liable for its debts.

For income tax purposes, the S corporation is treated like a partnership. Its income is considered to be that of the shareholders, not that of the corporate entity. Its losses can be used to offset income earned by its individual shareholders. For example, each of five equal shareholders of an S corporation with a $50,000 loss in a given year may use $10,000 of that loss to offset individual income they derived from other sources. Thus, if one of them had $50,000 in taxable income from other sources that year, that shareholder's net taxable income would be $40,000. As noted in the following Commentary, unlike the S corporation shareholder, the 20 percent owner of an LLC or partnership will not necessarily have a 20 percent loss; his or her percent of the firm's profits or losses may differ from his or her share of ownership.

The income of an ordinary for-profit corporation is treated differently; it is not considered income of its shareholders until they receive it as dividends. Assume that you are one of five equal shareholders of a corporation that earns $50,000 in a given year. The corporation may retain much of that money as working capital and distribute only a small portion, say $5,000, as dividends. Your share of those dividends, $1,000, would be the amount of your taxable income from the corporation. Income not distributed by the corporation may be retained for growth or future distribution. This cannot occur with the income of a partnership, S corporation, or limited liability company, because these entities must distribute all of their income to their partners or shareholders.

Commentary: The Limited Liability Company

By Jeffrey A. Tannenbaum

Robert H. Kane's start-up enterprise is a mouthful: Octagon Communications Limited Liability Co.

The name doesn't exactly have a ring to it. It's rather awkward on stationery and business cards. It even fails to convey the company's intended business: investments in rural cellular-telephone companies.

But loud and clear, the name conveys something else: a new form of ownership that Mr. Kane and his seven partners expect will serve them well. Their enterprise—to be based in Denver—is neither a traditional partnership nor a traditional corporation. Rather, under Colorado law, it is a "limited liability company," or LLC.

Mr. Kane and his partners expect to enjoy the best of both worlds: the tax advantages of a partnership and the legal safeguards of a corporation. Yet they face none of the drawbacks associated with forming a so-called Subchapter S corporation, which also is taxed much like a partnership. For example, S corporations can't have corporate shareholders, but LLCs can. . . . In 1977, Wyoming became the first state to authorize LLCs, but it took until 1988 for the Internal Revenue Service to confirm that the new Wyoming entities would be treated as partnerships for federal tax purposes.

To date, only five other states—Colorado, Florida, Kansas, Virginia and, most recently, Utah—have followed Wyoming in authorizing their own LLCs, according to an American

Bar Association survey.* But lawyers in many other states report growing interest because of the IRS ruling. Two ABA panels are studying the topic, as is the National Conference of Commissioners on Uniform State Laws, a group allied with the ABA. Meantime, moves are afoot to introduce LLC statutes in Arizona, Illinois, Maryland, Michigan, Nevada, Ohio, Oklahoma and Texas, the ABA survey found.

One appeal of LLCs is that, as with partnerships, any income flows through untaxed to the individual owners. Such owners don't avoid personal taxes, but they do avoid corporate taxes. Regular corporations face higher maximum taxes in the first place. And if the corporations pay dividends, owners are taxed again.

Flexibility of a Partnership

Of course, S corporations avoid double taxation—but they don't enjoy all the advantages of partnerships when it comes to juggling income and deductions. For example, the 20 percent owner of an S corporation normally must pay taxes on 20 percent of any income. By contrast, partnership members are free to divvy up any income and tax liability as they see fit. Thus, equal partners might change the allocations of profit or loss year to year to fit their individual tax needs. LLCs offer the same freedom.

With LLCs, as with regular corporations, only the company's assets, and not the owners' personal assets, are at risk in business-related lawsuits. In partnerships, so-called limited partners enjoy such protection, but general partners don't. And limited partners face restrictions on how active they can be in the business. LLCs are designed to protect all partners while imposing no limits on their activity.

Benefit for Foreigners

Proponents still say the LLC raises little risk for enterprises operating only in their home state or outside the U.S. And it's ideal for foreign investors—normally barred from S corporations.

LLCs don't limit the number or type of owners, as S corporations do, except for a two-owner minimum. But because of other restrictions, only closely held enterprises are suited to be LLCs. For example, if any owner leaves, the others must all formally agree to keep the enterprise going. . . . But even closely held companies face uncertainties on a number of technical and procedural issues, such as whether the conversion of a partnership into an LLC amounts to a "termination" under tax law, which might increase tax liability. IRS rulings are still awaited. In the meantime, warns Ms. Spudis, the Chicago lawyer, many LLC investors are entering uncharted territory.

*Texas also authorizes the formation of Limited Liability Companies.

Source: Jeffrey A. Tannenbaum, "Partnership, Corporation Aren't Only Ways to Start Out," *The Wall Street Journal*, May 14, 1991, p. B2.

Professional and Nonprofessional Corporations

The professional corporation—the use of the corporate form of business organization by people practicing the same profession—is a rather recent development. Physicians, attorneys, or accountants may organize their business activities as a professional corporation. A law firm known as Smith, James, and Jones, P.C. is a professional corporation. Usually, people who are not licensed to practice the particular profession are not allowed to be shareholders of such a corporation and the corporation is permitted to engage only in the activity for which its shareholders are licensed. Special state laws usually govern professional corporations.

A nonprofessional corporation is a corporation whose services do not require licensed professionals. Since dry cleaners are not licensed professionals, if the owners of a dry cleaning business form a corporation, it is considered a nonprofessional corporation.

Foreign and Domestic Corporations

Clearly, in the United States a corporation organized in France would be regarded as a foreign corporation. However, in the United States the terms *foreign* refers both to corporations incorporated outside the United States and to corporations incorporated outside a given state. Thus, Pennsylvania laws regard a corporation incorporated in Michigan as a foreign corporation.

Even if a corporation does business within a state, it may be regarded as a foreign corporation if it was incorporated in another state. Because General Motors was incorporated in Delaware, even Michigan, where its corporate offices are located, could regard it as a foreign corporation. However, although the classification of a corporation as foreign or domestic is generally based on its place of incorporation, many state laws and most laws of countries other than the United States, use a different criterion in classifying corporations as domestic or foreign. Often, that criterion is the location of the corporation's center of management. On this basis, most laws probably regard General Motors as a Michigan corporation.

THE ROLE OF CORPORATE PARTICIPANTS

The **shareholders** of a corporation are its owners. They have the power to sell or dissolve the corporation and to determine who will be responsible for managing it. The **directors** of a corporation are the managers of its business. They determine the corporation's overall strategy, and they select the **officers** who are in charge of conducting the corporation's day-to-day business.

The relationship among these corporate representatives is illustrated by Figure 13–1. In large corporations, different people occupy the roles of shareholders, directors, and officers. In smaller businesses, the same people may perform more than one of these functions. If this occurs, corporate records should clearly indicate the actions taken by the shareholders, directors, and officers, as they each have separate and distinct legal responsibilities in the corporation. Failure to keep accurate corporate records may result in the imposition of tax, contract, or tort liability on those who appear to be responsible for a corporation's business activities, regardless of their actual role in the corporation.

Shareholder Rights

Although *shareholders* own the corporation, in most large corporations they do not play an active role in corporate management. The shareholders in a large corporation perform several tasks. First, they elect the board of directors, whose members are entrusted with the management of the corporation. Second, they vote to approve or disapprove extraordinary transactions of the corporation. For example, shareholder approval is required if the corporation is to sell most of its assets, change its principal place of business, or merge with another corporation. Some shareholders are also seeking to require that the compensation of executive officers of corporations be established or approved by shareholders rather than by the board of directors.

Shareholders also have the right to inspect the books and records of the corporation and the right to sue the corporation in the event of improper action. For example, they may sue the corporation for agreeing to sell part of its assets if that action was not in their best interests. Finally, if the corporation is dissolved, the profits of the corporation are distributed to the shareholders.

FIGURE 13–1 Relationships among Corporate Officers, Directors, and Shareholders

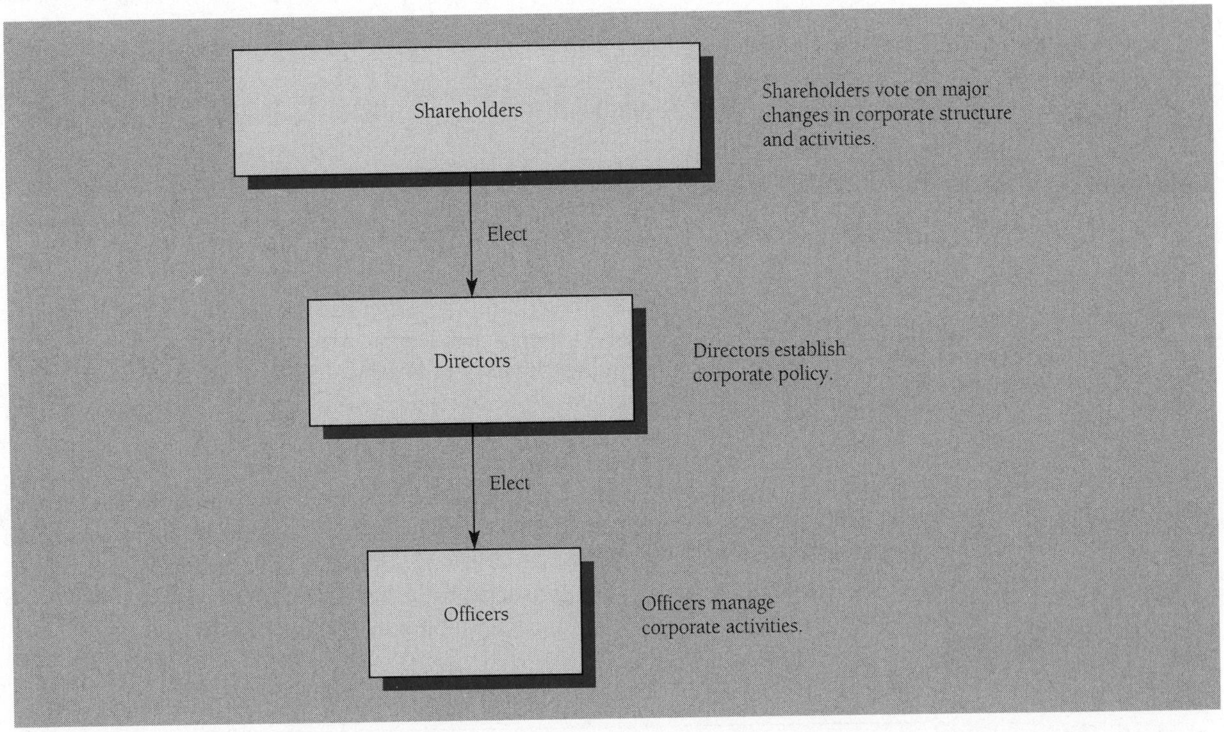

A shareholder who is unable to attend a shareholders' meeting can exercise his or her rights by means of a *proxy,* which gives someone else the right to vote for the shareholder at the meeting. Shareholder proxies are generally solicited by the corporate officers. In corporations with publicly held shares, most of the shareholders' votes are usually cast by proxies granted to these officers. Proxy fights occur when individuals or groups outside the corporation solicit the proxies of shareholders. During such fights, shareholders are asked to elect new members to the board of directors or to sell their shares to individuals or groups that are seeking to take over the management of the corporation.

A shareholder of one share of stock in a corporation is generally entitled to one vote. Thus, the holder of 100 shares of stock can cast 100 votes. If the corporation's bylaws permit cumulative voting, when a shareholder with 100 shares of stock is voting for three directors, the shareholder has 300 votes. This system permits a shareholder to cast 300 votes for one director or to give 100 votes to each of three directors. Cumulative voting is favored by those who seek to protect minority shareholders. These shareholders can cast all of their votes for one director, whereas the votes of the majority are being split among a group of directors. Most of the states require a corporation to conduct at least one shareholders' meeting each year; however, a few states, notably Delaware, have no such requirement.

Role of the Board of Directors

The board of directors is legally responsible for the management of corporate activities. If a corporation acts in an illegal or improper manner, the members of its board of directors can be held liable. The Revised Model Business Corporation Act requires that the business activities of a corporation be managed under the direction of its board of directors. The board usually delegates to corporate officers the responsibility for managing day-to-day corporate activities. It formulates and supervises management policies and strategies. Frequently, it authorizes some of its members to act for the entire board in certain matters. For example, an executive committee of the board of directors may make critical financial decisions and an audit committee may select and review the activities of auditors.

The board of directors interacts with the shareholders in several ways. It is responsible for calling shareholders' meetings, and it determines how large the dividends should be and when they should be paid to the shareholders. It is elected by the shareholders, and it must receive shareholder approval for mergers or other extraordinary corporate activities.

The board elects corporate officers and thereafter interacts with them to ensure the implementation of its policies. As members of the board, directors owe the duties of an agent to the corporation, including the duty of loyalty and the duty of reasonable care. Corporate officers or directors who neglect their duties can be held liable. However, many states shield directors from liability by applying the *business judgment rule.* Under this rule, directors are not held liable for errors in business decisions if they exercise reasonable business judgment. They are liable only for fraud, oppression, or arbitrary actions. Review the following commentary, which discusses the rise in the number of lawsuits against corporate officers and directors. Then consider the *Fireman's Fund* case, which decides whether an insurance bond insuring the corporation against liability based on a dishonest or fraudulent act by an employee applies to a director of the firm.

Commentary: Lawsuits against Corporate Officers

By Milo Geyelin and Ellen Joan Pollock

Lawsuits assailing the conduct of corporate officers and directors rose again last year, particularly in the trouble-plagued financial services industry, a new survey reports.

At the same time, companies found a tighter, more difficult market for insurance policies that protect against liability in such litigation. As a result, corporate officials are becoming increasingly exposed to personal liability in cases that allege poor performance or negligence. . . according to a survey by Wyatt Co., a Chicago-based consulting firm. . . .

"All industries are having much more difficulty obtaining adequate director and officer liability insurance for a reasonable premium," says Kenneth S. Wollner, a risk management consultant at Wyatt. "That trend is certainly led by banks, but it's a trend that's prevalent regardless of what kind of company you have."

Directors or officers at 26 percent of the companies surveyed said they were sued last year, up from 22 percent in 1989. The companies hardest hit are those with assets over $1 billion, according to the survey. Companies under that size have seen the frequency of lawsuits against directors and officers diminish, while larger companies have seen the rate grow "at a compound annual rate of 10 percent and 20 percent a year" since 1980.

Stockholders were most likely to sue last year, accounting for 51 percent of 852 claims analyzed by Wyatt. But the most frequent claim in suits against directors and officers was wrongful termination, which occurred in 12 percent of the cases. Overall, employee claims generally were responsible for 23 percent of claims, the second-largest category of suits, the survey found. . . .

Source: Milo Geyelin and Ellen Joan Pollock, "Suits against Corporate Officers and Directors Rose Again in 1990," *The Wall Street Journal*, January 15, 1991, p. B10.

Interstate Production Credit Association v. Fireman's Fund Insurance Co.

944 F. 2d 536 (9th Cir., 1991)
United States Court of Appeals

In 1971, Congress established the Farm Credit System to serve the credit needs of farmers and ranchers. Interstate Production Credit Association (IPCA) was organized to provide loans to its members under the Farm Credit Act. Fireman's Fund issued a 10-million dollar fidelity bond to IPCA's predecessor, Northwest Livestock Production Credit Association (NLPCA) to cover financial losses for "any direct financial loss through any dishonest or fraudulent act of any employee. . . ." The bond covered losses discovered at any time as long as they were discovered during the policy period.

John Courtright, the president and principal shareholder of the Courtright Cattle Company (CCC), was a member of the Board of Directors of NLPCA. The NLPCA began lending money to CCC, and Courtright individually guaranteed the loans. During the period of time covered by the bond, Courtright falsified loan documents by inflating CCC's cattle inventory. As a result of Courtright's fraud as an officer of CCC and his failure as a director of the NLPCA Board to disclose this dishonesty to the Board, IPCA alleged it lost over 10 million dollars. It sued Fireman's Fund to recover on the bond, but Fireman's claimed the bond covered only employees and not Courtright as a director. It also claimed that IPCA could not prove that its loss was caused by the actions of only one member of its Board of Directors, Courtright.

The trial court found that the bond did include Courtright as a director, but also found IPCA had not proved that Courtright caused its loss. Both parties appealed from that portion of the decision adversely affecting them.

Alarcon, Circuit Judge

The bond issued by Fireman's Fund defines the term employee as:

> . . . (1) a director, officer, or other employee of the insured while employed in, at, or by any of the insured's offices or premises covered hereunder . . . and a guest student pursuing studies in any of said offices or premises, and (2) a director or trustee of the insured, whether compensated or not, when performing acts coming within the scope of the usual duties of any officer or employee or member of any committee duly elected or appointed to examine or audit or have custody of the property insured.

The district court held that subsection one "covers directors while they are performing functions as directors." It rejected Fireman's Fund argument that the words "employed in, at, or by any of the Insured's offices or premises" should be read to limit coverage to services normally performed by officers or employees. The district court's interpretation "gives meaning to both . . . sections." The district court did not err in granting partial summary judgment to IPCA on this issue.

IPCA asserts that it lost over 10 million dollars in uncollectible loans because Courtright failed to disclose to the Board that CCC's collateral was fraudulently represented. Fireman's Fund contends that the bond does not cover Courtright's fraudulent representation, as an officer of CCC, because that conduct did not occur while he was performing the duties of a director. . . . It also argues that "the conduct of Courtright in performing functions as a director was not the cause in fact of or a substantial factor in causing the loss on the CCC loans." We disagree. Fireman's Fund ignores the fact that had Courtright informed the Board of his fraudulent representations concerning the collateral, the loans to CCC would not have been approved.

The bond provides that:

> For purposes of this bond, dishonest or fraudulent acts as used in insuring Agreement A, shall mean acts committed by an employee who *knowingly,* having authority to accept or approve an application for a loan or an extension thereof or an employee who *knowingly* furnishes information upon which the acceptance or approval of an application for a loan or an *extension* thereof is based, fraudulently, dishonestly,

> and *knowingly* alters or causes to be altered . . . material information on such application upon which the insured shall and does rely in making or obtaining a loan or an extension thereof. (Emphasis in original)

The terms of the bond require proof of a direct financial loss through any dishonest act of an employee. The agreement does not require that the director's dishonesty be the sole cause of a direct financial loss. Courtright's failure to disclose the fraud perpetrated in obtaining loans and loan extensions, for CCC caused a direct financial loss to IPCA.

Federal regulations and case law require a director to inform the corporation of any fraud that may adversely affect corporate decision making. Our view that a director has a fiduciary duty to disclose dishonest acts is supported by decisions from those circuits that have confronted similar issues. Each has concluded that an "employee's failure to disclose dishonesty in dealing with a corporation is covered under fidelity bonds with comparable terms."

The district court erred in concluding that the direct financial loss to IPCA that resulted from Courtright's failure to disclose his dishonest acts to the board of directors was not covered by the bond. The matter is remanded to the district court with directions to enter an order granting partial summary judgment in favor of IPCA on this issue.

Case Questions

1. What duty did Courtright have as a director of IPCA that he breached?
2. What fraudulent statements did Courtright make to the corporation? Would he be liable for this fraud? Why is Fireman's Fund held liable?

Role of the Officers

Corporate officers are the managers of the corporation's day-to-day business activities. They are responsible for carrying out the policies established by the board of directors. The board is responsible for determining the compensation paid to corporate officers and for detailing their duties. Corporate officers are agents of the corporation and owe the corporation a fiduciary duty of loyalty. It is wrong for a corporate officer to appropriate a corporate opportunity for personal gain. For example, if an opportunity arises for a corporation to purchase the stock of another corporation, a corporate officer who learns of the opportunity is prohibited from purchasing that corporation's stock as a personal investment unless his or her corporation consents.

Corporate officers also owe the corporation the duty to be diligent in carrying out corporate affairs. A corporate officer cannot be negligent or careless in performing the tasks of his or her office, but must use reasonable business judgment. For example, a corporate treasurer must take reasonable steps to safeguard and invest the corporate monies. It would be negligent for that officer to lend corporate funds to a friend involved in a risky business.

If, as an agent, a corporate officer uses reasonable care in acting on the corporation's behalf, then that officers' activities will also be the activities of the corporation. The corporation is obligated to reimburse any loss suffered by an officer who is sued by a third party for an act done on the corporation's behalf. Thus, if a shareholder sues the treasurer because a reasonable investment in the stock market did not produce the expected gain, the corporation would be obligated to pay the treasurer's legal expenses in defending that suit.

The rights and duties of corporate officers are often spelled out in an employment agreement. However, the law of agency also imposes duties on and grants rights to any corporate agents, including corporate officers. For example, agency law imposes on corporate officers the duty to disclose information that they receive in their capacity as corporate agents and it grants them the right to be indemnified or reimbursed for costs that they incur while acting on the corporation's behalf.

Commentary: Ethics and the Boardroom

In 1991 corporate scandals occurring in the United States, Japan, and the United Kingdom, indicate that unethical behavior and violation of fiduciary duties knew no boundaries.

In the United States, Salomon Brothers securities firm acknowledged that it had violated the agreement established for direct purchase of treasury notes. The government allows five or six firms to participate as direct purchasers of treasury notes; these firms then resell the notes to their clients and to other brokerage firms. Each participating firm agreed that it would purchase no more than 25 percent of the notes at any one sale. Salomon Brothers broke this agreement on several occasions, apparently purchasing 80 percent of the notes at one particular sale. Salomon Brothers breached its duty to the government and to the other firms by not disclosing its violation of the rules.

In Japan, several brokerage firms went to the extreme to ensure that their favored clients would continue to do business with them. These firms refunded the money lost on stocks purchased by their top customers. The losses of their other customers, however, were not refunded. Brokers as agents owe a duty of loyalty and a duty to use their best efforts for their clients. There is a clear breach of duty and conflict of interest when a broker represents that he or she acts on behalf of all clients but in fact gives preferential treatment to some without disclosing that fact to others or to the government.

In the United Kingdom, Robert Maxwell, chairman of Maxwell Enterprises and owner of newspapers on three continents (Australia, Europe, and North America) was found "dead in the water" near his yacht off the Canary Islands. After his death, authorities discovered that Maxwell had taken money belonging to public corporation pension accounts and transferred it to privately owned firms to keep them from falling into bankruptcy. His shell game, moving assets from one firm to another, was more extensive than anyone realized. The pension fund monies were there for the employees of the public firms, not for Maxwell's use with other firms. Maxwell's unethical actions certainly breached duties he owed to the expectant pensioners and no doubt also violated several laws.

ETHICAL DILEMMAS FOR CORPORATE MANAGEMENT

Corporate managers, officers, and directors have access to valuable and confidential corporate information regarding discoveries from corporate research and development, the design of products, plans about products, strategies about marketing, impending takeovers, and corporate financial performance. Managers who seek to use such information for personal gain breach their ethical obligations if they place their personal interests before the interests of shareholders.

In recent years, corporations have changed the composition of their boards of directors in order to increase the board's supervision of corporate managers. The boards of most publicly traded corporations have several members who are independent of management; these members work for other corporations, banks, customers, suppliers, universities, or labor unions. Such diversity of membership is intended to enhance the "open forum" character of board meetings. A strong executive is less likely to force subordinates to make unethical decisions if independent board members are present. Many corporations now have special subcommittees, mostly composed of independent members, that make decisions in areas of management compensation, litigation, and mergers. Independent board members arguably prevent insiders from taking advantage of their position to abuse shareholders or misappropriate corporate assets. However, is it ethical for inside managers to select only close friends as board members? Is this designed to merely give the appearance of independence? Many observers allege that the "independent" board members are too closely tied to the chief executive officer or other insiders to effectively monitor management. Furthermore, since such members often lack expertise in the corporation's line of business, they may not be able to effectively advise the corporation.

COMPARISON OF PROPRIETORSHIP, PARTNERSHIP, AND CORPORATION

Many small and medium-sized businesses face a choice between organizing as a sole proprietorship, partnership, or corporation. This concluding section examines the taxation, liability, control, and continuity treatment that the law gives each of these forms of business organization. Any of these four features may determine which form is most appropriate in a given situation. Table 13–1 provides a synopsis of the major attributes of the sole proprietorship, partnership, and corporate forms of business organization.

TABLE 13–1
Comparison of the Three Basic Forms of Business Organization

	Sole Proprietorship	Partnership	Corporation
Ease and expense of formation	No formalities or expenses are required other than those specific to the business to be operated.	No formalities or expenses are required other than those specific to the business to be operated. A written agreement among the partners is advisable.	Expense and time required to comply with statutory formality. Must receive charter from state. Usually required to register and pay fees to operate in states other than the state of incorporation.
Tax	Profits are taxed as ordinary income to the proprietor; losses are deducted by the proprietor.	A federal income tax return is filed by the partnership for informational purposes. Profits are taxed to each partner as ordinary income; losses are deducted by each partner. Profits and losses are shared equally unless the partnership agreement provides otherwise.	Profits taxed first as income to the corporation and a second time as dividends are distributed to owners. Losses are deductible only by the corporation.
Liability	Sole proprietor has unlimited personal liability.	Each partner has unlimited personal liability for partnership debts.	Liability of shareholders is limited to loss of capital contribution unless an extraordinary event requires piercing the corporate veil.
Control considerations	Sole proprietor has total control	Each partner is entitled to equal control unless the partners provide otherwise in the partnership agreement.	Separation of ownership and control. Owner generally has no control over daily management decisions.
Transferability of ownership	Transferable with sale of assets and business	Nontransferable unless the partners unanimously agree.	Freely transferable unless shareholder agreements provide otherwise.
Continuity	Limited to life of the proprietor.	Limited to life of the partners.	Unlimited.

Any small business, regardless of its form of organization, generally needs to obtain financing to begin its operations, to allow it to continue in difficult economic times, and to finance expansion. Table 13–2 depicts some of the sources of financing used by many small businesses.

Taxation

When individual tax rates are at or near historically low levels, taxation may lead a business to select the proprietorship or partnership form. Neither of these forms of business organization is taxed as an entity, as is a corporation. The profits of a proprietorship are taxed as ordinary income to the proprietor, and the losses of a proprietorship are deducted from the gains that the proprietor derives from other income sources. A partnership files a return on which it reports income or losses and distributions to the partners. The partners then report their individual shares of the partnership income on their separate returns; any tax liability due from a partner is based on his or her overall income.

Several tax benefits arise from selecting the sole proprietorship or partnership form rather than the corporate form. First, many of the states levy a separate franchise tax on the authorized shares of corporations doing business in the state. This tax is not imposed on sole proprietorships or partnerships.

Second, because the income derived by a proprietor or partner from the operation of a business is taxed only when received, it is not subject to double taxation (taxation of

TABLE 13–2
Sources of Financing for Small Businesses

1. PRIVATE SOURCES

   These include personal funds from relatives and friends. In addition, there may be some private pacement money available from venture capitalists, those willing to invest in a business in exchange for a guaranteed return or a partial ownership of the business. As venture capitalists want to have limited liability, they are more likely to invest in corporations, limited companies, or limited partnerships than in partnerships or proprietorships.

2. TRADE SOURCES

   A business may obtain funds from its suppliers by having the supplier make short-term or long-term credit available. The supplier will be guaranteed some future income and a new customer, and the business will obtain some needed credit.

3. INSTITUTIONAL SOURCES

   Firms needing capital may approach finance or leasing companies. Rates from these sources are generally higher than at commercial banks, but a continued source of funds may be obtained if the business continues to operate profitably. Firms may also obtain loans from commercial banks. Some banks specialize in short-term loans, whereas others offer either short- or long-term loans. Because the partner or proprietor is personally liable for loans made to the business, whereas the corporation is not, the owner of a small corporation may find that he or she will have to personally guarantee the repayment of loans made to the corporation.

4. GOVERNMENTAL SOURCES

   The Small Business Administration (SBA) may be helpful in obtaining financing. The SBA may make a loan to a bank or make a direct loan to the firm. These loans are usually long-term and at low interest rates.

5. OTHER SOURCES

   Insurance companies are a good source of financing for firms with substantial collateral, such as real estate, to secure the loan. Investment bankers may be a good source of financing for the well-known large corporation.

both the organization and the individual owner), as is corporate income distributed to a shareholder. For example, if a corporation earns $100 and distributes $25 of that amount to its shareholders as dividends, the corporation will be taxed on the $100 it earned and the shareholders will be taxed on the $25 they receive. Thus, a total of $125 is taxed. If a proprietorship or a partnership earns $100, that total is taxed to the proprietor or to all of the partners. In either case, the total amount subject to tax is only $100. As corporate and individual income tax rates vary over time, the prevailing tax rates must be examined to determine which form of business organization is most desirable from a tax viewpoint. Several proposals seek to remove or minimize this double taxation of corporate income distributed to shareholders as dividends. Readers may find this area of tax law changed in the near future.

Finally, because the income from a sole proprietorship or a partnership may be only a part of the proprietor's or partner's overall income, losses from other sources may reduce the business income subject to tax. However, because the corporation is a separate entity for tax purposes, the owner of a corporation cannot offset corporate profits with individual losses or use corporate losses to offset individual profits.

Because the corporation is a separate entity and the current individual income tax rates increase as the amount of income increases, forming a separate entity to pay a portion of the taxes due on certain activities can be beneficial. Splitting income between two entities, the corporation and the individual, may lower taxes. However, the current relatively low tax rate for individual income makes the formation of a separate corporate entity less desirable.

Liability

Liability considerations often result in the selection of the corporate form rather than the proprietorship or partnership form of business organization. The sole proprietor is liable for all of his or her business activities and obligations. All the members of a general partnership are liable for the debts, claims, or judgments of the partnership to the full extent of their total personal assets. Thus, the proprietorship or partnership form is usually not desirable for a business that is subject to significant tort liability exposure for injuries to customers, employees, or other parties. A firm manufacturing or selling chemicals, pesticides, or dangerous industrial machines would select the corporate form of organization because of its limited liability.

Control

The sole proprietor, of course, has total control of his or her business. Control in a partnership is relatively easy both to obtain and to maintain. The partnership agreement can establish the control that the initial partners are to exercise. Although majority rule usually controls the partnership's ordinary operations, a court will refer to the partnership agreement provisions if the partners indicate a contrary desire. When a partnership contains an even number of partners, it becomes essential to determine how deadlocks will be resolved. Because the admission of new partners generally requires the unanimous consent of all the existing partners, maintaining the control usually does not pose a problem for the partnership.

Control can be easy for the small corporation but difficult for the large one. This is because the shares of the small corporation are usually not freely traded. The existing shareholders can restrict the transferability of their shares by requiring that the corporation or existing shareholders be given the first option to purchase any shares from a person desiring to sell them. The large corporation issues so many shares that it usually cannot restrict their transferability. Thus, although the original owners of a corporation can take measures to ensure their ownership of enough shares to counteract any other shareholders, in recent years many corporate takeovers have been effected by outsiders who bought shares of selected publicly traded corporations.

Continuity

Continuity is a problem for both the proprietorship and the partnership. A sole proprietor's business must be liquidated on the owner's death unless it can be quickly sold to a new owner who will continue to operate it. Every time a partner dies, resigns, or leaves a partnership, the existing partnership is automatically dissolved, though a new one may be created to continue the business. Dissolution sometimes requires notification of all the creditors of the partnership. The withdrawing partner's capital must be paid off by the old partnership.

A partnership agreement can simplify some of the problems of partnership continuity. Transitions can be eased by the partnership's purchase of life insurance on the partners, with the partnership as the beneficiary, or by the maintenance of separate funds for payment to a withdrawing partner. Unlike dissolution of the proprietorship, dissolution of the partnership generally does not require it to liquidate or to cease doing business. However, the partnership must be able to pay off the withdrawing partner and prepare a new partnership agreement among the remaining partners.

Dissolution of a partnership can sometimes be handled internally by making adjustments in its financial and accounting records that do not adversely affect its business operations. Nevertheless, both the proprietorship and the partnership face continuity problems that must be dealt with. On the other hand, the corporation's existence is generally perpetual and its continuity is unaffected by the withdrawal of any one shareholder, key officer, or employee.

SUMMARY

Three main types of business organization are reviewed in this chapter: the proprietorship, the partnership, and the corporation. The proprietorship, which is the easiest to form, has no special legal status distinct from that of its owner. The partnership involves two or more persons who jointly carry on a business for profit. It is generally formed by a partnership agreement specifying the duties of the partners toward other partners and third parties.

Several other types of businesses are similar to the partnership. The joint venture and the limited partnership are used in special situations by persons who seek to combine partnership characteristics with attributes of other business organizations. Because a partner in a partnership may act as both its principal and its agent, he or she has duties and rights that define the relationships among the partners. The partners generally have authority to bind the partnership in normal business activities, and the partnership is liable for contracts made or torts committed by the partners.

The corporation is a desirable form of organization for many business activities. Essential characteristics of the corporation are its separate entity status, its limited liability, its ease of ownership transfer, and its perpetual life. A corporation is formed by filing articles of incorporation in a state office. Large for-profit private firms are the most noticeable corporations, but nonprofit corporations, professional corporations, public corporations, and closely held corporations, including limited liability companies and S corporations, are also common.

The bylaws of a corporation determine how it is organized. Shareholders, directors, and officers each perform distinct roles in the activities of the corporation. The shareholder-owners select the board of directors and vote to ratify or reject extraordinary corporate decisions. The directors are responsible for formulating and overseeing the corporation's management policies. The officers are responsible for the corporation's day-to-day operations.

In determining whether a proprietorship, a partnership, or a corporation is most suitable in a given situation, four factors are often examined. The taxation, liability, control, and continuity aspects of these forms of business organization generally are critical to a determination of the form that best fits the needs of a particular business.

KEY TERMS

sole proprietorship, p. 384
partnership, p. 385
franchise, p. 393
corporation, p. 394
separate entity, p. 396
limited liability, p. 396
limited liability company, p. 399
S corporation, p. 400
shareholders, p. 402
directors, p. 402
officers, p. 402

CHAPTER EXERCISES

1. Match each of the forms of business organizations listed in Column A with the appropriate statement in Column B.

A	B
1. Franchise	*a.* An artificial being created by the state
2. Propriertorship	*b.* Created when shareholders elect to be treated as partners for tax purposes
3. Partnership	*c.* An entity in which some partners are treated like shareholders for liability purposes
4. Limited partnership	*d.* Created by an agreement between two or more persons who agree to share its profits and losses
5. Corporation	*e.* Owned by one person who is personally liable for all of its losses
6. S corporation	*f.* A privilege granted or sold, such as the privilege of using a name or a process to sell products or services agreed upon between two parties
7. Joint venture	*g.* Two or more persons joined in a business activity that is limited to a specified period

2. A and B, two sisters, operate a decorating firm. They advertise under the firm name in the local newspaper and on letterhead stationery. Sister A recruits most of the firm's clients and contracts for its major jobs. When the time comes to divide the firm's profits, Sister B sues Sister A, claiming that they had formed a partnership and that the profits should be divided equally. Do you agree?

3. Joe and Tom are partners in the Classic Car business. While Joe is driving a customer in a Jaguar that is part of the inventory of the business, he is involved in an accident in which the customer is injured. The customer sues the partners individually and the partnership. Who can be held liable?

4. Jones, a limited partner in a fast-food franchise, invests $100,000 in the limited partnership. Explain (a) the requirements for the formation of the limited partnership, (b) whether the limited partner's interest may be transferred to his wife on his death, and (c) whether or to what extent the limited partner may be held liable for partnership debts.

5. John and Richard are wealthy businessmen in a high-income tax bracket. They wish to enter into a business venture with a high risk of potential product liability suits. They expect a loss for the first three years of the business, owing to significant capital expenses and the difficulty of entering the market. What form of business organization would be best for them? Explain.

6. A, B, and C are partners in a delivery business. The partnership owns three delivery trucks. Jones, a creditor of C, obtains a judgment against C and asks the court to issue a writ of execution and attach one of the delivery trucks. The court sells the

truck at an auction to pay off C's debt. Did Jones have the right to attach the partnership's delivery truck?

7. A and B are partners in a small business. B borrows $50,000 at the bank to purchase a new Mercedes for his personal use. Subsequently, B defaults on the loan amount and the bank repossesses the Mercedes. However, there is not enough value to pay off the remaining loan amount. May the bank take action against the partnership?

8. Roberta Goza owned 100 percent of the shares of the Alan Mills, Inc. corporation. She was in charge of the day-to-day operations of the corporation and wrote checks on the corporation's account to a business owned by her son and to herself. She says the transactions between herself and the corporation were legitimate business transactions. There is no evidence of any fraud or wrongdoing regarding any of those transactions. The corporation had signed promissory notes to Wright and then failed to pay. Can Wright hold Ms. Goza liable on the notes? *Wright v. Alan Mills, Inc.*, 567 So. 2d 1318 (Ala., 1990).

9. Figuerdo located undeveloped land in Orange County, Florida, that he thought would be a good investment. Figuerdo then formed a corporation under the laws of the Netherlands Antilles (a tax haven) to purchase the land. He told the investors that the cost of purchasing the land would be over $66,000 per acre and offered stock to investors in the corporation that then took title to the land. Meanwhile, Figuerdo made a tentative agreement to pay the owners approximately $43,000 an acre for the land. Figuerdo and the sellers agreed to have the documents show his cost of acquiring the land was $66,000 per acre instead of $43,000 and they split the difference between them. Once the investors found that Figuerdo had profited, they sued Figuerdo for the profits. Figuerdo then proved that the actual value of the land he acquired at the time of the trial had risen to well over $66,000 an acre. He asserts the investors have no claim because they did not lose money. Do you agree? *Tinwood N.V. v. SunBanks, Inc.*, 570 So. 2d 955 (1990).

10. In 1984, Wright Furniture Mills (Wright) sold furniture to the Bedtime Sleep Shop. The Shop was incorporated in 1983 and purchased by Sherill in 1985. Although Sherill did not keep great records of the corporation's activities, there is no evidence that Wright believed it was doing business with Sherill rather than with the Shop corporation. Wright sold its account receivable (the right to receive payment from the Shop) to Commonwealth Financial Corporation. That corporation sued Sherill individually for the corporation's debt. Can it collect? *Commonwealth Financial Corp. v. Sherill*, 398 S.E. 2d 438 (Ga. App., 1990).

11. Assume that you are an executive in a small office furniture firm. A former classmate whom you knew while studying at Alpha University asks you to become a member of the board of directors of the computer software firm he and another associate founded. After serving on the board for several years, you find that your former classmate and friend is making misstatements to banks and other potential investors in the firm regarding the firm's present work on several specialized projects. You also suspect that financial documents given to these parties by your friend, the chief operating officer of the firm, are incomplete.

    Do you discuss what you know and suspect with your friend, the corporate officer? Should you reveal this information to the banks and potential investors? If you were asked for your opinion regarding the status of the company and the integrity and ability of its officers by bank officials or potential investors, what would you say?

12. You and two friends want to form a partnership business that will import certain textiles from several companies in southeast Asia. One of these friends already has an import business dealing with several of these companies in different but related products. That friend wants to continue his own separate importing business. You worry that the Asian firms might sometimes deal with your friend in his own business rather than with the partnership. What ethical problems could confront your friend if he operates both businesses? What possible solutions could be recommended?

Chapter 14

SECURITIES REGULATIONS

KEY CONCEPTS

The securities laws provide fairness in the securities markets so firms can reliably raise capital. The Securities Act of 1933 regulates initial public offerings of new securities. The Securities Exchange Act of 1934 regulates the stock exchanges, brokers and dealers, insider trading, proxy solicitations, and tender offers.

The Securities Act of 1933 prohibits the sale of unregistered new securities. In addition to the traditional corporate stocks and bonds, securities include other novel investment contracts involving an investment of money into a common enterprise, where the investor is led to expect profits from the efforts of others.

Insider trading is the illegal use of misappropriated confidential information to trade in an issuer's securities. The practice is outlawed by § 16(b) of the Securities Exchange Act of 1934 for officers, directors and 10 percent shareholders. Additionally, insider trading is illegal as a form of securities fraud under Rule 10b-5 and other special statutes.

Proxy solicitors request shareholders' votes in directors' elections and on fundamental corporate changes. SEC proxy rules require solicitors to give shareholders accurate information to vote responsibly.

The Williams Act regulates how tender offers are conducted. This provides shareholders time to consider the tender offer's term and understand the tender offer bidder's intentions and financial capabilities.

INTRODUCTION: . . . PAST, PRESENT, FUTURE

Before the Great Depression, there was little regulation of the securities markets. *Laissez-faire* allowed the markets to police themselves. Investors were protected only by the state common law remedies for fraud and breach of contract. However, the unregulated market ideal was abandoned after the 1929 stock market crash. Congress, the states, and other nations' governments have the responsibility to reduce the kind of securities fraud rampant during the "Roaring Twenties."

Today, securities markets in the United States are probably the most efficient in the world providing the greatest liquidity of any market. This means there are usually enough buyers and sellers present to satisfy any trader's supply or demand. The U.S. securities markets provide better access to capital than any other securities market. However, the influence of markets in several other nations is growing rapidly.

Despite these strengths, the world's markets are still experiencing turmoil from the 1980s stock market crashes and the worldwide recession. Revelations of insider trading and financial fraud may hurt the credibility of the capital markets. Skepticism about the excesses of the highrolling, freewheeling 1980s has eroded investor confidence. Stock scandals in the United States, Japan, and Europe are constantly in the news. Many people believe that takeover activity is excessive. This has led to restrictions on takeover tactics, leveraged buyouts (LBOs), and numerous trading strategies. Regulators and the securities exchanges have installed computerized systems to track transactions by identifying the parties, their floor traders, the timing of actual trades, and the prices prevailing at that time. These enforcement mechanisms deter insider trading, financial fraud, and floor traders' conflicts of interest. Brokerage and investment banking firms are reducing staff worldwide to cope with lower projected activity in the 1990s.

In the future, the investment markets will become more globalized. Investors in one nation will quickly and easily make trades in other nations' markets. Twenty-four-hour trading will occur in many stocks somewhere in the world. Much of this new trading will occur electronically. Investment industry regulation over the activities of investment advisors, investment companies (mutual funds), financial planners, and investment bankers will probably increase. Regulators of the various nations' capital markets will adopt similar regulations. This will become a form of regulatory equilibrium as more stringent regulations ease and lax regulations increase. Nations with guarded markets will be unable to attract the cross-border flow of capital. Although drastically different securities laws in the United States are unlikely, periodic adjustments are inevitable as the world markets evolve.

OVERVIEW

This chapter reviews the securities laws and their effect on business efforts to raise capital. Businesses must take great care when issuing new securities, and when their securities are traded on the stock exchanges. The primary securities statutes are introduced in the first section. Next, the process of registering new securities for initial public offerings and disclosing corporate information is examined. Then, three contemporary problem areas are examined: insider trading, proxy solicitations, and tender offers. Insider trading regulation is intended to prevent corporate managers from abusing their fiduciary duties. Proxy regulation seeks to provide for corporate democracy. Finally, the tender offer regulations create a level playing field in contests for corporate control, thereby permitting rational shareholder action.

ETHICAL DILEMMAS IN THE SECURITIES MARKETS

Should management use its control over corporate affairs to hide its performance from shareholders and the public? Corporate information is owned by the firm and is ultimately produced for the benefit of shareholders. Material inside information may not be misappropriated for personal use by anyone, such as for a manager's inside trading. The securities markets, exchanges, and securities professionals serve the public by providing places for firms to raise capital and for investors to trade reliably and with confidence that the markets are fair. Actions that compromise these fiduciary duties show an unethical advantage over the beneficiaries of the trust and subvert the system. The securities laws legislate corporate morality. Managers have a disclosure duty so as to limit secrecy, making them more responsive to shareholders. This improves the integrity of the capital markets by making them appear to be a "fair game."

THE PRIMARY FEDERAL SECURITIES STATUTES

The United States has two main securities laws and several related amendments and ancillary laws. Other nations generally have some form of primary securities law, although they may differ widely in form and substance. For example, U.S. forces occupying Japan after World War II insisted that Japan's national legislature, the Diet, enact securities laws nearly identical to the U.S. law. However, Japan relies more heavily on consensus building than on governmental enforcement. Therefore, although insider trading is technically illegal in Japan and in most other nations, regulators have not always enforced their laws as rigorously as have U.S. regulators. As the world's investors realize that unregulated markets become rigged and unfair, capital will move into those markets with comprehensive and just securities laws.

Securities Act of 1933

The Securities Act of 1933 (1933 Act) is the original federal statute regulating the securities business. It was passed as part of President Franklin D. Roosevelt's New Deal. The 1933 Act requires firms that issue new securities to provide investors with financial information. These new securities must be registered with the Securities and Exchange Commission (SEC) as discussed later. Penalties are imposed for fraud and misrepresentation. The 1933 Act regulates **initial public offerings** (IPOs). For example, when Apple Computer "went public" its stock was registered before being sold to public investors.

Securities Exchange Act of 1934

Congress created the SEC in 1934 to administer the 1933 Act and an additional new securities law, the Securities Exchange Act of 1934 (1934 Act). The 1934 Act regulates the secondary trading markets for securities traded on an exchange, such as the New York Stock Exchange or the American Stock Exchange. The 1934 Act outlaws fraud in securities transactions, prohibits insider trading, and regulates corporate democracy (proxies and tender offers). Brokers, dealers, investment advisors, issuers, and exchanges must also register with the SEC. The 1934 Act requires continuous disclosure of pertinent corporate financial information (e.g., annual reports). The SEC is responsible for licensing, collecting disclosure information, and enforcing the various securities law requirements and prohibitions. Most other nations already have a regulator similar to the SEC, although these agencies' powers vary greatly. For example, as a result of the "kickback" scandals implicating several Japanese brokerage houses in 1991, Japan is seriously considering an agency independent of the Ministry of Finance to regulate its securities markets. By contrast, Canadian securities markets are regulated largely by Canadian provincial regulators, not by the Canadian central government.

INTERNATIONAL PERSPECTIVE: SECURITIES REGULATORS

The SEC is aggressively expanding its influence over international securities transactions through its Office of International Affairs. The International Securities Enforcement Cooperation Act of 1990 encourages the SEC to cooperate with other nations' securities regulators. The SEC has negotiated Memoranda of Understanding (MOU) with foreign securities regulators facilitating investigation of cross-border securities violations and enforcement actions in both nations. The SEC is actively engaged with these regulators to harmonize the differences between U.S. and foreign securities laws. Broad differences attract illegal activities to those nations with lax regulations. Most nations are beginning to recognize that this "race to the bottom" eventually results in harmful intermarket distortions causing investors to lose confidence that the capital markets are fair.

REGISTRATION OF SECURITIES

The initial public offering of new securities raises funds from the investing public to finance business operations. Underwriting is the process used to initially distribute a new issue of securities. Often, a closely held corporation like Apple Computer (the **issuer**) negotiates an underwriting contract with a group of underwriters, known as the *investment banking syndicate*. The underwriters may make a firm commitment to sell the whole issue. The syndicate takes the risk that the securities may not sell well because it promises to pay the issuer a specified amount of proceeds. Firms that are not yet well established may be unable to use this "wholesaling" form of underwriting. For such new firms, the underwriter acts only as a sales agent promising to make its "best efforts" to sell all the newly offered securities.

The 1933 Act broadly defines **underwriters** to include: (1) any person who has purchased from an issuer with a view to distribute the security, or (2) any person who offers or sells any security for an issuer in connection with a distribution. Underwriters must take great care because they may be liable for violating the 1933 Act. Unintentional liability is also possible if someone is inadvertently designated as an underwriter. Underwriting occurs whenever an individual or firm receives compensation for selling an issuer's securities for the issuer's benefit. This activity is restricted by the 1933 Act.

Registration Statement and Prospectus

The 1933 Act requires issuers to provide investors with sufficient financial information to make an informed investment decision. It requires issuers to provide a **prospectus**, illustrated in Figure 14–1. The prospectus is the primary sales and promotional tool in securities sales.

FIGURE 14–1

(b) Information contained herein is subject to completion or amendment. A registration statement relating to these securities has been filed with the Securities and Exchange Commission. These securities may not be sold nor may offers to buy be accepted prior to the time the registration statement becomes effective. This prospectus shall not constitute an offer to sell or the solicitation of an offer to buy nor shall there be any sale of these securities in any State in which such offer, solicitation or sale would be unlawful prior to registration or qualification under the securities laws of any such State.

NUVEEN

PROSPECTUS

Subject to Completion
May 3, 1989

10,000,000 Shares

Nuveen Performance Plus Municipal Fund, Inc.

Common Stock

Nuveen Performance Plus Municipal Fund, Inc. (the "Fund") is a newly organized, closed-end, diversified management investment company. The Fund's primary investment objective is current income exempt from Federal income tax, and its secondary objective is the enhancement of portfolio value through the selection of tax-exempt bonds and municipal market sectors that, in the opinion of the Fund's investment adviser, are undervalued. *See* "Investment Objectives and Policies." The Fund will seek to achieve its investment objectives by investing in a diversified portfolio of investment grade quality tax-exempt Municipal Obligations (as defined herein). No assurances can be given that the Fund's investment objectives will be achieved. The Fund's principal office is located at 333 West Wacker Drive, Chicago, Illinois 60606, and its telephone number is (312) 917-7825. Investors are advised to read this Prospectus and retain it for future reference.

The Fund's Board of Directors may in the future authorize the issuance of shares of preferred stock in order to provide leverage to the Common Stock, if the Board should determine that such leverage would be advantageous to the Common Shareholders under then existing and projected market conditions. No decision has yet been made by the Board to issue preferred stock, and the Fund does not anticipate the issuance of preferred stock under current market conditions. *See* "Special Leverage Considerations" and "Description of Capital Stock."

Prior to this offering, there has been no public market for the Common Stock. Application will be made to list the Common Stock on the New York Stock Exchange.

THESE SECURITIES HAVE NOT BEEN APPROVED OR DISAPPROVED BY THE SECURITIES AND EXCHANGE COMMISSION NOR HAS THE COMMISSION PASSED UPON THE ACCURACY OR ADEQUACY OF THIS PROSPECTUS. ANY REPRESENTATION TO THE CONTRARY IS A CRIMINAL OFFENSE.

	Price to Public	Underwriting Discounts and Commissions	Proceeds to the Fund(1)
Per Share	$15.00	$	$
Total(2)	$150,000,000	$	$

(a)

(1) Before deduction of expenses payable by the Fund, estimated at $

(2) The Fund has granted to the Underwriters an option, exercisable for 30 days from the date of this Prospectus, to purchase up to 1,500,000 additional shares to cover over-allotments, if any. To the extent that such option is exercised in full, the total Price to Public will be $172,500,000, total Underwriting Discounts and Commissions will be $, and total Proceeds to the Fund will be $. *See* "Underwriting."

The Common Stock is offered by the several Underwriters, subject to prior sale, when, as and if delivered to and accepted by them, and subject to the right of the Underwriters to reject any order in whole or in part. It is expected that delivery of the shares will be made at the offices of Alex. Brown & Sons Incorporated, Baltimore, Maryland, on or about , 1989.

Alex. Brown & Sons
Incorporated

John Nuveen & Co.
Incorporated

A. G. Edwards & Sons, Inc.

Blunt Ellis & Loewi
Incorporated

Dain Bosworth
Incorporated

Legg Mason Wood Walker
Incorporated

The date of this Prospectus is , 1989.

The preliminary (Red Herring) prospectus is identical to the formal prospectus except the price and date are omitted (a): A red colored warning is printed in the margins (b): and the final prospectus may be corrected or updated.

Prospectus

Any notice, circular, advertisement, letter, or communication, written or by radio or television which offers any security for sale or confirms the sale of any security.

Issuers must also file a *registration statement* with the SEC. Both of these documents must include or refer to the issuer's financial statements.

The *statutory* or *formal prospectus* is a specific document that contains basic information presumably of use in evaluating the securities. Fundamental information must be disclosed about the terms of the security and the issuer's financial condition.

Information Required in a Prospectus

1. Audited financial statements.
2. Five years of comparative financial information.
3. Management's discussion and analysis of financial condition.
4. Information describing the issuer's management.
5. A description of the security offered.
6. An explanation of how the proceeds will be used.

Well-established issuers may omit certain financial information by referring to it if contained in a current annual and quarterly report. The issuer must first negotiate with the underwriting syndicate and prepare the prospectus and registration statement. Thereafter, the *prefiling period* ends when the registration statement is filed with the SEC.

The Registration Process

Sales of securities are not permitted in the United States until the securities are registered with the SEC. *Sales* include contracts of sale or transfers of any interest in a security for value. "Gun-jumping" (preconditioning the market) during the prefiling period is prohibited to the issuer, its underwriter, and the investment banking syndicate. *Preconditioning* occurs when statements suggest a new securities offering is imminent. For example, press releases or speeches that predict, project, forecast, or estimate the new security's value are prohibited preconditioning because they can create demand before investors can adequately evaluate the issuer's financial statements. The issuer should continue to advertise its products and respond truthfully to inquiries by shareholders or securities analysts. The appearance of business as usual should be maintained during the prefiling period, however, since publicity about the expected new securities must be avoided.

The *waiting period* begins when the issuer files a registration statement with the SEC. No sales are permitted during this period. However, *statutory offers* to sell or buy are permitted as long as the offer only indicates the interest to sell or buy. Other permissible communications during the waiting period include: (1) *tombstone ads*—simple announcements with black borders resembling tombstones, usually appearing in the financial press, (2) the preliminary or *red herring prospectus* that conspicuously disclaims any formal offer, (3) *formal oral offers* that have not yet been accepted, and (4) the *summary prospectus* containing condensed information. All other forms of sales effort are illegal during the waiting period.

The effective date of the registration statement signals the beginning of actual sales during the *post-effective period.* This usually begins 20 days after the registration statement is filed unless the SEC accelerates the effective date or threatens to halt sales. A fully amended final prospectus must be sent along with all confirmations of sale, all deliveries of securities, written offers, and distributions of supplementary sales literature. The issuer, underwriters, dealers, and brokers are responsible to deliver a prospectus to all potential buyers. The initial sales period lasts for about 40 days or until all of the new

FIGURE 14–2
SEC Registration Process

	Prefiling Period	File with SEC	**Waiting Period** 20 days or until SEC accelerates effective date of registration statement	Registration effective	**Posteffective Period** 40 days or until all the securities have been sold to investors
Prohibited actions	No contracts to sell securities No announcements conditioning the market (gun jumping)		No contracts to sell securities		No preliminary or "red herring" prospectuses
Permitted/ required actions	Can contact investment bankers for advice Can negotiate with underwriters for possible participation in underwriting syndicate Must prepare registration statement, preliminary prospectus, and supporting documents for SEC filing Must maintain "business as usual" communications with security holders, customers, suppliers, the press, and securities analysts		Can publish or distribute statutory offers to buy or sell securities, including: Tombstone ads Preliminary prospectus Formal oral offers Summary prospectuses Distribution of preliminary "red herring" prospectus		Must forward formal prospectus before or with all confirmations of sales, deliveries of securities Must attempt to sell all of the newly registered securities unless registered as a shelf offering

issue is sold. The SEC's review of the registration statement does not ensure the accuracy of the issuer's claims nor does the SEC verify the securities as good investments. The three stages of SEC registration are illustrated in Figure 14–2.

Shelf Registration

Under traditional underwriting, the issuer must attempt to sell all the securities immediately after the registration becomes effective. However, *shelf registration* is an alternative process permitting the issuer to comply with the complex registration procedures well before the proceeds are needed. Thereafter, the preregistered securities are effectively held in inventory "on the shelf" until financing is needed and market conditions become optimal. Issuers often sell shelf securities directly to investors and avoid some underwriting costs.

INTERNATIONAL PERSPECTIVE: UNIVERSAL BANKING

Initial public offerings (IPOs) in some foreign nations do not follow the complex and costly process described above. For example, even though the securities laws of the European Community (EC) require IPO registration similar to the United States, the Germans have received an exception for their practice of "universal banking." The big German commercial banks are also investment bankers. They assemble an underwriting syndicate to sell IPO securities. Such dual purpose banking is illegal in the United States under the Glass-Stegall Act and is prohibited in many other nations. The Germans generally do not register new IPO securities. German disclosure law requires the issuer to provide much less information to potential shareholders than is required in the United States, particularly about management's activities. At this writing, there are efforts under way in the United States to permit universal banking. However, this U.S. banking reform process is complex and may never become the equivalent of German universal banking.

What Is a "Security?"

The securities laws regulate only those investments known as "securities." An abstract definition of a security might be: an intangible transaction or contract right requiring one party to make a future performance or payment to another party. Although the term security has acquired several colloquial meanings (i.e., collateral, reduced risk, or danger), a narrower meaning is used in the securities laws because of strict SEC regulation.

Security

The term *security* means any note, stock, treasury stock, bond, debenture, evidence of indebtedness, transferable share, investment contract, voting trust certificate, certificate of deposit for a security, fractional undivided interest in oil, gas, or other mineral rights, any put, call, straddle, stock option, warrant, or in general, any interest or instrument commonly known as a "security."

Generally, any instrument that is on the statutory list is a security covered by the securities laws. However, purely commercial, consumption, or consumer transactions are an exception. For example, exceptions apply to short-term commercial paper (corporate IOUs maturing in 9 months or less) and to notes that facilitate trade credit, facilitate sales of minor or consumer assets, or correct the seller's cashflow difficulties. Although the statutory wording seems to apply to *any* note, these exceptions extend to any note that bears a "family resemblance" to those intended for commercial or consumer purposes. *Reves v. Ernst & Young*[1] held that notes are securities depending on the following four factors: (1) the parties' purposes, (2) the seller's distribution plan, (3) the public expectation for securities law protection, and (4) whether another factor reduces the instrument's risk so the protection of the securities laws becomes unnecessary.

The factors just mentioned also determine which instruments are investment contracts and therefore regulated securities. Such instruments include: limited partnership interests, equipment trust certificates, some types of franchises, and pyramid selling schemes. How should a new type of investment contract be analyzed to determine whether it is a regulated security? The following case illustrates the elements of nontraditional securities, which include: (1) an investment of money, (2) in a common enterprise, (3) from which the investor is led to expect profits, (4) derived solely from the promoter's efforts.

---

[1]*Reves v. Ernst & Young*, 110 S.Ct. 945 (1990).

S.E.C. v. Howey
328 U.S. 293 (1946)
United States Supreme Court

Several investors purchased parcels of a common orange grove in Florida as part of the capital-raising efforts of the W.J. Howey Company. Each of the prospective purchasers was offered both a land sale contract and a service contract for planting, harvesting, and marketing the crop. Howey-in-the-Hills, a subsidiary of W.J. Howey, provided the cultivation services for 85 percent of the land sales. The 10-year service contracts granted Howey-in-the-Hills full and complete possession of the acreage. The various parcels of land were contiguous, and no fences or markers divided the investors' land. The harvested crop was pooled, and the purchasers shared profits in proportion to the land they owned. The average investors were nonresident professionals with no expertise in citrus growing. Most of the purchasers were patrons of an adjacent hotel that assisted in marketing these investments. The SEC challenged the sales program alleging the sale of unregistered securities.

Justice Murphy delivered the opinion of the Court.

Section 2 (1) of the Act defines the term "security" to include the commonly known documents traded for speculation or investment. This definition also includes "securities" of a more variable character, designated by such descriptive terms as "certificate of interest or participation in any profit-sharing agreement," "investment contract" and "in general, any interest or instrument commonly known as a 'security.' " The legal issue in this case turns upon a determination of whether, under the circumstances, the land sales contract, the warranty deed and the service contract together constitute an "investment contract" within the meaning of § 2 (1). An investment contract came to mean a contract or scheme for "the placing of capital or laying out of money in a way intended to secure income or profit from its employment." An investment contract for purposes of the Securities Act means a contract, transaction or scheme whereby a person invests his money in a common enterprise and is led to expect profits solely from the efforts of the promoter or a third party, it being immaterial whether the shares in the enterprise are evidenced by formal certificates or by nominal interests in the physical assets employed in the enterprise. It embodies a flexible rather than a static principle, one that is capable of adaptation to meet the countless and variable schemes devised by those who seek the use of the money of others on the promise of profits.

The transactions in this case clearly involve investment contracts as so defined. The respondent companies are offering something more than fee simple interests in land, something different from a farm or orchard coupled with management services. They are offering an opportunity to contribute money and to share in the profits of a large citrus fruit enterprise managed and partly owned by respondents. They are offering this opportunity to persons who reside in distant localities and who lack the equipment and experience requisite to the cultivation, harvesting and marketing of the citrus products. Such persons have no desire to occupy the land or to develop it themselves; they are attracted solely by the prospects of a return on their investment. Indeed, individual development of the plots of land that are offered and sold would seldom be economically feasible due to their small size. Such tracts gain utility as citrus groves only when cultivated and developed as component parts of a larger area. A common enterprise managed by respondents or third parties with adequate personnel and equipment is therefore essential if the investors are to achieve their paramount aim of a return on their investments. Their respective shares in this enterprise are evidenced by land sales contracts and warranty deeds, which serve as a convenient method of determining the investors' allocable shares of the profits. The resulting transfer of rights in land is purely incidental.

Thus all the elements of a profit-seeking business venture are present here. The investors provide the capital and share in the earnings and profits, the promoters manage, control and operate the enterprise. It follows that the arrangements whereby the investors' interests are made manifest involve investment contracts, regardless of the legal terminology in which such contracts are clothed. The investment contracts in this instance take the form of land sales contracts, warranty deeds and service contracts which respondents offer to prospective investors. And respondents' failure to abide by the statutory and administrative rules in making such offerings, even though the failure result from a bona fide mistake as to the law, cannot be sanctioned under the Act.

Case Questions

1. What are the four elements of an "investment contract"?
2. How did the Court rationalize including a land sale within the definition of a security?
3. What role was played in the Court's decision by the investors' need for the protection of the securities laws? Would the outcome have been different if the investors were sophisticated local citrus growers?

Later cases have refined the *Howey* concept when applied to novel and innovative instruments. For example, a security was offered when a seller issued warehouse receipts to each purchaser of aging scotch whiskey.[2] The receipts were to be repurchased later and the scotch blended by the seller for resale. The sale of all the common stock of a business to a buyer who intended to personally run the business was not considered exempt, rejecting the so-called *sale of business* doctrine.[3]

In several instances, courts have refused to find that a particular contract was a security. For example, an employee's interest in a noncontributory and compulsory pension plan is not a security. The so-called "stock," which permitted a tenant to lease a publicly subsidized co-op apartment, was not a security. These "stock certificates" lacked the traditional aspects of a security such as the right to vote, a share in profits, or the potential for capital gains appreciation.

INTERNATIONAL PERSPECTIVE: CROSS-BORDER TRADING

How do citizens of one nation trade on foreign stock exchanges or invest in securities of other nations' firms? Traditionally, U.S. citizens have invested in *American Depository Receipts* (ADRs), certificates that represent foreign securities held by a foreign trustee. ADRs are considered securities under the 1933 Act. Additionally, some foreign firms' securities are registered to trade directly on United States exchanges. The big brokerage firms from most industrialized nations have established foreign branch offices to execute trades ordered by customers in other nations. Trading links are developing between various foreign securities exchanges, permitting brokers to receive price quotes and last-sale information on a foreign nation's securities exchange. Outside the United States, the world's major stock exchanges include: Canada (Toronto and Montreal), United Kingdom (London), Japan (Tokyo), Hong Kong, Australia (Sydney), Germany (Frankfurt), France (Paris), Switzerland (Zurich), Italy (Milan), Netherlands (Amsterdam), Sweden (Stockholm), Belgium (Brussels), and Spain (Madrid). Other markets are emerging in much of the third world and Eastern Europe. The definition of a security varies somewhat among these nations.

[2] *S.E.C. v. Haffenden-Rimar Intl., Inc.*, 496 F.2d 1192 (4th Cir. 1974).

[3] *Landreth Timber Co. v. Landreth*, 471 U.S. 681 (1985).

Securities regulators often seek to regulate any local impact from a foreign broker's activities in the host nation. The regulator's power depends on how much direct involvement the foreign broker has in the host nation. Foreign brokers who solicit customers, provide investment advice, or execute orders for citizens of another nation are usually subject to licensing and regulation in the host nation. Securities regulators in most industrialized nations are negotiating MOUs with other nations' securities regulators. This may provide other nations' brokers some reciprocity or it may exempt foreign brokers altogether when dealing with local customers if they deal through a correspondent local broker. Dealing with foreign brokers is one of several risks inherent in trading foreign securities. Other risks include: changes in exchange rates, delays in settlement and clearance procedures (payment and delivery of security certificates), high withholding taxes, and high transactions costs.

Exemptions from 1933 Act Registration

The IPO registration process is extremely costly. There are fees for registration, accounting, legal services, and printing often causing months of delay. However, the security markets should be available to both small and large businesses. Therefore, the 1933 Act includes some *transactional exemptions* that reduce the cost for issues of small size and limited scope or distribution. Issuers must be careful not to lose an exemption because the sale of nonexempt unregistered securities is prohibited.

An exemption exists for "any *security exchanged* by the issuer with its existing security holders exclusively when no commission . . . is paid." This exemption affects three types of corporate reorganizations: (1) voluntary recapitalizations, (2) reorganizations made by the federal courts, bankruptcy courts, or authorized state agencies, and (3) securities issued in a merger, consolidation, or other transfer of assets approved by shareholders.

Intrastate Exemption The *intrastate* offering exemption allows a complete relaxation of all registration requirements. It recognizes the federalism principle by deferring to state securities laws. The SEC's Rule 147 exempts intrastate sales that meet these requirements. First, all purchasers must be residents of the state. Second, the issuer must be domiciled and doing business within the state. Third, the issuer must satisfy three 80 percent rules: (1) at least 80 percent of the issuer's gross revenues are derived in the state, (2) 80 percent of the issuer's assets are located in the state, and (3) 80 percent of the proceeds will be spent within the state. A restrictive legend must be placed directly on intrastate security certificates warning that resale is restricted in intrastate sales. For example, consider a Pennsylvania corporation, PennCorp, which manufactures asphalt used almost exclusively to resurface Pennsylvania highways. PennCorp may avoid expensive registration if it issues stock only to Pennsylvania residents and the three 80 percent limitations are satisfied.

Small Issue Exemption Because small businesses are generally limited to raising capital through bank loans, partnerships, government loan guarantees, or venture capital, the small issue exemption opens the capital markets to small firms. Regulation A, the short form, permits the issuance of \$1.5 million of securities without a complete registration statement. Only an *offering statement* is required, and it must include unaudited financial statements and a description of the issuer and the securities offered. An offering statement, prepared with less expense than a regular registration statement, must be delivered to all potential buyers solicited in a Regulation A sale.

Private Placement Exemption The market for the private placement of securities with large institutional investors is growing rapidly. Historically, this was a market mostly for small or risky firms that issued securities such as junk bonds. Today, this market is evolving to include healthy blue-chip corporations. Private placements permit more efficient capital raising and the avoidance of most SEC regulations. Many leveraged buyout loans and asset-backed securities are privately placed; they can be kept confidential, which is attractive to issuers suffering from adverse publicity.

Regulation D combines features of small issues with private placements. Generally, sales may be made to an unlimited number of *accredited investors,* parties with financial sophistication and sufficient net worth, experience, and knowledge of securities investments able to withstand the risk: such as certain institutional investors, corporations, employee benefit plans, the issuer's upper management, and certain "well-to-do" individuals.

Rule 504 permits unregistered offerings by non-public issuers for amounts up to $1 million if the issue is registered under state blue-sky law. Rule 505 limits offerings to $5 million, and Rule 506 has no upper dollar limit. Sales under both Rule 504 and 505 may be made to no more than 35 nonaccredited and any number of accredited investors.

There is no specific disclosure requirement when sales are made to accredited investors; however, the issuer must provide them with the information they request. Publicly traded issuers must provide their current annual reports when sales are made to nonaccredited investors. Nonpublic issuers must provide information similar to a registration statement. At this writing, the SEC has proposed some cost-saving deregulation of small offerings and private placements to encourage small business financing.

Integration of Exempt Offerings The securities sold in several separate exempt transactions could really be a single plan of financing. The SEC may *integrate* or combine several separate exempt offerings if they are made too close in time and the proceeds are used for the same general purpose. Consider the example of a Michigan corporation that issued $4 million of stock under Rule 505. Soon thereafter, it made a separate intrastate offering of $2 million in promissory notes to Michigan residents claiming the two offerings were separate. However, the proceeds of both sales were used to renovate a factory, so the SEC integrated the two offerings. Because the $6 million total exceeded the dollar limit of Rule 505, the two sales were unlawful after integration.

Resale Restrictions

There are *resale restrictions* on securities sold under any one of the exemptions just discussed. Resale restrictions discourage an issuer from circumventing the registration requirements. For example, the issuer might first sell new securities as exempt but really intend that the initial purchasers immediately resell them to the public. Unsuspecting investors would be deprived of adequate disclosure.

An initial buyer who intends to purchase only for a short time and resell immediately at a profit is considered an underwriter, triggering liability. Under Rule 144, initial purchasers may resell exempt securities only if they have *investment intent,* the desire to hold the securities for longer-term investment purposes. Initial purchasers of exempted securities must hold them for a minimum period of time, periodically reselling only small quantities. The SEC requires a boldface warning of resale restrictions on exempt securities.

INTERNATIONAL PERSPECTIVE: RULE 144A

The SEC is seeking to open the U.S. markets to foreign issuers who were traditionally reluctant to subject themselves to the more stringent U.S. securities laws. SEC Rule 144A is intended to make the U.S. private placement market more attractive to foreign firms seeking confidentiality by exemption from U.S. financial disclosure rules. To accomplish this, foreign firms must qualify under a transaction exemption so their securities may not be sold or traded by the public. Only *qualified institutional buyers* (QIB) may participate in the private placement market. The QIB is generally any institutional investor with securities investments over $100 million. Thrift institutions must meet more stringent standards because of the savings and loan financial disaster in the early 1990s. The United States' innovation in internationalization of the securities markets exerts competitive pressures on other nations to open their markets to foreign issuers and investors.

Securities Act Liabilities

There are remedies under the 1933 Act to encourage compliance with registration procedures. Investors may return nonexempt unregistered securities to the issuer and demand return of their investment. They may also bring private damage actions against those responsible for material omissions or misstatements. Persons subject to this liability include the issuer, its underwriters, control persons, and any individual who signs the registration statement, such as an officer, director, or auditor.

The *due diligence* defense may be used by defendants accused of making misstatements if they prove they reasonably believed the registration statement disclosures were true. Must the various responsible parties conduct a reasonable investigation to be protected by the due diligence defense? The following classic case illustrates the nature of fraud in initial public offers and the responsibilities of the various participants.

Escott v. BarChris Construction Corp.

283 F. Supp. 643 (S.D.N.Y. 1968)
United States District Court

Purchasers of the convertible debentures of BarChris Construction Corporation sued several persons, claiming that the BarChris registration statement was false and misleading. BarChris financed and built bowling alleys during the great expansion of the bowling alley industry. The public offering of debentures was necessary to deal with a cash flow problem that arose after the industry became overbuilt. Buyers of bowling alleys began to default on their payments to BarChris. There were significant errors and omissions in the financial statements concerning BarChris's cash flow, sales, income, earnings per share, assets, and liabilities.

McLean, District Judge

Russo

Russo was, to all intents and purposes, the chief executive officer of BarChris. He was a member of the executive committee. He was familiar with all aspects of the business. He was personally in charge of dealings with the factors. He acted on BarChris's behalf in making the financing agreements.

In short, Russo knew all the relevant facts. He could not have believed that there were no untrue statements or material omissions in the prospectus. Russo has no due diligence defenses.

Vitolo and Pugliese

They were the founders of the business who stuck with it to the end. Vitolo was president and Pugliese was vice president. Pugliese in particular appears to have limited his activities to supervising the actual construction work.

Vitolo and Pugliese are each men of limited education. It is not hard to believe that for them the prospectus was difficult reading, if indeed they read it at all.

But whether it was or not is irrelevant. The liability of a director who signs a registration statement does not depend upon whether or not he read it or, if he did, whether or not he understood what he was reading.

And in any case, Vitolo and Pugliese were not as naive as they claim to be. They were members of BarChris's executive committee. At meetings of that committee BarChris's affairs were discussed at length. They must have known what was going on. Certainly they knew of the inadequacy of cash in 1961. They knew of their own large advances to the company which remained unpaid. They knew that they had agreed not to deposit their checks until the financing proceeds were received. They knew and intended that part of the proceeds were to be used to pay their own loans.

Kircher

Kircher was treasurer of BarChris and its chief financial officer. He is a certified public accountant and an intelligent man. He was thoroughly familiar with BarChris's financial affairs. He knew of the customers' delinquency problem. He knew how the financing proceeds were to be applied and he saw to it that they were so applied. He arranged the officers' loans and he knew all the facts concerning them.

Kircher's contention is that he had never before dealt with a registration statement, that he did not know what it should contain, and that he relied wholly on Grant, Ballard and Peat, Marwick to guide him. He claims that it was their fault, not his, if there was anything wrong with it. He says that all the facts were recorded in BarChris's books where these "experts" could have seen them if they had looked. He says that he truthfully answered all their questions. In effect, he says that if they did not know enough to ask the right questions and to give him the proper instructions, that is not his responsibility.

Kircher has not proved his due diligence defenses.

Birnbaum

Birnbaum was a young lawyer, admitted to the bar in 1957, who, after brief periods of employment by two different law firms and an equally brief period of practicing in his own firm, was employed by BarChris as house counsel and assistant secretary in October 1960. Unfortunately for him, he became secretary and a director of BarChris on April 17, 1961, after the first version of the registration statement had been filed with the Securities and Exchange Commission. He signed the later amendments, thereby becoming responsible for the accuracy of the prospectus in its final form. He did not participate in the management of the company.

As a lawyer, he should have known his obligations under the statute. He should have known that he was required to make a reasonable investigation of the truth of all the statements in the unexpertised portion of the document which he signed. Having failed to make such an investigation, he did not have reasonable ground to believe that all these statements were true. Birnbaum has not established his due diligence defenses except as to the audited 1960 figures.

Auslander

Auslander was an "outside" director, i.e., one who was not an officer of BarChris. He was chairman of the board of Valley Stream National Bank in Valley Stream, Long Island.

In February and early March 1961, before accepting Vitolo's invitation [to accept a place on the board], Auslander made some investigation of BarChris. He obtained Dun & Bradstreet reports which contained sales and earnings figures for periods earlier than December 31, 1960. He caused inquiry to be made of certain of BarChris's banks and was advised that they regarded BarChris favorably.

Auslander was elected a director on April 17, 1961. The registration statement in its original form had already been filed, of course without his signature. On May 10, 1961, he signed a signature page for the first amendment to the registration statement which was filed on May 11, 1961. This was a separate sheet without any document attached. Auslander did not know that it was a signature page for a registration statement. He vaguely understood that it was something "for the SEC."

In considering Auslander's due diligence defenses, a distinction is to be drawn between the expertised and nonexpertised portions of the prospectus. As to the former, Auslander knew that Peat, Marwick had audited the 1960 figures. He believed them to be correct because he had confidence in Peat, Marwick. He had no reasonable ground to believe otherwise.

As to the nonexpertised portions, however, Auslander is in a different position. He seems to have been under the impression that Peat, Marwick was responsible for all the figures. This impression was not correct, as he would have realized if he had read the prospectus carefully. Auslander made no investigation of the accuracy of the prospectus. He relied on the assurance of Vitolo and Russo, and upon the information he had received in answer to his inquiries back in February and early March.

Section 11 imposes liability in the first instance upon a director, no matter how new he is. He is presumed to know his responsibility when he becomes a director. He can escape liability only by using that reasonable care to investigate the facts which a prudent man would employ in the management of his own property. In my opinion, a prudent man would not act in an important matter without any knowledge of the relevant facts, in sole reliance upon representations of persons who are comparative strangers and upon general information which does not purport to cover the particular case.

I find and conclude that Auslander has not established his due diligence defense with respect to the misstatements and omissions in those portions of the prospectus other than the audited 1960 figures.

The Underwriters and Coleman

The underwriters other than Drexel made no investigation of the accuracy of the prospectus. One of them, Peter Morgan, had underwritten the 1959 stock issue and had been a director of BarChris. He thus had some general familiarity with its affairs, but he knew no more than the other underwriters about the debenture prospectus. They all relied upon Drexel as the "lead" underwriter.

The facts as to the extent of the investigation that Coleman made may be briefly summarized. He was first introduced to BarChris on September 15, 1960. Thereafter, he familiarized himself with general conditions in the industry, primarily by reading reports and the prospectuses of the two leading bowling alley builders, American Machine & Foundry Company and Brunswick. These indicated that the industry was still growing. He also acquired general information on BarChris by reading the 1959 stock prospectus, annual reports for prior years, and an unaudited statement for the first half of 1960.

He obtained a Dun & Bradstreet report on BarChris on March 16, 1961. He read BarChris's annual report for 1960 which was available in March.

After Coleman was elected a director on April 17, 1961, he made no further independent investigation of the accuracy of the prospectus.

In any event, it is clear that no effectual attempt at verification was made. The question is whether due diligence required that it be made. Stated another way, is it sufficient to ask questions, to obtain answers which, if true, would be thought satisfactory, and to let it go at that, without seeking to ascertain from the records whether the answers in fact are true and complete?

The purpose of Section 11 is to protect investors. To that end the underwriters are made responsible for the truth of the prospectus. If they may escape that responsibility by taking at face value representations made to them by the company's management, then the inclusion of underwriters among those liable under Section 11 affords the investors no additional protection.

In order to make the underwriters' participation in this enterprise of any value to the investors, the underwriters must make some reasonable attempt to verify the data submitted to them. They may not rely solely on the company's officers or on the company's counsel.

A prudent man in the management of his own property would not rely on them.

It is impossible to lay down a rigid rule suitable for every case defining the extent to which such verification must go. It is a question of degree, a matter of judgment in each case. In the present case, the underwriters' counsel made almost no attempt to verify management's representations. I hold that was insufficient.

Case Questions

1. What is "due diligence"? How does it differ for insiders (e.g., officers, directors) and outsiders (e.g., underwriters, auditors)?
2. Why should the signatories and preparers of the registration statement be liable for omissions or misstatements? Does this raise the cost of initial public offerings?

Persons found guilty of intentional fraud in a securities offering are liable for both civil damages and criminal penalties. Under Section 12 of the 1933 Act, it is illegal to offer or sell an unregistered security, to fail to deliver a prospectus, or to use an illegal prospectus in making illegal offers or sales during the prefiling or waiting periods. These provisions are quite successful because most issuers are careful to follow the registration and prospectus delivery requirements.

INSIDER TRADING

The 1934 Act requires firms that are publicly traded on national securities exchanges or in the over-the-counter market to disclose material information. Fraud is outlawed in connection with purchases or sales of securities. In the 1980s, the SEC and the Justice Department focused enforcement attention on insider trading as an illegal form of fraud. *Insider trading* is the practice whereby a person's access to confidential and nonpublic information gives them an unfair advantage over others in trading a firm's securities. Their silence while trading with unsuspecting investors based on confidential information is a form of fraud by omission.

Commentary: The Controversy over Insider Trading

There is considerable controversy about insider trading. Insider trading opponents argue that it is an unfair practice. Insiders have an informational advantage that cannot be overcome by outsiders no matter how diligently they compete for information or conduct legitimate research. If insider trading proliferates, a widespread perception of unfairness will arise and the public will lose confidence in the capital markets. Opponents of insider trading point to the loss of confidence accompanying the Great Depression as evidence of this detrimental effect.

On the other side of this controversy are those who oppose restricting insider trading. They claim it is a victimless crime with no negative effect because the firm's shareholders can simply prohibit the practice. Some proponents argue that insider trading opportunities should be part of a corporate manager's implied compensation package. Some proponents argue that insider trading is beneficial by contributing to a more efficient market. They claim an insider's trading sends a "signal" to the market about the direction the firm's stock price should move. Insiders buy on good news and sell on bad news, so the market may infer traders have access to confidential nonpublic information by watching the insider's trading activity. This arguably makes the market a more accurate reflection of underlying value.

The proponents of insider trading apparently ignore the reality of shareholder democracy. Shareholders are probably unable to detect insider trading, and any corporate rule prohibiting it is ineffective. The victim of insider trading would probably insist on trading at a price adjusted for the insider's nonpublic information after the information became known publicly. If insider trading was considered an implied compensation or perk, this would encourage employees to manipulate the release of corporate information to enhance their profit opportunities by increasing the firm's price volatility. Some insiders could profit from the firm's misfortunes. Such market manipulation is inconsistent with an employee's fiduciary duty. Opponents of insider trading argue that management will be forced to release information more quickly if they cannot trade on inside information. Despite this controversy, most market professionals, Congress, the courts, the SEC, and the presidential administration oppose insider trading, making it illegal.

Short Swing Profits: Section 16(b)

Congress first restricted some forms of insider trading in Section 16(b) of the 1934 Act. *Short swing profits* made by specified insiders are illegal and belong to the corporation. These occur when the insider both purchases and sells the issuer's equity securities (stock) within any six-month period. Under §16(b), *insiders* are defined as officers, directors, and 10 percent shareholders. Section 16(b) requires that the illegal trading profits be paid to the issuer.

Insiders: Officers, Directors, and 10 Percent Shareholders Section 16(a) requires that insiders report trades in their company's equity securities to the SEC. These insider trading reports are intended to facilitate enforcement but are also available to the public. Some commentators have speculated that §16(a) reports are the most commonly violated provisions of the securities laws. The SEC addressed this problem by passing new reporting rules, which now require companies to disclose when their officers' or directors' reports are delinquent. Violations can be remedied by internal SEC administrative action.

Brokerages and banks often give "officer-like" titles to middle-level managers. However, if these employees do not perform significant corporate executive decision-making functions, they are not statutory insiders. The SEC now interprets the "officer" title to include the president, any vice president in charge of a principal business function, other officers of the issuer's parent or subsidiaries who perform policy-making functions for the issuer, the principal financial officer, and the principal accounting officer.

Some "interlocking directors" hold seats on the boards of two or more corporations. This may cause either corporation to be considered an insider of the other corporation, thereby restricting it from short swing trading in the other corporation's equity securities. Interlocking directors are considered "deputies" of both corporations because they may be a convenient conduit to transfer inside information.

There are similar definitional problems with 10 percent shareholders. For example, a shareholder could buy stock in the name of a spouse, minor child, or other relative living in the shareholder's household. Although it would appear the shareholder owned less than 10 percent, they would actually have *control* over more. To avoid this, the SEC has developed the concept of *beneficial ownership*. All the shares in which a related group has a pecuniary interest are presumed to be owned by one person. This presumption is rebuttable if the shareholder can prove no actual control was exercised over the relative's shares.

FIGURE 14–3 Short Swing Profit Liability

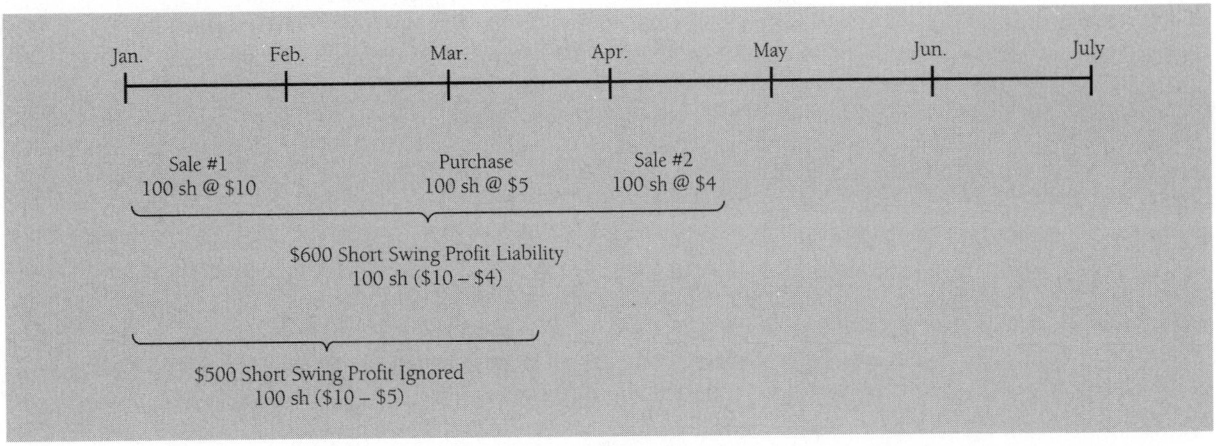

Short Swing Profit Liability A sliding six-month scale is applied to capture *any* two purchase and sale transactions within *any* six-month period. The purchase and sale requirement is satisfied by an actual transfer or even a contract to purchase or sell an equity security. Options and other derivative securities (e.g., warrants, convertible securities, stock appreciation rights) are considered purchased when they are acquired, so exercise or conversion is exempt; they are considered sold when the converted security is sold.

Short Swing Damages The corporation or any shareholder acting in its behalf may sue to recover an insider's trading profit. Damages are computed as the difference between the purchase and sale prices. These damages belong to the corporation, not to any shareholder personally. In computing short swing profits, the courts do not apply the FIFO (first-in, first-out) method of matching particular stock certificates. That is, the prices of shares purchased first are not compared with the prices of shares sold first to determine damages. Instead, the lowest purchase price and the highest sale price within any six-month period are matched, maximizing the measure of illegal trading profit.

Consider the example of an insider who sells 100 shares at $10 in January and purchases 100 shares in March at $5. Thereafter, the insider purchases another 100 shares in April at $4. The profit realized is $600 ($10 − $4 = $6 per share) even though the sale occurred first. The comparison between the $5 purchase and the $10 sale is ignored because the lower purchase price of $4 occurred within six months of the $10 sale (see Figure 14–3).

The computation of profit liability is intentionally maximized to hold insiders to a high standard of conduct by imposing a potent deterrent effect. The law prohibits sales before purchase because insiders could profit from bad news by "selling short" the issuer's securities. Although Section 16 is Congress' oldest prohibition of insider trading, much of the emphasis has shifted to insider trading illegal under SEC Rule 10b-5.

Insider Trading under the Common Law and Rule 10b-5

The common law developed a restriction against insider trading that combined the tort of deceit with the fiduciary duty concept even before Rule 10b-5 was used extensively. Insider trading was prohibited in certain "special circumstances." In the landmark 1909 case of *Strong v. Repide,*[4] a controlling stockholder failed to disclose pending merger negotiations when he purchased stock from minority shareholders.

The SEC originally passed **Rule 10b-5** in response to rumors that "the president of some company in Boston . . . is going around buying up the stock of his company from his own shareholders at $4 a share, and he has been telling them that the company has been doing very badly, whereas in fact the earnings are going to be quadrupled and will be $2 a share."[5] Rule 10b-5 has become the most pervasive antifraud provision in the securities laws.

SEC Rule 10b-5

It shall be unlawful for any person, directly or indirectly, by the use of any means or instrumentality of interstate commerce, or of the mails, or of any facility of a national securities exchange,

1. to employ any device, scheme, or artifice to defraud,
2. to make any untrue statement of a material fact or to omit to state a material fact necessary in order to make the statements made, in the light of the circumstances under which they were made, not misleading, or
3. to engage in act, practice or course of business which operates or would operate as a fraud or deceit upon any person, in connection with the purchase or sale of any security.

Rule 10b-5 requires corporate officers, directors, and any other insider to either *disclose* the inside information before they trade *or abstain* from trading altogether. This is the so-called *disclose* or *abstain* rule. This seemingly simple choice actually places the insider in a dilemma. The fiduciary duty of loyalty to the corporation would prohibit a corporate insider from revealing secret information before trading if disclosure would reveal important confidential corporate information.

This problem arose in a leading insider trading case, *SEC v. Texas Gulf Sulphur Company.*[6] The Texas Gulf Sulphur Company (TGS) made a substantial mineral discovery in Canada. In order to acquire the mineral rights on land surrounding the discovery site at favorable prices, TGS publicly denied rumors of the discovery. At the same time, some TGS employees who knew about the discovery purchased TGS stock. If these employees had disclosed the mineral discovery before purchasing TGS stock, they would have violated their fiduciary duty of confidentiality. These employees were guilty of illegal insider trading and TGS was guilty of securities fraud in making materially misleading disclosures. While TGS employees had no duty to inform surrounding landowners of the discovery before acquiring their mineral rights, a stronger duty applies to corporate insiders when trading in the securities markets.

---

[4]*Strong v. Repide,* 213 U.S. 419 (1909).

[5]Statement of Milton Freeman in American Bar Association, Section of Corporation, Banking and Business Law. Conference on Codification of the Federal Securities Laws, 22 Bus. Law. 793, 921–23 (1967).

[6]*S.E.C. v. Texas Gulf Sulphur Company,* 401 F.2d 833 (2d Cir. 1968).

ETHICAL DILEMMAS IN INSIDER TRADING

The disclose or abstain duty poses a false dilemma for managers in using the corporation's confidential inside information. If it is material financial information, management must disclose it to shareholders in periodic quarterly or annual reports. Before such reports are distributed, insiders must refrain from personal trading on it unless they first disclose the information. However, competitors can gain an advantage if such premature release reveals a corporate trade secret or strategic plan. Releasing sensitive confidential information is a breach of the manager's fiduciary duty. The profit incentive is strong, yet a manager cannot trade on the information without committing acts that are both illegal and an unethical breach of duty.

Under Rule 10b-5, insider trading is illegal in any type of security, debt, or equity, whether publicly traded or closely held. Defrauded sellers or purchasers may sue for civil damages, the SEC may bring enforcement actions and seek civil fines, and the Justice Department may prosecute insider traders by seeking fines and prison terms.

Elements of Rule 10b-5 Insider Trading Case

1. Identify the insider.
2. Hold liable persons receiving stock tips (i.e., tippees).
3. Determine the role of fiduciary duties in insider trading actions.
4. Determine the materiality of the misstatements or omissions.
5. Show reliance by the victims on the misrepresentations.
6. Show knowledge of the falsity of the statements by the misrepresentor.
7. Identify persons entitled to sue.
8. Measure the damages or penalty for insider trading.

Who is an "Insider"? Under Rule 10b-5, insiders include employees at lower levels in addition to officers and directors. Rule 10b-5 prohibits insider trading by *any* employee with access to confidential information. It also applies to certain tippees who receive inside information from insiders. The SEC established criteria for the identification of an insider in the leading case of *Cady, Roberts & Co.*[7] The trading restriction applies where: (1) a relationship gives access to information, (2) information is intended only for corporate purposes, and (3) it is used unfairly for the personal benefit of the insider.

A line of cases in the 1960s and 1970s expanded the insider concept beyond this definition. The *possession theory* or *parity of information* rule prohibited any trading by persons who had mere possession of nonpublic information. However, the Supreme Court reversed this trend in the *Chiarella*[8] case involving a financial printer's investment in

[7]In re *Cady, Roberts & Co.*, 40 SEC 907 (1961).

[8]*Chiarella v. United States*, 445 U.S. 222 (1980).

takeover targets. He had misappropriated these targets' identities from his employer. The court held that without evidence of wrongfulness, the mere possession of nonpublic information was not sufficient to prohibit trading. The Chiarella rule preserves the incentive for securities analysts to do research and investment analysis.

Tippee Liability There is a trend toward expanding insider trading liability to noninsiders. Often outside tippees receive inside information from a tip originating with an insider. What circumstances taint inside information so that outsider tippees may not trade on the information? The following case establishes the criteria for tippee liability.

Dirks v. SEC
463 U.S. 646 (1983)
United States Supreme Court

Dirks was a securities analyst for a New York broker-dealer firm. He received information from Secrist, a former officer of Equity Funding of America, that the assets of Equity Funding were vastly overstated as the result of fraudulent corporate practices. Secrist urged Dirks to investigate further. Dirks visited the corporate offices and interviewed several officers who denied any wrongdoing. However, some employees confirmed the fraud. Before Dirks notified the SEC, he openly discussed his findings with clients and fellow brokers at his firm, who in turn notified clients to liquidate nearly $16 million in Equity Funding holdings. During this period, the price of Equity Funding stock plummeted from $26 to $15. The New York Stock Exchange halted trading in Equity Funding, the SEC filed a complaint against it, and it eventually went into receivership. Dirks was censured for transmitting the inside information but was not disciplined more severely by the SEC because of his assistance in uncovering the fraud.

Justice Powell delivered the opinion of the Court.

In the seminal case of *In re Cady, Roberts & Co.,* the SEC recognized that the common law in some jurisdictions imposes on "corporate 'insiders,' particularly officers, directors, or controlling stockholders" an "affirmative duty of disclosure . . . when dealing in securities."

Unlike insiders who have independent fiduciary duties to both the corporation and its shareholders, the typical tippee has no such relationships.* In view of this absence, it has been unclear how a tippee acquires the *Cady, Roberts* duty to refrain from trading on inside information.

The SEC's position, as stated in its opinion in this case, is that a tippee "inherits" the *Cady, Roberts* obligation to shareholders whenever he receives inside information from an insider.

This view differs little from the view that we rejected as inconsistent with congressional intent in *Chiarella.*

Imposing a duty to disclose or abstain solely because a person knowingly receives material nonpublic information from an insider and trades on it could have an inhibiting influence on the role of market analysts, which the SEC itself recognizes is necessary to the pres-

*(Footnote 14) Under certain circumstances, such as where corporate information is revealed legitimately to an underwriter, accountant, lawyer, or consultant working for the corporation, these outsiders may become fiduciaries of the shareholders. The basis for recognizing this fiduciary duty is not simply that such persons acquired nonpublic corporate information, but rather that they have entered into a special confidential relationship in the conduct of the business of the enterprise and are given access to information solely for corporate purposes. When such a person breaches his fiduciary relationship, he may be treated more properly as a tipper than a tippee.

For such a duty to be imposed, however, the corporation must expect the outsider to keep the disclosed nonpublic information confidential, and the relationship at least must imply such a duty.

ervation of a healthy market. It is commonplace for analysts to "ferret out and analyze information," and this often is done by meeting with and questioning corporate officers and others who are insiders. And information that the analysts obtain normally may be the basis for judgments as to the market worth of a corporation's securities. The analyst's judgment in this respect is made available in market letters or otherwise to clients of the firm. It is the nature of this type of information, and indeed of the markets themselves, that such information cannot be made simultaneously available to all of the corporation's stockholders or the public generally.

The need for a ban on some tippee trading is clear. Not only are insiders forbidden by their fiduciary relationship from personally using undisclosed corporate information to their advantage, but they also may not give such information to an outsider for the same improper purpose of exploiting the information for their personal gain.

Thus, some tippees must assume an insider's duty to the shareholders not because they receive inside information, but rather because it has been made available to them *improperly.* And for Rule 10b-5 purposes, the insider's disclosure is improper only where it would violate his *Cady, Roberts* duty. Thus, a tippee assumes a fiduciary duty to the shareholders of a corporation not to trade on material nonpublic information only when the insider has breached his fiduciary duty to the shareholders by disclosing the information to the tippee and the tippee knows or should know that there has been a breach. As Commissioner Smith perceptively observed in *In re Investors Management Co.:* "[T]ippee responsibility must be related back to insider responsibility by a necessary finding that the tippee knew the information was given to him in breach of a duty by a person having a special relationship to the issuer not to disclose this information. . . ."

In determining whether a tippee is under an obligation to disclose or abstain, it thus is necessary to determine whether the insider's "tip" constituted a breach of the insider's fiduciary duty. . . . In some situations, the insider will act consistently with his fiduciary duty to shareholders, and yet release of the information may affect the market. For example, it may not be clear—either to the corporate insider or to the recipient analyst—whether the information will be viewed as material nonpublic information. Corporate officials may mistakenly think the information already has been disclosed or that it is not material enough to affect the market. Whether disclosure is a breach of duty therefore depends in large part on the purpose of the disclosure. This standard was identified by the SEC itself in *Cady, Roberts:* a purpose of the securities laws was to eliminate "use of inside information for personal advantage." Thus, the test is whether the insider personally will benefit, directly or indirectly, from his disclosure. Absent some personal gain, there has been no breach of duty to stockholders. And absent a breach by the insider, there is no derivative breach. As Commissioner Smith stated in *Investors Management Co.:* "It is important in this type of case to focus on policing insiders and what they do . . . rather than on policing information *per se* and its possession. . . ."

As the facts of this case clearly indicate, the tippers were motivated by a desire to expose the fraud. In the absence of a breach of duty to shareholders by the insiders, there was no derivative breach by Dirks. Dirks therefore could not have been "a participant after the fact in [an] insider's breach of a fiduciary duty."

We conclude that Dirks, in the circumstances of this case, had no duty to abstain from use of the inside information that he obtained. The judgment of the Court of Appeals therefore is *Reversed.*

Case Questions

1. When does a "tippee" inherit an insider's duty to "disclose or abstain" from trading?
2. What might have happened to analysts' incentive to investigate if the outcome in *Dirks* had been different?
3. What might constitute an "improper" motive for transferring inside information to an outsider?

The now famous *Dirks* footnote 14 established a new category of insiders: underwriters, accountants, lawyers, and other outside consultants who are *temporary insiders.* They owe a fiduciary duty to their employer and ultimately to the issuer. The corporation may expect its consultants to keep confidential any information discovered as part of the consultation.

A tippee inherits the insider's duty to disclose or abstain if the tippee knows or has reason to know of the insider's fiduciary breach in tipping the information. Dirks was not guilty as a tippee because Secrist, the insider, breached no fiduciary duty in revealing the Equity Funding fraud. A tippee is restricted from trading only if the insider conveyed the inside information *improperly*, such as when the insider expects a personal benefit from the tippee. For example, it is improper if there is an unspoken expectation that the tippee will return the favor in the future with another tip. This requirement was extended in *United States v. Chestman*,[9] which overturned the conviction of a remote tippee of inside information about a tender offer. Some commentators interpret *Chestman* as invalidating the tender offer insider trading rule (Rule 14e-3), and requiring that tippees become liable only if they had intent to deceive.

The Misappropriation Theory Under the **misappropriation theory**, it is irrelevant whether nonpublic information originates from inside or from outside the issuer whose shares are traded. It has been a common misconception that insider information can originate only from inside the issuer. However, secret information about tender offers is generally known only by outside takeover bidders, their consultants, and employees. Similar damage to the markets may occur with tender offer insider trading.

Any person, whether an insider or an outsider, who breaches their fiduciary duty by misappropriating nonpublic, confidential information may be liable for insider trading. Under the misappropriation theory, a financial printing firm employee who trades on information misappropriated from the employer is guilty of insider trading. Employees of law firms or investment banks that represent takeover participants are restricted from trading on nonpublic information learned from their employer. The misappropriation theory was established in *United States v. Newman*.[10] Employees at several investment banking firms traded on confidential takeover information they secretly exchanged before the information became public.

> "In a tender offer situation, the effect of increased activity in purchases of the target company's shares is to drive up the price of the target company's shares; but this effect is damaging to the offering company because the tender offer will appear commensurately less attractive and the activity may cause it to abort. The deceitful misappropriation of confidential information by a fiduciary, whether described as theft, conversion, or breach of trust, has consistently been held to be unlawful."

The Supreme Court has unanimously approved insider trading prosecution based on the misappropriation theory if the case is predicated on the federal mail and wire fraud statutes. However, the Supreme Court was evenly split, 4 to 4, in the famous *Wall Street Journal* "Heard on the Street" case, on whether misappropriation suits can be based on Rule 10b-5. Considerable attention in the late 1980s focused on the insider trading and securities fraud enforcement actions brought by the SEC and Justice Department against Dennis Levine, Ivan Boesky, Michael Milken, and the firm Drexel Burnham Lambert. In these cases, investment bankers and other Wall Street consultants established networks to regularly exchange inside information about companies involved in takeovers or restructuring. Although a few related convictions were reversed on technical grounds, there is widespread belief that these prosecutions have slowed the pace of insider trading. Figure 14–4 compares the two major insider trading prohibitions: Rule 10b-5 and §16(b).

---

[9]*United States v. Chestman*, 903 F.2d 75 (2d Cir. 1990).

[10]*United States v. Newman*, 664 F.2d 12 (2d Cir. 1981).

FIGURE 14–4
Insider Trading Comparison: Section 16(b) versus Rule 10b-5

	Section 16(b)	Rule 10b-5
Potential plaintiffs	Issuer or shareholder suing derivatively	SEC, Justice Department, and shareholders who trade contemporaneously with insider
Potential defendants	Statutory insiders: officers, directors, and 10% shareholders and deputies, nominees, or others performing officer-like or director-like duties	Any employee of the issuer, temporary insider, or misappropriator and certain tippees
Proof of access to and use of inside information	No proof required: access and use presumed for statutory insiders	Proof required: misappropriation or tippee status
Securities covered	Any registered equity security	Any security, registered or not
Disclosure required	Statutory insiders must report all changes in shareholdings within 15 days after any month in which a purchase or sale transaction occurs	Insider must publicly disclose inside information or abstain from trading
Tippee liability	No tippee liability	Tippee liable for insider trading if: Tippee knows or has reason to know that the tipper (insider) breached a fiduciary duty in tipping, and Tipper transferred tip for an improper purpose (i.e., personal benefit)
Damages recoverable	Match highest sale and purchase or purchase and sale within any six-month period	Disgorge illegal insider trading profit; SEC actions: ITSA treble penalty paid to U.S. Treasury; damages held in escrow for victims claimants
Criminal penalties	No criminal penalties; SEC may refer insider trading evidence to Justice Department	Justice Department may prosecute under rule 10b-5 or mail and wire fraud statutes; penalties of up to 10 years' imprisonment and $1 million fine for individuals, $2,500,000 fine for firms

Additional Insider Trading Laws

Between 1984 and 1990, Congress enacted three laws affecting insider trading prosecutions. The Insider Trading Sanctions Act of 1984 (ITSA) imposes a civil penalty of up to three times the insider's trading profit in enforcement actions brought by the SEC. The SEC has discretion to sue for the full treble penalty or for a lesser amount, which is payable into the federal treasury. ITSA actions are tried only by a judge, not a jury. The ITSA does not affect existing remedies under §16(b), Rule 10b-5, or Rule 14e-3. ITSA damages are the "profit gained or loss avoided" through illegal insider trading, computed as the difference between the insider's purchase price and the trading price right after the inside information is disclosed publicly.

The ITSA penalties are cumulative with other insider trading liabilities. For example, Ivan Boesky paid a double penalty under the ITSA and paid damages to investors who sold stock to him at lower prices than prevailed after public disclosure of the tender offers. Investors who traded contemporaneously with the insider are entitled to such damages. However, the statute of limitations applicable to civil insider trading cases for private damages requires these cases be brought within one year after the wrongful act is discovered. The SEC usually sets aside a fund for payment of disgorged profits to private insider trading victims. Boesky was also found guilty of criminal insider trading.

Congress further toughened the insider trading penalties and enforcement powers in the Insider Trading and Securities Fraud Enforcement Act of 1988 (ITSFEA). This law: (1) increases criminal penalties, (2) provides for payment of a bounty to informants, (3) requires brokers and dealers to supervise their employees to prevent tipping or insider trading, (4) establishes a statutory right for injured investors to sue for damages, and (5) gives the SEC authority to assist foreign investigations of international securities fraud.

The Enforcement Remedies and Penny Stock Reform Act of 1990 further expands the SEC's civil enforcement powers applicable to insider trading and other securities law violations. The SEC may seek money penalties and disgorgement in SEC administrative proceedings without prosecuting the defendants in federal court. Officers and directors may be debarred from practice before the SEC, effectively preventing their employment in that capacity for publicly traded companies. The SEC may issue cease and desist orders against repeat offenders. The Act significantly restructures the penny stock industry, giving the SEC powers over program trading and emergency enforcement powers over securities firms.

INTERNATIONAL PERSPECTIVE: INSIDER TRADING ABROAD

The insider trading laws in the United States are the most stringent in the world. Most nations have traditionally permitted insider trading as an innocent executive perk, or they simply ignore it or consider it no more than unethical. Insider trading enforcement in other nations is lax and few nations have cooperated fully with the SEC's enforcement of insider trading involving other nations. For example, in a 1983 case involving Santa Fe International Corp., the Swiss Supreme Court refused to adopt the misappropriation theory. Like the U.S. Supreme Court's *Chiarella* opinion, the Swiss find no direct fiduciary relationship between two strangers trading anonymously through brokers on the impersonal stock exchange.[11]

Some commentators have argued that the U.S. insider trading laws are excessively stringent, and that U.S. markets will therefore lose some trading volume to other nations' securities markets. However, there were damaging insider trading and securities fraud scandals in the early 1990s in the United Kingdom, Ireland, France, Germany, and Japan. This has aroused criticism that investors are not treated fairly in these markets because insider trading is not well regulated. Therefore, most nations are reevaluating their insider trading rules and prohibiting the practice. The SEC has negotiated bilateral accords with several nations to cooperate in insider trading enforcement.

PROXY SOLICITATIONS AND TENDER OFFERS

There is a market for corporate control in which individual financiers, takeover specialists, other corporations, and dissident shareholders struggle to own or control other corporations. The SEC is authorized to regulate how management and outsiders communicate and advocate shareholder action in proxy contests and how they implement a takeover through tender offers. The term proxy has several different meanings. In a gen-

[11] The *Santa Fe* case, 22 Intl. Leg. Mat. 785 (1983).

eral sense, *proxy* means the intangible agency or power of attorney a shareholder gives to another to vote. In corporate law, proxy refers to both the actual written ballot and to the person who actually votes. The 1934 Act confines the term proxy to "any proxy, consent, or authorization to vote shares." **Proxy solicitations** involve electioneering to convince shareholders to vote for particular proposals or director candidates, and that may affect corporate control. **Tender offers** involve outright takeover attempts, usually by nonmanagement persons who seek to purchase voting control directly from shareholders.

Proxy Solicitations

The proxy process is regulated by both state corporation statutes and the federal security laws. State law primarily regulates closely held corporations. The 1934 Act regulates proxy solicitations of shareholders in publicly traded corporations. The federal regulatory scheme attempts to maintain fairness by promoting full disclosure, prohibiting fraud, and facilitating shareholder proposals.

A proxy solicitation is usually made by either management or dissident shareholders (or both) to convince other shareholders to vote in a particular way. Proxy solicitations include a wide variety of communications and they trigger special duties under the 1934 Act. For example, proxy solicitations include any request to give or revoke a proxy, the furnishing of the proxy form itself, or advertising in newspapers, print or other media, and direct mail solicitations. They all must comply with the SEC's proxy rules.

Proxy Statements Any person soliciting proxies must file a *proxy statement* containing certain information to inform shareholders of the issues and of the solicitor's motives.

Information Required in a Proxy Statement

1. Identity of the solicitor.
2. Legal terms of the proxy itself.
3. Information concerning the election of directors.
4. Specific details about extraordinary corporate transactions (e.g., merger, recapitalizations).
5. The issuer's financial statements.

Management usually solicits proxies in directors' elections, so the SEC requires the issuer to distribute its latest annual report. This requirement has led to management's potential liabilities for proxy fraud if there are inaccuracies or misstatements in the annual report. If management decides not to solicit proxies for director elections, it must nevertheless distribute an *information statement* containing substantially the same information.

The proxy itself must be formatted much like a standard ballot, with a blank date line and boxes for each proposition permitting the shareholders' vote of approval, disapproval, or abstention (see Figure 14–5). A proxy solicited by the board of directors, or one permitting the directors to vote incomplete proxies must conspicuously state these facts directly on the proxy.

Shares are often held in *street name,* that is, in the name of a broker-dealer or nominee. These shares actually belong to the investor but are held in street name to facilitate quick settlement of trades, or the shares are held as collateral for margin loans when the investor

FIGURE 14–5

Proxy

P R O X Y

This Proxy Is Solicited on Behalf of the Board of Directors

The undersigned hereby appoints and and each of them, with full power of substitution, the proxies of the undersigned to vote all shares of Common Stock of which the undersigned is entitled to vote at the Annual Meeting of Stockholders of the corporation to be held at the principal corporate office, , on April , 19 , at 10:00 A.M. and at any adjournments or postponements thereof, with the same force and effect as the undersigned might or could do if personally present thereat.

1. ELECTION OF DIRECTORS ☐ FOR all nominees listed below *(except as marked to the contrary below)* ☐ WITHHOLD AUTHORITY to vote for all nominees listed below

(The Board of Directors recommends a vote FOR)

This proxy will be voted in the Election of Directors in the manner described in the Proxy Statement for the Annual Meeting of Stockholders
(INSTRUCTION: To withhold authority to vote for one or more individual members, write such name or names in the space provided below.)

---

2. PROPOSAL TO AMEND THE CERTIFICATE OF INCORPORATION of the Company to increase the authorized number of shares of Preferred Stock, $ 01 par value, from 1,000,000 to 10,000,000. (The Board of Directors recommends a vote FOR.)

   ☐ FOR ☐ AGAINST ☐ ABSTAIN

3. PROPOSAL TO RATIFY THE SELECTION OF , as independent public accountants for the corporation for the fiscal year ending December , 19 (The Board of Directors recommends a vote FOR)

   ☐ FOR ☐ AGAINST ☐ ABSTAIN

4. In their discretion, the Proxies are authorized to vote upon much other business as may properly come before the meeting. *(Continued on other side)*

(Continued from other side)

This proxy when properly executed will be voted in the manner directed herein by the undersigned stockholder. If no direction is made, this proxy will be voted FOR Proposals 1, 2 and 3.

Please sign exactly as name appears below. When shares are held by joint tenants, both should sign. When signing as attorney, executor, administrator, trustee or guardian please give full title as such. If a corporation, please sign in full corporate name by President or other authorized person. If a partnership, please sign in full partnership name by authorized person.

DATED________________________19

____
Signature

____
Signature if held jointly

PLEASE MARK, SIGN, DATE AND RETURN THE PROXY CARD PROMPTLY USING THE ENCLOSED ENVELOPE borrows to purchase securities. The issuer and broker-dealer must forward all proxy solicitation materials to the beneficial (actual) owner.

Proxy Contests *Proxy contests* are used increasingly in battles for control of corporations. Shareholders are best served by receiving accurate information from all proxy solicitors. Preliminary drafts of proxy solicitation materials must be filed with the SEC.

Corporate management has the most effective access to voting shareholders because management's proxy solicitation expenses are paid by the corporate treasury, and management alone possesses the lists of eligible shareholder voters. Dissident shareholders who oppose management have a more difficult time soliciting proxies. SEC regulations attempt to facilitate shareholder proxy solicitations in two ways. First, dissidents can pay for their own solicitation. Management has the option of either providing a shareholder list to dissident shareholder solicitors or mailing the dissidents' solicitation to shareholders at the dissidents' expense. The direct mailing alternative makes it difficult for dissidents to contact shareholders individually with follow-up electioneering.

Mandatory Shareholder Proxy Proposals The second shareholder solicitation method requires the corporation to pay expenses. Management must include certain shareholder proposals in management's own proxy mailing. This procedure is limited to use by small shareholders to give them at least some minimal voice in corporate elections.

An abuse of this process by small shareholders arose during the 1960s. Some politically active shareholders sought to air their personal political and social views. However, these views were arguably unconnected to the issuer's operations. For example, one shareholder opposed to the Vietnam War proposed to amend the corporate charter and prohibit it from producing napalm. The proxy process is not designed for such "political grandstanding," so the SEC tightened these requirements. Now, the dissident shareholder must have a serious financial interest in the corporation. This exists when the shareholder has held the shares for at least one year, owns at least 1 percent or $1,000 in market value of the voting securities, and can make only one proposal per year. If management desires, it can limit the dissident's proposal to no more than 500 words.

Sometimes management may omit a particular shareholder proposal if management determines the proposal violates the SEC guidelines in Rule 14a-8(c). Either the SEC or the shareholder may challenge the exclusion in the courts.

Management Exclusion of Shareholder Proposals: Rule 14a-8(c)

1. Proposal is illegal.
2. Proposal violates SEC proxy rules.
3. Proposal furthers a personal grievance.
4. Proposal is unrelated to the seller's business.
5. Proposal concerns issuer's ordinary business operations.
6. Proposal duplicates another pending proposal.
7. Proposal is moot.
8. Proposal attempts to censure a particular director.
9. Proposal requires declaration of a dividend.

Liability for Proxy Violations

Management, dissident solicitors, or others may be liable for violating the proxy rules. Proxy Rule 14a-9 is an antifraud provision prohibiting false or misleading proxy solicitation statements. The "total mix" of communications made to shareholders from all sources must be considered to determine if shareholders are intentionally misled. Proxy solicitors are also liable for negligent misstatements or omissions, a great potential liability.

The proxy rules exempt proxy solicitations by foreign issuers, issuers in bankruptcy or reorganization, and public utility holding companies. Most proxy rules do not apply to tombstone ads or to small solicitations of 10 or fewer persons. However, proxy misrepresentation is always illegal. Misstatements or omissions must be material (e.g., significant) to be actionable as proxy fraud or in any other securities fraud context. What types of misstatements might constitute proxy fraud? The following case discusses the fundamental threshold of proxy fraud materiality. It also sets the standard for materiality used in other securities fraud contexts.

T.S.C. Industries v. Northway

426 U.S. 438 (1976)
United States Supreme Court

After National Industries acquired 34 percent of TSC Industries' voting shares, five of National's nominees were placed in the TSC board of directors. The new board proposed to sell National all of TSC's assets and to buy out the remainder of TSC's shareholders with National preferred stock and warrants. A joint proxy statement was issued by both corporations, and all of the shareholders approved the transaction. Thereafter, TSC was liquidated and dissolved. Northway, a former TSC shareholder, sued, claiming that the proxy statement was false and misleading. The proxy statement failed to state that National's president was on the TSC board when proxies were solicited and that National might be deemed the "parent" corporation of TSC under SEC rules. However, the proxy statement indicated that National had substantial influence over TSC. The proxy statement was allegedly deficient in failing to note some " bad news" in a letter from an investment banker concerning the size of the "premium" that the TSC shareholders would receive in the exchange transaction. A final omission was that a mutual fund, on whose board a National employee sat, made large purchases of National before the exchange transaction. Northway alleged that disclosure of these factors might have indicated a conspiracy to manipulate National's price upward to make the transaction appear favorable to TSC shareholders. The Court of Appeals found the omissions to be "material."

Justice Marshall delivered the opinion of the Court.

The question of materiality, it is universally agreed, is an objective one, involving the significance of an omitted or misrepresented fact to a reasonable investor. Variations in the formulation of a general test of materiality occur in the articulation of just how significant a fact must be or, put another way, how certain it must be that the fact would affect a reasonable investor's judgment.

The Court of Appeals in this case concluded that material facts include "all the facts which a reasonable shareholder *might* consider important." This formulation of the test of materiality has been explicitly rejected by at least two courts as setting too low a threshold for the imposition of liability under Rule 14a-9.

We are aware, however, that the disclosure policy embodied in the proxy regulations is not without limit. Some information is of such dubious significance that insistence on its disclosure may accomplish more harm than good. The potential liability for a Rule 14a-9 violation can be great indeed, and if the standard of materiality is unnecessarily low, not only may the corporation and its management be subjected to liability for insignificant omissions or misstatements, but also management's fear of exposing itself to substantial liability may cause it simply to bury the shareholders in an avalanche of trivial information—a result that is hardly conducive to informed decisionmaking.

The general standard of materiality that we think best comports with the policies of Rule 14a-9 is as follows: An omitted fact is material if there is a substantial likelihood that a reasonable shareholder would consider it important in deciding how to vote. This standard is fully consistent with *Mills'* general description of materiality as a requirement that "the defect have a significant *propensity* to affect the voting process." It does not require proof of a substantial likelihood that disclosure of the omitted fact would have caused the reasonable investor to change his vote. What the standard does contemplate is a showing of a substantial likelihood that, under all the circumstances, the omitted fact would have assumed actual significance in the deliberations of the reasonable shareholder. Put another way, there must be a substantial likelihood that the disclosure of the omitted fact would have been viewed by the reasonable investor as having significantly altered the "total mix" of information made available. Rule 14a-9 is concerned only with whether a proxy statement is misleading with respect to its presentation of material facts. If, as we must assume on a motion for summary judgment, there was no collusion or manipulation whatsoever in the National and Madison purchases—that is, if the purchases were made wholly independently for proper corporate and investment purposes, then by Northway's implicit acknowledgment they had no bearing on the soundness and reliability of the market prices listed in the proxy statement, and it cannot have been materially misleading to fail to disclose them.

Case Questions

1. What is a "material" fact for purposes for the antifraud provisions of the securities laws?
2. Why does fraud liability arise only when misstatements or omissions are material? What danger is there if misstatements appear in a proxy statement?
3. Is the materiality standard a qualitative standard, or is it a quantitative, economic standard similar to the standards used by auditors? What is the difference?

Tender Offers

After the wave of conglomerate mergers in the 1960s, American financiers adopted the British practice of using the *takeover bid* or *tender offer.* A tender offer typically involves a public offering of cash and/or securities in exchange for a controlling interest in a target corporation. Thereafter, the bidder can restructure the target firm or merge it into the bidding firm. For example, Standard Oil Company of California (Chevron) took over Gulf Oil Co. by making a tender offer for all of Gulf's outstanding common shares.

Traditionally, tender offers occurred very quickly, leaving shareholders little time to evaluate the transaction. Before 1968, shareholders had little notice of tender offers and often became panicked into selling their shares without thinking carefully. Congress amended the 1934 Act in 1968 with the Williams Act to improve tender offer disclosure and slow the process so shareholders would have time to better reason through their decisions.

Reasons for Takeovers Many economists argue that the threat of takeovers disciplines existing management into acting more efficiently. Takeover targets are often characterized as undervalued firms with inefficient management. Takeover prices are often higher than the firm's stock price beforehand because the market expects the takeover bidder will better manage the target after the takeover. Proponents of freewheeling takeover activity insist it is beneficial and creates "new wealth."

FIGURE 14–6
Tender Offer Jargon

Tender Offer Jargon	Meaning
Saturday night special	Quick, surprise tender offer
White knight	Merger partner who helps target avoid a hostile takeover by an unfriendly bidder
Leveraged buy-out (LBO)	Takeover using target's borrowing power to buy target's shares; results in a few individuals or institutional investors owning target
Shark repellent	Defensive maneuver to avert hostile takeover
Poison pill	Large target debt liability that arises after takeover making target financially unattractive or the takeover becomes too expensive
Golden parachutes	Highly favorable management termination contracts; ousted management receives financial cushion if replaced after a takeover
Greenmail	Premium paid by target corporation to buy back a large block of stock from a hostile bidder
Standstill agreement	Agreement by hostile bidder not to attempt another takeover after payment of greenmail

There are other explanations for tender offers and takeovers. *Synergism* may result from a merger between two firms with complimentary products and facilities. The combination may be more valuable than the sum of its parts. This may result from *economies of scale* obtained when the merging firms eliminate unused administrative personnel or productive capacity. A *portfolio effect* may explain how the cash flows of two firms compliment each other after a merger by providing earnings stability. Despite these alleged benefits, many critics claim the real motive to merge comes from the psychological benefits of a larger firm and the profits made by leveraging the firm.

Opponents of increased tender offer activity argue that the resulting mergers make the industry anticompetitive. Before 1968, some institutional investors and large block shareholders took advantage of limited tender offers made for less than all outstanding shares. Wall Street participants allegedly crowded out small shareholders who did not learn of the tender offer until it was too late. Much of the tender offer jargon that built up around this period graphically illustrates the emotional and financial pressures surrounding a tender offer (see Figure 14–6).

Williams Act Notifications Requirements

The Williams Act amendments to the 1934 Act require disclosures designed to create a balance between the target management's power and the shareholder emotion precipitated by a quick tender offer announcement. A *Schedule 13D* gives an early warning to potential takeover targets and their shareholders. It identifies a possible takeover bidder who has accumulated a large block of the target's stock. Shareholders holding more than 5 percent of any equity security must make this disclosure when they acquire 2 percent or more of any registered equity security, and the purchase results in their ownership of 5 percent or more. Schedule 13D must disclose the purchaser's background and identity, the source and amounts of funds used, any present or likely future plans to control the target, the number of shares owned, and any contracts they have concerning the issuer's securities (e.g., options). An inadvertent and unintentional failure to file a Schedule 13D is not improper if the SEC is notified and the 5 percent shareholder does not immediately make a tender offer.

When a tender offer begins, the offeror must file a Schedule 14D-1 *tender offer statement* with the SEC, telephone it to the exchanges, and hand deliver it to the issuer. Schedule 14D-1 includes the same disclosures required in a Schedule 13D but must also describe the tender offeror's negotiations with the issuer, state the bidder's purpose, indicate the bidder's plans for the target, include certain bidder's financial statements, state the actual tender offer terms, and include any letters sent to shareholders or press releases used during the tender offer. Management must immediately advise shareholders in Schedule 14D-9 of management's opinion concerning the tender offer. Even if management supports the tender offer, the Williams Act regulations still apply because shareholders are still under pressure and management may be coerced to support the offer.

What Is a "Tender Offer"? *Tender offer* has no statutory or regulatory definition. Its meaning comes from cases and SEC interpretations. Tender offers usually involve a widespread public announcement and solicitation of shareholders, not privately negotiated stock purchases. Tender offer bidders usually attempt to acquire a large block of shares by paying a premium price over the prevailing market price. Tender offers remain open only for a short time and their terms are usually nonnegotiable, creating pressure to sell.

Although a corporation can be controlled with less than 100 percent ownership, the tender offer is usually made contingent on receiving all the shares the bidder seeks. The bidder can refuse to purchase any shares tendered unless the minimum amount sought is tendered. Some hostile bidders have terminated their undersubscribed tender offers and refused to purchase any shares tendered. Immediately thereafter the bidder may purchase a substantial block of the target's shares in large privately negotiated transactions. The SEC believes these *street sweeps* have the same impact as a tender offer.

Mechanics of the Tender Offer

Tender offers are usually publicly disclosed in the press. However, the tender offer must be separately and personally communicated to all shareholders. Usually the target corporation's management must distribute the tender offer documents. As in proxy solicitations, management may either provide a shareholder list to the offeror or it can mail the tender offer, but at the bidder's expense.

Tender offers must remain open for at least 20 days. If more shares are tendered than the bidder requests, all shares must be accepted pro-rata. This means all tendering shareholders may still own some of their original shares after acceptance if a limited tender offer is oversubscribed. Tendering shareholders may withdraw their shares within 15 business days after tender. During the tender offer it is illegal for the bidder to trade the target's shares on the stock market. Manipulation of the target's stock is also illegal and shareholders may not *short tender* by tendering borrowed shares.

Tender Offer Liabilities Violators of the tender offer rules may be held liable for fraud, failure to file the required schedules, or for commission of any manipulative acts. Although the Williams Act originally was passed to protect tendering shareholders, other parties such as the SEC, target corporations, or competing bidders may also enforce the rules.

State Tender Offer Regulations Most states, including Delaware, have passed some type of tender offer legislation. Some observers believe these statutes are really intended to retain the target corporation's employment and tax base within the state. Such laws may also attract businesses that seek protection from hostile tender offer bidders. Some of these state statutes interfere with the Williams Act and SEC rules. An Illinois antitakeover statute was invalidated in *Edgar v. MITE*[12] because it created delays inconsistent with the Williams Act. Should a state statute be valid if it is not specifically directed at regulating tender offers but directed instead at corporate shareholder democracy? The Indiana Control Share Acquisition Act discussed in the next case is the model followed by other state laws.

CTS Corp. v. Dynamics Corp. of America

107 S. Ct. 1637 (1987)
United States Supreme Court

The Indiana Control Shares Acquisition Act may be used by shareholders to prevent a tender offeror from voting shares acquired in a tender offer. The Act applies to any corporation incorporated in Indiana with 100 or more shareholders in which 10 percent of the shareholders are Indiana residents, 10 percent of the shares are held by Indiana residents, or 10,000 of the shareholders are Indiana residents. The Act focuses on the right that an acquiring person has to vote a controlling block of shares above any of three thresholds: 20 percent, 33⅓ percent, or 50 percent. An entity acquiring these "control shares" will have voting power only "to the extent granted by resolution approved by" majority vote of all the disinterested shareholders (i.e., those not controlled by the acquirer or management) in each class. Thereby, the Act permits disinterested shareholders to disapprove the acquirer's takeover at a special or regular shareholders' meeting. If the acquirer requests and pays the expenses, then management must call a special shareholders' meeting within 50 days to consider the acquirer's voting rights. If the shareholders at the meeting refuse to restore voting rights to the acquirer, the corporation may repurchase the shares, but it is not required to do so. If voting rights are restored, the acquirer may proceed with any plans to vote the shares for any purpose (e.g., merger, sale of assets). In March 1986, Dynamics Corporation announced a tender offer for 27.5 percent of CTS Corporation stock. Soon thereafter, Dynamics brought suit challenging that the Indiana Control Shares Acquisition Act was in conflict with the Williams Act.

Justice Powell, delivered the opinion of the Court.

The Indiana Act operates on the assumption, implicit in the Williams Act, that independent shareholders faced with tender offers often are at a disadvantage. By allowing such shareholders to vote as a group, the Act protects them from the coercive aspects of some tender offers. If, for example, shareholders believe that a successful tender offer will be followed by a purchase of nontendering shares at a depressed price, individual shareholders may tender their shares—even if they doubt the tender offer is in the corporation's best interest—to protect themselves from being forced to sell their shares at a depressed price. In such a situation under the Indiana Act, the shareholders as a group, acting in the corporation's best interest, could reject the

[12] *Edgar v. MITE Corp.*, 457 U.S. 624 (1982).

offer, although individual shareholders might be inclined to accept it. The desire of the Indiana Legislature to protect shareholders of Indiana corporations from this type of coercive offer does not conflict with the Williams Act. Rather, it furthers the federal policy of investor protection.

Dynamics nevertheless contends that the statute is discriminatory because it will apply most often to out-of-state entities. This argument rests on the contention that, as a practical matter, most hostile tender offers are launched by offerors outside Indiana. But this argument avails Dynamics little. "The fact that the burden of a state regulation falls on some interstate companies does not, by itself, establish a claim of discrimination against interstate commerce."

So long as each State regulates voting rights only in the corporations it has created, each corporation will be subject to the law of only one State. No principle of corporation law and practice is more firmly established than a State's authority to regulate domestic corporations, including the authority to define the voting rights of shareholders. Accordingly, we conclude that the Indiana Act does not create an impermissible risk of inconsistent regulation by different States.

Every State in this country has enacted laws regulating corporate governance. By prohibiting certain transactions, and regulating others, such laws necessarily affect certain aspects of interstate commerce. This necessarily is true with respect to corporations with shareholders in States other than the State of incorporation. Large corporations that are listed on national exchanges, or even regional exchanges, will have shareholders in many States and shares that are traded frequently. The markets that facilitate this national and international participation in ownership of corporations are essential for providing capital not only for new enterprises but also for established companies that need to expand their businesses. This beneficial free market system depends at its core upon the fact that a corporation—except in the rarest situations—is organized under, and governed by, the law of a single jurisdiction, traditionally the corporate law of the State of its incorporation.

These regulatory laws may affect directly a variety of corporate transactions. Mergers are a typical example. In view of the substantial effect that a merger may have on the shareholders' interests in a corporation, many States require supermajority votes to approve merger. By requiring a greater vote for mergers than is required for other transactions, these laws make it more difficult for corporations to merge. State laws also may provide for "dissenters' rights" under which minority shareholders who disagree with corporate decisions to take particular actions are entitled to sell their shares to the corporation at fair market value. By requiring the corporation to purchase the shares of dissenting shareholders, these laws may inhibit a corporation from engaging in the specified transactions.

It thus is an accepted part of the business landscape in this country for States to create corporations, to prescribe their powers, and to define the rights that are acquired by purchasing their shares. A State has an interest in promoting stable relationships among parties involved in the corporations it charters, as well as in ensuring that investors in such corporations have an effective voice in corporate affairs.

There can be no doubt that the Act reflects these concerns. The primary purpose of the Act is to protect the shareholders of Indiana corporations. It does this by affording shareholders when a takeover offer is made, an opportunity to decide collectively whether the resulting change in voting control of the corporation, as they perceive it, would be desirable. A change of management may have important effects on the shareholders' interests; it is well within the State's role as overseer of corporate governance to offer this opportunity. The autonomy provided by allowing shareholders collectively to determine whether the takeover is advantageous to their interests may be especially beneficial where a hostile tender offer may coerce shareholders into tendering their shares.

Whether the control shares statute "protects shareholders of Indiana corporations" or protects incumbent management seems to me a highly debatable question, but it is extraordinary to think that the constitutionality of the Act should depend on the answer. Nothing in the Constitution says that the protection of entrenched management is any less important a "putative local benefit" than the protection of entrenched shareholders, and I do not know what qualifies us to make that judgment—or the related judgment as to how effective the present statute is in achieving one or the other objective—or the ultimate (and most ineffable) judgment as to whether, given importance-level *x,* and effectiveness-level *y,* the worth of the statute is "outweighed" by impact-on-commerce *z.*

As long as a State's corporation law governs only its own corporations and does not discriminate against out-of-state interests, it should survive this Court's scrutiny under the Commerce Clause, whether it promotes shareholder welfare or industrial stagnation. Beyond that, it is for Congress to prescribe its validity.

Justice Scalia (concurring in part and concurring in the judgment)

I do not share the Court's apparent high estimation of the beneficence of the state statute at issue here. But a law can be both economic folly and constitutional. The Indiana Control Shares Acquisition Chapter is at least the latter. I therefore concur in the judgment of the Court.

Case Questions

1. How does the Indiana Control Shares Acquisition Act differ from previous state antitakeover laws?
2. What state interest is promoted by this Indiana statute?
3. Does the Indiana statute give anyone an advantage as compared with the balance of power under the Williams Act?

The states have a traditional role in structuring corporations and shareholder rights. Some statutes include defensive provisions in addition to the control share provisions mentioned above. For example, some laws require the target management to consider the interests of corporate constituencies other than shareholders. Some permit takeovers only at "fair prices" that are reviewable by the courts. Some statutes prohibit the bidder to merge with the target until after a long time elapses. These laws impede hostile takeovers and force the bidder to negotiate with the target's management and perhaps satisfy the target management financially.

ETHICAL DILEMMAS IN CORPORATE CONTROL CONTESTS

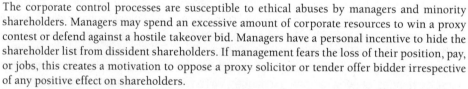

The corporate control processes are susceptible to ethical abuses by managers and minority shareholders. Managers may spend an excessive amount of corporate resources to win a proxy contest or defend against a hostile takeover bid. Managers have a personal incentive to hide the shareholder list from dissident shareholders. If management fears the loss of their position, pay, or jobs, this creates a motivation to oppose a proxy solicitor or tender offer bidder irrespective of any positive effect on shareholders.

It is arguably unethical for management to follow its self-preservation motive at the shareholders' expense. However, it is difficult to judge when management's opposition to an outsider is selfishly motivated. Similar ethical dilemmas exist for bidders who expect to be paid greenmail or minority shareholders who use the proxy process to simply air their personal political beliefs unrelated to the firm's financial success. The proxy and tender offer processes are designed to balance the powers and legitimate interests of management and shareholders. Unethical behavior in this area is possible even for those who comply with the law.

MISCELLANEOUS SECURITIES LAWS

The SEC administers several specialized laws in addition to its primary responsibility for the 1933 and 1934 Acts. In 1935, Congress passed the *Public Utility Holding Company Act* to correct abuses in the financing and operations of gas and electric utilities with pyramid-type capital structures. In 1939, Congress passed the *Trust Indenture Act* to prevent conflicts of interest by bond indenture trustees and to assure fair treatment of corporate bondholders. In 1940, two laws were passed to correct abuses by investment advisors and mutual funds. The *Investment Advisors Act* requires licensing of persons and firms who advise others about securities transactions. The *Investment Company Act* requires special registration and disclosures by mutual funds and money market funds. After the "back office" paperwork crisis that brokerage firms experienced in the late 1960s, Congress passed the *Securities Investor Protection Act* of 1970 (SIPA). The SIPA established the Securities Investor Protection Corporation, an insurance fund to protect investors' securities and accounts from their brokers' negligence or bankruptcy.

Two laws with an impact on the securities industry address social responsibility issues so they are discussed further in Chapter 22. Congress passed the *Racketeer Influenced Corrupt Organizations (RICO)* provision of the Organized Crime Control Act in 1970. Criminal and civil penalties are imposed for repeated federal crimes. The *Foreign Corrupt Practice Act* (FCPA) was passed in 1977 to prohibit foreign bribery.

SUMMARY

The 1933 Act and 1934 Act are intended to reduce fraud in securities trading. Issuers of new nonexempt securities must register the securities before any public sale by filing a registration statement and distributing the prospectus. Before registration, new securities may not be sold and the market may not be preconditioned. The SEC reviews the offering documents during the waiting period. Actual sales may commence during the post-effective period after clearance by the SEC. Shelf registration permits issuers to preregister securities long before sales are expected.

The securities laws apply only to "securities" such as stocks, bonds, notes, and options. The catchall phrase "investment contract" defines new investments as securities as needed. An investment contract is a security if a person invests money in a common enterprise or scheme and is led to expect profits will be derived primarily from the efforts of the promoter.

The costly registration process is exempted if securities are sold intrastate, in a private placement, or in small dollar volumes. Usually these securities may not be resold immediately to others. Issuers are liable in damages for securities fraud. There are criminal penalties for the illegal sale of unregistered securities.

Insider trading is prohibited if nonpublic, confidential information is misappropriated. Section 16(b) insiders (officers, directors, and 10 percent shareholders) must report their trading activity and refrain from making short swing profits. Rule 10b-5 prohibits securities fraud and restricts insider trading. Any person within or outside the issuer is prohibited from buying or selling securities based on inside information. Persons in possession of material, nonpublic, misappropriated information have the choice of disclosing the inside information or abstaining from trading. Tippees may not trade on misappropriated information or information improperly received from an insider.

Proxy solicitations are regulated requiring all solicitors to file a proxy statement stating various information about the solicitation. SEC rules provide two alternate methods for shareholder proxy solicitations. Small shareholders solicitations are included with management's solicitation at the corporation's expense. Larger solicitors pay their own expenses. There is liability for proxy fraud.

The 1968 Williams Act regulates tender offers. Takeover bidders and the issuer's management are placed on an even footing so shareholders can make reasoned choices about tendering. Tender offer disclosures are required including: (1) Schedule 13D by 5 percent shareholders, (2) Schedule 14D-1 by the tender offeror when the tender offer commences, and (3) Schedule 14D-9 by the target management. There are penalties for tender offer fraud, failure to disclose as required, or the commission of manipulative acts. The states may validly regulate the shareholder voting aspects of takeovers and tender offers.

KEY TERMS

initial public offering (IPO), p. 416
issuer, p. 417
underwriter, p. 417
prospectus, p. 418
Rule 10b-5, p. 432
Section 16(b), p. 430
insider, pp. 430, 433
misappropriation theory, p. 436
proxy solicitation, p. 439
tender offer, p. 445
RICO (Racketeer Influenced and Corrupt Organizations) provision, p. 449

CHAPTER EXERCISES

1. Under the Securities Act of 1933, there are three important periods that affect the offering of securities for sale. Name and describe these three periods.
2. Give three examples of transactions other than the sale of stock or bonds that involve the sale of a security. List several factors that indicate the existence of a "security."
3. What is the basic distinction between common law fraud and the statutory fraud provisions against insider trading? What is the importance of this distinction?
4. Claiming the intrastate exemption of the Securities Act of 1933, Jones Investment Company did not register its offering of shares with the SEC. Jones Investment is a Georgia corporation whose only offices are in that state. It sold shares only to Georgia residents. However, the funds were raised to finance the company's real estate developments in Florida. Is the intrastate exemption available to Jones investment?
5. Liability under Section 16(b) arises only if there is a purchase *and* a sale of equity securities within a six-month period. Profits are calculated by matching the lowest purchase price for a class of securities against the higher sales price. This yields the highest possible profit. Insiders may not offset their losses. Consider the following example, and calculate the short swing profits:
   On January 1, Insider purchased 100 shares of Atlantic stock at $30 a share.
   On February 28, Insider sold 100 shares of Atlantic stock at $20 a share.
   On April 15, Insider purchased 100 shares of Atlantic stock at $40 a share.
   On May 20, Insider sold 100 shares of Atlantic stock at $50 a share.
6. Rule 10b-5 of the Securities Exchange Act of 1934 is of fundamental importance in the law of securities regulation. State this rule in your own words, and describe its purposes.
7. John Smith is a junior executive of the Widget Company. In the course of his employment, he has accumulated $25,000 of its common stock (at its current market value of $12.50 per share), having first received a stock bonus eight years ago and having last made a purchase of 200 shares at $10 per share four months ago.

   During the last four months, since a new president was brought in from the outside, he has felt that the company was drifting downhill. Some rather weak executives have been hired, apparently because they were friends or relatives of the new president. A disappointment is in the offing because a new device that was rumored to be a breakthrough (and was prominently mentioned in the trade journals) is having production difficulties that will probably prevent it from being offered in the market for a long time to come.

   Smith thinks that when the facts about the new device are announced, Widget stock will go down several points. It is unlikely, however, to descend to its level a year ago for some time, perhaps not until its annual financial report is released in about seven months. Smith would like to sell his stock as soon as possible and would also like to advise some friends who have followed his lead and invested heavily in it to do so too. He asks you whether this is possible. Outline the issues in the case. Which statutes apply?
8. How would you apply the misappropriation theory to the fact pattern in Exercise 7? For example, suppose that John Smith passed on the information to his friends and that the friends tipped off other outsiders. Would this violate Rule 10b-5?

9. Congress has attempted to clarify insider trading enforcement with two statutes passed in the 1980s. List those statutes, and describe briefly what they cover.

10. James Jones has access to information on Atlantic Company that is not available to the general investor. He wants to buy stock in the company, and he is also preparing a proxy statement that is to be distributed to all of its shareholders. What standard should he apply to determine whether the information in his possession is "material," so that he cannot invest in his company prior to its public release. What standard should he apply to determine whether the information should be included in the proxy statement?

11. Contrast the analytical steps taken to evaluate the legal and ethical problems of the following securities markets activities:
a. Stock parking, the practice of acquiring and holding large blocks of the stock of potential takeover targets through friends, family, and business associates in order to conceal the identity of the acquirer.
b. Trading on inside information acquired from corporate employees of another firm by promising to return the favor with a tip of inside information on the trader's company.
c. Disclosure of false information about your companies' lower expected earnings for the next quarter in order to sell your holdings in the stock before the market price plunges.
d. Falsifying the accounting records of your company to show a false profit so that the company can float a new issue of bonds to secure financing that may help turn around the company's ill fortunes.
e. Failing to disclose in management's proxy solicitation which urges approval of a merger that the officers of the company currently own large amounts of corporate stock and have lucrative "golden parachutes" (huge severance pay bonuses). Approval of the merger will trigger the officers' rights to these stock profits and severance bonuses. However, the officers have not secured any advice on a fair merger price from an independent investment banker and the merger price is far below the company's true value.

Part 5

ANTITRUST LAW

This part introduces the federal laws designed to maintain a competitive environment. The Sherman and Clayton antitrust laws were passed as a result of experience with the natural tendency of business to collude for its perceived benefit. The antitrust laws provide a structure of regulation and legal rights that provides incentives for business to act consistently with the assumptions of the perfect competition model.

Antitrust analysis begins with the classification of the restraint in question. Collusion between competitors is a horizontal restraint of trade. Anticompetitive relationships between suppliers and resellers are vertical restraints. Chapter 15 discusses the analysis of monopolies and mergers, which is a process of determining the extent and influence of particular horizontal competitors in each product or service market. Chapter 16 examines more specific anticompetitive practices: price-fixing, resale price maintenance, division of markets, price discrimination, tying, and exclusive dealership. Finally, the FTC's powers to outlaw other types of unfair trade practices is examined.

Chapter 15

MONOPOLIES AND MERGERS

KEY CONCEPTS

Antitrust law is intended to maintain a competitive economy by prohibiting monopolistic practices or mergers that result in undue concentrations of market power.

There are three basic federal antitrust statutes. The Sherman Act outlaws monopolization and contracts in restraint of trade. The Clayton Act prohibits anticompetitive tendencies even before damaging effects occur. The Federal Trade Commission Act created the Federal Trade Commission and makes illegal unfair methods of competition and deceptive trade practices.

The antitrust laws exempt from prosecution many actions of the following industries: regulated financial institutions, the insurance industry, labor unions, and professional baseball.

Analysis of monopolization requires a finding of market power in a particular geographic and product market. Consumer buying habits and the geographic area affected by the alleged monopolist determine the geographic market. Consumer preferences and the interchangeability of substitute products determine the product market.

Mergers that tend to create a monopoly are prohibited. Horizontal mergers occur between competitors, vertical mergers occur between customers and suppliers, and conglomerate mergers occur between unrelated merger partners.

INTRODUCTION . . . PAST, PRESENT, FUTURE

After the Civil War, a period of industrial expansion revolutionized the U.S. economy. The corporate form of business became increasingly accepted, and capital markets expanded. Early investment bankers helped concentrate wealth, power, and productive capacity in the hands of a decreasing number of persons, and fewer and larger companies came to produce most U.S. goods. For example, Andrew Carnegie created the largest steel company, U.S. Steel, during this period. Small business, the heart of American capitalism, became unable to compete with larger firms, which had economies of large-scale production and installed laborsaving machinery that displaced many skilled craftsmen.

The work ethic and the equal opportunity theories underlying the U.S. Constitution have always been a dominant force in our economic environment. Americans believed that they had the "right" to pull themselves up by their own bootstraps according to their abilities and without undue governmental intervention. Thus, in the 19th century, business was regulated only by market competition. By the close of the 19th century, however, the new industrialism created a widening income disparity between classes threatening the new middle class and raising fundamental questions of fairness. Mechanized factories allowed the production of better goods in less time by less skilled workers. Skilled craftsmen and artisans lost economic power as large factories and concentrated businesses took over their markets. Many local businesses felt the shock of competition from more efficient production and began to mistrust big business.

Fewer and larger firms won larger market shares, resulting in a concentration of wealth and power. As their control of increasing amounts of money and increasing numbers of workers grew, the owners of these firms were able to dictate market prices. In response, a new political movement—*populism*—developed among the individualists, farmers, and small-business owners in the agrarian West. The populists claimed that large businesses were corrupt and oppressed those involved in the traditional economy.

Some large businesses brought on these criticisms by employing monopolistic practices. For example, the railroads came under federal regulatory power in 1888 because they paid secret rebates to some favored customers, resulting in price discrimination between shippers. Some large businesses temporarily priced their products below cost to eliminate competition, then later raised prices to recoup losses. Other large businesses bought out their competitors, creating monopolies. Standard Oil and U.S. Steel obtained the largest market shares in their industries by pressuring their customers, competitors, and suppliers. People considered such domination to be undesirable; without vigorous competition, a large company can arbitrarily set prices and production policies for its entire industry.

Big businesses prevented many of their small competitors from advertising, purchasing supplies, or selling to their customers. They threatened their suppliers and customers into boycotting small competitors. Critics argued that the success of big business was often due, not to increased efficiency, but to these abusive practices. Eventually public reaction to such practices led to passage of the antitrust laws.

Although the primary goal of the antitrust laws was to maintain a competitive economy, other goals, such as maintaining liberty, fairness, and opportunity, were also influential. The populists hoped that the system of small, independent business units would preserve the "American dream." They thought that further concentration of political and economic power would encourage the growth of power centers, reminiscent of feudalism, that might eventually rival the power of government. They considered the diffusion and decentralization of political and economic power to be necessary to preserve democracy. The populists believed that antitrust laws would encourage fairness and vigorous competition and ensure an equitable allocation of resources, thereby eliminating favoritism and prejudice.

The populists' discontent with industrial concentration highlighted how ineffective the common law was in dealing with monopolies. Since the common law was primarily state law, there was no uniformity among the states, and the outcome of litigation against large firms was unpredictable. Congress passed the *Sherman Antitrust Act* in 1890, deriving its principles from the state common law.

Today, antitrust laws are enforced by state and federal regulators and by private plaintiffs. The Federal Trade Commission and the Justice Department are responsible for monitoring the economic environment and maintaining competition. However, the courts and these regulators have been responding to new theories of competition that justify many acts previously considered anticompetitive.

As the reaction against the excesses of the 1980s intensifies, merger enforcement may be increased. The use of complex economic analysis to gauge the anticompetitive effects of suppliers' control over their distribution chains is expected to grow. Such analysis involves a structured set of inquiries requiring expert testimony by economists. Although the importance of antitrust laws is growing in the post-Reagan years, the increased interdependence of the world's economies will reduce the need for many traditional antitrust enforcement efforts. However, predatory acts will probably be prohibited for many years. A growing body of competition laws in other nations, particularly the EC, suggests that the policies of antitrust are spreading throughout the developed world.

OVERVIEW

Today, the economic efficiency argument dominates most descriptions of antitrust goals. The Supreme Court has stated this normative theory as the primary justification for the antitrust laws.

Economic Efficiency Theory Underlying the Sherman Act

The Sherman Act was designed to be a comprehensive charter of economic liberty aimed at preserving free and unfettered competition. . . . [I]t rests on the premise that unrestrained interaction of competitive forces will yield the best allocation of our economic resources, the lowest prices, the highest quality, and the greatest material progress.[1]

Under the economic efficiency theory, antitrust laws are justified as an incentive to innovate, maintain productive efficiency, and maximize the range and selection of goods. Monopolies are considered damaging because they impose limitations on production, heighten the danger of deterioration in quality, and give the monopolist power to fix prices and exclude competitors. These outcomes conflict with the basic premise that competition can provide incentives and disincentives consistent with maximum efficiency. Antitrust laws are justified as a way to maintain a competitive environment.

Economists recognize that the U.S. economy does not operate in a vacuum. The ability to compete efficiently with foreign producers, which are often subsidized by their gov-

[1] *Northern Pacific Railway Co. v. United States*, 365 U.S. 1 (1958).

ernments, may require some rethinking of the antitrust laws. Excessive enforcement of antitrust legislation could aid foreign competitors and damage domestic industry. The structures of particular industries, the efficiencies of scale within those industries, and the efficiency of foreign competition have become additional considerations in the application of antitrust law.

Antitrust laws affect the decisions of both upper management and line managers. Such statutes as the Sherman Act, the Clayton Act, and the Federal Trade Commission Act largely define the conduct of business. This chapter explores the history, content, economic theory, and criticisms of antitrust laws by first focusing on monopolies and mergers. As with other legal areas, the statutes provide only a starting point for gaining an understanding of antitrust law. The interpretive decisions of the courts and administrative agencies provide the critical details needed by management to avoid liability. Chapter 16 covers antitrust offenses omitted in this chapter: price discrimination, restraints of trade, and unfair trade practices.

U.S. ANTITRUST LAWS

The three major U.S. antitrust laws are summarized in Table 15–1.

The Sherman Act

The Sherman Act, passed in 1890, prohibits anticompetitive devices that restrain trade and erect the barrier of monopoly to any trade or other aspect of interstate commerce. Sections 1 and 2 of the Sherman Act are pertinent in this regard.

Sherman Act, Section 1: Restraints of Trade

Section 1 of the Sherman Act makes it an unlawful criminal act to enter into a "contract, combination . . . or conspiracy in restraint of trade."

Sherman Act, Section 2: Monopolization

Section 2 of the Sherman Act states that "every person who shall monopolize, or attempt to monopolize, or combine or conspire with any other person or persons, to monopolize any part of the trade of commerce among the several states, or with foreign nations shall be deemed guilty of a felony."

The Clayton Act

Initially, the federal courts were quite lenient in their interpretations of the Sherman Act. One early case held that manufacturing was not commerce so it could not be federally regulated.[2] Although that view was soon abandoned, it illustrates the courts' initial hostility to the Sherman Act. Congress responded to mounting criticism of this leniency by passing the *Clayton Act* in 1914. It was written in more specific terms, outlawing certain

[2]*United States v. E.C. Knight Co.*, 156 U.S. 1 (1896).

TABLE 15–1
Summary of Federal Antitrust Laws

Law	Effect	Enforcement*
Sherman Act (1890)	Illegal to enter contract, combination, or conspiracy in restraint of trade Outlaws monopolization, attempts to monopolize, or conspiracies to monopolize interstate commerce Criminal fines: for corporations, up to $1 million; up to $100,000 for noncorporations Prison sentences: up to three years for individuals	Justice Department: criminal and civil prosecutions FTC: no powers Private plaintiffs: civil damage suits State attorneys general: civil prosecutions
Clayton Act (1914)	Price discrimination declared illegal if it tends to create a monopoly or lessen competition Illegal to require another by contract to boycott a competitor if this substantially lessens competition or tends to create a monopoly (effectively prohibits tying and exclusive dealing) Prohibits mergers or purchase of assets if effect is to substantially lessen competition or create a monopoly Prohibits interlocking directorates	Justice Department: civil prosecutions FTC: civil prosecutions Private plaintiffs: civil damage suits
Federal Trade Commission Act (1914)	Creates FTC Empowers FTC to enforce FTC and Clayton acts Prohibits unfair methods of competition or deceptive trade practices	Justice Department: no powers FTC: civil prosecutions Private plaintiffs: no powers

*Enforcement is discussed later in this chapter.

acts. Whereas the Sherman Act requires proof of completed anticompetitive effects, the Clayton Act is violated if anticompetitive tendencies arise from conduct even before any actual damage occurs to competition. Sections 3 and 7 of the Clayton Act are discussed in this text. Section 3, covered in the next chapter, prohibits tie-in sales, exclusive dealing arrangements, and requirements contracts that "substantially lessen competition or tend to create a monopoly." Section 7, discussed in this chapter, prohibits interlocking directorates and mergers or stock acquisitions that result in a substantial lessening of competition. The Clayton Act also authorizes private damage suits for treble damages.

The Federal Trade Commission Act

The Federal Trade Commission Act, also passed in 1914, created the Federal Trade Commission (FTC). This act gives the FTC broad powers to prosecute "unfair methods of competition" and "unfair or deceptive acts or practices," and to enforce the Sherman and Clayton Acts. Thus, the act protects businesses from the predatory and anticompetitive acts of their competitors and it protects consumers from the deceptive acts of sellers.

Additional Antitrust Laws

In later years, Congress strengthened the antitrust laws three times. In 1936, price discrimination was specifically outlawed by the Robinson-Patman Act. In 1952, the Celler-Kefauver Amendment closed a loophole by extending the merger prohibition to corporate acquisitions in which the assets of another firm are purchased. In 1976, the Hart-Scott-Rodino Antitrust Improvement Act expanded the Justice Department's investigative powers. The Hart-Scott-Rodino Act requires public notice of mergers prior to their completion, and it permits the prosecution of antitrust violations by the attorneys general of the states for damages caused to state citizens.

State Antitrust Laws

Most states have antitrust laws that parallel the federal antitrust laws. Typically, state antitrust laws outlaw particular anticompetitive acts such as restraints of trade, price-fixing, exclusive dealing, and tying. In recent years, state attorneys general have increased enforcement efforts under both state and federal antitrust laws. For example, various state attorneys general combined to challenge a price-fixing scheme by several national insurance companies, alleging that the companies fixed premiums and colluded in refusing to offer certain types of insurance. Critics charge that some of this activism is politically motivated. Nevertheless, business must not be lulled into complacency over antitrust enforcement even if federal regulators relax their vigilance. State attorneys general and private parties may use state laws as an alternate basis for antitrust litigation, making enforcement less susceptible to ideological shifts in Washington.

INTERNATIONAL PERSPECTIVE ON COMPETITION LAWS

During the 20th century, most nations have had weaker antitrust enforcement than has the United States. Indeed, many nations promote domestic monopolies to compete more effectively with other nations' competitors. For example, a South Korean government agency, the "Office of Monopoly," promotes its home industries. Many educated people in developing nations are torn between the two extremes of monopoly and competition. On the one hand, popular nationalism motivates governments to grant monopolies in order to strengthen domestic industry. On the other hand, many of these supporters also denounce the inevitable decline in their personal standard of living caused by paying high monopoly prices. This tension has led to anticompetitive protectionist laws (e.g., discriminatory taxes, tariffs, quotas, excessive inspections) and hostility toward the competitive threat of large foreign firms and toward the application of U.S. antitrust laws. Nevertheless, the EC and some other successful industrialized economies are increasingly adopting new antimonopoly laws that resemble existing U.S. laws. The Treaty of Rome creating the EC includes prohibitions against collusion among competitors to fix prices, control production, allocate markets, or limit the development of products or geographic markets. Additionally, the EC business competition law prohibits tying, monopolization, and the use of discretionary supply contract terms.

The Sherman and Clayton acts have broad applicability to both domestic and foreign anticompetitive acts with an impact in the United States. From time to time, regulators, private parties, and commentators argue that U.S. antitrust laws should apply to foreign firms' anticompetitive practices. However, as discussed further in Chapter 21, U.S. courts examine several factors before applying U.S. antitrust law to foreign activity. Additionally, several principles of international law may restrict U.S. antitrust suits against foreign firms. For example, the *act of state* doctrine and *sovereign immunity* prevent U.S. courts from applying U.S. antitrust law when a foreign government's action sponsors the anticompetitive activity. This principle prevents a challenge of the collusion among Japanese firms promoted by MITI, Japan's Ministry of Trade and Industry. Under the principle of *comity* a foreign court will generally refuse to apply U.S. antitrust laws unless that nation has similar laws. Of course, a foreign firm's U.S. subsidiary may nevertheless be held liable for antitrust violations that have an anticompetitive impact in the United States.

Foreign nations can frustrate U.S. antitrust suits against their home industries with *blocking* laws that prohibit compliance with U.S. pretrial discovery requests. For example, it is common for antitrust plaintiffs to request numerous documents needed to prove their case against foreign firms charged with antitrust violations. Blocking laws often require precompliance notification to the foreign government, enabling its regulators to bar the production of documents. This can effectively frustrate the antitrust suit. The *extra-territoriality* of U.S. antitrust law under the Foreign Trade Antitrust Improvements Act of 1982 is discussed further in Chapter 21.

TRUSTS AND MONOPOLIES

As corporations develop, economic power becomes more concentrated, bringing productive capacity under the control of fewer persons. Concentration can also involve the creation of *pools,* in which groups of businesses agree to split up the available business among their members. For example, where markets are separated geographically, sales in each market may be allocated to a particular producer. This *division of markets* reduces competition among pool members. Because pooling contracts are illegal, however, pools lack effective methods for disciplining members that breach the pool agreement. A disciplinary problem of this kind weakened OPEC's efforts to control oil output and set worldwide oil prices. In the late 19th century, trusts provided more permanent and more enforceable bonds that did pools.

Characteristics of a Trust

A **trust** is an organizational form in which *trustors (settlors)* convey property to a *trustee* that actually holds legal title (ownership) to the assets transferred. The trustor or other beneficiary retains beneficial ownership of the property, but the trustee is responsible for making good decisions with regard to the trust property. The trust device is most justifiable when the beneficiaries have limited expertise in the investment or business property. However, actions undertaken by the early business trusts were eventually outlawed by the antitrust laws because their primary purpose was to restrain trade.

The early business trusts deprived shareholders, the trust beneficiaries, of their voting rights and consolidated corporate power in the hands of a few trustees. Stockholders of several competing corporations would transfer their stock to a board of trustees that in return issued *voting trust certificates.* These certificates were similar to stock because they were evidence of the trustor's beneficial ownership and they entitled the trustors to dividends.

Standard Oil Company was originally organized as a trust that drew together the major oil producers from Ohio (Sohio, now BP), New Jersey (Exxon), New York (Mobil), Indiana (Amoco), California (Chevron), and others. Later, under the antitrust laws, Standard Oil was broken up into separate companies. Eventually, all large business organizations that tended to crush competitors became known as trusts even if they were organized as corporations or did not use the trust form.

Market Structures

Traditional economic analysis defines five basic market structures: perfect competition, monopoly, oligopoly, monopolistic competition, and monopsony. This analytic model is used to predict the purchasing behaviors of consumers and the pricing and production behaviors of sellers.

Under **perfect competition**, a large number of buyers and sellers coexist and no individual firm or consumer has sufficient market power to influence prices or production quantity. It is assumed that under perfect competition there are low barriers to entry, uniform products, and perfect information concerning market conditions that is shared equally by all buyers and sellers. Of course, these unrealistic assumptions make perfect competition useful only as a model for economic analysis; as real-world markets are encountered, it becomes necessary to modify its implications. The securities markets and the markets for gasoline or groceries in larger cities come closest to the perfect competition model.

Monopoly describes a market dominated by one large seller. Typically, there are no close substitutes for the seller's product. Usually there are high *barriers to entry,* which are structures making it difficult for other firms to enter the market and produce similar products. Legal barriers to entry include patents, copyrights, franchises, and licenses limiting the use of the monopolist's technology. Natural barriers to entry include the need to purchase a large amount of assets to produce the product. Most utilities have limited monopolies in their service areas because it would be expensive to duplicate an electric utility's generators and distribution wiring. Their pricing and output decisions are regulated, however, to reduce their monopolistic tendencies.

Oligopoly conditions exist where there are a small number of sellers and high barriers to entry for new producers and where strong sellers have sufficient power to influence prices. The U.S. domestic steel market was long regarded as an oligopoly. The steel obtainable from most producers was virtually interchangeable. There was little price competition, but the steel producers competed with a subtle variety of features, service, or advertising. Prices tend to be higher and output lower in oligopolistic markets than under perfect competition, but they are less restricted in oligopolistic markets than in monopolistic markets.

Monopolistic competition involves markets in which a few sellers offer differentiated products that are somewhat substitutable. The automobile market is often regarded as a market of this kind. Each automaker can distinguish its models in consumers' minds, yet most autos are somewhat interchangeable for the purpose of basic transportation. Monopolistic competitors possess some market power and are slow to innovate.

Monopsony exists when a single buyer possesses monopoly buying power over prices charged; **oligopsony** exists when a few buyers have power over prices. For example, the employer in a company town stands in a monopsony position because it is the predominant buyer of labor in that town. It can set lower prices than under perfect competition.

These economic models are illustrated in Table 15–2; they form the basis for most traditional antitrust analysis.

ENFORCEMENT OF ANTITRUST LAW

There are four basic enforcing agents that may bring antitrust suits in the federal courts. First, the Department of Justice oversees antitrust enforcement. The Justice Department's Antitrust Division is the only enforcer with both criminal and civil enforcement powers. Justice is granted these powers under the Sherman Act and derives additional civil

TABLE 15–2

Basic Market Structures

Market Structure	Primary Characteristics	Effects	Examples
Perfect competition	Numerous buyers and sellers; low barriers to entry; perfect information; numerous substitutes; elastic demand	Allocative efficiency	U.S. financial markets; retail gasoline and grocery businesses
Monopoly	Single seller; high barriers to entry; no adequate substitutes; inelastic demand	Seller's market power: seller may raise price and lower output; abnormal monopoly profits; no innovation	Public utilities; patent or trade secret
Oligopoly	Few sellers; high barriers to entry; inadequate substitutes	Seller's market power: abnormal monopoly profit; slow innovation	Breakfast cereals
Monopolistic competition	Few sellers; high barriers to entry; substitutes "appear" distinguishable in consumers' minds	Seller's market power: abnormal monopoly profits; slow innovation	Aerospace, automobiles
Monopsony	Single buyer; high barriers to entry	Buyer has market power to set low prices	Single employer in a company town

enforcement powers under the Clayton Act. The Justice Department is directed by the attorney general, a cabinet member who is usually a close confidant of the president.

Second, the FTC may bring civil enforcement actions for violations of the Clayton Act. The FTC has sole enforcement authority of the FTC Act. The FTC is a quasi-independent regulatory agency headed by five commissioners appointed by the president and confirmed by the Senate. FTC composition and powers were discussed in Chapter 11.

Third, private parties injured by Sherman or Clayton Act violations may bring civil damage suits. A private party may also wait to sue until a government agency successfully prosecutes the violator. This tactic may increase the private plaintiff's chances for success because a successful government enforcement action is convincing evidence of the defendant's guilt. In certain limited situations, if several individuals have been harmed in a similar manner by the defendant's conduct, a *class action* suit may be instituted.

Fourth, state attorneys general may sue *parens patrie,* that is, on behalf of consumers harmed within their states. This enforcement activity has become well known in the 1980s and 1990s because of the concerted efforts of state attorneys general to prove anticompetitive acts in several industries such as insurance.

Congress has permitted many agents to bring antitrust suits in order to promote vigorous enforcement of the antitrust laws.

Criminal Penalties

The antitrust laws provide for substantial penalties to deter anticompetitive conduct. The Sherman Act permits the imposition of criminal sanctions on individuals, including fines of up to \$100,000 or prison sentences of up to three years, or both. Under the Sherman Act, corporations may be fined up to \$1 million. There are no criminal sanctions under the Clayton and FTC acts. Criminal convictions require proof of criminal intent, which means that the defendant must have had "knowledge of the probable consequences" of the anticompetitive action. The intent and burden of proof requirements make it difficult to obtain criminal convictions. Therefore, the predominant enforcement emphasis has shifted to civil suits and to the review and clearance of mergers by various government agencies.

Private Rights of Action

The Clayton Act grants standing to "any person . . . injured in his business or property by reason of anything forbidden in the anti-trust laws" (i.e., either Sherman or Clayton Act violations). Private plaintiffs may recover *treble damages* (three times the actual damage sustained) plus litigation costs, including reasonable attorneys' fees. Treble damages are similar to punitive damages because they give private parties a greater incentive to sue. Injured competitors, consumers, suppliers, state attorneys general, and even foreign governments may sue for treble damages.

Only direct purchasers may sue for treble damages. Indirect purchasers, those who purchase further down the distribution chain, are not directly injured by the anticompetitive action. In *Illinois Brick Co. v. Illinois,* the Supreme Court rejected the state's treble damage claim made for downstream consumers.[3] The suit alleged that concrete block manufacturers illegally fixed prices charged to building contractors. The added costs were allegedly "passed through" to the ultimate consumers through higher prices charged by the contractors. Despite the *Illinois Brick* rule, treble damages claims by such downstream indirect purchasers are permitted under some state antitrust laws.[4]

Civil Enforcement by Regulators

Both the FTC and the Justice Department use two enforcement devices to obtain innovative remedies. First, equitable relief may be obtained through an injunction to restrain and prevent future antitrust violations. This broad power permits the federal courts to restrain particular conduct, compel divestiture of subsidiaries, dismember monopolies and create more competitive industries, cancel a merger, order licensing of patents with reasonable royalty payments, and cancel existing contracts.

Second, *consent decrees* permit the government and the defendant to avoid trial by agreeing to a settlement. Typically, the defendant voluntarily agrees to cease its anticompetitive actions, neither admitting nor denying any violation of the law, and the court enters a permanent injunction against future violations and approves the settlement. Consent decrees avoid costly litigation and appeals. Subsequent damage suits by private plaintiffs may not take advantage of the consent decree as proof of violation. These plaintiffs must prove their cases independently following a consent decree, further encouraging such settlements.

Commentary: Approaches to Antitrust Enforcement

Although the laissez-faire economic theory has established the ethic that government should not intervene in markets to further competition, many observers believe that the shortcomings of business performance justify some government regulation. They argue that market-

[3] *Illinois Brick Co. v. Illinois,* 431 U.S. 720 (1977).

[4] *California v. ARC America Corp.,* 490 U.S. 93 (1989).

based systems often yield poor results, such as the natural tendency to develop monopolies. However, it is difficult to design a regulatory system that stops short of destructive interference with beneficial market activities.

Economists and antitrust lawyers have developed theories of *industrial organization* that attempt to explain the performance and shape of markets by describing the relations among firms competing in particular industries. Three basic approaches to government intervention have evolved from these theories: the structuralist approach, the conduct approach, and performance analysis.

The *structuralist approach* looks primarily at the organization of each industry to identify particular structural characteristics that tend toward anticompetitive effects. The structuralists closely examine the number of buyers and sellers as an indication of the degree of industry concentration. For them, the size and the geographic distribution of sellers indicate the extent of the sellers' market power. Next, the structuralists analyze the degree of differentiation among competing products to determine whether substitute products could be used. Finally, they determine whether potential competitors face excessively high barriers to entry that could stifle competition by restricting new competitors.

Adherents of the *conduct approach,* which occupies the middle ground, focus antitrust enforcement efforts on the actual behavior of firms. These analysts identify business practices that reveal inefficiencies or breakdowns in competition. They review the pricing and production policies of firms to ascertain the existence of anticompetitive practices. They search for the intentional commission of illegal acts, and they examine conduct in advertising, research, and innovation that is relevant to enforcement efforts.

The actual outcomes or end results of a firm's conduct are the focus of *performance analysis*. Performance analysts do not examine the potential for anticompetitive conduct, as do the structuralists, nor do they concentrate on the actual functioning of the market, as do the conduct analysts. Instead, performance analysts are concerned with how well the market performance meets the antitrust goals of economic efficiency. Their attention is directed toward the economic efficiency of industries, levels of technological innovation, reasonable profit performance, and reasonable barriers to entry. This requires a complex economic analysis of the costs, investments, returns on investment, innovations, and sales activities of particular industries.

The "proper" approach to antitrust enforcement has been the subject of a continuing debate among the proponents of these approaches. Big business often supports the performance analysts because their approach allows big business the greatest freedom of action. Performance analysts argue that small firms are unable to invest enough in research and development to remain efficient. In the long run, according to these analysts, technological developments will create new substitute products, thereby eliminating the large firm's short-term monopolies. However, structuralists offer considerable evidence that in many industries larger firms are less efficient than medium-sized firms. They argue that the large advertising and marketing expenses of many firms divert their scarce resources away from essential research and development expenditures.

Despite the antitrust enforcement debate, most commentators believe that monopolies are necessary in some industries to avoid inefficient duplication of facilities. For example, utilities operate most efficiently if only a single set of distribution facilities is built (e.g., power lines, telephone cables, and water, natural gas, and sewer pipes connected to consumers). For many years, the Justice Department was involved in costly antitrust litigation with AT&T. Eventually, a settlement was reached that permitted competition in long-distance service because the technology for the transmission of long-distance calls was no longer limited to wire. In addition, competition in the manufacture of phones and switching equipment has increased. In local phone connection and switching, however, the local service companies still retain their monopoly so as to avoid costly duplication of facilities. State regulatory agencies usually control prices and services to prevent monopolistic behavior where these "natural monopolies" exist.

Today, there are two schools of thought with regard to antitrust enforcement policy: the Harvard (or traditional) school and the Chicago school. The Harvard school prefers vigorous antitrust enforcement to maintain atomized competition among numerous independent businesses. It believes that concentration of economic power will nearly always lead to monopolistic behaviors and to less than optimal distribution of goods and services. By contrast, the Chicago school insists on using a separate economic analysis in every antitrust case. It would tolerate some monopolistic behaviors if the anticompetitive effects of these behaviors were short-term, if the monopolist competed internationally, or if the monopoly profits were used for innovation. This approach encourages natural monopolies that are more efficient than perfect competition and monopolies in which the monopolist may become the least-cost producer.

During most of the 20th century, the traditionalists have guided antitrust enforcement. Since the mid-1970s, however, adherents of the Chicago school have become more influential, primarily in the federal agencies responsible for antitrust enforcement and to a somewhat lesser extent in the courts.

ETHICAL DILEMMA: DETECTION AND ENFORCEMENT OF ANTITRUST LAW

Antitrust law represents a national ethical principle that encourages competition by having all of the participants in the economy strive for efficiency. Some people believe that this principle is similar to a basic work ethic. Arguably, monopolies and restraints of trade remove beneficial incentives for innovation or risk taking. Antitrust law may be viewed as a basis for economic ethics in a competitive society.

The criminal penalties for antitrust violations pose numerous ethical dilemmas for managers with decision-making authority. The difficulty of detecting some of these violations may encourage managers to engage in them and hope that the violations will go unnoticed. Most monopolies or mergers are too well publicized or too well known by competitors and customers to be ignored. However, if all of the parties to an agreement in restraint of trade maintain silence about the agreement, the results may be less obvious. These conditions may encourage the practices of secret price-fixing, division of markets, group boycotts, illicit trade association activities, and intimidation to enforce vertical restraints.

There is a national schizophrenia concerning antitrust enforcement. The two major intellectual schools of enforcement theory, the Harvard and Chicago schools, have had alternating successes in influencing the views of administrators, prosecutors, and the courts. This poses ethical dilemmas for business managers, who find it difficult to know what is required of them. It encourages companies to test the limits of the current mood of antitrust enforcement by going beyond what is apparently permissible.

Some commentators argue that smaller firms use the antitrust laws to intimidate larger firms. Ethical questions are clearly presented whenever the legal process is subverted for private gain in such ways.

Antitrust Exemptions

Antitrust regulation of some industries, such as insurance companies and financial institutions, is the responsibility of government agencies other than the FTC. This prevents duplicative and unnecessary antitrust enforcement in these industries. To ensure their survival, some industries are permitted to more freely use restraints of trade that would be illegal and anticompetitive in other industries. For example, the holders of patents, copyrights, and trademarks receive government-granted monopolies that are intended to encourage innovation by permitting the holders to exploit their intellectual property and receive monopoly profits. Congress and the courts have also granted antitrust exemptions to certain industries. These exemptions are narrowly construed under the policy of strict constructionism, which permits the courts little flexibility to exempt new variations of an activity unless they are almost identical to the exempt activity as originally defined.

Agricultural Cooperatives The Clayton Act specifically exempts nonprofit agricultural cooperatives organized to provide mutual assistance to farmers. The Capper-Volstead Act extended this exemption to "persons engaged in the production of agricultural products such as farmers, planters, ranchmen, dairymen, or nut and fruit growers." Fishermen's cooperatives are also exempt. The exemption applies only to "persons engaged in agricultural production" and not to packing houses or to associations involved in both production and distribution. The court's unwillingness to extend this exemption to packing houses illustrates strict constructionism.

Labor Organizations The National Labor Relations Act is considered a sufficient regulatory program for labor unions. The antitrust laws do not apply to most of the activities of labor unions as long as the unions are pursuing the welfare of their members. This exemption is limited, however, and the government may institute court action directly if labor unions conspire to restrain trade. Labor union activities that provide aid to nonlabor groups or that tend to create monopolies or control marketing are not exempt. For example, labor agreements that require the employer to avoid dealing with a supplier or a customer may be anticompetitive. Such agreements will be enforceable only if they are designed to protect a legitimate labor union interest.

State Action Since 1943, restraint of trade or monopolizations that result from valid governmental actions have been exempt from the Sherman Act under the **state action** exemption.[5] For example, state licensing of liquor stores or firearm sales often creates oligopolies restricting the number of sellers, an anticompetitive condition. These are not illegal restraints of trade, because the state licenses are for the public's protection. It is believed that adequate supervision provided by the state's regulations justifies the exemption.

For the state action exemption to apply, there must be a clearly defined state policy permitting or requiring the particular activity or restraint that causes the anticompetitive effect. The exemption does not apply to nongovernmental functions provided by the state itself. For example, the state action exemption was inapplicable (1) to alleged conspiracies by municipally owned utilities to exclude the services from utilities outside the municipality and (2) to a conspiracy between a city's sports stadium and its airport authority to exclude a particular brand of beer sold at both facilities. In another case, the Sherman Act was violated when the city of Boulder, Colorado, prevented a cable television company from expanding its service territory.[6] The state action exemption was inapplicable because the city's action was not taken pursuant to a valid and clearly articulated state policy.

Regulated Industries Prior to 1944, the insurance industry was not considered a part of interstate commerce, so antitrust regulation of insurance was prohibited. The new

---

[5] *Parker v. Brown,* 317 U.S. 341 (1943).

[6] *Community Communications Co. v. City of Boulder, Colorado,* 455 U.S. 40 (1982).

policy outlined by the McCarran-Ferguson Act in 1945 continued the special exemptions for insurance companies that were subject to state regulation of premium rates, for the selling and advertising of policies, and for insurance agent licensing. However, involvement in activities outside the sale of policies became subject to antitrust laws. For example, it may be illegal for an insurance company to boycott, coerce, or intimidate its competitors.

Stock exchanges have a limited form of antitrust exemption because they are considered necessary to support the regulatory framework of the securities laws. Bank and other financial institution mergers are exempt from antitrust laws because they are regulated by federal and state agencies, such as the Federal Reserve Board, the Comptroller of the Currency, the Federal Deposit Insurance Corporation, and the Office of Thrift Supervision.

Professions and Sports For many years, some professionals such as lawyers and engineers were also exempt from antitrust enforcement. However, there was no overwhelming justification for this exemption. As a result, local bar associations' "minimum-fee schedules" for attorneys' services are now considered illegal as price-fixing.[7] The ethical code of engineers once prohibited competitive bidding for engagements, but it effectively created an illegal agreement among competing engineers to refrain from discussing prices with potential customers.

Most professional sports involve restrictive actions among club owners, players' representatives, and owners of facilities (e.g., arenas and stadiums). For example, the limits on "free agency" prohibit players from moving between teams. Except for baseball, none of the professional sports are entitled to antitrust exemption. Football, boxing, basketball, and hockey are all subject to antitrust enforcement. The Supreme Court exempted professional baseball in 1922, 1953, and again in 1972. However, the baseball exemption is probably an aberration inconsistent with other laws.

Political Action Groups of businesses may join together to take mutually advantageous political action without violating the Sherman Act. The Supreme Court has refused to apply the Sherman Act to bona fide political activities of competitors even if their objective is noncompetitive legislation, regulations, or administrative action. The *Noerr-Pennington* doctrine is based on two First Amendment rights: freedom of speech and the right to petition the government for redress of grievances.[8] However, a *sham* exception to the Noerr doctrine has developed that does not protect intentional efforts to harass a competitor. For example, the purposeful interference with potential competitors' access to the courts or to regulatory agencies is not protected by Noerr. Conspiracy with a foreign government agency to restrain competition is also not protected.

MONOPOLIES

Monopolies are the original ills that the Sherman Act sought to cure. Monopoly power enables the monopolies to fix or control prices, reduce output, and exclude competitors. Under the Sherman Act, an illegal monopoly arises when monopoly power is intentionally exercised through such acts of monopolization.

---

[7]*Goldfarb v. Virginia State Bar,* 421 U.S. 773 (1975).

[8]*Eastern Railroad Presidents Conference v. Noerr Motor Freight, Inc.*, 365 U.S. 127 (1961).

Monopoly Power

The most fundamental question in a monopoly case concerns the existence of monopoly power exercised by the defendant. Economists define monopoly power on the basis of the *elasticity of demand*. Perfectly competitive markets are highly elastic; thus, when the price of a product rises, consumers can quickly switch their purchases to similar products. Conversely, when the price of a product falls, consumers can quickly shift to that product. The markets for investment securities and certain foodstuffs are elastic. There is seldom a significant level of monopolization in highly elastic markets.

Inelastic markets are markets in which consumer demand is relatively unresponsive to small price changes. The greater market power of firms in inelastic markets enables them to control prices to a greater extent. An *imperfect market*, characterized by inelastic demand, lends varying degrees of monopoly power to monopolists, oligopolists, and monopolistic competitors. Firms of these kinds may raise their prices without losing all of the customers because substitute products are not equivalent replacements. The market for component parts (such as microprocessor chips) patented or copyrighted by their manufacturers is often inelastic because buyers cannot easily use substitutes made by other manufacturers. Defining the relevant market is the first step in measuring monopoly power.

Relevant Market

Before the idea of a monopoly can make sense, the boundaries of the alleged monopoly's market must be defined. The monopolist's illegal use of market power must exist over (1) an identifiable geographic area and (2) a particular product. The plaintiff must define this **relevant market** in cases involving monopolies, mergers, and restraints of trade. The relevant market comprises all the producers of products or services that are functionally interchangeable and available to the same pool of consumers.

Geographic Market The monopolist's alleged illegal exercise of market power is relevant only to the specific geographic area within which that behavior affects competitors. Usually, evidence is presented concerning the buying patterns of existing consumers. If it is reasonable for consumers within a particular region to obtain the product or service produced within that region from any seller other than the alleged monopolist, then the region constitutes a geographic market. A particular geographic market may be local (e.g., a city, county, or metropolitan area), regional (e.g., a state or a number of states), or national. Generally, geographic markets are limited or bounded by the costs of transportation and by the ease with which consumers can gain access to other sellers. Within a particular geographic market, there may be *submarkets* in which a group of local sellers compete more directly. For example, neighborhood shops in commercial areas may comprise a submarket within a city's broader geographic shopping market.

Product Market The product market is determined by consumers' preferences and by their willingness to substitute physically different products for the same basic purpose or use. The issue is usually whether two products are perceived as reasonably interchangeable or substitutable. Courts examine the price, use, and quality of all reasonable substitutes and arrive at a determination concerning the cross-elasticity of demand between two allegedly similar products.

The determination of **cross-elasticity of demand** is a method of analysis that measures the relationship between two seemingly different goods or services. Cross-elasticity of demand is defined as the percentage change in the quantity demanded of one product divided by the percentage change of the substitute product's price. Where cross-elasticity is positive, the two goods compared are somewhat substitutable for each other and may be considered part of the same market (e.g., butter versus margarine). Negative cross-elasticity characterizes complementary products that are not substitutable for each other but are often purchased together (e.g., automobiles and tires). Cross-elasticity analysis is not a perfect method of determining product markets because consumers' willingness to substitute dissimilar products may change significantly at different price levels. For example, someone may be willing to ride a bus to work only if doing so is significantly cheaper than commuting in an automobile.

As more positive cross-elasticities are discovered between the monopolist's products and other products, the relevant market expands. On the other hand, if there are no reasonable substitutes (low cross-elasticities of demand) for the monopolist's product, then the size of the relevant product market will be small. A particular firm's market share in a market with many substitutes will usually be quite small, while a particular firm's market share in a market with few substitutes may be large. As a result, there is a natural tendency for plaintiffs to allege that few substitutes exist (low cross-elasticities), whereas defendants tend to allege that many substitutes exist (high cross-elasticities).

How might cross-elasticities analysis be used in a case involving a common household product such as food wrap? The following classic case illustrates the dilemma faced by courts attempting to define a relevant product market.

United States v. E.I. du Pont de Nemours & Co.

351 U.S. 377 (1956)
United States Supreme Court

Du Pont produced almost 75 percent of the cellophane (plastic food wrap) sold in the United States. Cellophane constituted less than 20 percent of all "flexible packaging material" sales. The Justice Department argued that cellophane and other flexible wraps (e.g., wax paper, aluminum foil) were neither substantially interchangeable in use (i.e., fungible) nor priced similarly. Under Section 2 of the Sherman Act, du Pont was charged with and convicted of monopolization of the cellophane market rather than the flexible packaging material market.

Justice Reed delivered the opinion of the Court.

If cellophane is the "market" that du Pont is found to dominate, it may be assumed it does have monopoly power over that "market." Monopoly power is the power to control prices or exclude competition. It seems apparent that du Pont's power to set the price of cellophane has been limited only by the competition afforded by other flexible packaging materials. Moreover, it may be practically impossible for anyone to commence manufacturing cellophane without full access to du Pont's technique. However, du Pont has no power to prevent competition from other wrapping materials. The trial court consequently had to determine whether competition from the other wrappings prevent du Pont from possessing monopoly power in violation of § 2. Price and competition are so intimately entwined that any discussion of theory must treat them as one.

If a large number of buyers and sellers deal freely in a standardized product, such as salt or wheat, we have complete or pure competition. Patents, on the other hand, furnish the most familiar type of classic monopoly. As the producers of a standardized product bring about significant differentiations of quality, design, or packaging in the product that permit differences of use, competition becomes to a greater or less degree incomplete and the producer's power over price and competition greater over his article and its use, according to the differentiation he is able to create and maintain. A retail seller may have in one sense a monopoly on certain trade because of location, as an isolated country store or filling station, or because no one else makes a product of just the quality or attractiveness of his product, as for example in cigarettes. Thus one can theorize that we have monopolistic competition in every nonstandardized commodity with each manufacturer having power over the price and production of his own product. However, this power that, let us say, automobile or soft-drink manufacturers have over their trademarked products is not the power that makes an illegal monopoly. Illegal power must be appraised in terms of the competitive market for the product.

Determination of the competitive market for commodities depends on how different from one another are the offered commodities in character or use, how far buyers will go to substitute one commodity for another. For example, one can think of building materials as in commodity competition but one could hardly say that brick competed with steel or wood or cement or stone in the meaning of Sherman Act litigation; the products are too different. This is the interindustry competition emphasized by some economists.

On the other hand, there are certain differences in the formulae for soft drinks but one can hardly say that each one is an illegal monopoly. Whatever the market may be, we hold that control of price or competition establishes the existence of monopoly power under § 2.

The Relevant Market—When a product is controlled by one interest, without substitutes available in the market, there is monopoly power. Because most products have possible substitutes, we cannot give "that infinite range" to the definition of substitutes. Nor is it a proper interpretation of the Sherman Act to require that products be fungible to be considered in the relevant market.

But where there are market alternatives that buyers may readily use for their purposes, illegal monopoly does not exist merely because the product said to be monopolized differs from others. If it were not so, only physically identical products would be a part of the market. To accept the Government's argument, we would have to conclude that the manufacturers of plain as well as moistureproof cellophane were monopolists, and so with films such as Pliofilm, foil, glassine, polyethylene, and Saran, for each of these wrapping materials is distinguishable.

An element for consideration as to cross-elasticity of demand between products is the responsiveness of the sales of one product to price changes of the other. If a slight decrease in the price of cellophane causes a considerable number of customers of other flexible wrappings to switch to cellophane, it would be an indication that a high cross-elasticity of demand exists between them; that the products compete in the same market. The court below held that the "[g]reat sensitivity of customers in the flexible packaging markets to price or quality changes" prevented du Pont from possessing monopoly control over price. The record sustains these findings.

We conclude that cellophane's interchangeability with the other materials mentioned suffices to make it a part of this flexible packaging material market.

Case Questions

1. What is cross-elasticity of demand? How is this measure used to determine the relevant market?
2. What approach should be used to determine market share in cases in which the defendant is the only producer of the product? Would your answer be different if the defendant holds a valid patent on the product?
3. How might the cross-elasticity analysis have been conducted differently if the Court had considered the different price ranges of the flexible wrapping products?

Refinement of the Product Market Analysis Although the Supreme Court's analysis in *du Pont* advanced the understanding of relevant product markets significantly, there are obvious flaws in this analysis. When considering all forms of flexible package wrap, the Court should have considered specific consumer preferences between any two products for a particular use. Some substitute products are clearly not substitutable for some uses. For example, only aluminum foil can be used in barbecue grilling, whereas microwave ovens usually require nonmetallic food wrap. The Supreme Court's inclusion of all aluminum foil sales in the market makes the impossible assumption that all aluminum foil users could switch to cellophane or wax paper for all uses of aluminum foil. A better analysis than that of the Supreme Court would provide for adjustments in the calculation of demand for substitute products that reflect reasonable estimates of the amount of nonsubstitutability. Nonsubstitutability helps explain why consumers are seldom indifferent in choosing between substitutes, a fact reflected in the calculation of cross-elasticity of demand. If this refinement in analysis had been used in the *du Pont* case, a smaller overall product market than *all* "flexible wrapping material" would have been used and du Pont might have been found closer to monopolization.

The cross-elasticity analysis used may be flawed for another reason. If a monopolist is already charging monopoly prices, consumers may be willing to switch to less perfect substitutes only if the substitutes are much lower in price. This suggests that imperfect substitutes are not acceptable if the price of the more perfect monopolized product is still at "reasonable" levels. In packaging sandwiches, for example, resealable plastic bags are generally considered superior to wax paper. If the two products are priced the same, most people will use plastic bags. Only if wax paper is significantly cheaper, will some people substitute it for plastic bags. In the *du Pont* case, the alleged substitutes were not perfectly substitutable. Thus, du Pont's control over the cellophane market was somewhat closer to monopolization of the flexible packaging material market than the Court held.

The *du Pont* case exemplifies how courts can expand the relevant market to protect alleged monopolists from prosecution. More recently, cross-elasticity analysis has been restricted somewhat, resulting in a narrower product market definition. For example, professional championship boxing matches have been considered a market distinct from other boxing matches because championship matches are considered the "cream" of the boxing business, appealing to a broader audience than other boxing matches. A similar analysis could be used to separate the major league baseball market from the minor league market. Gospel music has been considered a market distinct from popular music generally. In a case against IBM, a submarket for the leasing of large mainframes was differentiated from the market for the purchase of the same computers.

Market Share Once the court has defined the relevant product and geographic markets, it must determine the alleged monopolist's market power. Market power is typically measured as a percentage of the relevant market, called the **market share.** Market share requires the computation of a fraction: the numerator is the defendant's unit sales, the denominator is the total unit sales of all competitors. Unfortunately, there is no litmus paper test for determining what market share constitutes a monopoly. Such percentages as 90 percent, 85 percent, and 75 percent have usually been considered monopolies. Market shares of 20 percent or 50 percent are usually insufficient to constitute monopoly power. However, in the analysis of mergers, discussed later in this chapter, a lower market share is often considered sufficient to prohibit the merger.

Monopolization

The mere existence of monopoly power does not violate the Sherman Act. Indeed, some industries (e.g., utilities) are more efficient when operated as a monopoly. A monopoly becomes illegal when market power is used illegally. Thus, **monopolization** represents the intentional use of monopoly power to gain an illegal monopoly.

The *abuse theory of monopoly* is derived from the conduct approach to antitrust enforcement. Under this theory, monopolies are said to exist only where a firm with monopoly power abuses its market power by undertaking purposeful acts to harm competitors and consumers. Market power that is acquired by historical accident or is obtained or maintained by selling better products or using business savvy is not illegal as abusive. What inferences may be drawn from a producer's purposeful acts to forestall the entry of competitors into the market? The following case illustrates how the proof of monopolistic intent may be inferred from circumstantial evidence.

United States v. Aluminum Co. of America
148 F.2d 416 (2d Cir. 1945)
United States Court of Appeals, 2d Circuit

Up to the time of suit, Aluminum Company of America (Alcoa) was the only producer of "virgin" aluminum ingot (not from recycled scrap) in the United States. Alcoa argued that it was not a monopolist because markets existed for imported and recycled aluminum ingot. Alcoa also argued that it had not acquired its position of market dominance through illegal exclusionary acts. Although Alcoa's profit margins of about 10 percent were not considered a monopolist's profit, an illegal monopolization can exist even in the absence of such a profit. The Justice Department sought to have Alcoa dissolved, and it appealed from a trial court decision in favor of Alcoa.

L. Hand, Circuit Judge

Many people believe that possession of unchallenged economic power deadens initiative, discourages thrift and depresses energy; that immunity from competition is a narcotic, and rivalry is a stimulant, to industrial progress; that the spur of constant stress is necessary to counteract an inevitable disposition to let well enough alone. Such people believe that competitors, versed in the craft as no consumer can be, will be quick to detect opportunities for saving and new shifts in production, and be eager to profit by them. In any event the mere fact that a producer, having command of the domestic market, has not been able to make more than a "fair" profit, is no evidence that a "fair" profit could not have been made at lower prices. True, it might have been thought adequate to condemn only those monopolies which could not show that they had exercised the highest possible ingenuity, had anticipated every conceivable improvement, simulated every possible demand. No doubt, that would be one way of dealing with the matter, although it would imply constant scrutiny and constant supervision, such as courts are unable to provide. Be that as it may, that was not the way that Congress chose; it did not condone "good trusts" and condemn "bad" ones; it forbade all. Moreover, in so doing it was not necessarily actuated by economic motives alone. It is possible, because of its indirect social or moral effect, to prefer a system of small producers, each dependent for his success upon his own skill and character, to one in which the great mass of those engaged must accept the direction of a few.

It does not follow because "Alcoa" had such a monopoly, that it "monopolized" the ingot market; it may not have achieved monopoly; monopoly may have been thrust upon it. If it had been a combination of existing smelters which united the whole industry and controlled the production of all aluminum ingot, it would certainly have "monopolized" the market.

This notion has usually been expressed by saying that size does not determine guilt; that there must be some "exclusion" of competitors; that the growth must be something else than "natural" or "normal"; that there must be a "wrongful intent," or some other specific intent; or that some "unduly" coercive means must be used.

What engendered these compunctions is reasonably plain: persons may unwittingly find themselves in possession of a monopoly, automatically so to say; that is, without having intended either to put an end to existing competition, or to prevent competition from arising when none had existed, they may become monopolists by force of accident.

A market may, for example, be so limited that it is impossible to produce at all and meet the cost of production except by a plant large enough to supply the whole demand. Or there may be changes in taste or in cost which drive out all but one purveyor. A single producer may be the survivor out of a group of active competitors, merely by virtue of his superior skill, foresight and industry. In such cases a strong argument can be made that, although the result may expose the public to the evils of monopoly, the Act does not mean to condemn the resultant of those very forces which it is its prime object to foster. The successful competitor, having been urged to compete, must not be turned upon when he wins.

It would completely misconstrue "Alcoa's" position in 1940 to hold that it was the passive beneficiary of a monopoly, following upon an involuntary elimination of competitors by automatically operative economic forces.

There were at least one or two abortive attempts to enter the industry, but "Alcoa" effectively anticipated and forestalled all competition, and succeeded in holding the field alone. True, it stimulated demand and opened new uses for the metal, but not without making sure that it could supply what it had evoked. There is no dispute as to this; "Alcoa" avows it as evidence of the skill, energy and initiative with which it has always conducted its business; as a reason why, having won its way by fair means, it should be commended, and not dismembered.

The only question is whether it falls within the exception established in favor of those who do not seek, but cannot avoid, the control of a market. . . . It was not inevitable that it should always anticipate increases in the demand for ingot and be prepared to supply them. Nothing compelled it to keep doubling and redoubling its capacity before others entered the field. It insists that it never excluded competitors; but we can think of no more effective exclusion than progressively to embrace each new opportunity as it opened, and to face every newcomer with new capacity already geared into a great organization, having the advantage of experience, trade connections and the elite of personnel. Only in case we interpret "exclusion" as limited to manoeuvres not honestly industrial, but actuated solely by a desire to prevent competition, can such a course, indefatigably pursued, be deemed not "exclusionary." So to limit it would in our judgment emasculate the Act; would permit just such consolidations as it was designed to prevent.

In order to fall within § 2, the monopolist must have both the power to monopolize, and the intent to monopolize. To read the passage as demanding any "specific" intent, makes nonsense of it, for no monopolist monopolizes unconscious of what he is doing. So here, "Alcoa" meant to keep, and did keep, that complete and exclusive hold upon the ingot market with which it started. That was to "monopolize" that market, however innocently it otherwise proceeded.

We may start therefore with the premise that to have combined 90 percent of the producers of ingot would have been to "monopolize" the ingot market; and, so far as concerns the public interest, it can make no difference whether an existing competition is put an end to, or whether prospective competition is prevented.

Case Questions

1. What actions taken by Alcoa to interfere with the development of competitors could be termed "monopolization"? Would these actions have been legal if Alcoa did not already have a monopoly position?
2. How can intent to monopolize be proved? Which of Alcoa's actions were circumstantial evidence of intent?
3. How might a producer have market dominance "thrust upon" it? Does acquiring market dominance in this way justify holding a position of monopoly?

The types of monopolistic acts that constitute a monopoly vary considerably. Whenever a monopolist engages in predatory and coercive conduct in direct violation of the antitrust laws, monopolization intent can easily be inferred. However, acts considered legal in many circumstances may be illegal if the monopolist's market power is employed with monopolistic intent. For example, conduct that is intended to prevent the entry of competitors, such as systematically increasing production capacity in anticipation of new demand, is illegal. In another case, a policy of leasing but never selling a product was considered exclusionary and unlawful.

Predatory Pricing *Predatory pricing*, pricing below the producer's marginal cost, may also constitute deliberate and purposeful acts of monopolization. Although predatory pricing results in losses on sales, it often forces competitors out of business, thereby permitting later price increases to cover the earlier losses. If a monopolist lowers prices to undercut or restrict the entry of competitors, the intent to monopolize may be inferred. *Marginal cost* is the manufacturer's additional expense to produce one more unit beyond the number produced up to that point. *Average variable cost* is the average of all the variable expenses for all of the units produced. Some commentators have urged that pricing below average variable cost should be presumed predatory.

Predatory pricing is monopolistic if it tends to immediately eliminate rivals, thus creating a monopoly that enables the seller to recoup losses later. A similar tactic is to charge monopoly prices in one geographic or product market and to lower prices in a more competitive market. Discriminatory pricing allows the monopolist to undercut potential competition by taking temporary losses that are made up with profits taken at other times or profits made in other geographic or product markets.

Attempts to Monopolize

The Sherman Act prohibits "attempts to monopolize" even in cases in which the alleged monopolist does not possess clear monopoly power. The plaintiff must prove that the defendant employed methods, means, and practices that would, if successful, accomplish monopolization and that, though falling short of monopolization, nevertheless approached it so closely as to create a dangerous probability of monopolization.

The defendant in such cases must be proved to have had the specific intent of excluding competitors through the exercise of monopoly power. This "specific intent" requirement necessitates a higher burden of proof than is necessary in monopolization cases. As discussed earlier, however, intent may be inferred from unfair conduct. For example, inducing others to boycott a competitor's product, using discriminatory pricing, or refusing to deal with a particular customer are evidence of a specific intent of an attempt to monopolize. If two or more persons combine to do such acts, their agreement may also constitute a separate crime: the illegal *conspiracy* to monopolize.

MERGERS

Mergers have been receiving increasing attention from several perspectives. Mergers typically involve struggles between insiders and outsiders for corporate control. Many of these corporate control battles are fought in the securities markets and involve SEC regulation. Most mergers must be approved by shareholders, a process governed by state corporate law. However, mergers fundamentally involve antitrust law because they may result in the acquisition of monopoly power. Antitrust law poses a difficult question of industrial organization: Will the market structure resulting from a merger or an acquisition create an illegal monopoly?

Types of Mergers and Business Combinations

Mergers are only one of several ways for corporations to expand. Firms may raise capital to finance growth by generating cash flow internally or externally in the public securities markets. However, it is often quicker and easier to acquire an existing firm through a merger, consolidation, purchase of assets, or acquisition of a subsidiary. A *merger* brings together two independent firms, of which one survives and the other is dissolved. A *consolidation* combines two independent firms, which are terminated and replaced by a newly created combined entity. A *purchase of assets* involves the transfer of an acquired firm's assets to the acquiring firm without the necessity of dissolving either firm. In an *acquisition,* a firm acquired by another firm may operate as a separate division or subsidiary, though a merger may eventually result. For the purposes of antitrust analysis, all of these transactions are considered mergers.

Early interpretations of the Sherman Act held that mergers destroyed the competition that previously existed between the merged firms. Thus, most mergers were prohibited based simply on the concentration of power that would result. However, the courts eventually refused to use the Sherman Act to restrict mergers. Congress then passed the Clayton Act to specifically prohibit mergers tending to lessen competition.

Clayton Antitrust Act, Section 7

. . . no person engaged in commerce, or in any activity affecting commerce shall acquire, directly or indirectly, the whole or any part of stock or other share capital . . . [or] . . . the whole or any part of the assets of another person engaged also in commerce or in any activity affecting commerce, where in any line of commerce or in any activity affecting commerce in any section of the country, the effect of such acquisition may be substantially to lessen competition, or tend to create a monopoly.

Section 7 was amended in 1950 by the *Celler-Kefauver Act* to (1) prohibit noncompetitive market structures (e.g., oligopolies, monopolistic competition), (2) encourage internal growth and expansion, and (3) preserve local industrial control and small business viability. The Celler-Kefauver amendments also closed a major loophole in the Clayton Act by including sales of assets as covered activity. The amendments apply to all three of the basic merger variations—horizontal mergers between competitors, vertical mergers between suppliers and customers, and conglomerate mergers with firms in other industries.

Horizontal Merger Analysis

Although many mergers have aspects of a horizontal, vertical, or conglomerate nature, it is most useful to first examine **horizontal mergers**, or combinations of firms that compete at the same level of production in the same industry (see Figure 15–3). Regulation of horizontal mergers is the least controversial type of merger regulation and employs the basic method used in all merger analysis. Merger analysis is very similar to monopoly analysis because the court must determine the relevant market and market share controlled by the merged firms. A merger may be prohibited if it results in a substantial lessening of competition in the relevant market.

Relevant Geographic Market In a merger analysis, the court must first define the relevant "line of commerce." Each line of commerce has a geographic parameter and a product parameter. Mergers are prohibited when they tend to substantially lessen competition in a particular "section of the country." This requires the definition of product markets on a local, regional, or national basis, though geographic submarkets may also exist. Usually, an inquiry is undertaken into geographic substitutability for the particular region claimed as the relevant market. For example, evidence that buyers have shifted purchases between regions would tend to permit combination of the regions into a single market. However, if transportation costs increase, it becomes more difficult for customers

FIGURE 15–3 Horizontal Merger

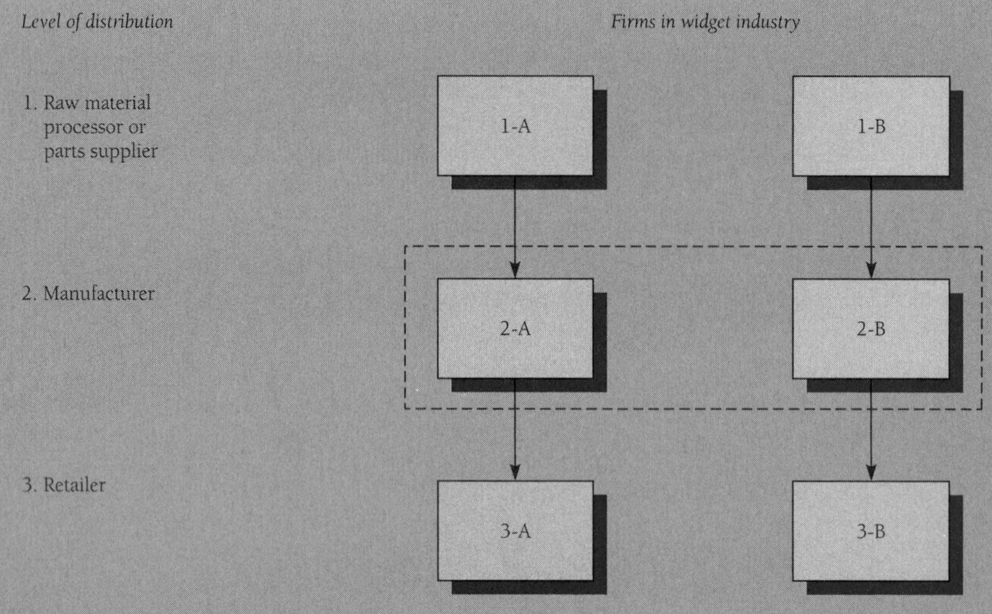

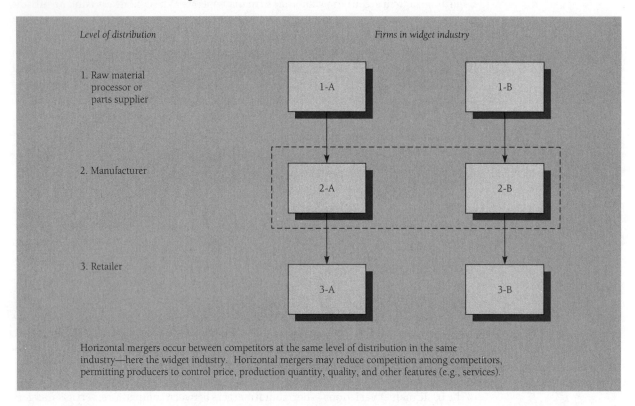

Horizontal mergers occur between competitors at the same level of distribution in the same industry—here the widget industry. Horizontal mergers may reduce competition among competitors, permitting producers to control price, production quantity, quality, and other features (e.g., services).

to switch between producers in different regions. When highly correlated changes in product prices occur in two neighboring regions, there is a strong inference that the regions may be geographically substitutable.

Relevant Product Market The next step involves an inquiry into the relevant product market. Substitute products and their cross-elasticities of demand are identified, and consumers' perceptions of product substitutability are examined. This requires analysis of the similarities and differences between the customary usage, design, and physical composition of allegedly similar products. Inquiries into the correlation of price movements between similar products may also shed light on their substitutability.

In merger cases, it is necessary to identify all of the major firms that produce in a relevant market and to compute their individual market shares. Firms may also be included if they are capable of (1) switching to produce the relevant product, (2) reconditioning other products to make them good substitutes for that product, or (3) vertically integrating into the relevant product market. As in monopolization cases, defendants have an incentive to expand the market definition so that their merger will appear insignificant.

Justice Department Merger Guidelines Since the 1982 revision of its merger guidelines, the Justice Department made its decisions to approve or oppose mergers on the basis of *market concentration,* an indication of the potential for exercise of monopoly power. Greater concentration is found where there are fewer firms, each with larger market shares; less concentration is found where more firms compete. As the number of firms grows, the market approaches perfect competition, an antitrust objective.

The *Herfindahl Index* calculates the degree of market concentration by summing the squares of each firm's individual market share. High Herfindahl numbers result if the market is dominated by monopolists with large market shares. For example, if just one firm in the relevant market had 75 percent of the market, the Herfindahl Index would be at least $75^2 = 5{,}625$. By contrast, if 10 firms in the relevant market each possessed a market share of 10 percent, the Herfindahl Index would be $10^2 + 10^2 + 10^2 + 10^2 + 10^2 + 10^2 + 10^2 + 10^2 + 10^2 + 10^2 = 10 \times 100 = 1{,}000$. The Herfindahl Index can range from 10,000 in the case of a pure monopoly (100^2) to less than 1 for a perfectly competitive market.

It is unlikely that the Justice Department will attack any mergers for which the Herfindahl Index remains below 1,000. If the index lies between 1,000 and 1,800, the Justice Department will challenge a merger that results in an increase of 100 or more Herfindahl points. If the index is above 1,800, it will challenge a merger that results in an increase of more than 50 points. Markets with Herfindahl indexes greater than 1,800 are considered highly concentrated. The Herfindahl Index does not have the force of law, but it is used by the Justice Department to indicate when prosecution should be undertaken. Clearly, the Justice Department can adjust its challenges to mergers by simply changing these thresholds. For example, it would be more lenient to raise the thresholds to 1,200 and 2,000 or more strict to lower them to 800 and 1,500.

Substantial Lessening of Competition Courts hearing merger cases must determine whether or not the resulting market share of the combined firms will probably lead to a substantial lessening of competition. Courts usually determine whether, as a preventive measure, a merger should be prohibited. Unlike court action under the Sherman Act, there is no necessity to prove attempts at predatory conduct or monopolistic acts. Probabilities, not "ephemeral possibilities," must be demonstrated by the party attacking the merger. The Justice Department considers the competitive impact of most mergers. Most parties will not pursue a merger if the Justice Department publicly opposes it.

The standard used by the federal courts to judge the anticompetitive effect of a merger is often different from the standard used by the Justice Department to bring suit. Courts prohibit mergers if the newly created firm "controls an undue percentage share" of the relevant market and results in "a significant increase in concentration." In one case, a prohibited merger would have resulted in a combined firm with a 30 percent market share. In another case, the absorption of a small, aggressive, and innovative firm by Alcoa was prohibited because the merger adversely affected competition.

In *United States v. Von's Grocery Co.*, the Supreme Court upheld a Justice Department challenge to a merger between two grocery store chains in the Los Angeles area: Von's and Shopping Bag.[9] The combined sales of the two chains would have been only 7.5 percent of the metropolitan Los Angeles grocery market. However, the court noted that these two firms had experienced tremendous growth and the "mom and pop" grocery stores were in steady decline. Merger analysis may consider industry trends toward consolidation to prevent a merger with short-term procompetitive effects but which would result in concentration permitting collusion in the future.

---

[9] *United States v. Von's Grocery Co.*, 384 U.S. 270 (1966).

FIGURE 15–4 Vertical Merger

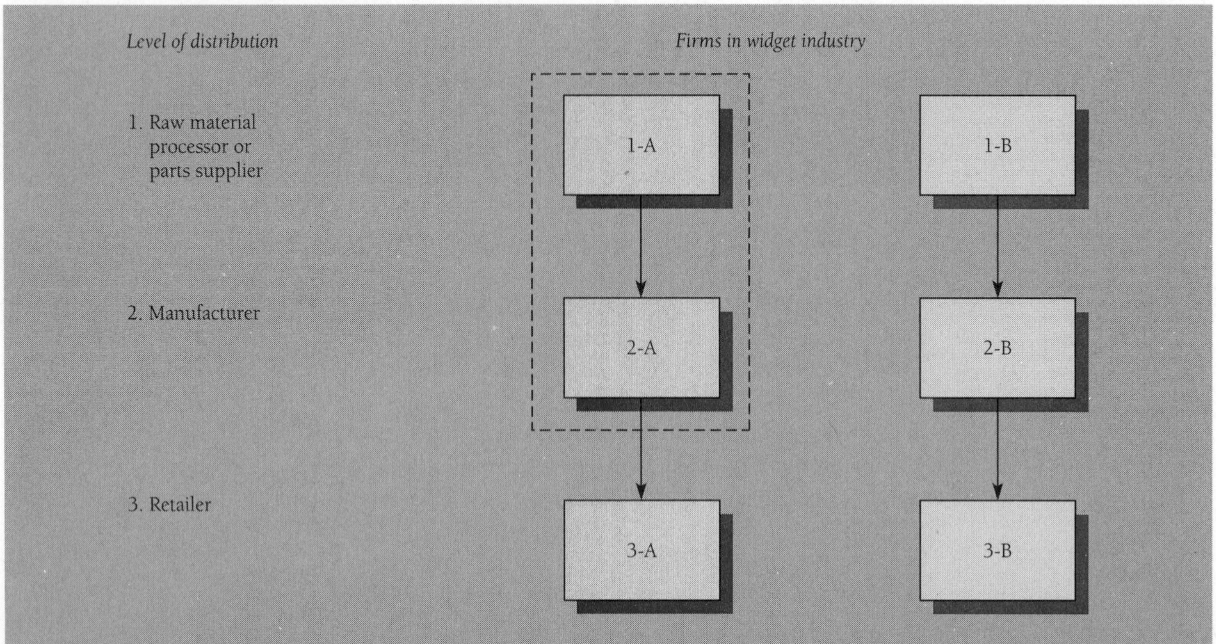

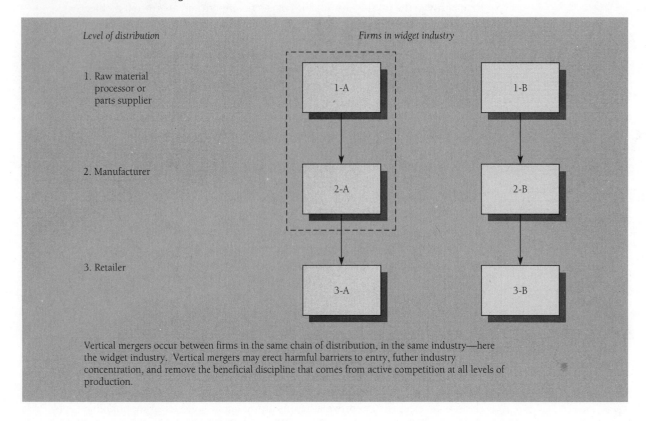

Vertical mergers occur between firms in the same chain of distribution, in the same industry—here the widget industry. Vertical mergers may erect harmful barriers to entry, futher industry concentration, and remove the beneficial discipline that comes from active competition at all levels of production.

Vertical Merger Analysis

Vertical mergers combine firms that stand in a supplier-customer relationship along the same chain of distribution, as illustrated in Figure 15–4. The term *vertical integration* has come to describe the result of expansion of producers into the retail or supplier levels. There is a natural tendency for businesses to control their customers and suppliers through vertical integration. Vertical mergers enable the resulting firm to squeeze out unintegrated competitors and to limit future competition by erecting barriers to entry. Vertically integrated firms tend to exclude their rivals from sources of supply or customers by causing a *supply squeeze*. They may also refuse to deal with nonintegrated firms and give preferential allocation of raw materials to their own subsidiaries. Vertically integrated firms may also discriminate in price, favoring their captive customers over nonintegrated competitors.

Mergers between companies attempting vertical integration are subjected to analysis similar to that of horizontal mergers. First, the relevant geographic and product markets are determined. Second, the probable effect of the merger on the foreclosure of competition due to acquisition of excessive market share is analyzed. Third, the courts analyze historical trends toward concentration, the nature and purpose of the merger, and any resulting barriers to entry.

Vertical mergers do not immediately result in more concentrated markets, so the analysis of a vertical merger's impact on competition is more difficult to perform than the analysis of a horizontal merger's impact. The court must focus more closely on the potential foreclosure of competition and resulting barriers to entry by new firms. Barriers to entry stemming from vertical integration become objectionable if they compel potential competitors to integrate vertically in order to compete effectively against the merged firm and thus make entry more difficult. Challenge of such mergers is controversial where vertical integration makes the industry more efficient.

The Justice Department will challenge a vertical merger if it facilitates collusion in a highly concentrated *upstream market* (concentration at the supplier level). For example, if suppliers own their retail outlets, then the prices of competing suppliers are easily discerned because these competing suppliers attempt to sell to the supplier's retail outlets. This can facilitate price-fixing among all suppliers. However, if there are independent and disruptive buyers, then suppliers may be forced to compete for the business of these buyers. Should a vertical merger be prohibited if it might reduce competition among suppliers? The next case illustrates how the potential loss of market discipline and the industry's trend toward concentration are used in the analysis of a vertical merger.

Brown Shoe Co. v. United States

370 U.S. 284 (1962)

United States Supreme Court

The Justice Department brought suit to block a merger between Brown Shoe Company, Inc. (Brown) and G.R. Kinney Company, Inc. (Kinney) as a violation of Section 7 of the Clayton Act. Both companies manufactured shoes and owned or controlled some retail outlets. The trial court found that the proposed merger would substantially lessen competition in the retail shoe market.

Chief Justice Warren delivered the opinion of the Court.

Economic arrangements between companies standing in a supplier-customer relationship are characterized as "vertical." The primary vice of a vertical merger or other arrangement tying a customer to a supplier is that, by foreclosing the competitors of either party from a segment of the market otherwise open to them, the arrangement may act as a "clog on competition," which "deprive[s] . . . rivals of a fair opportunity to compete." Every extended vertical arrangement by its very nature, for at least a time, denies to competitors of the supplier the opportunity to compete for part or all of the trade of the customer-party to the vertical arrangement. However, the Clayton Act does not render unlawful all such vertical arrangements, but forbids only those whose effect "may be substantially to lessen competition, or to tend to create a monopoly" "in any line of commerce in any section of the country."

We agree with the parties and the District Court that insofar as the vertical aspect of this merger is concerned, the relevant geographic market is the entire Nation. The relationships of product value, bulk, weight and consumer demand enable manufacturers to distribute their shoes on a nationwide basis, as Brown and Kinney, in fact, do. The anticompetitive effects of the merger are to be measured within this range of distribution.

Since the diminution of the vigor of competition which may stem from a vertical arrangement results primarily from a foreclosure of a share of the market otherwise open to competitors, an important consideration in determining whether the effect of a vertical arrangement "may be substantially to lessen competition, or to tend to create a monopoly" is the size of the share of the market foreclosed. On the other hand, foreclosure of a *de minimis* share of the market will not tend "substantially to lessen competition."

Between these extremes, in cases such as the one before us, in which the foreclosure is neither of monopoly nor *de minimis* proportions, the percentage of the market foreclosed by the vertical arrangement cannot itself be decisive. In such cases, it becomes necessary to undertake an examination of various economic and historical factors in order to determine whether the arrangement under review is of the type Congress sought to proscribe.

The present merger involved neither small companies nor failing companies. In 1955, the date of this merger, Brown was the fourth largest manufacturer in the shoe industry with sales of approximately 25 million pairs of shoes and assets of over $72,000,000, while Kinney had sales of about 8 million pairs of shoes and assets of about $18,000,000. Not only was Brown one of the leading manufacturers of men's, women's, and children's shoes, but Kinney, with over 350 retail outlets, owned and operated the largest independent chain of family shoe stores in the Nation. Thus, in this industry, no merger between a manufacturer and an independent retailer could involve a larger potential market foreclosure. Moreover, it is apparent both from past behavior of Brown, and from the testimony of Brown's President, that Brown would use its ownership of Kinney to force Brown shoes into Kinney stores. Thus, in operation this vertical arrangement would be quite analogous to one involving a tying clause.

Another important factor to consider is the trend toward concentration in the industry.

Brown argues, however, that the shoe industry is at present composed of a large number of manufacturers and retailers, and that the industry is dynamically competitive. But remaining vigor cannot immunize a merger if the trend in that industry is toward oligopoly. It is the probable effect of the merger upon the future as well as the present which the Clayton Act commands the courts and the Commission to examine.

The District Court's findings, and the record facts, many of them set forth in Part I of this opinion, convince us that the shoe industry is being subjected to just such a cumulative series of vertical mergers which, if left unchecked, will be likely "substantially to lessen competition."

We reach this conclusion because the trend toward vertical integration in the shoe industry, when combined with Brown's avowed policy of forcing its own shoes upon its retail subsidiaries, may foreclose competition from a substantial share of the markets for men's, women's, and children's shoes, without producing any countervailing competitive, economic, or social advantages.

Case Questions

1. What analytic steps should be taken in a vertical merger case?
2. What impact did the industry's trend toward vertical integration have on the Court's analysis?

Conglomerate Merger Analysis

Conglomerate mergers include all types of mergers that cannot be classified as horizontal or vertical; they are illustrated in Figure 15–5. Typically, they involve the acquisition of firms in other industries and other product lines at any level of production. *Product extension* conglomerate mergers allow a firm to acquire complementary product lines that can be used with existing products. For example, a computer manufacturer's acquisition of a software producer would be a product extension merger because software is used with computers. *Market extension* mergers enable the merging firm to operate in new geographic markets. Totally unrelated mergers are often referred to as *diversification mergers.* The diversified firm may smooth out its cash flows, permitting it to profit in other markets when its main market suffers a downturn.

Mergers that result in conglomerates appear to involve little or no anticompetitive effect. However, it is argued that conglomerate mergers tend to reinforce oligopoly conditions in some industries. This further weakens independent firms, eventually leading to the elimination of competition. Large, acquiring firms often bring financial resources and the goodwill of popular brand names to the merged firm. This makes it more difficult for independent firms to compete. After a conglomerate merger, the larger merged firm may use discriminatory and exclusionary practices to discipline smaller competitors into lessening competition.

FIGURE 15–5 Conglomerate Merger

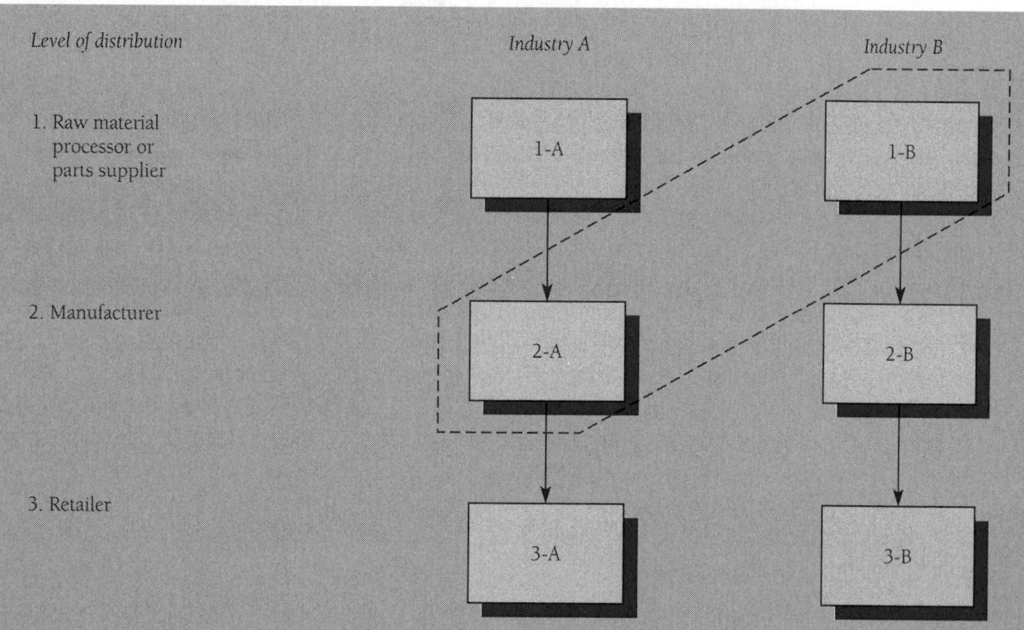

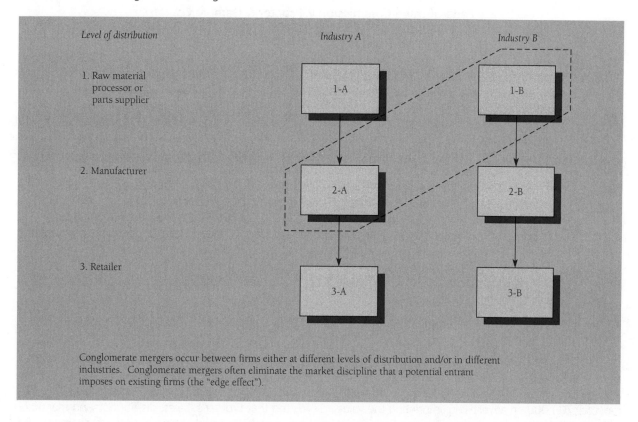

Conglomerate mergers occur between firms either at different levels of distribution and/or in different industries. Conglomerate mergers often eliminate the market discipline that a potential entrant imposes on existing firms (the "edge effect").

It is also argued that conglomerate mergers eliminate the *potential entrant,* or *potential competitor, effect.* As long as competitors perceive that outsiders may come into the market, market discipline impels them to remain efficient, pricing their products below monopoly levels. That is, if potential entrants are "waiting in the wings," an *edge effect* arises, causing the existing competitors to make more competitive production, pricing, and output decisions. If the potential entrant simply merges with an existing firm, this destroys whatever restraining effect its presence "at the edge" had on competitors in the given market. In other instances, the merger of a potential entrant may eliminate the probability of future procompetitive deconcentration. If, instead of merging, that firm entered the market on its own *(de novo),* it would reinforce competitive discipline by increasing the number of competitors.

In cases opposing conglomerate mergers, the plaintiff must first prove that the existing competitors perceived and were influenced by the potential entry of the outside merging firm. Second, the acquiring firm must have had reasonable means to enter the given market without merging. Third, the number of potential entrants cannot be excessive; otherwise, the elimination of only one potential entrant would not significantly reduce the competitive discipline.

What effect does a large potential entrant have on the marketing practices of existing firms? The next case illustrates the effect of a large conglomerate's financial resources on one product market.

Federal Trade Commission v. Procter & Gamble Co.

386 U.S. 568 (1967)
United States Supreme Court

In 1957, Procter & Gamble (P&G), a large, diversified consumer products firm, acquired the assets of Clorox Chemical Company, the largest manufacturer of fabric bleach. Clorox had nearly half of the fabric bleach market in most markets and larger shares in some markets. The top three bleach firms had 80 percent of the market; the remainder was held by some 200 small firms. P&G was a dominant producer of cleansers, soaps, and detergents and had the largest advertising budget of any consumer products firm. The FTC challenged the conglomerate merger as anticompetitive because P&G was considered a potential entrant into the bleach market. The FTC alleged that the presence of P&G in the bleach market through the acquisition of Clorox would (1) intimidate new entrants from entering the bleach market, (2) discourage active competition among existing competitors for fear of retaliation by P&G, and (3) reduce competition by eliminating P&G as the most likely new competitor. Liquid bleach was considered the product market, and the nation was considered the relevant geographic market (with several submarkets). The FTC appealed from an appeals court reversal of the trial court, which found the acquisition anticompetitive.

Justice Douglas delivered the opinion of the Court.

Since all liquid bleach is chemically identical, advertising and sales promotion are vital. In 1957 Clorox spent almost $3,700,000 on advertising, imprinting the value of its bleach in the mind of the consumer. In addition, it spent $1,700,000 for other promotional activities. The Commission found that these heavy expenditures went far to explain why Clorox maintained so high a market share despite the fact that its brand . . . retailed for a price equal to or, in many instances, higher than its competitors.

Prior to the acquisition, Procter was in the course of diversifying into product lines related to its basic detergent-soap-cleanser business. Liquid bleach was a distinct possibility since packaged detergents—Procter's primary product line—and liquid bleach are used complementarily in washing clothes and fabrics, and in general household cleaning.

The decision to acquire Clorox was the result of a study conducted by Procter's promotion department designed to determine the advisability of entering the liquid bleach industry. The initial report noted the ascendancy of liquid bleach in the large and expanding household bleach market, and recommended that Procter purchase Clorox rather than enter independently. Since a large investment would be needed to obtain a satisfactory market share, acquisition of the industry's leading firm was attractive. "Taking over the Clorox business . . . could be a way of achieving a dominant position in the liquid bleach market quickly, which would pay out reasonably well." The initial report predicted that Procter's "sales, distribution and manufacturing setup" could increase Clorox's share of the markets in areas where it was low. The final report confirmed the conclusions of the initial report and emphasized that Procter could make more effective use of Clorox's advertising budget and that the merger would facilitate advertising economies.

The Commission found that the substitution of Procter with its huge assets and advertising advantages for the already dominant Clorox would dissuade new entrants and discourage active competition from the firms already in the industry due to fear of retaliation by Procter. The Commission thought it relevant that retailers might be induced to give Clorox preferred shelf space since it would be manufactured by Procter, which also produced a number of other products marketed by the retailers. There was also the danger that Procter might underprice Clorox in order to drive out competition, and subsidize the underpricing with revenue from other products. The Commission carefully reviewed the effect of the acquisition on the structure of the industry, noting that "[t]he practical tendency of the . . . merger . . . is to transform the liquid bleach industry into an arena of big business competition only, with the few small firms that have not disappeared through merger eventually falling by the wayside, unable to compete with their giant rivals." Further, the merger would seriously diminish potential competition by eliminating Procter as a potential entrant into the industry. Prior to the merger, the Commission found, Procter was the most likely prospective entrant, and absent the merger would have remained on the periphery, restraining Clorox from exercising its market power. If Procter had actually entered, Clorox's dominant position would have been eroded and the concentration of the industry reduced. . . .

The liquid bleach industry was already oligopolistic before the acquisition, and price competition was certainly not as vigorous as it would have been if the industry were competitive.

The acquisition may also have the tendency of raising the barriers to new entry. The major competitive weapon in the successful marketing of bleach is advertising. Clorox was limited in this area by its relatively small budget and its inability to obtain substantial discounts. By contrast, Procter's budget was much larger, and, although it would not devote its entire budget to advertising Clorox, it could divert a large portion to meet the short-term threat of a new entrant. Procter would be able to use its volume discounts to advantage in advertising Clorox. Thus, a new entrant would be much more reluctant to face the giant Procter than it would have been to face the smaller Clorox.

Possible economies cannot be used as a defense to illegality. Congress was aware that some mergers which lessen competition may also result in economies but it struck the balance in favor of protecting competition.

It is clear that the existence of Procter at the edge of the industry exerted considerable influence on the market. First, the market behavior of the liquid bleach industry was influenced by each firm's predictions of the market behavior of its competitors, actual and potential. Second, the barriers to entry by a firm of Procter's size and with its advantages were not significant. There is no indication that the barriers were so high that the price Procter would have to charge would be above the price that would maximize the profits of the existing firms. Third, the number of potential entrants was not so large that the elimination of one would be insignificant. Few firms would have the temerity to challenge a firm as solidly entrenched as Clorox. Fourth, Procter was found by the Commission to be the most likely entrant. These findings of the Commission were amply supported by the evidence.

The judgment of the Court of Appeals is reversed and remanded with instructions to affirm and enforce the Commission's order.

Case Questions

1. What distinguishes a pure conglomerate merger from a product extension merger?
2. What is the market discipline that a potential entrant imposes on existing competitors? What competitive advantage is there to this discipline? How did P&G's acquisition of Clorox change this discipline?
3. What legal alternative could P&G have pursued to avoid the outcome of this suit? Why was this alternative considered better than P&G's acquisition of Clorox?

In recent years, some plaintiffs have argued that a conglomerate merger between an outsider and the lending seller in a concentrated industry is also anticompetitive. They have argued that if the outsider must merge to gain entry, it should acquire a smaller firm whose market position could be improved over time. This is known as a *toehold acquisition*. Such an acquisition is preferable because it might preserve the opportunity for deconcentration in an oligopolistic market.

Merger Defenses

When regulators or competitors challenge a merger, the merging firms may attempt to justify the transaction with a *merger defense*. For example, it is not uncommon for merging firms to claim that the merger will result in greater efficiency. Another merger justification is the *failing firm defense*. The defendant may argue that one of the merging firms will soon be unable to meet its financial obligations, making the merger necessary for the failing firm's survival. For this defense to apply, the failing firm must be unable to reorganize successfully under Chapter 11 of the bankruptcy laws. In addition, the failing firm must have made unsuccessful good faith efforts to find reasonable alternative merger partners that might reduce the concentration of market power held by firms in its industry. Another defense recognizes that purchases of another corporation's stock that are *solely for investment* and will not substantially lessen competition are justifiable.

Merger Enforcement Priorities and Procedures

The Justice Department's antitrust enforcement priorities have changed over the years. The attorney general, a cabinet-level officer reporting to the president, directs the Justice Department to pursue the antitrust philosophy of the president. Therefore, the Justice Department's prosecutorial fervor may vary with the economic theories of the presidential administration in power. By contrast, the FTC is a quasi-independent federal agency not directly under the president's control. Its prosecutorial efforts are more likely to reflect the philosophies of the various FTC commissioners, who may not have been appointed during the existing president's term. Finally, the attitude of the courts in cases brought by the public or by state attorneys general may reflect a set of priorities different from those of either the Justice Department or the FTC. As a result, antitrust enforcement continues to evolve and is not predictable with perfect certainty.

In recent years, merger regulation has not occurred through court decisions. Instead, proposed mergers have first been submitted for approval to the FTC, the Justice Department, or another agency closely involved with the industry in question. For example, airline or railroad mergers have been overseen by the Department of Transportation, and bank mergers have been overseen by federal banking regulators. Premerger negotiations have been subjected to scrutiny by federal agencies and the press, which affect merger activity by indicating approval or threatening a court challenge. Premerger notification is required if the acquiring firm has sales or assets exceeding $100 million and the target has sales or assets exceeding $10 million. Notice must be made at least 30 days before the merger and contain basic information to aid in the evaluation of the acquisition.

SUMMARY

Antitrust laws are intended to foster a competitive business environment, but they can profoundly affect the structure and conduct of business. The term *antitrust* arose from reactions to the trust form, under which many separate producers gave authority to a central management's use of anticompetitive practices. The Sherman Act was passed in 1890 to break up trusts. Markets with many producers and buyers are less likely to be affected by the anticompetitive practices of any one seller, so prices in such markets are more likely to be set by the market forces of supply and demand, and the distortions of centralized economic decision making are more likely to be limited.

There are two basic approaches to antitrust enforcement. The Harvard school uses a structuralist approach to define harmful anticompetitive practices. The Chicago school analyzes the performance of competitors and would restrain enforcement activity unless long-term anticompetitive effects are apparent. The compliance responses of business to antitrust law are often dictated by which school of thought controls the antitrust enforcement agencies.

The Sherman Act, passed in 1890, outlaws contracts in restraint of trade and conspiracies to monopolize. Lackluster enforcement of the Sherman Act led to passage of the Clayton Antitrust Act and the Federal Trade Commission Act in 1914. The Clayton Act outlaws anticompetitive actions that tend to create a monopoly and prohibits tie-in sales, exclusive dealing contracts, interlocking directorates, and certain mergers. The FTC Act created the FTC and gave it enforcement powers to define and prosecute unfair methods of competition and deceptive trade practices. Amendments now prohibit price discrimination, outlaw certain mergers accomplished through sales of corporate assets, and permit private parties and state attorneys general to sue. Persons convicted under the antitrust laws may be subject to civil and criminal penalties. Certain industries and activities are exempt from these laws—patents, copyrights, trademarks, agricultural cooperatives, labor unions, the insurance industry, political action, the stock markets, and baseball are all exempt to a certain degree.

The Sherman Act prohibits monopolies created when a defendant possessing monopoly power undertakes purposeful acts of monopolization. In order to be actionable, a monopolist's illegal market power must exist over a relevant market that has both geographic and product parameters. When two products have a high cross-elasticity of demand, they may be considered reasonably interchangeable as substitutes, expanding the product market. The alleged monopolist's percentage domination over a particular geographic and product market, called market share, is used to determine the existence of a monopoly. The intent to monopolize can be inferred from exclusionary conduct, predatory pricing, or attempts to monopolize.

Mergers are subject to antitrust law because they may result in the acquisition of monopoly power. The Clayton Act prohibits mergers, acquisitions, or sales of assets that tend to create a monopoly. This prohibition includes horizontal mergers between direct competitors, vertical mergers between suppliers and customers, and conglomerate mergers. Merger analysis is similar to the market share analysis used in monopolization cases. If a merger results in the acquisition of a market share large enough to create the probability of a substantial lessening of competition, the courts may prohibit the merger.

In vertical merger analysis, the courts consider historical trends toward concentration and the resulting barriers to entry. Vertical mergers may result in the imposition of discipline on suppliers or on customers' product pricing. Conglomerate mergers that eliminate the edge effect of a potential entrant may be illegal if competitors perceive the loss of the potential entrant's influence on market pricing and efficiency. If a single potential entrant has a reasonable means of entering the market on its own, then its merger with an existing firm may be anticompetitive.

Merging firms may attempt to justify their merger with a merger defense. Proof that a merger will result in greater efficiency, that one of the merged firms is failing and needs the merger to survive, or that the acquisition is for investment purposes may permit the merger.

KEY TERMS

trust p. 460
perfect competition, p. 461
monopoly, p. 461
oligopoly, p. 461
monopolistic competition, p. 461
monopsony, p. 461
state action, p. 465
relevant market, p. 468
cross-elasticity of demand, p. 468
market share, p. 471
monopolization, p. 471
horizontal merger, p. 475
vertical merger, p. 478
conglomerate merger, p. 480
potential entrant effect, p. 481
failing firm defense, p. 483

CHAPTER EXERCISES

1. Match the statutes and terms in Column A with the definitions in Column B.

1. Sherman Act	a. Exists where a single buyer possesses monopoly buying power over the prices charged.
2. Clayton Act	b. The federal antitrust laws do not cover activities mandated by state and local laws.
3. Federal Trade Commission Act	c. Makes illegal unfair methods of competition and deceptive trade practices.
4. State action exemption	d. Pricing below the producer's marginal cost.
5. Predatory pricing	e. Prohibits anticompetitive tendencies even before damaging effects occur.
6. Monopsony	f. Outlaws monopolization and contracts in restraint of trade.

2. Discuss three arguments for governmental intervention to ensure competition in the marketplace.

3. The three largest real estate brokerage firms in Atlanta conspire to fix real estate commissions. They are indicted by a federal grand jury. What punishments or penalties may be imposed on these firms if the case goes to trial?

4. Briefly discuss the prohibitions of the Sherman Act. Give two examples illustrating how a bank can wrongfully violate the Sherman Act.

5. Discuss the differences between the goals of those who would concentrate on "structure" in antitrust enforcement and the goals of those who would concentrate on "conduct" in such enforcement. How are "structure" and "conduct" used in Section 2 monopolization cases?

6. What kind of "conduct" is required for proof of a violation of Section 2 of the Sherman Act? Explain your answer fully.

7. Cola Company produces a cola soft drink that is much like Coke and Pepsi. After considerable effort, it obtained 62 percent of the cola market, and it is now charged with monopolization. The company contends that its market should be defined as the market for all soft drinks (root beer, orange drink, lemon-lime soda, etc.), of which it has only 6 percent. What are the relevant considerations in determining the market for Cola Company's soft drink?

8. A computer manufacturer designed a central processing unit that was demonstrably better than any other central processing unit on the market. It then designed peripherals (units that plug into the central processing unit) and redesigned the central processing unit so that no other peripherals could be used with it. A peripherals manufacturer sued the computer manufacturer for monopolization under Section 2 of the Sherman Act. Did the computer manufacturer violate the Sherman Antitrust Act? Discuss.

9. ABC Company, a manufacturer of love seats and sofas, acquires XYZ Company, which manufactures sleeper sofas. Such a merger is an example of:
   a. A vertical merger.
   b. A conglomerate merger.
   c. A horizontal merger.

   Choose the correct answer and explain.

10. Big Oil Corp. was approached by a chemical engineer, William Carbs, with a new fuel injection device that promises to revolutionize gasoline automobile engines. The system adds air and water to the gasoline fuel mix and completely atomizes the mixture as it is injected into the cylinder. This permits nearly compete combustion, increasing miles per gallon on average automobiles by over 35 percent. The system also reduces pollutants well below federal EPA standards, eliminating the need for catalytic converters on the exhaust. Big Oil had recently purchased a substantial number of platinum futures contracts on the expectation that the price would rise now that European nations are requiring catalytic converters containing platinum. If developed into a commercially, exploitable form, Carbs' invention would reduce the world's need for oil and platinum simultaneously. Big Oil acquired Carbs' small development corporation, including Carbs' patents. Thereafter Big Oil refrained from developing the fuel system altogether. Comment on the legal and ethical problems triggered by this merger.

11. The Justice Department challenged a merger between two waste disposal companies: Waste Management, Inc. and EMW Ventures, Inc. Both were large and dominant firms in this business. The merged firm would have a nearly 50 percent market share, with a Herfindahl Index of over 2,700. Barriers to entry were rather low, market entry by "mom and pop" waste disposal firms was easy—only a home office and a waste disposal truck were needed. On what basis could the merger be challenged? What defense might the firms offer to justify the merger? (*United States v. Waste Management, Inc.*, 743 F.2d 976 (2nd Cir. 1984).

Chapter 16

RESTRAINTS OF TRADE, PRICE DISCRIMINATION, AND UNFAIR TRADE PRACTICES

KEY CONCEPTS

The illegality of restraints of trade may be judged by either the per se rule or the rule of reason. Many horizontal restraints, including price-fixing, division of markets, group boycotts, and concerted refusals to deal, are per se offenses and, thus, are automatically illegal.

Vertical restraints of trade can occur between suppliers and customers. Such restraints, designed to protect the manufacturer's goodwill, typically involve restrictions on resale prices, maintenance of exclusive dealerships, territorial restrictions, and tying arrangements.

Price discrimination occurs when a seller charges different prices for goods of like grade and quality to different buyers and when this substantially lessens competition or tends to create a monopoly causing injury at the primary line (seller's level), the secondary line (buyer's level), or the tertiary line (buyer's buyer level).

The Federal Trade Commission Act outlaws unfair methods of competition and unfair or deceptive trade practices.

INTRODUCTION . . . PAST, PRESENT, FUTURE

The desire for decentralization of economic power was not satisfied by the courts' lackluster enforcement of the Sherman Act. Increases in the concentration of wealth and economic decision making around the turn of the 20th century aroused demands for more specific prohibitions of anticompetitive actions than were provided by the vague "monopolization" standard of the Sherman Act. Eventually, the courts and Congress acted to curb numerous horizontal and vertical anticompetitive abuses in restraint of trade by imposing the per se rule and outlawing specific practices under the Clayton and FTC acts.

Today, the most controversial areas of antitrust enforcement pertain to horizontal and vertical restraints of trade and price discrimination. The "new learning" of law and economics suggests that overzealous enforcement of trade restraint law may actually hinder competition. These advocates recommend shifting from the per se analysis discussed in this chapter to the rule of reason. In addition, restrictive interpretation of the price discrimination provisions may actually make markets less efficient by prohibiting quick pricing responses to changing market conditions. Fundamental changes in distribution channels, such as the rise in direct marketing and volume discounters, pit consumer choice against the traditional use of high-profit/high-service small local retailers.

In the future, many of the innovations in economic analysis imposed during the Reagan years may become more readily accepted. The Supreme Court might abandon per se analysis altogether and begin to analyze vertical restraints with the rule of reason on a case-by-case basis. Proof of antitrust violations will be increasingly subjected to structured economic analysis by regulators and the courts. Antitrust enforcement of restraints of trade will be much less sensitive to mere conjecture regarding anticompetitive effects. Instead, the size of relevant markets will be broadened to recognize internationalization, thereby suggesting a narrower impact of alleged domestic wrongdoing. The increasing need for competitiveness in global high-tech markets will permit joint research and development ventures heretofore considered conducive to collusion. However, it is unclear whether U.S. firms will adopt the Japanese custom of *Keiretsu* involving closer vertical relationships among suppliers and customers. Although Keiretsu strengthens related firms, it may be incompatible with the Western aversion to feudal relations.

OVERVIEW

Both the Clayton and Sherman Antitrust Acts apply to a wider range of anticompetitive practices than the monopolies and mergers previously discussed. This chapter examines restraints of trade resulting from horizontal relationships (between competitors) and vertical relationships (between suppliers and customers). Although some restraints are illegal in all instances, others have some economic justification, so the courts prohibit only unreasonable restraints of trade.

The first section discusses horizontal restraints such as price-fixing, division of markets, and group boycotts. The second section examines vertical restraints such as resale price maintenance, refusals to deal, exclusive dealing, tying, and franchising. The third section is devoted to price discrimination. The chapter concludes by reviewing the FTC's powers to prosecute anticompetitive actions.

HORIZONTAL COMBINATIONS AND RESTRAINTS OF TRADE

Horizontal restraints of trade arise when competitors in the same industry collaborate. They are considered the least justifiable restraints. Adam Smith, the famous laissez-faire economist, strongly urged that government should actively ensure competition in order to counteract the natural tendency of competitors to collude.

Adam Smith's Observations about Collusion

People in the same trade seldom meet together, even for merriment and diversion, but [that] the conversation ends in a conspiracy against the public, or in some contrivance to raise prices.

Early Supreme Court interpretations of the Sherman Act were so broad that "every contract, combination . . . or conspiracy in restraint of trade" was condemned. Later cases modified this approach by recognizing that some restraints were reasonable and therefore legal. Two different tests are used in examining horizontal and vertical restraints: the per se rule of illegality and the rule of reason. The **per se rule** requires a strict interpretation of the Sherman Act's "plain meaning." Per se violations leave no room for any defense or justification. The **rule of reason** emerged from the 19th-century judicial approach to contract law; it outlaws only unreasonable restraints of trade.

Rule of Reason

The Sherman Act, in Section 1, literally prohibits "every contract, combination . . . or conspiracy in restraint of trade." However, applying this provision too strictly is unwarranted because every contract restrains trade in some way. For example, when goods or services are purchased, they become unavailable to others and the buyer does not purchase them from a competitor. The Sherman Act was intended to encourage free market contracting, so it should not prohibit contracts that restrain some small amount of trade. Indeed, trade is restrained to an even greater extent by outputs or requirements contracts discussed in Chapter 8 or by exclusive dealing, exclusive supply contracts, and covenants not to compete. Yet the restraint of trade under these contracts is economically justifiable in most situations.

The rule of reason exception prohibits only contracts that are intended to restrict competition. In 1918, Justice Brandeis announced the proper inquiry for rule of reason analysis in *Chicago Board of Trade v. United States:*[1]

Rule of Reason Analysis of Restraints of Trade

The true test of legality is whether the restraint imposed is such as merely regulates and perhaps thereby promotes competition or whether it is such as may suppress or may even destroy competition. To determine that question, the court must ordinarily consider the facts peculiar to the business to which the restraint is applied; its condition before and after the restraint was imposed; the nature of the restraint and its effect, actual or probable. The history of the restraint, the evil believed to exist, the reason for adopting the particular remedy, the purpose or end sought to be obtained, are all relevant facts.

[1] *Chicago Board of Trade v. United States,* 246 U.S. 231 (1918).

The rule of reason permits courts to be more flexible by using a far less rigorous market share analysis than was used in monopolization or merger cases. This practice is justified because Section 1 of the Sherman Act requires no analysis of market power.

Per Se Violations

Over the years, the courts have encountered many antitrust cases justifying a return to the plain meaning of the Sherman Act. Certain types of agreements almost always produce unjustifiable and substantial restraints of trade. It is inefficient and time consuming to apply the rule of reason in each of these cases. As a result, certain types of business agreements, such as price-fixing, are designated *illegal per se,* so they are considered unreasonable in all instances. This means that the inquiry ends after the plaintiff or prosecutor proves the per se violation. Trials are shortened and simplified by avoiding unnecessary attempts to justify the restraint. The per se rule improves judicial efficiency and provides business managers with definite guidance. Per se offenses include price-fixing, division of markets, group boycotts, concerted refusals to deal, and tie-in relationships.

Initially, the courts must determine whether the conduct in question falls within a per se category. If it does, then no further analysis is necessary, and anticompetitive effect is presumed. For example, if two competitors agree to restrict competition, a per se violation arises.

If the conduct in question does not clearly fall within a per se category, the court must then carefully apply the rule of reason permitting the defendant to justify that conduct. For example, a particular restraint might make the market more competitive or increase market efficiency. To determine whether the restraint is legal, the court must balance its perceived anticompetitive effect against its benefits.

Price-Fixing among Competitors The most direct way for competitors to reduce competition is to agree to set artificial prices. Contracts to fix prices are illegal per se if they are among competitors at the same level of production. **Price-fixing** tends to eliminate competition and to pass on the costs of an inefficient oligopoly to consumers. Price-fixing is never justified by good intentions to set "reasonable" prices or eliminate "ruinous" competition.

The courts broadly interpret the per se prohibition of price-fixing. Agreements among competitors to fix minimum prices are illegal. For example, at one time state and local bar associations enacted minimum fee schedules requiring lawyers to charge a minimum price for particular services such as writing a will or drafting a contract. Today, such schedules are illegal per se as price-fixing. It is also illegal to set maximum resale prices even though fixing "low" prices might not seem harmful. Low prices drive out competitors and reduce nonprice competition for optional features, improvements, or additional services. The mere presence of a ceiling tends to stabilize prices. Illegal stabilization of prices also arises when automobile dealers agree to use negotiable list prices. Even where negotiable prices are not enforceable, they operate as a starting point for customer bargaining and tend to stabilize prices. Agreements among sellers to limit production or among buyers to limit purchases tend to manipulate prices and are illegal per se.

Credit terms are an inseparable part of a product's price, so fixing these terms is illegal per se. In one case, an agreement among beer distributors to eliminate trade credit to retailers was held to constitute illegal price-fixing, equivalent to an agreement to eliminate discounts. In another case, several plywood producers allegedly agreed to charge a uniform freight rate irrespective of the source of supply or the destination. This illegal scheme is known as *phantom freight* because it equalizes freight charges without reference to the actual distance transported. It eliminates competition based on the purchaser's closeness to the source of supply. Is an agreement among competitors to buy excess supplies of a commodity equivalent to a price-fixing arrangement? The next case is a classic illustration of the way price-fixing can be disguised and of how the Supreme Court analyzes its illegality.

United States v. Socony-Vacuum Oil Co., Inc.

310 U.S. 150 (1940)
United States Supreme Court

Numerous oil companies allegedly conspired to raise and maintain wholesale gasoline prices. These companies operated an organized program for discovering the amounts of surplus gasoline on the spot market, assigning portions of this surplus among the co-conspirators, and purchasing it at the going price. These intentional actions tended to stabilize and raise the wholesale and retail prices of gasoline. Wholesalers and consumers paid higher prices than they would have paid if competitive conditions had existed.

Justice Douglas delivered the opinion of the Court.

The elimination of so-called competitive evils is no legal justification for such buying programs. The elimination of such conditions was sought primarily for its effect on the price structures. Fairer competitive prices, it is claimed, resulted when distress gasoline was removed from the market. But such defense is typical of the protestations usually made in price-fixing cases. Ruinous competition, financial disaster, evils of price cutting and the like appear throughout our history as ostensible justifications for price-fixing. If the so-called competitive abuses were to be appraised here, the reasonableness of prices would necessarily become an issue in every price-fixing case. In that event the Sherman Act would soon be emasculated; its philosophy would be supplanted by one which is wholly alien to a system of free competition; it would not be the charter of freedom which its framers intended.

The reasonableness of prices has no constancy due to the dynamic quality of business facts underlying price structures. Those who fixed reasonable prices today would perpetuate unreasonable prices tomorrow, since those prices would not be subject to continuous administrative supervision and readjustment in light of changed conditions. Those who controlled the prices would control or effectively dominate the market. And those who were in that strategic position would have it in their power to destroy or drastically impair the competitive system. But the thrust of the rule is deeper and reaches more than monopoly power. Any combination which tampers with price structures is engaged in an unlawful activity. Even though the members of the price-fixing group were in no position to control the market, to the extent that they raised, lowered, or stabilized prices they would be directly interfering with the free play of market forces. The Act places all such schemes beyond the pale and protects that vital part of our economy against any degree of interference. Congress has not left with us the determination of whether or not particular price-fixing schemes are wise or unwise, healthy or destructive. It has not permitted the age-old cry of ruinous competition and competitive evils to be a defense to price-fixing conspiracies.

Under the Sherman Act a combination formed for the purpose and with the effect of raising, depressing, fixing, pegging, or stabilizing the price of a commodity in interstate or foreign commerce is illegal *per se*. Where the machinery for price-fixing is an agreement on the prices to be charged or paid for the commodity in the interstate or foreign channels of trade, the power to fix prices exists if the combination has control of a substantial part of the commerce in that commodity. Where the means for price-fixing are purchases or sales of the commodity in a market operation or, as here, purchases of a part of the supply of the commodity for the purpose of keeping it from having a depressive effect on the markets, such power may be found to exist though the combination does not control a substantial part of the commodity. In such a case that power may be established if as a result of the market conditions, the resources available to the combinations, the timing and the strategic placement of orders and the like, effective means are at hand to accomplish the desired objective. But there may be effective influence over the market though the group in question does not control it. Price-fixing agreements may have utility to members of the group though the power possessed or exerted falls far short of domination and control. Monopoly power is not the only power which the Act strikes down, as we have said. Proof that a combination was formed for the purpose of fixing prices and that it caused them to be fixed or contributed to that result is proof of the completion of a price-fixing conspiracy under § 1 of the Act.

Case Questions

1. What is the practical effect of the per se nature of the price-fixing prohibition on a defendant's attempt to justify the practice?
2. Is it necessary to have a monopoly in the relevant market before a price-fixing conspiracy is illegal? Why or why not?
3. What arguments are used to justify price-fixing?

In recent years, some restraints of trade involving incidental price-fixing have been judged under the rule of reason; in such cases, cooperation is deemed necessary to advance the market. For example, it is impractical for copyright owners of music to separately negotiate licensing fees for every performance of their works on television, radio, or in public. The Supreme Court applied the rule of reason to the blanket fee arrangement between the Broadcast Music, Inc. (BMI) and the American Society of Composers, Authors and Publishers (ASCAP) because these organizations provide clearinghouse services essential to effective licensing. Their arrangement does not restrain trade but, rather, actually encourages the licensing and enforcement of music copyrights.[2]

In another case, the rule of reason was used to judge a price-fixing scheme illegal. The National Collegiate Athletics Association's (NCAA) negotiated television contracts for all college football games between 1982 and 1985. However, television fees paid to schools were based neither on the size of the viewing audience nor on the popularity of the teams. The NCAA contracts with ABC and CBS limited the number of televised games and precluded price negotiation between the networks and schools. The NCAA scheme was invalid price-fixing under rule of reason analysis because both price and output were restrained, thereby effectively raising television fees above competitive prices with a system unresponsive to viewer demand. The per se rule was inapplicable because some horizontal restraint in athletics is essential to make the product available at all.[3]

Trade Association Activities The prohibition against price-fixing is so strong that competitors must carefully consider their collective activities. Many people believe that the exchange of price information among competitors makes price-fixing easier. Thus, even though there may not be any direct exchange of information among competitors, it may be an unreasonable restraint if a trade association provides a clearinghouse for the exchange of price information. However, many observers argue that to remain competitive in world markets, competitors should be permitted to "network" by joining legitimate trade associations that promote the collective success of their industry and improve product quality.

---

[2] *Broadcast Music Inc. v. CBS*, 441 U.S. 1 (1979).

[3] *NCAA v. Board of Regents of the University of Oklahoma*, 468 U.S. 85 (1984).

Despite the good intentions of trade associations some of them have acted as fronts for the distribution of price information. In the 1920s, for example, 365 hardwood manufacturers reported details of individual sales, production, inventories, and current price lists to one another through their trade association. An expert analyst constantly warned the association's members against overproduction. Eventually, hardwood prices increased sharply and the plan was found illegal. By contrast, the trade association of the maple flooring industry circulated information concerning average costs, freight rates, and past transactions but did not identify individual buyers or sellers. This exchange of information was not illegal because future prices were never discussed. In a more recent case, the paper box industry voluntarily exchanged price quotes that identified transactions with particular customers. The plan was held illegal because it tended to stabilize prices.

Exchange of information through trade associations is not illegal so long as it is not intended to lessen competition. For example, a cement manufacturers' association distributed a list of construction contractors that abused the free delivery of cement. The exchange was considered justifiable because it helped prevent fraud on the cement manufacturers. It has been suggested that trade associations can provide additional services for industry groups in the areas of political lobbying, public affairs, and the provision of access to information about suppliers and new production technologies.

Bidding rings may arise among construction contractors. Sometimes contractors preselect a different winner for each of several successive construction projects. The designated "losers" agree to bid higher than the selected winner, whose bid is rigged to be the "lowest." Although the selected winner's price may be lower than those of the other bidders, it is typically higher than the price that would have resulted from genuine competitive bidding. Bidding rings are considered illegal per se as a form of price-fixing. Legislation may be needed to remove the potential cloud over trade association activities if trade associations are to provide competitors with mutual benefits other than the exchange of price information. In Japan, it has been a common practice among construction contractors to consult each other before bidding on public works projects. This is allegedly a form of bid-rigging. The Japanese Fair Trade Commission, which is supposed to function like the U.S. FTC, has recently prohibited the practice, but only after the United States asserted that the practice effectively locked foreign firms out of the bidding.

When trade associations influence their members to standardize products, the result may be improved quality and safety, as well as interchangeability and simplicity, which clearly would benefit customers. However, standardization is anticompetitive if it becomes a hidden method of fixing prices or thwarting innovation. Some trade associations limit their membership. Although this may be pro-competitive if membership qualifications address integrity, quality, or reliability, such practice is anticompetitive if it restricts access to some valuable association facility. For example, most local real estate associations operate multiple listing services that compile listings and enhance members' opportunities to sell listed properties. Denying membership or limiting nonmember access to multiple listing services reduces competition, particularly in commission rates. Real estate commissions show price rigidity, with little discounting from the 6 percent to 8 percent range found throughout the nation.

ETHICAL DILEMMAS IN IMPOSING TRADE ASSOCIATION CODES OF ETHICS

Self-regulation by industry trade groups is gaining favor as an alternative to government regulation and litigation in resolving disputes. However, sometimes "industry codes" are disguised methods to fix prices or otherwise reduce competition. For example, the National Society of

Professional Engineers once prohibited its members from bidding competitively on design projects. The society contended that its prohibition supported professional ethics and maintained the quality of engineering services by discouraging engineers from cutting corners in their design work. Minimum fee schedules required by most local lawyers' bar associations were justified as necessary to ensure a minimum standard of effort, competence, and quality of lawyers' services. These organizations argued that without these restraints, some members would be forced by ruinous price competition to unethically cut corners, ultimately degrading the quality of services. Is it ethical for a profession to use codes of ethics to fix prices? Excessive discipline of a highly competitive member suggests that other members are really just suppressing competition. This is an ironic and unethical misuse of a professional association's powers over its members, particularly when such action is rationalized as an ethical rule.

Division of Markets Competitors may attempt to divide markets so that only certain producers serve particular regions or specified customers. Such territorial allocation or **division of markets** is illegal per se. Such agreements among horizontal competitors give the producer in each market segment an effective monopoly. Even if other competitors are selling in the affected region, the preferred firm is generally able to exert some market power. In one case, the joint exercise of buying power by a group of independent local grocers who formed a group buying chain was considered legal. However, the association also caused many members to limit the location of their stores to designated territories, creating an illegal division of markets. This division of markets was not justified by the grocers' intent to compete more effectively against larger chain stores.

Group Boycotts Individuals are usually free to deal with whomever they please. But when groups of competitors agree to boycott a certain individual or group, the action may be illegal. Although most courts consider **group boycotts** to be illegal per se, sometimes illegality is tested by the rule of reason.

It may be illegal for competing sellers to agree not to sell to a particular customer, reseller, or class of persons. A group of buyers with market power (monopsony or oligopsony) may also be involved in an illegal boycott if they agree to boycott certain sellers. In one case, an apparel manufacturers' trade association urged its members to boycott any retailers selling pirated designs (e.g., fake designer jeans). In another case, a National Football League rule required a team to compensate the former team of a free agent if the player changed teams. Both actions were illegal concerted refusals to deal. At one time, the American Medical Association had rules of ethics that prohibited doctors from participating in prepaid medical plans or from receiving a salary for practicing medicine. Those rules were illegal because they tended to destroy competition among professional groups.

Group boycotts are horizontal agreements used to force vertical restraints on suppliers or customers with whom a horizontal group is dissatisfied. Thus, some boycotts are legal under the First Amendment as legitimate noneconomic political expression. For example, no anticompetitive boycott was found when the National Organization of Women caused a boycott of convention hotels in states that had not ratified the Equal Rights Amendment. However, the Supreme Court found illegal per se a boycott by members of a Washington, D.C., trial lawyers association who refused to continue accepting court appointments to represent indigent defendants.[4] Ninety percent of the group's attorneys agreed to cease taking court appointments until the city doubled their fees. This

---

[4]*F.T.C. v. Superior Court Trial Lawyers Assn.*, 493 U.S. 411 (1990).

action was clearly motivated by desires for personal economic gain; thus, it was not protected as political speech.

Joint Ventures A *joint venture* is a form of partnership in which two entities (i.e., persons, partnerships, corporations) enter into a limited business activity together. Joint ventures are subject to rule of reason analysis because they are sometimes justifiable. If the purpose and effect of a joint venture are economic efficiencies, the joint venture is not illegal. The test is whether the restraint is really necessary to achieve the lawful purpose. The courts balance the joint venture's potential anticompetitive effects against its alleged efficiency. For example, the Associated Press is a cooperative wire service with thousands of members. Access to this service is often critical to effective competition. At one time, the bylaws of the Associated Press contained a veto clause that permitted any member to blackball a competitor seeking to become a member. Because this clause excluded competitors from the joint venture and posed a substantial barrier to entry for new firms in the newspaper business, it was held to be illegal under rule of reason analysis. The joint ownership of theaters by moviemaking companies was illegal because it was not making new releases freely available to nonmember theaters, thereby lessening competition.

INTERNATIONAL PERSPECTIVE ON JOINT VENTURES

Today, the development of increasingly complex technology may necessitate a pooling of resources and efforts from several competitors. Particularly in international competition, the primary vehicle for the import or export of technology is the joint venture. However, how can the antitrust law prohibitions against the competitive restraints of cooperative joint operations be reconciled with the need for international competitiveness? Does the threat of per se rule application discourage joint ventures?

International joint ventures are the most popular method to export products or technology to foreign markets. Firms unwilling or unable to make huge new investments to establish productive capacity in foreign nations often find that joint ventures with domestic firms are cost effective. Such joint ventures are not illegal when reasonable and limited in scope and duration. For example, Toyota was initially unwilling to commence automobile production in the United States without some assurance that it could produce quality products efficiently. Toyota joined with General Motors to convert an idle production facility in California to a plant where they jointly produce vehicles for NUMMI. NUMMI is a production joint venture that produces only Toyota Corollas and Geo Prisms for a limited time.

Congress passed the National Cooperative Research Act in 1984. The act reinforced the principle that research and development joint ventures are to be judged by the rule of reason, not the per se rule. Certainty about whether the rule of reason is applicable to production joint ventures still awaits new legislation.

Proof of an Illegal Agreement or Combination

Competitors agreeing to a horizontal restraint or price-fixing would probably avoid leaving a clear trail of evidence. Illegal contacts between co-conspirators would probably be hidden off the record. Clandestine tactics such as secret meetings or secret codes might be used. Because the Sherman Act's criminal provisions require proof beyond a reasonable doubt, it is difficult to prove guilt with direct evidence. Competitors' illegal concerted activity is usually inferred from circumstantial evidence. The participation of competitors in trade associations, conscious paralleling of competitors' price movements, and interlocking directorates can provide such evidence.

Conscious Parallelism In monopolistic competitive or oligopolistic industries, an illegal horizontal restraint of trade is seldom proved by direct evidence because competitors are careful not to meet or communicate directly. However, if businesses mimic the pricing behaviors of an industry leader, their **conscious parallelism** may obviate the need for an overt agreement. In 1939, the Supreme Court stated: "[i]t is enough that, knowing that concerted action was contemplated and invited, the distributors [of feature films] gave their adherence to the scheme and participated in it." This is the *Interstate formula,* which permits proof of an illegal agreement if there is conscious parallelism.[5] Conscious parallelism may also constitute an unfair method of competition under Section 5 of the Federal Trade Commission Act. When the highly complex contracts offered by several competitors to different customers are substantially similar, no proof of an actual illegal agreement may be necessary.

A more modern formulation recognizes that legal conduct may appear to be conscious parallelism. Businesses must often respond quickly to changes in market conditions or to new contract terms offered by their competitors. For example, changes in the price of crude oil often quickly lead to similar changes in the gasoline pump prices charged by independent gasoline retailers.

The American steel industry allegedly exhibited all the characteristics of conscious parallelism in the mid-1900s. Typically, the price leader, U.S. Steel, would raise or lower prices and the other steelmakers would follow suit within a matter of days or weeks. However, this pricing behavior was never successfully prosecuted.

Test of Conscious Parallelism

. . . the crucial question is whether the respondents' conduct . . . stems from an independent decision or from an agreement, tacit or expressed. But, this court has never held that proof of parallel business behavior conclusively establishes agreement.

Source: *Theatre Enterprises v. Paramount Film Distributor Corp.,* 346 U.S. 537 (1954).

Interlocking Directorates Section 8 of the Clayton Act outlaws certain **interlocking directorates,** that is, the same person sitting on the board of two competitors.

Clayton Act, Section 8: Interlocking Directorates

No person shall at the same time be a director in two or more corporations, any of which has capital . . . aggregating more than one million dollars . . . if such corporations are or shall have been theretofore, by virtue of their business and location of operation, competitors, so that the elimination of competition by an agreement between them would constitute a violation of any of the provisions of any of the antitrust laws.

[5] *Interstate Circuit, Inc. v. United States,* 306 U.S. 208 (1939).

The theory underlying the prohibition against interlocking directorates recognizes that a common director between competitors could provide a communication conduit for collusion. The FTC has been quite lax in enforcing this provision. In the few reported cases, directors have simply been permitted to resign one of their positions. By contrast, the Justice Department has been a more aggressive enforcer, extending the interlocking directorate provision to firms engaged in "related businesses." For example, an illegal interlocking directorate could exist if a single individual sat on the boards of a computer mainframe manufacturer and a manufacturer of computer software.

Exceptions The law concerning interlocking directorates is better known for its exceptions than for its prohibitions. First, interlocking directorates may exist between firms that are in a vertical relationship or in different industries (e.g., conglomerate interlocks). It is quite common for suppliers and customers to solidify their relationship by having common directors. Second, indirect interlocking directorates are permissible. For example, a bank employee may legally sit on the boards of two competing industrial firms. Third, a nondirector employee of one firm may sit on the board of a competing firm. For example, a nondirector employee of Firm A may sit on the board of directors of its competitor, Firm B, without violating Section 8. All these interlocks are actively used in Japanese *Keiretsu* firms.

Given the current trend toward holding directors liable for negligent decisions, it is an increasing challenge to attract competent and experienced directors. Therefore, vigorous enforcement of Section 8 could impair the overall quality of corporate management and directorships. It may also be inconsistent with the closer contacts firms may need to assure quality and technological compatibility from suppliers.

VERTICAL RESTRAINTS OF TRADE

Vertical restraints of trade are significantly different from restraints among competitors on a horizontal level. Vertical relationships intended to restrict certain activities along the chain of distribution may develop between manufacturers, wholesalers, retailers, and ultimately consumers. Vertical restraints of trade usually restrict resale prices, territorial or customer access, or the freedom to sell competing brands, or they require the purchase of less desirable goods in order to receive desirable ones.

Commentary: Vertical Restraint Controversy

Why should vertical restraints be illegal? Manufacturers and suppliers impose vertical restraints of trade to maximize their profits. Suppliers strive for long-term survival of their product line by limiting both the upper and lower bounds of retailers' profits. Abnormally high profits by retailers usually indicate a forthcoming decline in consumer purchases of an overpriced product. Retailers who receive abnormally low profits will probably exert less sales effort, advertise less, and provide poorer customer service. High prices create a quality image, whereas low prices suggest a cheap product image.

Vertical restraints induce the retailer to make the distribution process more efficient and favorable for the manufacturer. For example, retailers make greater sales efforts when their profit margins are larger. Higher profits permit retailers to hire trained sales and service technicians and to provide customers with better service and technical expertise. Retailers with higher profit margins can provide better promotional support, spending more on advertising, keeping larger inventories, providing a broader selection of goods, and devoting more display space to the manufacturer's products.

If the same goods are sold by both high-profit retailers and discount stores, the **free rider** problem may arise. Customers may learn about technically complex products from the more proficient sales personnel at high-priced retailers but then purchase the products from low-overhead discounters. The discounters "ride free" on the promotional and technical expenditures of the higher-profit retailers. If free riding becomes widespread, higher-profit retailers are forced out of business, leaving little technical expertise available. Manufacturers of complex products dislike free riding and argue that it is detrimental to customer satisfaction. The free rider problem has plagued the consumer electronics and personal computer markets in recent years.

Manufacturers or suppliers often impose vertical restraints to prevent widespread free riding. Manufacturers may require minimum resale prices, grant exclusive dealerships, or impose territorial restrictions on dealers to reduce cutthroat competition and foster retail prices that permit adequate levels of customer service. However, widespread vertical restraints reduce price competition.

Because of the free rider problem, some argue that it is better to enhance interbrand competition than intrabrand competition. *Intrabrand competition*—competition among sellers of the same brand—is eliminated by vertical restraints. Proponents insist that this enhances *interbrand competition*—competition among different brands of the same type of product—thereby making retailer service an important product feature. Consumers may select a different mix of service and price only by buying a competing brand from another dealer specializing in that brand.

Despite the arguments in their favor, vertical restraints that discipline retailers and reduce intrabrand competition are an exercise of market power by suppliers. If products do not need extensive customer service, vigorous intrabrand competition benefits consumers. Vertical restraints may be considered illegal under both the Sherman and Clayton Acts. Although some vertical restraints have been held illegal per se, there is a trend toward applying the rule of reason.

Vertical Price Restraint: Resale Price Maintenance

The most direct vertical restraint is the manufacturer's vertical price-fixing, an insistence that the retailer charge consumers a specified retail price. Whether the specified price is a minimum price or a maximum price, the courts originally considered this **resale price maintenance** a per se violation of the Sherman Act. However, increasingly they apply the rule of reason. Retailers have sought minimum prices as a hidden method of horizontal price-fixing, which they falsely allege is forced on them by the supplier's market power. A specified maximum retail price often becomes an unspoken minimum price, so that all retailers sell only at that price. What type of concerted activity may constitute illegal vertical resale price maintenance? The following case illustrates modern attempts to justify resale price maintenance as necessitated by state regulation.

California Retail Liquor Dealers Assn. v. Midcal Aluminum, Inc.

445 U.S. 97 (1980)

United State Supreme Court

A California statute required all wine producers to file fair trade contracts (price schedules) with the state showing the price at which wine must be sold. Although the state had no direct control over wine prices, wholesalers were subject to fine, license suspension, or revocation for selling below the posted prices. Midcal Aluminum, a wholesale distributor of wine, allegedly sold wines below the price posted by Gallo Winery. The California Court of Appeal ruled that the California wine-pricing system restrained trade in violation of the Sherman Act.

Justice Powell delivered the opinion of the Court.

California's system for wine pricing plainly constitutes resale price maintenance in violation of the Sherman Act. The wine producer holds the power to prevent price competition by dictating the prices charged by wholesalers. As Mr. Justice Hughes pointed out: such vertical control destroys horizontal competition as effectively as if wholesalers "formed a combination and endeavored to establish the same restrictions . . . by agreement with each other."

Thus, we must consider whether the State's involvement in the price-setting program is sufficient to establish antitrust immunity under *Parker v. Brown* . . . Several recent decisions have applied *Parker's* analysis. In *Goldfarb v. Virginia,* the Court concluded that fee schedules enforced by a state bar association were not mandated by ethical standards established by the State Supreme Court. The fee schedules therefore were not immune from antitrust attack. "It is not enough that . . . anticompetitive conduct is 'prompted' by state action; rather, anticompetitive activities must be compelled by direction of the State acting as a sovereign."

Petitioner contends that even if California's system of wine pricing is not protected state action, the Twenty-first Amendment bars application of the Sherman Act in this case. Section 1 of that Amendment repealed the Eighteenth Amendment's prohibition on the manufacture, sale, or transportation of liquor. The second section reserved to the States certain power to regulate traffic in liquor: "The transportation or importation into any State, Territory, or possession of the United States for delivery or use therein of intoxicating liquors, in violation of the laws thereof, is hereby prohibited."

These decisions demonstrate that there is no bright line between federal and state powers over liquor. The Twenty-first Amendment grants the States virtually complete control over whether to permit importation or sale of liquor and how to structure the liquor distribution system. Although States retain substantial discretion to establish other liquor regulations, those controls may be subject to the federal commerce power in appropriate situations. The competing state and federal interests can be reconciled only after careful scrutiny of those concerns in a "concrete case."

The federal interest in enforcing the national policy in favor of competition is both familiar and substantial.

> "Antitrust laws in general, and the Sherman Act in particular, are the Magna Carta of free enterprise. They are as important to the preservation of economic freedom and our free-enterprise system as the Bill of Rights is to the protection of our fundamental personal freedoms."

We have no basis for disagreeing with the view of the California courts that the asserted state interests are less substantial than the national policy in favor of competition. That evaluation of the resale price maintenance system for wine is reasonable, and is supported by the evidence cited by the State Supreme Court in *Rice.* Nothing in the record in this case suggests that the wine pricing system helps sustain small retail establishments. Neither the petitioner nor the state Attorney General in his *amicus* brief has demonstrated that the program inhibits the consumption of alcohol by Californians. We need not consider whether the legitimate state interests in temperance and the protection of small retailers ever could prevail against the undoubted federal interest in a competitive economy. The unsubstantiated state concerns put forward in this case simply are not of the same stature as the goals of the Sherman Act.

We conclude that the California Court of Appeal correctly decided that the Twenty-first Amendment provides no shelter for the violation of the Sherman Act caused by the State's wine pricing program. The judgment of the California Court of Appeal, Third Appellate District, is

Affirmed.

Case Questions

1. How can resale price maintenance impose barriers to competition?
2. How can a state statute or the existence of legitimate state control over the business involved have an effect on antitrust enforcement?

3. Would the state statute be a defense to prevent antitrust enforcement if the regulatory system were designed to further a compelling state interest? Would the control of liquor consumption through raising prices, rather than the restriction of competition to maintain wine producers' profits, be a sufficient state interest?

State Fair-Trade Laws Under pressure from small retailers, Congress reacted to the per se designation of resale price maintenance by permitting any state to legitimize it. In 1937, the Miller-Tydings Act legalized resale price maintenance if included in agreements between manufacturers and retailers. The Great Depression had led to a proliferation of chain stores that forced many small retailers and wholesalers out of business. Small businesses insisted that products should be sold at "fair prices," allowing a fair rate of return to all sellers. Miller-Tydings legitimized resale price maintenance, but only if the state passed a separate statute legitimizing it.

By the early 1950s, 45 states permitted resale price maintenance agreements. At the height of this activity, over 1,500 manufacturers enforced the fair-trade laws through agreements with retailers requiring them to charge at least the "list price." In 1952, the McGuire Act was passed extending resale price maintenance agreements even to retailers that never signed them, the so-called *nonsigner provisions.*

For years, many consumer goods, such as name-brand clothes, furniture, cameras, and consumer electronics, were not discounted. By the 1960s, however, mail-order houses began to proliferate in states without fair-trade laws. This eroded resale price maintenance, and the practice eventually became unpopular. Eventually, many manufacturers abandoned resale price maintenance, and by 1975 Congress had repealed both the Miller-Tydings and McGuire Acts, again permitting intrabrand competition. From time to time, legislation is introduced to reinstate or prohibit resale price maintenance; such efforts are underway at this writing.

Refusals to Deal After the return of a prohibition against resale price maintenance, manufacturers developed another form of discipline for retailers that do not observe minimum prices: the manufacturer's *refusal to deal.* In *United States v. Colgate,* the Supreme Court permitted certain refusals to deal so long as no contract agreement obligated the retailer to sell at specific prices.[6] The Colgate Company had merely announced publicly that it would refuse to deal with distributors that failed to participate in its announced resale price maintenance policy.

Later cases have severely limited the *Colgate* doctrine, though they have not overruled it. Under the modern view, a refusal to deal is illegal and coercive if there is any active harassment or monitoring of the retailer's pricing behaviors or if the manufacturer establishes a suspension or reinstatement system for retailers that fail to comply with resale price maintenance. For example, Parke Davis distributed its pharmaceuticals through wholesalers and drug retailers.[7] Its wholesale catalog announced a refusal to deal to sellers that sold below the announced prices; prices often included a 50 percent markup. Parke Davis's wholesalers ceased filling orders for several retailers who advertised discounted

[6] *U.S. v. Colgate,* 250 U.S. 300 (1919).

[7] *U.S. v. Parke Davis & Co.,* 362 U.S. 29 (1960).

prices on Parke Davis vitamins. The Supreme Court held that Parke Davis went beyond mere announcement of its refusal to deal to an illegal resale price maintenance combination or conspiracy.

INTERNATIONAL PERSPECTIVE ON VERTICAL RESTRAINTS

The Japanese often divert criticism about the market entry barriers to foreign consumer goods by apologizing for problems caused by their "unique" distribution system. Most retail shops are small and often receive restocking deliveries several times each day; the Japanese claim that this is a useful "just-in-time" inventory method. High prices are necessary for profitability at several wholesale levels lying between the manufacturer and the traditional mom-and-pop retailer. Japan has a strong anti–chain store law, making it difficult for large discounters to get started, expand, or continue operations. Widespread resale price maintenance is enforced through threats and intimidation by sellers, organized crime, and even discriminatory actions by regulators. Refusals to deal help to perpetuate this system. Today, the number of small stores is beginning to decline and discounters are on the rise. However, the Japanese resale price maintenance system effectively thwarts competition (both intrabrand and interbrand), discourages competitive imports, and passes huge overpricing on to consumers. Japanese consumer competition is tightly confined to perpetuate this system of inefficient small retailers, excessive levels of wholesale distributors, higher profits for all sellers, and a lower standard of living for Japanese consumers.

Consignments A *consignment sale* is a form of contingent transaction in which the manufacturer retains title to the goods (ownership) until the retailer resells them to the ultimate consumer. In a consignment, the consignee (retailer) is only an agent for the consignor-manufacturer. This obligates the retailer to make the sale only on the manufacturer's prescribed sale terms. Manufacturers may try consignments as a legal form of resale price maintenance. In an early case, General Electric Company sold light bulbs through retailers on consignment, setting the retail price and paying the retailers a commission. Because light bulbs were patented by General Electric, the court found this to be a legitimate agency relationship. General Electric retained title, risk of loss, and risk of price changes in the light bulb market, so no illegal price maintenance was established.

Today, the courts look more closely at consignments to assure that they are not disguised forms of resale price maintenance. After the General Electric patents expired, its consignment arrangements were held illegal per se under the Sherman Act. However, some consignment arrangements have legitimate purposes. For example, suppliers may seek to retain title to goods as collateral, particularly if the retailer is in financial trouble. If the consignee-retailer goes bankrupt, the manufacturer does not risk unpaid debts or losing the retailer's inventory.

Vertical Nonprice Restraints

Manufacturers are often dissatisfied with reliance on fair-trade laws. Some are unable to take advantage of resale price maintenance and seek other nonprice restraints to gain similar control over retailer behavior. One such device prevents retailers from selling to discounters for resale. Another device imposes territorial limitations prohibiting retailers from engaging in intrabrand competition. Both of these devices are vertical nonprice restraints. Nonprice restraints may have legitimate purposes, but, like other vertical restrictions, they can be used to enforce illegal resale price maintenance.

Exclusive Dealing The term *exclusive dealership* indicates some sort of restriction in the resale arrangement. Although the word *exclusive* often refers to fashionable or privileged status, in antitrust law it means two different things. First, the sole right to sell a manufacturer's products within a given region is known as an *exclusive distributorship*. This device may be used to exclude all other dealers from selling the manufacturer's products in the same region. The exclusive distributor could also sell competitors' products. Manufacturers generally have wide freedom to pick their retailers or wholesalers.

The exclusive distributorship may not always be justified. If there are few substitutes for a manufacturer's products, exclusive distributorships are probably unjustifiable because they may prevent all competition. Exclusive distributorships have been judged by the rule of reason, though some recent cases have held exclusive distributorships to be illegal per se. For example, it is illegal for one distributor to pressure the manufacturer to terminate sales to the only competing distributor.

The second way in which the term *exclusive* is used in antitrust law relates to *exclusive dealing*—requiring the buyer to resell only the products of a single manufacturer. Under Section 3 of the Clayton Act, it is specifically illegal to engage in exclusive dealing, which tends to create a monopoly or substantially lessen competition.

Clayton Act, Section 3: Exclusive Dealing

It shall be unlawful for any person engaged in commerce to lease or make a sale . . . of . . . commodities . . . on the condition, agreement or understanding that the lessee or purchaser thereof shall not use or deal in . . . commodities of a competitor . . . of the lessor or seller, where the effect of such . . . [agreement] may substantially lessen competition or tend to create a monopoly in any line of commerce.

Quantitative Substantiality Generally a manufacturer or supplier may not insist that a retailer refuse to carry the products of competitors. The legality of such exclusive dealing contracts is judged by the *quantitative substantiality* test. This test presumes that an exclusive dealing contract will have an adverse effect on competition when it covers a substantial dollar volume. Thus, a violation may exist with a far lower percentage of market control than would be considered a monopoly or merger violation. In recent cases, a trend has emerged to focus this test on the actual market share foreclosed rather than the simple dollar volume.

Adequate Representation A more subtle way to enforce an exclusive dealing arrangement is to rely on the protection of the *Colgate* doctrine by simply refusing to sell to nonexclusive dealers. Manufacturers seeking this protection have eliminated exclusive dealing language from their supply contracts. Instead, they insert an *adequate representation clause* that requires the retailer to make a substantial effort to market the manufacturer's products. This permits the manufacturer to terminate dealers that do not expend the required efforts in advertising, inventory maintenance, service, or sales calls stated in the supply contract's adequate representation clause.

Customer and Territorial Restrictions Manufacturers' efforts to restrict retailers from selling to particular customers or in specific territories are probably illegal. Arrangements that restrict retailers' sales to a geographic region or that require retailers to sell only to the particular customers on a list deny retailers the right to sell to others and are illegal. At first, such arrangements were considered illegal per se under the *Schwinn* rule.[8] In 1977, however, this rule was replaced with the rule of reason, so all vertical nonprice restrictions are now illegal only when they are unreasonable. The EC has banned territorial restraints in an effort to lower the barriers imposed by national borders within the EC.

Sometimes vertical nonprice restrictions actually enhance interbrand competition, so they may be valid. There are two important questions in the analysis of territorial or customer restrictions.

Tests for Vertical Nonprice Restrictions

1. Does the vertical restriction tend to limit competition?
2. Are there legitimate economic and business objectives for the vertical restriction?

Vertical nonprice restrictions may be illegal if there is little interbrand competition, if the manufacturer has considerable market power, or if high barriers to entry exist for new producers. Should these standards of reasonableness make it more difficult for plaintiffs to attack vertical nonprice restrictions? These factors and the trend toward rule of reason analysis are illustrated in the following case.

Continental T.V., Inc. v. GTE Sylvania, Inc.

433 U.S. 36 (1977)
United States Supreme Court

GTE Sylvania, a manufacturer of television sets, limited the number of retail franchises for a given area to strengthen its retail network. This program required franchised retailers to sell GTE Sylvania products only at particular locations. Continental, one of the most successful Sylvania retailers in San Francisco, complained when Sylvania granted another franchise to a retailer located near Continental. Thereafter, Continental canceled a large Sylvania order and advised Sylvania that it would sell its inventory of Sylvania products from a new store in Sacramento. Sylvania had refused to give Continental a franchise in Sacramento. It cut Continental's credit line substantially, prompting Continental to allege that Sylvania's territorial restrictions were illegal per se.

Justice Powell delivered the opinion of the Court.

Per se rules of illegality are appropriate only when they relate to conduct that is manifestly anticompetitive. As the Court explained in *Northern Pac. R. Co. v. United States*, "there are certain agreements or practices which because of their pernicious effect on competition and lack of any redeeming virtue are conclusively presumed to be unreasonable and therefore illegal without elaborate inquiry as to the precise harm they have caused or the business excuse for their use."

Vertical restrictions reduce intrabrand competition by limiting the number of sellers of a particular product competing for the business of a given group of buyers.

[8] *United States v. Arnold Schwinn & Co.*, 388 U.S. 365 (1967).

Location restrictions have this effect because of practical constraints on the effective marketing area of retail outlets. Although intrabrand competition may be reduced, the ability of retailers to exploit the resulting market may be limited both by the ability of consumers to travel to other franchised locations and, perhaps more importantly, to purchase the competing products of other manufacturers. None of these key variables, however, is affected by the form of the transaction by which a manufacturer conveys his products to the retailers.

Vertical restrictions promote interbrand competition by allowing the manufacturer to achieve certain efficiencies in the distribution of his products. These "redeeming virtues" are implicit in every decision sustaining vertical restrictions under the rule of reason. Economists have identified a number of ways in which manufacturers can use such restrictions to compete more effectively against other manufacturers. For example, new manufacturers and manufacturers entering new markets can use the restrictions in order to induce competent and aggressive retailers to make the kind of investment of capital and labor that is often required in the distribution of products unknown to the consumer. Established manufacturers can use them to induce retailers to engage in promotional activities or to provide service and repair facilities necessary to the efficient marketing of their products. Service and repair are vital for many products, such as automobiles and major household appliances. The availability and quality of such services affect a manufacturer's goodwill and the competitiveness of his product. Because of market imperfections such as the so-called "free rider" effect, these services might not be provided by retailers in a purely competitive situation, despite the fact that each retailer's benefit would be greater if all provided the services than if none did.

We conclude that the distinction drawn in *Schwinn* between sale and nonsale transactions is not sufficient to justify the application of a *per se* rule in one situation and a rule of reason in the other. The question remains whether the *per se* rule stated in *Schwinn* should be expanded to include nonsale transactions or abandoned in favor of a return to the rule of reason. We have found no persuasive support for expanding the *per se* rule. As noted above, the *Schwinn* Court recognized the undesirability of "prohibit[ing] all vertical restrictions of territory and all franchising . . ." And even Continental does not urge us to hold that all such restrictions are *per se* illegal. Accordingly, we conclude that the *per se* rule stated in *Schwinn* must be overruled. [The Court of Appeals application of the rule of reason is affirmed; Sylvania's territorial restriction is reasonable.]

Case Questions

1. What justifies a manufacturer's efforts to reduce intrabrand competition in favor of interbrand competition?
2. What impact has the debate between the per se rule of illegality and the rule of reason had on vertical nonprice restraints?

Dealer Terminations Manufacturers have the freedom to choose or terminate their dealers when the dealer is unsuccessful, breaches key provisions in the distributorship agreement (e.g., adequate representation), deviates from announced pricing, or the manufacturer changes its marketing strategy. However, the dealer termination power is not unlimited. Both federal and state laws protect against some types of arbitrary franchise termination. For example, the Automobile Dealer's Day in Court Act and the Petroleum Marketing Practices Act restrict arbitrary dealer terminations. State laws require manufacturers to exercise "good faith" or limit them to "just cause" terminations.

Recent antitrust cases permit dealer terminations where no concerted action is taken to maintain resale prices. *Monsanto Co. v. Spray-Rite Service Corp.*[9] reaffirmed per se analysis of resale price maintenance while subjecting vertical nonprice restrictions to the rule of reason. Should a manufacturer be permitted to terminate certain dealers if they fail to comply with the manufacturer's requirement for vertical nonprice factors? The following case permits somewhat wider latitude for manufacturers to terminate dealers.

[9]*Monsanto Co. v. Spray-Rite Service Corp.*, 465 U.S. 752 (1984).

Business Electronics Corp. v. Sharp Electronics Corp.

485 U.S. 717 (1988)
United States Supreme Court

Business Electronics was initially the exclusive dealer for Sharp calculators in the Houston market. Thereafter, Hartwell was added as a Sharp retailer. After continued discounting by Business Electronics, Hartwell threatened to quit selling Sharp products unless Sharp terminated the Business Electronics dealership. After Sharp terminated the dealership, Business Electronics sued Sharp for conspiracy in restraint of trade in violation of Section 1 of the Sherman Act. The Court of Appeals reversed a jury verdict for treble damages against Sharp.

Justice Scalia delivered the opinion of the Court.

Departure from the rule of reason standard must be justified by demonstrable economic effect, rather than formalistic line drawing. Departure from [the *GTE Sylvania* standard] must be justified by economic effect, such as the facilitation of cartelization, that interbrand competition is the primary concern of the antitrust laws, and that rules in this area should be formulated with a view towards protecting the doctrine of *GTE Sylvania.*

There has been no showing here that an agreement between a manufacturer and a dealer to terminate a "price cutter," without a further agreement on the price or price levels to be charged by the remaining dealer, almost always tends to restrict competition and reduce output. Without an agreement with the remaining dealer on price, the manufacturer retains both its incentive to cheat on any manufacturer-level cartel (since lower prices can still be passed on to consumers) and cannot as easily be used to organize and hold together a retailer-level cartel.

Any agreement between a manufacturer and a dealer to terminate another dealer who happens to have charged lower prices can be alleged to have been directed against the terminated dealer's "price cutting." In the vast majority of cases it will be extremely difficult for the manufacturer to convince a jury that its motivation was to ensure adequate services, since price cutting and some measure of service cutting usually go hand in hand. Accordingly, a manufacturer that agrees to give one dealer an exclusive territory and terminate another dealer pursuant to that agreement, or even a manufacturer that agrees to terminate another dealer for failure to provide contractually obligated services, exposes itself to the highly plausible claim that its real motivation was to terminate a price cutter. Manufacturers would be likely to forgo legitimate and competitively useful conduct rather than risk treble damages and perhaps even criminal penalties.

All vertical restraints have the potential to allow dealers to increase prices and can be characterized as intended to achieve just that. Vertical nonprice restraints only accomplish the benefits identified in *GTE Sylvania* because they reduce intrabrand competition to the point where the dealer's profit margin permits provision of the desired services. The term "restraint of trade" refers not to a particular list of agreements, but to a particular economic consequence, which may be produced by quite different sorts of agreements in varying times and circumstances. Economic analysis supports the view that a vertical restraint is not illegal per se unless it includes some agreement on price or price levels.

Affirmed

Case Questions

1. What additional conduct between Sharp and Hartwell would be required before their activity would have constituted a per se violation?
2. What was the likely competitive effect of Sharp's termination of Business Electronics? How would Hartwell have likely behaved after the termination?
3. How does this decision change communications in supplier-customer relations and enhance their mutual fortunes?

Tying Arrangements The Clayton Act has been interpreted to outlaw most tying arrangements. **Tying**, or tie-in agreements, requires customers to purchase certain commodities or goods. Typically, the seller refuses to sell a desirable, or *tying*, product, unless the customer agrees to purchase a less desirable, or *tied*, product. The tie-in relationship coerces buyers to purchase less desirable products if they want to obtain desirable ones. This effectively ties their main purchases to supplementary goods. A tie-in is ineffective unless the seller possesses some market power in the desirable or tying product, perhaps resulting from a patent or a secret process. The tying of only goods, not services or land sales, is illegal under the Clayton Act.

Tying usually arises in one of three types of relationships. First, the tied and tying products are used together in fixed proportions (e.g., nuts and bolts, tires on automobiles). Second, the tied product may be necessary for use with the tying product (e.g., computer cards or discs with a computer). Third, the products may be only loosely usable together and may even be used separately (e.g., seed and fertilizer). Tying may also be illegal under Sherman Act provisions where it applies more broadly to real estate, intangibles, and services in addition to goods.

Analysis of Tying For tying to be considered illegal, three elements must be established. First, there must be a tying product and a tied product. This requires evidence of the seller's sale of one product conditioned on the purchase of another. Second, the seller must have sufficient economic or market power to force the tie-in. This may be shown where buyers clearly prefer the seller's tying product. If several buyers agree to a coercive tie-in, the seller may be presumed to have market power. Third, the level of competition restricted in the tied (less desirable) product must be more than an insubstantial amount. This requires proof that there is a substantial amount of commerce in the tied product. For example, $500,000 of the salt market and $60,000 of the film market have been considered substantial irrespective of the market share purchased by the buyer.

Effects and Motives for Tying Tie-in relationships force buyers to purchase tied products in larger quantities than they would purchase if the tie-in did not exist. Without the tie-in, purchasers could probably obtain the tied product or a substitute more cheaply, perhaps from other sellers. Tying reduces the buyer's freedom to use the least cost vendor for each product. This probably permits the tying seller to charge near-monopoly prices for the tied product. Tying raises barriers to entry for potential producers of the tied product and reinforces the tying seller's near-monopoly in the tying product.

Sellers often use the tying relationship to extend their market power from the tying product to the tied products. Sometimes, manufacturers seek to protect their goodwill by restricting the use of tied products of allegedly inferior quality produced by outside vendors. Tying makes it possible to exercise a type of price discrimination by selling the tying product cheaply but receiving abnormally high profits from the tied product.

Justifications for Tying Although tying has been held to be illegal per se, the courts increasingly permit sellers to justify it, so some exceptions exist. In addition, the Justice Department has relaxed its stiff opposition to tying in recent years. In some instances, only one product actually exists, not two, so there can be no claim of tying. For example, both a picture tube and the accompanying television set or an automobile and its built-in radio can be viewed as single products. The real question here is whether there is a substantial market for the installation of the tied product into the tying product. There is only a replacement and repair market for television picture tubes, but a healthy and competitive installation aftermarket exists for car radios and stereos. Auto manufacturers may be guilty of an illegal tie-in of higher-priced and/or lower-quality car radios (tied product) to automobiles (tying product). Although some automakers permit buyers to delete standard equipment radios for a credit, at least one domestic automaker still makes it difficult to purchase stereos in the aftermarket by making its electrical system technically incompatible with aftermarket stereos.

In one case, U.S. Steel (now U.S.X.) insisted on selling high-priced prefabricated homes by providing low-cost loans. Homes and loans are obviously not a single product. However, consumers might be willing to pay higher prices for the less desirable prefabricated homes (the tied product) if they receive desirable low-cost loans (the tying product). Today, many automobile and appliance manufacturers have captive finance companies (e.g., GMAC, FOMOCO Credit, GE Credit) that validly provide low-cost financing without violating antitrust policies against tying.

Tying relationships can be justified if they result in economic efficiency. During start-up, for example, new businesses may need to assure the proper functioning of their complex products. However, once a business has become established, the tying relationship is no longer justified. For example, a cable TV antenna manufacturer required the purchase of service contracts with the purchase of its equipment. This tie-in was justified only until the business had become well established.

Tying relationships are also justified if the quality of the tied product is higher than that of competitors' similar products. The seller may claim that without the tie-in the goodwill it derives from the tying product will suffer. This argument is seldom successful. At one time, IBM required that only the IBM brand of computer punch cards be used with its computers. Although other vendors produced these punch cards at far lower prices, IBM argued that only the IBM punch cards could prevent fouling of the IBM card readers. The Bell System used a similar argument when it required that its customers use only Western Electric telephones and switching equipment. In both instances, the alleged low quality of competitors' products could be solved by other reasonable means, such as measurable design and performance specifications. For example, specifications concerning the thickness and resilience of computer punch cards are sufficient to prevent damage to IBM's leased computers. Likewise, specifications concerning the electronic characteristics of telephone instruments are sufficient to prevent damage to the Bell System's equipment. The quality control argument is weak if the company is well established and specifications can ensure the compatibility of the tied products with the tying products. How far may product tie-ins be legally used to maintain product quality and the firm's goodwill? The following case illustrates why franchises may use vertical restraints illegal for nonfranchise businesses. Franchises were also discussed in Chapter 13.

Principe v. McDonald's Corp.
631 F.2d 303 (4th Cir. 1980)
United States Court of Appeals

The Principes operated two McDonald's restaurant franchises in Virginia. McDonald's denied their request to acquire a third franchise on the ground that the additional franchise would impair the quality of the Principes' existing operations. Thereafter, the Principes sued McDonald's, alleging an illegal tying relationship. McDonald's required franchisees to pay royalties for use of the franchise and also required franchisees to rent the McDonald's store from McDonald's Systems, Inc.

Harry Phillips, Senior Circuit Judge

At the time this suit was filed, McDonald's consisted of at least four separate corporate entities. McDonald's Systems, Inc. controlled franchise rights and licensed franchisees to sell hamburgers under the McDonald's name. Franchise Realty Interstate Corporation (Franchise Realty) acquires real estate, either by purchase or long term lease, builds McDonald's hamburger restaurants, and leases them either to franchisees or to a third corporation, McOpCo. McOpCo, which is not a party to this suit, operates about one-fourth of the McDonald's restaurants in the United States as company stores.

McDonald's is not primarily a fast food retailer. While it does operate over a thousand stores itself, the vast majority of the stores in its system are operated by franchisees. Nor does McDonald's sell equipment or supplies to its licensees. Instead its primary business is developing and collecting royalties from limited menu fast-food restaurants operated by independent business people.

McDonald's develops new restaurants according to master plans that originate at the regional level and must be approved by upper management. Regional administrative staffs meet at least annually to consider new areas into which McDonald's can expand. Once the decision is made to expand into a particular geographic area, specialists begin to search for appropriate restaurant sites.

McDonald's uses demographic data generated by the most recent census and its own research in evaluating potential sites. McDonald's attempts to analyze and predict demographic trends in the geographic area.

This process serves a twofold purpose: (1) by analyzing the demographic profile of a given market area, McDonald's hopes to determine whether the residents are likely to buy fast food in sufficient quantities to justify locating a restaurant there; (2) by anticipating future growth, McDonald's seeks to plan its expansion to maximize the number of viable McDonald's restaurants within a given geographic area. Based on a comparison of data for various available sites, the regional staffs select what they believe is the best site in each geographic area. Occasionally no available site suits McDonald's requirements and expansion must be postponed.

As part of the planning process, McDonald's decides what type of store to build on each site and where to locate it on the land. Differences in lot size and shape necessitate adjustments in store and parking lot configurations. Projected market size dictates dining room size. Land elevation, sign restrictions, store visibility and local setback requirements control restaurant placement.

Meanwhile, Franchise Realty acquires the land, either by purchase or long-term lease, and constructs the store. Acquisition and development costs averaged over $450,000 per store in 1978. All McDonald's restaurants bear the same distinctive features with a few exceptions due to architectural restrictions: the golden arches motif, the brick and glass construction, and the distinctive roofline. According to the defendants, these features identify the stores as a McDonald's even where zoning restrictions preclude other advertising or signs.

As constructed, McDonald's restaurants are finished shells; they contain no kitchen or dining room equipment. Furnishing store equipment is the responsibility of the operator, whether a franchisee or McOpCo. McDonald's does provide specifications such equipment must meet, but does not sell the equipment itself.

Having acquired the land, begun construction of the store and selected an operator, McDonald's enters into two contracts with the franchisee. Under the first, the franchise agreement, McDonald's grants the franchisee the rights to use McDonald's food preparation system and to sell food products under the McDonald's name. The franchisee pays a $12,500 franchise fee and agrees to remit 3 percent of his gross sales as a royalty in return. Under the second contract, the lease, McDonald's grants the franchisee the right to use the particular store premises to which his franchise pertains. In return, the franchisee pays a $15,000 refundable security deposit (as evidence of which he receives a 20-year non-negotiable non-interest-bearing note) and agrees to pay 8.5 percent of his gross sales as rent. These payments under the franchise and lease agreements are McDonald's only sources of income from its franchised restaurants. The franchisee also assumes responsibility under the lease for building maintenance, improvements, property taxes and other costs associated with the premises. Both the franchise agreement and the lease generally have 20-year durations, both provide that termination of one terminates the other, and neither is available separately. The Principes argue McDonald's is selling not one but three distinct products, the franchise, the lease and the security deposit note. The alleged antitrust violation stems from the fact that a prospective franchisee must buy all three in order to obtain the franchise.

As evidence that this is an illegal tying arrangement, the Principes point to the unfavorable terms on which franchisees are required to lease their stores. Not only are franchisees denied the opportunity to build equity and depreciate their property, but they must maintain the building, pay for improvements and taxes, and remit 8.5 percent of their gross sales as rents. In 1978 the gross sales of the Hopewell store generated about $52,000 in rent. That figure nearly equaled Franchise Realty's original cost for the site and corresponds to more than a fourth of the original cost of the entire Hopewell restaurant complex. At that rate of return, the Principes argue, Franchise Realty will have recouped its entire investment in four years and the remainder of the lease payments will be pure profit. The Principes contend that the fact the store rents are so high proves that McDonald's cannot sell the leaseholds on their own merits.

Nor has McDonald's shown any need to forbid its licensees to own their own stores, the Principes say. Appellants contend that McDonald's is the only fast-food franchiser that requires its licensees not only to pay royalties but to lease their stores from the franchisor.

A separate tied product is the note that evidences the lessee's $15,000 security deposit, according to the appellants. The Principes argue the security deposit really is a mandatory contribution to McDonald's working capital, not security against damage to the store or breach of the lease contract. By tying the purchase of these $15,000 twenty year non-negotiable non-interest-bearing notes to that of the franchise, McDonald's allegedly has generated a capital fund that totaled over $45 million in 1978. It is argued that no one would purchase such notes on their own merits. The Principes assert that only by requiring franchisees to purchase the notes as a condition of obtaining a franchise has McDonald's been able to sell them at all.

As support for their position, the Principes rely primarily on the decision of the Ninth Circuit in *Siegel v. Chicken Delight, Inc.,* one of the first cases to address the problem of franchise tie-ins. Chicken Delight was what McDonald's characterizes as a "rent a name" franchisor: it licensed franchisees to sell chicken under the Chicken Delight name but did not own store premises or fixtures. The company did not even charge franchise fees or royalties. Instead, it required its franchisees to purchase a specified number of cookers and fryers and to purchase certain packaging supplies and mixes exclusively from Chicken Delight. These supplies were priced higher than comparable goods of competing sellers. A class composed of franchisees challenged the tying arrangement as a violation of the Sherman Act. . . . In the court's view, Chicken Delight had attempted "to extend trademark protection to common articles (which the public does not and has no reason to connect with the trademark)," a classic kind of illegal tying arrangement.

Without disagreeing with the result in *Chicken Delight,* we conclude that the court's emphasis in that case upon the trademark as the essence of a franchise is too restrictive. Far from merely licensing franchisees to sell products under its trade name, a modern franchisor such as McDonald's offers its franchisees a complete method of doing business. It takes people from all walks of life, sends them to its management school, and teaches them a variety of skills ranging from hamburger grilling to financial planning. It installs them in stores whose market has been researched and whose location has been selected by experts to maximize sales potential. It inspects every facet of every store several times a year and consults with each franchisee about his operation's strengths and weaknesses. Its regime pervades all facets of the business, from the design of the menu board to the amount of catsup on the hamburgers; nothing is left to chance. This pervasive franchisor supervision and control benefits the franchisee in turn. His business is identified with a network of stores whose very uniformity and predictability attracts customers. In short, the modern franchisee pays not only for the right to use a trademark but for the right to become a part of a system whose business methods virtually guarantee his success. It is often unrealistic to view a franchise agreement as little more than a trademark license.

Applying this standard to the present case, we hold the lease is not separable from the McDonald's franchise to which it pertains. McDonald's practice of developing a system of company-owned restaurants operated by franchisees has substantial advantages, both for the company and for franchisees. It is part of what makes a McDonald's franchise uniquely attractive to franchisees.

First, because it approaches the problem of restaurant site selection systematically, McDonald's is able to obtain better sites than franchisees could select. Armed with its demographic information, guided by its staff of experts and unencumbered by preferences of individual franchises, McDonald's can wield its economic might to acquire sites where new restaurants will prosper without undercutting existing franchisees' business or limiting future expansion. Individual franchisees are unlikely to possess analytical expertise, undertake elaborate market research or approach the problem of site selection from an area-wide point of view.

Second, McDonald's policy of owning all of its own restaurants assures that the stores remain part of the McDonald's system. McDonald's franchise arrangements are not static: franchisees retire or die; occasionally they do not live up to their franchise obligations and must be replaced; even if no such contingency intervenes, the agreements normally expire by their own terms after 20 years. If franchisees owned their own stores, any of these events could disrupt McDonald's business and have a negative effect on the system's goodwill. Buildings whose architecture identified them as former McDonald's stores would sit idle or be used for other purposes. Replacement franchisees would have to acquire new and perhaps less desirable sites, a much more difficult and expensive process.

Third, because McDonald's acquires the sites and builds the stores itself, it can select franchisees based on their management potential rather than their real estate expertise or wealth. Ability to emphasize management skills is important to McDonald's because it has built its reputation largely on the consistent quality of its operations rather than on the merits of its hamburgers. A store's quality is largely a function of its management.

Finally, because both McDonald's and the franchisee have a substantial financial stake in the success of the restaurant, their relationship becomes a sort of partnership that might be impossible under other circumstances. McDonald's spends close to half a million dollars on each new store it establishes. Each franchisee invests over $100,000 to make the store operational. Neither can afford to ignore the other's problems, complaints or ideas.

Case Questions

1. What characteristics of a tie-in relationship are present in the typical franchise relationship?
2. What is the franchisor's justification for requiring the franchisee to purchase a particular site, equipment, or supplies from the franchisor?
3. Which "products" were considered the tying and tied products in the *McDonald's* case?
4. How does McDonald's legally employ otherwise illegal territorial restrictions and exclusive distributorships?

Justice Department Vertical Restraint Guidelines

The Justice Department views vertical nonprice restraints more favorably than the courts do. It will prosecute criminal violations only if collusion among competitors or suppliers appears to accompany the vertical restraint. The Justice Department's view does not represent the law, but it does indicate the law's present direction and prosecutorial intent.

Justice Department policymakers believe that the prohibition of vertical nonprice constraints causes uncertainty and inefficiency in the distribution of goods. Before prosecuting such a restraint, the Justice Department undertakes a *structured rule of reason* analysis. This involves a complex economic analysis of the effect of the vertical restraint on the particular market involved. The guidelines assert that tying should be judged by the rule of reason unless the seller possesses market power in the tying product, the tying and tied products are separate, and the tying produces a substantial adverse effect on the market for the tied product.

PRICE DISCRIMINATION

Price discrimination is a seller's practice of charging different prices to different buyers for goods of like grade and quality. Where price discrimination substantially lessens competition or tends to create a monopoly, it is illegal under the Robinson-Patman Act. The FTC has enforcement powers under Robinson-Patman, and a private right of action exists for competitors or buyers damaged by a price discrimination.

In a perfectly competitive market, price discrimination would be impossible—a buyer faced with a higher price than that offered to others would simply buy from another seller. However, few markets are perfectly competitive. Some buyers or sellers have a certain degree of market power.

THE ETHICAL DIMENSIONS OF PRICE DISCRIMINATION

The Robinson-Patman Act prohibition against price discrimination was passed to protect small businesses competing with chain stores that had oligopsony or buyer's market power. Congress supported "atomized" markets despite evidence that such markets are inefficient in many areas of the economy. However, Congress sought to preserve small business and prevent secret rebates and kickbacks. The balance drawn by antitrust laws reflects a conscious legislative choice to discourage some forms of unethical behavior and to encourage and establish economic self-reliance as an ethical policy. Although some contemporary ethical systems make efficiency the sole basis for ethical judgments in economic matters, the antitrust laws exemplify a richer heritage that also includes popular societal norms to provide part of the basis for ethical judgments. However, critics claim that the Robinson-Patman Act has outlived its ethical and economic usefulness.

Conditions Leading to Price Discrimination

Price discrimination is usually sustainable only while buyers or sellers have imperfect information. Buyers are often ignorant of the prices paid by other buyers. If buyers had better information, they could simply boycott the seller charging higher prices. Price discrimination usually occurs when some buyers are given secret price concessions. Antitrust laws may impose conflicting and confusing standards. Whereas the Sherman Act prohibits active communication of price information among sellers to avoid the appearance of price-fixing, the Robinson-Patman Act suggests that the lack of price visibility may encourage price discrimination.

Proof of Price Discrimination

To establish a violation of the Robinson-Patman Act, a plaintiff or the FTC must prove the presence of the following elements:

Establishing Price Discrimination

1. Discrimination in price
2. Between two different purchases
3. Affects interstate commerce
4. Concerns sales of commodities of like grade and quality
5. Causes a substantial lessening of competition or a tendency to create a monopoly
6. Causes injury to competitors of the seller or the buyer or to their customers

The two discriminatory transactions must occur within a contemporaneous time period; transactions separated by an excessive amount of time are not contemporaneous.

The price discrimination is usually proved by reference to two different sales prices as stated in the contracts of sale, although nonprice terms may constitute discrimination. For example, preferential credit terms given to one buyer but not offered to others are a prohibited price discrimination. Quantity discounts that are theoretically open to all purchasers but are in practice denied to small buyers are also discriminatory.

Commodities of Like Grade and Quality The Robinson-Patman Act is inapplicable to intangibles, services, and mixed sales of goods and services. It is lawful to discriminate in the price charged for securities, mutual fund shares, patents, licenses, real estate leases, and consulting services. However, a price discrimination in intangibles or services could conceivably violate the Sherman Act as a restraint of trade or an attempt to monopolize. Such discriminations could also violate the FTC Act if they are found to be an unfair method of competition.

The goods sold must be of like grade and quality; that is, their physical and chemical composition must be similar. If buyers willingly substitute two seemingly different products as interchangeable, they may be of like grade and quality. Subtle differences in the brand names or labels of two similar products will usually not justify price discrimination if consumers perceive the two products as functionally similar in performance. Arguably, higher prices may be charged for name-brand goods, even if the seller manufactures a lower-quality, generic equivalent to account for cost differences in advertising or promoting a name brand.

Competitive Injuries from Price Discrimination

Price discrimination is prohibited if it substantially lessens competition or tends to create a monopoly or if it injures, destroys, or prevents competition. A critical element of proof is the actual injury to competition. Liability arises when any person either discriminates or knowingly benefits from a discrimination, thereby causing lost profits or missed business opportunities.

The level of the business suffering the injury must be identified. Injuries may occur at the seller's level, buyer's level, or the level of the customers of the buyer. Injuries at these levels are referred to as primary-line injuries, secondary-line injuries, and tertiary-line injuries, respectively (e.g., third-line injuries).

Primary-Line Injury Price discriminations tending to injure those in competition with the discriminating seller are *primary-line injuries.* A discriminating seller operating in two distinct geographic regions damages its competitors in the lower-priced region. The seller may discriminate between regions in order to drive competitors out of business in one region by charging higher than normal prices in another region where it has greater market power. It uses profits from the high-priced market to temporarily subsidize lower prices in the underpriced market. In Figure 16-1, Seller A has enough market power to charge a higher price in its primary market, Pennsylvania. This enables it to offer the same goods in Michigan at prices lower than Seller B can match. Injury to Seller B occurs at the primary line because B is a seller competing with A in Michigan.

Secondary-Line Injury Price discriminations between two buyers competing for the same customers may injure buyers, a *secondary-line injury.* If two buyers have different costs for the same goods, the buyer paying higher prices suffers because the buyer paying lower prices can pass the savings on to its customers. In Figure 16-2, Buyer B pays the seller a lower price and can pass this cost advantage on to its customers through lower

FIGURE 16–1 Primary-Line Injury

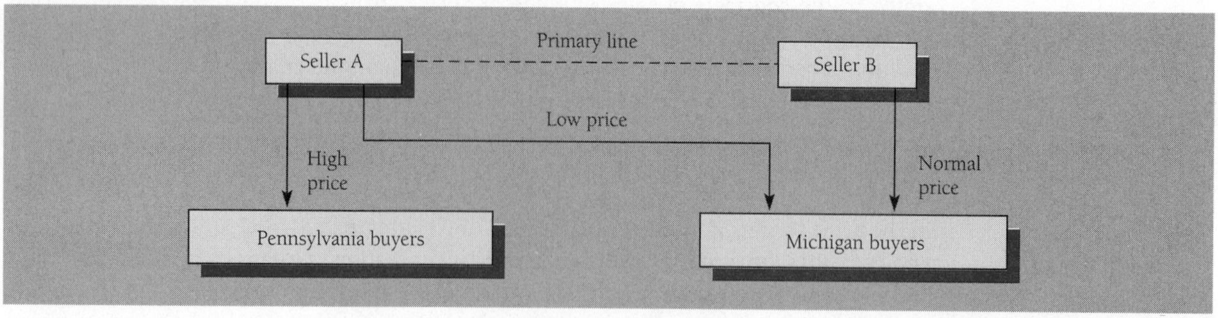

FIGURE 16–2 Secondary-Line Injury

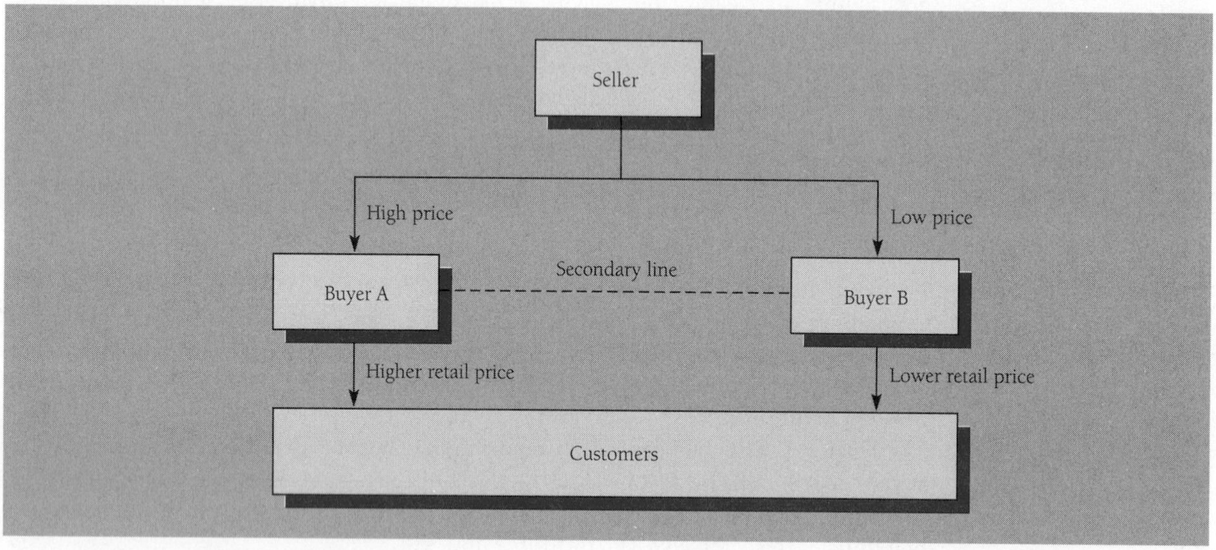

retail prices. If Buyer A cannot pass on its higher cost, it cannot compete effectively. Customers with a choice between A and B will prefer B's lower prices. However, if Buyer A and Buyer B were in distinct geographic markets, no secondary-line injury would occur because their two sets of customers could not practically choose one over the other. This condition existed in *Utah Pie Co. v. Continental Baking Co.*[10] Several national bakers sold pies in the Salt Lake City market at lower prices than they charged in other markets, suffering losses on many sales. The Supreme Court upheld a jury's conclusion that Utah Pie, a local baker, suffered secondary-line injury even though it was profitable at the time of suit. Price discrimination that slowly erodes competition due to a drastically declining price structure is sufficient evidence of past conduct to project future competitive injury in violation of Robinson-Patman.

[10]*Utah Pie Co. v. Continental Baking Co.*, 386 U.S. 685 (1967).

FIGURE 16–3 Tertiary-Line Injury

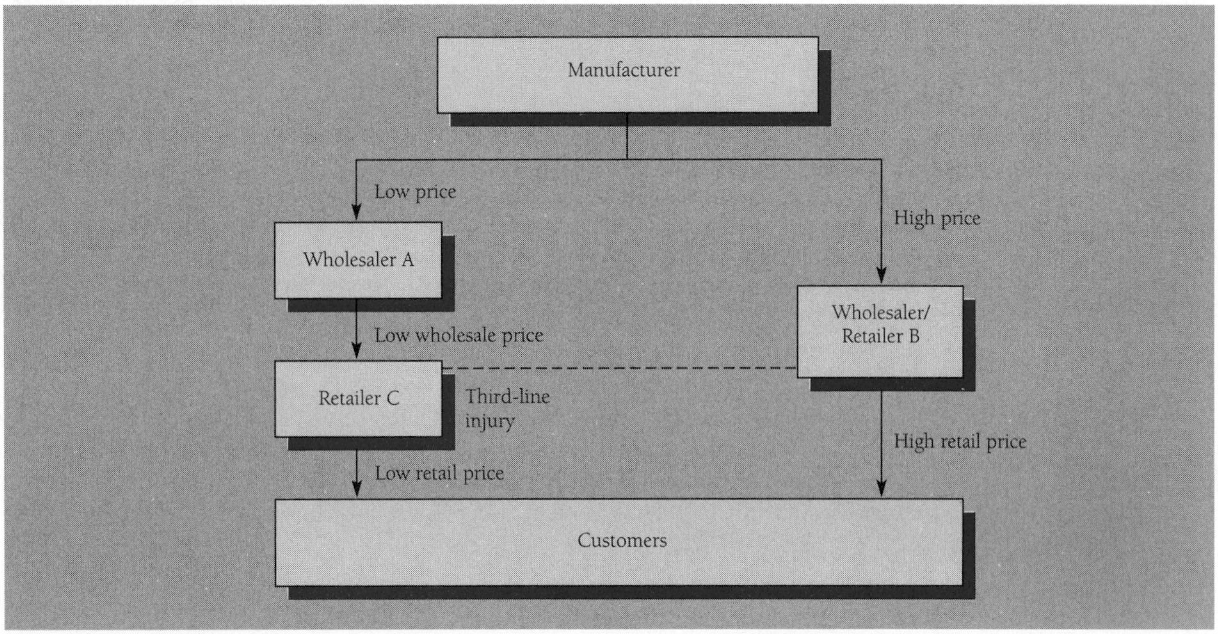

Tertiary-Line Injury A more controversial theory of price discrimination involves injury to the buyer's customers. Theoretically, injury may occur at any level of distribution, no matter where price discrimination occurs in a long chain of distribution. A *tertiary-line injury* may occur if customers of the buyers are injured by price discrimination because the cost savings are passed on through wholesalers to retailers. In Figure 16-3, a *third-line injury* occurs between the customers in two chains of distribution. The manufacturer has sold at a higher price to B, an integrated wholesaler/retailer which passes the higher costs on to customers as higher retail prices. Because Wholesaler A receives a lower price, it charges a low wholesale price to Retailer C, which passes the lower costs on as lower retail prices to customers. B's ability to compete with A and C is undermined in sales made to the same customer base. The third-line injury occurs between Wholesaler/Retailer B and Retailer C.

Price Discrimination Defenses

Price discrimination may be justified with an affirmative defense. The seller may attempt to show that the competitive effect of differential pricing was trivial, effectively rebutting evidence of competitive injury. For example, sales to a government may be made at prices different from nongovernment sales unless the government intends to resell in the retail market. Sales to a nonprofit institution are exempted so long as the institution does not resell in the retail market for profit. Export sales are exempted because the Robinson-Patman Act applies only to "commodities . . . sold for use, consumption, or resale within the United States." There are also three statutory defenses: changing conditions, cost differential, and meeting the competition in good faith.

Changing Conditions Section 2(a) of the Robinson-Patman Act provides a defense to allegations of illegal price discrimination when the market has changed so that prices previously charged are no longer realistic.

Robinson-Patman Act, Section 2(a): Changing Conditions Defense

. . . nothing herein shall prevent price changes from time to time in response to *changing conditions* affecting the marketability of the goods concerned, such as (but not limited to) actual or imminent deterioration of perishable goods, obsolescence of seasonal goods, distress sales under court process, or sales in good faith in discontinuance of business in the goods concerned.

The changing conditions defense is confined strictly to temporary situations in which the physical nature of the commodity requires a distress sale. A classic example is the lowering of retail automobile prices on the leftover inventory of the prior model year. After significant inventories of the new year's model arrive on dealer lots, conditions have changed sufficiently to permit lowering the price of the year-old "new" models.

Cost Differential Another defense provided in Section 2(a) recognizes that various sales contracts may have different costs.

Robinson-Patman Act, Section 2(a): Cost Differential Defense

. . . nothing herein contained shall prevent differentials which make only *due allowance* for differences in the cost of manufacture, sale, or delivery resulting from the differing methods or quantities in which such commodities are sold or delivered.

Although this justification would appear significant, in practice it has been difficult for sellers to rely on it. One problem is that there is no universal definition of costs. Robinson-Patman was designed to prevent predatory pricing in which one producer subsidizes low-priced sales from profits earned elsewhere and later raises prices above competitive levels after competitors have been driven from the market. Predatory pricing may be demonstrated through the circumstantial evidence of average variable costs. Price-cutting below average variable costs is strong evidence of predatory pricing.

Computation of average variable costs requires that an allocation be made of indirect costs (e.g., overhead), a complex and controversial process. The amount of overhead allotted to each unit in addition to average variable costs varies under different assumptions.

The cost differential defense is most often successful when discriminatory pricing is based on legitimate quantity discounts. The defense is more reliable when there are actual savings in packaging, handling, and transportation costs. Should "functional" discounts be permitted if some buyers provide these marketing functions? The next case illustrates how some sellers claim that discounts given to certain buyers represent legitimate savings when in reality, such discounts are destructive to those buyers who must pay higher prices.

Texaco v. Hasbrouck

110 S.Ct. 2535 (1990)
United States Supreme Court

Texaco supplied gasoline to both independent filling stations and to distributors that owned their own stations in the Spokane, Washington, area. Independent retailers paid Texaco a higher retail tank wagon price than was paid by groups of stations operated as a chain: Gull and Dompier. Gull sold Texaco gasoline through its own stations under the Gull tradename, and Dompier later entered the Spokane market selling Texaco gasoline through its own stations under the Texaco name. Texaco charged them lower "functional" discount prices than it charged the independents. Dompier's Texaco stations were restocked by Dompier's tanker trucks. However, Texaco prohibited the independents from hiring their own trucks to transport gasoline from Texaco at the lower discount price. The independents' sales volume fell significantly and Dompier's grew rapidly after it entered the market. The independents sued for treble damages, claiming that Texaco's pricing violated Robinson-Patman. Texaco claimed that its "functional" discounts were legitimate and as seller it was not responsible for the pricing behavior of its wholesale customers.

Justice Stevens delivered the opinion of the Court.

In order to establish a violation of the Act, respondents had the burden of proving four facts: (1) that Texaco sales to Gull and Dompier were made in interstate commerce; (2) that the gasoline sold to them was the same grade and quality as that sold to respondents; (3) that Texaco discriminated in price between Gull and Dompier on the one hand and respondents on the other; and (4) that the discrimination had a prohibited effect on competition.

In *F.T.C. v. Morton Salt Co.,* we held that an injury to competition may be inferred from evidence that some purchasers had to pay their supplier "substantially more for their goods than their competitors had to pay." Texaco, as supported by the United States and the FTC as *amici curiae,* argues that this presumption should not apply to differences between prices charged to wholesalers and those charged to retailers. Moreover, they argue that it would be inconsistent with fundamental antitrust policies to construe the Act as requiring the seller to control his customers' resale prices. The Report of the Attorney General's National Committee to Study the Antitrust Laws (1955) wrote:

> Suppliers granting functional discounts should not be held responsible for any consequences of their customers' pricing tactics. Price cutting at the resale level is not "the effect of" a differential that merely accords due recognition and reimbursement for actual marketing functions.
>
> On the other hand the law should tolerate no subterfuge. Where a wholesaler-retailer buys only part of his goods as a wholesaler, he must not claim a functional discount on all. Only to the extent that a buyer actually performs certain functions, assuming all the risk, investment, and costs involved, should he legally qualify for a functional discount.

In this case, there was no substantial evidence indicating that the discounts to Gull and Dompier constituted a reasonable reimbursement for the value to Texaco of their actual marketing functions. Indeed, Dompier was separately compensated for its hauling function, and neither Gull nor Dompier maintained any significant storage facilities.

The evidence indicates that Texaco affirmatively encouraged Dompier to expand its retail business and that Texaco was fully informed about the persistent and marketwide consequences of its pricing policies. Indeed, its own executives recognize that the dramatic impact on the market was almost entirely attributable to the magnitude of the distributor discount and the hauling allowance. Yet at the same time that Texaco was encouraging Dompier to integrate downward, Texaco was inhibiting upward integration by the respondents. The special facts of this case thus make it peculiarly difficult for Texaco to claim that it is being held liable for the independent pricing decisions of Gull and Dompier.

One would expect that most functional discounts will be legitimate discounts that do not cause harm to competition. A functional discount that constitutes a reasonable reimbursement for the purchasers' actual marketing functions will not violate the Act. Not every functional discount is entitled to a judgment of legitimacy, and it will sometimes be possible to produce evidence showing that a particular functional discount caused a price discrimination. When such anticompetitive effects are proved—as we believe they were in this case—they are covered by the Act.

Affirmed.

Case Questions

1. What level of injury was established in this case?
2. What kind of evidence is needed to prove the legitimacy of a discount? Can a functional discount be distinguished from a volume discount?

Meeting the Competition in Good Faith Section 2(b) of the Robinson-Patman Act also permits a seller to discriminate in price if the lower price "was made in good faith to meet an equally low price of a competitor." The price discriminator must have a reasonable belief that granting the lower price is necessary to win the sale. The lower price must exactly meet, but not beat, the competitor's price.

The problem of conflicting antitrust goals is also involved in satisfying the competition defense. Communications with competitors concerning price strongly suggest violation of price-fixing prohibitions. Good faith is crucial to the competition defense because price discrimination and price-fixing enforcement must be harmonized. Sellers may show good faith if they investigate the truth of a buyer's claim that a competitor charges a lower price. For example, some retailers require buyers to bring in the competitor's ad or estimate or prove that a lower price is available to the buyer.

When the necessity of meeting the price has ceased and market conditions return to normal, the seller must cease discriminatory pricing. To fall within the competition defense, sellers may discriminate only in meeting their own competition and may not discriminate to assist a customer in meeting its competition. The competitor's price must be met within a short time frame.

Seller and Buyer Liability

The Robinson-Patman Act applies to both buyers and sellers. It is unlawful for "any person . . . knowingly to induce or receive a discrimination in price." Thus, if the buyer has knowledge that the price it obtained was discriminatory, either the buyer or the seller may be held liable. However, if the seller has a defense, the buyer may utilize that defense. For example, the A & P foodstore rejected as too high a bid made by Borden to supply "private label" milk products to A & P. Borden made a revised lower bid in a good faith effort to meet the competition, so its price discrimination was justified by the "meeting the competition in good faith" defense. Because Borden had this defense, A & P was not liable as a buyer inducing a price discrimination.[11]

[11]*Great Atlantic and Pacific Tea Co., Inc. v. FTC*, 440 U.S. 69 (1979).

Indirect Concessions

The Robinson-Patman Act also prohibits price discriminations effected through indirect price concessions. It is unlawful for "any person to pay, grant, or receive any brokerage or allowance in lieu thereof except for services rendered in connection with the sale or purchase of goods." This provision prohibits a buyer from persuading a seller to pay a brokerage fee to a person who splits the payment with the buyer, an illegal form of kickback. Fictitious brokerage fees represent a secret discount. However, a brokerage fee is permissible if the buyer or a third party actually performs legitimate brokerage-type services, such as preparing documents or arranging transportation.

Robinson-Patman also prohibits the seller from discriminating in the provision of payments, services, or facilities, such as the provision of special assistance, allowances for advertising, or display materials, only to select customers. The disadvantaged buyer need only prove (1) that the promotional service or allowance was provided only to other purchasers or (2) that a competitor was favored in its "business stature." Such services are permissible if they are triggered at announced dollar volumes of purchases or are equally available to all buyers.

Discrimination in Freight Charges Price discrimination may also occur when shippers charge discriminatory freight rates. If the quoted sale prices in two sales are identical, but either customer pays more or less than the actual cost of shipment, then there is an indirect price discrimination. There is no discrimination if the buyer must pay all freight and delivery charges. However, some informal "delivered price" quotes include freight charges. If all buyers pay the same freight charges, as part of a uniform delivered price, then buyers geographically closer to the seller's plant pay higher freight charges per mile than do buyers located farther away.

Equal freight rates charged for unequal delivery distances may constitute *phantom freight*, an illegal price discrimination. Phantom freight is classified as (1) a single basing point system (if the freight is actually shipped from another place), (2) zone pricing (the same freight rates are imposed on all customers within a zone, regardless of the distance), or (3) a multiple basing point system (the nearest of several base points of origin governs the price charged for freight). In devising pricing, additional service provisions, freight rates, brokerage commissions, or any other nonprice allowances, consideration must always be given to the possibility that a buyer might argue that the practices used are discriminatory.

The Future Regulation of Price Discrimination

The Robinson-Patman prohibition against price discrimination is generally regarded as one of the most violated provisions of antitrust law. Many critics argue that this provision helps perpetuate an inefficient network of small retailers, reduces price competition, and simply raises consumer prices to uniform levels. However, it should be recognized that many of the international fair-trade laws, particularly the antidumping rules, are essentially price discrimination regulations. *Dumping*, as discussed in Chapter 21, is a foreign firm's practice of selling in another nation's market at prices lower than those prevailing in that firm's home market. The same arguments are made against both practices: dumping and price discrimination encourage cross-subsidies that drive out competitors, leaving the discriminator with a monopoly. For this and other reasons, Robinson-Patman will probably not be repealed.

UNFAIR TRADE PRACTICES

The Sherman and Clayton Acts do not cover a wide range of activities arguably resulting in unfair trade practices. Congress granted the FTC powers to remedy such practices in the FTC Act. Section 5 of the Federal Trade Commission Act gives the FTC extensive powers to prohibit "unfair methods of competition and unfair or deceptive acts or practices in or affecting commerce." Practices that are not clearly illegal under the antitrust laws may be ruled illegal by the FTC. The rulemaking power of the FTC permits it to fill in the gaps of the antitrust laws. In addition, most states have similar powers to prohibit some of these practices.

Federal Trade Commission Powers and Procedures

The FTC Act empowers the FTC to investigate and pursue complaints of unfair trade practices. The FTC often resolves such complaints with a *consent decree,* which requires the defendant to settle charges without admitting or denying them. Defendants must usually promise to refrain from the practice in the future. The FTC may also issue *cease and desist orders,* which are somewhat stronger than injunctions. Cease and desist orders require the defendant to stop an unfair trade practice and bear the stigma of a repeat offender.

FTC proceedings usually involve an internal hearing that is held before an administrative law judge. Appeals may be taken to the FTC commissioners and ultimately to the U.S. Court of Appeals and the U.S. Supreme Court. FTC orders may be enforced with contempt citations, including fines and imprisonment.

Federal Trade Commission's Informal Guidance

The FTC attempts to provide guidance on the manner in which it will exercise its powers. This gives businesses notice of what the FTC considers unfair trade practices. In addition, parties may request the FTC to issue an *advisory opinion* regarding the legality of specific proposed conduct.

From time to time, the FTC issues comprehensive industry *guidelines.* These guidelines create *safe harbors* for specific conduct. The FTC promises not to prosecute a business that conforms its transactions to the guidelines. However, FTC advisory opinions and guidelines do not have the force of law and may be reinterpreted by the courts. The FTC may also issue specific trade regulation rules that do have the force of law. For example, the courts sustained the FTC's requirement that gasoline retailers post octane numbers on gas pumps. The deceptive advertising aspects of this rulemaking power were discussed in Chapter 11.

The FTC uses standards of fairness in giving advisory opinions, issuing guidelines, promulgating rules, and prosecuting violations. The FTC often considers (1) whether public policy is offended by the alleged unfair trade practice; (2) whether the practice is immoral, unethical, oppressive, or unscrupulous; and (3) whether the practice causes substantial injury to consumers, competitors, or others in business.

In *FTC v. Brown Shoe Co.,* the FTC interpreted its mission as the extension of the philosophy of the Sherman and Clayton Acts.[12] Brown Shoe had promised special benefits

---

[12] *F.T.C. v. Brown Shoe Co.,* 384 U.S. 316 (1966).

to retailers that agreed not to sell other brands of shoes. The Supreme Court upheld the FTC's exercise of power to stop trade restraints in their incipiency, without proof that those restraints violated the Clayton or Sherman Acts.

SUMMARY

The rule of reason and the per se rule are used to judge the legality of restraints of trade. Under the rule of reason, the defendant's justification for a restraint of trade may be considered if it is clear that the restraint is not illegal per se. Only unreasonable restraints of trade are illegal under the Sherman Act. Horizontal combinations among direct competitors are illegal restraints of trade and the least justifiable of all such restraints. In certain repetitive and unjustifiable circumstances, restraints of trade are always considered illegal per se, these include: price-fixing, division of markets, group boycotts, concerted refusals to deal, and tying. Recently, several per se violations have been judged under the rule of reason.

Agreements among direct competitors to set prices at artificial levels are illegal per se. There is no justification for price-fixing even if the competitors are well intentioned, attempt to set maximum prices, or argue that the setting of prices is required by professional ethics. Fixing credit or freight terms is also illegal. Trade associations must be careful to avoid exchanges of price information that might facilitate price-fixing. Competitors that divide markets among one another commit a per se violation. Boycotts by groups of competitors are also illegal per se. Joint ventures are judged by the rule of reason.

Proof of conspiracies in restraint of trade is difficult because violators seldom leave an evidentiary trail. Circumstantial evidence often sustains the burden of proving criminal guilt beyond a reasonable doubt. Businesses that mimic the pricing behaviors of competitors under a tacit agreement may be committing illegal conscious parallelism.

Vertical restraints of trade impose tying arrangements and restrict resale prices, territorial access to markets, and the freedom to sell competing brands. Resale price maintenance agreements are illegal. A manufacturer's limited refusal to deal with retailers that refuse to follow suggested list prices may be legal if there is no harassment, price monitoring, or conspiracy. Legitimate consignment sales may impose resale price maintenance.

Vertical nonprice restraints may be illegal. Exclusive dealing contracts are illegal if they substantially lessen competition or tend to create a monopoly. Adequate representation clauses may permit manufacturers to drop retailers that fail to adequately promote their products. Vertical nonprice restrictions, such as customer or territorial restrictions, are judged by the rule of reason. Franchising is a method that may legally use many vertical restrictions to protect the franchiser from trademark infringement.

The Clayton Act prohibits tying in which sellers require customers to buy less desirable (tied) products in order to buy desirable (tying) products. Tying may be justified where there is actually only one product, where a start-up company needs to ensure its product quality, or where tied products of low quality would interfere with the tying product.

Price discrimination was made illegal by the Robinson-Patman Act. Under that act, it is illegal if (1) two different purchasers (2) in interstate commerce (3) pay different prices for (4) similar commodities and if (5) the price discrimination substantially lessens competition or tends to create a monopoly and (6) causes damage. Primary-line injury resulting from price discrimination occurs to competitors of the seller. Secondary-line injury occurs to the buyer paying the higher prices. Tertiary-line injury occurs to the customers of the buyer when the price discrimination occurs at the level of the buyer's buyer.

Sellers may justifiably discriminate in the prices they charge when market conditions change, legitimate quantity discounts are made, or lower prices of competitors are met in good faith. Both the seller granting the price discrimination and the buyer inducing it may be held liable.

The FTC Act fills in the regulatory gaps created by the federal Sherman and Clayton Acts and by the states' antitrust laws. Section 5 of the FTC Act prohibits unfair methods of competition and unfair and deceptive trade practices. The FTC may settle unfair trade practice claims with consent decrees or may prosecute in the courts.

KEY TERMS

rule of reason, p. 490
per se rule, p. 490
price-fixing, p. 491
division of markets, p. 495
group boycott, p. 495
conscious parallelism, p. 497
interlocking directorates, p. 497
free rider, p. 499
resale price maintenance, p. 499
tying, p. 507
price discrimination, p. 511

CHAPTER EXERCISES

1. Describe the source and nature of the rule of reason and the per se rule. Describe each of the per se categories.
2. The Goldfarbs contracted to buy a home in Virginia, and the mortgage company that was to lend them the money for the purchase required a title examination before the deal was closed. Only a licensed attorney could conduct such an examination. The Goldfarbs contacted 36 attorneys, all of whom indicated that their fee for such services was the one recommended by the Bar Association of Virginia. Generally, charging lower than the Bar Association's recommended fees was a ground for disciplinary action against attorneys. The Goldfarbs sued, claiming that the fee arrangement violated Section 2 of the Sherman Act. With what result, and why? *Goldfarb v. Virginia State Bar,* 421 U.S. 773 (1975).
3. Mutt and Jeff are both sole proprietors of building cleanup services in Atlanta. They have been friends for several years. Recently, they discussed an idea of mutual interest: the possibility of coordinating their pricing so that downtown office building managers didn't pit them against each other in bidding for cleanup jobs. Does this idea have any antitrust implications? If so, what would a competitor have to prove in order to show that it is illegal?
4. Is conscious parallelism the same thing as concerted action? What does the term *agreement* really mean?
5. What is the difference between horizontal and vertical restraints of trade?
6. The publishers of over 12,000 newspapers are members of the Associated Press (AP), which collects and assembles news and distributes news stories to its members. The bylaws of the AP prohibited its members from selling news to nonmembers and set up a system by which AP members could block nonmember competitors from joining. The United States filed a complaint charging that these provisions violated Section 1 of the Sherman Antitrust Act. With what result, and why? *Associated Press v. U.S.*, 326 U.S. 1, 1945.
7. Your company, Run Company, manufactures running shoes and sells them to sporting goods stores. *Runner Magazine* recently rated your WINGS brand "excellent" and your other brand, PLOP, "worthless." The sporting goods stores are clamoring for shipments of WINGS. You notify these retailers that if they want WINGS, they must order an equal quantity of PLOP. Why does your lawyer complain when he hears what you have done?
8. Your company, Run Company, needs shoelaces to make WINGS and PLOP running shoes. You persuade a shoelace manufacturer to sell you shoelaces at a price lower than the price it charges NIKE, your major competitor. Why does this trouble your lawyer?
9. What must one prove to establish a Robinson-Patman violation?
10. Allen sells his product in both Georgia and Florida, while Ben sells his competing product only in Florida. Allen lowers his price in Florida but leaves it the same in Georgia. Is this an example of a primary-line, secondary-line, or third-line injury? Why?
11. Seller A charges Buyers Y and Z a different price for its product. Buyers Y and Z, in turn, sell the product to other purchasers, but Buyer Z must charge a higher price than Buyer Y because of the higher price that is charged by Seller A. Is this an example of a primary-line, secondary-line, or third-line injury? Why?

12. Stacy Corporation produces a unique "add-on" software program that enhances spreadsheet analysis of differing budget alternatives. Usually, budget categories must be painstakingly replicated in most spreadsheets and the alternative assumptions of sales, expenses, interest rates, and overhead expense entered manually. Stacy's product, Budget-Ease, automatically projects different assumptions for the variables mentioned above, greatly reducing the time spent on projecting budget alternatives. However, Stacy insists that customers must purchase Stacy-Calc, the company's own spreadsheet program, in order to use Budget-Ease. Compare and contrast the legal and ethical analyses of this problem.

Part 6

EMPLOYMENT LAW

Part 6 reviews the various labor law concerns facing business. Public and private laws at both the state and federal level indirectly and directly address all employers' relationships with their employees. Chapter 17 covers the federal labor laws exclusively. These laws permit unionization of workers and require employers to bargain collectively with unions representing the employees.

Chapter 18 covers the federal and state regulations concerning workplace safety and various aspects of the employment relationship. Employers must take great care to maintain workers' safety and to provide pensions, periodic compensation, and compensation for extraordinary conditions such as unemployment and injuries.

The last area covered involves the federal laws pertaining to discrimination in employment decisions. Employers must make hiring, firing, promotion, and job tenure decisions based on the objective criteria of employees' real aptitudes and capabilities. Usually, employment decisions based on a person's race, sex, color, national origin, age, or disability are not sufficiently related to probable job performance to be justifiable. Decisions made on the employee's membership in a "suspect class" are discriminatory and expose the employer to liability.

Chapter 17

LABOR-MANAGEMENT RELATIONS

KEY CONCEPTS

Four federal statutes establish the basic regulatory structure for U.S. labor-management relationships: The Norris-LaGuardia Act, the National Labor Relations Act, the Labor-Management Relations Act, and the Labor-Management Reporting and Disclosure Act.

The National Labor Relations Board (NLRB) provides the forum that establishes labor's rights to self-organization. The NLRB processes unfair labor practice charges against both employers and unions.

Employers and unions are prohibited from interfering with union organization or committing other unfair labor practices.

The employer and the union must meet at reasonable times to bargain in good faith over mandatory bargaining topics, wages, hours, and other terms and conditions of employment. Bargaining is not required over other, permissive terms.

The National Labor Relations Act permits employees to engage in concerted activities, including peaceful picketing and striking for lawful mutual aid or protection.

Unless a valid state right-to-work law is in effect, unions may require the employer to maintain a union shop in which each covered employee must join the union or pay a union bargaining fee after a brief probationary period.

The union is the exclusive bargaining agent for all of the employees in the appropriate bargaining unit. It must represent all of the employees equally and fairly, irrespective of their union membership.

Employees' rights to picket are generally limited to primary sites—sites where the employer is located. Employees are generally entitled to reinstatement after unfair labor practice strikes but not after economic strikes.

Unions' elections must be conducted fairly, and the activities of union officials are subject to court review.

INTRODUCTION . . . PAST, PRESENT, FUTURE

Prior to the 20th century, the employment relationship was governed largely by private contracts. Employers negotiated face-to-face with prospective employees. But as businesses grew larger and employment relationships became more impersonal and complex, new employment problems emerged that the law of contracts and torts failed to address.

Tumultuous interactions between labor and management have occurred throughout the history of industrialization. Employers staunchly resisted employees' struggle to bargain collectively, thus slowing the growth of the U.S. trade union movement until the 1930s, when unions finally received widespread support from many sectors of the population. Labor appeared to need unity in order to increase its bargaining power against the monopsony power (buyer's monopoly) of employers. However, the power acquired by the American labor movement may have been too great, eventually causing a negative public reaction. After World War II, it appeared that the excessive political and economic influence gained by unions permitted them to intimidate their adversaries. The influence of Communists and organized crime over internal union politics also caused the pendulum of public sympathy to swing against unions, promoting Congress to pass tough laws curbing unions' undemocratic and bullying treatment of their members. Today, employers must bargain with unionized employees over such issues as working hours, retirement security, hiring and firing practices, and job health and safety. Employers must be aware of many complex statutes, administrative regulations, and judicial interpretations that affect the terms and conditions of employment.

The Taft-Hartley and Landrum-Griffin acts strike an important balance between the assurance of employees' organization rights and the potential for unions' abuse of power. The major constraints on union collective activity, picketing and strikes, apply to all union attempts to bring economic pressure on employers during labor disputes. Union officials must maintain accountability to the law and to the best interests of union members. Union officials who are unable to fairly conduct their legitimate activities can be removed.

In the future, labor unions will face numerous challenges to their traditional powers. Unionism is still strong in basic industries (e.g., automobile manufacturing, rubber, steel, mining, oil, chemicals), and unionism is spreading rapidly to white-collar workers. However, the total proportion of unionized employees has declined to 16 percent of the workforce. The traditional bargaining power of employees over their employer's business has diminished as assembly lines have been automated and many component parts are imported. Employers now often claim that because high wages diminish competitiveness, employees must scale back their wage demands to maintain their jobs. Employees may become disenchanted with unions and may increasingly prefer nonunion status, a trend now under way particularly in the U.S. Sunbelt. Despite the slow decline in the power of unions, even managers of nonunion facilities must avoid violations of the federal labor laws.

There is a growing trend toward state and federal legislation on matters traditionally bargained for by unions. It seems likely that legislation will continue to create statutory rights for employees, replacing much of the unions' role in protecting employee rights and improving working conditions. Such legislation is already in effect in the areas of discrimination, health and safety regulations, privacy, and compensation.

As many of their traditional bargaining concerns become the subject of direct legislation, the powers of unions may recede further. In addition, the perception that unions pursue unrealistic goals in an overly adversarial style may hasten their decline to a more limited role, decreasing the range of the issues settled by collective bargaining. Those issues may be legislated separately, with the influence of unions exerted only through lobbying. For example, unions may exert political pressure to limit the influx of immigrant labor, delay the creation of the North American Free-Trade zone in order to slow the loss of jobs to Mexico, and seek to limit wage reductions.

It may become difficult for unions to organize more workers in the traditional manufacturing sector, so unions may concentrate on white-collar and government employees. Despite the decline in the importance of unions, the potential for unionization continues to discipline the employment market, requiring both employers and unions to consider the impact that their bargaining decisions have on employees and the business' success.

OVERVIEW

This chapter discusses the law governing labor's relations with management. It begins with a historical overview of the social and economic pressures that led to the passage of various federal labor statutes and the creation of the National Labor Relations Board (NLRB). The NLRB oversees collective bargaining between labor and management, a process that begins when employees select a union to represent them. The chapter then focuses on the laws regulating union representation elections. These laws are intended to permit employees to organize and bargain collectively without coercion from the employer or any union. Next, the chapter discusses the process of collective bargaining between the employees' bargaining agent and the employer. It reviews the care required of both parties to avoid unlawful coercive conduct. Then, the chapter discusses the Taft-Hartley Act's limits on the power of unions to engage in certain concerted actions. Finally, it covers the Landrum-Griffin Act, which requires fair procedures in the election of union officials and prohibits union corruption. The Taft-Hartley and Landrum-Griffin Acts added to the federal labor law certain unfair labor practices by unions that had not been unlawful under the National Labor Relations Act.

THE BACKGROUND OF FEDERAL LABOR LAW

Contemporary labor law seeks to draw a balance between two goals. First, it encourages industrial peace and stability through collective bargaining and dispute settlement procedures. Second, it equalizes the balance of bargaining power between workers and management. Such a balance did not exist in the past. After the Civil War, industrial empires managed by a few powerful men dominated the American economy. The laissez-faire policies of the 19th century did little to protect the economic standing and job security of employees. The industrial revolution served only to widen the distance between employers and employees.

Many craft societies or guilds, the forerunners of unions, were formed in the early 1800s to aid skilled workers in refining their crafts. By the turn of the century, the American Federation of Labor (AFL) had increased the bargaining power of these workers. It granted member unions exclusive jurisdiction over a particular craft or a range of similar jobs. However, because the AFL never attempted to organize unskilled workers, this task was undertaken by another federation of unions—the Congress of Industrial Organizations (CIO).

Early Labor Conflicts

As early as 1806, the Pennsylvania state courts impeded unions by designating them as illegal combinations; union members were considered participants in a criminal conspiracy. By the mid-1800s, however, many courts shifted from the criminal conspiracy theory to issuing injunctions against union activities that were "inimical to the public welfare." Court orders prohibited strikes, the use of force to compel union membership, and union attempts to prevent replacement workers (i.e., scabs) from replacing strikers.

Interstate railroads became the first major battleground for unionization. The courts had prevented Congress from regulating most unionization because they did not consider manufacturing an interstate activity. In 1893, the American Railway Union organized railroad workers despite strong management resistance. When the Pullman Palace Car Company refused to negotiate with this union, a violent strike erupted. Congress appointed a federal strike commission that made a report favorable toward the growth of unions.

As the power of unions increased, many employers tried to slow their growth by using spies, blacklisting union sympathizers, and threatening reprisals against union members. Following an accelerated industrialization during World War I, management applied the "scientific management" techniques of industrial engineers. Time and motion studies were used to analyze job tasks and define "a fair day's work for a fair day's pay." During the roaring 20s, management argued that unions and collective bargaining were unnecessary, so AFL membership declined and the power of big business grew.

Development of Federal Labor Policies

The unions made some advances during World War I, when President Wilson's administration created the National War Labor Board. To prevent labor disputes from disrupting war production, employees were given the right to form unions and bargain collectively. However, these procedures were abandoned soon after the war ended. By 1926, only railroad workers had acquired permanent acceptance of their bargaining position.

During the 1930s, John L. Lewis established the CIO as an alternative umbrella labor organization that challenged the preeminence of the AFL. The CIO promoted two ideals in conflict with those of the AFL: (1) the representation of unskilled workers in the coal, steel, and other mass production industries; and (2) competition for some of the AFL's workers.

Although most unions adhered to anti-Communist philosophies, Communist party members became leaders of several CIO unions, a fact widely publicized in the 1940s. Congress reacted to this influence, and to a mounting public perception that unions were becoming too powerful, by passing the Taft-Hartley Act in 1947 and the Landrum-Griffin Act in 1959. These acts prohibit unions from engaging in certain unfair labor practices. The AFL and CIO merged in 1955, during the Eisenhower years, to maintain their diminishing power and to confront antiunion hostility in the president's administration.

INTERNATIONAL PERSPECTIVE: CONFRONTATION VS. COOPERATION BETWEEN UNIONS AND MANAGEMENT

Adversarial relations have dominated labor movement history in many nations, including countries in North America, Western Europe, and Southeast Asia. Under a *confrontational approach*, the parties bring economic pressure on their adversaries to influence the bargaining process. Proponents argue that confrontation produces an optimum compromise that becomes embodied in their collective bargaining agreement. However, some other nations, such as Japan and Germany, seek cooperation between unions and management. A *cooperative approach* involves unions in some management decisions, either formally, as in Germany, or informally, as in Japan.

In Germany, union representatives become involved in setting corporate policy under the *codetermination* system discussed later in this chapter. Although this system does not prevent strikes, it does force management to consider workers' well-being. The Japanese culture encourages cooperation and the appearance of harmony. Japanese labor relations manifest this tradition by confining unions to the role of craft refinement as practiced by the original craft guilds. Japan's lifetime employment system reduces adversarial relations between management and labor and encourages the two groups to share information. *Quality circles* are Japanese worker groups dedicated to increasing quality and eliminating production problems. Managers implement decisions after a consensus is developed in these worker groups.

FEDERAL LABOR STATUTES

Labor law is a federal regulatory scheme that largely displaces conflicting state law, so it eliminates most incentives for businesses to move to states with less restrictive labor law. Collective bargaining and union election relationships are governed solely by federal law, though there are gaps that the states may fill. For example, whenever labor disputes result in physical threats or actual violence, state or local police may intervene. If labor disputes bring about malicious defamation, trespassing, or intentional infliction of emotional distress, state tort law may apply. State unemployment benefit laws apply during labor disputes and may provide workers certain benefits. State legislatures may enact right-to-work laws, which permit employees to refrain from supporting unions.

Railway Labor Act

In 1926, Congress passed the Railway Labor Act (RLA), the first permanent federal legislation regulating labor-management relations. It gave railroad workers the right to organize into labor organizations and required railroad employers to bargain collectively. Later, the RLA was extended to cover airline employees.

Like the National Labor Relations Act, the RLA provides for noncoercive labor elections to select workers' bargaining representatives. The RLA created two regulatory boards to facilitate the settlement of labor disputes: the National Mediation Board (NMB) and the National Railroad Adjustment Board (NRAB).

The NMB operates much like the National Labor Relations Board, discussed later in this chapter. It decides representation questions, and it encourages settlement of labor disputes through mediation or recommends arbitration. In national transportation emergencies, it may propose that a presidential emergency board investigate and recommend whether a strike should be delayed.

The 1934 amendments to the RLA created the NRAB, an agency comprised of representatives from both the railroad companies and the railway unions. The NRAB mediates and arbitrates labor disputes about labor contract terms covering pay, work rules, and working conditions. The 1966 amendments gave the NRAB exclusive jurisdiction to render binding arbitration in many disputes.

Norris-LaGuardia Act

After Congress exempted labor activities from antitrust law in 1914, no comprehensive federal labor statute was passed until 1932. The Norris-LaGuardia Act of 1932 prohibits the federal courts from enjoining labor disputes unless unlawful acts are threatened or committed or a union strikes in violation of a valid no-strike agreement. *Labor disputes* include strikes, walkouts, labor union meetings, membership in labor unions, peaceful public assembly, publicity, payment of strike or unemployment benefits, and giving advice to others. Prior to 1932, federal injunctions against these activities demoralized strikers. Even if the strikers were later exonerated, injunctions usually undermined the impact of strikes.

The Norris-LaGuardia Act also outlaws *yellow-dog contracts*—contracts that require employees to refrain from joining a union or risk losing their jobs. Moreover, if violence occurs during a labor dispute, the Norris-LaGuardia Act requires proof that a union official participated in the violence before the union can be held liable for damages. Norris-LaGuardia does not require employers to negotiate with unions.

National Labor Relations Act

The National Labor Relations Act (NLRA or Wagner Act) has three important provisions forming the primary basis for modern labor law. First, Section 7 grants employees the right to form, join, or assist labor organizations; the freedom to bargain collectively with the employer; and the right to engage in concerted activity. Second, the NLRA requires employers to bargain collectively with the employees' certified bargaining representative (union). Third, the National Labor Relations Board (NLRB) was created as the principal regulatory body responsible for administering the act.

Later Enactments

Widespread dissatisfaction with union power, union corruption, and Communist influence in unions led to the passage in 1947 of the Labor-Management Relations Act (Taft-Hartley Act). This act defines certain unfair labor practices of unions: discrimination, refusal to bargain in good faith, excessive or discriminatory initiation fees, and other practices inhibiting workers' rights of organization.

In 1959, Congress again reacted to the power and misconduct of labor officials by passing the Labor-Management Reporting and Disclosure Act (Landrum-Griffin Act). The Landrum-Griffin Act requires fair, democratic procedures in the election of union officials. Disclosure provisions of the act are intended to eliminate embezzlement by union officials. Extensive financial disclosures must be made about all union transactions. Candidates for union office must disclose all of their transactions with the union. Additional federal laws addressing unionization of health care workers and public employees are discussed in Chapter 18. The federal labor laws administered by the NLRB are summarized in Table 17–1.

ROLE OF THE NLRB

During contract negotiations, the employer is represented by members of management, labor consultants, and labor lawyers who sit across the bargaining table from union representatives accompanied by their consultants and attorneys. Collective bargaining results only when both parties willingly negotiate in good faith over contract terms. This means that several activities must precede collective bargaining, including the grouping of employees into a bargaining unit, the election of a bargaining representative (union), and the employer's recognition of the union as the valid employee representative.

The National Labor Relations Act is intended to preserve a balance between the pressure on workers to select a particular union and the employer's pressures to resist

TABLE 17–1
Principal Federal Labor Laws

Date	Name of Law	Purposes and Provisions
1926	Railway Labor Act	Comprehensive coverage of collective bargaining between railroad or airline employers and unions representing their employees
1932	Norris-LaGuardia Act	Prevents federal courts from enjoining collective union activities (e.g., meetings, picketing, strikes) during labor disputes unless unlawful acts occur
		Outlaws yellow-dog contracts
		Permits unionization activities
1935	National Labor Relations Act (NLRA or Wagner Act)	Comprehensive coverage of collective bargaining for all employers not covered by Railway Labor Act
		Gives employees the right to form, join, or assist labor organizations
		Requires collective bargaining
		Created National Labor Relations Board (NLRB)
1947	Labor-Management Relations Act (Taft-Hartley Act)	Defines unfair labor practices of unions, such as discrimination and failure to bargain in good faith
1959	Labor-Management Reporting and Disclosure Act (Landrum-Griffin Act)	Requires fair and democratic procedures for elections of union officials
		Requires disclosure by union officials, unions, and employers to avoid embezzlement and conflicts of interest

unionization. The **National Labor Relations Board (NLRB)** certifies the selection of a particular union as the employees' bargaining representative. The NLRB is intended to provide a forum for worker protection from undue pressures by the employer or the union.

Organization of the NLRB

The NLRB is organized into two major divisions: the board itself and the Division of General Counsel. The board consists of five members appointed by the president with the "advice and consent" approval of the Senate. Each member serves a five-year term; the members' terms are staggered to provide continuity. Board members may be removed by the president only for "malfeasance in office or neglect of duty." Although the board may sit as a full panel of five members, it often expedites cases by delegating power to a three-member subpanel. Trial-like hearings about labor matters are first heard by one of the administrative law judges (ALJs) sitting in the various regional NLRB offices.

The Division of General Counsel is headed by an independent counsel, who is appointed for a four-year term by the president with Senate confirmation. This office has "final authority, on behalf of the Board, in respect to the investigation of the charges and issuance of complaints and with respect to the prosecution of complaints before the Board." The general counsel is independent of the NLRB.

NLRB Procedures

NLRB procedures are usually begun after one person files a charge that another person committed an unfair labor practice. Typically, field examiners investigate the matter, taking affidavits (sworn statements) to discover facts supporting or denying the charge. Even if the person filing the charge withdraws the complaint, the NLRB may continue prosecution. A charge must be filed within six months after the event in question; otherwise, the complaint is barred by the statute of limitations.

NLRB charges may be settled either in an informal settlement proceeding or at an ALJ hearing. The ALJ hearing is very similar to a court trial because the parties present their cases and the rules of evidence apply. An appeal from the ALJ hearing may be made to the whole board. In unfair labor practice cases, appeal beyond the NLRB may be taken to the appropriate federal Court of Appeals. In representation and election cases, however, appeal to the courts is prohibited because the NLRB has primary jurisdiction, making it the final authority in designating bargaining representatives.

The NLRB has a history of quasi-independence and near neutrality. However, many labor scholars argue that it became politicized during the Reagan administration years, favoring management and turning against even-handed treatment of labor disputes. Currently, the board is returning to the political center. Nevertheless, the lack of political balance for board appointees, as required for other quasi-independent agencies, suggests it will continue to vacillate with the politics of the presidential administration.

REPRESENTATION ELECTIONS

Representation elections are the predominant procedure used to select a particular union as the employees' bargaining representative. The NLRB has power to oversee representation elections through its regional directors.

Responsibilities of NLRB Regional Directors

1. Ordering elections.
2. Determining the appropriate bargaining unit.
3. Certifying the election results.
4. Deciding close representation questions.

The first step in a representation election is the filing of a petition with the NLRB, which evaluates the petition to ensure the satisfaction of statutory requirements. A hearing is then held to determine when the election should take place. After the election, the NLRB rules on its effect. For example, a fairly conducted election will probably be ruled valid. However, if there is evidence of coercion or threats, the NLRB may order a new election.

Employees often file petitions for a representation election and thereby assist an uncertified union in its organizational efforts. A union's petition must show support from at least 30 percent of the bargaining unit members. Employers who show that they reasonably believe that a union has employee support may also file petitions if the union has demanded recognition.

Types of Representation Elections

There are several types of representation elections. A *consent election* is held if the employer and the proposed union agree on which employees are in the bargaining unit and on the time and place of the election. A *contested election* arises if the employer and the prospective union disagree on these matters. A *"Globe election"* is held when a group of employees chooses between merging into a larger bargaining unit and operating separately.

A *certification election* is held when an employer willingly recognizes and bargains with a union that claims support from employees. Unions can also prove support by showing authorization or membership cards, membership applications, dues receipts or records, or petitions signed by employees. A certification election prevents rival unions from interfering with the certified union for one year following the election. A *decertification election* is held when employees become dissatisfied with an existing union and seek to remove it.

A *deauthorization election* permits employees to retain a certified union but remove a portion of its bargaining powers. For example, a certified union may be deauthorized from agreeing to a type of contract term that the membership does not want. A *runoff election* may be necessary when several competing unions are on one ballot and none of the top vote-getters receives a majority vote.

Appropriate Bargaining Unit

The **appropriate bargaining unit** includes all "employees" in a group who have similar interests in employment conditions and should be entitled to vote together as a unit. The unit should be represented by a single bargaining representative to ensure the fullest freedom of its members to exercise their rights. Eligible voters include any persons employed during the payroll period preceding the election, as well as most striking employees.

Bargaining representatives are selected for each appropriate bargaining unit. Employers must bargain with only a single bargaining representative for any group of workers. Of course, a large employer with many separate employee groups may have to bargain with several unions representing different bargaining units. For example, one union may represent production workers, another may represent truck drivers, and a third may represent maintenance workers. The NLRB selects the bargaining unit to ensure that the employees in it have similar economic interests, job classifications, and bargaining powers.

In determining the appropriate bargaining unit, the NLRB usually considers the similarity of interests among the employees within a potential bargaining unit; skills, wages, hours, and working conditions are considered the most important factors. Sometimes the NLRB also considers employees' desires, existing employee groupings, and collective bargaining history.

The National Labor Relations Act also requires that the employees within an appropriate bargaining unit have similarities at the level of the employer, the craft unit, or the plant unit or within a recognized subdivision of these levels. For example, professional employees may not be included with nonprofessionals unless a majority of the professionals consent. Similarly, plant guards, who must protect the employer's property, may not be included with other employees because during intense labor disputes there might be a conflict of interest between plant guards and those employees.

Alternative Union Selection Processes

Employer recognition occurs when an employer agrees to recognize a union after the union notifies the employer that it has the support of a majority of employees in a potential bargaining unit. The employer's decision to recognize the union may help avoid a costly and divisive election. For example, if the union has gained legitimate majority support by polling the employees, it may be better for the employer to voluntarily negotiate with the union than to insist on a certification election in which negative electioneering might harm the employer's goodwill. *Employee authorization* may be established if the union can show sufficient membership cards, authorization cards, petitions, or applications for membership. The signing of such a document by a majority of the employees shows sufficient employee support to require collective bargaining.

Unions may need an employee list to conduct an effective campaign. At a nonunion plant, employers often frustrate unionization by denying the union entry or an employee list. The *Excelsior* rule requires employers to give the union an employee list at least seven days prior to an election.

Even when a union receives petitions signed by enough employees to hold an election, it may not have enough employee support to win the election. A union's request for an Excelsior list must be satisfied if the union cannot reach all of the other employees without great expense. However, seven days is often insufficient time for effective electioneering, so some unions immediately cease campaign efforts after receiving the list, giving them more time to contact other employees. In such cases, the union must wait six months before beginning another election campaign.

ETHICAL DILEMMAS IN LABOR-MANAGEMENT RELATIONS

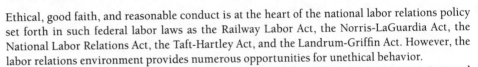

Ethical, good faith, and reasonable conduct is at the heart of the national labor relations policy set forth in such federal labor laws as the Railway Labor Act, the Norris-LaGuardia Act, the National Labor Relations Act, the Taft-Hartley Act, and the Landrum-Griffin Act. However, the labor relations environment provides numerous opportunities for unethical behavior.

The initial organization of an employer's facility may be subject to misrepresentations and intimidation either by the union seeking recognition or by an employer opposed to union representation. The National Labor Relations Act and the Taft-Hartley Act prohibit unfair labor practices that tend to deprive employees of reasonable "laboratory conditions" in making union selection decisions. It is unfair and probably unethical to use misrepresentations in electioneering. Employers that insist in bad faith that the business will fail if it becomes unionized or coerce employees with implied threats of a plant closing or economic reprisals may be using unethical means to avoid labor negotiations. Unions can be guilty of similar unfair electioneering tactics, particularly when coworkers intimidate other workers to gain support for the union.

EMPLOYER INTERFERENCE WITH UNION ORGANIZATION

Employers may not interfere with, restrain, or coerce employees who are exercising their self-organization rights. Employers have an incentive to disrupt union organization efforts, so certain specified employer acts are **unfair labor practices.** Unfair labor practices listed in Table 17–2 may inhibit employees' free choice of whether to unionize.

TABLE 17–2

Unfair Labor Practices of Employers

1. Interfering with employee efforts to form, join, or assist labor organizations.
2. Interfering with employees' concerted activities for mutual aid or protection.
3. Dominating a labor organization.
4. Supporting a labor organization.
5. Discriminating in hiring, firing, benefits, or other conditions of employment due to employee's union affiliation.
6. Discriminating due to employee's exercise of rights under the labor law.
7. Refusing to bargain collectively and in good faith with a duly certified labor organization.
8. Agreeing with a labor organization to conduct a secondary boycott.

Employer Unfair Labor Practices

Certain conduct by employers intimidates workers and thus upsets the ideal or "laboratory" conditions required for representation elections. Although employers may legitimately ask employees about the union's progress in organizing the workforce, an employer's intimidating interrogation is an unfair labor practice. This practice may be coercive if employees believe that the employer will retaliate against them if they support the union.

The employer's polling of employees is an unfair labor practice unless the employer simply seeks to verify whether a majority of the employees support the union. If employees are questioned, the employer must use secret ballots, so that employees are protected from employer reprisals. The employer's use of spies or informers during any phase of self-organization is prohibited. A representation election may be set aside if the employer engages in interrogation or surveillance or any other unfair labor practice. Limits on an employer's use of lie detectors are discussed in Chapter 18.

Interference with Solicitation of Employees A union usually begins a campaign to organize a particular group of employees by having union representatives from the national headquarters of a local union chapter visit employees and distribute literature to build support for unionization. These representatives may ask employees about their dissatisfaction with the employer and then attempt to build on any negative sentiments. In all but the smallest towns, where most employees know one another, it is difficult for union officials to contact employees effectively. Therefore, unions are usually forced to electioneer on or near the employer's property. However, the presence of nonemployees on the employer's land is a trespass that violates the employer's property rights.

Employers must tolerate *some* inconvenience during union organization and employees' concerted activities. However, they may impose reasonable nondiscriminatory restrictions. For example, if the congregation of too many nonemployees in work areas interferes with work or causes safety hazards, employers may restrict nonemployee union officials from trespassing in work areas. This effectively limits worksite solicitations to those made by employees sympathetic to the union. These employees may contact fellow workers during free time, before or after work, or during breaks and meals. Off-worksite solicitations may be made anytime and by anyone.

Employers may restrict the distribution of prounion literature and union authorization cards to nonworking areas, such as exits, parking lots, cafeterias, and rest rooms. They may also prohibit nonemployees and off-duty employees from soliciting on company premises. However, these restrictions may not discriminate against unions. For example, if the employer prohibits solicitation, that rule must apply for all other purposes, such as fund-raising by charities or membership drives by clubs; it may not simply target unionization. If the employer prohibits solicitation, reasonable alternatives for the distribution of union materials must be available.

Union Activities at Shopping Centers The Supreme Court has found union activities on private shopping center property to be a particularly troublesome problem since the union's free speech rights may conflict with the property owner's right to control the use of the property. For example, the employer may be a retail store located in the shopping center. Shopping centers are "dedicated to a public use," and the public access areas include the walkways, streets, and parking lots. Originally, under the *Logan Valley* rule, a union's free speech rights prevailed over the rights of a shopping center owner.[1] Therefore, such union activities as solicitation and picketing were permitted in shopping centers. More recently, however, the courts have limited these solicitation rights somewhat. In *Central Hardware Co. v. N.L.R.B.*, the mere fact that a large hardware store was open to the public did not mean that its private property was equivalent to a shopping center.[2] As long as alternative methods exist to communicate with retail store employees, unions have no constitutional right to enter on private property.

Shopping centers are unique in that they are owned by commercial land developers that lease space to retailers. In many communities, shopping centers have nearly replaced the public downtown shopping districts, where union activities are generally permitted. Union organizational efforts directed at an employer/retailer may intimidate the customers that shopping centers are intended to attract. How should an employer's rights be reconciled with employees' self-organization rights? The next case distinguishes between employee and nonemployee presence on the employer's premises.

Lechmere v. National Labor Relations Board

112 S.Ct. 841 (1992)

United States Supreme Court

Nonemployee members of the United Food and Commercial Workers Union attempted to organize employees of Lechmere, Inc. by handbilling car windshields in Lechmere's employee parking lot. Lechmere's manager ordered union organizers off the property, citing Lechmere's prohibition on solicitation or handbill distribution. The organizers relocated to a public grassy strip lying between the adjoining highway and Lechmere's parking lot to distribute prounion handbills as employees drove by. Approximately 20 percent of Lechmere's employees received prounion mailings after their addresses were identified by the Connecticut Department of Motor Vehicles from their license plate numbers. The union failed to organize Lechmere's employees and filed an unfair labor practice charge with the National Labor Relations Board (Board) charging that it had been illegally barred from Lechmere's private parking lot.

The Court of Appeals sustained an NLRB cease and desist order prohibiting Lechmere from enforcing the solicitation ban, and Lechmere appealed.

[1]*Amalgamated Food Employees Union, Local 590 v. Logan Valley Plaza, Inc.*, 391 U.S. 308 (1968).

[2]*Central Hardware Co. v. N.L.R.B.*, 407 U.S. 539 (1972).

Justice Thomas delivered the opinion of the Court.

Section 8(a)(1) of the NLRA makes it an unfair labor practice for an employer "to interfere with, restrain, or coerce employees in the exercise of rights guaranteed by § 7."

[In the *Babcock* case] we explained that the Board had erred by failing to make the critical distinction between the organizing activities of employees (to whom § 7 guarantees the right of self-organization) and nonemployees (to whom § 7 applies only derivatively). Thus, while "[n]o restriction may be placed on the employees' right to discuss self-organization among themselves, unless the employer can demonstrate that a restriction is necessary to maintain production or discipline, no such obligation is owed nonemployee organizers." As a rule, then, an employer cannot be compelled to allow distribution of union literature by nonemployee organizers on his property. As with many other rules, however, we recognized an exception. Where "the location of a plant and the living quarters of the employees place the employees beyond the reach of reasonable union efforts to communicate with them," employers' property rights may be "required to yield to the extent needed to permit communication of information on the right to organize."

To gain access, the union has the burden of showing that no other reasonable means of communicating its organizational message to the employees exists or that the employer's access rules discriminate against union solicitation. In practice, nonemployee organizational trespassing had generally been prohibited except where "unique obstacles" prevented nontrespassory methods of communication with the employees. So long as nonemployee union organizers have reasonable access to employees outside an employer's property, the requisite accommodation has taken place. It is only where such access is infeasible that it becomes necessary and proper to take the accommodation inquiry to a second level, balancing the employees' and employers' rights.

The exception to *Babcock's* rule is a narrow one. It does not apply wherever nontrespassory access to employees may be cumbersome or less-than-ideally effective, but only where "the location of a plant and the living quarters of the employee place the employees beyond the reach of reasonable union efforts to communicate with them." Classic examples include logging camps, mining camps, and mountain resort hotels. *Babcock's* exception was crafted precisely to protect the § 7 rights of those employees who, by virtue of their employment, are isolated from the ordinary flow of information that characterizes our society. The union's burden of establishing such isolation is "a heavy one," and one not satisfied by mere conjecture or the expression of doubts concerning the effectiveness of nontrespassory means of communication.

Because the employees do not reside on Lechmere's property, they are presumptively not "beyond the reach," of the union's message. Although the employees live in a large metropolitan area (Greater Hartford), that fact does not in itself render them "inaccessible" in the sense contemplated by *Babcock*. Their accessibility is suggested by the union's success in contacting a substantial percentage of them directly, via mailings, phone calls, and home visits. Such direct contact, of course, is not a necessary element of "reasonably effective" communication; signs or advertising also may suffice. Access to employees, not success in winning them over, is the critical issue—although success, or lack thereof, may be relevant in determining whether reasonable access exists. The union in this case failed to establish the existence of any "unique obstacles," that frustrated access to Lechmere's employees. The Board erred in concluding that Lechmere committed an unfair labor practice by barring the nonemployee organizers from its property.

The judgment of the First Circuit is therefore reversed, and enforcement of the Board's order denied.

Case Questions

1. How must an employer treat employees differently from nonemployee union officials in organizing the employer's workforce?
2. What unique inaccessibility problems trigger the *Babcock* rule permitting nonemployee trespass?
3. Is the difficult accessibility in this case sufficient for a union to communicate its message to employees?

Employer Electioneering

The First Amendment to the U.S. Constitution permits both employers and employees to exercise free speech by electioneering during union organization. However, there is a strong potential for misuse of that right by an employer because of its considerable economic power over employees. For example, an employer's antiunion sentiment may influence voting far more than statements of union organizers. Coercive employer statements may be unfair labor practices that the First Amendment does not protect. For example, an employer commits an unfair labor practice in threatening reprisal, or force, or in promising benefits to employees if they reject the union. The NLRB judges the employer's statements in their context by examining (1) the action threatened, (2) whether the threats could be taken seriously, and (3) how broadly the threats are communicated to workers.

Employees are a "captive audience," so the employer may give antiunion speeches at the worksite on company time; the employer is entitled to use its property, and employees' paid time as a forum to express its views. There is no requirement that the union be given equal time. Within the 24 hours preceding a representation election, however, both the employer and the union are prohibited from making speeches unless employees attend voluntarily. Less coercive, nonpersonal communications (literature, noncoercive radio messages) are permitted throughout this period.

Threats Employers must carefully word speeches to ensure that they are not coercive. Such statements as "I intend to deal hard with the union" or "You may be replaced if you strike" are not automatically coercive. However, predictions of future consequences if the union is certified are considered coercive unless they are reasonable forecasts of objective facts over which the employer has no control. Predictions based on factors within the employer's control are coercive because the employer has the power to implement such predictions unilaterally. For example, an employer's promise to close a plant down if the union is approved is coercive. By contrast, an employer's recitation of facts that occurred at other union plants, such as bombings, shootings, and violence, is not coercive if the employer remains willing to bargain with the union. Both unions and employers must avoid making misrepresentations.

Benefits Positive statements by either the employer or the union can also be coercive. If an employer attempts to confer economic benefits on workers just prior to an election, it looks like a bribe to influence the outcome. Promises of such benefits as paid holidays, vacation time, and higher overtime pay have been called the "iron fist in the velvet glove" because they remind employees that the employer controls their economic fortunes.

During the preelection campaign, the employer must maintain "business as usual" in its personnel policies. How can an employer effectively campaign against unionization if no representation election is held and the union gains support more secretly? The next case illustrates this dilemma and sets certain limits for employer electioneering.

N.L.R.B. v. Gissel Packing Co., Inc.

395 U.S. 575 (1969)

United States Supreme Court

The union waged an organizational campaign and obtained authorization cards from a majority of the employees, then demanded recognition by the employer. The employer refused to bargain, claiming that authorization cards were inherently unreliable, and carried out a vigorous antiunion campaign. After a hearing, the NLRB held that the employer had engaged in unfair labor practices and that the authorization cards were valid and entitled the union to recognition to bargain with the employer.

Chief Justice Warren delivered the opinion of the Court.

Almost from the inception of the Act, then, it was recognized that a union did not have to be certified as the winner of a Board election to invoke a bargaining obligation. It could establish majority status by other means . . . by showing convincing support, for instance, by a union-called strike or strike vote, or, as here, by possession of cards signed by a majority of the employees authorizing the union to represent them for collective bargaining purposes. The acknowledged superiority of the election process, does not mean that cards are thereby rendered totally invalid, for where an employer engages in conduct disruptive of the election process, cards may be the most effective—perhaps the only—way of assuring employee choice. . . .

The employers argue that their employees cannot make an informed choice because the card drive will be over before the employer has had a chance to present his side of the unionization issues. Normally, however, the union will inform the employer of its organization drive early in order to subject the employer to the unfair labor practice provisions of the Act; the union must be able to show the employer's awareness of the drive in order to prove that his contemporaneous conduct constituted unfair labor practices on which a bargaining order can be based if the drive is ultimately successful. Further, the employers argue that without a secret ballot an employee may, in a card drive, succumb to group pressures or sign simply to get the union "off his back" and then be unable to change his mind as he would be free to do once inside a voting booth. But the same pressures are likely to be equally present in an election, for election cases arise most often with small bargaining units where virtually every voter's sentiments can be carefully and individually canvassed. And no voter, of course, can change his mind after casting a ballot in an election even though he may think better of his choice shortly thereafter.

We do note that an employer's free speech right to communicate his views to his employees is firmly established and cannot be infringed by a union or the Board. Thus, an employer is free to communicate to his employees any of his general views about unionism or any of his specific views about a particular union, so long as the communications do not contain a "threat of reprisal or force or promise of benefit." He may even make a prediction as to the precise effects he believes unionization will have on his company. In such a case, however, the prediction must be carefully phrased on the basis of objective fact to convey an employer's belief as to demonstrably probable consequences beyond his control or to convey a management decision already arrived at to close the plant in case of unionization. If there is any implication that an employer may or may not take action solely on his own initiative for reasons unrelated to economic necessities and known only to him, the statement is no longer a reasonable prediction based on available facts but a threat of retaliation based on misrepresentation and coercion, and as such without the protection of the First Amendment. We therefore agree with the court below that "[c]onveyance of the employer's belief, even though sincere, that unionization will or may result in the closing of the plant is not a statement of fact unless, which is most improbable, the eventuality of closing is capable of proof." . . .

The Board found that petitioner's speeches, pamphlets, leaflets, and letters conveyed the following message: that the company was in a precarious financial condition; that the "strike-happy" union would in all likelihood have to obtain its potentially unreasonable demands by striking, the probable result of which would be a plant shutdown, as the past history of labor relations in the area indicated; and that the employees in such a case would have great difficulty finding employment elsewhere. In carrying out its duty to focus on the question: "[W]hat did the speaker intend and the listener understand?" the Board could reasonably conclude that the intended and understood import of that message was not to predict that unionization would inevitably cause the plant to close but to threaten to throw employees out of work regardless of the economic realities. In this connection, we need go no further than to point out (1) that petitioner had no support for its basic assumption that the union, which had not yet even presented any demands, would have to strike to be heard, and that it admitted at the hearing that it had no basis for attributing other plant closings in the area to unionism; and (2) that the Board has often found that employees, who are particularly sensitive to rumors of plant closings, take such hints as coercive threats rather than honest forecasts.

Case Questions

1. How can union supporters demonstrate that employee support for the union is sufficient to require the employer to bargain with it?

2. What problems are presented by the use of authorization cards as a method of union certification?
3. How must the employer approach electioneering in a certification election or other organization campaign?

Employers commit an unfair labor practice if they withhold customary periodic wage increases from employees who are attempting to unionize. However, the employer who announces that increased benefits will take effect after an election is not committing an unfair labor practice so long as the changes were planned prior to the election campaign. Just before the election at issue in *N.L.R.B. v. Exchange Parts,* the employer granted an additional "floating holiday."[3] At a dinner he held for employees, he lectured that the election would "determine whether [they] wished to hand over the right to speak and act for themselves." Later, he charged that the union had distorted the facts and reminded the employees of benefits that they had obtained without a union. "The company puts things in your envelope. . . . It didn't take a union to get you any of those things." The Supreme Court ordered a new election after the union lost. Elections should be held in an atmosphere uncontaminated by promises of benefits that are clearly intended to influence the outcome.

Employer Domination or Support of a Union

In the 1920s, some employers created *company unions* that were weak and favored the employer's goals. Employees were often unaware of the employer's secret support. However, employers are prohibited from dominating or interfering with labor organizations. For example, it is an unfair labor practice for employers to provide financial or other support to unions. The test of unlawful employer domination is whether the union is truly independent in representing employees in disputes arising with the employer.

Many types of employer activities may result in support or domination of a union. For example, if the employer or managerial supervisors solicit workers to join a particular union, then an unfair labor practice results. Undue assistance to a particular union may also be unlawful. For example, an unfair labor practice arises if the employer takes an active part in establishing a union by helping it to draft its bylaws or by actively opposing a competing union. In numerous instances, employers have given one union access to legal counsel, office space, secretarial services, printing services, and other financial support while denying such assistance to a competing union. These are unfair labor practices.

Union bylaws may not give the employer a voice or vote in the union's self-governance. Throughout the process of self-organization, the employer must maintain neutrality to avoid charges of domination, favoritism, or other interference with the employees' selection of a union.

INTERNATIONAL PERSPECTIVE: CODETERMINATION AND LABOR HARMONY

German law requires *codetermination,* a system permitting labor union representation on each employer's corporate boards to implement the German ideal of labor harmony. In the United States, this practice could be construed as an unfair labor practice if it encouraged the employer's

[3]*N.L.R.B. v. Exchange Parts,* 375 U.S. 405 (1964).

domination or support of the union. German corporate law requires two types of boards: the *supervisory board* and the *managing board*. Union representatives must constitute five of the eleven managing board members and one of the three supervisory board members. Shareholders elect five managing board members and an eleventh is elected by the other ten members to represent the public interest, mediate disputes, and cast tie-breaking votes. One management representative from sales and one from production also sit on the supervisory board.

The inclusion of various constituencies in corporate policy-making has arguably resulted in more peaceful industrial relations in Germany than in many other nations. Observers argue that Germany suffers less downtime from strikes, improved employee morale, and better working conditions than historically prevalent in the United States. Japanese unions also have harmonious relations with Japanese employers, a closeness that would probably violate the NLRA prohibition against employer domination of a union. The Japanese use *quality circles,* groupings of union employees and management supervisors to monitor quality control, provide a forum for discussing work refinement, and provide implementation of improvements. There are difficulties for United States firms in implementing similar techniques because of the history of adversarial labor relations. Considering the Japanese and German economic successes, policymakers could suggest some adaptations to the U.S. labor relations atmosphere.

Employer Discrimination

It is illegal for an employer to slow unionization by discriminating in hiring, firing, or job tenure. Employers may not grant promotions or pay raises to nonunion employees or withhold such benefits from union employees.

Business Purpose In most discrimination situations, the employer claims a business purpose for a particular hiring, firing, or promotion decision. That claim must be supported by strong, independent evidence showing that there is no anitunion motive. For instance, well-documented records of employee insubordination prior to union involvement is strong evidence. However, if a large percentage of discharged employees were engaged in union activities and had good work records, an antiunion motive may be inferred. Circumstantial evidence may also be derived from the timing of employee dismissals. If employees are fired during or immediately after unionization activities, the employer must show strong evidence that it had a reasonable basis for the dismissals.

Discrimination in hiring or firing on the basis of an employee's union affiliation is clearly unlawful. Decisions to lay off, demote, transfer, or change work assignments are illegal if they are based on antiunion considerations. In one case, an employer committed an unfair labor practice when it offered 20 years of seniority to strike-breaking employees.

Plant Closings An employer may lock employees out of the plant if there are valid economic justifications and if negotiations have reached an impasse. These *plant closings* bring economic pressure on the employees to settle by depriving them of income.

A more drastic action occurs when the employer's whole operation is closed permanently and moved to another locality. For example, an employer may want to slow unionization by starting new operations in an economically depressed region. If the employer moves only part of the business to a new location and the employer's purpose is to discourage unionization, the action is unlawful. By contrast, employers have an absolute right to terminate their entire business for any reason whatsoever (including antiunion sentiments). If sound economic considerations support movement of a plant, then the employer need not bargain over the move, and there is no unfair labor practice. This has been called the *runaway shop*. However, if the employer has a clear antiunion motive, it is an unfair labor practice to move a plant far enough to require the hiring of a new workforce. Also, notice of plant closings must be given to unions and employees under the WARN Act discussed in Chapter 18.

What if the runaway shop is one of several plants owned by the employer and the plant closing intimidates unionization at the employer's other plants? In the following case, the extent of the operations moved by the employer is explained in light of an alleged unfair labor practice.

Textile Workers Union v. Darlington Mfg. Co.

380 U.S. 263 (1965)
United States Supreme Court

Deering Milliken owned Darlington and several other textile companies. The Textile Workers Union successfully organized the Darlington textile mill even though Darlington had strongly resisted the organization effort. Soon afterward, Darlington was liquidated, the textile mill was closed, and the equipment was sold. After the Court of Appeals overturned the NLRB's determination that Deering Milliken had violated the NLRA by closing part of its business for a discriminatory purpose, the union appealed.

Justice Harlan delivered the opinion of the Court.

One of the purposes of the National Labor Relations Act is to prohibit the discriminatory use of economic weapons in an effort to obtain future benefits. The discriminatory lockout designed to destroy a union, like a "runaway shop," is a lever which has been used to discourage collective employee activities in the future. But a complete liquidation of a business yields no such future benefit for the employer, if the termination is bona fide. It may be motivated more by spite against the union than by business reasons, but it is not the type of discrimination which is prohibited by the Act. The personal satisfaction that such an employer may derive from standing on his beliefs and the mere possibility that other employers will follow his example are surely too remote to be considered dangers at which the labor statutes were aimed. Although employees may be prohibited from engaging in a strike under certain conditions, no one would consider it a violation of the Act for the same employees to quit their employment *en masse,* even if motivated by a desire to ruin the employer. The very permanence of such action would negate any future economic benefit to the employees. The employer's right to go out of business is no different.

We are not presented here with the case of a "runaway shop," whereby Darlington would transfer its work to another plant or open a new plant in another locality to replace its closed plant. Nor are we concerned with a shutdown where the employees, by renouncing the union, could cause the plant to reopen. Such cases would involve discriminatory employer action for the purpose of obtaining some benefit from the employees in the future. We hold here only that when an employer closes his entire business, even if the liquidation is motivated by vindictiveness toward the union, such action is not an unfair labor practice.

The closing of an entire business, even though discriminatory, ends the employer-employee relationship; the force of such a closing is entirely spent as to that business when termination of the enterprise takes place. On the other hand, a discriminatory partial closing may have repercussions on what remains of the business, affording employer leverage for discouraging the free exercise of § 7 rights among remaining employees of much the same kind as that found to exist in the "runaway shop" and "temporary closing" cases. Moreover, a possible remedy open to the Board in such a case, like the remedies available in the "runaway shop" and "temporary closing" cases, is to order reinstatement of the discharged employees in the other parts of the business. No such remedy is available when an entire business has been terminated.

Case Questions

1. What is a "runaway shop"? Why might such an action violate the NLRA?
2. What distinguishes an employer's right to discontinue operations from the prohibition against making partial closings?

Interference, Restraint, and Coercion by Unions

Unions, like employers, are prohibited from coercing employees in the exercise of their self-organization rights. However, unions have somewhat broader latitude than employers during organization. Unions must refrain from inflammatory racial or ethnic slurs during unionization and may express opinions so long as these are not coercive. On the other hand, such statements as "Those who do not join the union will eventually lose their job" and "We have ways of handling people that argue against the union" are unfair labor practices.

Threats of violence made against employees who fail to cooperate with the union are also unlawful. When a union directs violence against the employer and destroys company property it commits an unfair labor practice. In such a case, employees can reasonably infer that they are also threatened if they attempt to enter the plant.

Unions may be prohibited from other, more subtle forms of economic pressure. In one case, a union administered the employees' health fund, which was financed with contributions from all employees. The union acted unlawfully by threatening that only its members would receive benefit payments in an attempt to coerce nonmembers to join. In another case, the union's promise to waive or reduce union membership fees or dues was unlawful. Any union pressure on the employer to discriminate between union members and nonmembers is also illegal. Although picketing as such is not illegal coercion, it may be coercive if it is done on a massive scale that intimidates nonunion employees from approaching the worksite. For example, forcefully blocking plant entrances and exits is clearly unlawful. Unfair labor practices by unions are listed in Table 17–3.

TABLE 17–3
Unfair Labor Practices of Unions

1. Restraining or coercing employees who are exercising self-organization rights.
2. Coercing an employer to discriminate against nonunion employees.
3. Refusing to bargain in good faith with an employer if the union is certified as the employees' representative.
4. Engaging in illegal strikes, picketing, or secondary boycotts.
5. Charging excessive or discriminative dues in a union shop.
6. Featherbedding—requiring the employer to pay for work not actually performed.
7. Picketing to coerce the employer to recognize a noncertified union.
8. Agreeing with an employer to engage in a secondary boycott.

THE LABOR NEGOTIATION PROCESS

After an appropriate bargaining unit selects a particular union as its bargaining representative, both the employer and the union must bargain in good faith. **Good faith bargaining** is an interactive process in which each side makes offers and counteroffers in an effort to reach an agreement over wages, hours, and other terms and conditions of employment. The labor negotiation process fulfills the five basic functions for society, listed below. It reflects the overall social and economic pressure of the financial, product, and labor markets. The labor contracts negotiated during this process allow labor markets to reach economic equilibrium.

Functions of the Labor Negotiation Process

1. Establishes work rules.
2. Selects the form and mix of employee compensation.
3. Provides uniformity among competitors.
4. Sets priorities for both labor and management.
5. Permits economic pressures to shape labor-management relations.

Collective Bargaining and Negotiation

Collective bargaining is an interactive process between two parties that often have opposite goals. In many instances, gains made by one party represent losses for the other party, a zero-sum game. There are few opportunities for both parties to "win" on compensation issues. Typically, one party will compile a set of proposals into a first offer. For example, the union may select a team of representatives (the bargaining committee) who seek to improve or maintain the benefits currently received by employees.

The union's offer usually specifies an amount of compensation for each classification of employees, a designation of the work hours and overtime contingencies, a package of fringe benefits, and a classification of all the employees. Unions often seek to establish systems of seniority, grievance processes, protections against the loss of work to outside contractors or the cessation of business, and methods to schedule work and work shifts. Wage-related proposals include base salaries, cost-of-living and productivity increases, a wage scale rewarding seniority and higher levels of skill, and fringe benefits such as pension funds.

In most negotiations, the early offers from either party are more favorable to the offeror and less favorable to the opposing party. As a result, the opposing party may either decline the initial offer or make a counteroffer with terms more favorable to itself. Eventually, most negotiations result in a compromise in which the disagreements are reconciled by reaching some middle ground.

Bargaining Positions: Strengths and Weaknesses

It is customary for the negotiating teams representing management and the union to be well prepared for their first meeting. Elaborate financial statements and cost projections often accompany both the union's demand for higher wages and management's refusal to grant increases. The parties may study each other's negotiating history, particularly if past negotiators are again involved. Both parties should be well versed in the nuances of the labor law to avoid unfair labor practice litigation.

Because negotiations held on either party's "home turf" may provide a "home court advantage," neutral premises are often selected for negotiations. Negotiations are often held behind closed doors because a damaging and inflammatory atmosphere may result from public exposure or adverse publicity.

The parties often negotiate the noneconomic items first because their expectations are often closer on such items. For example, the existing grievance procedures, no-strike clauses, seniority provisions, and work assignments are usually acceptable to both parties. However, in recent years employers have increasingly found the prevailing work rules and assignments to be too costly. When absenteeism is high, production processes must be changed quickly. Restrictive work rules may permit overqualified workers to remain idle or prevent underqualified workers from moving into more complicated assignments. Many new contracts now remove these barriers to the employer's production flexibility.

Typically, each party's initial offer or counteroffer contains terms that are more favorable to itself than the terms it expects to achieve. For example, unions often demand higher salary raises than they realistically expect. By asking for "too much," each party is able to give up something during negotiations and thus appear to compromise. Most negotiators would be satisfied if they could reach agreement on a *fallback position,* getting somewhat less than their initial demands.

Astute third-party intermediaries (e.g., mediators) can facilitate cooperative negotiations and avoid adversarial relations. These persons act as conflict resolvers by reducing irrational feelings and pointing out the parties' unreasonable demands. They may generate alternative solutions or provide graceful retreats that permit the negotiators to save face. Such intermediaries also keep both parties focused on the important issues and remind them of the high costs of disagreement.

The teams representing both management and the union must have sufficient authority to bargain. The employer's representatives must have the authority to act as its agents in making offers or accepting union proposals. The authority requirement is less restrictive for union negotiators because the rank-and-file employees generally must approve the contract in a *ratification vote.* The employees may not immediately disavow their representatives after a certification election; this permits a newly elected union to establish itself.

A certified union has exclusive authority to represent all of the employees in the bargaining unit. Individual employees may not enter into separate bargains with the employer that are inconsistent with the collective bargaining agreement. For example, if the collective bargaining agreement covers all compensation issues, an individual union employee may not "cut a separate deal" to receive higher pay. Individual employees are considered third-party beneficiaries of the collective bargaining contract. In return for its exclusive bargaining right, the union must bargain fairly on behalf of all bargaining unit employees, both union members and nonmembers.

Duty to Bargain in Good Faith

The National Labor Relations Act (NLRA) requires that both the union and the employer must meet at reasonable times and confer in good faith with respect to wages, hours, and other terms and conditions of employment. It is an unfair labor practice for either party to refuse to bargain collectively. Neither party may engage in fictitious or surface bargaining if it has no real intent of reaching agreement. They must do more than just go through the motions of bargaining.

ETHICAL DILEMMA: IS "GOOD FAITH BARGAINING" AN ETHICAL STANDARD?

The bargaining process between a certified union and the employer presents ethical dilemmas. The law requires both sides to bargain in good faith. Fictitious or surface bargaining with no real intent to reach a compromise is probably unethical. The law requires bargaining with a sincere desire to agree. Hard bargaining in situations where the parties have irreconcilable differences is neither unlawful nor unethical. The basic question in bargaining is whether the parties intend to negotiate in "good faith," so this becomes the ethical standard.

Bad Faith Bargaining

Although bad faith is difficult to prove, it may be inferred. The parties should be willing to meet at reasonable times, put their agreement in writing, negotiate with each other, and bargain on mandatory subjects. These subjects include wages, hours, and other terms and conditions of employment. The total course of each party's conduct is carefully examined. For example, the offer of totally unreasonable proposals may indicate bad faith. It may be bad faith for the employer to offer and later withdraw a proposal before the union can evaluate it.

The parties are often required to furnish information potentially relevant to bargaining. For example, the employer may be required to provide financial statements to substantiate its inability to pay higher wages. However, the duty to disclose information is not unlimited because the information furnished might reveal confidential trade secrets. The union's need for such sensitive data may be balanced against the employer's need for confidentiality and the right to privacy.

Bad faith may be inferred from other bargaining conduct, such as the failure to offer meaningful counterproposals, the refusal to discuss economic terms until noneconomic issues are resolved, attempts to delay meetings or to move the meeting place to a burdensome location, the withdrawal of earlier concessions, the refusal to bargain until the opposing party has withdrawn an unfair labor practice charge, or the launching of an adverse publicity campaign. It may be difficult to distinguish between permissible "hard bargaining" and impermissible "surface bargaining."

Can either party simply impose its judgment of what is reasonable and refuse to bargain further? This "take it or leave it" position, disfavored by the law, is termed *Boulwareism,* after the GE executive who advanced it, as discussed in the following case.

N.L.R.B. v. General Electric Co.

418 F.2d 736 (2d Cir. 1969)
United States Court of Appeals

General Electric changed its bargaining tactics after a crippling strike in the 1940s. Lemuel R. Boulware, a GE vice president, approached bargaining as he would the marketing of a product. Comments on the levels and types of benefits expected by employees were collected from local plant managers. The cost effectiveness of these benefits was researched to formulate a "product" (i.e., bargaining proposals) acceptable to employees. GE then aggressively "sold" the proposals in an "avalanche" of publicity. GE stated that its proposals were firm, "fair offers," so that there was no need for union pressure or strikes. GE made this its "take it or leave it" approach. In the 1960 negotiations, GE heavily publicized the unreasonableness of the union's proposals and refused to honor the union's request for cost estimates. During the negotiations, GE unilaterally instituted a 3 percent wage increase for nonunion employees and implemented its insurance and pension proposals for all employees. A strike ensued, and GE publicly criticized the personal conduct of the union negotiators, threatening to lay off strikers who did not return to work. Eventually, the union capitulated to all of GE's proposals.

Irving R. Kaufman, Circuit Judge

Under the most favorable interpretation of the facts, GE's offhanded refusal to submit information on [the compensation] issue which it had itself raised, would amount to an unfair labor practice. This conclusion is fortified by GE's behavior in the prenegotiation meetings, when it demonstrated that it was capable of providing information—indeed even suggesting that it be provided—in a form different from that originally desired.

A union weighing wages against benefits, or one form of benefit against another, should receive answers to its genuine nonburdensome requests for cost information. If the Union were denied such data, it would be unable to bargain intelligently, and arrive at sensible and reasoned decisions, particularly those involving reallocation of benefits within GE's cost framework.

The terms offered at Schenectady and Pittsfield were in fact better than those made available to the national negotiators.

We agree with the Board that GE committed an unfair labor practice by failing to respect the IUE-GE Conference Board's status as exclusive bargaining representative.

Such tactics are inherently divisive; they make negotiations difficult and uncertain; they subvert the cooperation necessary to sustain a responsible and meaningful union leadership. The evil, then, is not in offering more. It is in the offer itself.

The Board, however, chose to find an overall failure of good faith bargaining in GE's conduct. Specifically, the Board found that GE's bargaining stance and conduct, considered as a whole, were designed to derogate the Union in the eyes of its members and the public at large. This plan had two major facets: first, a take-it-or-leave-it approach ("firm, fair offer") to negotiations in general which emphasized both the powerlessness and uselessness of the Union to its members, and second, a communications program that pictured the Company as the true defender of the employees' interests, further denigrating the Union, and sharply curbing the Company's ability to change its own position.

GE's reluctance to part with information was not limited to the specific instances complained of as an unfair labor practice. The record discloses that even before the general reopening of negotiations, GE displayed a patronizing attitude towards Union negotiators inconsistent with a genuine desire to reach a mutually satisfactory accord. During the early meetings devoted to employment security, GE's responses to the Union's detailed proposals were vague and uninformative, hardly calculated to apprise the IUE of GE's stand on any of the matters about which it wanted to negotiate. When the Union finished presenting its plan, GE, instead of offering counterproposals, or commenting specifically on the IUE's suggestions, offered a prepared lecture series on the general causes of economic instability, a response not at all designed to enlighten the Union on specific bargainable matters. This impression is reinforced by Moore's consistent refusal to permit the lecturing Employee Relations Managers to answer specific Union inquiries.

More crucial, perhaps, was the Company's persistent refusal, after publicizing its proposal, to estimate not only the cost of components of its offer, but the total size of the wage-benefit package it would consider reasonable. . . . The trial examiner found (as GE's bargaining philosophy required) that considerable cost studies had in fact been made, which would have been of substantial assistance to the Union. Without an estimate of the overall size of GE's offer, the Union was hamstrung in its efforts to decide which substitutions were reasonable, whether to press for more total benefits, or how much redistribution could be accomplished within GE's cost framework.

Case Questions

1. What duty does an employer have to provide data to the union during bargaining?
2. Does it seem sensible to put the best offer on the table early in negotiations?
3. Must negotiators deal with the authorized representatives of the opposition or can it go to lower-level leaders and make "side deals"?

If either party refuses to bargain, the National Labor Relations Board (NLRB) may order it to bargain or may issue a cease and desist order to refrain from bad faith bargaining. In unusual situations, the NLRB has ordered compensatory damages. In one case, for example, one party's refusal to bargain was so flagrant that the NLRB ordered the payment of litigation expenses to the innocent party. However, neither party may be forced to accept a particular agreement or provision. Nothing in the good faith bargaining obligation requires a party to make concessions.

When an employer experiences fundamental changes in its corporate structure, the question often arises whether existing labor contracts must be recognized. As discussed in Chapter 11, a firm in bankruptcy reorganization may have all of its contracts changed drastically, including its union contracts. Thus, the old labor contract may become unenforceable and employees may be required to accept a new, typically less favorable, collective bargaining agreement. However, when a corporation is merged with another corporation or its assets are purchased by another corporation, the surviving corporation must respect the terms of existing union contracts.

At first, the *N.L.R.B. v. Bildisco* case appeared to resolve a dilemma between the policy favoring collective bargaining and the bankruptcy law's protection from creditors.[4] However, many commentators feared that the case signaled a potential misuse of the Chapter 11 reorganization process to force unions to renegotiate labor contracts. As a result, Congress amended the bankruptcy law in 1984, effectively limiting the effect of *Bildisco*. The new law requires the bankruptcy judge's approval before an existing labor contract may be nullified. The bankruptcy judge must find that the labor contract modifications are "necessary" to the bankrupt's survival. Labor contracts may not be rejected unless (1) all creditors are treated fairly and equitably, (2) the union refused the bankrupt's proposed contract modification "without good cause," and (3) the equities favor rejecting the existing union contract.

Subjects of Bargaining

Managements and unions bargain over subjects that fall into three basic categories. The first category comprises **mandatory collective bargaining subjects**—"wages, hours, and other terms and conditions of employment, or the negotiation of an agreement, or any questions arising thereunder." The parties are required to bargain over these subjects because the employment relationship is directly affected by them. Bargaining on these subjects may continue to the point of impasse. Mandatory subjects include wages, merit increases, pension retirement benefits, vacations, rest periods, work assignments, seniority, no-strike provisions, and major grievances concerning working conditions. Safety rules and practices may also be considered mandatory subjects even though regulated under federal law. In one instance, Ford Motor Company was required to bargain over the prices it charged employees for food in its lunchrooms. Food prices were a significant part of the employment relationship, and the whole automobile industry bargained over them.

The second basic category of bargaining subjects comprises *permissive subjects*. These subjects are "bargainable," but only if both parties voluntarily agree to negotiate on them. Permissive subjects include company or union policies that only indirectly affect the employment relationship, modifications of an existing labor contract before it expires, public policies such as the employer's contributions to charities, the organization or size of the employer's corporation, the types of supervisors, general business practices, and

[4] *N.L.R.B. v. Bildisco*, 466 U.S. 513 (1984).

the location of production facilities. Neither party may refuse to bargain on mandatory subjects in an attempt to force bargaining on permissive subjects.

Some employers seek to reduce their operations and eliminate union jobs. If company supervisors perform production work and this deprives union members of overtime pay, the employer must bargain. Many employers have started to contract out work formerly performed by union employees on the premises. This practice, known as *outsourcing*, often leads to plant closure or to the sale or transfer of business operations. Employers have an incentive to reduce in-house work that an outsider paying lower wages can do more cheaply.

Managerial business judgments are considered mandatory subjects only to the extent that they directly affect the employment relationship. For example, managerial decisions to retrain or transfer employees or to give employees severance pay are usually considered mandatory subjects. In the *Fibreboard* case, an employer's unilateral decision to contract out maintenance work previously performed by employees was considered a mandatory subject.[5] The employer should have given the union an opportunity to help reduce the maintenance labor costs, particularly where there were no other alterations in the company's basic operations.

However, in *First National Maintenance*, the employer decided to discontinue certain operations.[6] First National had contracted to supply housekeeping and maintenance services to a nursing home. When it lost the contract, it decided to discontinue those operations altogether. Since the employer did not intend to replace the union employees it discharged, the cessation of operations was not considered a mandatory bargaining subject.

Either party may ask the other party to modify or terminate an existing agreement before its expiration date. However, neither party is required to bargain to modify an existing agreement. The party seeking a modification must notify the other party in writing at least 60 days before the agreement expires or 60 days before it wants the modifications to be effective and then bargain in good faith.

The third basic category of bargaining subjects comprises *illegal and prohibited subjects*. For example, the employer may not insist that the union bargain away its status as bargaining representative and the employer must recognize a certified union. Some subjects may never become part of any collective bargaining agreement. For example, no collective bargaining agreement may prohibit employees from distributing union literature on company property or require that employees become union members before they are hired.

Impasse

The parties must continue to bargain in good faith and attempt reconciliation until an impasse is reached. An *impasse* is a deadlock in which neither party can make an offer on terms any more favorable to the opposing party. The duty to bargain continues during a strike, shutdown, lockout, or layoff, as these are not impasses. After an impasse has been reached, the employer may solicit striking employees to return to work based on the old contract or any terms previously rejected by the union negotiators.

The employer's communications to strikers during an impasse must not be coercive. If the employer offers strikers a wage increase above the level that the employer offered

---

[5]*Fibreboard Paper Products Corp. v. N.L.R.B.*, 379 U.S. 203 (1964).

[6]*First National Maintenance Corp. v. N.L.R.B.*, 452 U.S. 666 (1981).

during negotiations, this may be an unfair labor practice because it tends to undermine the union's bargaining position. Impasses are seldom permanent in negotiations between several employers and a national or parent union representing several local unions. A temporary impasse does not necessarily signify a breakdown in negotiations, so the duty to bargain in good faith continues.

LABOR DISPUTE RESOLUTION: CONCERTED ACTIVITIES

The NLRA grants employees the right to engage in "concerted activities for the purpose of collective bargaining or other mutual aid or protection." When a particular union becomes the certified bargaining representative for a bargaining unit, employees must focus grievance activities through that union. Even unorganized employees with no certified union representative are entitled to engage in concerted activity. To gain legal protection for concerted activities, employees must act as a group and not merely as individuals. Thus, one employer committed an unfair labor practice by firing nonunion employees who walked off the job to protest extremely cold working conditions.

Some concerted activities are not protected under the labor laws. Concerted activities must be lawful, be advanced in good faith, and be directed toward a specific objective. The objective must be lawful and nonviolent, and it must not constitute a breach of the union contract. It must at least concern a work-related matter. For example, employees may become involved in political responses to labor legislation or be politically active in elections. The objectives of these activities are sufficiently "work-related" to gain protection. However, the employee's political freedom is balanced against the loyalty that employees must show to their employers. In one case, some employees discouraged the public from patronizing their employer. Since the employees failed to connect the boycott to a specific grievance or to benefits that they sought, their concerted activity was disloyal and unprotected.

Union Security Agreements

Concerted activities have greater economic impact on the bargaining process if the union is strong and the employees are not easily replaced. For many years, unions have sought to include provisions that strengthen the union in collective bargaining agreements. For example, all of the employees in the bargaining unit might be required to join the union or at least to pay union dues. Such *union security devices* must not be too restrictive.

Before 1947, many unions were successful in negotiating *closed shop* agreements requiring each new employee to join the union in order to work. Closed shop clauses gave unions extensive power over the pool of available workers and were effectively used to regulate and discipline union members. For fear of losing their jobs, unions members often blindly accepted the policy decisions of their union's officials without dissent. Today, closed shop agreements are illegal.

It is illegal for employers to hire only workers recommended by the union, because this is a disguised form of the closed shop agreement. However, it is permissible to have a system of *job referrals* from unions that operate a *hiring hall.* These unions provide employers with lists of qualified union members.

Union Shops The **union shop** agreement is a legal device that makes union membership compulsory *after* an employee is hired. Union membership may be required after the employee has worked a probationary period of at least 30 days, or after 7 days in the construction industry because work is often short-term and seasonal.

In a union shop, full-fledged union membership is not necessary. Instead, employees may only be required to pay dues and initiation fees, which must be reasonable. A *checkoff* provision requires the employer to deduct the union dues from employees' paychecks and then forward them to the union. If an employee has a bona fide religious objection to giving financial support to labor organizations, the employee may be required instead to pay an equivalent amount to a nonreligious, nonlabor, tax-exempt charity.

Agency Shop An *agency shop* does not require union membership, but only payment of a service fee or a bargaining assessment. This fee or assessment, which is used to cover union representation activity expenses, is often a smaller amount than regular union dues. Under a *maintenance of membership agreement,* union members may renounce their membership within a specified period after joining. For example, employees may decide to renounce union membership to avoid the union's discipline. However, nonunion members of the bargaining unit retain the benefits of union bargaining. Without these exceptions, the union could force the employer to discharge employees who are not union members or who refuse to pay dues, service fees, or initiation fees.

Right-to-Work Laws Section 14(b) of the Taft-Hartley Act permits state legislatures to prohibit certain union security agreements. State **right-to-work laws** may validly restrict or prohibit union or agency shops. More than 20 states, predominantly in the West and the South, have enacted some form of right-to-work law. Most of the states in the Midwest and the industrial Northeast permit union security agreements. Some observers argue that the right-to-work states are better able to attract new industry because in those states the unionization process is slower and unions are weaker. States may not override union security agreements that are valid under the Railway Labor Act.

Union's Duty of Fair Representation

The certified union has a special status as the "exclusive" bargaining representative of all the employees in the bargaining unit. The employer must bargain with the certified union. The certified union owes a duty of *fair representation* to all of the employees in the bargaining unit, including employees who voted against the union, are not union members, disagree with the union leaders, or are members of minority groups.

The duty of fair representation began in the 1940s and 1950s as a response to racial discrimination by some unions. In one case, a union induced the employer to give job referrals to U.S. citizens rather than Mexican nationals, even though both were in the bargaining unit.[7] It is an unfair labor practice for unions to discriminate against any employee on the basis of "invidious or arbitrary classifications" such as citizenship, sex, race, or national origin.

Although ordinary negligence does not constitute a breach of the fair representation duty, a union's gross negligence or its arbitrary or reckless disregard of an individual employee's rights may constitute a breach. What is the union's responsibility in maintaining industrial peace, and how does it fulfill that responsibility? The following case

[7] *N.L.R.B. v. International Longshoremen's Assn.*, 489 F.2d 635 (5th Cir. 1974).

illustrates the extent to which unions must protect employees' rights through grievance proceedings.

Bowen v. United States Postal Service

459 U.S. 212 (1983)
United States Supreme Court

Bowen was discharged from the U.S. Postal Service after an altercation with another employee. The national union declined to process his grievance through arbitration despite the recommendation of the local union chapter. The Court of Appeals affirmed the district court's determination that Bowen had handled his grievance arbitrarily. However, it reversed the money damage judgment assessed against the union.

Justice Powell delivered the opinion of the Court.

The Union contends that its unrelated breach of the duty of fair representation does not make it liable for any part of the discharged employee's damages. . . . This argument treats the relationship between the employer and employee, created by the collective-bargaining agreement, as if it were a simple contract of hire governed by traditional common-law principles. [The collective] bargaining agreement is much more than [a] traditional common-law employment terminable at will. Rather, it is an agreement creating relationships and interests under the federal common law of labor policy.

Of paramount importance is the right of the employee, who has been injured by both the employer's and the union's breach, to be made whole. In determining the degree to which the employer or the union should bear the employee's damages, the Court held that the employer should not be shielded from the "natural consequences" of its breach by wrongful union conduct. Were it not for the union's failure to represent the employee fairly, the employer's breach "could [have been] remedied through the grievance process to the employee-plaintiff's benefit." The union [must] bear some responsibility for increases in the employee's damages resulting from the breach. To hold otherwise would make the employer alone liable for the consequences of the union's breach of duty.

Fundamental to federal labor policy is the grievance procedure. It promotes the goal of industrial peace by providing a means for labor and management to settle disputes through negotiation rather than industrial strife. Adoption of a grievance procedure provides the parties with a means of giving content to the collective-bargaining agreement and determining their rights and obligations under it.

Although each party participates in the grievance procedure, the union plays a pivotal role in the process since it assumes the responsibility of determining whether to press an employee's claims. The employer, for its part, must rely on the union's decision not to pursue an employee's grievance. For the union acts as the employee's exclusive representative in the grievance procedure, as it does in virtually all matters involving the terms and conditions of employment. Just as a non-organized employer may accept an employee's waiver of any challenge to his discharge as a final resolution of the matter, so should an organized employer be able to rely on a comparable waiver by the employee's exclusive representative.

There is no unfairness to the union in this approach. By seeking and acquiring the exclusive right and power to speak for a group of employees, the union assumes a corresponding duty to discharge that responsibility faithfully—a duty which it owes to the employees whom it represents and on which the employer with whom it bargains may rely. When the union, as the exclusive agent of the employee, waives arbitration or fails to seek review of an adverse decision, the employer should be in substantially the same position as if the employee had had the right to act on his own behalf and had done so. Indeed, if the employer could not rely on the union's decision, the grievance procedure would not provide the "uniform and exclusive method for [the] orderly settlement of employee grievances," which the Court has recognized is essential to the national labor policy.

Nor will requiring the union to pay damages impose a burden on the union inconsistent with national labor policy. It will provide an additional incentive for the union to process its members' claims where warranted. This is wholly consistent with a union's interest.

Case Questions

1. What is the union's role in grievance proceedings?
2. May the union be held liable in damages to an employee for failing to discharge its duty of fair representation?
3. How does the grievance procedure serve to further federal labor policy?

Regulation of Strikes

Strikes are concerted activities of employees who stop work simultaneously to pressure their employer. No Supreme Court decision has ever squarely sanctioned the right to strike. However, several constitutional provisions are often cited to infer the right to strike. For example, the First Amendment ensures freedom of speech, press, and assembly; the Fifth Amendment prohibits the deprivation of life, liberty, or property without due process, and the Thirteenth Amendment prohibits slavery and involuntary servitude. The Constitution has been interpreted to protect employees involved in a strike over wages, hours or conditions of labor, the discipline or discharge of an employee, or the employment of nonunion labor, as well as employees striking in aid of others engaged in such a controversy. The right to "engage in concerted activity," conferred by the National Labor Relations Act, is also cited as guaranteeing the right to strike.

Strikes may be classified in many ways. *Illegal strikes* involve violence, discrimination against certain employees, violation of a cooling-off period, seeking to compel the acceptance of featherbedding or hot cargo provisions, or attempting to coerce recognition of a noncertified union when another union has already been certified. In illegal *sit-down strikes,* employees at the job site suddenly refuse to work. In such strikes, the employees typically occupy the employer's premises by sitting down at their workstations. Strikers engaging in violence may be discharged by an employer. Sporadic or disruptive shutdowns or partial work stoppages are also illegal. *Wildcat strikes* are illegal because the striking employees fail to give the employer the required advance notice and lack the approval of other union members.

It is an unfair labor practice for an employer to interfere with legitimate concerted activities such as strikes. Most strikers may not be fired for legal strike activities. However, the employer may hire temporary replacements because it may legitimately continue business operations during any strike. After a strike ends, a dispute often arises over the strikers' reinstatement. Strikers are entitled to reinstatement during or immediately after an *unfair labor practice strike,* a strike in protest against an employer's unfair labor practice, even if this means that temporary replacements must be fired. Such strikers must be paid " back wages" beginning on the date that they were fired for striking.

Economic strikes concern matters other than the employer's unfair labor practices. Economic strikers have no right to reinstatement if replacements are hired. They are entitled only to nondiscriminatory review of a reapplication for their old jobs. In addition, the employer may abolish the positions or the whole work unit of strikers if economic or business conditions radically change. For example, if the employer loses key customers because of the strike, the employer may shut down the struck plant permanently.

Economic strikes typically involve the efforts of employees to gain increased benefits or improved working conditions. Striking employees take the risk of permanent replacement if a strike is considered economic. By contrast, the employer hiring permanent replacements may risk breach of contract liability if the employer misjudges the strike to be economic rather than based on alleged unfair labor practices. Following most economic strikes, the union insists that the new contract include a term requiring nondiscriminatory reinstatement of all replaced strikers.

Commentary: The Controversy over Firing Economic Strikers

Strikes impose powerful economic pressures on management when they can shut down the employer's business, erase expected profits, or force the employer to breach contracts to its customers. However, the effectiveness of an economic strike varies by industry, by the skill levels of striking employees, and by the availability of qualified replacements. For example, compare the employers' ability to permanently replace professional athletes as opposed to flight attendants. After the failure of the 1987 National Football League strike over increasing players' "free agency" rights, all striking players were reinstated. With a few exceptions, all the "scab" replacement players who played during the strike were fired at the employers' option. This illustrates the power of unique and highly skilled employees to gain reinstatement. By contrast, some TWA flight attendants abandoned their strike and crossed the picket line as *crossover* replacements during their 1986 strike. When the strike ended, the Supreme Court refused to replace either crossovers or newly hired replacements with more senior strikers who had sought reinstatement.[8] Labor experts believe that this case gives employers a powerful counterbalance against the strike threat. More senior employees may hesitate to support a strike if they could lose seniority, or even their jobs, to crossover and newly hired replacements. This comparison also illustrates the weakness of a strike threat by less skilled employees or when sufficient qualified replacements are available in the labor pool.

Employers' newfound antistrike powers also tend to undermine the union's majority support by employees. For example, if a sufficient number of antiunion permanent replacements are hired, the union may lose its majority support by employees in the bargaining unit. Additionally, crossovers may lose faith in the union and cease to support it. A union risks its certified status and possibly the jobs (or seniority) of its members if the union misjudges the employer's resolve to fight a strike, whether many strikers will crossover, or the number of qualified replacements in the labor pool. Labor leaders are pressing Congress to pass one or more bills that would (1) limit the hiring of replacements during the first few weeks of economic strikes, (2) prohibit U.S. airlines or shipowners from hiring foreign replacement workers during a U.S. strike or lockout, or (3) prohibit the hiring of permanent replacements. The fate of these bills is uncertain.

Limitations on Strikes Unions must notify the employer at least 60 days before engaging in an economic strike and must offer to negotiate a new or modified contract. The 60-day notice is designed to prevent hasty decisions based on emotion or hysteria.

Strikes are illegal if they are intended to force the employer to discriminate against nonunion employees or to accept featherbedding clauses in collective bargaining agreements. *Featherbedding* agreements require the employer to pay for services that are not actually performed. In the 1950s, for example, many railroads complained that retraining firemen on diesel locomotives was featherbedding. Unlike the firemen who shovel coal

[8] *Trans World Airlines v. Indep. Fed. of Flight Attendants,* 489 U.S. 426 (1989).

on steam locomotives, firemen on diesel locomotives perform little real work. Today, the fireman's position has been eliminated altogether. Featherbedding is narrowly construed so that contracts requiring "make-work" jobs are enforceable if workers perform at least some minimal services.

Strikes to compel hot cargo agreements are illegal. *Hot cargo* clauses require the employer to terminate its business with another employer with which the union has a dispute. Thus, a collective bargaining agreement may not prohibit the employer from buying or reselling goods produced by nonunion employers.

Strikes called by a rival union that is seeking to organize an already unionized bargaining unit may also be illegal. It is an unfair labor practice for a union to strike or induce work stoppages in a bargaining unit if another union has already been certified to represent that bargaining unit. If a rival union desires to unseat and replace the currently certified union, that union must be ousted in a decertification election. Thereafter, the rival union may seek certification to replace the ousted union.

Rival unions sometimes get into *jurisdictional disputes* in which each union seeks to have certain jobs assigned to it. Striking to force assignment of such disputed jobs is an unfair labor practice. Although the NLRB usually decides jurisdictional disputes, some union contracts opt to have joint arbitration boards settle them. If a strike is legal, nonstriking employees may recognize the picket lines of striking employees and refuse to cross them unless they are restricted by a valid no-strike clause.

No-Strike Clauses Some labor contracts contain *no-strike clauses* that obligate the union to refrain from striking or from causing work stoppages or slowdowns during the life of the contract. A local union may be liable for breach of contract damages to individual employees or to the national or international union if it conducts a wildcat strike in violation of such a clause. Unions often agree to no-strike clauses in return for the employer's agreement to arbitrate grievances. Although the Norris-LaGuardia Act prohibits federal court injunctions against strikes, if there is an arbitrable grievance, unions may be enjoined from striking in violation of a valid no-strike clause.

National Emergency Strikes The Taft-Hartley Act includes a *cooling-off provision* that is intended to prevent severe strikes that might impair the national health or safety. If a threatened strike or lockout is expected to affect an entire industry, then the president of the United States is granted special powers. First, the president may appoint a board of inquiry to investigate the causes and circumstances of the labor dispute. The board investigates the facts and reports its recommendations. Thereafter, the president may direct the attorney general to seek a federal court injunction prohibiting the threatened activity. The issue at the trial is whether that activity will impair the national health or safety.

If an injunction is issued, the 80-day cooling-off period begins. During that period, the parties may freely engage in negotiations and, it is hoped, reach an agreement. The Federal Mediation and Conciliation Service aids the parties in their negotiations by attempting to reconcile their differences. However, if no agreement is reached, the strike or lockout may resume after 80 days. Congress is then left with the responsibility for curing the national emergency or its underlying causes.

In 1963, Congress used this power when railroad unions threatened to strike following an attempt by railroad companies to unilaterally change work rules. Congress averted a national transportation disaster by passing a law requiring compulsory arbitration over railroad work rules that temporarily required the retention of firemen on diesel locomotives and specified the minimum number of train crew members.

Regulation of Picketing

Picketing, if conducted in a peaceful manner and for a lawful objective, is another concerted activity protected by the Constitution. **Picketing** generally involves a gathering and patrolling of persons who intend to inform or disrupt others. It is typically done near the employer's place of business. Picketing may be enjoined as unlawful if it (1) violates federal law, (2) represents an unfair labor practice, or (3) violates state law—if, for example, it is not undertaken in a peaceful manner. Picketing may involve confrontations between the picketers and other employees of the picketed employer. Simply posting signs may not be sufficient to constitute confrontation, but confrontation may arise if the picketers remain close to the posted signs, because verbal or threatening exchanges are more likely.

Types of Picketing The picketing of an employer by its employees is considered *primary picketing* and receives the greatest degree of constitutional protection. *Stranger picketing*—that is, picketing by nonemployees—is protected only if it is done for a lawful purpose and in a peaceful manner. Whereas state law may regulate picketing by strangers, picketing as part of an uncertified union's campaign to organize the bargaining unit receives constitutional protection.

Secondary picketing takes place at a business site other than the site of the employer with which the picketing employees have a dispute. For example, a restaurant owner who wishes to build a new restaurant at a new site might hire a nonunion construction contractor. It is illegal secondary picketing for construction workers to picket at the site of the original restaurant to pressure the restaurant owner into bringing pressure on the contractor to hire union construction laborers. Other forms of secondary pressure are discussed later.

Limits on Picketing Mass picketing by large numbers of picketers may be illegal if it imposes implicit coercion on employees who are attempting to enter the worksite. The obstruction of plant entrances is illegal if it is intended to limit nonstrikers' access to the employer's premises. In *Carnegie-Illinois Steel Corp. v. United Steelworkers of America*, for example, several hundred strikers stood three deep across an entrance gate to the steel plant.[9] Workers and supervisors were denied access through the gate. The trial court stated: "Picketing which results in the intimidation and coercion of officers and employees . . . is not legal picketing." The state courts may enjoin mass picketing by employees if it intimidates other employees. Both the NLRB and the courts carefully examine the degree of violence that arises during a strike or picketing program. Minor and isolated instances of misconduct are probably not illegal under the NLRA.

It is unlawful for an uncertified rival union to picket an employer if the employer currently recognizes a certified union and a valid union certification election was held less than 12 months prior to the picketing. However, recognition and organizational picketing by a rival union before or after the 12-month period is permissible.

Informational picketing is designed to inform the employer's customers about a labor dispute. It may be legal even if it results in a consumer boycott of the employer. Infor-

[9] *Carnegie-Illinois Steel Corp. v. United Steelworkers of America*, 353 Pa. 420 (1946).

mational picketing becomes illegal when it disturbs deliveries or physically disrupts customer access to the employer's premises.

Regulation of Secondary Pressure

Secondary pressure is a union's concerted activity directed toward some other employer. An employer with which the union has no dispute is a *secondary employer.* For example, a union may seek to pressure the employer with which it has a dispute—the primary employer—by inconveniencing that employer's customers or suppliers, which are secondary employers. Secondary pressure exerted through picketing, strikes, or boycotts is generally prohibited.

A *secondary boycott* usually results from union pressure, threats, coercion, and other concerted activities aimed at a secondary employer. Such activities are illegal if the union strikes or refuses to handle goods or induces nonmembers to strike or refuse to handle goods. For example, although employees may legally strike or picket their own employer, picketing the employer's customers or suppliers is an illegal secondary boycott. Secondary boycotts intended to force a secondary employer to enter into a hot cargo agreement or to assign work to a rival union are also illegal. It is not an illegal secondary boycott to request employees of a neutral employer to refrain from crossing picket lines if the union in the primary dispute is certified and the strike is authorized.

The courts have adopted a case-by-case approach to define secondary activities. These activities are prohibited where an innocent secondary employer is forced into a labor dispute. In one case, longshoremen refused to handle grain shipments that were to be loaded onto ships headed for the Soviet Union. The longshoremen's action was part of a political protest against the Soviet Union's invasion of Afghanistan. The action was illegal because the longshoremen's refusal to work burdened secondary employers: shipowners, grain sales agents, and dock owners who had no direct labor dispute with the boycotting longshoremen.

Common Situs Problems A construction project located on a single worksite serviced by several subcontractor employers is known as a *common situs.* Picketing and strike activity at a common situs raises some ambiguity as to secondary pressure. When employees of one subcontractor picket a common situs, it may be difficult to determine which employer is the object of the concerted activity.

In the *Moore Drydock* case, the sailors' union struck against the owner of a ship that was being serviced at a drydock facility owned by a secondary employer.[10] The NLRB created the *Moore Drydock* rules to draw a balance between union interests and the interests of secondary employers. Picketing or strike activity at a secondary employer's situs may be restricted if the striking union has a secondary motive, as tested by the *Moore Drydock* rules, regardless of which employer owns the situs.

Employers often attempt to blunt the negative effects of common situs picketing by isolating the activities of primary employers. For example, the owner of a common situs may require each employer's workers to enter the premises through a separate gate and may confine the picketing of a primary employer to its assigned area so as to reduce intrusions on secondary employers. For these restrictions to apply, the primary employer must actually use only the designated gate. Construction sites involve similar problems for the landowner, lessees, the prime contractor, and the numerous subcontractors.

---

[10]In re *Sailors Union of the Pacific,* 92 NLRB 547 (1950).

Moore Drydock Rules

1. Picketing may occur only when the primary employer is engaged in its ordinary business activity.
2. The primary employer must be located at the secondary situs.
3. Picketing is limited to an area physically close to the situs of the primary employer.
4. Picketing signs must clearly state that the dispute is only with the primary employer.

Ally Doctrine In some instances, the secondary employer may not be neutral or innocent. A secondary employer economically linked to or aiding or abetting the primary employer is not protected from secondary pressure. For example, secondary pressure is legal if the secondary employer provides replacements for striking employees. A general contractor that hires temporary replacements from a subcontractor (the primary employer) to avoid work stoppage may validly be subjected to secondary pressure. A secondary employer may be considered an *ally* of the primary employer if its business operations are closely related to those of the primary employer. For example, a primary and secondary employer owned or controlled by the same parent corporation actually form two parts of the same business. Secondary picketing of such affiliated parties is permissible.

Consumer Boycotts Nothing prohibits a union from using nonpicketing means to advise the public about the products of the employer with which the union has a dispute. For example, a union's distribution of informational leaflets outside the primary employer's plant is permissible. Moreover, informational distributions conducted at a shopping mall are legal if the union is not picketing, patrolling, or engaged in other intimidating conduct. Such *handbilling* activity may advocate a consumer boycott of all the mall's stores even if the union's dispute is only with a contractor that is building a shop for a single mall tenant.[11]

A union's campaign to provide the public with information may be prohibited in certain more coercive situations. Under the *Tree Fruits* doctrine, such a campaign is illegal if it tends to cause a work stoppage or to interfere with deliveries to a secondary employer.[12] For example, a union that has a dispute with a food processor may choose to picket a supermarket that sells the food processor's products. The *Tree Fruits* doctrine permits this secondary picketing only if it causes no interference with suppliers' deliveries or customers' shopping. The secondary picketing permitted under *Tree Fruits* must be noncoercive and peaceful, and it must be designed only to induce customers to refrain from buying the boycotted product.

Remedies for Illegal Concerted Activities

Illegal strikes, boycotts, and picketing are remedied through the filing of unfair labor practice charges against the union. Such charges receive priority over all other NLRB cases. The regional director of the NLRB may immediately seek an injunction against the

---

[11] *DeBartolo Corp. v. Florida Gulf Coast Building and Construction Trades Council*, 108 S.Ct. 1392 (1988).

[12] *N.L.R.B. v. Fruit and Vegetable Packers and Warehousemen, Local 760*, 377 U.S. 58 (1964).

illegal activity. If violence is involved, the state or federal courts may issue injunctions. In some instances, the courts have ordered unions to pay damages to the secondary employer or to its customers or suppliers. For example, a union may be ordered to pay lost profits if its illegal secondary pressure had a direct and adverse impact on a secondary employer's sales.

Grievance Procedures and Arbitration

Employers often seek to include procedures in collective bargaining agreements for settling work floor disputes between workers and supervisors that could lead to strikes or picketing. Many collective bargaining agreements now include arbitration clauses delegating to independent and neutral third parties the authority to settle grievances in the final step of the proceedings.

The processing of a grievance usually begins with a hearing by lower-level managerial personnel. Eventually, the grievance may be reviewed or appealed to higher management levels and ultimately to an arbitrator. Typically, the union is responsible for processing employee grievances. Arbitrators are selected from neutral agencies such as the American Arbitration Association. In national emergencies, mediators of the Federal Mediation and Conciliation Service attempt to facilitate negotiations and to persuade the disputing parties to reach an agreement on their own. As noted in Chapter 4, unlike arbitrators, federal mediators may not issue binding decisions. Instead, they attempt to create a negotiation atmosphere conducive to settlement.

The Arbitration Process and Its Effects Arbitrators need not be lawyers, but they should be familiar with labor policies and labor disputes. They are paid jointly by the employer and the union, who together select the time and place for arbitration. The American Arbitration Association suggests the use of certain procedures for informal arbitration hearings, although the arbitrator selects the particular procedures used. While arbitration is being pursued, other forms of concerted activity or economic pressure are prohibited.

The arbitrator's authority is typically controlled by the collective bargaining agreement, which usually permits the arbitrator to settle disputes involving interpretation or application of contract provisions. This power is construed broadly, permitting the arbitrator to decide the facts but not to make rulings on questions of law. An arbitrator may decide only "arbitrable" issues. This condition often raises the legal question of whether the arbitrator has exceeded the authority granted. Although arbitrators, unlike judges, are not bound by precedents, they generally follow patterns derived from their own experience or from earlier awards between the same parties. The NLRB may refuse to review an arbitrator's award on appeal.

Basis for NLRB Refusal to Hear Arbitration Appeal

1. All of the parties had agreed to the arbitration.
2. The arbitration was conducted in a fair and regular manner.
3. The arbitrator decided only factual issues.
4. The arbitrator's award is not clearly repugnant to the purposes and policies of labor law.

Any party to a labor arbitration may appeal the award based on the arbitrator's incompetence or bias or on the violation of any of the four requirements listed above. The courts respect the awards of arbitrators so long as the parties followed the prescribed arbitration procedures and the union provided fair and adequate representation of the employee's interests. However, if a union delays the arbitration process or shows hostility toward the employee, a court may intervene or overturn an arbitration award.

INTERNAL UNION DEMOCRACY

Reports of union corruption led to the passage of two laws designed to balance the union's need for authority over its members against the members' rights to monitor the performance of union officials. The Taft-Hartley Act protects union employees from coercive discipline by union leaders. A union may validly discipline its members for conduct interfering with the union's economic well-being, such as engaging in wildcat strikes, working for wages below union scale, or spying for the employer. However, a union may not punish employees for pursuing their civic duties. For example, it may not punish an employee for testifying before judicial or congressional committees or for reporting violations of law by union members or officials.

It is an unfair labor practice for a union to induce an employer to discharge or deny promotions to an employee. However, a union may seek dismissal of an employee who fails to pay union dues as required by a valid union security agreement. Excessive or discriminatory initiation fees are prohibited. Unions have a legitimate right to prescribe membership rules, and they may enforce their own rules so long as there is no discrimination.

ETHICAL DILEMMAS FOR UNION OFFICIALS

Union officials face numerous ethical dilemmas in and out of the bargaining context. When union officials condone a wildcat strike or a walkout in which the employer is not given notice, they abuse the union's position of power. Violence in picketing and the intimidation of nonunion employees are also unethical, even if the union members believe in the importance of their objective. Illegal picketing and secondary boycotts that bring innocent employers into disputes or that intimidate retail customers are unethical.

In some instances, union officials have made personal use of union treasury pension funds or have used these funds for illegal political purposes. Such actions constitute an abuse of position and a clear breach of the officials' fiduciary duties.

The Landrum-Griffin Act: Labor's Bill of Rights

The Landrum-Griffin Act of 1959 created *Labor's Bill of Rights* to prevent abuses by union officials. Unions are prohibited from restricting a member's rights of free speech, assembly, or participation in union elections. Unions may increase dues, fees, and assessments only after reasonable notice and after all members are given an opportunity to vote by secret ballot. A union member must exhaust reasonable internal union procedures and remedies before suing a union official. Unions may not discipline a member for not paying dues until the member has been notified about specific charges and afforded time to prepare defenses in an impartial hearing.

Union Elections The early common law prohibited the courts from interfering with elections of union officials. The Landrum-Griffin Act modified this rule to guarantee fair union elections. It created minimum standards of voting and candidacy. First, all union members in good standing must be permitted to vote. Second, elections for local officers must be held at least every three years. Third, secret balloting procedures must be followed in local elections, though delegates to a national or international union convention may cast open votes. Secret local ballots preserve anonymity and help prevent coercion by coworkers. Fourth, a reasonable opportunity to nominate candidates must be given to all eligible voting members. Fifth, the qualifications for candidate eligibility must be reasonable. In *United Steelworkers of America v. Usery,* for example, a union eligibility rule required candidates for union office to attend at least half of all union meetings during the three years prior to an election.[13] This rule was considered unreasonable because it barred 97 percent of the union's members from candidacy.

Union elections must be designed to maximize the participation of union members. Candidates may not be denied access to membership lists or prohibited from distributing campaign literature. The Secretary of Labor and the federal district courts may overturn union elections in which these safeguards are absent. Legal problems in connection with union elections are often avoided by having independent and impartial nonunion election officials conduct the balloting and vote counting.

Union and Employer Disclosure Requirements The Landrum-Griffin Act attempts to control union corruption by requiring that unions, employers, and union officials disclose certain information. For example, a union must report to its members the names of officers, the union's financial condition, and certain election procedures. Financial transactions between a union officer or a union employee and the employer must be disclosed by the officer, employee, and employer. Violation of these reporting duties is punishable by fines of up to $10,000 and imprisonment of up to one year.

Duties of Union Officers Union officers, agents, shop stewards, and other employee representatives are considered fiduciaries. They owe a duty of the highest and utmost faith to the union and its members. Any misappropriation of union funds by these parties is illegal.

Litigation expenses of union officials may be paid by the union, but only if these officials are exonerated in the lawsuit. Unions are subject to damage suits or may be required to present an accounting of union transactions if there is good cause to suspect improprieties.

Trusteeship In certain circumstances, a local union chapter may lose control over its own affairs. For example, if local union officials become involved in corruption, misappropriation of union assets, failure to provide democratic procedures, or failure to carry out the union's legitimate objectives, the national or international union may impose supervision through a *trusteeship.*

Trusteeship is now regulated by the federal labor law because national union leaders used the process to prevent dissent by local chapters or officials and to plunder the treasuries of local unions. As a result, the Landrum-Griffin Act required trustees to file semiannual reports with the Secretary of Labor to ensure that the trusteeship process was not abused. Assessments imposed by the national union on local chapters may not be excessive.

---

[13] *United Steelworkers of America v. Usery,* 429 U.S. 305 (1977).

SUMMARY

Federal labor policies permit employees to bargain collectively with employers through their unions. Even where employees are not unionized, they may be entitled to damages for abusive or discriminatory discharge.

Several statutes provide nearly exclusive federal regulation of labor relations. The Clayton Act exempts collective labor action from the antitrust laws. The Railway Labor Act governs the collective bargaining of railroad and airline employees with their employers. The Norris-LaGuardia Act prohibits the federal courts from enjoining labor activities. The National Labor Relations Act requires employers to bargain collectively with certified unions and refrain from coercing employees during union organization activities.

The NLRB administers unfair labor practice and representation cases. Representation elections are the primary method for union selection. NLRB regional administrators order elections when an election petition is filed by employees in an appropriate bargaining unit, the unit comprising employees with similar legal rights and economic interests.

Both employers and unions may commit unfair labor practices by interfering with employees' rights to self-organize. An unfair labor practice arises if either the employer or the union makes coercive speech. Employers' promises of benefits to employees are also prohibited. Employers may not provide financial support for or dominate a particular union, discriminate against employees for antiunion motives, or provide benefits to employees opposing a union. Lockouts and plant closings are legal if they are not based on antiunion bias. Unfair labor practices are made by unions that threaten nonunion or nonsympathetic employees or that give employees economic incentives or threaten them with disincentives.

The employer may agree to bargain with a union that has claimed majority support or that presents authorization cards, petitions, or applications for union membership signed by a majority of employees. To aid the union in its efforts to reach the employees, the employer must give it a list of the employees' names (Excelsior list) at least 7 days before a representation election.

Collective bargaining negotiations must be conducted in good faith by both unions and management. Good faith bargaining is an interactive process in which the parties make offers and counteroffers until reaching a compromise on wages, hours, and other terms and conditions of employment. Both the employer and union negotiators must have authority to bargain. A union must bargain equally on behalf of all union and nonunion employees in the bargaining unit. A reasonable trial period must be given to a union certified within the previous year.

The obligation to bargain in good faith is violated if either party refuses to meet and confer over the mandatory subjects of bargaining: wages, hours, and other terms and conditions of employment. The parties may be required to provide information to each other. Neither party may adopt a "take it or leave it" approach, though neither party must accept any particular proposal or make concessions. The parties are not required to bargain over permissive subjects. The parties cannot bargain over prohibited subjects, such as a closed shop agreement, recognition of a certified union, or prohibitions of employee distribution of union literature. Existing agreements may be renegotiated if both parties consent.

The parties must bargain in good faith until an impasse is reached. Thereafter, the employer may solicit striking workers to return to work on terms no better than the last terms rejected by union negotiators.

Congress passed the Taft-Hartley Act in 1947 and the Landrum-Griffin Act in 1959 to control union corruption and curb unions' excessive power over workers. Employees may engage in concerted activities for mutual aid, but those activities must be lawful, made in good faith, nonviolent, directed toward work-related matters, and avoid violating the union contract.

Closed shop agreements are illegal. However, union hiring halls may provide employers with lists of qualified workers and union shops may legally require union membership or payment of dues after a probationary period. Almost half of the states have passed right-to-work laws restricting union shops. Agency shops require only the payment of a bargaining assessment.

The union must represent all employees in a bargaining unit equally and impartially. It is an unfair labor practice for the union to discriminate or cause the employer to discriminate against any employee on the basis of race, citizenship, sex, or union membership.

Strikes are concerted employee actions that temporarily halt work. Illegal strikes include strikes that are conducted during a national emergency; strikes that violate a no-strike clause or a cooling-off period; sit-down or wildcat strikes; and strikes that seek to coerce the employer into agreeing to prohibited practices.

The labor law protects employees who gather for informational purposes and conduct peaceful and lawful picketing. Mass picketing and violent picketing are illegal. Picketing an employer other than the primary employer is usually illegal secondary picketing. It is illegal for employees to picket an employer's customers. Where several employers utilize a common situs, picketing at some entrance gates may be prohibited. Picketers at a common situs must clearly identify the employer with which they have a dispute. Arbitration clauses are used to resolve grievances and reduce the probability of strikes or picketing. Arbitrators are independent hearing officers who determine disputed facts.

Unions may discipline members for not paying dues, engaging in wildcat strikes, working for less than scale wages, or spying for the employer. Members of a union may participate in political actions that are not in direct opposition to the union's best interests. The Landrum-Griffin Act requires that all union members in good standing be eligible to vote in union elections, that elections of local union officers be held at least every three years, that only reasonable qualifications be imposed on candidates for union offices, and that such candidates be provided with access to membership lists.

Extensive disclosures by unions, union officials, and employers are required; they include financial transactions between the employer and the union or its officials or employees. Officials of a union are fiduciaries owing the utmost and highest faith to the union and its members. The national union can replace local officials with trustees if the local officials become corrupt or fail to maintain democratic procedures.

KEY TERMS

National Labor Relations Board (NLRB), p. 532
representation election, p. 533
appropriate bargaining unit, p. 534
unfair labor practice, p. 535
good faith bargaining, p. 545
collective bargaining, p. 545
mandatory collective bargaining subjects, p. 549
union shop, p. 551
closed shop (agreement), p. 551
right-to-work laws, p. 552
strikes, p. 554
picketing, p. 557
secondary pressure, p. 558

CHAPTER EXERCISES

1. Identify whether each of the following activities is legal or illegal. Which statute applies in each situation?
   a. An employer requires an employee to sign a contract stating that he will refrain from joining a union if he is hired by the employer. Signing the contract is a condition of working for the employer.
   b. An employer is unionized, and the collective bargaining agreement between the employer and the union prohibits the discharge or discipline of employees without just cause. As part of its investigation of a theft, the employer attempts to interview an employee. The employee refuses to be interviewed unless his shop steward is present. Is the refusal protected? *N.L.R.B. v. Weingarten, Inc.* 420 U.S. 251 (1975).
2. Action Automotive, Inc., a retail automobile parts and gasoline dealer with stores in several Michigan cities, is a closely held corporation owned equally by the three Sabo brothers. The brothers serve as the corporation's officers, make all policy decisions, and retain ultimate authority for the supervision of every department. The union files a petition with the NLRB requesting a representation election. Action and the union agree to elections in two bargaining units—one comprising the employees at the company's nine retail stores and the other comprising the clerical employees at the company's headquarters. After the election, the union challenges the ballots of Diane and Mildred Sabo. Diane Sabo, the wife of Action's president, works as a general ledger clerk at the company's headquarters. Mildred Sabo, the mother of the

three Sabo brothers, is employed as a full-time cashier at a company store. Mildred lives with one of her sons, James Sabo, secretary-treasurer of the corporation, and she regularly sees or telephones her other sons and their families. Should the NLRB exclude Diane and Mildred Sabo from the collective bargaining units? Is it necessary that the NLRB find that the relatives enjoyed job-related privileges? *N.L.R.B. v. Action Automobile, Inc.*, 105 S.Ct. 984 (1985).

3. You are the plant manager for Westex Company. You are concerned that some employees are huddling near the rest room, whispering over their tables at lunch break, and passing notices around when they should be working. With regard to employees' solicitation on company property, you can't decide whether to draft a rule stating "No solicitation during working hours" or "No solicitation during working time." Does the wording make a difference? Which of these two choices is legal? Discuss.

4. You have recently been hired as the industrial relations supervisor of M & W Gear Company. Wilson McBride, the company president, seeks your advice on the following matter:

   The NLRB has just entered an order for a representation election to be held at M & W Gear on December 19. Approximately 40 percent of the employees signed union authorization cards, and these cards were duly presented to the board.

   For the past 10 years, the company has reevaluated the employees' pay rates around December 1. It has always announced the yearly pay raise at the annual Christmas party that it holds for the employees. At this year's Christmas party, to be held on December 15, McBride, aware of the upcoming union election, wishes not only to announce the yearly pay raise but also a new overtime rate and a new vacation schedule. Do you foresee any problems with all or part of his intended announcement? Why? How might you advise him?

5. Cabot Carbon Company established an in-plant employee committee system. The company prepared committee bylaws, which were then adopted by a majority vote of the employees. According to the bylaws, the committees were created to consider ideas and problems of mutual interest to the employees and management. The bylaws established a fixed term for committee membership, handled grievances at nonunion plants and provided for regular elections of employees to the committees. The NLRB challenged the establishment of the inplant committees, arguing that they were the equivalent of a company union. With what result, and why? *N.L.R.B. v. Cabot Carbon Co.*, 360 U.S. 203 (1959).

6. Sure-Tan, Inc. sent a letter to the Immigration and Naturalization Service (INS), asking it to check the immigration status of five employees who had supported the union at the company. INS agents discovered that the five employees were Mexican nationals working illegally in the United States. They were arrested, and they later accepted the INS grant of voluntary departure as a substitute for deportation. The union argued that Sure-Tan had in effect discharged the employees in retaliation for their support of the union. Did the employer commit an unfair labor practice by reporting the undocumented alien employees to the INS in retaliation for their participation in union activities? *Sure-Tan, Inc. v. N.L.R.B.* , 104 S.Ct. 2803 (1984).

7. The employees of an electrical business were trying to unionize the business. The owner of the business stated that he would never deal with a union and that he would go out of business if his workers voted one in. After the union won the representation election, the owner, true to his word, closed the business and sold all of its assets. Was the owner guilty of an unfair labor practice?

8. A majority of the employees of Linden Lumber Company signed authorization cards, and the union requested recognition by the company. The company refused to bargain, so the union filed an unfair labor practices charge. There was no allegation that the company had engaged in any unfair labor practice other than the refusal to bargain. Was the company guilty of a refusal to bargain in good faith? *Linden Lumber Company v. N.L.R.B.*, 419 U.S. 301 (1974).

9. A union shop agreement between the union and Western Airlines required all of Western's clerical workers to join the union within 60 days of employment. As the agreement was interpreted, these employees did not have to become formal union members, but they had to pay an "agency fee" equal

to the dues of members. The union, in turn, "rebated" to full membership a pro rata share of the dues to employees objecting. Certain employees objected to the plan, claiming that union expenditures left out of the rebate plan and paid for by the objecting employees went for the union's convention, litigation expenses, publications, social activities, and general organizing efforts. Were these activities "collective bargaining activities," and could the objecting employees be required to support them? *Ellis v. Brotherhood of Railway, Airline and Steamship Clerks, Freight Handlers, Express and Station Employees,* 104 S.Ct. 1883 (1984).

10. The union and the company were at a bargaining impasse. The major issue in dispute was whether to include an arbitration clause in their new contract. The company operated radio station WBT in Charlotte, North Carolina. Several union members picketed the radio station and distributed handbills attacking the company's method of operation and quality of programming. The handbills read: "Is Charlotte a second-class city? You might think so from the kinds of programs being presented over WBT. . . . There are no local programs being presented by WBT. . . . Why doesn't the company purchase the needed equipment to bring you the same type of programs enjoyed by other leading American cities?" The company fired the picketers. Was the firing an unfair labor practice? How did the use of handbills in this case differ from their use in a conventional strike? *NLRB v. Local 1229, International Brotherhood of Electrical Workers,* 346 U.S. 464 (1953).

11. You are the human resources director of Peachtree Company. Peachtree and the union reached an impasse in their bargaining over a new agreement, and the employees went on strike to bring pressure against the company. During the negotiations, the union demanded an increase of $2 an hour, but Peachtree would not agree to go higher than $0.75. The president of Peachtree asks you how to go about hiring replacements. What advice should you give? What will be the status of the striking employees and the replacement workers once the strike is over?

12. Jones has attended the union's meetings for the past three months. However, he has never been recognized or allowed to speak at these meetings. The union election is coming up, and Jones is concerned about the election procedures. Does he have any rights against the union? Explain.

13. J. Steve Peevens, CEO of Peevens Textiles, hated all unions. Although he believed his employees were treated fairly well, many employees sought union representation. J. Steve instructed his supervisors to conduct a negative publicity campaign against the United Textile Employees (UTE) union, which was attempting to organize the Peevens facility. In an effort to discredit the UTE, one supervisor falsified documents to wrongly show that UTE officials at other mills gambled with the pension funds of their union members.

    Compare and contrast the overlapping and separate ethical and legal analyses of these problems. What ethical and legal problems would exist for UTE officials if the allegations of Peevens' supervisor were true?

14. StrongSuit Airways operates the Western Air Shuttle, the high-volume passenger flight service between San Francisco, Los Angeles, and San Diego, California. To lower costs, Donald Strongsuit, the airline's owner and CEO, expected that when the new high-speed rail service commenced between these three cities, it would undercut fares on the Western Air Shuttle. He demanded that his flight attendants' union, the Amalgamated Flight Tenders (AFT) union, accept a 20 percent pay and benefit reduction two years before their contract was due to expire. Donald reasoned that the pay givebacks were necessary to remain competitive on the profitable western corridor passenger route. In response, AFT officials successfully enlisted the unions of the pilots and air traffic controllers which served all western U.S. airlines, as well as the unions of the locomotive engineers and switchmen for the passenger railroads in the region, to join in a sympathy strike. This effectively shut down all public passenger transportation between western corridor cities, except for automobile and bus service.

    Comment on the ethical and legal problems confronting the AFT officials in soliciting this form of secondary pressure. Is Donald ethically entitled to seek renegotiation of the AFT contract when the Shuttle confronts new competition from high-speed rail?

Chapter 18

TERMS AND CONDITIONS OF EMPLOYMENT

KEY CONCEPTS

Several federal laws regulate employment standards and compensation. The Fair Labor Standards Act regulates child labor and sets minimum wages, the standard workweek, and overtime compensation.

State laws set the eligibility qualifications for unemployment compensation. Federal tax and labor laws regulate retirement income from social security and private pension plans.

Workers' compensation systems are no-fault, employer-financed insurance programs that encourage employers to minimize worksite risks and provide the exclusive remedy for workers injured in the course of their employment.

The Occupational Safety and Health Act (OSHA) establishes safety standards by requiring most employers in interstate commerce to maintain safe working conditions.

Workplace safety problems are studied by the National Institute for Occupational Safety and Health (NIOSH), which makes recommendations to the OSHA Administration to regulate safety standards. Appeals from OSHA Administration determinations go to the Occupational Safety and Health Review Commission (OSHRC).

Laissez-faire principles generally apply to make employment-at-will the predominant employer-employee relationship. However, state and federal laws provide some job security from arbitrary terminations.

INTRODUCTION . . . PAST, PRESENT, FUTURE

Statutes governing the wages, hours, and character of the work force were among the first legal regulations of the employment relationship. These statutes were passed in response to the perception that employers took advantage of child workers, immigrants, and the poor. Employees worked long workdays but were provided bare subsistence wages. In the mid-19th century, some of the states passed laws intended to achieve "a fair day's work." However, such employment laws were challenged on the constitutional grounds that they deprived employers of their property without due process of law and that they unduly interfered with the right to contract. Few employment laws applied until the New Deal legislation of the 1930s, when Franklin D. Roosevelt and Congress pushed through legislation imposing minimum wages and maximum working hours.

Since the early 1900s, most states have enacted workers' compensation laws to provide workers with minimal injury compensation and meet the immediate cash needs of injured workers and their families. However, Congress responded to the perceived failure of the labor markets and workers' compensation laws to improve workplace safety. Comprehensive employment safety was provided in the Occupational Safety and Health Act (OSHA) of 1970. These laws cause employers to pass on the costs of making the workplace safe to consumers. It is argued that, on balance, safe workplaces generate more societal benefits than costs.

In an efficient employment market, employees are compensated for safety risks through adjustments in their income and work time. However, efficient markets arise only where the contracting parties have perfect knowledge about all the important factors of the transaction (e.g., the risks are known), and they voluntarily assume the risks. Employees fully informed of those risks might be willing to accept them if they were paid enough for doing so. However, the real-world labor markets have imperfections, both workers and employers are often ignorant about worksite risks. Employers have an incentive to withhold information about job risks. Both employers and employees have difficulty in identifying workplace risks or in analyzing the information available. Society suffers a burden if workers are injured, become unable to support their families, and productivity declines.

These imperfections of the labor market have led to the passage of major employment standards and safety laws. The centerpiece of employment standards legislation is the Fair Labor Standards Act of 1938 (FLSA). It is intended to stabilize the economy by (1) placing a floor under wages (the "minimum wage") and (2) encouraging broader-based employment of more workers by imposing a "standard workweek," with maximum regular working hours and higher pay required for overtime. Originally, the FLSA set the minimum wage at 25 cents per hour for a 44-hour workweek. It required that time and a half be paid for overtime worked beyond the 44-hour standard workweek (1.5 × standard wage). At this writing, the workweek is 40 hours and the minimum wage is $4.25 an hour, though federal legislation is expected to raise it soon. Proposals to raise the minimum wage have been made in Congress from time to time, and many employers have experimented with flexible workweek scheduling. By specifying particular hazards, OSHA supplements the financial incentives to achieve safety provided by state workers' compensation statutes.

In the future, many employment compensation and safety issues will be settled by means of uniform federal legislation rather than piecemeal state legislation. Legislation may address issues like mandatory medical insurance, rising minimum wages, a lower minimum wage for teenagers, child-care facilities or benefits, and parental or medical leave policies. Such legislation would add significantly to employers' costs or government spending, so public policy should reconcile the cost burden of the legislation with the need to attract competent employees.

Employment safety regulation has experienced varied enforcement under different presidential administrations. Safety regulation will probably receive greater emphasis in the future. Additional federal safety laws may require more extensive notification of workplace health risks. The costs of employment standards and safety regulation will probably increase for both employers and the federal government, with many employees securing greater benefits.

OVERVIEW

This chapter discusses the laissez-faire employment-at-will concept, the legal inroads that provide job security, and the state and federal laws covering employment standards and workplace safety. The Fair Labor Standards Act is discussed, which sets the standard workweek and regulates minimum wages and child labor. Next, the chapter considers the state systems assuring temporary unemployment compensation and the federal regulation of retirement income and pensions. The final major topic is state and federal legislation to assure workplace safety including state workers' compensation statutes and federal workplace safety law, the Occupational Safety and Health Act.

EMPLOYMENT AT WILL

Before the 20th century, employment contracts were based on laissez-faire economic theory. Broad freedom of contract was given to both employers and employees. Either party could terminate the employment relationship at any time and without any justification. Today, this freedom of contractual association is known as the **employment-at-will** doctrine. It is justified as a symmetrical laissez-faire relationship. The doctrine is justified for employees because it would be slavery to force individuals to work involuntarily for an employer. If employees have the right to quit, mutuality suggests the employer should have the right to fire them. It would be unfair to require the employer to accept substandard services from an employee or to retain an untrustworthy employee.

Rationale for the Employment-at-Will Doctrine

[Individuals] must be left, without interference, to buy and sell as they please, and to discharge or retain employees at will for good cause or for no cause, or even for bad cause, without thereby being guilty of an unlawful act per se. It is a right which an employee may exercise in the same way, to the same extent, for the same cause or want of cause as the employer.

Source: *Payne v. Western and Atlantic Railroad Co.*, 82 Tenn. 507, 518 (1884).

Erosion of Employment-at-Will

About 45 states have created tortlike remedies or contract law exceptions to the employment-at-will doctrine that protect employees from arbitrary dismissal. The first exception involves *abusive discharge* based on public policy. In many states, an employee may not be fired for refusing to obey a supervisor's order to violate the law or other clearly articulated public policies. For example, an employee may not be fired for reporting that the employer is committing crimes. This type of abusive discharge is often referred to as the *whistle-blower* exception. Another public policy favors employees' participation in the justice system through service on juries. Employees may be protected from discharge if their absence from work was necessary to perform a public responsibility, such as jury duty.

In some states, an employee's job is protected where the employer makes an express or implied guarantee of continued employment. For example, employers often issue written personnel policy guidelines or personnel manuals. The policies stated in these guidelines or manuals become implied terms of the employment contract. Many personnel manuals state that employees will be discharged only for "good cause" or "just cause." Some employers promise continued employment as long as employees "do the job." In such cases, the employer may be required to prove that the discharged employee was insubordinate, negligent, or performing poorly on the job. Some employers have responded to such restrictions either by removing "just cause" language from personnel manuals or by requiring that employees sign a document stating that they are employed-at-will or that the personnel manual is not part of the employment contract. However, the employee's rights may be reinstated by the employer's later oral promises of good faith, fair dealing, or removal only for just cause.

A few states have taken even stronger approaches. Some courts imply the covenant of good faith and fair dealing into employment contracts. In one case, a salesman was terminated just prior to becoming qualified for retirement benefits. Because the employer did not act in good faith, the court ordered payment of the benefits. Some of the states protect workers from sexual harassment. For example, a female employee may not be fired for refusing to submit to her supervisor's sexual advances. Such sexual harassment is also illegal under the federal equal employment laws, discussed in Chapter 19. Montana has an employment-at-will exception statute and there is a proposed Uniform Employment Termination Act.

Several other state and federal statutes prohibit employers from firing employees who exercise their statutory rights. All employees are protected from discharge if: (1) their wages are garnished, (2) they cooperate with government officials in legal proceedings brought against the employer for pollution or work safety violations, (3) they exercise self-organization rights under the labor laws or their rights under federal laws governing minimum wages or overtime pay, or (4) they refuse a lie detector test. Some of these topics are detailed later in this chapter.

As discussed in Chapters 12 and 21, many other nations prohibit terminations without just cause and then only after notice of several weeks or months. A few states are beginning to limit the employee's right to sue for punitive damages, reasoning that abusive discharge suits are based on breach of contract and not on tort law. Some state legislatures may balance the parties' conflicting rights by codifying the abusive discharge action but limiting the employee's remedies only to compensatory damages. What conditions justify a judicial intervention into the freedom of contract between employers and employees? The following case illustrates the judicial trend toward implying additional standards for discharge where employees know what job performance is expected.

Toussaint v. Blue Cross & Blue Shield of Mich.
292 N.W. 2d 880 (Mich. 1980)
Michigan Supreme Court

Toussaint served as a middle manager at Blue Cross for five years, then was discharged unexpectedly. His supervisors had assured him that his employment would have continued as long as he was "doing the job." When Toussaint inquired about job security, his supervisor handed him the Blue Cross Personnel Manual. The manual stated that it was company policy to release employees "for just cause only." Toussaint was unexpectedly fired after five years of good performance. He sued Blue Cross, claiming that his discharge had not been for good cause.

Levin, Justice

Employers are most assuredly free to enter into employment contracts terminable at will without assigning cause.

We see no reason why an employment contract which does not have a definite term—the term is "indefinite"—cannot legally provide job security. When a prospective employee inquires about job security and the employer agrees that the employee shall be employed as long as he does the job, a fair construction is that the employer has agreed to give up his right to discharge at will without assigning cause and may discharge only for cause (good or just cause). The result is that the employee, if discharged without good or just cause, may maintain an action for wrongful discharge.

Where the employment is for a definite term—a year, 5 years, 10 years—it is implied, if not expressed, that the employee can be discharged only for good cause and collective bargaining agreements often provide that discharge shall only be for good or just cause. There is, thus, no public policy against providing job security or prohibiting an employer from agreeing not to discharge except for good or just cause.

While an employer need not establish personnel policies or practices, where an employer chooses to establish such policies and practices and makes them known to its employees, the employment relationship is presumably enhanced. The employer secures an orderly, cooperative and loyal work force, and the employee the peace of mind associated with job security and the conviction that he will be treated fairly. No pre-employment negotiations need take place and the parties' minds need not meet on the subject; nor does it matter that the employee knows nothing of the particulars of the employer's policies and practices or that the employer may change them unilaterally. It is enough that the employer chooses, presumably in its own interest, to create an environment in which the employee believes that, whatever the personnel policies and practices, they are established and official at any given time, purport to be fair, and are applied consistently and uniformly to each employee. The employer has then created a situation "instinct with an obligation."

We all agree that where an employer has agreed to discharge an employee for cause only, its declaration that the employee was discharged for unsatisfactory work is subject to judicial review. The jury as trier of facts decides whether the employee was, in fact, discharged for unsatisfactory work. A promise to terminate employment for cause only would be illusory if the employer were permitted to be the sole judge and final arbiter of the propriety of the discharge. There must be some review of the employer's decision if the cause contract is to be distinguished from the satisfaction contract.

In addition to deciding questions of fact and determining the employer's true motive for discharge, the jury should, where such a promise was made, decide whether the reason for discharge amounts to good cause: is it the kind of thing that justifies terminating the employment relationship? Does it demonstrate that the employee was no longer doing the job?

An employer who agrees to discharge only for cause need not lower its standard of performance. It has promised employment only so long as the employee does the job required by the employment contract. The employer's standard of job performance can be made part of the contract. Breach of the employer's uniformly applied rules is a breach of the contract and cause for discharge. In such a case, the question for the jury is whether the employer actually had a rule or policy and whether the employee was discharged for violating it.

An employer who only selectively enforces rules or policies may not rely on the principle that a breach of a rule is a breach of the contract, there being in practice no real rule. An employee discharged for violating a selectively enforced rule or policy would be permitted to have the jury assess whether his violation of the rule or policy amounted to good cause.

Additionally, the employer can avoid the perils of jury assessment by providing for an alternative method of dispute resolution. A written agreement for a definite or indefinite term to discharge only for cause could, for example, provide for binding arbitration on the issues of cause and damages.

Case Questions

1. What reasons might motivate an employer to provide job security to an employee?
2. What questions does a jury decide in a case involving an employee's discharge for "good cause"?
3. Are employers really free to hire and fire at will?

Moral Dilemmas for Whistle-Blowers

Many workers from Japan and Europe have traditional as well as legal rights to be treated fairly in dismissal proceedings. In the United States, however, the employment-at-will doctrine generally permits employers to dismiss employees without any justification. The recent erosion of the employment-at-will doctrine in some states has reduced the employer's unilateral power over employees.

In one case, George Geary was fired by U.S. Steel after telling upper management that some tubular steel products were unsafe and unable to withstand normal operating stress. After several admonitions from his superiors, Geary continued to complain about these products. A Pennsylvania court upheld U.S. Steel's firing of Geary under the employment-at-will doctrine despite Geary's claim that an exception applied for so-called whistle-blowers.[1] This doctrine is still applied in many states. Since then a federal law to protect some types of whistle-blowing was enacted.

Plant Closing Law

Effective in February 1989, Congress constrained the freedom of many employers to decide exactly when plants might be closed down. The federal *plant closing law* requires employers to give notice of plant closings so that employees have an opportunity to adjust to the loss of employment and income. The Worker Adjustment and Retraining Notification Act of 1988 (WARN) requires employers of 100 or more employees to give at least 60 days' notice of a plant closing or layoff. Notice must be given for (1) *mass layoffs* of at least one third of the full-time work force or at least 500 employees at a single site and (2) permanent or temporary *plant closings* when 50 or more full-time employees will lose employment during any 30-day period. Notice must be given to unions representing the employees or to individual employees if they are nonunionized. In addition, local governments must be notified because of the adverse impact of mass layoffs and plant closings on the surrounding community.

Exemptions Several exemptions to the plant closing law reduce the 60-day notification period. First, notice may be reduced if the employer is actively seeking capital or new business necessary to continue the plant's operations and the employer believes in good faith that public notice would frustrate these efforts. Second, plant closings or mass layoffs caused by business circumstances that are not reasonably foreseeable permit reduction of the 60-day notification period. Third, no notice is required for closings due to natural disasters, such as floods, earthquakes, or drought. In these circumstances, the employer must give as much notice as is practical and explain why 60 days' notice was impossible. No notice is required when a temporary facility is closed or when a particular project has been completed and the employees knew that their employment was limited to that project. In addition, notice is not required for closings or layoffs during strikes or plant lockouts that are legal under the NLRA.

Employer Liability Employers in violation of the plant closing law are liable for back pay and benefits to each of the terminated employees. A penalty of $500 must be paid for each day that notice is not given to the local government if the employees are not paid within three weeks after the closing or layoff. These damages and penalties may be

[1]*Geary v. United States Steel,* 319 A.2d 174 (Pa. 1975).

reduced if the federal court hearing the case finds that the employer acted in good faith. The court may award attorney's fees to the prevailing party as part of the costs. The Department of Labor has rulemaking authority to interpret and enforce the law as necessary for such vague terms as what constitutes a single "facility."

Employee Privacy

Employers increasingly use tests and gather other information to predict the performance of new hires and existing employees. The equal employment laws discussed in Chapter 19 require that aptitude tests and other information used to project job performance must be directly related to the actual job tasks. Former employer references and information about individuals' lifestyle, habits, use of substances, and past behaviors may have a bearing on their honesty and general future performance. However, many people view some tests and background investigations as an excessive intrusion into their privacy. Some tests have questionable validity resulting from inaccurate testing procedures. The **employee privacy** controversy illustrates a growing tension between employer and employee rights.

Many employers require interviewees to take batteries of tests, including psychological, medical, drug, intelligence, and skills tests. Psychological testing may reveal an applicant's work ethic, criminal tendencies, ability to work with others, performance under stress, and aptitude for leadership. Intelligence and skills tests may reveal an applicant's knowledge and capabilities to perform the tasks necessary for the job. Medical tests may reveal an applicant's predisposition to certain diseases that require expensive treatment. For example, HIV tests for the AIDS virus are a controversial test procedure. Some employers have even considered genetic testing to predict an applicant's honesty, criminal tendencies, or future health care burden. The use of intrusive tests, particularly those without a scientific consensus on reliability, raises profound public policy, legal, and privacy issues. Similarly, a former employer may be liable for defamation if reference letters contain damaging false information.

Substance Abuse There is considerable empirical evidence that employees' abuse of certain substances can adversely impact their performance, productivity, health, and workplace safety. For example, tobacco use is strongly linked to lung cancer and emphysema. Whereas workplace smoking bans and hiring bans on smokers are probably legal, firing smokers may not be legitimate. Several hundred local ordinances regulate smoking in public places. The Occupational Safety and Health Administration, discussed later, may soon regulate workplace smoking. Alcohol and drug abuse is directly related to on the job accidents and diminished capacity, productivity, and public safety. Nearly all the Fortune 100 companies have drug testing programs, many for prospective new hires, usually performed through urinalysis or the assay of hair samples.

Drug testing poses numerous legal issues. Policies covering unionized employees must be negotiated with the union as a term or condition of employment. Random drug testing of existing employees may not be permissible. There are some exceptions for federal employees, where there is "reasonable suspicion" or "probable cause" that drug abuse has impaired the employee's job performance, and where the employee's job impacts public safety (e.g., operators of dangerous equipment, transportation workers: pilots, train engineers, air traffic controllers, bus drivers). The Drug-Free Workplace Act of 1988 requires private contractors supplying the federal government to establish and enforce drug-free policies, although the act neither requires drug testing nor rehabilitation services. These exceptions vary among the states, which have varying provisions that are still evolving.

Employers should take great care in establishing drug testing policies because the law is still unsettled. Employers should assure privacy and reliability of drug tests and maintain the confidentiality of test results. Additionally, employers should retest employees with positive tests, provide rehabilitation services to employees with positive tests, and sanction only repeat offenders.

Federal Lie Detector Prohibitions The Employee Polygraph Protection Act prohibits most employers' use of lie detectors unless there is reasonable suspicion of losses caused by employees. A lie detector test may be conducted if the employer provides a written statement showing a reasonable suspicion that the employee had access to damaged or missing material and was involved in the matter. The questions must relate only to the alleged misconduct and may not be the only basis for an employee's dismissal. Employers may not retaliate against employees who refuse to take a lie detector test. Violators are subject to liability for punitive damages, civil fines, and attorney's fees. Some exemptions exist for governments, government defense contractors, drug producers, and security protection companies.

THE FAIR LABOR STANDARDS ACT

The Fair Labor Standards Act (FLSA) applies to all employers engaged in interstate commerce. Typically, it covers employees in the manufacturing, transportation, and communications industries, as well as employees in any "enterprise" with gross annual sales in excess of $250,000. The FLSA does not apply to federal government employees or government contractors because similar but separate statutes establish labor standards for them.

The determination of which workers are treated as *covered employees* under the FLSA involves an important qualification test. For example, the act does not cover *independent contractors,* so their employers are not regulated by the FLSA. If an employer retains the right to control both the means used by the employee and the outcome obtained, then the FLSA applies. As discussed in Chapters 9 and 12, true independent contractors control their own work and most of their own scheduling; only the contract objective (outcome) is controlled by the contract with the employer.

Several exemptions have arisen from time to time under the FLSA. For example, a *white-collar provision* exempts "executive, administrative, and professional" employees. This exemption includes the traditional professions of law and medicine as well as artistic professions and positions that require the exercise of discretion and judgment. Certain workers in agriculture, commercial fishing, household domestic service, retail establishments, and white-collar jobs must be paid a salary to be exempt. If exempted by the secretary of labor, the wage rate paid to apprentices, handicapped workers, and students may be set below the minimum wage. Recent efforts to raise the minimum wage have been tied to establishing a statutory reduction in the minimum to achieve a "training wage."

Computation of the Minimum Wage

The FLSA sets standards and methods for the computation of minimum wages, overtime pay, and compensable time. The **minimum wage** paid may be reduced by an amount equal to "reasonable costs of food, lodging, and other facilities" furnished to the employee. When employees regularly receive more than $20 per month in tips, the employer may take these into account.

The overtime pay provisions require the payment of time and a half of the regular rate of pay for each hour worked in excess of the standard 40-hour workweek. For example, an employee working 45 hours at the minimum wage would receive $170 for the 40 hours at the regular pay rate ($4.25 × 40) and an additional $31.88 for the 5 overtime hours paid at time and a half (1.5 × $4.25 × 5) totaling $201.88. No overtime has to be paid if a 40-hour week contains workdays with more than eight hours. Overtime pay computation becomes more complex if the employee receives nonstandard compensation in addition to the hourly wage. For example, regularly earned bonuses or incentive pay must be included in the base pay rate to which the time and a half premium is applied. Overtime premiums do not apply to bonuses or expense reimbursements.

Transportation to and from the employer's place of business is not considered "compensable time." However, the minimum wage and overtime standards are applied to preliminary and postliminary activities. *Preliminary* activities might include the time that butchers spend sharpening knives or the time that workers assemble for transportation by the employer to the worksite. *Postliminary* activities might include cleanup or transportation by the employer from the worksite. Do the minimum wage provisions cover executive and administrative personnel? The next case illustrates that although overtime provisions are inapplicable to supervisors, it can be difficult to apply this exemption.

Donovan v. Burger King Corp.
675 F. 2d 516 (2d Cir. 1982)
United States Court of Appeals

Burger King's assistant managers usually performed managerial and supervisory functions. However, they also performed production activities during peak service hours at mealtime. They were not given any overtime pay for the hours they worked in excess of 40 hours per week. Burger King argued that these employees were exempt from the overtime record-keeping and pay provisions of the FLSA because they were genuine "executives." The Secretary of Labor sued, alleging violations of the FLSA provisions.

Ralph K. Winter, Jr. Circuit Judge

The "Long Test" Assistant Managers

Judge Sifton found as a fact that the Burger King Assistant Managers "spent at least half of their time doing the same work as the hourly employees." This was a direct consequence of a deliberate corporate policy at the regional level which dictated "ideal" ratios of hourly labor to production and thereby required Assistant Managers to serve as an "extra hand" during high volume meal periods. Were the Assistant Managers to abstain from production work, more hourly employees would be needed, "thereby 'blowing payroll'—that is, spending more than the store's budgeted amount for hourly labor."

The regulations provide a different test for employees earning at least $250 per week. Such employees are exempt if their "primary duty consists of management of the enterprise . . . or of a . . . subdivision thereof . . . and includes the customary and regular direction of the work of two or more employees. . . ."

We agree with Judge Sifton that the "short test" Assistant Managers have, as their "primary duty," managerial responsibilities. Five factors must be weighed in determining an employee's primary duty: (1) time spent in the performance of managerial duties; (2) relative importance of managerial and nonmanagerial duties; (3) the frequency with which the employee exercises discretionary power; (4) the employee's relative freedom from supervision; and (5) the relationship between the employee's salary and the wages paid employees doing similar non-exempt work.

The record fully supports Judge Sifton's finding that the principal responsibilities of Assistant Managers, in the sense of being most important or critical to the success of the restaurant, are managerial. Many of the employees themselves so testified and it is clear that the restaurants could not operate successfully unless the managerial functions of Assistant Managers, such as determining amounts of food to be prepared, running cash checks, scheduling employees, keeping track of inventory, and assigning employees to particular jobs, were performed.

Such employees also exercise discretionary powers, criterion (3). They schedule work time for employees according to estimates of business based on factors such as weather and local events and assign them to particular work stations. They have the power, which they exercise, to move employees from task to task and to see that they are performing their jobs. They represent management in dealings with employees when they are in charge of the restaurant and, while they do not exercise the power to hire and fire frequently, there are some instances thereof in the record. Given that the ten to twenty-five employees under their direction are teenagers, many on their first job, this supervision is a not insubstantial responsibility. Assistant Managers order supplies in quantities based on their judgments as to future sales and are responsible for dealing with the public. Finally, they must deal with case or inventory irregularities.

We do not understand the Secretary to dispute the existence of these powers and responsibilities so much as to disparage them as wholly dictated by the detailed instructions issued by Burger King. We fully recognize that the economic genius of the Burger King enterprise lies in providing uniform products and service economically in many different locations and that adherence by Assistant Managers to a remarkably detailed routine is critical to commercial success. The exercise of discretion, however, even where circumscribed by prior instruction, is as critical to that success as adherence to "the book." Burger King, of course, seeks to limit likely mistakes in judgment by issuing detailed guidelines, but judgments must still be made. In the competitive, low margin circumstances of this business, the wrong number of employees, too many or too few supplies on hand, delays in service, the preparation of food which must be thrown away, or an underdirected or undersupervised work force all can make the difference between commercial success and failure.

The record also shows that for the great bulk of their working time, Assistant Managers are solely in charge of their restaurants and are the "boss" in title and in fact. We take that fact to satisfy criterion (4), the relative lack of supervision. That the Restaurant Manager is available by phone does not detract in any substantial way from this conclusion. Being available for advice is in no sense the exercise of supervision.

Finally, the evidence in the record is that the employees doing exclusively non-exempt work were paid the minimum wage. Assistant Managers earning $250 or more were paid substantially higher wages even taking their longer hours into account. That fact satisfies criterion (5).

Case Questions

1. Why do FLSA provisions apply only to hourly employees and not to administrators, professionals, or supervisors?
2. Why did Burger King require assistant managers to perform the same work as hourly production workers?
3. What factors most clearly make these assistant managers exempt as "supervisors"?

Child Labor Provisions

The FLSA includes provisions intended to prevent the abuse of children's labor. During the early industrial revolution, child laborers worked 12 or more hours a day for pennies an hour. They often endured the dangerous and unhealthful aspects of mining and heavy industry. In 1938, child labor provisions were added to the FLSA prohibiting the shipment of goods in interstate commerce if produced by an employer involved in "oppressive child labor." Child labor laws are also designed to encourage school attendance.

There are exceptions to the FLSA child labor provisions. Generally, children under 13 may not be employed and the employment of children between the ages of 13 and 17 is restricted. For example, children 16 or 17 years old may not be employed in hazardous industries (mining, explosives, roofing, logging, excavation). Children 14 or 15 years old may work only in approved jobs (retail stores, food service establishments, gasoline service stations). Children may engage in agricultural employment if their parents give consent. Child actors may work with parental consent, but state laws often require an approved school-like tutorial training.

FLSA Administration

The Wage and Hour Division of the Employment Standards Administration was created under the FLSA as a part of the Department of Labor. The division's administrator, who is responsible for passing and interpreting its regulations and restrictions, is appointed by the president with advice and consent of the Senate. The division's administrative staff investigates alleged violations of the FLSA. If sufficient evidence exists, it may file lawsuits to enjoin future violations of the FLSA, collect damages on behalf of individual claimants, or bring criminal charges. Injured employees may also sue to collect unpaid minimum wages, overtime compensation, and penalty damages equal to twice the unpaid compensation. Both the federal and state courts may hear such suits against employers.

INTERNATIONAL PERSPECTIVE: VARIATIONS IN WORKTIME AND PRODUCTIVITY

Considerable controversy has arisen in the early 1990s about the worktime, vacation, leave, and productivity variations among the industrialized nations. On the one hand, some Japanese leaders have charged that American workers are lazy and illiterate. On the other hand, workers in most industrialized nations are legally entitled to longer annual paid vacations than are U.S. workers. Some measures put U.S. productivity at the top in the world, increasing steadily throughout the 20th century.

These seemingly contradictory facts raise significant questions about employment standards for the workweek, overtime, vacation time, family and maternity leave policies, childcare, and other related terms and conditions of employment. Should these matters be left to market forces permitting the employer and employee to negotiate terms and conditions of employment? Free market adherents argue that further regulation of employment terms would harm productivity and ultimately hurt U.S. competitiveness. Critics charge that the United States stands alone among the industrial nations in not mandating vacation, child care, and family leave benefits by law. They maintain that increased leisure and worktime flexibility may actually increase productivity; the German workers' high productivity is said to support this argument.

The Japanese, Koreans, and other Asian nationals have become known for working hard and putting in long hours. Some nations have adopted a survivalist and nationalistic work ethic to gain a competitive advantage against larger industrialized nations. Their work ethic provides the drive to enhance their collective competitive advantage and raises national productivity and strength. The Japanese workweek averages 45–46 hours compared to the American workweek of about 40 hours, whereas some European nations average less than 40 hours work per week.

Critics of Japanese work practices ask whether such long work hours can be sustained for several generations in the face of evidence that overwork eventually lowers productivity and job satisfaction while it raises harmful stress. Some critics charge the United States and Japan with pursuing what the Japanese call *karoshi,* or death by overwork. These critics suggest that increased leisure time would give workers time to "recharge their batteries," which would increase productivity.[2]

---

[2]See Juliet B. Schor, *The Overworked American: The Unexpected Decline of Leisure,* New York: Basic Books, 1992.

Vacation time seems to be important to workers: 70 percent of working Americans surveyed would willingly give up one day's pay to get an added vacation day. Certainly the German workforce at the end of World War II was successful in rebuilding its postwar economy. During this period, most German workers enjoyed up to 7 weeks of vacation per year. In the United States, some employers believe that concepts such as job sharing, flextime, compressed workweek, sabbaticals, telecommuting, maternity/paternity leave, and expanding part-time work raise the costs of administering the workforce. Adding extra employees initially raises the administrative expenses of training, unemployment compensation, workers' compensation, and tax withholding.

Resolution of this debate is necessary to determine whether competitive pressures force worldwide working conditions to adopt the hard work model followed in the United States and Japan or to follow the lead of some European nations in meeting employee desires for free time while perhaps increasing (or decreasing) national productivity.

UNEMPLOYMENT COMPENSATION

During the Great Depression, nearly a third of the work force became unemployed. Such tremendous hardship was suffered that Congress gave states an incentive to implement unemployment compensation. It devised a tax offset incentive system that reduces the social security withholding tax (FICA) in a state if the state imposes an unemployment compensation tax on employer's payrolls. All of the states have enacted unemployment compensation taxes. Employers usually support such statutes because employers must pay a 3 percent federal excise tax if the state has no unemployment compensation law.

Employer Qualifications

The **unemployment compensation** system provides benefits to the employees of covered employers. It applies to all employers with at least one employee working a minimum of 20 weeks per year and having a quarterly payroll of at least $1,500, including employers that are charitable, educational, and scientific nonprofit organizations. It also applies to former military service personnel. Employers must pay at least 3.4 percent of the first $6,000 of each employee's annual wages into a state-operated fund. Since the unemployment tax rate applies to only a portion of the annual wages of most employees, this amount is generally lower than the 3 percent excise tax mentioned above. Some states impose higher rates than 3.4 percent.

Employee Qualifications

The states may adopt one of a variety of unemployment compensation programs. Most states have set a maximum period during which the unemployed may collect benefits, but the length of that period varies with changing economic conditions. The total benefits payable to each unemployed worker are based on a percentage of that worker's average base earnings while employed. Typically, this is set as the highest pay rate earned by the worker during the previous one or two quarters, but is usually limited to $200 or $300 per week for 26 weeks. The worker must also have had earnings of a minimum amount in the preceding year to qualify. These limits are intended to prevent misuse of the unemployment compensation system by persons who have not had recent employment or whose employer has not paid into the system. Congress extended the benefit period twice during the 1991–1992 recession.

To qualify for benefits, the applicant must be actively seeking employment, be available and able to work, and follow the statutory procedure for claims processing. Applicants may be disqualified if they refuse to accept new employment, if they have quit without just cause, or if they have been fired either for serious misconduct or as the result of a labor dispute. Unemployment compensation is usually not available to fired striking workers.

Experience Rating

The circumstances surrounding the dismissal of employees affect the outcome of unemployment compensation hearings and the tax rate paid by employers. Employers that have low employee turnover rates may pay lower unemployment compensation premiums; this is known as *experience rating.*

Some state laws permit employers to disregard seniority systems as a method of limiting claims. During times of economic downturn, for example, a participating employer may retain a larger percentage of the workforce than might be permitted if the employer adhered strictly to union seniority systems. If seniority systems are circumvented in this way, all employees must work fewer hours and each employee collects unemployment compensation benefits for the lost time. Thereby, the employer avoids laying off trained workers and saves the cost of training replacements when the economy improves. Of course, the employer must pay higher regular unemployment compensation premiums to cover the additional benefits that its employees receive during economic downturns. Many employers find the trade-off between higher training costs and the temporarily higher unemployment compensation premiums to be favorable. However, some senior employees oppose even temporary loss of their seniority rights, hoping to force job dislocation on workers with less seniority.

ETHICAL DILEMMAS IN CIRCUMSTANCES SURROUNDING EMPLOYMENT SEVERANCE

A terminated employee's right to receive unemployment compensation depends on the circumstances of the severance. Employees who quit without good cause or are fired for misconduct are denied benefits. This rule can cause supervisors and employees to negotiate on how to characterize the termination: as a dismissal or resignation. In other circumstances, employees are sometimes given the choice of resigning rather than being dismissed to avoid disparaging their employment record. Is it ethical to collect unemployment compensation for an ineligible severance and thereby shift the costs of the employee's personal misconduct to the unemployment compensation system? Is it ethical to misrepresent the reason for a severance when an employee's misconduct is clearly pertinent to future employers? Both tactics pose an ethical dilemma for managers and employees.

RETIREMENT INCOME AND PENSIONS

Prior to 1935, very few workers had any form of old-age or retirement benefits except for personal savings. Many workers continued to work until they died or became disabled. In 1935, Congress passed the Social Security Act to prevent such severe economic hardship. Social security benefit payments are intended to supplement the income of retirees.

Social security covers nearly all American workers. Unlike the European retirement systems, however, it generally does not apply to persons who have never worked. The social security system is compulsory, requiring employers to withhold social security payments from the paychecks of most employees. Each employer must match the amount withheld, which effectively doubles the social security tax. The actual name of the social security system is Old-Age, Survivors, and Disability Insurance (OASDI). In recent years, private pension systems have also developed as an important supplementary source of retirement benefits.

Social Security

Social security taxes are paid into the Social Security Trust Fund under provisions of the **Federal Insurance Contributions Act (FICA).** The Internal Revenue Service (IRS) is responsible for collecting these taxes. This responsibility is similar to its responsibility for withholding periodic federal income tax payments from employees' paychecks.

FICA withholding does not become part of a savings or investment fund that is eventually repaid directly to the retiree. Instead, the system is designed on a "pay-as-you-go" basis. Contributions from current employees immediately pay benefits to current retirees. Contrary to the common misconception that these contributions are held for employees until they retire, the system remains solvent only while current contributions exceed current benefits payments. As the number of retirees increases and the number of paying employees remains constant or decreases, the solvency of the system may periodically come into question. This problem is magnified by cost-of-living adjustments (COLAs), which increase social security payments if inflation triggers an increase in the consumer price index.

Social Security Taxes Nearly all employees must pay the compulsory FICA tax. To compute that tax, the wage base must be determined and then the appropriate tax rate applied to it. The FICA tax is levied on each employee's earnings, which are known as the *wage base*. This amount equals the employee's actual pretax earnings up to a statutory maximum that has steadily increased in recent years; the maximum is $55,500 in 1992. The FICA tax is paid only on amounts up to the statutory maximum; amounts earned in excess of the maximum are exempt from the tax. The *tax rate* is a percentage that is applied to the wage base to determine the amount of tax withheld. The tax rate is 6.2 percent in 1992, but that has increased over the years and it may continue to increase. Both the employer and the employee who earns $25,000 in 1992 and the employer will have paid 6.2 percent of that wage base into FICA (0.062 × $25,000 = $1,550.00). The FICA withholdings of employees who earned more than $55,500 in 1992 were limited to $3,441.00 (0.062 × $55,500) because the FICA tax applies only up to $55,500 in earnings.

Self-employed persons must also pay FICA taxes. When self-employed persons make their quarterly estimated federal tax payment in lieu of withholding and file their annual federal income tax return, they pay their FICA tax to the IRS in addition to their federal income tax. The FICA tax paid by self-employed persons is nearly double that paid by employed persons because self-employed persons pay all the FICA taxes, including the employer's contribution. In 1991, the FICA tax of self-employed persons was 15.3 percent up to the statutory maximum.

Social Security Benefits The social security system provides retirement income primarily to those who have actively participated in the workforce. A worker's eligibility and amount of benefits are based on the worker's income level and on the work credits given while employed. *Fully insured* employees receive full old-age and survivors benefits. To qualify, the employee must have worked at least one fourth of the time since 1950 or since reaching the age of 21, whichever is lowest. This is determined by giving the employee credit for each quarter of a year (three-month period) in which the employee was paid at least $50 by an employer or made at least $100 if self-employed. In addition, the employee must have worked a number of calendar quarters that equals or exceeds the number of years since attaining the age of 21 or since 1950, whichever is less.

Reduced benefits are available to employees who worked at least 6 calendar quarters in the previous 13 quarters if this time period ends in retirement, disability, or death. This results in *currently insured status*. Another type of reduced benefits may be paid to persons with *disability status*. Reduced benefits are paid if an employee worked for at least 20 quarters within the 40 quarters preceding disablement.

Benefits can be paid monthly to retired persons after age 62 according to their base pay during their work life. Spouses and children of deceased workers may receive half of the retired worker's benefit amount. The amounts paid tend to be a higher percentage of the base pay for lower-income workers and a lower percentage for upper-income workers. Social security recipients with annual incomes of over $25,000 pay federal income tax on half of their social security benefits.

Disability benefits may be paid to any former employee with a medically determined physical or mental impairment. The Social Security Administration, the agency responsible for benefit payments, automatically recognizes several severe impairments, such as loss of limbs or sight. An impairment not regularly recognized may qualify if the impairment is expected to be fatal or to last for more than a year. New impairments are determined on a case-by-case basis. Disability payments under social security are determined by criteria different from those used in determining disability under workers' compensation. Some disabled persons may receive both social security and workers' compensation payments.

Medicare Benefits Since 1965, health insurance for the aged and disabled has been available for all qualified persons in the system known as *Medicare*. Hospital insurance pays for many hospital expenses. Persons over 65 years of age may qualify for such insurance even if they are not eligible for social security. Optional supplementary and medical insurance coverage is available to beneficiaries who pay additional premiums. Since Medicare does not pay enough to defray all medical costs, an active private insurance system has arisen to supplement Medicare coverage. For 1992, both employers and employees each contribute 1.45 percent of each employee's wage base as a Medicare payroll tax up to the $125,000 cap.

Private Pension Plans

Although private pension plans have existed for over a century, their growth as a major source of retirement benefits has occurred mainly in the last 50 years. Historically, pension payments were made largely at the employer's discretion. Employers often terminated or reduced pension benefits at will. These payments were considered gratuitous rewards given only to faithful employees, not as part of a regular and mandatory compensation package.

Many private pension plans were discriminatory and unpredictable, so Congress passed the *Employee Retirement Income Security Act (ERISA)* in 1974, to standardize retirement plans. ERISA regulates eligibility for pension benefits and the taxation of pension plan earnings and benefit payments. Private pension plans that meet ERISA requirements are entitled to tax-free treatment in the years that employers and employees contribute to the plans.

The Plan Administrator's Fiduciary Duties Qualified pension plans must be administered by a person responsible for handling the pension funds. This person is a fiduciary who must carefully invest the funds and act only in the beneficiaries' best interest, using the skill and care of a reasonably prudent person. Pension administrators must diversify their investments to minimize the risk of large losses. They must disclose certain information to the Labor Department and to the plan's beneficiaries: the terms of the plan, annual financial reports, and annual summaries of each beneficiary's interest.

Vesting and Participation Before ERISA was passed, pension plan beneficiaries could lose all their benefits under certain circumstances. For example, a beneficiary whose employment was terminated prematurely or interrupted by a temporary layoff could have benefits denied or severely limited. As a result, ERISA established the **pension vesting** concept requiring that the beneficiary's interest become irrevocable after employment for a minimum time period. Pension plans need not give an irrevocable right to the employer's contributions to beneficiaries until they have worked for the employer for at least 10 years, though many plans permit vesting in a shorter time. Of course, the employee has a right to eventually receive all of his own contributions. Vesting in partial amounts for fewer than 10 years of service may also occur if the plan permits.

Many ERISA plans are *defined benefit plans*. Such plans provide specific payment amounts based on the employee/beneficiary's age and length of service. By contrast, a *defined contribution plan* requires each employee or employer to make a particular contribution. This allows for the payment of different retirement benefit amounts depending on the plan's investment successes during the employee's work life.

ERISA established the Pension Benefit Guaranty Corporation (PBGC) to insure pension plans. PBGC funds underwrite the payment of vested benefits to beneficiaries of plans that are terminated prematurely. If a terminated pension plan has insufficient assets to satisfy the beneficiaries' future claims, then the employer may be liable to PBGC for deficiencies. The PBGC provisions apply only to defined benefit plans and not to retirement annuities.

Other Retirement Plans Individuals operating small businesses may establish less formal pension plans called *Keogh Plans*. In addition, some individuals may contribute limited amounts per year into individual retirement accounts (IRAs). IRA earnings are tax-free until their withdrawal during retirement. Additional withholdings from wages that are also sheltered from taxation may be paid into deferred payment annuities (DPA or 401(k) plans). The tax advantages of these plans were reduced drastically by the 1986 Tax Reform Act. The benefits paid by all pension plans, Keogh plans, IRAs, and DPAs are taxable whenever the beneficiary withdraws them. Payments into such plans are subject to substantial penalties for early withdrawal. However, the enactment of proposals to encourage the national savings rate may reinstate some IRA tax advantages.

WORKERS' COMPENSATION

Workers' compensation developed because the common law system of negligent torts imposed tremendous barriers on employee suits for injury compensation. Employees had the difficult burden of proving their employer's negligence. Three common defenses to negligence suits imposed further difficulties on injured workers. First, the *fellow servant doctrine* prevented an injured employee's suit where a fellow employee negligently contributed to the injury. Second, the *assumption of risk* defense prevented suits where the injured employee voluntarily accepted the job's risks. An injured employee who was aware of the jobsite risks was barred from recovering for the injury. Finally, the *contributory negligence* defense barred an injured employee's suit if the employee in any way contributed to creating the dangerous condition. Because this negligence "fault system" provided very limited remedies, the states created no-fault, employer-financed workers' compensation systems. Workers' compensation benefits are "exclusive remedies" preventing employee's suits against their employers for compensatory, pain and suffering, or punitive damages.

Workers' compensation laws create a form of compulsory insurance. Depending on the particular state's law, an employer may self-insure, purchase private insurance, or participate in a state-managed fund. Employers that take effective steps to minimize job risks may pay reduced premiums. The risk-adjusted employer premiums of this *merit rating system* provide employers with another incentive to maintain a safe work environment.

Workers' Compensation Coverage

The first issue in a workers' compensation claim is whether the employee's injury is work related. Employees are covered by workers' compensation only while on the job; off-the-job injuries are covered by traditional tort law. Workers' compensation is applicable where the employer has the right to control the employee, so independent contractors are not covered by workers' compensation. Instead, independent contractors have full access to the tort system. If the employer may control only the outcome but not the means used by a particular person, the person is an independent contractor. This determination is similar to the "scope of employment" problem discussed in Chapters 9 and 12 under the respondeat superior doctrine.

Most workers' compensation benefits are restricted to injuries occurring "in the course of and arising out of employment." Employees en route to or from the workplace are usually not covered by workers' compensation. This *going and coming rule* restricts workers' compensation coverage to the time that the employee is at the employer's worksite if the worksite is located at a fixed and limited place. Workers' compensation provides coverage only after the employee arrives at the employer's premises. An employee is covered after parking in the employer's lot, while walking to a locker room to put on safety gear, and while being shuttled by the employer to the jobsite.

Problems may arise if employees must leave the employer's workplace as part of their job. Where employees are required to leave the premises to eat lunch, they are covered under workers' compensation. Employees required to travel away from the employer's premises are usually covered by workers' compensation. If a worker is hurt by a coworker's intentional act, some states distinguish between assaults, which are not covered by workers' compensation, and simple horseplay, which is covered. In *Murray v. Industrial Commission of Illinois,* the court overturned the Industrial Commission's decision that Murray's injuries were not work related.[3] Murray's coworker hit him behind the knees, causing them to buckle, so that he slipped on oil on the floor. Murray's horseplay injuries were compensable under workers' compensation.

---

[3] *Murray v. Industrial Commission of Illinois,* 516 NE.2d 1039 (Ill. App. 3d Dist. 1987).

United Parcel Service v. Fetterman

336 S.E.2d 892 (Va.1985)
Supreme Court of Virginia

Randall Fetterman, a UPS driver, was required to load, unload, and deliver packages as part of his job duties for UPS. While unloading packages one day, Mr. Fetterman noticed his shoe was untied so he raised his foot to the back of the truck and bent over to tie the shoe. Mr. Fetterman immediately noticed an acute back pain; he had suffered an accidental lumbosacral strain. The deputy commissioner of the Virginia Industrial Commission denied Mr. Fetterman's unemployment claim holding that his injury did not arise out of employment because it was not traceable to employment as a proximate cause and was not a natural incident of the work. Mr. Fetterman's claim was reinstated by the full commission prompting UPS and its insurer to appeal.

Per Curiam

An accident arises out of employment where there is a causal connection between the claimant's injury and the conditions under which the employer requires the work to be performed. Under this test, an injury arises "out of" the employment when it has followed as a natural incident of the work and has been a result of the exposure occasioned by the nature of the employment. Excluded is an injury that comes from a hazard to which the employee would have been equally exposed apart from the employment. The causative danger must be peculiar to the work, incidental to the character of the business, and not independent of the master-servant relationship. The event must appear to have had its origin in a risk connected with the employment and to have flowed from that source as a rational consequence.

The injury did not arise out of the claimant's employment. Under these circumstances, the act of bending over to tie the shoe was unrelated to any hazard common to the workplace. In other words, nothing in the work environment contributed to the injury. Every person who wears laced shoes must occasionally perform the act of retying the laces. The situation of a loose shoelace confronting the claimant was wholly independent of the master-servant relationship.

Award reversed, application dismissed

Case Questions

1. Should loose shoelaces or other clothing be considered workplace hazards? What if a loose shirttail became caught in a workplace conveyer dragging an employee into certain injury?
2. Would your answer to the question above be different if the employer supplied special protective gear or clothing and an accident similar to Mr. Fetterman's was caused by his reaching to tighten/straighten it?

Workers' Compensation Benefits

Workers' compensation benefits are paid out of the workers' compensation insurance fund directly to the employee or the employee's family. Typically, these benefits include medical payments and disability or death benefits. Medical payments are made for the services of physicians and nurses, hospitalization, and the use of rehabilitation equipment. Disability benefits indemnify employees for wages lost during their convalescence and usually range between one half and two thirds of the employee's normal wages.

Specific *scheduled benefits* are paid for the loss of certain bodily functions. Such benefits are established to reflect the likely extent and duration of the disability. For example, *temporary total disability* prevents the employee from working at all for a while. *Temporary partial disability* prevents the employee from performing certain activities for a while. Such disability might affect only eyesight, hearing, or the use of an arm or leg.

Permanent partial disability prevents the employee from performing certain activities for the remainder of his or her work life. Finally, *permanent total disability* prevents the employee from ever working again. Permanent disabilities include such total losses as both eyes, hands, or legs or total paralysis. It also includes less drastic losses where impairment prevents work.

Death benefits are usually limited; they are paid to the employee's next of kin to cover only burial expenses (typically about $2,000). A few states pay substantial death benefits to replace the decedent's lost wages for surviving family members. Life insurance is usually still necessary to adequately replace the employee's lost income for survivors.

Compensable Injuries

Loss of limb or bodily functions is a clear indication of compensable injury. However, some other conditions and maladies are more controversial. In early cases, occupational diseases were not covered by workers' compensation.

Physical Injuries Today, workers' compensation benefits apply to *occupational diseases* but not to the ordinary diseases of life. Ordinary diseases are contracted away from the jobsite or communicated by coworkers. The precise cause of an employee's disease is difficult to prove unless specific job hazards are positively linked to the disease. For example, it is difficult to prove that cancer is caused by occupational exposure because the disease often takes so long to develop and its cause is difficult to pinpoint. Cancer and allergic reactions are compensable only if the employee proves job-related exposure and causation.

Mental Injuries The causation of mental injuries is quite difficult to prove. Courts have been increasingly providing benefits for diseases caused by the pressures of employment. Before ordering payment, most courts require that a physical impact accompany any alleged mental injury. For example, anxiety depression resulting in numbness of hands and feet, high blood pressure, and vertigo are compensable physical injuries. These injuries must arise out of and in the course of employment, causing total and permanent incapacity due to the traumatic and repetitious activities of the job.

Mental injuries resulting from a physical blow or trauma are also covered. Should the ordinary strain of work without physical injury or eventual physical effect be covered under workers' compensation? The following case exemplifies how the courts place limits on work-related anxiety and depression claims.

Joseph Albanese's Case

389 N.E.2d 83 (Mass. 1979)
Supreme Court of Massachusetts

Joseph Albanese was a "working foreman" at Atlantic Steel Company for 20 years. After unionization in 1969, Atlantic Steel eliminated overtime pay. This often required Albanese to "go out into the shop and prod the men to expedite the work." He was also required to relay unpopular information to employees, causing considerable friction. Joseph's supervisor often reversed these decisions, undercutting Joseph's authority. After a heated discussion over one employee's claim to overtime pay, the plant manager again changed a decision to not pay overtime and told him to pay the employee anyway. Albanese immediately "became distressed, developed chest pains, nausea." He did not work thereafter and continually experienced pains, sweatiness, shortness of breath, headaches, and depression. His condition was later diagnosed as "a chronic anxiety state mixed with depression and somatized reaction and . . . neurocirculatory asthenia." Albanese's workers' compensation claim was granted by the hearing examiner, reversed by the review board, and then reinstated by the Massachusetts Superior Court.

Abrams, Justice

On appeal, the insurer does not dispute the fact that Albanese has become disabled as a result of a mental or emotional disorder, but argues that Albanese's condition is the result of gradual "wear and tear" and thus is not a compensable personal injury under the statute as interpreted by this court.

However, subsequent to the board's decision and to the proceedings in the Superior Court we held that "the term 'personal injury' also permits compensation in cases involving mental disorders or disabilities causally connected to mental trauma or shock arising 'out of the employment looked at in any of its aspects.' . . . There is no valid distinction which would preclude mental or emotional disorders caused by mental or emotional trauma from being compensable."

The insurer concedes that "the lack of a sudden episode does not of itself disqualify an employee's claim for personal injury." Instead, the insurer argues that in Albanese's case there is no evidence of shock or stress greater than ordinary and hence Albanese's disability is solely the result of general wear and tear.

Contrary to the insurer's claim of general wear and tear, the board did not find that Albanese's injury was the result of general stress or the wear and tear of working. The reviewing board found as fact both the existence of a series of specific stressful episodes and a causal nexus between Albanese's working conditions and his emotional disorder. Thus his injury is not "[a] disease of mind or body which arises in the course of employment, with nothing more, [and which] is not within the act'."

Based on the board's findings, we conclude that Albanese's injury was not the result of everyday stress or "[b]odily wear and tear resulting from a long period of hard work." Rather, it resulted from a series of identifiable stressful work-related incidents occurring over a relatively brief period of time, compared with his twenty-year employment. Therefore, Albanese is entitled to workmen's compensation for his disability.

Case Questions

1. What is a compensable or personal injury under the workers' compensation rulings?
2. Is there an exception from workers' compensation claims for the ordinary stress or wear and tear of working? Why?

Administration of Workers' Compensation

Most of the states have established a separate administrative agency to administer the workers' compensation statute. These agencies have such titles as the state *industrial commission* or the state *workers' compensation bureau* or *board*. The agencies perform legislative, executive, and judicial functions, adjudicating workers' compensation claims and managing the receipt and disbursement of funds.

Injured workers begin processing their claims by applying for benefits at the state administrative agency. Typically, a claims examiner investigates to verify the extent of the compensable injury. Most of the legitimate claims are quickly certified, with payment following almost immediately. However, if the agency disallows claims, contested cases are heard by a hearing officer in an informal proceeding. After review in the agency, novel questions and the coverage of new diseases are usually appealed through the state court system. Benefits must be paid after a claim is proved.

Commentary: The Rising Costs of Workers' Compensation

There are fundamental problems with the workers' compensation system, bringing it close to collapse in several states. Thousands of claims remain unpaid and employers' costs are skyrocketing. Premiums averaged 2.3 percent of payroll in 1990 and up to 40 percent of payroll in some dangerous industries. Some employers are relocating from high cost to lower cost states. Insurers are paying out 10 percent more in claims than they received in premiums; some insurers have gone bankrupt. Many state boards deny requests to raise premiums, pressuring some insurers to eliminate coverage. Injured employees find it harder to receive compensation promptly and completely so they are forced to litigate claims. The pressure to increase productivity forces employers to speed up the work and to introduce new and complex production systems with unknown dangers. Job-related deaths are still high in several industries: construction, mining, agriculture, fishing, forestry, transportation, and public utilities.

A proliferation of abuses by claimants also raises workers' compensation costs. For example, because claimants are generally free to use a physician of their choice, some claimants make false claims that are supported by sympathetic physicians who will readily certify a serious disability. Some workers make false claims for injuries that occur outside their jobs that are not fully covered by other insurance. Some retirees make workers' compensation claims to supplement their retirement income.

Reformers argue that more rigid and responsive state administration would speed payments, reduce uncertainty and litigation, and thereby reduce system costs. Costs might be better controlled by adapting a technique from HMOs and preferred provider health care systems: restricting the employee's right to choose any physician. Increasing employees' co-payment and deductible payments could also help minimize the "moral hazard" and thereby reduce fraud.

OCCUPATIONAL SAFETY AND HEALTH ACT

In the 1950s and 1960s, there was a growing public sentiment that workers' compensation and other incentives to reduce workplace risks were ineffective to stop industrial accidents. This pressure accelerated as new manufacturing technologies introduced new and incalculable risks. For example, microwaves, atomic energy, lasers, new chemicals, and high-speed processing machinery significantly reduced the safety of workplaces. The problem was heightened by the inadequacy or absence of workplace safety regulations in most states.

Congress reacted in 1970 by passing the **Occupational Safety and Health Act (OSHA)**. The act is intended to "insure so far as possible every working man and woman in the nation safety and healthful working conditions to preserve our human resources." The act applies to any employer with at least one employee engaged in a business affecting interstate commerce. Exemptions exist for industries regulated under other safety laws. For example, the Coal Mine Safety Act, Railway Safety Act, and Nuclear Regulatory Act regulate the unique safety risks of those industries. Domestic household employees and the religious activities of religious organizations are also exempt.

Administration of OSHA

OSHA created three new federal agencies: the Occupational Safety and Health Administration (OSHA Administration), the National Institute for Occupational Safety and Health (NIOSH), and the Occupational Safety and Health Review Commission (OSHRC). The OSHA Administration is authorized to implement the act by promulgating regulations and setting safety standards. The agency also inspects employers' premises for compliance with its safety standards. The OSHA Administration is responsible to the Department of Labor, a cabinet-level department controlled by the president.

NIOSH is responsible for conducting research into health and safety hazards and for recommending new regulations and safety or health standards to the OSHA Administration. It is also responsible for educating and training employers and employees to make the workplace safe. NIOSH is housed in and has responsibility to the Department of Health and Human Services.

OSHRC is an independent commission that conducts appeals from determinations made by the OSHA Administration. It is not directly controlled by any cabinet-level department, by another regulatory agency, or by the presidential administration. Its independence is designed to reduce bias that might be exerted by employers, employee groups, or the political system. OSHRC members are appointed by the president for staggered six-year terms and must be confirmed by the Senate.

Congress intended that the three agencies created by OSHA increase workplace safety by involving both employers and employees in the process. In addition to other responsibilities, both employers and employees must keep records and report on the procedures used to investigate and remedy job-related injuries and illnesses.

The Employer's Duty of Safety

OSHA requires employers to provide a safe work environment and prevent unreasonably hazardous conditions that arise from the employment relationship. There must also be a general recognition in the industry in question that such hazards exist and could cause serious physical harm. Finally, it must be feasible, within the limits of modern technology, to prevent harm from the hazards. OSHA establishes an employer's *general duty* to make a safe workplace. The OSHA Administration may also promulgate specific health and safety standards. These standards impose a *specific duty* on employers to modify particular workplace safety and health conditions.

Health and Safety Standards

NIOSH is responsible for conducting research into workplace hazards and eventually suggesting recommendations for "legally enforceable regulations governing conditions, practices, or operations to assure safe and healthful workplaces." The OSHA Administration is not bound to accept NIOSH suggestions and may promulgate regulations on its own initiative. In OSHA's first year of existence, Congress required the OSHA

Administration to adopt nearly 4,400 "consensus standards" drawn from existing federal regulations and from voluntary industry codes. However, many of these standards were already obsolete, leading to criticism of the OSHA Administration.

Design versus Performance Standards Throughout the 1970s, the OSHA Administration replaced the original consensus standards with more stringent *design standards,* which provide minimum specifications for safety equipment. For example, a design standard for a face mask might require construction from particular substances and a minimum thickness. However, experience shows that design standards stifle innovation, preventing the use of more effective or less costly means for achieving the same protection.

The recent trend in OSHA regulations has been to provide *performance standards,* which focus on a level of protection (end) rather than a particular device (means) to achieve the necessary protection. Performance standards would permit any type of face mask as long as the particular design sufficiently reduced the substance to be filtered.

Safety versus Health Regulations Another trend in OSHA regulations has been away from the primary focus on safety regulations and toward protecting employee health. Unsafe conditions are obvious dangers because they cause sudden and obvious disability. However, *delayed manifestation diseases* are becoming linked to low-level workplace exposure to hazardous or toxic substances. OSHA's performance standards now tend to provide increased protection from health hazards, overlapping the environmental regulations discussed in Chapter 20.

Health and Safety Rulemaking Process The OSHA Administration follows the same rulemaking procedure imposed on federal regulatory agencies discussed in Chapter 6. Typically, an investigative study conducted by NIOSH reveals a safety or health hazard. NIOSH then recommends action to the OSHA Administration. If the OSHA Administration agrees that a safety or health hazard exists, it drafts a proposed regulation and publishes it in the *Federal Register.* This begins a comment period that permits the affected industry and other interested parties to make known their views about the adequacy or feasibility of the proposed rule and that may result in revisions (see Figure 18-1 on p. 593).

Cost-Benefit Analyses All new OSHA regulatory proposals must provide societal benefits greater than the expected costs. The president's Office of Management and Budget (OMB) interacts with the OSHA Administration to assure the accuracy and relevance of this analysis. OMB also assures that OSHA rule proposals are consistent with policies of the president's administration.

It may be impossible to completely eliminate certain harmful substances from the work environment. This becomes a particularly difficult problem where the OSHA Administration, NIOSH, or commenting parties insist that there is no safe exposure level for a substance. Such a problem arose when OSHA attempted to reduce the level of occupational exposure to Benzyne, a known cancer-causing carcinogen. The OSHA Administration had set safe levels of Benzyne exposure at no more than 1 part per million (ppm). Benzyne exposures above 10 ppm had been scientifically linked to blood disorders, leukemia, and other cancers. However, there was no reliable evidence that reductions in the standard from 10 ppm to 1 ppm would result in significant health improvements. The Supreme Court held, in *Industrial Union v. American Petroleum Institute,*[4] that the

---

[4]*Industrial Union v. American Petroleum Institute,* 448 U.S. 607 (1980).

OSHA Administration must determine that a particular level of exposure to a hazardous substance posed a "significant risk" of material health impairment before imposing specific limits on exposure.

A similar controversy arose over workers' exposure to cotton dust, which can cause "brown lung" disease. In *American Textile Manufacturers Institute v. Donovan,* the Supreme Court required only a feasibility analysis rather than a more stringent cost-benefit analysis.[5] Today, Executive Order 12,291 requires a full cost-benefit analysis before most new OSHA regulations are imposed.

Variances

Employers may avoid compliance with safety and health standards if a variance is granted. An employer unable to comply immediately with a new OSHA standard may seek a *temporary variance* if more time is needed to implement the standard. To qualify, the employer must assure that all available and feasible safety measures are in place until full compliance can be obtained. A *permanent variance* may be granted to an employer that proves that alternative safety or health measures provide at least equal levels of workplace safety. Employees may contest the grant of either type of variance. Although compliance costs are considered in setting standards initially, they are not considered in granting variances.

Strict compliance may also be excused if the safety or health equipment interferes with production. Isolated instances of employee misconduct or violation of safety rules may justify temporary noncompliance with OSHA's standards. For example, some employees may refuse to wear heavy masks or protective clothing if it is uncomfortable or causes excessive perspiration.

OSHA Enforcement Procedures

The OSHA Administration enforces OSHA and the agency's own regulations by collecting information submitted by employees and employers and from on-site inspections. The OSHA Administration may issue citations for violations and assess penalties for more serious violations.

Record-Keeping and Reporting Requirements OSHA requires employers to report unsafe incidents, accidents, fatalities, lost workdays, job transfers and terminations, medical treatments, and restrictions of work. These reports must be filed with the secretary of labor. Detailed logs of all recordable incidents must also be maintained. Employers with fewer than 11 employees are exempt from record-keeping. OSHA must be notified within 48 hours following an accident if it results in a fatality or in the hospitalization of more than four employees. OSHA requires employers to post information regarding OSHA rights and obligations for all employees to review.

OSHA Inspections The OSHA Administration also conducts on-site inspections. The Supreme Court has said that only businesses with a long history of close regulation (e.g., the liquor industry, sellers of firearms, sellers of foods and drugs) may be subject to warrantless searches. Therefore, surprise OSHA inspections violate the Fourth Amendment's protection against unreasonable searches and seizures. Employers may legally

---

[5]*American Textile Manufacturers Institute v. Donovan,* 452 U.S. 490 (1981).

refuse OSHA Administration inspectors access to search their premises unless the inspectors have a search warrant issued by a federal magistrate. This principle, established in *Marshall v. Barlow's, Inc.*, was discussed in Chapter 6.[6]

The employer's worksite may be inspected if the OSHA Administration inspector has a search warrant, the violation is in "plain view," or the employer consents. Typically, the employer or one of its representatives accompanies the OSHA inspector during the visit. The OSHA inspector may confer directly with employees unless an employee representative accompanies the inspector (e.g., a union shop steward); in that case, any conferring must be with the representative.

OSHA Administration inspectors may conduct four types of investigations. First, *accident investigations* usually follow reports of fatalities and catastrophes. Second, *employee complaints* trigger one third of all investigations. Third, *programmed inspections* are conducted in industries with a history of dangerous hazards. Inspections are typically routine in industries with higher-than-average injury reports. Fourth, the OSHA Administration often conducts *follow-up inspections* where it has previously issued citations for violations of safety standards.

OSHA Citations The OSHA Administration may issue written citations and impose penalties for violations of safety standards. The penalties may involve monetary fines, and the employer is usually required to remove the violation. The area director of the OSHA Administration also issues citations and imposes penalties. These penalties may vary according to the size of the business, the employer's good faith and safety record, and the severity of the violation. Citations must be posted prominently near the location of the violation to give employees notice.

OSHA Violations and Penalties OSHA violations have several levels of seriousness, and this permits the OSHA Administration to impose different penalties. *De minimis violations* have no direct relationship to safety, so the employer is usually notified and no penalty is imposed. For example, the lack of private toilet facilities or waste containers and the availability of only used paper cups are considered *de minimis* violations.

Nonserious Violations A *nonserious violation* relates to job safety, but is unlikely to cause death or serious physical harm. A monetary penalty for nonserious violations may be levied at the discretion of the director of the OSHA Administration. Examples include a hazard of tripping due to poor housekeeping and a failure to provide instructions for the use of machinery.

Serious Violations Violations that pose a substantial probability of death or serious physical harm are *serious violations*. Repeat violations and violations that might lead to imminent danger of likely death or serious physical harm carry penalties of up to $10,000 and/or up to six months in jail. Willful repeated violations carry a $20,000 fine and up to one-year imprisonment.

Protection from Employer Retaliation Employers are forbidden to discharge or discriminate against employees who report safety violations. The secretary of labor is empowered to investigate and determine whether employer retaliation has occurred. Should an employer be required to reinstate a fired employee and give back pay or other relief to

[6]*Marshall v. Barlow's, Inc.*, 436 U.S. 307 (1978).

FIGURE 18–1 OSHA Procedures

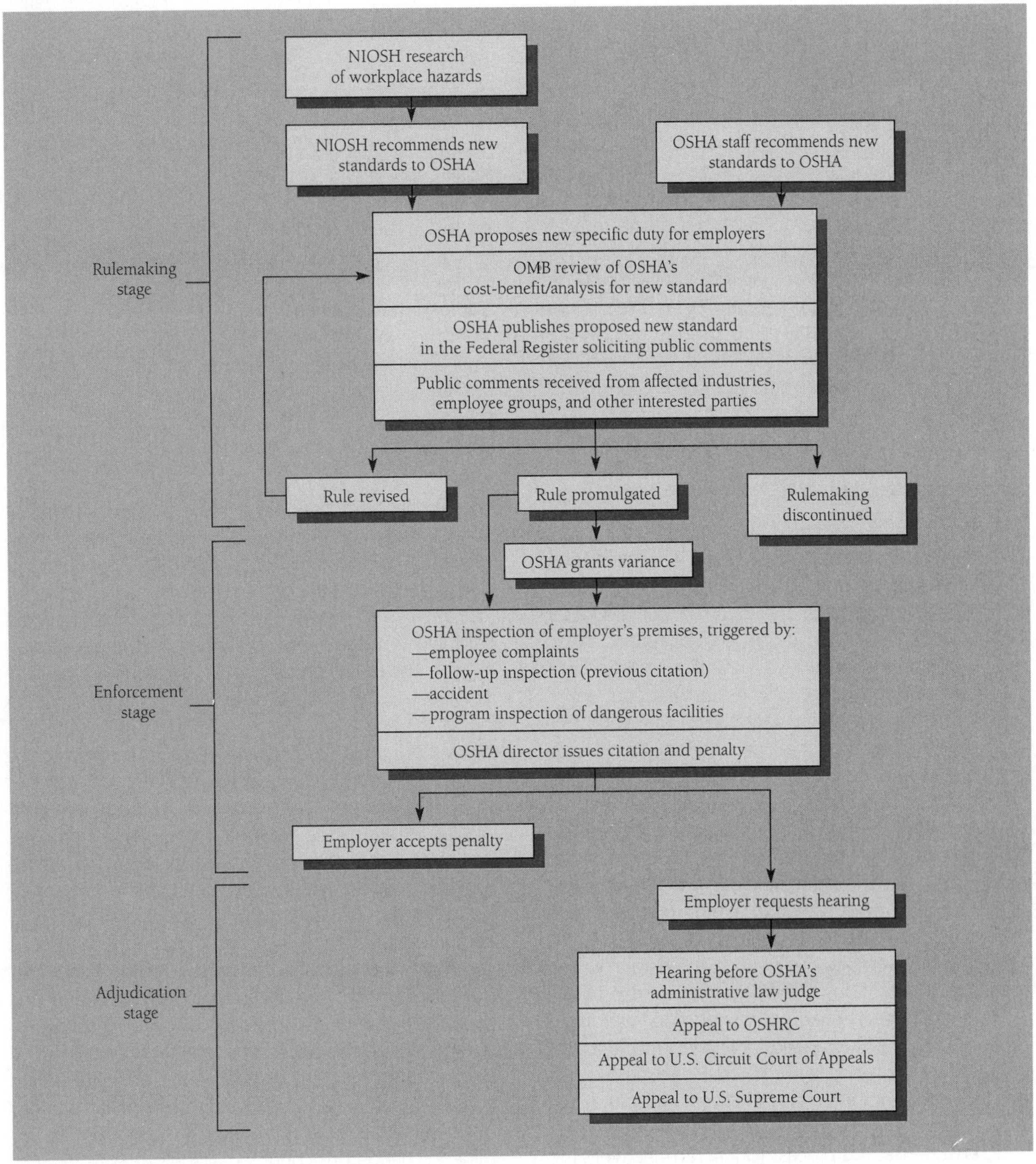

replace benefits of which a wrongfully discharged employee has been deprived? The following case illustrates how OSHA protects employees who report safety or health violations.

Whirlpool Corp. v. Marshall

445 U.S. 1 (1980)
United States Supreme Court

The secretary of labor adopted a regulation interpreting the employee retaliation law. The new regulation permitted employees to refuse an assigned task if a reasonable apprehension existed that death or serious injury would result from its performance. Two Whirlpool employees refused to perform assigned maintenance work, fearing that a wire mesh used to prevent objects from falling from an overhead conveyer was unsafe. The employees were sent home without pay for insubordination, and their refusal to work was noted on their records. The Court of Appeals reversed the district court's finding that the regulation was invalid.

Justice Stewart delivered the opinion of the Court.

The Act itself creates an express mechanism for protecting workers from employment conditions believed to pose an emergent threat of death or serious injury. Upon receipt of an employee inspection request stating reasonable grounds to believe that an imminent danger is present in a workplace, OSHA must conduct an inspection. In the event this inspection reveals workplace conditions or practices that "could reasonably be expected to cause death or serious physical harm immediately or before the imminence of such danger can be eliminated through the enforcement procedures otherwise provided by" the Act, the OSHA inspector must inform the affected employees and the employer of the danger and notify them that he is recommending to the Secretary that injunctive relief be sought. At this juncture, the Secretary can petition a federal court to restrain the conditions or practices giving rise to the imminent danger. By means of a temporary restraining order or preliminary injunction, the court may then require the employer to avoid, correct, or remove the danger or to prohibit employees from working in the area.

To ensure that this process functions effectively, the Act expressly accords to every employee several rights, the exercise of which may not subject him to discharge or discrimination. An employee is given the right to inform OSHA of an imminently dangerous workplace condition or practice and request that OSHA inspect that condition or practice. He is given a limited right to assist the OSHA inspector in inspecting the workplace and the right to aid a court in determining whether or not a risk of imminent danger in fact exists. Finally, an affected employee is given the right to bring an action to compel the Secretary to seek injunctive relief if he believes the Secretary has wrongfully declined to do so.

In the light of this detailed statutory scheme, the Secretary is obviously correct when he acknowledges in his regulation that, "as a general matter, there is no right afforded by the Act which would entitle employees to walk off the job because of potential unsafe conditions at the workplace." By providing for prompt notice to the employer of an inspector's intention to seek an injunction against an imminently dangerous condition, the legislation obviously contemplates that the employer will normally respond by voluntarily and speedily eliminating the danger. And in the few instances where this does not occur, the legislative provisions authorizing prompt judicial action are designed to give employees full protection in most situations from the risk of injury or death resulting from an imminently dangerous condition at the worksite.

As this case illustrates, however, circumstances may sometimes exist in which the employee justifiably believes that the express statutory arrangement does not sufficiently protect him from death or serious injury.

Such circumstances will probably not often occur, but such a situation may arise when (1) the employee is ordered by his employer to work under conditions that the employee reasonably believes pose an imminent risk of death or serious bodily injury, and (2) the employee has reason to believe that there is not sufficient time or opportunity either to seek effective redress from his employer or to apprise OSHA of the danger.

The regulation clearly conforms to the fundamental objective of the Act—to prevent occupational deaths and serious injuries.

The regulation thus on its face appears to further the overriding purpose of the Act, and rationally to complement its remedial scheme. In the absence of some contrary indication in the legislative history, the Secretary's regulation must, therefore, be upheld, particularly when it is remembered that safety legislation is to be liberally construed to effectuate the congressional purpose.

Case Questions

1. Would OSHA be effective if employers could threaten employees with discipline or dismissal for seeking its protection?
2. Is an employee's refusal to work under unsafe conditions the best method for discovering workplace hazards?

In recent years, the business community has leveled considerable criticism against the OSHA Administration's enforcement of OSHA. One basic problem involves the lack of efforts by employees to minimize their own exposure to risks. Employees often defeat the effectiveness of safety equipment or refuse to wear safety clothing. Improvements in the training and supervision of employees may be needed in this area. Some other countries have approached the problem by requiring the installation of state-of-the-art technology, periodic inspections by environmental engineers, the testing of exposure to toxic substances, and the training of safety personnel. Others have suggested a tax on employers for unsafe conditions.

State Occupational Safety Laws

There are numerous additional state and federal laws with an impact on safety and health conditions in the workplace. Numerous "right-to-know" laws have been enacted requiring employers to inform employees of the toxic, carcinogenic, or potentially harmful chemicals and other substances used in the workplace. The OSHA Administration has made these disclosures uniform by requiring employers to develop Material Safety Data Sheets for all of the chemicals they use. In addition, employers must post notices of the chemicals used in each facility and educate employees on safe methods of handling chemicals. OSHA funds state safety regulation programs.

There has been significant controversy over OSHA's preemption of state criminal laws. Local prosecutors in Illinois, Texas, and New York have brought criminal charges (e.g., murder, negligent homicide, assault, reckless endangerment) against high-level company officials for work-related injuries and deaths. Greater local prosecutorial activity is expected until either Congress strengthens the OSHA Administration's criminal penalties or the Supreme Court or Congress clarifies whether OSHA leaves any room for state law.

SUMMARY

Laws regulating the employment relationship began to supplement private contracts as businesses grew in size and relationships became more impersonal. With some exceptions employment is continued only at the will of both the employer and the employee.

With narrow exceptions, federal legislation now

prohibits the use of lie detector tests by the employer. The plant closing law requires employers to give employees 60 days' notice of mass layoffs or plant closings. The 60-day period may be reduced in special cases.

The Fair Labor Standards Act (FLSA) requires employers in interstate commerce to pay a minimum wage and establishes a standard 40-hour workweek. It applies only to employees, not to independent contractors or professionals. Overtime is computed at time and a half of the regular wage rate for compensable time over 40 hours per week. In response to child labor abuses that began with the industrial revolution, child labor is significantly restricted.

State unemployment compensation statutes allow employees with an established record of employment to withdraw benefits for a fixed time period unless they are not seeking employment or were fired for serious misconduct or during a strike. Employers with low employee turnover rates may pay lower premiums into state insurance funds than are paid by employers with higher turnover rates.

The social security system was developed to supplement retirees' income. Employers are required to withhold social security taxes from employees' wages and pay them to the IRS. These payments provide benefits to current retirees. Limited medical benefits are paid under Medicare to older persons even if they do not qualify for social security.

Private pension plans are a significant source of retirement income. ERISA regulates such plans by standardizing their vesting provisions, payments, contributions, and taxability. Additional retirement devices, such as Keogh plans, IRAs, and deferred payment annuities, receive special tax treatment to encourage retirement savings by working individuals.

Workers' compensation and OSHA regulations are intended to give employers an incentive to reduce workplace dangers and to compensate employees for workplace injuries. Workers' compensation is a compulsory, no-fault, employer-financed insurance system that covers the injuries of employees while they are "on the job" at the worksite. Injuries of independent contractors or employees while en route to work are excluded. Money benefits are paid to the injured employee or to the deceased employee's family for medical expenses, lost wages, loss of bodily functions, or death if the injury is clearly linked to a worksite danger. There is often too much uncertainty about the cause of physical or mental diseases for the workers' compensation system to provide benefits. State workers' compensation agencies process claims by investigating to verify the extent of the compensable injury.

The Occupational Safety and Health Act of 1970 applies to all employers in interstate commerce with at least one employee unless an exemption applies. The OSHA Administration establishes safety standards, NIOSH researches safety hazards, and the OSHRC provides an independent process for appeals from OSHA Administration determinations. OSHA regulations impose duties on both employers and employees to follow OSHA procedures and maintain a safe workplace.

The OSHA Administration sets health and safety standards on its own initiative and after NIOSH research suggests a need. New OSHA regulations have been increasingly based on performance standards that encourage innovation to achieve a given level of protection. As physical safety hazards have been eliminated, emphasis has turned to the prevention of the delayed manifestation occupational diseases. New regulations must be feasible, must be directed against verifiable and significant health risks, and must provide societal benefits greater than the costs of implementation.

The OSHA Administration may grant variances that permit employers to use alternative methods of compliance. Employers must compile detailed accident records and submit them to the OSHA Administration so that it can monitor compliance. An OSHA Administration inspector may visit the employer's worksite only if the employer consents or if the inspector has a search warrant. OSHA Administration investigations usually follow an accident or an employee complaint. Reinspections occur after citations for noncompliance have been issued and may occur regularly in certain dangerous industries. Fines and abatement orders are issued by the area directors of the OSHA Administration. OSHA violations have several levels of seriousness. Employers may not retaliate against employees who report violations.

KEY TERMS

employment-at-will, p. 570
employee privacy, p. 574
minimum wage, p. 575
unemployment compensation, p. 579

social security, p. 581
Federal Insurance Contributions Act (FICA), p. 581
pension vesting, p. 583
workers' compensation, p. 583
Occupational Safety and Health Act (OSHA), p. 588

CHAPTER EXERCISES

1. Galvcoat Metals Co. uses numerous toxic chemicals in its metal coatings business. Technicians recently discovered that applications of increased concentrations of sulfuric acid (SO_2) improved the preparation of the sheets of raw steel for the electroplating process applied by Galvcoat. However, management considered the new technique to be a "trade secret process," so it refused to disclose the higher SO_2 concentrations to employees or to provide additional protective gear as required by OSHA regulations. This failure to disclose helped to conceal why Galvcoat metals performed better than competitors' products. This enabled Galvcoat to charge higher prices for its "superior" products. However, Galvcoat paid for none of the additional safety expenses needed to protect workers from the higher concentrations of SO_2.

   Comment on the ethical and legal problems presented here.

2. Hauck sued his former employer, Sabine Pilot Service, for wrongful discharge, claiming that he was discharged for refusing to pump the bilges of the boat on which he worked. He had been told by an official of the U.S. Coast Guard that pumping bilges into the water was illegal. Sabine Pilot Service claimed that Hauck was discharged for insubordination and for refusing to swab the deck and not following through on other duties. Should Hauck be able to recover on a claim of the tort of wrongful discharge? Discuss the application of the employment-at-will doctrine. *Sabine Pilot Service, Inc. v. Hauck*, 687 S.W.2d 734 (1985).

3. TWA, a major commercial air carrier, trained all TWA flight attendants at its training academy, located in Kansas. Flight attendant positions were highly desirable, and TWA received thousands of applications for these positions each year. It carefully selected trainees from a large group of applicants. During the four-week training period, most of the trainees resided in dormitory-like accommodations located on the grounds of the training academy. They did not receive any wages from TWA at that time, but TWA did provide them with meals, lodging, and good ground transportation.

   Trainees were not permitted to work on regular commercial flights or to supplement the work of regular flight attendants until they had completed the training course. Completion of the course qualified them as flight attendants, but TWA did not guarantee that all of the successful trainees would be hired upon graduation. Were the TWA flight attendant trainees "employees" within the meaning of the Fair Labor Standards Act? *Donovan v. Transworld Airlines, Inc.*, 726 F.2d 415 (1984).

4. What qualifications must an employee meet in order to receive unemployment compensation?

5. GMAC, which provided financing for buyers of General Motors automobiles, had employees at each of its offices whose job was to collect overdue accounts and repossess cars. These employees put in long and irregular hours, and they usually worked on their own and without direct supervision. The upper management of GMAC regularly encouraged the accurate reporting of hours worked. However, lower-level supervisors set strict limits on the number of hours that could be reported. These supervisors gave the collection employees substantially more work than could be done in a 40-hour week but generally permitted them to report only 40–42 hours. On the average, the collection employees actually worked about 53 hours per week. The U.S. Department of Labor filed a suit claiming that GMAC had violated the overtime provision of the Fair Labor Standards Act. With what result, and why? *Brennan v. GMAC*, 482 F.2d 825 (1973).

6. Explain why the common law system of negligence torts imposed tremendous barriers on employee suits for injury compensation.

7. Communication Workers of America (CWA) recommended a nationwide strike of Bell Telephone in 1971. In New York State, the strike continued

for seven months. Since the state's unemployment insurance law provided no exemption for striking workers, the 38,000 striking CWA members in New York State filed for and received unemployment compensation. The amounts they received were charged back to the employer under the state's system of establishing employer contributions. Bell Telephone filed suit, claiming that the New York law had been preempted by the National Labor Relations Act. Did the National Labor Relations Act implicitly prohibit the state of New York from paying unemployment compensation to strikers? *New York Telephone Co. v. New York Department of Labor,* 440 U.S. 519 (1979).

8. A collective bargaining agreement between General Tire and the union included a supplemental unemployment benefits plan (SUB) administered by General Tire and designed to supplement unemployment insurance benefits to laid-off employees. General Tire had the right to terminate the plan when the agreement expired, provided that the assets remaining in the plan were used to pay benefits until they were exhausted. Adams and the other plaintiffs were laid-off union members who had been receiving benefits under the plan. When the collective bargaining agreement expired and the union called a strike, General Tire suspended all SUB payments. Was this a breach of its fiduciary duty? *Adams v. Rubber Co.,* 794 F.2d 164 (1986).

9. What relationship exists between workers' compensation and OSHA safety and health efforts?

10. Jane was an employee of Oxford Industries. One day, she noticed that the safety guard on the cutting machine she operated was dislocated. If her hand slipped, she could suffer a serious injury. Jane reported the matter to her foreman, but nothing was done about it. Finally, out of anger and fear, she walked off the job, refusing to work until the safety guard on the cutting machine was repaired. The company immediately fired her. Does Jane have a remedy?

Chapter 19

EQUAL EMPLOYMENT OPPORTUNITIES

KEY CONCEPTS

Most of the equal opportunity laws are based on federal statutes passed during the 1960s and 1970s. Other sources include portions of the U.S. Constitution, state law, presidential executive orders, and post–Civil War statutes.

The Equal Pay Act of 1963 prohibits unequal pay between males and females performing jobs that require equal skills, effort, and responsibility under similar working conditions.

The Civil Rights Act of 1964 prohibits employment discrimination on the basis of race, color, religion, national origin, or sex. Illegal discrimination may arise from disparate treatment, disparate impact, or a pattern or practice.

Limited discrimination is lawful if based on narrow exceptions: bona fide occupational qualification, performance on professionally developed aptitude tests, or pursuant to a valid and nondiscriminatory seniority system.

The Equal Employment Opportunity Commission (EEOC) has issued guidelines prohibiting sexual harassment in the workplace.

The EEOC enforces the antidiscrimination laws by rulemaking, investigation, and adjudication. Most EEOC complaints are settled nonjudicially through conciliation.

The Civil Rights Act of 1991 expanded some private rights to damages for unlawful discrimination and placed the burden of proving that unintentional discrimination is a business necessity on the employer.

The Americans with Disabilities Act (ADA) prohibits employment discrimination against qualified but disabled workers and requires employers to provide them reasonable accommodation and ready accessibility to the workplace.

INTRODUCTION . . . PAST, PRESENT, FUTURE

Although several constitutional provisions are aimed at preventing discriminatory treatment of U.S. citizens, considerable discrimination existed throughout the first half of the 19th century. During the Reconstruction period that followed the Civil War, the Fourteenth Amendment was adopted and Congress passed civil rights laws in 1866 and 1871. These measures were designed to correct the discriminatory abuses of the pre–Civil War period. The *Civil Rights Act of 1866* gives all persons the same right to make and enforce contracts, to sue, and to give evidence at trial. It recognizes that the full and equal benefit of all laws must be given to all people. However, it prohibits only racial discriminations; it does not specifically cover discrimination based on religion or sex. As a result, pervasive discrimination has continued through the 20th century.

The only major antidiscrimination measure that was adopted between the Reconstruction period and the 1960s was the Nineteenth Amendment, which gave women the right to vote. Evidence suggests that there is still extensive discrimination in the housing and labor markets.

Unequal opportunities and discriminatory practices in employment, promotions, working conditions, and compensation systems work against minorities and women. Some economists argue that this failure to reward productive activity misallocates labor resources and causes imperfect labor markets. In addition, it relegates potentially productive workers to less skilled jobs, leaving an important pool of talent unused. In response to the economic and moral arguments against discrimination, Congress has passed several more antidiscrimination laws since the 1960s. Today, these laws significantly affect all employment decisions of managers.

In the future, there may be additional workplace and political conflicts over how coworkers' and managers' attitudes cause discrimination. Major steps have already been taken to eliminate housing and job-entry discrimination; in the future, the more insidious stereotyping and discriminatory attitudes will be addressed. However, these sources of discrimination are difficult to prove, so the initial approaches to eliminating them may appear to unfairly favor certain minority groups and may therefore arouse resentment. Until the public willingly accepts more widespread nondiscriminatory attitudes, the effectiveness of legal controls may be limited.

OVERVIEW

This chapter focuses on federal laws relating to equal employment opportunities. The *Equal Pay Act of 1963* prohibits sexual discrimination in pay for work that requires "equal skill, effort, and responsibility." The best-known antidiscrimination law is the *Civil Rights Act of 1964,* which prohibits failing to hire or to provide housing on the basis of race, color, religion, sex, or national origin. This act effectively extends civil rights protections to a broad spectrum of categories of protected persons. The *Age Discrimination in Employment Act of 1967* extends the protections of the Equal Pay Act and the Civil Rights Act to persons between the ages of 40 and 70. The *Vocational Rehabilitation Act of 1973* extends many antidiscrimination protections to the handicapped and was substantially supplemented by the *Americans with Disabilities Act of 1990.* The *Civil Rights Act of 1991* expands the damages remedies and reverses several Supreme Court cases that had narrowed civil rights.

From time to time, the President issues *executive orders* that are administered by the *Office of Federal Contract Compliance Programs.* Some of these orders prohibit discrimination by contractors that perform work for the federal government. The unwary employer that does not comply with the antidiscrimination statutes, executive orders, and administrative agency regulations and rulings may be exposed to significant legal liability. State fair employment practice acts in approximately 45 states supplement federal laws, but their provisions are quite varied.

EQUAL PAY ACT

The Equal Pay Act amended the Fair Labor Standards Act by prohibiting unequal pay for equal work by either sex. The Equal Pay Act is enforced by the Equal Employment Opportunity Commission (EEOC). It does not apply to discrimination in hiring, promotions, or firing on the basis of sex, which is regulated by the Civil Rights Act of 1964. If one of two substantially similar jobs is held by a male and the other by a female, the employer is prohibited from paying the two employees at different rates. For this prohibition to apply, the two jobs must require "equal skill, effort, and responsibility . . . [if] performed under similar working conditions." A recurring issue under the Equal Pay Act is the content analysis of jobs. Employers must specify a *job description* for each job, so that if two jobs are substantially similar, the equality of the pay given for performing them can be determined.

Permitted Pay Differentials

The Equal Pay Act does not apply to pay differentials resulting from factors other than sex, such as the differentials that result from bona fide seniority systems, bona fide merit systems, or the quantity or quality of output. For example, *shift differentials*—pay differentials based on the time of a work shift—are usually valid. However, such differentials may be illegal if there are no shift differences in working conditions and one shift is staffed predominantly by males and another by females.

New workers involved in training programs may be rotated through several departments and perform work substantially similar to that done by workers permanently assigned to the departments. Pay differentials between such trainees and permanent workers are not illegal so long as the training programs are open equally to both sexes.

Comparable Worth From time to time courts are urged to reexamine an old theory of equal pay known as **comparable worth.** Under this theory, male and female workers who are not performing substantially equal jobs under the same working conditions may nevertheless be required to receive equal pay. The comparable worth theory arose during World War II in an effort to equalize pay. It has resurfaced because of longtime discriminatory patterns that have forced females into clerical and service positions, reserving positions of higher pay for males. Arguably, the comparable worth theory could also apply to wage comparisons based on suspect classifications other than sex.

Analyses of job classifications often indicate that two very different jobs have roughly equal levels of responsibility and difficulty. Members of one sex may predominantly hold a lower-paying job whose worth is comparable to that of another job predominantly held by members of the opposite sex. Some people insist that the courts should order equalization in the pay for two such jobs. For example, a salesperson and an administrative assistant performing different tasks may have equal responsibilities and skills. If they receive different pay for their work, a comparable worth program would adjust the pay structure to reflect the inherent equality of the two jobs.

Many economists have argued that a comparable worth system limits the free market's operations in setting prices according to the demand for particular jobs and the supply of qualified applicants. Therefore, enforcement of pay scales between different jobs could distort the allocation of resources. In *County of Washington v. Gunther,* the Supreme Court suggested that Title VII of the Civil Rights Act of 1964, not the Equal Pay Act, might form the basis for comparable worth systems if the gender-based discrimination is intentional.[1] More recently, the lower federal courts have been less receptive to the comparable worth theory. However, Canada, some states, and several local governments have comparable worth statutes for government workers. Any attempt by the state legislatures to apply the comparable worth doctrine to private employers will affect the whole employment market. Although the doctrine has not yet been firmly established, employers must be aware of its development in the courts and legislatures.

THE CIVIL RIGHTS ACT OF 1964

Title VII of the Civil Rights Act of 1964 has the greatest impact on the employment relationship of all the discrimination laws. It prohibits discrimination by employers with 15 or more employees, by unions that bargain with such employers or operate hiring halls, and by employment agencies. Title VII makes it illegal to discriminate in hiring, firing, compensation, or the terms, conditions, or privileges of employment if based on race, color, religion, national origin, or sex. Any classification of employees based on these *protected classes* is prohibited if it deprives persons in these classes of employment opportunities. Liability will attach to employers whose discrimination results in (1) disparate treatment, (2) disparate impact, (3) or a pattern or practice of discrimination.

Generally, *discrimination* is the practice of choosing or differentiating among alternatives based on distinguishable characteristics. Discrimination becomes illegal when employment decisions are based on bias or prejudice about a person's membership in a protected class. Illegal discrimination arises when applicants or employees are separated by class, constructively discharged by class (resignation prompted by harassment), paid differently by class, or subjected to different standards for personal characteristics by class (e.g., personal conduct, appearance, lifestyle).

Title VII does not require an employer to hire or promote any particular person. Of course, employers may legitimately discriminate among job applicants on the basis of their ability to perform or their prospects for success. It is important to recognize that Title VII outlaws only "discrimination" predicated on race, sex, religion, color, and national origin. Discriminations based on measurable differences in qualifications closely related to job performance are necessary, justifiable, and legal. The three theories of illegal discrimination—disparate treatment, disparate impact, and pattern or practice—are summarized in Figure 19–1.

Disparate Treatment

Title VII prohibits discriminatory policies of an employer, union, or employment agency that treat one group of employees or job applicants more favorably than a protected class. An illegal **disparate treatment** occurs when an employer intentionally conducts discriminatory hiring, promotion, or firing policies.

[1]*County of Washington v. Gunther,* 452 U.S. 161 (1981).

FIGURE 19–1

Theories of Unlawful Discrimination under Title VII of the Civil Rights Act of 1964

Discrimination Theory	Disparate Treatment Theory	Disparate Impact Theory	Pattern or Practice Theory
Statement of theory	Employer, union, or employment agency announces and/or uses intentional discriminatory policies that are more favorable to one group than to a protected class.	Employer, union, or employment agency uses job selection standards that appear neutral, yet result in a disparate impact on a protected class.	Employer, union, or employment agency's track record reveals a pattern or practice of discrimination affecting a protected class of persons rather than a specific individual.
Proof required	Intent to discriminate. Inferences are allowed from circumstantial evidence. Employment of a qualified applicant from a protected class is rejected, and job remains unfilled afterward. Burden of proof shifts to employer to justify actions.	No proof of discriminatory intent required. Adverse effect on protected class; statistical proof may be used. Employer unable to justify the employment practice as job related. Evidence of disparate treatment unavailable.	No proof of discriminatory motive required. Inference from statistical analysis: Compare the percentage of suspect class members in the employer's workforce with its percentage in job applications and among the general public. Employer's work force contains a substantially lower percentage of suspect class members than of members of other groups.
Examples	Biased hiring, firing, and promotion practices. "Blacks need not apply." "This is a man's job."	General intelligence or achievement tests covering background rather than specified job skills. Unjustified height restrictions or high school diploma requirement.	Qualified persons in the protected class deterred from applying due to employer's reputation for discrimination. Low utilization of protected class applicants. Pay differences between members of protected class and members of other groups in comparable jobs. Similar pattern or practice of discrimination by other employers.

Establishing a Prima Facie Case of Disparate Treatment

To establish a prima facie case of disparate treatment, a plaintiff must prove:

1. Membership in a protected class.
2. Qualification for the job sought.
3. Rejection despite adequate qualifications.
4. That the position remained open after the plaintiff was rejected.

Proof of such a discrimination would be easy if the employer overtly stated, for example, "blacks need not apply" or "this is a man's job." Today, overt practices are rare. Disparate treatment typically results from more subtle conduct, so courts accept inferences based on circumstantial evidence.

In a disparate treatment trial, the plaintiff must first establish a prima facie case. Once the plaintiff establishes the prima facie case (the basic elements) the burden of proof shifts to the defendant, who must prove that there was a legitimate reason for the disparate treatment. Often the plaintiff may rebut this justification by showing statistical evidence of a pattern of discrimination by the employer, which also constitutes disparate treatment. What if an employer has a mixture of legal and illegal discriminatory reasons for an employment decision? The next case illustrates the Supreme Court's analysis of such a situation.

Price Waterhouse v. Hopkins

109 S.Ct. 1775 (1989)
United States Supreme Court

Ann Hopkins, a senior manager at the Washington, D.C., office of the Price Waterhouse accounting firm was proposed by the partners in her office for a promotion to partner in 1982. However, her candidacy was held over for reconsideration to the following year and thereafter dropped. Only 7 of a total of 662 Price Waterhouse partners nationwide were women, and Hopkins was the only woman of 88 partner candidates that year. Both her supporters and opponents indicated that Hopkins was "overly aggressive, unduly harsh, difficult to work with, and impatient with staff." Ms. Hopkins was described as "macho" and "overcompensating for being a woman." She was advised to take a "course at charm school" and to walk, talk, and dress "more femininely, wear make-up, have her hair styled, and wear jewelry." Price Waterhouse claimed that the decision was based primarily on legitimate interpersonal factors. The trial court held that Price Waterhouse had unlawfully discriminated against her on the basis of sex by consciously giving credence to sexually stereotyped comments.

Justice Brennan delivered the opinion of the Court.

In passing Title VII, Congress made the simple but momentous announcement that sex, race, and national origin are not relevant to the selection, evaluation, or compensation of employees. The statute does not purport to limit the other qualities and characteristics that employers may take into account in making employment decisions. The critical inquiry in this case is whether gender was a factor in the employment decision at the moment it was made. Title VII was meant to condemn even those decisions based on a mixture of legitimate and illegitimate considerations.

To say that an employer may not take gender into account is not the end of the matter. Title VII preserved the employer's remaining freedom of choice. The employer shall not be liable if it can prove that, even if it had not taken gender into account, it would have come to the same decision. In saying that gender played a motivating part in an employment decision, we mean that, if we asked the employer at the moment of the decision what the reasons were and if we received a truthful response, one of those reasons would be that the applicant or employee was a woman. An employer who acts on the basis of the belief that a woman cannot be aggressive has acted on the basis of gender. We are beyond the day when an employer could evaluate employees by assuming or insisting that they match the stereotype associated with their group.

An employer who objects to aggressiveness in women but whose positions require this trait places women in an intolerable and impermissible Catch-22:

out of a job if they behave aggressively and out of a job if they do not. Title VII lifts women out of this bind. Price Waterhouse invited partners to submit comments; some of the comments stemmed from sexual stereotypes; the Policy Board's decision on Hopkins was an assessment of the submitted comments; and Price Waterhouse in no way disclaimed reliance on the sex-linked evaluations. The defendant may avoid a finding of liability only by proving by a preponderance of the evidence that it would have made the same decision even if it had not taken the plaintiff's gender into account. [After remand on whether Price Waterhouse would have made the same decision without considering sex stereotyping, the trial court ordered that Ms. Hopkins be made a partner.]

Case Questions

1. How can an employer avoid liability in mixed-motive decisions? What standard is used to judge how the decision was made?
2. Would it be relevant to Price Waterhouse's decision if client comments indicated that Hopkins's aggressive behavior was inappropriate or if clients requested she be replaced on their assignment?

Disparate Impact

Title VII allows the plaintiff to bring a legal action even if direct or circumstantial evidence of disparate treatment is unavailable. A violation may be found if it can be shown that a **disparate impact** resulted from the employer's hiring policies or evaluation process. Violations may result where hiring standards and employment practices fail to deal adequately with a suspect class, resulting in a disparate impact.

Sometimes the use of apparently neutral employment policies causes disparate impact. Certain achievement tests or job qualifications may appear neutral, yet cause a disparate impact on a particular class. For example, height restrictions often result in the exclusion of females or Asians. General intelligence tests often discriminate in favor of those whose background is most closely tested. Some argue that the Scholastic Aptitude Test (SAT) discriminates against blacks. Some courts have enjoined the use of allegedly biased tests in employment or admission decisions.

Unless physical requirements or general intelligence tests are directly related to necessary job qualifications, they may result in a disparate impact. Both disparate impact cases and the pattern or practice cases discussed next may be proved by statistical evidence. Usually a comparison is made between a segment of the employer's workforce and the pool of qualified applicants available for work in that segment. However, such comparisons are susceptible to error from numerous arbitrary classifications. For example, who should be placed in the pool of potential applicants for comparison with the employer's workforce? The next case illustrates how a prospective employee could be treated unfairly by an employer's use of overinclusive or underinclusive classifications.

Wards Cove Packing Co. Inc. v. Antonio

109 S.Ct. 2115 (1989)
United States Supreme Court

Wards Cove Packing operates its Alaskan salmon canneries with employees who are divided into two basic groups: (1) lower paid and unskilled "cannery jobs" held predominately by nonwhites, and (2) higher paid and skilled "noncannery jobs" held mostly by whites. Certain "cannery" employees claimed that the company violated Title VII of the Civil Rights Act of 1964 by discriminating in hiring and promotions that caused a disparate impact on nonwhites. The alleged discriminatory acts included: nepotism, rehire preferences, lack of objective hiring practices, separate hiring channels, and the practice of not promoting from within. These practices allegedly caused a racial stratification, denying nonwhite employees employment opportunities on the basis of race. The United States Court of Appeals reversed the District Court's dismissal of the employees' claims holding that once employees make out a prima facie case of disparate impact, the burden of proving that no discrimination occurred shifts to the employer. The employer then appealed to the Supreme Court.

Justice White delivered the opinion of the Court.

In holding that respondents [employees] had made out a prima facie case of disparate impact, the court of appeals relied solely on respondents' statistics showing a higher percentage of nonwhite workers in the cannery jobs and a lower percentage of such workers in the noncannery positions. Although statistical proof can alone make out a prima facie case, the Court of Appeals' ruling here misapprehends our precedents and the purposes of Title VII, and we therefore reverse.

The "proper comparison [is] between the racial composition of [the at-issue jobs] and the racial composition of the qualified . . . population in the relevant labor market." . . . With respect to the skilled noncannery jobs at issue here, the cannery work force in no way reflected "the pool of *qualified* job applicants" or the "*qualified* population in the labor force." Measuring alleged discrimination in the selection of accountants, managers, boat captains, electricians, doctors, and engineers—and the long list of other "skilled" noncannery positions found to exist by the District Court by comparing the number of nonwhites occupying these jobs to the number of nonwhites filling cannery worker positions is nonsensical. If the absence of minorities holding such skilled positions is due to a dearth of qualified nonwhite applicants (for reasons that are not petitioners' fault), petitioners' selection methods or employment practices cannot be said to have had a "disparate impact" on nonwhites.

The Court of Appeals' theory, at the very least, would mean that any employer who had a segment of his work force that was—for some reason—racially imbalanced, could be hauled into court and forced to engage in the expensive and time-consuming task of defending the "business necessity" of the methods used to select the other members of his work force. The only practicable option for many employers will be to adopt racial quotas, insuring that no portion of his work force deviates in racial composition from the other portions thereof; this is a result that Congress expressly rejected in drafting Title VII.

The Court of Appeals also erred with respect to the unskilled noncannery positions. Racial imbalance in one segment of an employer's work force does not, without more, establish a prima facie case of disparate impact with respect to the selection of workers for the employer's other positions, even where workers for the different positions may have somewhat fungible skills (as is arguably the case for cannery and unskilled noncannery workers). As long as there are no barriers or practices deterring qualified nonwhites from applying for noncannery positions, if the percentage of selected applicants who are nonwhite is not significantly less than the percentage of qualified applicants who are nonwhite, the employer's selection mechanism probably does not operate with a disparate impact on minorities. Where this is the case, the percentage of nonwhite workers found in other positions in the employer's labor force is irrelevant to the question of a prima facie statistical case of disparate impact.

Moreover, isolating the cannery workers as the potential "labor force" for skilled noncannery positions is at once both too broad and too narrow in its focus. Too broad because the vast majority of these cannery workers did not seek jobs in skilled noncannery positions; there is no showing that many of them would have done so even if none of the arguable "deterring" practices existed. Thus, the pool of cannery workers cannot be used as a surrogate for the class of qualified job applicants because it contains many persons who have not (and would not) be noncannery job applicants. Conversely, if respondents propose to use the cannery workers for comparison purposes because they represent the "qualified labor population" generally, the group is too narrow because there are obviously many qualified persons in the labor market for noncannery jobs who are not cannery workers.

[On] the question of causation the law was correctly stated by Justice O'Connor's opinion last term in *Watson v. Forth Worth Bank & Trust:*

> "[W]e note that the plaintiff's burden in establishing a prima facie case goes beyond the need to show that there are statistical disparities in the employer's work

force. The plaintiff must begin by identifying the specific employment practice that is challenged. . . . Especially in cases where an employer combines subjective criteria with the use of more rigid standardized rules or tests, the plaintiff is in our view responsible for isolating and identifying the specific employment practices that are allegedly responsible for any observed statistical disparities."

Title VII plaintiff does not make out a case of disparate impact simply by showing that, "at the bottom line," there is racial *imbalance* in the work force. As a general matter, a plaintiff must demonstrate that it is the application of a specific or particular employment practice that has created the disparate impact under attack. Such a showing is an integral part of the plaintiff's prima facie case in a disparate impact suit under Title VII.

Here, respondents have alleged that several "objective" employment practices (e.g., nepotism, separate hiring channels, rehire preferences), as well as the use of "subjective decision making" to select noncannery workers, have had a disparate impact on nonwhites.

Some will complain that this specific causation requirement is unduly burdensome on Title VII plaintiffs. But liberal civil discovery rules give plaintiffs broad access to employers' records in an effort to document their claims. Also, employers falling within the scope of the Uniform Guidelines on Employee Selection Procedures are required to "maintain . . . records or other information which will disclose the impact which its tests and other selection procedures have upon employment opportunities of persons by identifiable race, sex, or ethnic group[s]." This includes records concerning "the individual components of the selection process" where there is a significant disparity in the selection rates of whites and nonwhites. Plaintiffs as a general matter will have the benefit of these tools to meet their burden of showing a causal link between challenged employment practices and racial imbalances in the work force; respondents presumably took full advantage of these opportunities to build their case before the trial in the District Court was held. . . .

If respondents establish a prima facie case of disparate impact with respect to any of petitioners' employment practices, the case will shift to any business justification petitioners offer for their use of these practices. This phase of the disparate impact case contains two components: first, a consideration of the justifications an employer offers for his use of these practices; and second, the availability of alternate practices to achieve the same business ends, with less racial impact.

The judgment of the Court of Appeals is reversed, and the case is remanded.

Case Questions

1. What is the proper comparison of racial composition in disparate impact cases?
2. When employees make out a prima facie case of disparate impact, what further inquiries become necessary?

Although this case placed on the employee the burden of proving a specific employment practice caused a disparate impact on a particular class, the Civil Rights Act of 1991 shifted this burden to the employer. The act is discussed more fully later in this chapter.

Pattern or Practice of Discrimination

Where the employer's discrimination affects a whole class of persons rather than a specific individual, suit may be based on the **pattern or practice theory**. Evidence of such systematic discrimination is usually circumstantial and derived from statistical inference as discussed in the previous case. The employer's pattern or practice of discrimination is usually revealed by comparing the percentage of persons from a protected class in the employer's workforce with the percentage of persons from that class in the pool of available qualified applicants. It may be inferred that significantly lower percentages of employees from the protected class result from a pattern or practice of discrimination. Congress refrained from setting a definitive percentage for comparison, leaving it to the courts to establish standards on a case-by-case basis.

An employer may rebut the inference of pattern or practice discrimination with evidence of serious methodological flaws in the statistical comparison used. The *Wards*

Cove Packing case, for example, illustrates how a faulty comparison might result from the selection of an inappropriate population for comparison with the employer's workforce. The general population may contain an insufficient number of trained applicants from the protected class in question. Perhaps due to living and commuting patterns, the relevant population has a profile different from that of the employer's workforce.

If a plaintiff successfully proves that an employer is involved in a pattern or practice of discrimination, a presumption arises in favor of all job applicants in the protected class. Some of the people in that class may have been deterred from applying for jobs with the discriminating employer. A pattern or practice suit is strengthened when the plaintiff proves disparate impact or disparate treatment as evidence of the employer's discriminatory policy.

Certain personnel policies are especially likely to lead to a pattern or practice suit. These include low utilization of available minorities, disparate pay treatment of minorities or women, and disparate pay for minorities in comparable jobs. Some employers are large and influential enough to encourage other employers to mimic their pattern or practice discrimination. Such parallelism tends to broaden the disparate impact of the discrimination. If an employer with high turnover rates fails to hire available members of minorities, then EEOC guidelines suggest that there is a pattern or practice of discrimination.

Protected Classes

Title VII of the Civil Rights Act of 1964 prohibits discrimination in employment practices on the basis of membership in a protected class. A **protected class** is a demographic variable or classification of persons who have historically been subjected to discrimination in hiring. The protected classes include race, religion, national origin, and sex. An employment practice is prohibited if it discriminates against an applicant on the basis of his or her membership in a protected class and this results in disparate treatment, disparate impact, or a pattern or practice of discrimination.

Race Both the Civil Rights Act of 1866 and the Civil Rights Act of 1964 are intended to prohibit racial discrimination. Although the original focus of these acts was to prohibit discrimination against blacks, both of the acts also apply to all other races. All persons are members of a particular race, religion, or sex and have a particular national origin, so the antidiscrimination laws should apply to both whites and blacks. Thus, *reverse discrimination* may be illegal; this occurs when preference is given to members of protected classes that historically suffered discrimination. This principle was established in 1978 in a famous Supreme Court case, *Regents of the University of California v. Bakke.*[2] In that case, the University of California admitted minority applicants whose admission test scores were lower than that of Bakke, a white applicant. Reverse discrimination is discussed later in the "Affirmative Action" section.

Religion A fundamental concern addressed in the Constitution is discrimination based on religious practices and beliefs. The separation of church and state and the First Amendment freedoms of religion form a protected zone for religious beliefs. In addition, the 1964 Act prohibits employment discrimination on the basis of religion.

The term *religion* is easiest to define when it refers to standard denominations. From the standpoint of the law, however, the term also includes sets of ethically or morally

---

[2]*Regents of the University of California v. Bakke,* 438 U.S. 265 (1978).

based beliefs that are sincerely held. Thus, in addition to protecting the traditional religions—Christianity, Judaism, Islam, Buddhism, and Hinduism—Title VII protects such beliefs as atheism and agnosticism.

A recurring problem in religious discrimination cases is the extent of an employer's *accommodation* for religious observance by employees. Where an employee's religious practices tend to interfere with the employer's business, a delicate balance must be drawn between hardships on the business and hardships on the employee's beliefs. Where an employer convincingly demonstrates that accommodating an employee's religious beliefs would impose undue hardship on the business, discrimination on the basis of religion is permitted. How can an employee's observance of the Sabbath be reconciled with a union's seniority system and an employer's need for 24-hour shift schedules? The following case illustrated this problem.

Trans World Airlines, Inc. v. Hardison

432 U.S. 63 (1977)
United States Supreme Court

Hardison worked for TWA maintenance, which operated 24 hours a day. The union collective bargaining agreement gave the most senior employees some choice of job and shift assignments. Hardison used his seniority to opt out of work on Saturday, his Sabbath. However, his seniority dropped after his transfer to another department, forcing him to work Saturdays. TWA discharged Hardison after he refused to do so. Hardison sued for an injunction under Title VII, claiming that the discharge constituted unlawful religious discrimination. Both the trial court and the Court of Appeals agreed with Hardison; TWA appealed to the Supreme Court.

Justice White delivered the opinion of the Court.

The Court of Appeals held that TWA had not made reasonable efforts to accommodate Hardison's religious needs under the 1967 EEOC guidelines in effect at the time the relevant events occurred. In its view, TWA had rejected three reasonable alternatives, any one of which would have satisfied its obligation without undue hardship. First, within the framework of the seniority system, TWA could have permitted Hardison to work a four-day week, utilizing in his place a supervisor or another worker on duty elsewhere. That this would have caused other shop functions to suffer was insufficient to amount to undue hardship in the opinion of the Court of Appeals. Second—according to the Court of Appeals, also within the bounds of the collective-bargaining contract—the company could have filled Hardison's Saturday shift from other available personnel competent to do the job, of which the court said there were at last 200. That this would have involved premium overtime pay was not deemed an undue hardship. Third, TWA could have arranged a "swap between Hardison and another employee either for another shift or for the Sabbath days." In response to the assertion that this would have involved a breach of the seniority provisions of the contract, the court noted that it had not been settled in the courts whether the required statutory accommodation to religious needs stopped short of transgressing seniority rules, but found it unnecessary to decide the issue because, as the Court of Appeals saw the record, TWA had not sought, and the union had therefore not declined to entertain, a possible variance from the seniority provisions of the collective-bargaining agreement. The company had simply left the entire matter to the union steward who the Court of Appeals said "likewise did nothing."

We disagree with the Court of Appeals in all relevant respects. It is our view that TWA made reasonable efforts to accommodate and that each of the Court of Appeals' suggested alternatives would have been an undue hardship within the meaning of the statute as construed by the EEOC guidelines.

It appears to us that the [seniority] system itself represented a significant accommodation to the needs, both religious and secular, of all of TWA's employees. As will become apparent, the seniority system represents a neutral way of minimizing the number of occasions when an employee must work on a day that he would prefer to have off. Additionally, recognizing that weekend work schedules are the least popular, the company made further accommodation by reducing its work force to a bare minimum on those days.

Any employer who, like TWA, conducts an around-the-clock operation is presented with the choice of allocating work schedules either in accordance with the preferences of its employees or by involuntary assignment. Insofar as the varying shift preferences of its employees complement each other, TWA could meet its manpower needs through voluntary work scheduling.

It was essential to TWA's business to require Saturday and Sunday work for at least a few employees even though most employees preferred those days off. Allocating the burdens of weekend work was a matter for collective bargaining. In considering criteria to govern this allocation, TWA and the union had two alternatives: adopt a neutral system, such as seniority, a lottery, or rotating shifts; or allocate days off in accordance with the religious needs of its employees. TWA would have had to adopt the latter in order to assure Hardison and others like him of getting the days off necessary for strict observance of their religion, but it could have done so only at the expense of others who had strong, but perhaps nonreligious, reasons for not working on weekends. There were no volunteers to relieve Hardison on Saturdays, and to give Hardison Saturdays off, TWA would have had to deprive another employee of his shift preference at least in part because he did not adhere to a religion that observed the Saturday Sabbath.

Title VII does not contemplate such unequal treatment. The repeated, unequivocal emphasis of both the language and the legislative history of Title VII is on eliminating discrimination in employment, and such discrimination is proscribed when it is directed against majorities as well as minorities.

To require TWA to bear more than a *de minimis* cost in order to give Hardison Saturdays off is an undue hardship. Like abandonment of the seniority system, to require TWA to bear additional costs when no such costs are incurred to give other employees the days off that they want would involve unequal treatment of employees on the basis of their religion. By suggesting that TWA should incur certain costs in order to give Hardison Saturdays off, the Court of Appeals would in effect require TWA to finance an additional Saturday off and then to choose the employee who will enjoy it on the basis of his religious beliefs. While incurring extra costs to secure a replacement for Hardison might remove the necessity of compelling another employee to work involuntarily in Hardison's place, it would not change the fact that the privilege of having Saturdays off would be allocated according to religious beliefs.

Case Questions

1. What kind of accommodations could be made to permit employees' observance of religious holidays?
2. How much economic hardship must an employer undergo to provide religious accommodation?
3. How does the collective bargaining agreement balance employer economic hardship against employee religious accommodation?

National Origin Discrimination based on the country in which a person was born or from which the person's forebears came is *national origin* discrimination. Refusing to hire persons whose surnames are typical of a particular national origin is an example of such discrimination. It is sometimes legal for employers to indirectly discriminate against aliens or noncitizens. For example, some jobs may require fluency in English, particularly those involving communication with customers, suppliers, or fellow employees. However, if fluency in English is not required by business necessity, then making it a qualification may be prohibited if this has an adverse impact on certain groups, such as Hispanics.

Sex It is illegal to discriminate on the basis of sex. This prohibition was originally designed to correct the stereotypical societal roles of the sexes, which tended to discriminate against females. However, the prohibition protects both females and males. Although the Nineteenth Amendment granted women voting rights in 1919, women have made other significant advances only recently. These advances probably result from several factors: (1) the Civil Rights Act of 1964, (2) the evolution of the economy from a manufacturing base to a service base, and (3) a blurring of the distinctions between sex roles. A clear trend of the 20th century has been the enlargement of the economic activities of women. Today, women comprise approximately 40 percent of the workforce.

Pregnancy Discrimination. Congress passed the Pregnancy Discrimination Act in 1978 to assure women of protection against employment discrimination during pregnancy. Over 70 percent of all women who become pregnant were working during that time; half return to work after the newborn reaches three months of age and almost three-fourths return by the child's first birthday. The act prohibits employers from requiring that pregnant employees take leaves of absence if they are still qualified to do the job. Pregnancy leaves may not be treated differently from other temporary disability leaves. Employers may not specify the length of postdelivery leaves of absence. Pregnant women may not be denied a promotion or job assignment on the basis of their pregnancy. The act applies to both married and unmarried employees and to both females and males. For example, if the employer provides family medical coverage, it cannot provide lesser pregnancy benefits to spouses of male employees than are provided to female employees.

Fetal Protection Policies. In more hazardous jobs, employers are becoming concerned that pregnant employee exposure to toxic substances or radiation could lead to liability for infertility, miscarriages, or birth defects. Some employers have reacted defensively by refusing employment or terminating the jobs of women of child-bearing age. However, in *International Union v. Johnson Controls* the Supreme Court found that such practices were discriminatory on the basis of sex.[3] Unfortunately, this places a substantial and uncertain burden on employers to discover and monitor the workplace for numerous toxic agents, to inform employees, and to undertake costly protective measures. Employers' potential liability for such injuries is still incalculable yet potentially substantial.

Sex-Plus Discrimination. *Sex-plus discrimination* occurs when an employer requires additional qualifications of one sex but not of the other. For example, one airline required that female flight attendants be unmarried, yet hired married male flight attendants, an illegal sex-plus discrimination. Similarly, permitting one sex to retire earlier, smoke on the job, or receive desirable overseas assignments while denying such rights to employees of the other sex is illegal discrimination.

Age Discrimination on the basis of an employee's age is not a prohibited activity under Title VII, but the Age Discrimination in Employment Act of 1967 was amended in 1978 to protect persons between the ages of 40 and 70 from some forms of age discrimination. The act is enforced by the EEOC. It applies to both public and private employers of 20 or more employees. Numerous age discrimination claims have been brought by middle-aged professional white males often dismissed in favor of equally qualified but lower paid younger workers.

Some employers prefer younger workers to older ones because seniority systems tend to raise wage costs with age. Some employers insist on the perceived strength and appearance of younger workers. However, researchers find that older workers usually have more experience and may be more loyal than younger workers. Where an employer imposes physical fitness standards that are directly related to job activities, a pattern or practice of discrimination against older workers may be justified. For example, where public safety is involved, performance tests may be used even if this results in the hiring of fewer persons over 40 (e.g., as bus drivers, pilots, fire fighters, or police officers).

---

[3] *International Union v. Johnson Controls*, 111 S.Ct. 1196 (1991).

Although it once seemed justifiable to require all employees to retire sometime between the ages of 65 and 70, federal law now prohibits this. Employees in policy-making positions who have extensive employer-financed pension benefits, however, may be forced to retire by age 70.

Handicaps and Disabilities Title VII did not originally include handicapped workers as a protected class. In 1973, however, Congress passed the Vocational Rehabilitation Act, which requires employers that receive federal contracts to consider handicapped job applicants. Employers covered by the act must consider hiring a handicapped applicant if a job can be performed after a *reasonable accommodation* has been made, permitting the minimum level of performance. Note that employers are not required to hire unqualified handicapped workers.

Handicaps are physical or mental impairments that substantially limit one or more of a person's major life activities. Handicaps that result from diabetes, epilepsy, deafness, disfigurement, heart disease, cancer, retardation, blindness, paraplegia, quadriplegia, alcoholism, or drug abuse are protected by the act. So long as a handicap does not adversely affect successful job performance, the employer may not take it into consideration in offering employment. For example, persons with communicable diseases may be "handicapped" under the Vocational Rehabilitation Act and receive its protections. In *School Board of Nassau County Florida v. Arline,* Gene Arline was discharged from her position as a school teacher after her inactive tuberculosis again became active.[4] The Supreme Court held that because the risk of transmitting the disease was slight, Arline was still qualified as a teacher. Employers must make reasonable accommodation for diseased employees to continue employment. Courts have only started to deal with the many difficult questions raised by discrimination against AIDS victims.

The **Americans with Disabilities Act of 1990** (ADA) expands the coverage of the Rehabilitation Act to most private employers. The definition of *disability* is broadened to include additional mental and physical handicaps. The ADA makes all Title VII remedies and procedures applicable to persons with disabilities. This means discrimination in employment decisions based on an applicant or employee's disability is prohibited. Only valid tests or measures of performance directly relevant to the particular job tasks may be considered.

The ADA also imposes a duty on employers and operators of public facilities to provide reasonable accommodation to the disabled; employers must make work stations usable by handicapped employees so long as no undue hardship is imposed. Operators of public facilities such as motels, hotels, restaurants, theaters, passenger trains and busses, and retail stores must ensure that their premises accommodate the disabled with reasonable access and use. Although many firms have made these accommodations without great cost, some critics claim that the ADA may cost U.S. businesses $20 million per year during the early transition years.

ETHICAL DILEMMAS IN EMPLOYMENT DISCRIMINATION

Is it ethical for a manger to permit personal prejudices or preferences to influence promotion or hiring decisions? Discrimination in promotion or hiring poses ethical dilemmas because managers must use their personal discretion. Decisions based on conflicts between the manager's

[4]*School Board of Nassau County Florida v. Arline,* 480 U.S. 273 (1987).

personal bias and the optimal use of human resources based on past and expected performance create an ethical problem. Most employees expect employment decisions to be based on merit and not on the employee's race, color, national origin, sex, religion, handicap, or age. Equality of opportunity is the essence of fairness as set out in the Declaration of Independence, the Constitution, and a number of constitutional amendments, including the Bill of Rights.

Another ethical issue has emerged from affirmative action programs. Some statutes and labor union contracts require hiring and promotion decisions to bring minority participation into balance with the overall population. Many opponents claim that these are reverse discrimination quotas. Is it ethical to correct the discriminatory abuses of many years in a much shorter time span? Does affirmative action redress past wrongs, or does it unfairly treat the qualified applicants who are not selected?

Statutory Exceptions to Title VII

There are three major statutory exceptions to prohibited discrimination under Title VII. These exceptions permit employers to discriminate against employees on the basis of sex, age, national origin, and religion, and sometimes on the basis of race. The exceptions are: (1) bona fide occupational qualification, (2) professionally developed aptitude tests, and (3) valid nondiscriminatory seniority systems.

Bona Fide Occupational Qualification The first major statutory exception to Title VII permits an employer to discriminate where religion, national origin, or sex is a **bona fide occupational qualification** (BFOQ). Discrimination is permitted if an applicant's membership in one of these protected classes is a **business necessity**, where employment of persons from other groups would undermine the business. The employer must prove that hiring persons outside the BFOQ class entails more than mere inconvenience. Race discrimination is never justified by a BFOQ.

Religious institutions may validly require that candidates for certain jobs have certain religious characteristics. For example, churches may hire only ordained ministers and kosher butcheries may require Jewish butchers. Female models may be required to display women's fashions. Fluency in a particular language may be necessary for tour guides or for persons working with the public or with coworkers.

BFOQs are not granted easily by the courts, and the employer must show absolute business necessity to invoke these exceptions. For example, airlines may not insist on female flight attendants even though females may be superior to males in providing reassurance to anxious passengers, giving courteous personalized service, or making flights more pleasurable. Similarly, the preference of gourmet restaurant customers for male waiters does not justify a BFOQ for males only. Ethnic restaurants may not insist on waiters or waitresses of a particular national origin by arguing that this makes for a better ambience.

A valid BFOQ requires female locker room attendants in a female exercise club. By contrast, it is discriminatory to exclude female sportswriters from the male locker rooms of professional sports teams. This is probably because sportswriters spend only short times in the locker room while nearly all locker room attendants' time is spent there.

Professionally Developed Ability Tests The second major exception to the prohibitions of Title VII permits employers to discriminate on the basis of an applicant's performance on professionally developed ability tests. The employer may require certain education qualifications or require demonstration of the skills needed on the job. These qualifications must be directly related to the job and constitute a business necessity. The qualifications or tests must be validated as accurate and reliable predictors of job performance. These requirements have made it difficult for employers to use tests that are not scientifically designed or have not been proven to offer direct evidence of successful job performance.

Disparate impact analysis and the necessity of validating qualification tests were originally established in *Griggs v. Duke Power Co.*[5] That case invalidated the requirement that janitorial workers possess a high school diploma or pass an intelligence test. The Wonderlick Aptitude test used by the employer tended to reward the experiences of whites over blacks. The test had no bearing on success in the janitorial job in question but only to a generally "intelligent work force." As a result of the *Griggs* case, today tests must be validated as significantly related to successful job performance. Tests that disqualify members of a protected class at a rate substantially higher than the rate at which they disqualify other persons may not be used unless the test's validity is established, a complex task for industrial psychologists.

The EEOC has issued guidelines to assist employers in designing valid tests. Tests that have an adverse impact on a protected class must be validated by any one of three test validation methods. The first requires that *criterion validity* be established. Tests with criterion validity demonstrate a strong statistical relationship between test results and observed job performance. *Content validity* exists when the test contains a representative sample of the job tasks that are part of the job description. *Construct validity* exists when the test measures the characteristics that are considered useful on the job. For example, a typing test would exhibit both criterion and content validity for a typist's position. The test would identify good typists when typing is the primary job activity. Construct validity might exist for a test to establish a police officer's emotional stability or leadership ability. A psychological test that demonstrates these traits might serve this purpose.

The EEOC guidelines require employers to publish *job descriptions* that carefully catalog the tasks required for each job. The employer may use only tests that validly discriminate between applicants who can successfully accomplish the tasks listed in a job description. This restriction leads to a more careful analysis of job requirements and to greater precision in specifying job characteristics.

Seniority System The third major Title VII exception permits job discrimination pursuant to a bona fide seniority system if it is not designed to discriminate. In decisions to lay off, promote, or give merit raises, employers may legitimately discriminate in favor of more senior employees if the union contract includes a seniority provision. Such provisions are intended to eliminate favoritism and permit the employer to retain its more experienced employees.

Some seniority systems may tend to perpetuate the effects of discrimination because the newest workers were typically hired under conditions of less discrimination than existed when many of the older workers were hired. During times of economic downturn, more recently hired workers are laid off first even though they represent higher percentages of protected class members. As a result, seniority systems tend to frustrate the goals of the antidiscrimination laws. How should the antidiscrimination laws and the goals of the National Labor Relations Act be reconciled? The following case illustrates that bona fide seniority systems prevail over discrimination laws.

---

[5] *Griggs v. Duke Power Co.*, 401 U.S. 424 (1971).

International B'hd of Teamsters v. United States

431 U.S. 324 (1977)
United States Supreme Court

The United States brought suit against the Teamsters Union and a trucking company employer, alleging a pattern or practice of discrimination against blacks and persons with Spanish surnames. These persons were hired in lower-paying and less desirable driving jobs than those of the long-haul and over-the-road drivers. The collective bargaining agreement between the employer and the Teamsters provided for a seniority system that perpetuated and locked in the effects of past discrimination. The district court ordered a complex subsectioning of the labor force to reduce this discrimination. The Court of Appeals reversed the district court's decision, eliminating the new seniority system. Instead, it gave minority workers retroactive seniority to blacks and Hispanics to secure the better jobs. The union appealed to the Supreme Court.

Justice Stewart delivered the opinion of the Court.

The primary purpose of Title VII was "to assure equality of employment opportunities and to eliminate those discriminatory practices and devices which have fostered racially stratified job environments to the disadvantage of minority citizens." To achieve this purpose, Congress "proscribe[d] not only overt discrimination but also practices that are fair in form, but discriminatory in operation." Thus, the Court has repeatedly held that a prima facie Title VII violation may be established by policies or practices that are neutral on their face and in intent but that nonetheless discriminate in effect against a particular group.

Were it not for § 703 (h), the seniority system in this case would seem to fall under the *Griggs* rationale. The heart of the system is its allocation of the choicest jobs, the greatest protection against layoffs, and other advantages to those employees who have been line drivers for the longest time. Where, because of the employer's prior intentional discrimination, the line drivers with the longest tenure are without exception white, the advantages of the seniority system flow disproportionately to them and away from Negro and Spanish-surnamed employees who might by now have enjoyed those advantages had not the employer discriminated before the passage of the Act. This disproportionate distribution of advantages does in a very real sense "operate to 'freeze' the status quo of prior discriminatory employment practices."

Although a seniority system inevitably tends to perpetuate the effects of pre-Act discrimination in such cases, the congressional judgment was that Title VII should not outlaw the use of existing seniority lists and thereby destroy or water down the vested seniority rights of employees simply because their employer had engaged in discrimination prior to the passage of the Act. . . .

The seniority system in this litigation is entirely bona fide. It applies equally to all races and ethnic groups. To the extent that it "locks" employees into non-line-driver jobs, it does so for all. The city drivers and servicemen who are discouraged from transferring to line-driver jobs are not all Negroes or Spanish-surnamed Americans; to the contrary, the overwhelming majority are white. The placing of line drivers in a separate bargaining unit from other employees is rational, in accord with the industry practice, and consistent with National Labor Relations Board precedent. It is conceded that the seniority system did not have its genesis in racial discrimination, and that it was negotiated and has been maintained free from any illegal purpose. In these circumstances, the single fact that the system extends no retroactive seniority to pre-Act discriminates does not make it unlawful.

Because the seniority system was protected by § 703 (h), the union's conduct in agreeing to and maintaining the system did not violate Title VII. On remand, the District Court's injunction against the union must be vacated.

Case Questions

1. How could a seniority system have a discriminatory effect?
2. Does the Civil Rights Act permit seniority systems that might arguably have a discriminatory effect?
3. How can a seniority system be designed to avoid a claim of discrimination?

Sexual Harassment

Title VII does not specifically outlaw **sexual harassment**. However, making submission to sexual harassment a condition of employment may be prohibited as discriminatory. Due to the difficulties in distinguishing between nonoffensive social gestures and unlawful sexual harassment, it can be hard to fairly judge behavior in this area. If an employee has been promoted or given pay raises as the result of sexual relations with a supervisor, then an unlawful sexual harassment has caused discrimination on the basis of sex. Employees who quit a job as the result of sexual harassment may also maintain an action as a *constructive discharge* on the basis of sexual harassment.

The EEOC has issued guidelines on sexual harassment. These apply the general principles of Title VII to employers and supervisors irrespective of whether the sexually harassing acts are authorized. An employee experiences harassment when unwelcome sexual advances are encountered, requests for sexual favors are received, or verbal or physical conduct of a sexual nature is received. If the surrounding circumstances either explicitly or implicitly make submission to the sexual advances a term or condition of employment, the action is illegal. This is the so-called quid pro quo sexual harassment. A right of action arises if an employee is not granted a promotion or a pay raise because a less qualified person who granted sexual favors was promoted instead.

Even less blatant actions may constitute sexual harassment. Sexual innuendos that create an intimidating, offensive, or "hostile working environment" may be prohibited. In *Meritor Savings Bank v. Vinson*, a bank employee repeatedly submitted to her supervisor's sexual advances out of fear of losing her job.[6] Although the employer had a policy against sexual harassment and there was a grievance procedure, the Supreme Court found that a sexually harassing atmosphere existed. Employers that know or should know about the sexually harassing acts of employees may be held responsible and liable for damages if they fail to take appropriate corrective action.

The EEOC regards prevention as the best way to eliminate sexual harassment and encourages employers to take all necessary steps to sensitize employees to the problem; many firms conduct seminars or discussion groups on sexual harassment or use video enactments of sexually harassing behavior. How should an employer be required to "unpoison" a work atmosphere affected by sexual harassment? The following case illustrates how sexual insults may be harassing and the employer ordered to remedy the situation.

Bundy v. Jackson

641 F.2d 934 (D.C. Cir. 1981)
U.S. Circuit Court of Appeals

Sandra Bundy served the District of Columbia Department of Corrections as a vocational rehabilitation specialist, finding jobs for former criminal offenders. On numerous occasions, Bundy received sexual advances from her supervisors. For example, Burton continually called her into his office, requesting that she spend the workday afternoon with him at his apartment and asking about her sexual interests. Gainey made sexual advances and asked her to join him at a motel and in the Bahamas. When she reported these events to Swain, her supervisor, he dismissed her complaints, saying, "Any man in his right mind would want to rape you." After these events, Bundy's supervisors began

[6] *Meritor Savings Bank v. Vinson*, 477 U.S. 57 (1986).

to criticize her performance. She had never received such criticism previously. Her supervisors created the impression that they were impeding her promotion because she had offended them by resisting their advances.

Wright, Chief Judge

We thus have no difficulty inferring that Bundy suffered discrimination on the basis of sex. Moreover, we have no difficulty ascribing the harassment—the "standard operating procedure"—to Bundy's employer, the agency. Although Delbert Jackson himself appears not to have used his position as Director to harass Bundy, an employer is liable for discriminatory acts committed by supervisory personnel.

Here, however, Delbert Jackson and other officials in the agency who had some control over employment and promotion decisions had full notice of harassment committed by agency supervisors and did virtually nothing to stop or even investigate the practice.

We thus readily conclude that Bundy's employer discriminated against her on the basis of sex. What remains is the novel question whether the sexual harassment of the sort Bundy suffered amounted by itself to sex discrimination with respect to the "*terms, conditions, or privileges of employment.*" Numerous cases find Title VII violations where an employer created or condoned a substantially discriminatory work *environment,* regardless of whether the complaining employees lost any tangible job benefits as a result of the discrimination.

Bundy's claim on this score is essentially that "conditions of employment" include the psychological and emotional work environment—that the sexually stereotyped insults and demeaning propositions to which she was indisputably subjected and which caused her anxiety and debilitation, illegally poisoned that environment.

The relevance of these "discriminatory environment" cases to sexual harassment is beyond serious dispute. Racial or ethnic discrimination against a company's minority clients may reflect no intent to discriminate directly against the company's minority employees, but in poisoning the atmosphere of employment it violates Title VII. Sexual stereotyping through discriminatory dress requirements may be benign in intent, and may offend women only in a general, atmospheric manner, yet it violates Title VII. Racial slurs, though intentional and directed at individuals, may still be just verbal insults, yet they too may create Title VII liability. How then can sexual harassment, which injects the most demeaning sexual stereotypes into the general work environment and which always represents an intentional assault on an individual's innermost privacy, not be illegal?

The employer can thus implicitly and effectively make the employee's endurance of sexual intimidation a "condition" of her employment. The woman then faces a "cruel trilemma." She can endure the harassment. She can attempt to oppose it, with little hope of success, either legal or practical, but with every prospect of making the job even less tolerable for her. Or she can leave her job, with little hope of legal relief and the likely prospect of another job where she will face harassment anew.

The Final Guidelines of Sexual Harassment in the Workplace (*Guidelines*) issued by the Equal Employment Opportunity Commission on November 10, 1980, offer a useful basis for injunctive relief in this case. Those Guidelines define sexual harassment broadly:

> Unwelcome sexual advances, requests for sexual favors, and other verbal or physical conduct of a sexual nature constitute sexual harassment when (1) submission to such conduct is made either explicitly or implicitly a term or condition of an individual's employment, (2) submission to or rejection of such conduct by an individual is used as the basis for employment decisions affecting such individual, or (3) such conduct has the purpose or effect of unreasonably interfering with an individual's work performance or creating an intimidating, hostile, or offensive work environment.

The Guidelines go on to reaffirm that an employer is responsible for discriminatory acts of its agents and supervisory employees with respect to sexual harassment just as with other forms of discrimination, regardless of whether the employer authorized or knew or even should have known of the acts, and also remains responsible for sexual harassment committed by nonsupervisory employees if the employer authorized, knew of, or should have known of such harassment. The general goal of these Guidelines is *preventive.* An employer may negate liability by taking "immediate and appropriate action."

Applying these Guidelines to the present case, we believe that the Director of the agency should be ordered to raise affirmatively the subject of sexual harassment with all his employees and inform all employees that sexual harassment violates Title VII of the Civil Rights Act of 1964, the Guidelines of the EEOC, the express orders of the Mayor of the District of Columbia, and the policy of the agency itself. The Director should also establish and publicize a scheme whereby harassed employees may complain to the Director immediately and confidentially. The Director should promptly take all necessary steps to investigate and correct any harassment, including warnings and appropriate discipline directed at the offending party, and should generally develop other means of preventing harassment within the agency.

Case Questions

1. What factors might create an atmosphere of coercive sexual harassment?
2. What is the legal result of the creation of a discriminatory environment?
3. What duties do the EEOC guidelines impose on employers and supervisors in regard to sexual harassment?

ETHICAL DILEMMAS INVOLVING SEXUAL HARASSMENT

Blatant forms of sexual harassment pose ethical dilemmas. Sexual harassment clearly arises if supervisors abuse their positions to gain sexual favors from subordinates. Requests for such favors are usually made under the implied or overt threat that the supervisor will make adverse promotion, hiring, or firing decisions unless the subordinate complies with them. Hearings on the confirmation of Supreme Court Justice Clarence Thomas exposed the disparity between male and female perceptions about what sexual harassment is and how it tips the balance of power to the harasser.

Despite the appearance of clear prohibitions, there is much ambiguity in less clear-cut cases. For example, norms have only begun to emerge concerning the extent to which joking behavior leads to the creation of a chilling and harassing work atmosphere. What kinds of behavior should expose firms and supervisors to damage liability? What "tasteless" behaviors are serious enough to be unethical? Are there workable standards for identifying a chilling atmosphere? Are such standards generally recognized or capable of precise measurement? Any form of discrimination that is not based on clear performance measures may be unethical. Wherever a supervisor abuses a position of authority to make decisions that are based on the supervisor's biases but are unconnected with performance and economic efficiency, an ethical dilemma arises.

ENFORCEMENT OF THE ANTIDISCRIMINATION LAWS

The **Equal Employment Opportunity Commission** (EEOC) was created by the Civil Rights Act of 1964 and was granted additional powers by the Equal Opportunity Act of 1972 and the ADA in 1990. The EEOC may investigate, conciliate, and litigate grievances filed by existing and prospective employees who claim violation of the various employment discrimination laws. It is also authorized to issue rules implementing the antidiscrimination laws. Approximately 45 states have similar fair employment practice laws with widely varying provisions. They typically establish a state Fair Employment Practices Commission with powers paralleling those of the EEOC.

Record-Keeping Requirements

The EEOC requires record-keeping and disclosure to provide evidence for pattern or practice and disparate impact suits. Employers, union, and employment agencies covered by the record-keeping regulations must keep biographical and demographic records concerning all applicants for new positions and concerning promotions, demotions, transfers, layoffs, and pay rate changes.

These records must be made available whenever an employment discrimination suit arises. Each year, employers must audit their minority populations. A notice must be posted describing the various rights available under Title VII so that employees know how to pursue these rights.

EEOC Investigations

An EEOC right of action is first triggered when an aggrieved employee perceives that an unlawful discrimination has occurred. If the state in which the alleged discrimination occurred has an antidiscrimination statute, the aggrieved employee must initially file charges with the state agency. If the state agency takes no action for 60 days, the employee may file charges with the federal EEOC. EEOC filings must be made within 180 days after the discriminatory act or within 300 days if the state antidiscrimination law requires a local filing first. This is a shorter statute of limitations than exists for most other legal rights.

The EEOC must notify the employer of the discrimination charges and then investigate the incident by visiting the employer's premises and questioning the employer and employees. It may subpoena any documents relevant to the investigation. If reasonable cause exists for believing that a Title VII violation has occurred, the EEOC then notifies the employer of its intent to seek a form of mediated settlement known as *conciliation.* Otherwise, the EEOC dismisses the charges and advises the aggrieved employee that it will not pursue them but that the employee may proceed. This "right to sue letter" permits the employee to file suit within the next 90 days in federal district court or state court.

Conciliation

Most EEOC complaints are settled by the alternative dispute resolution process known as *conciliation.* Typically, a confidential proceeding is conducted between the EEOC and the employer in the absence of the aggrieved person. During this proceeding, the EEOC represents the aggrieved person. If the EEOC presents convincing evidence of a discriminatory pattern or practice or a resulting disparate impact, then both the employer and the EEOC may voluntarily agree to a remedy.

A conciliation agreement is binding on both parties; neither party may turn to the courts except to enforce the agreement. If no agreement is reached, the EEOC regional office may have its litigation counsel bring suit in a federal district court. Remedies awarded by the court may include the victim's reinstatement into the old job, back pay, litigation costs, attorney's fees, or some affirmative action. Figure 19–2 illustrates these EEOC procedures. In private damage actions, compensatory and punitive damages may be granted for intentional discrimination.

Affirmative Action

The Civil Rights Act of 1964 specifies certain remedies, but in some cases the courts have implied additional rights and permitted proactive antidiscrimination remedies. These remedies may require employers to use more positive approaches to reduce the underlying

FIGURE 19–2 EEOC Procedures

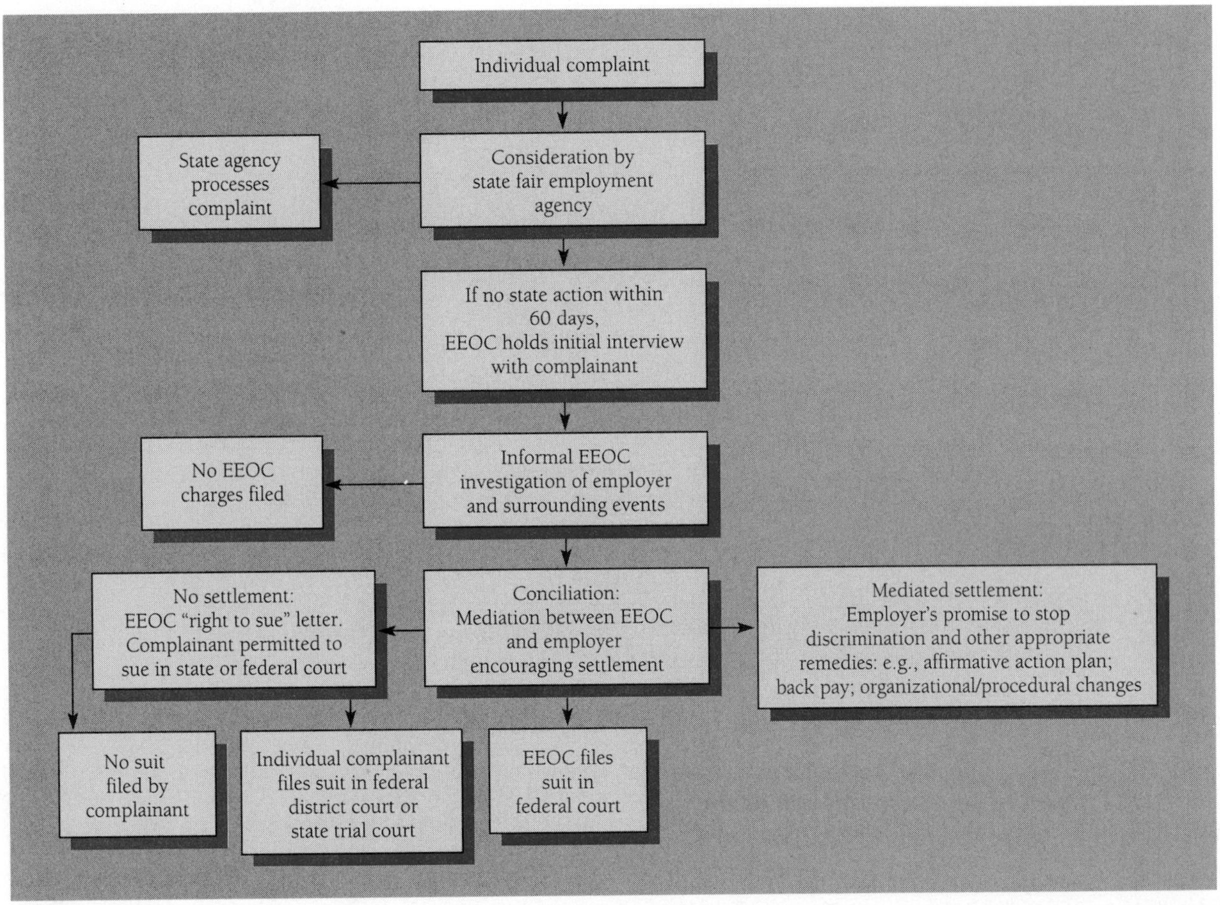

conditions leading to discrimination by actively encouraging the employment of minorities and women.

In its conciliation process, the EEOC has often taken more "affirmative action" to achieve equal employment opportunities. **Affirmative action** programs actively recruit minorities and may establish goals and timetables for greater employment participation among certain employers by members of suspect classes that have historically suffered patterns of discrimination. Affirmative action plans are also adopted voluntarily or can result from a negotiated collective bargain with unions. Affirmative action plans are required for most federal contractors.

Affirmative action programs can lead to charges of *reverse discrimination.* Qualified white male applicants are sometimes displaced by less qualified women or members of minorities who are given preference in hiring by these programs. Some affirmative action programs have been invalidated because they unnecessarily "trammeled" nonminority employees in hiring, firing, or promotion decisions. For example, provisions in labor union contracts giving minorities preference to avoid layoffs violate the equal protection clause of the Fourteenth Amendment. Hiring quotas foreclose only one of many employment opportunities to the better-qualified applicant. However, layoff preferences impose the entire burden of achieving racial equality on the particular individuals laid off. This disruption of these individuals' lives is unacceptable, and other means of achieving equality, such as affirmative action hiring plans, should be used.

Should the courts approve privately negotiated affirmative action plans between employers and unions to achieve racial balance? The type of program that may receive court approval is illustrated in the next case.

United Steelworkers of America v. Weber

443 U.S. 193 (1979)

United States Supreme Court

The 1974 master collective bargaining agreement between Kaiser Aluminum & Chemical Corporation and the United Steelworkers of American (USWA) included an affirmative action plan to eliminate conspicuous racial imbalances. The enrollees in Kaiser's in-plant craft-training programs were almost exclusively white. The affirmative action plan was to reserve 50 percent of the openings in these programs for blacks until the percentage of black craftworkers in the Kaiser workforce came up to the percentage of blacks in the local labor force. In the first year, seven blacks and six whites were selected for the training program at one plant on the basis of seniority. However, the most senior black selected had less seniority than several white workers who had been rejected for the program, including Weber. Weber claimed reverse discrimination on the basis of race because he was rejected for the training program. The Court of Appeals affirmed the district court's finding of reverse discrimination in the affirmative action plan, and the Steelworkers union appealed to the Supreme Court.

Justice Brennan delivered the opinion of the Court.

Respondent [Weber] argues that Congress intended in Title VII to prohibit all race-conscious affirmative action plans. Respondent's argument rests upon a literal interpretation of §§ 703 (a) and (d) of the Act. Those sections make it unlawful to "discriminate . . . because of . . . race" in hiring and in the selection of apprentices for training programs.

Respondent's argument is not without force. But it overlooks the significance of the fact that the Kaiser-USWA plan is an affirmative action plan voluntarily adopted by private parties to eliminate traditional patterns of racial segregation.

Congress' primary concern in enacting the prohibition against racial discrimination in Title VII of the Civil Rights Act of 1964 was with "the plight of the Negro in our economy." Before 1964, blacks were largely relegated to "unskilled and semi-skilled jobs." Because of automation the number of such jobs was rapidly decreasing.

As a consequence, "the relative position of the Negro worker [was] steadily worsening. In 1947 the non-white unemployment rate was only 64 percent higher than the white rate; in 1962 it was 124 percent higher."

Congress feared that the goals of the Civil Rights Act—the integration of blacks into the mainstream of American society—could not be achieved unless this trend were reversed.

Given this legislative history, we cannot agree with respondent that Congress intended to prohibit the private sector from taking effective steps to accomplish the goal that Congress designed Title VII to achieve. The very statutory words intended as a spur or catalyst to cause "employers and unions to self-examine and to self-evaluate their employment practices and to endeavor to eliminate, so far as possible, the last vestiges of an unfortunate and ignominious page in this country's history," cannot be interpreted as an absolute prohibition against all private, voluntary, race-conscious affirmative action efforts to hasten the elimination of such vestiges. Nothing contained in Title VII "shall be interpreted to *require* any employer . . . to grant preferential treatment . . . to any group because of the race . . . of such . . . group on account of" a *de facto* racial imbalance in the employer's work force. The section does *not* state that "nothing in Title VII shall be interpreted to *permit*" voluntary affirmative efforts to correct racial imbalances. The natural inference is that Congress chose not to forbid all voluntary race-conscious affirmative action.

We need not today define in detail the line of demarcation between permissible and impermissible affirmative action plans. It suffices to hold that the challenged Kaiser-USWA affirmative action plan falls on the permissible side of the line. The purposes of the plan mirror those of the statute. Both were designed to break down old patterns of racial segregation and hierarchy. Both were structured to "open employment opportunities for Negroes in occupations which have been traditionally closed to them."

At the same time, the plan does not unnecessarily trammel the interests of the white employees. The plan does not require the discharge of white workers and their replacement with new black hirees. Nor does the plan create an absolute bar to the advancement of white employees; half of those trained in the program will be white. Moreover, the plan is a temporary measure; it is not intended to maintain racial balance, but simply to eliminate a manifest racial imbalance. Preferential selection of craft trainees at the Gramercy plant will end as soon as the percentage of black skilled craftworkers in the Gramercy plant approximates the percentage of blacks in the local labor force.

Case Questions

1. What is the purpose of an affirmative action plan?
2. How does the Supreme Court balance the protections of the Civil Rights Act against the freedom of contract?
3. How long must affirmative action plans persist?

Periodic review of an affirmative action plan that permits revisions to account for its success may be a redeeming feature. In *Johnson v. Transportation Agency, Santa Clara, California*, the court held that plans should be limited to "attaining" racial balance, but not intended to maintain permanent numerical quotas.[7] Government- or court-sponsored plans may constitutionally employ racial classifications essential to remedy unlawful treatment of minorities. Plans should consider neutral alternative remedies and maintain the plan's flexibility by waiving quotas when no qualified minority candidates are available.

Minority set-asides are another device challenged as reverse discrimination. Such programs involve government quotas requiring that a certain minimum percentage of federal contracts or other valuable government privileges be reserved for minority groups. For example, a federal program that reserved at least 10 percent of subcontracts on certain federal construction projects for minority business enterprises was held constitutional.[8]

The future for set-aside programs is unclear. Some state government programs have been invalidated where race-neutral alternatives existed. The Federal Communication Commission (FCC) has a "multicultural" broadcast license program that gives preference to minority or women applicants for TV and radio broadcast licenses. The FCC's program is designed to promote diversity in programming, station ownership, and management to enhance viewers' rights. Although a 1990 decision supported the concept,[9] a 1992 decision invalidated a license granted in that program because preference was given to the applicants due to their gender.[10]

---

[7] *Johnson v. Transportation Agency, Santa Clara, Calif.*, 480 U.S. 616 (1987).

[8] *Fullilove v. Klutznick*, 448 U.S. 448 (1980).

[9] *Metro Broadcasting, Inc. v. F.C.C.*, 110 S.Ct. 2997 (1990).

[10] *Lamprecht v. F.C.C.* 958 F.2d 382 (D.C. Cir. 1992).

Executive Order Program

Since the passage of the Civil Rights Act of 1964, several presidents have issued executive orders dealing with discrimination by the federal government or by private employers that contract with the federal government. Executive Order 11,246 requires that all contracts between the federal government and federal contractors include a provision prohibiting discrimination on the basis of race, color, creed, or national origin. More recently, executive orders have also prohibited age and sex discrimination. Federal contracts must also include a provision requiring nondiscriminatory hiring practices. If discriminatory practices are proved, federal contracts may be canceled or suspended and contractors declared ineligible for future contracts.

Executive Order 11,246 and 11,375 created the Office of Federal Contract Compliance Programs. This agency oversees the affirmative action programs required of most federal contractors. The larger federal contractors must develop affirmative action programs to remedy imbalances among protected classes in their workforce. Typically, a federal contractor must analyze its minority employee profile as compared to that of the workforce in general or of the population at large. To implement the affirmative action programs, federal contractors often establish goals and timetables for hiring from protected classes.

Other Remedies

State statutes, court decisions, and other federal laws establish enforcement mechanisms to supplement the EEOC enforcement, state agency enforcement, affirmative action programs, and the executive order program techniques just discussed. For example, the EEOC has negotiated court-approved *consent decrees* with employers charged with widespread discriminatory practices. The employer typically agrees to adopt new employment practices often involving affirmative action plans. EEOC and state agency remedies include *reinstatement* for an individual dismissed or constructively discharged by the discrimination. *Back pay* (with interest) is often ordered to compensate for earnings lost by the individual while he or she was denied the job or promotion. Awards of *retroactive seniority* are also made from the time of the discrimination.

The *Civil Rights Act of 1991* authorized recovery of punitive damages for intentional, malicious, or reckless indifference to the discrimination laws. Claimants may also receive compensatory damages, other than back pay, that can include future income losses, pain and suffering, mental anguish, and other noneconomic damages. However, punitive and compensatory damages are capped, or limited in dollar amount, in all but race discrimination suits. These caps are scaled according to the size of the discriminating employer's work force, as indicated in Figure 19–3.

The Civil Rights Act of 1991 changed other aspects of employment discrimination litigation. In disparate impact cases, the employer has the burden of proving that its employment practices are job related and have a business necessity when they have an unintended disparate impact. This reverses the Supreme Court's shift of the burden of proof in unintentional discrimination cases to the employee, as discussed earlier in the *Ward's Cove Packing* case. An employer's claim that a particular employment practice is a business necessity is not a defense to an intentional discrimination. The new law permits either party to demand a jury trial. The law also prohibits "test norming," the adjustment of test scores or providing different test score cutoffs to favor a protected class.

FIGURE 19–3

Damage Caps under Civil Rights Act of 1991

Number of Employees	Upper Limit on Damages (Compensatory and Punitive)
0 – 14	No damages allowed
15 – 100	$ 50,000
101 – 200	100,000
201 – 500	200,000
over 500	300,000

Commentary: The New Civil Rights Law and "Quotas"

The Civil Rights Act of 1991 raises considerable controversy because it represents a hard-fought compromise. Proponents argue that the act's expanded remedies and procedural provisions were necessary to regain civil rights lost in some court decisions. Opponents argue that it constitutes a "quota" bill, despite the act's explicit prohibition against quotas. They claim that by making it easier for workers to challenge employment practices and qualification tests with a disparate impact, the act will force employers into making hiring, promotion, and retention decisions based on quotas. The law may adversely affect smaller businesses because they have fewer resources to develop valid tests or other screening procedures. The new punitive damage provisions may lead to the filing of frivolous claims with a "settlement value," thus further intimidating businesses into adopting quotas to steer clear of discrimination litigation.

The act's proponents object that applying the damage caps to sex or disability discrimination suits is unconstitutional. There are already proposals to remove the damage caps and a court test seems inevitable. A real danger is that employers may move away from general aptitude tests altogether even though such tests are better than interviews, references, education, or experience in predicting future job performance.

Despite the controversy, the new act will probably have its biggest impact on promotion and retention, for which traditional decisions may be difficult to justify to juries. The prospect of costly litigation and possibly excessive jury awards may also cause employers to require the use of arbitration for internal promotion and retention employment discrimination disputes.

IMMIGRATION REFORM AND THE ANTIDISCRIMINATION LAWS

In 1986, Congress amended the immigration laws and thoroughly revised U.S. immigration policy. The law now prohibits the employment of illegal aliens and imposes stricter responsibilities on employers to verify whether their employees are illegal aliens. The law granted amnesty to illegal aliens residing continuously in the United States between 1982 and 1986. It also imposed additional equal employment responsibilities on employers. Antidiscrimination provisions in this law affect employment practices.

General Provisions

Employers are prohibited from hiring, recruiting, or referring for a fee any known illegal alien. Employers must verify the work eligibility of all employees hired after November 6, 1986, by examining original documents that "reasonably appear genuine." Form I–9

(Employment Eligibility Verification Form) must be filed with the Immigration and Naturalization Service (INS) within three days after every new employee is hired. Verification is required for all full-time, part-time, temporary, and casual employees, but not for independent contractors. The status and documents of aliens with amnesty must be verified. I–9 forms must be retained for three years so that the Labor Department or the INS may inspect them. Employers are subject to civil fines for failing to verify all newly hired employees, for failing to retain I–9 forms, or for hiring illegal aliens.

Antidiscrimination Provisions

Discriminatory hiring practices prohibited under Title VII are explicitly restated in the antidiscrimination provisions of the immigration law. Congress included the "Frank Amendment" out of concern that the law might engender or excuse employment discrimination on the basis of national origin or citizenship. The EEOC intends to vigorously enforce Title VII against employers that attempt to avoid immigration law compliance by simply refusing to hire individuals who look "foreign" or speak with a foreign accent. It is an unfair employment practice to discriminate on the basis of national origin or to hire only U.S. citizens.

The antidiscrimination provisions of the immigration law do not apply to employers of 3 or fewer persons; they apply to employers of 4 to 14 persons. Title VII prohibits employers of 15 or more persons from national origin discrimination, and the immigration law requires them to refrain from discrimination on the basis of citizenship.

Employers should avoid employment practices that may violate Title VII and the immigration law's antidiscrimination provisions. Refusals to hire or decisions to fire should not be based on race, color, national origin, sex, religious preference, accent, height or weight requirements, fluency in English, citizenship, tests revealing national origin, or physical appearance.

INTERNATIONAL PERSPECTIVES ON EMPLOYMENT DISCRIMINATION

Few other nations show as much concern for equal employment opportunities as does the United States. Many observers cite cultural diversity and the diverse immigrant ancestry as the driving force behind the economic and social successes of the United States. By contrast, many nations seek to remain "ethnically pure" by consciously resisting integration with other races or people of other national origins. For example, critics charge that the low-paying and undesirable jobs in Japan are relegated to immigrants from other Asian nations. Some sociologists argue that the Japanese presume that their economic success is due to their racial homogeneity.

Other nations have similar discriminatory policies or practices. For example, Northern Ireland, a predominantly Protestant nation, still has no comprehensive prohibition against religious discrimination. Israel permits only Jews to vote in national elections. The Israeli Jewish clergy determines who is a Jew and, therefore, who can vote. The role of women in Japan, in the Muslim world, and in most other nations is far more restricted than is the role of women in the United States.

Although many nations have adopted antidiscrimination laws in recent years, these laws are presently rather ineffective because they are poorly enforced. However, the EC has adopted an equal pay policy and will soon permit the free movement of workers, licensed professionals, and the self-employed throughout the EC. While it is difficult to attain and maintain diversity and equal opportunity without discrimination or bigotry, the United States demonstrates the potential for the ultimate success of such policies.

SUMMARY

Equal opportunity laws are intended to prevent discrimination against protected individuals. The Equal Pay Act prohibits paying the sexes unequally for the performance of equal work. Employers must establish accurate job descriptions that permit the comparison of work performed. Comparable worth theories would equalize the pay of different jobs with different tasks but with roughly equal responsibility and difficulty.

Title VII of the Civil Rights Act of 1964 prohibits employment discrimination in hiring, firing, promotion, and the terms of employment based on race, color, religion, national origin, or sex. It prohibits disparate treatment—discriminatory policies that treat one group of employees or job applicants more favorably than a protected class. Disparate impact arises when apparently neutral selection criteria have adverse effects on a protected class. Pattern or practice discrimination affects a whole protected class. It may be proved by statistical inferences from comparisons between the proportion of protected class members in the general population and those in the employer's workforce.

Discrimination based on membership in a protected class, such as race or religion, is prohibited. Here, the term religion includes not only the traditional denominations but also any set of sincerely held ethically or morally based beliefs. Employers must make some accommodation for employees' religious observances. Discrimination against persons due to their national origin is illegal unless such discrimination is required for the performance of a specific job. It is illegal to discriminate on the basis of sex, either male or female. Some discrimination against handicapped persons and persons between the ages of 40 and 70 is also illegal.

There are three exceptions that permit employers to legally discriminate against members of a protected class. First, discrimination is permitted if there is a bona fide occupational qualification, though race is never a BFOQ. Second, employers may discriminate on the basis of professionally developed aptitude tests if these are validated as accurate predictors of job performance. Third, employers may discriminate when a valid union contract imposes a seniority system for employees in a bargaining unit.

Sexual harassment is the unlawful requirement of requiring submission to sexual advances or the creation of a hostile sexual environment. Although sexual harassment is not specifically outlawed by Title VII, it is illegal to make submission to sexual advances a condition of employment. EEOC guidelines have separately outlawed sexual harassment. Employers may be held liable for not monitoring the activities of supervisors guilty of sexual harassment.

The EEOC is responsible for enforcement of the antidiscrimination laws through investigation, rulemaking, and adjudication. It requires extensive recordkeeping to facilitate such enforcement. Although most EEOC complaints are settled through conciliation, the EEOC or the victim may also sue in a federal court.

In some cases, affirmative action programs may be validly used to achieve greater employment participation for protected classes that have historically suffered patterns of discrimination. Federal contractors are not allowed to discriminate and must implement such affirmative action programs.

Immigration law prohibits the hiring of illegal aliens. To avoid violation of Title VII and the antidiscrimination provisions of the new immigration law, most employers are required to document the work eligibility of all their newly hired employees.

KEY TERMS

comparable worth, p. 602
disparate treatment, p. 603
disparate impact, p. 606
pattern or practice theory, p. 608

protected class, p. 609
Americans with Disabilities Act (ADA), p. 613
bona fide occupational qualification (BFOQ), p. 614
business necessity, p. 614
sexual harassment, p. 617
Equal Employment Opportunity Commission (EEOC), p. 619
affirmative action programs, p. 621

CHAPTER EXERCISES

1. List the defenses that are available to an employer under the Equal Pay Act. Why are certain pay differentials permitted?
2. Ace Airlines required an applicant for flight officer to have a college degree for employment. Joan Jones, a female who did not have a college degree but was otherwise qualified for this position, applied for the position and was denied employment. She filed a complaint with the EEOC. At the hearing, Ace Airlines testified: "All flight officers undergo a rigorous training program on being hired and then are required to attend intensive refresher programs at six-month intervals in order to remain at peak performance ability. Possession of a college degree indicates that the applicant is able to understand and retain the concepts and information imparted in a classroom atmosphere and is more apt to cope with these programs than a person without a college degree." Will Joan win? Discuss the issues that the court should consider.
3. Weeks, a woman, worked for the telephone company in Georgia for 19 years before requesting that she be given the job of switchman. She was told that women were not eligible for this job because it was strenuous and because it required the employee to be on 24-hour call. A Georgia statute prohibited women from being employed in a job that required them to lift over 30 pounds. Weeks claimed that her employer had illegally discriminated on the basis of sex. The telephone company contended that sex was a BFOQ for the job. Was this a violation of Title VII? *Weeks v. Southern Bell & Telegraph Co.*, 408 F.2d. 228 (1969).
4. The Los Angeles Department of Water and Power provided an employee retirement program in which benefits were funded by employer and employee contributions and computed on the basis of monthly salary and years of service. Because standard mortality tables showed that the average female would live longer and thus receive more benefits than the average male, female employees were required to make monthly contributions that were almost 15 percent higher than the contributions of male employees. Manhart, a female employee, filed a class action suit alleging that this differential contribution requirement constituted sex discrimination in violation of Title VII of the 1964 Civil Rights Act. With what result, and why? *Los Angeles Department of Water and Power v. Manhart*, 435 U.S. 702 (1978).
5. Do the following fact situations present a legal problem? Why or why not?
   a. X company is laying off employees, starting with the employees who have least seniority. The first group to be laid off consists of 25 white women and 15 black men and women.
   b. A company refuses to hire male receptionists, maintaining that business callers, mostly male, want to see a "pretty face" in the reception area.
   c. X company has traditionally hired males to do its assembly-line work. The assembly-line positions include some jobs that require lifting and some that do not. Males are rotated between these jobs, all male assembly-line workers being on the same pay scale. The company has recently started to hire women for the assembly line, but they work only in nonlifting positions. For this reason, they are paid a lower wage scale than the men. The female assembly line workers sue.
6. Coburn was 43 years old and had worked for Pan Am for 17 years when he was discharged due to a reduction in workforce caused by Pan Am's financial difficulties. The airline argued that, on the basis of a fair and nondiscriminatory evaluation process to assess productivity, it had concluded Coburn was the least productive employee in his peer group. Pan Am's policies with regard to the layoffs were formal and rigorous and they were applied uniformly. Did Pan Am discriminate against Coburn on the basis of age? What are the

elements of an age discrimination case? *Coburn v. Pan American World Airways,* 711 F.2d 339 (1983).

7. Philbrook's religious beliefs required him to miss six workdays each year. The Ansonia Board of Education allowed him to use three personal leave days and to take the other three days as unauthorized leave for which he received no pay but was not otherwise disciplined. The school board refused Philbrook's request to allow him to pay for a substitute teacher and not have his pay docked. Did the school fulfill its duty to accommodate Philbrook's religious beliefs? *Ansonia Board of Education v. Philbrook,* 107 S. Ct. 367 (1986).

8. Ms. Rawlinson applied for a position as a correctional counselor in a male maximum security prison in Alabama. The Alabama Board of Corrections adopted a rule forbidding women to be employed in "contact" positions requiring close physical proximity to inmates. Ms. Rawlinson sued under Title VII. With what result, and why? *Dothard v. Rawlinson,* 433 U.S. 321 (1977).

9. In 1983, the Richmond city council adopted an ordinance requiring that minority subcontractors (MBEs) receive 30 percent of the dollar amount of each city construction contract. MBEs were defined as businesses 51 percent owned or controlled by "blacks, Spanish-speaking [persons], Orientals, Indians, Eskimos or Aleuts." At public hearings on the proposed set-aside program, it was noted that although Richmond's population was 50 percent black, only .67 percent of the city's prime construction contracts had been won by minority firms during the previous five years. J. A. Croson Company, a mechanical plumbing and heating firm, attempted to bid on a project for urinals and water closets in the city jail. Despite efforts to find a minority subcontractor, Croson ultimately submitted a bid without minority participation, seeking a waiver of the set-aside requirement on the ground that no qualified minority subcontractor was available. A minority firm, however, tardily submitted a somewhat higher bid than Croson's. The city denied Croson's waiver request and resolved to rebid the project. Croson sued in federal court, claiming that the Richmond ordinance was unconstitutional on its face. With what result, and why? *City of Richmond v. J. A. Croson,* 488 U.S. 469 (1989).

10. Supervisors may place their coworkers and subordinates into uncomfortable ethical dilemmas by attempting to cover up discriminatory bias in job decisions. This may be an unspoken expectation for those involved in evaluating candidates for new jobs or for promotion to conform their judgments to the supervisor's discriminatory bias.

    Is it ethical for such coworkers and subordinates to submit to these pressures or to alter their honest hiring/promotion evaluations and documents to substantiate the supervisor's false claim that hiring was nondiscriminatory?

Part 7

GOVERNMENT REGULATION AND SOCIAL POLICIES

The chapters in Part 7 concern businesses' responsibilities toward society. Each chapter focuses on an area of regulation that has recently gained importance. As environmental problems multiply, businesses have responsibilities to address them and minimize the risk they present. Chapter 20 notes the myriad federal statutory laws which seek to regulate activities that cause air, water, and land pollution.

Chapter 21 focuses on laws affecting international business. Long important for large businesses, the globalization of production facilities, financial resources, and marketing opportunities of international trade have affected small- and medium-sized firms from the United States and abroad. Joint ventures with firms in Poland, Czechoslovakia, Russia, and even China are increasing rapidly as a result of changes occurring in the legal systems of these formerly Communist countries. The European Community (EC) further integrated its markets in 1992 and as international offices and facilities increase, businesses will need to understand the legal environment and the laws of international activities.

The final chapter concerns business ethics and corporate social responsibility. What is the responsibility of a business firm toward society? What nonlegal duties do business organizations have toward society? Do corporate codes of conduct effectively cause officers and employees to act ethically? Most Americans believe businesses have an obligation to help society, despite the possible reduction in corporate profit. This chapter ends the text because it concerns responsibilities that surpass legal obligations. Businesses' adherence to strict ethical standards and concern for society may lessen the need for further government regulation.

Chapter 20

ENVIRONMENTAL LAW

KEY CONCEPTS

Environmental law refers to state land use control laws and federal regulatory programs that are designed to prevent further deterioration of the quality of land, water, and air.

Environmental impact statements are comprehensive studies of the impact that proposed major federal actions will have on the quality of the environment. These statements must be submitted to the president and the Council of Environmental Quality and disclosed to the public.

The Environmental Protection Agency is the federal regulator responsible for enforcement of the Clean Air Act, the Clean Water Act, and the Solid Waste Disposal Act.

The Clean Air Act establishes air quality standards for moving and stationary air pollution in the United States. Federal action on new sources of pollution must be coordinated with the state implementation plans. New plants in seriously polluted areas are required to install the best available pollution control technology.

The 1990 Clean Air Amendments impose alternative fuel requirements on automobile manufacturers and establish some deadlines for dealing with acid rain. Ozone smog problems in specific cities must be reduced as early as 1993.

The Clean Water Act, which is intended to prevent water pollution, requires a permit for any person or firm that seeks to make discharges into bodies of water.

INTRODUCTION . . . PAST, PRESENT, FUTURE

In the past, only nuisance, trespass, zoning, and land use laws sought to regulate actions affecting the environment. The dumping of solid, liquid, and gaseous products into streams and harbors, on land, and into the air was largely unregulated. Medical science was unaware of the effects on health of waste, pollution, and decaying products. Centuries ago, the London smog was in evidence when soft coal became a common fuel. Venice has encountered serious water and air pollution problems for centuries. For decades, the water from lakes and rivers near many cities throughout the world has been virtually undrinkable due to the wastes dumped into them by residents and business firms.

The first federal legislation aimed at water pollution was the River and Harbors Act of 1886. This act established a permit system for the discharge of such refuse as sewage, rubbish, or litter into navigable waters. Although it focused on items that could obstruct navigation in the nation's primary waterways, it also became a means for attacking some sources of water pollution.

Modern water pollution law originated in the 1948 Water Pollution Control Act, which sought to eliminate all discharges of pollutants into the nation's waterways. After this act had been amended on several occasions, the Clean Water Act, a comprehensive plan for maintaining and restoring the quality of the nation's waterways, was adopted in 1972.

Environmental law now comprises pervasive federal regulation. The Clean Water Act, Clean Air Act, Superfund legislation, Solid Waste Disposal Act, and Toxic Substances Control Act are recent statutory laws intended to address environmental problems. Yet environmental law seems ineffective. Billions of dollars can clean up only a few of the hundreds of sites that present critical environmental problems. The states charged with providing regional sites for hazardous waste disposal respond: "Not in my back yard" (NIMBY). Oil spills, illegal dumping, and acid rain all threaten the fragile ecosystem.

Recent global environmental tragedies include the oil spill from the *Exxon Valdez* tanker in Alaska, Iraq's deliberate spilling of oil in the Persian Gulf and setting ablaze oil wells in Kuwait during the Persian Gulf War, and the massive cutting of trees and clearing of land in the Brazilian rainforests.

Other environmental problems may be very significant for greater environmental damage, such as that done to U.S. and Canadian lakes and streams by acid rain resulting from power plant emissions. The potentially devastating consequences of a *greenhouse effect,* the warming of the lower atmosphere caused by emissions of carbon dioxide, are being studied. The depletion of the ozone layer, caused at least in part by the use of fluorocarbons, has led to state and federal regulation and international agreements mandating the gradual decrease of their use. Some environmentalists say the existing efforts are still "too little, too late."

Environmental law is increasingly important for business managers. A growing number of criminal actions are being brought against polluting firms and their managers for intentional violations of environmental laws. Most of the major environmental laws contain criminal enforcement provisions, and a governmental crackdown on environmental crimes has begun. In the last decade, over 500 indictments have been brought by the environmental section of the Justice Department. The Environmental Protection Agency reported that in 1989, federal courts examining environmental cases handed out prison terms totaling about 37 years and over $11 million in fines. Five years earlier, the jail time for environmental violations totaled about two years, and total fines were less than $200,000.[1]

OVERVIEW

The environment consists of all of the surrounding physical conditions and influences that affect the development of living things. Environmental law regulates our interaction with the surrounding air, water, and land through limitations imposed by law. Despite the deregulation movement of the 1980s, public concern over the deteriorating environment is increasing, not decreasing.

Serious environmental threats to human health have become too common and too dangerous to ignore. The laissez-faire attitude toward the use of the environment that prevailed throughout the first half of the 20th century led to the dumping of wastes in waterways, the burning of low-grade coal, and lead emissions from millions of cars. Pollution problems and environmental regulations aimed at addressing them are neither merely national in scope nor totally recent in origin.

Mexico City's rapid urbanization has created some of the most acute pollution problems in the world. In Estonia, a republic of the former Soviet Union, the emissions from a cement factory descend from the air and cake village rooftops. The waste from the four million inhabitants of Athens, Greece, is dumped untreated into the Mediterranean Sea. Air pollution in some cities in the former East Germany has been measured at 50 times higher than national standards. The greenhouse effect and the depletion of the ozone layer are environmental concerns that affect the entire planet.

This chapter examines recent laws regulating the use and abuse of the environment in the United States. Unlike many other fields of law, environmental law is primarily statutory and federal in scope; the common law plays only a minor role in American environmental regulation. Although pollution differs from region to region, its effects do not stop at state or national borders. The chapter focuses first on the most important federal environmental statute: the National Environmental Policy Act. Next, it takes up other important federal statutory laws dealing with air, water, and land pollution. Then, it considers more specific environmental concerns—nuclear power and wildlife protection. Finally, it discusses the role of the states and local communities in enforcing environmental laws.

THE NATIONAL ENVIRONMENTAL POLICY ACT

The 1970 National Environmental Policy Act (NEPA) makes it federal policy to consider the environmental impact of various activities. It also establishes the Council of Environmental Quality, which gathers information on the environment, reviews and recommends changes in federal policies, and makes annual reports on environmental conditions. NEPA lists numerous general purposes. These purposes include the following: to declare a national policy that will encourage productive and enjoyable harmony be-

---

[1]See "Environmental Crime Can Land Executives in Prison These Days," *The Wall Street Journal*, September 10, 1990, p. A1, col. 1.

tween man and his environment; to promote efforts that will prevent or eliminate damage to the environment and the biosphere and stimulate the health and welfare of man; and to enrich our understanding of the ecological systems and national resources important to the nation.

The Environmental Protection Agency (EPA) was created in 1970 to coordinate the federal government's environmental policies. Congress recognized that the problems of air pollution, water pollution, and solid waste disposal were interrelated. Subsequent laws addressed control of pesticides, ocean dumping, and hazardous waste problems. The EPA is headquartered in Washington, D.C., but it also has 10 regional offices throughout the country. Although the EPA is the nation's primary federal agency, the Nuclear Regulatory Commission (one of the litigants in the *Metro Edison* case) and the Department of Interior also have specific environmental responsibilities.

Environmental Impact Statements

The NEPA **environmental impact statements** are studies of the effects that certain proposed federally financed or approved projects will have on the environment. Such statements have to be prepared for major projects that are likely to have a significant effect on the quality of the human environment. When the federal government plans to build a dam or power plant, the appropriate federal agency must prepare an environmental impact statement. State roads or prisons built with federal funds also require the preparation of such a statement. Private companies that receive federal contracts or that are granted permits to cut timber or drill for oil on federal property may be required to assist in preparing environmental impact statements.

The Content of an Environmental Impact Statement

A significant provision of NEPA requires the preparation of an environmental impact statement before any major federal action is taken that can significantly affect the quality of the human environment. Such a statement must contain the following information:

1. The environmental impact of the proposed action.
2. Any adverse environmental effect that can be avoided should the proposed action be implemented.
3. Alternatives to the proposed action.
4. The relationship between local short-term use of the environment and the maintenance and enhancement of long-term productivity.
5. Any irreversible and irretrievable commitments of resources that would be involved should the proposed action be implemented.

Environmental impact statements are submitted to the president and the Council on Environmental Quality and disclosed to the public. What concerns must be addressed in such statements? The following case involves the start-up of one of the nuclear power plants near Three Mile Island, Pennsylvania.

Metro Edison v. People Against Nuclear Energy

406 U.S. 766 (1983)
United States Supreme Court

Metropolitan Edison (Metro) owned two nuclear power plants at Three Mile Island, near Harrisburg, Pennsylvania. In March 1979, one of these plants, TMI–2, suffered a serious accident that damaged its nuclear reactor. After the accident, the Nuclear Regulatory Commission (NRC) ordered Metro to also keep TMI–1, the other plant, shut down until a determination was made as to whether it could be operated properly. The NRC then published a notice of a hearing regarding several safety-related issues. The notice stated that NRC had not determined whether to consider psychological harm and other indirect effects of the accident in deciding whether to permit the renewed operation of TMI–1. People against Nuclear Energy (PANE) contended that restarting TMI–1 would cause severe psychological damage to persons in the area, but the NRC decided not to consider such evidence at its hearing. PANE argued that the National Environmental Protection Act required agencies to consider various effects on health in making a decision. Metro intervened on the side of the NRC. The Court of Appeals found for PANE, and Metro appealed to the Supreme Court.

Justice Rehnquist delivered the opinion of the Court.

The issue in these cases is whether petitioner Nuclear Regulatory Commission (NRC) complied with the National Environmental Policy Act of 1969 (NEPA), when it considered whether to permit petitioner Metropolitan Edison Co. to resume operation of the Three Mile Island nuclear power plant near Harrisburg, Pa. Both plants were licensed by the NRC after extensive proceedings, which included preparation of Environmental Impact Statements.

All the parties agree that effects on human health can be cognizable under NEPA, and that human health may include psychological health. The Court of Appeals concluded that these propositions were enough to complete a syllogism that disposes of the case: NEPA requires agencies to consider effects on health. An effect on psychological health is an effect on health. Therefore, NEPA requires agencies to consider the effects on psychological health asserted by PANE.

PANE, using similar reasoning, contends that because the psychological health damage to its members would be caused by a change in the environment (the renewed operation of TMI–1). NEPA requires the NRC to consider that damage. Although these arguments are appealing at first glance, we believe they skip over an essential step in the analysis. They do not consider the closeness of the relationship between the change in the environment and the "effect" at issue.

Section 102(C) of NEPA directs all federal agencies to "include in every recommendation or report on proposals for legislation and other major Federal actions significantly affecting the quality of the human environment, a detailed statement by the responsible official on—

"(i) the environmental impact of the proposed action, [and]

"(ii) any adverse environmental effects which cannot be avoided should the proposal be implemented. . . ."

To paraphrase the statutory language in light of the facts of this case, where an agency action significantly affects the quality of the human environment, the agency must evaluate the "environmental impact" and any unavoidable adverse environmental effects of the proposal. The theme of section 102 is sounded by the adjective "environmental": NEPA does not require the agency to assess every impact or effect of its proposed action, but only the impact or effect on the environment. We think the content of the statute shows that Congress was talking about the physical environment—the world around us, so to speak.

The statements of two principal sponsors of NEPA illustrate this point:

> "What is involved [in NEPA] is a congressional declaration that we do not intend, as a government or as a people, to initiate actions which endanger the continued existence or the health of mankind: That we will not intentionally initiate actions which do irreparable

> damage to the air, land and water which support life on earth." (remarks of Sen. Jackson). "We can now move forward to preserve and enhance our air, aquatic, and terrestrial environments . . . to carry out the policies and goals set forth in the bill to provide each citizen of this great country a healthful environment." (remarks of Rep. Dingell).

To determine whether section 102 requires consideration of a particular effect, we must look at the relationship between that effect and the change in the physical environment caused by the major federal action at issue. This requirement is like the familiar doctrine of proximate cause from tort law. The issue before us, then, is how to give content to this requirement. This is a question of first impression in this Court. The federal action that affects the environment in this case is permitting renewed operation of TMI–1. The direct effects on the environment of this action include release of low-level radiation, increased fog in the Harrisburg area (caused by operation of the plant's cooling towers), and the release of warm water into the Susquehanna River. The NRC has considered each of these effects. Another effect of renewed operation is a risk of a nuclear accident. The NRC has also considered this effect.

PANE argues that the psychological health damage it alleges "will flow directly from the risk of [a nuclear] accident." But a risk of an accident is not an effect on the physical environment. A risk is, by definition, unrealized in the physical world. In a causal chain from renewed operation of TMI–1 to psychological health damage, the element of risk and its perception by PANE's members are necessary middle links. We believe that the element of risk lengthens the causal chain beyond the reach of NEPA.

For these reasons, we hold that the NRC need not consider PANE's contentions.

Case Questions

1. According to PANE, what law required the NRC to consider PANE's evidence? How did the Court interpret this law?
2. Did the NRC have to assess the possible damages caused by the risk of nuclear accident when considering the restarting of TMI–1?

AIR POLLUTION

The first federal statute dealing with air pollution was passed in 1955. Then, the Clean Air Act was passed in 1963 and amended in 1970, 1977, and most recently in 1990. That act requires the EPA to set national ambient air (atmospheric air as opposed to air inside buildings) quality standards (NAAQS) for such pollutants as carbon monoxide, hydrocarbons, lead, nitrogen oxide, ozone, and sulfur dioxide. Originally, each state was required to develop a state implementation plan (SIP) to achieve a level of air pollution below the maximum level specified by EPA standards. States also were required to inform the EPA about the methods used to achieve the standards for each industrial plant and meet the attainment dates. If a state's plan was found to be inadequate, the EPA had authority to withhold federal funds, halt construction of new sources of air pollution, or take steps to implement alternative plans.

The EPA controls both mobile and stationary sources of pollution. Mobile sources of pollution account for over 50 percent of the air pollution in the United States. Motor vehicles are subject to emission and fuel standards established by the EPA. The use of unleaded gasoline has diminished the amount of lead in the air. Manufacturers' installation of pollution control devices has lessened the emission of carbon monoxide and hydrocarbons (a source of smog) from cars, trucks, and buses. Stationary sources of pollution, such as industrial plants, are more difficult to control. Heavily industrialized areas were unable to attain air quality standards set by the EPA.

The Pre-1990 Clean Air Act

At first, the Clean Air Act prohibited new plants or modifications to existing ones in *nonattainment areas*—areas not meeting the EPA standards. Strict enforcement could have halted new construction in practically all industrial areas. The 1977 amendments to the act addressed this problem by allowing new construction or modification if state permits were first obtained. The permit requirements varied depending on the air quality in the area of the proposed addition or change.

New construction in areas with clean air—air of better quality than that specified by the national standards—could be undertaken as long as the resulting increase in pollutants did not cause these areas to exceed the allowable maximum. New industrial plants in these areas were required to install the **best available technology.** In areas with more air pollution than the national standards allowed, firms wishing to construct new facilities were required to meet stricter standards.

Pollution Control Standards in Polluted Areas

1. The facility must use technology designed to obtain the lowest achievable emissions rate.
2. The firm must prove that all of the other major sources of pollution within the state that are under the firm's control meet the state implementation plan (SIP).
3. The increased emissions from the new facility may not exceed the allowance for growth identified in the SIP, or, alternatively, there must be a more than equal reduction in the emission of similar pollutants from other plants in that area. The second option is known as the *emissions offset policy.*

In 1981, the EPA regulations permitted the states to adopt a plantwide definition of the term *stationary source of pollutants.* Thus, even if individual machines or emission points within a plant failed to meet the established standards, a firm could meet permit requirements if the total pollutants emitted from the plant did not increase. This **bubble concept** treats all of the pollution-producing devices within a plant as a single unit—as if they were all under one bubble. Industry favors expansion of the bubble concept to permit the combining of numerous facilities and communities. The bubble concept allows companies or facilities to market their "pollution permit rights" to firms that do not meet existing pollution standards. Is the bubble concept consistent with the National Environmental Protection Act? The next case established the bubble concept as a precedent in determining a "stationary source."

Chevron, USA, Inc. v. Natural Resources Defense Council, Inc.

467 U.S. 837 (1984)
United States Supreme Court

In 1977, Congress passed amendments to the Clean Air Act that required the states to address stationary sources of air pollution. Under the act, the Environmental Protection Agency (EPA) was to establish modified standards with regard to air pollution from stationary sources that the states had to meet. The EPA's standards allowed the states to treat all air pollution-emitting devices within the same industrial grouping as a single "source." The EPA published a regulation containing the plantwide definition, referred to as the *bubble concept.* The Natural Resources Defense Council filed a petition in the Court of Appeals for a review of that rule, and the Court of Appeals set aside the EPA rule. Chevron had an industrial plant that would be adversely affected if the proposed rule was not adopted, so it appealed to the Supreme Court.

Justice Stevens delivered the opinion of the Court.

The question presented by this case is whether EPA's decision to allow States to treat all of the pollution-emitting devices within the same industrial grouping as though they were encased within a single "bubble" is based on a reasonable construction of the statutory term "stationary source."

Section 109 of the 1970 Amendments directed the EPA to promulgate National Ambient Air Quality Standards (NAAQS's), and section 110 directed the States to develop plants (SIP's) to implement the standards within specified deadlines. In addition, section 111 provided that major new sources of pollution would be required to conform to technology-based performance standards. Section 111(e) prohibited the operation of any new source in violation of performance standards.

Section 111(a) defined the terms to be used in setting and enforcing standards of performance for new stationary sources. It provided: "For purposes of this section:
"(3) The term 'stationary source' means any building, structure, facility, or installation which emits or may emit any air pollutant."

Nonattainment

The 1970 legislation provided for the attainment of primary NAAQS's by 1975. In many areas of the country, particularly the most industrialized states, the statutory goals were not attained. The Clean Air Act Amendments of 1977 were a lengthy, detailed, technical, complex, and comprehensive response to a major social issue. A small portion of the statute expressly deals with nonattainment areas. Most significantly for our purposes, the statute provided that each plan shall: "(6) require permits for the construction and operation of new or modified major stationary sources."

The 1977 Amendments contain no specific reference to the "bubble concept." Nor do they contain a specific definition of the term "stationary source," though they did not disturb the definition of "stationary source" contained in section 111(a)(3) of the Act. Significantly, the EPA expressly noted that the word "source" might be given a plantwide definition for some purposes and a narrower definition for other purposes. In 1981 a new administration took office and initiated a "Government-wide reexamination of regulatory burdens and complexities." The EPA concluded that the term should be given the same definition in both nonattainment and PSD (Preventing Significant Deterioration) areas.

Statutory Language

The definition of the term *stationary source* in section 111(a)(3) refers to "any building, structure, facility, or installation" which emits air pollution. The definition in section 302(j) sheds virtually no light on the meaning of the term "stationary source."

The meaning of a word must be ascertained in the context of achieving particular objectives, and the words associated with it may indicate that the true meaning of the series is to convey a common idea. The language may reasonably be interpreted to impose the requirement on any discrete, but integrated, operation which pollutes. This gives meaning to all of the terms—a single building, not part of a larger operation, would be covered if it emits more than 100 tons of pollution, as would any facility, structure, or installation. Indeed, the language itself implies a bubble concept of sorts: each enumerated item would seem to be treated as if it were encased in a bubble.

In this case, the Administrator's interpretation represents a reasonable accommodation of manifestly competing interests and is entitled to deference: the regulatory scheme is technical and complex, the agency considered the matter in a detailed and reasoned fashion, and the decision involves reconciling conflicting policies. We hold that the EPA's definition of the term "source" is a permissible construction of the statute which seeks to accommodate progress in reducing air pollution with economic growth. The Judgment of the Court of Appeals is reversed.

Case Questions

1. What did the 1977 amendments to the Clean Air Act require the states to do regarding stationary sources of pollution?
2. What did these amendments say regarding the term *stationary source of pollution*?
3. What was the Court's most important reason for agreeing with the EPA's interpretation of the term *stationary source*?

FIGURE 20–1 Target Cities of the Clean Air Act

A total of 96 cities and communities with the worst ozone smog problems have been targeted to meet stricter federal standards.

- Cities with marginal problems must meet the standards by November 1993:

Albany, N.Y.	Fayetteville, N.C.	Knoxville, Tenn.	Paducah, Ky.
Allentown, Pa., nearby N.J.	Greenbrier County, W.Va.	Lake Charles, La.	Poughkeepsie, N.Y.
Altoona, Pa.	Greenville-Spartanburg, S.C.	Lancaster, Pa.	Scranton, Pa.
Birmingham, Ala.	Hancock County, Maine	Lewiston, Maine	South Bend, Ind.
Buffalo, N.Y.	Harrisburg, Pa.	Lexington, Ky.	Stockton, Calif.
Canton, Ohio	Indianapolis, Ind.	Lincoln County, Maine	Sussex County, Del.
Columbus, Ohio	Johnson City-Kingsport-Bristol, Tenn.	Manchester, N.H.	Tampa, Fla.
Erie, Pa.	Johnstown, Pa.	Montgomery, Ala.	Waldo County, Maine
Essex County N.Y.	Kansas City, Mo.-Kan.	Norfolk, Va.	York, Pa.
Evansville, Ind., nearby Ky.		Owensboro, Ky.	Youngstown, Ohio-Sharon, Pa.

- Cities with moderate problems which must meet the standards by November 1996:

Atlantic City, N.J.	Detroit	Miami	San Francisco-Oakland-San Jose
Bowling Green, Ky.	Grand Rapids, Mich.	Modesto. Calif.	Santa Barbara, Calif.
Charleston, W. Va.	Greensboro, N.C.	Nashville, Tenn.	Smyth County, Va.
Charlotte, N.C., nearby S.C.	Jefferson County, N.Y.	Pittsburgh, Pa.	St. Louis, nearby Ill.
Cincinnati, nearby Ky. and Ind.	Kewaunee County, Wis.	Portland, Maine	Toledo, Ohio
Cleveland	Knox County, Maine	Raleigh-Durham, N.C.	Visalia, Calif.
Dallas	Louisville, Ky., nearby Ind.	Reading, Pa.	Worcester, Mass.
Dayton-Springfield, Ohio	Memphis, Tenn., nearby Ark. and Miss.	Richmond, Va.	
		Salt Lake City	

- Cities with serious problems which must meet the standards by November 1999:

Atlanta	El Paso, Texas	Parkersburg, W. Va., nearby Ohio	Sacramento, Calif.
Bakersfield, Calif.	Fresno, Calif.	Portsmouth, N.H., nearby Maine	Sheboygan, Wis.
Baton Rouge, La.	Hartford, Conn.	Providence, R.I.	Springfield, Mass.
Beaumont, Texas	Huntington, W. Va., nearby Ky. and Ohio		Washington, nearby Md. and Va.
Boston, nearby N.H.			

- Cities with severe problems which must meet the standards by November 2005:

* Baltimore	Houston	* New York, nearby N.J. and Conn.	Philadelphia, nearby N.J., Del. and Md.
Chicago, nearby Ind. and Wis.	Milwaukee	San Diego	
	Muskegon, Mich.		

*These cities have until 2007 to meet the standards

- The city with extreme problems which must meet the standards by November 2010:

Los Angeles

The 1990 Amendments to the Clean Air Act

Reduction of Ozone and Carbon Dioxide (SMOG) The 1990 Amendments to the Clean Air Act impose additional requirements for the nation's urban areas that were not in compliance with the standards for ozone and carbon monoxide. Ninety-six cities were given deadlines for meeting the federal standards. Those classified as having marginal or moderate problems have until 1996 to meet the federal standards. Areas that are worse than moderate must reduce their smog by 15 percent by 1996. The goal is that all but nine areas meet the standards before the year 2000. Figure 20–1 depicts the target cities.

Acid Rain The 1990 Amendments also addressed the acid rain problems for the first time. The emission of sulfur dioxide from over 100 power plants in 21 states must be reduced by 5 million tons by 1995 (a two-year extension is possible in some cases). Further reductions must be accomplished by the year 2000. A bonus system allows companies whose emissions are cleaner than that allowed by law to sell their rights to emit more sulfur dioxide to other companies who are having difficulty meeting the standards.

Toxic Emissions Toxic air pollution is also significantly affected. While the pre-1990 law had identified and regulated only 7 chemicals, the firms which emit 189 chemicals must use their best technology to reduce emissions by 90 percent before the end of the decade.

Alternative Fuels Finally, the most striking legacy of the 1990 Clean Air Amendments will probably be the use of alternative fuels. The law requires that by 1998 fleets of 10 or more cars must run 80 percent cleaner than 1990 autos; trucks must be 50 percent cleaner. By 1995, all gasoline in the nation's nine smoggiest cities will have to be cleaner-burning, with 15 percent less hydrocarbons and toxic pollutants. Car manufacturers must produce at least 150,000 super-clean cars and light trucks a year, cars and trucks that run on methanol, electricity, or other alternative fuels.

Another provision inserted into the 1990 Clean Air Amendments made it unlawful to tamper with existing devices on automobile exhaust systems that were installed to reduce the emission of carbon monoxide and hydrocarbons. Several arguments are presented by the muffler center that was sued by the EPA. Note the law provides for a fine of up to $2,500 per violation. Do you think such a fine is too stiff?

United States of America v. Economy Muffler & Tire Center, Inc.

762 F. Supp. 1242
U.S. District Court (Virginia, 1991)

Economy Muffler operates an automobile repair shop in Richmond, Virginia, that routinely services motor vehicle exhaust systems. On 32 occasions during the past five years, Economy Muffler service personnel replaced three-way catalytic converters with two-way catalytic converters on a total of 51 motor vehicles.

Two-way catalytic converters contain platinum and palladium, chemical substances that reduce the emissions of carbon monoxide and hydrocarbons. Three-way catalytic converters also contain rhodium, a chemical substance that reduces the emissions of nitrogen oxides. Since the early 1980s, most passenger cars sold in the United States have been equipped with three-way converters, in accordance with Environmental Protection Agency (EPA) emission control standards.

Economy Muffler representatives regularly received and signed certificates, also known as "statement forms," labeled "Notice[s] to Professional Installers." The statement forms contained the following excerpt from the Section 203(a)(3)(B) enforcement policy published by the EPA at 51 Fed. Reg. 28118 on August 5, 1986:

> In order not to be considered a violation of Section 203(a)(3) of the Clean Air Act, the [**3] converter must:
>
> 3. Be the same type of converter as the original (i.e. oxidation, three-way, or three-way plus oxidation).
> 4. Be the proper converter for the vehicle application as determined and specified by the Catalog.

On December 3, 1990, the United States sued Economy Muffler, charging violations of Section 203(a)(3)(B) of the Clean Air Act of 1990, and seeking penalties of up to $2,500.00 for each violation. The trial court's decision follows.

Richard L. Williams, District Judge

Section 203(a)(3)(B) of the Clean Air Act of 1990, known as "the tampering provision," prohibits "any person engaged in the business of repairing [or] servicing . . . motor vehicles" from "knowingly . . . removing or render[ing] inoperative any device or element of design installed on or in a motor vehicle . . . in compliance with regulations under this title." In *United States v. Haney Chevrolet, Inc.,* (1974), a Florida District Court held that a service manager violated Section 203(a)(3)(B) by removing an automobile's original carburetor and accompanying idle speed solenoid and installing a new carburetor without the idle speed solenoid. The Court reasoned that the transmission control spark system and the idle speed solenoid are emission control devices or elements of design within the meaning of the statute. The replacing of the original carburetor with a different carburetor that lacked the idle speed solenoid rendered the solenoid inoperative. The same reasoning is applicable here. Three-way catalytic converters contain rhodium, a "device" or "element of design" without which a motor vehicle's exhaust system cannot reduce emissions of nitrogen oxide. Replacing a three-way converter with a two-way converter effectively removes rhodium or renders it inoperative and is therefore subject to civil penalties under the Clean Air Act.

The legislative history of the Act suggests that Congress intended the statute to be interpreted in this manner. The Senate Report explains that the provision does not prohibit the use of aftermarket parts "except where the use of such parts or the service performed would adversely affect the emission control system of the vehicle." Installing a two-way converter in place of a three-way converter adversely affects a vehicle's emission control system by destroying its capacity to prevent the harmful emission of nitrogen oxides.

The EPA has consistently interpreted the statute to bar the replacement of three-way catalytic converters with two-way catalytic converters. The tampering enforcement policy published by the EPA on August 6, 1986, and reproduced on statement forms distributed to repair shops specifically requires that a replacement converter "be the same type of converter as the original." As the agency responsible for Clean Air Act enforcement, the EPA's interpretation of the statute is entitled to "considerable deference."

Defendant argues that the tampering policy imposes a new set of legal obligations not contained in the statute and, for this reason, should have been enacted or promulgated as regulations in accordance with the Administrative Procedure Act's notice and comment rulemaking requirements. The defendant's characterization of the EPA enforcement policy is inaccurate. The tampering enforcement policy falls under Administrative Procedure Act Section 553(b)(3)(A), which exempts interpretive rules, general statements of policy, and rules of agency organization, *procedure,* and practice from the APA's rulemaking requirements.

Economy Muffler also claims that its employees did not knowingly violate the Clean Air Act because they were not aware of the Act's requirements with respect to converters. In adopting the 1977 amendments to the Clean Air Act, the House Committee on Interstate and Foreign Commerce endorsed the construction of the term "knowingly," given by the Federal District Court in *United States v. Haney Chevrolet, Inc.* The Court in Haney accepted the well-settled view that "an act is done knowingly when it is done voluntarily or intentionally, and not by mistake."

The term "knowingly" modifies the verbs "remove" and "render" and applies not to the law but to the offensive act. Both the United States Supreme Court and the Fourth Circuit Court of Appeals have established that the inclusion of the term "knowingly" in an environmental statute does not "carve out an exception to the general rule that ignorance of the law is no excuse."

Finally, Economy Muffler challenges the statute as void for vagueness. In reviewing a business regulation for vagueness, "the principal inquiry is whether the law affords fair warning of what is proscribed." Fair warning is interpreted more loosely in the context of economic regulation because businesses, which face economic demands to plan behavior carefully, can be expected to consult relevant legislation in advance of action. The company president's claim that he and other employees were unaware of the legal requirements even though they had received and signed dozens of statement forms bearing the text of the enforcement policy strains credibility. For these reasons, the defendant's motion for summary judgment is *denied* and the government's motion for partial summary judgment is *granted.*

Case Questions

1. Why does replacing a three-way converter with a two-way converter violate the Clean Air Act?
2. How did the EPA notify firms like Economy Muffler that replacing converters would violate the Clean Air Act? Do you agree with the court that the employees did knowingly violate the Act?

INTERNATIONAL PERSPECTIVE: AIR POLLUTION PROBLEMS

Canadian government leaders have long sought to have more control over the acid rain that falls on Canada from the northeastern and midwestern United States. The 1990 Clean Air Amendments indicate that the United States has decided to take some action to address this regional problem.

Scientists claim that fires in the Amazon Basin caused by burning of the rainforest are destroying not just the region but perhaps the planet. The loss of trees and foliage also reduces the photosynthesis capacity to take in carbon dioxide. Approximately 7 percent of the carbon dioxides that are said to be responsible for global warming are spewed from the Amazon region.

At a 1990 London conference, almost 60 nations agreed to eliminate by the year 2000 the production of chlorofluorcarbons (CFCs) and other chemicals that damage the ozone layer. Data examined by some scientists in early 1992 suggest even that response may not be strong enough. There is evidence that the ozone layer is breaking up over the Arctic far faster than had been anticipated. Accordingly, many nations are now ready to eliminate the CFCs by 1995 instead of waiting until the year 2000.

International agreements are the only way to address some of these worldwide environmental problems. The environmental and international legal environment concerns covered in this and the next chapter are likely to be increasingly intertwined in the coming years.

WATER POLLUTION

The Clean Water Act requires a permit before pollutants can be discharged into navigable waters from any point source, regardless of whether the discharge existed prior to the legislation. Criminal sanctions may be imposed if pollutants are discharged without a permit.

Permits are required for any private or public source of discharge into navigable waters. A firm with a discharge permit must monitor its own performance regarding the discharge of pollutants and report the results to the state and the EPA. The states have the option of administering the permit program themselves or allowing the EPA to do so.

For both private and public organizations discharging pollutants into the nation's waters, the Clean Water Act establishes two standards: the *best practicable technology (BPT)* and the *best available technology economically achievable (BAT)*. All plants were required to install water pollution control devices representing the best practicable pollution control technology by 1977. Such factors as the cost of the equipment, the amount of time required to install it, and the severity of the pollution were considered in determining whether a firm had complied with this requirement.

The Clean Water Act provided that a more stringent standard of best available technology economically achievable had to be met by 1987. Firms must now install the most effective water pollution control equipment available. Less effective alternatives are not acceptable even if they are significantly less expensive.

The Federal Water Pollution Control Act establishes minimum water quality standards, but it also allows the states to adopt more stringent standards. Once the EPA has approved such state standards, those standards must be met by all persons in the state that seek permits. Are the states free to consider any factors they choose in establishing more stringent state water quality standards? Consider the excerpt from the *Homestake Mining* case, which examined water quality standards established in South Dakota:

> The FWPCA states that "standards shall be established taking into consideration" the various factors listed. The applicable federal regulation states that "the State should take into consideration" the various factors. It must, therefore, be determined what the phrase "taking into consideration" requires.
>
> Nothing in the statute seems to indicate that the states must give equal weight to all the factors listed. The *Weyerhaeuser* case indicates that the amount of weight to give each individual factor is within the State's discretion.
>
> In *United States Steel Corporation v. Train,* the Court dealt with the issue of more stringent state standards. The Court held that the FWPCA was not designed to inhibit the states from adopting more stringent standards and in forcing industry to create more effective pollution control technology. Furthermore, the Court held that EPA has no authority to set aside or modify state standards which are more stringent than those mandated by the Act.
>
> The FWPCA clearly indicates that the states are to play a significant role in the reduction of water pollution. The statute itself and the case law make it clear that the states can adopt more stringent standards and can force technology. South Dakota was not required to consider economic and social factors, and thus its failure to do so does not invalidate its water quality standards. EPA's approval of those standards was not arbitrary and capricious or violative of the Act.[2]

LAND POLLUTION

Pollution of the earth is caused by the disposal of toxic and nontoxic solid wastes. Millions of tons of solid wastes are generated each year and are disposed of in open dumps or landfills. Trash from residences and small businesses is usually taken by disposal companies to county or municipal landfills. However, some solid wastes are burned by the individuals or firms generating them. The largest portion of solid wastes comes from agricultural operations. Solid wastes generated by mining operations are another significant factor in land pollution. Solid waste disposal is not only a land pollution problem. Burning solid wastes contributes to air pollution, and dumping solid wastes in or near sources of water may contaminate waterways, lakes, and streams. Many sources of pollution fit into more than one pollution category.

Until very recently, the federal government gave less attention to solid waste disposal than to air and water pollution. Today, however, three federal statutes are concerned with land pollution: the Solid Waste Disposal Act, the Toxic Substance Control Act, and the Comprehensive Environmental Response, Compensation, and Liability Act (Superfund).

---

[2]*Homestake Mining Co. v. U.S. Environmental Protection Agency,* 477 F. Supp. 1279 (S.D. 1979).

Solid Waste Disposal Act

The Solid Waste Disposal Act was enacted in 1965 and amended in 1970. Its purpose is to assist states and municipalities in addressing waste disposal problems. Grants from the federal government are made for waste disposal studies and for the construction of facilities that turn solid waste into energy. Several events occurring in the 1970s focused the attention of Congress on the need for more specific regulation of the use and disposal of certain types of wastes. For example, the land and water contamination caused by the improper disposal of chemical wastes in New York State's Love Canal and by the improper disposal of an insecticide in Virginia received significant attention.

Resource Conservation and Recovery Act In 1976, the *Resource Conservation and Recovery Act (RCRA)* amended the Solid Waste Disposal Act, creating a federal permit system. All businesses that use, transport, or store hazardous wastes are required to comply with its standards. **Hazardous wastes** are wastes that contribute significantly to a serious, irreversible illness or pose a hazard to human health when improperly managed. Firms that generate such wastes must keep records of their disposal. Hazardous wastes must be packaged and labeled. If they are transported off-site for disposal, a manifest must identify the nature and quantity of the wastes and the names of both the transporter and the firm receiving them. The transporter must make entries on the manifest and is responsible for intentional or accidental waste discharges occurring during transportation. Firms generating hazardous wastes must submit annual reports.

Facilities for the disposal of hazardous wastes must have a permit. Such permits are issued only if certain performance standards are met. A disposal facility of this kind must sign the manifest it receives from the transporter of hazardous wastes and return the manifest to the generator of the wastes. Each disposal facility has an EPA identification number. Representative samples of the hazardous wastes must be analyzed before the wastes are stored or treated. EPA inspectors are authorized to enter the disposal facilities at reasonable times to conduct inspections or review records. Currently, only 15 states have commercial dumps for hazardous waste. Although several of these states have attempted to limit out-of-state waste from being dumped at their facility, federal courts have consistently found such laws to interfere with the freedom of interstate commerce. Restrictions in Alabama, Ohio, and South Carolina have been struck down by courts in the last several years. For example, in a 1991 South Carolina case, the federal court of appeals judges wrote in their unanimous ruling, "The effect of every state designating particular limits and bars for out-of-state waste would be catastrophic. . . . Such barriers threaten national economic union."[3]

Hazardous and Solid Waste Amendments In 1984, the *Hazardous and Solid Waste Amendments* amended RCRA to increase the EPA's regulatory powers. Many small waste generators that were exempt form RCRA are now required to use the manifest system for tracking the use, transport, and disposal of hazardous wastes. The 1984 amendments also established a timetable for the gradual elimination of landfills as sites for the disposal of many hazardous substances. Beginning in 1987, existing landfills were required to use specific equipment to limit the harmful effects of leakage. A regulatory program for underground storage tanks was established, and the protection of groundwater is now being addressed by a national commission.

---

[3]See Milo Geyelin and Jeff Bailey, "Court Says South Carolina Can't Stop Waste Disposal There from Out of State," *The Wall Street Journal*, September 25, 1991, p. A16.

The scope of the 1984 amendments indicates the increasing concern with land pollution from hazardous waste disposal. How does an environmental concern covered by one statute affect environmental concerns covered by other statutes? Although the following case deals primarily with land pollution, it also deals with water pollution and public nuisances.

O'Leary v. Moyer's Landfill, Inc.

523 F. Supp. 642 (Pa. 1981)
United States District Court

The plaintiffs were citizens who claimed that the defendants' disposal practices included the addition of pollutants to U.S. waters in violation of the Clean Water Act and open dumping in violation of RCRA. They also sued under several state pollution control laws.

Louis H. Pollack, District Judge

The complaint alleges the landfill's responsibility for: (1) the discharge of leachate (i.e., contaminated liquid) into nearby Skippack Creek; (2) the contamination of water used by the landfill's neighbors for drinking and other purposes; (3) the release of mal odors and loose trash; and (4) the illegal inclusion of toxic wastes among the waste materials accepted for disposal.

Plaintiffs' claims under the Clean Water Act and RCRA are brought under the "citizen suit" provisions contained in each statute. Plaintiffs' claims under RCRA are brought under both the "hazardous waste" and the "solid waste" provisions. The complaint seeks declaratory judgment and enforcement of RCRA's requirement that notification be given to EPA of the storage or disposal of hazardous waste and enforcement of the proscription of "open dumping" of solid waste.

This Act prohibits the unlicensed discharge of any pollutant. The definitions define an "open dump" as a facility that does not comply with the requirements there set forth. The hazardous waste provisions of RCRA require any operator of a site for the storage or disposal of hazardous waste to give notice of the activity to EPA or the state before undertaking the activity. Hazardous wastes include the carcinogens found to be escaping in the landfill's leachate (the solution that results when soluble waste is dissolved). Indeed, leachate from hazardous waste is an important target of RCRA. And the regulatory definition of a "discarded" waste, which in turn includes materials "disposed of," points directly to contaminated leachate.

A material is "disposed of" if it is discharged, deposited, injected, dumped, spilled, leaked, or placed into or on any land or water so that such material or any constituent thereof may enter the environment or be emitted into the air or discharged into ground or surface waters. The evidence of toxic chemicals in leachate from Moyer's Landfill is compelling evidence that those chemicals were "discarded" at the landfill.

However, defendants accurately note that such chemicals, even if discarded, are not "hazardous" unless the chemicals were "commercial chemical product" or "off specification" commercial product. These categories encompass the commercially pure grade of the chemical, any technical grades of the chemical that are produced or marketed, and all formulations in which the chemical is the sole active ingredient.

It is fairly clear from EPA's comments to the regulations that the limitation to commercial product was meant to exclude materials that simply contained such a chemical but which were not themselves the product. Plaintiffs adduced no evidence that the discarded toxic chemicals were materials disposed of in their commercial form rather than, for example, materials which were the residue of other waste. Accordingly, I cannot conclude that the landfill is a noncomplying hazardous waste site.

[Discussion of the violation of the Clean Water Act is omitted.]

The findings underlying my conclusion that pollutants have been discharged into the waters of the United States under the Clean Water Act also lead me to conclude the pollutants have been discharged into Commonwealth waters, which include "any and all rivers, streams, creeks . . . " within this state. Accordingly, I find the defendants have violated the Pennsylvania Clean Streams Act.

Plaintiffs have advanced other claims under the state statutes, which declare a violation of their provisions to be a "public nuisance." Public nuisances may be civilly prosecuted by private plaintiffs only if these plaintiffs allege and prove specific injury "over and above the injury suffered by the public generally." A private nuisance may be abated when the plaintiff's use and enjoyment of his land are substantially diminished by defendant. While plaintiffs have urged findings of both public and private nuisance, there is insufficient evidence showing significant contamination of plaintiffs' drinking water, and there is virtually no evidence showing that the existing contamination of drinking water is a result of the landfill operations.

I have concluded that defendants are in violation of the Clean Water Act and the Resource Conservation and Recovery Act. The accompanying Order (1) declares the defendants to be in violation of the Clean Water Act and the Resource Conservation and Recovery Act; (2) directs defendants forthwith to repair all damaged elements of the existing leachate collection system; and (3) directs the parties, after consultation with EPA and DER; promptly to submit a proposed further Order outlining the long-range steps defendants will be required to take to halt all leachate leakage from the landfill at the earliest possible date.

Case Questions

1. What was the basis for the court's finding that the defendants had violated the federal Clean Water Act?
2. What was the basis for the court's finding that the defendants had not violated the RCRA?

The Toxic Substances Control Act

Congress enacted the Toxic Substances Control Act in 1976 to identify, test, and control chemicals that were believed to pose an unreasonable risk of injury to health or the environment. Many chemicals that are manufactured for useful purposes, such as dioxins, PCBs, and Agent Orange, pose grave dangers to human health and to the environment for years after they have been discarded. Initially, the EPA was charged with developing a comprehensive list of all manufactured chemicals, including thousands of chemicals used in industry and agriculture.

The Toxic Substances Control Act requires manufacturers to test toxic chemicals. The EPA can halt the manufacture of high-risk substances and can issue regulations concerning the manufacture, distribution, commercial use, or disposal of toxic chemical substances. The Toxic Substances Control Act does not cover pesticides because these are regulated under the Pesticide Control Act. It provides that pesticides which are classified for restricted use may be applied only by certified persons.

Over 100 nations have signed an international agreement on toxic waste exports. The international accord requires the government of any country exporting toxic waste to obtain written permission from the government of any country to which the waste is to be shipped. Both industrial and developing countries are concerned about toxic waste exports. The waste from industrial countries has often found its way to developing countries that have been willing to accept it in exchange for much-needed hard currency. Although developing countries may not have the technical know-how to safely dispose of the waste they accept, they realize it is dangerous. The treaty provides them with greater assurance that there will not be secret dumping of foreign waste in their territory.

Ocean Dumping The Marine Protection Research and Sanctuaries Act of 1972 is a U.S. law that establishes a permit system to regulate dumping of materials into the ocean. The Ocean Dumping Ban Act banned the dumping of industrial waste after 1991. Internationally, over 60 countries have signed the 1990 London Dumping Convention. The signatory nations agreed to abide by a 1995 global ban on ocean dumping of industrial waste.

The Comprehensive Environmental Response, Compensation, and Liability Act of 1980 (Superfund)

Until 1980, most of the environmental laws enacted by Congress were aimed at preventing future environmental problems. However, the Superfund legislation was intended to create a fund for the identification and cleanup of hazardous waste disposal sites. The money for the fund is raised through taxes levied on manufacturers of certain dangerous chemicals.

Approximately \$1.6 billion was used over a five-year period from 1980 to 1985, mostly for cleaning up hundreds of emergency oil and tank car spills. By the end of that period, less than 2 percent of the 679 sites on the national priority list had been cleaned up. In 1986, Congress provided an additional \$8.5 billion for cleanup during the 1986–1990 period. In 1990, another \$5.1 billion was authorized for 1990–1994. It is estimated that over the next 50 years more than \$100 billion will be required to clean up waste sites.

The Right to Know Act Congress also amended the Superfund law in 1986 when it passed the Emergency Planning and Community Right-to-Know Act. The act was passed in response to the chemical plant disaster in Bhopal, India, that resulted in over 3,000 deaths. The act requires companies to notify the government if they release any extremely hazardous chemicals into the environment. Inventories of hazardous substances must be submitted to the government, and state and local planning to deal with emergencies is required.

Compensation and Liability Provisions An important aspect of the Superfund legislation is its compensation and liability provisions. Owners and operators of polluting facilities or vessels, as well as those who generate, treat, and dispose of hazardous waste, are held strictly liable for all cleanup costs. These costs include the government's response costs and the damage to natural resources. Owners who cooperate in cleanup and whose acts are not willfully negligent have limited liability. A due diligence defense exists if commercial developers run tests and examine EPA records and title documents to discover previous toxic dumping.

The imposition of liability on the "owner and operator" of polluted sites caused banks to severely limit their commercial real estate lending. After complaints from businesses that were affected by the "credit crunch" brought about by the Superfund liability provisions, the EPA made some modifications in the liability portions of the law.

Superfund Law Creates a Credit Crunch: EPA Reacts

The provision of the Superfund law that imposes liability on the owner of property for the costs of any cleanup of hazardous waste has caused significant problems for banks and some firms seeking bank loans. Courts have ruled that financial institutions can be held liable under the Superfund Law as an "owner or operator" of a polluted site by virtue of lending money to the owner of the tainted property or being able to affect hazardous waste disposal decisions. These decisions prompted bankers to refuse credit to some high-risk industries with significant real estate assets.

Bankers sought clarification of their liability particularly when they obtained a security interest (such as a mortgage) on property but did not participate in managing that property.

The EPA responded with a rule that allows lenders to engage in a variety of activities, including protecting their security interests and requiring the cleanup of a facility during the life of a loan, without incurring Superfund liability.

See Eleanor Erdevig, "Lenders and Environmental Policies," *Economic Perspective,* The Federal Reserve Bank of Chicago, November–December 1991, p. 2.

The Superfund legislation does not make polluters liable for injuries to private persons, though such persons may bring private suits in state courts under common law rules. In addition, persons injured by hazardous waste may make a limited claim for compensation from the Superfund if the owner of the hazardous waste site is unknown. Figure 20–2 depicts the major federal environmental laws, while several other federal environmental laws are noted in the next section. Some states have laws providing compensation for hazardous waste victims. Other state and local environmental concerns are discussed in the final section of the chapter.

OTHER FEDERAL ENVIRONMENTAL CONCERNS

Two other environmental concerns that have been addressed by significant federal legislation are nuclear energy and wildlife preservation. In the early days of nuclear energy, the federal government had a monopoly on its use and would not allow its use for civilian purposes. More recently, the federal government's concerns with nuclear energy have focused on nuclear accidents and nuclear waste. Since wildlife is regarded as subject to federal regulation under the commerce clause, the state laws affecting wildlife are subject to preemption by federal laws. Some of the federal laws that seek to protect wildlife from both governmental and private interference are noted in this section.

FIGURE 20–2
Major Federal Environmental Laws

Act	Coverage
Clean Air Act	Protects ambient (outdoor) air quality through national ambient air quality standards, state implementation plans, and controls on both stationary (point source) and moveable (automotive) sources.
Clean Water Act (Federal Water Pollution Control Act)	Protects quality of surface water by setting water quality standards and limiting industrial and municipal discharges into those waters by a permit system
Comprehensive Environmental Response Compensation and Liability Act (Superfund)	Identifies and provides funding for cleanup of hazardous waste sites; imposes liability for cleanup on those who generate, treat, and dispose of hazardous waste.
Marine Protection, Research, and Sanctuaries Act	Regulates dumping of all materials into ocean waters.
Resource Conservation and Recovery Act (RCRA)	Establishes a regulatory system for the generation, transportation, and disposal of hazardous waste; also deals with solid waste problems.
Toxic Substance Control Act	Requires testing of toxic chemicals and provides for regulation of those chemicals that pose an unreasonable risk to health or the environment.

Nuclear Power and Nuclear Waste

Nuclear power is a controversial source of energy in the United States and, to a lesser extent, throughout the rest of the world. Although it has the potential for supplementing fossil sources of energy such as coal and oil, significant dangers are posed by the possibility of nuclear radiation, nuclear accidents, and terrorist acts against nuclear power plants. Nuclear power currently provides approximately 10 percent of the energy used in the United States, over 30 percent of the energy used in Japan and Great Britain, and close to 65 percent of the energy used in France.

The Regulation of Nuclear Power Plants Nuclear power has been heavily regulated by the federal government since the beginning of the atomic age during World War II (1941–1945). The Atomic Energy Act was amended in 1954 to authorize the Atomic Energy Commission (now the Nuclear Regulatory Commission) to license a variety of private, commercial uses for nuclear energy. In 1959, Congress permitted the states to establish restrictions regarding the location of nuclear power plants and the disposal of nuclear wastes. Under the Clean Air Act, the states may also establish limits for the emission of radioactive particles by nuclear power plants. Some states have such restrictive standards with regard to the use of nuclear power that nuclear power plants cannot be constructed in them.

Since the 1986 disaster at the Chernobyl, Russia, nuclear power facility, it has been clear that a nuclear accident can cause substantial damage and injury to thousands of people. Although the most disastrous consequences are felt by those close to the accident site, radiation in the atmosphere and in the food supply adversely affects the lives of millions of people in distant locations.

Regulation of Nuclear Waste The accumulation of nuclear wastes is a second concern associated with nuclear energy. Radioactive wastes are created as the fissions of uranium release energy in nuclear reactors. Since those wastes may take centuries to become harmless, the need for safe storage or disposal sites is critical. In 1982, Congress passed the *Nuclear Waste Policy Act* to establish a national plan for the disposal of highly radioactive nuclear wastes. The construction of several appropriate storage facilities is to begin in the 1990s. The cost of constructing and operating the facilities will be paid for by fees levied on nuclear energy generators.

Wildlife Protection

Numerous federal laws seek to protect wildlife. The most comprehensive of these laws is the *Endangered Species Act.* This act, enforced by the Environmental Protection Agency and the Department of Commerce, protects endangered and threatened animal species. It prohibits the taking of any animal on the endangered species list. Harassing, harming, pursuing, hunting, shooting, trapping, collecting, and capturing are considered the taking of an animal. Federal projects must not adversely affect endangered species or their habitats. It is a federal offense to buy, sell, or possess any species listed as endangered or threatened or any product made from such a species. For example, the Endangered Species Act prohibits the sale or purchase of garments made from some furs or of products made from reptile skins.

The Migratory Bird Treaty Act, the Fishery Conservation and Management Act, and the Marine Mammal Protection Act are among the federal laws designed to protect wildlife. The states also enact laws to protect wildlife within their borders. The granting of state hunting and fishing permits is often dependent on the need to protect state fishing and gaming resources.

ETHICAL DILEMMA: YEW TREES—ENVIRONMENT VERSUS MEDICINE

Sometimes protecting the environment isn't easy. Thirty thousand women in the United States struggle with ovarian cancer; 12,000 are likely to die of the disease this year. An experimental drug, taxol, has achieved a very good response rate in advanced ovarian cancer cases. But, taxol is derived from a rare Pacific yew tree. Because only a small amount of taxol is available from each tree, tens of thousands of the trees, which grow in old forests and provide refuge to some endangered wildlife, would have to be cut down to meet the demand for the drug. Conservationists oppose large-scale sacrificing of the trees, while medical researchers say the yew trees' taxol is the most promising chemotherapy to appear in a decade. How should we decide what action to take?

STATE AND LOCAL CONCERNS

State Environmental Protection Laws

Most states have detailed legislation requiring environmental impact statements regarding actions by state or local governments that will affect environmental quality. This legislation generally also requires private industrial and commercial firms to prepare such statements regarding actions of this kind on their part. Some states are addressing environmental concerns that are more appropriately handled on a state level. Solid waste bans for yard waste, mandatory use of recyclable materials, and higher limits for automobile emissions are among the proposals being addressed by the states.

West Michigan Environmental Action Council, Inc. v. Natural Resources Commission of the State of Michigan

275 N.W.2d 538 (1979)
Supreme Court of Michigan

The Michigan Department of Natural Resources (DNR)* sold oil and gas leases covering 500,000 acres of state land, including part of a state forest. After filing an environmental impact statement, the DNR permitted Shell Oil Company and several other oil companies to drill exploratory wells in a portion of the state forest. The plaintiffs filed a complaint under the Michigan Environmental Protection Act, claiming DNR's agreement with the oil companies did not properly consider the environmental impact of the drilling on wildlife, particularly the elk. The trial court upheld the agreement, and the plaintiffs appealed to the Supreme Court of Michigan.

*The Department of Natural Resources was governed by the Natural Resources Commission. For purposes of this case, the Commission and the DNR are treated as one.

Moody, Justice

Perhaps the single most revealing piece of evidence is the Environmental Impact Statement for Potential Hydrocarbon Development in the Pigeon River County State Forest, prepared by the DNR. Many of the EIS's conclusions directly apply to the effects of exploratory drilling.

Testimony before the trial court indicated that six of the ten proposed sites were not adjacent to any road, requiring that roads be built to such sites. The EIS cites studies in Montana which concluded that "[e]lk avoid roads even when there is no traffic." The EIS also observed that "[w]hether the elk will return to their former range following completion of the last seismic survey work is unknown."

Some quantification of the adverse impact of exploratory drilling on the elk can be gained from comparing the EIS's Matrix for Proposed Hydrocarbon Development in the Southern Portion of the Forest with Dr. Inman's testimony. Dr. Inman, who participated in the development of the EIS, testified that a slow recovery time is considered to be 40 to 50 years or more, a short recovery time less than 20 years, and a great recovery time is 100 years or more.

The Environmental Impact Matrix defines a significant adverse impact as "a change in the element that is impacted from its present status to a status that may take a long time for recovery, at least during the duration of the project." Applying Dr. Inman's definitions of what constitutes a slow recovery time to the matrix predictions, it would appear that elk would avoid the impacted areas for 40 to 50 years.

We recognize that virtually all human activities can be found to adversely impact natural resources in some way or other. The real question before us is, when does such impact rise to the level of impairment or destruction? The DNR's environmental impact statement recognizes that "[e]lk are unique to this area of Michigan" and that the herd is "the only sizable wild herd east of the Mississippi River. Several attempts to introduce elk elsewhere in Michigan have been unsuccessful."

It is estimated that the herd's population, which numbered in excess of 1,500 in 1963, now probably lies between 170 and 180. Expert testimony has established that the Pigeon River Country State Forest, particularly unit 1 in which the exploratory drilling is to take place, provides excellent habitat for elk and that the elk frequent this area. Furthermore, it is clear from the record that available habitat is shrinking.

In light of the limited number of the elk, the unique nature and location of this herd, and the apparently serious and lasting, though unquantifiable, damage that will result to the herd from the drilling of the ten exploratory wells, we conclude that defendants' conduct constitutes an impairment or destruction of a natural resource. Accordingly, we reverse the remand to the trail court for entry of a permanent injunction prohibiting the drilling of the wells.

Case Questions

1. Why would the exploratory drilling damage the elk?
2. If it is impossible to drill without adversely affecting some animals, would drilling ever be permitted?

Antilitter Laws

A few states have enacted laws aimed at reducing the litter along state highways. Litter is frequently in the form of disposable beverage bottles or cans. Some states have passed *bottle laws* requiring purchasers to pay a cash deposit on all beverage containers. The purchaser receives a return of the deposit for empty containers returned to any authorized center. Usually, stores selling beverages must also handle returns and refund the deposit. The states with bottle laws have significantly decreased roadway litter.

Nuisance, Trespass, and Land Use Laws

Nuisance Laws Common law nuisance statutes have long been used by state and local governments to deal with environmental problems. A **nuisance** is a substantial and unreasonable interference with the use and enjoyment of a person's interest in property. A public nuisance causes damage to the property of many people or to public facilities, whereas a private nuisance is a use of property that deprives other property owners of their right to use and enjoy their property. Both public and private nuisances are discussed in Chapter 7.

Trespass A **trespass** is an unlawful interference with the property of another. The person who sets foot on the property of another is a trespasser, but so is the firm that causes soot, dust, or other particles to intrude onto the land of another. Trespass invades the property owner's exclusive right of possession, whereas a nuisance interferes with the property owner's use and enjoyment of the property. If the cement dust from a nearby factory is deposited on another's land, a trespass has occurred because something else is now on that land. Since trespass and nuisance often overlap, it is generally less important to determine which exists than to determine whether either has occurred.

Land Use Laws Zoning ordinances and land use regulations have recently begun to play a larger role in the addressing of environmental problems. As Chapter 7 indicates, municipalities enact zoning ordinances to control the use of land. State laws may require municipalities to prepare land use plans or allow them to determine how differing uses of land will be accommodated.

SUMMARY

Environmental laws regulate human interaction with the surrounding air, water, and land. These laws impose limitations on the use of products and manufacturing processes that can adversely affect the natural environment. Most of the environmental laws in the United States are fairly recent federal laws. The 1970 National Environmental Policy Act declared a national policy of protecting the environment. Its most significant provision requires that an environmental impact statement be prepared before any major federal action that will significantly affect environmental quality. The Environmental Protection Agency is responsible for enforcing federal laws regulating air, water, and land pollution.

The Clean Air Act is the primary federal statute directed at air pollution. It establishes standards for air quality, and it requires each state to develop a plan for achieving an air pollution level lower than those standards. The 1990 Amendments to the Clean Air Act concern smog, acid rain, toxic emissions, and alternative fuels. The Water Pollution Control Act seeks to eliminate water pollution, and the Clean Water Act requires permits for discharges of pollutants into navigable waters from any source. Like the Clean Air Act, the Clean Water Act establishes standards that are to be met and allows the states to administer a permit program.

Three federal statutes address land pollution. The Solid Waste Disposal Act, as amended by the Resource Conservation and Recovery Act, establishes a permit system regulating the use, transport, or storage of hazardous wastes. The Toxic Substances Control Act regulates the manufacture, distribution, commercial use, and disposal of chemical substances that pose an unreasonable risk of injury to health or the environment. The Superfund legislation of 1980 provides money for the identification and cleanup of hazardous waste disposal sites. It places liability for cleanup costs associated with the treatment or disposal of hazardous wastes on the waste generator or landowner. Nuclear power and wildlife protection are important environmental issues addressed by other federal laws.

Although the most significant environmental legislation is found at the federal level, state and local laws also seek to protect the environment. State environmental protection laws are modeled on, and permitted by, the National Environmental Policy Act. Special state resources are also protected by state laws. A few states have enacted bottle laws that require deposits for cans or bottles of beverages sold in the state; such laws seek to reduce litter from these containers by encouraging their return and recycling. The common law doctrines of nuisance and trespass are also used to deal with environmental problems. Zoning ordinances at the local level also regulate land use.

KEY TERMS

environmental impact statement, p. 635
best available technology, p. 638
bubble concept, p. 638
hazardous waste, p. 645
nuisance, p. 652
trespass, p. 653

CHAPTER EXERCISES

1. Discuss the purpose of the National Environmental Policy Act. Why is government regulation of the environment important to the business community?
2. Your firm has been hired to build a new federal post office near a large in-town neighborhood. A group of in-town residents oppose the building of the new government facility. What factors must you consider in an environmental impact statement (EIS)?
3. What is the difference between an individual machine emission point source and a "bubble concept" source?
4. What does it mean to say that the Clean Air Act is "technology forcing"? What purpose does technology forcing serve?
5. What are three requirements that are a part of the 1990 Clean Air Act? Which one(s) do you think will have the greatest effect on business prices?
6. As part of its mushroom farming business, Frezzo Brothers, Inc. produces compost to provide a growing base for mushrooms. The Frezzos were discharging pollutants through the runoff overflow of pollutants from their mushroom farm. The government brought criminal actions against their firm. May criminal sanctions be used as a means of enforcement under the Clean Water Act? What must one prove for there to be criminal liability? *United States v. Frezzo Brothers, Inc.*, 602 F.2d. 1123 (1979).
7. What are hazardous wastes? How does the EPA regulate hazardous wastes?
8. What is the Superfund, and what is its importance to business? How does it affect bank lending?
9. The city of Chicago enacted an ordinance banning the use of detergents containing phosphates. Procter & Gamble lost $4.8 million in sales in the Chicago area during the first five months following the enactment of this ordinance because a number of Chicago-area wholesalers that sold in midwestern states other than Illinois refused to carry phosphate-based detergents. Procter & Gamble sued, alleging that the ordinance resulted in an impermissible interference with interstate commerce. Do you think that state and local governments should have the power to regulate such products as phosphates? *Procter & Gamble v. City of Chicago*, 501 F.2d. 69 (1975).
10. Why has the federal government enacted extensive legislation in the environmental area? Do you favor international regulation instead of national regulation? Federal regulation instead of state regulation? Why?
11. Water pollution caused by oil spills in the waters of Alaska, Texas, and Delaware occurred in 1989. In the summer of 1988, numerous beaches on the eastern coast of the United States were inundated with medical debris that apparently had been discarded from hospitals or medical clinics.

    In some cases, the polluter responsible for an oil spill is a corporation that has little insurance or assets and is thus unable to pay for the cleanup costs. In a few cases, the waste disposal firm is responsible for the pollution.

    In other cases, it is impossible to trace the debris dumped into an open sea to one or more polluters. In these cases, what should be the government policy? Should the government absorb the cost of cleanup? Should the cost be spread among all manufacturers of certain products, or to all waste disposal firms, even if many are not polluters? What if the cost of cleanup to private industry or to a particular polluting firm will cause that firm to go bankrupt or to reduce employment? Is the benefit derived from having the firm pay for its pollution worth the cost to society of having the firm go out of business? Will enforcing pollution laws make U.S. firms less competitive with foreign firms that may not have to bear such costs? If so, should the laws still be strictly enforced?

Chapter 21

THE LEGAL ENVIRONMENT OF INTERNATIONAL BUSINESS

KEY CONCEPTS

Laws from several sources can affect international business transactions. Although laws in the country of source are generally the most important, laws of other countries that have extraterritorial effect must also be considered. Regional and international organizations are also sources of laws that affect international business transactions.

International trade is affected by laws that regulate exports because of security concerns or scarcities of goods and by laws and policies that promote exports through tax benefits and governmental assistance.

Tariffs, quotas, and product bans restrict imports. Exchange controls affect trade because they regulate the foreign currency that is needed to pay for goods.

Licensing may offer a cost-effective method of conducting international business without investing in foreign facilities.

As a result of national regulations and of the desire to minimize risk and to benefit from the unique contributions of foreign firms, joint ventures are becoming more common than direct investments in international activities.

Numerous legal questions must be answered before a foreign investment is made. Tax, labor, antitrust, and investment laws should be consulted. Foreign investments are also affected by the independence of a country's courts and by the nature of its economic, political, and legal environments.

INTRODUCTION . . . PAST, PRESENT, FUTURE

International trade has existed for thousands of years. The law merchant began in the 17th century as a private law to govern commercial transactions between merchants from different countries. The Uniform Commercial Code (UCC), applicable to the sale of goods in the United States, and the United Nations Convention on Contracts for the International Sale of Goods (CISG), are present-day successors to the law merchant.

Today, a combination of national, regional, and international laws govern international business activities. Laws in the country of source regulate the import of goods, determine the acceptability of provisions in licensing agreements, and affect the organization and operation of joint-venture or direct-investment facilities. Laws in the country of origin may be given extraterritorial application so as to affect foreign business activities that have an impact on commerce in that country.

Organizations such as the European Community (EC), the Association of Southeast Asian Nations (ASEAN), the Gulf Cooperation Council (GCC), the Organization of Petroleum Exporting Countries (OPEC), and the Andean Common Market (ANCOM) have emerged in recent decades as regional sources of law. Some regional organizations are concerned with particular problems (OPEC's concern with the world price for petroleum products), or with certain types of international transactions (ANCOM's regulation of foreign investments), whereas others have a variety of institutions that make laws in numerous fields (the EC).

OVERVIEW

International business has become so important to nations and business firms that some study of its scope and character is essential. Until recent decades, the United States had a somewhat self-sufficient economy, so that international business activities received little attention. American consumers are now well aware of many imported products. For example, many of us eat Chinese food, drink French wines, operate German machinery, and drive Japanese cars. In addition, U.S. businesses export such products as farm machinery, computers, and airplanes, and U.S. farmers export wheat, corn, lettuce, citrus products, and many other crops. International investment, by contrast, is just beginning to receive widespread attention. Worldwide investment by U.S. corporations that build factories in such countries as Mexico, France, and Japan is one side of the international investment picture; the other side is the opening of new manufacturing facilities by Japanese, German, or Korean firms in South Carolina, Tennessee, Pennsylvania, or Michigan. Both sides of international trade and investment deserve attention from the legal perspective.

The first section of this chapter discusses the current status of international trade and investment. Conflicts between international business firms and the nations that seek to regulate their conduct are noted. International business activities may be regulated by national, regional, and international laws. The second section focuses on the sources of laws and on the special problems that arise when one nation attempts to apply its laws to events occurring outside its borders. The third section examines the laws that most directly affect international trade. Trade may involve the export or import of products or services, or it may involve the licensing of patents, trademarks, copyrights, or know-how to foreign manufacturers or distributors that make or sell products or services internationally. The final section discusses laws that affect foreign investments through joint ventures and direct investments by single firms.

FIGURE 21–1 European free trade association members

FIGURE 21–2 Trends in World Trade

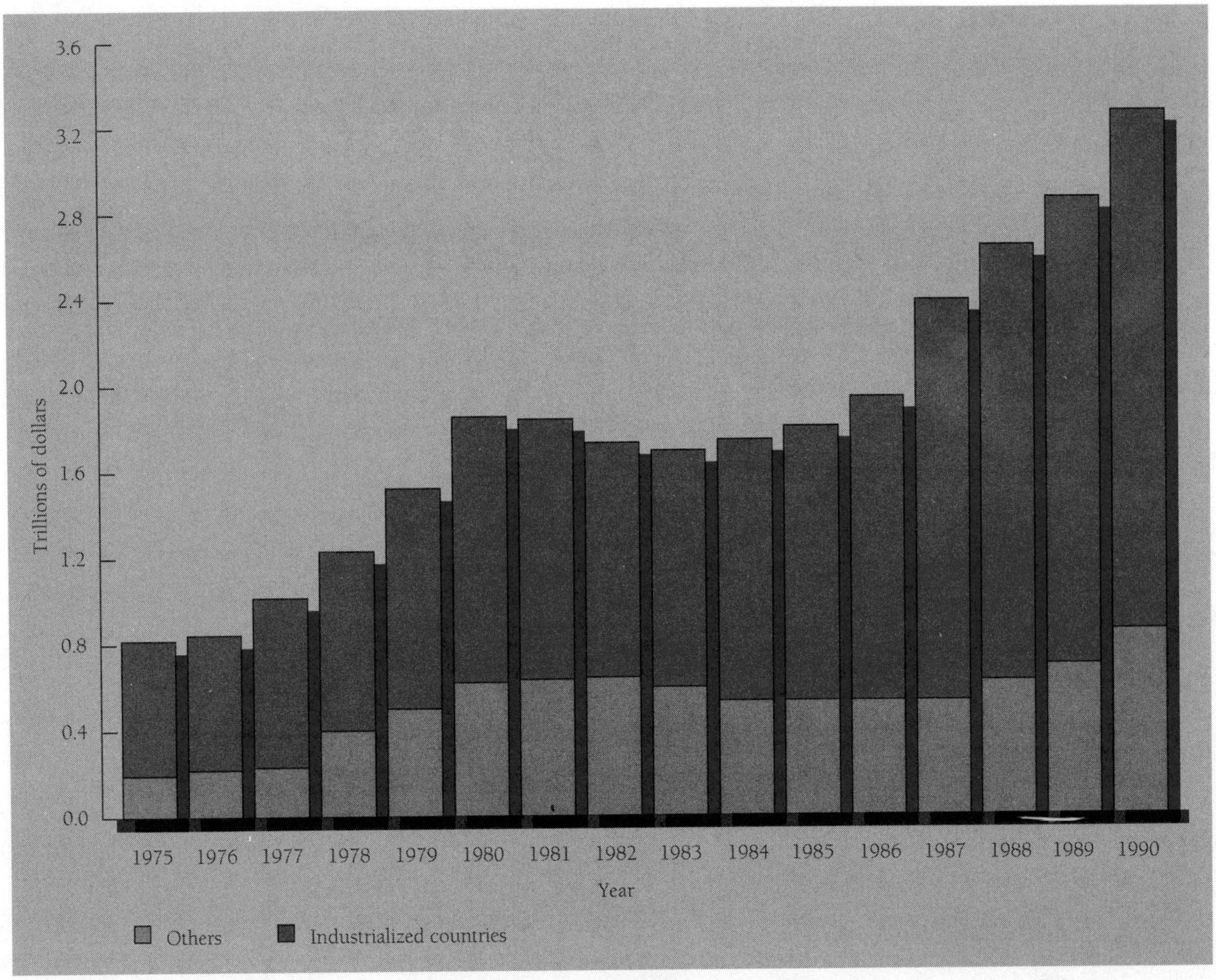

Source: *Direction of Trade Statistics: 1980–1989 Yearbooks 1980-1988,* Washington, D.C.: International Monetary Fund 1989; and International Financial Statistics: 1991, Washington, D.C.: International Monetary Fund 1991.

CONDUCTING INTERNATIONAL BUSINESS

International Trade

The United States has long played an important role in world trade development, but the countries of the European Community (EC) rank first in the value of trade (imports and exports) conducted with other countries and regions.[1] (Figure 21–1 shows the location of the EC countries.) In recent decades, countries on the Pacific Rim have intensified their

---

[1]As of 1992, the countries of the European Community include Belgium, the Netherlands, Luxembourg, France, Germany, Italy, Ireland, the United Kingdom, Denmark, Greece, Spain, and Portugal. Several other countries, once members of the European Free Trade Association (EFTA), have agreed to merge with the EC in 1993; they include Austria, Finland, Iceland, Norway, Sweden, and Switzerland.

involvement in world trade. Japan has been in the forefront of world trade for many years. Taiwan, South Korea, Singapore, and Hong Kong have become world trade centers, and China has been seeking to significantly increase its international trade.

The volume of world trade in goods and services in 1990 was almost four times the volume in 1975. Figure 21–2 indicates both the trend and source of world trade from 1975 to 1990.

International Investment

Although international trade is generally more visible, international investment has been increasing and has reached significant levels in many countries. Foreign investment occurs when individuals or firms purchase securities (typically stocks or bonds) of foreign firms. If the amount of the investment by the purchaser gives that person or firm at least 10 percent ownership of the foreign firm, the investment is known as a **direct investment**.

FIGURE 21–3 Foreign Investments in the United States: 1980 and 1989

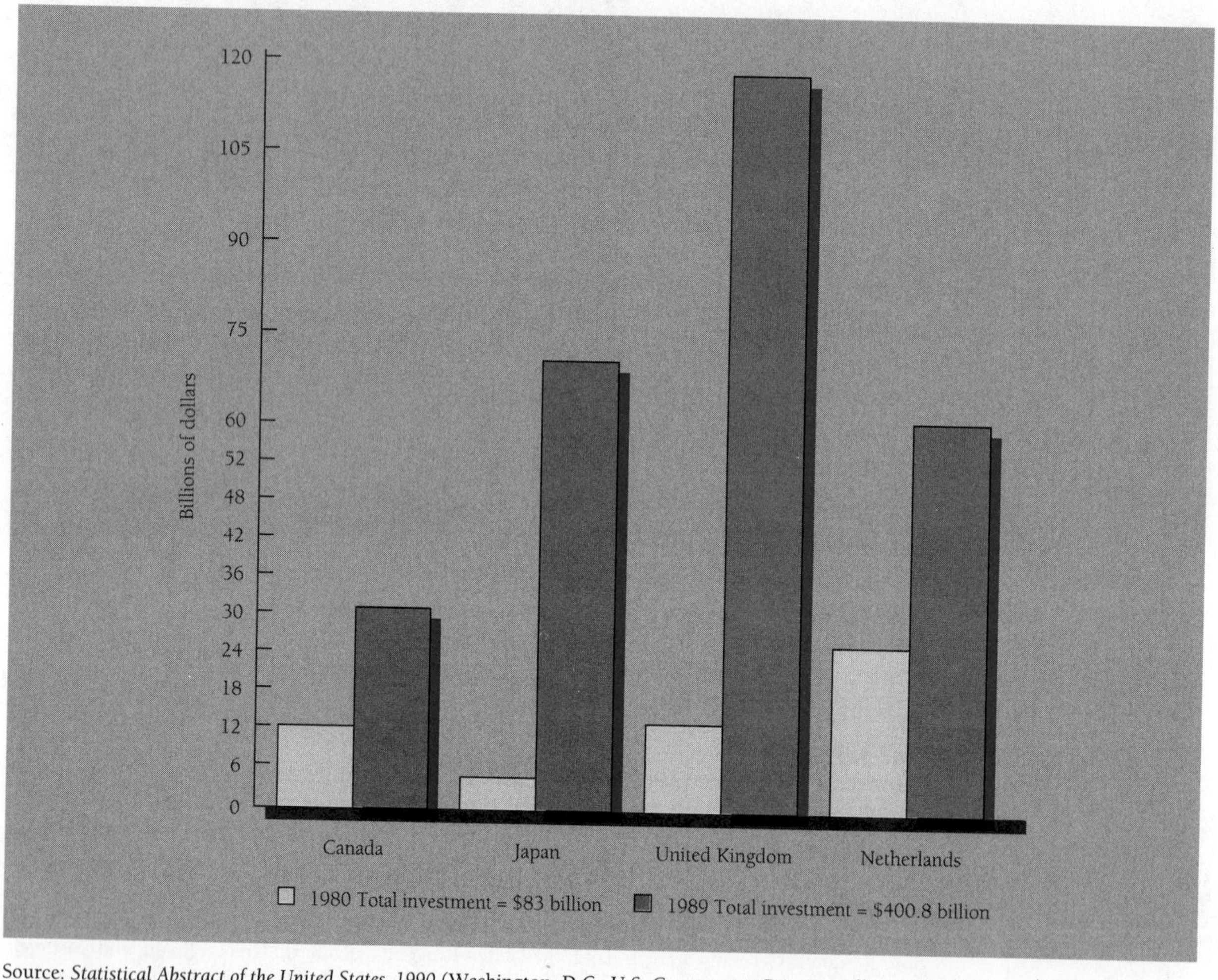

Source: *Statistical Abstract of the United States, 1990* (Washington, D.C.: U.S. Government Printing Office, 1990), U.S. Department of Commerce, Bureau of the Census, p. 777.

FIGURE 21–4 U.S. Investments Abroad: 1980 and 1989

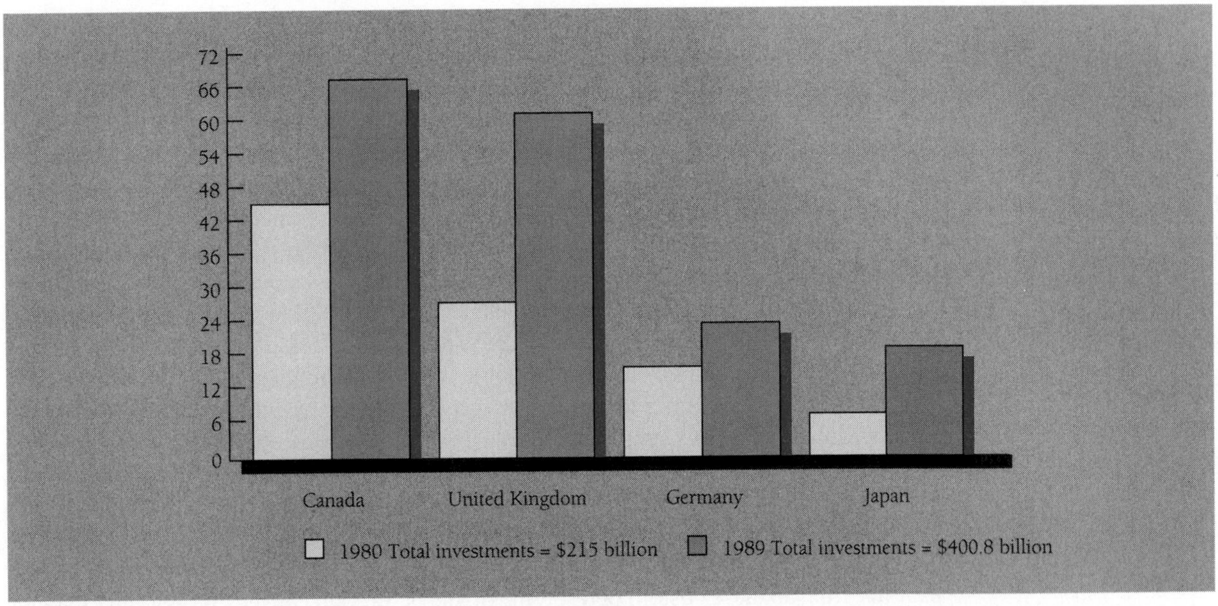

Source: *Statistical Abstract of the United States, 1990* (Washington, D.C.: U.S. Government Printing Office, 1990), U.S. Department of Commerce, Bureau of the Census, p. 797; Business America, April 22, 1991, U.S. Department of Commerce, p. 7.

A purchase of foreign securities that results in the purchaser owning less than 10 percent of that firm is known as a **portfolio investment.**

In recent years, foreign firms have made significant direct investment in EC countries, the United States, Mexico, and several countries in eastern Europe. For the United States, the amount of investment by foreign firms, known as foreign direct investment in the United States (FDIUS) has recently surpassed the level of direct investment abroad (DIA) by U.S. firms. Figure 21–3 illustrates the origin of foreign investment in the United States, and Figure 21–4 depicts the major countries in which U.S. firms invest.

Nations and International Business Firms

Different nations have different policies and laws regarding the conduct of business by foreign-based firms. As early as the 1950s, some governments began to realize that their goals could conflict with the goals of the local business subsidiaries of foreign corporations. Consequently, some nations imposed a variety of laws, administrative rules, and investment codes on foreign investors. By contrast, other nations welcomed foreign investors because they provided many people with jobs and economic improvement. These nations modified their tax laws, currency exchange regulations, and administrative policies to attract multinational enterprises.

Countries also vary in the manner in which they regulate how their own firms conduct their international business activities. For example, although exports are generally encouraged, they are sometimes restricted. Moreover, within any one country, some national laws may promote international business, whereas others seek to restrict its influence.

SOURCES OF LAW

A domestic or national legal problem is approached by attempting to fit the facts into a known legal framework. When doing business in the United States, a business manager assumes the existence of legal rules established by legislatures or administrative agencies and interpreted by the courts. However, the national or regional laws governing foreign transactions may be based on social, political, and economic values different from those of the United States. Moreover, the role of law and even the type of legal system in other countries are often quite different from the U.S. legal environment.

For example, in the countries of the European Community, some laws originate at the national or local level while directives and regulations come from the Commission of the Community. The legal systems in Poland, Czechoslovakia, and the republics in the Commonwealth of Independent States (CIS) are changing rapidly. A new legal order has not yet replaced the old system. For example, the new republics of Estonia, Latvia, and Lithuania are each seeking to attract foreign investment by offering tax incentives to firms willing to build facilities there. Only a few years ago, the republics were not a source of law of concern for foreign business firms. In the Middle East and in countries such as Malaysia and Indonesia, one must be cognizant of the influences of the Islamic religion on the legal system. The Islamic sources of law affect both the substantive and procedural laws in many countries. To complicate matters, many rules are unpublished customs. For example, the Japanese custom of resolving disputes through consensus between financial regulators and financial firms makes it difficult for foreign firms to compete because the rule are not "transparent." Just as the foreign investor in the United States is faced with a new and complex legal environment when doing business here, the legal environment in other countries will differ from that to which U.S. businesses are accustomed.

National, Regional, and International Laws

When a firm engages in international business, its activities are regulated by national, regional, and international laws. The dominant source of the laws that affect international business is national law.

National Laws The laws of different countries often have conflicting aims. Countries frequently regulate overlapping aspects of business transactions. Some countries seek to resolve conflicting rules by entering into *bilateral treaties,* agreements with both national and international effect. Treaties are an important source of law that should be consulted before transacting international business.

Absent treaty provisions resolving conflicts between different national laws, a business should assume that a transaction could be subject to the law of more than one nation. In some situations, the laws of a nation can regulate activities or transactions occurring outside its geographic boundaries (*extraterritorial*). In such situations, a business must seek to comply both with the law of the nation where the transaction occurs and with the national law that is given extraterritorial effect.

Regional Laws The regional coordination of policies by different nations is a fairly recent development affecting the conduct of international business. *Regional organizations* provide a larger framework for the regulation of business activities than do individual nations. They are more cohesive, though smaller, groups of nations than the groups found in international organizations. Regional organizations take a variety of forms. Some nations cooperate for rather limited and specific purposes. The member nations of the Organization of Petroleum Exporting Countries (OPEC) seek to stabilize the price at which oil is sold. Many of those nations do not cooperate with one another in other matters affecting international business. The five South American countries that are members of the Andean Common Market (ANCOM) agree to a common policy under which foreign investments will be permitted within that region.[2] The EC is the most important of the regional organizations. Its role as a lawmaker affecting international activities is discussed later in the chapter.

International Law In some cases, the nations of the world have given lawmaking powers to *international organizations*. For example, such organizations as the International Monetary Fund, the General Agreement on Tariffs and Trade, and the United Nations sometimes have significant effects on the international legal environment. Recent international conferences about the law of the sea, environmental problems, trade barriers, and monetary matters provide examples of the continuing development of new international laws that affect business activities.

National Law and Legal Systems

The national law of the country in which a firm is doing business usually has a greater impact on the firm's activities than do any other types of law. The laws of most countries, despite much variation, can be classified as belonging to one of three major legal systems. The socialistic legal system is no longer considered significant for international business activities because it has been discarded in recent years by many of the countries that followed it.

Major Legal Systems

1. Civil law or code law system, as in France.
2. Common law legal system, as in the United States.
3. Islamic legal system, as in Pakistan.

Despite the variety of legal systems found among the countries of the world, the recognized legal sources within most countries are customs, judicial practices, and legislation. Significant differences, however, lie in how each legal system uses these sources of law. For example, judicial decisions are recognized as a primary source of law in a nation with a common law legal system. In such a nation, courts may interpret legislative acts and declare them void if they conflict with the nation's constitution. By contrast, civil law or code law legal systems give a more limited role to courts. For example, because in France only laws derived directly from the *code civil* are considered primary sources of law, French court decisions have a lower status than legislative enactments as a source of law.

There are also important differences in the application of substantive laws. For example, even though contract laws occupy an important role for individuals and business firms in many countries, the details of a particular contract may differ significantly. Consider the United States, where a contract is apt to include language for every contingency. The approach of businesspeople and their lawyers is to use the contract as the written

[2]These countries include Bolivia, Venezuela, Colombia, Ecuador, and Peru. Chile was a member until it withdrew in 1977.

expression of everything the parties have agreed to do. In Germany, however, contracts do not need to include all the terms agreed to. If there are standard practices and ways of conducting business in a certain industry, the parties are expected to know and abide by those practices; reference to them is not found in a contract. Still further, in Japan, the parties undertaking the same type of business activity might not even make a written contract. If a contract is prepared, it likely will be less extensive than its counterpart in the United States or Germany and if conditions change, the parties will expect to renegotiate the contract, regardless of what the contract provides. The contract terms are less important than is the relationship between the parties and the expectations which arise from that relationship.

Legal institutions have varying degrees of independence and authority in different countries. Even where the letter of the law seems to be similar, its interpretations, application, and enforceability can differ greatly. For example, the dozens of countries that have a legal system based at least in part on Islamic law differ in their interpretations of the Shari'a and Koran.

Extraterritoriality of National Laws

A conflict may occur between national laws if attempts are made to extend the effects of one country's law beyond that country's boundaries, thereby creating *extraterritorial law.* For example, both the U.S. income tax and antitrust laws have extraterritorial application. If a U.S. corporation derives income from export sales to Germany, license royalties from Brazil, or dividends from a Japanese subsidiary, all of these sources of income are subject to the U.S. income tax. There may be double taxation of such income because the country where the income is earned, the country of source, generally seeks to tax income earned within its boundaries. However, credit provisions in the U.S. tax laws and bilateral treaty agreements between the United States and many other countries may reduce or even eliminate this potential double taxation.

Another example of an extraterritorial law is found in the Sherman Act, the keystone of U.S. antitrust law, discussed in Chapter 15.

Extraterritorial Language of the Sherman Antitrust Act

Every contract, combination or conspiracy in restraint of trade or commerce . . . with foreign nations is declared to be illegal.

In 1945, Judge Learned Hand made it clear that the Sherman Act applied to restrictive practices of non-U.S. firms acting abroad if their practices were intended to affect and did affect imports into the United States:

> It is settled law . . . that any state may impose liabilities, even upon persons not within its allegiance for conduct outside its borders which the state reprehends.[3]

How does a U.S. court determine whether U.S. antitrust laws should apply to a restrictive agreement occurring outside the borders of the United States that could affect U.S. commerce? The following case discusses the possible extraterritorial application of a U.S. law.

[3] *United States v. Aluminum Co. of America,* 148 F.2d 416, 419 (2d Cir. 1945).

Timberlane Lumber Co. v. Bank of America

749 F.2d 1378 (1984)
Court of Appeals, Second Circuit

Timberlane Lumber Company, whose primary business is the purchase and distribution of lumber in the United States, formed a partnership with two Honduran corporations to develop alternative sources of lumber for delivery to the United States from Honduras. It eventually purchased an interest in an existing but financially unstable lumber mill owned by the Lima family. Before the Timberlane purchase, a part of the ownership of the Lima firm had been transferred to Bank of America. Timberlane filed this antitrust action, alleging that Bank of America refused to sell its share in the Lima enterprise because it wanted to protect its interests in competing lumber mills by driving Timberlane out of the Honduran lumber market. The district court dismissed the action, but in the case referred to as Timberlane I, the Court of Appeals vacated the district court's holding and announced a three-part test for determining whether the United States would assert federal jurisdiction over claims alleging illegal antitrust behavior outside the United States.

On remand, the district court again dismissed the antitrust claim of Timberlane, which again appealed.

Sneed, Judge

Timberlane I's test undertakes three separate inquiries: (1) the effect or intended effect on the foreign commerce of the United States; (2) the type or magnitude of the alleged illegal behavior; and (3) the appropriateness of exercising extraterritorial jurisdiction in light of considerations of international comity and fairness.

The district court applied Timberlane's analysis and concluded that jurisdiction should not be exercised in this case. Although we agree with the district court's conclusion, we do not expressly approve all of its analysis. Therefore, we discuss each part of the inquiry as set forth in Timberlane I.

1. "Does the alleged restraint affect, or was it intended to affect, the foreign commerce of the United States?"

The first part of Timberlane I's analysis requires "that there be some effect—actual or intended—on American foreign commerce before the federal courts may legitimately exercise subject matter jurisdiction under [the antitrust] statues." On appeal, Bank of America does not deny that Timberlane has met this requirement. "[B]y alleging the ability and willingness to supply cognizable markets with lumber that they allege would have been competitive with that already in the marketplace, they have satisfied this prong of the circuit's test."

2. "Is it of such a type and magnitude so as to be cognizable as a violation of the Sherman Act?"

The only issue under the second part of the inquiry is whether the magnitude of the effect identified in the first part of the test rises to the level of a civil antitrust violation, i.e., conduct that has a direct and substantial anticompetitive effect. In this case Timberlane alleges that Bank of America conspired with its Honduran subsidiaries to prevent Timberlane from milling lumber in Honduras and exporting it to the United States. Our review of the complaint reveals that Timberlane has alleged an injury that would state a claim under the antitrust laws against Bank of America. Thus, it satisfies the second part of the analysis.

3. "As a matter of international comity and fairness, should the extraterritorial jurisdiction of the United States be asserted to cover it?"

Under the third part of Timberlane I's analysis, the district court must determine "whether the interests of, and links to, the United States—including the magnitude of the effect on American foreign commerce—are sufficiently strong, vis-à-vis those of other nations, to justify an assertion of extraterritorial authority." This determination requires that a district court consider seven factors. This district court here found that the undisputed facts required that jurisdiction not be exercised in this case. We agree. To support our conclusion each factor will be examined.

a. "The degree of conflict with foreign law or policy."

We must determine whether the extraterritorial enforcement of United States antitrust laws creates an actual or potential conflict with the laws and policies of other nations. Timberlane argues that no conflict exists between United States and Honduran law. We disagree.

Although Honduras does not have antitrust laws as such, it does have definite policies concerning the character of its commercial climate. To promote economic development and efficiency within its relatively undeveloped economy, the Honduran Constitution and Commercial Code guarantee freedom of action. The Code specifically condemns any laws prohibiting agreements (even among competitors) to restrict or divide commercial activity. On balance, we believe that the enforcement of United States antitrust laws in this case would lead to a significant conflict with Honduran law and policy. This conflict, unless outweighed by other factors in the comity analysis, is itself a sufficient reason to decline the exercise of jurisdiction over this dispute.

b. "The nationality or allegiance of the parties and the locations of principal places of business of corporations."

Next we should consider the citizenship of the parties and witnesses involved in the alleged illegal conduct. In this case, with only one exception, all of the named parties are United States citizens or nationals. But it is also true that "[a]ll of the crucial witnesses to the incidents were either Honduran citizens or residents." We believe, therefore, that the citizenship of the parties weighs slightly in favor of the exercise of jurisdiction.

c. "The extent to which enforcement by either state can be expected to achieve compliance."

The weighing of this factor yields no clear answer. Of course, any judgment against Bank of America could easily be enforced in a United States court. Whether such a judgment could be enforced as easily in Honduras is less certain. We believe that the enforcement factor tips slightly in favor of the assertion of jurisdiction.

d. "The relative significance of effects on the United States as compared with those elsewhere."

A more definitive answer emerges when we compare the effect of the alleged illegal conduct on the foreign commerce of the United States with its effect abroad. The insignificance of the effect on the foreign commerce of the United States when compared with the substantial effect in Honduras suggests federal jurisdiction should not be exercised. We believe that the relative significance of effects in this case weighs strongly against the exercise of jurisdiction.

e. "The extent to which there is explicit purpose to harm or affect American commerce."

Timberlane has not demonstrated that Bank of America had any particular interest in affecting United States commerce.

f. "The foreseeability of such effect."

Aside from the fact that American commerce has not been substantially affected, Timberlane has not shown that Bank of America should have foreseen the consequences of its actions. We do not believe that a reasonable investor would have foreseen the minimal effect that has occurred here. This weighs against the exercise of jurisdiction.

g. "The relative importance to the violations charged of conduct within the United States as compared with conduct abroad."

Finally, a court should consider the location of the alleged illegal conduct in order to assess the appropriateness of the exercise of extraterritorial jurisdiction. In this case both parties agree that virtually all of the illegal activity occurred in Honduras. This factor clearly weighs against the exercise of jurisdiction.

h. Resolving the Seven Factor Test.

It follows that all but two of the factors in Timberlane I's comity analysis indicate that we should refuse to exercise jurisdiction over this antitrust case. The potential for conflict with Honduran economic policy and commercial law is great. The effect on the foreign commerce of the United States is minimal. The evidence of intent to harm American commerce is altogether lacking. The foreseeability of the anticompetitive consequences of the allegedly illegal sections is slight. Most of the conduct that must be examined occurred abroad. The factors that favor jurisdiction are the citizenship of the parties and, to a slight extent, the enforcement effectiveness of United States law. We do not believe that this is enough to justify the exercise of federal jurisdiction over this case.

Affirmed.

Case Questions

1. Explain the court's answer to the first two questions of the "three-part test" used to determine whether the court should consider the antitrust claim of Timberlane.
2. Which of the seven factors reviewed by the court led it to conclude that it should not consider Timberlane's claim?

National Laws and Foreign Governments

In the United States, international business activities are conducted primarily by private corporations. In some other countries, international business activities are conducted solely by governments or by corporations that governments own and manage. If contracts between private business firms and governmental organizations arise, two legal concepts may affect the resolution of disputes. One of the concepts, the sovereign immunity doctrine, is based in international law and is accepted, in one form or another, by practically all countries. The other concept is the act of state doctrine. This concept originated in the Supreme Court of the United States and serves as a guide to the determination of whether the judiciary, rather than the executive or legislative branch of government, should seek to resolve certain legal problems.

Should U.S. law be applied extraterritorially to acts of foreign governments if those acts hurt the economy of the United States? As the following case indicates, both the sovereign immunity and the act of state doctrines respect the sovereignty of foreign countries, even when their actions are contrary to U.S. interests.

Intern. Ass'n of Machinists v. OPEC

649 F.2d 1354 (1981)

Court of Appeals, Ninth Circuit

The members of the International Association of Machinists and Aerospace Workers (IAM) were disturbed by the high price of petroleum and petroleum-derived products in the United States. They believed that price-fixing by the Organization of Petroleum Exporting Countries (OPEC) caused this burden on the American public. Accordingly, IAM sued OPEC and its member nations in December 1978, alleging that their price-setting activities violated U.S. antitrust laws. The district court entered judgment in favor of the defendants, holding that it lacked jurisdiction and that IAM had no valid antitrust claim; the IAM appealed to the Court of Appeals.

Choy, Circuit Judge

IAM is a nonprofit labor association. Its members work in petroleum-using industries, and like most Americans, they are consumers of gasoline and other petroleum-derived products. They object to the high and rising cost of such products.

OPEC is an organization of the petroleum-producing and exporting nations of what is sometimes referred to as the Third World. The OPEC nations have organized to obtain the greatest possible economic returns for a special resource which they hope will remove them from the ranks of the underdeveloped and the poverty-plagued. OPEC was formed in 1960 by the defendants Iran, Kuwait, Saudi Arabia, and Venezuela. The other defendants, Algeria, Ecuador, Gabon, Indonesia, Libya, Nigeria, Qatar, and the United Arab Emirates, joined thereafter.

OPEC achieves its goals by a system of production limits and royalties which its members unanimously adopt. After formation of OPEC, it is alleged, the price of crude oil increased tenfold and more. Whether or not a causal relation exists, there is no doubt that the price of oil has risen dramatically in recent years, and that this has become of international concern.

Supporters of OPEC argue that its actions result in fair world prices for oil and allow OPEC members to achieve a measure of economic and political independence. Without OPEC, they say, in the rush to the marketplace these nations would rapidly deplete their only valuable resource for ridiculously low prices. Detractors accuse OPEC of price-fixing and worse in its deliberate manipulation of the world market and withholding of a resource which many world citizens have not learned to do without.

In the international sphere each state is viewed as an independent sovereign, equal in sovereignty to all other states. It is said that an equal holds no power of sovereignty over an equal. Thus the doctrine of sovereign immunity; the courts of one state generally have no jurisdiction to entertain suits against another state. This rule of international law developed by custom among nations. Also by custom, an exception developed for the commercial activities of a state. The former concept of absolute sovereign immunity gave way to a restrictive view. Under the restrictive theory, immunity did not exist for commercial activities since they were seen as nonsovereign.

In 1976, Congress enacted the FSIA [Foreign Sovereignty Immunity Act] and declared that the federal courts will apply an objective nature-of-the-act test in determining whether activity is commercial and thus not immune: "The commercial character of an activity shall be determined by reference to the nature of the course of conduct or particular transaction or act rather than by reference to its purposes." The trial judge reasoned that, according to international law, the development and control of natural resources is a prime governmental function. The opinion cites several resolutions of the United Nations' General Assembly, which the United States supported, and the United States Constitution, which treat the control of natural resources as governmental acts. While we do not apply the doctrine of sovereign immunity, its elements remain relevant to our discussion of the act of state doctrine.

The act of state doctrine declares that a United States court will not adjudicate a politically sensitive dispute which would require the court to judge the legality of the sovereign act of a foreign state. This doctrine was expressed by the Supreme Court in *Underhill v. Hernandez* (1897):

> Every sovereign State is bound to respect the independence of every other sovereign State, and the courts of one country will not sit in judgment on the acts of the government of another done within its own territory.

The doctrine recognizes the institutional limitations of the courts and the peculiar requirements of successful foreign relations. To participate adeptly in the global community, the United States must speak with one voice and pursue a careful and deliberate foreign policy. The political branches of our government are able to consider the competing economic and political considerations and respond to the public will in order to carry on foreign relations in accordance with the best interests of the country as a whole. The courts, in contrast, focus on single disputes and make decisions on the basis of legal principles.

When the courts engage in piecemeal adjudication of the legality of the sovereign acts of states, they risk disruption of our country's international diplomacy. The principle of separation of powers is central to our form of democratic government. Just as the courts have carefully guarded their primary role as interpreters of the Constitution and the laws of the United States, so have they recognized the primary role of the President and Congress in resolution of political conflict and the adoption of foreign policy.

The doctrine of sovereign immunity is similar to the act of state doctrine in that it also represents the need to respect the sovereignty of foreign states. The two doctrines differ, however, in significant respects. The law of sovereign immunity goes to the jurisdiction of the court. The act of state doctrine is not jurisdictional. Rather, it is a prudential doctrine designed to avoid judicial action in sensitive areas. Sovereign immunity is a principle of international law, recognized in the United States by statute. It is the states themselves, as defendants, who may claim sovereign immunity. The act of state doctrine is a domestic legal principle, arising from the peculiar role of American courts. It recognizes not only the sovereignty of foreign states, but also the spheres of power of the co-equal branches of our government. Thus a private litigant may raise the act of state doctrine, even when no sovereign state is a party to the action. The act of state doctrine is not diluted by the commercial activity exception which limits the doctrine of sovereign immunity. While purely commercial activity may not rise to the level of an act of state, certain seemingly commercial activity will trigger act of state considerations.

The decision to deny access to judicial relief is not one we make lightly. There is no question that the availability of oil has become a significant factor in international relations. It is clear that OPEC and its activities are carefully considered in the formulation of American foreign policy. The remedy IAM seeks is an injunction against the OPEC nations. The possibility of insult of the OPEC states and of interference with the efforts of the political branches to seek favorable relations with them is apparent from the very nature of this action and the remedy sought.

A further consideration is the availability of internationally accepted legal principles which would render the issues appropriate for judicial disposition. While conspiracies in restraint of trade are clearly illegal under domestic law, the record reveals no international consensus condemning cartels, royalties, and production agreements. We are reluctant to allow judicial interference in an area so void of international consensus. The act of state doctrine is applicable in this case. The courts should not enter at the will of litigants into a delicate area of foreign policy which the executive and legislative branches have chosen to approach with restraint. The decision of the district court dismissing this action is affirmed.

Case Questions

1. Did the court find that OPEC's sovereign immunity prevented it from deciding this case?
2. Would it have mattered if the OPEC governments had conducted their oil sales through private corporations that they owned instead of through governmental agencies?
3. Compare and contrast the sovereign immunity doctrine with the act of state doctrine.

INTERNATIONAL TRADE

International organizations such as the International Monetary Fund (IMF), the General Agreement on Tariffs and Trade (GATT), and the United Nations (UN) make rules that affect both trade and investment. Bilateral treaties, such as the recent U.S.-Canada Free Trade Agreement, and multilateral treaties, such as the Law of the Sea Convention, are both national and international sources of law.

Since past GATT negotiations have removed many of the tariff barriers to trade, international trade negotiations during the next few years are likely to emphasize the removal of nontariff barriers affecting both goods and services. It is likely that China, the republics in the Commonwealth of Independent States, and several eastern European countries will be among the areas where the greatest increase in trade is experienced. As countries continue to associate in regional organizations and develop free-trade linkages through multilateral treaties, foreign investment will increasingly be subject to regional developments and legal changes, rather than national laws.

The Sale of Goods

Export—the selling of a domestically manufactured product to a foreign purchaser—is the most common and least complex method of conducting international business. The manufacturer or seller is the exporter; the purchaser is the importer.

All commerce and trade requires a stable legal environment. Special laws and customs known as *law merchant* govern the sale and movement of goods. These laws spread through England and other countries centuries ago, and they remain in effect today. In recent years, the international community has agreed on a common body of international sales law, the United Nations Convention on the International Sale of Goods (CISG). The Convention was drafted by representatives from countries with common law, civil law, and socialist legal systems, and it embodies principles from each. This treaty has been adopted by over two dozen countries, including the United States, and is being reviewed in many others. The CISG applies to contracts for the commercial sale of goods between parties whose places of business are in different nations that have agreed to the terms of the convention.

There are some clear differences between the sales law terms under the CISG and those under the UCC, which applies to sales occurring within the United States. For example, no writing is required for the sale of goods under the CISG, but the UCC requires a writing if the goods sold are valued at $500 or more. Further, whereas the UCC limits a party's right to disclaim implied warranties that arise with the sale of goods, the CISG allows disclaimers of implied warranties. This difference occurs because international sales generally take place between more sophisticated and experienced sellers and buyers and, unlike the UCC, the CISG's provisions do not apply to consumer sales.

Documents Used in International Sales Transactions

The sale of export goods between countries entails risks that differ greatly from those encountered when the sale occurs within national boundaries. The documentary sale has developed to accommodate the needs of both the buyer and the seller in an international sale. The seller doesn't want to release the goods until payment is received from the buyer and the buyer doesn't want to pay until the goods have arrived and been inspected. Standardized documents and terms are used to ensure that three objectives are met: (1) each party knows who pays the costs of transporting and insuring the goods while en route to their destination, (2) the buyer will obtain good title to the goods when they are received, and (3) the seller is sure that payment will be made when the title for the contracted goods is transferred.

Transportation Terms The terms under which goods will be transported must be agreed to by the parties. Transportation terms are a part of most sales contracts, whether the sales occur domestically or internationally. In international transactions, the costs, insurance, and freight expenses for sending goods (**CIF**) are generally quoted as one price to the buyer. For example, if a Chicago seller agrees to deliver chairs to a buyer in Paris, the seller will determine the costs of the goods, the insurance needed while they are in transit, and the shipping or freight charges and give the total price to the buyer for the goods CIF to Paris.

In some cases, the contract will call for the seller to ship the goods to a certain spot, beyond which the buyer must pay for their transport to the ultimate destination. For example, if the contract prices the chairs free on board (**FOB**) to Chicago, the seller will deliver the goods free to where they are placed on board by a common carrier (truck, railroad, airplane, etc.) in Chicago, and the French buyer must pay for the freight and insurance costs to transport them to Paris.

There are other alternatives for shipping goods from one country to another. The *C & F contract* requires the seller to prepay the freight expenses but the buyer pays the costs of insurance while goods are in transit. Under an *FAS contract,* the seller places the goods free alongside ships, or a specific ship, in a port, and the buyer assumes the risk of loss and pays all freight charges from that point.

The Bill of Lading A second objective is to ensure that the buyer obtains good title to the goods. A **bill of lading** is a contract between a carrier and the firm or person shipping the goods. It describes the terms agreed to regarding the transport and delivery of the goods and acts as a receipt for the goods by the carrier. The bill of lading is a document of title that permits the owner of the goods to transfer them even though the goods are not in the owner's possession.

The bill of lading document has two forms. Under a *straight bill of lading,* the carrier must deliver the goods only to the person named in the bill of lading. The straight bill of lading does not represent a transferable title to the goods. However, if a *negotiable bill of lading* is used, title to the goods may be transferred by the owner endorsing it to another party such as a bank or the buyer of the goods. The goods themselves do not have to be delivered to transfer ownership; a negotiation of the bill of lading document transfers title to the goods. Thus, while goods are in transit on a ship or in a truck covering long distances, the title to the goods may be transferred numerous times. For example, the ownership of oil in tankers leaving the Persian Gulf may be transferred more than a dozen times before it reaches its ultimate destination.

The Letter of Credit A third objective is to make sure the seller is paid when the title to the goods is transferred. A **letter of credit** is used to reduce the risk of nonpayment. Most common is a transaction in which the buyer contracts with a bank to pay for the goods being sent by the seller. The seller, who may not be ready to offer credit terms to an unknown buyer in a foreign country, will insist on a letter of credit. Thus, a bank's credit is substituted for that of the buyer. For example, the buyer's bank issues a letter of credit and agrees with the buyer to pay the seller, provided that the seller gives it certain documents, primarily the bill of lading, within a specified time.

Generally, there are three aspects to a letter of credit transaction. First, a contract exists for the sale of goods between the buyer and the seller. Second, a contract exists between the buyer and a bank. The buyer agrees to pay the bank to issue a letter of credit on its behalf to the seller. Third, a bank that issues a letter of credit may be liable directly to the seller who is the beneficiary of the letter of credit.

In some cases, the letter of credit does not create an obligation from the bank to the seller. Instead, the bank only provides a banking service by sending an *advising letter of credit* to the seller. The bank informs the seller of the terms that the buyer desires regarding the number of items, description of goods, packaging requirements, and so forth. Once the seller reviews the terms suggested in the letter of credit and determines to go ahead with the transaction, it will contact a bank (the seller's negotiating bank), which will send the letter of credit to the buyer's issuing bank. That issuing bank is the one who reviews the seller's bill of lading and other documents submitted to it. If those documents fully comply with the terms established in the letter of credit, the buyer's issuing bank will make payment to the party who delivers the bill of lading document, whether that is the seller, the shipper, the seller's agent, or a party to whom the seller transferred the bill of lading. That bank will turn over the bill of lading document to the buyer, who then uses it to claim the goods.

In some cases, the seller may not be satisfied with the assurance of the foreign bank. It may be unsure of the soundness of that bank or fear that the country where the bank is located may impose restrictions on the transfer of foreign currency by its banks. In these situations, the seller will ask for a *confirming letter of credit,* which makes the bank issuing it liable on the letter of credit. Thus, a U.S. seller may insist that a Turkish buyer obtain a confirming letter of credit from a U.S. bank. That bank would agree that as soon as it receives the documents specified in the letter of credit, payment would be made by the bank to the seller. The documents would be sent to the confirming bank by an issuing bank in the buyer's country and, if the documents received are in order, the confirming bank will be paid by the issuing bank, who in turn is paid by the buyer. Figure 21–5 depicts a confirming letter of credit transaction in which the seller's bank agrees to assume liability on the letter of credit.

FIGURE 21–5

ORIGINAL
Date: April 6, 1992

Call 828-8327 concerning inquiries on Documents submitted under this letter of Credit

DOCUMENTARY CREDIT—IRREVOCABLE	CREDIT NUMBER: of Issuing Bank 0/00/000 Our No. 0000000
FOR ACCOUNT OF: Taiwan Steel Products Co., Ltd. Taipei Taiwan	CORRESPONDENT: First Bank Taipei Taiwan
BENEFICIARY: John Doe Exporters, Inc. Chicago, Illinois U.S.A.	AMOUNT: Six Thousand and 00/100 U.S. Dollars U.S. $6,000.00 EXPIRY June 15, 1992

IN ALL COMMUNICATIONS WITH US, PLEASE MENTION OUR REFERENCE NUMBER

Gentlemen:

We have received from the above named bank a cable dated April 5, 1976 requesting us to inform you that they have opened in your favor their irrevocable Credit particulars of which are as follows:

Available by your drafts at sight ON US

Accompanied by the following documents (full sets required unless otherwise specified):

Signed commercial invoice in triplicate, describing the merchandise as mentioned below, stating that goods shipped conform with purchase order No. 0/00/0 dated March 5, 1992.

Packing list in triplicate.

Insurance policy or certificate in duplicate covering all risks including war risks.

Full set of clean on board ocean bills of lading issued to shipper's order and blank endorsed, marked "Freight Prepaid" and notify International Forwarders, Keelung.

Evidencing shipment from U.S. Port to Keelung, Taiwan not later than May 25, 1992 of the following merchandise: 200 sets of Cookware at the price of $30.00 per one set CIF Keelung, Taiwan.

Partial shipments permitted.

Transshipments prohibited.

Drawings under this letter of credit must be presented for negotiation not later than ten days after the date of issuance of the bills of lading.

☐ This credit is not confirmed by us and therefore carries no engagement on our part, but is simply for your guidance in preparing and presenting drafts and documents.

☒ This credit is confirmed by us and we undertake that all drafts drawn and presented in accordance with the terms of the credit will be honored by us.

The above mentioned correspondent engages with you that all drafts under and in compliance with the terms of this Credit will be duly honored on delivery of documents as specified.

If the Credit has been opened by cable, this advice is subject to correction upon receipt of the mail confirmation. Drafts must be marked "Drawn under First Bank, Taipei, Taiwan, Letter of Credit No. 0/00/000 " and presented at our office on or before the above indicated expiry date.

The credit is subject to the Uniform Customs and Practice for Documentary Credits [1974 revision the International Chamber of Commerce Publication No. 290

Should the terms of the above mentioned Credit be unsatisfactory to you, please communicate with your customers and request that they have the issuing bank send us amended instructions. Original Credit must be returned with documents for negotiations.

Yours very truly

J. Smith
FOR CASHIER

G. Black
FOR CASHIER

Laws Affecting Exports

Laws may encourage or discourage exports. Laws may discourage the export of products that are scarce in the exporting country. For example, U.S. export quotas have been imposed on wheat and soybeans during crop shortages. Laws may also discourage exports out of concern over their possible misuse by the importer. For example, the United States restricts the export of military equipment and technologically advanced computer hardware because these may have adverse military uses.

Despite these concerns, laws usually encourage exports because the penetration of foreign markets by domestic producers helps a country's balance of trade. Governmental assistance and tax benefits are among the means used to encourage exports.

License Regulations for Exports Businesses should investigate the domestic laws of their home country to be certain that the goods in question may be freely exported. Laws may require prior approval before particular goods are allowed to leave the country. Such laws generally prohibit the export of these goods to any country. However, certain export controls target specific countries. For example, U.S. computer parts may be freely exportable to many countries but not to Iraq.

Governmental Assistance for Exports Numerous governmental programs assist exporters. In addition to providing exporters with tax assistance, discussed more fully in the following section, governments frequently provide them with a great deal of valuable information. Publications of the U.S. Department of Commerce, for example, assist potential exporters in identifying countries and firms that seek certain products. The Department of Commerce also assists U.S. exporters in contacting foreign representatives. In addition, the department sponsors exhibits and trade shows in U.S.-owned trade centers throughout the world. Many U.S. firms participate in these events to facilitate meetings with foreign business people who are interested in U.S. products.

The Export Trading Company Act of 1982 also assists exporters. This act assures U.S. firms that their export activities are not illegal under U.S. antitrust laws. A firm must first file information regarding its export activities. If the firm meets certain conditions, it will be immune from antitrust prosecution by the U.S. government. The Export Trading Company Act also permits U.S. banks to invest capital and make loans to *trading companies,* entities that seek to export U.S. goods and services. The intent of the law is to encourage the formation of such companies.

Several governmental organizations make financial assistance available to exporters. The Export-Import Bank (EX-IM) offers medium- and long-term loans and credit guarantees. The loans are made directly to exporters and to commercial banks that relend them to exporters.

Tax Assistance for Exports Exports are encouraged because they provide jobs and revenue for the economy. Special programs often give tax assistance to exporters. For example, the turnover or value-added tax (VAT) levied in many European countries is often refunded to the seller if the goods are sold for export. Thus, the cost of goods purchased inside these countries will be less for the foreign buyer than for the local buyer (as long as the rebate of the tax is passed along to the ultimate purchaser). In the United States, the Foreign Sales Corporation Act of 1984 exempts from U.S. tax 15 percent of the income of foreign sales corporations. A foreign sales corporation (FSC) must be located outside the United States in a country with a tax information exchange agreement. Most of the income of the FSC must be derived from qualified export transactions.

Laws Affecting Imports

Legal controls are often imposed on products by both the importing country and the exporting country. Importing countries may want to protect domestic products from competition with foreign products. Some importing countries may simply lack the capital necessary to pay for imports.

Legal restrictions against imports range from prohibitions declaring that certain products cannot be imported, to quotas limiting the number of products imported, to tariffs taxing imported products, to various forms of discrimination against foreign goods or in favor of domestic goods. Although each nation may adopt its own import policy, a nation's commitment to international trade agreements, such as the General Agreement on Tariffs and Trade (GATT), limits the restrictions that it may impose.

Prohibitions on Imports The United States prohibits the import of certain products. For example, the Trading with the Enemy Act grants the president the power to restrict all imports from countries considered enemies of the United States. Some U.S. laws restrict the import of products, such as certain firearms or narcotics, regardless of the country of origin. Brazil prohibits the import of small computers and light passenger airplanes, and Taiwan keeps out chemicals used in making drugs if those chemicals can be produced domestically.

Quotas on Imports A *quota* limits the quantity of a product that may be imported, so it is less restrictive than an outright prohibition but more restrictive than merely taxing the product. The GATT prohibits certain quotas. Quotas, which are widely regarded as an effective form of restricting imports, are frequently disguised as "voluntary" agreements between trading partners. The EC has pressured Japan to limit its shipments of quartz watches, stereo equipment, and computer-controlled machine tools. The United States has obtained similar promises from Japan to limit its auto exports and from European and South American countries to limit their exports of steel.

Tariffs **Tariffs** are taxes on imported products. They are invariably discriminatory because domestic products are not subject to the same taxes. Usually, tariffs are levied to protect infant industries from the better-developed industries of foreign countries. Tariffs may be levied on an *ad valorem* basis (the tariff represents a percentage of the value or price of the item imported) or on a *flat rate* basis (the tariff is levied on each unit imported, such as a barrel of oil, a foot or meter of pipe, or a pound of nails).

Other Duties In addition to tariffs, two other duties may be imposed on imports that are regarded as unfairly traded goods. *Antidumping duties* are imposed when goods are *dumped,* or sold in the importing country at a price lower than that in their home market. Article VI of the GATT permits the importing nation to impose an antidumping duty that is equal to the difference between the sales price of the imported product and the price of a comparable product in the home market.

In the United States, the International Trade Administration first determines that foreign merchandise is being sold in the United States at less than fair value (LTFV). Then, the International Trade Commission determines whether a domestic industry is materially injured or is threatened with a material injury. The International Trade Commission's determinations may be appealed to the federal Court of International Trade, which in turn can be reviewed by the federal Court of Appeals.

Countervailing duties are assessed to counteract foreign subsidies of imported products that materially injure competing domestic products. The foreign subsidy may be in the form of tax rebates, favorable financing terms, or other special governmental assistance. According to the GATT, where the subsidy causes or threatens to cause material injury to a domestic industry, countervailing duties may be levied as long as they do not exceed the amount of the subsidy. For countries that are not members of the GATT, U.S. law permits the imposition of countervailing duties whether or not a U.S. firm is injured by the subsidy.

Nontariff Barriers **Nontariff barriers** consist of governmental policies and practices that discriminate against imports or in favor of exports. It is difficult to enumerate all of the major types of nontariff barriers, but they include prohibitions, quotas, import licensing controls, foreign exchange controls, import fees, financial deposit requirements for imported producers, and product testing and certification requirements.

Nontariff barriers can be classified into nontariff barriers effective upon entry (barriers that affect goods as they come into a country) and nontariff barriers effective subsequent to entry (programs, practices, and policies of an importing country that discriminate against imported goods already in the country).

Nontariff Barriers Effective upon Entry Import licensing controls require importers to obtain a governmental license to import products. The license may require payment of a fee, completion of extensive documentation regarding the products and their manufacturing firms, or approval by regulatory agencies. An import license may be available only if a business has certain export "credits" with which to purchase the imported products. In some Latin American countries, import licenses often take months to process, and chosen officials are given complete discretion to approve such licenses. Standards, procedures, and guidelines for determining an official verdict may be unknown or nonexistent, and given the absence of such criteria, court appeals may be pointless.

Nontariff Barriers Effective Subsequent to Entry Nontariff barriers effective subsequent to entry include governmental procurement policies, internal tax policies, subsidy programs, and other practices giving domestic industries an advantage. For example, the "Buy America" Act prohibits the purchase of foreign goods by federal agencies if domestic equivalents are available at comparable prices or if national security interests are involved.

The United States requires all imported items to carry a marking that identifies their *country of origin.* This requirement is intended to ensure that the American consumer knows that such items were produced in foreign countries. No import that lacks a marking of this kind is permitted, so this nontariff barrier is effective upon entry. Since marking all imports with the country of origin gives American consumers the choice of selecting American-made alternatives, the marking requirement is also a nontariff barrier effective subsequent to entry.

Licenses

In addition to exporting, another method of conducting international trade uses licensing agreements. A **license** is a certificate or document that gives the licensee permission to produce or distribute the licensor's product under the licensor's name. For example, a patent license is a written authorization to make or use the patented article for a limited time in a designated territory.

Terms of a Licensing Agreement A license agreement generally contains the grant of a license from the licensor, details the conditions of its use, establishes other assistance that the licensor may provide to the licensee, fixes the compensation payable to the licensor, determines the governing law, and establishes methods for resolving disputes.

The grant of the licensee usually states the nature of the license being granted and expresses limitations on its use by the licensee. For example, confidentiality requirements are usually imposed on the licensee, particularly where trade secrets, rather than patents, are being licensed. The licensor will try to require confidentiality over a long period of time, whereas the licensee will seek a shorter period. In addition, both parties will be concerned about how to treat new technologies that are developed under the agreement. The licensor will seek the right to use any new related "know-how" that the licensee develops. The licensee will want to ensure that updated information and improvements developed by the licensor are transferred so that the licensee can maintain its competitive position.

Manufacturing and marketing limitations may also be imposed on a licensee. For example, a licensee may be allowed to manufacture or sell products only in certain locations. Permitted use limitations may restrict the applications for which licensed technology may be used. For example, licensed plastics manufacturing technology might be allowed to be used for cups, boxes, and other containers, but not for automotive products.

In addition to granting the license, the licensor may also agree to provide training assistance, marketing programs, or manufacturing guidance. Training of personnel may be more necessary at the beginning of the licensing period, but in some cases periodic review of updated and emerging uses for the technology is also included. Marketing assistance may consist of advertising prepared by the licensor or perhaps a financial contribution to advertising prepared or purchased by the licensee. Manufacturing guidance in laying out the manufacturing or assembly processes to use may be necessary for some licensed products.

As compensation for the use of the license, the licensee generally pays a royalty to the licensor. The royalty must be at a rate that allows both the licensee and the licensor to make a fair return on their investment in developing and using the licensed technology. The parties to any license agreement also must determine the frequency of the royalty period, whether royalties are determined on net or gross income, and designate the currency of payment. Some countries restrict the methods used to determine royalties. For example, in India, the government, which must approve all licensing agreements, will not allow the licensor to require a minimum guaranteed royalty to be paid. Instead, royalties must be tied to income earned: if no income is earned, no royalty is due.

The determination of the governing law may be difficult. In some situations, the country where the licensee is located will not approve contracts where the law of the licensor's country is selected. In most countries, however, the parties are free to select the governing law, and the courts of each nation will enforce the law selected by the parties. Although each party often prefers its law, the critical question concerning applicable law is whether the governing law effectively recognizes and protects intellectual property. Some countries fail to adequately protect all forms of intellectual property, and others take no steps to discourage piracy of transferred technology. In those situations, a gray market of goods in the licensor's country may develop as competitors for goods produced by the appropriate licensee.

The Gray Market In the United States, *gray-market goods* are produced abroad and bear trademarks identical to the U.S. trademark, but they are imported into the United States outside of authorized channels of distribution and without the consent of the trademark owner. The gray market is most active in goods that have high brand recognition. Watches, perfumes, pharmaceuticals, sporting goods, luggage, and handbags are common gray-market goods. Gray-market goods present a problem to a U.S. licensor when the goods, produced outside the United States at a lower cost than comparable goods produced domestically, make their way back into the country and compete with the licensor's goods. The prices of the gray-market goods undercut the prices of the U.S. products, which are made comparatively higher by either the high quality associated with the product or the fluctuation of international currency values. In addition, the producer of gray-market goods does not have to pay the royalties that the licensor uses to recoup its initial investment.

Despite the concerns of the trademark holder, the law regarding gray-market goods is not all one-sided. Consumers and some retailers argue that the gray market allows goods of quality comparable with well-known brands to be purchased at significantly lower prices. U.S. courts have not been decisive in answering gray market problems. Most foreign jurisdictions allow the entry of gray-market goods. In the EC, the use of intellectual property law provisions and licensing agreements to block trade in gray-market goods has been repeatedly denied by the European Court of Justice.

Taxation of Licenses The tax treatment of licensing agreements concerns both the licensor and the licensee. Both the licensor's country and the country in which the licensee manufacturers, uses, or sells the licensed product will probably seek to tax a share of the royalties stipulated in the licensing agreement. In the absence of tax treaties, royalties are usually subject to income tax in the licensee's country, which is the *country of source* for the activity giving rise to royalties. The tax authorities in the country of source generally withhold the tax due from royalty payments that the licensee makes to the licensor. Royalty income is generally taxed a second time in the licensor's country, the *country of origin*.

Tax treaties may either exempt royalty income from taxation in one of the countries or give the licensor credit for income tax paid in the country of source. Generally, if the licensor has a permanent establishment (branch, office, factory, or warehouse) in the country of source, royalty income is taxed only there.

ETHICAL DILEMMAS AND INTERNATIONAL BUSINESS LAW

Many ethical questions are raised when a firm does business internationally. Is it ethical for the manufacturer of gray-market goods to knowingly sell them, misleading consumers to believe that the goods are genuine? Is it ethical for a firm to import gray-market goods or for consumers to knowingly buy them?

Should a product that is banned in one country be sold in other countries? This question poses ethical dilemmas when manufacturers are faced with substantial inventories of products that the legal institutions, regulators, or consumers in one country have determined are too dangerous to sell. Should managers take advantage of people in less developed countries who may lack information and awareness of possible hazards associated with products?

Such ethical dilemmas have arisen for food producers when adulterated fruit juices are sold to foreign countries or when poor parents of foreign infants are not properly advised about how to prepare infant formula mixes. Similarly, is it ethical to contract with governments in poor countries to dispose of trash or toxic waste in those countries? What if the disposing firm has reason to believe that money paid to foreign officials will not be used to protect people from the hazards associated with the product?

Another area that poses ethical dilemmas for firms doing international business concerns the payment of money to foreign officials. Although most countries have laws against bribery, sometimes significant differences exist regarding customary and acceptable practices affecting payments made to officials. A payment made for services performed by a government official may be ethically and legally proper in one country but not in another. Firms engaging in international business must be aware of the legal and ethical standards in the country where the business activity is performed. In the United States, the Foreign Corrupt Practices Act (FCPA), which amends the securities laws, outlaws foreign bribery by all domestic concerns. The FCPA is discussed in greater detail in Chapter 22.

International Dispute Resolution

The careful drafting of licensing agreements and other international contracts may eliminate many disputes, but some cannot be avoided. For example, disputes may arise over the method of transferring new production techniques or over the licensee's adherence to required quality standards. To resolve such disputes, the parties could submit their disagreements to national courts or use mediation. In international transactions, however, many disputes are often resolved by arbitration.

You will recall from Chapter 4 that arbitration differs from mediation. Whereas mediation is a voluntary, nonbinding dispute resolution method, arbitration is a binding procedure. Firms that frequently engage in international business transactions often select arbitration at the time they enter into contracts because it is quicker and less complicated than litigation and because the decisions are binding on the parties involved.

Significant international consensus exists regarding the enforceability of both the agreement to arbitrate and the arbitrator's award. Over 70 countries have signed the United Nations Convention on the Recognition and Enforcement of Foreign Arbitral Awards. A variety of bodies are used to determine the rules and processes for international arbitration. These include the American Arbitration Association, the International Chamber of Commerce in Paris, the Euro-Arab Chamber of Commerce, and the United Nations Commission for International Trade Law (UNICTRAL).

The **UNICTRAL** rules were developed in 1985 by the United Nations, which attempted to take into account concerns from all legal systems in all parts of the world. The model law developed by UNICTRAL can be applied to all international commercial arbitration, whether administered on an individual case basis or by an established institution (such as the AAA or the International Chamber of Commerce).

Courts have limited roles regarding arbitration under the UNICTRAL rules. They can select a neutral arbitrator if the parties do not, refer the parties to arbitration, review challenges to the arbitrators, and set aside arbitration awards for a few specific reasons. According to the model law, an arbitration is international in nature if it meets the requirements noted below.

Requirements for an Arbitration to be International Pursuant to UNICTRAL Provisions

1. Parties have their place of business in different countries at the time the arbitration agreement is concluded.
2. Parties agree that the subject matter of the arbitration relates to more than one country.
3. The place of arbitration as determined by the arbitration agreement is outside the countries in which the parties have their place of business; or the place where a substantial part of the commercial relationship is performed, or the place with which the subject matter of dispute is most closely connected, is outside the countries in which the parties have their place of business.

In the past two decades, the U.S. Supreme Court has decided several cases regarding the enforceability of arbitration agreements. Two of those cases are excerpted here. In *Scherk v. Alberto-Culver,* the court reviewed a contract between a U.S. firm, Alberto-Culver, and a German citizen, Scherk, who owned companies in Germany and Liechtenstein. In this case, the court specifically notes the international nature of the transaction in which the U.S. firm agreed to purchase businesses operating primarily in Europe.

Scherk v. Alberto-Culver Co.

417 U.S. 506 (1974)
United States Supreme Court

In order to expand its overseas operations, Alberto-Culver, an American manufacturer based in Illinois, purchased from petitioner, a German citizen, three enterprises owned by him and organized under the laws of Germany and Liechtenstein, together with all trademark rights of these enterprises. The sales contract, which was negotiated in the United States, England, and Germany, signed in Austria, and closed in Switzerland, contained express warranties by petitioner that the trademarks were unencumbered and a clause providing that "any controversy or claim (that) shall arise out of this agreement or the breach thereof" would be referred to arbitration before the International Chamber of Commerce in Paris, France, and that Illinois laws would govern the agreement and its interpretation and performance. Subsequently, after allegedly discovering that its trademarks were subject to substantial encumbrances, Alberto-Culver sued Scherk contending that Scherk's fraudulent representations concerning the trademarks violated the Securities Exchange Act of 1934. The District Court refused to decide the case because it held that the arbitration clause was enforceable. The Court of Appeals affirmed and Scherk appealed to the Supreme Court.

Justice Stewart delivered the opinion of the Court.

The United States Arbitration Act, reversing centuries of judicial hostility to arbitration agreements, was designed to allow parties to avoid "the costliness and delays of litigation," and to place arbitration agreements "upon the same footing as other contracts . . . . " Accordingly, the Act provides that an arbitration agreement such as is here involved "shall be valid, irrevocable, and enforceable, save upon such grounds as exist at law or in equity for the revocation of any contract. . . ."

Alberto-Culver's contract to purchase the business entities belonging to Scherk was a truly international agreement. Alberto-Culver is an American corporation with its principal place of business and the vast bulk of its activity in this country, while Scherk is a citizen of Germany whose companies were organized under the laws of Germany and Liechtenstein. The negotiations leading to the signing of the contract in Austria and to the closing in Switzerland took place in the United States, England, and Germany, and involved consultations with legal and trademark experts from each of those countries and from Liechtenstein. Finally, and most significantly, the subject matter of the contract concerned the sale of business enterprises organized under the laws of and primarily situated in European countries, whose activities were largely, if not entirely, directed to European markets.

Such a contract involves considerations and policies significantly different from those found controlling in *Wilko.* In *Wilko,* quite apart from the arbitration provision, there was no question but that the laws of the United States generally, and the federal securities laws in particular, would govern disputes arising out of the stock-purchase agreement. The parties, the negotiations, and the subject matter of the contract were all situated in this country, and no credible claim could have been entertained that any international conflict-of-laws problems would arise. In this case, by contrast, in the absence of the arbitration provision considerable uncertainty existed at the time of the agreement, and still exists, concerning the law applicable to the resolution of disputes arising out of the contract.

Such uncertainty will almost inevitably exist with respect to any contract touching two or more countries, each with its own substantive laws and conflict-of-laws rules. A contractual provision specifying in advance the forum in which disputes shall be litigated and the law to be applied is, therefore, an almost indispensable precondition to achievement of the orderliness and predictability essential to any international business transaction. Furthermore, such a provision obviates the danger that a dispute under the agreement might be submitted to a forum hostile to the interests of one of the parties or unfamiliar with the problem area involved.

A parochial refusal by the courts of one country to enforce an international arbitration agreement would not only frustrate these purposes, but would invite unseemly and mutually destructive jockeying by the parties to secure tactical litigation advantages. In the present case, for example, it is not inconceivable that if Scherk had anticipated that Alberto-Culver would be able in this country to enjoin resort to arbitration he might have sought an order in France or some other country enjoining Alberto-Culver from proceeding with its litigation in the United States. Whatever recognition the courts of this country might ultimately have granted to the order of the foreign court, the dicey atmosphere of such a legal no-man's-land would surely damage the fabric of international commerce and trade, and imperil the willingness and ability of businessmen to enter into international commercial agreements.

An agreement to arbitrate before a specified tribunal is, in effect, a specialized kind of forum-selection clause that posits not only the situs of suit but also the procedure to be used in resolving the dispute. The invalidation of such an agreement in the case before us would not only allow the respondent to repudiate its solemn promise but would, as well, reflect a "parochial concept that all disputes must be resolved under our laws and in our courts. . . . We cannot have trade and commerce in world markets and international waters exclusively on our terms, governed by our laws, and resolved in our courts."

For all these reasons we hold that the agreement of the parties in this case to arbitrate any dispute arising out of their international commercial transaction is to be respected and enforced by the federal courts in accord with the explicit provisions of the Arbitration Act. Accordingly, the judgment of the Court of Appeals is reversed and the case is remanded to that court with directions to remand to the District Court for further proceedings consistent with this opinion.

Case Questions

1. The court sends the case back to the District Court. Will the dispute between the parties be brought to an arbitration panel for resolution? What substantive law will that panel follow? What procedural rules will it follow? Where will the arbitration hearing take place?
2. Why does the Court determine that an arbitration agreement may be needed more in international business transactions than in domestic situations?
3. What reasons does the court give for enforcing this agreement to arbitrate the parties' dispute?

Although the *Alberto-Culver* case clearly indicated that arbitration agreements, and particularly international arbitration agreements, generally were to be enforced, the unique nature of the U.S. antitrust laws were thought to possibly provide an exception. Are the U.S. antitrust laws so tied to U.S. public policy that only judges, not arbitrators, are able to interpret them? That was the argument advanced by the Soler Chrysler-Plymouth dealer in the following case, which occurred more than a decade after the *Alberto-Culver* case.

Mitsubishi Motors v. Soler Chrysler-Plymouth

473 U.S. 614 (1985)
United States Supreme Court

Mitsubishi Motors (MM) is a Japanese corporation that manufactures automobiles and has its principal place of business in Tokyo, Japan. It is the product of a joint venture between Chrysler International S.A. (CISA), a Swiss corporation wholly owned by Chrysler Corporation and Mitsubishi Heavy Industries Inc., a Japanese corporation. The aim of the joint venture was the distribution through Chrysler dealers outside the continental U.S. of vehicles manufactured by MM and bearing Mitsubishi or Chrysler trademarks. Soler is a Puerto Rican corporation with its prime place of business in Puerto Rico.

Soler made an agreement with CISA and MM to sell cars in Puerto Rico, including an agreement to arbitrate all disputes "which arise between Mitsubishi and Soler of or in relation to . . . this Agreement or for the breach thereof." The disputes were to be "finally settled by arbitration in Japan in accordance with the rules and regulations of the Japan Commercial Arbitration Association."

Initially, Soler did a good business, but in 1981 it ran into difficulty selling the required number of cars provided by the agreement. Attempts to work out the difficulties failed, and Mitsubishi sued Soler in the U.S. District Court for Puerto Rico and asked the Court to refer the dispute to the Japan Commercial Arbitration Association. Soler claimed Mitsubishi and CISA had conspired to divide the market in restraint of trade in violation of the U.S. antitrust laws. It argued its antitrust claim could not be resolved by arbitration.

Justice Blackmun delivered the opinion of the Court.

We granted *certiorari* primarily to consider whether an American court could enforce an agreement to resolve antitrust claims by arbitration when that agreement arises from an international transaction. . . . The "liberal federal policy favoring arbitration agreements" manifested in by the [Arbitration] Act as a whole, is at bottom a policy guaranteeing the enforcement of private contractual arrangements: the Act simply "creates a body of federal substantive law establishing and regulating the duty to honor an agreement to arbitrate." By agreeing to arbitrate a statutory claim, a party does not forgo the substantive rights afforded by the [antitrust] statute; it only submits to their resolution in an arbitral, rather than in a judicial forum. It trades the procedures and opportunity for review of the courtroom for the simplicity, informality, and expedition of arbitration. . . .

There is no reason to assume at the outset of the dispute that international arbitration will not provide an adequate mechanism. To be sure, the international arbitral tribunal owes no particular allegiance to the legal norms of particular states; hence, it has no direct obligation to vindicate their statutory dictates. The tribunal, however, is bound to effectuate the intentions of the parties. Where the parties have agreed that the arbitral body is to decide a defined set of claims which includes, as in these cases, those arising from the application of American antitrust law, the tribunal therefore should be bound to decide the dispute in accord with the national law giving rise to the claim. . . .

As international trade has expanded in recent decades, so too has the use of international arbitration to resolve disputes arising in the course of trade. The controversies that international arbitral institutions are called upon to resolve have increased in diversity as well as in complexity. . . . If they are to take a central place in the international legal order, national courts will need to "shake off the old judicial hostility to arbitration," and also their customary and understandable unwillingness to cede jurisdiction of a claim arising under domestic law to a foreign or transnational tribunal. To this extent, at least, it will be necessary for national courts to subordinate domestic notions of arbitrability to the international policy favoring commercial arbitration.

Accordingly, we "require this representative of the American business community to honor its bargain" . . . by holding this agreement to arbitrate "enforce[able] in accord with the explicit provisions of the Arbitration Act."

Case Questions

1. Does the United States have a federal policy regarding arbitration agreements? What is that policy and where is it found?
2. Does the Court indicate that the arbitration panel will be able to review claims based on the U.S. antitrust law even if the panel has no special knowledge of that law?
3. Do you think the Court believes it is likely that arbitration will continue to be used as a method to resolve international contract disputes?

INTERNATIONAL INVESTMENTS

Legal constraints on exporting and licensing often make international investment a more desirable method of engaging in international business. If significant barriers to international trade exist, investment may be the only means of selling products in a foreign market. Local laws may erect discriminatory barriers against foreign products that only the establishment of plants in those countries can overcome. For example, many U.S. firms have made investments in European countries to bypass the tariff barriers imposed by the EC.

Crucial business factors may also make investment preferable to exporting or licensing. The on-site locations obtained through investment enable foreign firms to market goods more effectively. In particular, the transportation expenses incurred in exporting often make trade arrangements so costly that investment may be the only profitable means of selling internationally. These factors help explain why many companies that export

FIGURE 21–6 Comparison of Direct Investment and Joint Venture

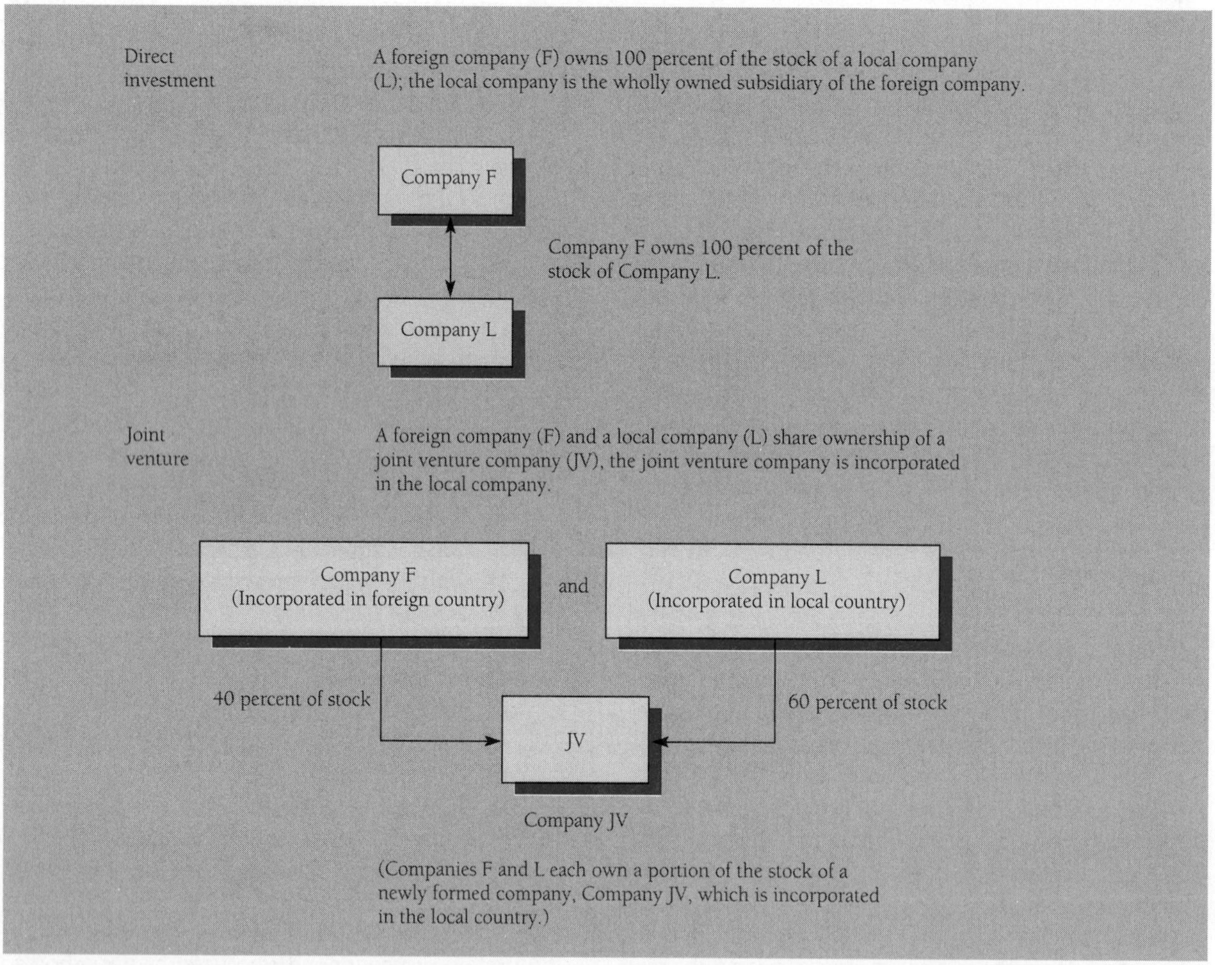

TABLE 21–1
Sources of Law Affecting International Business Investment in Germany by a U.S. Firm

Type of Law	Specific Legal Source
Laws of country in which investment is made (country of source)	German laws
Laws of regional organization	EC laws
Extraterritorial laws of country of origin	U.S. tax or antitrust laws
Treaty agreements between countries	U.S.–German treaty on double taxation
Relevant rules of international institutions	Rules of General Agreement on Tariffs and Trade (GATT)

goods to the United States from Japan, Korea, and other Asian countries have begun to produce these goods in the United States.

Joint ventures and direct investments are becoming widely used methods of engaging in international transactions. *Joint ventures* have two or more active participants and usually involve the establishment of a separate corporation in the host country. *Direct investments* are investments in foreign facilities by a single firm. In a joint venture, each party shares in contributions and ownership. For example, a foreign firm may contribute capital and management experience, while a local firm may contribute raw material resources and local marketing expertise. A comparison of joint ventures with direct investments is shown in Figure 21–6.

The laws of the countries in which the operations are conducted must be closely examined to determine the benefits of international investment, whether through direct investments or joint ventures. However, as Table 21–1 illustrates, international investment is also affected by certain rules of international law, extraterritorial aspects of the laws of the country of origin, treaty obligations between the country of origin and the country of source, and relevant rules of international institutions.

Joint Ventures in International Business

Joint ventures are commonly used by companies engaged in international business. Mitsubishi Motors, for example, is a joint venture between Chrysler International (CISA) and Mitsubishi Heavy Industries, Inc. As discussed in Chapter 13, the joint venture is a form of partnership that is limited in scope. The parties to a joint venture do not agree to merge all of their activities but instead agree to cooperate in some areas while perhaps continuing to compete in others.

Joint venture arrangements have recently replaced direct investments in wholly owned subsidiaries as the most prevalent method for establishing foreign manufacturing facilities. In many countries, investment codes prohibit many types of direct investments and require that a specific percentage of a joint venture be owned by local individuals, firms, or government units. In such countries, the joint venture may be the only means of foreign investment.

Absent legal restraints requiring the use of joint ventures, this method of international investment may be preferable where direct investment is too expensive. Political and business risks may be so great that it may be best to share them. There may be critical ingredients of business success, such as access to local capital, political contacts, personnel, and local suppliers, that only a local partner can provide.

In some countries, laws require that the government itself be a part owner of any joint venture. Such an arrangement has both advantages and disadvantages. If a government is a part owner, the joint venture is generally assured that governmental agencies will grant needed licenses and regulatory approval. However, governmental participants may lack business experience or may be subject to removal if they fall out of favor with the ruling party.

The unique legal problems associated with the international joint venture are primarily those that affect its organization and its relations with the firms that created it. A number of legal sources must be consulted to determine the profitability of the venture. These are discussed further in the next section.

Direct Investments in International Business

Direct investment is the most involved method of conducting international business. Most nations have mixed views about granting foreign firms the right to participate directly in economic activities within their borders, and the policies adopted on this score vary according to political and economic considerations. A country's historical experiences with foreign investors, its level of economic development, its need for foreign capital and technology, and its political ideology are important factors. Numerous legal questions must be answered before a foreign investment is made.

Legal Questions Affecting Foreign Direct Investments

1. What are the country's investment laws or policies?
2. Which form of business organization is most appropriate for an investment?
3. Are there exchange controls affecting movement of money into or out of the country?
4. What is the taxation policy of the source country?
5. Do labor laws require worker representation on a company's board of directors or the hiring of a certain percentage of the labor force from the source country?
6. Is expropriation or nationalization a possibility?
7. What are the antitrust policies, and how have they been developing?
8. Is intellectual property (patents, trademarks, and copyrights) protected?

Highlights from several legal areas illustrate the primary importance of the laws of the source country. These considerations influence decisions regarding both direct investments and international joint ventures.

Investment Laws and Policy The impact of foreign investment laws is probably the first area that should be investigated. Many countries attempt to attract foreign investors by creating a favorable legal environment, including incentives to invest in particular industries, in stipulated depressed localities, or in special programs. Such incentives are often implemented by means of tax holidays, increased depreciation, or other benefits aimed at making the country's tax rate favorable for foreign investors. Ireland and Scotland have recently attracted numerous manufacturing operations largely through tax incentives.

Many countries try to stimulate some foreign investments while restricting and controlling others. Analysis of the overall objectives of a country's investment code—as well as detailed analysis of its provisions—is required to determine whether the country's policy of promoting and encouraging foreign investments is counteracted by the restrictions and regulations found in more specific laws.

Forms of Business Organization The choice of a particular form of business organization for international investment often has critical tax consequences. For a U.S. firm, the U.S. tax laws, the tax laws of the country of source, and tax treaties between the United States and the country of source may influence which form is chosen.

One option is to organize a foreign corporation that is a separate subsidiary of the domestic corporation. Typically, a *subsidiary* is incorporated under the laws of the country where its business activity is to take place, thereby increasing the likelihood that it will be treated as a local company. Such subsidiaries are separate legal entities and are not usually considered part of the parent corporation. In some cases, however, such as the chemical disaster in Bhopal, India, involving the Union Carbide Company and its Indian subsidiary, Union Carbide, Ltd., the parent company may be held liable for the activities of its subsidiary.

The Internal Revenue Code encourages U.S. corporations to establish *foreign sales corporations (FSCs)*. The parent firm that establishes an FSC subsidiary owns all the shares of the subsidiary's stock. Thus, the FSC is essentially a "shell" or "paper" corporation. The parent firm sells its export products to the FSC, which then resells them to foreign buyers. For this reason, the FSC, not the parent firm, derives income from export sales. Taxes may be 15 percent less on the sales of an FSC than on sales made directly by the parent corporation.

Another option is to establish a foreign branch of the domestic corporation. *Foreign branches* of U.S. corporations are not independent entities but a part of the parent corporation. The choice between the branch and subsidiary forms is often based on the activities to be conducted. If an initial loss is anticipated for a foreign venture, a branch may be preferable since that loss may offset other income of the corporation. On the other hand, if a foreign venture is taxed at a lower rate in the country of source than in the country of origin, a separate corporation may be preferable. Liability concerns may also affect the choice of organizational form. Figure 21–7 illustrates the differences between the foreign subsidiary and branch forms.

Exchange Controls Foreign direct investment decisions may be affected by currency exchange controls designed to limit the investing firm's right to withdraw profits, interest, dividends, or portions of the invested capital. Some protection against the most severe restrictions is available to U.S. corporations pursuant to treaty provisions. Firms may also secure insurance protection against the risk of inability to convert investment receipts from the local currency into dollars.

Tax Considerations Foreign direct investors must examine both direct and indirect taxes. Many countries derive most of their income from indirect taxes, such as sales taxes, turnover taxes, or excise taxes. Indirect taxes are easier to collect than direct taxes and are less dependent on a high level of taxpayer income. Thus, for example, almost 50 percent of France's taxes are indirect taxes.[4]

Municipal or state taxes, as well as national taxes, must be reviewed to determine the total tax burden. In Switzerland, for example, the municipal or canton taxes on corporate income are far more significant than the Swiss federal tax.

Tax treaties play an important role in determining the tax burden of some transactions. As previously stated, tax treaties may alleviate the double taxation imposed by conflicting or overlapping tax laws of the country of source and the country of origin.

---

[4]*Price Waterhouse Information Guide: Doing Business in France* (Price Waterhouse World Firm Limited, 1990), p. 116.

FIGURE 21–7 Comparison of Foreign Subsidiary and Branch Organizations

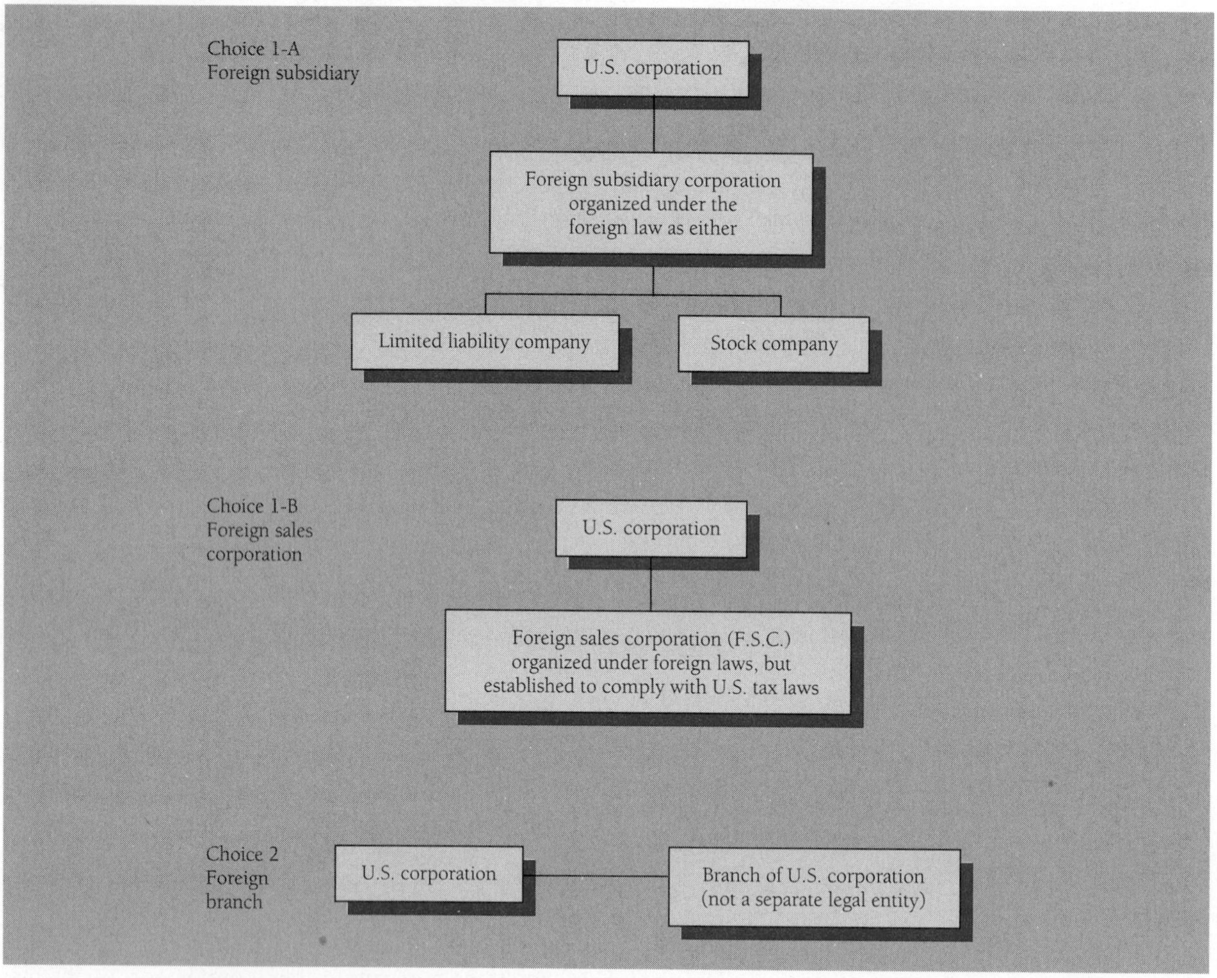

Labor Laws Labor costs are generally a significant part of the cost of doing business and therefore influence most foreign investments. International investments are affected not only by minimum or prevailing wage laws but also by legal provisions regarding hours of work, workers' compensation, retirement benefits, and vacation bonuses. In most European countries, for example, bonuses of one month's pay generally are required by legislation or practice for salaried and hourly workers. In Japan, bonuses of at least one month's pay or more are awarded to most workers in July and December, and these bonuses may be as high as six months' pay. Severance payments accompanying notice of termination are expected or legislated in many countries.

In some countries, workers have a vested right to their jobs; Mexican and Colombian laws restrict an employer's right to discharge workers except under specifically prescribed conditions. Local laws often require foreign workers to obtain work permits, such as work visas or green cards in the United States. Further, laws may require that local nationals comprise a minimum percentage of the labor force. All foreigners working in Saudi Arabia must obtain work permits, and all companies in Saudi Arabia that employ foreigners must employ 75 percent Saudi nationals and pay at least 51 percent of their total payroll to Saudi nationals.[5] Indian law required Union Carbide to have Indian managers at its Bhopal facility.

Safety of Investment from Expropriation or Nationalization Expropriation or nationalization occurs when a government takes over the ownership and management of private firms. Although the terms are often used interchangeably, the government pays compensation to the former owner when *nationalization* takes place; no compensation is paid when *expropriation* occurs. In 1982, France nationalized many of the banks operating in France, both foreign and domestically owned; in the 1960s and 1970s, Cuba expropriated many of the foreign banks operating there.

If sizable investments are contemplated, legal protection against the risk of expropriation should be considered. Such protection may be available from a variety of sources. The local investment code may have express nonexpropriation guarantees. Treaties signed by some foreign countries with the United States indicate agreement as to the standard for "reasonable compensation." Certainly, the insurance protection offered through such U.S. agencies as the Export-Import Bank, the Foreign Credit Insurance Association, and the Office of Private Investment Controls should be examined if there is any danger regarding the safety of expropriation or nationalization. In any event, firms should analyze the risk of expropriation before investing in politically unstable foreign countries.

Antitrust Laws Firms operating in the United States, whether of domestic or foreign origin, have long been aware of the possible effects of the antitrust laws on their operations. The U.S. antitrust laws, discussed in Chapters 15 and 16, are intended to preserve a relatively free system of competition by controlling anticompetitive practices and by regulating the growth and use of economic power.

Countries other than the United States have also enacted antitrust laws, though U.S. antitrust law has had more influence on international business transactions than the antitrust law of any other country. Antitrust laws were enacted in most of the major European countries after World War II. Those national laws were subsequently supplemented and to some extent replaced by Article 85–90 of the Treaty of Rome, which created the European Community. Article 85–90 of that treaty prohibits practices and agreements that restrict or distort competition within the EC or among its member states. Furthermore, the EC has clearly indicated that Article 85–90 also applies to extraterritorial activities that affect trade or commerce in the member states even if one of the parties to such activities is a nonmember of the EC.

Patents, Trademarks, and Copyrights Intimately connected with antitrust law is the legal protection afforded trademarks and patents. Whereas antitrust law is antimonopolistic, patent law gives a limited monopoly to certain processes, products, or designs, and trademark law gives a limited monopoly to symbols or words. Trademarks designate the source of origin of a product, while patents give their owner a monopoly over a product's manufacture, sale, or use.

A country cannot give extraterritorial effect to its patent laws; therefore, a patent confers rights that are protected only within the boundaries of the country in which the

---

[5]*Price Waterhouse Information Guide: Doing Business in Saudi Arabia* (Price Waterhouse World Firm Limited, 1991), p. 81.

patent is issued. Thus, a U.S. patent and a Canadian patent, even when granted for the same invention, create separate and distinct rights that may differ in scope and effect in each of the issuing countries.

U.S. courts have held that a foreign patent confers no rights on its owner with respect to acts done in the United States. Under U.S. patent laws, inventors are not required to use their patents or to permit others to use them; no taxes are due to maintain their patents. In some other nations, however, these obligations must be performed to maintain a patent's validity.

The principal international agreement relating to patents and trademarks is the International Convention for the Protection of Industrial Property (Paris Union), of which the United States and over 80 other countries are members. This agreement creates uniformity by allowing applicants in one member country to apply subsequently for protection in other member countries. A person in one member country who files an application in another member country within six months of the original filing date is entitled to priority based on the original filing date.

The oldest multilateral treaty for the protection of copyrights is the Berne Convention. Over 70 countries, including all of the EC countries, are members. A literary, artistic, or musical work whose publication first occurs in a member country qualifies for protection in other member countries. The Universal Copyright Convention is another major multilateral copyright treaty. It provides for national treatment of copyright holders of member countries if the copyrighted work was written by a citizen or resident of a country that is a party to the treaty or was first published in a member country. The United States is a member of the Uniform Copyright Convention but not of the Berne Convention.

SUMMARY

International business is conducted through international trade or investment. International trade has increased dramatically over the last several decades. In recent years, many Pacific Rim countries have accounted for an increasingly larger portion of international trade. International investment occurs when businesses from one country open offices, plants, and factories in other countries. Although foreign investment by U.S. firms continues to be a significant part of total foreign investment, foreign firms invest a greater amount in the United States.

A variety of laws affect firms engaged in international business. The organization and operation of international business is subject to national, regional, and international laws, but national laws have the greatest effect. If the country of source has a legal system with which the business person is unfamiliar, its laws should be closely reviewed. Common law, civil law, and Islamic law are the main categories of legal systems.

Some laws of the country of origin may have extraterritorial effect. The antitrust and income tax laws of the United States have effect outside its territory. Regional laws may be superimposed on national laws. Thus, business operations are affected, for example, by the regional laws of the European Community and the Andean Common Market. International organizations and agreements such as the International Monetary Fund, the United Nations, and the General Agreement on Tariffs and Trade, are also a part of the international legal environment.

International trade is affected by laws that encourage or restrict exports and by laws that restrict imports. Laws restricting exports are intended to preserve scarce resources or regulate access to vital national products and information. Laws encouraging exports often take the form of subsidies or tax incentives. Laws affecting imports include prohibitions, quotas, tariff barriers, and nontariff barriers. Although the tariff barriers of many developed countries have been reduced, a variety of nontariff barriers remain in place in many countries. International trade occurs not only through the export of products but also through the licensing of patents, trademarks, and know-how. Licensing agreements usually require the licensee to pay the licensor a royalty in exchange for information on or use of a product developed by the licensor. The parties to any international licensing agreement need to consult the laws of the country of origin, where the licensor is located, and the laws of the country of source, where the licensee is located. International contract disputes are generally submitted to arbitration rather than court litigation.

International investment occurs either through joint ventures by two or more firms or through one firm's direct investment in a foreign country. In either case, the laws of the country in which the investment is made have the greatest weight. However, extraterritorial laws of another country may also be of some concern. Many countries have an investment code that details the treatment given to the investments of foreign firms. Laws that affect the appropriateness of specific forms of business organization should be consulted. The tax laws of the country in which an investment is contemplated should be carefully examined.

Clearly, the safety of any international investment must be determined before the investment is made. Labor laws, antitrust laws, and patent and trademark laws vary significantly among countries. The international legal environment for business investment is affected by the laws of the country of source, extraterritorial laws of the country of origin, and applicable regional and international laws.

KEY TERMS

direct investment, p. 660
export, p. 669
CIF, p. 670
FOB, p. 670
bill of lading, p. 670
letter of credit, p. 671
tariff, p. 674
nontariff barrier, p. 675
license, p. 675
UNICTRAL, p. 678

CHAPTER EXERCISES

1. What are the sources of law that affect most international business transactions?
2. Assume that a firm is doing business in three countries: one with a common law legal system, one with a civil law legal system, and one with a system based primarily on Islamic law. What particular aspects of the laws affecting the firm are likely to vary significantly among these countries?
3. Assume that the United States, France, and Germany have signed the CISG Treaty, but Portugal and Mexico have not done so. Baachus Wines, a U.S. importer of wine and beer, contracts with a French winery to buy French wines. A dispute arises regarding the quality of the wines sent to Baachus. Does the CISG apply? What if the contract is for German beer? What if Portuguese wine is being purchased? Would your answer to these questions be different if Baachus wanted the products delivered to its Mexican office?
4. What are gray-market goods? Give three examples of goods that might be gray-market goods. How do these goods affect firms engaged in international business?
5. What is a letter of credit? How is it used in international business? Are all letters of credit the same? Explain.
6. A U.S. firm is thinking of opening a new manufacturing facility in Poland. Before it makes a direct investment in that country, it seeks your advice as to which types of laws it should review to determine if it should make the investment. Assume that Poland welcomes foreign investment of the type planned by this firm. What advice would you give?
7. The United Kingdom imposes quality standards on domestic producers of milk and dairy products. It has also passed a regulation prohibiting the import of pasteurized milk and unfrozen dairy products as a measure to protect its people from milk that may not meet its standards. Other European Community member countries protest that the regulation does not provide a method whereby their milk and dairy products can pass the health and safety standards that the U.K. imposes on its producers. Does the EC regulation violate the "free movement of goods" provisions of the Treaty of

Rome governing the EC countries or the directives of its Commission prohibiting national laws interfering with that free movement? *Re The Importation of Pasteurized Milk and Cream: EC Commission v. United Kingdom, European Court of Justice,* (1988), 2 CMLR 11.

8. A U.S. firm sells caustic soda to a firm in India under a CIF contract. The soda was loaded on the ship, but a labor strike made it impossible for the ship to leave the U.S. port where it was docked. As a result, the soda arrived in India six months late, and the Indian buyer sues. Who wins? Does it matter if the seller knew before the soda was loaded that a labor strike might occur? *Badwahr v. Colorado Fuel and Iron Corp.*, 138 F. Supp. 595 (1955).

9. Union Carbide Corporation owned 50.9 percent of Union Carbide India, where a leak of toxic methyl isocyanate killed more than 2,000 people in 1984. A lawsuit on behalf of the victims was filed in the United States against Union Carbide Corporation, the parent corporation, claiming that it had effective control over Union Carbide India. What factors would a court consider in determining whether a parent corporation has control over another corporation? If the parent corporation in this case had "control," should it be held liable for the injuries that occurred in India?

10. Griffin is the holder of both a U.S. and an Italian patent for a composting machine. Griffin granted an exclusive license to Longwood to make and sell the machine in the U.S. and an exclusive license to Carminati for Italy and other countries in the European Community. Keystone purchased three machines from Carminati; he used one in his business in the U.S. and sold the other two to U.S. purchasers. Griffin claims Keystone violated its and Longwood's patent rights. Keystone said that as he bought the machine from one who had a license to sell it, he could do whatever he wanted with the machines. Is Keystone correct? See *Griffin v. Keystone Mushroom Farm, Inc.*, 453 F. Supp. 1283 (1978).

Chapter 22

THE SOCIAL RESPONSIBILITY OF BUSINESS

KEY CONCEPTS

Ethical standards, religious precepts, and community mores provide managers with some guidance in making ethical decisions. These principles are normative because they suggest ideal goals for conduct. Criminal laws are proscriptive because they prohibit certain conduct.

Corporations have duties to their various stakeholders, the entities affected by corporate decisions. There is wide agreement that shareholders are corporate stakeholders. There is a growing recognition that other groups, including customers, suppliers, employees, the financial community, and neighbors close to the firm's facilities, deserve the consideration of managers.

Business may exert significant political influence through its financial support of candidates, legislation, and ballot issues. The Federal Elections Campaign Act requires political contributors and candidates to disclose their campaign-financing activities. In addition, there are limits on contributions by individuals, corporations and political action committees (PACs).

Codes of professional responsibility have been adopted by nearly all professions and many business groups. General codes of corporate honor do not exist, however, so managers are faced with the significant challenge of supplying guidance for employees to recognize ethical dilemmas and choose the right course of conduct.

INTRODUCTION . . . PAST, PRESENT, FUTURE

Public concern with the social responsibilities of business has increased greatly in recent decades. During the 1950s, the public began to consider the view that the role of corporations should go beyond maximizing their shareholders' welfare. During the 1960s and 1970s, concern over the scandals of Watergate and the weapons used in the Vietnam War heightened the public's demand that business become more socially responsible.

Seventy percent of Americans polled in one survey believed that "business has an obligation to help society, even if it means less profit."[1] Another survey indicated that "most respondents have overcome the traditional ideological barriers to the concept of social responsibility and have embraced its practice as a legitimate and achievable goal of business."[2] The recent banking, savings and loan, insider trading, stock manipulation, Iran-Contra, government securities, and defense contractor scandals have reinforced public demands on both business and government.

In the future, business must recognize that significant new scandals or evidence of widespread unethical behavior will be met with strong political pressure. Unless business managers act in good faith, laws to re-regulate may be enacted hastily amid an atmosphere of overreaction. Business can avoid ill-conceived regulatory reactions to unethical behavior by instilling ethical standards in all employees. The adoption of ethical codes, the close supervision of employees, and strict enforcement of ethical standards will go far to alleviate the threat of new regulation.

OVERVIEW

Much of the criticism of the unethical behavior of business concerns fraud, collusive conduct, corporate crimes, and bribery. Two major issues arise in this context. First, business activities have been judged increasingly on the basis of their ethical content. Second, since business activities have an impact on many aspects of society, the social responsibility of business is constantly scrutinized.

Business managers who consider social responsibility in making decisions are more likely to avoid sanctions when society cracks down on unfair or unethical activity. Legal and ethical principles reflect an evolution in society's expectations through the setting of public policy. Society's reactions cause public issues that require constant attention by managers.

In order to facilitate the learning process, business decision making is usually presented as a separate subject from the laws affecting business. However, few business decisions can be so neatly and simply compartmentalized. Business transactions and the relations among firms are becoming increasingly complex. Therefore, the study of business social responsibility should be viewed as a complex and multifaceted set of constraints and opportunities that influence nearly every aspect of business. Any important decision may have contractual, regulatory, employment, financing, or competitive considerations. Each of these may be affected by various aspects of social responsibility:

---

[1]"Mounting Public Pressure for Corporate Social Responsibility," in *ORC Public Opinion Index* (Princeton, N.J.: Opinion Research Corporation, January 1974), reprinted in Lyman E. Ostlund, "Attitudes of Managers toward Corporate Social Responsibility," *California Management Review* (Summer 1977), p. 25.

[2]Steven N. Brenner and Earl A. Molander, "Is the Ethics of Business Changing?" *Harvard Business Review* (January-February 1977), pp. 57, 59.

resolution of ethical dilemmas, avoidance of criminal liability, the need for stakeholder analysis, political interaction, and self-regulation. As you review the following materials on the social responsibility of business, consider how these matters may impact business decision making. It is important to integrate this form of analysis into the wide range of legal and business issues developed in this course and in other business courses.

WHITE-COLLAR CRIME

Society increasingly believes it is wrong for business to generate undesirable side effects as a result of its economic activity. Unique temptations and opportunities encourage some business crimes. Criminal acts are often blended with legitimate transactions, thereby permitting the corporate criminal to avoid detection. Enforcement is frustrated because existing laws do not address all aspects of corporate crime. Many laws target individual conduct or organized crime groups while ignoring the unique attributes of business crime. Increasingly, however, new laws specifically address **white-collar crime** (i.e., illegal, nonviolent behavior by business employees) and **corporate crime** (i.e., illegal behavior intended to benefit business firms).

As white-collar crime becomes more prevalent, prosecutors more actively apply these laws to business activities. Consequently, managers should work to understand criminal law and its procedures and should diligently direct their firms' attorneys to review proposed transactions to avoid unintended criminal exposure. This section discusses the criminal law process, some common types of crime applicable to business, and special crimes of increasing concern to business. As you study white-collar crime, you should also review the material concerning the legal process and the defendant's constitutional rights under the Bill of Rights, previously discussed in Chapters 2 through 5.

Ethics and the Criminal Law

For many centuries, both religious principles and laws have been a primary source of ethical guidance. Religious precepts and ethical standards outline the ideal behavior of persons. These standards are often called *normative* principles because they suggest ideal goals for conduct. Laws, by contrast, are *prescriptive* because they do more than suggest normative or "ought to" standards; they require, or prescribe, minimal levels of conduct.

Criminal law is usually *proscriptive* in that it forbids certain actions that society views as unacceptable. Society constantly makes choices between flexible ethical standards and the less flexible criminal laws. This dilemma poses both threats to free choice and opportunities for responsive businesses. Nearly every business decision can be analyzed for ethical impact. Careful ethical choices by managers can avert legal regulation and preserve freedom of action.

Corporate Crime

Law has not proven to be a sufficiently effective control over aberrant corporate behavior.[3] Some structural and procedural aspects of law reduce its effectiveness as a motivator of corporate responsibility. For example, business crimes tend to affect much larger financial

---

[3]See Christopher D. Stone, *Where the Law Ends: The Social Control of Corporate Behavior* (New York: Harper Colophon Books, 1975).

interests than do personal crimes. In addition, judges tend to be more lenient with corporate wrongdoers than with "common" criminals.

Several explanations have been given for the law's leniency toward corporate criminals. Corporate officers are usually upstanding community members with reputations for responsibility. They can usually afford to hire the best lawyers. Defendants charged with corporate crime often claim that their actions were motivated not by personal greed or hatred, but by the goal of business survival.

Many corporate crimes involve fraud or labor, environmental, or manufacturing violations that are not immediately obvious. Unlike the more common "street crimes" of murder or larceny, corporate crimes often go undetected because their effects may not surface for some time. Since the emphasis of most law enforcement was traditionally directed toward the more immediate and personal crimes involving the use of force, corporate crime was shielded from attention.

Criminal Procedure

The criminal procedure followed by state and federal law enforcement officials varies according to which governmental units have jurisdiction over the activity and according to the seriousness of the alleged crime. Criminal prosecutions differ from civil cases because the plaintiff is a local prosecutor, state attorney, or United States attorney protecting the public, rather than a private party vindicating a personal right. Private citizens, however, often do report business crimes to prosecutors and seek to initiate prosecution. The commission of a criminal act initially prompts an investigation and arrest by the police or by other law enforcement officials. Thereafter, law enforcement officials may continue the investigation, question the accused and potential witnesses, seize documentary or other hard evidence, bring a criminal charge (also called an affidavit, complaint, accusation, or information) against the person or persons implicated in the crime.

Pretrial Procedures After charges are filed, the accused defendant makes the first appearance before a judge or other magistrate at an *arraignment*. The defendant may then file a *plea:* not guilty, guilty, or *nolo contendere* (no contest, no admission of guilt but submitting to court resolution). A defendant who does not plead not guilty may be immediately sentenced. Indigent defendants may be assigned a free public-defender attorney in accordance with the constitutional right to counsel. Bail may be set to ensure that the defendant will appear at the trial. Bail is often provided by a bail bondsman, or, in some cases, may be waived if the judge believes the defendant will not flee, thereby releasing the defendant on his or her own recognizance. The defendant may waive the right to a preliminary hearing or review by the grand jury. The U.S. Constitution requires that the defendant be given an appearance before a judge without unreasonable delay and the defendant must receive a speedy trial.

Before any criminal trial is held, there are prescreening processes to prevent law enforcement officials from abusing the criminal process or bringing false charges against innocent accused defendants. At a *preliminary hearing,* the prosecutor must demonstrate the existence of probable cause that the evidence connecting the defendant to a crime is sufficient to "hold the defendant over" for prosecution. A *grand jury,* consisting of numerous local citizens, performs a similar function by issuing an *indictment* when there is sufficient evidence against the defendant. Some states use only one of these prescreening processes, although both may be used in some serious cases. Many defendants agree to settle the charges in a *plea bargain agreement,* pleading guilty to a lesser offense or to only some of several charges. This process conserves public resources when the defendant understands that the prosecution could win a conviction on some charge.

The Criminal Trial Criminal trials follow a sequence similar to civil trials: (1) a jury is impaneled, (2) both sides make opening remarks, (3) the prosecution presents its case-in-chief (i.e., examination and cross-examination of witnesses, presentation of tangible evidence), (4) the defense presents its case-in-chief, (5) both sides make closing remarks, (6) the judge instructs the jury with the applicable law, (7) the jury deliberates, and (8) the jury renders its verdict. Criminal verdicts must usually be unanimous; otherwise the result is a "hung jury," necessitating either another trial or the defendant's release.

The defendant may be sentenced immediately if the law requires mandatory sentences. However, sentencing may be postponed in capital crimes or where sentencing guidelines give the judge discretion in passing sentence. In such cases, a later hearing is held after further evidence is presented regarding the seriousness of the crime and the defendant's background and likelihood of recidivism (return to crime). Generally, the defendant may appeal a conviction. Appeal may be automatic if capital punishment is ordered. The appeals court may permanently dismiss the charges or order a new trial. Unless the trial court made an error, the constitutional protection against double jeopardy prohibits a second trial on the same charges.

Proof of Criminal Guilt

Criminal prosecutors must usually prove two elements of an alleged crime to gain a conviction. First, a *criminal act* defined by the criminal code must have been committed by the defendant. Second, the defendant must have had the *intent* to commit the criminal act. You probably recall that each of these elements must be proved *beyond a reasonable doubt*, a much higher burden of proof than the *preponderance of the evidence* standard used to evaluate civil offenses.

Corporate criminal prosecutions are further limited by the difficulty of assessing individual responsibility. Because businesses are large organizations that perform complex acts in which many persons have a part, the legal determination of criminal intent is problematic. It is difficult to assign direct responsibility for the overall effect of such complex behavior. If an administrative agency's investigation discovers violations of the law, how is the criminal intent of a whole corporation determined? Which individuals in a large business organization should be held responsible if a business fails to adhere to critical safety or health regulations? The following case illustrates this dilemma of corporate criminal enforcement.

United States v. Park
421 U.S. 720 (1975)
United States Supreme Court

Park was the chief executive officer of Acme Markets, Inc., a national retail grocery chain headquartered in Philadelphia. Acme employed approximately 36,000 employees who worked at 874 retail outlets and 12 warehouses. Acme pleaded guilty to numerous charges of violating the Food, Drug, and Cosmetic Act by failing to maintain sanitary conditions at some food warehouses. During 1971, for example, a food safety inspector found rodent infestation in the Baltimore warehouse. After Acme received FDA citations, the FDA inspector commented that "there was still evidence of rodent activity in the building and in the warehouses and we found some rodent-contaminated lots of food items." Park testified that although all Acme employees were theoretically under his control, the company had an "organizational structure for responsibilities for certain functions" and assignments "to individuals who, in turn, have staff and departments under them." When Park received notice of the FDA inspections, he conferred with the Acme department responsible for sanitation, which was investigating and attempting to correct the unsanitary conditions. Although Park believed that there was nothing more he could have done to remedy the problem, he conceded that sanitation was ultimately his responsibility, despite delegation of that responsibility to other managers. Park was found guilty of a criminal violation of the Food, Drug, and Cosmetic Act.

Chief Justice Burger delivered the opinion of the Court.

The rule that corporate employees who have "a responsible share in the furtherance of the transaction which the statute outlaws" are subject to the criminal provisions of the Act was not formulated in a vacuum. Cases under the Federal Food and Drugs Act of 1906 reflected the view both that knowledge or intent were not required to be provided in prosecutions under its criminal provisions, and that responsible corporate agents could be subjected to the liability thereby imposed. Moreover, the principle had been recognized that a corporate agent, through whose act, default, or omission the corporation committed a crime, was himself guilty individually of that crime. The principle had been applied whether or not the crime required "consciousness of wrongdoing," and it had been applied not only to those corporate agents who themselves committed the criminal act, but also to those who by virtue of their managerial positions or other similar relation to the actor could be deemed responsible for its commission. . . . It was enough in such cases that, by virtue of the relationship he bore to the corporation, the agent had the power to prevent the act complained of.

Thus, the Court has reaffirmed the proposition that "the public interest in the purity of its food is so great as to warrant the imposition of the highest standard of care on distributors." In order to make "distributors of food the strictest censors of their merchandise," the Act punishes "neglect where the law requires care, or inaction where it imposes a duty." "The accused, if he does not will the violation, usually is in a position to prevent it with no more care than society might reasonably expect and no more exertion than it might reasonably exact from one who assumed his responsibilities."

Similarly, Courts of Appeals have recognized that those corporate agents vested with the responsibility, and power commensurate with the responsibility, to devise whatever measures are necessary to ensure compliance with the Act bear a "responsible relationship" to, or have a "responsible share" in, violations. . . . This is by no means necessarily confined to a single corporate agent or employee—the Act imposes not only a positive duty to seek out and remedy violations when they occur but also, and primarily, a duty to implement measures that will insure that violations will not occur.

. . . The Act, in its criminal aspect, does not require that which is objectively impossible. The theory upon which responsible corporate agents are held criminally accountable for "causing" violations of the Act permits a claim that the defendant was "powerless" to prevent or correct the violation to "be raised defensively at a trial on the merits."

Congress has seen fit to enforce the accountability of responsible corporate agents dealing with products which may affect the health of consumers by penal sanctions cast in rigorous terms, and the obligation of the courts is to give them effect so long as they do not violate the Constitution.

The Government established a prima facie case when it introduced evidence sufficient to warrant a finding by the trier of the facts that the defendant had, by reason of his position in the corporation, responsibility and authority either to prevent in the first instance, or promptly to correct, the violation complained of, and that he failed to do so. The failure thus to fulfill the duty imposed by the interaction of the corporate agent's authority and the statute furnishes a sufficient causal link. . . .

We conclude that, viewed as a whole and in the context of the trial, the charge was not misleading and contained an adequate statement of the law to guide the jury's determination.

Case Questions

1. Is criminal intent required in corporate crime prosecutions?
2. Why should managers be responsible for criminal violations?
3. Does this decision unfairly expose all employees to potential criminal liability?

BUSINESS CRIMES

Although a business crime could be defined as any crime committed by or against a business, here it includes only those business activities that have a criminal impact. This section discusses the more common, nonviolent business crimes: embezzlement, computer crime, mail and wire fraud, racketeering, and bribery. Of course, there may be criminal sanctions for violating many of the legal or regulatory laws discussed previously: committing some intentional torts; the infringement of a patent, copyright, or trademark; unfair or deceptive trade practices; antitrust violations; securities fraud; environmental pollution; or tax evasion.

Embezzlement

Embezzlement is the wrongful appropriation of property entrusted to an individual. Embezzlement differs from larceny in that the embezzler is given rightful possession of the misappropriated property; a thief has no rightful possession of stolen property. Therefore, embezzlement is committed by persons who are entrusted with another's property: agents, brokers, consultants, accountants, attorneys, or corporate officials. Consider, for example, cashiers, who receive currency from customers as payment for goods or services. A cashier can rightfully possess the cash during working hours, even though it really belongs to the employer. Thus, it is embezzlement for a cashier to take money from the cash register while on the job. By contrast, it is larceny for a cashier to steal cash out of the employer's unguarded safe because the cashier has no right to possess that money.

Computer Crime

Because computers are an integral part of nearly every business, numerous computer crimes are now possible. These include embezzlement by computerized funds transfer; industrial espionage or misappropriation of confidential computer files; theft of valuable computer-use time; sabotage through tampering with computer files or destroying data, programs, or hardware; and fraud in making misrepresentations in computer-collected data. Computer crimes are difficult to detect because the more artful "hackers" carefully cover their tracks to prevent an "audit trail" from revealing their illegal activities. Firms must be vigilant in using effective computer security controls (e.g., access to computer hardware, requiring passwords and ID codes). Until recently, the enforcement of computer crime has simply required the extension of existing law. The states are, however, increasingly customizing computer laws to accommodate the special problems involved. The next case illustrates the problems of adapting existing law to either white-collar crime in general or computer crime in particular. The problems confronted by this case have prompted the passage of computer crime codes in some of the states.

State v. McGraw

480 N.E.2d 552 (Ind. 1985)
Indiana Supreme Court

The City of Indianapolis leased computer services at a flat-rate fee, which was irrespective of how much actual on-line processing time was used. McGraw, a city employee, was given authorization to access the system from a terminal on his desk. City employees were forbidden to make unauthorized use of city property. McGraw began moonlighting by selling the direct marketed product NaturSlim to his coworkers. He used the city's computer system to keep the associated business records: correspondence, client lists, inventory records, and so on. McGraw was reprimanded for making sales during office hours and was eventually terminated for poor job performance. After his discharge, McGraw requested a former coworker to make a printout of his personal business records and to delete all associated computer files from the city's system. The former coworker provided the printout to McGraw's supervisor, thereby initiating an investigation into McGraw's criminal theft of computer time. The state appealed the trial court's dismissal of his conviction for the theft.

Prentice, Judge

It is fundamental that penal statutes must be construed strictly against the State. They may not be enlarged by implication or intendment beyond the fair meaning of the language used and may not be held to include offenses other than those which are clearly described, notwithstanding that the court may think the legislature should have made them more comprehensive. The Act provides: "A person who knowingly or intentionally exerts unauthorized control over property of another person with intent to deprive the other of any part of its value or use commits theft, a class D felony."

It is immediately apparent that the harm sought to be prevented is a deprivation to one of his property or its use—not a benefit to one which, although a windfall to him, harmed nobody. The Court of Appeals focused upon Defendant's unauthorized use of the computer for monetary gain and upon the definition of "property" as used in the statute. We think that it would be more accurate to say that the information derived by use of a computer is property. Having determined that Defendant's use was property, was unauthorized and was for his monetary benefit, it concluded that he committed a theft. Our question is, "Who was deprived of what?"

There is no evidence that the City was ever deprived of any part of the value or the use of the computer by reason of Defendant's conduct. Defendant's unauthorized use cost the City nothing and did not interfere with its use by others. He extracted from the system only such information as he had previously put into it. He did not, for his own benefit, withdraw City data intended for its exclusive use or for sale. Thus, Defendant did not deprive the City of the "use of computers and computer services" as alleged. We find no distinction between Defendant's use of the City's computer and the use, by a mechanic, of the employer's hammer or a stenographer's use of the employer's typewriter, for other than the employer's purposes. Under traditional concepts, the transgression is in the nature of a trespass, a civil matter—and a de minimis one, at that. Defendant has likened his conduct to the use of an employer's vacant bookshelf, for the temporary storage of one's personal items, and to the use of an employer's telephone facilities for toll-free calls. The analogies appear to us to be appropriate.

Intent is a mental function and, absent an admission, it must be determined by courts and juries from a consideration of the conduct and natural and usual consequences of such conduct. There was no evidence presented from which the intent to deprive, an essential element of the crime, could be inferred. A companion statute to the theft statute, proscribing conversion, [states] as follows: "A person who knowingly or intentionally exerts unauthorized control over property of another person commits criminal conversion, a class A misdemeanor."

The only difference between the statutory definitions of theft and criminal conversion is that the definition for conversion omits the words "with intent to deprive the other of any part of its value or use." At most, the evidence in this case warranted a conviction for criminal conversion.

The decision and opinion of the Court of Appeals are ordered vacated, and the judgment of the trial court is affirmed.

Pivarnik, Judge (dissenting).

I must dissent from the majority opinion. In the first place, intent is clearly shown in that Defendant used the City computer system for his personal business, well knowing that he was doing so and well knowing that it was unauthorized. I think the Court of Appeals properly focused upon Defendant's unauthorized use of the computer for monetary gain and upon the definition of property as used in the statute. Time and use are at the very core of the value of a computer system. To say that only the information stored in the computer, plus the tapes and discs and perhaps the machinery involved, are the only elements that can be measured as the value or property feature of that system is incorrect.

It is irrelevant that the computer service was leased to the City at a fixed charge and that the tapes or discs upon which the imparted data was stored were erasable and reusable. The fact is the City owned the computer system of all the stations including the defendant's. The time and use of that equipment at that station belonged to the City. Thus, when the defendant used the computer system, putting on data from his private business and taking it out on printouts, he was taking that which was property of the City and converting it to his own use, thereby depriving the City of its use and value. I therefore would allow the Court of Appeals opinion to stand.

Case Questions

1. What is the wording and perspective taken in the Indiana statutes, which are not readily adaptable to the type of computer crime in this case?
2. How could a new statute be written to specifically eliminate the ambiguities inherent in applying traditional criminal law to computer crime?

Mail and Wire Fraud

Federal statutes make it a criminal offense to perpetrate fraud by communicating misrepresentations in the mail or over the telephone, telegraph, radio, television, or other means of electronic communication. These laws prohibit the use of the mail or wire to conduct an intentional scheme or artifice to defraud in order to obtain money or property. Most businesses communicate to potential clients or customers by mail, over the phone, and increasingly by some electronic means (e.g., electronic data interchange, computer modem, satellite). If any such communication is used in the fraud, or even as a mere incidental part of perpetrating the fraud, the businessperson may be liable for mail and wire fraud. These crimes carry stiff penalties of fines up to $1,000 and imprisonment for up to five years per count. Elaborate fraudulent schemes may contain numerous counts, each of which are punishable separately. The racketeering laws discussed in the next section create additional civil and criminal liability whenever these successive similar crimes form a pattern of racketeering activity based on a mail or wire fraud.

Mail and wire fraud is often combined with the prosecution of other regulatory crimes. For example, the mail and wire fraud statutes were used in the infamous insider trading case involving *The Wall Street Journal's* "Heard on the Street" columnist. The Supreme Court decisively outlawed the participants' insider trading under the misappropriation theory when prosecuted under the mail and wire fraud statutes.[4] Therefore, insider trading is illegal as mail or wire fraud if confidential information is misappropriated and trades are made by mail or co-conspirators are tipped by phone. These activities would also be illegal under Rule 10b–5 of the Securities Exchange Act of 1934.

---

[4] *Carpenter v. United States*, 108 S.Ct. 316 (1987).

Racketeer Influenced and Corrupt Organizations (RICO)

A portion of the Organized Crime Control Act of 1970 is known as **RICO** (the Racketeer Influenced and Corrupt Organizations provision). RICO permits private plaintiffs to sue for civil treble (triple) damages against persons found guilty of racketeering activities. Among other violations, the RICO provision specifically includes securities fraud as a *predicate offense*. RICO outlaws a pattern of illegal activities that include: securities law violations, murder, arson, extortion, drug dealing, fraud, bribery, loan sharking, and other enumerated state and federal crimes.

A RICO action requires the private plaintiff to prove the following essential elements to win triple damages: (1) the defendant committed at least two prohibited acts (2) that constituted a pattern (3) of racketeering activity (4) by which the defendant (5) invested in, maintained an interest in, or participated in (6) an enterprise (7) that affected interstate or foreign commerce. The federal courts have expanded RICO coverage to include many activities that were not traditionally considered part of organized crime.

It is unlawful to invest proceeds derived from racketeering activities. In one case, the proceeds from the sale of a firm tainted by securities fraud were invested in another firm, triggering a RICO claim. In another case, a fraud by general partners who sold their brokerage business constituted RICO activity. The pattern of racketeering activity outlawed by RICO may be proved, for example, by the artificial inflation of a company's market price. Nearly half of the states have passed RICO-type statutes. The state laws combined with the expansive federal RICO provision make significant liabilities possible in business litigation. In addition, the RICO criminal procedures provide for stiff penalties and permit the defendant's assets to be frozen during the prosecution. This tactic has allegedly been used to bully investment banking firms accused of stock manipulation and securities fraud into settling RICO charges.

ETHICAL DILEMMAS IN ACCUSING RACKETEERS

RICO and state racketeering laws are susceptible to unethical abuse. Courts have permitted private plaintiffs and prosecutors to broaden RICO's reach into crimes or activities of legitimate businesses that were never part of the traditional mobster-type organized crime. Recent cases have charged racketeering in contract disputes, securities investments, religious protests, retirement village mismanagement, and commodities speculation. Such more common business disputes are often based on broad-reaching predicate offenses like mail and wire fraud.

Congress intended RICO to provide civil plaintiffs the treble damage incentive to aid law enforcement efforts against racketeers and thereby prevent the use of illegal racketeering profits to finance legitimate businesses. When racketeering operations exist, other legitimate businesses are placed at a considerable competitive disadvantage and may suffer injuries. However, RICO's powerful penalties and vagaries give this "super crime" an increasingly abusive profile. For example, plaintiffs and prosecutors may threaten RICO suits to bludgeon settlements from defendants even if they are chargeable with only two of the prohibited predicate offenses. The Supreme Court may have slowed the RICO misuse somewhat in *H.J. Inc. v. Northwestern Bell Telephone Co.* by requiring better proof of a relationship between the predicate offenses, such as the same or similar purpose, results, participants, victims, or methods of commissions.[5] There is no "pattern" from two isolated events that do not pose a threat of continuity.

[5] *H.J. Inc. v. Northwestern Bell Telephone Co.*, 109 S.Ct. 2893 (1989).

RICO's special powers and penalties promise treble damages and attorney's fees to civil plaintiffs. Criminal conviction can carry fines of up to $25,000 and/or imprisonment for up to 20 years per violation. RICO and other criminal statutes authorize judges to order the defendant to forfeit any property acquired with the illegal racketeering profits. This permits prosecutors to request a pretrial freeze or seizure of the defendant's assets. This powerful settlement inducement was allegedly used to bring down the "junk bond king" Michael Milken and his investment banking employer Drexel, Burnham, Lambert. Financial firms like Drexel would have difficulty operating if their capital were frozen while they awaited the outcome of a lengthy RICO trial. Therefore, Drexel settled the RICO claims to avoid such a financial squeeze. The subsequent fall of the junk bond market imperiled the solvency of numerous banks, thrifts, insurance companies, and retirement annuity companies that were too heavily invested in junk bonds.

Critics charge that RICO's pretrial forfeitures are unreasonable. However, defendants charged with street crimes commonly submit to pretrial forfeitures such as arrest, jail, or high bail. Similarly, in drug offenses brought under the Comprehensive Crime Control Act of 1984, defendants' vehicles may be confiscated. Forfeitures deter defendants from fleeing or disposing of assets and become permanent only if the defendant is ultimately convicted.

Business managers must be aware of their potential personal and corporate liability under RICO. These threatening powers create a strong "settlement value" and incentive to win treble damages or for a prosecutor's desire for political visibility. The use of RICO's considerable powers constitutes an ethical dilemma for prosecutors and plaintiffs. They must weigh RICO's adverse consequences for individuals and firms against the benefits to society from punishing and deterring genuine racketeering.

Bribery and the Foreign Corrupt Practices Act

Following the Watergate scandal, which led to President Nixon's resignation, the public focused inquiry on the misuse of corporate funds for unethical and illegal purposes. In the mid-1970s, the SEC investigated several questionable payments by domestic firms, including bribery of domestic and foreign officials, campaign contributions, and kickbacks. Subsequently, in 1977, Congress passed the **Foreign Corrupt Practices Act (FCPA)**, which it later clarified with the Foreign Corrupt Practices Act Amendments of 1988. The FCPA outlaws foreign bribery and establishes accounting standards to prevent bribery. Among other things, the FCPA was intended to prevent bribery because it is unethical. In addition, the FCPA tends to restore investors' confidence in corporations whose securities are traded in the financial markets. The FCPA outlaws foreign bribery by all *domestic concerns*. Bribery in domestic settings is also a criminal offense under various state and federal laws.

Domestic Concern

. . . any individual who is a citizen, national, or resident of the United States; and any corporation, partnership, association, joint-stock company, business trust, unincorporated association, or sole proprietorship which has its principal place of business in the United States, or which is organized under the laws of a state of the United States or a territory, possession, or commonwealth of the United States.

Prohibited Bribery The FCPA antibribery provisions outlaw any corrupt payments, offers to pay, and offers to give anything of value to foreign officials to influence their decisions. *Foreign officials* include persons with discretionary powers (rather than ministerial or clerical responsibilities), foreign political parties, and candidates for foreign public office. The FCPA is intended to prevent any gifts made with the intent of influencing a decision by the recipient to grant foreign business to a domestic concern.

Grease or facilitating payments are not considered bribes under the FCPA. *Grease* is usually a payment made to a lower-echelon foreign agent with no discretionary powers. In some foreign countries, for example, customs officials routinely expect a "gratuity" to expedite the clearance of incoming goods. If a domestic concern made such a payment to facilitate the clearance of perishable goods through foreign customs, the payment would probably not be an illegal bribe. Where such payments are legal in the foreign country involved, they are not considered illegal bribes. Similarly, bona fide promotional expenditures and contract performance expenses, including lodging for foreign officials, are not illegal.

Accounting Standards The FCPA accounting standards provisions are intended to prevent the accumulation of funds for use as bribes. These provisions apply only to publicly traded firms, requiring them (1) to maintain accurate records and (2) to maintain a system of internal accounting controls. *Internal accounting controls* are procedures for reconciling and overseeing corporate books and assets. These procedures provide reasonable assurance that transactions are executed as authorized and that assets are adequately safeguarded. Records must be reconciled so that accurate financial statements can be prepared. When independent auditors find weaknesses in a firm's accounting system and internal controls, the firm should remedy them. As an important method of supervising employees to avert the misuse of corporate funds, accounting controls reinforce corporate ethics.

Two SEC rules support these accounting provisions. First, it is unlawful to falsify accounting records. Second, misrepresentations to an accountant are prohibited. The FCPA accounting standards and the SEC rules reinforce the FCPA as an ethical code.

FCPA Enforcement The FCPA gives enforcement powers to both the SEC and the Department of Justice (DOJ). The DOJ conducts criminal investigations, prosecutes criminal bribery, and may seek injunctions. The SEC has civil enforcement powers over publicly traded firms and enforces the accounting standards provisions of the FCPA. Publicly traded corporations that violate the FCPA bribery provisions are subject to fines of up to \$2 million, and individual violators are subject to fines of up to \$100,000 and/or imprisonment for up to five years. The SEC may assess civil penalties of up to \$10,000 for individuals. The employer may not pay an individual violator's fine. Most of the cases brought by the SEC have been settled by *consent decree.* Usually, the publicly traded corporation and the individual defendants consent to certain undertakings without admitting or denying guilt. The 1988 amendments give the attorney general power to issue guidelines to assist firms in complying and the power to issue opinions on the legality of specific proposed conduct by domestic concerns. The Enforcement Remedies Act of 1990 gives the SEC considerably greater enforcement powers.

INTERNATIONAL PERSPECTIVE: ETHICS AND FOREIGN BRIBERY

The FCPA represents a confluence of important international management and policy issues. These include ethical dilemmas, the clash of cultures, the conduct of foreign contract negotiations, growing uniformity in accounting and auditing standards, and whether U.S. practices should be exported abroad. Bribery contradicts the basic assumptions underlying the perfect competition model by diverting transactions from freely negotiated market outcomes into sub-optimal transactions based on factors other than price, service, and quality. Bribery receives varying degrees of acceptance in other nations. Firms may be induced to bribe foreign officials to gain business in nations where prohibitions against bribery receive inconsistent enforcement or where bribery is tolerated either by the culture or by self-interested government officials. These foreign officials act unethically when other nations' firms must bribe them to gain business. The officials' personal profiteering occurs at the expense of their citizens and their own nations.

Nearly all nations outlaw bribery. Therefore, bribery becomes possible only where there are primitive control systems and lax accountability or intentional efforts to hide the corruption. The FCPA has established a higher standard in law and accounting by requiring internal corporate accountability. Critics charge the FCPA is simply an effort to export U.S. ethics. Further, they argue that it is an ill-conceived plan because firms from nations without tough antibribery laws will simply fill the foreign orders that U.S. firms cannot win through bribery. Yet, although there is conflicting evidence, U.S. exports seem to have grown steadily since the FCPA passage.

The FCPA appears to be exporting accountability as U.S. accounting and auditing standards are implemented worldwide. Some major U.S. accounting firms have merged with foreign accounting firms so these accounting practices are multi-national. U.S.-trained auditors supervise audits of foreign firms and expect FCPA-style accounting controls. This eventually raises the ethical standards intrinsic in the foreign firms' accounting systems. Among the industrialized nations, only Spain fails to require independent auditors, although this will likely change as the EC requires greater uniformity among publicly traded firms. Generally accepted auditing practices will eventually become standardized as the world's capital markets merge. Capital will be attracted mainly to markets with accountable firms, which investors will perceive as carrying a lower risk.

Perquisites: Ethical and Legal Analysis

The accounting standards provisions of the FCPA have been used in ethical contexts other than foreign bribery. They have been applied to upper management in situations involving excessive perquisites, or perks. *Perks* are profits or benefits that an employee receives in addition to regular compensation. Perks arguably help to more closely identify the personal interests of employees with the interests of the firm, and some say that they can help "perk up" the performance of employees.

However, upper management may be tempted to abuse its position by giving itself excessive perks. Accountability for the use of corporate assets by executives is often more relaxed than is accountability for their use by other employees. An executive's misuse of corporate assets is a classic case of unethical behavior. Does an executive's personal use of perks conflict with the firm's interests? The following case illustrates that accountability for excessive use of perks may be maintained under the FCPA even if state law fails to address such ethical abuses.

In re Playboy Enterprises, Inc.

S.E.C. Admin. Proc. File No. 3–5951 (1980)
Securities and Exchange Commission

The SEC held an administrative hearing concerning Playboy Enterprises, Inc. to determine whether certain perks given to its president, Hugh Hefner, were excessive. In addition to Hefner's use of the Playboy mansion, described below, Hefner, his family, and his friends had extensive use of limousine service, personal tax and legal consulting services, insurance policies, flights on the Playboy DC-9 jet plane *Big Bunny,* automobile use, hotel and Playboy club charges, and loan guarantees. Although Hefner personally paid for some of these expenses, many were paid from the Playboy corporate treasury.

Hefner, the company's founder, is Chairman of the Board of Directors and Chief Executive Officer. Since Playboy became a publicly held company, Hefner has owned approximately 72 percent of the company's common shares issued and outstanding. The company has approximately 25,000 other stockholders of record.

The federal securities laws require registrants to fully disclose, among other things, all forms of remuneration provided to their officers and directors, as well as company transactions in which officers, directors or 10 percent shareholders have a direct or indirect material interest. Possible conflicts of interest and the use of corporate assets for the personal benefit of officers or directors are required to be disclosed in a wide variety of filings with the Commission, including prospectuses, proxy statements and annual reports to the Commission. Since becoming a public company in 1971, Playboy has in significant respects failed to make disclosures required of it in these vital areas of required disclosure to its stockholders and the investing public in general.

Playboy's Audit Committee determined that the total amount of all such benefits received over a period of approximately eight years was in excess of $2 million.

Playboy's Audit Committee determined that Hefner should have been charged $212,749 for his basic accommodations for the period 1971–1978, $65,199 more than the amounts he paid for rent during this period.

The Chicago Mansion consists of two separate buildings. The principal building is a four-story, 54-room stone structure containing 13 apartments and bedrooms; a number of common areas, including a large ballroom and restaurant-type kitchen; and a six-car garage. After purchasing the building, Playboy added a swimming pool (with adjacent "underwater bar"), sauna, and recessed grotto. Playboy also converted first-floor space into a game-room and exercise room, and installed a wide assortment of electronic gadgetry, consisting of a variety of audio/visual equipment and extensive security apparatus.

The second, 20-room building comprises three additional bedrooms, a board room, an office for Hefner, and additional office and storage space. A dormitory with room for thirty Playboy Club Bunnies occupies the top floor of the two buildings. Improvements consisted of general refurbishing and the installation of a single-lane bowling alley on the building's lower level. Playboy's improvements to the Chicago Mansion, completed over the period from 1959 to 1977, cost approximately $3.2 million. Playboy absorbed the total cost of operating the Chicago Mansion, less Hefner's rent and rent by the Playboy "Bunnies" residing in the dormitory. The total amount spent by Playboy on operating costs for the Chicago Mansion during the period 1971 to 1978 was approximately $9.15 million.

Hefner's accommodations comprised a master bedroom suite, consisting of a bedroom, bathroom, living room and sitting room. Located on the first floor and accessible through Hefner's bathroom is the "Roman Bath," an elaborate bathing/sleeping area. Adjoining the suite are a study, library/work area and conference room, which were available to Hefner for use as office space.

Playboy Mansion West [PMW] consists of a 30-room Tudor-style stone structure set on 5½ wooded acres. The main floor consists of a two-story hall, living room (with built-in movie screen and antique pipe organ), library, dining room, breakfast room, and kitchen/servants' dining area. The second floor comprises a master bedroom suite, five furnished guest rooms, and four offices. Above the master bedroom is an attic, converted to an office for Hefner. The master bedroom suite consists of a bedroom, bathroom, and dressing area. The bedroom contains an extensive array of audio/visual equipment, which is monitored through a small electronics control room. Two one-story outbuildings within the Mansion complex serve as a separate guest house and a game house. On the landscaped Mansion grounds are a lighted tennis court, a barbecue area, a swimming pool with a bathhouse/cabana/sauna and grotto, an animal shelter, and a greenhouse/aviary. The grotto, a cavern with underwater access and multiple sitting areas, contains individualized Jacuzzi systems and a stereophonic sound system.

Playboy undertook substantial renovation of PMW. [T]he first stage [of] improvements totaled approximately $5 million, [and] the [second stage] is $2.6 million, of which $1,035,000 is attributable to Hefner's quarters. PMW operating costs during the period 1971 through 1978 were approximately $11.5 million.

Personal guests of Hefner have stayed at the Mansions for extended periods of time. They included Hefner's family members, Hefner's girlfriends, and other friends and associates. The expenditure of corporate funds on these personal guests served no business purpose to the company. All Mansion guests enjoyed a wide variety of services and amenities. In addition to meals and beverages, they received the use of extensive recreational facilities, including swimming pools, a bowling alley, game rooms, and a tennis court. Playboy's Audit Committee found that, out of at least 21,949 overnight guest "stays" at the Mansions, some 6,020 such stays were personal to Hefner and thus should be reimbursed to the company.

Playboy has spent substantial amounts on sophisticated video equipment, commercial films, blank films, and tape cassettes for on-premises taping. This equipment is used by Hefner primarily for business purposes and much of it is located in his bedroom suite at PMW. The equipment purchased by Playboy has included four wide-screen projection systems, five video-replay/recorder units, three color TV monitors, and three low-light cameras. On occasion, Hefner has used some of this equipment for purely personal purposes. Playboy has also purchased an extensive collection of erotic films and cassettes, which the Audit Committee found to serve the company's editorial needs.

Hefner hosted frequent parties at the Chicago Mansion and PMW [including] an open bar and buffet dinner followed by the screening of a movie or prize fight. A 1974 management study showed that the direct cost of such parties ranged from $1,000 to $7,000 per party.

Playboy has taken and continues to take the position that such expenditures are "promotional" in nature and thus benefit the company's business activities. . . . The Commission has taken into consideration the argument that expenditures on parties and social gatherings given by Hefner at the Mansions and the substantial expenditures on lavish improvements to the Mansions are business-related because they are designed to promote the Playboy "image" and thus produce a benefit to Playboy, albeit one of indeterminate value. This argument has been accepted in large part by Playboy's Audit Committee, which concluded that, while Playboy's promotional success "is not solely or even primarily attributable to activities at the Mansions," management had a reasonable basis for believing that promotion of the Mansions was part of a "highly successful corporate strategy."

Finally, the argument that expenditures on Hefner are "promotional" in nature and thus are business-related has no application to the undisclosed benefits to company executives who are not in the "public eye" and thus whose receipt of benefits at corporate expense could not be deemed part of some sort of promotional program. Playboy lacked an adequate system of internal accounting controls for distinguishing between business and nonbusiness expenditures at the Mansions and between reimbursable and nonreimbursable expenses of officers. . . . Playboy's Annual Reports since 1972 have omitted disclosure of management remuneration and affiliated transactions. Playboy's proxy statements have inadequately disclosed the matters discussed. No disclosure of the benefits received by persons other than Hefner was made. . . .

[Playboy settled the SEC charges by making forthright disclosure of these perks, reinforcing its internal control over these assets, electing an additional outside director, and having these matters audited independently.]

Case Questions

1. What legal and ethical safeguards exist to prevent the misuse of corporate assets?
2. Is there any justification for a corporation's provision of the benefits described in this case to its president?
3. Does this case represent a misuse of the FCPA in an area that has little or no connection with foreign bribery?

Limitations on the general effectiveness of criminal sanctions have led many people to advocate that business must assume more responsibility. For example, commentators on corporate social responsibility advocated that modifications be made to the *theory of the firm* to avoid further government regulation. This view is the result of society's changing expectations for business performance. Exclusive reliance on the profit motive, laissez-faire capitalism, and Adam Smith's invisible hand is currently under attack. The broader side effects of business behaviors have come under increasing scrutiny.

Some observers advocate *re-regulation,* insisting that society should not need to prove any definitive causal relationship between business behaviors and societal problems before it imposes protective regulations. These observers assert that the needs and rights of diverse communities, groups, individuals, and future generations should be considered in all business decisions. Opponents of this view believe that competitive pressures make it difficult for any single firm to be the first to make socially responsible decisions. According to them, firms that undertake socially responsible behavior when their competitors do not will sustain at least a temporary competitive disadvantage. There has been actual re-regulation or pressures to re-regulate in recent years in several industries: cable television, employment and labor relations, banking, thrifts, insurance, and transportation, as well as in the treatment of environmental pollution.

CORPORATE SOCIAL RESPONSIBILITY

There have been various stages in the development of the social responsibility of American business. Before the 20th century, the corporate form was seldom used. Without the limited liability of the corporate form, business owners were personally liable for the debts of their businesses. The discipline on business was felt directly by owners who had no shield from personal liability. As the limited liability concept became more widespread during the 1800s, the next stage of business responsibility developed. Passive investors were encouraged to provide the capital needed for industrial expansion. As the use of the corporate form widened, the ownership and control of business were separated. This created new ethical dilemmas, or *moral hazards,* for business managers in their relations with shareholders. It also tended to insulate managers from many of the adverse effects of their decisions.

Laissez-faire capitalism and the industrial revolution brought in such side effects as monopolistic practices. The Great Depression ushered in another stage of social responsibility. Society made increasing demands on business to control the undesirable side effects of competition. This movement persists today, suggesting that business should become more active in planning to avert excessive regulation.

Corporate Stakeholders

In performing strategic planning, business should be aware of the diverse expectations of numerous groups. Business can actively identify its stakeholders and attempt to understand their reaction to and influence on corporate actions. **Corporate stakeholders** are entities that are affected by the firm's decisions. Society actively monitors the impact that business has on its stakeholders. For many of these stakeholders, there are significant measures of business performance other than the firm's profitability.

Identifying Stakeholders Numerous parties that have direct or indirect contact with business may consider themselves corporate stakeholders. Consumers, customers, wholesalers, employees, and retailers are the predominant stakeholders because they contract with the corporation. Participants in the distribution chain expect the corporation to act responsibly in satisfying their concerns. They evaluate the corporation's responsibility by the quality of its products or services, by its work environment, and by its honesty in describing products. Similarly, employees and suppliers expect fair dealing and prompt payments. These audiences usually receive considerable attention from firms.

FIGURE 22–1 Corporate Stakeholder Influences

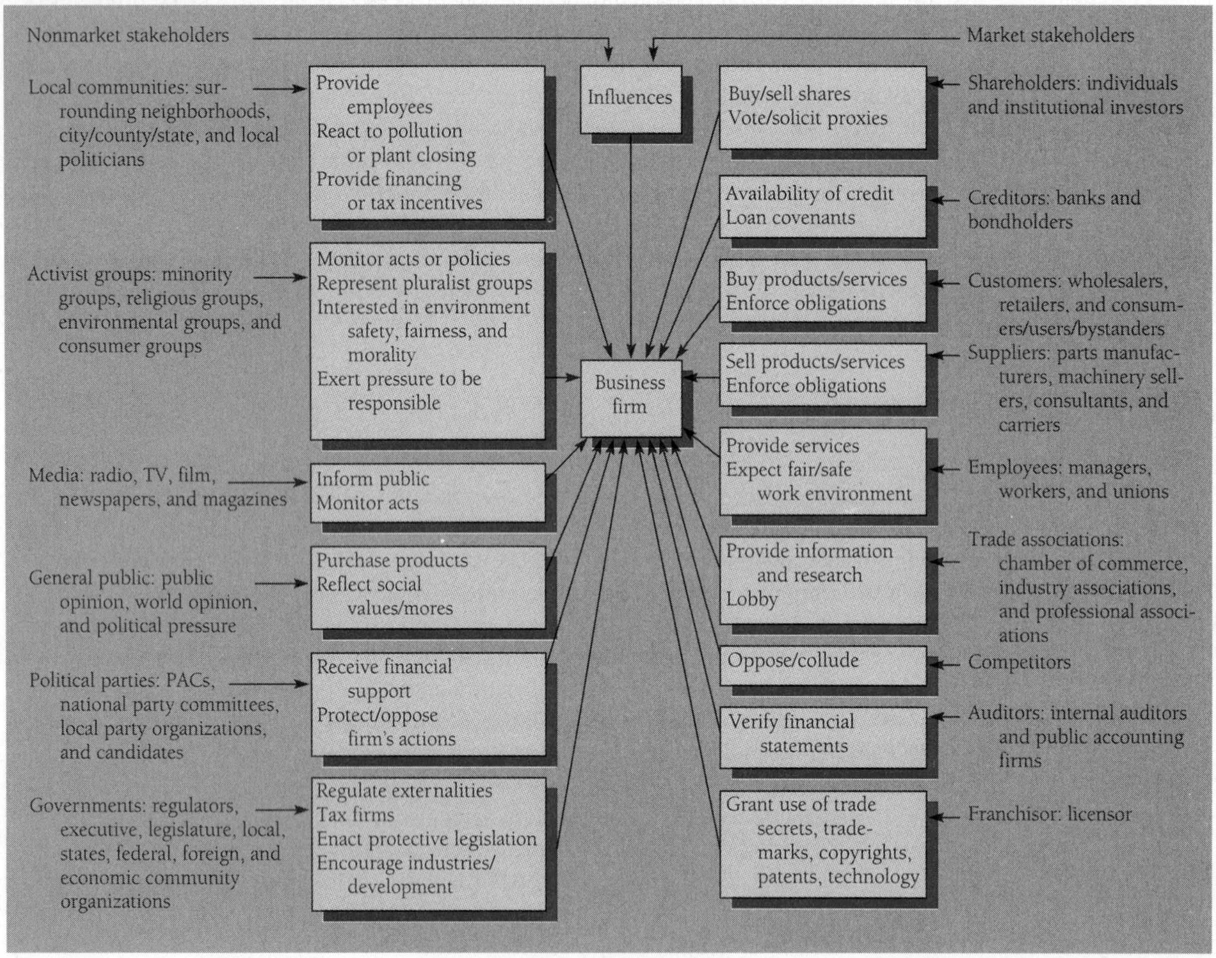

The financial community is another audience that demands the attention of corporations. It consists of shareholders, creditors, investment advisers, investment bankers, and potential investors. Firms must provide sufficient and accurate information concerning their financial status and prospects. Contributors of capital may use the legal system to remedy irresponsible behaviors of firms. If a firm's management becomes unresponsive, shareholders can take over the firm or use its proxy process to oust its management or change its policies.

Another audience is the local community near the firm's facilities. For example, nearby homeowners and businesses can pressure the firm through the legal system, deny needed zoning or operating permits, and influence the public with adverse publicity. Firms should monitor the attitudes of their major audiences and modify their policies to avoid detrimental reactions by these stakeholders. Figure 22–1 suggests how these stakeholders interact with business.

Stakeholders' Expectations and Influence Business is expected to refrain from having a negative impact on various stakeholders. Some stakeholders expect business to generate

FIGURE 22–2 Social Issue Life Cycle

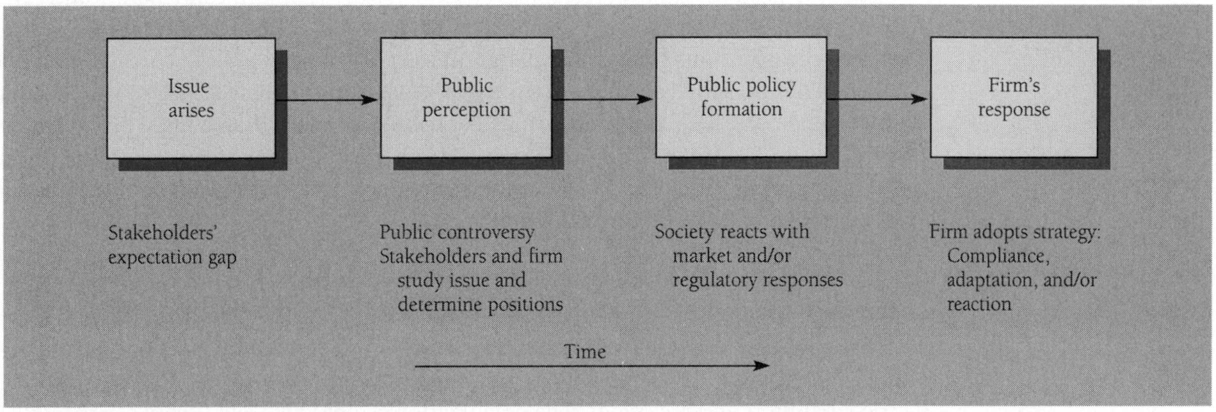

favorable benefits or positive externalities. For example, corporate philanthropy, economic growth, freedom from pollution or industrial accidents, and beneficial research are often considered responsibilities of business. If some audiences of a firm have sufficient political or economic power to pressure it to act in a "responsible" manner, then the firm should consider their influence in its decision making. To avert costly regulation, business managers must understand the complex power structure of government and the relationships among the participants in government who affect the legal environment of business.

Successful corporations often take an active role in managing issues to maintain a good reputation for social responsibility. This necessitates an understanding of the issue's life cycle, as depicted in Figure 22–2.

Campaign Finance Laws and Political Action Committees

Advocacy during political campaigns or referenda is a primary method by which business can exert political influence. Today, federal elections are often won by the candidates who spend the most. Political consultants and pollsters, television advertisements, and electioneering visits to voters' communities are very costly. Many businesses are able to make large political contributions. Numerous observers argue that such contributions pervert the political process by making politicians beholden to business.

In the late 19th century, some businesses made large direct money contributions in elections. Society believed that the political influence of these businesses was excessive, so in 1907 Congress passed the Tillman Act, which prohibited corporations from directly contributing to candidates in federal elections. Some of the states passed similar laws. To bypass the Tillman Act, some business executives were paid large bonuses that they were expected to use as political contributions. Corporate staff, facilities, and consultants have sometimes been provided to candidates. In recent elections, some candidates have had their debts canceled or have been given free rental cars or secret contributions.

Federal Election Campaign Act In 1971, Congress reinforced the Tillman Act with the Federal Election Campaign Act (FECA). The FECA established the Federal Election

Commission (FEC) to administer the campaign finance laws. The FEC requires disclosure of political contributions, receipts, and expenditures by both contributors and candidates. The FECA permits the formation of political action committees to solicit campaign contributions from particular groups.

The FECA prohibits individuals from contributing more than $1,000 to the election of any federal candidate. Individuals may contribute no more than $5,000 per year to a political action committee or $20,000 per year to the national committee of a political party. An aggregate limit of $25,000 per year is imposed on contributions by an individual to all recipients of political contributions.

PACs **Political action committees (PACs)** are groups formed by corporations, labor unions, trade associations, and other special interest groups. A PAC officially exists when it receives political contributions from more than 50 people and either spends or receives over $1,000 per year. PACs must file regular financial reports with the FEC, identifying their contributors and recipients. The organization establishing a PAC may pay the PAC's expenses for rent, salaries, or postage without violating the FECA. PACs advocate policies favorable to their members. They channel contributions received from management, employees, stockholders, or other members to the causes or candidates they believe support their best interests.

PACs may not contribute more than $5,000 to any one federal candidate during primary elections. They may contribute another $5,000 to the same candidate during the general election. PACs may give up to $15,000 per year to national party committees and up to $5,000 per year to other PACs. Although corporations with several facilities may establish separate PACs for each facility, the contributions of these PACs are combined in determining whether they have remained within the contribution limits.

After a presidential candidate has received federal matching funds for an election campaign, PAC contributions are prohibited. However, PACs may make an unlimited amount of "independent" expenditures called "soft money," in favor of particular candidates or causes. These expenditures must not be made with the candidate's cooperation or knowledge. Therefore, PACs may independently buy TV ads to promote a candidate. This technique was used effectively in 1982 in a negative campaign that ousted several key members of Congress. The PAC chairperson or treasurer may be subject to criminal prosecution for violations. The PAC system is coming under criticism for controlling legislation favorable to their industries' interests. PAC activities may be further limited in the future. Some critics seek to prohibit PACs altogether and to limit soft money expenditures.

THE DIVERGENT GOALS OF BUSINESS AND SOCIETY

Laissez-faire capitalism is founded on freedom of contract. Traditional theories of capitalism hold that a corporation's sole social responsibility is strict adherence to the profit motive, which will result in the best allocation of goods and services. Competition leads to the success of efficient firms and the failure of inefficient ones. Free choice determines the types and quantities of goods produced. Management is motivated to succeed by heeding market signals and influences. However, today firms need not follow this ideology so strictly. Firms may recognize there are market failures such as externalities. The needs of various societal interests may be considered in making corporate decisions. The following sections acknowledge an evolution from strict laissez-faire and the emergence of corporate codes of conduct.

Externalities

Firms produce some costs and benefits that the firms themselves do not absorb. These are side effects that some economists call **externalities.** Some observers believe that externalities are caused by failures of the free market model. Government regulation is usually intended to control negative externalities. Pollution is the classic modern example of an externality that society believes should be controlled by government. The costs of pollution would not be paid by the polluter or passed on to consumers unless regulations required that the costs of pollution control be internalized. This problem illustrates the natural dilemma of managers who must pursue profits yet face government regulation if that pursuit results in socially irresponsible behaviors.

Corporate Philanthropy

Many firms seek to act responsibly by giving educational or research grants or engaging in other philanthropic efforts. In some early court decisions, judges prohibited philanthropy as an improper corporate goal. Is a corporation permitted to intentionally provide societal benefits? Some Ford shareholders questioned Henry Ford's goals of corporate social responsibility. Henry Ford owned a controlling interest in the common stock of Ford Motor Company. As the company expanded and its automobile became immensely popular, it was able to pay large quarterly dividends and a total of $41 million in special dividends. In October 1915, however, Henry Ford declared that special dividends would no longer be paid. He publicly declared his ambition to "employ still more men, to spread the benefits of this industrial system to the greatest possible number, to help them build up their lives and their homes."[6] Thereafter, Ford put the greatest share of its profits back into the business. The Dodge brothers, who together owned one tenth of all Ford Motor Company stock, sued the company, complaining that a dividend should be paid. The Michigan Supreme Court established the "goal of the firm" by stating:

> A business corporation is organized and carried on primarily for the profit of the stockholders. The powers of the directors are to be exercised in the choice of means to attain that end, and does not extend to change in the end itself, to the reduction of profits, or to the nondistribution of profits among stockholders in order to devote them to other purposes.
>
> It is not within the lawful powers of a board of directors to shape and conduct affairs of a corporation for the merely incidental benefit of shareholders and for the primary purpose of benefiting others.

The judicial attitude toward corporate philanthropy has evolved since the early 20th century; today, many firms make charitable contributions. A firm's ultimate successes may be enhanced by its reputation for responsible acts. Philanthropy may actually be in a firm's best interests if it leads to favorable public impressions of the firm. In an early 1950s case, a group of stockholders alleged that a corporation's donation of $1,500 to Princeton University was beyond the corporation's powers.[7] However, such gifts are upheld because they legitimately advance the corporation's interests, as quoted next.

---

[6] *Dodge v. Ford Motor Co.,* 170 N.W. 668 (Mich.1919).

[7] *A.P. Smith Mfg. Co. v. Barlow,* 98 A.2d 581 (N.J.1953).

Justification for Corporate Philanthropy

"[i]ndividual stockholders' . . . interests rest entirely upon the well-being of the . . . corporation, [and these stockholders] ought not be permitted to close their eyes to [the corporation's] high obligation as a constituent of our modern social structure."

Universities provide educated employees and research discoveries that are used directly by business. However, philanthropic contributions are permissible even if business receives less direct benefits. Over half the states, including Delaware, have adopted "corporate constituency" takeover legislation permitting corporate boards to consider the effect of its operations on surrounding communities, customers, suppliers, and others. In *Schlensky v. Wrigley* a minority shareholder in the Chicago Cubs sued Philip K. Wrigley and the Cubs' corporate directors, claiming management was not maximizing shareholder wealth.[8] Wrigley Field, the Cubs' home park, had no field lights, which prohibited night games. However, all other major league teams played most home games at night to maximize attendance. Without night games, the Cubs allegedly could not maximize attendance, limiting their profitability. The Illinois court sustained the board's decision, stating:

> It appears to us that the effect on the surrounding neighborhood might well be considered by a director who was considering the patrons who would or would not attend the games if the park were in a poor neighborhood. Furthermore, the long-run interest of the corporation in its property value at Wrigley Field might demand all efforts to keep the neighborhood from deteriorating.

Of course, the lights now at Wrigley Field are further hastening the demise of baseball as a "day sport," a fear voiced by Philip K. Wrigley. Today, modern constituency statutes would not even require that a board connect the firm's financial interests so directly to the condition of the surrounding community.

Codes of Responsibility and Ethics

Regulatory responses are often initiated when self-regulation efforts are perceived as insufficient or nonexistent. Government initiates many of these responses, but there has also been a trend toward the imposition of **ethical codes** by firms. Although professional codes may not be given the force of law, they may nevertheless become an issue in trials. The determination of professional malpractice liability often depends on professional standards. For example, an auditor's failure to follow generally accepted auditing standards, a real estate agent's violation of his association's code of ethics, or a lawyer's violation of the code of conduct usually represents malpractice.

Some industry groups have also adopted codes of responsibility. For example, many advertisers, broadcasters, many trade associations, and purchasing managers voluntarily abide by codes of conduct. Typically, these codes require professionals to be loyal to their clients' interests and to avoid conflicts of interest. The professional must exercise his or her best efforts for every client. Confidential relationships with clients should be maintained, and due care should be exercised in all efforts made on behalf of clients.

[8]*Schlensky v. Wrigley,* 237 N.E.2d 776 (Ill.1968).

Unfortunately, "business" has never been considered a separate profession and has not yet developed a comprehensive and universal code of conduct for general application. Some firms have developed specific in-house codes with varying degrees of success. A "model" code of business responsibility, developed by Charles E. Harris of the Florida Bar, is reproduced below.[9] The *canons* are general statements of broad applicability. The ethical principles focus attention on more specific behaviors.

Code of Business Responsibility

Canon 1. A Professional Manager Should Assist in Maintaining the Integrity and Competence of the Business Community.

Ethical Principles

EP 1.1. The public and shareholders of this Company have a right to expect that the business of this Company will be efficiently and competently performed by our officers and employees. A professional manager should strive for excellence in performing his or her duties.

EP 1.2. A professional manager should maintain a high level of integrity in business conduct and should encourage other managers to do likewise. A manager should refrain from all illegal conduct in personal and business affairs. In doing so, the manager should support and obey both the language and the spirit of the law, avoiding efforts to circumvent the law by devious means or questionable interpretations. A professional manager should be able to rely upon the opinions of lawyers, accountants, and other outside experts, but should not shirk the final responsibility of making the business decisions associated with those opinions.

EP 1.3. A professional manager should disclose, as may be necessary and appropriate, any illegal or unethical business activities by any director, officer, or employee that are likely to have an adverse effect upon the business reputation or affairs of the Company. Although the manager should respect the Company's organizational structure if possible, the integrity and interests of the Company, its shareholders, and our business community may dictate that the manager report such illegal or unethical activity directly to the Company's audit committee, board of directors, or legal counsel, or, as a last resort, to appropriate governmental authorities.

Canon 2. A Professional Manager Should Preserve the Confidential Nature of Business and Customer Information.

Ethical Principles

EP 2.1. A professional manager should ensure that all confidential and proprietary information relating to the Company, its shareholders, and its existing and prospective customers and suppliers, acquired in the course of duty, is used solely for Company purposes and is not provided to unauthorized persons or used for the purpose of furthering a private interest or making a personal profit.

EP 2.2. A professional manager should ensure that all material nonpublic information concerning the securities, financial condition, earnings, and other performance of the Company remains confidential, unless and until it is fully and properly disseminated to the public.

EP 2.3. The obligation of a professional manager to preserve the confidential nature of business and customer information continues after termination of the manager's employment with the Company.

Canon 3. A Professional Manager Should Place the Interests of the Company ahead of Any Private Interests and Should Disclose the Facts in Any Situation where a Conflict of Interest May Appear.

[9]Charles E. Harris, "Restructuring a Workable Business Code of Ethics," *University of Florida Law Review*, 30 (1978), p. 310. Reprinted with the permission of the University of Florida Law Review. Copyright 1978.

Ethical Principles

EP 3.1. A professional manager should ensure that none of his or her outside personal, business, or investment activities unreasonably conflict with the interests of the Company. In all situations where an actual or potential conflict of interest exists or may appear to others to exist, the manager should disclose all details of the activity and conflict.

EP 3.2. A professional manager should not use his or her position with the Company for personal gain. Likewise, a professional manager should separate personal interests and considerations from activities and decisions relating to the Company and its affairs.

EP 3.3. Except where expressly authorized by the terms of the manager's employment agreement or compensation arrangements with the Company, a professional manager should not directly or indirectly solicit or accept any fee, commission, entertainment, gift, gratuity, property, discount, or loan for himself or herself or his or her affiliates or immediate family as compensation for performing duties with the Company or for making, or causing the Company to make, any business decision.

EP 3.4. Except where expressly authorized by the Rules of Conduct, a professional manager should not directly or indirectly solicit or accept any fee, commission, entertainment, gift, gratuity, property, discount, or loan for himself or herself or his or her affiliates or immediate family from any existing or potential customer, competitor, or supplier of the Company.

EP 3.5. Except where expressly authorized by the Rules of Conduct, neither a professional manager nor his or her affiliates or immediate family should directly or indirectly solicit or receive any bequest or legacy from any customer, competitor, or supplier of the Company, or serve as executor, personal representative, trustee, or guardian of an estate, trust, or guardianship established by a customer, competitor, or supplier of the Company.

Canon 4. A Professional Manager Should Avoid Even the Appearance of Impropriety in Business Matters.

Ethical Principles

EP 4.1. Continuation of the American free-enterprise system requires that the public have confidence in this system and, particularly, in the ethical conduct of its business leaders. Consequently, a professional manager should strive to promote public confidence in our business system by avoiding not only ethical impropriety but also the appearance of ethical impropriety in business matters.

EP 4.2. A professional manager should exercise prudence and restraint in personal financial affairs, including speculative investments and margin accounts, in order to avoid debts or other financial obligations that are, or might appear to be, significantly out of proportion to the manager's financial statement and personal or family financial condition.

EP 4.3. Although a professional manager should be encouraged to participate freely and actively in the political process, the manager should ensure that such activities are separated from those of the Company. Except where expressly permitted by the Rules of Conduct, no Company assets, funds, or loans should be used for political purposes. All contributions for political purposes should be made pursuant to law and accurately reflected in the Company's books.

EP 4.4. Except for campaign contributions and lobbying expenditures designated as such and authorized or permitted by applicable law in the jurisdiction for which the election is held, no fee, commission, property, bribe, or any other compensation should be offered or paid directly or indirectly by a professional manager to, for, or on behalf of any elected, appointed, or ruling government official or head of state, in the United States or abroad, for the purpose of influencing in any way any decision by or within the influence of such official or head of state.

EP 4.5. If a professional manager has previously performed government or public service, or is presently performing such service, the manager should not perform activities for the Company in connection with any specific matter for which the manager had or has substantive responsibility as a government or public servant.

Canon 5. A Professional Manager Should Be Honest in Dealing with the Public and with the Company's Officers, Directors, Employees, Experts, and Customers.

Ethical Principles

EP 5.1. A professional manager should be open and honest in his business relationships with other officers and employees of the Company, the board of directors of the Company, and the lawyers, accountants, and other professionals retained by the Company. In this regard, honesty requires the furnishing of all information that the manager has that would be material to a given decision. The failure to furnish information that is known or thought to be necessary, or the provision of information that is known or thought to be inaccurate, misleading, or incomplete, is unacceptable.

EP 5.2. In order to preserve confidence in the information and advertising disseminated by our nation's businesses, a professional manager should strive to ensure that all information, advertising, and other statements released to the public by the Company are not misleading and do not omit to state any material fact necessary to make the information, advertising, or statements not misleading under the particular circumstances involved.

In recent years, numerous corporations have instituted codes of ethics for their employees. These codes are usually enforced with disciplinary sanctions or discharge for serious violations. Typically, corporate codes of conduct prohibit employees from taking or making bribes or kickbacks. They usually prohibit conflicts of interest, illegal political contributions, and other general violations of the law. Other prohibitions that appear less frequently in such codes include misappropriation of inside information and insider trading, bribery, falsification of records, antitrust or FCPA violations, and work for other firms.

Legal Effect of Corporate Codes of Conduct

The accelerating trend toward corporate codes of conduct may be due to several factors. First, codes are sometimes adopted to appease regulators. For example, some defense contractors found guilty of overcharging the U.S. government have agreed to develop, implement, and strongly enforce codes of conduct in order to retain their defense contracting business. In other industries, codes have been instituted under consent decrees made with various regulators. Second, codes probably improve the firm's public image.

The proliferation of codes poses questions about their legal effect on the criminal, tort, and regulatory liability of both employers and employees. If strictly enforced, codes may sometimes reduce legal obligations. The *respondeat superior* doctrine of tort law holds the master vicariously (indirectly) liable for a servant's torts committed within the scope of employment. *Respondeat superior* is often applied in criminal prosecutions to punish a firm for its employees' crimes. However, several factors may influence leniency among prosecutors, judges, and juries if the firm cooperates in the investigation and/or strictly enforces its code of conduct. Comment C to the Restatement of Agency (Second) Section 230 suggests there should be a corporate code exception from employer liability when employees violate the code:

> [The corporate code prohibition] accentuates the limits of the servant's permissible action and hence makes it more easy to find that the prohibited act is entirely beyond the scope of employment.

Although codes generally parallel the law, they may actually trigger additional legal obligations. In the insider trading context, a corporate code or other work rules that prohibit insider trading actually triggers the misappropriation theory. This means that employees who violate corporate codes prohibiting misappropriation of information may be liable for insider trading or for revealing confidential nonpublic information. Investment banking firms that enforce such codes may avoid some vicarious liability for their employees' insider trading. For example, the firm's liability is reduced if *Chinese wall* procedures are implemented to prevent the leak of inside information from the firm's underwriting division to its brokerage division. Other provisions of the securities laws eliminate vicarious liability if firms have effective compliance programs and the firms act in *good faith* with no knowledge of the illegal activities of the person(s) they control (e.g., employees). Should a jury consider leniency for a firm which strictly enforces its code of conduct? The following case illustrates this problem.

United States v. Beusch
596 F.2d 871 (9th Cir. 1979)
United States Courts of Appeals

The California subsidiary of Deak & Co., the world's largest foreign currency exchange dealer, and its president, Beusch, were convicted of 377 misdemeanor violations of the Bank Secrecy Act. Deak failed to report these money shipments to the Treasury Department, as required by the Act for transactions over $5,000 received in cash from outside the United States. Beusch had initiated contact with two Filipinos who sent numerous large cash shipments to Deak for further dispersal throughout the world. Deak appealed the conviction, contending the trial jury was improperly instructed to hold the firm vicariously liable for the violations of its employee, Beusch.

James M. Carter, Circuit Judge.

Deak's final contention is that one of the instructions given to the jury prior to its deliberation was erroneous because, in effect, it imposed strict liability on Deak for Beusch's acts in spite of the requirement of specific intent. The challenged instruction reads as follows:

> "A corporation may be responsible for the acts of its agents done or made within the scope of its authority, even though the agent's conduct may be contrary to the corporation's actual instruction or contrary to the corporation's stated policies."

We have examined all of the instructions related to vicarious responsibility and find that, read in context, the challenged instruction does not mean what Deak says it means. It does not impose strict liability on Deak without proof of intent. Rather, it suggests that a corporation *may* be liable for acts of its employees done contrary to express instructions and policies, but that the existence of such instructions and policies may be considered in determining whether the employee in fact acted to benefit the corporation. Merely stating or publishing such instructions and policies without diligently enforcing them is not enough to place the acts of an employee who violates them outside the scope of his employment. It is a question of fact whether measures taken to enforce corporate policy in this area will adequately insulate the corporation against such acts, and we see no reason to disturb the jury's finding in this regard.

Case Questions

1. Does the law require the court to consider the firm's efforts to enforce its corporate code? What weight is given the firm's enforcement efforts?
2. What can a firm do to prove it made enforcement efforts as a mitigating factor in vicarious criminal liability?

U.S. Sentencing Guidelines A variation of the approach suggested in the *Beusch* case was adopted in the U.S. Sentencing Commission Guidelines, effective November 1991. Firms with a strictly enforced compliance program or corporate code of conduct may receive credits that reduce the firm's criminal sentence as low as 15 percent of the potential penalty for their employees' violations. To qualify, such programs must be reasonably designed, implemented, and enforced in such a way as to be generally effective in preventing and detecting criminal conduct. This "mitigation" of the corporate penalty depends on whether the firm (1) reported the violation voluntarily, (2) instituted an effective compliance program (code of conduct and enforcement) before and after the violation, (3) had no high-level policy-setting official with knowledge of the violation, (4) cooperated fully with the government's investigation, and (5) accepted responsibility and took prompt reasonable steps to remedy the harm. The sentencing guidelines add force to the trend to adopt and enforce corporate codes of conduct.

SUMMARY

Society increasingly expects business firms to act in a socially responsible manner. Managers seeking to avoid society's negative reactions should use ethical analysis in making decisions. Ethical principles create normative standards for ideal behavior. They contrast with the proscriptive standards of criminal law, which impose a required minimum base for behavior.

Procedural and personal biases involved in the prosecution of corporate crimes make the law less effective as a deterrent to corporate crimes. Therefore, a greater role exists for proactive social responsibility analysis by decision makers to avert additional government regulation. Ultimately, a firm's chief officers are responsible for compliance with the law and may be held criminally liable.

Business must identify its audiences and consider the effect that its decisions will have on various stakeholders. Some businesses participate actively in public affairs and practice issues management. These interactive processes of social responsibility identify emerging issues, monitor their development, and suggest action in the firm's interest.

The influence of business on the political process is often criticized, so campaign finance laws were passed to diffuse their financial influence. Limits on political contributions and the development of PACs tend to spread rather than concentrate this influence, though their growing influence is again under public scrutiny.

Some people see a natural difference between the profit motive of business and society's perception of its best interests. Since business can externalize its costs, society reacts through regulation that forces it to internalize them. Some people believe that the only legitimate goal for corporations is to maximize their profits and thereby enhance the welfare of their shareholders. Increasingly, business is held responsible to society. Philanthropic acts are legitimate corporate actions because they indirectly enhance corporate interests.

An important trend toward borrowing ethical codes from the learned professions has been developing in business. Many firms and trade associations have been attempting to ward off new regulation by imposing self-regulation. This promotes the public's perception of business/social responsibility. Increasingly, the ethical codes adopted by business have addressed such matters as employee conflicts of interest, misappropriation of corporate assets or information, insider trading, falsification of records and disclosures, misuse of confidential information, quality control, antitrust or environmental violations, and illegal billing, expense, and time card practices. Well-enforced codes may help shield firms from criminal liability. In making business decisions, employees should keep all the sources of ethical/legal analysis in mind: ethical principles, codes of ethics, criminal laws, and civil laws.

KEY TERMS

white-collar crime, p. 694
corporate crime, p. 694
RICO, p. 701
Foreign Corrupt Practices Act (FCPA), p. 702
corporate stakeholders, p. 707
political action committees (PACs), p. 710
externalities, p. 711
ethical code, p. 712

CHAPTER EXERCISES

1. Discuss why the law has not proven to be the most effective control over aberrant behavior.
2. What does the term *corporate social responsibility* mean to you as a business manager?
3. Discuss how the corporate stakeholders in your industry affect the doctrine of corporate social responsibility.
4. There are thousands of political action committees (PACs) in existence. Candidates for Congress increasingly look to these special interest groups for campaign financing. What is the role of PACs, and how does this role relate to the Federal Election Campaign Act?
5. What are the two main sections of the Foreign Corrupt Practices Act of 1977?
6. McClean and Uriarte were employees of International Harvester Company. International Harvester supplied equipment and acted as a subcontractor to Crawford Enterprises, which had contracted to build a plant for the National Petroleum Company of Mexico. McClean and Uriarte were indicted for violating provisions of the Foreign Corrupt Practices Act and for bribing officials of the National Petroleum Company. They filed motions to dismiss the charges against them on the grounds that the failure to convict their employer was a bar to their prosecution. Does the Foreign Corrupt Practices Act permit the prosecution of an employee if his employer has not been, and cannot be, convicted of similarly violating the act?
7. List structural changes that have been suggested to control irresponsible corporate behavior.
8. The text points out that many companies have codes of responsibility and ethics to govern the behavior of their key executives and employees. How do companies enforce such codes?
9. Nestlé Corporation used questionable marketing practices to sell baby formula in Third World countries. Some mothers in these countries watered the formula to make it go further. As a result, babies were unable to receive adequate nutrition. Certain groups urged a consumer boycott of Nestlé's products, claiming that Nestlé contributed to causing malnutrition and even death of babies in lesser developed countries. As Nestlé's vice president for marketing, how would you respond to this accusation?
10. Draft a code of ethics for your company.

Appendix A

The Constitution of the United States of America

We the People of the United States, in Order to form a more perfect Union, establish Justice, insure domestic Tranquility, provide for the common defence, promote the general Welfare, and secure the Blessings of Liberty to ourselves and our Posterity, do ordain and establish this Constitution for the United States of America.

Article I

Section 1 All legislative Powers herein granted shall be vested in a Congress of the United States, which shall consist of a Senate and House of Representatives.

Section 2 The House of Representatives shall be composed of Members chosen every second Year by the People of the several States, and the Electors in each State shall have the Qualifications requisite for Electors of the most numerous Branch of the State Legislature.

No Person shall be a Representative who shall not have attained to the age of twenty five Years, and been seven Years a Citizen of the United States, and who shall not, when elected, be an Inhabitant of that State in which he shall be chosen.

Representatives and direct Taxes shall be apportioned among the several States which may be included within this Union, according to their respective Numbers, which shall be determined by adding to the whole Number of free Persons, including those bound to Service for a Term of Years, and excluding Indians not taxed, three fifths of all other Persons.[1] The actual Enumeration shall be made within three Years after the first Meeting of the Congress of the United States, and within every subsequent Term of ten Years, in such Manner as they shall by Law direct. The Number of Representatives shall not exceed one for every thirty Thousand, but each State shall have at Least one Representative, and until such enumeration shall be made, the State of New Hampshire shall be entitled to choose three, Massachusetts eight, Rhode-Island and Providence Plantations one, Connecticut five, New York six, New Jersey four, Pennsylvania eight, Delaware one, Maryland six, Virginia ten, North Carolina five, South Carolina five, and Georgia three.

When vacancies happen in the Representation from any State, the Executive Authority thereof shall issue Writs of Election to fill such Vacancies.

The House of Representatives shall chuse their Speaker and other Officers; and shall have the sole Power of Impeachment.

Section 3 The Senate of the United States shall be composed of two Senators from each State, chosen by the Legislature thereof,[2] for six Years; and each Senator shall have one Vote.

Immediately after they shall be assembled in Consequence of the first Election, they shall be divided as equally as may be into three Classes. The Seats of the Senators of the first Class shall be vacated at the Expiration of the second Year, of the second Class at the Expiration of the fourth Year, and of the third Class at the Expiration of the sixth Year, so that one third may be chosen every second Year; and if Vacancies happen by Resignation, or otherwise, during the Recess of the Legislature of any State, the Executive thereof may make temporary Appointments until the next Meeting of the Legislature, which shall then fill such Vacancies.[3]

No Person shall be a Senator who shall not have attained to the Age of thirty Years, and been nine Years a Citizen of the United States, and who shall not, when elected, be an Inhabitant of that State for which he shall be chosen.

The Vice President of the United States shall be President of the Senate, but shall have no Vote, unless they be equally divided.

The Senate shall chuse their other Officers, and also a President pro tempore, in the Absence of the Vice President, or when he shall exercise the Office of President of the United States.

The Senate shall have the sole Power to try all Impeachments. When sitting for that Purpose, they shall be

---

[1]Changed by the Fourteenth Amendment.
[2]Changed by the Seventeenth Amendment.
[3]Changed by the Seventeenth Amendment.

on Oath or Affirmation. When the President of the United States is tried, the Chief Justice shall preside: And no Person shall be convicted without the Concurrence of two thirds of the Members present.

Judgment in Cases of Impeachment shall not extend further than to removal from Office, and disqualification to hold and enjoy any Office of honor, Trust or Profit under the United States: but the Party convicted shall nevertheless be liable and subject to Indictment, Trial, Judgment and Punishment, according to Law.

Section 4 The Times, Places and Manner of holding Elections for Senators and Representatives, shall be prescribed in each State by the Legislature thereof; but the Congress may at any time by Law make or alter such Regulations, except as to the Places of chusing Senators.

The Congress shall assemble at least once in every Year, and such Meeting shall be on the first Monday in December, unless they shall by Law appoint a different Day.[4]

Section 5 Each House shall be the Judge of the Elections, Returns and Qualifications of its own Members, and a Majority of each shall constitute a Quorum to do Business; but a smaller Number may adjourn from day to day, and may be authorized to compel the Attendance of absent Members, in such Manner, and under such Penalties as each House may provide.

Each House may determine the Rules of its Proceedings, punish its Members for disorderly Behaviour, and, with the Concurrence of two thirds, expel a Member.

Each House shall keep a Journal of its Proceedings, and from time to time publish the same, excepting such Parts as may in their Judgment require Secrecy; and the Yeas and Nays of the Members of either House on any question shall, at the Desire of one fifth of those Present, be entered on the Journal.

Neither House, during the Session of Congress, shall, without the Consent of the other, adjourn for more than three days, nor to any other Place than that in which the two Houses shall be sitting.

Section 6 The Senators and Representatives shall receive a Compensation for their Services, to be ascertained by Law, and paid out of the Treasury of the United States. They shall in all Cases, except Treason, Felony and Breach of the Peace, be privileged from Arrest during their Attendance at the Session of their respective Houses, and in going to and returning from the same; and for any Speech or Debate in either House, they shall not be questioned in any other Place.

No Senator or Representative shall, during the Time for which he was elected, be appointed to any civil Office under the Authority of the United States, which shall have been created, or the Emoluments whereof shall have been encreased during such time; and no Person holding any Office under the United States, shall be a Member of either House during his Continuance in Office.

Section 7 All Bills for raising Revenue shall originate in the House of Representatives; but the Senate may propose or concur with Amendments as on other Bills.

Every Bill which shall have passed the House of Representatives and the Senate, shall, before it become a Law, be presented to the President of the United States; If he approve he shall sign it, but if not he shall return it, with his Objections to that House in which it shall have originated, who shall enter the Objections at large on their Journal, and proceed to reconsider it. If after such Reconsideration two thirds of that House shall agree to pass the Bill, it shall be sent, together with the Objections, to the other House, by which it shall likewise be reconsidered, and if approved by two thirds of that House, it shall become a Law. But in all such Cases the Votes of both Houses shall be determined by yeas and Nays, and the Names of the Persons voting for and against the Bill shall be entered on the Journal of each House respectively. If any Bill shall not be returned by the President within ten Days (Sundays excepted) after it shall have been presented to him, the Same shall be a Law, in like Manner as if he had signed it, unless the Congress by their Adjournment prevent its Return, in which Case it shall not be a Law.

Every Order, Resolution, or Vote to which the Concurrence of the Senate and House of Representatives may be necessary (except on a question of Adjournment) shall be presented to the President of the United States; and before the Same shall take Effect, shall be approved by him, or being disapproved by him, shall be repassed by two thirds of the Senate and House of Representatives, according to the Rules and Limitations prescribed in the Case of a Bill.

Section 8 The Congress shall have Power To lay and collect Taxes, Duties, Imposts and Excises, to pay the Debts and provide for the common Defence and general Welfare of the United States; but all Duties, Imposts and Excises shall be uniform throughout the United States.

To borrow Money on the credit of the United States;

To regulate Commerce with foreign Nations, and among the several States, and with the Indian Tribes;

To establish an uniform Rule of Naturalization, and uniform Laws on the subject of Bankruptcies throughout the United States;

To coin Money, regulate the Value thereof, and of foreign Coin, and fix the Standard of Weights and Measures;

To provide for the Punishment of counterfeiting the Securities and current Coin of the United States;

---

[4]Changed by the Twentieth Amendment.

To establish Post Offices and post Roads;

To promote the Progress of Science and useful Arts, by securing for limited Times to Authors and Inventors the exclusive Right to their respective Writings and Discoveries;

To constitute Tribunals inferior to the supreme Court;

To define and punish Piracies and Felonies committed on the high Seas, and Offences against the Law of Nations;

To declare War, grant Letters of Marque and Reprisal, and make Rules concerning Captures on Land and Water;

To raise and support Armies, but no Appropriation of Money to that Use shall be for a longer Term than two Years;

To provide and maintain a Navy;

To make Rules for the Government and Regulation of the land and naval Forces;

To provide for calling forth the Militia to execute the Laws of the Union, suppress Insurrections and repel Invasions;

To provide for organizing, arming, and disciplining, the Militia, and for governing such Part of them as may be employed in the Service of the United States, reserving to the States respectively, the Appointment of the Officers, and the Authority of training the Militia according to the discipline prescribed by Congress;

To exercise exclusive Legislation in all Cases whatsoever, over such District (not exceeding ten Miles square) as may, by Cession of particular States, and the Acceptance of Congress, become the Seat of the Government of the United States, and to exercise like Authority over all Places purchased by the Consent of the Legislature of the State in which the Same shall be, for the Erection of Forts, Magazines, Arsenals, dock-Yards, and other needful Buildings;—And

To make all Laws which shall be necessary and proper for carrying into Execution the foregoing Powers, and all other Powers vested by this Constitution in the Government of the United States, or in any Department or Officer thereof.

Section 9 The Migration or Importation of such Persons as any of the States now existing shall think proper to admit, shall not be prohibited by the Congress prior to the Year one thousand eight hundred and eight, but a Tax or duty may be imposed on such Importation, not exceeding ten dollars for each Person.

The Privilege of the Writ of Habeas Corpus shall not be suspended, unless when in Cases of Rebellion or Invasion the public Safety may require it.

No Bill of Attainder or ex post facto Law shall be passed.

No Capitation, or other direct, Tax shall be laid, unless in Proportion to the Census of Enumeration herein before directed to be taken.[5]

No Tax or Duty shall be laid on Articles exported from any State.

No Preference shall be given by any Regulation of Commerce or Revenue to the Ports of one State over those of another: nor shall Vessels bound to, or from, one State, be obliged to enter, clear or pay Duties in another.

No Money shall be drawn from the Treasury, but in Consequence of Appropriations made by Law; and a regular Statement and Account of the Receipts and Expenditures of all public Money shall be published from time to time.

No Title of Nobility shall be granted by the United States: And no Person holding any Office of Profit or Trust under them, shall, without the Consent of the Congress, accept of any present, Emolument, Office, or Title, of any kind whatever, from any King, Prince, or foreign State.

Section 10 No State shall enter into any Treaty, Alliance, or Confederation; grant Letters of Marque and Reprisal; coin Money; emit Bills of Credit; make any Thing but gold and silver coin a Tender in Payment of Debts; pass any Bill of Attainder, ex post facto Law, or Law impairing the Obligation of Contracts, or grant any Title of Nobility.

No State shall, without the Consent of the Congress, lay any Imposts or Duties on Imports or Exports, except what may be absolutely necessary for executing its inspection Laws: and the net Produce of all Duties and Imposts, laid by any State on Imports or Exports, shall be for the Use of the Treasury of the United States; and all such Laws shall be subject to the Revision and Controul of the Congress.

No State shall, without the consent of Congress, lay any Duty of Tonnage, keep Troops, or Ships of War in time of Peace, enter into any Agreement or Compact with another State, or with a foreign Power, or engage in War, unless actually invaded, or in such imminent Danger as will not admit of delay.

Article II

Section 1 The executive Power shall be vested in a President of the United States of America. He shall hold his Office during the Term of four Years, and, together with the Vice President, chosen for the same Term, be elected, as follows

Each State shall appoint, in such Manner as the Legislature thereof may direct, a Number of Electors, equal to the whole Number of Senators and Representatives to which the State may be entitled in Congress: but no

[5]Changed by the Sixteenth Amendment.

Senator or Representative, or Person holding an Office of Trust or Profit under the United States, shall be appointed an Elector.

The Electors shall meet in their respective States, and vote by Ballot for two Persons, of whom one at least shall not be an inhabitant of the same State with themselves. And they shall make a List of all the Persons voted for, and of the Number of Votes for each; which List they shall sign and certify, and transmit sealed to the Seat of the Government of the United States, directed to the President of the Senate. The President of the Senate shall, in the Presence of the Senate and House of Representatives, open all the Certificates, and the Votes shall then be counted. The Person having the greatest Number of Votes shall be the President, if such Number be a Majority of the whole Number of Electors appointed; and if there be more than one who have such Majority, and have an equal Number of Votes, then the House of Representatives shall immediately chuse by Ballot one of them for President; and if no Person have a Majority, then from the five highest on the List the said House shall in like Manner chuse the President. But in chusing the President, the Votes shall be taken by States, the Representation from each State having one Vote; A quorum for this purpose shall consist of a Member or Members from two thirds of the States, and a Majority of all the States shall be necessary to a Choice. In every Case, after the Choice of the President, the Person having the greatest Number of Votes of the Electors shall be the Vice President. But if there should remain two or more who have equal Votes, the Senate shall chuse from them by Ballot the Vice President.[6]

The Congress may determine the Time of chusing the Electors, and the Day on which they shall give their Votes; which Day shall be the same throughout the United States.

No Person except a natural born Citizen, or a Citizen of the United States, at the time of the Adoption of this Constitution, shall be eligible to the Office of President; neither shall any Person be eligible to that Office who shall not have attained to the Age of thirty five Years, and been fourteen Years a Resident within the United States.

In Case of the Removal of the President from Office, or of his Death, Resignation, or Inability to discharge the Powers and Duties of the said Office, the Same shall devolve on the Vice President, and the Congress may by Law provide for the Case of Removal, Death, Resignation or Inability, both of the President and Vice President, declaring what Officer shall then act as President, and such Officer shall act accordingly, until the Disability be removed, or a President shall be elected.[7]

The President shall, at stated Times, receive for his Services, a Compensation, which shall neither be encreased nor diminished during the Period for which he shall have been elected, and he shall not receive within that Period any other Emolument from the United States, or any of them.

Before he enter on the Execution of his Office, he shall take the following Oath or Affirmation:—"I do solemnly swear (or affirm) that I will faithfully execute the Office of President of the United States, and will to the best of my Ability, preserve, protect, and defend the Constitution of the United States."

Section 2 The President shall be Commander in Chief of the Army and Navy of the United States, and of the Militia of the several States, when called into the actual Service of the United States; he may require the Opinion, in writing, of the principal Officer in each of the executive Departments, upon any Subject relating to the Duties of their respective Offices, and he shall have Power to grant Reprieves and Pardons for Offences against the United States, except in Cases of Impeachment.

He shall have Power, by and with the Advice and Consent of the Senate, to make Treaties, provided two thirds of the Senators present concur; and he shall nominate, and by and with the Advice and Consent of the Senate, shall appoint Ambassadors, other public Ministers and Consuls, Judges of the supreme Court, and all other Officers of the United States, whose Appointments are not herein otherwise provided for, and which shall be established by Law; but the Congress may by Law vest the Appointment of such inferior Officers, as they think proper, in the President alone, in the Courts of Law, or in the Heads of Departments.

The President shall have Power to fill up all Vacancies that may happen during the Recess of the Senate, by granting Commissions which shall expire at the End of their next Session.

Section 3 He shall from time to time give to the Congress Information of the State of the Union, and recommend to their Consideration such Measures as he shall judge necessary and expedient; he may, on extraordinary Occasions, convene both Houses, or either of them, and in Case of Disagreement between them, with Respect to the Time of Adjournment, he may adjourn them to such Time as he shall think proper; he shall receive Ambassadors and other public Ministers; he shall take Care that the Laws be faithfully executed, and shall Commission all the Officers of the United States.

Section 4 The President, Vice President and all civil Officers of the United States, shall be removed from Office on Impeachment for, and Conviction of, Treason, Bribery, or other high Crimes and Misdemeanors.

---

[6]Changed by the Twelfth Amendment.

[7]Changed by the Twenty-fifth Amendment.

Article III

Section 1 The judicial Power of the United States, shall be vested in one supreme Court, and in such inferior Courts as the Congress may from time to time ordain and establish. The Judges, both of the supreme and inferior Courts, shall hold their Offices during good Behaviour, and shall, at stated Times, receive for their Services, a Compensation, which shall not be diminished during their Continuance in Office.

Section 2 The judicial Power shall extend to all Cases, in Law and Equity, arising under this Constitution, the Laws of the United States, and Treaties made, or which shall be made, under their Authority;—to all Cases affecting Ambassadors, other public Ministers and Consuls;—to all Cases of admiralty and maritime Jurisdiction;—to Controversies to which the United States shall be a party;—to Controversies between two or more States;—between a State and Citizens of another State;[8]—between Citizens of different States;—between Citizens of the same State claiming Lands under Grants of different States, and between a State, or the Citizens thereof, and foreign States, Citizens or Subjects.

In all Cases affecting Ambassadors, other public Ministers and Consuls, and those in which a State shall be Party, the supreme Court shall have original Jurisdiction. In all the other Cases before mentioned, the supreme Court shall have appellate Jurisdiction, both as to Law and Fact, with such Exceptions, and under such Regulations as the Congress shall make.

The Trial of all Crimes, except in Cases of Impeachment, shall be by Jury; and such Trial shall be held in the State where the said Crimes shall have been committed; but when not committed within any State, the Trial shall be at such Place or Places as the Congress may by Law have directed.

Section 3 Treason against the United States, shall consist only in levying War against them, or in adhering to their Enemies, giving them Aid and Comfort. No Person shall be convicted of Treason unless on the Testimony of two Witnesses to the same overt Act, or on Confession in open Court.

The Congress shall have Power to declare the Punishment of Treason, but no Attainder of Treason shall work Corruption of Blood, or Forfeiture except during the Life of the Person attainted.

Article IV

Section 1 Full Faith and Credit shall be given in each State to the public Acts, Records, and judicial Proceedings of every other State. And the Congress may by general Laws prescribe the Manner in which such Acts, Records and Proceedings shall be proved, and the Effect thereof.

Section 2 The Citizens of each State shall be entitled to all Privileges and Immunities of Citizens in the several States.

A Person charged in any State with Treason, Felony, or other Crime, who shall flee from Justice, and be found in another State, shall on Demand of the executive Authority of the State from which he fled, be delivered up, to be removed to the State having Jurisdiction of the Crime.

No Person held to Service or Labour in one State, under the Laws thereof, escaping into another, shall, in Consequence of any Law or Regulation therein, be discharged from such Service or Labour, but shall be delivered up on Claim of the Party to whom such Service or Labour may be due.[9]

Section 3 New States may be admitted by the Congress into this Union; but no new State shall be formed or erected within the Jurisdiction of any other State; nor any State be formed by the Junction of two or more States, or Parts of States, without the Consent of the Legislatures of the States concerned as well as of the Congress.

The Congress shall have Power to dispose of and make all needful Rules and Regulations respecting the Territory or other Property belonging to the United States; and nothing in this Constitution shall be so construed as to Prejudice any Claims of the United States, or of any particular State.

Section 4 The United States shall guarantee to every State in this Union a Republican Form of Government, and shall protect each of them against Invasion; and on Application of the Legislature, or of the Executive (when the Legislature cannot be convened) against domestic Violence.

Article V

The Congress, whenever two thirds of both Houses shall deem it necessary, shall propose Amendments to this Constitution, or, on the Application of the Legislatures of two thirds of the several States, shall call a Convention for proposing Amendments, which, in either Case, shall be valid to all Intents and Purposes, as Part of this Constitution, when ratified by the legislatures of three fourths of the several States, or by Conventions in three fourths thereof, as the one or the other Mode of Ratification may be proposed by the Congress; Provided that no Amendment which may be made prior to the Year One thousand eight hundred and eight shall in any Manner affect the first and fourth Clauses in the Ninth Section

---

[8] Changed by the Eleventh Amendment.

[9] Changed by the Thirteenth Amendment.

of the first Article; and that no State, without its Consent, shall be deprived of it's equal Suffrage in the Senate.

Article VI

All Debts contracted and Engagements entered into, before the Adoption of this Constitution, shall be as valid against the United States under this Constitution, as under the Confederation.

This Constitution, and the Laws of the United States which shall be made in Pursuance thereof; and all Treaties made, or which shall be made, under the Authority of the United States, shall be the supreme Law of the Land; and the Judges in every State shall be bound thereby, any Thing in the Constitution or Laws of any State to the Contrary notwithstanding.

The Senators and Representatives before mentioned, and the Members of the several State Legislatures, and all executive and judicial Officers, both of the United States and of the several States, shall be bound by Oath or Affirmation, to support this Constitution; but no religious Test shall ever be required as a Qualification to any Office or public Trust under the United States.

Article VII

The Ratification of the Conventions of nine States, shall be sufficient for the Establishment of this Constitution between the States so ratifying the Same.

Done in Convention by the Unanimous Consent of the States present the Seventeenth Day of September in the Year of our Lord one thousand seven hundred and eighty seven and of the Independance of the United States of America the Twelfth. In witness whereof We have hereunto subscribed our Names.

♦ ♦ ♦ ♦ ♦

The first ten amendments are known as the "Bill of Rights."

Amendment I (Ratified 1791)

Congress shall make no law respecting an establishment of religion, or prohibiting the free exercise thereof; or abridging the freedom of speech, or of the press; or the right of the people peaceably to assemble, and to petition the Government for a redress of grievances.

Amendment 2 (Ratified 1791)

A well regulated Militia, being necessary to the security of a free State, the right of the people to keep and bear Arms, shall not be infringed.

Amendment 3 (Ratified 1791)

No Soldier shall, in time of peace be quartered in any house, without the consent of the Owner, nor in time of war, but in a manner to be prescribed by law.

Amendment 4 (Ratified 1791)

The right of the people to be secure in their persons, houses, papers, and effects, against unreasonable searches and seizures, shall not be violated, and no Warrants shall issue, but upon probable cause, supported by Oath or affirmation, and particularly describing the place to be searched, and the persons or things to be seized.

Amendment 5 (Ratified 1791)

No person shall be held to answer for a capital, or otherwise infamous crime, unless on a presentment or indictment of a Grand Jury, except in cases arising in the land or naval forces, or in the Militia, when in actual service in time of War or public danger; nor shall any person be subject for the same offence to be twice put in jeopardy of life or limb; nor shall be compelled in any criminal case to be a witness against himself, nor be deprived of life, liberty, or property, without due process of law; nor shall private property be taken for public use, without just compensation.

Amendment 6 (Ratified 1791)

In all criminal prosecutions, the accused shall enjoy the right to a speedy and public trial, by an impartial jury of the State and district wherein the crime shall have been committed, which district shall have been previously ascertained by law, and to be informed of the nature and cause of the accusation; to be confronted with the witnesses against him; to have compulsory process for obtaining Witnesses in his favor, and to have assistance of counsel for his defence.

Amendment 7 (Ratified 1791)

In Suits at common law, where the value in controversy shall exceed twenty dollars, the right of trial by jury shall be preserved, and no fact tried by a jury, shall be otherwise re-examined in any Court of the United States, than according to the rules of the common law.

Amendment 8 (Ratified 1791)

Excessive bail shall not be required, nor excessive fines imposed, nor cruel and unusual punishments inflicted.

Amendment 9 (Ratified 1791)

The enumeration in the Constitution, of certain rights, shall not be construed to deny or disparage others retained by the people.

Amendment 10 (Ratified 1791)

The powers not delegated to the United States by the Constitution, nor prohibited by it to the States, are reserved to the States respectively, or to the people.

Amendment 11 (Ratified 1795)

The Judicial power of the United States shall not be construed to extend to any suit in law or equity, commenced or prosecuted against one of the United States by Citizens of another State, or by Citizens or Subjects of any Foreign State.

Amendment 12 (Ratified 1804)

The Electors shall meet in their respective states, and vote by ballot for President and Vice-President, one of whom, at least, shall not be an inhabitant of the same state with themselves; they shall name in their ballots the person voted for as President, and in distinct ballots the person voted for as Vice-President, and they shall make distinct lists of all persons voted for as President, and of all persons voted for as Vice-President, and of the number of votes for each, which lists they shall sign and certify, and transmit sealed to the seat of the government of the United States, directed to the President of the Senate;—The President of the Senate shall, in the presence of the Senate and House of Representatives, open all the certificates and the votes shall then be counted;—The person having the greatest number of votes for President, shall be the President, if such number be a majority of the whole number of Electors appointed; and if no person have such majority, then from the persons having the highest numbers not exceeding three on the list of those voted for as President, the House of Representatives shall choose immediately, by ballot, the President. But in choosing the President, the votes shall be taken by states, the representation from each state having one vote; a quorum for this purpose shall consist of a member or members from two-thirds of the states, and a majority of all the states shall be necessary to a choice. And if the House of Representatives shall not choose a President whenever the right of choice shall devolve upon them, before the fourth day of March next following, then the Vice-President shall act as president, as in the case of the death or other constitutional disability of the President.[10]—The person having the greatest number of votes as Vice-President, shall be the Vice-President, if such number be a majority of the whole number of Electors appointed, and if no person have a majority, then from the two highest numbers on the list, the Senate shall choose the Vice-President; a quorum for the purpose shall consist of two-thirds of the whole number of Senators, and a majority of the whole number shall be necessary to a choice. But no person constitutionally ineligible to the office of President shall be eligible to that of Vice-President of the United States.

Amendment 13 (Ratified 1865)

Section 1 Neither slavery nor involuntary servitude, except as a punishment for crime whereof the party shall have been duly convicted, shall exist within the United States, or any place subject to their jurisdiction.

Section 2 Congress shall have power to enforce this article by appropriate legislation.

Amendment 14 (Ratified 1868)

Section 1 All persons born or naturalized in the United States, and subject to the jurisdiction thereof, are citizens of the United States and of the State wherein they reside. No State shall make or enforce any law which shall abridge the privileges or immunities of citizens of the United States; nor shall any State deprive any person of life, liberty, or property, without due process of law; nor deny to any person within its jurisdiction the equal protection of the laws.

Section 2 Representatives shall be apportioned among the several States according to their respective numbers, counting the whole number of persons in each State, excluding Indians not taxed. But when the right to vote at any election for the choice of electors for President and Vice President of the United States, Representatives in Congress, the Executive and Judicial officers of a State, or the members of the Legislature thereof, is denied to any of the male inhabitants of such State, being twenty-one[11] years of age, and citizens of the United States, or in any way abridged except for participation in rebellion, or other crime, the basis of representation therein shall be reduced in the proportion which the number of such male citizens shall bear to the whole number of male citizens twenty-one years of age in such State.

Section 3 No person shall be a Senator or Representative in Congress, or elector of President and Vice President, or hold any office, civil or military, under the United States, or under any State, who, having previously taken an oath, as a member of Congress, or as an officer of the United States, or as a member of any State legislature, or as an executive or judicial officer of any State, to support the Constitution of the United States, shall have engaged in insurrection or rebellion against the same, or given aid or comfort to the enemies thereof. But Congress may by a vote of two-thirds of each House, remove such disability.

Section 4 The validity of the public debt of the United States, authorized by law, including debts incurred for payment of pensions and bounties for services in suppressing insurrection or rebellion, shall not be questioned. But neither the United States nor any State shall

[10]Changed by the Twentieth Amendment.

[11]Changed by the Twenty-sixth Amendment.

assume or pay any debt or obligation incurred in aid of insurrection or rebellion against the United States, or any claim for the loss or emancipation of any slave; but all such debts, obligations and claims shall be held illegal and void.

Section 5 The Congress shall have power to enforce, by appropriate legislation, the provisions of this article.

Amendment 15 (Ratified 1870)

Section 1 The right of citizens of the United States to vote shall not be denied or abridged by the United States or by any State on account of race, color, or previous condition of servitude.

Section 2 The Congress shall have power to enforce this article by appropriate legislation.

Amendment 16 (Ratified 1913)

The Congress shall have power to lay and collect taxes on incomes, from whatever source derived, without apportionment among the several States, and without regard to any census or enumeration.

Amendment 17 (Ratified 1913)

The Senate of the United States shall be composed of two Senators from each State, elected by the people thereof, for six years; and each Senator shall have one vote. The electors in each State shall have the qualifications requisite for electors of the most numerous branch of the State legislatures.

When vacancies happen in the representation of any State in the Senate, the executive authority of such State shall issue writs of election to fill such vacancies: *Provided,* That the legislature of any State may empower the executive thereof to make temporary appointments until the people fill the vacancies by election as the legislature may direct.

This amendment shall not be so construed as to affect the election or term of any Senator chosen before it becomes valid as part of the Constitution.

Amendment 18 (Ratified 1919; Repealed 1933)

Section 1 After one year from the ratification of this article the manufacture, sale, or transportation of intoxicating liquors within, the importation thereof into, or the exportation thereof from the United States and all territory subject to the jurisdiction thereof for beverage purposes is hereby prohibited.

Section 2 The Congress and the several States shall have concurrent power to enforce this article by appropriate legislation.

Section 3 This article shall be inoperative unless it shall have been ratified as an amendment to the Constitution by the legislatures of the several States, as provided in the Constitution, within seven years from the date of the submission hereof to the States by the Congress.[12]

Amendment 19 (Ratified 1920)

The right of citizens of the United States to vote shall not be denied or abridged by the United States or by any State on account of sex.

Congress shall have power to enforce this article by appropriate legislation.

Amendment 20 (Ratified 1933)

Section 1 The terms of the President and Vice President shall end at noon on the 20th day of January, and the terms of Senators and Representatives at noon on the 3d day of January, of the years in which such terms would have ended if this article had not been ratified; and the terms of their successors shall then begin.

Section 2 The Congress shall assemble at least once in every year, and such meeting shall begin at noon on the 3d day of January, unless they shall by law appoint a different day.

Section 3 If, at the time fixed for the beginning of the term of the President, the President elect shall have died, the Vice President elect shall become President. If a President shall not have been chosen before the time fixed for the beginning of his term, or if the President elect shall have failed to qualify, then the Vice President elect shall act as President until a President shall have qualified; and the Congress may by law provide for the case wherein neither a President elect nor a Vice President elect shall have qualified, declaring who shall then act as President, or the manner in which one who is to act shall be selected, and such person shall act accordingly until a President or Vice President shall have qualified.

Section 4 The Congress may by law provide for the case of the death of any of the persons from whom the House of Representatives may choose a President whenever the right of choice shall have devolved upon them, and for the case of the death of any of the persons from whom the Senate may choose a Vice President whenever the right of choice shall have devolved upon them.

Section 5 Sections 1 and 2 shall take effect on the 15th day of October following the ratification of this article.

Section 6 This article shall be inoperative unless it shall have been ratified as an amendment to the Constitution by the legislatures of three-fourths of the several States within seven years from the date of its submission.

---

[12]Repealed by the Twenty-first Amendment.

Amendment 21 (Ratified 1933)

Section 1 The eighteenth article of amendment to the Constitution of the United States is hereby repealed.

Section 2 The transportation or importation into any State, Territory, or possession of the United States for delivery or use therein of intoxicating liquors, in violation of the laws thereof, is hereby prohibited.

Section 3 This article shall be inoperative unless it shall have been ratified as an amendment to the Constitution by conventions in the several States, as provided in the Constitution, within seven years from the date of the submission hereof to the States by the Congress.

Amendment 22 (Ratified 1951)

Section 1 No person shall be elected to the office of the President more than twice, and no person who has held the office of President, or acted as President, for more than two years of a term to which some other person was elected President shall be elected to the office of the President more than once. But this Article shall not apply to any person holding the office of President when this Article was proposed by the Congress, and shall not prevent any person who may be holding the office of President, or acting as President, during the term within which this Article becomes operative from holding the office of President or acting as President during the remainder of such term.

Section 2 This Article shall be inoperative unless it shall have been ratified as an amendment to the Constitution by the legislatures of three-fourths of the several States within seven years from the date of its submission to the States by the Congress.

Amendment 23 (Ratified 1961)

Section 1 The District constituting the seat of Government of the United States shall appoint in such manner as the Congress may direct:

A number of electors of President and Vice President equal to the whole number of Senators and Representatives in Congress to which the District would be entitled if it were a State, but in no event more than the least populous State; they shall be in addition to those appointed by the States, but they shall be considered, for the purposes of the election of President and Vice President, to be electors appointed by a State; and they shall meet in the District and perform such duties as provided by the twelfth article of amendment.

Section 2 The Congress shall have power to enforce this article by appropriate legislation.

Amendment 24 (Ratified 1964)

Section 1 The right of citizens of the United States to vote in any primary or other election for President or Vice President, for electors for President or Vice President, or for Senator or Representative in Congress, shall not be denied or abridged by the United States or any State by reason of failure to pay any poll tax or other tax.

Section 2 The Congress shall have power to enforce this article by appropriate legislation.

Amendment 25 (Ratified 1967)

Section 1 In case of the removal of the President from office or of his death or resignation, the Vice President shall become President.

Section 2 Whenever there is a vacancy in the office of the Vice President, the President shall nominate a Vice President who shall take office upon confirmation by a majority vote of both Houses of Congress.

Section 3 Whenever the President transmits to the President pro tempore of the Senate and the Speaker of the House of Representatives his written declaration that he is unable to discharge the powers and duties of his office, and until he transmits to them a written declaration to the contrary, such powers and duties shall be discharged by the Vice President as Acting President.

Section 4 Whenever the Vice President and a majority of either the principal officers of the executive departments or of such other body as Congress may by law provide, transmit to the President pro tempore of the Senate and the Speaker of the House of Representatives their written declaration that the President is unable to discharge the powers and duties of his office, the Vice President shall immediately assume the powers and duties of the office as Acting President.

Thereafter, when the President transmits to the President pro tempore of the Senate and the Speaker of the House of Representatives his written declaration that no inability exists, he shall resume the powers and duties of his office unless the Vice President and a majority of either the principal officers of the executive department or of such other body as Congress may by law provide, transmit within four days to the President pro tempore of the Senate and the Speaker of the House of Representatives their written declaration that the President is unable to discharge the powers and duties of his office. Thereupon Congress shall decide the issue, assembling within forty-eight hours for that purpose if not in session. If the Congress, within twenty-one days after receipt of the latter written declaration, or, if Congress is not in session, within twenty-one days after Congress is required to assemble, determines by two-thirds vote of both Houses that the President is unable to discharge the powers and duties of his office, the Vice President shall continue to discharge the same as Acting President; otherwise, the President shall resume the powers and duties of his office.

Amendment 26 (Ratified 1971)

Section 1 The right of citizens of the United States, who are eighteen years of age or older, to vote shall not be denied or abridged by the United States or by any State on account of age.

Section 2 The Congress shall have power to enforce this article by appropriate legislation.

Amendment 27 (Ratified 1992)

No law, varying the compensation for the services of the Senators and Representatives, shall take effect, until an election of Representatives shall have intervened.

Appendix B

Securities Act of 1933*

Section 2 When used in this title, unless the context requires—

(1) The term "security" means any note, stock, treasury stock, bond, debenture, evidence of indebtedness, certificate of interest or participation in any profit-sharing agreement, collateral-trust certificate, preorganization certificate or subscription, transferable share, investment contract, voting-trust certificate, certificate of deposit for a security, fractional undivided interest in oil, gas, or other mineral rights, any put, call, straddle, option, or privilege on any security, certificate of deposit, or group or index of securities (including any interest therein or based on the value thereof), or any put, call, straddle, option, or privilege entered into on a national securities exchange relating to foreign currency, or, in general, any interest or instrument commonly known as a "security," or any certificate of interest or participation in, temporary or interim certificate for, receipt for, guarantee of, or warrant or right to subscribe to or purchase, any of the foregoing.

Section 3 (a) Except as hereinafter expressly provided the provisions of this title shall not apply to any of the following classes of securities:

◆ ◆ ◆ ◆ ◆

(2) Any security issued or guaranteed by the United States or any territory thereof, or by the District of Columbia, or by any State of the United States, or by any political subdivision of a State or Territory, or by any public instrumentality of one or more States or Territories, or by any person controlled or supervised by and acting as an instrumentality of the Government of the United States pursuant to authority granted by the Congress of the United States; or any certificate of deposit for any of the foregoing; or any security issued or guaranteed by any bank; or any security issued by or representing an interest in or a direct obligation of a Federal Reserve Bank. . . .

(3) Any note, draft, bill of exchange, or banker's acceptance which arises out of a current transaction or the proceeds of which have been or are to be used for current transactions, and which has a maturity at the time of issuance of not exceeding nine months, exclusive of days of grace, or any renewal thereof the maturity of which is likewise limited.

(4) Any security issued by a person organized and operated exclusively for religious, educational, benevolent, fraternal, charitable, or reformatory purposes and not for pecuniary profit, and no part of the net earnings of which inures to the benefit of any person, private stockholder, or individual;

◆ ◆ ◆ ◆ ◆

(11) Any security which is a part of an issue offered and sold only to persons resident within a single State or Territory, where the issuer of such security is a person resident and doing business within, or, if a corporation, incorporated by and doing business within, such State or Territory.

(b) The Commission may from time to time by its rules and regulations and subject to such terms and conditions as may be described therein, add any class of securities to the securities exempted as provided in this section, if it finds that the enforcement of this title with respect to such securities is not necessary in the public interest and for the protection of investors by reason of the small amount involved or the limited character of the public offering; but no issue of securities shall be exempted under this subsection where the aggregate amount at which such issue is offered to the public exceeds $5,000,000.

Section 4 The provisions of section 5 shall not apply to—

(1) transactions by any person other than an issuer, underwriter, or dealer.

(2) transactions by an issuer not involving any public offering.

*This material is excerpted from the Securities Act of 1933, as amended.

(3) transactions by a dealer (including an underwriter no longer acting as an underwriter in respect of the security involved in such transactions), except—

(A) transactions taking place prior to the expiration of forty days after the first date upon which the security was bona fide offered to the public by the issuer or by or through an underwriter,
(B) transactions in a security as to which a registration statement has been filed taking place prior to the expiration of forty days after the effective date of such registration statement or prior to the expiration of forty days after the first date upon which the security was bona fide offered to the public by the issuer or by or through an underwriter after such effective date, whichever is later (excluding in the computation of such forty days any time during which a stop order issued under section 8 is in effect as to the security), or such shorter period as the Commission may specify by rules and regulations or order, and
(C) transactions as to securities constituting the whole or a part of an unsold allotment to or subscription by such dealer as a participant in the distribution of such securities by the issuer or by or through an underwriter.

With respect to transactions referred to in clause (B), if securities of the issuer have not previously been sold pursuant to an earlier effective registration statement the applicable period, instead of forty days, shall be ninety days, or such shorter period as the Commission may specify by rules and regulations or order.

(4) brokers' transactions, executed upon customers' orders on any exchange or in the over-the-counter market but not the solicitation of such orders.

◆ ◆ ◆ ◆ ◆

(6) transactions involving offers or sales by an issuer solely to one or more accredited investors, if the aggregate offering price of an issue of securities offered in reliance on this paragraph does not exceed the amount allowed under section 3(b) of this title, if there is no advertising or public solicitation in connection with the transaction by the issuer or anyone acting on the issuer's behalf, and if the issuer files such notice with the Commission as the Commission shall prescribe.

Section 5 (a) Unless a registration statement is in effect as to a security, it shall be unlawful for any person, directly or indirectly—

(1) to make use of any means or instruments of transportation or communication in interstate commerce or of the mails to sell such security through the use of medium of any prospectus or otherwise; or

(2) to carry or cause to be carried through the mails or in interstate commerce, by any means or instruments of transportation, any such security for the purpose of sale or for delivery after sale.

(b) It shall be unlawful for any person, directly or indirectly—

(1) to make use of any means or instruments of transportation or communication in interstate commerce or of the mails to carry or transmit any prospectus relating to any security with respect to which a registration statement has been filed under this title, unless such prospectus meets the requirements of section 10, or

(2) to carry or to cause to be carried through the mails or in interstate commerce any such security for the purpose of sale or for delivery after sale, unless accompanied or preceded by a prospectus that meets the requirements of subsection (a) of section 10.

(c) It shall be unlawful for any person, directly or indirectly, to make use of any means or instruments of transportation or communication in interstate commerce or of the mails to offer to sell or offer to buy through the use or medium of any prospectus or otherwise any security, unless a registration statement has been filed as to such security, or while the registration statement is the subject of a refusal order or stop order or (prior to the effective date of the registration statement) any public proceeding of examination under section 8.

Appendix C

Securities Exchange Act of 1934*

Section 3 (a) When used in this title, unless the context otherwise requires—

♦ ♦ ♦ ♦ ♦

(4) The term "broker" means any person engaged in the business of effecting transactions in securities for the account of others, but does not include a bank.

(5) The term "dealer" means any person engaged in the business of buying and selling securities for his own account, through a broker or otherwise, but does not include a bank, or any person insofar as he buys or sells securities for his own account, either individually or in some fiduciary capacity, but not as part of a regular business.

♦ ♦ ♦ ♦ ♦

(7) The term "director" means any director of a corporation or any person performing similar functions with respect to any organization, whether incorporated or unincorporated.

(8) The term "issuer" means any person who issues or proposes to issue any security; except that with respect to certificates of deposit for securities, voting-trust certificates, or collateral-trust certificates, or with respect to certificates of interest or shares in an unincorporated investment trust not having a board of directors or the fixed, restricted management, or unit type, the term "issuer" means the person or persons performing the acts and assuming the duties of depositor or manager pursuant to the provisions of the trust or other agreement or instrument under which such securities are issued; and except that with respect to equipment-trust certificates or like securities, the term "issuer" means the person by whom the equipment or property is, or is to be, used.

(9) The term "person" means a natural person, company, government, or political subdivision, agency, or instrumentality of a government.

Section 10 It shall be unlawful for any person, directly or indirectly, by the use of any means or instrumentality of interstate commerce or of the mails, or of any facility of any national securities exchange—

(a) To effect a short sale, or to use or employ any stop-loss order in connection with the purchase or sale, of any security registered on a national securities exchange, in contravention of such rules and regulations as the Commission may prescribe as necessary or appropriate in the public interest or for the protection of investors.

(b) To use or employ, in connection with the purchase or sale of any security registered on a national securities exchange or any security not so registered, any manipulative or deceptive device or contrivance in contravention of such rules and regulations as the Commission may prescribe as necessary or appropriate in the public interest or for the protection of investors.

Section 16 (a) Every person who is directly or indirectly the beneficial owner of more than 10 per centum of any class of any equity security (other than an exempted security) which is registered pursuant to section 12 of this title, or who is a director or an officer of the issuer of such security, shall file, at the time of the registration of such security on a national securities exchange or by the effective date of a registration statement filed pursuant to section 12(g) of this title, or within ten days after he becomes such beneficial owner, director, or officer, a statement with the Commission (and, if such security is registered on a national securities exchange, also with the exchange) of the amount of all equity securities of such issuer of which he is the beneficial owner, and within ten days after the close of each calendar month thereafter, if there has been a change in such ownership during such month, shall file with the Commission (and if such security is registered on a national securities exchange, shall also file with the exchange) a statement indicating his ownership at the close of the calendar month and such changes in his ownership as have occurred during such calendar month.

*This material is excerpted from the Securities Exchange Act of 1934, as amended.

(b) For the purpose of preventing unfair use of information which may have been obtained by such beneficial owner, director, or officer by reason of his relationship to the issuer, any profit realized by him from any purchase and sale, or any sale and purchase, of any equity security of such issuer (other than an exempted security) within any period of less than six months, unless such security was acquired in good faith in connection with a debt previously contracted, shall inure to and be recoverable by the issuer, irrespective of any intention on the part of such beneficial owner, director, or officer in entering into such transaction of holding the security purchased or of not repurchasing the security sold for a period exceeding six months. Suit to recover such profit may be instituted at law or in equity in any court of competent jurisdiction by the issuer, or by the owner of any security of the issuer in the name and in behalf of the issuer if the issuer shall fail or refuse to bring such suit within sixty days after request or shall fail diligently to prosecute the same thereafter; but no such suit shall be brought more than two years after the date such profit was realized. This subsection shall not be construed to cover any transaction where such beneficial owner was not such both at the time of the purchase and sale, or the sale and purchase, of the security involved, or any transaction or transactions which the Commission by rules and regulations may exempt as not comprehended within the purpose of this subsection.

(c) It shall be unlawful for any such beneficial owner, director, or officer, directly or indirectly, to sell any equity security of such issuer (other than an exempted security), if the person selling the security or his principal (1) does not own the security sold, or (2) if owning the security, does not deliver it against such sale within twenty days thereafter, or does not within five days after such sale deposit it in the mails or other usual channels of transportation; but no person shall be deemed to have violated this subsection if he proves that notwithstanding the exercise of good faith he was unable to make such delivery or deposit within such time, or that to do so would cause undue inconvenience or expense.

Appendix D

The Sherman Act*

Section 1 Trusts, etc., in restraint of trade illegal; penalty Every contract, combination in the form of trust or otherwise, or conspiracy, in restraint of trade or commerce among the several States, or with foreign nations, is hereby declared to be illegal. Every person who shall make any contract or engage in any combination or conspiracy hereby declared to be illegal shall be deemed guilty of a felony, and, on conviction thereof, shall be punished by fine not exceeding one million dollars if a corporation, or if any other person, one hundred thousand dollars, or by imprisonment not exceeding three years, or both said punishments, in the discretion of the court.

Section 2 Monopolizing trade a felony; penalty Every person who shall monopolize, or attempt to monopolize, or combine or conspire with any other person or persons, to monopolize any part of the trade or commerce among the several States, or with foreign nations, shall be deemed guilty of a felony, and, on conviction thereof, shall be punished by fine not exceeding one million dollars if a corporation, or, if any other person, one hundred thousand dollars, or by imprisonment not exceeding three years, or by both said punishments, in the discretion of the court.

Section 7 The word "person," or "persons," wherever used in this Act shall be deemed to include corporations and associations existing under or authorized by the laws of either the United States, the laws of any of the Territories, the laws of any State, or the laws of any foreign country.

*This material is excerpted from the Sherman Act, as amended.

Appendix E

The Clayton Act*

Section 3 Sale, etc., on agreement not to use goods of competitor It shall be unlawful for any person engaged in commerce, in the course of such commerce, to lease or make a sale or contract for sale of goods, wares, merchandise, machinery, supplies, or other commodities, whether patented or unpatented, for use, consumption, or resale within the United States or any Territory thereof or the District of Columbia or any insular possession or other place under the jurisdiction of the United States, or fix a price charged thereof, or discount from, or rebate upon, such price, on the condition, agreement, or understanding that the lessee or purchaser thereof shall not use or deal in the goods, wares, merchandise, machinery, supplies, or other commodities of a competitor or competitors of the lessor or seller, where the effect of such lease, sale, or contract for sale or such condition, agreement or understanding may be to substantially lessen competition or tend to create a monopoly in any line of commerce.

Section 4 Suits by persons injured; amount of recovery Any person who shall be injured in his business or property by reason of anything forbidden in the antitrust laws may sue therefor in any district court of the United States in the district in which the defendant resides or is found or has an agent, without respect to the amount in controversy, and shall recover threefold the damages by him sustained, and the cost of suit, including a reasonable attorney's fee. . . .

Section 7 Acquisition by one corporation of stock of another No person engaged in commerce or in any activity affecting commerce shall acquire, directly or indirectly, the whole or any part of the stock or other share capital and no corporation subject to the jurisdiction of the Federal Trade Commission shall acquire the whole or any part of the assets of another corporation engaged also in commerce, where in any line of commerce in any section of the country, the effect of such acquisition may be substantially to lessen competition, or to tend to create a monopoly.

No person shall acquire, directly or indirectly, the whole or any part of the stock or other share capital and no corporation subject to the jurisdiction of the Federal Trade Commission shall acquire the whole or any part of the assets of one or more corporations engaged in commerce, where in any line of commerce in any section of the country, the effect of such acquisition, of such stocks or assets, or of the use of such stock by the voting or granting of proxies or otherwise, may be substantially to lessen competition, or to tend to create a monopoly.

This section shall not apply to persons purchasing such stock solely for investment and not using the same by voting or otherwise to bring about, or in attempting to bring about, the substantial lessening of competition. Nor shall anything contained in this section prevent a corporation engaged in commerce from causing the formation of subsidiary corporations for the actual carrying on of their immediate lawful business, or the natural and legitimate branches or extensions thereof, or from owning and holding all or part of the stock of such subsidiary corporations, when the effect of such formation is not to substantially lessen competition.

Section 8 Interlocking directorates and officers. . . No person at the same time shall be a director in any two or more corporations, any one of which has capital, surplus, and undivided profits aggregating more than $1,000,000, engaged in whole or in part in commerce, other than banks, banking associations, trust companies, and common carriers subject to the Act to regulate commerce approved February fourth, eighteen hundred and eighty-seven, if such corporations are or shall have been theretofore, by virtue of their business and location or operation, competitors, so that the elimination of competition by agreement between them would constitute a violation of any of the provisions of any of the antitrust laws. The eligibility of a director under the foregoing pro-

*This material is excerpted from the Clayton Act, as amended.

vision shall be determined by the aggregate amount of the capital, surplus, and undivided profits, exclusive of dividends declared but not paid to stockholders, at the end of the fiscal year of said corporation next preceding the election of directors, and when a director has been elected in accordance with the provisions of this Act it shall be lawful for him to continue as such for one year thereafter.

Appendix F

The Federal Trade Commission Act*

Section 5 Unfair methods of competition unlawful; prevention by Commission—declaration Declaration of unlawfulness; power to prohibit unfair practices.

(a)(1) Unfair methods of competition in or affecting commerce, and unfair or deceptive acts or practices in or affecting commerce, are declared unlawful. . . .

Penalty for violation of orders, injunctions and other appropriate equitable relief.

(b) Any person, partnership, or corporation who violates an order of the Commission to cease and desist after it has become final, and while such order is in effect, shall forfeit and pay to the United States a civil penalty of not more than $10,000 for each violation, which shall accrue to the United States and may be recovered in a civil action brought by the Attorney General of the United States. Each separate violation of such an order shall be a separate offense, except that in the case of a violation through continuing failure or neglect to obey a final order of the Commission each day of continuance of such failure or neglect shall be deemed a separate offense. . . .

*This material is excerpted from the Federal Trade Commission Act, as amended.

Appendix G

The Robinson-Patman Act*

Section 2 Discrimination in price, services, or facilities

(a) Price: selection of customers.

It shall be unlawful for any person engaged in commerce, in the course of such commerce, either directly or indirectly, to discriminate in price between different purchasers of commodities of like grade and quality, where either or any of the purchasers involved in such discrimination are in commerce, where such commodities are sold for use, consumption, or resale within the United States or any Territory thereof or the District of Columbia or any insular possession or other place under the jurisdiction of the United States, and where the effect of such discrimination may be substantially to lessen competition or tend to create a monopoly in any line of commerce, or to injure, destroy, or prevent competition with any person who either grants or knowingly receives the benefit of such discrimination, or, with customers of either of them: *Provided,* That nothing herein contained shall prevent differentials which make only due allowance for differences in the cost of manufacture, sale, or delivery resulting from the differing methods of quantities in which such commodities are to such purchasers sold or delivered: *Provided, however,* That the Federal Trade Commission may, after due investigation and hearing to all interested parties, fix and establish quantity limits, and revise the same as it finds necessary as to particular commodities or classes of commodities, where it finds that available purchasers in greater quantities are so few as to render differentials on account thereof unjustly discriminatory or promotive of monopoly in any line of commerce; and the foregoing shall then not be construed to permit differentials based on differences in quantities greater than those so fixed and established: *And provided further,* That nothing herein contained shall prevent persons engaged in selling goods, wares, or merchandise in commerce from selecting their own customers in bona fide transactions and not in restraint of trade: *And provided further,* That nothing herein contained shall prevent price changes from time to time where in response to changing conditions affecting the market for or the marketability of the goods concerned, such as but not limited to actual or imminent deterioration of perishable goods, obsolescence of seasonal goods, distress sales under court process, or sales in good faith in discontinuance of business in the goods concerned.

(b) Burden of rebutting prima-facie case of discrimination.

Upon proof being made, at any hearing on a complaint under this section, that there has been discrimination in price or services or facilities furnished, the burden of rebutting the prima-facie case thus made by showing justification shall be upon the person charged with a violation of this section, and unless justification shall be affirmatively shown, the Commission is authorized to issue an order terminating the discrimination: *Provided, however,* That nothing herein contained shall prevent a seller rebutting the prima-facie case thus made by showing that his lower price or the furnishing of services or facilities to any purchaser or purchasers was made in good faith to meet an equally low price of a competitor, or the services or facilities furnished by a competitor.

(c) Payment or acceptance of commission, brokerage or other compensation.

It shall be unlawful for any person engaged in commerce, in the course of such commerce, to pay or grant, or to receive or accept, anything of value as a commission, brokerage, or other compensation, or any allowance of discount in lieu thereof, except for services rendered in connection with the sale or purchase of goods, wares, or merchandise, either to the other party to such transaction or to an agent, representative, or other intermediary therein where such intermediary is acting in fact for or in behalf, or is subject to the direct or indirect control, of any party to such transaction other than the

*This material is excerpted from the Robinson-Patman Act, as amended.

person by whom such compensation is so granted or paid.

(d) Payment for services or facilities for processing or sale.

It shall be unlawful for any person engaged in commerce to pay or contract for the payment of anything of value to or for the benefit of a customer of such person in the course of such commerce as compensation or in consideration for any services or facilities furnished by or through such customer in connection with the processing, handling, sale, or offering for sale of any products or commodities manufactured, sold, or offered for sale by such person, unless such payment of consideration is available on proportionally equal terms to all other customers competing in the distribution of such products or commodities.

(e) Furnishing services or facilities for processing, handling, etc.

It shall be unlawful for any person to discriminate in favor of one purchaser against another purchaser or purchasers of a commodity bought for resale, with or without processing, by contracting to furnish or furnishing, or by contributing to the furnishing of, any services or facilities connected with the processing, handling, sale, or offering for sale of such commodity so purchased upon terms not accorded to all purchasers on proportionally equal terms.

(f) Knowingly inducing or receiving discriminatory price.

It shall be unlawful for any person engaged in commerce, in the course of such commerce, knowingly to induce or receive a discrimination in price which is prohibited by this section.

Section 3 Discrimination in rebates, discounts, or advertising service charges; underselling in particular localities; penalties It shall be unlawful for any person engaged in commerce, in the course of such commerce, to be a party to, or assist in, any transaction of sale, or contract to sell, which discriminates to his knowledge against competitors of the purchaser, in that any discount, rebate, allowance, or advertising service charge is granted to the purchaser over and above any discount, rebate, allowance, or advertising service charge available at the time of such transaction to said competitors in respect of a sale of goods of like grade, quality, and quantity; to sell, or contract to sell, goods in any part of the United States at prices lower than those exacted by said person elsewhere in the United States for the purpose of destroying competition, or eliminating a competitor in such part of the United States; or to sell, or contract to sell, goods at unreasonably low prices for the purpose of destroying competition or eliminating a competitor.

Any person violating any of the provisions of this section shall, upon conviction thereof, be fined not more than $5,000 or imprisoned not more than one year, or both.

Appendix H

National Labor Relations Act*

Section 2 When used in this Act—

(2) The term "employer" includes any person acting as an agent of an employer, directly or indirectly, but shall not include the United States or any wholly owned Government corporation, or any Federal Reserve Bank, or any State or political subdivision thereof, or any person subject to the Railway Labor Act, as amended from time to time, or any labor organization (other than when acting as an employer), or anyone acting in the capacity of officer or agent of such labor organization.

(3) The term "employee" shall include any employee, and shall not be limited to the employees of a particular employer, unless the Act explicitly states otherwise, and shall include any individual whose work has ceased as a consequence of, or in connection with, any current labor dispute or because of any unfair labor practice, and who has not obtained any other regular and substantially equivalent employment, but shall not include any individual employed as an agricultural laborer, or in the domestic service of any family or person at his home, or any individual employed by his parent or spouse, or any individual having the status of an independent contractor, or any individual employed as a supervisor, or any individual employed by an employer subject to the Railway Labor Act, . . . or by any other person who is not an employer as herein defined.

(11) The term "supervisor" means any individual having authority, in the interest of the employer, to hire, transfer, suspend, lay off, recall, promote, discharge, assign, reward, or discipline other employees, or responsibly to direct them, or to adjust their grievances, or effectively to recommend such action, if in connection with the foregoing the exercise of such authority is not of a merely routine or clerical nature, but requires the use of independent judgment.

(12) The term "professional employee" means—

(a) any employee engaged in work (i) predominantly intellectual and varied in character as opposed to routine mental, manual, mechanical, or physical work; (ii) involving the consistent exercise of discretion and judgment in its performance, (iii) of such a character that the output produced or the result accomplished cannot be standardized in relation to a given period of time; (iv) requiring knowledge of an advanced type in a field of science or learning customarily acquired by a prolonged course of specialized intellectual instruction and study in an institution of higher learning or a hospital, as distinguished from a general academic education or from an apprenticeship or from training in the performance of routine mental, manual, or physical processes; or

(b) any employee, who (i) has completed the courses of specialized intellectual instruction and study described in clause (iv) of paragraph (a), and (ii) is performing related work under the supervision of a professional person to qualify himself to become a professional employee as defined in paragraph (a).

Section 7 Employees shall have the right to self-organization, to form, join, or assist labor organizations, to bargain collectively through representatives of their own choosing, and to engage in other concerted activities for the purpose of collective bargaining or other mutual aid or protection, and shall also have the right to refrain from any or all of such activities except to the extent that such right may be affected by an agreement requiring membership in a labor organization as a condition of employment as authorized in section 8(a)(3).

Section 8 (a) It shall be an unfair labor practice for an employer—

(1) to interfere with, restrain, or coerce employees in the exercise of the rights guaranteed in section 7;

(2) to dominate or interfere with the formation or administration of any labor organization or contribute financial or other support to it: *Provided,* That subject to rules and regulations made and published by the Board, an employee shall not be prohibited from permitting employees to confer with him during working hours without loss of time or pay;

---

*This material is excerpted from the National Labor Relations Act, as amended.

(3) by discrimination in regard to hire or tenure of employment or any term or condition of employment to encourage or discourage membership in any labor organization: *Provided,* That nothing in this Act, or in any other statute of the United States, shall preclude an employer from making an agreement with a labor organization . . . to require as a condition of employment membership therein on or after the thirtieth day following the beginning of such employment or the effective date of such agreement, whichever is the later, (i) if such labor organization is the representative of the employees as provided in section 9(a), in the appropriate collective-bargaining unit covered by such agreement when made, and (ii) unless following an election held as provided in section 9(e) within one year preceding the effective date of such agreement, the Board shall have certified that at least a majority of the employees eligible to vote in such election have voted to rescind the authority of such labor organization to make such an agreement: *Provided further,* That no employer shall justify any discrimination against an employee for nonmembership in a labor organization (A) if he had reasonable grounds for believing that such membership was not available to the employee on the same terms and conditions generally applicable to other members, or (B) if he had reasonable grounds for believing that membership was denied or terminated for reasons other than the failure of the employee to tender the periodic dues and the initiation fees uniformly required as a condition of acquiring or retaining membership;

(4) to discharge or otherwise discriminate against an employee because he has filed charges or given testimony under this Act;

(5) to refuse to bargain collectively with the representatives of his employees, subject to the provisions of section 9(a).

(b) It shall be an unfair labor practice for a labor organization or its agents—

(1) to restrain or coerce (A) employees in the exercise of the rights guaranteed in section 7: *Provided,* That this paragraph shall not impair the right of a labor organization to prescribe its own rules with respect to the acquisition of retention of membership therein; or (B) an employer in the selection of his representatives for the purposes of collective bargaining or the adjustment of grievances;

(2) to cause or attempt to cause an employer to discriminate against an employee in violation of subsection (a)(3) or to discriminate against an employee with respect to whom membership in such organization has been denied or terminated on some ground other than his failure to tender the periodic dues and the initiation fees uniformly required as a condition of acquiring or retaining membership.

(3) to refuse to bargain collectively with an employer, provided it is the representative of his employees subject to the provisions of section 9(a);

(4) (i) to engage in, or to induce or encourage any individual employed by any person engaged in commerce or in an industry affecting commerce to engage in, a strike or a refusal in the course of his employment to use, manufacture, process, transport, or otherwise handle or work on any goods, articles, materials, or commodities or to perform any services; or (ii) to threaten, coerce, or restrain any person engaged in commerce or in an industry affecting commerce, where in either case an object thereof is—

(A) forcing or requiring any employer or self-employed person to join any labor or employer organization or to enter into any agreement which is prohibited by section 8(e);

(B) forcing or requiring any person to cease using, selling, handling, transporting, or otherwise dealing in the products of any other producer, processor, or manufacturer, or to cease doing business with any other person, or forcing or requiring any other employer to recognize or bargain with a labor organization as the representative of his employees unless such labor organization has been certified as the representative of such employees under the provisions of section 9: *Provided,* That nothing contained in this clause (B) shall be construed to make unlawful, where not otherwise unlawful, any primary strike or primary picketing;

(C) forcing or requiring any employer to recognize or bargain with a particular labor organization as the representative of his employees if another labor organization has been certified as the representative of such employees . . . ;

(D) forcing or requiring any employer to assign particular work to employees in a particular labor organization or in a particular trade, craft, or class rather than to employees in another labor organization or in another trade, craft, or class, unless such employer is failing to conform to an order or certification of the Board determining the bargaining representative for employees performing such work:

Provided, That nothing contained in this subsection (b) shall be construed to make unlawful a refusal by any person to enter upon the premises of any employer (other than his own employer), if the employees of such employer are engaged in a strike ratified or approved by a representative of such employees whom such employer is required to recognize under this Act: *Provided further,* That for the purposes of this paragraph (4) only, nothing . . . shall be construed to prohibit publicity, other than picketing, for the purpose of truthfully advising the public, including consumers and members of a labor organization, that a product or products are produced by an employer with whom the labor organization has a primary dispute and are distributed by another employer, as long as such publicity does not have an effect of inducing any individual employed by any person other than the primary employer in the course of his employment to refuse to pick up, deliver, or transport any goods, or not to perform any services, at the establishment of the employer engaged in such distribution:

(5) to require of employees covered by an agreement authorized under subsection (a)(3) the payment, as a condition precedent to becoming a member of such organization, of a fee in an amount which the Board finds excessive or discriminatory under all the circumstances. In making such a finding, the Board shall consider, among other relevant factors, the practices and customs of labor organizations in the particular industry, and the wages currently paid to the employees affected;

(6) to cause or attempt to cause an employer to pay or deliver or agree to pay or deliver any money or other thing of value, in the nature of an exaction, for services which are not performed or not to be performed; and

(7) to picket or cause to be picketed, or threaten . . . or cause to be picketed, any employer where an object thereof is forcing or requiring an employer to recognize or bargain with a labor organization as the representative of his employees, or forcing or requiring the employees of an employer to accept or select such labor organization as their collective bargaining representative, unless such labor organization is currently certified as the representative of such employees:

(A) where the employer has lawfully recognized in accordance with this Act any other labor organization and a question concerning representation may not appropriately be raised under section 9(c) of this Act;

(B) where within the preceding twelve months a valid election under section 9(c) of this Act has been conducted, or

(C) where such picketing has been conducted without a petition under section 9(c) being filed within a reasonable period of time not to exceed thirty days from the commencement of such picketing: *Provided,* That when such a petition has been filed the Board shall forthwith, without regard to the provisions of section 9(c)(1) or the absence of a showing of a substantial interest on the part of the labor organization, direct an election in such unit as the Board finds to be appropriate and shall certify the results thereof: *Provided further,* That nothing in this subparagraph (C) shall be construed to prohibit any picketing or other publicity for the purpose of truthfully advising the public . . . that an employer does not employ members of, or have a contract with, a labor organization, unless an effect of such picketing is to induce any individual employed by any other person in the course of his employment, not to pick up, deliver or transport any goods or not to perform any services.

Nothing in this paragraph (7) shall be construed to permit any act which would otherwise be an unfair labor practice under this section 8(b).

(c) The expressing of any views, argument, or opinion, or the dissemination thereof, whether in written, printed, graphic, or visual form, shall not constitute or be evidence of an unfair labor practice under any of the provisions of this Act, if such expression contains no threat of reprisal or force or promise of benefit.

(d) For the purposes of this section, to bargain collectively is the performance of the mutual obligation of the employer and the representative of the employees to meet at reasonable times and confer in good faith with respect to wages, hours, and other terms and conditions of employment, or the negotiation of an agreement, or any question arising thereunder, and the execution of a written contract incorporating any agreement reached if requested by either party, but such obligation does not compel either party to agree to a proposal or require the making of a concession: *Provided,* That where there is in effect a collective-bargaining contract covering employees in an industry affecting commerce, the duty to bargain collectively shall also mean that no party . . . shall terminate or modify such contract, unless the party desiring such termination or modification—

(1) serves a written notice upon the other party to the contract of the proposed termination or modification sixty days prior to the expiration date thereof, or in the event such contract contains no expiration date, sixty days prior to the time it is proposed to make such termination or modification;

(2) offers to meet and confer with the other party for the purpose of negotiating a new contract or a contract containing the proposed modifications;

(3) notifies the Federal Mediation and Conciliation Service within thirty days after such notice of the existence of a dispute, and simultaneously therewith notifies

any State or Territorial agency established to mediate and conciliate disputes within the State or Territory where the dispute occurred, provided no agreement has been reached by that time; and

(4) continues in full force and effect, without resorting to strike or lockout, all the terms and conditions of the existing contract for a period of sixty days after such notice is given or until the expiration date of such contract, whichever occurs later.

The duties imposed upon employers, employees, and labor organizations by paragraphs (2), (3), and (4) shall become inapplicable upon an intervening certification of the Board, under which the labor organization or individual, which is a party to the contract, has been superseded as or ceased to be the representative of the employees subject to the provisions of section 9(a), and the duties so imposed shall not be construed as requiring either party to discuss or agree to any modification of the terms and conditions contained in a contract for a fixed period, if such modification is to become effective before such terms and conditions can be reopened under the provisions of the contract. Any employee who engages in a strike within any notice periods specified in this subsection, or who engages in any strike within the appropriate period specified in subsection (g) of this section, shall lose his status as an employee of the employer engaged in the particular labor dispute, for the purposes of sections 8, 9, and 10 of this Act, but such loss of status for such employee shall terminate if and when he is reemployed by such employer. Whenever the collective bargaining involves employees of a health care institution, the provisions of this section 8(d) shall be modified as follows:

(A) The notice of section 8(d)(1) shall be ninety days; the notice of section 8(d)(3) shall be sixty days; and the contract period of section 8(d)(4) shall be ninety days.
(B) Where the bargaining is for an initial agreement following certification or recognition, at least thirty days' notice of the existence of a dispute shall be given by the labor organization to the agencies set forth in section 8(d)(3).
(C) After notice is given to the Federal Mediation and Conciliation Service . . . the Service shall promptly communicate with the parties and use its best efforts, by mediation and conciliation, to bring them to agreement. The parties shall participate fully and promptly in such meetings as may be undertaken by the Service for the purpose of aiding in a settlement of the dispute.

(e) It shall be an unfair labor practice for any labor organization and any employer to enter into any contract or agreement, express or implied, whereby such employer ceases or refrains or agrees to cease or refrain from handling, using, selling, transporting, or otherwise dealing in any of the products of any other employer, or to cease doing business with any other person, and any contract or agreement entered into heretofore or hereafter containing such an agreement shall be to such extent unenforceable and void: *Provided,* That nothing in this subsection (e) shall apply to an agreement between a labor organization and an employer in the construction industry relating to the contracting or subcontracting of work to be done at the site of the construction, alteration, painting, or repair of a building, structure, or other work: *Provided further,* That for the purposes of this subsection (e) and section 8(b)(4)(B) the terms "any employer," "any person engaged in commerce or any industry affecting other producer, processor, or manufacturer," "any other employer," or "any other person" shall not include persons in the relation of a jobber, manufacturer, contractor, or subcontractor working on the goods or premises of the jobber or manufacturer or performing parts of an integrated process of production in the apparel and clothing industry: *Provided further,* That nothing in this Act shall prohibit the enforcement of any agreement which is within the foregoing exception.

(f) It shall not be an unfair labor practice under subsections (a) and (b) of this section for an employer engaged primarily in the building and construction industry to make an agreement covering employees engaged (or who, upon their employment, will be engaged) in the building and construction industry with a labor organization of which building and construction employees are members (not established, maintained, or assisted by any action defined in section 8(a) of this Act as an unfair labor practice) because (1) the majority status of such labor organizations has not been established under the provisions of section 9 of this Act prior to the making of such agreement, or (2) such agreement requires as a condition of employment, membership in such labor organization after the seventh day following the beginning of such employment or the effective date of the agreement, whichever is later, or (3) such agreement requires the employer to notify such labor organization of opportunities for employment with such employer, or gives such labor organization an opportunity to refer qualified applicants for such employment, or (4) such agreement specifies minimum training or experience qualifications for employment or provides for priority in opportunities for employment based upon length of service with such employer, in the industry or in the particular geographical area: *Provided,* That nothing in this subsection shall set aside the final proviso to section 8(a)(3) of this Act: *Provided further,* That any agreement which would be invalid, but for clause (1) of this subsection, shall not be a bar to a petition filed pursuant to section 9(c) or 9(e).

(g) A labor organization before engaging in any strike, picketing, or other concerted refusal to work at any health care institution shall, not less than ten days prior to such action, notify the institution in writing and the Federal Mediation and Conciliation Service of that intention, except that in the case of bargaining for an initial agreement following certification or recognition the notice required by this subsection shall not be given until the expiration of the period specified in clause (b) of the last sentence of section 8(d) of this Act. The notice shall state the date and time that such action will commence. The notice, once given may be extended by the written agreement of both parties.

Section 9 (a) Representatives designated or selected for the purposes of collective bargaining by the majority of the employees in a unit appropriate for such purposes, shall be the exclusive representatives of all the employees in such unit for the purposes of collective bargaining in respect to rates of pay, wages, hours of employment, or other conditions of employment: *Provided,* That any individual employee or a group of employees shall have the right at any time to present grievances to their employer and to have such grievances adjusted, without the intervention of the bargaining representative, as long as the adjustment is not inconsistent with the terms of a collective-bargaining contract or agreement then in effect: *Provided further,* That the bargaining representative has been given opportunity to be present at such adjustment.

(b) The Board shall decide in each case whether, in order to assure to employees the fullest freedom in exercising the rights guaranteed by this Act, the unit appropriate for the purposes of collective bargaining shall be the employer unit, craft unit, plant unit, or subdivision thereof: *Provided,* That the Board shall not (1) decide that any unit is appropriate for such purposes if such unit includes both professional employees and employees who are not professional employees unless a majority of such professional employees vote for inclusion in such unit; or (2) decide that any craft unit is inappropriate for such purposes on the ground that a different unit has been established by a prior Board determination, unless a majority of the employees in the proposal craft unit vote against separate representation; or (3) decide that any unit is appropriate for such purposes if it includes, together with other employees, any individual employed as a guard to enforce against employees and other persons rules to protect property of the employer or to protect the safety of persons on the employer's premises; but no later organization shall be certified as the representative of employees in a bargaining unit of guards if such organization admits to membership, or if affiliated directly or indirectly with an organization which admits to membership, employees other than guards.

(c)(1) Whenever a petition shall have been filed, in accordance with such regulations as may be prescribed by the Board—

(A) by an employee or group of employees or an individual or labor organization acting in their behalf alleging that a substantial number of employees (i) wish to be represented for collective bargaining and that their employer declines to recognize their representative as the representative defined in section 9(a), or (ii) assert that the individual or labor organization, which has been certified or is being currently recognized by their employer as the bargaining representative, is no longer a representative as defined in section 9(a); or

(B) by an employer, alleging that one or more individuals or labor organizations have presented a claim to be recognized as the representative defined in section 9(a); the Board shall investigate such petition and if it has reasonable cause to believe that a question of representation affecting commerce exists shall provide for an appropriate hearing upon due notice. Such hearing may be conducted by an officer or employee of the regional office, who shall not make any recommendations with respect thereto. If the Board finds upon the record of such hearing that such a question of representation exists, it shall direct an election by secret ballot and shall certify the results thereof. . . .

(2) In determining whether or not a question of representation affecting commerce exists, the same regulations and rules of decision shall apply irrespective of the identity of the persons filing the petition or the kind of relief sought and in no case shall the Board deny a labor organization a place on the ballot by reason of an order with respect to such labor organization or its predecessor not issued in conformity with section 10(c).

(3) No election shall be directed in any bargaining unit or any subdivision within which, in the preceding twelve-month period, a valid election shall have been held. Employees engaged in an economic strike who are not entitled to reinstatement shall be eligible to vote under such regulations as the Board shall find are consistent with the purposes and provisions of this Act in any election conducted within twelve months after the com-

mencement of the strike. In any election where none of the choices on the ballot receives a majority, a run-off shall be conducted, the ballot providing for a selection between the two choices receiving the largest and second largest number of valid votes cast in the election.

(4) Nothing in this section shall be construed to prohibit the waiving of hearings by stipulation for the purpose of a consent election in conformity with regulations and rules of decision of the Board.

(5) In determining whether a unit is appropriate for the purposes specified in subsection (b) the extent to which the employees have organized shall not be controlling.

(d) Whenever an order of the Board made pursuant to section 10(c) is based in whole or in part upon facts certified following an investigation pursuant to subsection (c) of this section and there is a petition for the enforcement or review of such order, such certification and the record of such investigation shall be included in the transcript of the entire record . . . and thereupon the decree of the court enforcing, modifying, or setting aside . . . the Board shall be made and entered upon the pleadings, testimony, and proceedings set forth in such transcript.

(e)(1) Upon the filing with the Board, by 30 per centum or more of the employees in a bargaining unit covered by an agreement between their employer and a labor organization made pursuant to section 8(a)(3), of a petition alleging they desire that such authority be rescinded, the Board shall take a secret ballot of the employees in such unit, and shall certify the results thereof to such labor organization and to the employer.

(2) No election shall be conducted pursuant to this subsection in any bargaining unit or any subdivision within which, in the preceding twelve-month period, a valid election shall have been held.

Appendix I

Title VII of Civil Rights Act of 1964*

Section 701 [j] The term "religion" includes all aspects of religious observance and practice, as well as belief, unless an employer demonstrates that he is unable to reasonably accommodate to an employee's or prospective employee's religious observance or practice without undue hardship on the conduct of the employer's business.

(k) The terms "because of sex" or "on the basis of sex" include, but are not limited to, because of or on the basis of pregnancy, childbirth or related medical conditions; and women affected by pregnancy, childbirth, or related medical conditions shall be treated the same for all employment-related purposes, including receipt of benefits under fringe benefit programs, as other persons not so affected but similar in their ability or inability to work, and nothing in Section 703(h) of this title shall be interpreted to permit otherwise. This subsection shall not require an employer to pay for health insurance benefits for abortion, except where the life of the mother would be endangered if the fetus were carried to term, or except where medical complications have arisen from an abortion: *Provided,* That nothing herein shall preclude an employer from providing abortion benefits or otherwise effect bargaining agreements in regard to abortion.

Section 703 (a) It shall be an unlawful employment practice for an employer—

(1) to fail or refuse to hire or to discharge any individual, or otherwise to discriminate against any individual with respect to his compensation, terms, conditions, or privileges of employment, because of such individual's race, color, religion, sex, or national origin; or

(2) limit, segregate, or classify his employees or applicants for employment in any way which would deprive or tend to deprive any individual of employment opportunities or otherwise adversely affect his status as an employee, because of such individual's race, color, religion, sex, or national origin.

(b) It shall be an unlawful employment practice for an employment agency to fail or refuse to refer for employment, or otherwise to discriminate against, an individual because of his race, color, religion, sex, or national origin, or to classify or refer for employment any individual on the basis of his race, color, religion, sex, or national origin.

(c) It shall be an unlawful employment practice for a labor organization—

(1) to exclude or to expel from its membership, or otherwise to discriminate against, any individual because of his race, color, religion, sex, or national origin;

(2) to limit, segregate, or classify its membership or applicants for membership or to classify or fail to refuse to refer for employment any individual, in any way which would deprive or tend to deprive any individual of employment opportunities, or would limit such employment opportunities or otherwise adversely affect his status as an employee or as an applicant for employment, because of such individual's race, color, religion, sex, or national origin; or

(3) to cause or attempt to cause an employer to discriminate against an individual in violation of this section.

(d) It shall be an unlawful employment practice for any employer, labor organization, or joint labor-management committee controlling apprenticeship or other training or retraining, including on-the-job training programs, to discriminate against any individual because of his race, color, religion, sex, or national origin in admission to, or employment in, any program established to provide apprenticeship or other training.

(e) Notwithstanding any other provision of this title, (1) it shall not be an unlawful employment practice for an employer to hire and employ employees, for an employment agency to classify, or refer for employment, any individual, or for any employer, labor organization, or joint labor-management committee controlling apprenticeship or other training or retraining programs to admit or employ any individual in any such program, on the basis of his religion, sex, or national origin in those cer-

*This material is excerpted from Title VII of the Civil Rights Act of 1964.

tain instances where religion, sex, or national origin is a bona fide occupational qualification reasonably necessary to the normal operation of that particular business or enterprise, and (2) it shall not be an unlawful employment practice for a school, college, university, or other educational institution or institution of learning to hire and employ employees of a particular religion if such school, college, university, or other educational institution or institution of learning is, in whole or in substantial part, owned supported, controlled, or managed by a particular religion or by a particular religious corporation, association, or society, or if the curriculum of such school, college, university, or other educational institution or institution of learning is directed toward the propagation of a particular religion.

(f) As used in this title, the phrase "unlawful employment practice" shall not be deemed to include any action or measure taken by an employer, labor organization, joint labor-management committee, or employment agency with respect to an individual who is a member of the Communist Party of the United States or of any other organization required to register as a Communist-action or Communist-front organization by final order of the Subversive Activities Control Act of 1950.

(g) Notwithstanding any other provision of this title, it shall not be an unlawful employment practice for an employer to fail or refuse to hire and employ any individual for any position, for an employer to discharge an individual from any position, or for any employment agency to fail or refuse to refer any individual for employment in any position, or for a labor organization to fail or refuse any individual for employment in any position, if—

(1) the occupancy of such position, or access to the premises in or upon which any part of the duties of such position is performed or is to be performed, is subject to any requirement imposed in the interest of the national security of the United States under any security program in effect pursuant to or administered under any statute of the United States or any Executive order of the President; and

(2) such individual has not fulfilled or has ceased to fulfill that requirement.

(h) Notwithstanding any other provision of this title, it shall not be an unlawful employment practice for an employer to apply different standards of compensation, or different terms, conditions, or privileges of employment pursuant to a bona fide seniority or merit system, or a system which measures earnings by quantity or quality of production or to employees who work in different locations, provided that such differences are not the result of an intention to discriminate because of race, color, religion, sex, or national origin; nor shall it be an unlawful employment practice for an employer to give and to act upon the results of any professionally developed ability test provided that such test, its administration or action upon the results is not designed, intended, or used to discriminate because of race, color, religion, sex, or national origin. It shall not be an unlawful employment practice under this title for any employer to differentiate upon the basis of sex in determining the amount of wages or compensation paid or to be paid to employees of such employer if such differentiation is authorized by the provisions of Section 6(d) of the Fair Labor Standards Act of 1938 as amended (29 U.S.C. 206(d)).

(i) Nothing contained in this title shall apply to any business or enterprise on or near an Indian reservation with respect to any publicly announced employment practice of such business or enterprise under which a preferential treatment is given to any individual because he is an Indian living on or near a reservation.

(j) Nothing contained in this title shall be interpreted to require any employer, employment agency, labor organization, or joint labor-management committee subject to this title to grant preferential treatment to any individual or to any group because of the race, color, religion, sex, or national origin of such individual or group on account of an imbalance which may exist with respect to the total number or percentage of persons of any race, color, religion, sex, or national origin employed by any employer, referred or classified for employment by any employment agency or labor organization, admitted to membership or classified by any labor organization, or admitted to, or employed in, any apprenticeship or other training program, in comparison with the total number or percentage of persons of such race, color, religion, sex, or national origin in any community, State, section, or other area, or in the available work force in any community, State, section, or other area.

Section 704 (a) It shall be an unlawful employment practice for an employer to discriminate against any of his employees or applicants for employment, for an employment agency, or joint labor-management committee controlling apprenticeship or other training or retraining, including on-the-job training programs, to discriminate against any individual, or for a labor organization to discriminate against any member thereof or applicant for membership, because he has opposed any practice made an unlawful employment practice by this title, or because he has made a charge, testified, assisted, or participated in any manner in an investigation, proceeding, or hearing under this title.

(b) It shall be an unlawful employment practice for an employer, labor organization, employment agency, or joint labor-management committee controlling apprenticeship or other training or retraining, including on-the-job training programs, to print or cause to be printed or published any notice or advertisement relating to employment by such an employer or membership in or any classification or referral for employment by such a labor organization, or relating to any classification or referral for employment by such an employment agency, or relating to admission to, or employment in, any program established to provide apprenticeship or other training by such a joint labor-management committee indicating any preference, limitation, specification, or discrimination based on race, color, religion, sex, or national origin, except that such a notice or advertisement may indicate a preference, limitation, specification, or discrimination based on religion, sex, or national origin when religion, sex, or national origin is a bona fide occupational qualification for employment.

GLOSSARY

absorption doctrine principle derived from the Fourteenth Amendment under which the Bill of Rights and other protections of the U.S. Constitution are applied to actions by state governments

abusive discharge employment-at-will theory permitting an employee's right of action against an employer that arbitrarily dismisses the employee for refusing to violate the law or for providing evidence of the employer's illegal wrongdoing

accord and satisfaction an agreement and the performance according to the Agreement that resolves disputed claims under a previous contract

accredited investors sophisticated investors with sufficient net worth and experience to "fend for themselves" by negotiating adequate information from issuers of exempt offerings, thus justifying relaxation of public disclosure requirements

acquisition purchase by one firm of the stock of another firm in order to operate that firm as a separate division or subsidiary

act of state the act of a foreign state occurring in that state. U.S. Courts will not examine the validity of such acts absent a specific treaty or legislative directive to do so

actual authority authority given by a principal to an agent

adequate representation clauses supplier contract clauses requiring a retailer to make substantial promotional efforts to sell a manufacturer's products

adjudicatory activities agency activities that determine facts and make judgments on the basis of evidence presented, such as conducting hearings that are like trials

administrative agency governmental body that is not a legislative, executive, or judicial unit

administrative law laws governing the activities and procedures used by administrative agencies

Administrative Procedure Act specifies the methods to be followed by federal administrative agencies in performing their activities

administrative processes methods by which administrative agencies perform a variety of activities

ad valorem tariff import taxes based upon a percentage of the value or price of the item imported

adversarial system method of litigation that places the responsibility for developing and proving a claim on the parties rather than the judge

advice and consent U.S. Constitutional requirement for U.S. Senate review and confirmation of Presidential appointees; e.g., judges, cabinet heads, independent regulators

advising letter of credit a letter of credit in which a bank informs the seller of the terms on which the buyer insists, regarding the number of items, description of goods, and packaging requirements. The advising letter does not obligate the bank to make any payments

affectation doctrine view that under the commerce clause of the U.S. Constitution Congress has the power to regulate any interstate or intrastate activity that has an appreciable direct or indirect effect on interstate commerce

affirmative action contractual or statutory program in which an employer establishes goals, quotas, and timetables to achieve greater employment participation by members of protected classes

affirmative defense defendant's response to a complaint in which a legal justification for the defendant's conduct is provided

agency coupled with an interest agency in which the agent has a property interest in the agency's subject matter

agency relationship relationship between two people that arises when one of them agrees to act on behalf of the other

agency shop union security device in the employer's contract requiring bargaining assessment (dues payment) by all employees rather than full union membership

agency theory economic theory that evaluates the costs associated with an agent's breach of fiduciary duty

agent person who acts on behalf of or represents another person

all or nothing rule the rule that prohibits any recovery by the plaintiff from the defendant if the defendant proves any contributory negligence by the plaintiff

ally doctrine exception to the prohibition against secondary pressure where the secondary employer is economically linked to the primary employer

alter ego the term used to describe a corporation that fails to conduct business as a distinct corporate entity separate and distinguishable from the shareholders

alternative dispute resolution the methods used to resolve disputes that are used as alternatives to adversarial litigation

ADR American depository receipts. These receipts are certificates representing foreign securities that are trading in U.S. markets

annual percentage rate of interest standardized computation, required by the Truth-in-Lending Act, of the interest cost of credit

answer the defendant's response to the plaintiff's complaint, admitting or denying each essential segment of the complaint

anticipatory breach (anticipatory repudiation) notice of inability to perform as promised, made prior to the time for performance, which permits the innocent party to sue immediately for nonperformance or freely find performance from another contractor

antidumping duties duties imposed on dumped goods, that is, goods sold in the importing country at a price lower than their price in the home market

Anti-Federalists political movement of the late 18th century that advocated states' rights and a weak central or federal government

antitrust federal laws designed to maintain competition and prevent monopolistic concentration of economic power

apparent authority authority from the principal that creates the appearance of authority for third parties even though no actual authority exists

appellant party bringing an appeal of a case to a higher court

appellate jurisdiction reviewing court's right to hear and review legal issues in a case originating in another court

appellee party defending an appeal of a case to a higher court

appropriate bargaining unit all employees working for a particular employer who share similar employment conditions and are therefore entitled to vote together as a unit

arbitration method of dispute resolution in which a person or a panel of people other than a judge make a decision after hearing from the parties and witnesses

arraignment initial court appearance in which the person who is accused of a crime enters a plea of innocence or guilt

Articles of Confederation constitutional document specifying a confederation structure for the United States, in effect between the Revolutionary War and ratification of the present U.S. Constitution (1781–89)

articles of incorporation documents filed with a state department that provide required information regarding the name, place of business, activities, and officers of a corporation

assignee person to whom an assignment is made

assignment transfer of existing contract rights to a new obligee; transfer of all of one's rights in property to another

assignor person who makes an assignment to another person

assumption of risk the voluntary exposure to a known and appreciated danger; a defense used in a strict liability case

attachment execution of a security agreement, the contract that is the first step in establishing a secured transaction; court order authorizing the seizure and sale of a defendant's property

attempt the unsuccessful or incomplete attempt to commit crime; an attempt to commit a crime is treated as a separate crime

attorney at law person who acts for someone else in legal matters

attorney-client privilege the privilege under law that protects the information given to the attorney in confidence by the client. The attorney cannot be compelled to testify regarding privileged information

auction without reserve auction terms prohibiting the seller from withdrawing goods from the block provided that at least one good faith bid is made

auction with reserve auction terms permitting the seller to withdraw goods prior to sale, before the auctioneer knocks them down to the highest bidder

average variable cost average of all the variable expenses needed to produce the number of units under analysis

bailee person to whom bailment property is transferred

bailment transfer of personal property to another person for a specific purpose

bailor person who transfers bailment property to someone else

bait and switch deceptive trade practice in which a seller advertises inexpensive merchandise, the "bait" (often available in insufficient quantities), intending to actively "switch" consumers to alternative higher-profit merchandise

bankruptcy uniform federal process to permit debtor relief and debtor liquidation for the benefit of creditors

bankruptcy stay bankruptcy court bar to creditors' pursuance of remedies against debtors in default pending the bankruptcy proceeding

barriers to entry structures that make it difficult for new sellers to enter a market

basis of the bargain buyer's reliance on warranty of the seller

battle of the forms inevitable nonconformity between offers and acceptances, purchase order forms and confirming invoices, that led to enactment of UCC 2–207 to preserve contracts despite lack of a mirror image

beneficial ownership SEC implication that one person controls all of the shares owned by an affiliated group

benefits conferred requirement of implied-in-law contracts that the party seeking quasi-contractual remedies must have given the other party a valuable benefit

best available technology standard established, as of 1987, by the Clean Air Act for new plants and by the Clean Water Act for new water pollution equipment

best practicable technology Clean Water Act standard for water pollution control devices installed by 1977

beyond a reasonable doubt burden of proof imposed on the society in a criminal case

bilateral contract contract in which two parties exchange promises

bilateral treaty agreement between two countries in which conflicting rules are resolved

bill of lading document issued by a transporter of goods in which the transporter generally agrees to deliver the goods described to whoever has the document

Bill of Rights first 10 amendments to the U.S. Constitution, which protect fundamental freedoms and liberties

blocking laws laws that one nation uses to block foreign laws that might have extra territorial application in that nation

bona fide occupational qualification (BFOQ) justification for discrimination in which an applicant's membership in a particular protected class is necessary for successful operation of the employer's business

bottle laws state laws requiring purchasers to pay a cash deposit on all beverage containers

Boulwareism take-it-or-leave-it bargaining position first advanced by a General Electric manager named Boulware

brief short summary of a case that makes it easier to review its important aspects; written presentation that a party uses to argue a point or appeal a decision

bubble concept approach under which all the pollution-producing devices of a plant are treated as a single unit—as if they were all under one bubble

burden of proof the necessity of proving certain facts in dispute on an issue; the burden of proof imposed differs in criminal and civil suits

business ethics application of traditional ethical analysis to business decisions

business judgment rule rule holding that corporate officers and directors are not liable for errors based on the exercise of reasonable business judgment

"but for" test a test used in a negligence case to view the defendant's actions to see whether "but for" those actions the injury to the plaintiff still would have occurred

bylaws rules of a corporation that govern its internal management actions

case of first impression case in which no legislation, administrative regulations, or prior cases provide a solution for the problems presented

case or controversy U.S. Constitutional requirement of genuine adversary interests necessary for access to federal and most state court adjudication

categorical imperative ethical principle, developed by Kant, holding that certain actions are unethical in all instances, that there is no justification for ever taking specified actions (*examples:* "Thou shall not kill," the Golden Rule)

caveat emptor "let the buyer beware"

cease and desist orders administrative and judicial remedies, similar to court-ordered prohibitory injunctions with stronger deterrent effect, that order that specific conduct will not occur in the future

challenge for cause request to disqualify a juror due to lack of impartiality

chancery courts established in England and carried over to the United States that allow the judge or chancellor to make decisions based on justice and equity as well as law

charitable subscription substitute for consideration, like promissory estoppel the promisor's promise induces the promisee's detrimental reliance, when promisee is a charitable institution

circuit courts of appeal appellate courts in the federal court system

citation information in a case heading that tells where the case may be found and when it was decided

civil law that part of the law that concerns wrongs against persons in society

closing event at which the parties to the sale of real property exchange documents

closing statements concluding remarks of the parties at the end of a trial

Code of Federal Regulations official compilation of agency rules and notices

codetermination the requirement that there be labor representation on corporate boards of directors

comity the international law principle that one nation should give effect to the judgment of courts of other nations, even though there is no legal obligation to recognize those judgments

commercial speech speech by business to inform and advertise to the public

common law case law resulting from court decisions

common law legal system legal system in which the courts are recognized as creators of law

common situs single site or location where several construction contractors and subcontractors operate and picketing activity may cause prohibited secondary pressure on employers with which the picketing union has no dispute

company union union dominated or supported by the employer, which therefore cannot adequately represent the organizational rights of the employees

comparable worth equal pay theory that requires equal pay for jobs with similar responsibilities rather than similar tasks

comparative negligence doctrine that weighs the relative negligence of the plaintiff and the defendant before determining recovery (see **contributory negligence**)

compensatory damages damages that compensate an injured party for losses actually suffered, such as medical expenses and lost wages

complaint document used to initiate a civil lawsuit, gives the plaintiff's version of the facts and includes a request for relief from the court

composition agreement substitute for consideration in which several creditors of a single debtor agree to relaxed debt repayment; enforceable without any new consideration from the debtor

computer crime any illegal act requiring knowledge of computer technology or involving the use of a computer

concurrent powers constitutional powers possessed by both the federal government and the state governments (*example:* taxation)

conditional acceptance offeree's termination of an offer by modification of terms; operates like a counteroffer

conditions express or implied contract terms in which certain events or conditions are prerequisites to one or both parties' duty to perform

condominium property ownership under which an owner is granted individual control over a specific area while sharing common areas with other owners

conduct approach antitrust enforcement approach that seeks to prohibit anticompetitive behaviors

confederation government in which a loose aggregation of independent and distinct local or state governments are tied together by a weak central government

confirming letter of credit a letter of credit usually issued by a seller's bank which makes that bank liable when it confirms the letter of credit issued by the buyer's bank

conflict of law rules the general principals courts use to determine which laws should be referred to when a conflict exists between the laws of several states affecting the parties and their dispute

conflicts of law rules that determine which state's law applies in multistate transactions or occurrences

conglomerate mergers mergers that cannot be classified as horizontal or vertical; usually combine firms in different industries and sometimes combine firms at different levels of production

conscious parallelism tacit agreement among competitors to mimic one another's pricing behaviors

consent decree administrative remedy in which charges are filed against an alleged law violator, who soon thereafter consents to a court-ordered injunction against further wrongdoing and other undertakings

consequential damages additional damages due to the innocent party's special circumstances that flow naturally from a breach (*example:* lost profits or income)

consequential ethical theory analysis of the outcomes and results of decisions rather than the means used; Machiavellian view that "the ends justify the means" (*examples:* utilitarian, egoist theories)

consideration test of contract seriousness that requires each party to give up something new in making mutual assent; benefit to the promisor or detriment to the promisee

consignment sale contingent sale in which the manufacturer retains title to goods until the retailer actually sells them to ultimate customers; may permit the supplier's control over sale terms

consolidation combination of two formerly independent firms in which both are dissolved and a new firm is created

construct validity justification for a job-testing method that measures identifiable candidate characteristics considered useful in performing the job in question

content validity justification for a job-testing method that uses a representative sample of the tasks that applicants must perform successfully on the job in question

contract legally enforceable set of counterpromises between parties for which duties and rights are recognized

contract clause provision of the U.S. Constitution that prohibits states from passing laws relieving the obligation of existing contracts

contributory negligence conduct by the plaintiff that is a contributory factor in causing his or her injury and thus bars recovery (see **comparative negligence**)

cooperative property owned by an association or a corporation that leases specific units to individual tenants who are shareholders or owners of the association or corporation

copyright legal protection granted for the original work of authors, musicians, and painters that restricts copying without the owner's consent

corporate crime illegal behavior intended to benefit business firms

corporate opportunity doctrine the doctrine that requires a corporate officer or agent to offer to the corporation any opportunity before that officer or agent uses the opportunity for personal benefit

corporation legal entity separate and distinct from its shareholder-owners

corrective advertising court-ordered remedy for deceptive advertising that requires the advertiser to confess to previous misleading statements

counterclaim that part of the defendant's answer in which it is alleged that the plaintiff wronged the defendant

counteroffer offeree's counterproposal made in response to the offeror's offer; rejects the original offer and substitutes a new proposal

countervailing duties duties assessed to counteract foreign subsidies on imported products that materially injure competing domestic products

country of origin in an international sales or investment transaction, the country that is the origin of the product or technology being transferred

country of source in an international sales or investment transaction, the country that is the source of income being generated

course of dealing precedents established between parties that have previously contracted together

course of performance precedents established between parties that have repeatedly performed a single contract

covenant not to compete contract provision prohibiting one party from competing against the other; enforceable only if reasonable and necessary to protect interests in an employment or sale of business contract

cover UCC buyer's remedy that permits the buyer to purchase substitute goods if the seller defaults and to collect damages equal to the additional price paid

creditor under the Truth-in-Lending Act, one that regularly extends or arranges for consumer credit

creditor third-party beneficiary third-party beneficiary that receives the right through transfer from a debtor and may enforce the duty against both the obligor and the promisee

criminal law that part of the law that concerns wrongs against society

criterion validity justification for a job-testing method that indicates which applicants will perform successfully or unsuccessfully in the job

cross-elasticity of demand economic analysis of the substitutability between two products usable for similar purpose; the percentage change in the quantity demanded for one product divided by the percentage change in the price of the alleged substitute

cross-examination questioning of a witness by the party opposed to the party that produced the witness

cure UCC seller's remedy that permits the seller to substitute conforming goods if these are delivered before the time allowed for performance

deauthorization election election in which the members of an appropriate bargaining unit vote on whether to remove some of the bargaining powers of a currently certified union

debtor relief laws state laws, passed when the Articles of Confederation were in effect, that released all debts

deceit tort of fraud

deceptive advertising advertising, illegal under the Wheeler-Lea Act, capable of deceiving the typical ordinary consumer

decertification election election in which the members of an appropriate bargaining unit vote on whether to remove a currently certified union

deductive reasoning reasoning from the general to the specific, as from a code provision to a specific problem

deed document used to transfer the ownership of real property

deep pocket theory theory of suing the party with the most financial resources, say a business firm rather than its agent

defamation publication of an untrue statement that injures a person's reputation

default judgment court's order in a case where the defendant has not responded to the allegations in the plaintiff's complaint

defendant the party being sued in a lawsuit

defined benefit plan pension plan that provides specific retirement benefit payments based on the employee-beneficiary's age and length of service at retirement

defined contribution plan pension plan to which each employee makes specific contributions and whose benefit payments may vary according to the investment successes of the plan

delayed manifestation product liability injury that goes undetected, sometimes for many years

delayed manifestation diseases diseases and medical conditions stemming from exposure to defective and dangerous products or hazardous and toxic substances in the workplace that arise slowly over time

delegation transfer of an existing contract duty to a new obligor; transfer of power by one governmental body to another

deposition transcribed testimony that a witness under oath gives outside court

design standards OSHA standards specifying particular equipment designs to ensure health and safety

direct examination questioning of a witness by the party on whose behalf the witness has been called

direct investment an investment by a corporation or an individual in a foreign firm that gives them at least a 10 percent ownership in that firm

direct marketing mail-order sales of goods

directors managers of a corporation who are responsible for establishing its policies

disability physical or mental handicap necessitating certain accommodation in the workplace and public accommodations

disaffirm cancellation right of a victim of fraud, misrepresentation, duress, or undue influence; the right of an incapacitant to cancel

discharge in bankruptcy elimination of most debts in bankruptcy

disclose or abstain rule rule that gives insiders the choice of disclosing inside information before trading or abstaining from trading altogether

discovery procedures procedures used by one party in a lawsuit to discover relevant information in the exclusive knowledge or possession of the other party or that party's witnesses

discretionary activities agency activities that are not subject to judicial review

disparate impact theory of job discrimination in which the plaintiff proves that the employer's apparently neutral hiring and promotion policies actually had an adverse impact on a protected class

disparate treatment theory of job discrimination in which the plaintiff proves that the employer treated members of one protected class differently than it treated members of another protected class

diversification merger conglomerate merger between firms in totally unrelated industries

diversity of citizenship federal courts' jurisdiction over cases between citizens of different states or countries

division of markets competitors' restraint of trade in allocating customers or geographic markets to avoid competition; competitors' allocation of customers or geographic markets to particular sellers, prohibited as anticompetitive

domestic corporation a corporation that is regarded as a citizen in the state (or nation) in which the court is located. Thus, a Michigan corporation is a domestic corporation under Michigan law

donee third-party beneficiary third-party beneficiary that receives a contract right as a gift but who may enforce the duty only against the obligor

double jeopardy legal provision that bars trying individuals twice on the same criminal charges

due diligence nonnegligent conduct of underwriters, auditors, and management during the preparation for registration of an initial public offering

due process requirement of the U.S. Constitution that all persons and business entities receive fair treatment in trials, hearings, and the like and that legislation be fairly drawn

dumping a firm's sale of goods at a lower price in a foreign market as compared to the price in the firm's home market. Dumping violates international trade agreements and justifies the levy of antidumping duties

duress contract defense where one contracting party entered into an unfavorable bargain because the other contracting party used coercive threats of force

easement nonpossessory interest in land that permits its owners to make limited use of some portion of another's land

economic due process variant of substantive due process, now inapplicable, that was used to invalidate economic regulation of business

economic duress contract defense where one party threatened breach of an existing contract unless the other party assented to an unfavorable bargain

economic strike strike concerning matters other than an employer's unfair labor practices; participants in such strikes generally not entitled to reinstatement unless this is required by the renegotiated contract

edge effect discipline on existing competitors imposed by a potential entrant into a market

egoist ethical theory analysis with the goal of maximizing the decision maker's welfare (*examples:* personal power, wealth, pleasure)

elasticity of demand measure of how quickly and easily consumers can switch to similar products to satisfy the same need if prices change

electronic funds transfer paperless electronic movement of money through the banking system, often through the use of ATM machines and by telephone transfer

eminent domain governmental taking of privately owned real property for a public interest; adequate compensation required

Employee Retirement Income Security Act (ERISA) federal law administered by the Department of Labor and the Internal Revenue Service, imposing requirements on private pension plans seeking to qualify for federal tax benefits

employer and independent contractor relationship between an employer and a person who contracts to act for the employer but whose conduct is not subject to the employer's control

employment-at-will principle that permits either the employer or the employee to terminate an employment contract without the other's consent and without breach of contract

enabling acts statutes that establish administrative agencies and specify their powers

enabling legislation the legislation that grants authority to an agency to perform specific activities

Endangered Species Act the Act enforced by the EPA and the Department of Commerce that protects endangered and threatened animal species

enumerated powers powers that the U.S. Constitution specifically delegates to the federal government (*example:* regulation of interstate commerce)

environmental impact statement document that must be submitted to the EPA before any major federal action is taken that can significantly affect the quality of the human environment

Equal Employment Opportunity Commission (EEOC) federal agency responsible for administration of the anti-discrimination laws

equal protection provision of the U.S. Constitution prohibiting arbitrary classifications in legislation that unfairly penalize groups of persons

estate the interest that a person has in real or personal property

ethical analysis process of evaluating conduct in which the evaluator identifies the right and wrong consequences of actions

ethics field of philosophy that examines motives and actions from the perspective of moral principles

European Community regional organization of 12 European countries that have established several regional institutions and formed a regional market free of tariffs

excelsior list list of employees' names that an employer must provide to a union attempting to organize the employer; must be given to the union at least seven days before the representation election is scheduled

exclusive dealing agreement requiring a retailer to sell only a particular manufacturer's products

exclusive distributorship right of a retailer to be the sole seller of a manufacturer's products

exculpatory clauses contract provisions relieving one party of liability; unenforceable if their purpose is to relieve that party from the consequences of wanton or willful misconduct; must be communicated

executed contract contract whose duties have been fully performed

execution process process for enforcing a defaulted loan in which a court order directs the sheriff to take and sell enough of the debtor's property to provide proceeds that will discharge the debt to the creditor

executive orders orders issued by the chief executive of a government

executory contract contract whose duties have not yet been fully performed by one or more of the parties

exhaustion of remedies requirement that a person seeking judicial review of an agency's activities first seek a remedy from the agency

experience rating adjustments in unemployment compensation insurance premiums for employers with low employee turnover rates

export domestically manufactured product sold to a foreign purchaser

express contract contract arising from the parties' expression of mutual assent—gestural, oral, or written

express warranty contractual promise relating to the future performance of goods that arises from (1) an affirmation of fact or promise regarding the goods, (2) a description, (3) a sample, (4) technical specifications, or (5) a model used by the seller in making representations to the buyer

expropriation takeover of certain firms by the government, usually without adequate payment to their former owners

externalities costs or benefits resulting from a firm's activities that are absorbed, not by the firm, but by outsiders

extraterritorial law law of a governmental entity regulating conduct or activities that occur outside its borders

failing firm defense defense to a conglomerate merger that the firm must be acquired to save it from bankruptcy

Fair Labor Standards Act (FLSA) federal law defining standardized workday, workweek, overtime pay computation, and the minimum wage

fair use doctrine copyright law provision that allows limited copying of protected materials

federal district courts trial courts in the federal court system

Federal Insurance Contributions Act (FICA) federal law that established the procedures for payments of social security contributions (FICA withholding)

federalism ideology regarding the optimal placement of various governmental powers, either those of a central, federal government or those of governments at a more local level, such as states and municipalities; the division of legal power in the United States among federal, state, and local governments

Federalists political movement of the late 18th century that advocated a strong central or federal government

federal question jurisdiction of the federal courts to hear cases involving federal laws

Federal Register the place where proposed and promulgated rules adopted by federal administrative agencies are published

Federal Trade Commission (FTC) agency responsible for the enforcement of federal laws on antitrust, consumer credit, deceptive advertising, and deceptive trade practices

fellow servant doctrine negligence defense used by employers to avoid liability to an injured employee when another employee contributed to the injury

fiduciary duties to a principal imposed by law on an agent, such as the duties of loyalty and due care

fiduciary relationship relationship in which the fiduciary (agent) is required to place the interests of the principal above its own interests

financing statement document filed to establish a creditor's priority over other creditors with a security interest in the collateral

firm offer under the UCC, no consideration required for the time stated if an offer is made by a merchant in a signed writing; valid for no longer than three months

fixtures personal property that becomes real property through attachment to land or buildings

flat rate tariff import taxes levied on each unit imported, such as a barrel of oil, pound of nails, or ton of grain

force majeure contract provision that specifies the conditions releasing one or both of the parties to the contract from their obligations

foreign branch foreign establishment that is legally a part of its parent firm

foreign corporation a corporation that is not regarded as a citizen of the state in which the court is located. Thus, Michigan corporations and Mexican corporations are both foreign corporations to Pennsylvania courts

foreign sales corporation subsidiary formed under U.S. law used by a U.S. corporation to sell its exports

forum non conveniens the concept that a court with jurisdiction to hear and decide a case may decline to decide a case if it determines that it is not a convenient place or forum for the parties, witnesses, and court

forum state state in which suit is brought

fourth-line injury price discrimination injury at the purchaser's level

franchise privilege granted or sold, such as the privilege of using a name, process, trademark, or copyright

franchisor person or firm that develops a product or service and licenses its use by others

fraud intentional misrepresentations permitting the victim to rescind the contract

fraudulent transfers sales or gifts for unfair value that a bankrupt makes to close friends, relatives, or associates

Freedom of Information Act the law that seeks to increase the accountability of federal agencies to the public by mandating that most agency files and documents be open to public inspection

free rider person or business that benefits from the expenditures of competitors on certain services, advertising, and promotional activities

full faith and credit clause clause of the U.S. Constitution requiring each state to recognize the laws and legal processes of all the other states

full performance complete and satisfactory performance of a contractual duty

full warranty special consumer rights, stipulated by the Magnuson-Moss Warranty Act, that require reasonable replacement or repair of products without charge

fundamental rights rights protected by the U.S. Constitution, such as the rights of voting, interstate travel, and certain pretrial and trial procedures in criminal legal actions

gambling contract creating a risk with no prior existence for the purpose of shifting that risk to the players; illegal unless permitted by statute

garnishment statutory procedure used by creditors to collect unpaid debts out of debtors' wages; a court order that a third party pay a plaintiff some of a defendant's money

general creditors creditors with no security interest or collateral to secure their loans

going and coming rule exception to workers' compensation coverage for accidents that employees incur while en route from or to the worksite

good faith bargaining interactive proposals for a contract between an employer and a bargaining unit of unionized employees

grand jury group of citizens that investigates possible criminal activity

gratuitous agency an agent who is not compensated for activities performed on the principal's behalf

grease payments payments made to lower-level officials who have no discretion to grant business; not bribes under the Foreign Corrupt Practices Act

greenhouse effect warming of the lower atmosphere caused by emissions of carbon dioxide

greenmail premium over the market value of the shares held that is paid to a potential corporate raider

group boycotts collusive agreements not to buy from or sell to certain customers

handicap physical or mental impairment that substantially limits one or more major life functions

hazardous wastes wastes that contribute significantly to serious, irreversible illnesses or pose hazards to human health when improperly managed

hearsay testimony testimony based on what one person hears another person say

Herfindahl index measure of the degree of market concentration; computed by summing the squares of the market shares of all competitors

highly material terms under UCC 2–207, terms in the parties' communications that must be exactly mirrored in the acceptance or the acceptance will be considered a counteroffer

hiring hall union-operated list of qualified job candidates among whom the employer agrees to hire

historical facts facts or circumstances noted in the plaintiff's complaint that led to the claimed wrongful act of the defendant

holder in due course special legal status afforded to transferees of commercial paper (negotiated checks or notes) that insulates them from real defenses

horizontal merger combination of two competing firms at the same level of production

horizontal restraint of trade collaboration among competitors to restrain trade

hot cargo agreement agreement with a union requiring a secondary employer to cease dealing in the goods of the primary employer with which the union has a dispute

hung jury result in a case in which fewer than the required number of jurors agree on a verdict

illegal bargaining subjects subjects that are legally excluded from bargaining between unions and employers

illegality defense to a contract whose primary objective or likely performance will involve the commission of an illegal act

illusory promise performance of a party is optional, subject to his or her wish, will, or desire; a promise that provides insufficient consideration

impasse bargaining deadlock in which neither party can make further proposals more favorable to the other side

imperfect market a market in which some form of market power is held by producers or consumers

implied contract contract arising from mutual assent inferred from the conduct of the parties

implied-in-law contract contract-like duties and remedies imposed by the law to achieve fairness

implied powers Constitutional powers of Congress that are inferred from the necessary and proper clause

implied warranty of fitness for a particular purpose quality warranty that arises whenever the buyer relies on the seller's selection decision

implied warranty of merchantability quality warranty of goods sold by a merchant; must be acceptable in the trade, fit for ordinary purposes, be within permitted variations, be adequately packaged and conform to the package promises

import product of foreign manufacture that has been bought by a domestic purchaser

incidental beneficiary third party with no rights in the contract because the contracting parties did not identify this party or intend that this party receive any benefit

incorporators persons who apply for the incorporation of a corporation

indemnification payment of expenses or damages from a legally responsible party

independent contractor person or firm that works for but is not subject to the control of another person or firm

indictment grand jury finding that sufficient evidence exists to hold a criminal trial against the accused

individual retirement accounts (IRAs) retirement savings-investment accounts whose holders receive limited tax benefits

inductive reasoning reasoning from the specific to the general, as from prior cases to a general legal principle

industrial organization view held by economists of various market models and of the proper antitrust theories applicable to them

industry guides FTC regulations providing industrywide guidance on unfair and deceptive trade practices

inelastic markets markets in which consumer demand is relatively unresponsive to changes in price

inferior courts lower-level trial courts that hear specific minor cases

informal actions agency activities other than rulemaking or adjudication (*examples:* administering programs, providing assistance, issuing permits)

informational picketing picketing designed to inform the public about a labor dispute

information statement document, filed in lieu of a proxy statement with the SEC, that identifies the proxy solicitor, states the legal terms of the proxy, and provides information relevant to a grant of proxy—director candidates, issuer financial statements, details about the resolutions up for vote

insider employee of an issuer or a consultant to an issuer with access to confidential information

insider trading purchases or sales of an issuer's securities, timed to take advantage of confidential information, by management, employees, or others who owe a fiduciary duty to the issuer

instructions judge's statement to the jury of the law applicable to a case

insurable interest nexus between a person buying insurance and the property or person insured, ownership of the property, or the right to possess it

intangible property personal property that does not have a physical existence

integration formal contract that the trial judge rules is sufficiently complete to trigger the parol evidence rule

integration of exempt offerings SEC technique for combining several exempt offerings that are actually based on a single plan of financing if these are made too close in time

intellectual property intangible property that has been created primarily by mental rather than physical effort

intentional tort civil wrong based on an intentional act

interbrand competition competition among sellers of similar products made by different manufacturers

interlocking directorate illegal condition in which a single director sits on the boards of two competitors

internal accounting controls procedures for reconciling the authorization of transactions with the actual receipt or disbursement of assets

international organizations organizations that most nations have granted some law-making powers

interrogatories written questions that the opposing party must answer under oath

interstate commerce commercial intercourse affecting trade between the states. The U.S. Constitution grants Congress power to regulate interstate commerce

***inter vivos* gift** gift of personal property made while the donor is living

intrabrand competition competition among sellers of the same product brand and models

intrastate activities carried on wholly within one state

intrastate offering exemption exemption from SEC registration of an initial public offering of securities within one state

investment banking syndicate group of investment banking firms that participate in selling an initial public offering of new securities sold by a corporate issuer

investment intent investor's good faith intention to hold securities sold in an exempt offering for a sufficient time to permit the inference of long-term investment purposes

involuntary bankruptcy petition initiation of bankruptcy process at the creditor's discretion

irrevocable offer offer that the offeror may not revoke

issues management public affairs activities engaged in by a firm to avoid negative influences from the environment

job description inventory of job tasks showing the content analysis of a job

joint tenancy with rights of survivorship co-ownership of property in which the interest of one co-owner is transferred to the other co-owners on the co-owner's death

joint venture form of partnership designed for a limited and narrow objective—an investment having two or more active participants; commonly used in international business transactions

judgment judge's determination that concludes a trial

judgment notwithstanding the verdict (NOV) judge's determination that reverses the jury's verdict

judgment-proof a term used to describe a defendant who is uninsured or unable to pay any monies due under a judgment for the plaintiff

judicial review power of a court to review actions of administrative agencies

jurisdiction court's power to hear and decide cases

jurisdictional dispute dispute between rival unions vying for control over certain job classifications

jurisdictional facts statements in the plaintiff's complaint that indicate the relationship between the parties and their controversy and the court

jurisdiction of the person court's right to hear a case involving the parties; usually, a defendant must be served a summons

jurisdiction of the subject matter court's right to hear the type of case being tried

justice ethical goal of law—the achievement of fairness and equity, whose content is usually derived from political, economic, and social values

Kantian or universal theory the ethical theory that suggests that actions are moral only if those actions could be undertaken by everyone

Keogh plan pension plan conferring income tax benefits on self-employed persons

Koran Muslim holy book, which contains God's revelations to the prophet Mohammed

Labor-Management Relations Act (Taft-Hartley Act) federal labor law designating certain unfair union labor practices

Labor-Management Reporting and Disclosure Act (Landrum-Griffin Act) federal labor law establishing fair and democratic union elections and regulating the actions of union officials

laissez-faire economic philosophy that stresses the virtues of governmental noninterference and free markets

Lanham Act federal statute under which patents and trademarks are registered

law binding standards or guidelines for actions or behavior in a society

law merchant European trading customs dating from the Middle Ages that evolved into the modern UCC

leading object rule exception to the statute of frauds that permits the enforceability of oral contracts of guarantee in which the promisor is protecting a personal interest; also called the *main purpose doctrine*

lease contract granting the right to use and/or possess real property or goods for a term of time

leasehold tenant's possessory interest in real property

legal environment of business study of the laws, processes, and legal institutions that affect business activities

legislative history method that courts use to interpret legislation—looks at the legislative process leading to the legislation

legislative oversight committees committees of Congress or state legislatures that exercise some control or review powers over certain administrative agencies

legislative veto power power of the legislature to veto the rules of administrative agencies

legislature body of persons having the authority to make laws for a political unit

lemon laws state statutes requiring refund of the purchase price or replacement of certain consumer goods if these prove to be unrepairable after repeated attempts

lender liability liability imposed on lenders for fraud or incompetent interference with the businesses of troubled debtors

letter of credit document that a bank uses to substitute its credit for that of a buyer in an international sales transaction: if confirmed, the bank must pay the seller if the letter's terms are met; if advising, the bank does not incur liability

LBO leveraged buyout, an acquisition of a firm financed in part by using the acquired firm's borrowing power

libel written defamation

license permit allowing one person to use another person's land for a limited purpose; a permit to manufacture or sell a patented product; or document that gives its holder, such as a foreign manufacturer or distributor, the right to make or distribute a product in a certain territory or country

lien one person's nonpossessory, collateral-type interest in another person's property

limited liability the liability of a corporate shareholder is limited to the amount of his or her investment

limited liability company a form of business organization that offers its owners limited liability and yet taxes the owners' earnings, not the company earnings. It is similar to the "Subchapter S" corporation

limited partnership a business organizational form that involves two or more partners, at least one of whom contributes capital but does not participate in the management of the partners' business

line of credit contract between a bank and a borrower obligating the bank to lend the borrower up to a specified amount at the borrower's request

liquidated damages provision that specifies the amount of damages in the event of a breach of contract; the damages must not be a penalty, and they must be difficult to forecast at the time of contracting

loan covenants contract clauses that restrict a defaulting debtor's discretion in financial matters

long arm statute state law that gives courts jurisdiction over parties outside the state

Magna Carta declaration by King John of England in 1215 granting fundamental rights; it is a forerunner of U.S. Constitutional freedoms

mailbox rule acceptances, if made by a reasonable means of communication, effective upon dispatch even if they are lost in the mail or if a rejection or revocation arrives before the acceptance arrives

main purpose doctrine exception to the statute of frauds that permits the enforceability of oral contracts of guarantee in which the promisor is protecting a personal interest; also called the *leading object rule*

malpractice liability of professionals (e.g., lawyers, doctors, accountants, engineers) for negligent or otherwise insufficient services harming the client

mandatory bargaining subjects wages, hours, and other terms and conditions of employment that unions and employers must bargain over in collective bargaining

marginal cost manufacturer's additional expenses to produce one unit more than the number already produced

market concentration measure of the potential for the exercise of market power

market extension merger merger enabling the acquiring firm to expand into new markets

market share percentage of the relevant market held by the firm in question

market share liability concept relieving plaintiffs from providing proof of the precise manufacture of a defective product (*example:* liability for delayed manifestation diseases resulting from a dangerous drug according to the market share held by drug companies at the time the drug was sold)

mass layoff firing of at least one third of the full-time workforce or of at least 500 employees at a single site; triggers the employer's notification duty under the Worker Adjustment and Retraining Notification Act

master or **principal** a person who has a right to control the business acts of another person

master-servant relationship or **employer-employee relationship** relationship between an employer and an employee whose physical conduct is subject to the employer's direct supervision

material breach failure of a contracting party to fully perform as promised; triggers the other party's right to suspend counterperformance

material terms acceptance terms that would cause surprise; to become part of a UCC contract, require agreement of the parties

mechanic's lien interest of a person who provides services that improve another person's real or personal property

mediation method of dispute resolution in which a person or a panel of people other than a judge recommends a decision after hearing from the parties and witnesses

Medicare federal health insurance program that pays some medical expenses of persons over 65 years of age and of certain indigent persons

MOU memoranda of understanding. An international cooperation agreement among regulators from two or more nations

memorandum written contract that is minimally sufficient to satisfy the statute of frauds

mercantile terms abbreviations used in goods shipments that designate the parties' duties with regard to payment, risk of loss, insurance, transportation, and loading or offloading

merchants persons who deal in goods of the kind sold in the transaction; persons who hold themselves out as experts in commercial transactions

merger combination of two formerly independent firms, of which one survives and the other is dissolved

merit rating adjustments in workers' compensation insurance premiums for employers with lower numbers of employee accidents

Michigan Register the place where proposed and promulgated rules adopted by the state of Michigan administrative agencies are published

mini FTC acts state laws paralleling the FTC Act and federal antitrust laws

minitrial method of dispute resolution that features the informal presentation of a dispute to senior executives or an independent outsider

mirror image rule requirement in common law contracts that the terms of the acceptance be exactly the same as the terms of the offer

misappropriation wrongful use of confidential information for personal securities trading in violation of a fiduciary duty

misrepresentation defense to contract liability where the victim justifiably relied on misrepresentations of material facts made by the other party

misuse product liability defense similar to assumption of risk that relieves the defendant of liability if the plaintiff misused the product; a form of assumption of risk based on improper product use

mitigation of damages duty of the innocent party to minimize the damages resulting from the other party's breach

mock up false demonstration in product advertisement

monopolistic competition market dominated by a few large sellers, each of which has some market power over prices and supply, that offer functionally similar but differentiated products

monopolization intentional acts to obtain and maintain an illegal monopoly

monopoly market dominated by one large seller with market power to dictate prices and supply

monopoly power seller's power to control price and supply due to its relative size as a supplier

monopsony market dominated by one large buyer with market power over demand

morality human behavior found to be good and just

moral reasoning the process of moving from premise to conclusion in determining the right course of action

mortgage document giving a lender an ownership interest in property owned or being purchased by another party

mortgagee lender that finances the purchase of real property by lending money to the purchaser

mortgagor purchaser of real property who borrows from a lender

motions requests to the court for some type of court order; may be made by either party at various stages of litigation

motion to direct the verdict request to have the judge instead of the jury decide a case because the evidence so clearly favors one of the parties

mutual assent parties' agreement to form a contract, usually through the acceptance of a valid offer

mutual mistake defense to a contract where both parties are mistaken about the identity, existence, or character of the subject matter

National Institute for Occupational Safety and Health (NIOSH) federal agency responsible for conducting research on worksite health and safety hazards and for recommending regulations

nationalization takeover of certain firms by a government, usually after agreeing to pay the firms' former owners

National Labor Relations Act (Wagner Act) keystone of federal labor law—permits unionization and concerted employees activities, requires collective bargaining with certified unions, created National Labor Relations Board (NLRB)

National Labor Relations Board (NLRB) federal administrative agency responsible for the administration of federal labor laws

National Mediation Board (NMB) regulatory agency responsible for administration of the Railway Labor Act

National Railroad Adjustment Board (NRAB) federal agency responsible for mediating, arbitrating, or otherwise settling labor disputes under the Railway Labor Act

necessaries necessities of life—for example, food, clothing, and shelter; an incompetent is liable for the reasonable value of necessaries

necessary and proper U.S. Constitutional provision granting Congress the legislative power to implement all its other granted powers

negligence per se standard employed when the plaintiff uses the defendant's violation of a criminal law as proof of the defendant's negligence

negligent tort wrong based on a careless act or fault by the defendant

negotiable bill of lading a documentary receipt for goods that allows the title to the goods to be transferred (negotiated) by the owner endorsing it to another party such as a bank or buyer of the goods

New Deal economic and regulatory reconstruction program to revive U.S. economy during the Great Depression

nolo contendre in a criminal case, the plea entered by a defendant that does not contest the charge but that neither admits nor denies guilt

nonattainment areas areas not meeting EPA air pollution standards; new construction in these areas is restricted by the Clean Air Act

nonconsequential ethical theory analysis of the means used to implement decisions (*example:* the categorical imperative)

noneconomic damages damages such as pain and suffering that are needed to compensate for injuries that have not cost the injured party any direct economic loss

nonsigner provisions provisions of some fair trade laws that required all resellers to adhere to a resale price maintenance agreement even if they did not sign the agreement

nontariff barriers all import restrictions other than tariffs

normative principles ethical concepts that suggest ideal goals for conduct

Norris-LaGuardia Act federal anti-injunction act; prohibits federal courts from enjoining strikes or other labor disputes as well as yellow-dog contracts, which bar employees from joining unions

no-strike clause union contract provision that prohibits a union from striking; usually given in return for the employer's agreement to arbitrate disputes

Nuclear Waste Policy Act the 1982 Act that establishes a national plan for the disposal of highly radioactive nuclear wastes

nuisance substantial and unreasonable interference with the use and enjoyment of a person's interest in property

objective theory of contracts theory that the offers or acceptances of parties are determined by a reasonable interpretation of the parties' communications as judged by an objective observer

obligee recipient of a contract obligation or duty

obligor contracting party that owes an obligation or duty under the contract

Occupational Safety and Health Act (OSHA) federal statute regulating safety and health hazards in the workplace

Occupational Safety and Health Administration (OSHA Administration) federal agency responsible for administering the OSHA

Occupational Safety and Health Review Commission (OSHRC) independent federal agency responsible for deciding appeals from the rulings of the OSHA Administration

offer proposal to contract containing all of the necessary terms; conveys a power to contract to the offeree

offeree recipient of an offer

offering statement form of registration statement that is used for exempt small issues under Regulation A

offeror original author of a contract proposal or offer

officers persons who are in charge of corporation's day-to-day business

oligopoly market dominated by a few sellers that have the power to dictate prices and supply

oligopsony market dominated by a few large buyers, each of which has some market power over demand

omission failure to provide all of the facts necessary for an accurate understanding; considered deceptive if practiced by advertisers or issuers of securities

opening statement initial overview of a case that is given in a trial

option contract offer that is made irrevocable by the offeree's payment of consideration

ordinances laws and regulations of municipal bodies

original jurisdiction trial courts' right to hear a case involving factual and legal determinations

overruling an objection judge's decision to allow the presentation of evidence

Paperwork Reduction Act the federal law that requires federal agencies to consider and seek to minimize the paperwork costs on businesses affected by regulation

Pareto optimality condition that arises when decisions or events result in net increases in society's benefits without making anyone worse off

parol evidence rule rule that prohibits the parties to a written contract from presenting evidence at trial that would alter, add to, or subtract from the contract if the contract is a formal integration

partnership association of two or more persons who carry on as co-owners of a business for profit

part performance doctrine exception to the statute of frauds for oral sales of real estate where the seller knows that the buyer took possession of the land, part of the purchase price was paid, and the buyer made valuable improvements

patent original, novel, useful, and nonobvious invention recognized and protected by law

pattern or practice theory of job discrimination based on circumstantial or statistical evidence of discrimination against a protected class

peremptory challenge request to disqualify a juror that is not based on a legal reason

perfect competition condition in which there are large number of buyers and sellers, no single seller or buyer has market power, and prices are set by supply and demand for functionally identical products

perfection final step that provides public notice establishing priority over the collateral in a secured transaction

performance analysis antitrust enforcement approach that focuses on the actual outcomes of allegedly anticompetitive conduct

performance standards OSHA standards specifying acceptable protection or exposure levels for health and safety protective devices

perks profits or benefits received by an employee in addition to regular compensation

permanent variance OSHA Administration order permitting an employer to use alternative safety or health measures that provide equal levels of safety

permissive bargaining subjects topics of bargaining that unions and employers are allowed to bargain over but may not insist on bargaining over

perpetual life the term which signifies that a corporation's existence continues and is not dependent on the lives of its owners

per se rule conduct in restraint of trade that is always illegal, for which no justification exists

petit jury trial jury that determines the facts and renders a verdict in a lawsuit

phantom freight disguised price-fixing technique that equalizes the freight charges among all buyers irrespective of the actual freight charges

picketing gathering and patrolling by persons to inform others of a labor dispute

pierce the corporate veil the action of a court that pierces the shield protecting an individual officer or shareholder of a corporation from liability and holds the individual personally liable for corporate debts

plain meaning a method that courts use to interpret legislation; looks at the common meaning of words or phrases

plaintiff person who initiates a lawsuit and claims that his or her rights have been infringed

planned unit developments (puds) large planning developments that permit a mixture of land uses in one area despite the limitations imposed in other areas

plant closing permanent or temporary layoff of 50 or more employees during any 30-day period; triggers employer's notification duty under the Worker Adjustment and Retraining Notification Act

plea bargain an agreement between the prosecutor and a criminal defendant, usually substituting a guilty plea on a lesser offense for the one for which the person was originally charged

police powers constitutional powers of the states and local governments to regulate in order to promote public health, safety, morals, and the general welfare

political action antitrust exemption given for legitimate concerted political activities of competitors

political action committee (PAC) groups of like-minded political contributors who concentrate their resources for candidates and causes that support the interests of their members

portfolio investment an investment by an individual or a corporation in a foreign firm that gives them less than a 10 percent ownership in that firm

posteffective period time after which the registration of an initial public offering of securities becomes effective, during which sales and solicitations are permitted

potential entrant firm whose ability to enter a market exerts competitive discipline on existing competitors

prayer for relief statement in the plaintiff's complaint that indicates the requested court remedy

precedent a previous decision relied upon by a court for authority in making a current decision

preconditioning prohibited promotional activity during the prefiling period before an initial public offering of securities

predatory pricing pricing below a producer's marginal cost

preempt concept that gives priority to federal law in the event of a conflict between federal law and state law

preexisting legal duty rule rule that a party's promise to make the same performance that it is already obligated to perform is insufficient as consideration

preferential transfers payments made by a debtor within 90 days before bankruptcy filing that give a creditor a greater percentage of the debtor's assets than the creditor would obtain under bankruptcy; rescindable by the bankruptcy trustee

prefiling period time preceding an issuer's filing of a registration statement

preliminary hearing pretrial criminal tribunal that is held to determine the sufficiency of evidence to hold a trial

preponderance of the evidence burden of proof generally imposed on the plaintiff in a civil case

prescriptive principles legal concepts that require minimum levels of conduct

pretrial conference meeting held prior to trial at which an effort is made to resolve the issues still in dispute

price discrimination seller's illegal practice of charging different prices for commodities of like grade and quality

price-fixing agreement of competitors to restrain trade and eliminate competition by artificially establishing prices high enough to provide profit for all of them

primary-line injury price discrimination injury at the supplier level

primary picketing picketing by employees at their employer's facilities

principal person who gives authority to another person to act on his or her behalf

principal-agent relationship relationship between a principal and its agent, who has the authority to carry out a broad range of activities on the principal's behalf

priority secured right of creditors to have their claims fully satisfied before any part of the claims of other creditors is satisfied

priority creditors unsecured creditors that are given priority over other unsecured creditors for specially defined claims (*examples:* bankruptcy administration costs, limited amounts of the wages and pensions of the bankrupt's employees, and customer deposits)

prior restraint effect of laws that prohibit or regulate the content of speech or press before utterance

private law law that concerns the relationships between firms and individuals in a society

private nuisance use of real property that interferes with others' use of their property

private placement exempt offering of securities made in private sales to sophisticated (accredited) investors and a few nonaccredited investors

privileges and immunities clause clause of the U.S. Constitution that prohibits states from discriminating against citizens of other states; not applicable to corporations

privity contract direct contract relationship between buyer and seller necessary to bring product liability suit; now largely abandoned

privity of estate mutual or successive relationship to the same rights in property

procedural due process constitutional requirements of fair pretrial handling and fair trial and appeal procedures

procedural law that part of the law that details the means or methods by which rights and duties will be enforced

prohibited powers governmental powers that the U.S. Constitution bans federal and state governments from exercising (*example:* establishment of religion)

promisee recipient of a contract promise

promisor maker of a contract promise

promissory estoppel substitute for actual consideration in which the promisor makes a promise that is expected to induce the promisee's reliance and detrimental reliance

promissory note document that evidences a debt, such as that by a purchaser of real property to a lender

property bundle of rights that people have in things

property interest legally enforceable relationships between people or businesses and certain things

property tax tax levied by states and municipalities on tangible personal and real property

proscriptive principles criminal law concepts that forbid certain behaviors

prospectus any notice, circular, advertisement, letter, or communication that offers or confirms a security sale

protected class demographic classification of persons historically subject to job discrimination (*examples:* age, sex, religion, national origin, color, race)

proximate cause negligence standard used to establish the causal relationship between a defendant's breach of duty and a plaintiff's injury

proxy right that a shareholder gives someone to vote for the shareholder at a corporate meeting

proxy solicitation efforts of management or insurgent shareholder groups to gain proxies from sufficient shareholders to win a corporate election of directors or passage of a resolution

proxy statement document filed with the SEC identifying the proxy solicitor, stating the legal terms of the proxy, and providing information relevant to a grant of proxy—director candidates, issuer financial statements, details about the resolutions up for vote

public law law that concerns the relationship between people and their government

public nuisance use of real property that interferes with the public's use of property

puffing statements of opinion that are usually too vague to be misrepresented as facts, thus relieving the party that makes them of misrepresentation or fraud

punitive damages additional damages awarded to punish the wrongdoer for willful misconduct; intended to punish the wrongdoer, not to compensate for the injured party's loss

purchase money security interest credit sale transaction secured by the property purchased

purchase of assets transfer of the assets of an acquired firm to an acquiring firm

QIB qualified institutional buyer: An institutional investor with substantial financial means who may participate in the private placement resale market

quantitative substantiality test of the legality of exclusive dealing based on whether the contract covers a substantial dollar volume of business

quasi contract contract-like duties imposed in law as implied-in-law remedies for a party that has conferred a benefit on another party that is thereby unjustly enriched

quasi-strict scrutiny test of equal protection that invalidates legislation with unjustifiable classifications based on sex or legitimacy. This standard occupies the middle ground between the strict scrutiny and the rational basis tests

quitclaim deed deed to real property that transfers the seller's interest but does not guarantee the seller's title

quota limit on the quantity of a product that may be imported

RICO racketeer influenced corrupt organizations. A crime of repeated and related underlying federal crimes by organized crime.

ratification intentional acceptance of a contract that was made while an agent was incompetent and is valid only after the incapacity of the agent has been removed; conduct of a principal that approves an act of an agent who originally acted without authority

ratification vote authorization by a union's members, required to validate a contract negotiated by the union with the employer

rational basis test test of equal protection that validates legislation by demonstrating a rational connection between a statute and a permissible government purpose

real property land and everything attached to it, including the air above the surface and the minerals below the surface

recall manufacturer's program to notify consumers of defective goods and to make repairs

record official document that indicates what happened at trial

recording process of entering documents that involve an interest in real property in the public record

red herring preliminary prospectus with red border warning that it does not solicit sales of securities; may be used only during the waiting period

redlining creditors' illegal practice of refusing credit in depressed neighborhoods

refusal to deal supplier's practice of cutting off supplies to retailers that violate suggested retail or minimum pricing

regional organizations groups of nations in a given area that cooperate in one or more organizations

registration statement document, filed with the SEC, that registers the sale of a public offering of securities

regulatory licensing statute licensing statute whose objective is to protect the public from unscrupulous or unskilled professionals; renders contract with such professionals void at the victims' insistence

rejection offeree's termination of an offer by direct repudiation and refusal

relevant market the first step in assessing monopoly power in a particular product line within a particular geographic region

remittitur reduction of damage award on appeal

rent-a-judge method of dispute resolution, usually not legally binding, that uses a retired judge or lawyer acting as a judge as the decision maker

reorganization bankruptcy process that permits corporations to continue operations without liquidation

reorganization plan privately negotiated arrangement among shareholders and creditors to receive less than their original claims in order to preserve a bankrupt corporation

reply the response by the plaintiff to the defendant's Answer either admitting or denying the new facts raised by that Answer

reporters books that contain a collection of cases from the same state, region, or federal court

representation election predominant procedure used by employees to certify a particular union as their bargaining representative

re-regulation movement to replace the deregulation of the 1980s, typically with more narrowly targeted regulatory programs

resale price maintenance agreement between a supplier and a customer requiring the customer to resell the supplied product at a minimum or higher price

resale restrictions SEC rules prohibiting the resale of securities too soon after they have been sold in an exempt offering, intended to prevent the issuers of exempt offerings from circumventing registration

reserved powers constitutional powers retained by the states (*example:* police power)

res ipsa loquitur "the thing speaks for itself"; the presumption that negligence occurred because the accident would not have occurred otherwise

res judicata prohibition of further trial litigation once a competent court with proper jurisdiction has made a final decision

respondeat superior concept that holds a principal liable for the torts of an agent if those torts were committed within the agent's scope of authority

Restatement of Contracts collection of contract principles as rephrased by legal scholars

restrictive covenant private agreement restricting the use of real property

revenue-raising licensing statute licensing statute whose objective is the raising of governmental revenue; violation of statute has no effect on the legality of contracts

reverse discrimination discrimination arising from affirmative action plans designed to reverse historic patterns of racial or sex-based discrimination; employment practice that favors members of a suspect class who historically received discriminatory treatment

reversionary interest landlord's interest in real property leased to a tenant

revocation offeror's withdrawal and termination of an offer before acceptance

right-to-work laws state laws, permitted by the Taft-Hartley Act, that prohibit union or agency shops from mandating union membership by employees in the bargaining unit

ripeness requirement that agency activities be final before there is any judicial review

risk of loss legal burden allocated between contracting parties—if the buyer has the risk, the purchase price must be paid even for lost goods or goods damaged in transit; if the seller has the risk, the buyer need not pay for lost or damaged goods

rulemaking administrative agency activity that is legislative in nature; agency rules generally have the same legal validity as legislative acts

rule of reason restraint of trade that is judged by its reasonability; justification for the restraint of trade may be acceptable

Rule 10b–5 provision of the 1934 Securities Exchange Act that prohibits fraudulent omissions and disclosures, insider trading, and market manipulation

runaway shop employers' practice of closing a facility and reopening the same operation elsewhere to escape dealing with unions; practice may be illegal if its motivation is to break a union

run with the land restrictive covenants that are imposed on subsequent purchasers

sale act of selling or exchanging property

scab replacement workers who cross picket lines during strikes or other labor disputes

Schedule 13D disclosure, filed with the SEC, giving notice that shareholdings have reached 5 percent of a class of equity securities

secondary boycott threats, coercion, or other union activity directed at an employer with which the union has no dispute

secondary employer employer that is targeted for union concerted activities, but with which the union has no dispute

secondary-line injury price discrimination injury at the purchaser level

secondary picketing picketing, generally prohibited, at a business site other than the site of the picketers' employer

secondary pressure union activity directed at an employer with which the union has no dispute; usually intended to enlist the assistance of the secondary employer

secured creditor creditor with a security interest that provides collateral for a loan

secured transactions contract granting a legally enforceable lien on collateral, usually to secure a loan

Securities and Exchange Commission (SEC) federal agency responsible for regulating the securities markets

security note, stock, Treasury share, bond, investment contract, or any interest or instrument commonly known as a *security*

security agreement signed writing in which a debtor grants a security interest to a creditor

seniority relative employment time entitling longer-term employees to certain benefit and working condition preferences

separate entity the concept that a corporation is a legal person, separate and distinct from its shareholder/owners

separation of powers split of authority in the U.S. legal system among the executive, judicial, and legislative branches

servants or **agents** persons whose business acts are subject to the control of another person

sex-plus discrimination discriminatory policy in which an employer requires additional qualifications of one sex

sexual harassment illegal conduct by an employer, a supervisor, or coworkers in which submission to sexual relations is made a part of the job or a "chilling atmosphere" exists on the jobsite

shareholders owners of a corporation

Sherman Act first antitrust law, passed in 1890; outlawed monopolization

shift differentials pay differences for the same job classification based on the time of the workshift

short tender tender of borrowed shares to a tender offer; largely a prohibited activity

sit-down strike strike in which employees occupy the employer's premises

slander oral defamation

slapp suits strategic litigation against public participation. Suits seeking to deter public interest groups from seeking restrictive legislation/regulation or negative publicity about business activities

small claims court special court that hears minor cases and uses simplified procedures

social regulation administrative agency regulations that are designed to benefit society

social security (OASDI) federal retirement income supplement funded by current employee contributions (FICA)

sole proprietorship business that is owned and managed by one person for a profit

sovereign immunity the international law concept which holds that sovereign governments are immune from suit in the courts of other nations. The immunity generally does not apply to a government's commercial actions

special manufactured goods exception to the UCC statute of frauds that permits enforcement of an oral contract for the manufacture or procurement of goods not suitable for sale in the seller's ordinary course of business

specific performance contract remedy in which the court orders the obligor to perform as promised

spoliation unlawful destruction of evidence; permits a rebuttable presumption that the information is true

stakeholders persons and entities that are directly and indirectly affected by the decisions of a business

standards that part of an enabling act that specifies the activities to be performed and establishes the objectives to be pursued

standing requirement imposed on people seeking review of agency activities that focuses on whether the person seeking review has sufficient interest to question a given activity

stare decisis "let the decision stand"; the doctrine in common law legal systems that requires courts to follow the precedents established by the prior decisions of higher courts

state action governmental intervention into the processing of rights or discipline sufficient to invoke constitutional rights such as due process; exemption under the antitrust laws for actions resulting from valid governmental actions

stationary source of pollution nonmovable pollution source such as a factory or an item of equipment

state-of-the-art defense manufacturer's claim that a product includes all known safety improvements; defense to a product liability suit

statute of frauds requirement of written contracts in sales of an interest in land, guarantee contracts, contracts not to be performed within one year, and UCC sales of goods with a value of $500 or more

statute of limitations the legislation which requires court cases to be filed within a limited period commencing with the date a wrong occurs or is (or should be) discovered

statute of repose time limitation on product liability suits which limit the time products must remain defect-free (e.g., 10 years)

statutory laws laws that have been formally adopted by legislative bodies

statutory preclusion provision in a statute that prohibits judicial review of certain agency activities

statutory purpose method that courts use to interpret legislation—looks at the purpose of the policy behind the legislation

straight bankruptcy complete liquidation of most of the debtor's assets for distribution to creditors

straight bill of lading documentary receipt for goods which provides the carrier must deliver the goods only to the person named in the bill of lading

stranger picketing picketing by nonemployees

street name stock beneficially held for an investor in the name of the investor's broker

strict constructionism ideology of constitutional interpretation according to which the legislature is a better place than the courts to inaugurate new laws, that the courts should be limited to interpretation and minor modifications of existing laws

strict liability liability without fault, such as that imposed on a person engaged in inherently dangerous or ultrahazardous activities

strict scrutiny test of equal protection that invalidates legislation violating certain fundamental rights or discriminating against persons in suspect classes

strike concerted activity in which employees stop work simultaneously to bring pressure on the employer to settle a labor dispute

structuralist antitrust enforcement approach that seeks to prohibit particular anticompetitive structural characteristics

sublease a transfer of less than a tenant's full remaining interest in leased premises

subpoena court order requiring a witness to appear before a court to give testimony

subpoena duces tecum court order requiring the production of documents for use as evidence at trial

subrogation insurer's right to reimbursement of damages paid to victim/claimant from wrongdoer

subsidiary a corporation which is totally or partially owned and controlled by another (parent) corporation

substantial performance slightly defective but adequate performance qualifying the performing party to receive payment, with allowance for the reduction in value due to the defects in performance

substantive due process constitutional prohibition against vague legislation or regulations

substantive law that part of law that defines rights and imposes duties

substituted service of process service of summons in a legal suit when the defendant is unavailable for direct personal delivery (*examples:* publication in newspaper, delivery to secretary of state, registered mail delivery)

successor liability liability of a purchased firm which is inherited by the purchasing corporation

summons court order giving the defendant notice of a lawsuit

supremacy clause grant, by the U.S. Constitution, of governmental power to the federal government that displaces any exercise of state governmental power

SQ3R study method consisting of these steps: survey, question, read, recite, and review

suspect classes demographic classifications of persons who deserve protection from discrimination

sustaining an objection judge's decision to prohibit the presentation of evidence

taking governmental appropriation of private property that generally requires payment of "just" compensation to owner

tangible property personal property that has a physical existence

tariff tax on imported goods that is levied on an ad valorem basis (percentage of the value of a product) or at a flat rate (a specified amount on each unit of a product)

temporary insiders outsiders with a fiduciary relationship to the issuer; prohibited from insider trading

temporary variance OSHA Administration order permitting an employer to delay compliance with a health or safety standard until the equipment necessary for full compliance is available

tenancy in common co-ownership of property that transfers the interest of a co-owner to his or her heirs on the co-owner's death

tender offer public announcement offering to purchase some portion of the outstanding shares of a publicly traded issuer

tender offer statement Schedule 14D–1 disclosure, filed with the SEC, that a tender offer is commencing

tertiary-line injury price discrimination injury at the purchaser's level

third-party beneficiary contract outsider that may enforce certain contract duties

time is of the essence contract term that prohibits late performances

time/price differential sale of goods in which case prices are listed separately from prices for deferred payment; typically, usury laws do not apply to such sales

tippee outsider who receives information improperly conveyed by an insider; trading is then prohibited

title ownership of property; need not be evidenced by a certificate of title

Title VII section of the Civil Rights Act of 1964 that prohibits discrimination based on an employee's membership in a protected class

toehold acquisition to avoid excessive concentration, acquisition of only a small firm by an outsider that must make an acquisition to enter a market

tombstone ads simple announcements of securities offerings or merger transactions, often with stark black borders, that appear in the financial press

tortfeasor person who commits a tort

tort law legal system's recognition of an injured party's right to seek compensatory damages for personal injuries

TQM total quality management. A firm's policies that seek to attain or maintain high-quality goods and services

trademark distinctive mark on goods that distinguishes them from the goods of competitors

trade regulation rules FTC regulations prohibiting unfair and deceptive trade practices

trade secret valuable formula, process, or compilation of information that is not known to the public

trading companies entities that seek to export goods and services

treble damages statutory award of damages equal to three times the amount of the actual damage; have a function similar to that of punitive damages

***Tree Fruits* doctrine** exception to the prohibition against secondary pressure where an authorized strike is in progress and picketing employees request employees of neutral (secondary) employers to refrain from crossing the picket line

trespass unlawful interference with another's property

trust organizational form in which a trustor conveys legal title to property to a trustee that makes decisions about the property; beneficial ownership is retained by the trustor or given to others

trusteeship replacement of officials of a local union who have been involved in corruption by a trustee appointed by the national or international union

tying requirement of the supplier that the buyer purchase a tied, or undesired, product in order to purchase a tying, or desired, product; generally illegal under the rule of reason

unconscionability basis for court reformation of a contract that is so one-sided or oppressive as to "shock the conscience"

underwriters persons that purchase securities with a view to distributing them to the public

undisclosed principal principal whose existence and identity are unknown to third parties

unemployment compensation state insurance system that is intended to provide replacement income for unemployed workers

unfair labor practice one of numerous specified actions by an employer or a union that impedes the self-organization rights of employees

unfair labor practice strike strike in protest of an employer's unfair labor practice; the strikers are generally entitled to reinstatement thereafter

unilateral contract contracts formed by the act or performance that one party makes in return for the promise of the other party

union shop provision in the contract between a union and an employer that requires all employees to join the union

unjust enrichment requirement of implied-in-law contracts; the party from whom a quasi-contractual remedy is sought must have unfairly received valuable benefits

unsecured creditor creditor whose loan has no security interest or collateral to secure it

usages of trade customary business understandings unique to a particular line of business in which special meanings are given to ordinary terms

use taxes sales taxes levied on the purchaser if the seller resides out-of-state

usury laws state laws that set maximum rates on the interest charged on consumer loans

utilitarian theory the ethical theory that determines moral right and wrong by examining the consequences of a given action. Morally correct actions produce the greatest good for the greatest number

valid contract agreement that meets all of the legal requirements

values personal or organizational preferences and perceptions of morality that underlie an individual's attitude toward means and ends

value systems generalized principles that guide a person's evaluation of decisions or specific instances of conduct

verdict jury's decision in a lawsuit

vertical integration result of vertical mergers or of expansion along the same chain of distribution

vertical merger combination of two firms that stand in a supplier-customer relationship

vertical price-fixing resale price-fixing between a manufacturer and a distributer/wholesaler or between a distributor and a retailer

vertical restraints of trade restraints of trade arising from contracts between suppliers and customers along the chain of distribution

vesting ERISA requirement that a pension beneficiary's interest become irrevocable after a minimum employment period

vicarious liability liability of one person or firm based on the actions of another person or firm

voidable contract contract that may be canceled by a party victimized by fraud, misrepresentation, incapacity, duress, undue influence, or mistake

void contract agreement that is invalid and unenforceable due to an illegal objective or the insanity of a party

voir dire "to speak the truth"; this phrase signifies the questioning of potential jurors

voluntary bankruptcy petition initiation of a bankruptcy process at the debtor's discretion

voting trust certificates receipts, given to trustors that create a corporate voting trust as evidence of beneficial ownership

wage base employee earnings subject to the FICA tax rate

waiting period time following the filing of a registration statement for an initial public offering of securities and preceding the effective date; sales are permitted after this period

warranty product seller's affirmation of fact or promise of performance

warranty deed deed to real property that guarantees that the title is free of liens and encumbrances

white-collar crime illegal, nonviolent behavior by businesses and their employees

wildcat strike strike unauthorized by the union or the bargaining unit

workers' compensation state insurance plans that provide cash benefits for workers injured while on the job

work rules job descriptions that designate the authorized employee tasks in an appropriate bargaining unit

zoning ordinances laws, enacted pursuant to the public powers, that restrict the use of real property

INDEXES

CASE INDEX

Cases appearing in italic type are excerpted in the text; others are discussed or cited.

D

E

F

G

H

I

SUBJECT INDEX